KERUX COMMENTARIES

MATTHEW

KERUX COMMENTARIES

MATTHEW

A Commentary for Biblical Preaching and Teaching

DARRELL L. BOCK
TIMOTHY D. SPRANKLE

Matthew: A Commentary for Biblical Preaching and Teaching

Published by Kregel Ministry, an imprint of Kregel Publications, 2450 Oak Industrial Dr. NE, Grand Rapids, MI 49505-6020.

Italics in Scripture quotations indicate emphasis added by the authors.

The Hebrew font, NewJerusalemU, and the Greek font, GraecaU, are available from www.linguistsoftware.com/lgku.htm, +1-425-775-1130.

Cataloging-in-Publication Data is available from the Library of Congress.

ISBN 978-0-8254-5825-5

Printed in China

25 26 27 28 29 / 5 4 3 2 1

Contents

PUBLISHER'S PREFACE TO THE SERIES

Since words were first uttered, people have struggled to understand one another and to know the main meaning in any verbal exchange.

The answer to what God is talking about must be understood in every context and generation; that is why Kerux (KAY-rukes) emphasizes text-based truths and bridges from the context of the original hearers and readers to the twenty-first-century world. Kerux values the message of the text, thus its name taken from the Greek *kērux*, a messenger or herald who announced the proclamations of a ruler or magistrate.

Biblical authors trumpeted all kinds of important messages in very specific situations, but a big biblical idea, grasped in its original setting and place, can transcend time. This specific, big biblical idea taken from the biblical passage embodies a single concept that transcends time and bridges the gap between the author's contemporary context and the reader's world. How do the prophets perceive the writings of Moses? How does the writer of Hebrews make sense of the Old Testament? How does Clement in his second epistle, which may be the earliest sermon known outside the New Testament, adapt verses from Isaiah and also ones from the Gospels? Or what about Luther's bold use of Romans 1:17? How does Jonathan Edwards allude to Genesis 19? Who can forget Martin Luther King Jr.'s "I Have a Dream" speech and his appropriation of Amos 5:24: "No, no, we are not satisfied, and we will not be satisfied until 'justice rolls down like waters, and righteousness like a mighty stream'"? How does a preacher in your local church today apply the words of Hosea in a meaningful and life-transforming way?

WHAT IS PRIME IN GOD'S MIND, AND HOW IS THAT EXPRESSED TO A GIVEN GENERATION IN THE UNITS OF THOUGHT THROUGHOUT THE BIBLE?

Answering those questions is what Kerux authors do. Based on the popular "big idea" preaching model, Kerux commentaries uniquely combine the insights of experienced Bible exegetes (trained in interpretation) and homileticians (trained in preaching). Their collaboration provides for every Bible book:

- A detailed introduction and outline
- A summary of all preaching sections with their primary exegetical, theological, and preaching ideas
- Preaching pointers that join the original context with the contemporary one
- Insights from the Hebrew and Greek text
- A thorough exposition of the text
- Sidebars of pertinent information for further background
- Appropriate charts and photographs
- A theological focus to passages

- A contemporary big idea for every preaching unit
- Present-day meaning, validity, and application of a main idea
- Creative presentations for each primary idea
- Key questions about the text for study groups

Many thanks to Jim Weaver, Kregel's former acquisitions editor, who conceived of this commentary series and further developed it with the team of Jeffrey D. Arthurs, Robert B. Chisholm, David M. Howard Jr., Darrell L. Bock, Roy E. Ciampa, and Michael J. Wilkins. We also recognize with gratitude the significant contributions of Dennis Hillman, Fred Mabie, Paul Hillman, Herbert W. Bateman IV, and Shawn Vander Lugt who have been instrumental in the development of the series. Finally, gratitude is extended to the two authors for each Kerux volume; the outside reviewers, editors, and proofreaders; and Kregel staff who suggested numerous improvements.

—Kregel Publications

PREFACE TO MATTHEW

Anyone who has written a commentary knows they stand on the shoulders of their commentary partners. I wish to explain how I have done this commentary to try to make it useful to users beyond what I have written. I have tracked major commentaries on Matthew fairly carefully. In spots where I had to be brief, I have often noted the work of others where I am signaling either a more complete discussion (usually indicated by a discussion that is more than a page long) or the best discussion of the question from someone else. This means you can use my discussion as a starter and locator for other discussions if you wish to have more detail. A teacher's or preacher's time in preparation is precious, so I have structured things this way to help readers manage their own study and pursue their own interests.

I have used the charts section mostly to highlight cultural background and texts that show parallel thinking, especially in Jewish texts. These are often ignored or underappreciated. By highlighting their presence one can see how they help show the thinking of the ancient period. They also help to explain what I call "cultural scripts," shorthand ways to refer to important customs or understandings that the writer and reader appreciate because they share the culture. Bible citations are from the NET. Apocryphal citations are from the NRSV. Pseudepigraphical texts are from James Charlesworth's two-volume works (*Old Testament Pseudepigrapha*). Mishnah texts are from the Neusner edition but sometimes have the formatting stripped out for a shorter layout, something I have done with other texts as well on occasion. Nonbiblical Dead Sea Scrolls are either from the Wise, Abegg, and Cook volumes (*The Dead Sea Scrolls: A New Translation*) or, when it is clear where text breaks are, from the volumes of Parry, Tov, and Clements (*The Dead Sea Scrolls Reader*). Josephus is from the Whiston translation, which is not the best but is more widely available than others. Philo is from C. D. Yonge's translation. Apostolic fathers are from Michael Holmes's translation. The New Testament Apocrypha used Craig Evans's translation. In most cases abbreviations have been used for resources, but in a few cases where the work is less known, the title is spelled out.

—Darrell L. Bock

EXEGETICAL AUTHOR'S ACKNOWLEDGMENTS

To Mark Bailey, Brother in the Lord, Friend, Colleague, and Supervisor:
Special friends are a true gift from the Lord. I wish you well in your retirement and all the Lord's best. Thank you for years of faithful service.

I once again have to thank my colleagues at Dallas Theological Seminary and the Hendricks Center for the support that allows me time to work on projects like this. Their friendship and example inspire my own work and teach me much about our walk with God. Deep appreciation goes as well to Kregel, especially Herb Bateman for shepherding through the many formats Kerux has had while I worked on the commentary portion of the text. Thanks also goes to Shawn Vander Lugt and his team of editors for taking this work through its final paces and saving me in many places. I'd also like to pay tribute to Mark Bailey, whose service as president of Dallas Seminary for almost two decades served all of us so well. The volume is dedicated to him as a token of my appreciation for all of his work over these many years.

—Darrell L. Bock

PREACHING AUTHOR'S ACKNOWLEDGMENTS

To those who have played a pivotal role in my discipleship to Jesus

The call to discipleship is communal. Jesus invites us to follow him with others. We walk and learn together. We serve and grow together. Like Peter, Andrew, James, and John, my experience is similar. So many men and women have shaped me, but the following people have played a pivotal role.

My father brought the family to church after his conversion. I first heard the gospel and prayed a Sinner's Prayer during a worship service. He helped start this journey. Bev and Tom invited me into their home, brought me to youth group, and helped me personalize my faith in Jesus. In high school, my core group of friends formed a weekly Bible study called The Young Disciples of Christ. During this phase, Jesus's call to vocational ministry became clear. At Grace College, David Plaster, Herb Bateman, and D. Brent Sandy instilled a love for Scripture. During a spiritual dry spell, Dr. Plaster encouraged me, "Any time you get stuck in your faith, read the Gospels." I've clung to that advice for twenty years. During my two years in Phoenix, Ed Waken taught me to love people, serve faithfully, and talk about Jesus freely. His saying, "Strong disciples make strong churches," still rings true. Steve Porter guided my doctoral studies on discipleship, giving language to our rich, multifaceted relationship with Jesus. For the past eighteen years, my church family at Leesburg Grace has been a great cloud of witnesses. They regularly hear me say, "The story of Jesus is happening here: Let's share it!" Finally, my wife Liz and children (Claire, Margot, and Sensi) are my inner circle. Of all my traveling companions, they show me the most grace, provide the most joy, and give the most love.

In Christ,
Timothy D. Sprankle

OVERVIEW OF ALL PREACHING PASSAGES

Matthew 1:1–25

EXEGETICAL IDEA
Through the announced birth of Jesus through a virgin, God executed a promised divine plan to bring a savior and deliverer from sin who is God with us.

THEOLOGICAL FOCUS
God's long-standing promise to the world through Abraham and David comes in a virgin-born Jesus.

PREACHING IDEA
God's family plans are perfectly conceived.

PREACHING POINTERS
Matthew opens his biography of Jesus with an impressive lineage of the Savior and Messiah. A number of false messiahs appeared in Judea during the mid-60s A.D., who were a challenge to believers in Judea as well as those near the homeland of Jesus. The Roman emperor was also presented as the ultimate savior. Thus, there was the need to establish Jesus as qualified to be Israel's Messiah and fit the hope of Jewish promise. Matthew traces Jesus's roots through a list that includes Jewish household names (Zerubbabel, David, and Abraham), surprising characters (Rahab, Ruth, and Tamar), and lesser-known figures from the postexilic period. The inclusions, omissions, and structure of Matthew's genealogy hinted to his Jewish audience that God's covenantal promises to Abraham and David had reached a climax. Furthermore, God's plan had transgressed borders; he was reaching all the nations with a message of salvation embodied in the miraculous birth of Jesus. Matthew also makes it clear that the promise extended to both men and women. For the original readers near Jesus's homeland, Matthew's introduction inspired hope and assurance in God's sweeping plan of salvation.

Today people in the Western world have rediscovered an interest in family roots. The rise of genetic testing and online ancestry programs has sent people digging into their backgrounds. Lineage and places of origin are important to many Americans. People realize their past shapes their future. Blood disease may run in the family. Chemical abuse or mental illness may mark our forefathers. Or perhaps, a generational chain of doctors, lawyers, or police officers may narrow our career path. Exploring one's background often reveals happy surprises, family secrets, and signs of God's fingerprint in shaping a person. This passage assures us that in Jesus God's family plans are perfectly conceived.

Matthew 2:1–23

EXEGETICAL IDEA

After Gentiles worshiped the newborn king, God used dreams to direct the magi away from Herod and Joseph to take the child to Egypt to protect him.

THEOLOGICAL FOCUS

Through a look at Scripture and divinely directed acts (here: stars and dreams), believers see God's protective and providential directions emerge for those who obey.

PREACHING IDEA

Follow God's directions to enlist his protection.

PREACHING POINTERS

Matthew introduces new characters into the birth narrative of Jesus. Their respective responses to the child represent typical reactions to Jesus throughout the gospel. The magi traveled long and far to honor the child. They followed a star, searched the Scriptures, and heeded a dream, each as a demonstration of Gentile sensitivity to God's plans. Herod and the Jewish leaders opposed God's plans. Tragically, Herod conspired against God, killing Jewish children to eradicate rivals to his throne. Fortunately, God's plans cannot be thwarted. God used Scriptures and stars, angels and dreams, foreigners and faithful servants like Joseph to keep his plan on track. For Matthew's original readers, this narrative affirmed God's protective plan and prompted them to evaluate their response to Jesus.

Today a rising tide of opposition faces God and his people. In large sections of the global South and East, rival religions and government officials oppose the church. In the West, New Atheists and secular lobbyists attack Christian institutions, deeming their practices outdated and oppressive. Cancel culture and the threat of "hate crimes" against churches for their sexual ethic are recent examples. Even the swell of apathetic, religious sentiment infecting the culture pushes back against the uniqueness of Jesus, sovereignty of God, and authority of Scripture. This opposition toward God's plan and people is nothing new. Jesus has dodged rivals since his infancy. The church has faced enemies since its inception. God's plan prevails. This passage teaches us to follow God's directions to enlist his protection.

Matthew 3:1–12

EXEGETICAL IDEA

Fulfilling Scripture and in preparation for the kingdom, John the Baptist offered a baptism for forgiveness of sins, warned the Jewish leaders to flee God's coming wrath, and announced one to come who would bring the Spirit and judgment.

THEOLOGICAL FOCUS

John the Baptist's ministry points to an accountability before God that all people have, while promising them forgiveness and enablement should they respond to the one to come.

PREACHING IDEA
Heed voices that invite us back into God's favor.

PREACHING POINTERS
Matthew introduces John the Baptist, a critical character in the announcement of God's coming kingdom through Jesus. His bold proclamation, ascetic appearance, remote location, and large following depict him as a remarkable figure. More importantly, Matthew identifies John as a fulfillment of the messenger promised in Isaiah 40. John's message pointed away from himself to a stronger one who would come but not be universally accepted. The Baptist's message reverberated with messianic hope and eschatological judgment. He called Jewish people to repent, and promised God's forgiveness in return. He warned them that their Jewish heritage (i.e., children of Abraham) and religious affiliation (e.g., Pharisee, Sadducee) did not exempt them from God's wrath. For the original audience, John's voice served as a wakeup call: "Turn your hearts back to God; good things are coming."

Today's church needs a voice like John's, calling us to turn back to God. We need a renewed vision of God's inbreaking kingdom. Sadly, the evangelical church in the West has settled for a blend of pop religion and politics. We like preaching that serves as a pick-me-up and policies that protect our "moral majority." In many ways, our thinking mirrors that of the Jewish people in John the Baptist's day. We boast about doctrinal and denominational purity like they did about birthright. Likewise, we preach behavior modification rather than heart change. When we ignore voices like John's—strong, visionary, incisive, and Christocentric—we reject God's invitation to a life flooded with forgiveness and spiritual power. This passage grabs our ear, teaching us to heed voices that invite us back into God's favor.

Matthew 3:13–17

EXEGETICAL IDEA
John the Baptist baptized the divinely endorsed beloved Son Jesus, who himself accepted baptism to affirm John's eschatological message and identify with Israel's need.

THEOLOGICAL FOCUS
The divine endorsement of Jesus as King and Servant points to the need to respond to him, as God calls him to begin his work.

PREACHING IDEA
The divine voice deserves the last word on Jesus.

PREACHING POINTERS
Jesus traveled a significant distance to meet John the Baptist in the wilderness. John saw in Jesus the stronger one to come and attempted to reverse roles with him. Jesus would not be dissuaded. He came to identify with the sinful people of Israel, while maintaining a vision of righteousness—the ethic of the inbreaking kingdom. In the end, he received John's support and

a divine endorsement when the Father spoke, rent the heavens, and sent the Spirit to enable him. This powerful, intimate scene launched Jesus into his career as God's long-awaited, beloved, and well-pleasing Son and Servant.

Opinions about Jesus are as numerous as people who voice them. Some view Jesus as a magician, political subverter, kindly moralist, best friend, merely a prophet like others, or a memorable rabbi. Others view Jesus as a hippie, liberal, or lunatic. Historians undertake "quests" to discover the real Jesus of history. Theologians distill Jesus into doctrinal statements. Church councils debate the nature of Jesus. Children learn from an early age that Jesus is a prophet, priest, and king. These voices say more about those who speak than about Jesus himself. The authoritative voice, the last word, the ultimate claim about Jesus belongs to his Father—who loved him, endorsed him, and enabled him with his Spirit. The divine voice deserves the last word on Jesus.

Matthew 4:1–11

EXEGETICAL IDEA

Jesus's faithfulness and commitment to God rebuffed Satan's temptations, showing Jesus's qualifications to represent humanity because he succeeded where Adam and Israel had failed.

THEOLOGICAL FOCUS

Jesus's successful overcoming of temptation means he can reverse what Adam did and qualifies him to represent all humanity.

PREACHING IDEA

Temptation is a proving ground for our love of God.

PREACHING POINTERS

On the heels of his baptism—a scene depicting his solidarity with Israel and divine endorsement—Jesus followed the Spirit's lead into the wilderness for forty days. Known as a place of testing and temptation, Jesus faced an ancient enemy of God and his people: the devil, Satan. A dramatic scene unfolded, where the devil dangled before Jesus three tests to reject God's provision, protection, and delegated power. In each instance, Jesus affirmed the Hebrew Scriptures and modeled loyalty to God. The original audience would have heard echoes of Eden and the exodus, where Adam fell prey to the devil's original test and Israel doubted God's passage into the promised land. Jesus stood above his forerunners, embodying for Israel and all humankind loyal, flawless love for God.

Temptation did not cease with Jesus's victory in the wilderness. His followers from every age have faced various tests. Today temptations lure us to doubt God, distrust his provision, disobey his commands, and give in to timeless deceptions. The diabolical voice whispers, "Do it. You deserve it. Go get what God won't give." Married couples are tempted to reject their vows, divorce, and kindle new romances with other partners. Employees are tempted to take credit for work ideas they borrowed from others or claim hours they never worked.

Politicians are tempted to use their power to manipulate others and maintain their platforms. Businesspeople are tempted to cut ethical corners or take advantage of others for the sake of the bottom line. All of us risk making other people invisible because they are not like us. In a global pandemic, all people with access to grocery stores are tempted to stockpile to ensure their maximum comfort. Fortunately, whenever we resist these temptations, we reaffirm our trust in God. In fact, this passage indicates temptation is a proving ground for our love of God.

Matthew 4:12–25

EXEGETICAL IDEA

As Jesus drew crowds through powerful acts and teaching, the early Galilean ministry represented light that called for repentance as the kingdom of heaven came near, inviting disciples to follow him as a top priority.

THEOLOGICAL IDEA

To embrace Jesus is to turn to the kingdom of heaven and follow him as a life priority.

PREACHING IDEA

Priorities change when Jesus calls your name.

PREACHING POINTERS

After successfully overcoming Satan's temptation, Jesus emerged in public life as a light. His words and deeds reveal the powerful nature of God's inbreaking kingdom. He healed the sick, cast out demons, and called people to leave their sinful ways and embrace God's good news. The message of God's kingdom would have appealed to Matthew's audience. Facing political turmoil in their time and hearing from supposed messianic figures, the evidence of Jesus's powerful word and deed would have been persuasive. In the call of the first followers, the original audience would have heard a timely invitation to realign their priorities and commit themselves to Christ Jesus.

For too many of us, our operating system is governed by a single priority: self. Our personal wants and needs easily become our own greatest priority. We live by what feels good, eases pain, expands comfort, offers security, and advances popularity. Even altruistic priorities—serving the needy, loving our families, giving to charity, fighting injustice—can mask our greatest priority of serving self and seeking praise. Fortunately, Jesus modeled a life of self-denying, self-giving, self-sacrificial service. And he invited men and women to join him as students in his school of kingdom priorities. This sermon teaches that priorities change when Jesus calls your name.

Matthew 5:1–12

EXEGETICAL IDEA

Jesus shared nine virtues of kingdom participants and declared them blessed with great kingdom reward, both now and in the future.

THEOLOGICAL FOCUS

Jesus encourages his disciples by assuring them of their blessing and rich reward for reflecting the virtues of those who follow him in a way that honors God.

PREACHING IDEA

Rest assured: God rewards those who reflect his character.

PREACHING POINTERS

Jesus's first discourse, the renowned Sermon on the Mount, introduced his disciples to the virtues of living as kingdom citizens. Jesus's ethic contrasted with the world's by prizing poverty, humility, mercy, and peace. Tied to this ninefold ethic was the promise of reward from God, who guaranteed entrance, sustenance, and satisfaction in the kingdom; each virtue is punctuated by the memorable word "blessed." For Matthew's audience, this assurance of blessing would have come as welcome news. Allegiance to Jesus in an age where messianic speculation, resistance to Rome, and persecution for believers was rising would have been challenging. The Beatitudes offered a word of assurance to stay the course, develop character, and trust Jesus's kingdom claims.

Followers of Jesus in our day need assurance and resolve to live ethically. The world provides an ever-shifting moral target. It praises sexual expression while mocking sexual purity. It encourages relentless consumption while vilifying environmental exploitation. It leverages public shame to destroy careers and cancel churches while muttering Jesus's prohibition against judgment. It debates justice in ways that do not bring us closer to possessing it or remove the lack of equity in an unjust world. In this vortex of confusing and unforgiving ethics, Christ-followers can feel guarded, threatened, or tempted to adopt worldly character to blend in. Jesus's first words in his famed sermon address these feelings and inspire confidence. This message implores us to rest assured, God rewards those who reflect his character.

Matthew 5:13–20

EXEGETICAL IDEA

As salt and light, disciples were to season the world with a righteousness that shone forth, fulfilled the ethical intent of the law, and reflected the kingdom of God.

THEOLOGICAL FOCUS

The disciple's call is to live in a way that shows the character of God, drawing people to the Father.

PREACHING IDEA

Be a force for good, to show the heart of God.

PREACHING POINTERS

Jesus intended his disciples to be the greatest witness to the heavenly Father's character, integrity, and glory. He called them to shine God's goodness like a light. He called them to saturate the world with moral excellence. He implored his followers to go beneath the surface of the law, beyond external compliance, to its heart for justice, mercy, and humility. For Matthew's audience, this mission came at a critical time, warning those pulled toward extremes of antinomianism and staunch legalism. He reminded them of the Messiah's middle way of exceeding righteousness from the heart.

Today's church desperately needs a fresh hearing of Jesus's mission statement. Moral decay infects our age. Injustice casts a shadow over our society. However, legislation and moral teaching bring limited change. Greater change comes when followers of Jesus embrace his call to live as change agents. This passage forces today's disciples to inspect their own hearts, analyze their motives, and critique their behavior. Two timeless metaphors—salt and light—focus this passage on the disciple's duty to benefit the world by action, not bludgeon it by accusation. Simply put, this message teaches we should be a force for good, to show the heart of God.

Matthew 5:21–48

EXEGETICAL IDEA
Jesus's exposition of the law pointed to the heart, promoting healthy relationships with everyone, including enemies, and was not merely to be followed in an external way.

THEOLOLGICAL IDEA
True application of the law asks "What kind of righteousness does it seek?"—and then goes there.

PREACHING IDEA
Elaborate love goes above and beyond the law.[1]

PREACHING POINTERS
In the next portion of his Sermon, Jesus offers six case studies for living the heart of the law. His disciples must heed his authoritative voice, not simply subscribe to the teachings and traditions of his day. Matthew's audience would have been familiar with the Mosaic law. They would have heard scribal and Pharisaical interpretations of it. Murder, adultery, and false testimony were known prohibitions. Divorce and retaliation were commonly debated topics. Love for neighbor was a timeless ethic. Jesus did not counter them as much as he elaborated on them, showing how every ethical encounter is an opportunity for love. For Matthew's audience, this message both established Jesus's authority as a superior teacher and clarified the particulars of living the heart of the law.

Religion always attracts moralists and legalists. People love to know the letter of the law so they can recite it. They love to know the line that marks sin from acceptable behavior so they can toe it. Few want to get away with murder, but many are willing to hold a grudge. The depraved heart looks for loopholes and exceptions in the law, so it can make the rules work in its favor,

1 Pennington (2007, 40) uses similar prepositions to describe the already–not yet ethic of the Sermon on the Mount: "Biblical virtue ethics is also 'from above' (based on divine revelation) and 'from beyond' (based on the hope of the coming eschaton)."

rather than work out its salvation with fear and trembling. We put in just enough hours at work to merit our paycheck. We study just enough for a passing grade. We tell enough of the story to make it "truthy." We spend enough time with our family, avoiding glaring sins, so they cannot accuse infidelity. Meanwhile, we miss the law's ultimate aim: love of God and neighbor. This passage illustrates how elaborate love goes above and beyond the law.

Matthew 6:1–18

EXEGETICAL IDEA

Jesus urged that alms, prayer, and fasting be directed sincerely to the Father with a spirit of dependence and trust rather than before people.

THEOLOGICAL FOCUS

Jesus seeks a sincere integrity to the worship we perform, offered to and for God alone.

PREACHING IDEA

Sincere devotion avoids the spotlight.

PREACHING POINTERS

Jesus did not make strong distinctions between public and private life. Elaborate love and sincere devotion were genuine marks of faith for his disciples in every sphere of life. Jesus wanted his followers to show the same earnestness in their private giving, praying, and fasting as they did in their public displays of forgiveness, purity, fidelity, honesty, and mercy. His rationale was simple: the heavenly Father sees all and rewards sincerity. For Matthew's audience, the social pressure to perform religious acts for public honor had not abated. In fact, rising pressure to rally against Rome may have further stirred Jewish fervor. Matthew reminded them to practice piety for God alone.

"Authenticity" is a buzzword in our age. Its counterparts—genuine, real, sincere—promote a similar virtue. The world wants us to "be ourselves" without filters, to practice full-blown self-expression; social media platforms make it simple. We post staged family moments on Facebook. We capture shameless confessions on Snapchat. We unleash our inner performer for our growing TikTok audience. The cellphone is a mobile spotlight; we are the stars. Rewards come in comments, likes, shares, and followers. Sadly, shameless self-expression can creep into our religious performance. We can give, pray, serve, and sacrifice so the world (or our parents and pastors) takes notice. Such a motive is, in fact, *in*authentic. Piety for public approval misses the point. Giving, praying, and fasting please God. This sermon reminds us that sincere devotion avoids the spotlight.

Matthew 6:19–34

EXEGETICAL IDEA

Jesus urged seeking heavenly treasure by being careful about what we see and think, avoiding the pursuit of material things over God, and trusting God to give us what we need so we avoid worrying in this life.

THEOLOGICAL FOCUS
The disciple is to live a disciplined life, focused on the inbreaking kingdom and honoring and trusting God.

PREACHING IDEA
Entrust your overwhelming cares to God's overwhelming care.

PREACHING POINTERS
As Jesus's masterful sermon continued, he moved from the disciples' private devotion to God's daily provision. More people in Jesus's day were overwhelmed by worry than wealth. Goods were limited; jealousy and greed were common. Thus, Jesus taught the need to keep one's eye and heart pure by focusing more on God's provision than their stockpile of supplies. For Matthew's audience, the rising pressures of persecution surfaced the threat of suffering and material loss. They likely needed to double down on their trust in God's provision and inbreaking kingdom.

Today consumer options abound in the West. How we shop, where we eat, what we wear, and how we customize our products to express our individuality and fit our mood seems endless. Furthermore, diverse currency and credit options remove barriers for buying homes, cars, and knee replacements. Ironically, our material prosperity has not alleviated our worries. In fact, anxiety is epidemic. We worry about the safety of our homes. We worry about the legitimacy of our warranties. We worry about the purity of our water and additives in our meat. We worry about the style of our clothes, smoothness of our skin, and future of our children. Our cares cascade into full-blown panic. This message implores us to entrust our overwhelming cares to God's overwhelming care.

Matthew 7:1–12

EXEGETICAL IDEA
Jesus urged treating others with prayerful love and an absence of hypocritical judgment—by being honest about our own faults before helping others, regarding what is holy with care, asking for good things from a gracious God, and treating others as we wish to be treated.

THEOLOGICAL FOCUS
Treating others sensitively and seeing ourselves realistically reflects our calling and requires being spiritually discerning.

PREACHING IDEA
Train your eyes to empathize through honest self-reflection.

PREACHING POINTERS
As Jesus wrapped up the core section of the Sermon on the Mount, he closed with a series of maxims about relating to others and God. Jesus called for honesty and self-reflection rather than launching a social campaign for moral reform. Throughout the sermon, the Master

Teacher reminded his disciples of the heart of the law—sincere devotion to God and elaborate love for others—as well as the heavenly Father's intimate attention to their needs. He affirmed their blessed status and missionary role in God's inbreaking kingdom. The cumulative effect of these themes should produce humility, discernment, and prayerfulness. Matthew's audience may have been prone to criticizing others, showing a lack of discretion about holy matters, and being presumptuous about God's provision due to their religious standing. Jesus's teaching provided an opportunity for earnest self-reflection.

In today's post-Christian culture, Jesus's prohibition against judgment rules the day. "Do not judge" is the banner under which people flaunt their sexual choices, justify consumer habits, defend divorce, allow for abortion, endorse vulgar speech, and excuse addictive behavior. It is claimed that judgment displays rank ignorance of cultural and chemical factors that cause people to do what they do; everyone has a story, reason, or excuse for their decisions. Moreover, judgment threatens their personal pursuit of happiness, which is the aim of life in the secular age. Although these claims may be overstated, they do underscore complex and unseen factors that feed into another person's actions. Properly understood, Jesus's call to inspect oneself before casting stones (or pearls) trains our eyes to gaze inward before glaring outward. In fact, this message compels us to train our eyes to empathize through honest self-reflection.

Matthew 7:13–29

EXEGETICAL IDEA
Jesus underscored the importance and consequences of a proper response to his message and authority by speaking of the narrow gate, fruit on the tree, knowing others, and the house built on a good or bad foundation.

THEOLOGICAL FOCUS
Responding by doing what Jesus says leads to fruit and wisdom in life.

PREACHING IDEA
Following Jesus leads to true flourishing.

PREACHING POINTERS
Jesus taught among many types of teachers in his day. Other rabbis trained their disciples. Groups of scribes, Pharisees, and elders instructed the Jewish populace. Even itinerant teachers stirred up crowds. A teacher's credibility, however, was not determined by the size of their audience but the soundness of their words. Matthew reminded his original audience of Jesus's profound wisdom. His vivid imagery—two gates, two trees, and two foundations—grips the imagination. The conclusion to the sermon gave a final call to its hearers to inspect their hearts and reject messianic pretenders, which was especially relevant for those facing persecution and political pressures in Matthew's day. Only Jesus's words offered wisdom for the day and confidence for the coming day of judgment.

There is no shortage of advice in our information age. It buzzes from blogs and social media sites. TV screens and newspaper columns shout it. People post their opinions, offer self-help insights, provide motivational tips, and share DIY instructions for projects ranging from "build your own changing table" to "how to bake eggplant lasagna." Anyone can become an expert these days; all they need to do is drive enough traffic to their website. Unfortunately, the wisdom of our age is not only self-focused but also fleeting. Our "best life now" may get worse tomorrow. Fortunately, Jesus's teaching has endured the ages and prepares us for eternity. We should put it to work. This message reminds us that following Jesus leads to true flourishing.

Matthew 8:1–22

EXEGETICAL IDEA

Jesus's healings and exorcisms showed his ability to cleanse and the value of faith in the fulfillment of the promise to bear our infirmities. This section highlights why discipleship under pressure is a priority.

THEOLOGICAL FOCUS

Jesus's miracles reveal his authority and lay a basis for a total faith commitment to the ways of God in discipleship.

PREACHING IDEA

Forget your comforts and follow Christ.

PREACHING POINTERS

On the heels of the Sermon on the Mount, Jesus descended the hill and began to serve. His words did not stand alone but came with deeds to show what he meant. Not only was Jesus a master teacher but also a burden-bearer and miracle worker. Matthew wove together three miracles—cleansing a leper, healing a centurion's servant, and ridding Peter's mother-in-law of a fever—that signaled Jesus's authority. Moreover, Jesus's powerful and compassionate work affected all types of people. Matthew's audience would have taken note of the inclusive nature of the Son of Man's ministry. Likewise, they would have heard the high demands Jesus placed on would-be disciples. Due to increasing social pressures in Matthew's day, these statements on the cost of discipleship were timely.

Today the cost of discipleship remains steep. In many parts of the world, the church remains underground, not afforded the comforts of public gatherings or personal confessions of faith. Even in the United States, the aggressive push of secularism and "safe places" has made it more difficult for Christians to share their convictions without facing repercussions, like getting "canceled" or publicly shamed. Followers of Jesus are no longer afforded the comforts from the days when they constituted the majority. This, however, may be a blessing in disguise. Seeking and securing comforts easily becomes selfish. Showing compassion can be costly. In fact, Jesus modeled compassion to those needing spiritual and physical comforts regardless of their social status. We should do the same. This passage encourages us to forget our comforts and follow Christ.

Matthew 8:23–9:17

EXEGETICAL IDEA

Jesus's calming of the storm, the exorcism of the Gadarene demoniac, and the healing of the paralytic showed the fulfillment of his calling to provide forgiveness, although many would not embrace it despite the evidence God gave through him.

THEOLOGICAL FOCUS

As Jesus provides evidence that God is at work through him, people are forced with a choice to accept or reject him.

PREACHING IDEA

Let the evidence of Jesus's actions address your inner skeptic.

PREACHING POINTERS

The mighty works of Jesus begin to pile up in the next section. Matthew linked three miracles together to showcase the scope of Jesus's power and recipients of his healing touch. He stopped a storm and awed his disciples. He cast out demons and unnerved pig farmers. He forgave a paralytic and fixed his legs, which aggravated scribes. Moreover, Jesus called a despised tax collector to discipleship and dined with his unsavory friends, leading to a final conflict about his choice of company and eating habits. The original audience would have felt the tension Jesus created by the evidence of his powerful works and perplexing words. Matthew provided the evidence for them to examine and respond with faith toward this merciful, miracle-working Son of Man.

In our secular age, many people treat miracles as ancient folklore. They view Jesus's healings, exorcisms, and command of nature as unscientific accounts of preliterate cultures. While a degree of chronological snobbery exists, these people cannot be blamed. We are trained to be skeptics (Lewis 1963 is a solid discussion of miracles; Keener 2012). We know marketing promises more than any product can offer. We know politicians play politics. We know history exalts winners, silences losers, and tells only one side of the story. We know "innocent until proven guilty" does not apply equally to all ethnicities. Finally, we know no truth is absolute (except for this one), so unless it feels right or the evidence compels us, we are under no obligation to believe. In the face of such uncertainty, this passage admonishes us to let the evidence of Jesus's actions address our inner skeptic.

Matthew 9:18–38

EXEGETICAL IDEA

Jesus's works of healing as Son of David brought the Pharisees' negative reaction that he healed by demonic power, even as Jesus issued a call to pray for more harvest laborers.

THEOLOGICAL FOCUS

Jesus's show of kingdom authority often meets with opposition, even as he asks for prayer for more laborers.

PREACHING IDEA
Jesus's compassion deserves a positive reaction.

PREACHING POINTERS
Jesus continued to display miraculous powers in the next passage. For the third time, Matthew bundled a triad of miracles (one is a double miracle), followed by a short teaching. Though his description is brief, the narrative showcases Jesus's compassion and rising fame. He healed an unclean woman, resuscitated a girl, restored sight to two blind men, and cast out a demon. Jesus did not discriminate in exercising his power; however, he did manifest caution, aware that too much attention to his charismatic gifts might incite mixed reactions. The Pharisees validated this concern; their hard hearts prohibited them from holding a positive view of Jesus. Instead, they accused him of colluding with the prince of demons. Matthew wanted his audience to consider Jesus's compassion and respond positively. He wanted them to prayerfully join Jesus the Messiah in proclaiming God's kingdom.

The compassion of Jesus remains a compelling characteristic in our day. It is a heartfelt, measured response toward others as he sees their suffering. Our compassion often discriminates and easily burns out. On one hand, group polarization has hardened us. We hesitate to cross political, religious, gender, or racial lines; we do not want to be polluted by their propaganda. Compassion is too soft a word for our polarized world, so it meets with a worldly skepticism. Nevertheless, it is a virtue Jesus valued. On the other hand, the constant stream of sad stories and suffering fatigues us. We see images and read stories of hurricane destruction, Afghan refugees, race riots, lost jobs, dead pets, and loneliness. Compassion is too great a need for our groaning world. Fortunately, what we lack in compassion, Jesus fully embodies. This passage reminds us that Jesus's compassion deserves a positive reaction.

Matthew 10:1–11:1

EXEGETICAL IDEA
As Jesus called his disciples to trust in a priority mission for the kingdom to Israel, he predicted opposition alongside enablement from God, who knew what was taking place.

THEOLOGICAL FOCUS
God oversees the word-and-deed mission Jesus's disciples undertake even though there is opposition to it.

PREACHING IDEA
Go public and don't panic: God's got your back.

PREACHING POINTERS
Matthew recorded Jesus's second sermon, a summons to mission. Calling the twelve disciples by name, Jesus prepared them for entering villages and encountering fellow Israelites with news of the inbreaking kingdom of God. As with Jesus, wonderful works would validate their words. Like Jesus, they would face opposition—religious, political, and familial. To help his disciples overcome this opposition, Jesus promised the Spirit's empowerment and Father's

protection. For Matthew's audience, this message offered assurance of God's care in the face of rising political tensions. Moreover, the sermon served as a fresh summons to proclaim Jesus's kingdom message until his return.

Opposition toward Jesus and his message persists today. In numerous countries the church remains underground; persecution is aggressive and overt. In the West, animosity toward believers continues to rise. We are flagged for our political views, moral standards, and theological positions about gender, creation, and eternal judgment, to name a few. Moreover, faith in the West primarily remains a private matter. People may vote their beliefs at the polls or share them on social media, but rare is the follower of Jesus who deliberately, personally, and articulately shares his or her faith. Indeed, most disciples keep quiet, afraid they might sound pushy, awkward, hateful, or inarticulate in proclaiming Jesus. This passage confronts such fear head-on with a personal call to join Jesus's mission. He still says, "Go public and don't panic: God's got your back."

Matthew 11:2–30

EXEGETICAL IDEA
The special nature of the current time, shown by John's relationship to Jesus, made the rejection by Israel's cities an act worthy of judgment but also offered opportunity for spiritual rest to those who embraced Jesus.

THEOLOGICAL FOCUS
The way in which John the Baptist's ministry mirrors Jesus's and the new era's presence offers a choice between judgment and spiritual rest.

PREACHNG IDEA
Only Jesus can recharge our spiritual batteries.

PREACHING POINTERS
Spiritual giants and sinful cities have something in common: their response to Jesus is paramount to their future hope. John the Baptist, whom Jesus acknowledged as a spiritual giant, began to question his understanding of Jesus during his imprisonment. His initial fervor waned as Jesus failed to meet his expectations of Messiah. Jesus sent word through John's disciples that God indeed was doing something new through him. The cities of Chorazin and Bethsaida took John's uncertainty a step further by rejecting Jesus and sealing their condemnation. On the other hand, children depicted those who received Jesus's embrace. They embodied the trust and reliance desired of disciples who take up Jesus on his offer of rest. For Matthew's original audience, this section continued to reveal Jesus's nature and mission, as well as the benefits of embracing him. To those burdened by sin, self-reliance, and religious duty, he would give lasting relief.

Life wears us down. It is fast-paced with constant inputs and endless obligations. Media and entertainment mask our problem. Multitasking, time management, and medication only take us so far. We need more than sleep and mindfulness techniques. Our souls need rest. Fortunately, Jesus's invitation to rest remains available to those willing to embrace him. Unfortunately, this is more difficult than it may seem. Our doubts keep Jesus at a distance. Our sin pushes him away. The lack of embrace leads to languishing energy. This sermon reminds us that only Jesus can recharge our spiritual batteries.

Matthew 12:1–21

EXEGETICAL IDEA
Jesus's response to Sabbath controversies, including acts of healing, showed him to be the promised Servant and Lord of the Sabbath, despite the objections of some.

THEOLOGICAL FOCUS
Jesus shows himself to be Lord of the Sabbath and the fulfillment of a long-awaited promise.

PREACHING IDEA
Serving others matters more than saving time.

PREACHING POINTERS
Controversy with the Pharisees continued to escalate. In consecutive scenes, Jesus tested conventional teaching about the Sabbath. First, he allowed his hungry disciples to graze on the Sabbath, defended them against accusation, and declared himself Lord of the Sabbath. Second, he healed a man in the synagogue with a hand deformity, appealed to rabbinic logic, and made a case for doing good on the Sabbath. For his original readers, Matthew linked these stories to Isaiah's portrait of the Suffering Servant. He described Jesus as the prophetic embodiment of these ancient promises. Matthew presented Jesus as Suffering Servant and Lord of Sabbath, granting him authority to subvert traditional Sabbath practice for the good of others.

Time is our greatest asset in the age of efficiency. Although we have equal amounts of it, the best of us makes the most of our time. We don't want to waste time or lose it. We're willing to bank time or borrow it. Saving time is a virtue. We hallow it, hedge it, and hate to get interrupted or delayed. Consider the collective sigh at the airport when they announce your flight will depart an hour late! Our protectiveness of time parallels the Pharisaic practice of Sabbath, which was riddled with restrictions. Time is a gift. It should free us to feast, enjoy fellowship, and serve others. Knowing Jesus is the master of time means we are not enslaved by it. This sermon reminds us that serving others matters more than saving time.

Matthew 12:22–50

EXEGETICAL IDEA
In the face of choices about Jesus and the good, Jesus urged his audience to see that his presence pointed to the kingdom's arrival and doing God's will.

THEOLOGICAL FOCUS
Jesus defends the nature of activity coming from him as coming from above and warns of the serious consequences of rejection.

PREACHING IDEA
Pick Jesus's side when people are polarized.

PREACHING POINTERS
Opposition against Jesus continued to intensify. Religious teachers contested his words and deeds at every turn. They accused him of collusion with the devil. They requested signs to authenticate his identity. Even his family members betrayed disbelief in his messianic identity. Jesus was a polarizing figure. Nonetheless, he did not entertain their criticisms but responded with wisdom and prophetic rebuke. He came to reveal God's kingdom and redeem God's people. Matthew's sequence of stories stressed the gravity of rejecting Jesus. His words and deeds spoke for themselves. The demand for additional evidence or desire to remain neutral were subtle forms of denying him.

Polarization plagues our age. Partisanship has turned politics into a circus. Churches and denominations have divided over sexual ethics, theological disagreements, and musical styles. Many friends and families have experienced the loss of relationship following miscommunication or a difference of opinion. In an age of polarization, neutral ground vanishes and people on opposite sides of an issue become enemies. Jesus and his disciples were not strangers to such strife. Their strong stance for God provoked strong opposition. Those who stand for Jesus today feel similar stress. Thus, this sermon reminds us to pick Jesus's side when people are polarized.

Matthew 13:1–23

EXEGETICAL IDEA
As one of the kingdom's mysteries revealed to the disciples, Jesus's parable of the soils showed the different reactions people have to the kingdom's offer and explained the obstacles that get in the way of responding.

THEOLOGICAL FOCUS
The parables extend Jesus's teaching to disciples who have access to the mysteries tied to God's kingdom with its call for receptive hearts.

PREACHING IDEA
When God speaks, be a good listener.

PREACHING POINTERS
After rebuking religious leaders and redefining family as those who did God's will, Jesus returned to the seashore for his third discourse. This teaching comprised a series of parables, explanations, and intimate instructions to his disciples about the dynamics of the kingdom of God. The first parable used agricultural imagery—seed, soils, and fruit—to illustrate good and bad responses to Jesus's message. When pressed by his disciples for clarity, Jesus quoted Isaiah 6:9–10 to explain his purpose of revealing truth to receptive people while concealing it from those with hardened hearts. Neutrality toward Jesus was not an option. For the original audience, Jesus's invitation to discipleship lingered, while judgment for rejecting him loomed ever larger.

The parables of Jesus have maintained their simplicity, mystery, and ability to captivate listeners. The parable of the soils is no exception; it presses modern hearers to reflect on their level of receptivity to Jesus. Despite our ready access to Bibles, commentaries, sermons, devotionals, Christian literature, and podcasts, we can be poor listeners. Rather than putting Jesus's teaching into practice, we doubt it, forget it, or get too busy to do what we hear him say. We must learn to fight deception, danger, and distractions that keep us from responding to Jesus's invitation to discipleship. This passage says, "When God speaks, be a good listener!"

Matthew 13:24–58

EXEGETICAL IDEA
Jesus's kingdom parables showed that the kingdom would start small and end up large, involved a judgment coming at the end, and was so precious that one should give up all to get it, all in a context where many still rejected him because of spiritual blindness.

THEOLOGICAL FOCUS
Despite all that the kingdom offers and the certainty that it will be universal in scope one day, people still reject the offer of God's grace.

PREACHING IDEA
Stay tuned: God's plan is full of surprises!

PREACHING POINTERS
Jesus's teaching on the mysteries of the kingdom continued. Following The parable of the soils and his private explanation to the disciples, Jesus rattled off six more stories, pictured through key metaphors: wheat and tares, mustard seed and leaven, treasure and pearl, and a massive catch of fish. The parables, ripe with Old Testament allusions, pointed to God's slow and steady growth of his kingdom. This work is inclusive and pervasive but not universally accepted because of the sacrifice involved in those who receive it. In fact, Jesus's subsequent rejection in Nazareth underscored for Matthew's audience the need to listen, watch, and respond to Jesus's subversive and surprising ministry as Son of God.

God continues to move in mysterious ways. He follows his own timeline. He works at his own pace. He includes unlikely people in his plan and leverages unfortunate events for our good. In short, God is full of surprises. Our task is to trust and stay attuned to his activity. We get to watch and see him work deathbed conversions. We get to watch and see him grow the underground church in Communist countries. We get to watch and see him turn selfish people into sacrificial disciples. And we get to watch and see him crush unresolved evil with unwavering justice. Someday his kingdom will indeed arrive in full. Thus, this sermon teaches us to stay tuned: God's plan is full of surprises.

Matthew 14:1–12

EXEGETICAL IDEA

Herod's execution of John the Baptist led him to think Jesus was working with powers from a raised John.

THEOLOGICAL FOCUS

Some are perplexed about who Jesus is and are struggling to explain his power.

PREACHING IDEA

Exposing corruption may leave you exposed.

PREACHING POINTERS

Matthew briefly shifts the spotlight from Jesus to John the Baptist. Both figures spoke against corrupted power, religious hypocrisy, and marital infidelity; their preaching packed a punch and impressed crowds. Thus, Jesus and John the Baptist became a threat to Herod Antipas, the political icon of the region. Matthew recounts the personal tension between John the Baptist and Herod Antipas stemming from the prophet's confrontation of the king about his unlawful marriage to his sister-in-law. Herod imprisoned John and eventually executed him at the public request of his stepdaughter at a party. For the original audience, both Herod's cowardice and corruption of power were obvious. Sadly, this served as one more story of how godless authority figures oppose godly truthtellers.

Corruption of power is a timeless problem. From persecutions by Herod the Great and Nero to papal abuses near the Reformation to mass murders by Stalin, Hitler, and Pol Pot to the modern misconduct of Watergate, Enron, #MeToo abusers, and rogue police officers, stories of corruption are readily available. These examples illustrate Lord Acton's famous insight: "Power corrupts. Absolute power corrupts absolutely." Sadly, anyone with power may go to great lengths to preserve it, including a spouse, parent, pastor, or boss. Worse, those who push back against abuse of power often suffer more abuse. This is no reason to remain silent in the face of injustice. It is, however, a reality check: exposing corruption may leave you exposed.

Matthew 14:13–36

EXEGETICAL IDEA

Jesus's miracles around the lake showed that he could prevail over nature as well as provide for and direct those who turn to him.

THEOLOGICAL FOCUS

Jesus's actions show the comprehensive scope of his power.

PREACHING IDEA

Whatever we need, Jesus can exceed it.

PREACHING POINTERS
Jesus's control over nature contrasted with Herod Antipas's political might. Herod used his power to hurt others; Jesus used his power to help others. Jesus fed five thousand hungry travelers in the wilderness, rescued his disciples in a sea storm, and healed many with illnesses. Whereas self-protection marked the way of Herod, compassion defined the way of Jesus. He expected his disciples both to experience his power and to extend it, as evident in their distribution of bread and Peter's walking on water. Matthew here continues to describe Jesus's unique identity (Bock 2020b). His original audience would have seen him as the Son of God and Messiah who met their needs.

Meeting our needs comes easy today. We satisfy our need for food at grocery stores, fast-food, and whatever snacks we can find in the kitchen. We satisfy our need for protection through savings accounts, insurance policies, and protective headgear. We satisfy our need for physical health through exercise, surgery, rest, and a healthy diet. Modern methods in food production, finances, and medicine can make us feel like masters of the natural world. This, of course, is an illusion. We can predict the weather but cannot control it. We can treat cancer but cannot prevent it. We can mass-produce food but cannot distribute it to the masses. We are limited in our ability to meet needs. Jesus is not. This passage shows that whatever we need, Jesus can exceed it.

Matthew 15:1–20

EXEGETICAL IDEA
In a dispute with the Pharisees and scribes over handwashing purity issues, Jesus charged his opponents with hypocrisy and taught that real defilement came out of the heart, when it perverted relationships.

THEOLOGICAL FOCUS
Jesus teaches that real defilement is not a matter of legal practice but of heart relations.

PREACHING IDEA
More laws don't lead to better lives.

PREACHING POINTERS
The Pharisees return to the scene. They arrive from Jerusalem, armed with a fresh point of contention: Jesus's disregard for purity laws. His response was equally charged, accusing them of elevating tradition over Torah and lip service over love. The offensive interchange led to a follow-up explanation with his confused disciples about getting to the root of impurity. The heart, not the hands, was the source of sin. Matthew's audience would have been familiar with oral customs added to the written Torah, as well as the weight they carried. Moreover, purity laws were a chief distinctive of the Jewish people. Jesus's dismissal of handwashing would have been a surprising claim of divine authority.

Too many people approach the Bible as a moral blueprint or game plan for their lives. They highlight the commands and underline the prohibitions, hoping that following the rules will lead to God's favor (or, at least, protect them from harm). This kind of thinking exposes an unhealthy view of the law as a guarantee of the good life. The logic extends: more laws mean a better life for more people. Families have household rules that build upon the Bible. (*Always pray before you eat!*) Churches develop corporate practices that build upon the Bible. (*Stand and sing three hymns. Then sit for a three-point sermon.*) Christian institutions design conduct policies that build upon the Bible. (*Students will refrain from dancing or drinking alcohol.*) And while these efforts may be well-meaning, too often our so-called biblical rules become more sacred than Scripture. Meanwhile, in an effort to manage behavior, we fail to address our defiled hearts. This passage reminds us that more laws don't lead to better lives.

Matthew 15:21–39

EXEGETICAL IDEA
The continuing and expanding compassion of Jesus in the face of opposition showed itself in his exorcism of the Canaanite woman's daughter, his healing of the crowds, and his feeding of the four thousand–plus.

THEOLOGICAL FOCUS
Jesus extends a ministry of God's compassion to new groups even in the face of opposition, while a woman shows an exemplary faith of humble non-entitlement.

PREACHING IDEA
Desperation draws Jesus to us.

PREACHING POINTERS
As opposition toward Jesus continued to escalate, he again withdrew. This pattern repeats throughout Matthew's gospel. In his current retreat, Jesus and his disciples first migrated to Gentile territory and encountered a desperate Canaanite woman with a demonized child. Her bold faith persuaded Jesus to heal her child. Jesus interacted with and responded to one who many would have regarded with disdain, even as the enemy—a Gentile woman. After returning to an unnamed mountain in Galilee, Jesus healed many needy people before feeding a hungry crowd. The scene pulses with Old Testament imagery foreshadowing the messianic age. For Matthew's readers, these stories and summaries narrated the deep compassion of Jesus and wide reach of his ministry. Rising opposition would not suppress his expansive love to desperate people.

There is no shortage of needy people today. Despite the promises of late modernity to overcome human suffering through education, economics, medication, and technology, global suffering remains. Child trafficking, dirty water, ethnic persecution, gender inequality, and war plague our world. Citizens of the United States are not exempt from suffering. Despite priding ourselves on liberty, equality, and opportunity, signs of desperation are evident: increasing rates of single-parent homes, obesity, drug abuse, and suicide, mental health crises, the vanishing middle class, rising crime and houseless populations in cities. We live in desperate times, and our diversions, distractions, and digital solutions cannot save us. Fortunately, this sermon reminds us that desperation draws Jesus to us.

Matthew 16:1–12

EXEGETICAL IDEA
The result of Jesus's confrontation with Jewish leaders was a call to recognize the divine vindication of him by the sign of Jonah and the destructive teaching of the leaders.

THEOLOGICAL FOCUS
Jesus contrasts what is at stake in the choice between the Jewish leaders and himself.

PREACHING IDEA
Sharpen your spiritual dullness.

PREACHING POINTERS
Matthew combines two conversations to stress the importance of thinking clearly about Jesus. First, the Sadducees and Pharisees requested a sign from Jesus. Their inquiry was a test. Jesus knew it and replied with a rebuke and a veiled reference to Jonah. Next, Jesus warned his disciples against letting the religious teachers corrupt their thinking. The disciples slowly caught Jesus's meaning because his reference to yeast provoked a tangential discussion about their lack of bread. He spoke harshly of their weak faith before explaining his comment about the Sadducees and Pharisees. For Matthew's original audience, these conversations stressed the importance of clear thinking about Jesus. His words and deeds provided sufficient evidence of his identity and authority.

Discernment is essential for navigating today's complex world. We have more access to more information than at any moment in history. However, the deluge of data has not made us more loving, wise, or faithful followers of Jesus. Sadly, our learning has led many away from Jesus. Consider the explosion of faith deconstruction stories—tales of people who have rejected historic Christianity and biblical authority for a feeble faith in a reconstructed Jesus or hollow faith in humanity. While every faith deconstruction story is different, each one is affected by the yeast of secular, postmodern thinking. Secular people may not search for signs, but they look for patterns, meaning, and coherence. Truthfully, they are looking for God—we all are—but spiritual dullness prevents them from admitting it. This sermon encourages us to sharpen our spiritual dullness.

Matthew 16:13–28

EXEGETICAL IDEA
Peter's confession of Jesus as the Christ led to the revelation of a suffering Messiah in whose way the disciples were to follow, even as the church shared in his prevailing authority.

THEOLOGICAL FOCUS
Jesus affirms the disciples' confession of Jesus as the Christ, and yet tells them that he—and they—will suffer.

PREACHING IDEA
A true confession comes at a cost.

PREACHING POINTERS
Jesus withdrew from Galilee with his disciples. This excursion allowed him space to question his disciples. He asked them about others' perceptions of him: others called him a prophet. He asked them about their own perception of him: Peter called him the Christ. This confession revealed Peter's understanding; however, his picture of Messiah was incomplete. Thus, Jesus filled in the detail about suffering, an experience each disciple would share by following in his footsteps. From the outset of his gospel, Matthew has provided hints of Jesus's messianic mission. This pericope clarifies that mission by predicting Jesus's suffering, death, and resurrection. The original audience would have heard Jesus's suffering as a summons to self-denial.

In the secular age, self-denial is a sin. Self-indulgence and self-expression are virtues. Digital media allows for nonstop streaming and shopping. The consumer is king! Social media allows for unlimited posting and scrolling of our overstated lives. Influencers are modern-day royalty! Sadly, secularism has dethroned Jesus and installed the self in his place. In this tragic reversal, Jesus exists to serve us and meet our desire for happiness. To resist self-rule, we must see Jesus for who he really is: Messiah, Son of David, and Suffering Servant. Jesus is not merely one religious great among others. He is unique in the purposes of God. This sermon reminds us that a true confession comes at a cost.

Matthew 17:1–20

EXEGETICAL IDEA
Jesus's preview of glory, the promise of suffering, and the failure of the disciples to heal the demon-possessed boy showed their need for a deeper faith as Jesus's destiny approached.

THEOLOGICAL FOCUS
The nature of who Jesus is requires disciples to pay closer attention to him and their faith.

PREACHING IDEA
Learning from Jesus is a lifelong journey.

PREACHING POINTERS
Matthew combines two stories, both featuring the disciples' immaturity. First, God revealed Jesus's identity in sight—radiant face, white robes, beside Moses and Elijah—and sound—"This is my beloved Son. Listen to him!" During the transfiguration, Peter made a foolish comment, proving he had more to learn about Jesus's uniqueness and redemptive mission. Second, Jesus encountered a distressed father who begged for help with his ailing son after the disciples had failed to heal him. Jesus rebuked the unbelieving crowd, the destructive demon, and his ineffective disciples. For the original audience, the combination of stories would have provoked an increase in faith by listening more closely to Jesus and trusting his power at work in them.

To be a disciple is to be a learner; it is implied in the name. This was true in Jesus's day and is true in ours. We all have room to grow in our knowledge. Not only do we have gaps in our knowledge, but we are also prone to cognitive bias and fallacious thinking. Our brains like shortcuts. Thus we oversimplify, stereotype, cherry-pick data, and outsource our research to the first page of results on any Google search. Perhaps these mental tricks work when we are trying to learn about the ten-day forecast, date for Easter in 2027, or filmography of Tom Hanks. However, when trying to learn about Jesus—a subject of inexhaustible and glorious nature—we are all novices. This sermon teaches that learning from Jesus is a lifelong journey.

Matthew 17:22–27

EXEGETICAL IDEA

After predicting his death and resurrection, Jesus explained and performed a miracle to show that although children of the kingdom were exempt from paying the temple tax, they would pay it.

THEOLOGICAL FOCUS

Despite being separated from the world, disciples will participate in earthly life.

PREACHING IDEA

Engage your world as long as you live in it.

PREACHING POINTERS

Jesus predicted his death and resurrection a third time. His fate in Jerusalem loomed, but not before another stop in Capernaum to give further instructions to his disciples. Back in his hometown, Peter encountered a tax collector, who inquired about Jesus's payment of the temple tax. This led to a private conversation between Jesus and his disciples about their heavenly status and earthly responsibilities. This tension between heavenly and earthly citizenship, as well as exemption and engagement, would have resonated with Matthew's audience. Although their Jewish roots and Christian loyalties pulled them in different directions, this passage reminded them that religious freedom does not give them the right to withdraw.

From the outset of Jesus's earthly ministry, his followers have had to manage tensions of their dual citizenship. As heavenly citizens, we pledge loyalty to Jesus alone, obey the laws of God, and find our identity in Christ, not in ethnic, gender, or socioeconomic markers. As earthly citizens, we pay taxes, volunteer in our towns, follow federal laws, and vote for national leaders. Unfortunately, managing these tensions has proven challenging. At times we have become overzealous in trying to bring the kingdom of God to earth through proselytizing indigenous people, legislating morality, or launching bloody crusades. On other occasions, Christians have withdrawn, crossing oceans to establish religious freedom or creating subcultures replete with schools, camps, clothes, candles, and media. Jesus's calling finds a happy medium between withdrawal and culture war—engagement. Indeed, this sermon implores us to engage our world as long as we live in it.

Matthew 18:1–20

EXEGETICAL IDEA
After proclaiming that humility and trust defined greatness, Jesus urged accountability for holiness by warning the one who causes stumbling, urging the regaining of the wayward believer, and introducing a process for dealing with and disciplining stubborn, sinful believers.

THEOLOGICAL FOCUS
Jesus teaches on community relations, balancing accountability with forgiveness.

PREACHING IDEA
Messy people need more structure to shape up.

PREACHING POINTERS
Matthew introduces Jesus's fourth discourse. In this block of teaching, Jesus focused on the role of humility, accountability, and forgiveness in shaping a healthy community. The discourse is packed with surprising imagery—millstones, dismemberment, and wandering sheep—as well as terms of endearment: children, little ones, brothers. Sadly, shaping a healthy community is no easy task. Obstacles to community abound. For Matthew's original audience, the discourse identified pride, stumbling blocks, and persistent sin. Such obstacles undermine the community's shared pursuit of holiness. Thus, Jesus spoke firmly about pursuing childlike faith, purging sin, and confronting persistent sinners with a deliberative process that would keep the community pure.

Jesus's message remains relevant for today's church. Christian communities are messy. At every level—from denominations to local churches to elder boards to small groups—we struggle with pride, stumbling blocks, and persistent sin. Look no further than the last few years of pastoral scandals, pandemic policies, or denominational spats about female leaders. Our dysfunction disrupts spiritual health. According to Jesus, the key to developing healthy communities is confronting our messes, not covering them up. Healthy communities create structures where candor is welcomed, feedback is expected, and accountability is ingrained. Although external structures cannot change a stubborn heart, they can mitigate messes in a spiritual community. This passage emphasizes that messy people need more structure to shape up.

Matthew 18:21–35

EXEGETICAL IDEA
God's forgiveness of us makes forgiving others imperative, something Jesus emphasized by calling for repeated forgiveness through a saying and a parable.

THEOLOGICAL FOCUS
The example of God's forgiveness of us should make us forgiving.

PREACHING IDEA
Messy people need more grace.

PREACHING POINTERS
Jesus's teaching about accountability provoked a question about forgiveness. Peter spoke for the group, asking if forgiving seven offenses extended enough grace. Jesus dwarfed Peter's number with an absurd figure: seventy-seven acts of forgiveness. Then he told a story about a Gentile king's absurd accounting as an illustration of God's abundant grace. The parable concluded with a warning: God's grace endured for those who extended it to others. For Matthew's original audience, the message of forgiveness replaced their right to revenge. Jesus repeatedly subverted the law of retribution with a call to mercy.

We live in a messy moment. Political parties are polarized. Voices on social media convey mean and hateful comments. Disagreement in the church leads to division. Even friends and family members quickly sever ties at misunderstandings and petty offenses. In this combative age, the need for mercy, grace, and forgiveness is undeniable. Sadly, people today are quicker to practice self-protection, social distancing, and ghosting than to show grace to someone who hurt them. We need a fresh hearing of Jesus's radical call to forgiveness. This sermon reminds us that messy people need more grace.

Matthew 19:1–12

EXEGETICAL IDEA
Jesus affirmed marriage as a lifelong bond between a man and a woman, while divorce was the result of hardness of heart and was only permissible for immorality. This led the disciples to say it might be better not to marry. Jesus acknowledged that only some were able to live that way.

THEOLOGICAL FOCUS
The design of marriage was to be a permanent bond before God between a man and woman, making divorce a violation of that promise.

PREACHING IDEA
Marriage maximalists strive for God's design.

PREACHING POINTERS
After concluding his fourth discourse, Jesus changed locations and entertained another challenge from the Pharisees. In their latest encounter, Jesus responded to questions about divorce. Two schools of thinking dominated the debate—a strict camp (i.e., Shammai) and a looser group (i.e., Hillel). The Pharisees wanted to trap Jesus by mapping his marital ethic into the controversial topic. However, Jesus transcended the debate by taking them back to God's original design for marriage in Genesis. Marriage had a good and beautiful beginning; it was a sacred bond, neither meant to be broken nor promised to all people. Matthew's original audience would be familiar with disagreements about marriage, divorce, and singleness. Moreover, they would again see Jesus's respect for God's law and exceeding righteousness on display.

Marriage ethics have tanked in the last half century and we have strayed from God's design. Upon closer scrutiny, Western sentiments toward marriage appear lukewarm, evident in delayed marriages, decreases in marriages, and increases in sexual expression and identity. We are marriage minimalists. Not only is God's standard for marriage countercultural, it is viewed by our age as outdated and oppressive. Sadly, our pursuit of sexual happiness at the expense of sexual holiness has led to brokenness within and outside of the church.[2] Being marriage minimalists is less beneficial than we think. This passage reminds us that marriage maximalists strive for God's design.

Matthew 19:13–30

EXEGETICAL IDEA
After noting that the kingdom belonged to people who are like children, and while asking that one leave all behind and follow him, Jesus observed that wealth often blocked one from coming to the kingdom and following him.

THEOLOGICAL FOCUS
Jesus discusses humility and then has a conversation with a rich man that shows how wealth can be an obstacle to the pursuit of God.

PREACHING IDEA
Wealth is worthless if it keeps us from Jesus.

PREACHING POINTERS
Jesus did not subscribe to the value system of his day. He preferred humility to honor, sacrifice to status, allegiance to wealth. These insights emerged from controversies with his disciples and a rich young man about eternal life. Misunderstandings about wealth, status, and God's favor were common among Matthew's readers. The original audience lived during a time when wealth was not widely distributed and often mistaken as a sign of divine reward. By extension, poverty was a punishment. Jesus's teaching countered these misconceptions and assured them of future reward for those who followed him.

In our day, wealth is power, privilege, and opportunity. Wealth can buy elections. Wealth provides purchasing power to secure a home in a safe cul-de-sac and lease a reliable car for daily commutes to work. Wealth can jump-start a child's academic and athletic journeys. Wealth is wonderful for those who have it. Except for this fact: one's wealth is never enough. As Rockefeller famously said, "A little bit more" would satisfy him. To paraphrase The Beatles: money can't buy you love. And most importantly, Jesus told us that eternal life has no sticker price. Thus, this sermon teaches that wealth is worthless if it keeps us from Jesus.

---

2 Those who have been through a divorce already know how painful it is and that it has consequences. It is usually others, who have not been through it, who need the help. A preacher will have to work hard to balance biblical standards and truth with pastoral awareness of the havoc divorces cause. Solid theological and exegetical treatments of this passage and of the issue in general are Blomberg 1990; Instone-Brewer, 2002; and Instone-Brewer 2003.

Matthew 20:1–16

EXEGETICAL IDEA
Jesus's parable of the hired workers showed God's grace by highlighting that all who come receive the same benefits no matter when they come—something all were to appreciate about grace.

THEOLOGICAL FOCUS
Grace gives the same access to God's benefits, no matter when we come to him.

PREACHING IDEA
There's plenty of grace for last place.

PREACHING POINTERS
Matthew recounted another parable of Jesus. The story of the generous manager is unique to Matthew. It described a manager hiring groups of laborers from dawn to the end of the day but paying them an equal wage. His generosity surprised the earliest group of workers, who expected a greater amount for their longer shift. Their reaction exposed a faulty understanding of grace as merited rather than received. For the original audience, benefaction and grace were built into everyday economics (Keener 2009, 481–83). Moreover, the caution against envy would have challenged their desire for greater reward at the expense of others. Again, Jesus illustrated his heavenly Father's inclusive and extravagant nature.

God's grace is an inexhaustible resource. This is good news. And it is good news for all people, since God's grace extends to anyone willing to receive it. Those born into Christian families in Midwestern suburbs can receive grace. Those who unexpectedly encounter Christ in a liberal university can receive grace. Those who first meet Christ through a dream and break from their Muslim upbringing can receive grace. And those who respond to a chaplain's gospel presentation within hours of their death can receive God's grace. We neither earn nor inherit grace. God mercifully extends it up to the eleventh hour. This sermon communicates that there's plenty of grace for last place.

Matthew 20:17–28

EXEGETICAL IDEA
Announcing his coming suffering, Jesus issued a call to be a servant for those asking about kingdom rank, with the example being his death as a ransom.

THEOLOGICAL FOCUS
Jesus reconfigures how rank in the world should work by pointing to the example of being a servant.

PREACHING IDEA
Service over status is the way of Jesus.

PREACHING POINTERS

Matthew records Jesus's third and most detailed passion prediction. His arrival in Jerusalem will upset the social order and will lead to his gruesome death. News of Jesus's death and resurrection does not penetrate his disciples' delusions of grandeur. In fact, the mother of James and John requests seats of honor for her sons. Rather than a crown, Jesus warned they would share his call to service and cup of suffering. For the original audience, these themes remained relevant. In a culture obsessed with honor, the status of a servant forced them to rethink their lust for status.

The drive for status is timeless. Although today's status symbols may differ from Jesus's era, the want for power, prestige, rank, and honor remain. In the modern era, status shows up in the size of one's popularity or platform. Influencers have status. We rank people based upon their beauty, athleticism, or physical strength. Athletes and celebrities have status. We herald successful CEOs, entrepreneurs, and politicians. The rich have status. Meanwhile, those who keep houses, care for the elderly, teach children, wait tables, and work retail rarely make headlines. Service is not a status symbol in our culture. This sermon comes as a corrective. Service over status is the way of Jesus.

Matthew 20:29–21:11

EXEGETICAL IDEA

The healing of two blind men in Jericho who cried out to the Son of David illustrated Jesus's messianic authority, something that Jesus's entry into Jerusalem also declared.

THEOLOGICAL FOCUS

Jesus's actions point to him as the promised king of eschatological hope, something his power to heal underscores.

PREACHING IDEA

Don't overlook Jesus's public service announcement.

PREACHING POINTERS

As he headed from Jericho to Jerusalem, Jesus enacted his penultimate healings. Two blind men cried out for mercy, calling him the Son of David. Although the crowds rebuked the men, Jesus restored their sight. When his march to Jerusalem continued, Jesus enlisted his disciples to procure a donkey and colt for his entrance to the city (Zech. 9:9). The scene is packed with messianic imagery. A band of travelers cheered him along, waving branches, tossing coats, and shouting "Hosanna" (Ps. 118). The original readers would have noticed Jesus's change of strategy. He went public. In Jerusalem, he would claim his messianic identity, confront religious hypocrisy, and suffer Roman brutality. Matthew's audience observed the return of Israel's king. With his return, tensions would rise.

Many Westerners consider faith a private matter. They value it so long as it does not infringe on them. They want to keep church and state separate. They want to keep Christ out of Christmas. They are comfortable with "prayers and wishes" when crises arrive; however, they cringe when they see teams huddle in prayer before a football game or families bow to bless their food in a restaurant. Public announcements of Christian faith cause tension. They expose cultural beliefs and values at odds with God's kingdom (e.g., might vs. meekness, dominance vs. service). To make a public announcement of faith is to pledge allegiance to King Jesus, not political parties and consumer brands. This sermon encourages us not to overlook Jesus's public service announcement.

Matthew 21:12–22

EXEGETICAL IDEA
By cleansing the temple and cursing the fig tree, Jesus symbolically purged the nation and warned them of judgment.

THEOLOGICAL FOCUS
Jesus shows his authority by challenging the nation's worship and spiritual state.

PREACHING IDEA
Purity is priority when we gather to worship God.

PREACHING POINTERS
The population in Jerusalem swelled for Passover. Pilgrims came from all directions to worship at the temple. Jesus was among them; however, when he found the outer court of the complex littered with merchants selling sacrificial animals to travelers for profit, he responded indignantly. He overturned tables, rebuked religious leaders, and quoted prophets in protest. Then tension built as Jesus healed crowds, received praise, and cursed a fig tree in subsequent scenes. For Matthew's audience, Jesus's actions showed his authority over nature and religious leaders. He could curse a fig tree and condemn priests who failed to perform their God-given tasks. Jesus's public opposition was profoundly offensive to Jerusalem's brass. This scene precipitated his coming crucifixion.

For too many churches, contemporary worship gatherings have become performances. They are timed and designed for efficiency and entertainment. The countdown clock ticks off seconds before the show begins. Video announcements run like commercials. The worship band blasts music for a crowd shrouded in darkness. The preacher dashes out during a slick bumper video and delivers an inspiring talk with a few practical takeaways. After a closing prayer, people vacate their seats, shuffle through the doors, and exit the building until next week's service. We act more like consumers than worshipers. The formative elements of church life—prayer, confession, fellowship, communion, giving, service—get sacrificed on the altar of performance. Unfortunately, high production value does not translate to holiness. Precision does not make us pure. This sermon renews Jesus's vision for corporate worship: exalting God. Purity is priority when we gather to worship God.

Matthew 21:23–46

EXEGETICAL IDEA
In a series of controversies and parables that were leading the leadership to seek to arrest him, Jesus emphasized the value of obeying God and showed how the kingdom program was being passed on to others because his authority came from God.

THEOLOGICAL FOCUS
The authority of Jesus and the danger of opposition to him are shown in final controversies tied to Jesus's presence in Jerusalem.

PREACHING IDEA
There's no higher authority than heaven.

PREACHING POINTERS
Tensions in Jerusalem continued to rise during Jesus's final week. After Jesus cleared the temple, religious leaders confronted him, demanding an explanation for his bold actions. Jesus responded with a question and two stories that exposed their rejection of heavenly authority. The parable of the Two Sons illustrated God's desire for obedience over lip service. The parable of the Wicked Tenants illustrated the religious leaders' preference for self-rule over submission to God. Matthew tethered these three narratives together to highlight how Jerusalem's elite could not accept Jesus's authority. For the original audience, their rejection of Jesus justified God's shifting focus to tax collectors, sinners, and Gentiles who would respond in faith.

Respect for heavenly authority remains low today. Since the Enlightenment, humans have steadily replaced God with mammon, technology, medicine, and politics. These tools provide for us the illusion that we are masters of our own fate and rulers of our private domains. We can reassign sex through surgery. We can control birth dates and euthanize the elderly. We can harness nuclear energy and produce food with 3D-printers. We no longer think the sky is the limit. We have no limits. This, of course, is the myth of progress. It is bound to fail because human striving will never replace God's strength. This sermon reminds us that there's no higher authority than heaven.

Matthew 22:1–14

EXEGETICAL IDEA
The refusal of some to attend the son's wedding, and of others not to be appropriately responsive, meant that many of the first to be invited would be excluded, while others would be brought into blessing.

THEOLOGICAL FOCUS
Jesus tells yet another parable about the consequences of rejection that also shows the program will go forward with others.

PREACHING IDEA
Honor your RSVP to be with King Jesus.

PREACHING POINTERS
Jesus continued to give the religious leaders in Jerusalem reason to fear him. His parable of the Wedding Feast completed a series of three that illustrated good and bad responses to God's kingdom program. In this story, the king's original guests had backed out; however, since the tables had been set and food had been prepared, the king would not let all the expenses go to waste. He extended the invitation to anyone who would respond. Many came, but one stood out for his filthy dress. He was banished from the banquet. The parable illustrates three different responses to Jesus: outright rejection (i.e., original guests), uncommitted interest (i.e., poorly dressed guest), and true allegiance (i.e., those who came dressed for the party). For the original audience, these three types of responses gave a warning (Davies and Allison 1997, 188–89; Turner 2008, 521), coaxing them to reflect and reaffirm their response to Jesus.

We live in an age averse to commitment. Despite our loaded schedules, we are always looking for better options. Opportunities abound. We can choose between sports and school events, work and family obligations, social and religious gatherings. Deciding can be exhausting. Worse, making a commitment does not alleviate the fear of missing out (FOMO). Saying "yes" to one invitation necessarily means "no" to another. So we keep our options open, wait until the last minute to commit, and look for an "easy out" of an obligation. While our half-hearted responses may pass for family dinners and pickup basketball games, they do not bode well for discipleship to Jesus. Rather, this text teaches we should honor our RSVP to be with King Jesus.

Matthew 22:15–46

EXEGETICAL IDEA
A series of controversies showed a very competent Jesus who was not a revolutionary, believed in resurrection as taught in Torah, taught loving God and neighbor as the Great Commandment, and challenged the leaders to understand why the Messiah was called Lord by David.

THEOLOGICAL FOCUS
Though rejected, Jesus shows himself fully qualified to lead God's program through his understanding of hope, ethics, and the promise of God.

PREACHING IDEA
Jesus passes every quality control test imaginable.

PREACHING POINTERS
Jesus provoked opposition from several fronts in Jerusalem. In a series of oral tests, Jesus responded to questions from Herodians, Sadducees, and Pharisees before posing a question of his own. The first group tried to surface his zealous motives with a question about taxes; the second group challenged his treatment of the law; and the final opponent asked Jesus about ethics. While each controversy stands alone, they collectively illustrate Jesus's competency

as Messiah. Matthew's audience would have marveled at Jesus's understanding of Scripture, wisdom, and ability to sidestep rhetorical traps.

In the age of Big Data, we test everything. We do medical testing: DNA, white blood counts, and cholesterol. We do academic testing: ACT, SAT, MCAT. We test personalities: Myers-Briggs, DISC, and various internet inventories (e.g., Which Hogwarts House would you be in?). We test our water for chemicals, our basements for mold, and our vehicles for carbon emissions. With our endless need to rank, rate, understand, and make improvements, there is no shortage of testing. This compulsion to test applies to Jesus. People still test his words, deeds, and the biblical claims about him. Fortunately, his reputation as a teacher, ethicist, and debater stands the test of time. This sermon reminds us that Jesus passes every quality control test imaginable.

Matthew 23:1–39

EXEGETICAL IDEA
After denouncing the scribes and Pharisees for hypocrisy, pride, blocking the way to blessing, misuse of oaths, neglecting mercy, and working against what the prophets represented, Jesus pronounced judgment against Israel until she recognized the one who comes in the Lord's name.

THEOLOGICAL FOCUS
Jesus issues a full indictment of the nation's leadership for spiritual failure and announces judgment against the nation until she recognizes who God has sent.

PREACHING IDEA
Shallow religion needs a sharp rebuke.

PREACHING POINTERS
After responding to a series of tests, Jesus preached his final public message—and it was not a pleasant one. Summoning his inner prophet, Jesus lambasted the religious leaders for their pride, hypocrisy, and poor direction of God's people. With a series of woes, Jesus made his case for reform in Jerusalem. He preached passionately; as a faithful Jew, he lamented the shallow spirituality of his own people. Matthew's audience would have understood Jesus's zeal for religious integrity—honesty, mercy, and covenant faithfulness. They would have sensed the seed of hope buried in his rebuke—namely, that those who followed Messiah's leadership would escape the trap of bad religion.

Shallow religion is an age-old problem. Worse yet, throughout history religion has been weaponized. It has sparked tribal feuds, justified witch trials, silenced victims of abuse, and preyed on desperate people hoping to find healing by funding televised preachers. All religions are prone to hypocrisy, scams, and crowd control. As Marx opined, "Religion is . . . the opium of the people." Christianity is not immune. One of the favorite labels critics throw at Christians is "hypocritical" (Kinnaman and Lyons 2012, 27). Clergy scandals in recent years have only bolstered these claims. Fortunately, Jesus's tough talk to religious leaders encourages all of us to take a close look at our religious commitment. Indeed, shallow religion needs a sharp rebuke.

Matthew 24:1–35

EXEGETICAL IDEA
Jesus proclaimed judgment on the temple and discussed the signs that would accompany the return of the Son of Man for judgment and vindication of the righteous.

THEOLOGICAL FOCUS
Jesus depicts signs that show the nation's coming judgment and the return of the Son of Man.

PREACHING IDEA
Assurance of God's plan builds endurance to the end.

PREACHING POINTERS
In his final discourse, Jesus provided a map of things to come. This sermon drew from Old Testament prophets, apocalyptic images, and Jesus's concern that his followers remain committed to God in the face of oncoming chaos. Surely Jesus's disciples listened with rapt attention as he assured their vindication and doubled down on God's program. Although Jesus did not provide date and times, the sequence of events and hyperbolic language combined to describe events both in days to come and the last days (i.e., typological-prophetic). Matthew's audience would have heard Jesus's predications, especially the destruction of the temple in A.D. 70, as key puzzle pieces in God's big picture. They would have anticipated the fulfillment of these events and endured in faith awaiting Jesus's climatic return.

Jesus's dramatic and cryptic discourse has given the church much to speculate about concerning end times, timelines, and headlines. Views about the rapture and return of Christ are manifold. Efforts to predict precise dates are pointless. Even Jesus punted when it came to telling the time. However, disciples can rest in this fact: God's plan continues to unfold. War between nations in our time do not thwart God's plan. Contested elections in the United States or economic instability across the globe have not thwarted God's plan. God will complete the puzzle. He will execute his plan. He will bring the end. Until then, we watch, wait, and remain faithful in our chaotic times as his witnesses. This sermon insists that assurance of God's plan builds endurance to the end.

Matthew 24:36–25:30

EXEGETICAL IDEA
Jesus called for a faithful and alert walk until he returns, stressing the accountability that would come with his return and noting the uncertainty of when that would be.

THEOLOGICAL FOCUS
Jesus issues a call to be alert for the end and to be faithful in the meantime.

PREACHING IDEA
Get ready. Stay ready. Christ is coming soon.

PREACHING POINTERS
Jesus's final discourse concluded with a series of parables focusing on staying watchful and faithful until his return. These stories emphasized the uncertainty of the timing (e.g., "like a thief in the night") and functioned as a warning to his audience. Simply being among the crowd of disciples was no guarantee of eternal reward. Rather, these memorable parables—of servants, maidens, and stewards—described two types of responses to Jesus: faithful or listless. For Matthew's audience, this theme of separation resounded. Listeners would not want to be caught unprepared, resulting in judgment and rejection. Instead, as they waited for Jesus's return, they would have remained faithful.

Predictions of disaster have become background noise in our day. Threats of inclement weather sound on the radio. News reporters cover the latest outbreak of the newest virus. We hear stories of increasing gun violence, pollution, and fraud. With each prediction of disaster, we receive directions on how to prepare. Readiness is our best defense when trouble looms. This principle applies to the spiritual life. Though we cannot predict suffering, persecution, or the day of Jesus's return, we can prepare for it. And we should, because it is inevitable. This sermon challenges us to get ready and stay ready, for Christ is coming soon.

Matthew 25:31–46

EXEGETICAL IDEA
In the parable of the Sheep and the Goats, Jesus showed that part of what will be assessed in the judgment is how one responded to those tied to Jesus.

THEOLOGICAL FOCUS
Jesus shows the tie between faith, ethics, and the treatment of his own.

PREACHING IDEA
Care for our kin is care for the King.

PREACHING POINTERS
In the concluding illustration from the Olivet Discourse, Jesus declared his reign, described his judgment, and divided people into two groups: sheep and goats. These iconic categories represented those who respond to Jesus's authority in compassionate acts to other Christ-followers (i.e., sheep), and those who failed to care for others (i.e., goats). In his explanation, Jesus provided six examples of caring for downtrodden Christians. Not only was this care commended for its benefit to other believers, but it also affected Jesus, who felt solidarity with his spiritual siblings. For Matthew's audience, this teaching reached a group of people under pressure for their faith convictions. They not only needed assurance that King Jesus would vindicate their faithfulness but also the compassionate care of other Christ-followers to sustain their faith.

Despite its prominent place in history, the church has no shortage of enemies today. In the West, opponents scrutinize its beliefs, criticize its hypocrisy, and blame it for myriad inequalities. In communist states, the church is targeted for its teaching and is forced underground. In Islamic nations, churches suffer loss of liberty, land, and life. Jesus feels these attacks; our pain is his pain. However, these critical times are a proving ground for the body of Christ to care for its own. The church does not need local government, foreign aid, or philanthropic organizations to sustain it. Jesus commissioned the church to be a community of care; our aid is his aid. This sermon shows that care for our kin is care for the King.

Matthew 26:1–35

EXEGETICAL IDEA
Prepared for death by an anointing and explaining that his sacrificial death was inaugurating a covenant dealing with sin and forgiveness, Jesus predicted betrayal and denial.

THEOLOGICAL FOCUS
Jesus prepares his disciples for his death by explaining what it means.

PREACHING IDEA
Godless plots cannot stop God's plan.

PREACHING POINTERS
On the heels of his final discourse, Jesus predicted his death again. In a dramatic series of stories, Matthew detailed the religious leaders' secret plot to kill Jesus, Jesus's anointing with oil by a woman in Bethany, Judas's betrayal, the inaugural communion meal, and Peter's bold claim of faith followed by Jesus's prediction of repeated denial. These responses to Jesus displayed a range of responses to Jesus likely common in Matthew's day—from faithful to confused to fed up to opposed. Even more central to the narrative than how people responded to Jesus was what he taught about salvation. In a novel interpretation of the Passover meal, he set his death—broken body and poured-out blood—as pivotal to the new covenant promise of forgiveness. Matthew's audience would have appreciated the symbolism of the Lord's Table and weight of Jesus's sacrifice.

God's plans are not relegated to days long past. He controls yesterday, today, and tomorrow. His purposes will prevail. His redemptive aims will not be waylaid by global threats like AI, political forces, economic upheaval, or rival religions. Nor will our pathetic grasping for autonomy ever overthrow God. All efforts to redefine morality, identity, and reality are "plots that will fail" (Ps. 2:1). Fortunately, God's plan included provision for our godless plots. Jesus gave his life—his broken body and blood poured out—to secure our forgiveness. This sermon reminds us that godless plots cannot stop God's plan.

Matthew 26:36–56

EXEGETICAL IDEA
As a result of Judas's betrayal and after committing himself to God's will to accept his death, Jesus refused to fight and was arrested as a common criminal in fulfillment of Scripture.

THEOLOGICAL FOCUS
God's plan leads to Jesus's arrest and his accepting the way of God in suffering for others.

PREACHING IDEA
The higher the pressure, the harder we pray.

PREACHING POINTERS
Jesus and his disciples left the comfort of the upper room for the crucible of Gethsemane, where his predictions of suffering, betrayal, and scattered disciples would be fulfilled. He invited Peter, James, and John to join him in prayer, but they repeatedly fell asleep. In this emotionally laden scene, Matthew captures Jesus in a poignant moment of human pathos. God's "cup" brimmed with suffering; Jesus desired a different drink. Thus, he prayed, and by praying he surrendered his will to his Father's plan. Moments later, Judas arrived with an armed mob to betray Jesus. Rather than resisting arrest or calling an army of angels to his side, Jesus accepted his divine appointment to suffer while his disciples fled in the night. For the original audience, this passage underscored the contrast between Jesus's steady, surrendered life and the disciples' flighty faith.

Prayer has never lost its power or importance for God's people. Through prayer God brings healing, provides clarity, breaks strongholds, changes hearts, builds confidence, and moves the proverbial mountain. Prayer is effective. Sadly, we often take prayer for granted. We remain in a prayerless slumber until a crisis rouses us. We receive a letter from a collections agency and start praying. We wait for results from a blood test and keep praying. We watch our adult child get deployed to an unnamed location in the Middle East and intercede with intensity. Prayer not only seeks God's aid, but it also surrenders our will. This sermon teaches that the higher the pressure, the harder we pray.

Matthew 26:57–75

EXEGETICAL IDEA
Alongside Peter's three denials, Jesus predicted his exaltation by God in response to a question about being the Messiah, a view the Jewish leaders took to be blasphemy.

THEOLOGICAL FOCUS
Jesus's claim to be the seated Son of Man produces a choice about him, either blasphemy or exaltation—a dispute Jesus predicts God will resolve in resurrection.

PREACHING IDEA
With God as his witness, Jesus can't lose.

PREACHING POINTERS
The godless plot of the religious leaders moved forward. Jesus stood trial before them. A parade of witnesses presented hollow claims of Jesus's subversive teaching. Then the high priest questioned Jesus directly about his messianic identity. Jesus bore witness to his unique heavenly authority: God would exalt him and seat him in heaven. In this claim, Jesus sealed his fate. The

priest condemned Jesus for blasphemy. Meanwhile, his intrepid disciple, Peter, stood outside the court denying inquiries about knowing Jesus. After a third denial, the rooster crowed and Peter wept. Matthew captured the drama of this midnight mock trial. Despite the false charges and denials, Jesus stood firm knowing God was his witness. The original audience would read this section having to decide whether they would side with God's verdict on Jesus or popular opinion.

Jesus remains on trial today. False witnesses misrepresent him. They call him a social justice warrior, revolutionary, or political liberal. The challenge here is that Jesus is some of this, but that is not all he is. Sometimes there is a grain of truth that still misleads. Others call him mystical, magical, or ascetic. Others simply reject Jesus. They ignore his teachings. They view his crucifixion as nothing more than a tragic death, made more tragic by his followers who insist it was necessary to pay for sin and appease God's wrath. Sadly, this impulse to deny Jesus lives in all of us. Peter's bravado is a cautionary tale. Many of us go mute about Jesus when our comfort or reputation is on the line. Few of us brim with confidence when questioned about our faith. All of us fail to represent Jesus's love, mercy, and sacrifice. Fortunately, his verdict does not rest on our virtue. This sermon reminds us that with God as his witness, Jesus can't lose.

Matthew 27:1–31

EXEGETICAL IDEA
With Judas acknowledging Jesus's innocence and the Jewish leaders and crowd applying pressure, Pilate sent Jesus to be crucified.

THEOLOGICAL FOCUS
Under pressure, Pilate sentences Jesus to an unjust death, despite his sense that Jesus is innocent.

PREACHING IDEA
Cowards cave when crowds rage.

PREACHING POINTERS
The religious leaders handed Jesus over to Pilate for his death sentence. Only the Roman governor had the authority to execute Jesus for sedition. Matthew's retelling of Jesus's second (and more official) trial shifts focus from the religious leaders to Judas to Pilate to the crowds. Each perspective provides a contrasting perspective on Jesus's innocence. Judas felt remorse and hanged himself. Religious leaders remained opposed to Jesus and convinced the crowd to call for Barabbas's release. Pilate thought Jesus was innocent but conceded to the crowd. The scene concludes with Roman guards mocking and beating Jesus before leading him to his death. For the original audience, the cast of characters and their responses to Jesus would have highlighted the scandal of his death: an innocent man silently suffered while the mob went mad, and a governor gave into its pressure.

Mob justice is not just an ancient problem. In fact, with the rise of social media, mob justice has experienced a revival. Online masses can immediately form and shame people for anything ranging from shoe styles to political opinion to sexual misconduct. In our age, pastors get canceled addressing the rights of a fetus in being pro-life, following government mandates during a pandemic, speaking up for injustice to minorities, and platforming women during a worship service. Mob justice has plagued higher academia. Students protest "dangerous" guest speakers and demand the resignation of faculty who "trigger" them. A raging crowd stormed the U.S. Capitol building to try and overturn the 2020 presidential election results. Once these masses gain momentum, they become a terrifying force. "Both sides" do it. Few will stand in their way. This sermon illustrates that cowards cave when crowds rage.

Matthew 27:32–66

EXEGETICAL IDEA

Amid mocking, scriptural fulfillment, and heavenly portents that witnesses observed, Jesus was crucified as king of the Jews, confessed as God's Son, given a burial, and had his tomb guarded to prevent the body being stolen.

THEOLOGICAL FOCUS

Jesus dies as king of the Jews and God's Son, in fulfillment of God's plan.

PREACHING IDEA

The cross is a cosmic witness to the work of God.

PREACHING POINTS

Matthew reached a climax in God's redemptive story. Jesus, the promised Son—born of a virgin and sent as a ransom for sins—mounted the cross and died. Matthew describes two types of witnesses: mockers and confessors. Crowds, religious leaders, and criminals mocked him. The centurion, female disciples, and Joseph of Arimathea confessed him. Added to this kaleidoscope of cameos, Matthew describes the cosmic witness affected by Jesus's death: darkness, earthquake, torn veil, and open graves. Jesus's suffering was profound but not without purpose. The Son of God fulfilled Scripture. And the preservation of his body in Joseph's tomb remained a point of interest to his followers and the religious authorities, who anticipated God had not finished the work he began in Jesus. For Matthew's audience, themes of fulfillment, opposition, salvation, and witness came to a head. The cross was a turning point in human history.

The cross remains a core image of Christian faith. Whereas other ancient iconography has lost its potency, the cross is a timeless witness to God's work. The cross testifies to Jesus's suffering, divine forgiveness, and scriptural fulfillment. Today many believers wear cross tattoos, earrings, and pendants to express their faith in Jesus. Likewise, crosses mark Protestant church buildings or adorn pulpits and stages. A cross is the most common etching on the front of a Bible. Perhaps the ubiquity of the cross numbs us to its original brutality. Alas, Jesus sacrificed dearly for our sins. The cross is a profound witness. A wordless and wonderful witness. Or, as this sermon indicates, the cross is a cosmic witness to the work of God.

Matthew 28:1–20

EXEGETICAL IDEA
Despite the guards, God raised Jesus, who commissioned his followers to make disciples in all the world and affirmed he would be with them until the end of the age.

THEOLOGICAL FOCUS
The resurrection is God's vindication of Jesus as Son, leading to a commission to take the gospel into the world and make disciples.

PREACHING IDEA
Our mission: Reach out. Bring in. Build up. Repeat.

PREACHING POINTERS
In the final chapter, the risen Jesus appeared and commissioned his followers to continue his kingdom-building work. Matthew describes the empty tomb, opened by an earthquake and visited by various witnesses—angels, women, and Jesus himself. Jesus spoke to the women, giving them orders for the eleven disciples to return to Galilee. Meanwhile, the soldiers tasked with guarding the tomb were dumbfounded and afraid. They reported to the high priests who, by helping them fabricate a story of Jesus's body being stolen, inadvertently testified to the empty tomb. Finally, Jesus met his disciples to reassure them and deliver what has become known as the Great Commission. Matthew recorded these final words as a mandate for his readers and for followers of Jesus in every age. Under Jesus's authority, the church must fulfill her disciple-making mission throughout the world.

Jesus's mandate to make disciples remains relevant today. Without the Great Commission, we grow insular. Church growth experts often envision a bell curve when describing the life cycle of a local congregation. When a church launches, it looks outward. It reaches new people, raises them up, and develops them for ministry. As the body grows, it creates more structures, systems, and programs geared toward those within. Then the church reaches a tipping point. Its mission becomes self-preservation: feeding and maintaining its structures, systems, and programs. Within a few decades, the church begins to decline. The mission of reaching the lost and least is long forgotten. Instead of making disciples, the church drifts into being a social club for spiritual clones. This sermon is an echo of Jesus's timeless mandate to reach out, bring in, build up, and repeat in our disciple-making mission.

ABBREVIATIONS

GENERAL ABBREVIATIONS

A.D.	in the year of our Lord (*anno Domini*)
B.C.	Before Christ
B.C.E.	before the Common Era
C.E.	Common Era
DSS	Dead Sea Scrolls
Eng.	English translation
HB	Hebrew Bible
LXX	Septuagint
NT	New Testament
MT	Masoretic Text
OT	Old Testament

TECHNICAL ABBREVIATIONS

agcy.	agency
ap.	apposition
b.	born
ca.	circa
cf.	compare (*confer*)
chap(s).	chapter(s)
col(s).	column(s)
cond.	condition(al)
d.	died
des.	descriptive
e.g.	for example
esp.	especially
et al.	and the rest
i.e.	that is (*id est*)
n.	note
s.v.	see under
trans.	translated by
v(v).	verse(s)
vol.	volume

BIBLICAL SOURCES

Old Testament

Gen.	Genesis
Exod.	Exodus
Lev.	Leviticus
Num.	Numbers
Deut.	Deuteronomy
Josh.	Joshua
Judg.	Judges
Ruth	Ruth
1 Sam.	1 Samuel
2 Sam.	2 Samuel
1 Kgdms.	1 Kingdoms (LXX)
2 Kgdms.	2 Kingdoms (LXX)
1 Kings	1 Kings
2 Kings	2 Kings
3 Kgdms.	3 Kingdoms (LXX)
4 Kgdms.	4 Kingdoms (LXX)
1 Chron.	1 Chronicles
2 Chron.	2 Chronicles
Ezra	Ezra
Neh.	Nehemiah
Esther	Esther
Job	Job
Ps./Pss.	Psalm(s)
Prov.	Proverbs
Eccl.	Ecclesiastes
Song	Song of Songs
Isa.	Isaiah
Jer.	Jeremiah
Lam.	Lamentations
Ezek.	Ezekiel
Dan.	Daniel
Hos.	Hosea
Joel	Joel
Amos	Amos
Obad.	Obadiah

Old Testament (continued)

Jonah	Jonah
Mic.	Micah
Nah.	Nahum
Hab.	Habakkuk
Zeph.	Zephaniah
Hag.	Haggai
Zech.	Zechariah
Mal.	Malachi

New Testament

Matt.	Matthew
Mark	Mark
Luke	Luke
John	John
Acts	Acts
Rom.	Romans
1 Cor.	1 Corinthians
2 Cor.	2 Corinthians
Gal.	Galatians
Eph.	Ephesians
Phil.	Philippians
Col.	Colossians
1 Thess.	1 Thessalonians
2 Thess.	2 Thessalonians
1 Tim.	1 Timothy
2 Tim.	2 Timothy
Titus	Titus
Philem.	Philemon
Heb.	Hebrews
James	James
1 Peter	1 Peter
2 Peter	2 Peter
1 John	1 John
2 John	2 John
3 John	3 John
Jude	Jude
Rev.	Revelation

EXTRABIBLICAL SOURCES

Old Testament Apocrypha

Tob.	Tobit
Jdt.	Judith

Old Testament Apocrypha (continued)

Wis.	Wisdom of Solomon
Sir.	Wisdom of Jesus the Son of Sirach (Ecclesiasticus)
Bar.	Baruch
1 Macc.	1 Maccabees
2 Macc.	2 Maccabees
1 Esd.	1 Esdras
3 Macc.	3 Maccabees
2 Esd.	2 Esdras
4 Macc.	4 Maccabees

Old Testament Pseudepigrapha

1 En.	1 Enoch (Ethiopic Apocalypse)
2 Bar.	2 Baruch (Syriac Apocalypse)
2 En.	2 Enoch
3 Bar.	3 Baruch
3 En.	3 Enoch
4 Ezra	4 Ezra = 2 Esdras
Adam and Eve	Life of Adam and Eve
Apoc. Ab.	Apocalypse of Abraham
Apoc. Ezek.	Apocalypse of Ezekiel
As. Mos.	Assumption of Moses = Testament of Moses
Ep. Arist.	Epistle/Letter of Aristeas
Jos. Asen.	Joseph and Aseneth
Jub.	Jubilees
L.A.B.	Pseudo-Philo
Liv. Pro.	Lives of the Prophets
Mart. Ascen. Isa.	Martyrdom and Ascension of Isaiah
Pss. Sol.	Psalms of Solomon
Sib. Or.	Sibylline Oracles
T. 12 Patr.	Testaments of the Twelve Patriarchs
T. Ash.	Testament of Asher
T. Benj.	Testament of Benjamin
T. Dan	Testament of Dan
T. Gad	Testament of Gad
T. Iss.	Testament of Issachar
T. Jos.	Testament of Joseph
T. Jud.	Testament of Judah
T. Naph.	Testament of Naphtali
T. Reu.	Testament of Reuben
T. Sim.	Testament of Simeon
T. Levi	Testament of Levi
T. Zeb.	Testament of Zebulon
T. Ab.	Testament of Abraham
T. Adam	Testament of Adam

Old Testament Pseudepigrapha (continued)

T. Isaac	Testament of Isaac
T. Jac.	Testament of Jacob
T. Job	Testament of Job
T. Mos.	Testament of Moses = Assumption of Moses
T. Sol.	Testament of Solomon

Classification of the Dead Sea Scrolls

1Q	Cave 1, Qumran
4Q	Cave 4, Qumran
11Q	Cave 11, Qumran
a, b, c, etc.	manuscript identifiers
Ap	Apocalypse (e.g. 4QMessAp)
apocr	apocrypon (e.g., 1QapGen)
ar	Aramaic (e.g., 1QapGen ar)
frag	fragment
Mess	Messianic (e.g. 4QMessAp)
ord	ordinances (e.g., 4Qorda)
p	pesher (e.g., 1QpHab)
pap	papyrus (e.g., 4QpapParaKings)
Q	Qumran
tg	targum (e.g., 11QtgJob)

Dead Sea Scrolls

Number	*Abbreviation*	*Name*
1QM	1QWar Scroll	Milḥamah *or* War Scroll
1QH		Hymns/*Hoyadot*
1QpHab		Pesher Habakkuk
1Q20	1QapGen ar	Genesis Apocryphon
1Q28	1QS	Rule of the Community
1Q28[a]	1QSa	Rule of the Congregation
1Q28[b]	1QSb	Rule of Blessings
3Q15		Copper Scroll
4Q159	4Qord[a]	Ordinances[a]
4Q161	4QpIsa[a]	Isaiah Pesher[a]
4Q174	4QFlor	Florilegium
4Q175	4QTest	Testimonia
4Q242	4QpNah.	Nahum Pesher Prayer of Nabonidus
4Q252	4QCommGen A	Commentary on Genesis A; Patriarchal Blessings
4Q265		Miscellaneous Rules
4Q266	4QD[a]	Damascus Document[a]
4Q286		Ber[a]
CD	Damascus Document	Cairo Genizah copy of the Damascus Document

Dead Sea Scrolls (continued)

Number	*Abbreviation*	*Name*
4Q381		Non-Canonical Psalms B
4Q385		psEzek[a]
4Q510		Songs of the Sage
4Q521		Messianic Apocalypse
4Q544	4QAmram[b] ar	Visions of Amram[b]
4Q546	4QAmram[d] ar	Visions of Amram[d]
11Q13	11QMelch	Melchizedek
11Q17	11QShirShabb	Songs of the Sabbath Sacrifice
11Q19	11QT[a]	The Temple Scroll[a]

Mishnah/Talmud/Tosefta

ʾAbot.	Avoth
ʿArak.	ʿArakhin
b.	Babylonian Talmud (tied to tractate)
B. Bat.	Baba Batra
B. Mesiʿa	Baba Mesiʿa
B. Qam.	Baba Qamma
Ber.	Berakot
Demai	Demai
Giṭ.	Giṭṭin
Ḥag.	Ḥagigah
Kelim	Kelim
Ker.	Keritot
Ketub.	Ketuboth
Maʿaś	*Maʿaserot*
Maʿaś Š	Maʿaser Sheni
Mak.	Makkot
Mid.	Middot
Mo'ed Qat.	Moʾed Qatan
Ned.	Nedarim
Neg.	Nega'im
Nid.	Niddah
ʾOhol.	Ohalot
Pe'ah	Peʾah
Pesaḥ.	Pesaḥim
Qidd.	Qiddushin
Šabb.	Shabbat
Sanh.	Sanhedrin
Šeb.	*Sheviʾit*
Šheb.	Šhevu'ot
Šheq.	*Šheqallim*
Soṭah	Sotah
Taʿan.	Taʿanit

Mishnah/Talmud/Tosefta (continued)

Yad.	Yadayim
Yebam.	Yebamot
Yoma	Yoma
Zabim	Zavim

Midrashim, Midrash Rabbah (Rabbinic Works)

ʾAbot. R. Nat.	*ʾAbot de Rabbi Nathan*
Cant. Rab.	Canticles Rabbah
Exod. Rab.	Exodus Rabbah
Eccl. Rab.	Ecclesiastes Rabbah
Gen. Rab.	Genesis Rabbah
Mek.	*Mekilta*
Midr. + biblical book	*Midrash on* + biblical book
Num. Rab.	Numbers Rabbah
Pesiq. Rab.	*Pesikta Rabbati*
Qoh. Rab.	Qoholet Rabbah
Sipre	*Sifre*

Apostolic Fathers

1 Clem.	1 Clement
2 Clem.	2 Clement
Jewish believer(s) tradition	Early Christian missionary; mid-first to early second century (likely turn of the century)
Did.	*Didache*
Ignatius	Syrian bishop of Antioch, church father; ca. A.D. 50–ca. 110
Eph.	*To the Ephesians*
Magn.	*To the Magnesians*
Pol.	*To Polycarp*
Smyrn	*To the Smyrnaeans*
Mart. Pol.	*Martyrdom of Polycarp*

Classical and Ancient Christian Writings (Greek and Latin Works)

Aristophanes	Greek Athenian playwright; 446–386 B.C.
Av.	*Birds (Aves)*
Aristotle	Greek philosopher, scientist; 384–322 B.C.
Eth. Eud.	*Eudemian Ethics*
Pol.	*Politica*
Babrius	Second century A.D. Greek author
Cicero	Roman statesman; 106–43 B.C.
Div.	*De divination*
Off.	*De Officis*
Dio (Cassius)	Roman historian; c. A.D. 164–235
Rom. Hist.	

Classical and Ancient Christian Writings (Greek and Latin Works (continued)

Diogenes Laertius	Greek philosopher; A.D. 180–240
Life	
Epictetus	Greek Stoic philosopher; A.D. 55–135
Diatr.	*Diatribai (Dissertationes)*
Eusebius (of Caesarea)	Bishop and church historian; ca. A.D. 264–ca. 340
Hist. Eccl	*Ecclesiastical History* (*Historia Ecclesiastica*)
Firmacus Maturnus	Latin writer; A.D. 306–337
Math.	*Mathesis*
Irenaeus	Bishop of Lyon, Greek theologian; ca. A.D. 130–ca. 200
Haer.	*Against Heresies* (*Adversus haereses* [*Elenchos*])
Josephus	Roman-Jewish historian; A.D. 37–100
A.J.	*Jewish Antiquities* (*Antiquitates judaicae*)
B.J.	*Jewish War* (*Bellum Judaicum*)
C. Ap.	*Against Apion* (*Contra Apionem*)
Vita	*The Life* (*Vita*)
Justin Martyr	Church Father; A.D. 100–165
1 Apol.	*First Apology*
Dial.	*Dialogue with Trypho*
Juvenal	Roman poet; ca. A.D. 55/60–ca. 127
Sat.	*Satitrae*
Menander	Athenian dramatist; c. 342–292 B.C.
Origen	Christian theologian, biblical scholar; ca. A.D. 185–ca. 254
Cels.	*Contra Celsum*
Philo (of Alexandria)	Jewish philosopher; ca. 20 B.C.–A.D. 50
Abr.	*On Abraham (De Abrahamo)*
Decal.	*The Decalogue* (*De decalogo*)
Flacc.	*Against Flaccus* (*In Flaccum*)
Legat.	*On the Embassy to Gaius* (*Legatio ad Gaium*)
Mos.	*Life of Moses* (*De vita Mosis*)
Plant.	*On Planting* (*De plantatione*)
Sacr.	*On the Sacrifices of Cain and Abel* (*De sacrificiis Abelis et Caini*)
Spec.	*On the Special Laws* (*De specialibus legibus*)
Virt.	*On the Virtues* (*De virtutibus*)
Philostratus	Greek Sophist, ca. A.D. 170–247
Vit. Apoll.	*Vita Apollonii*
Plato	Greek philosopher; 427–347 B.C.
Leg.	*Laws* (*Leges*)
Resp.	*Republic (Respubica)*
Pliny the Elder	Roman statesman, polymath; A.D. 23–79
Nat.	*Natural History* (*Naturalis historia*)
Pliny the Younger	Roman magistrate; A.D. 61–ca. 113
Ep.	*Epistalae*

Classical and Ancient Christian Writings (Greek and Latin Works (continued)

Plutarch	Greek biographer, essayist; ca. A.D. 46–120
Ant.	*Antonius*
Mor.	*Moralia*
Porphory	Greek-Phoenician Neoplatonic philosopher; A.D. ca. 234–ca. 305
Vit. Pyth.	*Vita Pythagorus*
Sextus	Christian wisdom writer of late second and early third century A.D.
Sentences	
Suetonius	Roman biographer, historian; A.D. 69–122
Aug.	*Divus Augustus*
Tib.	*Tiberius*
Vesp.	*Vespasian*
Tacitus	Roman senator, historian; A.D. 56–120
Ann.	*Annales*
Hist.	*Historiae*
Varro	Roman scholar; 116–27 B.C.
Rust.	*De re rustica*
Virgil	Roman poet; 70–19 B.C.
Aen.	*Aeneid*

New Testament Apocrypha

Prot. Jas.	*Protoevangelium James*
Ps-Mt.	*Gospel of Pseudo-Matthew*

Papyri

P.Oxy.	*The Oxyrhynchus Papyri*

New Testament Manuscripts bear their normal abbreviations.

PERIODICALS

ABSA	Annual of the British School at Athens
ABW	*Archaeology in the Biblical World*
AUSS	*Andrews University Seminary Studies*
BA	*Biblical Archaeologist*
BAR	*Biblical Archaeology Review*
BASOR	*Bulletin of the American Schools of Oriental Research*
BBR	*Bulletin for Biblical Research*
Bib	*Biblica*
BJRL	*Bulletin of the John Rylands University Library of Manchester*
BR	*Biblical Research*
BSac	*Bibliotheca Sacra*
BZ	*Biblische Zeitschrift*
CBQ	*Catholic Biblical Quarterly*
CJT	*Canadian Journal of Theology*

CSion	*Cahiers Sioniens*
CTJ	*Calvin Theological Journal*
DRev	*Downside Review*
DSD	*Dead Sea Discoveries*
ETL	*Ephemerides Theologicae Lovanienses*
ExpT	*Expository Times*
FM	*Faith and Mission*
GTJ	*Grace Theological Journal*
HTR	*Harvard Theological Review*
HUCA	*Hebrew Union College Annual*
HvTSt	*Hervormde Teologiese Studies*
JAAR	*Journal of the American Academy of Religion*
JANES	*Journal of Ancient Near Eastern Society*
JAOS	*Journal of the American Oriental Society*
JBL	*Journal of Biblical Literature*
JETS	*Journal of the Evangelical Theological Society*
JJS	*Journal of Jewish Studies*
JNSL	*Journal of Northwest Semitic Languages*
JSJ	*Journal for the Study of Judaism in the Persian, Hellenistic, and Roman Periods*
JSNT	*Journal for the Study of the New Testament*
JSOT	*Journal for the Study of the Old Testament*
JTS	*Journal of Theological Studies*
MMJT	*McMaster Journal of Theology*
Mus	*Muséon: Revue d'études orientales*
Neot	*Neotestamentica*
NovT	*Novum Testamentum*
NTS	*New Testament Studies*
PEQ	*Palestine Exploration Quarterly*
RB	*Revue Biblique*
ResQ	*Restoration Quarterly*
RevExp	*Review and Expositor*
RevQ	*Revue de Qumran*
RHPR	*Revue de d'Histoire et de Philosophie*
RTR	*Reformed Theological Review*
SJT	*Scottish Journal of Theology*
ST	*Studia Theologica*
SwJT	*Southwestern Journal of Theology*
ThEd	*Theological Educator*
TJ	*Trinity Journal (new series)*
TynBul	*Tyndale Bulletin*
TZ	*Theologische Zeitschrift*
TZT	*Tübinger Zeitschrift für Theologie*
USQR	*Union Seminary Quarterly Review*
VT	*Vetus Testamentum*

WTJ	*Westminster Theological Journal*
ZAW	*Zeitschrift für die alttestamentliche Wissenschaft*
ZNW	*Zeitschrift für die neutestamentliche Wissenschaft und die Kunde der älteren Kirche*

SERIES

AB	Anchor Bible
AmCNT	American Commentary on the New Testament
AnBib	Analecta Biblica
ANTC	Abingdon New Testament Commentaries
ANTF	Arbeiten zur neutestamentlichen Textforschung
BECNT	Baker Exegetical Commentary on the New Testament
BZNW	Beihefte zur Zeitschrift für die neutestamentliche Wissenschaft
CBC	Cambridge Bible Commentary
CBSC	Cambridge Bible for Schools and Colleges
ConBNT	Coniectanea Biblica: New Testament Series
CSHJ	Chicago Studies in the History of Judaism
DJD	Discoveries in the Judaean Desert
Ebib	Études bibliques
EC	Epworth Commentary
ECNT	Exegetical Commentary on the New Testament
EKKNT	Evangelisch-katholischer Kommentar zum Neuen Testament
EuroHoch	Europäische Hochschulschriften
FRLANT	Forschungen zur Religion und Literatur des Alten und Neuen Testaments
HNT	Handbuch zum Neuen Testament
HNTE	Handbook for New Testament Exegesis
ICC	International Critical Commentary
JSJSup	Supplements to the Journal for the Study of Judaism
JSNTSup	Journal for the Study of the New Testament Supplement Series
JSOTSup	Journal for the Study of the Old Testament Supplement Series
JSPSup	Journal for the Study of the Pseudepigrapha Supplement Series
KCB	Kregel Charts of the Bible
KEK	Kritisch-exegetischer Kommentar über das Neue Testament (Meyer-Kommentar)
KNT	Kommentar zum Neuen Testament
LEC	Library of Early Christianity
LNTS	Library of New Testament Studies
NAC	New American Commentary
NCBC	New Cambridge Bible Commentary
NIBC	New International Biblical Commentary
NICNT	New International Commentary on the New Testament
NIGTC	New International Greek Testament Commentary
NTD	Das Neue Testament Deutsch
NTL	New Testament Library

NTM	New Testament Message
PCNT	Paideia Commentaries on the New Testament
PNTC1	Pelican New Testament Commentaries
PNTC2	Pillar New Testament Commentary
RCRD	Rule of the Community and Related Documents
SBLDS	Society of Biblical Literature Dissertation Series
SBLMS	Society of Biblical Literature Monograph Series
SBLSS	Society of Biblical Literature Supplement Series
SBT	Studies in Biblical Theology
SD	Studies and Documents
SNTSMS	Society for New Testament Studies Monograph Series
SP	Sacra Pagina
TBC	Torch Bible Commentaries
THKNT	Theologischer Handkommentar zum Neuen Testament
THNTC	Two Horizons New Testament Commentary
TNTC	Tyndale New Testament Commentaries
TSAJ	Texts and Studies in Ancient Judaism
WBC	Word Biblical Commentary
WC	Westminster Commentaries
WUNT	Wissenschaftliche Untersuchungen zum Neuen Testament

REFERENCES

ABD	Freedman, D. N., ed. 1992. *Anchor Bible Dictionary*. 6 vols. New York: Doubleday.
BAGD	Bauer, W., W. F. Arndt, F. W. Gingrich, and F. W. Danker. 1979. *Greek-English Lexicon of the New Testament and Other Early Christian Literature*. 2nd ed. Chicago: University of Chicago Press.
BDAG	Danker, F. W., W. Bauer, W. F. Arndt, and F. W. Gingrich. 2000. *Greek-English Lexicon of the New Testament and Other Early Christian Literature*. 3rd ed. Chicago: University of Chicago Press.
BDF	Blass, F., A. Debrunner, and R. W. Funk. 1961. *Greek Grammar of the New Testament and Other Early Christian Literature*. Chicago: University of Chicago Press.
DJG	Green, Joel, Scot McKnight, and I. Howard Marshall, eds. 1992. *Dictionary of Jesus and the Gospels*. Downers Grove, IL: InterVarsity Press.
PG	Patrologia Graeca [= *Patrologiae Cursus Completus*: Series Graeca]. 162 vols. Paris.
SB	Strack, H., and P. Billerbeck. 1922–1961. *Kommentar zum Neuen Testament aus Talmud und Midrasch*. 6 vols. Munich: Beck.
TDNT	Kittel, G., and G. Friedrich, eds. 1964–1976. *Theological Dictionary of the New Testament*. Trans. G. W. Bromiley. 10 vols. Grand Rapids: Eerdmans.

BIBLE TRANSLATIONS

ESV	English Standard Version
LXX	Septuagint
NASB	New American Standard Bible
NET	New English Translation
NIV	New International Version
NRSV	New Revised Standard Version

INTRODUCTION TO MATTHEW

OVERVIEW OF MATTHEW

Author: Matthew

Place of Writing: Churches near the homeland of Jesus

Original Readers: Jewish congregations with questions

Date: mid- to late 60s A.D.

Historical Setting: The continuing split from Judaism

Occasion: The causes of the split, defense of the faith

Literary Genre: Ancient biographies

Theological Emphases: Jesus is the promised one of God according to Scripture, so its prophetic claims are in line with the Jewish hope of saving deliverance. Matthew traces the rise of hostility between Jesus, the community he formed, and the mass of more traditional Jews.

AUTHORSHIP OF BOOK

The first mention of the author of the first gospel came to us from Papias by way of the early church historian Eusebius, who wrote in the early quarter of the fourth century (c. A.D. 325). In the early second century, Papias, a bishop who knew John, wrote a five-volume work called *Expositions of the Sayings of the Lord* about conversations he likely had had decades earlier.

Papias

According to Eusebius, Papias was a very early believer who lived in Hieropolis and had contact with Philip's daughters. There is also mention of John the Presbyter and Aristion. Whether John was the same figure as the apostle or another early John is debated. This makes Papias a third-generation Christian, writing at the end of the first and the early second centuries. What we know of this writing comes mainly through Eusebius. Papias held to a millennium view, something Eusebius criticizes him for believing. However, when it came to the Gospels, he was said to be in touch with old traditions about their origins. For details on his life and writings, see Shanks 2013.

This places Matthew's gospel in the first century. What Papias says about Matthew is that he "collected the oracles in the Hebrew language, and each interpreted them as best he could" (Eusebius, *Hist. Eccl.* 3.39.14–16 [trans. Lake]). Eusebius notes that this work from Papias still existed in his time. We have since lost these volumes. Irenaeus, in the late second century, wrote, "Matthew also among the Hebrews published a written gospel in their own dialect" (*Haer.* 3.1.1 [trans. Davies and Allison 1988, 8 with original]).

There are issues in what is said here. Our gospel of Matthew is in Greek. It gives no evidence of being a translated work. This has led to discussion (Davies and Allison 1988, 12–17). Also, Papias mentions oracles, which may not refer to a gospel (Nolland 2005, 2), although that is clearly how Irenaeus understood the tradition. One option is that the reference to the Hebrew *dialect* (the literal term) is not so much a reference to the language as the style and manner of the gospel. It is laid out in a Jewish kind of way (Evans 2012, 2; details on Papias, Shanks 2013). Another possibility is that the roots for Jesus's teaching in the gospel, of which there are five blocks (Matt. 5–7; 10, 13, 16–18, 23–25), go back to earlier collections in which Matthew had a part as well. It is important to note that Irenaeus said the gospel was for a Hebrew audience in their own dialect, but that there were some Jews who were Hellenistic in emphasis versus working in a Semitic language and so a linguistic transition probably took place very early. Other key attestations include the *Didache* with its reference to the Lord's Prayer in 8:2 (though this may be through church tradition as well).

It is unlikely that the Gospels that came to be read in the church circulated anonymously. Even though the authors never named themselves in the work, the delivery and use of this important material would likely have come with an indication of its roots (Hengel 2000, 48–56). The evidence includes the superscriptions that introduced the gospel in early manuscripts. There is no indication of any dispute about a connection to Matthew in these ancient sources. The claim that the church supplied the author to give the work apostolic status and picked Matthew later has little to commend it. Outside of a connection to this gospel, Matthew

St. Matthew and the Angel.
Painting by Rembrandt.

had no important status among the Twelve. All we know is that he was a tax collector (Matt. 9:9; called Levi in Mark 2:14 and Luke 5:27, as having two names was not unusual in the period, e.g., Saul/Paul, Simon/Peter). Other apostles were more prominent (France 1989, 66–74). Matthew is not even named in the book of Acts. It is quite likely the tradition in this case knew who it was identifying and why, because otherwise there is little reason in these few facts to have connected him to writing a gospel. As a former tax collector, he was well qualified to write such a gospel, since his previous vocation would have been controversial for many Jews. That "minority" status made him well suited to be aware of controversy within the Jewish context.

There are only two solid questions challenging this link to Matthew. First is the claim that an apostolic author would not use a non-apostolic source (Mark) as Matthew's gospel does and then write in his name for Levi, as another person, in Matthew 9:9 (Konradt 2020, 17). However, the association of Mark's gospel with Peter's teaching is an adequate reply to part of this objection. It is also not clear Levi is a distinct person from Matthew as it may be a second name for Matthew (see below on Matt. 9:9). Second is Nolland's claim that the link from Papias's remark about Matthean oracles to the gospel is really a broken link (Nolland 2005, 3). Nolland argues that there is no clear way to get from Papias's claim about Hebrew oracles to a reference to the Greek gospel as being from Matthew. He concludes that the solid tradition after that reference is mistaken in this case. However, this point undervalues the case Hengel makes for early attestation for the unique *kata* phrase that names an author, as well as the likelihood that such attributions would be rooted in knowledge of the source of the gospel (Hengel 2000, 48–53). It is likely that such a known link allowed the gospel to come into early prominence in the church as a source for early worship settings.

PLACE OF WRITING AND ITS SIGNIFICANCE

We really do not know where this gospel was written. Antioch, Syria, or Galilee are suggestions. What these suggestions share is a gospel written in or near the homeland of Jesus, Judea. Antioch in Syria is the most frequent suggestion (Davies and Allison 1997, 138–46; Keener 2009, 41–42). Antioch had a well-established Jewish population that would fit the mix of themes we see in this gospel. It also is a key sending church for mission in Acts (Acts 13). Our first attestation to this gospel appears in three allusions to Matthew from Ignatius who was a bishop there (Ignatius, *Eph.* 19:1–3 and Matt. 2; Ignatius, *Smyrn.* 1:1 and Matt. 3:15; Ignatius, *Pol.* 2:2 and Matt. 10:16). Despite this possibility, we simply do not know the location of its writing. Yet, we can say that Matthew wrote his gospel for churches near the Judean homeland. This means his gospel was in close touch with some of the earliest disputes the emerging church had with its Jewish neighbors. Since the church had originated out of Judaism, these disputes show the new community fighting to establish its legitimacy and identity, whether it had totally separated from the Jewish community yet or not (Culpepper 2021, 2–3, argues that question is not clear). In part, Matthew is claiming to be a legitimate extension of Jewish hope in line with promises God had made long ago. In this emphasis, Matthew parallels Luke, but with an additional layer of Jewish concerns to pursue.

ORIGINAL READERS AND LEGITIMIZATION

The early church was a controversial social entity. It not only proclaimed a human savior figure as divine in the context of Jewish hope but it also combined Jew and Gentile into a single social entity. Moreover, the origins of the movement in Judaism made it surprising that many Gentiles were present. This kind of diverse racial mix alongside the change in practice about the law (for at least some in that community) meant that the authentic Jewish roots of the movement could be questioned. Matthew wrote his gospel for the churches near the homeland of Jesus to explain this transition as a legitimization document. Matthew showed the nature of the Jewish rejection of Jesus's actions and teaching involved ignoring signs of authority Jesus consistently presented. Matthew also argued that the thrust of the law was aimed at creating a certain kind of heart where mercy was desired over sacrifice. Behind these transitions was an authority that Jesus possessed as Son that allowed him to speak authoritatively about the law. What Judaism often tied to a response of faithfulness to the law had now become a response to Jesus and his teaching. Matthew's core claim was that Jesus's bringing of the Spirit and the nature of God showing support for the kinds of salvific acts Jesus had executed pointed to the long-awaited arrival of the new era with its fresh teaching in new wineskins. Those new wineskins were not only about the makeup of the new community but also about how this broader ethnic makeup also impacted practices. That opportunity also meant all nations were accountable to respond to the invitation, with blessing coming to those who did and with judgment coming to those who rejected the invitation.

One of Matthew's key objectives was to defend the gospel and church as rooted in promises tied to Israel and her hope. Matthew defended the new movement as a legitimate expression of Jewish expectation and realization. The cause for the hostility within Judaism was its rejection of this hope and the denial of the evidence for it. The growing separation from the synagogue was not a result of intent by Christians but was the result of a forcing out. Interestingly, Acts covers the same ground through a look at the aftermath of Jesus's career. Matthew may have provided a note of reassurance to those of the faith that their presence in the community reflected their embracing God's will, reinforcing a Christian faith under pressure. By defending the new faith's legitimacy, Matthew also proclaimed that hope and gave an apologetic response to those who challenged its presence (Blomberg 1992, 34–37).

DATE OF WRITING

Two issues impact the date of the gospel of Matthew: the date of Mark and whether Matthew alluded to the destruction of Jerusalem in A.D. 70. Some see the burning of the city in Matthew 22:1–4 as a reference to this event. However, the idea of Jerusalem being overrun by Gentiles as a result of covenantal unfaithfulness is an idea that reaches back to Deuteronomy. In addition, the precedent for the city's destruction and burning existed in events tied to exile in connection with such a judgment (2 Kings 25:9; 2 Chron. 36:19; Neh. 1:3; 2:3, 13, 17; Isa. 64:11). If Jesus saw the nation as unfaithful to covenant hope by rejecting him as the sent one, then this kind of a judgment could be predicted simply as a theological reflection on events. This explanation as a factor for dating is not persuasive.

The date of Mark is also much discussed and becomes relevant, as most see Mark as the first gospel written with Matthew using it. The date of Mark is variously placed. Some date it as early as the late 50s because it is said Acts was written in the early 60s; one can then work back to Mark being before the gospel of Luke. Others contend we cannot determine the date of Luke-Acts by when Acts ends. They look for Mark's setting in a time when persecution became an issue for the church. This fits the early to mid-60s and runs through the decade with the writing of Matthew following Mark's gospel. Also discussed is whether Matthew knew and used Luke, but the differences between Matthew and Luke make that unlikely. Major differences include how the infancy materials differ between these two gospels as well as how the Sermon on the Mount material differs between them in terms of placement of material. Another option after the more common view of Marcan priority is Matthean priority. This view was popular in the early church, but now taken as less than likely. Mark's outline dominates all three gospels. So it likely comes first or last in the sequence of the three gospels. Yet Mark does not appear to be the last of the three gospels as the explanation for this phenomena would require if Matthew were written first. Another option for Matthew's dating places it later in the first century. Those who place Mark at the end of the decade or just after the fall of Jerusalem push Matthew as a gospel following Mark to the 80s, on the premise that a work written close to the fall of Jerusalem would have mentioned it more directly. So we have a date that suggests either the mid- to late 60s for Matthew, written shortly after Mark, or a date in the 80s far enough away from the catastrophic destruction to limit mention of it. Some texts in Matthew appear to show the temple as still present and active (Matt. 5:23–24; 17:24–27; 23:16–22). This would favor a pre-70 date (France 2007, 19; Nolland 2005,

12). In that case, Matthew likely belongs in the mid- to late 60s, though some argue for a late-first-century date (Culpepper 2021, 26; Konradt, 2020, 23, and 2023, 24, in the 80s).

HISTORICAL SETTING

Painting of Saint Mark Writing from the Mouth of Saint Peter by Pasquale Ottini.

Assuming the 60s date, the believers near the homeland of Jesus, to whom Matthew wrote, lived when Nero was the emperor of Rome. Nero began his rule October 13, A.D. 54, at barely the age of fourteen (Tacitus, *Ann.* 13.1; Suetonius, *Nero* 8). The first five to eight years of his reign were mostly calm as he followed the guidance of his mother, Agrippina the Younger; his tutor, Seneca; and a leading Praetorian prefect, Sextus Afranius Burrus. Agrippina was forced to retire in A.D. 56 and was put to death by Nero in A.D. 59 supposedly for insanity as well as her raising opposition to him, while the other two counselors remained until A.D. 62. As he assumed more power starting around A.D. 62, his rule became more power-hungry and erratic. Suetonius breaks his account at chapter 20 of Nero to turn to the emperor's more problematic period of rule. Nero developed a reputation as a tyrant and by the mid-60s had become controversial as a ruler. Revolts emerged throughout the empire, including in Judea. That revolt began in A.D. 67 and culminated in the destruction of Jerusalem and the temple in A.D. 70. His reign came to an end on June 9, A.D. 68, when he became the first emperor to be condemned to death by trial, even though it was *in absentia*. He is said to have committed suicide. Notoriously known for cruelty, he was responsible for the death of Agrippina his mother, Octavia his wife, his aunt Domitia, as well as for the rape then murder of a male relative, Aulus Plautius—just to name a few (Suetonius, *Nero* 33–35). Yet, Nero is best known for the burning of Rome in July A.D. 64 (Tacitus, *Ann.* 15.38–39; Suetonius, *Nero,* 38). During his latter part of his reign, the "Peace of Rome" (*Pax Romana*) was in jeopardy due to the Jewish riots in Judea wreaking havoc against Rome's presence (Bateman 2017, 51–79). Some consider the Neronian persecution mentioned in Mark and Hebrews as reactions to the Jewish uproar in Judea (Bruce 1990, 376; Hengel 1985, 30). So Nero generated problems in both Rome and Judea. This ferment reached the locations where Matthew was writing, and Jews were reacting against Roman rule in the midst of the chaos that resulted near the end of Nero's reign. These realities possibly impact the background to the Gospels but may also explain some positive remarks about accepting Roman rule in earlier Christian epistles, such as Romans 13. By the book of Revelation, views about the Roman government appear to have changed. The internal tension within Jewish groups also would be a major context if Matthew was written in the 80s, while the Roman role would be less significant, other than the continuing desire to be shed of Roman authority—something that finally crops up in the early second century with the Bar Kokhba rebellion.

Dates of the Emperors from Augustus Through the Julio-Claudian Dynasty

Augustus 27 B.C–A.D. 14
Tiberius A.D. 14–37
Caligula A.D. 37–41
Claudius A.D. 41–54
Nero A.D. 54–68

OCCASION

The purpose of this gospel is as an apologetic, as legitimization, and as proclamation. Starting with the infancy material, Matthew made the case that Jesus was the promised one of God according to Scripture and its prophetic claims. He traced the rise of hostility between Jesus, the community he formed, and the mass of more traditional Jews. Matthew described the rejection Jesus met from Jewish leaders, especially the scribes and Pharisees. Matthew defended that Jesus supported the law, especially in its ethical thrust and intent. A severe opposition to him and his followers arose because of Jesus's actions and self-claims, alongside his handling of issues of Sabbath, healings, and other acts tied to issues of purity and the law. Matthew claimed such objections to Jesus ignored all the signs within this ministry that God was working through him, which at the least challenged some Jewish tradition. This opposition became so great that it led to Jesus's death and crucifixion. Even this suffering was predicted in the Hebrew Scripture. Jesus's cause was vindicated by God through the resurrection, which exalted him to a place with God. This act made it imperative that people respond to what Jesus offers, the promise of life with God among his newly formed people, with Jesus's work on the cross and God's vindication of him in resurrection clearing the way for that offer. The Jewish focus of Matthew suggests that the Jewish Christians and those Jews they might interact with were the primary readers of this gospel originally. It may be that events in Judea, both rising opposition from many Jews and between Jews and Rome, also motivated this gospel, contending that Jesus provided an alternative in dealing with Rome. The true Messiah and rule were to be found in the kingdom of God and its initially realized promise, not Rome (most contended for by Carter 2004). Matthew may well have been equipping fellow Jewish believers in Christ with how to tell the story of Jesus and how to interact with their Jewish neighbors, including how hostility emerged between them, as Matthew demonstrated Jesus had a genuine connection to the hope of the Hebrew Scripture.

STRUCTURE AND LITERARY GENRE

Matthew built his gospel around five discourse blocks: Matthew 5–7, 10, 13, 16–18, 23–25. Each discourse has a key role in introducing important Matthean themes: the law in 5–7, mission in 10, kingdom in 13, the church in 18, and condemnation of Jewish leadership and the hope of vindication in 23–25. The gospel largely follows Mark's outline of Jesus's ministry from Galilee to Jerusalem. The infancy material sets two key notes: Jesus's coming fulfilled the promises of Scripture, and God directed events tied to Jesus. God's direction was seen in how dreams control the key movement of people in the opening to the gospel. God was at work in the events tied to Jesus. Matthew is known as the Jewish gospel, but it also is filled with significant hints of Gentile involvement, starting with Gentile women and the magi in the infancy section.

In terms of genre, all the Gospels mirror ancient *bios* or biography (Burridge 1992). This is not to say they are like modern biographies where family background and physical traits are common. Rather, it is to stress that what the person said and did is what gets highlighted, particularly if the goal is to present the person as exemplary. In this case it is not only Jesus who is exemplary but that he has a unique role in God's plan and promise for deliverance.

Matthew's Teaching Blocks	
Matthew 5–7	Sermon on the Mount
Matthew 10	Mission Charge
Matthew 13	Kingdom Parables
Matthew 18	On the New Community
Matthew 23–25	Rebuke of Jewish Leaders and Olivet Discourse

SOURCES FOR THE GOSPEL

Most New Testament scholars hold to Marcan priority, namely that Mark was the first gospel written. Formal introductions to the New Testament cover these issues in some detail and point to these discussions (Carson and Moo 2005; Köstenberger, Kellum, and Quarles 2016). Significant alternate options do exist, namely the Farrer hypothesis that sees Mark as written first, then Matthew, and then Luke using Matthew, and the Griesbach hypothesis that has Matthew coming first followed by Luke and then Mark. This commentary argues that Mark was the first gospel written, that Luke and Matthew did not use each other but shared a teaching source or sources of some kind, and that Matthew also had access to unique materials.

Mark

It is commonly regarded that Mark was a source for Matthew, as around 90 percent of that gospel shows up in Matthew. Despite the claim by Papias that Matthew was the first gospel written, as fully noted above, the fact that this claim comes with the idea of a linguistically Jewish version makes that claim problematic, since the gospel we have does not give evidence of having such an origin or of being a translation. Those who contend that an apostle like Matthew would not use a gospel from a non-apostolic source ignore the association Mark had with Peter. The outline of Mark is mostly followed by Matthew in such a way that Mark is seen as either first or last of the three Synoptics. Mark being last of the Synoptics is unlikely given what Mark omits from both of the other gospels, nor is it likely Mark is a "Reader's Digest" version of the other gospels, as he is normally longer in those passages where there is overlap. This all suggests Mark came first.

It is sometimes suggested that Matthew is a kind of anti-Markan and anti-Pauline gospel (Culpepper 2021, 4–6, with a helpful list of noted differences). This construal has too much of the old Tübingen school about it, placing Matthew with James and taking the difference of emphasis on the law with Paul as reflective of the two supposedly deeply competing approaches. It is better to see this gospel as written to a primarily Jewish believing audience where there is regard for the law, in part to reach out to Jewish unbelievers. This mix of respect for Jewish context and for more freedom in a Gentile setting—which is Mark's setting—is seen in Acts with differences existing between Paul and James without seeing a full rift where one rejects the other. Jesus's handling of the law was controversial enough to gain a more traditional Jewish reaction. This shows Jesus did have some differences in how the law was seen even in a strictly Jewish context. The claim that Jesus saw the law as applying to Gentiles says too much, and it is a key to arguing for the extent of the difference here. Context of ministry makes a difference, and that is what the distinct emphases and sensitivities show (Gurtner et al. 2011).

The "Q" Source

Matthew also shares some kind of a source(s) and/or a tradition stream with Luke that focuses on Jesus's teaching. This source has commonly been called "Q." This represents around 200–225 verses of these two gospels that overlap. The key supposition here is not simply a posited source as some claim, as the positing of a source is the most probable result of a set of likelihoods. The first is that neither Matthew nor Luke used the other's gospel. That claim is likely if one considers the different ways the infancy material is handled and the way things like the Sermon on the Mount appear. Second is the nature of the shared 200–225 verses. In this material, a third of it is very close in wording between the gospel versions, another third is somewhat close, and the final third debatable whether it arose from the same source. If the two gospels did not use each other (point 1), then by default this material, so close in so much of it, must have come from some common source (point 2). Given the existence of oral tradition sources alongside written sources (something Luke 1:1–2 gives attestation to), it is hard to see Q only as a single written entity. But the amount of material involved does give a strong suggestion of a shared Jesus tradition involving a teaching source or sources, and even a mix of written and oral materials.

Assumptions Behind a Source/Tradition Like Q

- The original context for passing information on was oral.
- Jesus's teachings would have been gathered orally and/or in written form in the churches while being overseen by the apostles.
- Matthew and Luke share around 225 verses of teaching.
- Matthew and Luke did not use each other's gospels (just look at their differences).
- These shared verses must have come from somewhere, and a deposit of Jesus's teaching in the churches—either oral, written or a mix—and used for worship, is a likely source.
- Once this material became incorporated in apostolically sanctioned gospels, the need for it no longer existed and it disappeared.

"M" Material

As an apostle and as one who would have been prominent in the church, Matthew also would have access to unique material, some of which highlighted the church's roots to Jewish contexts—issues that were of special concern to Matthew. This is often labeled "M" material.

So, three primary sources for Matthew beyond his own experiences are Mark's gospel, Q teaching material, and unique Matthean material (called M). The list of texts tied just to Matthew is extensive. Common is a list of unique citations of the Hebrew Scripture and several parables that only he presented to us. The list of M texts or key sayings is as follows:

1:1–17 Genealogy Through Solomon and David to Abraham
1:18–25 Angel Appears to Joseph
2:1–12 Birth in Bethlehem and Magi
2:13–25 To Egypt and Then to Galilee
3:14–15 John: I Have Need to be Baptized by You
4:13–16: Galilee of the Gentiles
4:23–24 Galilee Teaching Summary
5:1–2, 7–9 Sermon on Mount—Introduction and Some Blessing
5:14, 16 You Are the Light of the World
5:17, 19 Came to Fulfill the Law
5:20–24, 27–30, 32–38, 47 Antitheses
6:1–7 On Alms, Prayer
6:15–18 Forgive, On Fasting
6:19 Do Not Store Treasure on Earth
6:34 Do Not Worry About Tomorrow
7:2 Standard by Which You Judge
7:6 Pearls to Swine
7:14 Narrow Is the Gate
7:15 Watch Out for False Prophets
7:17–20 Good, Bad Tree and Fruit
7:22 Lord, Lord

8:6–7 My Servant/I Will Heal
8:17 Isaiah 53:4 Citation
8:18 Other Side of the Lake
9:27–31 Heals Two Blind Men
9:32–33 Demon-Possessed Mute
10:6 Go to the Lost Sheep of Israel
10:23 Not Finished Until You Go Through All Towns of Israel
10:25 Disciple Like Teacher, Called Beelzebul
10:36 Man's Enemies a Member of the Household
10:40–42 Whoever Receives You
11:1 Teaching Summary
11:20 Begins Criticizing Cities
11:24 More Tolerable for Sodom (Than Capernaum)
11:28–30 Come to Me, You Weary, and Find Rest
12:5–7 Priests on Sabbath, Mercy Not Sacrifice
12:11–12 Sheep Pulled Out on Sabbath
12:17–21 Isaiah 42:1–4 Citation
12:34 Offspring of Vipers Rebuke
12:36–37 Give an Account for Every Word
13:14–15 Long Citation of Isaiah 6:9–10
13:24–30 Parable of the Wheat and Tares
13:35 Psalm 78:2 Citation
13:36–43 Interpretation of Wheat and Tares
13:44 Parable of the Hidden Treasure
13:45–46 Parable of Pearl of Great Price
13:47–50 Parable of the Dragnet
13:51–52 Parable of the Old and New
13:53–54 Transition to Synagogue Visit
14:28–32 Peter Walks on Water
15:13 Every Plant Not Planted by Father Uprooted
15:23–25 Cannanite-Phoenician Woman Exchange
16:2 Red Sky, Fair Weather
16:11 Beware of Yeast of Pharisees and Sadducees
16:17–19 Jesus Commends Simon bar Jonah
17:6–7 Disciples Throw Themselves to Ground at Transfiguration
17:24–27 Temple Tax Discussion
18:4 Humble Yourself Like a Child
18:10 Do Not Disdain the Little Ones
18:14 Little Ones Not to Be Lost
18:15–20 Discipline in the Community
18:21–22 Forgive Seven/Seventy-Seven Times
18:23–35 Parable of the Talents
19:10–12 Better Not to Marry
20:1–15 Parable of the Workers
21:4–5 Zechariah 9:9 Citation
21:14–16 Healing Summary and Psalm 8:2 Citation
21:28–32 "Who Obeys?" Parable
21:41 Evil Men Destroyed for Rejection
21:43 Kingdom Given to Those Who Produce Fruit
22:1–2, 4, 6, 8–14 Introduction and Wedding Banquet Parable
22:33–34 Crowds Amazed, Intro to Great Commandment Query
22:40 All the Law and Prophets Depend on This
23:2–3 Moses's Seat
23:5–6 Phylacteries, Tassels, Banquets
23:8–12 One Teacher, Greatest Is Servant, Exalted and Humbled
23:15 Woe, Cross Land and Sea
23:16–22 Swear by Temple
24:9–13 Handed Over for Persecution and False Prophets
24:40 Two Men in the Field
24:42–44 Be on the Alert, Don't Know the Time
25:1–10 Parable of the Ten Virgins
25:16–20, 22–23, 27, 30 Parable of the Talents
25:31–46 Parable of the Sheep and Goats
26:1 Introduction to Passover
26:25 Judas Denies
26:53–54 Could Call Twelve Legions, Must Be Fulfilled
27:3–10 Regret of Judas
27:19 Dream of Pilate's Wife
27:24–25 Pilate Washes His Hands
27:43 Mocking of Jesus Seeking Deliverance
27:51–53 Earthquake with Veil Rent and Tombs Opened
27:62–66 Chief Priests and Pharisees Request Tomb Guards

28:3–4 Guards React to Angel
28:9–10 Jesus Greets the Women
28:11–15 Guards Report Empty Tomb and Stolen Body Claim
28:16–20 Appearance in Galilee, Great Commission

THEOLOGICAL EMPHASES

The program of God. The infancy material opens with numerous narrative remarks about how the birth of Jesus fulfills Scripture. The point is to argue that the program of God is unfolding. Matthew's way of doing this differs from Luke's. In Luke, the participants in the events provide the language of fulfillment and Scripture. In Matthew, these are narrative remarks in many cases. This fulfills the legitimization going on in the book, with the citation of Scripture playing a major role throughout the gospel. Culpepper (2021, 9, citing Davies and Allison 1988, 29–57) says there are twenty-one citations and fifty allusions peculiar to Matthew in the account. The proper ancestry to Jewish hope is shown in these links that continue throughout the gospel. As Konradt (2020, 2) says, "The community of Christian believers is the true custodian of the theological traditions of Israel."

The unique Jesus. Jesus not only stands at the center of God's activity, but he also performs divine acts showing who he is. In the Synoptics, it is common for the emphasis in Christology not to be found in what Jesus says about himself but by what he does. Matthew is no exception to this. Jesus forgives sin, has authority over the Sabbath, calms the wind and waves, rules over the definition of purity, controls the temple, and can change Torah liturgy (at the Last Supper). These are but a sample of examples. Beyond this, he is the only teacher (Byrskog 1994). Unlike Jewish reliance of a set of authoritative rabbis, Jesus's teaching alone is what counts. His teaching on the kingdom of God in Matthew 13 will lay out the distinctives of his work, including a time between the kingdom's arrival and the reckoning it will bring to all one day. The idea of a Messiah who suffers takes the disciples some time to grasp. Matthew highlights Jesus as Son of David, Son of Man, and Son of God, but it is Jesus's suffering that most fail to grasp about the way the promise comes.

The discourse teaching blocks. In many ways, the discourse teaching blocks reveal Matthean theological interests. How Jesus fits into Jewish ethical and eschatological expectation is seen in the Sermon on the Mount. The law is meant to aim at the heart motive. A disciple performs piety before God, not as a matter of public display. There is a mission the church has that has an element of urgency to it, whether we think of the initial mission to Israel in Matthew 10 or of the Great Commission to the world. The kingdom comes in two steps, an offer and a later time of accountability. Matthew 13 shows a claim made on all the people of the world whether they recognize it or not. One is either of God or the devil regarding how one responds to Jesus, and the seed sown of the kingdom is an essential part of that story. The visible presence and power of the kingdom is seen in the fruit of God's people, but a claim on all lives means accountability at the end. Matthew 18 shows kingdom people being accountable to each other but also characterized by a forgiving spirit that does not forget that every believer is a beneficiary of forgiveness. Matthew 23 is a kind of negative example of what piety is not—a Sermon on the Mount in reverse. This is how not to walk with God, as Jesus challenges the non-example of the Pharisees. Love and mercy stand at the center of how relationships are to be pursued and provide the contrast (Matt. 9:13; 12:7; 22:34–40). Torah is most honored by this core heart ethic. Matthew 24–25 shows the eschatological thrust of Matthew and the vindication and deliverance of the saints while holding the unrighteous accountable. The tie between belief and action is also affirmed as the judgment looks at evidence for an active faith that has borne fruit.

Jewish concerns, with an eye to Gentiles. Matthew spends much time on issues tied to Judaism. The antitheses and discussion of practices of piety in the Sermon on the Mount reflect Jewish concerns. The constant debates with Pharisees do the same. The emphasis that Jesus's mission focused on a mission to Israel also makes this point. The crowds appear open and their allegiance is sought within the gospel. They are distinguished from authorities who challenge and reject Jesus. Even in the eventual seeming rejection of Jerusalem, Matthew holds out hope that one day Israel will respond to Jesus (Matt. 23:39; 24:30; 28:19). Yet Gentiles are not missing in the gospel. The genealogy mentions Gentile women. The magi are Gentiles. The centurion has an exemplary faith. The Syro-Phoenician woman is blessed by Jesus. A soldier confesses Jesus as Son of God at his crucifixion. The movement of the gospel to all the nations is previewed in these encounters.

The challenge of discipleship and the community. How those who follow Jesus will live is also a theme in the gospel (Konradt 2020, 11–15). Discipleship will be demanding, even radical, with nothing else coming first. The bearing of the cross is a requirement. The world will not embrace them just as it did not embrace Jesus. Believers will be a new community that needs to live distinctly in accountability to each other, while being ready to be a forgiving community, something the discourse in Matthew 18 will develop. This new community stands out as the place where the activity of God is most evident. Only Matthew uses the word "church" among the Gospels. It shows an emerging identity, distinct from the Jewish community and in tension with them. Peter is the key foil for how the understanding of the disciples develops. He alternates between doing well and doing poorly (Wilkins 2004, 31). He is an example of a learner of new ways. Konradt (2020, 13) notes, "For Matthew, the church is the community of salvation being formed in Israel and beyond, throughout all peoples of the world, qualified by their confession of Jesus as the Son of God (16:16) and their life in accord with his teaching (28:20a)." There is no supersession here, but a broad incorporation.

The Great Commission. At the end of the gospel comes the call that is one of its key applications. Where the earlier mission was focused on Israel (Matt. 10:6), now the call is to go into all the world (28:19). Given the account Matthew has rendered, the call is to rest in who Jesus is and what he provides and to go into all the world to make disciples who will follow what Jesus has taught. This new faith, rooted in promises of old, is not to be a privatized experience. It is a message of hope to be taken to all the world. The calling is to live and proclaim what Jesus has revealed about God's plan and kingdom, knowing that Jesus is with them as believers. They are to proclaim and live in the ways of God.

CONCLUSION

Determining the circumstances under which an ancient document was written is a little like trying to put together a puzzle when some of the pieces are missing. We only have small pieces of information. What we have alludes to works that have been lost. Nonetheless, the information we do have points in one direction: that Matthew in some way stands behind the first gospel. The text itself does not name him, but everything said about the roots of this gospel point in this direction. This gospel proclaims a resurrected Jesus, Son of David, Son of Man, and Son of God as at the center of a promised kingdom program. His suffering and death seem surprising, but they also are a part of this plan. What the Hebrew Scripture had hoped for is what Jesus brings. The kingdom program has a future wrapped up in a return of the crucified but now vindicated Messiah. Upon his return, all people will be held accountable for how they have responded to God and the raised Son. The conflict with other Jewish groups is about the claim that a ruling Jesus brings a theology of hope tied to Jewish promise. That authority makes no one immune from what Jesus offers. There is no default righteousness apart from him. To draw others to this message means disciples must live before God from the heart, in the Spirit through both word and deed. Their communities will face pressure and pushback from the world. The draw will be in how distinctively the community cares for itself, lives in unique ways, and still reaches out to the world in a manner that shows the offer of forgiveness and restoration to new life that is wrapped up in what the church calls the gospel, or good news. To tell the story of that gospel is what Matthew does. That gospel account calls Matthew's readers to live out and reflect that gospel to a world in need of hope.

OUTLINE

Matthew is divided into four major divisions with fifty-one preaching units.

INTRODUCTION TO JESUS AND JOHN THE BAPTIST (1:1–4:11)

- The Birth and Genealogy of Jesus (1:1–25)
- The Magi Show Gentile Respect, While Herod Shows Hostility (2:1–23)
- John the Baptist Announces the Kingdom (3:1–12)
- John Baptizes Jesus (3:13–17)
- Jesus Overcomes Three Satanic Temptations (4:1–11)

MESSIAH CONFRONTS ISRAEL IN GALILEE AND MEETS REJECTION (4:12–12:50)

- Jesus Comes as Light, Preaches the Kingdom, and Calls Disciples (4:12–25)
- The Beatitudes: Blessed Are Those Who . . . (5:1–12)
- Disciples as Salt and Light: Jesus Issues a Call to Righteousness (5:13–20)
- Jesus Issues a Call for a Greater Righteousness (5:21–48)
- Teaching on Alms, Prayer, and Fasting (6:1–18)
- Seek the Kingdom and Live Without Worry (6:19–34)
- Be Careful About Judging, Self-Discerning, and How You Treat Others (7:1–12)
- Jesus Teaches on the Narrow Gate, False Prophets, and Heeding Him (7:13–29)
- Jesus Heals a Leper, a Centurion's Slave, and Peter's Mother-in-Law (8:1–22)
- Jesus Calms the Storm, Exorcizes Demons, and Heals a Paralytic (8:23–9:17)
- Jesus Heals a Woman, a Daughter, Two Blind Men, and a Mute Man (9:18–38)
- Jesus Sends the Disciples on a Mission to Israel (10:1–11:1)
- Jesus's Ministry Shows Itself to Be from God (11:2–30)
- The Sabbath Acts Point to Jesus's Authority (12:1–21)
- A Warning About Not Doing God's Will (12:22–50)

KINGDOM, PROVISION-ACCEPTANCE-CALL, AND REJECTION BY ISRAEL (13:1–20:28)

- On the Kingdom and Its Mysteries, Part 1 (13:1–23)

- On the Kingdom and Its Mysteries, Part 2 (13:24–58)
- Herod Struggles to Figure Out Who Jesus Is and Slays John the Baptist (14:1–12)
- Jesus Feeds 5,000 and Calms the Storm (14:13–36)
- Jesus Discusses Defilement and Purity as a Matter of the Heart (15:1–20)
- Jesus Heals and Cares for People, Including a Gentile Woman (15:21–39)
- Jesus Contrasts the Results of His Ministry with Those of the Jewish Leaders (16:1–12)
- Peter Confesses Jesus as the Christ (16:13–28)
- The Transfiguration and the Disciples' Failure to Heal a Young Boy (17:1–20)
- Jesus Predicts His Suffering and Reminds Disciples of Their Obligations (17:22–27)
- Jesus Teaches About Community, Accountability, and Forgiveness, Part 1 (18:1–20)
- Jesus Teaches About Community, Accountability, and Forgiveness, Part 2 (18:21–35)
- Jesus Discusses the Design of Marriage and the Impact of Divorce (19:1–12)
- Jesus Discusses Childlike Faith and the Challenge of Wealth (19:13–30)
- Jesus Tells the Parable of the Hired Workers (20:1–16)
- Jesus Predicts His Suffering and Presents His Service as an Example (20:17–28)

REJECTION AND VINDICATION OF THE MESSIAH-SON IN JERUSALEM (20:29–28:20)

- Jesus Performs a Healing and Presents Himself to Jerusalem (20:29–21:11)
- Jesus Purges the Temple and Curses a Fig Tree (21:12–22)
- Disputes and Parables Show Jesus's Authority and Warn the Opposition (21:23–46)
- The Parable of the Wedding Banquet (22:1–14)
- Facing Challenges Dealing with Politics, Theology, and Ethics (22:15–46)
- Jesus Issues an Indictment of Woes Against the Scribes and Pharisees (23:1–39)
- Jesus Describes the Signs That Point to the Nation's Judgment (24:1–35)
- Jesus Tells Parables About the End-Time Judgment (24:36–25:30)
- The Parable of the Sheep and Goats (25:31–46)
- Jesus Predicts Betrayal and Denial (26:1–35)
- Jesus Is Arrested as a Common Criminal and Does Not Fight Back (26:36–56)
- Jesus Accepts the Claim of Being Messiah and Peter Denies Him (26:57–75)
- Jewish Leaders and a Crowd Pressure Pilate to Sentence Jesus to Crucifixion (27:1–31)
- Jesus Is Crucified and Buried (27:32–66)
- God's Resurrection of Jesus Vindicates the Son (28:1–20)

FOR FURTHER READING

For further discussion on issues tied to the introduction to Matthew, any thorough New Testament introduction will be of help. I note here additional resources for historical background issues.

Charlesworth, James H., ed. 2006. *Jesus and Archaeology.* Grand Rapids: Eerdmans.

Green, Joel, Jeanine K. Brown, and Nicholas Perrin, eds. 2013. *Dictionary of Jesus and the Gospels.* 2nd ed. Downers Grove, IL: InterVarsity Press.

Green, Joel, Scot McKnight, and I. Howard Marshall, eds. 1992. *Dictionary of Jesus and the Gospels.* Downers Grove, IL: InterVarsity Press.

Hengel, Martin. 2000. *The Four Gospels and the One Gospel of Jesus Christ: An Investigation of the Collection and Origin of the Canonical Gospels.* Harrisburg, PA: Trinity Press International.

Jeremias, Joachim. 1969. *Jerusalem in the Time of Jesus: An Investigation into Economic and Social Conditions during the New Testament Period.* London: SCM.

Levine, L. I. 2000. *The Ancient Synagogue: The First Thousand Years.* New Haven, CT: Yale University Press.

Schürer, E. 1973–87. *The History of the Jewish People in the Age of Jesus Christ (175 B.C.–A.D. 135).* Rev. ed. Edited by G. Vermes, F. Millar, and M. Black. 4 vols. Edinburgh: T & T Clark.

Shanks, Monte. 2013. *Papias and the New Testament.* Eugene, OR: Pickwick.

Key resources for the study of Matthew, especially commentaries, carry an asterisk in the References section that concludes this volume.

INTRODUCTION TO JESUS AND JOHN THE BAPTIST (1:1–4:11)

This unit opens the first section of Matthew, extending to Matthew 4:11. The material includes the infancy material, the ministry of John the Baptist including Jesus's baptism, and the temptations of Jesus. God is driving a program involving a Son sent to bring the kingdom. The virgin birth shows the Son is sent, as does the fulfillment of Scriptures which points to a divine program. The mood of conflict and opposition is present from the start, a beginning distinct from Luke's more praiseful infancy material. While Luke gives the perspective of Mary, the perspective here focuses on Joseph. John the Baptist prepares the way with his call to repentance. Jesus is endorsed by God as Son and Servant at the baptism. He shows himself to be qualified as faithful Son at the temptations. Jesus succeeds at the point Adam and Israel had failed. The genealogy of this unit announces the arrival of the promised Davidic king and is connected to the promise tied to Abraham. It is rooted in several narrative notes that cite the Hebrew Scripture to show the promise was a part of God's plan. Although those to whom the message is given largely oppose the movement, God is at work keeping his promises and bringing deliverance, a restoration that is to reach into all the world.

Five preaching units comprise the section. The first two cover the infancy material. The remaining three introduce how John the Baptist's ministry set up the divine endorsement of Jesus at the baptism and how Jesus resisted the devil—an initial example of how to be faithful to God.

Matthew 1:1–25

EXEGETICAL IDEA

Through the announced birth of Jesus through a virgin, God executed a promised divine plan to bring a savior and deliverer from sin who is God with us.

THEOLOGICAL FOCUS

God's long-standing promise to the world through Abraham and David comes in a virgin-born Jesus.

PREACHING IDEA

God's family plans are perfectly conceived.

PREACHING POINTERS

Matthew opens his biography of Jesus with an impressive lineage of the Savior and Messiah. A number of false messiahs appeared in Judea during the mid-60s A.D., who were a challenge to believers in Judea as well as those near the homeland of Jesus. The Roman emperor was also presented as the ultimate savior. Thus, there was the need to establish Jesus as qualified to be Israel's Messiah and fit the hope of Jewish promise. Matthew traces Jesus's roots through a list that includes Jewish household names (Zerubbabel, David, and Abraham), surprising characters (Rahab, Ruth, and Tamar), and lesser-known figures from the postexilic period. The inclusions, omissions, and structure of Matthew's genealogy hinted to his Jewish audience that God's covenantal promises to Abraham and David had reached a climax. Furthermore, God's plan had transgressed borders; he was reaching all the nations with a message of salvation embodied in the miraculous birth of Jesus. Matthew also makes it clear that the promise extended to both men and women. For the original readers near Jesus's homeland, Matthew's introduction inspired hope and assurance in God's sweeping plan of salvation.

Today people in the Western world have rediscovered an interest in family roots. The rise of genetic testing and online ancestry programs has sent people digging into their backgrounds. Lineage and places of origin are important to many Americans. People realize their past shapes their future. Blood disease may run in the family. Chemical abuse or mental illness may mark our forefathers. Or perhaps, a generational chain of doctors, lawyers, or police officers may narrow our career path. Exploring one's background often reveals happy surprises, family secrets, and signs of God's fingerprint in shaping a person. This passage assures us that in Jesus God's family, plans are perfectly conceived.

THE BIRTH AND GENEALOGY OF JESUS (1:1–25)

LITERARY STRUCTURE AND THEMES (1:1–25)

This unit opens the first section of Matthew extending to Matthew 4:11. The material includes the infancy material, the ministry of John the Baptist, including Jesus's baptism, and the temptations of Jesus. God is driving a program involving a Son sent to bring the kingdom. The ties to David and Abraham points to Jewish promise through the covenant commitment to each of those figures of the past (Gen 12:1–3; 2 Sam. 7:7–17). The virgin birth shows that the Son is sent, as does the fulfillment of Scriptures, all pointing to a divine program. John the Baptist prepares the way with his call to repentance. Jesus is endorsed by God as Son and Servant at the baptism. He shows himself to be qualified as faithful Son at the temptations. Jesus succeeds at the point Adam and Israel had failed. The genealogy of this unit announces the arrival of the promised Davidic king and is connected to the promise tied to Abraham. This opening unit shows how Jesus is sent by God directly and is qualified to be Messiah because he is in the right royal legal line. The ministry of John the Baptist affirms this in the baptism that takes place, while also showing what people who respond to Jesus need to be prepared to do—namely, be open to turning to God's way (repentance).

Matthew opens his gospel drenched in promise. This unit comes in two parts: a genealogy (vv. 1–17) and a birth announcement (vv. 18–25). Matthew opens with Jesus's genealogy, to confirm his legitimate Messianic connection divinely rooted in the promises made to Abraham and David (vv. 1–17). Matthew reinforces Jesus's divinely directed birth with the angelic announcement of Jesus's birth (vv. 18–25). The key structure of the genealogy involves three units of fourteen generations each. The heading highlights two key figures of the past, David and Abraham, and grounds the birth in promises made to them and in two key Hebrew Scripture covenants named after them. The nature of the listing shows that those on the fringe will be included and that the program will include women and Gentiles. The birth announcement fits the common pattern in a biblical birth announcement and served to direct a pious Joseph to accept the child and Mary into his family even though Joseph was not the biological father of the child. The obedience of Joseph in the scene is exemplary, but the main point is that God had initiated what was about to take place through Jesus. The child's arrival pointed to God being with his people and opening the door to salvation through the forgiveness of sins into a delivered life. Through the announced birth of Jesus through a virgin, God executed a divine plan to bring a savior and a deliverer from sin into life, a plan rooted in promises tied to a regal line running through David and back to the original patriarch Abraham.

Women and Gentiles

The women named are Tamar, Rahab, Ruth, and the wife of Uriah (Bathsheba). In some cases, there is action related to these women that is unseemly, as Tamar was mother to a child out of wedlock, Rahab was a prostitute, and David sinned horribly against the wife of Uriah. The indirect mention of Bathsheba probably means she is not blamed for the act but David is. Ruth did nothing wrong but may be suspect because of how she came to be tied to Boaz. Rahab and Ruth, at the least, were Gentiles. Amazingly by God's grace, all of these irregular connections were a part of the line that led to Messiah (Blomberg 1992, 55–56). Technically these women were not all immoral, as Ruth was righteous and Rahab did nothing wrong with reference to Israel but believed God was behind the conquest. In fact, these two women were highly regarded in Israel's history. Still, Mary's alleged irregular birth also may fit here, with several of these women's pasts serving as a foil. John 8:48 shows such charges were tied to Jesus, even though they were not true.

Regardless of how many of the women were Gentiles, at least two of them were. So Matthew had his eye on the world, not just Israel (Garland 1995, 18). Perhaps the indirect reference to Bathsheba as the wife of Uriah, known as Uriah the Hittite, points to this theme. How Israel blesses the world is the key storyline, as the promise to Abraham in Genesis 12:1–3 looked to blessing the world. God was restoring what had been lost in humanity's dysfunctional turning away from God noted in Genesis 1–11. God redeems sinners of all races through what he has promised to do through Messiah.

EXPOSITION (1:1–25)

With the rise of false messiahs in Judea and Judeans who desired to break with Rome to re-establish Israel as an independent kingdom, not to mention the claims of some Roman emperors to be a savior-deliverers, Matthew reaffirmed Jesus's regal roots to Jewish believers living in or near the homeland. Both the genealogy and the angelic announcement to Joseph root Jesus's family tree in hope by pointing back to Abraham and David, while citing the example of "God with us" in the prophecy of Isaiah 7:14. This opening is also saturated with grace. In a move unusual for a genealogy, four women are noted alongside Mary. One need not assume all the women present in the listing are there to make the same point, but this is often assumed in the discussion. Osborne (2010, 63–64) is right to see various points at play in their presence. So, through the announced birth of Jesus through a virgin, God executed a promised divine plan to bring *the* savior and deliverer from sin who is God with us.

The Genealogy (1:1–17)

Through the announced birth of Jesus through a virgin, God executed a divine plan rooted in promises tied to a regal line running through David and Abraham.

1:1. Matthew opens his genealogy with a title (Robertson 1934, 793; Wallace 1996, 50). Three names dominate: Jesus Christ, David, and Abraham. Yet the order is reversed here from unsual recounting; it moves from oldest to youngest (vv. 2–16; Davies and Allison 1988, 149). His descending genealogy moves from Abraham to Jesus. Luke's genealogy ascends in the opposite direction, moving from Jesus to Adam (Luke 3:23–38).

Matthew's use of "genesis" (γενέσεως) points to a beginning or an arrival, an origin (BDAG s.v. "γένεσις" 3:192–93). The title looks not only at the genealogy, but also to Jesus's arrival onto the scene of history as part of God's promised plan. It was not farfetched for Matthew to render this "the book of Genesis." He saw an allusion back to the start of this divine promise story in the book of Genesis. The word "genesis" reappears in 1:18 as a literary bracket, making a larger scope possible, even likely. The resumption does not point to a break with what goes before in the genealogy, but a connection. The genealogy looks back at Jesus's roots, before his arrival, while 1:18 picks up the story and moves it forward. The "new" part of the long divine story is the arrival of Jesus, the Messiah, but Matthew was looking at the fulfillment and the completion of a story long promised, not a new drama.

Matthew's genealogy opens with regal overtones, by mentioning David. Yet Jesus's birth was distinct in the humble arrival of this divinely sent king in contrast to the era of pomp that accompanied the Roman emperor (Wilkins 2004, 54–55). This birth involved a humble Jewish family tucked away in a far corner of the Roman Empire (much like the Samoan Islands are a part of America but are not much in the news about America).

Birth Narrative Distinctives

Where Mark begins with John the Baptist, Luke focuses on Mary's experience, and John ignores the birth to point to Jesus's preexistence, Matthew looks at the line of promise and the perspective of Joseph. This pious, engaged man was asked to adjust to God's surprising action and did so with a response of faith. The distinct perspectives reflect the way in which the Gospels often complement each other.

Matthew extends the longed-for promise back to divine commitments made to the other two figures named in the verse. David, Israel's king, received the promise of a dynastic line in 2 Samuel 7:8–16. This hope grew into the expectation of a kingdom built not by hands but by God, as the book of Daniel presents it. A deliverer portrayed in various ways was anticipated by Jewish people of the time. He was seen as a king, as in Isaiah 9–11. He was seen as a figure of heavenly authority, as in Daniel 7:9–14. In later Judaism, he was seen as a military figure bringing victory from the nations (Pss. Sol. 17–18) or as a celestial figure who judged with God (1 En. 37–71). Variations on this idea include the "sprout of Jesse" (Isa. 11:10) and "shoot of David" (Jer. 23:5; 33:15; Zech. 3:8; 6:12; 4Q252 [4Q252 Patr. Bless.] 3; 4Q174 [4Q Flor] 1:11–12; 4Q161 frags. 7–10, 22; 4 Ezra 12:32; Davies and Allison 1988, 156). These various expectations, all of them about power and none about suffering, may be the reason the title is not so prevalent in Jesus's ministry. Jews had missed as part of the hope the portrait of suffering that came with it from Isaiah 52:13–53:12. For Matthew and other Jewish authors, the starting point for this hope was the promise to David. That promise came with a variety of expressions, which Jesus brought together in one unified hope (Bateman et al. 2012).

Matthew highlights Jesus as the Son of David, using the expression nine times (1:1, 20-of Joseph; 9:27; 12:23; 15:22; 20:30, 31; 21:9, 15; plus, twice as son with David clearly in view, 22:42, 45). Luke also emphasized this about Jesus in his birth account (Luke 1:27, 32–33; 2:4, 11). In fact, the New Testament makes this point about Jesus being David's son again and again (Acts 2:30–36; 13:23; Rom. 1:3; 2 Tim. 2:8; Rev. 22:16; McNeile 1915, 1).

Behind God's commitment to David stood the example of Abraham. He received the promise of a nation coming from his seed and the hope that through that descendant the world would be blessed (Gen. 12:1–3; also Gen. 18:18; contra Nolland 2005, 72, who does not see such an implication). For the nation, the Abrahamic covenant involved the hope of a people, peace, and land. However, beyond that there was the expectation that blessing would spring forth to the world through the line Abraham would father. This hope came to be seen in the one special seed, Jesus, through whom God's promise was said to come (Gal. 3:1–4:6, esp. 3:16). Matthew sought to tell the story of the unique figure in God's plan, Jesus, the Christ. Matthew's title in verse 1 indicates the note that Jesus's arrival was the start of a big, long-planned gospel program reaching back to the beginning of God's restoring work through promsies to Abraham. Here, in contrast to the Jewish leadership, was where the promise and hope resided (Konradt 2020, 26). The genealogy both affirms and legitimizes the new movement as rooted in God's plan.

1:2. Matthew begins by tracing the line of Jesus from Abraham. Many of the names are found in genealogical lists from 1 Chronicles 1–3 in the Septuagint, as well as Ruth 4:18–22.

Throughout the genealogy, "was the father" (ἐγεννησεν) is key (BAGD s.v. "γεννάω" 1a, 193). The presentation of generations in groups of fourteen was intentionally rhetorical. The first group of fourteen begins with Abraham and ends with David (v. 6). It is the line for the nation of Israel that is presented here as Abraham fathers Isaac, Isaac begets Jacob, and Jacob fathers Judah and his brothers, an allusion to the twelve tribes of Israel. The story of Genesis chapters 12–50 is in view here. The listing reinforces the title of the opening verse. Both Isaac and Jacob were born after some difficulty (Gen. 12–27), so the emergence of this family was seen as a work of God's grace.

1:3. Matthew then moves to the children Perez and Zerah (Ruth 4:18; 1 Chron. 2:4) of Judah through Tamar (Gen. 38), as well as to Hezron (Num. 26:21; Ruth 4:18; 1 Chron. 2:5) and Aram (= Ram in some translations; Ruth 4:19; 1 Chron. 2:9, 25). Tamar is not described in Genesis in a way that makes her ethnicity clear, but many commentators think she is presented in a way that makes it likely she was a Gentile (e.g., Davies, and Allison 1988, 170, "a Canaanite"). The period from Perez to Amminadab (Matt. 1:3–4) covers 450 years in four generations. We know nothing else about Hezron and Aram.

1:4. Matthew continues his genealogy by naming Aram, Amminadab (Exod. 6:23), Nashon (Num. 1:7; 2:3; 7:12–17; 10:14), and Salmon (Ruth 4:19–20). Luke 3:33; 1 Chron. 2:9–11 differs here as Amminadab is named the son of Admin and a grandson of Arni (it may be that Admin in Luke abbreviates or is a variation on Admminadab; so one option from Nolland 2005, 78, who also sees an inadvertent repetition here as another option). This also might reflect the skipping of generations already noted when Matthew is compared with Luke. In this case, the father and son really share a same name, and the difference distinguishes them and makes clear we do not have a repeated name. The situation here is complex as there are also variant names in the manuscripts at this point in Luke. Nashon was known as "prince of the sons of Judah" (1 Chron. 2:10; Davies and Allison 1988, 172). Outside of the listing in genealogies, Salmon is otherwise unknown.

Portrait of a Woman as Ruth.
Painting by Francesco Hayez.

1:5. Matthew then names four male figures—Salmon, Boaz, Obed, and Jesse—who also come from 1 Chronicles 2:11–12 and Ruth 4:21–22. Matthew's mention of Rahab is a fresh detail. This looks to be the harlot from Joshua 2 and 6 who hailed from Jericho (Heb. 11:31; James 2:25). It is not clear where the source for this detail is from, especially since there appears to be a time gap of up to two hundred years between the two figures (Nolland 2005, 78 n. 49).

To have fathered someone in this list may not always mean the next generation (Hendrikson 1973, 116). The role of Ruth is not so surprising given both the book of Ruth and its own genealogy which is paralleled in Matthew's listing. These events link David to Bethlehem. Obed only appears in genealogies. Jesse also is noted in 1 Samuel 16–17 and is tied to David in several texts (1 Sam. 20:27, 30; Isa. 11:1, 10; Sir. 45:25; Rom. 15:12; Eighteen Benedictions 15; *Midr. on* Ps. 21.2; Targum on Isa. 11:1; Davies and Allison 1988, 174).

1:6. Matthew's naming of Jesse, David, Solomon, and the wife of the Hittite reflects 1 Chronicles 2:13–15; 3:5, 10, and Ruth 4:22, as well as accounts noting Bathsheba from 2 Samuel 11:26; 12:10, 15, and especially the narrative from those two chapters. This is Matthew's last parallel with the genealogy of Ruth 4. First Chronicles 3:10–15 is the parallel from Solomon to Josiah as the kings of Judah become the focus. Matthew calls Bathsheba the wife of the Hittite probably to underscore the Gentile relationship. David, as the fourteenth name, ends the first section of fourteen names. Matthew identifies David as the king with an emphatic double use of the Greek article: the David the king, something English translations may not reflect. This is a royal genealogy (McNeile 1915, 2). The term "king" appears twenty-two times in Matthew, more than in any other New Testament book, but only six uses refer to Jesus (Matt. 2:2; 21:5; 27:11, 29, 37, 42; Morris 1992, 24). These appearances cluster at the end of the gospel, as do uses of "Messiah."

Matthew begins a new listing of fourteen generations with Solomon (1 Kings 1–11; 1 Chron. 22–28; 2 Chron. 1–9), extending to the Babylonian captivity. His name will appear again in the next verse. The note about a third woman, Bathsheba, "wife of Uriah," appears. David's involvement with her is seen as the most noteworthy of David's failings, adultery plus murder (1 Kings 15:5). The placement of such a combination in the messianic line shows God's grace. Samuel described how David succeeded Saul as king after Saul's failure to obey God at Gilgal (1 Sam. 13). In anticipation of that kingship, Samuel anointed David as king (1 Sam. 16).

1:7. Matthew moves from King David to naming four subsequent Judean kings: Solomon, Rehoboam (1 Kings 11:43; negative: 14:21–30; 2 Chron. 12:13–14), Abijah (negative: 1 Kings 14:31; 15:1–8; positive: 2 Chron. 13:1–22), and Asa (positive: 1 Kings 15:8–24; 2 Chron. 14–16), whom Matthew calls *Asaph* in the better manuscripts (cf. the mansucripts p1vid, א, B). These were the kings of the south, from the tribe of Judah. Many were described as evil kings, while some like Abijah and Asa had mixed reviews. Still the line of promise marched on through the generations. Some commentators suggest Asaph is a name introduced to point to Levitical temple musicians, but this is merely speculative (Davies and Allison 1988, 175; Nolland 2005, 79–80). The fact that Josephus calls this king *Asanos* shows he was known by a variety of names.

1:8. Matthew continues the line of Judean kings from Asaph (= Asa) to Jehoshaphat (a mostly positive rule: 1 Kings 15:24; 22:41–50; 2 Chron. 17–20), Joram (1 Kings 22:50; negative: 2 Kings 8:16–24; 2 Chron. 21:1–20), and Uzziah. A curse on the house of Ahab may be involved here where judgment fell on three generations so names were excluded (Exod. 20:5; Nolland 2005, 80 and n. 62; on Uzziah being given a mixed assessment, 2 Chron. 26). Such omissions in genealogical listings are not unusual (compare Gen. 46:21 with 1 Chron. 8:1–4; 1 Chron. 5:33–36 with Ezra 7:3; Ezra 5:1 with Zech. 1:1; Davies and Allison 1988, 176–77; Gundry 1982, 16).

1:9. From Uzziah we move to Jotham (mixed positive and negative: 2 Kings 15:32–38; 2 Chron. 27:1–9), Ahaz (negative: 2 Kings

16:1–20; 2 Chron. 28:1–27), and Hezekiah (very positive: 2 Kings 18–20; 2 Chron. 29–32).

1:10. Manasseh had a reputation as an evil king, who repented at the end of his life (2 Kings 21:1–18; 2 Chron. 33:1–10). The better reading of the Greek manuscripts for the next king (Amon) is "Amos," as it is the more difficult reading, making it unlikely to be the reading to be produced by a correcting scribe, and is fairly widely attested. Josiah was seen as a righteous king who led a reform, including a renewal around the rediscovery of the Law (2 Chron. 34–35).

List of Good, Mixed, and Evil Kings from Rehoboam with Noted Breaks (*)

Rehoboam—evil
Abijah—mixed
Asaph (Asa)—good
Jehoshaphat—good
Joram—evil
* (three skipped)
Uzziah—mixed
Jotham—mixed good and evil
Ahaz—evil
Hezekiah—good
Manasseh—evil, repents
Amon—evil
Josiah—good
* (two skipped)
Jeconiah—evil

This reflects the topsy-turvy history of Israel.

1:11. Matthew moves from Josiah to Jeconiah, also known as Jehoiachin (negative: 2 Kings 24:8–17; 2 Chron. 36:9–10). By doing so, he skips Jehoahaz and Jehoiakim. The reference to "his brothers" alludes to Zedekiah at the least (1 Chron. 3:16; 2 Chron. 36:10). The mention of brothers also may be a way to bracket with the reference to the royalty of Judah, where the last mention of brothers takes place, suggesting the end of functioning kingship. Here were the last true kings of the nation. At this point, Matthew ends the second list of fourteen, and the Babylonian captivity points to the end of listings (beyond verse 12) that have parallels in the Hebrew Scripture.

1:12. The final group of fourteen follows with the Jeconiah to Christ sequence. The reference to deportation points to exile and the judgment of the nation for covenantal unfaithfulness (2 Chron. 36:15–21, rooted in Deut. 28–32). The reality of deportation showed the need for a savior-deliverer. The fact that Rome occupied Israel when Jesus was born and when Matthew wrote also points to the national need for a savior. Shealtiel comes next (Ezra 3:2, 8; Neh. 12:1). He was known as the father of Zerubbabel (on Zerubbabel: Hag. 2:23—signet ring and chosen; Zech. 4:2, 14—lampstand and anointed [Osborne 2010, 67]; Matthew's remark appears supported by Ezra 3:2, 8; 5:2; Neh. 12:1; Hag. 1:1, 12, 14; 2:2, 23). Zerubbabel became a messianic-like figure as the Israelite vassal governing in Jerusalem.

1:13–15. Matthew then cites nine names with no parallels anywhere: Abiud, Eliakim, Azor, Zadok, Akim (Achim in some translations), Eliud, Eleazar, Matthan, and Jacob. Matthew's sources for these names are unknown. Yet these nine names covered around five hundred years. By contrast, Luke has eighteen names in this period, showing Matthew's selectivity in his listing (Bruner 2004a, 15). Prominent Jewish families did keep genealogies. For example, Josephus mentions his own family records (*Vita* 6; *C. Ap.* 1.28–36; *Mishnah, Qidd.* 4:5–6; France 2007, 39 and n. 41; Jeremias 1969, 275–90; Keener 2009, 76). Eusebius also discusses genealogies (*Hist. Eccl.* 3.12.19; 3.20.1–6; 3.32.3–6; Nolland 2005, 85 and n. 94).

1:16. Matthew ends the listing from Jacob to Joseph with a key mention of Mary, the wife of Joseph from whom was fathered Jesus who was called the Christ. Two things were important to Matthew. First, the relative pronoun makes the connection to Mary the point of emphasis since "whom" (ἧς; NET) is feminine. While Mary bore the child, Joseph was not the biological father. This was a virgin birth. Matthew makes that point explicit in verses 18–25. Second, Matthew's listing comes with an *inclusio*, as the name of Jesus Christ opens the listing in the title of verse 1 and closes it here.

1:17. Matthew concludes here with a listing of three sets of fourteen. As noted while going through the list, Matthew skips some generations (see sidebar of the list of Israel's kings). Matthew's point is rhetorical. There is most likely a *gematria* (a number play) on the name of David, based on the consonants in Hebrew which add up to fourteen. The two divisions in the listing are at David and the Babylonian captivity. Toussaint (1980, 41) suggests that there is a covenantal connection here, since the Abrahamic covenant belongs to the first period, the Davidic covenant belongs to the second, and the new covenant belongs to the third. Only forty-one names appear, suggesting a name should be counted twice (perhaps Jeconiah as pointing to both Jehoiakim and Jehoiachin—Nolland 2005, 86; Wilkins 2004, 64; or David—Konradt 2020, 28).

Matthew, by means of a genealogy, gives the legal line of Jesus through Joseph as son of David and Abraham. This Davidic connection through Joseph in this scene stands in contrast to Luz (1989, 111), who says how Jesus became related to Joseph is left open and is part of the historical difficulties of the genealogy that make it unusable today. However, the passage that follows the genealogy (vv. 18–25) explains the connection and how Jesus came into Joseph's house as a legal heir of the house of David and Abraham (Davies and Allison 1988, 185; on how vv. 18–25 connect, France 2007, 45–47, and especially France 1981). Despite questions about sources, the transparent presence of skipping in the list, and a distinct list of names at points from Luke's, Matthew makes an ancient claim to the Davidic line that is reflective of Jesus's roots that the church embraced.

Osborne (2010, 68–70) says this unit makes five points: (1) the Messiah is here; (2) the kingdom is here; (3) God's providence is at work; (4) outcasts and the downtrodden are included; and (5) there is a mission to the world. Given how women in particular were marginalized in the first century, their inclusion in the genealogy also makes a statement about their importance.

The Angelic Birth Announcement (1:18–25)

The word to Joseph points to God's divine plan involving a Christ who is God with us, a deliverer from sin into life.

1:18. In his second key unit, Matthew moves from the genealogy to the story of how the unusual birth was communicated to Joseph. Strictly speaking, the birth involved a virgin conception. God acted to conceive a child in a woman with no previous experience. Paradoxically as it sounds, it was a unique birth: a virgin gave birth to a child with a unique origin. Joseph lacked knowledge of this conception and so was understandably disturbed by the situation of his betrothed being pregnant without his involvement.

Matthew portrays the birth of Jesus as a fulfillment of Isaiah 7:14 (cf. 1:23). While ancient parallels to divine births do not involve virgin conception, they do describe crassly how a divinity or god impregnated the human mother. In contrast, Luke presents the birth announcement from Mary's perspective. So the birth, or better, conception, of Jesus is said to have been "in the following manner" (οὕτως ἦν).

This scene is actually the first of five historical events in Matthew's infancy account tied to Scripture (Blomberg 1992, 56; France 2007, 40–45; Keener 2009, 81–83). This scene, according to Matthew, was the first to be directed by divine activity, involving here both angelic announcement and the use of dreams. Dreams will be repeatedly used in these early chapters. Matthew highlights the fact that God moved and acted to bring about his plan. This also explains how Jesus was of David's line, having been accepted as Joseph's son and legal heir (Garland 1995, 21).

The angelic announcement to Joseph came while he and Mary were still betrothed and before she moved in with him to be his wife. He reacted as anyone would initially, thinking of some likely immoral act on the part of his betrothed. Mary was likely a very young teenager at this time, about thirteen or so. Joseph was likely older, probably between eighteen and twenty. It was during the betrothal time that, disturbingly, she was found to be pregnant. Although the narrator says the pregnancy was by the Holy Spirit (ἐκ πνεύματος ἁγίου), Joseph did not know this at the start of the scene.

While the Spirit gave life, Matthew provides few details about the cultural context for the conception. Betrothal would have made Mary a part of Joseph's family and would have involved a period of up to a year before the wedding for a virgin, while a widow could be married in thirty days (Davies and Allison 1988, 199). According to Deuteronomy 22:23–24, Mary could have been punished as an adulteress in a way a virgin woman without attachment would not (Deut. 22:28–29; cf. *m. Ketub.* 1:2; 4:2; 5:2; Turner 2008, 65). There was a contract and an exchange of gifts as a pledge. Though only engaged, Mary was considered socially tied to Joseph. This was why Joseph contemplated some type of legal dismissal. Nonetheless, with the betrothal, Mary was in an in-between social state as she was connected to her fiancé Joseph, but not fully his until she was married and moved into his house. This in-between status was evident in that a young girl's marriage contract rights belonged to her father and not to her if the marriage was not yet consummated and her betrothed died (see Tob. 7:13; *m. Ketub.* 4:2–3; Wilkins 2004, 73–75). If she married her "betrothed" (μνηστεύω) by moving into his house, then the contract was hers to make if her husband died. This is Matthew's only use of the verb that means to be betrothed (BDAG s.v. "μνηστεύω" 656; also in Luke 1:27; 2:5).

1:19. Matthew describes Joseph as a pious Jew. He was righteous in terms of following the law and did not want to shame his betrothed spouse. The clause provides the motivation of Joseph's intended actions and shows the character of Jesus's parents (Osborne 2010, 75). It is not concessive as Joseph does not act despite being righteous, but because he is "righteous" (contra Turner 2008, 65; on the meaning of δίκαιος, see Davies and Allison 1988, 202). The note portrays Joseph as having compassion in the midst of his seeming moral dilemma. He had decided to give Mary the required bill of divorce, called a *git,* in secret, that is, privately (Tosato 1979; *m. Ketub.* 1:4; also 9:4, 8), because seemingly she had acted unfaithfully. Such a divorce would be required (Bockmuehl 1989; Wilkins 2004, 75). This is a better explanation than that he wanted to put her aside because he knew she was pregnant by the Spirit and so regarded her as sacred (but so Gundry 1982, 22).

1:20. While Joseph was still contemplating what to do, he had a dream. This was the first of several dreams where God directed events in Matthew (2:12, 13, 19, 22; also 27:19). This was not unusual, given the use of dreams in the Old Testament (Gen. 28:12; 37:5–9; Num. 12:6; Judg. 7:13; Dan. 2:3; 4:5; 7:1; Osborne 2010, 76). An angel instructed Joseph as a son of David to not fear to take Mary as his wife, that is, to consummate the marriage and take Mary into his home. The reason was simple: the child Mary carried was "from" (ἐκ) the Holy Spirit, a repeat of the idea noted in verse 18. This repetition makes the point emphatically. If viewed as analogous to Luke's angelic announcement, this was not *the* angel of the Lord, but *an* angel (so correctly Davies and Allison 1988, 206; Turner 2008, 68).

1:21. Matthew presents the birth announcement in a manner typical of other divine birth announcements (Gen. 16:11; 17:19; Isa. 7:14; Luke 1:13, 31). There often was a call not to fear and then in all cases instructions about the son to be born with a specific name. Matthew's language about the birth of the son anticipates the citation of Isaiah 7:14 in verse 23. The child's name would be "Jesus" (Ἰησοῦν), as the angel also told Mary in Luke 1:31, meaning "Yahweh saves." The name points to the calling, because the child would save people from their sins. As Nolland (2005, 99) points out, this was normally attributed as a responsibility of God. The language is close to Psalm 130:8, where Yahweh delivers from sin. The mention of sin shows the issues surrounding deliverance are not political but moral and spiritual. The name Jesus was a Hellenized version of Joshua. When Joseph names the child, he says the child is mine and is a part of my family, lineage, and heritage (*m,* B. Bat. 8:6; Culpepper 2021, 38).

The "people" mentioned here in verses 19–21 are often seen as Israel, since the picture is of a regal, legal relationship to one descended from David. In that case, it may well refer to the faithful remnant, since only they would benefit from the offer of forgiveness because they accepted what Jesus had done (Turner 2008, 68). In Matthew, "people" (λαός) refers to Israel (1:21; 2:4, 6; 4:16, 23; 13:15; 15:8; 21:23; 26:3, 5, 47; 27:1, 25, 64). However, Bruner (2004a, 31) argues it is both Israel and the church, but without giving a reason other than to claim a double sense and cites Chrysostom, *Homilies* 4:13. Davies and Allison (1988, 210) appeal to Matthew 21:43, but the term for "people" there is different (ἔθνος). More persuasive is the observation that the genealogy looks at Gentiles in the line, suggesting a broader referent (Wilkins 2004, 77). The intention of the term is likely broader than ethnic Israel, although Jesus did come to call his kin back to God. The reference to people here is to God's people, whoever embraces the one God sent and responds to the opportunity his coming represents.

1:22–23. Matthew validates his narration with the first of five Old Testament citations used in chapters 1–2. He places the citations in a narrator's comments. It is best to see these verses in the same way and not as a continuation of the announcement (Turner 2008, 68). Matthew, then, argues that what God will do through Jesus is a part of a prophesied program from God.

Matthew's first citation is Isaiah 7:14. It points to the special character of Jesus's birth through a virgin and in such a way that "God is with us." Matthew notes that this verse was fulfilled by this divine act. "Fulfilled" (πληρόω) means to complete something, in this case, with reference to Scripture (BDAG s.v. "πληρόω" 4a, 827–29). This promise from God came "through" (διὰ) the prophet, with the preposition pointing to intermediate means. Matthew commonly uses this kind of a formula pointing to fulfillment (2:15, 17, 23; 4:14; 8:17; 12:17; 13:35; 21:4; 26:56; 27:9). Morris (1992, 30) points out that Matthew's use of "all" in v. 22 is not common to Matthew, but appears only twice, here and in 26:56.

Definition of a Typological-Prophetic Text and Isaiah 7:14

A typological prophetic text includes a pattern prophecy where a near-term event mirrors a later ultimate fulfillment. The pattern is in the parallel. Example types include creation-new creation, exodus-new exodus, and day of the Lord as locust plague and then as day of judgment. Sometimes the ultimate fulfillment is a greater example than the original. So in the OT a birth by a virgin at the time of announcement becomes in the NT a birth by a woman who is a virgin at conception. The difference is the escalation. "God with us" is also escalated as the OT event shows God with us; while now in the NT, Jesus is God with us in the flesh—a point Matthew develops and which emerges more clearly throughout his whole gospel.

The fulfillment here is probably typological-prophetic in that in Isaiah's time a current virgin had a child and that by the time that child was of age, Ahaz's kingship had been judged. The announcement of such a child and the sign the child reflected showed God was with the people. In like manner, but with typical typological escalation, now a virgin (παρθένος) conceived supernaturally and gave birth to a child who truly was God with us—the meaning of the name Immanuel. In speaking of the name Emmanuel here, we are not thinking about what Jesus was called, but a naming of who he was and is in terms of his significance (a theme Matthew likes; 17:17; 18:20; 26:29).

Matthew will spend his entire gospel filling out what Jesus's birth means: (1) God's activity was present in Jesus (2) who himself showed authority like that of God (Matt. 9:3–6; 18:20; 28:20). Yahweh was saving by means of this child who was God with us.

1:24–25. Matthew manifests Joseph's righteousness again when Joseph obeyed the angel's command and took Mary to be his wife (v. 20). The couple also showed restraint in that there were no sexual relations between them until the son had been born. In a second act of obedience, the couple named the child Jesus (v. 21).

God acted to bring this special child into the world, explaining the unique nature of his conception. He was part of a program of promise that meant God was at work to save his people from their sins. This Jesus would be a savior. The special nature of the birth was both predicted in Scripture and pointed to the special nature of the time in God's revealed program. Pious parents raised the child and were responsive to God's call and leading. They also belonged to the promised line of David. They would now follow God's directions in receiving the child that included acts of protection God would provide. The primary actor in Matthew 1 is the God who executed the divine plan to send Jesus to earth to restore what had been lost because of sin.

THEOLOGICAL FOCUS

The exegetical idea (through the announced birth of Jesus through a virgin, God executes a promised divine plan to bring a savior and deliverer from sin who is God with us) leads to this theological idea: God's long-standing promise to the world through Abraham and David comes in a virgin-born Jesus.

First, God's long-standing promise is prominent. Whether one looks at the motley crew that makes up the genealogy of Jesus, considers the special nature of Jesus's birth, or looks at how Joseph is informed of what is taking place, it is God who acts in grace to save God's people from their sins through a deliverer sent. Jesus's human credentials and social standing link him to David and Abraham. The promise of Scripture in covenant and in texts like Isaiah 7:14 show God's plan.

Second, the virgin birth of Jesus tells us much about humanity and its need but tells us more about the God who steps in to provide what we as humans lack, supplying what we need. The chapter then is less about a miracle and more about God, who uses the unusual means to get our attention about what is taking place. This is why miracles are called "signs" in Scripture. They do not exist for their own ends but point to God's character and actions authenticating what is taking place. The theological idea of this text is that God has sent the Son in a miraculous way to meet the human need of a savior from sin in line with his promises.

The virgin birth of Jesus also makes it important to see the Trinity at work. It is God who executes the plan. He does so through the sending of Jesus, while the Spirit is the creative source that leads to incarnation. This interplay will be important in key spots in Matthew, even appearing at the end of the gospel in the baptismal formula about the Father, Son, and Spirit. The unity and triunity of God acting in concert reveals energy of God toward humanity and the restoration of the creation. The Spirit as the source of life is also an important picture in the passage. The virgin birth is an act of God's Spirit. The Scripture shows the program and anticipates it.

Finally, we also see how God works to overcome the impact of sin, shown so vividly through the names that occupy the genealogy. The sin that led to exile and deportation for a nation causes God to send a savior to bring about deliverance and reconciliation.

The noting of the women shows that God acts because of sin and in spite of sin. Sin drives God to send a savior, and that savior comes through a line of descendants whose stories are riddled with sin and failure. Humanity cannot fix the problem of sin and brokenness on its own. God is about redeeming what has been lost and restoring what has gone awry. God also notes the lowly, those whom society often ignores. The listing of women points in this direction, since women often were excluded from such listings.

In the midst of unfaithfulness, God does find some faithful people, folks like Joseph and Mary. God uses them and their faithfulness in obedience even at the risk of public shame. It is easy to forget that in the claim that God was responsible for this child's birth, many would see a story made up to mask a different, more shameful event. Joseph and Mary take this on, because their loyalty to God is the priority.

This birth announcement says much about God, about God's relationship to people, about how people should respond, and what they might have to both gain and risk to follow God.

PREACHING AND TEACHING STRATEGIES

Exegetical and Theological Synthesis

Matthew demonstrates God's providence and power over Jesus's birth. Not only did the Messiah's birth fulfill covenantal promises to Abraham and David, but it also suspended natural law to secure a virgin birth. The genealogy rooted Jesus in human history. Joseph's dreams revealed news from the heavens. Certainly, the coming Messiah bridged heaven and earth.

Moreover, the opening scene of Matthew's gospel underscores the gravity of sin. Former generations of faithful people remained incapable of lifting the stain of sin from humanity. God had to intervene. Enter Jesus: Savior, Immanuel, the Messiah.

Finally, human agents played a part in God's powerful, providential plan to redeem creation. The genealogy comprises likely and unlikely figures whose faith paved the way for Jesus's arrival. Joseph demonstrated nobility, dedication, and obedience to God. Mary gave silent assent to bear the Christ child. God's plans typically incorporate human players; our obedience is critical.

Preaching Idea

God's family plans are perfectly conceived.

Contemporary Connections

What does it mean?

What does it mean that God's family plans are perfectly conceived? First, we must distinguish between spiritual family and biological family. Jesus made this distinction in several core teachings on discipleship. When he called his first disciples, they left their families to be with him (Matt. 4:18–22). Jesus left his biological family outside a social gathering, while redefining family as those who do the will of God (12:46–50). More starkly, Jesus called disciples to hate father and mother, brother and sister, if it were to impede their love for him (Luke 14:26). In a beautiful contrast, during his execution, Jesus connected John and his mother as a spiritual family set (John 19:26–27). In other words, through Jesus God works to make a new, multiethnic, spiritual family of faith.

A Sampling of Family Imagery in the NT

John speaks of believers as children of God (John 1:12–13; 3:3–8; 14:18; 1 John 3:1; 5:1).

Paul speaks to believers as brothers and sisters, born of the Spirit (Rom. 8:12–17; Gal. 4:4–7; see also nearly every epistolary greeting and closing, e.g., Col. 1:2 and 4:15).

Paul describes the church as a household (Gal. 6:10; Eph. 2:19).

Paul presents himself as a parental figure (1 Cor. 4:17; Gal. 4:19; 1 Thess. 2:5–12; 2 Tim. 1:2).

General epistles employ family language (Heb. 3:1–5; James 1:2; 2:1, 5; 2 Peter 1:10).

Second, the perfect conception of God's plan speaks specifically to Jesus's incarnation. Paul summarized this well in his letter to the Galatians: "But when the appropriate time had come, God sent out his Son, born of a woman, born under the law" (4:4). Matthew verifies Jesus's perfect conception by stylizing his genealogy, as well as presenting it as a miraculous fulfillment of Isaiah's prophecy. As a full-fledged member of the human race (John 1:14), Jesus could empathize with our weaknesses, face temptations, suffer in the flesh, and obey everything commanded by God without sinning (Heb. 5:7). Thus, perfection not only marked his miraculous conception but also his entire messianic career.

Is it true?

Is it true that God's plans for his family are perfectly conceived? Indeed, God is perfect and perfection marks all his plans. However, this does not mean God's family plans exempt us from all pain, difficulty, or suffering. In fact, God often uses painful trials or adverse circumstances to grow his family. A brief glimpse of Jesus's genealogy underscores this fact. Many of the names on the list recall stories of barrenness and waiting, deceit and murder, death and longing. Jesus's family of origin was far from perfect, yet God worked a perfect plan despite generations of sin.

Furthermore, we must insist on seeing God's perfect family plan as his initiative to draw all peoples to himself through Jesus the Messiah. Matthew has in mind the grand narrative of redemption, not the personalized portraits of our families. God does not sit down with us for a family-planning session to reveal whether we will be married or single, have seven children or none, live close to the grandchildren, or spend our twilight years in a retirement community. Many people have gone off the rails trying to divine God's mind for the fine-tuned details of their lives.

Nonetheless, Matthew makes clear to readers of *any* generation that God knows *all* generations. He is familiar with our faces and family names. He knows our backstories and coming attractions. He knows sin is an age-old problem, and Jesus's advent sets in motion the perfect remedy. God will perfect what he started in his spiritual family.

Now what?

How should we respond to God's perfectly conceived family plan? First, we revel in his merciful character and mighty power. Sadly, we often skim the list of names in the genealogy, giving little attention to their stories. Moreover, we allow the commercialized Christmas season to taint the wonder of Jesus's birth narrative. God overcame generations of sin, Joseph's religious decorum, and Mary's virgin womb to conceive Jesus in perfection. He chose the right people at the right time to fulfill promises dating back millennia. God's ability to execute a plan should astound us.

Second, our awe in God's plans should bring assurance. Matthew describes a God who fulfills promises and keeps covenants. His stylized genealogy shows God's willingness to work with imperfect and ethnically diverse people to conceive a perfect family plan. His editorial remarks detail God's desire to be with us, to save us, to put an end to sin. We can trust this God.

Finally, Matthew's opening chapter should stir introspection. It might move us to consider family events that shaped us. It might surface our fragile trust in God's faithfulness. It might reveal our tendency to reduce God's plan to a personalized path to getting hitched or pregnant. Or Jesus's genealogy and birth may remind us of the people who introduced us to God and invited us to join his family. For we did not conceive our own salvation; life in God's family came by his initiative.

Creativity in Presentation

In recent years, online tools have made it easier for people to track down their family history. Websites like ancestry.com allow you to trace your family line through some unexpected twists and turns. My (Tim's) brother-in-law discovered the Native American blood in his family lines was a myth. Genetic testing services like 23andMe help you unravel mysteries of your DNA, perhaps exposing a greater risk for diabetes. Whether these biological research tools uncover good surprises or sobering details, they feed a swelling interest in family backgrounds. Consider highlighting one of these tools as a way of surfacing our growing engagement with family roots.

Another way to illustrate family plans is to show a picture of a family tree. Some family trees might look orderly, like an organization chart. Others, however, would be riddled with divisions, splits, and new lines. (Sadly, the "family tree" of my denomination reflects the latter.) In the West, many of us struggle to trace our family lines more than a few generations. Only three years ago, when helping my daughter with a family tree project, did I officially learn my paternal grandfather's name: Aloise. Until that assignment, I introduced myself as "Timothy, son of Frederick, son of, well, I'm not sure, but we called him 'Bud.'" Giving your people a chance to turn to a neighbor in the worship service and introduce themselves using the names of successive generations of paternal grandfathers may be humorous, sad, or telling.

Our technological culture promises to perfect our family plans in the future. Not only have we seen a drastic reduction in infant mortality in the last century, we've also found ways around infertility. Though no method is foolproof—and infertility will remain ever complicated by emotional pain—in vitro fertilization, intrauterine insemination, and surrogate pregnancy offer some innovative forms of family planning. Technology, however, has overreached by trying to produce designer babies, at first by removing genetic diseases, but eventually genetic enhancements will be sought out: intelligence, looks, physical strength. Science fiction warns us that our godlike aim to perfect family planning will go awry. Consider contrasting our scientific errors in family planning with God's perfectly conceived plan for Jesus.

Examples from Film and Literature Where Designer Babies Go Awry

- Bean, the protagonist in *Ender's Shadow* (Card 1999) doesn't fit in or feel human.
- Babies in Huxley's dystopian *Brave New World* (1932) are produced in test tubes.
- Children are aborted who do not meet certain thresholds in *The Giver* (Lowry 1993).
- In *Gattaca* (1997, directed by Andrew Niccol), society is sorted into two classes based upon their genetics.
- The Jurassic (*Park* and *World*) series, conceived by Michael Crichton, shows the disastrous effects of designer dinosaurs.

One final way to illustrate the rich history of family planning is to identify one or two families within your church with three (or more) generations represented. Having a brief interview of one grandparent, one parent, and one child could demonstrate the integration of faith and family. Each person could describe a favorite song or memory from their time in the church. The grandparent could offer a blessing for the younger generations. The parent or child could honor the grandparent for their faithfulness in serving and giving. The interview should be practiced and well guided to keep family members from rambling. Filming the interview may prove more effective, keeping answers precise and the tone positive.

Regardless of the creative elements you choose, be sure the preaching communicates that God's long-standing promise to the world through Abraham and David comes in a virgin-born Jesus. God's family plans are perfectly conceived and a contrast to all of our frailties.

- God places everyone in an imperfect family (1:1–17).
- God conceived a perfect plan to save us (1:18–25).

DISCUSSION QUESTIONS

1. How does Matthew's genealogy contrast with Luke's version?
2. What role do Abraham and David play in Matthew's genealogy? How do the four women factor into Matthew's theology?
3. Matthew provides his first of five Old Testament "fulfillment" texts in Jesus's birth narrative. What type of fulfillment does he suggest and what does this mean?
4. How would Joseph have felt hearing news of Mary's pregnancy?
5. Where have you seen God's providence in your life? How has he used unlikely people or unexpected events to shape you?

Matthew 2:1–23

EXEGETICAL IDEA

After Gentiles worshiped the newborn king, God used dreams to direct the magi away from Herod and Joseph to take the child to Egypt to protect him.

THEOLOGICAL FOCUS

Through a look at Scripture and divinely directed acts (here: stars and dreams), believers see God's protective and providential directions emerge for those who obey.

PREACHING IDEA

Follow God's directions to enlist his protection.

PREACHING POINTERS

Matthew introduces new characters into the birth narrative of Jesus. Their respective responses to the child represent typical reactions to Jesus throughout the gospel. The magi traveled long and far to honor the child. They followed a star, searched the Scriptures, and heeded a dream, each as a demonstration of Gentile sensitivity to God's plans. Herod and the Jewish leaders opposed God's plans. Tragically, Herod conspired against God, killing Jewish children to eradicate rivals to his throne. Fortunately, God's plans cannot be thwarted. God used Scriptures and stars, angels and dreams, foreigners and faithful servants like Joseph to keep his plan on track. For Matthew's original readers, this narrative affirmed God's protective plan and prompted them to evaluate their response to Jesus.

Today a rising tide of opposition faces God and his people. In large sections of the global South and East, rival religions and government officials oppose the church. In the West, New Atheists and secular lobbyists attack Christian institutions, deeming their practices outdated and oppressive. Cancel culture and the threat of "hate crimes" against churches for their sexual ethic are recent examples. Even the swell of apathetic, religious sentiment infecting the culture pushes back against the uniqueness of Jesus, sovereignty of God, and authority of Scripture. This opposition toward God's plan and people is nothing new. Jesus has dodged rivals since his infancy. The church has faced enemies since its inception. God's plan prevails. This passage teaches us to follow God's directions to enlist his protection.

THE MAGI SHOW GENTILE RESPECT, WHILE HEROD SHOWS HOSTILITY (2:1–23)

LITERARY STRUCTURE AND THEMES (2:1–23)

The unit has two core scenes: the magi coming to worship Jesus (vv. 1–12) and Herod's reaction in seeking to murder the child. Divine protection spoiled the dire plan, so the child went to Egypt and then returned to Nazareth after Herod's death (vv. 13–23). Matthew frames these two units with four scriptural citations that show how God's direction and plan were tied to the events. God's hand was everywhere as the event's main player overcame a ruler who thought he had great power. A key to this passage is the character contrast between the magi and Joseph on one side as responsive to God and Herod on the other as rejecting the divine program. Two themes dominate the unit: God's protection, and the magi showing that Gentiles will be responsive to what God is doing. The tragedy of the scene is the missed opportunity for the Jewish leader, priests, and scribes.

EXPOSITION (2:1–23)

Political figures often strive to rival God's kingdom plan. Herod was no exception. So, Matthew recounts a time when after Gentiles worshiped the newborn king, God directed Joseph to take the child to Egypt to protect him from Herod's resistance to God's program. This section reassures readers that God's providential protection enabled the program around Jesus to unfold.

The Magi Honor Jesus (2:1–12)

After Gentiles worshiped the newborn king, God used dreams to direct the magi away from Herod and Joseph to take the child to Egypt to protect him.

2:1–2. Jesus's birth in Bethlehem during the days of Herod the Great caused a cosmic stir that was noticed in lands to the East. The locale in the East is not given. Persia, Babylon, and Arabia are all suggested, but there is no way to decide (Davies and Allison 1988, 228).

"Magi" is a term out of Persia and Babylonia for priests and wise men who engaged in astrology (BDAG s.v. "μάγος" 1, 608; Keener 2009, 99; cf. Dan. 1–2). Their vocation was to interpret cosmic signs when something caught their attention. There is no indication that they were kings (correctly, Morris 1992, 36; contra the hymn "We Three Kings"). When they saw the star arise, they headed in the direction it was leading them. By the time they reached Herod, they had already interpreted that the king of the Jews must have been born, as that is what they asked information about so they could worship him. To refer to the king as of the "Jews" meant they did see themselves as guests honoring a foreign king. In the context of Matthew, this positive act was something indicating cultural respect from people who came from the foreign East to give a king exalted honors (on the term for "worship," 2:2, 8, 11; 8:2; 9:18; 14:33; 15:25; 20:20; 28:9, 17). The catalyst for this act was that God had shown in the skies that something unusual was taking place. The magi had listened to the creation. This question of the magi is the only place where they speak in the chapter. Everywhere else they portray a responsive faith.

We are not told how many magi came. The number three is associated with the fact they give three gifts later in the scene, but that is simply an inference (Hendriksen 1973, 152). Eastern tradition has twelve magi (Wilkins 2004, 94, who notes the traditional Western names of the three come from a sixth-century Ravenna, Italy, mosaic located in a church). We also are not told how they came to sense all of this. The focus is strictly that they came realizing who was portended by the star (Hendriksen 1973, 155). The timing of this event is after the events narrated in Luke, since by the time the magi arrive Mary and Joseph are in a house (Blomberg 1992, 61–62). In other words, the magi and shepherds were not before the manger at the same time, as traditional scenes often portray. The attempt to slay children under the age of two also points in the direction of a later scene for the magi, but how much later is unclear since Herod was trying to be sure he got the child in his purge.

The Timing of This Event

The arrival of the magi before Herod is why the birth of Jesus is said to fall between 6 and 4 B.C., since Herod died in 4 B.C. The death is said to have taken place during an eclipse of the moon, a detail that allows us to date its chronology (Josephus, *A. J.* 17.167). A recalculation of errors in the calendar of the sixth-century monk responsible for our calendar (Dionysius Exiguus), led to A.D. 1 being set back to 4 B.C. (Blomberg 1992, 62). Although Jesus should have been born in the year 1, as the intent was to set a calendar by his birth, the errors led to the recalculation to the time around Herod's death (Matt. 2:19). The temper Matthew describes in Matthew 2:16 fits the way Josephus (*A.J.* 17) portrays Herod's temper as well.

Normally such astrologers were seen negatively (Isa. 47:13; Ezek. 21:21; Acts 7:42; 8:9–24; 13:6–11), but in this case their vocation led them to pursue the truth. As was sometimes the case, people outside the faith saw things well. The otherwise negative portrayal is an argument for the historicity of this text, as the criterion of embarrassment meant the church would have been unlikely to have made up such a story about characters who were normally seen negatively (Bruner 2004a, 59–60; France 2007, 65). The birth took place somewhere near the end of Herod's reign (he was born in 73 B.C. and ruled from 37 to 4 B.C.; Gundry 1982, 26).

Matthew relates an intense Gentile sensitivity to what God was doing by reading the signs in the creation. This stood in contrast to the Jewish leaders' reaction of hostility or indifference, a picture of how many reacted to the news about Jesus. The reference to "his star" likely pointed to a sign that itself pointed to the Jewish king (as in OT and Jewish texts: Num. 24:17; 4Q266 [Damascus Document] 7.18–21; 4Q175 [4Q Testimonia] 9–13). Suetonius (*Vesp.* 5) records that the expectation of a ruling king from Judea did circulate through the East (Wilkins 2004, 94). The movement of the star later and over a period of time probably pointed to a nonnatural phenomenon and a direct sign from God. So this was likely not a comet, planetary conjunction, or nova (so correctly France 2007, 68–69). Nor is an angel likely, since Matthew seems to be clear when they are the source of revelation (but so Wilkins 2004, 96, as one plausible option). Here was openness to God and a sensitivity to God to go where God directed. Is there an echo of Psalm 87:4 here (so Bruner 2004a, 56)? It is natural to expect the magi to go to the capital to find a king.

Jesus's birth in Bethlehem, for Matthew, explained how Jesus as Messiah would fulfill Scripture even though he came from Nazareth. He was born in the promised messianic city as Micah 5:2 showed. There is multiple attestation to this birth, as the accounts in Matthew and Luke are independent (for historicity, Bruner 2004a, 55–56). There is no good reason to doubt this as the place of Jesus's birth. There is little to gain by claiming a birthplace that was false in these documents. It would seriously undercut the claims in the book, which were written early enough for people to remember such a detail. Stars would later play a role in the Olivet Discourse on the end and in the crucifixion (Matt. 24:29; 27:45, but there these were terrible omens about coming judgment in contrast to the positive indication it serves with Jesus's birth, Davies and Allison 1988, 235).

The Place of Jesus's Birth

Unlikely are efforts to see roots in Creco-Roman or Jewish backgrounds as responsible for a created event detail of the presence of stars in Matthew's account especially given the fact the Mosaic parallel is late in Exod. Rab. 1 (Hill 1972, 80–81, opts for a Mosaic background; Hill also notes Cicero, *Div.* 1.47; Suetonius, *Aug.* 94; and the later Parthian magi who visit Nero in A.D. 66, Tacitus, *Ann.* 14.22; that stars could point to a king, Dio, *Rom. Hist. 45.7*—Caesar received among the immortal indicated by a star or comet in the sky*;* Suetonius, *Nero* 36—a comet portends Nero's death; Firmicus Maturnus, *Math.* 6.1; 8.31; Culpepper 2021, 43; Davies and Allison 1988, 233–34; for a defense of the core historicity of the scene, Hagner 1993, 25–26; Yamauchi 1989). What this material does show is that readers might understand that such a birth points to a significant figure, possibly counter to honor given to the emperor (Konradt 2020, 40).

2:3. The news troubled Herod. A study of his career from Josephus shows that he was very nervous about succession and protecting his rule, even slaying his sons and favorite wife to protect his power (*A.J.* 15.228–42; see also much of *A.J.* 17). He was nervous in part because he was a "half Jew" (*A.J.* 14.403; Herod's father was Idumean, that is, an Edomite). Herod had such a violent reputation that Caesar Augustus was alleged to have said it was better to be Herod's pig than Herod's son (Grundmann 1975, 84; Macrobius, *Saturnalia* II.4, 11). The expression "all in Jerusalem" is surely hyperbole and points simply to the disruption the announcement caused within Herod's circle, perhaps including some of the priestly leaders (Turner 2008, 81; so also perhaps, Matt. 21:10 and 27:24–25). They did not want a new leader. This was the start of Herod's downward spiral in the chapter. He will go from being troubled to anger, from anger to murder (Matt. 5:21–26). Lack of faith kills in the end.

2:4. The query leads Herod to call the chief priests and scribes to inquire about where the Christ is predicted to be born (on this combination of faith leaders, Matt. 20:18; 21:15). Normally Herod was hostile to this group, executing many of them at the start of this reign (Josephus, *A.J.* 14.175), but now he needs help to craft his response to this seeming threat to his rule. The wise men need the help of others. As is often the case in spiritual things, the Scripture supplies what they lack in knowledge as members of the world. This query involves the ruling families and those who had become students of the Scripture (Ezra 7:6, 11; Sir. 38–39), especially Torah (on the two groups of priests and scribes, Davies and Allison 1988, 239–40). This was not a full meeting of the Sanhedrin, but of a different group, as the reference to scribes looks to a distinct combination. The verb "to inquire" (*punthanomai*) points to the pursuit of a question or consultation (BDAG s.v. "πυνθάνομαι" 1, 897–98). Out of twelve uses of this term in the NT, this is the only use in Matthew. The priests with the scribes would know where in Scripture to look for such an answer, given the longing for a divinely sent deliverer.

2:5–6. The question led them to Micah 5:2 (5:1 in MT and LXX). The answer is Bethlehem in Judea, called Judah twice in verse 6. The text does not match the MT or LXX. It is more targumic (an "interpretation," so Davies and Allison 1988, 242). Judah stands in for the less clear, archaic

Ephrathah (Gundry 1982, 29). Judah points back to the tribe of the king (Matt. 1:2).

There were other Bethlehems in Israel, but the location, just a few miles south of Jerusalem, is the expected and predicted site. Again, we get an introductory formula that speaks of what God said as written through (*dia*) the prophet. The text points to a ruler who emerges from Bethlehem. This city will not lack status as it will not be among the least of the land. This non-lack of status is highlighted by the addition of "by no means."

This ruler shall shepherd the people Israel. Matthew is still focused on the promise to the nation. The reference to shepherding is yet another allusion to David, who became king after being a shepherd (2 Sam. 7:8, see especially the LXX which has both "shepherd" and the term for "ruler"; the combination virtually reproduces 2 Sam. 5:2 and 1 Chron. 11:2; Ps. 78:70–71; Luke 1:32–33 has the theme explicitly). Bethlehem had been his home (1 Sam. 16:1; 17:12, 15; Turner 2008, 82). The citation is a mixture of Micah 5:2 (first three lines) and 2 Samuel 5:2 (last line), a fusion of texts not uncommon in Judaism (Osborne 2010, 89). The savior (Matt. 1:21) is also a ruler and shepherd. This answer of the locale was common in Judaism of the time (John 7:42; Targum on Mic. 5:1—"Out of you shall come forth before me the Messiah"; McNeile 1915, 16; also Justin, *1 Apol.* 34). So was the expectation of a coming shepherd-ruler to restore Israel (Ezek. 34:4–16; Pss. Sol. 17–18; 4 Ezra 13:34–50; 2 Bar. 77–86; Sanh. 10:3—only about restoration in the resurrection to come; Davies and Allison 1988, 243). The NT also highlights this idea (John 10:11; Heb. 13:20; 1 Peter 5:2–4; John 21:16; Wilkins 2004, 98). The allusion to shepherd from the reference to Bethlehem refers to the guidance and protection for the people alongside the deliverance that the idea of ruler conveys. The fact there was no follow-up to welcome this news and respond to it in the upper echelons of the nation portends what will come at the end of the gospel. There was no rush to embrace the possible Messiah, only indifference and hostility (Garland 1995, 27; Tousaaint 1980, 51, calls the leaders' response to Herod "pitifully apathetic").

Matthew is noting that Jesus was born in the right place to be Messiah, but the event was not invented to make the point (so correctly, Hagner 1993, 29). There was little point in publicly claiming a birthplace that was wrong for Jesus in a time when people would have known this fact, something someone could challenge. The birthplace is attested outside of Matthew and Luke as early as the second century and was not disputed, something that surely would have been done if the locale were wrong (Keener 2009, 103; Jerome, *Letter 58 to Paulinus,* looks back in time and alludes to the second century building of a pagan site at the traditional site of Jesus's birth).

2:7–8. Herod did two things after he determined the location of the birth in the context of his being troubled (see v. 3). First, he "secretly" (*lathra*) called the magi into a meeting and asked when the star had appeared. He wished "to determine exactly" (*ēkribōsen*) how old the child likely was. This verb looks to a kind of precise determination, to do something with care (BDAG s.v. "ἀκριβόω" 39). Some time had passed since Jesus had been born. Again, this scene was later than the one Luke depicts of the shepherds' visit. Second, Herod told the magi that they when they found the child to let him know, so he also could worship the child (see v. 2 for the magi's desire to worship). They are "to search carefully" (*ēxetasate*) for him (BDAG s.v. "ἐξετάζω" 1, 349). The verb portrays Herod as especially concerned, giving an appearance of caring when in fact his desire was completely different. The later murdering of children will show the rank hypocrisy of Herod in making this request. Subsequent events in Matthew 2:16 will show this desire to be a ruse. Herod's effort to kill boys two years and under was probably excessive in scope of age as a way to be sure the child was eliminated. Herod wanted to destroy the threat to his rule. The secret meeting was apparently at night, as the star guided the magi when they departed (Gundry 1982, 30). We will meet a similar meeting later in the gospel, with the Jewish leaders' plot to kill Jesus and arrest him in secret (Matt. 26:3–5).

2:9. The magi departed and were led by the star to the place where the child was. Jesus is simply called "the child" in this chapter (Matt. 2:8, 9, 13, 14, 20, 21). He is in the hands of his parents and the care of a supervising God. Only at Matthew 2:15 is he called "Son."

It was the very specific and lingering function of the star that suggests we are not dealing with the description of a natural phenomenon ("patently miraculous," so Hill 1972, 83). The star "was leading" (imperfect tense) before it "stopped" (aorist tense) over the exact location (Turner 2008, 95 n. 10). The divine guidance is a key motif in the scene. The magi followed where God led. The star contrasted God's direction as well with Herod's sinister desire to foil God's act. Wilkins (2004, 99) suggests the star's supernatural activity was consistent with angelic guidance, which is possible. If so, Matthew does not say it directly, but only leaves it implied. The closest analogy is the pillar of fire in the wilderness during the exodus (Keener 2009, 104; Exod. 13:21).

2:10. The magi were thrilled to find the home as they "rejoiced exceedingly" (*echarēsan charan*) upon arriving at the child's home. The construction is emphatic in its emotion, as the idea of joy is repeated in a cognate accusative and is a Hebraism. It indicates in this case the presence of an emotion raised to a high level. Luke also has notes of joy with Jesus's birth (Luke 1:14, 44, 46; 2:10, 14, 20; Hagner 1993, 30).

2:11. The magi fulfilled their wish to worship the child as they fell to the ground in honor and presented the child with their gifts. Only the child with the mother is now in view. He is the focal point. Homes at this time would have been connected to their stables, so France (2007, 75) argues that this is the same house Luke has in mind. But this is not certain at all. We may well be at a much later time frame and the family may have found better housing in the meantime.

This act of worship would be the normal full prostration of getting down on one's knees and bowing the head to the ground. The act offered honor and indicated respect and submission. The precious gifts of gold, frankincense, and myrrh pictured bequeathing something special in honor of the king's presence (Wilkins 2004, 100; Gen. 43:11–15; 1 Sam. 9:7–8; 1 Kings 10:1–2; France 2007, 76, speaks of "luxury gifts"). That is all it represents, despite an array of efforts to see more symbolism. Frankincense was probably a reference to incense and was used for all kinds of occasions beyond worship. Gold was valuable, and the two fragrances were found in the best perfumes (Wilkins 2004, 101). The OT expresses hope of such gifts from foreign kings for Israel (1 Kings 10:2; Ps. 72:10–11, 15; Isa. 60:3–6; Osborne 2010, 91). Worship is a key theme in Matthew (2:2, 11; 8:2—leper; 9:18—ruler; 14:33—disciples; 15:25—Canaanite woman; 20:20—mother of James and John; 26:6–13—unnamed woman who anoints Jesus; 28:9—women at the tomb; 28:19—disciples; Garland 1995, 27). In this specific context, we are probably looking at a display of honor, not full worship of God. They had come to honor a king, and kings received such high honor in the East. Matthew, of course, sees even more implications in this act as the rest of his gospel shows. Bruner (2004a, 63–64) sees full worship as the point of the act, but I prefer to see it as an implication of it, given the magi's roots and cultural backdrop. Keener (2009, 105) speaks appropriately of "divine honor of some sort" that someone from the East would give to a ruler. That understanding may well be implied by the fact Jesus is a unique king.

2:12. A dream of divine guidance intervened again, as the magi were warned not to tell Herod where the child was. The verb *chrēmatizō* used here is often used of a divine revelation (BDAG s.v. "χρηματίζω" 1bα, 1089). If the dream was of the pattern of others in this narrative section (Matt 1:20; 2:19; Wilkins 2004, 101), then an angel had directed them. If not, then this warning was seen as more direct, perhaps because the danger was greater (Osborne 2010, 91). In response, the magi take another route home. Herod was left uninformed of the exact location of the child. Everything said about the magi in this text shows Gentiles who were sensitive to and responding to what God was doing. The contrast in their heart response to what was coming from Herod could not have been greater.

This completes the first act of Matthew 2. God's sovereignty drove the events that guided the sensitive Gentiles into Jewish territory to worship the new king. Beyond God's direction, there are three contrasting character types in the scene. Herod showed the power of deceit and a stubborn heart that refused to see God at work and simply sought to preserve his own position and power. Such self-absorption and self-interest would lead from lying to murder. Likewise, the Jewish leaders were indifferent to the inquiry. They failed to appreciate what God was doing or to even care. If such lack of appreciation continued to be nurtured, such indifference could grow into rejection. That is what the gospel will show. Finally, we see Gentiles sensitive to God and open to God's direction. This led to respect for what God was doing. Readers of the narration are asked to reflect on which character type they are to be most like.

Osborne (2010, 92–93) speaks of the following themes in this unit: divine providence, worship of the Christ, Jesus as one honored in the world, conflict with rejection of Jesus, and the magi as seekers open to God.

Joseph Flees with Jesus to Egypt and Returns to Nazareth (2:13–23)

2:13–14. Another dream directed Joseph's next steps and protected the child. This scene contrasts in tone with Matthew 2:1–12. There the magi's desire was to worship the child; here Herod wishes to eliminate him. The present tense, literally "appears" (*phainetai*), may indicate that the dream warning Joseph came very close to the time of the magi's departure (BDF §321).

The angel knew what Herod was thinking, even though the text has given no indication yet of what Herod's plan was. The king intended to kill the child. Jesus was in danger from a king just as Moses had been (Exod. 1:22–2:6), but the deliverance here was by fleeing through a warning versus a parent's cleverness sparing Moses with a providential landing in Pharaoh's house. Joseph, with the child, fled a king, while Moses ended up in the king's house. Thus, the Moses story was not the basis for the Jesus story. We know from Josephus how violently Herod worked to protect his kingship. The decision to kill children in Bethlehem fits what we know of him.

So the angel told Joseph to take his family to Egypt. Joseph not only responded but did so immediately, leaving at night for Egypt. He was still the focus for the family's actions. A quick departure was necessary because Jerusalem was so close to Bethlehem. The Egyptian border and key parts of the country were some eighty to one hundred and fifty miles away, although it is likely the family went further into that nation. This trip would have taken up to a week. Egypt was a common location for Israelites to flee when there was trouble (1 Kings 11:40; 2 Kings 25:26; Jer. 41:16–18; 43:1–7; Josephus, *A.J.* 12.387; 14.21; 15.46; *B.J.* 7.409–10; Davies and Allison1988, 259). Its population at the time is said to be one-third Jewish (France 2007, 79 n. 9). Jesus began his life as a refugee, foreshadowing the rejection that would come (Keener 2009, 109).

Joseph is told he also would be informed when he could return. The scenario is like 1 Kings 11:40. God had his eye on this child and the program tied to him.

2:15. This trip to and from Egypt was a part of a prophetic read of Hosea 11:1, which Matthew now cites. The introductory formula matches Matthew 1:22. Matthew cites the text in a version closer to the Hebrew than the LXX, which has a reference to calling his children, pointing to a reference to the nation. Davies and Allison (1988, 262) speak of the influence of Numbers 24:8 on the text, given how Numbers 24:7 and 17 were sometimes seen as messianic (v. 17—a star from Jacob and a scepter from Israel). The fact that the angel anticipated a return in his remarks shows that one should not debate whether the text referred to the departure or the return. The trip to and from Egypt was the point (Osborne 2010, 99). Magi from the east came to the land, and the family went farther west to Egypt. The story of Jesus extended beyond Israel.

This text should be read typologically, as a pattern fulfillment. In the original context there was a look back to the exodus from which God called the nation, described as a "son" (Blomberg 1992, 67; Evans 2012, 58; France 2007, 80–81; Howard 1986; Toussaint 1980, 55; Turner 2008, 90–91; Wilkins 2004, 110–12). However, the context of Hosea 11:8–12 goes on to speak of hope for the nation (Carson 1984, 92), so a second exodus motif is not a stretch for Matthew to apply here, especially since the messianic redemption is also paralleled to the exodus frequently (Isa. 40:3–4; Ezek. 20:33–44; Hos. 2:14–15; Zech. 10:10). The prophetic fulfillment came with the common formula about what the Lord spoke through the prophet. This detail about the birth becomes part of an exodus-Moses typology where Israel is again redeemed as God promised through the work to come from the sent Son. Jesus, the Son, represents what is best for the nation, just as Israel was the son Hosea originally referred to in his prophecy. What God did in delivering the nation through Moses, he now will do for the world, delivering through his Son. The world is in view in the story as well. In this move from nation as Son to Jesus as Son also is found the escalation common in typological-prophetic texts as initial salvation became the initial realization of promise with more to come. This is Matthew's first use of the term "son" for Jesus. It appears in a context where Jesus is compared to the status of the nation. "My son" points to a special relationship. Jesus reflected and represented Israel, and he still does. Matthew will wait to develop the idea of son until Matthew 3:13–4:11.

Matthew loves to cite Scripture. Garland (1995, 28) notes that Matthew has forty-two explicit citations, as compared to nineteen each in Mark and Luke and fourteen in John. Culpepper (2021, 9), cited in the introduction above, has a different number for the citations: twenty-one citations and fifty allusions. Garland may be naming citations and explicit allusions. Some are predictive (like Matthew 2:6), others typological (Matthew 2:15), while others point to a theme (Matthew 2:23).

2:16. Herod determined that the magi had left without telling him about the child's location. He was angry, very angry. Note the contrast with the magi's joy in Matthew 2:10. The text makes this clear with the expression *ethmuōthē lian* (*lian* means "very"; BDAG s.v. "ἐθυμόω" "angry," 462). One could say he was enraged. There is irony in the term "tricked" (*enepaichthē*), because it means to deceive someone (BDAG s.v. "ἐμπαίζω" 2, 323). Herod had tried to deceive the magi, saying he had good intentions for the child, but ended up getting an eye-for-eye-and-tooth-for-tooth exchange by being successfully deceived back. Turner (2008, 93) correctly notes that in the end Herod was angry at God, not the magi, for the direction to note the child's birth had come from him. This frustration pictures the futility of opposing God and his providence, as Psalm 2:1–2 teaches (Acts 4:24–28).

Herod worked to protect a threat he saw to his rule. We have already noted how this behavior fit what Josephus tells us about how Herod protected his power. Even family members and a favorite wife were not spared. So Herod sent his soldiers to kill all the children under two in Bethlehem and the region. The verb "killed" (*aneilen*) looks to the violent removal of someone (BDAG s.v. "ἀναιρέω" 2, 64). Estimates say this would only have been a handful of children since Bethlehem was a small village. Wilkins (2004, 112 n. 7) notes the population of the city was not more than a thousand, so the number slain is put between ten and thirty. He also contends that Bethlehem was so small and the number so few it is not surprising no other record of the event exists, especially since these children had no social status. Still, the loss of life is shocking and tragic, showing the lengths some would go to protect their own self-interest.

Here was an opportunity for Israel, but all Herod could think of was his own power. By slaying all the children two and under, Herod was trying to make sure that he had eliminated the child. The time was figured from the timing the magi had given him, although it is likely he added some time just to be sure. The event is historical and not a creation from scriptural reflection.

2:17–18. The slaying paralleled another time in Israel's history, leading to yet another typological or patterned reference to fulfillment. Matthew presents a word from Jeremiah with the common introductory formula speaking of God's word being fulfilled through the prophet and then citing Jeremiah 31:15. The aorist passive participle "what was spoken" (*to rēthen*) points to God as the ultimate speaker. Only one detail is different in the formula. "In order to be fulfilled" is not present but simply, "Then . . . was fulfilled." Some suggest this might be to spare God blame for the event, but the variation may only be stylistic. The citation is typological and not an exclusive prediction. It is the result of a human decision which Matthew likens to the pain of suffering in the exile. God was not to blame, regardless of the wording. God did not act here but Herod did, unlike what took place with the other citations in the infancy material where God was acting (Davies and Allison 1988, 266). This is the first time Matthew names the prophet he cites.

The picture is of lamentation. The cited text is slightly closer to the Hebrew version than the LXX of Jeremiah 38:15, which is the LXX parallel (Davies and Allison 1988, 268–70; Morris 1992, 46 n. 53). Jeremiah described the mourning and weeping that met the nation going into exile when children lost their lives. It is discussed whether in view is exile in the north (Nolland 2005, 125, with anticipation in the south) or south (Wilkins 2004, 113; Jer. 40:1–2), or both (Bruner 2004a, 70; Hendriksen 1973, 184). Likely the pain of exile in general was in view, since Jeremiah spoke with an eye to the impending judgment on the south.

Ramah is a locale around five miles north of Jerusalem and would have been one of the first places passed as people left Jerusalem for exile. There are other distinct traditions that connect Rachel with Bethlehem, through a reference to Ephrathah in association with her death (Gen. 35:19; Blomberg 1992, 68). The ancestral mother Rachel was said to have wept, not willing to be consoled. This was a personification of the mothers of Israel and the national pain tied to exile (Turner 2008, 93). In parallel to that, the messianic child's arrival was intended to bring peace, but the destructive reaction of rejection had brought lying, murder, and death instead. Damage to people is what happens when people reject what God is doing.

Interestingly, this tragic verse in Jeremiah falls in a larger context of hope, so the patterned type may include the idea that although the rejection is painful now, hope is still present (Carson 1984, 95). Nolland (2005, 173) sees Herod as picturing a foreign power and its rejection, not that of Israel, but this association is unlikely. Herod was portrayed in the Matthean narrative as residing in Jerusalem as head of the nation of Israel. He might not represent the entire nation, but he did show that her current leadership, of mixed race, had no interest in God sending a Messiah.

2:19–21. Yet another dream directed Joseph back to Israel, just as had been promised in verse 13. In fact, these verses virtually mirror verses 13–14. Now came a dream where an angel directed Joseph to return with his family because Herod had died. Herod suffered a particularly gruesome, slow, and painful death from disease (Josephus, *A.J.* 17.168–81). Herod died at sixty-nine years old in 4 B.C. (Wilkins 2004, 114). This was the fourth of five dreams in these opening two chapters (Matt. 1:20; 2:12, 13, 19, 22). God was still directing events.

The reference to "those who sought the child's life" had Herod primarily in mind and those who helped him execute his power (either Hagner 1993, 39—his servants who are no longer in power; or Osborne 2010, 101—his soldiers). This description echoes Exodus 4:19–20 (Davies and Allison 1988, 271). Another possible explanation for the plural is that it was a "generalizing plural," where an important individual is portrayed in the plural (BDF §141; Turner 2008, 97; Wallace 1996, 403–6). It is reasonable to think of this as referring to Herod's death and the death of the power of others tied to him as a judgment of these acts (Morris 1992, 47). A major figure has an entourage tied to him. What is made clear is that it was safe to return. The full reference to the land of Israel is the only such reference in the New Testament.

Joseph was obedient again to the dream and returned. The brief exile because of rejection was over. We do not know how long the family was there, but most estimates involve no more than a year.

Five Appeals to Scripture in the Matthean Infancy Account

Matthew 1:22: "through the prophet would be fulfilled"; Isaiah 7:14, virgin birth, Immanuel

Matthew 2:5–6: "it is written this way by the prophet"; Micah 5:2 [5:1 HB], born in Bethlehem

Matthew 2:15: "through the prophet was fulfilled"; Hosea 11:1, out of Egypt God called his son

Matthew 2:17: "what was spoken by Jeremiah the prophet was fulfilled"; Jeremiah 31:15, Rachel weeping for her children

Matthew 2:23: "what had been spoken by the prophets was fulfilled"; likely sound wordplay on theme of Isaiah 11:1/*Netzer-Branch*/Nazarene

2:22–23. Back in Israel, Joseph received more guidance through the final dream in these infancy events. Joseph feared Herod's son, Archelaus. He was not alone. Many in Israel had not wished him to be a ruler. Josephus (*B.J.* 2.1–13 and *A.J.* 17.200–344) covered his whole rule, including a slaying of three thousand Passover participants (France 2007, 91). *Antiquities* 17.188 showed that Archelaus came to inherit a part of Herod's rule as a result of a late change to Herod's will (Suetonius, *Tib.* 8).

In the midst of Joseph's concern, yet another dream directed him to take the family to the district of Galilee, and they ended up in Nazareth. Matthew calls Nazareth a city but simply is using the term in a generic way as a living place, not as a description of size (with Davies and Allison 1988, 274; contra Luz 1989, 148; see Luke 1:26; 2:4, 39). There is no other record of it in the Hebrew Scripture, Josephus, Mishnah, or Talmud. It was a very small town with an estimated population of not more than five hundred (France 2007, 91; Keener 2009, 113; *ABD* 4:1050). It was located fifteen miles west of the southern tip of the Sea of Galilee. The locale of Galilee becomes a focus in Matthew 4:12–16, which appeals to Isaiah 9:1. It was a hill's view away from the more important ancient city of Sepphoris. This conclusion to the infancy material explains how Jesus ended up in the northern portion of Israel and, as a result, ministered there.

This locale also fulfilled Scripture, although exactly what was in view is much discussed. The idea that Jesus shall be called a Nazarene is said to fulfill Scripture. The introductory formula again appeals to what God said through the prophets. The plural reference to prophets may be a hint that we have a theme and not a text (Davies and Allison 1988, 275). It appears that in this case Matthew did not have a specific passage in mind, since there is nothing like what was said here in the Hebrew Scripture. Rather we have an idea, perhaps wrapped up in a wordplay. But what is the wordplay?

Most often suggested is a variation on the word for "branch," which was seen as a messianic image, referring to a branch from the root of Jesse (Gundry 1982, 40; Nolland 2005, 130–31; Wilkins 2004, 116–19, in combination with Nazareth as a humble locale of reproach, see below; Carson 1984, 97, also has this combination; Keener 2009, 114–15). The term *netzer* means "branch" and sounds like "Nazarene," so it is often suggested as the point of connection (Isa. 11:1; with another term for the same idea—*semah*: Jer. 23:5; 33:15; Zech. 3:8; 6:12). Jerome notes this view (Luz 1989, 150 n. 45). This does bring in a Davidic connection and involves a passage close to the already cited Isaiah 7:14. Isaiah 11 is also widely used in the early church. However, this is not the only suggestion.

Although not clear as to the exact point of the reference, Isaiah 11 and the idea of "branch" seems the most likely, especially given the Davidic and messianic themes that resonate in Matthew. It was not unusual for a teaching point to be seen in a wordplay in Jewish exegesis. Perhaps the low reputation of the city was also in play here. We should not limit our readings of these ancient texts to things that fit later Western constraints.

The Five Dreams of Matthew's Infancy Account

Matthew 1:20: To Joseph, about taking Mary as a wife

Matthew 2:12: To the Magi, about not returning to Herod

Matthew 2:13: To Joseph, to go to Egypt

Matthew 2:19: To Joseph, to return from Egypt to Israel

Matthew 2:23: To Joseph, to go to Galilee, not Judea

THEOLOGICAL FOCUS

The exegetical idea (After Gentiles worshiped the newborn king, God used dreams to direct the magi away from Herod and Joseph to take the child to Egypt to protect him) develops into this theological idea: God's protective and providential directions emerge for those who obey through a look at Scripture and divinely directed acts (here: stars and dreams).

The thrust of this scene comes in the divine direction and protection that included God's creation pointing to the nature of the child. Both the star and dreams with the involvement of angels showed the importance of the newly arriving king. God's direction was multilayered, guiding the magi and protecting the family. The Scripture also pointed to the plan and gave it detail.

The three reactions to God's plan are also given attention. First, Matthew portrays

Joseph as the patriarchal head of the family, with God using dreams to direct the protection of the family and the child. Joseph obeyed and went where God directed. The magi also were sensitive to the direction coming from creation and responded to the divine guidance through Scripture and dreams. They serve as positive examples of responding to God. Second, and in contrast, stand the Jewish leadership. They simply pointed to what Scripture said about the promised child's birthplace and did nothing else. They seemed to reflect an indifference to what God was doing, when they should have been more interested in responding. Third, there was the hostile reaction of Herod, whose self-interest led to deceit, lying, and murder. God's presence always surfaces an array of responses.

The presence of Jesus always will produce a variety of responses in the Gospels. God supported his chosen one, so God directed people to him and protected him. As an example, Joseph points to those who follow God's direction in obedience. The magi point in the same direction and show a respect Jesus generates from many, in appreciation of who he is. Many in the world are indifferent to Jesus even among those who might be expected to know better. That is the image of the Jewish leadership. Finally, there is the angry, self-focused approach of Herod, who only wanted to eliminate any sense of God's presence and acts. In this history of the birth of the child, we see in microcosm the world's reaction to God's act in Jesus. There is a conflict between an appreciation of God's presence in his acts to save and a rejection driven by evil desire that results in an odd juxtaposition of worship and murder. The reality of Jesus's coming forced, and forces, a choice. Matthew affirms that we are to be more like Joseph and the magi, in contrast to the indifference of the leadership or the hostility of Herod. Being open to seeing what God is doing helps to take us to that response.

PREACHING AND TEACHING STRATEGIES

Exegetical and Theological Synthesis

The exegetical section describes how King Herod clung tightly to his authority. He protected it by snuffing out potential threats. Rumors of a Jewish king stirred his jealousy for control and sparked his murderous rage. He is not the only king to preemptively defend his throne. The prophets and psalmists mocked kings and princes for presuming to have unquestioned authority (e.g., Ps. 2; Isa. 13; Ezek. 34; cf. John 19:11). Typically, power is a gift that people are quicker to receive than relinquish.

With a beautiful contrast, however, the magi paid homage to the Jewish king. They trekked across the country to give Jesus iconic gifts. Their sensitivity to divine leading—by stars and dreams—conveys God's openness to high-status Gentiles. In fact, God's redemption plan includes people from diverse cultures, economic strata, and vocations, as long as they remain loyal to Jesus.

Joseph again serves as a model of loyalty, trusting God and obeying his leading. By aligning his life with divine revelation, Joseph ensured the safety of his son. Obedience to God does not guarantee us from a life free from pain (e.g., Job), but biblical obedience spares us from some unnecessary suffering.

Preaching Idea

Follow God's directions to enlist his protection.

Contemporary Connections

What does it mean?

This preaching idea affirms the doctrine of God's control and care. He rules over the created realm, directing the wind and waves, stars and seasons, human life and animal kingdom (e.g., Pss. 104; 139). No god, political figure, or technological advance can rival him (Ps. 2; Isa. 43:10–13; Dan. 2:20–23). He is never taken by surprise. No matter what, his will comes to pass (Prov. 19:21; Rom. 11:33–36).

Underscoring his sovereign control is loving care. Biblical history resounds with stories of providential protection: Joseph's rescue and rise to power in Egypt, Israel's exodus from Egypt, Joshua's conquest of the promised land, Naomi's deliverance from poverty, David's numerous escapes from countless enemies, Daniel's safety in the lion's den, Peter's angelic release from jail, and Paul's list of near-death experiences. Sparing Jesus from Herod fits God's historic pattern of protecting his people.

Divine acts of protection continue today. People can recount miraculous recoveries from cancer or a car crash, noting the power of prayer in their rescue. Persecuted people tell tales of escaping the clutches of Muslim raids or dodging threats from corrupt political leaders. God has protected others from death from overdose, complications in delivery, or demonic oppression. As a modern hymn proclaims, "No power of hell, no scheme of man, can ever pluck me from his hand."

Our responsibility is to follow God's directions. This means we trust his sovereign control and loving care. It also means we obey his revealed will in Scripture and nudges in our lives. Heeding God's directions for sexual purity can protect us from relational brokenness and disease. Heeding his directions for honesty can protect us from stealing credit from coworkers and losing our jobs. His moral will has built-in protections.

Is it true?

Is it true that following God's direction enlists his protection, even today? Yes, but it does not ensure it. God's plan does not include a provision to protect his people from any and all harm. For example, he protected Jesus from Herod's purge but not Pilate's death sentence. He protected Peter from Agrippa I (Acts 12), but the apostle later died a martyr. God does not guarantee unconditional, physical protection for all persons but promises long-term spiritual salvation for believers (Rom. 8:31–39). Stephen suffered martyrdom for his faith and Paul was beaten (Acts 7; 2 Cor. 11:16–33). Even Jesus was crucified, but ultimately was vindicated in resurrection, so one of the ways God protects us is by the preservation of life we have in the coming promise of the hope of life.

Here's the problem: claiming God's universal protection by citing verses like Psalm 91 and Isaiah 54:17 misunderstands the Scriptures. It makes God a cheap dealer of health and wealth. Furthermore, it overlooks God's use of hardship to shape his people (Gen. 50:20; Rom. 8:28).

OT Examples of God Using Hardship to Shape His People

He used hardship to show Job his sovereignty before restoring his fortunes (Job 38–42).

He used hardship to shape Joseph and reduce the harm of famine (Gen. 50:20).

He used hardship to shape Naomi's faith and family line (Ruth 4:13–22).

He used hardship to judge Judah for covenant unfaithfulness in Jeremiah's day (Jer. 25).

He used hardship to get the attention of listless workers in Haggai's day (Hag. 1:7–11).

In fact, sometimes the very act of following God's directions gets his people in hot water. A faithful spouse may follow God's direction to honor marriage, only to have her partner cheat on her. A missionary may follow God's direction to "preach the word" and end up beaten, imprisoned, or killed. Church leadership may follow God's direction to protest racial injustice and watch many disgruntled members leave their congregation. Living God's way is costly. Yet vindication awaits us in the judgment to come, so the protection may come ultimately and not in the present (Rom. 8:31–39).

Now what?

First, we must trust God can protect us, which is not as easy as it sounds. Few of us will face maniacal threats such as the one Herod posed to Jesus. Nonetheless, a coworker may spoil our reputation. A disease may wreck our health. A major loss or personal failure may challenge our self-worth. A natural disaster may destroy our home. When divine protection is needed, Scripture provides many helps to shore up faith. In addition to the examples in the sidebar, the Psalms model prayers for protection. Examples abound of David and company begging God to protect them. More importantly, these writers view God as their shelter, rock, refuge, and dwelling place (Pss. 7; 11; 16; 18; 23; 62; 91; 144). We bolster our faith by committing these prayers to memory and praying them in times of danger.

Second, we must follow God's directions. Obedience is a telltale sign of our trust in God. When we follow God's directions, we communicate to him our loyalty and belief that he knows what is best for us. We do not treat his moral directions as burdensome, but as a light and delight (Pss. 1:2; 19:7–11; 119:105; 1 John 5:3). When he directs us to share our faith, use our spiritual gifts, give charitably, or change careers, heeding these nudges may protect us from guilt, missed opportunities, or discontentment.

Finally, we stay attuned to God no matter how frightening the circumstances. Fear has a way of focusing our emotions on present threats instead of divine truths. We tend to fight, fly, or freeze. Like Joseph and the magi, we must listen for God's direction. He led them by stars, dreams, angels, and Scripture. We can expect him to speak through Scripture, wise counsel, conscience, and promptings from the Holy Spirit. God has led many to global mission fields where danger looms. He has prompted others to make financial sacrifices, decline medical treatments, or confront injustice. His plan must take priority, even if it counters cultural norms. We may have to rest in the ultimate vindication to come.

Creativity in Presentation

I (Tim) regularly refuse adding extended warranties or protections to my purchases. This, however, does not mean I refuse to protect my stuff. Every time I buy a new cell phone, I protect it with a screen guard and shock-absorbent case. (How many times has my smart phone leapt from my back pocket and plummeted to the floor?) Some protective brands are more notable than others. OtterBox and LifeProof cases make phones seem like they cannot be wrecked. My niece nullified her claim when she submerged her iPhone in a hot tub. Share how some of your best protective measures (Scotchgard, car wax, helmets) have proven unable to keep you and your stuff from stains, scratches, cracks, dings, and dents.

Directions help protect us in many areas of life; perhaps this is a measure of God's common grace. Consider compiling a list of directions (or warnings) that might protect us from harm. A few examples may suffice. Following the directions to drive hands-on (don't text and drive) and wear a seatbelt may protect you from injury. Following laundry directions (wash like colors in cold water) may protect the whole load of laundry from turning pink or a particular garment from shrinking. Following directions on microwaveable food may protect you from starting a fire, burning your mouth, or ruining the snack. If these directions protect us from minor suffering, following God's directions may spare us from greater suffering.

C. S. Lewis's *The Horse and His Boy* (1970, 155–160), closes with a memorable dialogue between Aslan and Shasta. The Great Lion responds to the tearful boy who tells his "unfortunate" story. Aslan explains how during the boy's perilous past, the lion protected him. He says, "I was the lion who forced you to join with Aravis.

I was the cat who comforted you among the houses of the dead. I was the lion who drove the jackals from you while you slept. I was the lion who gave the Horses the new strength of fear for the last mile so that you should reach King Lune in time. And I was the lion you do not remember who pushed the boat in which you lay, a child near death, so that it came to shore where a man sat, wakeful at midnight, to receive you." This extended quotation illustrates how God protects us, not from all pain but from ultimate wreckage.

Finally, contemporary stories of God's protection may have an impact on your audience. A decade before I assumed the role as pastor of my church, an arsonist broke into the building and set it on fire. Some of our people viewed this as an opportunity for our church to dissolve. Others determined we press on. Three years later, we erected a new building, recognizing God had protected us and that an arsonist couldn't wreck us. One of our missionary partners in the Central African Republic told a miraculous tale of God's protection. Two rebels held him at gunpoint and forced him to drive them across the country on his motorbike. When they approached their destination, they threw the missionary off his bike, pointed a rifle at him, and pulled the trigger. The gun would not fire. Spooked, the rebels fled. God protected this faithful missionary. Perhaps a story more proximate to your people would better illustrate God's protective power.

In the end, the sermon should emphasize that God's protective, providential direction of Jesus's birth takes place through dreams in fulfillment of Scripture as he engages Joseph and the magi to forestall Herod's reaction to the birth. No one can wreck God's plan or his commitment ultimately to protect us.

- Jesus evokes a mixed response (2:1–12).
- Jesus evades a murderous plot (2:13–23).

DISCUSSION QUESTIONS

1. How do the magi contribute to themes from Matthew's opening chapter?
2. How does Matthew's presentation of Herod the Great align with Josephus's?
3. What are the various responses to Jesus embodied in this chapter?
4. How would you define worship? What role does obedience play in worship?
5. What do we learn about God's modes of communication in these two stories? Are his modes of communication the same today? Explain.
6. How does God protect his people today? How should we respond when his people suffer pain, loss, and persecution?

Matthew 3:1–12

EXEGETICAL IDEA

Fulfilling Scripture and in preparation for the kingdom, John the Baptist offered a baptism for forgiveness of sins, warned the Jewish leaders to flee God's coming wrath, and announced one to come who would bring the Spirit and judgment.

THEOLOGICAL FOCUS

John the Baptist's ministry points to an accountability before God that all people have, while promising them forgiveness and enablement should they respond to the one to come.

PREACHING IDEA

Heed voices that invite us back into God's favor.

PREACHING POINTERS

Matthew introduces John the Baptist, a critical character in the announcement of God's coming kingdom through Jesus. His bold proclamation, ascetic appearance, remote location, and large following depict him as a remarkable figure. More importantly, Matthew identifies John as a fulfillment of the messenger promised in Isaiah 40. John's message pointed away from himself to a stronger one who would come but not be universally accepted. The Baptist's message reverberated with messianic hope and eschatological judgment. He called Jewish people to repent, and promised God's forgiveness in return. He warned them that their Jewish heritage (i.e., children of Abraham) and religious affiliation (e.g., Pharisee, Sadducee) did not exempt them from God's wrath. For the original audience, John's voice served as a wakeup call: "Turn your hearts back to God; good things are coming."

Today's church needs a voice like John's, calling us to turn back to God. We need a renewed vision of God's inbreaking kingdom. Sadly, the evangelical church in the West has settled for a blend of pop religion and politics. We like preaching that serves as a pick-me-up and policies that protect our "moral majority." In many ways, our thinking mirrors that of the Jewish people in John the Baptist's day. We boast about doctrinal and denominational purity like they did about birthright. Likewise, we preach behavior modification rather than heart change. When we ignore voices like John's—strong, visionary, incisive, and Christocentric—we reject God's invitation to a life flooded with forgiveness and spiritual power. This passage grabs our ear, teaching us to heed voices that invite us back into God's favor.

JOHN THE BAPTIST ANNOUNCES THE KINGDOM (3:1–12)

LITERARY STRUCTURE AND THEMES (3:1–12)

This unit weaves together several core themes of the gospel, as it shows how John the Baptist prepared the way for Jesus.

The narrative here moves like a series of snapshots. Each of the four scenes is crisply presented. The first unit frames the chapter with John's call to repent because the kingdom of heaven was drawing near (vv. 1–2). Second, Scripture frames what comes next. John's ministry realized the promise of Isaiah 40:3 of one crying in the wilderness for the nation to prepare for God's coming. That preparation involved repentance for the forgiveness of sins as the nation had a need to be restored back into connection with God (vv. 3–6). John is described in verses 1–6, while his message is the point in verses 7–12 (Osborne 2010, 108). Third, the message involved a challenge extended to the religious leaders of the nation, the Pharisees and Sadducees. They had come to observe John but had the same need for repentance. They were not to presume they were blessed, as God could bring sons from anywhere. They were as accountable to God as anyone was. Thus, they also had the need to bring fruit worthy of repentance (vv. 7–10). Fourth and finally, the narrative turns its attention to Jesus. He is narratively framed as the stronger one to come who would bring the Spirit and fire, a picture of purging enablement and judgment. John, even as a prophet, was not worthy to be his slave. That is how great the One to come was (vv. 11–12).

Three themes dominate. First, the coming of the promised kingdom means accountability to God that demands a humble turning to him. Second, this ministry is something Scripture promised would come. John is a part of God's program to prepare for the coming of the Lord and the salvation God brings. Third, the call for preparation means not going through religious motions but a sincere turn of the heart toward God and his ways.

The parallels to this text are Mark 1:1–8 and Luke 3:1–9, 15–17. There also is a section in Matthew 3:7–10 from Matthew's shared tradition with Luke 3:7–9, often called Q. This Q unit on John the Baptist is somewhat exceptional, since Q mostly reflects Jesus's teaching, not that of another. Luke has even more detail in having two additional units that cover John's ethical call (Luke 3:10–14) and the reasons for his arrest in challenging Herod (Luke 3:18–20).

EXPOSITION (3:1–12)

John the Baptist's Ministry (3:1–12)

Fulfilling Scripture and in preparation for the kingdom, John the Baptist offered a baptism for forgiveness of sins, warned the Jewish leaders to flee God's coming wrath, and announced one to come who would bring the Spirit and judgment.

3:1–2. "In those days" is just a vague reference to the timing of John's ministry, placed somewhere between A.D. 27 and 29 (Carson 1984, 99). Hoehner (1977, 29–44) has details tied to the more precise Luke 3:1, which names rulers to make the timing more specific. The decision with regard to dates is tied to whether one places the crucifixion at A.D. 30 or 33. One then works back from that event about four years, given what John's gospel says about the length of Jesus's ministry. Some see an eschatological significance in the words (Hagner 1993, 47; Isa. 10:20; Amos 9:11; Zeph. 1:15; Zech. 12:3–4). However, the phrase occurs in normal contexts as well (Gen. 6:4; Exod. 2:11), so it is hard to see it as a technical term (Davies and Allison 1988, 288). We have jumped over several years, around thirty or more total, about which we know nothing tied to Jesus. Only Luke 2:41–52 tells us anything about the intervening time, recounting a visit to the temple when Jesus was twelve. This shows the selectivity of a gospel focusing on what we need to know in order to appreciate Jesus's ministry.

Matthew is noting that while Jesus was still in Nazareth, John appeared. Jesus will show up in Matthew 3:11. John is described as a baptist and a preacher. The idea of an eschatological prophet came in many shapes in ancient Judaism (Deut. 18:18—a prophet like Moses; Mal. 4:5—Elijah). Matthew ties John to the salvation-announcing prophet of Isaiah 40. John's preaching took place in the Judean wilderness in the area of the Jordan River, probably more to the south than the north. Wilderness had many associations in Judaism, as did crossing the Jordan. These locales are tied to stories associated with Israel's salvation and the giving of the law. So John's location points to a new exodus (Jer. 2:2–3; Ezek. 20:33–38; Hos. 2:14–15; Pss. Sol. 11:1; Keener 2009, 117). Qumran also connected Isaiah 40:3 to their own labor (1QS 8:13–14; 9:20). Whether John was at Qumran as a former member of that community is debated.

Was John at Qumran?

It is debated whether or not John was a member of the Qumran community. The eschatological thrust was similar, but there were also key differences because John was not a separatist as that community was (Osborne 2010, 109). Josephus presents John as a moral prophet (*A.J.* 18.116–19). Prophets often had a countercultural dimension to them as John had. What was a little unusual is that rather than the prophet going to the people, here John was gathering attention outside of where people normally were (Nolland 2005, 136). His activity is most often tied to the lower Jordan valley. A full detailed study of John the Baptist can be found in work by Robert Webb (1991), with special attention to the historicity of the baptism in Bock and Webb (2009, 95–150).

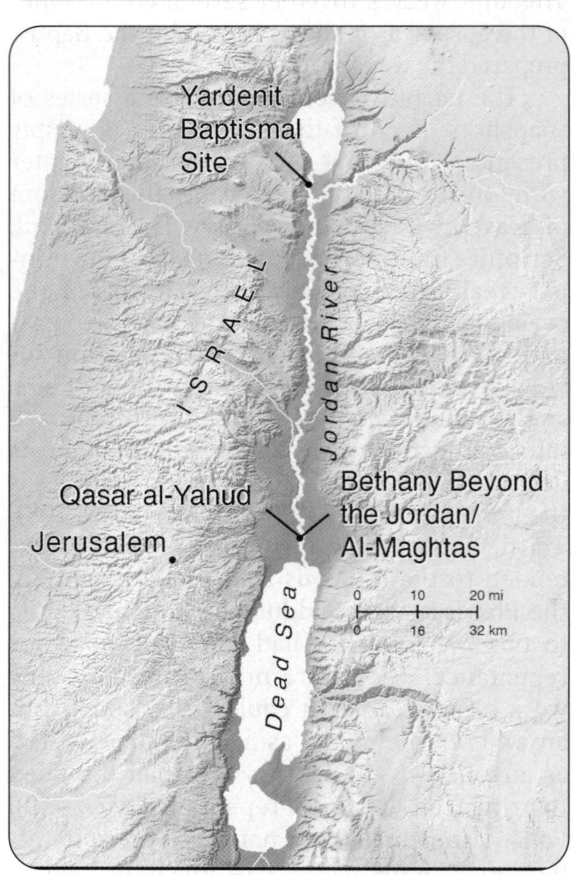

Possible Baptismal Sites of John.
Map of Yardinit (Northern Location)
and Qasr el Yahud (Southern Location).

John's message came in two related parts as well. The people (1) needed to repent, (2) as God's new era of promised rule in the kingdom of heaven approached.

Repentance pictured a need that God's people had as a community to turn back to God. Beyond God's people, all need to repent (Rom. 3:9–20). The term itself in Greek means to change one's mind, but it also can reflect the Hebrew idea of turning, a change of direction out of sense of regret for a wrong action or attitude (BDAG s.v. "μετάνοια" 2, 640–41; in Judaism, see Keener 2009, 120). The term pictures a change of orientation. That attitude leads into a change of practice. Later, Jesus offered a similar call (Matt. 4:17). He instructed the disciples to issue a similar call when he sent them out in mission (Matt. 10:7). The very fact that Rome was in their land would indicate to a Jewish person that judgment for unfaithfulness to God and covenant might be present. Among the curses of Deuteronomy 28–32 was the risk of being overrun by other nations. So repentance would be a solution. This scenario pointed to a kind of spiritual exile from which deliverance was needed. That exile was both corporate and individual. John urged acts of individual fruitfulness from their repentance, even as he called all, including the religious leaders (Matt. 3:7–10) to respond. In fact, the challenge of the religious leaders may well show how deep the issue was, for often in Israel the spiritual condition of the nation was read by how its leaders were doing spiritually. Often this was the king, but it could be the priests as well as Ezekiel 34 shows. They were to prepare their hearts and lives for God's coming (Wilkins 2004, 132).

This idea of repentance was also quite prominent at Qumran (Grundmann 1975, 92, who notes numerous texts; Hagner 1993, 47, points to CD [Damascus Document] 19:16: 4:2; 6:5). John's baptism was a once-for-all declaration by the persons being baptized that they were spiritually prepared in heart, mind, and soul for God to come with an expressed openness to his message.

"Kingdom of heaven" is Matthew's term for kingdom of God (thirty-three times, as he only uses "kingdom of God" in a few texts—Matt. 12:28; 19:24; 21:31, 43; perhaps 6:33). The two terms are synonymous here, as Matthew has "kingdom of heaven" in texts where the parallels in the other gospels have "kingdom of God." Though the expression "kingdom of God" is almost absent in the Hebrew Scripture, the idea of a grand rule of God that leads to peace is expressed in many texts (2 Sam. 7:13–14; Isa. 1:24–28; 9:6–7; 11:1–10; 64–66; Jer. 23:5–6; 31:31–34; Ezek. 37:24; Dan. 2:44; 7:13–14; Carson 2010, 128). The expression depicts God's dynamic rule, where his presence shows itself in a community of people responsive to him. In Judaism, all kinds of ideas clustered around the kingdom: Israel regathered and restored, justice restored, the nations judged, God's people ruling, righteousness established, the righteous vindicated, evil removed, and the world transformed into what could be called a new heavens and earth (Osborne 2010, 110; 1 En. 45; 2 Bar. 36–40, 45, 72–75; T. Jud. 25; 4 Ezra 13). That promised comprehensive, restorative rule had not yet come, so it is distinct from general claims of God's sovereignty in texts like the Psalms, where God rules in the context of being Creator. This call for the kingdom's arrival is God acting as restorer.

Kingdom

The term also has the suggestion of a realm, whether seen as a people in a land or as a gathered community over which God has a direct relationship or both. The image of a millennium represents the former type of realm in the context of consummative hope, while the church pictures the latter as believers are portrayed as citizens of heaven (Phil. 3:20–21), while also being exiles on earth (1 Peter 1:1).

The kingdom of heaven is connected to the restorative connection of promise and redemption that is in view. God as redeemer is in view. Matthew's mention of heaven reflects a circumlocution for God—that this kingdom is ruled from above, from heaven, transcending any form of rule rooted in the earth and politics, particularly any rule in a fallen world (Pennington 2007). There is a spiritual dimension to this rule, as John announced, that makes it distinct from the exercise of power that often drives earthly rule, pointing to a limitation of what earthly politics and powers can give to humanity. John was announcing the approach of this distinct, longed-for kingdom. It was near. When the one who was to come arrived, it would be here (Matt. 12:28). This is why texts of fulfillment of God's Word and promise are cited, as the kingdom was in the process of coming (France 2007, 103). Later, Jesus would handle this declaration with care because what some expected with this hope was not exactly what he brought, at least not at the start. When John said the kingdom was near, he meant it was almost here, as the one to come would bring it with him. The kingdom's coming was not merely an offer of it with a potential for it all to come, but was its arrival at its beginning, as with this initial phase came forgiveness, salvation, and the Spirit that brings life. This was another reason that Matthew, in telling Jesus's story, cites the fulfillment of Scripture as the fulfillment of long-standing promises.

3:3. Scripture again appears, as it will frequently do in these chapters (Matt. 3:3, 17; 4:4, 6, 7, 10, 15–16, with notes about fulfillment, here and 4:16; Blomberg 1992, 71). The introductory formula here is crisp, "For he is the one about whom the prophet Isaiah had spoken." Scripture explained what was taking place.

Isaiah 40:3 was an important text that was widely used to describe the hope of the eschaton. Matthew cites wording like the LXX. The picture is of clearing a highway in honor of God's coming to the people, starting from the land's edge. The metaphor in the LXX is that a voice in the wilderness calls on the nation to be ready for the Lord's coming in salvation. A modern image might be the laying down of a red carpet for the arrival of a dignitary. Only here the preparation is personal, not merely physical.

Readiness involved an open and prepared heart, ready to follow God. That was what John's baptism signified. The Lord showed up in the stronger one to come that the Lord sent, and God's program arrived in that one.

The point is that John prepared the way for the Lord God (France 2007, 105; contra Morris 1992, 54, who sees the Lord as Jesus). The change from God's ways in the LXX to his ways in Matthew's citation at the end of the verse might allow for a reference to Jesus here (Davies and Allison 1988, 293), but in Matthew God acted through Jesus. The change also may reflect a pious Jewish hesitation to address directly a reference to God. There is ambiguity here, but the Father drives the kingdom program (Hagner 1993, 48, does not make a choice). The previous six references to Lord in Matthew refer to God; most are a mention of an angel of the Lord, some are after Jesus was born (Matt. 1:20, 22; 24; 2:13, 15, 19). The Father sent the Son to represent him. In his coming through Jesus, God's kingdom from heaven arrived. That is the point of linking verse 2 with verse 3. All of this is rooted in a new exodus motif and an already–not yet character for the kingdom. The kingdom idea Jesus taught involves an "already" element, here in him and the giving of the Spirit as a result of forgiveness, and a "not yet" come in fullness element, when full *šālôm* and righteousness appear in the world (Bock 2002, 565–93).

3:4. The description of John follows, noting his ascetic lifestyle, a life that was separated from the usual luxuries of life, a life of the poor (Keener 2009, 118). John's style was different than the one Jesus would have (Matt. 11:18–19), but they both pointed to God's work.

John's cloths are "camel hair" (BDAG s.v. "κάμηλος" 506), with a leather belt for the waist. He did not wear tog-like clothing. His diet was locusts and honey, the most basic of menus. "Locusts" refers to the migratory grasshoppers

(BDAG s.v. "ακρίς" 39) that are still eaten today by the poor in areas like Arabia and Syria. These were not carob pods. This was the only kosher insect (France 2007, 106; Lev. 11:20–23; CD [Damascus Document] 12:14–15; 11QTa [11QTemple] 48:3–5). The "honey" came either from bees or plants (BDAG s.v. "ἄγριος" 15). This lifestyle is like that of Elijah (2 Kings 1:8; Mal. 4:5) and another figure of the time, Bannus (Josephus, *Vita* 11).

3:5–6. Those who responded to John came from Jerusalem, Judea, and the whole region of Jordan. This is a way of saying he impacted the nation of Israel and drew their attention. The reference to the Jordan probably pointed to visitors from Perea as well. The reference to "all" for Judea and the Jordan is hyperbolic and looks to a large number of respondents. The imperfect verbs for those who were coming (*exeporeueto*) and those who were being baptized (*ebaptizonto*) point to a repeated and continual stream of people participating in the rite (Hagner 1993, 49). They came to be baptized in the Jordan River and confess their sins. By doing so, they were participating in John's unique eschatological washing, saying they sought God's forgiveness and were ready for God's program to come, a redirection of their lives in tune with God's direction and calling. John's ministry was creating a distinction within Israel, with some responding to God and others not. Davies and Allison (1988, 298) observe that in Matthew this distinction of groups within Israel is often not noticed when Matthew's view of Judaism is described as negative. Some Jews *were* responding to God. Nolland (2005, 140) contrasts these responses to John here to the negative responses from within Israel in Matthew 2. Josephus mentions John the Baptist as preaching baptism as well (*A.J.* 18:117).

Judaism possessed washings for ritual purity (Exod. 19; Lev. 15; Num. 19; Isa. 1:16–17; Jer. 4:14; Ps. 51:7–9) or for proselyte baptism (Pusey, 1984). Such washings were usually self-administered. John's baptism was mediated versus being self-administered, making it unusual. John's baptism also appeared to have been a once-for-all declaration of being ready for God to come, making it a special kind of eschatological washing versus the repeated washings of Judaism. So, although this background about washings in Judaism helps us to see the kind of thing John is doing, what he did was unique.

"Confessing their sins" meant a public, humble declaration of wrongs committed before God (*exomoloumenoi tas hamartias autōn*). Thus, there was the need to seek forgiveness. The fact the baptisms took place in a river looks at immersion (BDAG s.v. "βαπτίζω" 2a, 164–65; Turner 2008, 109, notes Jewish washings also involved immersion; *Did.* 7). Confession has roots in the Old Testament (Lev. 5:5; 16:21; 26:40; Num. 5:6–7; Ezra 10:1; Neh. 9:2; Osborne 2010, 112). The timing of this confession is not clear other than being connected with the baptism. Did confession come before entering the water or as one was about to be baptized, or did the act represent the confession? Mark 1:4 speaks of a "baptism of repentance," but to confess sin, whether in word or act, in response to a call to repent (Matt. 3:2) says the same thing. Those who argue forgiveness of sins is limited to Jesus in Matthew are correct but overextend the point when they suggest this corrects Mark's reference to John's baptism for the forgiveness of sins (Mark 1:4), as John's action is linked to a readiness for what is to come in Jesus (contra Konradt 2020, 47–48).

3:7. John also confronted the Jewish leaders from the Pharisees and Sadducees. One article introduces both groups, showing their unity of need in light of what John says (Wallace 1996, 279). They are described as coming "to" (*epi*) the baptism, but not said to be baptized by him. So either they did not actually respond, were just present, or their participation was less than sincere, something the following rebuke also suggests (Wilkins 2004, 136 n. 18; Yamasaki 1998, 86).

John challenged them with an ironic rebuke about who had warned them to flee the coming wrath. Addressing them as a brood of "snakes" (BDAG s.v. "ἔχιδνα" 420) shows John questioned the sincerity of their coming. At the least, we have a challenge to make sure the leaders were there for the right reasons or (if they were getting baptized) were not merely engaging in an act for appearances' sake only. Matthew 21:23–27 suggests the Pharisees were not responsive to John, as does Luke 7:30, adding scribes to the mix. The combined expression naming both groups reappears later with Jesus (Matt. 12:34; 23:33).

This term for snakes often referred to vipers, which were poisonous (Isa. 11:8; 14:29; 30:6; Nolland 2005, 143 n. 38). This group of seemingly righteous leaders was really quite dangerous, even deadly. So Matthew intensifies the challenge to them, suggesting they were not really present because they agreed with the need for forgiveness, but either to court popularity or keep an eye on John (Wilkins 2004, 136). It was appropriate to challenge religious leaders most, since they often influenced others. It is common in the Gospels that the harshest rebukes are dealt to those who should know better. A warning about sincerity points to needs all are to seek. The picture of fleeing wrath like a snake describes running away from a fire in the desert. This kind of desert fire chased snakes from their holes, like tree serpents fleeing those destroying a forest (Keener 2009, 123). John's warning represents a danger to avoid. So with irony John asked who warned them about the challenge he was raising. Luke's version of this saying has John challenging everyone in the crowd (Luke 3:7). The call for sincerity is like what was said at Qumran (1QS 5:13–14; Davies and Allison 1988, 301).

Sadducees and Pharisees were two very different groups (Saldarini 1994; Josephus, *A.J.* 18.11–17). The Sadducees were aristocrats who cooperated with Rome, assimilating to the power reality with as little pushback as possible. They held the key positions of power in Jerusalem and were the high priestly party. They paid less attention to legal issues than the Pharisees and did not like the developing oral tradition. Sadducees did not believe in angels or resurrection. The Pharisees were pious, religiously driven people, who were called "the separated ones" to show their commitment to live distinctly holy lives. They sought to build a "fence around the law" (*m. 'Abot.* 1:1). Matthew refers to the Pharisees twenty-nine times, more than any other NT writer. By contrast the Sadducees are only referred to seven times by Matthew. The Pharisees carefully studied the law and developed the oral legal tradition (Morris 1992, 56–57). They were not enamored with Rome, but still worked within the society. They were more popular and respected than the Sadducees and apparently had larger numbers than the Sadducees.

In the question about fleeing wrath, John was noting that God's wrath aimed at injustice and immorality, as well as arrogance. John was about to address arrogance in the assumption that Jewish birthright meant having God's pleasure. Such a challenge is like those of the OT prophets (Amos 2:4–8; 6:1–7; Carson 1984, 103). Bruner (2004a, 92) says the wrath of God "is not the irritability of God; it is the love of God in friction with injustice." So the warning is about fleeing God's final judgment (Isa. 13:9; Dan. 7:9–11; Zeph. 1:15; 2:2–3; Mal. 4:1; Hagner 1993, 50). Judgment is a part of accountability to God as Creator and as the one who brings the kingdom that leads into holiness, righteousness, and peace. John's message was an act of grace to warn "people that doom is pending and certainly will overtake them unless they repent and believe" (Hendriksen 1973, 206).

3:8–9. John's exhortation made two points and then gave a rationale for the exhortation. The exhortation is introduced with the inferential particle *oun*. In this context it means "so" or "then." If they really wished to flee the coming wrath, then this was what must be done. Matthew stresses the crowd's response to John in contrast to the leaders' (contrast Matt. 3:5–6 with 3:7).

The first call was to make fruit worthy of repentance (Acts 26:20 shows Paul making a similar point). The idea of fruit-bearing is frequent in Matthew (Matt. 3:10; 7:16–20; 12:33; 13:8, 23, 26; 21:19, 33–34; Turner 2008, 113). Fruit in the singular looked at the product as a singular whole (Bruner 2004a, 95). John was not interested in the mere participation in a rite. Rather, he hoped that there was a resolve that participating in a baptism would open one up to God. The expectation was that behavior would change as a result of orienting oneself to the program which allowed getting a fresh and cleansed start, with past spiritual debts canceled. Matthew's version is more compact than Luke's. This was not merely a generic national call to have Israel steer away from national sin (Nolland 2005, 144). There was an individual dimension to this call. Repentance is the other side of faith; one turns and trusts God and his ways (Blomberg 1992, 78). That trust in turn will yield a responsiveness to God and produce good fruit.

The second call was a warning to not merely rely on birthright as guaranteeing blessing. It may have suggested that an objection to John's call was that blessing already came to a group of people because of their connection to Abraham and covenant. John was fighting against such a sense of entitlement. The late Jewish text *Genesis Rabbah* 48:8 expresses this idea: "In the hereafter Abraham will sit at the entrance of Gehenna, and permit no circumcised Israelite from descending therein," reflecting a note elsewhere in Judaism. That this inheritance is not a guarantee was John's point. They should not even begin to think in this way (Wallace 1996, 723–25, on this force to the grammar here). Even their thoughts should not be turned in this direction. Having Abraham as a father was not an insurance policy on being welcomed by God (a variation of this idea is Sirach 5:5—"Do not be so confident of forgiveness that you add sin to sin"). God can make children out of whomever he wishes. Romans 4 makes the point that having a faith like Abraham's faith in God is what connects one to God, not ancestry. John the Baptist made that point by observing that God could make children for Abraham out of the stones of creation if he wished. When Scripture wishes to drive home an idea, the personification of creation is often used like this (Luke 19:40). There is a wordplay here involving the Hebrew words for "son" (*bēn*) and "stone" (*eben*).

One should recall that the original Abraham gave birth to a nation out of a divine promise to produce a seed out of barrenness (Gen. 17:17; 18:10–14; Isa. 51:1–2, "rock from which you were hewn"; Rom. 4:17). God had made a people out of a non-people. Galatians 3 expresses a similar idea when it discusses the inclusion of Gentiles into blessing. Matthew's citing of John's remark may have anticipated a similar idea. In Romans 4 and Galatians 3 it is the likeness to Abraham's faith, not his ancestry, that is emphasized.

3:10. The reason one should pay attention to John's message is that the new era's arrival reminds one of the accountability to God that comes with being his creature, an accountability that will end in judgment (Matt. 25:46). The need for a gospel also communicates a need for forgiveness, because one faces the prospect of sin and judgment otherwise. Love and wrath go together because love also loves justice and righteousness (Bruner 2004a, 95, speaks of holy love). In other words, without the prospect of judgment there would be no need for a gospel. The picture pointing to judgment is one of an axe that can cut down a tree. The axe lies there "already" (*ēdē*) to stress the idea of immediacy. This adverbial term is thrown forward in the verse for emphasis.

Trees that do not bear good fruit are to be cut down and cast into the fire. The figure is common (Matt. 7:19; 12:33—tree and fruit only; Isa. 6:13; 10:15–19, 33–34; 32:19; Jer. 11:16; 17:10—gives the principle; 46:22; Ezek. 31:12; Dan. 4:14; Isa. 5:2—good fruit; Jer. 2:21; NT: Gal. 5:22; Phil. 1:11; James 3:18; McNeile 1915, 27). The appeal here is rooted in the idea that there is accountability to the creator God. The fruit that is worthy (ἄξιον) of repentance is good fruit. A useless tree that does not bear such fruit will be removed at the time of judgment (Matt. 5:22; 7:19; 13:40, 42, 50; 18:8–9; 25:41; all uniquely Matthean texts except for the verses in Matt. 18). The present tenses of the three verbs in the imagery of this verse highlight vividly the proximity of judgment wrapped up in the choice John asked his hearers to make (Davies and Allison 1988, 310–11; especially on fire and judgment in Judaism).

The idea of a judgment that is associated with works runs through the New Testament, even in texts where a faith based in Christ is present, indicating that a response of faith to grace produces works (Matt. 7:15–27; 12:50; 21:28–32; Acts 26:20; Rom. 2:6; 14:12; 1 Cor. 3:12–15; 1 Peter 1:17; Rev. 2:23; 22:12; on grace and works: Eph. 2:8–10, esp. 2:10; Titus 2:11–14; James 2:14–26).

3:11. Attention turns to the one to come. John contrasted his baptism of repentance with that of the one to follow. Only Matthew's version notes repentance here, and the phrase *eis metanoian* speaks of association with repentance (BDAG s.v. "εἰς" 10a, 291; Hagner 1993, 51; Turner 2008, 115). John baptized with water, but the one to come would baptize with the Spirit and fire. One other point is not insignificant. John said he was not worthy "to carry" (*bastasai*) the sandals of the stronger one (BDAG s.v. "βαστάζω" 3a, 171). In other words, he was not worthy to be the slave of the one to come. Later Jewish texts make it clear that to be a slave is an act of dishonor (*Mek.* on Exodus 21:2; *Ketub.* 96a; *Sipre* on Numbers 15.41; SB 1:121; France 2007, 113 n. 64). John was not even worthy of such dishonor before the one to come. It was a statement of intense humility, given John was a prophet. Mark and Luke's parallels speak of untying the sandal. The ambiguity may reflect the Aramaic which can mean either carrying or untying (Hill 1972, 94). The image of untying is fundamentally the same, performing one of the most demeaning of tasks for a slave. John was a prophet, so this is a significant point. The one to come would be of another order than John, even though a prophet was a person of high stature. If the one to come points to Psalm 118:26 and refers to the one who comes in name of the Lord, then Messiah is in view. The background for the separation to come is discussed. A reference to the "powerful one" could look back at Isaiah 11:1–2 (also 1 En. 49:3; Davies and Allison 1988, 314–15; Pss. Sol. 17:37).

The sign of the new era is the purging work of the Spirit and fire, an "eschatological fire" (so Davies and Allison 1988, 316; one baptism, Webb 1991, 292–98; 1QS 4:20–22; especially Dunn 1970, 11–12). The eschatological act is seen as one comprehensive moment. There is an internal work of the Spirit that is a baptism. Water washes, but the Spirit enables or tests one to survive the judgment and only enters a cleansed vessel. Purging was clear from the image of making a separation in the next verse. The giving of the Spirit is an act of God (Isa. 44:3; 59:21; Ezek. 36:27; 37:14; 39:29; Joel 2:29; Zech. 12:10; Keener 2009, 130) and is tied to judgment as well (Isa. 4:4; 40:24; 41:16; Jer. 4:11–16; 23:19; 30:23; Ezek. 13:11–13; 1QSb 5:24–25; Davies and Allison 1988, 317).

Mark 1:8 only mentions the Spirit and his treatment does not explicitly discuss judgment, but the fact that John sought repentance and alluded to the new era means that accountability and judgment were not completely absent. Mark simply is emphasizing the bringing of the Spirit.

3:12. The purging points to a distinguishing judgment where wheat and chaff are on the threshing floor to be cleared. Wheat is gathered and placed into a storehouse. The chaff is set aside to be burned with an unquenchable fire, an allusion back to Matthew 3:10. The picture may be of the winnowing fork tossing grain in the air to make the separation as the heavier good grain falls straight down (Wilkins 2004, 138). Threshing floor imagery is also common for judgment (Ps. 1:4; Isa. 17:5–6, 13; 33:11; 41:15–16; Jer. 15:7; Hos. 13:3; Joel 3:13; Amos 8:1–2; Zeph. 2:2; 1QM 14:1; T. Ab. 12 A; Keener 2009, 129 nn. 161–62). What is left in the end and survives the judgment is a faithful remnant (France 2007, 116).

In sum, John's message is that preparing for the arrival of the new era requires a humble turning to God in repentance and being ready for the purging work of the one to come who brings the Spirit. That Spirit makes a separation between people. In turning to God, one is ready to walk in a manner that seeks to bear fruit for God. This is necessary because the coming of the new era also points to a time of accountability to God. The gospel offers hope and division at the same time. The gospel is simultaneously about both hope and judgment. The vastly different result emerges from the choice of how one responds to its offer.

THEOLOGICAL FOCUS

The exegetical idea (fulfilling Scripture and in preparation for the kingdom, John the Baptist offered a baptism for forgiveness of sins, warned the Jewish leaders to flee God's coming wrath, and announced one to come who would bring the Spirit and judgment) leads to this theological idea: John the Baptist's ministry points to an accountability before God all people have, while promising them forgiveness and enablement should they respond to the one to come. As forerunner, John the Baptist warned the Pharisees and Sadducees to flee the coming wrath—not assume birthright means salvation—and announced the sign of the Messiah and new era rooted in the one who would bring the Spirit of God.

How does one prepare for the new era? Preparation involves responding to John's ministry and his call to repent. This response to God's coming points to an awareness that one cannot fix oneself. It understands the need for forgiveness and possesses the humility to have such a recognition. This attitude appreciates that before the living creator God, one has an accountability that one cannot meet without divine aid and enablement. We are all his creatures whether we accept that reality or not. We cannot work our way to fellowship with God and fix ourselves. So we turn to God in repentance, seeking forgiveness in the way God offers it. Everything the New Testament says about the gospel being a gift points in this direction of God graciously meeting our need when we recognize it.

The characters in this unit also show an array of responses to God's program. First, we see a faithful minister in John. He showed a humility that recognized the greatness of the one God sent and that faithfully challenged a world in need of what God offers. He clearly articulated that people need to come to God in a spirit of repentance that turns to God and seeks to have fruit that is worthy of that turning to him. He rejected any approach to God that says God owes us or that we are entitled to salvation from him. Second, there was the candidate John sought. He or she comes to God humbly seeking forgiveness and placing one's spiritual fate in God's gracious hands. Third, there was the possibility of hypocrisy, as is seen in John's warning to the Pharisees and Sadducees. Often with hypocrisy comes a mistaken sense of entitlement, as if salvation does not involve a personal engagement with God on his terms but can simply be inherited by birthright. Hypocrisy is ultimately rooted in the arrogance that one can live independently of God. John declared that this was not at all correct. Realizing corporate and individual accountability to the Creator God in judgment prevents such a false view of salvation with its assumption of automatic, entitled blessing. Jesus identified with and supported John's understanding of the new era and what it requires, as the next scene shows.

PREACHING AND TEACHING STRATEGIES

Exegetical and Theological Synthesis

The exegetical section highlights human sinfulness, the need for repentance, and God's gracious offer to receive those who humbly acknowledge their spiritual poverty. At the center of this narrative stands the bold, faithful, and enigmatic Baptist, who takes up the mantle foretold by Isaiah, preparing the way for Jesus by announcing his coming. John welcomed penitent sinners but rebuked pretenders, namely, the religious leaders who assumed God's favor by reason of their Jewish heritage. He exposed a human tendency toward entitlement and warned of future judgment.

While John ushered in a new era of salvation history, hinting both at the Messiah's coming and the Spirit's enablement, the Baptist echoed an age-old refrain from the prophets: turn back to God. Sinful attitudes and actions direct us away from God. Rebellion comes in myriad forms: idolatry and injustice, doubt and denial, selfishness and pride, hate and hypocrisy. Some sinful choices are glaring—murder, adultery, and slander—but many remain subtle—exaggeration, envy, and anxious thinking.

John reminded the crowds that they could not change by pure force of will. Repentance both acknowledges the need for change and signals the desire for change. True renewal, however, requires the Holy Spirit. Only a life enabled by the Spirit will persevere and prove genuine in the coming judgment.

Preaching Idea

Heed voices that invite us back into God's favor.

Contemporary Connections

What does it mean?

What does it mean to heed voices that invite us back into God's favor? Who are these voices and how do they speak their invitation? First, we must acknowledge John the Baptist's *special role*. Jesus considered him the greatest of men born among women (Matt. 11:11). Matthew depicts him in a special, providential role as the Messiah's forerunner, quoting Isaiah 40:3. We are not John the Baptist *redivivus*.

We can, however, hear his tone and enduring truth in those who echo his message. John warned of judgment, called for repentance, and offered forgiveness. Countless faithful voices from church history have echoed his invitation into God's favor. Authors of NT letters and sermons recorded in Acts record voices that invite us back into God's favor. Patristic (Ignatius, Justin Martyr) and Puritan (Jonathan Edwards, John Owen) writers provide voices that invite us back into God's favor, as well as Reformers (Martin Luther, John Calvin), and revival preachers (John Wesley, Billy Graham). Local church pastors, conference speakers, and contemporary authors (John Piper, Elyse Fitzpatrick) likewise invite us back into God's favor.

However, we would be foolish to limit our inviting voices to professional clergymen and dead theologians. Some of the most common voices who speak God's favor into our lives include parents, grandmothers, Sunday school teachers, high school mentors, Christian friends, extended family members, and social media connections. Through modeling and timely words, they remind us of God's call to repentance and his offer of forgiveness. To use Paul's words, they "do the work of an evangelist"

(2 Tim. 4:5 NIV) by giving voice to the gospel. Heeding them means hearing them out and responding in trust.

Is it true?

Is it true we should heed voices that invite us back into God's favor? Absolutely. Anyone who needs a history lesson to compel them should turn to the OT prophets. Israel's constant rejection of voices inviting them back into God's favor landed them in exile, homeless and hopeless. Of course, calls to repentance resounded in the NT as well. John the Baptist gave the first invitation, echoed by Jesus, Peter, Paul, and numerous other voices. Failure to heed the voice, they warned, would not bode well in future judgment.

Voices of God's favor still speak today. We are wise to heed their invitation to come back to him, even if the threat of exile does not apply. In fact, most sinful choices have built-in, negative consequences. Sexual sin may lead to emotional baggage, unwanted pregnancy, or shame. Dishonesty may lead to false expectations or fracture relationships. Pride may lead to entitlement and a critical spirit. Injustice leads to division and hostility. Greed leads to forms of oppression and abuse. Ultimately, all sin distances us from God and covers us in shame. When we heed the voices that call us back to God, his forgiveness—not our lust, lies, selfishness, or ego—gets the last word.

As mentioned above, these voices come in various tones. We are wise to heed spiritual counsel from parents, pastors, and counselors. We are wise to heed spiritual rebuke from close friends and mentors. We are wise to heed spiritual encouragement from thoughtful authors, speakers, and podcasters. Each of these voices is a manifestation of the still, small voice of God who whispers in accordance with his inspired Word (1 Kings 19:12; 2 Tim. 3:16).

Now what?

Heeding voices that invite us back into God's favor comprises three steps: listen, obey, and repeat. First, we must listen for these voices God has providentially and strategically placed in our lives. They are all around us—in our homes, behind pulpits, online, in books, at work, on the radio—playing diverse roles in our lives. We know them by their tone: they teach, reprove, correct, and train us for righteousness (2 Tim. 3:10–17). We know them by their testimony: they love God and others and live what he commands. We know them by the gospel truth they speak.

Next, heeding means putting what we hear into action. Perhaps we need to obey a pastor's challenge to address a false belief about ourselves or God. Perhaps we need to take the counsel of an accountability partner and end a relationship that has led to sexual compromise. Perhaps we need to respond to a father's rebuke about spiritual sloth and make time for prayer and corporate worship. Knowing God has providentially and strategically placed these voices in our lives so we can enjoy his favor should motivate our willingness to heed.

Finally, as people who experience God's favor, we should want to extend the invitation to others. We can be a voice that calls people back to God to our family, friends, and other followers of Jesus. We can be this voice to sinners, hypocrites, neighbors, and enemies. The offer of forgiveness is a public good secured by the stronger one whom John preceded. Jesus gave his life to show God's favor for the world. We can at least move our lips to extend his invitation.

Creativity in Presentation

Reality television shows featuring vocal talents have proliferated in the past decade. *American Idol* (and other national versions), *The Voice*, and *X Factor* are among the most popular. Each show allows judges and viewers to weigh in on their favorite voice. Some of the winners have advanced to musical stardom (e.g., Carrie Underwood, Kelly Clarkson, Cassadee Pope, and Leona Lewis). Similarly, Susan Boyle wowed audiences in *Britain's Got Talent*.

Boyle's appearance underwhelmed compared to other contestants, but her voice transcended other singers when she performed "I Dreamed a Dream" from *Les Misérables*. Consider using a commercial from one of these TV programs or a clip of Boyle's performance on YouTube. Mention our love for compelling voices, saying, "When a powerful voice resounds, we naturally take notice."

Some of the more impactful voices in Christian history have been revival preachers (e.g., George Whitfield, John Wesley) and evangelists (e.g., Dwight Moody, Billy Graham). While a short biographical sketch of these figures may be helpful in the sermon, a testimony from someone Whitefield by their voice may prove more effective. In his biography *Unbroken* (Hillenbrand 2014), Louis Zamperini shares his reluctant trip to a Billy Graham crusade. The former Olympic athlete and WWII prisoner of war had been medicating his pain with alcohol when his wife dragged him to the event. Graham's voice penetrated Zamperini's heart, moving him on a deep journey of forgiveness toward his ruthless Japanese captor, "The Bird." After heeding himself the invitation to come back to God's favor, Zamperini showed that very favor to his enemy. Although the biography and movie of Zamperini's life understate his conversion and evangelistic career, the WWII survivor himself became a voice for God's favor in public speeches and interviews, as captured online.

Of course, voices that invite us to come back to God's favor are often closer than we think. Leverage stories of grandparents or parents serving as a voice of God's favor. In *Because He Loves Me*, Elyse Fitzpatrick (2008, 10) writes about her role as a grandmother, speaking God's favor to her numerous grandchildren. Likewise, years ago I was part of a wedding party where the maid of honor had a tattoo on her forearm that read, "You are. So be." When I asked her about it, she explained the phrase: her father had repeated it to her throughout her childhood to help her overcome anxiety. Her father invited her to release her anxiety by remembering God's unconditional embrace of her as a beloved daughter.

We all have stories of friends or family, mentors or ministry workers, whose voices invited us back into God's favor. (Hopefully, as pastors and teachers, each of us are one of those voices!) Of course, we may share personal stories of voices that invited us back to God's favor. We may even consider those voices we failed to heed, and the fallout from our neglect. Moreover, a SurveyMonkey poll or Facebook survey from your congregation may surface specific examples of impactful voices in their lives. Following up with a few people for detailed stories and permission to use them might infuse the sermon with relevant illustrations of the importance of heeding voices that invite us back to God.

By the time you finish the sermon, you want to be certain you have clearly articulated the truths below. John the Baptist's ministry points to an accountability before God that all people have, while promising them forgiveness and enablement when they respond to the one to come. This reality is true whether we recognize it or not. Therefore, we should heed voices who invite us back into God's favor.

- It's time to come back to God (3:1–2).
- A new voice offers an old invitation to come back to God (3:3–6).
- Coming back to God is a conscious choice (3:7–10).
- A time will come when God's invitation expires (3:11–12).

DISCUSSION QUESTIONS

1. How did John's voice align with the surrounding voices of renewal in his day? How was his message different? Be specific.

2. What role does Isaiah 40:3 play in Matthew's presentation of John? How does this fit a broader use of Scripture in Matthew's gospel?

3. How would you define baptism and repentance? How are they different today than in John's day?

4. What is the evangelical equivalent of Jewish birthright? In other words, what beliefs, activities, or traditions do we assume merit God's favor?

5. Who are the key voices in your life who invite you back into God's favor? Give an example of a voice you heeded, and one you failed to heed.

6. Are there ways God invites us back into his favor, other than personal voices? Explain.

Matthew 3:13–17

EXEGETICAL IDEA

John the Baptist baptized the divinely endorsed beloved Son Jesus, who himself accepted baptism to affirm John's eschatological message and identify with Israel's need.

THEOLOGICAL FOCUS

The divine endorsement of Jesus as King and Servant points to the need to respond to him, as God calls him to begin his work.

PREACHING IDEA

The divine voice deserves the last word on Jesus.

PREACHING POINTERS

Jesus traveled a significant distance to meet John the Baptist in the wilderness. John saw in Jesus the stronger one to come and attempted to reverse roles with him. Jesus would not be dissuaded. He came to identify with the sinful people of Israel, while maintaining a vision of righteousness—the ethic of the inbreaking kingdom. In the end, he received John's support and a divine endorsement when the Father spoke, rent the heavens, and sent the Spirit to enable him. This powerful, intimate scene launched Jesus into his career as God's long-awaited, beloved, and well-pleasing Son and Servant.

Opinions about Jesus are as numerous as people who voice them. Some view Jesus as a magician, political subverter, kindly moralist, best friend, merely a prophet like others, or a memorable rabbi. Others view Jesus as a hippie, liberal, or lunatic. Historians undertake "quests" to discover the real Jesus of history. Theologians distill Jesus into doctrinal statements. Church councils debate the nature of Jesus. Children learn from an early age that Jesus is a prophet, priest, and king. These voices say more about those who speak than about Jesus himself. The authoritative voice, the last word, the ultimate claim about Jesus belongs to his Father—who loved him, endorsed him, and enabled him with his Spirit. The divine voice deserves the last word on Jesus.

JOHN BAPTIZES JESUS (3:13–17)

LITERARY STRUCTURE AND THEMES (3:13–17)

This unit describes one of the most crucial events in Jesus's ministry: his baptism by John and the divine confirmation that accompanied it. When Jesus arrived, John sensed his own need to be baptized by Jesus. However, Jesus needed to endorse what John represented. Jesus also wanted to identify with the people's need for righteousness, so John was told to proceed with his baptizing of Jesus. The climactic movement in the narration is the divine voice endorsing Jesus as the Spirit came upon the beloved Son. This relationship of Jesus to God and this enablement explains why he is the stronger one to come. With this act, Jesus was ready to embark on the ministry that would bring the kingdom of heaven (vv. 13–17). The passage is a vision-call scene. Throughout this chapter, everything John did pointed to Jesus as the one who would bring the new era.

This material has parallels in Mark 1:9–11 and Luke 3:21–22 and some overlap with John 1:32–34. Mark and Luke share a reference from the voice to Jesus using the second person, "You are my beloved Son." Matthew has, "This is my beloved Son," pointing to the significance of what was largely a private experience of Jesus in terms of the voice. Only John's gospel tells us John also saw the Spirit descending like a dove, but there is no indication John heard the voice. Mark and Luke stress that Jesus beheld the heavens open. Mark is explicit that the event was focused on Jesus and what he saw. This was the divine call and confirmation to begin the new ministry.

The climactic scene with John had Jesus receive baptism to identify with John's ministry and his call to the nation to repent. The result was a commendation of Jesus from God as Son and Servant. The language of Scripture is central as regal and servant motifs are combined from Psalm 2:7 and Isaiah 42:1. Everyone had spoken in the gospel up to this point. Now God spoke and showed how important Jesus is, showing him to be a Spirit-anointed sent one.

Jesus is the one who will bring what is offered. His work of bringing the Spirit and fire is so great that even a prophet like John was not worthy to serve him. Jesus is in a class all his own. He is far more than a prophet. He is the unique anointed one of God, at the center of all God will do to save.

EXPOSITION (3:13–17)

This passage focuses on one climactic endorsement. It completes the John the Baptist section and turns the attention solely on Jesus. The endorsement came from God, as represented in the voice from heaven. Jesus is affirmed as the beloved Son, which in context means the stronger one to come. The imagery of the voice's description reflects both a regal role as Son and a servant role as a beloved one. He was symbolically equipped with the Spirit, so that Father, Son, and Spirit were all active in the scene. Jesus identified with Israel and her need by accepting baptism. The people needed cleansing. For all the endorsing that Scripture and Jesus perform for John, the Baptist himself pointed to Jesus, who was marked out as the unique and beloved Son-Servant by God. In effect, God showed Jesus it was time to begin his active ministry. Jesus did so with a divine stamp of approval.

The relationship between John and Jesus is a key topic in the Gospels. Matthew emphasizes how John knew Jesus was the one to come, and this event explains why. God's divine endorsement of Jesus as Servant-Son marked him out as far superior to the forerunner prophet. What Luke takes two chapters to show (Luke 1–2), Matthew does explicitly in this act and by the affirmation from the previous scene.

John Baptizes Jesus as the Spirit Descends and God Speaks (3:13–17)

John the Baptist baptized the divinely endorsed beloved Son Jesus, who himself accepted baptism to affirm John's eschatological message and identify with Israel's need.

3:13. This verse makes a transition into John's baptism of Jesus. The scene contains Matthew's portrayal of Jesus's first intentional act in the gospel. Jesus showed up at the Jordan from Galilee (Matt. 2:22). He came on a trip of about seventy miles to participate in John's baptism. The verb for "arriving" recalls Matthew 2:1 and 3:1. Jesus came without regal pomp from the edge of Israel (Wilkins 2004, 139). This event was not a creation of the early church. It is unlikely the church would have made up such an event with an implication that Jesus might have sinned, when they did not see him that way. This historical observation involves applying the criterion of embarrassment and argues for the core historical authenticity of the event (Keener 2009, 131).

3:14–15. The exchange in these two verses is unique to Matthew. John "tried to prevent" (*diekōluen*) Jesus from accepting his baptism because John sensed a need for Jesus to baptize him. The inclusion and juxtaposition of the Greek pronouns makes the description more emphatic: "I have need by you to be baptized" is the Greek word order at the start of the verse. John knew Jesus was a greater figure than he. He knew, as one who announced and offered forgiveness, where real forgiveness came from. The humility of John in Matthew 3:11 is reinforced here in his appreciation of who Jesus was. Grammatically, this verb speaks of an attempt to do something that was not completed, what is called a conative imperfect (BDF §326; Wallace 1996, 550). So John tried to prevent Jesus from being baptized but eventually did not stop him. It is not clear from Matthew alone how John came to see Jesus as he did, since Matthew does not appeal to the kind of background Luke 1 gives us about their familial relationship. Luke likely supplies in part what Matthew lacks (Luke 1:5–25, 39–56; Turner 2008, 118; contra Davies and Allison 1988, 323, who do not see a historical recollection in Luke). John 1:33 tells us John testified to Jesus as Messiah and the one to come as a result of what he saw take place at the baptism. The act is probably confirmatory of anything John had heard about Jesus from his family and was John's firsthand experience of the connection. In John's gospel, the divine voice left no doubt for the Baptist about how to identify Jesus's role.

Jesus replied that John should leave it alone and go ahead with baptizing him, since Jesus's baptism by John would "fulfill all righteousness." The term "righteousness" is frequent in Matthew (Matt. 3:15; 5:6, 10, 20; 6:1, 33; 21:32). Most of these uses come in the Sermon on the Mount and have a legal-ethical context. This use seems distinct (France 2007, 120; Hagner 1993, 56; Wilkins 2004, 140). What exactly this means has been much discussed. Actually, the baptism began Jesus's ministry that accomplished sending this righteousness to Israel thus extending what John was committed to doing, bringing the people to righteousness and pointing the way to Jesus (Nolland 2005, 153–54). This is the best explanation for what Jesus meant. At the core of the explanation is an endorsement of John's message and ministry as Jesus identified with the needs of God's covenant people (Robert Webb in Bock and Webb 2009, 95–150, especially 143). In identifying with the sin of the people, he associated with sinners and their need to deal with sin (Isa.

53:11–12). So John consented to, and baptized, Jesus. John obeyed as Joseph had, even though he was not entirely able to appreciate all that was taking place. Jesus embraced an eschatological orientation to God's plan and humbly identified with those he came to save. This eschatological embrace means that Jesus shared John's view about how people are accountable to God and that there will be a judgment to come. There is a compelling need for the righteousness God supplies through the kingdom program Jesus brought.

3:16–17. As Jesus came up from the water, the heavens divided and he saw the Spirit of God descending like a dove from above (in Mark "the Spirit"; in Luke "the Holy Spirit"). Note how it was Jesus who saw all of this. Nothing is said about anyone else being aware of what was taking place. Only John 1:33 tells us John also saw this, but John the evangelist also gave no indication that John the Baptist heard anything.

The Spirit is compared to a dove, so the picture is not of a dove descending, but of a movement of the Spirit like a dove (Nolland 2005, 155, speaks of the Spirit looking like a dove, but the word order slightly favors a figure for movement here; Luke 3:22 is parallel). The dove element probably points to the idea of a messenger, but there is an array of suggestions for the point of connection, none of which is a clear choice. The association of the Spirit with the one to come reflects the Hebrew Scripture (Isa. 11:1; 42:1; 61:1). The Spirit came to rest on him. The heavens opening was a disclosure of what goes on beyond earth, a heavenly perspective that pointed to divine involvement and reflected an apocalyptic, revelatory genre and event (Isa. 64:1; Ezek. 1:1; John 1:51; Acts 7:56; Rev. 4:1; Turner 2008, 119).

Next was a voice from heaven declaring, "This is my beloved Son (*ho huois mou ho agapētos*), in whom I am well pleased." Mark and Luke have a more direct statement to Jesus, "You are my beloved Son, with whom I am well pleased." The difference is between Matthew's "this" (*houtos*) and Mark's and Luke's "you" (*su*). The point is the same with one distinct nuance. Jesus is God's beloved Son—the nuance is how this is presented. Matthew's wording shows the significance for all of the direct address from Mark and Luke. Jesus was being marked out as the One. Nolland (2005, 156) argues the heavenly court heard the voice since there was no indication of a public crowd nor of their reaction in this specific scene (contra Osborne 2010, 124–25, who sees a public event; Carson 2010, 137, sees John as hearing the voice). Matthew is pointing to the public significance of the act and has in view a heavenly declaration. The text is not so clear on who heard this voice, although the parallels limit the hearing to Jesus and perhaps John. John's gospel has John see the descent of the Spirit (John 1:31–34). Matthew's emphasis is on the experience of Jesus (Morris 1992, 66). Matthew does not give us any other potential witnesses to the voice, except perhaps John the Baptist himself.

God had marked out Jesus at this time, issuing a call that describes his role. The voice identifies Jesus, with a combination of descriptions from Psalm 2:7 and Isaiah 42:1, as a regal, specially born Son and as the chosen Servant, a proclaimer and bearer of salvation. The idea of being pleased with the Son points to the connection with servant imagery. "Son" anticipates the temptation scene of Matthew 4:1–11 where Jesus's sonship is the issue. Matthew 12:18 will also use Isaiah 42:1 to point to Jesus as Servant. Psalm 2 and Isaiah 42 are messianic texts in some expressions of Judaism (4Q174 [4QFlor.] 10–14; Targum on Isa. 42:1; Blomberg 1992, 82). The idea of the beloved might also appeal to Genesis 22:2 and point to an identification with Israel as another special son. The voice endorsed Jesus as God's sent one, while the Spirit showed the enablement Jesus had. The tradition behind the scriptural usage is debated.

This event does not reflect an adoptionism or a provision of the Spirit Jesus had lacked, because Matthew sees Jesus as a divinely enabled Son from birth (Matt. 1:20; Blomberg 1992, 82; Wilkins 2004, 142–43). The voice probably reflected a contrast to the *Bat Qol* of Jewish teaching, where in this scene God's voice is portrayed as present instead of the "daughter of the voice" (Davies and Allison 1988, 335–36; Turner 2008, 120; contra Hill 1972, 97). Being marked out by God, Jesus was ready to minister and carry out his calling. The roots of a Trinitarian view of God's activity should be seen here, as all three persons are active in this event.

The action revealed a key part of Matthew's Christology. Jesus was special, far greater than a prophet. He was the Son and Servant, with a call to fulfill righteousness for God's people. John showed a humble attitude and appreciation for the greatness of the one to come. Key to the new era is the Spirit. Jesus's baptism also served as an endorsement of John's message, with a recognition of the accountability we all have to God. Judgment comes with the gospel, but forgiveness comes with repentance. All of this means that the way into blessing and God's presence requires responding to God and the special one he sent. Placed in the context of the previous scene, this response means that it is not our works nor our ancestry nor our social status that brings salvation. God showed his support for Jesus by getting creation to react with the opening of the heavens and sending the Spirit, all the while speaking and appealing to scriptural promise.

THEOLOGICAL FOCUS

The exegetical idea (John the Baptist baptized the divinely endorsed beloved Son Jesus, who himself accepted baptism to affirm John's eschatological message and identify with Israel's need) leads to this theological focus: the divine endorsement of Jesus as King and Servant points to the need to respond to him, as God calls him to begin his work.

What does God give to meet the needs of the new era? He sends his beloved Son. Jesus is the one to come who is in a category far distinct from prophet. Even though many in the world want to make Jesus a prophet, this sells him far short of who he is. He is the unique Son who brings the enablement we lack to walk with God. He brings the Spirit. The Spirit's coming is also an act of divine purging that separates humanity. The washing Jesus brings comes with the new era's offer of the indwelling Spirit. Matthew's narrative will develop this theme, especially in the turn of the story that takes place in Matthew 16–17 with Peter's confession at Caesarea Philippi.

Our response to God requires we turn and embrace what God offers by grace through Jesus (Eph. 2:8–10). In that turning to God is a recognition of a need God supplied to enable us to fellowship with him and walk in God's ways. John the Baptist set the table for that response in his ministry, a ministry Jesus's baptism also endorsed.

As the unique Son whom God is pleased to use, Jesus is the stronger one who brings a purging that also involves the Spirit of God (Acts 2:14–36). That cleansing and purging, which one needs to embrace and seek, leads one into the enablement from God to walk with him and experience participation in the new era Jesus brings. The world may want to make Jesus one prophet among many in the religious pantheon, but that is not how to respond to his coming. God spoke here to show Jesus is unique, at the center of the one program of God that saves. No one else who has occupied the planet is like him in God's plan.

PREACHING AND TEACHING STRATEGIES

Exegetical and Theological Synthesis

In the exegetical section, Jesus surprised John by requesting baptism. His insistence on fulfilling righteousness proved his desire to identify fully with the people of Israel. Their sin did not repel him but compelled him to assume his vocation as Son and Servant. Coming out of the water, Jesus received divine endorsement and enablement. The heavens opened, the Father spoke, and the Spirit descended. God's voice echoed promises from Psalm 2:7 and Isaiah 42:1, implying Jesus as the fulfillment of these roles. Voices of the prophets, the Baptist, heavenly Father, and Holy Spirit coalesce to announce an inbreaking kingdom in the earthly ministry of Jesus.

Sadly, this initial, clear proclamation of Jesus as Son and Servant fell many times on deaf ears during his ministry. Religious tradition deafened people. Sinful rebellion deafened people. Political ambition deafened people. Acute physical, social, and psychological need deafened people. And inattentive, preoccupied, selfish tendencies deafened people. These conditions described the people Jesus met during his public ministry tour. They describe us today. We must all reckon with the climactic question Jesus asked his disciples at Caesarea Philippi: "But who do you say that I am?" (Matt. 16:15).

Preaching Idea

The divine voice deserves the last word on Jesus.

Contemporary Connections

What does it mean?

Simply put, we should put greater stock in what the heavenly Father said about Jesus than his lethal enemies or misguided fans. In his day, the religious leaders accused Jesus of blasphemy and cried for his death. In our day, *TIME* magazine annually questions the historical reliability of the Gospels, and it always coincides with Lent and Advent seasons. The Jesus Seminar has rated and reviewed the sayings and doings of Jesus with a color-coding system. Former evangelicals like Bart Ehrman have promoted a hermeneutic of suspicion about Jesus. Renewed interest in the gnostic gospels (e.g., writings by Elaine Pagels), suggests that ancient voices about Jesus were suppressed. Even popular fiction, like Dan Brown's *Da Vinci Code*, raises questions about Jesus's relationship and progeny with Mary. Enemies of Jesus exist in every age; their voices must not get the last word.

Nor should we give the last word to Jesus's misguided fans. Evangelicals, in our simple enthusiasm, can reduce Jesus to a few likeable traits. We tout the gentleness of Jesus. We stress the strength of Jesus. We focus on the faithfulness of Jesus. None of these emphases is wrong; however, we must beware of the human tendency to avoid complexity. For example, voices that highlight the compassion of Jesus may overlook his biting words toward Pharisees. People who teach on the piety and spiritual practices of Jesus may understate his ordinary habits of walking, eating, and telling stories.

That God deserves the last word on Jesus means we trust his first words about Jesus: "This is my one dear Son; in him I take great delight." These first words are lasting words, repeated at the Transfiguration (Matt. 17:5). They set the tone and direction for the ministry of Jesus—who identifies with sinners, cares about righteousness, ushers in the kingdom, and lives in loving obedience to his Father and firm reliance on the Spirit. Heeding the divine voice keeps us from becoming Jesus's lethal opponents or misguided fans.

Is it true?

Is it true the divine voice deserves the last word on Jesus? Absolutely. We cannot let culture make ultimate claims about Jesus with its hermeneutic of suspicion. We cannot let preachers, professors, or denominations make ultimate claims about Jesus with their tendency to overlook complexity or to feed bias.

Unfortunately, our partial knowledge of Jesus means we often craft him in our own image. We envision Jesus much like ourselves, just with a little more wit, wisdom, patience, and compassion and less envy, irritation, and selfish preoccupation. In *The Blue Parakeet*, McKnight

(2008, 49, 220–223) has confirmed this bias in an assessment he uses with his undergraduate students.

This, of course, does not mean great teachers, pastors, authors, mentors, parents, or peers have nothing to teach us about Jesus. As Paul taught, we learn Christ through the imitation of others (1 Cor. 11:1). John made a similar claim: since most people haven't seen Jesus, we learn him from fellowship with others (1 John 1:3). Every one of us reflects Jesus—his character and teaching—in some measure, but none of us fully knows him (1 Cor. 13:12; cf. John 3:2). Thus, we must continually return to the Father's divine endorsement of Jesus. His first words are lasting word that must shape our view of Jesus.

Now what?

How should we respond to this divine voice? How do we ensure the heavenly Father gets the last word on Jesus? First, we must acknowledge rival voices. As mentioned above, culture, church, and personal bias can all cloud our understanding of Jesus. We must become more aware of who speaks to us about Jesus and what they say. Are we listening to skeptical voices? Liberal voices? Chauvinistic voices? Conservative voices? Trendy voices? Our own voice? When we take inventory of these voices, we can learn to filter their limited presentation of Jesus.

Second, we must tune our ear to the divine voice. Not only do we listen to the words the Father spoke, but also to their tone and implication as he uttered important imagery from the Hebrew Scriptures. "My Son" indicates the Father's personal relationship with Jesus, the promised King of David's line. "Beloved" connotes God's choice of Jesus; he is special, unique, and prized by God. "In whom I am well pleased" endorses Jesus's role as Spirit-empowered Servant, evident in the Spirit's descent. Even the rending of the heavens in this baptismal scene hints that God wanted an angelic audience to enjoy Jesus's coronation. Whatever else we hear (or think) about Jesus, we must run it through the grid of God's first words to make sure they are the last word.

Finally, granting the divine voice the last word on Jesus recognizes his authority. Our posture, like the Baptist's, is one of anticipation, obedience, and surrender. We may not be worthy to untie the strap of Jesus's sandal, but we are invited to follow his footsteps. Remarkably, this divinely endorsed Son and Servant stooped low enough to wash his disciples' feet before laying his life down for them. His is worthy of our allegiance. Hence, when the heavenly Father says, "Listen to him [my Son]!" (Matt. 17:5), we should heed him.

Creativity in Presentation

First words in literature can set the tone that lasts the rest of the book. In *Write Better*, Le Peau (2019, 9–24) opens with a plea to "Find an Opening." To justify his claim that "Beginnings matter," he provides numerous examples of first lines in nonfiction and fiction writing. He includes Dickens's sprawling introduction to *A Tale of Two Cities*, "It was the best of times, it was the worst of times . . . "; and Bradbury's terse start to *Fahrenheit 451*, "It was a pleasure to burn." Cite a few of your own favorite "first lines" from literature that set a lasting tone for the rest of the book and make the link to the Father's first words about Jesus setting a lasting tone for the rest of Matthew.

Parents play an unrivaled role in shaping their children. Sometimes a single word or repeated phrase becomes a "script" for the rest of their children's lives. Scazzero (2015, 75–79) helps people identify these "scripts" to develop "emotionally healthy spirituality." My wife's mother told her, "You're my favorite favorite." My parents repeatedly asked me, "What's your backup plan?" instilling the notion that I would likely face failure. Other scripts include, "You're worthless"; "You are. So be"; "Look for the good"; "We all know life's not fair, so there's no need to fuss." These scripts have a lasting impact on the son or daughter who hears it. Even

Isaac's blessing of Jacob (Gen. 27:27–29; 28:1–5), Jacob's blessing of Judah (Gen. 49:8–12), and David's final prayer for Solomon (1 Kings 2:1–4) provide a last word with lasting effect from a father to his son. God's endorsement of Jesus was a powerful script with lasting effect.

John Ortberg (2014, 21–22) recounts an intriguing story about Dallas Willard a former mentor and professor of philosophy at University of Southern California. During a lecture, a student challenged Willard with "an insulting . . . and wrong" objection. Willard whom Ortberg described as "the smartest man I ever knew," had a public opportunity to decimate the student and prove his professorial intellect. He didn't. Instead, he ended the class. Perplexed, Ortberg asked Willard to explain his logic. "I was practicing the discipline of not having the last word," Willard replied. The sentiment affirms the power of last words and the human tendency to get the final punch in a verbal spar. When it comes to the character, mission, and identity of Jesus, the Father gets the last word.

Finally, we all intuitively know the force of last words in stories and ceremonies. Consider the iconic ending to fairy tales: "And they lived happily ever after." Less dramatic stories and films may conclude with a simple, "The End." On his daily radio broadcast, Paul Harvey signed off by saying, "And now you know . . . the rest of the story." America's trusted and beloved news anchor Walter Cronkite always said, "And that's the way it is." New Year's Eve parties end with kissing, singing "Auld Lang Syne," and bold resolutions for the coming year. Wedding ceremonies close with, "It is my pleasure to introduce to you Mr. and Mrs. So-and-So." Worship services end with a doxology, "Now to him who is able to keep you from stumbling . . ." (Jude 24 NKJV). Share a few of your favorite closing lines or last words. Give special pomp to the closing doxology the weekend you preach this text.

As you add creative elements to your sermon, keep in mind the core theological and homiletical ideas. John the Baptist's ministry points to an accountability before God that all people have, while promising them forgiveness and enablement should they respond to the one to come. The divine voice deserves the last word on Jesus.

- Jesus insists on identifying with us (3:13–14).
- Jesus receives his identity from God (3:16–17).

DISCUSSION QUESTIONS

1. What compelled Jesus to travel so far for his baptism? What does he mean by "righteousness"?
2. How does John respond to Jesus's request for baptism? Why?
3. How does Matthew's version of the baptism differ from that of the other gospels? What does Matthew emphasize?
4. What does this passage teach about the Trinity? What does it not say?
5. Why does the timing of God's endorsement and enablement of Jesus's ministry matter? What would this event have communicated to Jesus? Matthew's readers?
6. What voices in your life speak truth about Jesus? What misleading voices about Jesus have you, your church, or our culture given too much attention to?

Matthew 4:1–11

EXEGETICAL IDEA

Jesus's faithfulness and commitment to God rebuffed Satan's temptations, showing Jesus's qualifications to represent humanity because he succeeded where Adam and Israel had failed.

THEOLOGICAL FOCUS

Jesus's successful overcoming of temptation means he can reverse what Adam did and qualifies him to represent all humanity.

PREACHING IDEA

Temptation is a proving ground for our love of God.

PREACHING POINTERS

On the heels of his baptism—a scene depicting his solidarity with Israel and divine endorsement—Jesus followed the Spirit's lead into the wilderness for forty days. Known as a place of testing and temptation, Jesus faced an ancient enemy of God and his people: the devil, Satan. A dramatic scene unfolded, where the devil dangled before Jesus three tests to reject God's provision, protection, and delegated power. In each instance, Jesus affirmed the Hebrew Scriptures and modeled loyalty to God. The original audience would have heard echoes of Eden and the exodus, where Adam fell prey to the devil's original test and Israel doubted God's passage into the promised land. Jesus stood above his forerunners, embodying for Israel and all humankind loyal, flawless love for God.

Temptation did not cease with Jesus's victory in the wilderness. His followers from every age have faced various tests. Today temptations lure us to doubt God, distrust his provision, disobey his commands, and give in to timeless deceptions. The diabolical voice whispers, "Do it. You deserve it. Go get what God won't give." Married couples are tempted to reject their vows, divorce, and kindle new romances with other partners. Employees are tempted to take credit for work ideas they borrowed from others or claim hours they never worked. Politicians are tempted to use their power to manipulate others and maintain their platforms. Businesspeople are tempted to cut ethical corners or take advantage of others for the sake of the bottom line. All of us risk making other people invisible because they are not like us. In a global pandemic, all people with access to grocery stores are tempted to stockpile to ensure their maximum comfort. Fortunately, whenever we resist these temptations, we reaffirm our trust in God. In fact, this passage indicates temptation is a proving ground for our love of God.

JESUS OVERCOMES THREE SATANIC TEMPTATIONS (4:1–11)

LITERARY STRUCTURE AND THEMES (4:1–11)

This scene is a controversy account involving Satan and Jesus. It is shared in much briefer form in Mark 1:12–13, and is like Luke 4:1–13 but with a different sequence. The existence of two versions may well suggest that shorter and longer versions were known in the church. Mark may well be alluding to a well-known longer version. Luke and Matthew have the order of the second and third temptations reversed. Matthew has the tighter connectives, so it looks as if Luke is the one who changed the order (e.g., only Matthew has the final dismissal of Satan after the third temptation). Luke consistently calls the opponent the devil, while Matthew switched up his description of the adversary.

This must have been an experience Jesus told to his disciples; it is neither a myth nor merely creative haggadic midrash (Carson 1984, 111; Hagner 1993, 63; Keener 2009, 136 n. 184; contra Davies and Allison 1988, 352–53). Though four OT texts are cited, they are not the point; Jesus's character is. The showing of kingdoms from a mountain probably describes a type of visionary experience.

The controversy revolved around how one should serve God and self. It also was a challenge to how Jesus would live as Son of God. Satan tempted Jesus in three scenes to go his own way and abandon the path God called him to live. The tests were that Jesus (1) should provide for himself, (2) examine to see if God was loyal and would protect, and (3) accept power from Satan by abandoning his commitment to worship God. Jesus rebuffed each test with Scripture, showing a core commitment to God (James 4:7; 1 Peter 5:9). One was to live by God's word, avoid testing God and his loyalty, and worship and serve God alone. Jesus allowed nothing to sever his connection to and dependence upon God as he sought to follow God's calling and direction for him. The independence Satan sought and preached was the way of death. The temptations progressed from a wilderness scene to the temple to the world's kingdoms with a call to worship Satan. The challenges involved symbolism about personal need (bread), the nation (temple), and the world (kingdoms; Toussaint 1980, 75). The defection Satan desired was not subtle, but total. Jesus refused to go in that self-defeating direction. The way in which Jesus gave himself to God stood in contrast to how power was seen in the ancient world, where looking after oneself was key.

The three challenges were each met with Scripture that communicated core values. The point was not merely the citing of Scripture but the truth in Scripture that directed the heart. In the end, when the angels came to minister to Jesus, we see a figure whose utter loyalty to God qualified him to represent humanity in a way Adam had failed to do when the first man went independently of God's direction (Gen. 3). Jesus also succeeded where Israel failed. He was worthy to be her Messiah. This was a single confrontation scene, with Jesus emerging victorious through faithfulness.

The key themes point to Jesus's qualifications to represent the nation and humanity in light of that faithfulness. The text also shows that loyalty to God and his ways is how to defeat temptation. Because Jesus understood this, he succeeded where Adam and Israel failed. Jesus's use of Scripture showed what knowing God's public revelation can mean. Embracing God's Word can protect us from straying.

The Three Temptations in Matthean Order

Bread: Self-Provision

Temple Jump: Test God's Protection

Receive Kingdoms by Worshiping Satan: Defect from Loyalty to God

Jesus's Three Replies

Deut. 8:3: Man Lives Not by Bread Alone

Deut. 6:16: One Should Not Test God

Deut. 6:13: One Should Worship God Alone

EXPOSITION (4:1–11)

Jesus Overcomes Three Satanic Temptations (4:1–11)

Jesus's faithfulness and commitment to God rebuffed Satan's temptations, showing Jesus's qualifications to represent humanity because he succeeded where Adam and Israel had failed.

4:1–2. In this scene we move from one end of the transcendent spectrum to the other, from the divine voice to the devil's diverting whispers. It was the Spirit who led Jesus into this encounter. It was a test of allegiance that took place in the desert after forty days of fasting. Matthew alone speaks of the devil's entrance after forty days of fasting, while Luke sees the entire period as the diabolical test, since the fasting set up the test (Luke 4:2). The fast would have involved no food in this period. Esther 4:16 speaks of a three-day fast involving no food or drink for three days and nights. This suggests choices did exist about food and drink and that some fasts ran through the day but not the night (Judg. 20:26; 1 Sam. 14:24; 2 Sam. 1:12). This may explain why bread is mentioned in the first temptation.

The character of the hero is being tested (Nolland 2005, 161). The path Jesus took was reinforced here (Morris 1992, 72). In deep hunger and human need, Jesus was asked to turn from God and his path and seek refuge in ways other than loyalty, prayer, and dependence. The verb πειράζω (*peirazō*) can mean "tempt" or "test." Since the devil was the origin of the expression and was the key actor in the event, the meaning "tempt" is best here. God permitted this, but the experience was a real opportunity to betray God (BDAG s.v. "πειράζω" 4, 792). God does not tempt but can test (Gen. 22:1; James 1:13). There is a touch of double entendre here, yet in the end Satan drove the narrative and attempted to tempt Jesus.

The expression "the devil" looks at a slanderer (BDAG s.v. "διαβόλος" 2, 226; Morris 1992, 73; Job 1). This was one of several terms Matthew uses for the devil. What Satan did here fits that character of a slanderer who is opposed to God. The association of demons and the desert was common (Evans 2012, 81).

"To fast" is a spiritual exercise designed to focus one on God (BDAG s.v. "νηστεύω" 672). It could involve taking only water and only fasting in the daytime (Turner 2008, 126). The choice to fast could reflect grief (Deut. 9:9; 2 Sam. 1:12; 12:22; Dan. 10:3; Zech. 7:5; Bar. 1:5) or preparation for prayer (Josephus, *A.J.* 20.89). Pharisees might have fasted twice a week as a sign of piety (Luke 18:12; *Did.* 8:1; Pss. Sol. 3:8; DJG, "Fasting," 233–34). Moses fasted for forty days and nights in getting the Law (Exod. 34:28; also Elijah, 1 Kings 19:8). The wilderness is the place where Israel had failed (Blomberg 1992, 83; Deut. 8:2).

4:3–4. Satan knew Jesus's power as Son. The first-class conditional clause ("if you are the Son of God") reflects a kind of baiting in the hopes

Jesus would not be the right type of son. There is some discussion about whether the "if" assumes a condition of reality and that Satan views Jesus as the Son, so it should be translated "since"; but that is not the point here (correctly Turner 2008, 127–28). Whatever Satan was seen as thinking about Jesus, he was trying to undercut that connection, even questioning God's earlier endorsement of Jesus.

In this verse Satan is called "the one who tempts." He challenged Jesus to feed himself by turning the stones to bread. If God could make children from stones (Matt. 3:9), then surely the Son can make bread from them. The temptation is for the Son to act independently from God, which hints at a lack of trust in God. This challenge was about Jesus using all of his attributes to make the path easier for himself. In taking on the limits of humanity, Jesus had chosen to enter into the human experience fully. Satan wanted him to take a shortcut from life in a demanding and fallen world. Jesus was to use his power to sustain himself and take him away from the focus on God that the fast in the wilderness had been designed to foster. In contrast to Adam, who was tempted while having access to almost everything in the garden, Jesus had access to little during his temptation (Morris 1992, 75).

Jesus's reply was succinct as he drew on the words of Scripture to formulate a response. He cited Deuteronomy 8:3, a text that communicates that life is more than sustenance from bread. Life is about more than core material provision. Life is lived in connection with God's way as expressed in every word that comes from God's mouth as a reflection of his will. This core spiritual connection to God is something that never should be broken. The issue was not about miraculous power as Messiah, as no one else was present. A spiritual connection to and a dependence on God were the values most evidently displayed in all that Jesus did throughout this scene. God's ways would be Jesus's ways. Jesus was called in this mission to depend on God. Nothing would tear that asunder. Spirituality is not something we create or make up; it is found, nurtured, and fed in the revelation and relationship that comes with and from God. It is that which gives life. Submission and obedience to it sustained Jesus, an example from the representative man about how to live (John 4:34; Osborne 2010, 133). The resources he used are also available to us (Morris 1992, 75).

The text also shows Jesus was not a magician (Keener 2009, 139). He did not use his power to draw attention to himself. Rather, he was one who served and followed God's way, even with deprivation, no matter what else he could do.

4:5–6. The second temptation took Jesus to a high point at the temple. Matthew returns to the use of the name "devil" for the tempter (so also in vv. 8, 11 with "Satan" intervening in the rebuke from Jesus in v. 10). The Greek term used here describes the "edge" of something, better a "wing," so an edge of the temple is what is being described (BDAG s.v. "πτερύγιον" 895; Robertson 1934, 756; Wallace 1996, 208). The devil proposed that Jesus leap off the edge and test God's protection of him. Turner (2008, 129) portrays it as request to take a misguided leap of faith. This was likely the southeast corner of the temple that had a height of some three hundred to four hundred feet over the Kidron Valley (Josephus, *A.J.* 15.411–12). Wilkins (2004, 159) speaks of a height of four hundred and fifty feet. The other option is the edge of the temple itself, a height of almost fifty meters or about one hundred forty-five feet (France 2007, 132).

The devil even used Scripture to invite Jesus to take the plunge, citing Psalm 91:11–12, a text that promises protection to those who are cared for by God, those who take shelter in God. The image is of angels keeping one's foot from striking the rock. Satan's use of this text was hyperliteral, even though he omitted the explanation "to guard you in all your ways" to make the point. It is clear from the rest of the citation that this protection was what was evoked. Again, no crowd was present, so the point was not to impress anyone (correctly, France 2007, 133, who also reminds us this likely was a vision, an idea defended by Hendriksen 1973, 231–32). Bruner (2004a, 129) says it well, "But the ambience of the miracle seems less an evangelistic meeting for others than a confirmation class for Jesus." Appeals to a public manifestation at the temple roof by the King, as the later *Pesiq. Rab.* 36 described, fall out of consideration (Davies and Allison 1988, 367; SB 1:151). The challenge was strictly a matter of testing how Jesus would relate to God, even in private. To accept the challenge and take the leap would have involved a manipulation of God, forcing him to act (Morris 1992, 76). In many ways, this was a taunt by the devil that would be mirrored in similar challenges by others at the cross (Matt. 27:40, 43; Konradt 2020, 55).

Model of Temple (and Temptation) Site Today.

4:7. Jesus replied with Scripture as well. Deuteronomy 6:16 teaches that one should not put the Lord God to the test. Jesus would not presume on God's protection by forcing his hand artificially. The act would have reflected distrust, because of the way the situation demanded God respond. It asked, "Will you save me, God? Then show it right now." Such testing of God's goodness and care was not a proper way to relate to God. Those reading Matthew already know that God had protected Jesus through the events of Matthew 2 (Nolland 2005, 165). There was no need to test God. So what God taught Israel when she rebelled at Massah (Meribah), Jesus applied (see Exod. 17:1–7; Ps. 95:7–11; 1 Cor. 10:9; Heb. 3:7–19; Turner 2008, 129). There Israel demanded water from God. Here Jesus trusted God.

4:8–9. The final temptation offered the world to Jesus. It was the "most brazen" offer of all (Blomberg 1992, 85). It asked Jesus to violate the first commandment (Turner 2008, 130). Satan dropped all pretense of what he was after here. Satan sought nothing less than a full defection from God through an independent claim to power. Such independence represented the core sin since Adam's fall. Here the devil took Jesus to a high mountain to show him all the kingdoms of the world and their glory. There was no mountain that could literally provide such a vista, so this is a reason many commentators speak of the temptations as involving some form of a vision (Blomberg 1992, 85 n. 81). The appeal here was to power and independence. To gain it, Jesus would have to sell his soul to the devil and worship the one who is opposed to God and his will. He would have to avoid the cross and service as the Servant God called him to be at the baptism (Carson 1984, 114; Wilkins 2004, 160, speaks of a shortcut). He also would have to ignore God's commitment to give the Son the nations (Ps. 2:8, the verse following the one used at the baptism; Hagner 1993, 68). Jesus would not follow such a path of denial. He would fulfill the mission God gave to him. It was a Faustian wager that Satan placed before Jesus.

To fall down and offer worship recalls the language of Matthew 2:2. It is discussed whether or not this was an offer the devil actually could make. At best, this was a "delegated authority" (France 2007, 135; Keener 2009, 141–42; Dan. 10:13, 20–21; John 12:31; 14:30; 16:11; 2 Cor. 4:4; 1 John 5:19; no such power, Gundry 1982, 58). At worst, it was an outright lie. Clearly Jesus was being challenged to rebel against the one true God. It also is likely the offer was not genuine but a lie, much like the one the Serpent gave Eve in the garden when he said a bite of the fruit would not lead to death. Death comes when we sever ourselves from life in communion with God. Jesus gave a similar warning not to do this when he taught, "What does it benefit if a person gains the whole world but forfeits his life [soul]?" (Matt. 16:26; Nolland 2005, 167).

4:10. Jesus dismissed Satan in a remark unique to Matthew's version. This is one of the reasons Matthew's order looks more original and Luke is viewed as having reversed the order of the temptations. The dismissal was offered in a command, telling Satan to "be gone" (BDAG s.v. "ὑπάγω" 1028, 1). The Aramaic word "Satan" means "the adversary." It may be that the offer's offense caused Jesus to say, in effect, "Enough!" The reason Jesus replied as he did is found in Deuteronomy 6:13. The word order is important there: "The Lord your God" comes first. It is only he who should be worshiped and served. The title at the start of the verse says it all. There is only one Lord to be worshiped. The single addition to the whole citation is the addition of the word "only," adding emphasis about the only one who is to be served. The loyalty to be given to God in terms of worship is unique. The *Shema* of Deuteronomy 6:4 is echoed in the addition. There is only one God to worship. Jesus would not betray that relationship, nor would he alter that ordering of honor.

4:11. So the devil left him, having failed in the attempt to lure Jesus into sin and unfaithfulness. Jesus's authority emerged in successfully commanding the devil to depart. He was more powerful than Satan. Jesus's faithfulness maintained his connection to God and his love (Grundmann 1975, 103). Luke 4:13 notes it was but for a time that the devil left Jesus alone, while Matthew portrays ongoing battles between Jesus and the forces of evil. These incidents involved exorcisms, the misdirected suggestions of his disciples, and the cross (Matt. 16:23; 26:36–46; see also Matt. 5:37; 6:13; 12:28–29; 13:19, 38; Turner 2008, 130).

Then the angels came and "were ministering" to Jesus. This detail parallels Mark 1:13 but is not noted in Luke. In his timing God ensured the Son was cared for. What Jesus did not demand in the second temptation was now provided (McNeile 1915, 42). First Kings 19:5–8 has the reverse order. There the angels fed Elijah and then he fasted for forty days (Davies and Allison 1988, 374). The second verb in the imperfect ("were ministering") pictures a sustained support of Jesus, so food and more was in view (Ps. 78:25; Carson 2010, 143; Nolland 2005, 169 n. 62). It also can be rendered "began to minister" to show the start of this ongoing ministry. Hebrews 1:14 describes angels as ministering spirits (note other angel texts in Matt. 13:39, 41, 49; 16:27; 18:10; 22:30; 24:31, 36; 25:31, 41).

Jesus now had shown he was resolute in faithfulness in contrast to Adam and Israel. Jesus was both a representative of man and a representative of the nation. Wilkins (2004, 162–66) in discussing the text's application highlights that Jesus survived the temptations out of a core response from his humanity, showing true faithfulness. He was Spirit-led, which means being responsive to the Spirit. Self-control, strengthened by relying on the Spirit, won over self-indulgence. This response was rooted in an unbreakable connection to God that drew on what the Father provided. Jesus's action provided an example for Matthew's readers about how to deal with challenges of the devil to disobey God.

Jesus's Temptations versus the Tests of Others

Adam	Do Not Eat the Fruit	Disobeyed and Experienced Death
Israel	Trust God in the Wilderness	Failed, Grumbled, and Worshiped Golden Calf
Jesus	Bread, Jump, Worship Satan	Threefold Success

THEOLOGICAL FOCUS

The exegetical idea (Jesus's faithfulness and commitment to God rebuffed Satan's temptations, showing Jesus's qualifications to represent humanity because he succeeded where Adam and Israel had failed) leads to this theological truth: Jesus's successful overcoming of temptation means he can reverse what Adam did and qualifies him to represent all humanity. Jesus showed his unflinching allegiance to God by affirming his unbending loyalty to God. He cited God's Word in the face of Satan's attempts to tempt him to unfaithfulness. The use of Scripture showed his trust in God and the Word of God.

Two key theological themes dominate this scene. The first is that one resists temptation when loyalty and allegiance are high priorities in life. Jesus resisted the devil because he valued God and the relationship he had to him with such priority that he would do things, even hard things, God's way. Jesus would not presume upon God and would make sure God had his exclusive loyalty. Scripture was the means he used to communicate those values. What God had asked Israel to learn, Jesus reflected in dealing with Satan. Independence from God was the sin at the center of all these temptations. Jesus knew his mission, his calling to depend on God, and that serving God alone was the only proper response. He kept true to all of these values.

A second key theme involves Jesus's success in resisting the devil. This victory showed him to be qualified in ways Adam and Israel failed with faithlessness, making him both representative for man and representative for the nation. Throughout his ministry, Jesus responded consistently to God with a faithfulness like that which he had just displayed. Jesus showed himself to be qualified and ready for the demands of the ministry he would undertake. He showed himself to be a faithful Son. He is an example of one in fellowship with God, even in the midst of challenge from the devil.

The scene is built around characters who are on opposite ends of the spectrum as far as loyalty to God. The classic battle of good versus evil is present. The devil sought to undercut God's unique glory and did so through appeals for Jesus to show his independence from the Creator. He attempted to deceive by making demands that turned God into Jesus's servant versus Jesus being his servant. Jesus reflected a complete commitment to God and his will. Jesus met his needs by seeking what God said. God is not to be presumed upon to act in ways we might force upon him. Rather, God is to remain the sole object of worship and service. He is to drive what we do and think as we live our lives. We are to be dependent on him. Jesus's sense of values and allegiance to God, reflected in what Scripture taught, protected him from the devastating consequences of denying God. A failure would have denied his calling and damaged his true self. That is always the effect of sin. As Hagner (1993, 70) says about faithfulness, "The goal of obedience to the Father is accomplished, not by triumphant self-assertion, not by exercise of power and authority, but paradoxically by the way of humility, service and suffering." This is all done out of loyalty and love for God, not to mention in fulfillment of the first commandment (Deut. 6:5–8; Osborne 2010, 135).

Attributes of Jesus at the Temptations

Faithfulness to God
Dependence on God
Reliance on God's Word
Trust in God's Ways
Total Allegiance to God
Repudiation of the Devil

PREACHING AND TEACHING STRATEGIES

Exegetical and Theological Synthesis

The exegetical section explained Jesus's triumph in the face of temptation. Unlike Adam who rejected God in Eden, and Israel who denied God on their way to the promised land, Jesus remained steady, loyal, and trusting. Even in his vulnerable state, hungry and alone in the wilderness, Jesus denied the devil's three temptations and proved his unrivaled love for God. Fueling Jesus's love for the Father was a mind saturated in the Scriptures (Deut. 8:3; 6:16, 13). With his entire heart, soul, and might, Jesus committed himself to God.

While we may not show the steadfastness of Jesus, we can learn from his example. Scripture must fuel our love for God. The very act of revelation suggests God's desire to be known and loved. Reading, studying, memorizing, teaching, and applying Scripture all nurture our relationship with God.

Moreover, a growing awareness of the biblical narrative, key redemptive themes, and good intentions behind God's commands—to bless and prosper, to guide and protect—helps us see through the devil's deceptions. Satan would have us believe God withholds, punishes, and commands arbitrarily. He oversells our potential ("you will be like God," Gen. 3:5) and understates the fallout of sin ("Surely you will not die," Gen. 3:4). Knowing Scripture builds our awareness of God's goodness and Satan's tactics.

Preaching Idea

Temptation is a proving ground for our love of God.

Contemporary Connections

What does it mean?

What does it mean that temptation is a proving ground for our love of God? First, we must reiterate that it is Satan who tempts us, not God (James 1:13). God may test us, as he does Abraham (Gen. 22:1) or Israel (1 Cor. 10:11), to prove our trust and allegiance, but he never deceives us with false promises, dangles sin before us, or baits us into disobedience. These are tactics of the devil, whose schemes are well known (2 Cor. 2:11; Eph. 6:11). He preys on our selfish, fleshly desires, which take on a life of their own (James 1:14–15).

Second, though temptation comes with demonic force, God always provides an escape route (1 Cor. 10:13). Jesus followed this way of escape his entire earthly life (Heb. 4:15; cf. Matt. 26:36–44). He did not overcome temptation by accessing magical powers or divine attributes, but rather by harnessing his singular devotion for the heavenly Father. He proved love of God mattered more than personal comfort, security, power, or any other offer the flesh, devil, or world could serve him (1 John 2:15–17).

Finally, we must realize our temptation comes from the same source and follows a path similar to Jesus's wilderness challenge. And every temptation we overcome proves we choose God over comfort, God over security, God over power, God over injustice, God over selfish desire, or God over any other offer. Saying "no" to harmless gossip proves our love for God. Saying "no" to selfishly skimping on a tip proves our love for God. Saying "no" to feeding racial bias proves our love for God. In essence, obedience to God says, "I love you" (1 John 5:3).

Is it true?

Is it true that temptation is a proving ground for our love of God? Indeed, Jesus's life bore this out. His perfect penitence displayed perfect love. Again and again, he said in essence, "I only say and do what the Father leads me to say and do" (John 5:17–23; 8:28; 12:49–50). He spoke of abiding in the Father's love (John 15:9–10; 17:26), who from the beginning of his earthly ministry called him "beloved" (Matt. 3:17). He summarized all ethical teaching of the Hebrew Scriptures in the command to love God with one's whole being (Matt. 22:36–37; cf. Deut. 6:4–6), a passage he alluded to during his temptation.

If we think this came easily to Jesus, we overlook his critical decisions and personal suffering in the Gospels (Matt. 16:21–23; 19:3;

22:35; 26:36–44; cf. John 6:15). His disciples, crowds, and religious leaders each tested Jesus's loyalty to God and his plan. Moreover, the author of Hebrews stressed the lifelong reality of Jesus's temptations, trials, and sufferings (Heb. 2:14–18; 4:15; 5:7–8; 12:1–3). For Jesus, every day was a proving ground for his love for God. This is true for us, as well.

We prove our love for God when we stick with our marriages during hard years, for giving up prioritizes comfort over God's call to fidelity (Matt. 5:31–32). We prove our love for God when we admit a mistake, for a lie prioritizes saving face over God's call to honesty (Matt. 5:37). We prove our love for God when we show compassion toward someone who tries to force their opposing political, religious, or sexual ideology on us; for such a judgment prioritizes pride over God's call to love others (Matt. 5:44; 7:1). On the other side of every temptation, we have evidence for our greatest love: either God or self.

Now what?

Without oversimplifying the challenge or complexity of temptation, we can help prove (and improve) our love of God with the following four movements: (1) know God's Word; (2) discern the temptation cycle and the devil's tactics; (3) seek accountability in our vulnerability; and (4) seek to serve God and love others. Each of these is illustrated below.

Know God's Word: Jesus quoted three passages from Deuteronomy when Satan tempted him. His model should inspire diligence in hiding God's Word in our hearts. Spiritual transformation, in fact, results from the renewal of the mind. What better way to bolster our minds than memorizing Scripture, so we can "take every thought captive to make it obey Christ" (2 Cor. 10:5). Any number of verses may prove helpful in battling temptation, but the sidebar provides key passages to trust God and his resources while under fire.[1]

Memory Verses for Facing Temptation

Passages About God's Provision, Power, and Protection in Temptation

Psalm 91; Proverbs 3:5–6; Matthew 6:13; 1 Corinthians 10:13; 2 Corinthians 12:9–10

Passages About Guarding and Inspecting the Heart

Psalms 26:2–3; 27:14; 139:23–24; Proverbs 4:23; Matthew 5:8; Ephesians 3:14–19

Passages About Our Primary Call to Love God

Exodus 20:2–7; Deuteronomy 6:4–6; Psalm 27:4; Matthew 22:36–40; 1 John 5:3

Passages About Temptation, Spiritual Warfare, and Satan's Tactics

2 Corinthians 10:1–5; Ephesians 6:11–18; James 1:12–15; 1 Peter 5:8–9; 1 John 2:15–17; 4:1–6

Discern the temptation cycle: According to James, temptation follows a predictable path. First, we see the bait; then, we follow the lure; next, we entertain the offer; finally, we give way to sinful desire (James 1:12–15). The example of envy may be helpful. The *bait* to envy may be the sight of a new car or happy family photo posted online. *Following the lure* of envy would entail fixating on other people's goods (their better car, family, job, etc.) and underappreciating our own lives (our clunker vehicle, struggling marriage). *Entertaining the offer* of envy means we start to plot how to get our hands on the good of others or rid them

1 This list, of course, is not exhaustive. Moreover, for those battling a particular temptation, a biblical text about that topic may be most helpful. For example, for one struggling with keeping their mouth shut, they might memorize Psalm 19:14 or meditate on Jesus's silence when falsely accused by the crowds and questioned by Pilate.

of theirs. In a culture of plenty, this may mean buying our own car even if it exceeds our income. If scarcity is a reality, envy may result in us harming those who have more (by theft, curse, gossip, etc.). Finally, giving way to desire is acting on the mental plot we hatched: we sign a contract at the Toyota dealer or jam a nail in our coworker's rear tire.

Discern the devil's tactics: Throughout the temptation cycle, the devil will whisper to us. First, he speaks deceptions that cause us to doubt God's goodness and question his provision. Next, he goads us with self-justification ("It's no big deal. Everyone does it. You deserve it."). Then, once we act, Satan showers us with shame and accusations ("You're worthless, sinful, unforgivable.").

Seek accountability: The devil likes to isolate us, so we cannot rely on the aid of other believers (1 Peter 5:8–9). Accountability is spiritual friendship that invites daily encouragement, regular confession, and honest rebuke. Followers of Jesus are not intended to walk alone, but to bear one another's burdens, pray for one another, and point one another to the transforming grace of Jesus when they are in the grip of sin (Gal. 6:1–5; Heb. 3:12–15; 12:1–13; James 1:2–5; 5:16, 19–20; 1 John 1:9). Because human accountability will not be perfect, we keep our eyes fixed on Jesus, the author and perfector of our faith, who intercedes for us in our weakness (Heb. 4:15; 12:1–3).

Serve God and love others: This is nothing more than the Great Commandment: to love God fully and love one's neighbor (Matt. 22:34–40; Mark 12:28–34). This is to include our enemies, as that is what makes Christian love distinct (Matt. 5:43–48; Rom. 12:19–21).

Creativity in Presentation

The Great British Baking Show is a charming series that gathers twelve amateur bakers beneath a tent to prove their abilities. Each week they perform three challenges—signature, technical, and showstopper—bakes that test their creativity, skill, and culinary knowledge. Two iconic judges—Paul Hollywood and Mary Berry—scrutinize their bakes based on appearance, texture, and taste. Every episode they crown one contestant "Star Baker" and send another home. The overlaps between the show and Jesus's temptation are numerous: contestants face three challenges, Paul Hollywood plays the part of a diabolical judge, and every contestant aims to prove they are stellar (not exactly what Jesus was after, but it gets at Satan's question). Moreover, one of the keys to baking well is a process called "proving." Each baker has access to a "proving drawer," which gives dough a place to rise more quickly in a controlled environment. Under-proofed bread is not ideal; it leaves the baker (and eater) with a dense middle. Consider showing the trailer from the TV series, bringing in a loaf of bread, and setting various cooking instruments on stage (a chef's hat, mixing bowl, spatula, kids' Easy-Bake Oven, etc.). Let your congregation know that Jesus excelled at every challenge, impressed the diabolical judge, and properly proved something better than bread: his love for God.

The imagery of three tests as a proving ground appears in film and fairy tales. In *Indiana Jones and the Last Crusade* (directed by Steven Spielberg, 1989), the title character (played by Harrison Ford) must pass three biblically inspired challenges before getting his hands on the Holy Grail, the famed cup of Christ. The stakes are high. If he fails any test, he will die. If he cannot secure the cup, his father (played by Sean Connery) will die from a bullet wound. For the first test he must bow before getting decapitated. As he kneels he says, "Only the penitent man will pass." For the second test, he must honor the Lord's covenant name, YHWH, or fall to his death. And for the final test, he must take a leap of faith, crossing a chasm on an invisible bridge. Though the tests aren't perfect parallels to Jesus's, they illustrate the need to revere God and trust his provision. Another film built around the formula of three proving tests is *Pan's Labyrinth* (directed by Guillermo del Toro, 2006), in which a little girl must prove she is a princess by (1) facing a toad monster, (2) refusing food from a banquet table, and (3) offering a sacrifice. The film is haunting, and aesthetically marvelous and wonderfully illustrates the resolve under trials with the protagonist offering her life as a substitute sacrifice for others and proving herself a genuine princess.

The rush to create a vaccine for the coronavirus illustrated the importance of proving the efficacy of a drug. By the end of 2020, three pharmaceutical companies had developed a product ready for the public. Drug testing requires millions of dollars in research and development, including studies on human subjects, to produce a proven vaccine. No one wants an unproven vaccine with uncertain side effects coursing through their veins. Even more damning, an unproven Savior and Messiah offers no remedy to the pandemic of sin.

Companies test and try their products before presenting them to the public. They make prototypes of new machinery or first editions of new software. Restaurants practice soft openings. Writers, pastors, and comedians test their material on small audiences before releasing them to large crowds. The test site for military personnel to experiment with new weapons and devices is literally called the "proving ground." Every time a professional or organization runs a trial before "going public," they create a proving ground of their own. Before "going public," Jesus experienced his own proving ground.

Ultimately, the sermon should convey these truths: Jesus's successful overcoming of temptation means he can reverse what Adam did and qualifies him to represent all humanity. Thus, temptation is a proving ground for our love of God.

- The Spirit empowers us through temptation (4:1–2, 11).
- Satan entices us by temptation (4:3, 5–6, 8–9).
- Scripture anchors us in times of temptation (4:4, 7, 10).

DISCUSSION QUESTIONS

1. What is the difference between a test and temptation? Which of these words best describes this scene?
2. How does it help you to know that Jesus was "tempted in every way just as we are, yet without sin" (Heb. 4:15b)? Be specific.
3. How does the exegetical section describe true "spirituality"? How does Jesus model this?
4. Where else does Scripture record the devil tempting people? What do these narratives tell us about the devil and his tactics?
5. What role does Scripture play as we face temptation? What are key passages that have helped stand firm in temptation?
6. How can the church nurture a safe and honest culture of accountability?

MESSIAH CONFRONTS ISRAEL IN GALILEE AND MEETS REJECTION (4:12–12:50)

The initial phase of Jesus's ministry focuses on Galilee and moves to a decisive rejection of him by many in Israel. After declaring the kingdom was near and calling disciples, Jesus's work is dominated by a consistent exchange of ministry activity and two discourse blocks (Sermon on the Mount, and mission discourses). At the core of this unit are three distinct pieces comprising three miracles each, with a set of sayings following them. At the unit's end is a series of controversies surrounding the Sabbath and where Jesus's capability to heal came from, above or below. Demonstrations of Jesus's power, followed by teaching, meet with positive response by some and resistance by many. Jesus's actions show what is going on and the teaching explains it.

This section comes in four parts. The first unit begins a series of scenes introducing Jesus's Galilean ministry and a sequence that shows how rejection of Jesus emerged. That story of conflict runs through Matthew 12. Matthew 4:12–25 opens a second major section of Matthew extending to Matthew 12:50. Matthew mixes ministry actions, block discourses (Matt. 5–7, 10), and various thematic sections as he reviews Jesus's time in Galilee. Miracles pointing to who Jesus is are also common in this unit. In spots Matthew uses a series of triads to present the material in memorable ways. However, in saying this, Matthew has other structural notes to his gospel than the break here and at the plot turn at Matthew 12:50. Matthew also ends each discourse block with a repeatable phrase "when Jesus finished" at the conclusion. This sets up some key subsections of Jesus's ministry (so correctly Davies and Allison 1988, 386–87; France 2007, 144). The outline we give for the gospel is tied to a mix of structural markers and to major plot shifts. The break here is seen in that Matthew presents Jesus beginning his active ministry. Jesus showed himself to be qualified by Matthew 4:1–11. Now the ministry begins in earnest in fulfillment of Scripture.

The Refrain That Completes Matthew's Discourse Blocks

Block: Matthew 5–7; Matthew 7:28: "When Jesus finished saying these things"
Block: Matthew 10; Matthew 11:1: "When Jesus had finished instructing his twelve disciples"
Block: Matthew 13; Matthew 13:53: "Now when Jesus finished these parables"
Block: Matthew 18; Matthew 19:1; "Now when Jesus finished these sayings"
Block: Matthew 23–25; Matthew 26:1: "When Jesus had finished saying all these things"

Often the Gospels portray their Christology versus calling it out explicitly. The tension mounts as the unit proceeds. Displays of divine power and authority meet with counterclaims of power from satanic sources. The unit closes with Jesus stating that his family are those who hear and do the will of his Father. The issue emerging from the gospel is a question to ponder: Who reflects the hope and promise of God given long ago? Matthew contends that Jesus is the hope and the way.

Matthew 4:12–25

EXEGETICAL IDEA

As Jesus drew crowds through powerful acts and teaching, the early Galilean ministry represented light that called for repentance as the kingdom of heaven came near, inviting disciples to follow him as a top priority.

THEOLOGICAL IDEA

To embrace Jesus is to turn to the kingdom of heaven and follow him as a life priority.

PREACHING IDEA

Priorities change when Jesus calls your name.

PREACHING POINTERS

After successfully overcoming Satan's temptation, Jesus emerged in public life as a light. His words and deeds reveal the powerful nature of God's inbreaking kingdom. He healed the sick, cast out demons, and called people to leave their sinful ways and embrace God's good news. The message of God's kingdom would have appealed to Matthew's audience. Facing political turmoil in their time and hearing from supposed messianic figures, the evidence of Jesus's powerful word and deed would have been persuasive. In the call of the first followers, the original audience would have heard a timely invitation to realign their priorities and commit themselves to Christ Jesus.

For too many of us, our operating system is governed by a single priority: self. Our personal wants and needs easily become our own greatest priority. We live by what feels good, eases pain, expands comfort, offers security, and advances popularity. Even altruistic priorities—serving the needy, loving our families, giving to charity, fighting injustice—can mask our greatest priority of serving self and seeking praise. Fortunately, Jesus modeled a life of self-denying, self-giving, self-sacrificial service. And he invited men and women to join him as students in his school of kingdom priorities. This sermon teaches that priorities change when Jesus calls your name.

JESUS COMES AS LIGHT, PREACHES THE KINGDOM, AND CALLS DISCIPLES (4:12–25)

LITERARY STRUCTURE AND THEMES (4:12–25)

This unit opens the larger section with the note that ministry in Galilee was a fulfillment of Scripture. Jesus's message echoed that of John the Baptist. That kingdom message needed disciples who would capture others for the kingdom. As a result, Jesus called four men to start this process. Such discipleship meant that the old life of fishing was transformed into fishing for people. Jesus ministered in word and deed to show what the kingdom was about, redeeming the needy and lost. His fame spread.

This unit has a parallel with Mark 1:14–20 and 1:29–34. It also is like Luke 4:14–15 and 4:38–41, but Luke's call of the four disciples is told through a distinct scene and event in Luke 5:1–11. Matthew's citation of Isaiah 9:1–2 is unique to his gospel.

This unit is a discipleship call (vv. 18–22) bounded on both ends by ministry summaries (vv. 12–16, 23–25) and a message summary (v. 17). We see Jesus had a ministry that was not only a word, but was a ministry of action that supported what the word claimed God was doing. The combination is important as one reinforces the other. If either element was missing, the impact would be lost. This is an important theme for all ministry. It was this kind of combination ministry with a wide scope to heal and exorcize that explained Jesus's ability to draw disciples to help him in the task of catching people for God. Even though miracles were involved, do not miss the deeper point. Jesus's actions served people and showed God's care for them. Kingdom and action, hope and service stood at the ministry's center. Even as the message challenged people to repent, it also invited them to see and experience God's care and compassion. God's power was on display to serve and help the people called to turn to God. Here there was no word alone. No word or teaching was allowed to ring hollow by an absence of application. Word and deed reinforced each other as Jesus preached and engaged those around him. Jesus showed them how God had brought light to the people, in order to meet the needs they had before God.

Key themes include a kingdom call that rooted Jesus's ministry in eschatological hope of restoring the people of God, a discipleship that involved mission and evangelism, and an effective combination of word and action that undergirded the message given to people. The combination of word and deed showed that God's rule was present. Deliverance was both preached and shown as a mission strategy. Word and action did not compete nor conflict with each other, nor are they opposed to each other as if social engagement and preaching were in distinct categories, but word and deed flowed together to make one consistent message about God, his presence, and his care.

EXPOSITION (4:12–25)

The verses from Isaiah 9:1–2 really explain this unit. Jesus appeared as a light in Galilee and gathered initial followers through a ministry showing his authority, an authority God underwrote. Here was the true messenger of God who brought the long-promised deliverance of God to those seated in darkness. The imagery mirrors what Luke 1:76–79 also proclaims.

Introduction and Summary: Jesus Comes as Light (4:12–25)

As Jesus drew crowds through powerful acts and teaching, the early Galilean ministry represented light that called for repentance as the kingdom of heaven came near, inviting disciples to follow him as a top priority.

4:12–13. The account picks up after the temptation and has an unspecified time gap. It jumps to Herod Antipas's arrest of John the Baptist and notes that as a result Jesus withdrew to his homeland in Galilee. Matthew saves the details of this story for later in Matthew 14:1–12. John's gospel has a period of ministry in Judea before this (John 2:13–3:21), as well as other events (John 1:19–2:12 and 3:22–4:42). Matthew chooses to start the story in the central place of Jesus's ministry in the north of Israel in the region of Galilee. This locale also was Jesus's home and the place he seemed to have garnered much initial significant attention. The expression in Matthew "he withdrew" often is tied to acts where danger was present (Turner 2008, 132; BDAG s.v. "ἀναχωρέω" 1b, 75; Matt. 2:12–14, 22; 4:12; 12:15; 14:13; 15:21). Jesus was still in Herod's territory, but away from the direct locale of John's arrest. Still, a retreat may not be in view, since he was still in Herod's region (Osborne 2010, 141). This was not a full withdrawal, but it was a relocation that may have created distance from danger. The next verse makes it clear Jesus initially returned to Nazareth and then moved on.

This region of Galilee was fertile and had two great cities, Tiberius and Sepphoris, which surprisingly never show up in the New Testament. This may suggest Jesus ministered primarily in rural areas. Recent archaeological work has shown that many faithful Jews lived in the region (Chancey 2002; Freyne, 1988; Keener 2009, 146). However, they seem to have been independent of influence from the Pharisees. The region was more Jewish than Gentile, but it did have an ethnic mix (Judg. 18:7, 28; 2 Kings 15:29; 17:24–27; 1 Macc. 5; Turner 2008, 133).

From Nazareth, his home, Jesus moved to Capernaum in the region of Zebulon and Naphtali, by the Sea of Galilee. The name meant "village of Nahum" (*Kefar Nahum*). Their territory is delineated in Joshua 19:10–16 (Zebulon) and 19:32–39 (Naphtali). Located on the northern edge of the land, it had always been a buffer region, and thus the first to be attacked from the north, as with Assyrians (1 Kings 15:29 in 732 B.C.), leading to a large Gentile presence. The naming of the two tribes and the description of its being by the sea make up the word links into the citation of verses 15–16. Hagner (1993, 73) connects this "by the sea" description to the Roman road that ran through Bethsaida and Capernaum. Nazareth was in Zebulon and Capernaum was in Naphtali (Nolland 2005, 171). Capernaum was where Jesus would make his headquarters, traditionally associated with Peter's house.

The Sea of Galilee was some 8¾ by 12¼ miles in width and length and 682 feet below sea level (on the dimensions, Carson 2010, 148). The reference to sea that the road or way ran along may refer to the Mediterranean Sea (Davies and Allison 1988, 382, speak of this sense as possible). More likely is a reference to the Sea of Galilee, as in Matthew 4:18. Capernaum was almost on the northern edge of the Sea of Galilee, just to the west of that northern tip and about two miles west of the Jordan River. It was a fishing village and had an estimated population of a few thousand. The range is a thousand to twelve thousand with most estimates in the middle of this range (France 2007, 141 and n. 12; Josephus, *A.J.* 403; *B.J.* 3.519). Agriculture was the other main economic means of gaining a livelihood. Capernaum had a toll collection booth (Matt. 9:9–10). Morris (1992, 81) places the village's size as eight hundred by two hundred and fifty meters. It is likely that Peter's house was in this village, a site that can be visited today (Laughlin 1993).

Photo of the Remains of Peter's House in Capernaum Today.

4:14–16. Matthew sees this locale in Galilee, Zebulon and Naphtali, as a fulfillment of Scripture. He introduces this note of fulfillment with a standard introductory formula using the passive "was spoken" that looks to God as the ultimate speaker. Matthew names the prophet Isaiah and speaks directly of fulfillment. This is like the formula in Matthew 1:22, except the prophet is named as in Matthew 2:17 and 3:3 (Isaiah also is named in Matt. 8:17; 12:17).

The text comes from Isaiah 9:1–2 (= 8:23–9:1 MT, LXX), just before the promise of a great king from the line of David is announced. The passage fits into Israel's history in the midst of the spiritually dark period of Ahaz. Isaiah 9:6 notes a great king is to come in this bleak context. The text also points back to messianic hope of Matthew 1–2.

The main picture is of a great light that shines on people dwelling in darkness, a light that shows the way, a way that has been prepared for by John the Baptist and now is ready to be followed. Luke 1:78–79 also associates Jesus's coming with a light by referring to Messiah as the morning sun lightening up the new day (also John 1:4–5, 9; 8:12). The verb "rises" (ἀνατέλλω) in Matthew 5:45 and 13:6 refers to sunlight arising over the horizon, so the image of a new day dawning is likely present in 4:16 (BDAG s.v. "ἀνατέλλω" 2b, 73). The mention of "the shadow of death" in the citation indicates we are thinking of a spiritual condition and need here, a core premise for why the gospel is good news. Jesus's ministry delivers from spiritual death and meets a basic human need.

The reference "beyond the Jordan" looked to its location north of the main portion of the river and may reflect the perspective of Gentiles who traveled there and crossed the river to pass through the area (Blomberg 1992, 88). Messiah may have been expected to spend much time in Jerusalem as king, but the mention of this text from Isaiah tells us Jesus was ministering in a location that would be tied to the light of salvation and, eventually, would include Gentiles (Davies and Allison 1988, 379–80; Keener 2009, 146; Nolland 2005, 172; John 7:41–42, 52). That ministry to Gentiles was simply foreshadowed here because Jesus himself ministered mainly to the lost house of Israel (Matt. 10:6).

4:17. Jesus began to teach at this point. That expression introduces a structural break in Matthew, as in Matthew 16:21 and 26:16. But this was not an indication of the major structural units of Matthew as some suggest (correctly Carson 2010, 145–46). Other literary indicators point to other breaks in Matthew's literary structure (see above, section introduction to

Matthew 4:12–12:50 and the chart there on refrains to discourse blocks).

Jesus's message matched that of John the Baptist in Matthew 3:2. The call was to repent, for the kingdom of heaven was near. Contextually, the Greek term ἤγγικεν speaks either of approach or arrival. Its nearness yielded an urgency to repent. The verb "to repent" is not as common a term tied to Jesus in Matthew as in Luke (Matt. 3:2; 11:20–21; 12:41; 13:15; plus two uses of the noun, 3:8, 11; in contrast to Luke with fourteen uses of the noun and verb). In effect, the call was to recognize that you needed to join God's program. Meeting that need meant a change of heart, seeking what God was offering on his terms. The way one has lived was not the way to live. The invitation was to come into God's rule provided through Christ.

There is not a distinction to be made here between an earthly kingdom and a spiritual kingdom (Bock 2016, 60–90, on the concept of the kingdom). Nor should one force a choice between a specific locale for rule (realm) and divine activity. The themes present here are a both–and, not and either–or. The following constrastive dualisms do not apply to the kingdom John and Jesus preached. The announced kingdom is both spiritual and earthly. It involves heaven and earth. It is spiritual and a realm. It is a place (but not always tied to a specific land) and a dynamic where God's presence and rule is effectively at work in a way that will be transnational. The reason we say it is not always tied to a land here is because Israel was already in the land. This was the kingdom program God had promised and many of these hoped-for elements (deliverance, forgiveness, the Spirit in us) have come near with Jesus, meaning these features have arrived. This early form of the kingdom spread into the world as a result of evangelism. It became a space across the world, yet within it, that one is invited into in order to experience God's work in community as a testimony to the world. The kingdom does not take over the world until the consummation when Jesus returns. Rather, in its current form, it coexists in the midst of the world as an enclave of God's presence among those who are his own, those who choose to enter in by faith (Matt. 13:36–43). John the Baptist noted Jesus would bring the Spirit as an indication of Jesus's superiority to John, as an indication of the arrival of the new era, and with entry into its enabling power accomplished through God's rule (Matt. 3:11–12; Luke 3:15–17).

But what about the kingdom? Has it come near or has it arrived? Morris (1992, 83) observes that the nearness of the kingdom was both something here and yet to come. With Jesus, it approached and arrived, but there also is much more to come. The kingdom's coming was and is a program of events and it did not come in one moment (Davies and Allison 1988, 390). Jesus announced the kingdom. Entry into God's rule in response to Jesus led into all it would bring over time. The announcement showed it was near. So, in this Matthew 4 context the kingdom is near, but also very close to being here (Davies and Allison 1988, 392: "on the point of arrival"; an already–not yet, Wilkins 2004, 175 and n. 15). Those who heard Jesus were to repent; this did not bring the kingdom but allowed them to participate in what was coming with his life and ministry (Bruner 2004a, 139). The kingdom is a realm where God acts and people enter and participate (Bruner 2004a, 140).

Those Who Heard

One needs to distinguish between who benefits from the kingdom and who is accountable to it. The repentance/faith *response* brings one into the *benefits* of the kingdom, although the *accountability to all* comes in the consummation of the kingdom, and that accompanying judgment means the kingdom's authority and claim on people *is present whether an individual responds or not*. The timing of the kingdom's arrival should be tied to teaching like that in Isaiah, since this prophet has already been used twice to point to fulfillment of these events

(Nolland 2005, 176; Isa. 24:23; 52:7). The kingdom's arrival is the fresh dawn of light arising on the horizon that Matthew 4:16 just noted. The kingdom is dawning with Jesus, but the full light is yet to come as he ultimately brings the rest of the promise.

4:18–20. Jesus's call of four disciples involved two short scenes that have exactly the same structure. It has a parallel in Mark 1:16–20. It is a call story (Davies and Allison 1988, 394, presents the case for core historicity). Jesus spotted two pairs, called them to follow him, and they left behind what they were doing to follow him. Both pairs involved fishermen. Jesus was calling people from everyday life to join his cause. That Capernaum fishermen were involved is not surprising, since that was a chief vocation for a town on the edge of the Sea of Galilee.

To be a disciple was to be a learner under a chosen master teacher. In fact, "learner" is what the Greek word for "disciple" means (BDAG s.v. "μαθητής" 1 and 2bα, 609–10). This intense life learning required following. There was something incarnational and life-engaging that was a part of such instruction. Discipleship was about far more than mere information and could not be contained in a classroom. So the men had to follow Jesus in life to get it (Keener 2009, 150–54; Wilkins 1988). In this sense the disciple was more than a learner, but was an adherent (Keener 2009, 148 n. 218). In contrast to Judaism where a pupil chose his rabbi, Jesus chose his own disciples (*m. 'Abot.* 1:16; Hengel 1981, esp. 17, 32–33, 50–57; Morris 1992, 84 n. 50). A model for this kind of call is that of Elijah to Elisha (1 Kings 19:19–21), not Cynic philosophers (so correctly Keener 2009, 154).

The first pair was Peter and Andrew. Peter became the lead apostle, dominating the early chapters in the book of Acts. He is named twenty-three times in Matthew with this name, with five references to Simon and two other instances involving both names together as here (Matt. 10:2 is the other dual name text). His confession in the middle of each of the Synoptic Gospels that Jesus is the Christ provides a key pivot in all three of those gospels. Andrew is far less prominent, mentioned only twelve times in the New Testament. In this gospel, he is only here and in the listing of the Twelve in Matthew 10:2 (so also in Mark 1:16 and 3:18). Mark 13:3 has him as one of the disciples who heard the Olivet Discourse. Luke 6:14 is his only appearance in that gospel in the listing of the Twelve. John refers to him the most. Andrew was responsible for bringing Peter to Jesus (John 1:40, 42, 44) and was involved in two conversations with Jesus (John 6:8; 12:22). Acts 1:13 lists him among the Twelve. The John 1 scene probably preceded this call in Matthew, so Jesus was not making a random invitation to people he just met (Blomberg 1992, 90). John 1:44 tells us these brothers were from Bethsaida, but they labored in Capernaum.

Jesus spotted these two working their nets and called them to follow him. The "nets" were circular hand nets that had weights on the edges (BDAG s.v. "ἀμφίβληστρον" 55). They were tossed into the sea and dragged up to gather the fish. The Greek adverb is an interjection ("come"), an exhortative particle that introduces a call (BDAG s.v. "δεῦτε" 220). The full phrase of invitation was simply "come after me." The promise was that he would make them "fishers" (ἁλιεύς) of humanity, capturing or gathering people for the kingdom (BDAG s.v. "ἁλιεύς" 44). The expression "fishers of men" echoes Jeremiah 16:16, but the context here is positive, so it is not the same idea as that prophet's judgment scene. Is it a reversal of that judgment because of the gospel that Jesus alluded to here? That is quite possible. If so, then the opportunity to end spiritual exile is over for those who respond. Such a calling is praised in the Old Testament (Prov. 11:30; Dan. 12:3; Hendriksen 1973, 248).

Photo of Ginosar First-Century Fishing Boat.

The men's response was immediate: they left their nets to follow Jesus. The action reflected a break in their routines and the immediate undertaking of a new mission in life. Matthew likes the word "to follow," using it twenty-five times (Matt. 8:22; 10:38; 16:24; 19:21, 28; Hagner 1993, 77; BDAG s.v. "ἀκολουθέω" 2 and 3, 36–37). The calling of Jesus was "disruptive" of life (Nolland 2005, 179), "a decisive break with business as usual" (Davies and Allison 1988, 397), and a "total reordering of priorities in life" (Garland 1995, 48). Their vocation was no longer all they did nor their primary mission in life (Osborne 2010, 150). As village fishermen the disciples were among the lower middle class. This vocation still reflected a better life condition than most citizens as they were not among the abject poor. So this move would have been a challenge to them in terms of making a living (Keener 2009, 151–52). They "left everything" to follow Jesus (Matt. 19:27).

4:21–22. Jesus repeats the call with James and John, sons of Zebedee. They were mending their nets with their father. The Greek term καταρτίζω means to fix something (BDAG s.v. "καταρτίζω" 1a, 526). Matthew simply says Jesus called them and gives no more content, unlike the call to come with Andrew and Peter. The response was the same. They immediately left the boat and their father to follow him. To make this move with their father present was an added note to this second calling, as compared with the earlier called pair.

John was a prominent disciple. Matthew mentions him less than do Mark and Luke (Matt. 10:2; 17:1; Mark 1:19, 29; 3:17; 5:37; 9:2, 38; 10:35, 41; 13:3; 14:33; Luke 5:10; 6:14; 8:51; 9:28, 49, 54; 22:8, plus nine times in Acts). He is traditionally seen as the author of John's gospel as well as the three epistles of John and Revelation. Those books were likely written in the 90s of the first century. As such, he was the second most-known apostle after Peter. James appears in the same passages in Matthew as John. He also is noted nine times in the same texts as John in Mark. He appears five times in Luke, again always with John except in Luke 9:49 where John is alone. James is named twice in Acts (Acts 1:13; 12:2). One can see the brothers are often cited together. This includes three more times as the sons of Zebedee (Matt. 20:20; 26:37; 27:56). The two are not named individually in John's gospel, but many see John as the beloved disciple of that gospel. They do appear as the sons of Zebedee in John 21:2 (Davies and Allison 1988, 400–401). James was slain by Herod Agrippa I, as Acts 12:2 notes, around A.D. 43–44. Both of these brothers stood with Jesus for a long time.

These callings showed Jesus beginning to gather followers to teach and help him in his mission. The Twelve are named in Matthew 10:2–4. The success of his effort came in the fact that the early church was planted and sustained by these leaders and others like them. They ended up following in the full commitment Jesus would teach them to have (Matt. 8:18–22; 10:21–22, 34–37; 12:46–50; France 2007, 148).

4:23. The subunit starting here marks a transition. It introduces and summarizes Jesus's impact in Galilee and sets the stage for the discourse to come. As such, it could end this unit or introduce the next one.

Jesus came into all of Galilee. Three activities appear in this summary account. Matthew likes to work in threes, as three elements will dominate his presentation in Matthew 8–9. Jesus (1) taught in the synagogues, (2) preached the gospel of the kingdom, and (3) healed the people's diseases and maladies. Word and deed came together as the message of hope was enveloped in a ministry of compassion. The disciples taught and healed in their mission as well (Matt. 10:1, 6). This summary is like what we see in Mark 1:39 and 3:7–12, as well as Luke 4:44 and 6:17–18. This account shows the impact of Jesus and sets the stage for the kind of audience Jesus's discourses drew.

Synagogues were Jewish places of worship and prayer (Keener 2009, 156–57). In the synagogue, Torah was read, along with linking scriptural texts, and messages were preached. Jesus went to his people in the very places where God was proclaimed, a custom noted in several texts (Matt. 9:35; 13:54; Mark 1:21; Luke 4:15–30; 6:6; 13:10; John 8:59; 18:20). Davies and Allison (1988, 413) say there were three themes tied to the synagogue for Matthew: the place Jesus taught, a locale of persecution (Matt. 10:17; 12:9–14), and a locale for hypocrisy (Matt. 6:2, 5; 23:6). Tension with Jews and the synagogue may explain the reference here to "their" synagogues, pointing to a break with Judaism by the time Matthew wrote (Luz 1989, 205). The alternative is that it simply means the synagogues of Galileans, which also is possible (Nolland 2005, 182–83). That alternative meaning might suggest Matthew was not from Galilee.

The message of the kingdom's coming is noted in Matthew 4:17, but the wording here may reflect Isaiah 52:7 about how delightful the feet are of the one who announces the gospel. The term "gospel" appears four times in Matthew (Matt. 9:35; 11:5; 24:14; 26:13). Mark has seven uses and Luke none.

The ministry Jesus offered found support in the restorative ministry of healing he performed. Josephus, the first-century Jewish historian, reports that Jesus did unusual works, which is probably an allusion to this aspect of Jesus's ministry (*A.J.* 18.63–64). A similar word-and-deed sequence surfaces in Luke's opening description of Jesus's ministry in Luke 4:14–44, though Luke elaborates on it with two detailed scenes, where Jesus preached in Nazareth and then healed in Capernaum. Jesus's compassion and mercy framed his message and set the stage for the Sermon on the Mount that followed. The acts backed up the message and gave it credibility by showing the words were not empty claims but reflected practice, avoiding any charge of hypocrisy.

4:24. The report about Jesus spread as far as Syria. It is discussed if this was the large Roman province or a smaller area northeast of Galilee (Nolland 2005, 183). It is not entirely clear. Either way, this was a Gentile area.

Matthew notes the range of Jesus's healing as the sick and those suffering the pains of disease were brought to him. Included were those with seizures (Matt. 17:14–18), paralytics (Matt. 9:1–8), and the demon-possessed (Matt. 8:16, 28, 33; 9:32; 12:22). Two terms are particularly vivid: βάσανος for "pains," which often means "torture" or "torment" (BDAG s.v. "βάσανος" 2, 168), and σεληνιάζομαι for "seizures" or "epilepsy," which literally means "moonstruck" (BDAG s.v. "σεληνιάζομαι" 919). Jesus healed them all, showing the scope of his authority. The messianic era was to lack sickness (Isa. 29:18; 35:5–7; 2 Bar. 73:2–3; Jub. 23:28–30; 4 Ezra 8:53; Davies and Allison 1988, 416; also, exorcism was important here, 4Q510 1.4). The healings pointed to the new era and showed who Jesus was (Matt. 11:4–5; also Matt. 8:16–17 with its citation of Isa. 53:4). It showed Satan being defeated (Turner 2008, 139) and pointed to the kingdom's arrival (Evans 2009).

4:25. A great crowd came to follow Jesus. They came from Galilee, the Decapolis, Jerusalem, Judea, and the other side of the Jordan. Jerusalem falls in the middle of the list. The audience would have been primarily Jewish, but the noting of the Decapolis and beyond the Jordan points to others coming as well since that region was primarily Gentile. The Decapolis comprised ten cities from Damascus in the north to Philadelphia in the south, including Gadara and Gerasa (McNeile 1915, 48; on the Decapolis, Parker 1975). All these sites were east of the Jordan except for Scythopolis (= Beth Shem). It was seen as part of the biblical land of Israel by Jews, but it had a largely Gentile population, something the healing of the Gadarene demoniacs in Matthew 8:28–34 showed since the people there were raising pigs, unclean animals for Jews. Jesus's ministry was introduced to show he was having an impact. In Matthew, the crowds are seen as open to Jesus in contrast to the opposition of the Pharisees (Matt. 9:33–34; 15:1–11; 23:1–4), but they will turn against him in the end (Matt. 26:47, 55; 27:20, 24).

THEOLOGICAL FOCUS

The exegetical idea (as Jesus drew crowds through powerful acts and teaching, the early Galilean ministry represented light that called for repentance as the kingdom of heaven came near, inviting disciples to follow him as a top priority) leads to this theological one: to embrace Jesus is to turn to the kingdom of heaven and follow him as a life priority.

God was at work through Jesus, and the promised one chose to use disciples in mission. Those themes are at the core of this text. There was a message about the kingdom's presence as light. There was a need that God could and desired to fix, pictured in how Jesus ministered with care and compassion. There were the messengers who sought to let others know where help could be found. That ministry focused on a word but did not stop there, so that what the messengers did made evident how those who represented God ministered, reinforcing their message. So Jesus served through healing and pointed to life by doing so. The lesson is that the message of the kingdom comes with a mission that reflects that message and the hope of life, extending down to actions that underscore the message.

Jesus was showing who he was in fulfillment of Scripture. He is light. That light draws disciples to help in the task of drawing others into the light. That light shows itself in kingdom preaching and ministers in a way that shows God at work, reversing the effects of disease and the devil. The combination points to life in the new era. These three scenes point to a mission and commitment that Jesus brought. He shared that mission with others as he pointed the way to God's salvation.

We see mission and what mission takes. Mission involves bringing light to a needy world. Such ministry is a message and a demonstration of acts that support that message. It is holistic in scope. Jesus ministered in this way in his earthly ministry; his disciples would do so later. The church is to model the approach of this original era. Receiving light means recognizing a need God only can supply. Repentance points to a need to have sins forgiven, something we cannot do for ourselves but only God can do for us. The ground for this forgiveness eventually involved Jesus's work on the cross. A response to this mission brings one into the kingdom of God, to experience the life and rule God supplies in the new era. In Jesus, that kingdom opportunity arrives.

The kingdom's coming means there is an urgency to respond to it and a need to make it a priority in life. We also have the picture of the four disciples who left their current vocation behind to follow Jesus. God's ways are worth that commitment. To seek to bring people into the kingdom is like the effort to catch fish. This was the goal of those disciples who joined Jesus. When one considers the length of life for some of these disciples, one lived a long life (John), others were martyred (Peter and James), but their commitment was total either way.

PREACHING AND TEACHING STRATEGIES

Exegetical and Theological Synthesis

The exegetical section describes Jesus's radiant beginning to his earthly ministry. He journeyed from wilderness to Galilee to announce God's inbreaking kingdom and to shine a light of compassion. Jesus matched powerful deed with preached word, calling people to realign their priorities (i.e., repent) in light of the coming kingdom of heaven. Jesus bore witness to the kingdom in his ability to heal sickness and exorcise demons.

Not only were Jesus's actions and announcements powerful, but his ministry was personal. He healed sick individuals. He freed demon-possessed persons. And he called actual, named fishermen to a life of discipleship. Peter and Andrew, James and John left family and fishing boats to follow Jesus. Embedded in this personal call was a promise of relationship ("follow me") and transformation ("I will make you fishers of men."). Embracing this personal call of Jesus does not come without risks, but the eternal rewards are astounding. Thus, these first followers provide an inspiring example.

Finally, the passage hints at Jesus's inclusive reach. The gospel reached areas populated by Jews and Gentiles. Crowds of possessed, sick, and curious came to him. He turned no one away. Because controversy ever looms in the background of Matthew, we cannot feel at ease with Jesus's early popularity. Not everyone who came to him became a disciple. Too many were satisfied with a passing glance or quick fix to their infirmities.

Preaching Idea

Priorities change when Jesus calls your name.

Contemporary Connections

What does it mean?

What does it mean that priorities change when Jesus calls your name? We all live with an implicit set of priorities. The areas of our lives that control our time, attention, energy, affection, and finances often put a spotlight on our priorities. Like Jesus's first followers, our careers and families are core priorities. That they left boats, nets, coworkers, and father on the shore displayed radical reprioritization. They put Jesus first when he called their names. The call to repentance is an invitation to change.

New priorities in the life of discipleship to Jesus include a renewed sense of mission, a renewed commitment to righteousness, and a new set of social bonds. Jesus calls us to become fishers of men—to be his witnesses, living as salt and light in a world in desperate need of the news of his inbreaking kingdom. He calls us to transcend religious duty, social mores, and self-righteousness, motivated by the superior ethic of love for God and neighbor. And he calls us to walk with other followers of Jesus, carrying their burdens, holding them accountable, and inspiring them to honor Jesus in everyday life.

A change of priorities includes both dramatic and day-to-day examples. Some will respond to Jesus's call by leaving an unhealthy dating relationship, breaking with a negative friend group, leaving the corporate world to teach in the inner city, or canceling credit cards to avoid all debt. More ordinary measures of change may comprise limiting time on mobile devices to curb their addictive nature, waking a half-hour early to spend time in a daily prayer office, confessing a sin to a friend to destroy the power of secrecy, or making a habit to attend church weekly. Because each of us inhabits a different life stage and set of responsibilities, our reshuffling of priorities will require personal discernment.

Is it true?

Is it true that when Jesus calls your name your priorities should change? Without question. The life of discipleship is marked by consistent change. God *immediately* changes our status—from sinner to saint. He *ultimately* changes our eternal destination—from eternally separated to forever alive in his presence. And throughout our earthly sojourn, he *consistently* helps us change our spiritual condition—taking off the old and putting on the new as we work out our salvation with fear and trembling (Eph. 4:22–24; Phil. 2:12–13). It is in this ongoing work of sanctification that our priorities change.

Now what?

How should we respond to Jesus's calling? What changes should we make? First, those who have neither heard nor heeded the initial call to discipleship should listen up. Jesus still calls followers today: "Come, follow me." The invitation to life with Jesus includes intimacy and mission: "I will make you fishers of people." All humans at their core want purpose and relational connection. We must emphasize that Jesus's call offers deep intimacy and profound purpose.

Second, those who have initially responded to Jesus's call should realize they have a long road to walk (and massive footsteps to follow). It begins by daily renewing one's commitment to Jesus (Luke 9:23). Thus, every day the disciple must put Jesus's priorities above her own. This may begin by affirming each morning, "Jesus, you are my first priority. Today, I carry my cross and follow you. Your will, not mine, be done." Some variation of this prayer can set the tone for the day. Then, as the day unfolds, reviewing this daily commitment (at lunch, at dinner, before bed) may help keep priorities in order.

Third, a thorough priority assessment may expose rivals to Jesus as one's top priority. A priority assessment should scrutinize several areas of life: time, money, attention, and talk. We might ask:

- What have I been spending most of my time doing in recent days? What is my favorite part of the day? The week? What interruptions to my schedule are most frustrating? What will I protect in my daily routine or annual calendar? What am I likely to reschedule/cancel?
- What gets my greatest attention/focus? What do I think about first in the day? Last in the evening? When my mind wanders, where does it go?
- What do I spend the most money on? What am I saving up for? What do these purchases signify to me?
- What topics dominate in conversatins with my family? Friends? What do I post about most often on social media?
- How is my priority for Jesus evident in my use of time and money? How is my priority for Jesus evident in my attention and talk?

Because priorities change based on our stage of life and set of responsibilities, we are wise to reassess them occasionally. Moreover, you might seek feedback from a spouse, close friend, or coworker. Hearing how they perceive your priorities could be insightful.

Creativity in Presentation

Casting directors use the term "callback" in theater to let an actress know she has made it to round two or three in determining the cast for a play. The actress receives a callback if she looks and sounds close enough to the role that she deserves another hearing. For the callback, she hears her name (via phone call, email, or text) and gears up to prove herself. She may have to memorize a monologue, perform a song, or do a dance. Ultimately, the director determines the casting, but would-be actors try to impress. Jesus's selection process for the disciples provides a striking contrast. Matthew does not explain the potential Jesus sees; the four fishermen have prepared no impressive monologue, song, or dance. And yet they need no callback to respond dramatically.

You may consider your call to the church where you have served or currently serve as pastor. Protestant churches often give an official "call" to a pastor. Prior to the call, they have vetted him, checking his credentials, speaking to his references, listening to samples of his teaching, perusing his social media, and interacting with him through interviews. Like theatre (or sports or most career placement), the call is tied to skill and ability. This contrasts sharply with Jesus's call of the disciples, who do not come with great credentials, numerous references, a preaching portfolio, a social media footprint, or formal interviews with Jesus. For Matthew's version, the call was the interview.

The long-standing daily gameshow *The Price Is Right* provides a delightful picture of people responding to hearing their name called. Every person in the live studio audience submits their name; they are all potential contestants. Audience members become players if their name is called. Then they get a chance to wager a guess on a manufactured item to compete for bigger prizes. The show begins with the announcer calling four names: "Peter the Rock . . . come on down. Andrew the Meek . . . come on down. John the Beloved . . . come on down. James the Thunderous . . . come on down." Once called, players erupt from their seats, rush down the aisles, and genuflect on the stage. Perhaps, the first four disciples responded similarly when Jesus said, "Come on down." When you zero in on the preaching idea, you might insert names of people from your congregation, as though Jesus were calling, and say, "[Congregant name] . . . come on down."

To illustrate changing priorities, you might provide an enlarged list of common priorities: family, finances, health, security, friendship, and entertainment. You might even poll people on Facebook or with a Google poll in advance of the sermon to ask your congregation to rate their priorities. Encourage them to answer honestly rather than ideally, considering what they give the most time, money, attention, and talk to. Based upon your anecdotal evidence, post the top priorities on a PowerPoint slide, whiteboard, or flip chart. As you describe changing priorities, you can display an updated chart with Jesus as the top priority, or simply flip the chart on its head.

Since the passage of Scripture describes Jesus's first followers in boats by the sea, consider decorating the stage with fishing gear. Although modern fishing equipment looks different, it provides a visual aid for all that Peter, Andrew, James, and John left behind. You may be able to find a canoe, oars, nets, poles, tackle boxes, life jackets, and an old man to sit on stage pretending to be Mr. Thunder (Zebedee).

Example of Changing Our Priorities

Priorities of Today's Disciples	Changed Priorities
Happiness Relationships (family, friends, fans) Money/status Comfort/security Health/beauty Career/success Popularity Entertainment/recreation	Jesus Everything else in submission to Jesus

By the end of the sermon, you should have clearly communicated that to embrace Jesus is to turn to the kingdom of heaven and follow him as a life priority. Or, simply put, priorities change when Jesus calls our name.

- Transitions are good times for great change (4:12–17).
- Jesus's call compels great change (4:18–22).
- Jesus's work causes great change (4:23–25).

DISCUSSION QUESTIONS

1. How are Jesus's and John the Baptist's ministries similar? How do they differ?
2. What does Jesus mean by "kingdom of heaven"? How is it "near" or "at hand"?
3. What did the first four disciples give up to follow Jesus? How does their call differ from the typical discipleship relationships in their day?
4. What is a personal invitation you have rejected? What is one that you accepted?
5. What is clear evidence of repentance? Is repentance ongoing? Explain.
6. What priorities dominate your life? How has Jesus called you to reorganize them?

Matthew 5:1–12

EXEGETICAL IDEA
Jesus shared nine virtues of kingdom participants and declared them blessed with great kingdom reward, both now and in the future.

THEOLOGICAL FOCUS
Jesus encourages his disciples by assuring them of their blessing and rich reward for reflecting the virtues of those who follow him in a way that honors God.

PREACHING IDEA
Rest assured: God rewards those who reflect his character.

PREACHING POINTERS
Jesus's first discourse, the renowned Sermon on the Mount, introduced his disciples to the virtues of living as kingdom citizens. Jesus's ethic contrasted with the world's by prizing poverty, humility, mercy, and peace. Tied to this ninefold ethic was the promise of reward from God, who guaranteed entrance, sustenance, and satisfaction in the kingdom; each virtue is punctuated by the memorable word "blessed." For Matthew's audience, this assurance of blessing would have come as welcome news. Allegiance to Jesus in an age where messianic speculation, resistance to Rome, and persecution for believers was rising would have been challenging. The Beatitudes offered a word of assurance to stay the course, develop character, and trust Jesus's kingdom claims.

Followers of Jesus in our day need assurance and resolve to live ethically. The world provides an ever-shifting moral target. It praises sexual expression while mocking sexual purity. It encourages relentless consumption while vilifying environmental exploitation. It leverages public shame to destroy careers and cancel churches while muttering Jesus's prohibition against judgment. It debates justice in ways that do not bring us closer to possessing it or remove the lack of equity in an unjust world. In this vortex of confusing and unforgiving ethics, Christ-followers can feel guarded, threatened, or tempted to adopt worldly character to blend in. Jesus's first words in his famed sermon address these feelings and inspire confidence. This message implores us to rest assured, God rewards those who reflect his character.

THE BEATITUDES: BLESSED ARE THOSE WHO . . . (5:1–12)

LITERARY STRUCTURE AND THEMES (5:1–12)

This unit of beatitudes is laid out in a strict parallelism of nine units. First there is the setting (vv. 1–2). With each of the nine beatitudes, there is the announcement of blessing, the virtue, and then the reward (vv. 3–12). Virtue and reward are closely related to each other in a unified theme, since a reward is paired to each character trait.

The parallel to this unit is in Luke 6:20–23, but Luke only has three beatitudes and contrasts them immediately with three woes that Matthew does not have. As is common with the parallels with Luke, the third gospel's version is more compact. Konradt (2020, 66) sees the additional beatitudes as not traceable back to Jesus but a reflection either of the tradition or Matthew. How one can claim this is not clear, though he says their construction is based on Old Testament texts. Nothing about these additional virtues is out of character with Jesus and the style of his own ministry. It is not clear why Old Testament allusions are beyond what Jesus would have done as a messenger from God. The way righteousness is read reflects less of the early church's idea of imputed righteousness and more of the idea of a practiced righteousness.

The opening unit of beatitudes focuses on character, as does much of the sermon. To be blessed is to be happy or fortunate. The premise of these beatitudes is that God is pleased with those who have such a character. The call offers a note of congratulations. Jesus's opening remarks set the tone for the kind of people he seeks and is calling to God's kingdom. It is a "manifesto on the values of the kingdom of heaven" (France 2007, 159). It is kingdom-Torah, focused on the heart. There are differences with Moses, especially that Jesus does not mediate God's will as an intermediary and speaks with a direct kind of authority (Garland 1995, 52). Garland (1995, 54–59) sees in the unit the following breakdown: the disposition toward God, verses 3–6; the disposition toward others, verses 7–10; the situation of the church, verses 11–12. It is better not to mention the church yet in discussing this, since it has not yet been introduced in the gospel and the kingdom comprises more than the church in terms of figures past and structures yet to come (the millennium and/or new heavens and new earth). What we have in verses 11–12 is the reaction of the world to kingdom saints, but otherwise the breakdown is helpful. The world is always in tension with the kingdom, so the situation of reaction to the kingdom is in view at the unit's conclusion.

These values are not the ones normally elevated in the world, for the core virtues of humility and dependence on God are most prominent. Ancient Greek philosophers saw humility as weakness (MacIntyre 1988, 163). These are blessings, not entrance requirements, but they come to the person as gifts from God because of the heart's turn to him so that God supplies these virtues to his own (Turner 2008, 146–47). Repentance turns to God in faith and shapes us, leading into blessing.

The structure of these blessings is to name the virtue and then mention the reward. The remarks are designed to inspire and encourage. The rewards reflect the eschatological reversal that runs through the benefits God supplies and the disciple seeks. God honors those who walk in the ways he desires. So God desires those who are poor in spirit, who mourn, who are meek, who hunger and thirst for righteousness, who are merciful, who are clean in heart, who are peacemakers, who are persecuted for righteousness' sake, and who are despised and persecuted. Here are the nine virtues Jesus commends.

The Nine Beatitudes in Matthew and the Four in Luke (Luke noted after /)

Poor in spirit/poor
Mourn/ weep*
Meek
Hunger and thirst for righteousness/hunger
Merciful
Pure in heart
Peacemakers
Persecuted for righteousness' sake/hated, excluded, and rejected
Despised

*Weep comes after hunger in Luke.

These aspects of character are not entrance requirements for the kingdom but are words of assurance to the person who has responded to God, given that the text follows the passage where disciples have already been called (Talbert 2004, 47). Neither is this text a political manifesto, but a reflection of virtue, ethics, character that God has produced in those who respond to and follow him (Talbert 2004, 47–48).

Beatitudes have a precedent in the Psalter and wisdom literature (Guelich 1982, 63–65; Pss. 1:1–2; 32:1–2; 40:4; Prov. 3:13; 8:34; Dan. 12:12). There is a rich theology revolving around blessings in the Hebrew Scripture (Culpepper 2021, 86). They were a call to character by reminding listeners of what pleases God. The term μακάριος means "happy," "favored," "fortunate," so "blessed" (BDAG s.v. "μακάριος" 2a, 610–11). These nine beatitudes are balanced in structure. The virtue is named that yields blessing and the reward is stated. That reward is the mirror opposite of what was suffered (known as eschatological reversal) and so is a reward for faithfulness. A discussion of character leads off the teaching about the kingdom. Given the earlier call to repentance, there now is a recognition of character not based on power and strength but rooted in a humble spirit of dependence on God. There also is a recognition that the world will not accept people who live so distinctly. The distinct way disciples live reminds others that God is there and challenges the way the world lives.

Jesus previewed the end at the beginning of his teaching. This is the character God honors. How one got to this way of living is not explained in this starting point. Jesus simply set out the goal and reward for being there. Those who ally themselves with Jesus are to understand where he is taking them. Jesus always discussed the entire package of what the kingdom offered. He presented the entire journey, not just its start. He wanted people to understand what they were signing on for and where that would take them. To repent and embrace the way of God was to begin a life journey of transformation. Salvation was not about a single moment of faith but a life of faith. We may be saved in a moment of embracing faith, but the life of that faith is designed to lead us into transformation as we develop these attributes.

EXPOSITION (5:1–12)

Jesus introduced the kingdom, offering a call to a completely different kind of life that God seeks from those who walk in his ways and often suffer for it in a broken world. In these nine virtues, Matthew reveals Jesus's awareness of such injustice and argues that God will reward those who turn to him and embrace the distinctive way of life that is part of kingdom citizenship.

Jesus shared nine virtues of kingdom participants and declared them blessed with great kingdom reward, both now as kingdom participants and in the future with reward.

5:1–2. This scene opens with the setting. It was on a mount, where Jesus saw the crowds and gathered them to hear his kingdom exhortation. He sat as he taught them. The entire sermon takes about seven minutes to read, so it is likely we have a distillation of much more that was said. Matthew refers to Jesus going up to a mountain in two other places (Matt. 14:23, where he prays; 15:29, where he heals; Hagner 1993, 85). Otherwise, there are mountains tied to temptation (Matt. 4:8), transfiguration (Matt. 17:1), eschatological discourse (Matt. 24:3), and resurrection (Matt. 28:16). Anyone familiar with the Sea of Galilee knows this is not a mountain in the classic sense but a raised area or hill in a plateau area (Blomberg 1992, 97). Crowds and disciples were both taught here.

Photo of Traditional Site of Sermon on the Mount, Outside of Capernaum.

5:3. The term "beatitude" comes from the Latin *beatituto* and points to being happy. These beatitudes were a series of congratulatory statements (Guelich 1982, 67).

The first beatitude describes the "poor in spirit" (πτωχοὶ τῷ πνεύματι). The spirit in view here is the human spirit (Nolland 2005, 199). The concept appeares in texts like Isaiah 61:1 (also Isa. 57:15; 66:2; also Ps. 34:6; on poor, BDAG s.v. "πτωχός" 3, 896; Prov. 16:19; Isa. 66:2; Zeph. 2:3). Luke simply refers to the poor, contrasted to the rich in Luke 6:20 and 24. Material blessing was not a guaranteed sign of divine approval, but a heart turned toward him was (Wilkins 2004, 206). However, Luke's section also speaks of those who were persecuted, so this was the pious poor. These were the *ʿănāwîm* of the Old Testament (Guelich 1982, 68–71). They suffered for following God and being set aside by the world. This was not a spiritualized poor, but those who suffered for their stand with God. They suffered and longed for God to act (Nolland 2005, 200, points to the parallel with the use of the term at Qumran and their hope, 1QH 8:12–15; 1QM 11:8–15; 14:7). They were genuinely poor and literally suffered for it, but also were pious. This pious connection is seen in the later beatitudes in Matthew 5:10–12. Culpepper (2021, 87–88) notes how Roman culture had little patience for the poor, as poverty was seen as the fault of their own laziness. Appian in *Civil Wars* 2.17.120 says, "Moreover the distribution of corn to the poor, which took place in Rome only, drew thither the lazy, the beggars, the vagrants of all Italy."[1] So alms were discouraged. Contrast Leviticus 23:22: "When you gather in the harvest of your land, you must not completely harvest the corner of your field, and you must not gather up the gleanings of your harvest. You must leave them for the poor and the resident foreigner. I am the Lord your God." One is reminded of Galatians 6:10: "let us do good to all people, and especially to those who belong to the family of faith."

The reward was that the kingdom of God belonged to them. The kingdom belonged to them *even now,* not just in the future. The present tense of the verb ἐστιν ("is") here is important. Jesus brought the kingdom. God's rule and offer started now. This humble spirit is what God honors. They recognized their need for

1 Appian, *The Civil Wars.* ed. H. White (New York: MacMillan, 1899).

God and turned to him. God's rule came to such people as a gift and could manifest itself in such people. They gladly accepted God's rule (France 2007, 165). It makes sense that the list starts here, because this virtue represents the core that leads to the others. It is what a prepared heart reflects as a result of repentance. The present tense is bracketed by Matthew 5:10. Even in the midst of persecution that came because of such a humble heart, the kingdom of God belonged to such as these. Davies and Allison (1988, 446) see a look to the future, but do admit that some blessing exists even now. The exhortation is not about politics, but it does deal with social status. It also affirms a spiritual dimension to those God responds to with blessing. This core virtue reflects an openness to be shaped by God. It is a fundamental orientation to being a disciple and a learner of God's ways.

5:4. The second beatitude describes those who mourn. The background is likely Isaiah 61:2. Those who mourn experience and identify with the suffering that is part of a fallen world. They see the sin that resides in injustice and are sad. They see persecution with its suffering and are sad. Osborne (2010, 166) sees sin and persecution as being in view, something the entire context supports.

The reward is that comfort is coming. In the end, mourning will be reversed. Pain will disappear. Comfort is a theme of messianic hope (Isa. 49:13; 51:12; 66:13; Jer. 31:13; Guelich 1982, 81). In fact, Messiah came to be known as "the Comforter" (*Menahem*; SB 1:195). The comfort is described in a passive verb form, an example of God supplying the comfort. Isaiah 40, a text Matthew has already used, opens with such a call to comfort.

5:5. The third beatitude is for the meek. It is unique to Matthew's version. This matches the poor in spirit. This overlap may explain why Luke lacks it. The roots here are Psalm 37:11, where *ʿănāwîm* are present. It is not about timidity, but one who was an object of injustice and did not strike back. This person is humble, gentle, genuinely dependent on God, and not aggressive (Blomberg 1992, 99; Morris 1992, 98). This person exhibits "a poise of not having to assert oneself," a spirit that is what the world values (Bruner 2004a, 166).

The reward is that these shall inherit the earth, a promise that shows that the blessing to come also involves this world and life. God will complete the promise within the history that started the human saga. This is a future hope in contrast to the hope of Matthew 5:3.

5:6. The fourth beatitude describes those who hunger and thirst for righteousness. Here the character turn is toward a life of virtue, what the epistles describe as a life of integrity and purity ("right relationship with God and others," Guelich 1982, 87). It involves personal righteousness and justice, as in the other beatitudes (Carson 2010, 164). They hunger and thirst for righteousness because this virtue is hard to find in a fallen world full of injustice. They long for a world of just social order and the personal righteousness such justice requires. Psalm 107:5 and 9 may be in view (Turner 2008, 151). Matthew loves to discuss this term. Such character is both a gift from God and a way of living (Guelich 1982, 84–87). This is one of the things the gift of the Spirit or law in the heart does as a part of the new covenant. It is a gift, is ethical, and eschatological because Jesus gives it (Luke 1:53; John 14–16). To hunger and thirst for this is to seek it like one seeks and needs food and drink or as one seeks wisdom in the OT (Prov. 2:1–4). It sustains and does so regularly. This is like what Jesus said in Matthew 4:4: their food is the will of God. Everything about these first four beatitudes shows people who turn to God and are dependent on him. They do not earn salvation and commendation; they rely on and look to God and his ways for it (Bruner 2004a, 167–68). To merely equate these virtues with right conduct minimizes the call to repentance and turning to God that is the prerequisite for what is said here. It also bypasses the promised offer of the Spirit as a purging baptism (Matt. 3:2, 11; 4:17). These texts set the context for what is said here. Matthew 6:33 also gives what drives this attitude, to seek his kingdom.

The reward is that the righteous will be filled in the end. They will not lack in terms of character. They will be fed to the full with this divinely rooted righteousness (Pss. 132:15; 146:7; Isa. 49:10; 55:1; 65:21–22).

5:7. As we turn to how others are to be treated in the next three blessings, we come to the fifth beatitude. Jesus noted how the "merciful" are blessed (BDAG s.v. "ἐλεήμων" 316). The term is rare, appearing in the New Testament only in Hebrews 2:17 besides here. As seen in the Old Testament, mercy is being kind to people in need and who may well not deserve it (Exod. 33:19—mercy a function of being gracious; 1 Kings 18:47; 2 Chron. 33:20–21; Ps. 51:5; Prov. 11:17; 14:21; 17:5; 19:11; 20:6; 28:22; Hos. 4:1, 6:6; Mic. 6:8). It does not calculate if there will be a payback (Nolland 2005, 203). It involves pardon and kindness (Guelich 1982, 88). It takes into account where another is coming from and is empathetic to that. Concrete acts of kindness were known as alms. Here it is primarily pardon, but both ideas are in the sermon (Matt. 5:43–48; 6:1–4).

This mercy reflects the character of God according to Luke 6:36, although a different, synonymous term for mercy is used there (BDAG s.v. "οἰκτίρμων" 700). Matthew 18:21–35 places this idea in a parable that urged one to be quick to forgive, while Matthew 6:2–4, 12, 14–15 also teaches it (Blomberg 1992, 100; Turner 2008, 153, adds Matt. 9:27, 36; 15:22; 17:15; 20:30). Mercy is extended because one appreciates that we all need mercy and that God extends it to those who are willing to receive it (1 Peter 3:18; Carson 1978, 23–24; Garland 1995, 56; Morris 1992, 100). This recognition makes one slow to judge as well (Matt. 7:1–5; Guelich 1982, 90). Jesus stressed mercy as a key attribute of the disciple, and Matthew picks up that emphasis.

The reward is that mercy will be received by the one who shows mercy. This point is made in an opposite way from the parable in Matthew 18:23–35. The Pharisees are portrayed as lacking this trait (Matt. 9:13; 12:7; 23:23). The one not showing mercy by refusing to offer forgiveness will not receive mercy. Similar in force as a positive exhortation are Matthew 5:43–48; 9:13; 12:7; and 25:31–46. James 2:13 says this more negatively about the person who lacks mercy. All these texts point to another core Christian virtue.

5:8. Purity in heart is the sixth beatitude. In Scripture, the heart is the center of emotions and being (Gen. 27:41; Deut. 28:47; Ps. 27:8; Prov. 6:18; 27:11; Davies and Allison 1988, 456; Garland 1995, 57). It is like a pure conscience (Pss. 24:3–4; 73:1; 1 Tim. 1:5; Heb. 12:14). This is part of what is connected to the pursuit of righteousness. Here is a call to be holy. The inner condition of the heart is in view, an internal integrity (Matt. 6:21–24; 7:16–20; 13:45–46; 22:37; James 3:17–18; 4:8; Turner 2008, 152). It is illustrated in 6:1–18 (Davies and Allison 1988, 456). "Heart" is an important term for Matthew (Matt. 5:28; 6:21; 9:4; 11:29; 12:34; 13:15, 19; 15:8, 18–19; 18:35; 22:37; 23:26). Matthew 23:25–26 is the opposite idea, as is Matthew 27:6. The danger of what the heart can produce appears in Matthew 15:19. The heart and what goes on inside is at the core of what follows in the exhortations of Matthew 5:20–48.

The reward here is to see God (Pss. 11:7; 17:15; 42:3; Isa. 6:5). This was what purity permitted in Jewish thinking. Only the pure and cleansed went into the temple. The person who shared God's character also experienced his fellowship. This experience is promised in the salvation to come (Isa. 52:6; 60:16; Jer. 24:7; 31:31–34; so also in the NT: 1 John 3:2; Rev. 22:4; Turner 2008, 152).

5:9. The seventh beatitude, being a "peacemaker," also yields blessing. This is not referring to a mere desire for peace, but to those who help bring it (BDAG s.v. "εἰρηνοποιός" 288; Carson 1978, 26). Again, the issue is being a person who does not escalate violence but seeks to quell it. Matthew 5:23–24 is the example text. Judaism also held to this value. Second Enoch 52:11[ms. A] has a blessing for the one who cultivates the love of peace ("Blessed is he who imparts peace and love"). In the Old Testament, *šālôm* is the term for "peace," and it refers to the condition of wholeness and harmony (Blomberg 1992, 100). This beatitude would have shocked the Zealots, who wanted to fight to gain freedom (Carson 1984, 135). This virtue leads to seeking a genuine reconciliation that yields peace. Much of the work of salvation is about reconciliation at a corporate level (Eph. 2:11–22).

Such an effort reflects God's character and shows one to be a son of God. The language here is like Hosea 2:1 LXX. In Judaism, the righteous were said to be sons of God (Wis. 2:13, 18; Strecker, 1988, 41). In the Mishnah, *Peah* 1:1 one of the things that brings benefit in this life and in the world to come is bringing peace between a man and his fellow man (McNeile 1915, 52). Luke 6:35 makes this observation about those who loved their enemies, did good, and lent money expecting nothing in return (also Matt. 5:43–48, esp. 44–45; Guelich 1982, 91). To share God's character is a compliment to the one who walks with God. The picture is of being recognized as a person of the covenant and reflecting that in one's actions. The triad of beatitudes just completed are mercy, purity, and peace, three key characteristics that reflect God (Bruner 2004a, 179). Grace takes us into God and his character, so we are God's people by grace and are led to imitate him with works that reflect his character (Eph. 2:8–10; Titus 2:11–14).

This verse has some tension with Matthew 10:34, where Jesus says he came not to bring peace but division (Davies and Allison 1988, 458). However, that verse is really a remark about how people react to Jesus versus his intention. The fact is that Jesus brought a division of opinion depending on how people reacted to him (Luke 2:34).

5:10. The eighth beatitude extends to those who are persecuted for righteousness's sake. There is a transition here. The remaining beatitudes deal with how the world treats disciples. This beatitude is unique to Matthew. The shift is evident by a move from a second-person address in beatitudes one through seven to the third person in this beatitude and the next.

A perfect passive participle (οἱ δεδιωγμένοι) names the category: "those who have been persecuted" (BDAG s.v. "διώκω" 2, 254). The passive points to the world as the source of persecution, while the perfect points to a state of existence that abided (Osborne 2010, 169). Persecution is another theme in Matthew (Matt. 10:23; 13:21; 23:34).

This verse shows the "pious poor" nature of the entire list and parallels the last beatitude. They suffered on account of righteousness, standing up for the way of God. Here righteousness is a virtue of action, not a gift. It still is rooted in trust of God and receiving what his way offers (1 Peter 3:14 in the context of the promise of the book). It also goes with the final beatitude and stresses right up front the cost of following God. Some will not like the call for commitment to God and his righteousness (Luke 6:26; John 3:19–20; 15:18–25; Acts 14:22; 2 Tim. 3:12; 1 Peter 4:13–14; Carson 2010, 165). Judaism also sensed this reaction to their commitment to the one God (Keener 2009, 171; Wis. 1:16–5:23; 2 Macc. 7:9; 14:38; 4 Macc. 9:29; 2 Bar. 52:6; Davies and Allison 1988, 459).

The reward is that the kingdom of God belongs to them. In a sense, this is not a reward, in the strictest sense of that term, since it comes with the orientation to be a part of God's program, making it more a word of assurance. It does, however, note that there is a benefit in responding. The present tense returns as this is the last reward noted, so it brackets with the first beatitude's reward, which makes the same point. One does not retaliate but trusts God for a just response.

5:11–12. The ninth beatitude is for those who are insulted, persecuted, and slandered with all sorts of evil things said falsely because of their allegiance to Jesus ("on account of me": ἕνεκεν ἐμοῦ). It is the expression parallel to "on account of righteousness" in the previous verse. This personalizes the beatitude and tightens the association of the kingdom with Jesus. You cannot have one without the other. They are to bear the name of Jesus by following his path and teaching. The term for "insult" also appears in 1 Peter 4:14 (BDAG s.v. "ὀνειδίζω" 1, 710). Verbal abuse is in view (Guelich 1982, 94), as the later reference to verbal slander by referring to speaking evil also shows (1 Peter 3:14–17).

Instead of simply noting a reward, there is a reaction that should come, being exceedingly glad and rejoicing (Rev. 19:7; on the term for "exceeding gladness," BDAG s.v. "ἀγαλλιάω" 4). Reward is a repeated theme in Matthew (Matt. 5:46; 6:1, 2, 5, 16; 10:41–42; 20:1–15; 24:45–47; 25:20–23, as well as 6:4, 6, 18; 19:27–29; 25:34–40; France 2007, 172–73). There is mention that the reward in heaven is great, with a reason given using γὰρ ("for"). The point is important because the previous beatitude notes a present benefit for persecution, while this note looks to the future (Matt. 6:1, 19–21).

The prophets were treated in the same way. Thus, through their faithfulness to God and Jesus, the disciples would join a company of witnesses who went before them and pointed to such faithfulness (1 Kings 18:4; 2 Chron. 24:21; Neh. 9:26; Jer. 20:2; Amos 7:10–12; Matt. 21:35; 23:32–37; Heb. 11:32–40). Jesus notes to all who listen that suffering and rejection will come from following him. There are no surprises here; the world will push back—expect it. The way of the cross was put right up front in the presentation of the kingdom. First Peter 4:12–14 is similar in force (Hagner 1993, 95). The reward here is not earned on one's merit but is a recognition of faithfulness for drawing on what God has provided (Guelich 1982, 95–96).

Character Virtues of the Matthean Beatitudes Showing a Spiritual Dimension of Faith versus a General Description

Poor in Spirit
Those Persecuted for Righteousness' Sake
Those Who Are Despised, Persecuted, and Slandered Because of Jesus

THEOLOGICAL FOCUS

The exegetical idea (Jesus shared nine virtues of kingdom participants and declared them blessed with great kingdom reward, both now as kingdom participants and in the future with reward) leads to this theological one: Jesus encourages his disciples by assuring them of their blessing and rich reward for reflecting the virtues of those who follow him in a way that honors God.

As Davies and Allison (1988, 466) argue, the announcement of the kingdom of God opens with blessings, not requirements. It "will bring eschatological comfort, a permanent inheritance, true satisfaction, the obtaining of mercy, the vision of God, and divine sonship" (Davies and Allison 1988, 466). This is an invitation with a preview of what God will give. The kingdom is about an opportunity, but it also issues a call for a different kind of character than is common in the world. Reliance on God, trust in his way of justice, a lack of retaliation, hesitation about power that takes advantage of others, and humility are at its core. Such attributes reflect a commitment to righteousness and holiness. The kingdom and Jesus go together. The rule of God transforms the way we live in the world by giving us a picture of a different kind of person and way of living.

The theological thrust in this unit describes followers who respond in such a way that God's grace transforms them and leads into blessing. Jesus stressed the character that God seeks to form in those who belong to his kingdom. These disciples do not live in a world of independence and power. They are humble, suffer, and are willing to live against the flow of the world's values. They pursue righteousness, holiness, humility, peace, and justice, and often suffer for their choices through those who do not appreciate their divinely encouraged values. This way of life stands out in stark contrast to the way the world lives. It shows God has been at work in the life of disciples. These attributes are what disciples are to reflect in how they live and engage with the world.

As a result, God honors such faithfulness. These disciples belong to the kingdom, will inherit the earth, and are sons and daughters of God in terms of character. They are promised justice and peace to the full, a recognition that will come one day and be abiding in character. People who seek to be blessed by God are told from the start that this is the kind of person God seeks for his kingdom. The teaching stands as an encouragement that even though the world does not appreciate who they are and how they live, God does see their legacy and will honor their commitment to him. This is the character God seeks to build in those who follow him and experience his blessing.

PREACHING AND TEACHING STRATEGIES

Exegetical and Theological Synthesis

The exegetical section highlights both the promise of reward and ethical expectations for disciples. Followers of Jesus reflect his way in the world. He did not come as an agenda-driven judge or glory-seeking king, but as a humble servant. Jesus not only paved the way for God-pleasing service but also provided an invitation into kingdom living. His ethic made no false promises. He acknowledged persecution, conflict, hunger, sorrow, and poverty; however, he assured his disciples that present conditions were not the best reading of divine reward. Those who embodied his ethic would experience the inbreaking kingdom and God's pleasure, in some form, until the kingdom fully arrived.

The beatitudes strike an important balance between virtuous living and divine reward. Headlining each ethical statement, Jesus spoke a word of blessing—happiness, favor, fortune, or congratulations. God's favor precedes the ethic. God's favor precedes the reward. Lapsing into a view of divine retribution becomes too easy—if I obey, God blesses; if I rebel, God punishes—but the Sermon on the Mount does not feed this errant thinking. Regardless of their current obedience streak, all believers are blessed.

On the other hand, ultimately, apprentices of Jesus are destined to become like their Master (Matt. 10:25). They mimic his mercy, humility, and purity. They reflect his stalwart faith and commitment to serve. Even today Jesus's ethical example and imperatives stand in bold contrast with the world's self-seeking, self-gratifying, stock-up-and-throw-stones ethic. When disciples feel like they are losing because they choose Christlike character, they must cling to the hope of heavenly reward.

Preaching Idea

Rest assured: God rewards those who reflect his character.

Contemporary Connections

What does it mean?

What does it mean that God rewards those who reflect his character? What aspects of God's character should we reflect? The virtues embedded in the Beatitudes reflected Jesus's way of being in the world. He was a humble, righteous, suffering servant. The list of Christian virtues in the Beatitudes, which is by no means exhaustive, includes being humble, sensitive to sin, righteous, merciful, peace-making, pure, and steadfast in suffering. Humble followers of Jesus are not constantly promoting themselves on social media. Disciples who are sensitive to sin may have a specific social evil (e.g., sex trafficking, racism, oppression, injustice) that makes them weep. Those who are steadfast in suffering do not let "cancel culture" and public shaming silence their love for Jesus. God loves seeing his character manifested in the lives of his people.

However, reflecting God's character does not guarantee instant and immediate reward. We must beware of divine-retribution theology. Virtuous living does not exempt us from high blood pressure and economic recession. Nor do our personal, moral failures cause lightning to strike. Our heavenly Father is not prone to retaliation or manipulation. Rather, he delights to give good gifts (Matt. 7:11; James 1:17).

The rewards for virtuous living in the Beatitudes are rich. They transcend the common graces of everyday life—food, clothing, and desirable weather (Matt. 5:3–12; cf. 6:4, 6, 18)—and reinforce Jesus's teaching on divine generosity (Matt. 5:45; 6:25–34). Reflecting God's character results in assurance, comfort, satisfaction, mercy, peace, and vision. Because these are eschatological rewards, disciples will not likely feel their full weight in the present. However, a merciful mother dedicated to loving her rebellious teenager is likely to have a deeper appreciation for God's mercy. Likewise, a recently converted businessman may be rewarded for his new taste for integrity with a deeper sense of vocation.

Is it true?

Is it true that God rewards those who reflect his character? Can we rest assured in this? This beautiful collection of blessings is true. However, as mentioned above, we must caution against a mechanistic view of God. There is a subtle gap between *assumption* and *assurance.* Living by assumption can lead us to treat God like a vending machine. We put in our coins (e.g., righteousness, purity) and wait for the prize (e.g., satisfaction, vision). We limit God by our conditional statement: "If I live virtuously, then God rewards me." Not only does this assume God must act according to our expectation, but we are likely to overstate our own virtue. This too is a dangerous assumption.

Assurance, on the other hand, respects God's timing and our sinful tendencies. We always have room to grow in our reflection of Jesus's humility, integrity, righteousness, mercy, purity, and steadfastness. In our pursuit of the virtuous life, God maintains our motivation by the foretaste of perfect comfort, perfect satisfaction, and perfect peace. We will experience the fullness of these rewards when the kingdom fully comes.

Jesus knew his followers needed this assurance, so he preached it. Matthew knew his readers needed this assurance, so he recorded it. Followers of Jesus today need assurance as well. The ethics of the world do not align with kingdom virtues. Selfish people gain fame; greedy people maintain an economic edge; injustice often prevails; and angry people get attention. Meanwhile, the meek get bullied, the pure get mocked, and peacemakers get double-crossed. A disciple must fight the allure of fleeting rewards and stay assured of eternal rewards.

Now what?

The response to the beatitudes is twofold. First, the passage calls for a character evaluation. These nine virtues should serve as a mirror to our way of being in the world, our imitation of Christ. We should approach self-evaluation slowly and mercifully. The poor in spirit are always open to being shaped by God. A rushed and inflated self-examination will do little good. Hence, we may methodically pray through the Beatitudes on a weekly or monthly basis, asking, "God, have I been poor in spirit, mourning, meek, righteous, merciful, pure, peacemaking, and steadfast in persecution?" Pausing between each virtue to reflect and listen would give this exercise a chance to take effect. Then we should confess the lacking virtues, celebrate the proven virtues, and consider ways to foster growth in virtue. This practice requires patience and focus; each session may take five to fifteen minutes.

Praying for Growth in Christian Character

Your time set aside to pray for growth in Christian character may benefit from the following:

- A quiet location, free from visual or audible distractions
- A focal text from Scripture (e.g., the Beatitudes, Matt. 5:3–12; fruit of the Spirit, Gal. 5:22–23; Phil. 1:9–11; and Col. 1:9–12; 3:5–16)
- A fixed time (e.g., first Monday of the month, every Wednesday morning, at bedtime)
- A few key questions:
  - How does Jesus model this character trait?
  - How does our world twist this character trait?
  - What factors (internal/external) make this character trait hard to demonstrate?
  - What is something specific I can do this week to grow in this character trait?
- A firm commitment to reflect Jesus's character in the world

Second, the Beatitudes call for assurance. While the rewards Jesus tied to each virtue remained distant realities, his ninefold repetition of "blessed" affirmed a present state of favor. Disciples must realize, know, and remain convinced that they are favored by God *now*. His love is certain. His sovereign care is certain. His salvation is certain. His forgiveness of sins and invitation to the kingdom are certain. No matter our present circumstances, we are wise—no, blessed!—if we rehearse these Beatitudes. Moreover, future reward is certain, as well. Matthew has already made a strong case for God's stunning ability to keep his promises (cf. 1:1–25). Thus we can rest assured in the full advent of the kingdom, full comfort, full inheritance, full satisfaction, and so on. Rather than dwell on the miseries of our modern age, we find assurance by seeking first the kingdom (Matt. 6:33) and reminding ourselves, "We are blessed. We are blessed. We are blessed."

Creativity in Presentation

Simon and Garfunkel wrote a song inspired by the Beatitudes. "Blessed" (from the *Sounds of Silence* album) borrows imagery from Jesus, adding some of their own striking phrases. For example, they sing, "Blessed are the sat upon, spat upon, ratted on. . . . Blessed are the meth drinkers, pot sellers, illusion dwellers." If this doesn't grab your congregation's attention, they're not listening! Consider playing the song and commenting on its distorted tone. The artists seem unable to cope with the sorrow in the world, not having an eschatological outlook to lift their eyes from the "forsakenness" they see all around them. As a moving contrast, you might coordinate with the worship team to play the song "Blessed Assurance" at the close of the service, reminding folks that because Jesus was forsaken, we can be assured that we're blessed.

Jesus's ethics differed from the Greco-Roman values of his day. They contrast with our day, as well. Though rather subjective, it could be helpful to compile a list of the top nine virtues of our age. You could research these online, utilize a Gallup or Barna study,[2] or run your own (nonscientific) poll of people in your church. It is likely that people will list virtues they think the pollster wants to hear, but if you begin with a list of options, you can steer the discussion a bit. See the sidebar for a limited list of worldly virtues.

2 For example, Barna's 2016 publication, *The Porn Phenomenon: The Impact of Pornography in a Digital Culture*, reports many young Americans view recycling as a higher virtue than abstaining from pornography.

A Limited List of Worldly Virtues		
PERSONAL VIRTUES	**RELATIONAL VIRTUES**	**CULTURAL VIRTUES**
Self-expressive/independent Vulnerable Outraged Self-aware Real Influential	Tolerant Inclusive Nondiscriminating Commited Networked Connected	Wealthy Tribal Green Socially active Relevant Driven

Once you hone your list to nine, try and pair them to one of the character traits from the Beatitudes. You could display these on a slide, whiteboard, or notepad for reference. Using contrasting colors or fonts would emphasize the difference. Announcing each worldly virtue with the phrase "Blessed are the . . ." would reinforce the irony of Jesus's original, ninefold ethic.

Personal stories of character and reward can help the homiletical idea stick. In my (Tim's) early years of elementary school, I was a nightmare for the teachers. My education preceded the proliferation of labels (e.g., ADHD) and meds (e.g., Ritalin). I could neither sit still nor stay silent in class. I was combative with teachers and classmates. Negative consequences did not moderate my behavior, so my mother tried the carrot. Each week she promised the reward of a new toy if I could tame myself in class. It worked, for the most part, because Friday was never too far away. God's rewards are far more distant, but will last much longer than a cheap, plastic action figure. Find a similar story of motivation-by-reward from your childhood or parenting.

Finally, we should note that anticipated-but-unpredictable rewards have a powerful effect on human behavior. This phenomenon has been noted with gambling addicts, who keep feeding the machine because they know they will *eventually* be rewarded. Employers have found similar results when providing anticipated-but-unpredictable rewards for their workers: a random Starbucks gift card, a company hat, a flex day (Pink 2011, 64–67). Social science studies suggest these anticipated-but-unpredictable rewards result in more job satisfaction than the predictable end-of-the-year bonus. God's blessings come in small doses to disciples who stay focused on their task. These are but a foretaste of the full reward to come.

No matter what creative elements you adopt and adapt, be sure your sermon communicates that Jesus encourages his disciples by assuring them of their blessing and rich reward for reflecting the virtues of those who follow him in a way that honors God. Hence, we should rest assured; God rewards those who reflect his character.

- The stage is set for a powerful sermon (5:1–2).
- Jesus announces our blessed assurance (5:3–12).
- Jesus encourages virtuous living (5:3–12).
- Jesus promises future reward (5:3–12).[3]

3 This message could systematically work through each of the nine Beatitudes (eight and night overlapping) individually. To best explain the Preaching Idea, however, the suggested outline offers a broad overview of the Beatitudes by looking at three key themes (assurance, virtue, and eschatological reward).

DISCUSSION QUESTIONS

1. How does understanding the Beatitudes as wisdom literature help us interpret Jesus's blessing statements correctly? How can they be misinterpreted?

2. Which of the virtues listed would have sounded odd to Matthew's audience? Which virtues sound odd to a contemporary audience?

3. When can we expect God to give out these eschatological rewards? In what ways does he reward his people in the present?

4. What worldly virtues have seeped into your church? How can you expose them?

5. What are different ways to motivate people to live virtuously? How do you guard against fueling new forms of legalism when cheering for virtue?

6. Which eschatological rewards do you find most appealing? Why?

Matthew 5:13–20

EXEGETICAL IDEA

As salt and light, disciples were to season the world with a righteousness that shone forth, fulfilled the ethical intent of the law, and reflected the kingdom of God.

THEOLOGICAL FOCUS

The disciple's call is to live in a way that shows the character of God, drawing people to the Father.

PREACHING IDEA

Be a force for good, to show the heart of God.

PREACHING POINTERS

Jesus intended his disciples to be the greatest witness to the heavenly Father's character, integrity, and glory. He called them to shine God's goodness like a light. He called them to saturate the world with moral excellence. He implored his followers to go beneath the surface of the law, beyond external compliance, to its heart for justice, mercy, and humility. For Matthew's audience, this mission came at a critical time, warning those pulled toward extremes of antinomianism and staunch legalism. He reminded them of the Messiah's middle way of exceeding righteousness from the heart.

Today's church desperately needs a fresh hearing of Jesus's mission statement. Moral decay infects our age. Injustice casts a shadow over our society. However, legislation and moral teaching bring limited change. Greater change comes when followers of Jesus embrace his call to live as change agents. This passage forces today's disciples to inspect their own hearts, analyze their motives, and critique their behavior. Two timeless metaphors—salt and light—focus this passage on the disciple's duty to benefit the world by action, not bludgeon it by accusation. Simply put, this message teaches we should be a force for good, to show the heart of God.

DISCIPLES AS SALT AND LIGHT: JESUS ISSUES A CALL TO RIGHTEOUSNESS (5:13–20)

LITERARY STRUCTURE AND THEMES (5:13–20)

This unit has two short metaphors and one mission statement that serves as an exhortation (Wilkins 2004, 212). It concludes with an exhortation about what God sought from disciples. These snapshots about the believer's mission and character set a tone for what kingdom life should be. There are parallels to the salt imagery in Mark 9:49–50 and Luke 14:34–35. The parallel is conceptual as there is very little verbal overlap between Matthew and these texts. The image of light not being placed under a bushel also has parallels in Luke 11:33 and Mark 4:21. The passage in Matthew 5:17–20 is unique to Matthew as is the city on a hill image. Luke 16:17 and Mark 13:31 are close to Matthew 5:18 but are in distinct contexts.

Jesus used a series of metaphors to explain the disciples' calling. The mission was to be salt and light. Salt was useful as long as it seasoned and preserved. Light was made to shine and not be covered up. So disciples were to be God's effective representatives in the world in a way that showed their distinctive character.

Matthew 5:17 is a mission statement of Jesus (Deines 2004, esp. 447–51). He came to fulfill the law. He did so by drawing others to be responsive to God, so that the law was fulfilled, not abolished. Those who followed Jesus were to walk down the same path of responsiveness to God. The result was an individual and corporate righteousness that was about more than external conforming to a standard. It was about a heart that reflected God's character. So what Jesus said here, he would fill out with examples to follow, where the standard of the law was not merely what its wording precluded, but what character trait was being sought after in its wording (Matt. 5:21–48). The key theme was one that focused on the community's character and mission.

In Matthew 5:17–20 we have a core claim: Jesus came to fulfill the law, not destroy it. We have a supportive idea that the law was valid until the creation passed away and all was fulfilled. The first application was that the law was to be taught and those who taught it were great in the kingdom. A second application was that the righteousness that would bring entry into the kingdom required a righteousness greater than that of the scribes and Pharisees (Davies and Allison 1988, 481). A debated issue is what exactly about the law was in view here. The focus was the law as it related to the development of genuine righteousness as the examples in Matthew 5:21–48 show. It was not focused on the individual stipulations of the law as much as what the law was driving toward in terms of overall character, with Jesus as the key landing place (Deines 2004, 269–80). For this unit serves as the introduction to the examples that follow in Matthew 5:21–48. This does mean that identifying the next section as the six "antitheses" could misname its intent. The contrasts in Matthew 5:21–48 were designed to show what the law was really seeking. The law that Jesus fulfilled did not look to meeting a minimal external standard but made a greater demand to test the heart's core orientation, reflecting a genuine, deep-seated righteousness.

EXPOSITION (5:13–20)

Jesus introduced what disciples are to be and placed it against the common measuring standard for righteousness in Judaism—the law—asking the disciples to be a preservative and to shine out the way of God. Jesus argued that reflecting such righteousness represented the fulfillment of the law. This was not to be measured by stipulations as such, but that every jot and tittle of the law met its match when people's hearts reflected what the law was after in terms of who followers of God were. This would have been controversial for some in Judaism, but the illustrations in 5:21–48 were designed to drive home Jesus's point stated in principle form here. Matthew is showing Jesus was not antinomian or a deceiver at all. Such a charge against him would be false.

As salt and light, disciples were to season the world with a righteousness that shone forth, fulfilled the ethical intent of the law, and reflected the kingdom of God.

5:13. The address to "you" in this verse and the next looks back to the Beatitudes and shows that the disciples were addressed. The second-person plural pronoun "you [all]" (ὑμεῖς) is in an emphatic Greek position as the pronoun leads off both sentences in each verse (Luz 1989, 249). The comparison of kingdom life to salt was discussed because salt has many points of potential comparison. Probably no specific point was in view (Hagner 1993, 99). The point of the image was how salt was a benefit in many ways (Pliny, *Nat.* 31.102: "Nothing is more useful than salt and sunshine"). In most cases, salt combated deterioration (Hendriksen 1973, 282). Jesus's emphasis was on the usefulness of the salt. It had an impact. So a disciple was to be useful. Preservation, seasoning, cleansing, and potential for helping growth were likely all in view. In being the salt of the world, the mission's scope was said not just to be Israel but the entire world (Osborne 2010, 175). Gentile mission is supposed here because of mention of the world. That point extends through verse 16.

What Salt Can Do

- Season
- Preserve
- Purify
- Fertilize

If salt lost its saltiness, it could not regain it. Literally the verb here means "to become foolish" (BDAG s.v. "μωραίνω" 2, 663), suggesting this kind of salty life with impact was a wise way to live (France 2007, 175). If salt no longer functioned as it should, then it was useless and would be tossed out. So the point was to be what you were designed to be, or else you were expendable. What is not so clear is who did the tossing out. Was it God, or was it those among whom its usefulness was designed to function? That point is left unexplained.

The picture was of contributing to that which was wholesome in a society, of preserving its character and keeping the world a "seasoned" place with a good taste. Morris (1992, 104) speaks of being a moral antiseptic. "Disciples are to make the world a better place" (France 2007, 173). "The worse the world becomes and the more its corruption proceeds apace, the more it stands in need of Jesus's disciples" (Carson 1978, 30). The impure salt of Palestine, mixed with gypsum, could lose its saltiness, unlike genuine salt (*TDNT* 1:229). When that happened, it was useless. When it was useless, it no longer had any value.

5:14. The picture of light is an extension of the image of what the Messiah was to the world (Matt. 4:16; John 8:12; 9:5). So those who were a part of his kingdom shared in this role to be light. Light pictured ethical integrity (Matt. 3:8) and was associated with salvation and the mission of God's people as seen in the servant (Isa. 42:6; 49:6; 60:3). Light illumined and was designed to function openly. It was not hidden or covered. In fact, light exposed, it did not conceal, like the city on a hill that could not be covered. Part of being the light was to live in a manner that was distinct from the world and its values. To shine in the midst of darkness was to be distinct. There was an implied critique of the world and of the spiritual leadership of others in this remark. Disciples were needed in the world because light and leadership were lacking otherwise. It may even be that the city on a hill was designed to compare with Jerusalem, which also had a raised locale (Turner 2008, 155). However, the image was generic, as the reference was not to "the" city.

5:15. Jesus then considered the image of a lamp as light. One does not light a lamp and then set it under a bushel to block its light. The lamp would have been an ancient terra-cotta oil lamp.

Photo of a Sample of Ancient Terra-Cotta Lamps.

Technically, the "bushel" would have been a peck measure or measuring bowl that alternatively could be used to cover a lamp, or better, extinguish the lamp (BDAG s.v. "μόδιος" 656). This measure contained about 8.75 liters of space (= 16 sextarii). No, one did not cover the lamp, but it went on a lampstand to light up the entire house. The image not only pictured light as exposing but assumed that light engaged in the world. It shone forth in public.

The passage assumes one does not cover light. Garland (1995, 60) says, "God does not provide a lamp to enlighten the world only to snuff it out with a basket. God sends light to enlighten."

5:16. Jesus made the application, "in the same way" (οὕτως). Disciples were to let their light shine in front of people, so that their good works were evident. A disciple was to be useful and productive. These works were not something to be trumpeted, as Matthew 6:1–18 will make clear. They were simply there as a way of life. But good works were not the only or even main goal of letting one's light shine—the glory of the Father was. The same people who saw and appreciated the good works also thanked God for what was done. These were acts of compassion along with acts that led to peace (Grundmann 1975, 140), as Matthew 5:21–48 will show. Being light brought honor to God. Thus, images of salt and light pictured two related characteristics of disciples that also had an element of tension within them, for in each case their function was not to be extinguished. Disciples were distinct from, yet engaged with, the world. The issue was not control in the sense of power, but an effective presence whose moral quality and integrity had an impact. Osborne (2010, 176) speaks of lifestyle evangelism being in view here (2 Cor. 4:6; Phil. 2:15; Titus 2:8; 1 Peter 2:12, 15). A closeted faith or a self-service approach to life is excluded here (Davies and Allison 1998, 478).

5:17. In a mission statement, Jesus turned his attention to the teaching of the law and the prophets. What Jesus was doing was not a denial or a negation of what Torah taught. Jesus was not antinomian. He explained that he had not come to abolish the law and the prophets. The key term here is καταλῦσαι (BDAG s.v. "καταλύω" 3a, 521–22). The meaning of this term is not so much "to abolish," a sense this word can have, but not "to destroy" (Matt. 24:12; 26:61; 27:40 of the temple). The term when used of a text can mean to annul or repeal, but in effect that is to destroy the text's authority. Jesus was arguing we should not ignore what God has revealed. Even though it may seem Jesus was doing things differently, Jesus did not come to destroy or cancel out what the law and the prophets sought to achieve. What Jesus taught underscored what the law and prophets taught. What Jesus meant here is shown in the illustrations he gives in Matthew 5:21–48. His goal was not to undercut the law, nor was it merely to follow an external standard. It was to urge one to walk with a heart that lived instinctively in light of what the law and prophets taught.

The combination of law *and* prophets may also be important (Nolland 2005, 218). The inclusion of the law and prophets in Matthew 7:12 shows that what was in view was the way of life they together represented. Jesus was in continuity with them in terms of a way of life. Jesus was not thinking of the law as mere statutes or stipulations, but the law was seen through the eyes of the prophets with a call to walk humbly and ethically with God (Mic. 6:8). This perspective included the prioritization that God desired mercy and not sacrifice in the law. The direction of God was to be applied wisely and with depth, not merely as a kind of external measure. There also was an eschatological-promise dimension to the law as tied to the prophets (Matt. 11:13). All of this was likely in play in these remarks (on this text, see Banks 1974).

Jesus sought to fulfill the law and the prophets and not cancel it out. He fulfilled it in the sense that he showed what the law was driving at in terms of the heart (Talbert 2004, 61). Jesus eschatologically brought God's program that made the law's realization possible. The view that the law would be better understood in the eschaton existed in Judaism as well (1 Macc. 4:46).

The law also appears as a unit here. There was no subdividing it into civil and ceremonial (correctly Blomberg 1992, 103). The next verse makes it clear the law was to accomplish something, so law pointing to realization was in view. This remark was about how the law pointed us to righteous character, as the following examples in Matthew 5:21–48 show. That sacrifices were no longer important is argued in other NT works such as Hebrews. That circumcision was no longer important is seen in works like Acts 15 and remarks by Paul in 1 Corinthians 7:19. So there were cultic features of the law that were impacted by what Jesus did and said (Mark 7:19). A text like Galatians 3 also makes this point. Even Matthew makes similar points about the limitation of the law in spots (Matt. 5:32, 34, 39; 15:11; France 2007, 180). France (2007 183) goes on to say it this way: "If in the process it may appear that certain elements of the law are in fact for all practical purposes 'abolished,' this will be attributable not to the loss of status as the word of God but to their changed role in the era of fulfillment, in which it is Jesus, the fulfiller, rather than the law which pointed forward to him, who is the ultimate authority."

5:18. Jesus proclaimed the validity of the law by noting that not one iota of the law should pass away until all the law aimed for was realized. It would abide as long as the creation. The context here is important because Jesus was speaking of how the law pointed to promise and practice. One can think of law in terms of statutes or in terms of its goal of reflecting God's peculiar people who shared in hope, provision, and promise living righteously as a result of God's kingdom benefits. It is mainly the latter versus statutes that serves as the context here.

The reference to jot and tittle pictures the end of certain Semitic letters, which by just removing an edge can change the letter and as a result the word it evokes (Nolland 2005, 220; e.g., dalat (ד) versus resh (ר)). The figure means that the law in its entirety would be realized, down to the last point. The duration of God's word was something that often accompanies a major affirmation about God's will and revelation (Isa. 54:10; Jer. 31:35–36).

5:19. Greatness in the kingdom was determined by how one handled these commandments. If the law abides, as was just claimed in verse 18, then one should keep it and teach others to do so. To loosen or relax one of the least of the ethical standards as represented in the law was to be least in the kingdom. However, the one who did follow the law in this sense and taught others to follow it would be called great in the kingdom. Note the stress here was on not just teaching the law but living out the commandments. Nothing in what Jesus brought or taught altered the ethical dimensions of what the law and prophets sought from God's people. Everything about what was said here argued that the expression "until heaven and earth pass away" (v. 18) looked to something still future. God's ways were still to be followed until the end of history.

5:20. Jesus's point was about ethical or genuine righteousness. That can be seen in his conclusion. One's righteousness must exceed that of the scribes and Pharisees in order to enter God's kingdom. The law was designed not for its own ends, but to lead people into righteousness, to reveal God's standards of living, to be a monitor and litmus test for the heart. The goal of the law was to lead into righteousness. That also was the goal of the kingdom Jesus brought. What this core righteousness looked like was what Jesus developed in the six following illustrations of how to work with the law (Matt. 5:21–48). To see what Matthew 5:17–20 means, we have to look at those examples. It is too often the case in exposition that these verses get cited in a prooftext manner, while excluding those explanatory texts. The examples show an intensification of what the wording of the law pointed to but driving toward the righteousness the law sought. In many ways, the six "antitheses" are actually six "explanations." In that intensified sense, Jesus fulfilled the law and the prophets and showed what the law was really aiming at, developing a righteous heart. Righteousness in this context was "Christian character and conduct in accordance with the demands of Jesus—right intention, right word, right deed" (Davies and Allison 1988, 499). Entering the kingdom meant exactly that. It ultimately took seeking to become righteous in faith to enter the kingdom of God. This is something God helps us to do over time. The expression here meant entering the kingdom in its consummation, after the judgment.

THEOLOGICAL FOCUS

The exegetical idea (as salt and light, disciples were to season the world with a righteousness that shone forth, fulfilled the ethical intent of the law, and reflected the kingdom of God) points toward this theological idea: the disciple's call is to live in a way that shows the character of God, drawing people to the Father.

The merit of God's way and will is the point of the passage, as well as the affirmation that what Jesus was bringing did not alter the standards of God's ways. This means that disciples have a certain calling and character. They are to be a force for good in society, engaging it in ways that preserve society's ethical character. They are to be light by living in a way that shows what real character is. That means that living God's way matters and that such values are the goal of the teaching among those who follow God. Disciples should espouse and live out values that follow in such paths. The result is a genuine righteousness that is to be the hallmark of those who are in the kingdom, behavior distinct from that of the world. This last part of the Sermon on the Mount's introduction affirms this calling. It shows what the aim of Jesus's program was and is. It is not just about salvation, but about what salvation brings. It brings a call to be a new kind of person, living life as God designed it to be lived. It is a life restored to its original intent to image God, to glorify God by how we live, how we manage the affairs of the earth, and what we value. The result is that those in God's creation honor him by living this way.

Jesus's message is not about a freedom that leads to antinomianism. His teaching reflects an effort to fulfill what the law sought from God's people. The emphasis here is on behavior, values, and ethics. This ethical core informs the calling disciples have to be salt and light. That emphasis on behavior and relationships can be seen from the examples that follow in Matthew 5:21–48. Jesus is concerned about a personal integrity that connects to how one relates to God and to others, whether friend or enemy. In fact, how we treat the enemy is what makes it so distinctive (Luke 6:27–36). Instruction should be responsive to the character aims of the law. The result is a righteousness that emanates from within, a heart that beats for God's will and ways. Such faithfulness does not ask what is the least one can do to be obedient, but what best represents God's presence and character.

PREACHING AND TEACHING STRATEGIES

Exegetical and Theological Synthesis

The exegetical section emphasizes the calling of God's people to reflect his character to the world. This was not a new calling but was embedded in Israel's mission to live as a counter-community: a royal priesthood and light to the nations (Exod. 19:3–4; Isa. 42:6; 49:6; 51:4). That she failed in her task is an understatement. John accused religious leaders of putting more stock in their ethnic identity than their ethical performance (Matt. 3:9–10). Jesus rebuked their hypocrisy; their heartless legalism was a pious show (see Matt. 5:21–48; 15:1–20; 23:1–36).

We rob the goodness from "good works" when we do them for the wrong reasons. Jesus's motivation is clear: Good works bolster our witness for God. The most impactful witness will combine words and works. Social activism without any spoken words does not necessarily draw attention to God. Spoken words without activism can come across as insincere (James 2:14–17; 1 John 3:16–18). Long before theologians debated the "faith or works" disjunction between Paul and James, Jesus answered it with a simple: both.

Lest we create another unnecessary disjunction—sincere lawlessness or legalistic duty—Jesus's call for exceeding righteousness likewise bridges the gap. He revealed his supreme respect for the law by insisting his desire to fulfill it. Not feeling like doing the right thing does not exempt us from the obligation to do it. Sometimes good works precede the warm feelings. Sometimes no warm feelings follow. Either way, feelings are often overrated in following Jesus and expose the fickleness of our wandering hearts.

Preaching Idea

Be a force for good, to show the heart of God.

Contemporary Connections

What does it mean?

Believers are often at their best in showing the heart of God when they lend their hands to causes of justice, mercy, and compassion. The early church shared her material wealth with those in need and distributed bread to widows (Acts 4:32–35; 6:1–6). She was known for mobilizing in crisis, caring for abandoned children, burying the dead, and boarding those in need of shelter (Hellerman 2009, 97–119). In more recent times, Christians like William Wilberforce advocated for the abolition of slavery, Martin Luther King Jr. peacefully protested for equal treatment of people of color, and Franklin Graham currently deploys people and resources to fight poverty and help people recover from natural disasters through Samaritan's Purse. In a world with so much bad news, opportunities to do good not only abound but resound. We need to be and exemplify a positive community. Such acts of caring engagement help disciples shine a spotlight on God.

Being a force for good may be a personal endeavor or group effort. Churches preach on the importance of loving neighbor, community service, and maintaining a good testimony at work, online, and among others. They provide community outreach events, short-term mission trips, or partnerships with local schools or non-profit organizations where their members can do good (e.g., homeless shelters, food banks, mentoring programs).

Local nonprofits and faith-based organizations give their full attention to doing good in the world. These include mission agencies, crisis-response networks, global food and water suppliers, and organizations that fight slavery or advance development.

Examples of Force-for-Good Organizations

Samaritan's Purse
World Vision
International Justice Mission
Destiny Rescue
Doctors without Borders
Water for Good
Clean Water

Moreover, many profitable businesses, driven by a desire to show God's heart, have shifted into being forces for good by dedicating part of their proceeds to providing clean water, shoes for children in poverty, or free medical clinics. The diversity of good works is astounding. When matched with godly character, good works are truly radiant.

Is it true?

Is it true we should be a force for good to show the heart of God? Absolutely. Not only did Jesus stress this fact, but the apostle Paul assured believers that they were God's "workmanship, created in Christ Jesus for good works, which God prepared beforehand so that we would walk in them" (Eph. 2:10 NASB). Doing good is in the DNA of every disciple.

However, three cautions are in order. First, we must not be bullish about doing good. When we demand people receive our help, it often hurts our witness and the people we aim to serve (Corbett and Fikkert, 2014). We must not be bullheaded, hasty, or messianic in our efforts to help. Rather, we must match godly character with good works.

Second, we must realize our limits. We can proclaim the kingdom and live as signposts of its coming, but we will not bring it by our good works. Many believers have experienced the sting of defeat after their enthusiastic service returned void. Our good works cannot bring God's kingdom.

Third, we must pay attention to where the spotlight shines. Jesus called disciples to show the heart of God, not to show off. Sometimes church service projects turn into publicity stunts, where (true story) workers spend as much time posing for pictures as they do cleaning up debris from a tornado. When our good works merely expose our attention-seeking hearts, people discount the goodness of the work and do not see God.

Now what?

Being a force for good to show the heart of God will look different for each church and congregation. It requires perspective, prayerful discernment, and personal involvement. Perspective means keeping in mind our part in Jesus's kingdom mission. His invitation to mission implies that we play an important role in showing God's heart to the world, but we must not overreach. Disciples are ambassadors, not saviors; we do not generate light but reflect it.

Prayerful discernment helps us identify where to serve as a force for good. Opportunities for good in our world are endless. We can easily feel overwhelmed by all the needs, resulting in mild paralysis. Or countless needs may cause us to furiously serve until our knuckles bleed. Prayerful discernment helps us commit to works of good where our giftings, resources, and energies best match the need. Individuals and churches should each ask God where he wants them to spread salt and shine his light.

Furthermore, having a focal point for doing good does not exempt us from doing random acts of goodness.

Once a person or congregation has discerned where to be a force for good, they should start doing. Regular involvement will have a greater impact than random acts of good. Thus, disciples should seek out service opportunities or organizations that allow for recurring responsibilities. Weekly mentoring programs, seasonal help at a retirement community, and occasional labor with Habitat for Humanity are examples. Because showing the heart of God is the goal, we must not overlook decisions we make each day to practice hospitality to strangers, charity in conversations, kindness online, and humility among extended family and coworkers. A steady display of good character creates a positive force we cannot possibly calculate.

Creativity in Presentation

Kids can be a force for good. In 2013 *Sports Illustrated Kids* covered a story about a fourteen-year-old, Will Thomas, who raised $100,000 for U.S. veterans by making twenty thousand basketball jump shots. In the interview, Elizabeth Jennings, the sister-in-law of a deceased veteran said, "You don't see a lot of good like this very often."[1] When Katherine Commale was five years old, she began to raise money for mosquito nets to slow malaria in Africa. Ten years later, her efforts afforded her a trip to Taiwan where she was received as a "hero" for doing good. A 2018 feature story in the *Philadelphia Inquire*r reports the girl first appealing to her Sunday school class and eventually moving to the United Nations.[2] While these stories are dramatic and powerful, each pastor could pull from smaller local examples of good from within their congregation. I (Tim) immediately think of an elementary school student named Jacob who reached out to kids with special needs or who struggled socially. He befriended anyone and everyone as a force for good.

Christian efforts at justice can be a force for good. When Martin Luther King Jr. led a peaceful march from Selma, Alabama, to the state capitol in Montgomery, the sea of people embodied a force for good. A moving clip from their march can be found in the film *Selma* (directed by Ava DuVernay, 2014). Every October, Life Chains assemble across the United States, where pro-life proponents link arms and observe silence in defense of the unborn. Images from a Life Chain could be compelling. If these causes are too political for your congregation, consider a good work or justice cause someone from your church engages in. Ask her for a live or recorded interview, where she can share her reasons for getting involved, her passion for the task, the good she sees God doing, and the importance for Christians to be a force for good. Such causes may include clean water, combating human trafficking, crisis response, microfinancing, literacy/career training, medical missions, or foster/orphan care.

To help your people take Jesus's metaphors home, consider the following two ideas. Purchase (or get a donation from a fast-food restaurant) hundreds of 0.6-gram salt packets. Distribute two to everyone in attendance. During the sermon have them break open one packet and taste the salt. Say something like, "This is you. You are salt." Then hold up a twenty-six-ounce salt container, describing it as the collective force of the church. If my math is correct (show me grace, I'm a pastor), one

---

1 See Eli Burnstein, "How a 14-Year-Old Used His Jump Shot to Support the Troops," *Sports Illustrated Kids* (June 13, 2013), accessed Jan. 19, 2021, https://www.sikids.com/the-arena/operation-hawkeye.

2 See Kathy Bocella, "Downington Girl Who Raised Millions for Malaria Nets Treated as a Hero in Taiwan," *Philadelphia Inquirer* (June 30, 2018), accessed Jan. 19, 2021, https://www.inquirer.com/philly/education/katherine-commale-downingtown-girl-malaria-nets-prevention-taiwan-hero-20180630.html.

container equals 1,180 little packets. Declare, "This is us. We are salt. The earth needs you. The earth needs us."

You can pull off a similar illustration using finger flashlights. These gadgets sell for nothing online, but don't feel compelled to buy one for each person in attendance. However, you will want to arrange in advance to have a few people turn on their lights as you cue them. When describing our dark world and calling disciples to shine, you can dim the lights in the auditorium. Have the first volunteer illumine his or her light. Then the second. Then the third. Eventually, invite all those with flashlights (cell phones would work too) to set their lights ablaze. Have people look around the room. Consider saying, "We are light. Darkness fades when we all shine. The world needs you. The world needs us."

Ultimately, the sermon should emphasize that the disciple's call is to live in a way that shows the character of God, drawing people to the Father. Thus, we should be a force for good, to show the heart of God.

- Be a force for good where you live (5:13–16).
- Be a force for good to show God's heart (5:17–20).

DISCUSSION QUESTIONS

1. What is the range of meaning for Jesus's two governing metaphors?

2. How do "good works" relate to public faith? How do social justice movements of the day help or hurt Jesus's call to do good?

3. What role does evangelism or verbal testimony play in our public faith?

4. In what social causes has the church historically had a positive impact? Where are we lacking?

5. What was Jesus's relationship to the Old Testament Law? How did he model his teaching from 5:17–20?

Matthew 5:21–48

EXEGETICAL IDEA

Jesus's exposition of the law pointed to the heart, promoting healthy relationships with everyone, including enemies, and was not merely to be followed in an external way.

THEOLOLGICAL IDEA

True application of the law asks "What kind of righteousness does it seek?"—and then goes there.

PREACHING IDEA

Elaborate love goes above and beyond the law.[1]

PREACHING POINTERS

In the next portion of his Sermon, Jesus offers six case studies for living the heart of the law. His disciples must heed his authoritative voice, not simply subscribe to the teachings and traditions of his day. Matthew's audience would have been familiar with the Mosaic law. They would have heard scribal and Pharisaical interpretations of it. Murder, adultery, and false testimony were known prohibitions. Divorce and retaliation were commonly debated topics. Love for neighbor was a timeless ethic. Jesus did not counter them as much as he elaborated on them, showing how every ethical encounter is an opportunity for love. For Matthew's audience, this message both established Jesus's authority as a superior teacher and clarified the particulars of living the heart of the law.

Religion always attracts moralists and legalists. People love to know the letter of the law so they can recite it. They love to know the line that marks sin from acceptable behavior so they can toe it. Few want to get away with murder, but many are willing to hold a grudge. The depraved heart looks for loopholes and exceptions in the law, so it can make the rules work in its favor, rather than work out its salvation with fear and trembling. We put in just enough hours at work to merit our paycheck. We study just enough for a passing grade. We tell enough of the story to make it "truthy." We spend enough time with our family, avoiding glaring sins, so they cannot accuse infidelity. Meanwhile, we miss the law's ultimate aim: love of God and neighbor. This passage illustrates how elaborate love goes above and beyond the law.

---

1 Pennington (2007, 40) uses similar prepositions to describe the already–not yet ethic of the Sermon on the Mount: "Biblical virtue ethics is also 'from above' (based on divine revelation) and 'from beyond' (based on the hope of the coming eschaton)."

JESUS ISSUES A CALL FOR A GREATER RIGHTEOUSNESS (5:21–48)

LITERARY STRUCTURE AND THEMES (5:21–48)

This unit is built around six examples and a summary. The examples involving murder and adultery are without parallels in the Gospels. The imagery of being placed into jail in the discussion of murder is like Luke 12:57–59, but that context is distinct, not involving personal reconciliation but making reconciliation with God. Conceptual parallels to plucking out the eye and cutting off the hand are in Mark 9:43–47, which is like Matthew 18:8–9. The topic of divorce has several texts where the theme comes up but in ways distinct from what is expressed here. In those other texts there is a contrast between a permission to divorce and a call not to divorce (Matt. 19:3–12; Mark 10:11–12; Luke 16:18). The discussion of oaths is without a direct parallel elsewhere, though Matthew 23:16–22 takes up the topic again. Other parallels exist from Luke 6:29–30, 34, with the examples tied to nonretaliation. The call to love the enemy is paralleled in Luke 6:27–28, 32–33, 35–36, where Luke goes on to speak of lending and doing good, while also appealing to the example of God. *Didache* 1:3–4 also parallels the last example. Hagner (1993, 133) sees enough differences with this Lucan parallel to speak of distinct traditions at work here.

The unit primarily consists of six examples. The core form is to introduce a current saying, and then Jesus says, "But I say to you." This is often followed by an example or illustration. This is done in two sets of three, as the first three categories express the contrast more fully. Jesus came "not to abolish, but to uphold and expound Torah on the basis of the authority which is his" (Loader 1997, 173). The changes Jesus introduced by his authority pressed the law to be realized from the heart. In some cases, a command was directly cited, as was the case with murder and adultery. In these cases, it is clear we are getting an exposition on the law. In other cases, such as with oaths, we are getting a form of traditional teaching, even if it is rooted in the law. In every case, however, Jesus deepened the wording of the law by pointing to the heart issue that law raised. This is not so much a corrective, so that we are dealing with antitheses, as it is an elaboration that seeks to allow the law to speak not to a legal sanction but to the heart. The key theme of the unit revolves around the heart characteristic to which each illustration drives, as righteousness is the goal.

The responses were variously stated. In the first three, we see legal instructions, while in the last three we have straightforward prohibitions (Guelich 1982, 177). These responses were inwardly directed, went beyond specific rules to principles, sought to discover God's will, and pushed for an ideal and deeper level of righteousness (France 2007, 197).

The Six Antitheses/Explanations

- Not murder, but anger
- Not adultery, but lust
- Not divorce, but fidelity
- Not an oath, but truthfulness
- Not eye for eye, but vulnerability and generosity
- Not hating the enemy, but loving the neighbor and enemy

EXPOSITION (5:21–48)

Jesus simply described the righteousness the kingdom sought. He did so through a detailed exposition of what the law was after. There is no antinomianism here, nor any disrespect to the law. Jesus's exposition of the law pointed to the heart, promoting healthy relationships with everyone, including enemies, and was not merely to be followed in an external way.

5:21. Jesus's first example dealt with murder, as he cited the commandment about not killing (Exod. 20:13; Deut. 5:17). Jesus noted the commandment and then observed that it carried a sanction of judgment for one who violated it. The exact wording of the prohibition is not in the Old Testament, but the sentiment is (Exod. 21:12; Lev. 24:17; Num. 35:12; Deut. 17:8–13; Davies and Allison 1988, 511). This idea of murder and judgment was not merely a rabbinic idea. The prohibition comes out of the recognition that life is sacred as people are made in God's image (Gen. 1:26–27; 9:6). The Scripture distinguishes between premeditated murder, which this commandment treated, and manslaughter (Deut. 19:4–6, 8–10), as well as treating the right to self-defense or the government's right to bear the sword (Exod. 22:2; Rom. 13:4).

5:22. The expression "but I say" (ἐγὼ δὲ λέγω) is why many call these six examples the "antitheses." Jesus stated a law and/or tradition and then responded in contrast to it. The response, however, was more of an elaboration than a contradiction to the law, especially given what Jesus said in Matthew 5:17–20 (Wilkins 2004, 240–41). So the name "antitheses" for the list can be a little misleading (Turner 2008, 165, is clear here). Jesus also pointed to his own authority by speaking of what "I" say. This authority disturbed some but reflected his right to determine what the law meant. Jesus was and is Lord of the law, relocating authority over Torah to himself (Bruner 2004a, 208; Davies and Allison 1988, 508; France 2007, 198–99; Hagner 1993, 111; Moo 1984; Turner 2008, 167–68; for the authority this represents, Bock 2020; Bock and Simpson 2016, 104–9). The intensification may well have represented fulfilling every jot and tittle of the law (Matt. 5:18), pointing to the real goal of the law.

In this particular case, Jesus pointed to the real issue not merely being murder but unresolved anger and hateful speech because these things tear down a person like murder does (1 John 3:15). Sanction or legal liability came when one remained angry with a brother. It is important to note that the issue here was harbored anger, as the illustration showed. It was not about a righteous anger that is directed toward injustice or unrighteousness as the prophets discussed (Carson 2010, 182–83).

Beyond anger, careless speech was also condemned by Jesus. Such speech expressed itself in either an insult ("raca") or in belittling that brother ("fool"). It may be that anger can lead ot careless speech. Sirach 22:24 reads, "The vapor and smoke of the furnace precede the fire; so insults precede bloodshed." Talbert (2004, 70) has several Jewish texts that are conceptually parallel. The term "raca" means empty headed or good for nothing, so an insult is in view (BDAG s.v. "ῥακά" 903). Even in such cases one was liable to the council that regulated human affairs and to God's judgment represented by Gehenna as a place of fire (Josh. 15:8; 18:16; 2 Kings 23:10; 2 Chron. 28:3; 33:6; Jer. 7:31–32; Rev. 19:20: 20:14–15; 1 En. 90:24). The punishments were not reflective of an escalation, as the violations were seen as equal. Konradt (2020, 80–82) stresses that the violations (murder, anger, and insult) are equal in their consequences and are not to be seen merely as a sequence that escalates. They are merely varied in pointing to applications applying to the reactions of men and God respectively.

Who was the brother? Was it someone in the Christian community? This seems somewhat unlikely since the sanction included the council, which would be a Jewish institution. Just as the prohibition to murder was not limited to those in the community, insults probably worked the same way. The broad example to follow makes this conclusion likely. This was a prohibition against "every expression of human alienation from and hostility towards another" (Nolland 2005, 231). This exhortation would be especially true in the community but was not limited to it (Gal. 6:10). The brother was someone with whom one had either a spiritual or social bond.

5:23–24. Jesus turned to two illustrations in the following verses. One involved worship at the temple, where Matthew retained a reference to its presence. The second was a legal situation. One looked at a brother, while the other involved an adversary (Carson 2010, 183), showing that Jesus's exhortation was broad, applying across the board (Davies and Allison 1988, 519).

In the worship context, one should not bring an offering to the altar if one knew that a brother had something against him. The idea here is that one had a just claim against you (Hill 1972, 122). One was not to sort out whose fault it was (Turner 2008, 169). All situations were covered in this discussion. Two contrasting situations were treated, whether one was angry with another as in verses 21–22 or the reverse as here, where the fault may lie elsewhere. Regardless, reconciliation was the goal. This is a theme Matthew likes (Matt. 18:6, 10, 12–17, 21–35; also Matt. 6:14–15; Mark 11:25; Rom. 12:18; in the early church, *Did.* 14:2).

In such a case, the gift was to be left at the altar and the brother was to go and be reconciled before completing the offering. The expression "be reconciled" looked to bringing a relationship back into harmony (BDAG s.v. "διαλλάσσομαι" 232). This is the only use of this verb in the New Testament. Here we see Jesus's priority for the disciple was regarding the quality of relationships. One should not pretend to be walking well with God and not be concerned with how one relates to others. Judaism had similar teachings (Isa. 58:2–7). Sirach 34:23 says, "The Most High is not pleased with the offerings of the ungodly, nor for a multitude of sacrifices does he forgive sins." Sirach 34:29 also declares, "When one prays and the other curses, to whose voice will the Lord listen?" Something similar is present in the Mishnah *Yoma* 8:9, "For the transgressions between man and his fellow, the Day of Atonement atones, only if the man will regain the good will of his friend." Jesus placed the responsibility to set things right on the one who may well have done wrong. The text was an example in principle versus being taken literally in that if one were in Galilee or the diaspora it would not apply in its specifics to a temple setting, as it would have taken days to go and find the brother and return to the temple for the sacrifice (Osborne 2010, 191, speaks of an "exaggeration for effect").

Parallel Jewish Teachings on Seeking Reconciliation

Sirach 34:23: "The Most High is not pleased with the offerings of the ungodly, nor for a multitude of sacrifices does he forgive sins."

Sirach 34:29: "When one prays and the other curses, to whose voice will the Lord listen?"

Mishnah, Yoma 8:9: "For the transgressions between man and his fellow, the Day of Atonement atones, only if the man will regain the good will of his friend."

5:25–26. A second illustration followed that filled out the need to be reconciled. One should make friends with one's accuser when one could (Prov. 6:1–5; 25:7b–10). The expression "reach agreement" looked at settling the case with a plaintiff (BDAG s.v. "εὐνοέω" 409) and only appears in the New Testament here. Without such an effort at reconciliation, the alternative was that one would be handed over to the judge and put in prison. Once you were convicted, you would have to pay the very last penny. This was expressed emphatically (οὐ μὴ): you "shall not" come out until you pay it back. A quadrans was a small amount of currency, often translated "penny" to show the force. It equaled two lepta and was a very small unit of money, being 1/64 of a denarius, or a day's wage. The lepta was the smallest level of Roman coin. The point of selecting a smaller level of coin was to say that every last penny to make restitution would be required of the one who did not reconcile, leaving justice to do its work. The normal penalty was twice the value of what was stolen (Nolland 2005, 234).

The assumption in the illustration was that the one bringing the gift had done something wrong that had left him at risk of arrest. The call was to set things right. One should not remain angry and leave the wrong uncorrected. Grudges were not to remain. Relationships were to be restored (Wilkins 2004, 244). It is not so clear this payback was intended in an eschatological direction, as the similar Luke 12:57–59 reflects. This is a distinct context and is personal in focus (correctly Carson 1978, 43), although ultimately God is aware of such violations as well. The picture points ultimately to accountability before God.

The way Jesus juxtaposed his reading of the law with the law was provocative (Davies and Allison 1988, 521). Who could speak so directly of what the law required beyond the wording of the law? This point about the authority Jesus displayed is inherent in the entire exposition of these six examples.

5:27. The second example of deepening the law came from the example involving the prohibition of adultery. There is no parallel to it elsewhere in the Gospels. Jesus began by citing the commandment that one should not commit adultery (Exod. 20:14; Deut. 5:18). As with murder, this was not an exposition of tradition but a direct citation of the law. The point of this law was to protect the integrity of the family unit. Adultery was a crime with victims, not a private act. It was not about consenting adults, as it often is portrayed today, but it was an attack on vows and relationships previously entered into that led to the family's formation and stability. The act was a betrayal of the spouse and any children under the parents' care. As such, it was not merely an individual nor a private act. In these remarks, Jesus lifted up the importance of marriage and the exclusive commitment to another it represented.

Bruner (2004a, 219) notes that anger and lust are both about power and controlling others, by hatred or desire. These are not innocent emotions. The texts on anger and lust also show how deep sin is. Sin resides in the heart's misdirected desires. We have a deep need for what God can supply by his grace.

5:28. Jesus deepened the issue of when the violation occurred. He explained the law's point and dealt with the root sin the law addressed. This is not an antithesis, but an elaboration. There can be adultery without physical contact. To look on a woman to lust after her was also a violation of the marriage vow, reflecting unfaithfulness to the original spouse. The Greek here could mean to look at a woman to lust after her or to draw her into lust (Carson 2010, 184–85; Haacker 1977).

The issue was permitting the look to become a leer. One thinks of James 1:14–15, as sin comes when temptation is allowed to conceive. The entire act of lust points to a dual violation, for there is adultery against the spouse, but there also is making the other woman who is lusted after an accomplice in the act, objectivizing her. So the violation involves three people: the one committing the adultery, the one who wittingly or unwittingly was brought in to share it, and the spouse who was betrayed. God is also in the mix as the marriage vows were before him. When one stares lustfully, the "other person is no longer really a unique human being; she or he is now simply kindling tinder, a thing; a way for one to enjoy oneself, to express oneself, to feel one's powers" (Bruner 2004a, 220).

In the larger culture, men were generally allowed to pursue outside relationships as long as the women involved were not married, but women were not supposed to engage in such relationships, a precept which if followed would have also prevented many such situations from arising (Morris 1992, 117). The difference discloses the patriarchal bent of the ancient society. Jesus's remarks placed the onus on the man in response (Garland 1995, 67).

Judaism also made this kind of association (Davies and Allison 1988, 522), but in a less direct, culpable manner than Jesus did here. Two texts in the Testaments of the Twelve Patriarchs made this association. Testament of Issachar 7:2 says, "I have not had intercourse with any other woman other than my wife, nor was I promiscuous by lustful look." Testament of Isaac 4:53 reads, "Do not look at a woman with a lustful eye." Similar ideas existed also in the Greco-Roman world. Sextus, *Sentences* 233 declares, "Know that you are an adulterer even if you think of committing adultery." Those with a deep ethical sense knew that the heart was corrupted even when the letter of the law was not violated, but Keener (2009, 186) notes many Greco-Roman texts affirmed lust as healthy. Jewish texts saw it as a real threat. Job 31:1 says it this way, "I have made a covenant with my eyes; how then could I entertain thoughts against a virgin?" Sirach 9:8 has, "Turn away your eyes from a shapely woman, and do not gaze at beauty belonging to another; many have been seduced by a woman's beauty, and by it passion is kindled like a fire." Similar to Sirach 9 is Proverbs 6:25: "Do not lust in your heart for her beauty, and do not let her captivate you with her alluring eyes." Sirach 23:6 advises, "Let neither gluttony nor lust overcome me, and do not give me over to shameless passion." Sirach 41:21 speaks of gazing at another man's wife as a cause of shame. It may well be that the tenth and seventh commandments are combined here, since one should not covet another's wife (Turner 2008, 170). The term "to lust/desire" (ἐπιθυμέω) also appears in the tenth commandment (Guelich 1982, 193; Exod. 20:17; Deut. 5:21). The idea of coveting another's wife had a note of taking possession of someone, showing the idea of power being at the heart of lust. Responsibility to avoid this sin was not placed on the woman but on the one who reacted to her inappropriately.

Parallel Jewish and Greco-Roman Teachings on Lust

Testament of Issachar 7:2: "I have not had intercourse with any other woman other than my wife, nor was I promiscuous by lustful look."

Testament of Isaac 4:53: "Do not look at a woman with a lustful eye."

Sirach 9:8: "Turn away your eyes from a shapely woman, and do not gaze at beauty belonging to another; many have been seduced by a woman's beauty, and by it passion is kindled like a fire."

Sirach 23:6: "Let neither gluttony nor lust overcome me, and do not give me over to shameless passion."

***Sextus, Sentences* 233**: "Know that you are an adulterer even if you think of committing adultery."

Jesus's remark again came with the authoritative "I say to you." He did not use "the Lord says" as a prophet would. Jesus's remarks tackled the *laissez-faire approach* to sexuality with a direct challenge and an authority like that of the Word of God itself (Bruner 2004a, 220).

5:29–30. Two parallel illustrations follow that are hyperbole, involving the eye and the hand. The right eye and hand involved the natural favored side and thus were seen as the more valuable (Grundmann 1975, 161). Since the eye led one to act, Jesus referred to eyes and hands as the tools that carried out the sin. In each case, they were a "cause of stumbling," that is, they were the means through which sin was carried out (BDAG s.v. "σκανδαλίζω" 1a, 926). Matthew frequently used the concept of stumbling as a reference for sin (Matt. 11:6; 13:21, 41; 15:12; 16:23; 17:27; 18:6–7, 8–9; 24:10; 26:31–33; France 2007, 205). Jesus said it was better to separate oneself from these members than to end up in hell. Radical sacrifice was required to avoid sin (Hagner 1993, 121; Turner 2008, 170). The point of the hyperbole was that one should distance oneself from that which causes one to go into sin (so also Philo, *Plant.* 36–38; Talbert 2004, 76).

The verse also highlighted the accountability to God for such acts. Such sin rendered people culpable before the God who judges. Matthew 18:9 is parallel conceptually (Mark 9:47). This point about judgment showed how serious such sin was. A similar idea is found in Colossians 3:5–6, where one was to "put to death whatever in your nature belongs to the earth" that led to death. In fact, Colossians may well be a rendering of the principle Jesus made here with its explicit application. One was responsible for how one's body acted and what it did (Davies and Allison 1988, 526).

These first two examples dealt directly with the law, not tradition. They also did not revoke the law, but did "radicalize and internalize" it (Meier 1976, 136). Anger and lust were just as serious flaws as murder and adultery. They attacked others in similar ways.

5:31. Jesus now turned to the issue of divorce as his third topic. From here on in the listing we deal with acts, not just attitudes (Hagner 1993, 122). This verse merely cites Deuteronomy 24:1 and 3, which notes that with a divorce, one can provide a writ of divorce, freeing the spouse from the marital bond and its obligations. The writ was a form of legal protection and provision for the divorced woman (Talbert 2004, 63). The cause was "something offensive in her" according to Deuteronomy. This writ in the first century came with a statement of the right to remarry (*Giṭ.* 9:1–3; see chart below for 9:1). It was not permitted for the divorcing husband to remarry the ex-wife. Grounds for divorce in Judaism were debated, with Rabbi Shammai limiting divorce to immorality of various sorts, including certain shameful public acts (like letting one's hair down in public), while Hillel allowed it for spoiling a meal and Akiba for finding a more beautiful woman (*Giṭ.* 9:10). Generally only men could get a divorce in Second Temple Judaism, although in some contexts the opposite may have been possible (Philo, *Spec.* 30; Josephus, *A.J.* 15.259–60; the Elephantine community; Papyrus Se'elim 13; Talbert 2004, 80). For Jesus, the complaint was that divorce was not merely "a matter of course" (Loader 1997, 175). It was not a given right. Nor should the women be seen as property who could be cast aside, since the vow had value and represented a breach of a commitment made to another person before God that had continual moral weight (Grundmann 1975, 163).

This topic of divorce has several parallels: Matthew 19:3–12, Mark 10:11–12, and Luke 16:18. There are a few differences in these accounts, but the main difference involves Matthew's inclusion of sexual immorality as an exception for the prohibition of divorce that Mark and Luke do not mention. The law of divorce reflected a flaw in human relationships and did not need to be invoked. In that sense Jesus intensified the law as in the previous examples. Marriage was designed to be permanent and stable. The intensification makes it likely the remark, including the exception, does go back to Jesus, despite opinions to the contrary. This teaching did radicalize the law by asking someone to honor his vow, even though conditions for divorce were present in the law. More than this, Paul knew Jesus's teaching, as he made clear in 1 Corinthians 7, and an absolute statement by Jesus with no qualifications would well have kept Paul from including unbeliever desertion as an additional exception, unless exceptions existed going back to Jesus. Better to see the emphasis of Mark and Luke on no qualifications as stressing the main point Jesus was making: marriage was supposed to be for life.

In sum, there are four results when all these texts are put together (McNeile 1915, 65): (1) the man who divorces (except for immorality) and marries another commits adultery; (2) the woman who divorces her husband and marries another commits adultery (Mark 10:11–12); (3) the man who marries a divorced woman commits adultery; (4) the man who divorces his wife (except for immorality) forces her to commit adultery. Note how the assumption here was that the woman was likely to remarry, which was the social reason one gets a divorce to begin with, because that divorce put one into a position to remarry.

Example of a Divorce Writ from Mishnah, *Giṭṭin* 9:1 (Neusner, ed.)

A. He who divorces his wife and said to her, "Lo, you are permitted [to marry] any man except for so-and-so"—
B. R. Eliezer permits [the woman to be divorced on such a condition].
C. And sages forbid it.
D. What should he do [in such a circumstance]?
E. He should take it back from her and go and give it to her again, and say to her, "Lo, you are permitted to marry any man."
F. But if he wrote it into the body of the document.
G. even if he blotted it out,
H. [the writ remains] invalid.

5:32. Jesus's response remarked that divorce for any cause other than πορνεία ("immorality") will lead into adultery on the assumption of a remarriage.

The meaning of the exception has been much discussed. Is it adultery only, any form of sexual immorality, or is it a reference to a particular type of sin like incest? The term itself is most often a general reference to all forms of sexual immorality (BDAG s.v. "πορνεία" 854; Janzen 2000; Nolland 2005, 245; Osborne 2010, 200). It was broader than adultery, which had its own specific word. It also was the word normally used for female activity, so both genders are brought into the remarks here (Bauer 1980; Blomberg 1992, 111). Adultery applied to the act of either partner. Incest seems too technical a reference and has no support in the subsequent reading of the early church. So the exception was most likely a reference to a variety of forms of infidelity, with adultery being the most common example. Except in such cases of infidelity, divorce led into adultery with a remarriage likely. Jesus's real point was that marriage was designed to be permanent, as the discussion in Matthew 19:1–12 shows. It was important to note that Judaism required divorce for adultery (*Yebam.* 2:8; *Sotah* 5:1; Bockmuehl 1989). Jesus merely excluded that requirement from applying to his remarks about marriage. Even in such a case, for Jesus, a choice to remain in the marriage was present.

The act of divorce forced another to commit adultery. The point was important. Divorce had consequences for others. The assumption here was that one would remarry as the divorce writ permitted it. There was no such thing as a "no consequences" divorce. In addition, to marry a divorced woman was to commit adultery. In each case, the original vow and commitment was seen to still be in force and each spouse was seen to have value so that the oath before God to each other should be kept. In Mark 10:11, the act of divorce led the one who divorces into adultery because he or she also was seen as likely to remarry. That a real exception is in view is likely. In fact, the best way to think of this saying is that Jesus "probably intended [this saying] to be more haggadic than halakic; that is, its purpose was not to lay down the law but to reassert an ideal and make divorce a sin, thereby disturbing then current complacency" toward divorce (Davies and Allison 1988, 532). This kind of reading fits the way in which hyperbole has been working throughout the sermon. The point was to gain the embrace of a righteous standard versus writing more law (Keener 2009, 190–92).

5:33. Jesus's fourth topic involved oaths. It has no parallel in the other gospels. It may be no accident that this followed the urging to keep a marriage vow. Here the cited law taught not to break an oath, but to fulfill the vows one made to God. Vows prohibited the use of something, while an oath required someone to do something (Guelich 1982, 213). The command about oaths came from ideas in texts like Exodus 20:7, Leviticus 19:12, Numbers 30:3–15, and Deuteronomy 23:21–23, but without matching the wording of any of these texts. Oaths tied to the name of God were discussed in Deuteronomy 6:13 and 10:20. Sometimes oaths were required in the law (Exod. 22:11; Num. 5:19–21; France 2007, 214). So this was a summary of oath commands versus being a single citation (Wilkins 2004, 247). As such, it was still law and not tradition that is being cited. The law made a point about integrity, keeping your word and vows. Jesus heightened this demand in ways others also affirmed (Philo, *Decal.* 34–35 is similar in force). Philo went on to speak of how swearing brought suspicion of a person's trustworthiness and that those who swore an oath a lot raised the issue of false swearing (Talbert 2004, 85; Philo, *Decal.* 84, 92). So Jesus's prohibition of oaths got at this problem. The language of keeping vows parallels Psalm 50:14.

Josephus speaks of the integrity of the Essenes by saying, "They say that one who is not believed without an appeal to God stands condemned already" (Wilkins 2004, 247; Josephus, *B.J.* 2.135). Sirach 23:9–11 reads, "Do not accustom your mouths to oaths; nor habitually utter the name of the Holy One, for as a servant who is constantly under scrutiny will not lack bruises, so also the person who always swears and utters the Name will never be cleansed from sin. The one who swears many oaths is full of iniquity, and the scourge will not leave his house." James 5:12 basically repeats Jesus's teaching. Qumran had a hesitation about most oaths, although one was required for entrance into the community (CD 15:1–6; 1 QS 5:7–8; 6:27; 11QTa 53–54; Turner 2008, 173). So what Jesus said fit into the ethos of first-century Judaism.

A Jewish Parallel on Oaths

Sirach 23:9–11: "Do not accustom your mouths to oaths; nor habitually utter the name of the Holy One, for as a servant who is constantly under scrutiny will not lack bruises, so also the person who always swears and utters the Name will never be cleansed from sin. The one who swears many oaths is full of iniquity, and the scourge will not leave his house."

5:34a. Jesus's response was not to take an oath at all, because one's word should be good enough so that oaths were not necessary (see Matt. 5:37). If someone was honest and was known for it, what need was there for oaths? Jesus then proceeded through a list of things not to swear by as one took an oath: by heaven, by earth, toward Jerusalem, and by one's own head (other substitutes appear in Matt. 23:16–22).

5:34b–36. Jesus noted four substitutes one should not swear by as a way of circumventing an oath. Now sometimes a substitute was given because God's name was no longer pronounced out of respect for God. At other times God was not directly invoked to keep the oath from being binding. Either way, to invoke an oath in a name other than God's did not change the nature of the oath as binding. So Jesus began by saying one should not invoke heaven, because it is God's throne. The pointing to God was a reminder that he is watching and we are accountable to him. Creation is connected to him. Jesus's point was not so much to abrogate the law (but so Meier 1976, 152–56) as to treat the law on oaths as unnecessary by making the requirement for honesty stricter (Loader 1997, 176).

It had become common to avoid the point of an oath by invoking something other than God. So important was this area to Judaism that entire tractates of the later Mishnah were named "oaths" (*Ševu'ot*) and vows (*Nedarim*). Jesus was simplifying all of this. There was no such thing as a nonbinding oath (Davies and Allison 1988, 536). He also was suggesting that to invoke something associated with God as a way around an oath was to dishonor God by suggesting a separation from God, a secularization that does not really exist (Hagner 1993, 128). Jesus's connecting these circumlocutions for God to him meant that making this invocation should be binding, so it was better not to do it and just let your yes or no mean what it said. The role of all his explanations in Matthew 5:34b–36 was to show God was still involved with these less sacred categories. Heaven as God's throne is an OT idea (Ps. 11:4; 99:5; Isa. 66:1; Lam. 2:1). Earth was the realm over which he ruled as Creator (also Isa. 66:1). Jerusalem was the city of his rule and presence. These images were all connected to God as the great king (Pss. 47:2; 48:2; 95:3). Literally the reference was to swear "toward" (εἰς) Jerusalem, but the idea was still to invoke a substitute for God. It may picture the idea of facing toward Jerusalem as one made the oath (Hill 1972, 126; McNeile 1915, 68; Tosefta, *Ned.* 1). An oath in one's own name was also futile because one did not control life. One cannot make their hair black or white (note Matt. 6:27; 10:31). So to invoke oneself was to invoke someone with no authority over the accountability of the oath. Jesus said that all of this was best avoided.

Negating an Oath by Swearing by:

- Heaven
- Earth
- Jerusalem
- One's own head

The text perhaps should not be overinterpreted to be an absolute prohibition as much as a counter-exhortation to be honest as the next verse shows (France 2007, 216–17; Nolland 2005, 252; Wilkins 2004, 248). Not only did Matthew 5:37 point in this direction but other texts show oaths being undertaken, even by God (Luke 1:73; Acts 2:30; Rom. 1:9; 2 Cor. 1:18, 23; Gal. 1:20; Phil. 1:8; 1 Thess. 2:5, 10; Heb. 6:13–20; Rev. 10:6). Jesus himself responded to an oath in Matthew 26:63–64.

5:37. So Jesus urged that our affirmations alone should be good enough. One's yes should mean yes, just as one's no should mean no. There is discussion of the double reference to yes and no invoking a kind of oath, but that seems unlikely given the contrast that was involved here throughout the sermon.

Anything more said was coming "from the evil one" or "from evil." The expression (ἐκ τοῦ πονηροῦ) is ambiguous because as either a neuter or masculine, it can refer to abstract evil or the evil one. To add to the integrity of what one said moved in the direction of deception and was not worthy of the kingdom of God, but reflected evil, even perhaps the devil (John 8:44, where the devil is the father of lies; see also Matt. 5:39; 6:13; 13:19, 38). If Matthew 13:19, 38–39 are guides, then Jesus has personalized this remark. But Matthew 5:39 looks like a reference to evil. By alluding to the evil either way, Jesus connected this integrity to loyalty toward God.

5:38. The issue of private retaliation was Jesus's fifth topic. Here he cited the idea of an eye for an eye and a tooth for a tooth.

You got what you gave. The citation recalls Exodus 21:24, Leviticus 24:20, and Deuteronomy 19:21. Jesus's topic involved a legal setting and the issue was about gaining justice. These OT texts were referred to as the *lex talionis*, or law of retaliation, an old idea of justice going back to the law of Hammurabi ## 196–200 from the eighteenth century B.C. The equality in the retribution of the eye-for-eye law was designed to prevent seeking an excessive punishment or disproportionate revenge in the pursuit of justice (Guelich 1982, 224; Turner 2008, 174). These laws sought "proportional justice" applied to "cases of physical harm" (Nolland 2005, 255, who argues this was the goal more than preventing excessive punishment). Jewish culture came to allow the altering of the physical punishment with a monetary recompense (Josephus, *A.J.* 4.280). It was a common cultural teaching (Jub. 4:31–32; 11QTa 61:10–12). The underlying issue was personal retaliation or vengeance.

5:39. Jesus's response was that one does not respond in kind. One resisted evil with good. Other texts also make this point. Leviticus 19:18 says not to take vengeance nor hold a grudge against a countryman, but to love one's neighbor. Deuteronomy 32:35 leaves vengeance to God. Proverbs 20:22 says not to repay evil but to wait on the Lord for deliverance. Proverbs 24:29 says not to pay back in kind. Isaiah 50:6 describes enduring persecution and rejection as giving the back to those who strike and the cheek to those who pull out the beard. At Qumran, 1QS 10:18–19 speaks of pursuing evil with good. The teaching left its mark on the church, as 1 Peter 2:20–23 shows. The idea reaches back to the meek, merciful, and peacemakers of the Beatitudes. Blomberg (1992, 113) notes that the goal is to break the normal "chain of evil action and reaction that characterizes human relationships."

OT Texts on Not Taking Vengeance and Leaving It to God

Leviticus 19:18: "You must not take vengeance or bear a grudge against any of your people, but you must love your neighbor as yourself."

Deuteronomy 32:35: "I will get revenge and pay them back at the time their foot slips; for the day of their disaster is near, and the impending judgment is rushing upon them!"

Proverbs 20:22: "Do not say, 'I will pay back evil!' Wait for the Lord, so that he may vindicate you."

Proverbs 24:29: "Do not say, 'I will do to him just as he has done to me; I will pay him back according to what he has done.'"

Resistance of evil in terms of personally retaliating to an act was be avoided. One could well say: do not resist the evil person's act in terms of retribution. First Thessalonians 5:15 says not to repay evil for evil, but evil with good. In this context, the remark was not about resisting the evil one (correctly Hagner 1993, 131, versus Bruner 2004a, 250). In effect, Jesus was abrogating the *lex talionis* (Guelich 1982, 224; Meier 1976, 157–61). There was more than intensification of the law here. To apply it this way was to not seek recompense, even though it was merely a denial of exercising one's rights. This contrast, along with the one on oaths, ended up restricting what the law allowed. One might have the right to do something, but that did not mean it was wise to use that right. The assumption behind letting revenge go was that God would perform justice one day. To respond this way was an act of faith.

Four illustrations followed to make Jesus's point comprehensively. They involved an insult, going to court, being drafted by a soldier, and being asked for money either through begging or borrowing (by splitting the last example, Turner 2008, 175, speaks of five illustrations). In moving beyond the original saying's legal context, Jesus showed he was presenting a general ethic (Nolland 2005, 257–58). Parts of Luke 6:27–36 overlap with this teaching (especially vv. 29–30, 34). *Didache* 1:4–5 is very close to this passage as well. Davies and Allison (1988, 539–40) argue the writer of *Didache* knew Matthew. Luke and Matthew were aware of the same teaching too. So what Jesus taught here left an impact. The intent was probably to break a cycle of violence.

The first illustration involved a slap on the right cheek, a sign of rejection (B. Qam. 8:6). One remained vulnerable and so the other cheek was left exposed. Insult and rejection, possibly involving persecution, were in view. Isaiah 50:4–9 comes to mind here (Job 16:10; Lam. 3:30). One did not seek such suffering but remained open to it. So one was unselfish and willing to suffer the loss of personal rights (Heb. 10:34). One was not to trade insult for insult. There was to be no counter-self-assertion. Jesus was not renouncing the Old Testament here; he is advocating not exercising a right it permits (correctly Keener 2009, 196).

This exchange took place at a personal level. The call was to be personally magnanimous in the face of insult, litigation, exploitation, and being taken advantage of (Bruner 2004a, 252). Justice from God and legal enforcement through social institutions like the state, which has the right of the sword, were not addressed in these examples. This was also not dealing with situations where the injustice involves others and standing up for them (Bruner 2004a, 205). The law and the pursuit of social justice have their place. One can be a policeman or a soldier (Carson 1978, 49–51; Talbert 2004, 92–93). Jesus was focused here on personal self-assertion and rights, applying the text in this larger, personal-relational context, not merely in the context of legal matters (Betz 1995, 277–85; Loader 1977, 177).

5:40. The second illustration involved being sued for a tunic (inner garment) and probably assumed it was for good cause. This was a specific legal setting, indicated by the term κριθῆναι ("to sue"), and was not a case where there was robbery (BDAG s.v. "κρίνω" 568, 5aβ). One then offered the cloak (outer garment) as well. The normal procedure was to offer the inner garment for collateral against the claim made for an outer garment; nothing more was required, as a person had the right to an inner garment (Exod. 22:26; Deut. 24:13; Carson 1984, 156). The point was that rather than responding in kind, with a countersuit, one was to remain vulnerable. The allusion was to the two garments men wore, an outer and inner garment. This "inner garment" could also act as a cover from the evening cold and was protected from being taken in a legal context (BDAG s.v. "ἱμάτιον" 2, 475; Guelich 1982, 222; Wilkins 2004, 250). This act of offering the inner garment involved a suspension of the pursuit of one's rights. It was clearly a hyperbolic illustration designed to make the point vividly about the nonassertion of rights (Talbert 2004, 91). Jesus experienced this in his own suffering to come (Matt. 26:67; 27:35). First Corinthians 6:7 also applies the idea expressed here, yet another example of an epistle applying the ideas here concretely.

5:41. The third illustration was if someone forced you to go a mile with them, you were ready to go two. The forcing to go a mile or two was about being impressed for service by a soldier. The key term here is "to force." It looked to being pressed into service for something or being requisitioned (BDAG s.v. "ἀγγαρεύω" 7). Matthew 27:32 and Mark 15:21 are examples. This looked to a citizen who is faithful, an important remark in the context of Roman presence and occupation, since a mile was a Roman way of measuring distance (Hill 1972, 128). This is something a Zealot would never have done. The response reflected a willingness to go beyond what was asked.

5:42. The fourth illustration was that one gave to someone who begged and offered to someone who sought to borrow. One acted on the side of generosity and availability. This is a theme in the Old Testament, since many passages point to such generosity, especially when it comes to almsgiving (Exod. 22:25; Lev. 25:36–37; Deut. 15:7–11; Prov. 28:27; Davies and Allison 1988, 547). One did not seek equity but went the extra step to reach out to another. All the illustrations moved in this direction. The disciple was to be generous and non-retaliatory.

OT Texts on Care for the Poor and Resources

Exodus 22:25: "If you lend money to any of my people who are needy among you, do not be like a moneylender to him; do not charge him interest."

Leviticus 25:36–37: "Do not take interest or profit from him, but you must fear your God and your brother must live with you. You must not lend him your money at interest and you must not sell him food for profit."

Deuteronomy 15:7–8: "If a fellow Israelite from one of your villages in the land that the Lord your God is giving you should be poor, you must not harden your heart or be insensitive to his impoverished condition. Instead, you must be sure to open your hand to him and generously lend him whatever he needs."

Proverbs 28:27: "The one who gives to the poor will not lack, but whoever shuts his eyes to them will receive many curses."

More important than the specific examples here was the general emphasis being called for by the accumulation of the examples. One needs to recognize the hyperbole present, or else one is left to walk the streets unclothed if one presses the second example (correctly Keener 2009, 195–96). Jesus was teaching about a certain kind of character, not writing more law. He was forcing his disciples to think in unselfish and non-retaliatory terms. This is an exposition about the heart. The examples all point to the greater righteousness he urged at the end of the discussion in Matthew 5:48 (France 2007, 218).

5:43. The sixth and final topic of Jesus's exposition dealt with love and hate. The command to love the neighbor was from Leviticus 19:18 (Matt. 19:19; 22:39; Rom. 13:9–10; Gal. 5:14). James 2:8 calls this the royal law. In Leviticus, it is clear that a neighbor was one's own countryman or kin. This raised the issue of whether there was such a thing as a non-neighbor. What Jesus said will make clear that such exclusion was not a reflection of God's will. A sense of ethnic or ethical loyalty or patriotism might have created such a distinction, but Jesus was not going to go there.

The call to hate your enemy has no specific text. One perhaps can find texts that reflect its attitude, such as Psalm 137:8–9, but no text directly says to hate your enemy (texts that show a rejection of the enemy are Deut. 7:2; 20:16; 23:3–4, 7; 30:7; Pss. 26:4–5; 139:19–22). Jesus was citing a prevalent attitude among humans. So strong was this that loving one's enemy is complained about in 2 Samuel 19:6–7. The "us and them" nature of the command is clear. It was this division that Jesus would reconfigure. On the other side, one has to note spots in the Old Testament where there is a move in a more conciliatory direction (Exod. 23:4–5; Prov. 24:17, 29). So, although one could and did move in a direction to reject the enemy; it was not a given in the Old Testament.

OT Teaching on Care for the Neighbor

Exodus 23:4–5: "If you encounter your enemy's ox or donkey wandering off, you must by all means return it to him. If you see the donkey of someone who hates you fallen under its load, you must not ignore him, but be sure to help him with it."

Proverbs 24:17: "Do not rejoice when your enemy falls, and when he stumbles do not let your heart rejoice."

Proverbs 24:29: "Do not say, 'I will do to him just as he has done to me; I will pay him back according to what he has done.'"

When it came to love, prayer, and care, there was to be no us and them. Jesus heightened or surpassed the call to love only one's neighbor and countryman to a call to love all. There were no non-neighbors, something Luke taught in presenting Jesus's parable of the Samaritan (Luke 10:25–37). This was the better righteousness of Matthew 5:20 (Davies and Allison 1988, 550). When Jesus called for love of the enemy, he was not revoking the law, since there was no such specific command (Meier 1976, 138–39). He was reversing a common attitude. In doing so, he also set up the mission to Gentiles, who often were seen as enemies, given they were polytheists as well as often hostile to Israel (Hendriksen 1973, 313).

The next unit starting in v. 44 is full of pairs with two commands, two acts of the Father, two types of people repeated in a pair itself and tied to two rhetorical questions (Davies and Allison 1988, 548). All of this made the unit easier to recall, given it was said in an oral culture. So, we have the old commands, Jesus's response, a reason, rhetorical reflection, and a conclusion that both completed this exhortation and also completed the entire exposition for the kind of character God required.

5:44–45. Jesus's response was to love even the enemy and pray for those who persecuted you. The "us and them" was dissolved in this response. Gundry (1982, 97) notes Jesus's remarks as a whole challenge to anger, lust, divorce, oaths, standing up for your rights, and hatred. This involved a love for those outside the circle, seeking to draw them nearer to God and seeking to reduce the tension that comes from being on the opposite side. The command to love is in a present tense (ἀγαπᾶτε), calling for an ongoing love. The plural for enemies made the command wide in scope. As the following verses made clear, this love involved doing good for, praying for, and greeting those who were your enemies. Jesus was not calling for a mere inner feeling but for concrete, applied action. This idea is presented throughout the New Testament (Luke 23:34; Acts 7:60; Rom. 12:14, 17–20; 1 Cor. 4:12–13; Gal. 6:10; 1 Thess. 5:15; James 2:8; 1 Peter 3:9). Davies and Allison (1988, 551) also note OT, Jewish, and Greco-Roman parallels to the call to show concern for enemies, such as Exodus 23:4–5, or the example of God's care for the Ninevites in Jonah 4:10–11, but this was not as explicit and comprehensive as what Jesus called for here, as they also note (also Exod. 23:4–5; Lev. 19:33–34; Deut. 10:18–19; Prov. 25:21–22; Sir. 4:10; T. Zeb. 7:2). The scholarly discussion of this entire unit notes many parallels to all the ideas expressed, but the combination and force of what Jesus said and how emphatically he said it is unique to him.

When it comes to praying for those who persecute you, two examples from the New Testament stand out: Luke 23:34 and Acts 7:60. Jesus did what he taught and so did Stephen. Old Testament and Jewish precedent also existed for this idea (Ps. 35:11–14; T. Jos. 18:2; 1QapGen ar 20:28–29; Talbert 2004, 95).

Matthew 7:12 comes back to this idea in the form of what came to be called the Golden Rule. As the illustration that follows argues, all are cared for and served by what God does. God has the sunshine for all (Ps. 145:9) and brings the rain to the evil and good and to the righteous and unrighteous (Wis. 15:1—God's mercy on all). The order is chiastic: evil, good, just, unjust. God cares for all of humanity. So by caring for all, one shows sonship in a character that mirrors the Father. God the Creator is the standard for our own character, as Matthew 5:48 also says in wrapping up both this topic and capping off the entire discussion of Matthew 5:21–48 (France 2007, 224;

Nolland 2005, 263; also Eph. 5:1–2; 1 John 4:7–12; 1 Peter 1:13–25). This also showed the way to peace as Matthew 5:9 describes, but the call to love was not contingent on a response. That was because it was to reflect God's character and take the initiative to love.

Now such love does not mean ethical indifference, as Matthew 23 shows Jesus confronting those he loves (France 2007, 226). Love engages not only with acceptance and a greeting but with reflection and challenge for that which is really best for people. One should not confuse love with an unqualified acceptance of all a person does or says. Toleration can sometimes reflect indifference or dismissal of someone. Love is more discriminating and discerning than merely turning a blind eye to things that are destructive or that undercut human well-being. Jesus's concept "of love is apparently not at the level of simply being nice to people or allowing error to go unchallenged. Love is not incompatible with controversy and rebuke" (France 2007, 226). The old adage that God loves the sinner but hates the sin applies here (Wilkins 2004, 253). It is a mistake to equate acceptance of a person with acceptance of an act that a person performs that is damaging to others and himself. There also is a difference between relating to all as made in the image of God, which is the basis for this call to love, and accepting their actions they take that can be challenged. The application is to serve and pray for enemies and do good to them, but this does not mean nonengagement at those points where a loving challenge might be appropriate.

5:46–47. Jesus asked a set of rhetorical questions around two actions that called for disciples to be distinct from the world by how they lived. He asked, if you only love those who love you and only greet brothers, how is that different from tax collectors and Gentiles? It is not, because even tax collectors and Gentiles do this. The use of ὀυχί in the question expected a positive reply. The clear implication is that disciples are to be different. In fact, the scope of this love including enemies is what makes the disciples different. Without it, there is nothing distinctive about the community's love. Matthew 5:20 has disciples doing more than the scribes and Pharisees, while these verses have them doing more than ordinary people. There is no reward, or better credit, in doing what everyone does. The idea here is not eschatological, but practical (Osborne 2010, 213).

The remark worked with cultural stereotypes in that tax collectors and Gentiles were not respected as people (*Sanh.* 3:3; B. Qam. 94b). So the example was that if those who lived differently and poorly did these minimal things, what was so distinctive about that? Jesus urged his audience to look different from the world by how they loved. The tax collectors were the tax farmers who collected the indirect taxes for the Romans and, as Jews, were seen as collaborators with the Romans and so were despised (Davies and Allison 1988, 558; Donahue 1971; BDAG s.v. "τελώνης" 999). The use here fits the negative cultural perception of these groups within Judaism, which Jesus was using for illustrative purposes, but Jesus involved himself with tax collectors (Matt. 9:10–11; 10:3; 11:19; 21:31–32; Luke 18:9–14; 19:1–10). There was no contradiction here in referring to tax collectors in this way. Neither was there a contradiction in using Gentiles as an illustration here from a cultural perspective, "taking advantage of their bad popular image," even though Jesus urged outreach to Gentiles (Nolland 2005, 269). His use of this perspective said that if even those whom we do not see as exemplary live this way, then what kind of a standard is that? He taught and insisted that disciples should be better than that. He also called Gentiles to come to God and change the way they live in the process.

The idea of greeting others was common in Judaism as a sign of general respect (*m. 'Abot.* 3:13; 4:15; Davies and Allison 1988, 559). Jesus's example then picked out those who hold to a low standard. The greeting was not a mere hello, but a kind of well-wishing toward others, "spending time in a warm exchange" (BDAG s.v. "ἀσπάζομαι" "to greet," 1a, 144). In parts of Judaism, greeting Gentiles was seen as wise to maintain an environment for peace (*m. Giṭ.* 5:9: "Greetings may be offered to Gentiles in the way of peace") or as an appropriate courtesy to another human (*m. 'Abot.* 4:15: "Be first in greeting every creature"). The Jewish greeting was of peace or *šālôm*, so it was a kind of invocation (Morris 1992, 133). However, at Qumran, hating those opposed to the light was commanded (1QS 1:9–11).

5:48. Jesus concluded this section of the sermon with a summation of both this sixth point and the list as a whole. A disciple's character was to reflect the Father. One was to be perfect or wholly mature, as God is. One was to be perfect as the Father is perfect. God's children were to reflect the values of the head of the house. The exhortation here is like Leviticus 19:2, to be holy as God is, and Deuteronomy 18:13, to be "blameless" before God, which the LXX renders with the term Matthew uses (τέλειος). This use shows the force of the term as pointing to a person who is whole or without flaws, mature, loving without limits. It was not sinlessness but a moral integrity and "approximating God's benevolence: that is the point" (Davies and Allison 1988, 562; Turner 2008, 177; 1 Cor. 2:6; 14:20; Phil. 3:15). Godliness mirrored God, revealing his character and presence to others.

Application: Examining Heart Integrity

Moving from murder to dealing with anger
Moving from adultery to dealing with lust
Moving from divorce to keeping our commitments
Moving from taking oaths to having a word that needs no oath
Moving from legal equity and retaliation to vulnerability and generosity
Moving from hating enemies to loving and praying for them

THEOLOGICAL FOCUS

The exegetical idea (Jesus's exposition of the law pointed to the heart, promoting healthy relationships with everyone, including enemies, and was not merely to be followed in an external way) leads to this theological focus: true application of the law asks "What kind of righteousness does it seek?"—and then goes there.

The ethical standards that are to drive the disciple include reflecting God's character, having a pure heart that seeks reconciliation, integrity, purity, generosity, vulnerability, truth, and a way of life that is distinct from the way the world lives. That distinctiveness emerges and stands out when disciples love their enemies.

This unit is about the law, gospel, ethics of disciples and the kingdom, as well as picturing Jesus's authority. Jesus showed his sense of authority by the way he independently handled the law. This was not a rabbinic-like figure, who listed what other rabbis said. Here was a Jesus who said, "But I say to you." What we also see is an intensification of the law, getting at the righteousness the law was driving at. Ethics for a disciple in the kingdom examines the heart and not the mere standard that the wording of the law sets. As a result, we move from murder to anger, from adultery to lust, from divorce to keeping our commitments, from taking oaths to having a word that needs no oath, from legal equity and retaliation to vulnerability, generosity, and graciousness. We move from hating enemies to loving and praying for them. The moves here point to the attitude that drives action. Jesus's goal here was not to put forward a new set of legal rulings. That reading of these examples misses the way Jesus illustrated his points. Rather, he was driving at positive core attitudes that are to be at the heart of the disciple by being in and from the heart.

Three key standards drive the disciple in this ethical call: God's character, a pure heart, and a way of life that is distinct from the way the world lives. Jesus appeals to all three levels in making his point. To live in the way Jesus calls for here is to reflect God's character, mirror his righteousness, and possess integrity that is greater than that of the scribes and Pharisees. That differentiation also is distinct from how tax collectors and Gentiles live, a picture of how the walk of faith is to contrast with the way of the world. Disciples are to set a greater standard than the one the world has. All of this comes from an approach to life that doesn't ask "What is the least I can do, or what can I get away with doing?," but that gives rise to actions that reflect a true, pure heart. Jesus taught that this is where the law was always trying to take people. His approach showed what God desires, while also exposing how often we come up short of this goal. Thus, we have a deep need to turn to and depend on God. The depth of character God desires of those who seek to walk with him requires we turn to him and the resources he gives to enable us to live in this distinctive way.

PREACHING AND TEACHING STRATEGIES

Exegetical and Theological Synthesis

The exegetical section elaborates on the need for elaborate love. Furthermore, it explains a timeless temptation to leverage the law for our benefit. Jesus did not appeal to such fanciful thinking. These six elaborations are bookended by a call to moral excellence—the kind that exposes the Pharisees' shallowness (Matt. 5:20) and praises God's perfection (5:48). In other words, disciples of Jesus cannot separate their witness (i.e., salt and light) from their works (i.e., forgiveness, purity, honesty, charity, love).

Of course, Jesus's elaboration of the law brings two more temptations to the surface. First, the literalist listens merely to the "jots and tittles" of his application. He hears Jesus speaking in extremes and sharpens his knife to gouge out his eye, restrains his tongue from any words but "yes" and "no," and plods down the street in his boxer briefs, having given the rest of his clothes to charity. The literalist fails to understand the role of hyperbole in stoking our imagination. His fixation on details misses the point. Every church is filled with literalists—some earnestly grappling for truth, others simply grasping for control.

Second, the perfectionist knows Jesus has elevated the law and, by golly, she will prove she can attain it. Her life is marked by feats of triumph and periods of defeat. Failure will not hold the perfectionist captive too long; she will arise, work hard, press on, and meet her goal. She may be driven by holy discontent, but more likely she is trying to erase disappointment from her life and/or earn God's love. Somewhere along the line, the perfectionist becomes a modern-day Pharisee, holding her superior performance over others. We can strive for perfection, but we do not achieve it ourselves (Phil. 3:12). Hence Jesus came to fulfill all righteousness for us and clothe us in his perfection (2 Cor. 5:21).

Preaching Idea

Elaborate love goes above and beyond the law.

Contemporary Connections

What does it mean?

What is elaborate love? How does it go above and beyond the law? The apostle Paul provides a stunning description of elaborate love in 1 Corinthians 13. It is patient, kind, not jealous, not braggy or arrogant, not rude; it is selfless and forgiving, seeks good, shows trust, and is trustworthy. The catalogue is not only elaborate, but Paul contrasts genuine love with spiritual performance. When speaking in tongues, giving to charity, and making sacrifices merely fulfill a legal requirement—when they are loveless duty—they amount to nothing (1 Cor. 13:1–3). Paul called the Corinthians to get above and beyond duty.

When we consider Jesus's six elaborations and Paul's elaborate love treatise, we can make connections to our own context. And we might speak more in terms of duty than law. Below are six contemporary examples that coincide with Jesus's six elaborations.

1. *Anger*: When an older brother apologizes to the younger sister he just slugged simply because Mom told him to, he is appeasing his mother, not showing elaborate love.
2. *Lust*: Elaborate love not only avoids pornography, but it also sets up safeguards through personal accountability and internet filters to keep one's mind pure.
3. *Marital fidelity*: A husband goes above and beyond his marital duty to remain faithful when he actively shows affection to his wife (e.g., cuddles; buys flowers; talks with her; pays exclusive, undistracted attention to her when she talks). Living separate lives under the same roof does not get above and beyond the law.
4. *Honesty*: A person shows elaborate love by avoiding the trend to exaggerate her accomplishments and airbrush her flaws on social media. Her posts will include honest captions and imperfect images of her normal, unheroic life.
5. *Non-retaliation*: Instead of getting in the last and loudest word in an argument, one who shows elaborate love approaches conflict as an empathetic listener. Our noisy and divisive world could truly benefit from the above-and-beyond ethic of empathetic listening.
6. *Love of enemies*: Those who show elaborate love will not demonize those who oppose them, whether the topic is politics, race, gender, religion, or sports. Even in disagreement, they will respect their opponents' humanity and show them dignity. Some will even rise above the conflict and befriend their enemies.

Is it true?

Is it true that elaborate love goes above and beyond the law? Yes, this is the nature of elaborate love. But not every expression of love is elaborate, in the sense that it flows from deep emotional reservoirs. Sometimes love is sheer duty. Sadly, in our age, many discredit dutiful acts of love because they set emotional expression above and beyond relational obligation. In fact, some may ask, "If I have to work so hard to show love—if it feels more like forced than free-flowing—should I do it?" This question reflects the roots of romanticism, which puts a higher premium on spontaneous emotional expression than planned and deliberative action. Romanticism has pressed us into a cultural moment where unless something "feels good" and genuine, it has no moral weight. We prefer emotional expression to elaborate love. In fact, we have conflated the two concepts, resulting in an elaborate love of self. Even when loving "feelings" are absent, we are responsible to fulfill God's legal requirements. This love is distinctive in its approach and scope.

Now what?

Once we come to terms with the idea that elaborate love goes above and beyond the law, we would do well to review Jesus's six elaborations. They become a starting point for self-assessment. Anytime the biblical text serves as a mirror for our soul, we want to invite the Spirit to sensitize our conscience, expose sin, affirm our status as children of God, and renew us (John 16:8–11; Rom. 8:16; Gal. 5:16–24; Eph. 4:23).

We can process through the six elaborations in two systematic ways: assessing our relationships and presenting our bodies. First, we note Jesus's teaching begins with family relationships (e.g., brother, spouse) and works toward social relationships (e.g., neighbor, enemy). Both our intimate and peripheral connections matter to God. Because all people deserve elaborate love, we might work through the spheres of relationship in our lives, asking, "How can I show elaborate love to . . . ?"

Spheres of Relationships		
Family	**Close Relations**	**Loose Relations**
Spouse Children Parents Siblings In-laws Extended	Friends Accountability partners Small group members Mentor/mentee Counselor Teammate/partner	Neighbor Coworker Government/service workers Entertainers/media Strangers Enemies

In addition to the spheres of relationship, we might present our bodies to God as instruments of righteousness (Rom. 6:12–14; 12:2). In his six elaborations, Jesus mentioned the eyes, hands, mouth, head, and cheek. Implied are the mind, genitalia, and feet. Our whole body contributes to, or undercuts, elaborate love. Working from head to toes, we might present our members to God for loving service.

Finally, self-assessment should result in changed behavior and obedience. It is not enough to say, "My love is lacking in these relational spheres. My eyes and hands do not contribute to elaborate love." No, we must, by the Spirit's power, take steps of obedience. Elaborate love goes above and beyond introspection; it results in daily interactions: forgiveness, purity, fidelity, honesty, mercy, and hospitality. Choosing to work on one of Jesus's elaborations will get us moving in the right direction.

Creativity in Presentation

Songs have a way of sticking in people's heads, especially when a pastor unexpectedly breaks out with a beloved tune. One risky idea that requires some technical savvy would be taking the instrumentation from Soft Cell's catchy 1982 hit "Tainted Love" and parodying it with words from Jesus's six elaborations. The following lyrics pair with the first minute of the song.

Sometimes I feel I've got to . . . stop my hate . . .
I've got to . . . turn my cheek . . .
From the pain that comes from my enemies
The way of law
Seems to go nowhere
It can't make me right
So I try and try; can't sleep at night

Once I did the law
Now I go above
This elaborate love you've shown me
I give with all my heart you know
So take my hands and eyes and coat
Oh, elaborate love
Elaborate love

Perhaps a more palatable option would be to play Third Day's "Love Song" from their debut album (1996). The lyrics describe Jesus's "above and beyond" sacrifice—climbing Mount Calvary, keeping every promise, walking on the raging sea, and dying on the cross—to secure our salvation. This song may work to close the message, assuring your people that Jesus perfectly embodied elaborate love. Many lyric videos, even some with scenes from *The Passion of the Christ*, are available on YouTube.

A simple but effective way of illustrating the "above and beyond" the law is to set up six boxes, crates, stepladders, or platforms on the stage. Below each prop, in large letters, display the key law Jesus addressed—murder, adultery, divorce, false testimony, retaliation, hate. As you describe the common understanding of the law, stand on the ground level. When you explain Jesus's elaboration, advance to the raised platform or prop. This slight transition will provide a strong visual cue.

Stories, of course, give each of the elaborations flesh and bone. While the sermon may not allow for a story for each of the six elaborations, carefully select two or three that suggest a case study in elaborate love. This language of case studies helps people think contextually. For those elaborations you glossed over, encourage your people to make their own case studies as a follow-up exercise. Below is a list of case studies for the six elaborations.

Case Studies on Jesus's Six Elaborations

Do not hate: The first sibling pair in Scripture gives an example of anger opening the door to fratricide. Cain murders Abel after God has given him warning. He has noted Cain's seething emotions. Nonetheless, Cain executes his murderous plot. When confronted, Cain asks, "Am I my brother's keeper?" He should have been, but it turned out he was his brother's killer (Gen. 3:1–16).

Do not lust: In the movie *Fireproof* (directed by Alex Kendrick, 2008), firefighter Caleb Holt (played by Kirk Cameron) wants to turn around his struggling marriage. To aid his effort, he follows a forty-day challenge called "The Love Dare," which gives daily prompts to pursue his wife. One of them is to eradicate pornography from his life. In a memorable scene, Caleb takes his computer outside and beats it with a baseball bat to "cut off" that means of enticement.

Do not divorce: Gary Thomas (2000, 45–51) records the testimony of Dr. John Barger, who after years of domineering his wife, decisively turned toward her in love after she miscarried their child. The event changed him, but their marriage required many years of hard work, communication, and forgiveness to rebuild. Once they reached a point of security, his wife faced a cancer diagnosis that took her life. Death, not divorce, parted them.

Say yes and no: John Ortberg (2002, 169–72) describes "impression management," a common tactic where we embellish or qualify our words to win favor with others.

Go the extra mile: Dr. Martin Luther King Jr. insisted on nonviolence in his civil rights efforts. The march to Selma left many people battered and bruised. Bus boycotts and sit-ins resulted in injuries and incarcerations. King said, "Force begets forces, hate begets hate, toughness begets toughness. And it is all a descending spiral, ultimately ending in destruction for all and everybody. Somebody must have sense enough to and morality enough to cut off the chain of hate and the chain of evil in the universe. And you do that by love." While this teaching could equally fit the next elaboration on loving our enemies, King's non-violent ethic fits this fifth elaboration well.

Love your enemies: In 1947, Corrie Ten Boom preached a message of forgiveness and afterward was approached by a Nazi guard from Ravensbrück concentration camp—the place where Corrie had suffered and her sister had died. The guard stretched out his hand and asked for Corrie's forgiveness. After a moment of struggle and silent prayer, Corrie put her hand in his and granted him his request (1980, 53-55).

As you adapt the creative ideas for your message, keep the main truth in mind: true application of the law asks "What kind of righteousness does it seek?"—and then goes there. Or, more simply, elaborate love goes above and beyond the law.

- Elaborate love uproots hate (5:20–26).
- Elaborate love denies lust (5:27–30).
- Elaborate love champions fidelity (5:31–32).

- Elaborate love tells the truth (5:33–37).
- Elaborate love resists revenge (5:38–42).
- Elaborate love loves everyone (5:43–48).

DISCUSSION QUESTIONS

1. Why is it better to see Jesus's six treatments of the law as elaborations rather than antitheses?
2. How does Jesus's teaching compare with the various streams of rabbinic thought?
3. How does the Second Temple wisdom literature potentially inform Jesus's treatment of the law?
4. What makes behavior modification more attractive than effecting heart change?
5. Consider Matthew 5:48. How does it relate to the final elaboration? The whole set of six?
6. Of the six elaborations, which is the most difficult for you? For the culture you live in? What makes that elaboration so challenging?

Matthew 6:1–18

EXEGETICAL IDEA

Jesus urged that alms, prayer, and fasting be directed sincerely to the Father with a spirit of dependence and trust rather than before people.

THEOLOGICAL FOCUS

Jesus seeks a sincere integrity to the worship we perform, offered to and for God alone.

PREACHING IDEA

Sincere devotion avoids the spotlight.

PREACHING POINTERS

Jesus did not make strong distinctions between public and private life. Elaborate love and sincere devotion were genuine marks of faith for his disciples in every sphere of life. Jesus wanted his followers to show the same earnestness in their private giving, praying, and fasting as they did in their public displays of forgiveness, purity, fidelity, honesty, and mercy. His rationale was simple: the heavenly Father sees all and rewards sincerity. For Matthew's audience, the social pressure to perform religious acts for public honor had not abated. In fact, rising pressure to rally against Rome may have further stirred Jewish fervor. Matthew reminded them to practice piety for God alone.

"Authenticity" is a buzzword in our age. Its counterparts—genuine, real, sincere—promote a similar virtue. The world wants us to "be ourselves" without filters, to practice full-blown self-expression; social media platforms make it simple. We post staged family moments on Facebook. We capture shameless confessions on Snapchat. We unleash our inner performer for our growing TikTok audience. The cellphone is a mobile spotlight; we are the stars. Rewards come in comments, likes, shares, and followers. Sadly, shameless self-expression can creep into our religious performance. We can give, pray, serve, and sacrifice so the world (or our parents and pastors) takes notice. Such a motive is, in fact, *in*authentic. Piety for public approval misses the point. Giving, praying, and fasting please God. This sermon reminds us that sincere devotion avoids the spotlight.

TEACHING ON ALMS, PRAYER, AND FASTING (6:1–18)

LITERARY STRUCTURE AND THEMES (6:1–18)

These three subunits are exhortations on piety—alms (vv. 2–4), prayer (vv. 5–15), and fasting (vv. 16–18)—with the principle stated in verse 1. The section on prayer includes a model prayer for disciples known as the Lord's Prayer but is better called the Disciples' Prayer (vv. 9–15). The location of the apostrophe in that name is important. It is a prayer that is said as a community for the community. It is not a private prayer. Disciples are to pray for each other and intercede for a spirituality that is rooted in mutual dependence before God and a graciousness with each other. Jesus presented the three topics through a contrastive style of what not to do followed by what to do. The teaching emphasized what God desires and rewards. Genuine piety is only concerned with God knowing and seeing what we do. Though three topics are covered, it is prayer that gets the most attention.

Most of this unit lacks synoptic parallels. An exception is the Disciples' Prayer. Luke 11:2–4 is quite similar, but in that passage the prayer emerged in a distinct context and with a distinct wording. It may well be we are dealing with distinct traditions about the roots of the prayer and/or its repetition as a teaching point. The variation in the prayer shows the point is in the emphasis and not exact wording.

This triad of acts repeats a three-part structure that Matthew likes and has no parallel in Mark or Luke. The pattern of development is similar in all three sections, although the section on prayer is far more developed since Jesus gives a model prayer for disciples (France 2007, 233). Each unit has what not to do, followed by what is to be done. The issue of reward as a motivation is also present. Each unit notes that a self-directed display has its reward only on earth, while that done in secret is rewarded by the Father. So, we have situation (6:2, 5, 16), prohibition (6:2, 5, 7–8, 16), reason (6:2, 5, 16), command (6:3, 6, 7, 17) and result (6:4, 6, 18; Turner 2008, 179).

The key theme was on the action's integrity, much like the concern of Matthew 5:21–48. It was not done for self-interest or for drawing attention to oneself. It was done for the relationship being nurtured, whether it be in helping others out or in one's walk with God. It was a spiritual act in the deepest sense since God was the one who saw it and the one before whom it was done. All of these actions were to take place in faith. God was the one who saw and would reward. So, the actions not only pointed to authenticity but to faith and trust. It is important to recall Matthew 5:16, where if others saw good acts and glorified God, then this was good. So there was a public dimension to such acts that was praiseworthy as long as the attention pointed to God and his goodness and was not self-directed (France 2007, 234). It was not the acting generously in public that was the concern, but doing it only to be seen by people (Nolland 2005, 273).

EXPOSITION (6:1–18)

Taking on another angle on righteousness and integrity, Jesus discussed acts of piety that were not to be for public display but for God. Such acts were not to be done to draw attention to oneself but were best done in private for God, as the audience of one. Jesus's teaching served as a contrast to common, more public displays of some of his opponents. The sermon's theme of a distinct way of faith emerges from these contrasts.

Jesus urged that alms, prayer, and fasting be directed sincerely to the Father with a spirit of dependence and trust rather than before people.

6:1. Jesus turned to issues of piety and began by stating the principle with regard to what is called "righteousness" (δικαιοσύνη), acts that are described as acts of "mercy" (ἐλεημοσύην) or often called "alms" in Matthew 6:2–3 (BDAG s.v. "δικαιοσύνη" 3b, 247–48; BDAG s.v. "ἐλεημοσύην" 1, 315). Other acts of righteousness in the section are prayer and fasting. This triad of acts is seen elsewhere in Judaism. Tobit 12:8–10 says, "Prayer with fasting is good, but better than both is almsgiving with righteousness. A little with righteousness is better than wealth with wrongdoing. It is better to give alms than to lay up gold. For almsgiving saves from death and purges away every sin. Those who give alms will enjoy a full life, but those who commit sin and do wrong are their own worst enemies" (Wilkins 2004, 271). The term "righteousness" took an attribute of character and now placed it on gracious actions such a character produces. Character and deed fit together. This kind of use has precedent in the Old Testament (Ezek. 3:20; 33:13; Dan. 9:18). The verse gave the general principle that guides Matthew 6:1–18. Jesus desired a righteousness that expressed itself in concrete care and caring for others and their spiritual welfare (Keener 2009, 206–7). So, the giving of alms, prayer, and fasting to focus on God were all reflections of a righteous character. How we see God and how he impacts us also affects how we relate to others.

The act of giving alms or showing mercy was commended in Judaism (Deut. 15:7–11; Ps. 112:9; Tob. 1:3; 4:7, 16; 12:8–10; Sir. 7:10; 29:8; T. Job 9:8). Relief for the poor also was highlighted in the Torah (Lev. 19:9–10; Deut. 14:28–29; 24:19–21; 26:12–13), as well as in the prophets (Isa. 3:15; 10:1–2; Amos 2:6–8; 5:11). Kindness to those who need aid is something God desires. Such kindness is not about politics or ideology, but about reaching out to one's neighbor.

Relief to the Poor, Foreigner, Orphans, and Widows in the OT

Leviticus 19:9–10: "When you gather in the harvest of your land, you must not completely harvest the corner of your field, and you must not gather up the gleanings of your harvest. You must not pick your vineyard bare, and you must not gather up the fallen grapes of your vineyard. You must leave them for the poor and the resident foreigner. I am the Lord your God."

Deuteronomy 14:28–29: "At the end of every three years you must bring all the tithe of your produce, in that very year, and you must store it up in your villages. Then the Levites (because they have no allotment or inheritance with you), the resident foreigners, the orphans, and the widows of your villages may come and eat their fill so that the Lord your God may bless you in all the work you do."

Deuteronomy 24:19–21: "Whenever you reap your harvest in your field and leave some unraked grain there, you must not return to get it; it should go to the resident foreigner, orphan, and widow so that the Lord your God may bless all the work you do. When you beat your olive tree you must not repeat the procedure; the remaining olives belong to the resident foreigner, orphan, and widow. When you gather the grapes of your vineyard you must not do so a second time; they should go to the resident foreigner, orphan, and widow."

Deuteronomy 26:12–13: "When you finish tithing all your income in the third year (the year of tithing), you must give it to the Levites, the resident foreigners, the orphans, and the widows so that they may eat to their satisfaction in your villages. Then you shall say before the Lord your God, "I have removed the sacred offering from my house and given it to the Levites, the resident foreigners, the orphans, and the widows just as you have commanded me. I have not violated or forgotten your commandments."

Giving in secret was also an idea discussed in Judaism. In the later Babylonian Talmud, it is said that a person who gave in secret was greater than Moses (B. Bat. 9b). The remark assumed the unusual nature of the act and thus praised it. This commendation by Jesus and in Judaism was because such an act came from the heart and reflected meeting a need not out of obligation but out of consideration for others. Jesus emphasized that such acts not be for display. They were not to be done before people in a way that drew attention to the person. Acts done in a manner where their goal was not outwardly directed but done for the self were not rewarded by God. "Right deeds must be accompanied by right intention." Davies and Allison (1988, 575) note that the pride of show was a malignancy on true religion as God looked on the heart (1 Sam. 16:7). Disciples were to shine as light before people according to Matthew 5:16, but the goal was not to gain attention to themselves but to make sure their attention was directed to God (Konradt 2020, 99–100). Matthew 23:5 is the contrastive, negative example. Jesus was in line with what the best in Judaism taught here. The Letter of Aristeas 169 teaches that one was to show righteousness to all people while being mindful of God. Mishnah *'Aboth* 1:2 has Rabbi Simeon of the third century B.C. teach, "By three things is the world sustained: by the law, by temple-service, and by acts of generosity" (France 2007, 235 n. 27).

The exposition was very Jewish, since we have a principle followed by examples of what it looks like. This was called a *kelal* (Davies and Allison 1988, 577; Osborne 2010, 218). So Jesus commanded that one should take care that such acts of kindness and other acts of piety were not for public display and acclamation. In other words, acting for public acclaim was to be avoided.

6:2. Jesus applied the point with an example using the giving of alms, known as acts of mercy. He switched to the second-person singular here from the second-person plural of the previous verse, personalizing the application. When alms were undertaken, Jesus said not to do it by drawing others' attention to it, by "blowing one's horn." There were to be no parades of praise and honor as one gave to draw attention to the self in the act. This public display was done by hypocrites, people whose seemingly generous actions covered their real motives, which were to receive credit and draw attention to themselves. Jesus often used the term "hypocrite" in Matthew (BDAG s.v. "ὑποκριτής" 1038). Matthew uses the term thirteen times versus four uses for Mark and none for Luke or John (Matt. 6:2, 5, 16; 7:5; 15:7; 22:18; 23:13, 15, 23, 25, 27, 29; 24:51; often of scribes and Pharisees). It points to an actor, one who played at doing one thing but really was doing something else. The goal of the act was not mercy and lovingkindness but to garner praise, whether in the synagogues or in the streets. The Father would not respond to such self-directed acts of pseudo-kindness. The idea of having only this reward appears again in Matthew 6:5 and 16, so it was a refrain that God would not honor acts that were really designed to garner self-glorification. The expression "paid in full" made the point that the only reward would be the temporary public praise (Quarles 2011, 176; BDAG s.v. "ἀπέχω" 1, 102). Man's praise was all they would get.

6:3–4. Jesus continued the shift to the individual, staying in the singular. He treated how to give such aid in a way that pleases God. Jesus argued not to let one part of the body know what the other is doing. This was a picture and metaphor for acting in such a nonpublic way that even the person himself did not see what was taking place. The point was to act only before God and in private, not drawing attention to oneself. The best gift was an anonymous gift. The illustration also showed that the act was done for its own sake, not for an ulterior motive. This made it a sincere act of mercy. It was the genuineness of the action that God would honor (also in Tob. 4:10; 12:8; 14:10). Jesus said in Matthew 6:4 that such acts are to be done in secret. God should be the one bringing honor to the person who gives and not others. The verse may suggest we need to give more thought to how we raise funds, motivate those who might give, and honor those who respond positively.

The aim of giving alms in a way that one hand did not know what the other was doing was so that the gift would be secret. It was what God thought that mattered. He would see the act done in a discreet way and would give a reward. The reward is not named, but some form of commendation apparently is in view. God's response was a replacement for human praise, in contrast to the person giving with an eye to human response. Other ideas are that God himself, a good conscience, or increased holiness was the point of the reward. Faithfulness to God and pleasing him versus people seem to be most apt in this context. Sincere worship was a theme in Judaism as well (*m. 'Abot.* 1:13; 5:13; T. Job 9:7–8).

The expression about the Father's reward is a refrain in this unit, as it also appears in Matthew 6:6 and 18. One is to live and serve in a way that pleases God and shows faith in him. The giving Jesus urged shows one trusts that God will see and reward the one who gives quietly. God as the one who sees the heart is a theme in the Old Testament and Judaism. Thus this theme appears in 1 Samuel 16:7, Proverbs 24:12, and Testament of Gad 5:3, which reads, "The person who is just and humble is ashamed to commit an injustice, not because someone else will pass judgment on him but out of his own heart, because the Lord considers his inner deliberations" (Davies and Allison 1988, 584). He is called "the Father" to the disciple in all three texts in this unit that mention reward (Matt. 6:6, 18). Nowhere else in Matthew, Mark, or Luke is an application stated in a father/son linkage (Davies and Allison 1988, 584).

6:5. When Jesus turned to prayer, he began with the negative example involving Jews and returned to a second person plural making the point for the community. Gentiles were in view in the next negative example Jesus gave in Matthew 6:7. The Jewish background may have been the two or three regular times of prayer in the Jewish day: in the morning, afternoon at 3 p.m., and the evening (Dan. 6:10; *Did.* 8:3—mirrors the Jewish model; Josephus, *A.J.* 14.65, speaks of morning and three p.m.; Levine 2000, 510–23). Jews also prayed at other times (*m. Ber.* 1:1–2—the Shema is to be recited at the start of the day and at its close; 3:4—for meals; 4:1; France 2007, 238; Quarles 2011, 178). Everything stopped for the afternoon prayer. One was to pray in a way not to be seen by others, whether in the synagogue or street corners. The negative theme surfaced again in Matthew 23:5–7. Standing to pray was common (1 Sam. 1:26; Neh. 9:4; Jer. 18:20), while bowing or kneeling was left to special circumstances (1 Kings 8:54; Ezra 9:5).

Prayer is conversation between a person and God, so what others saw about it did not matter. Prayer's goal is fellowship and communion with God, not self-promotion (Blomberg 1992, 117). The point was that public yet private prayer could be a contradiction in terms, by drawing undue and inappropriate attention to oneself. The context is slightly distinct from corporate prayer that is shared in a community and is inherently public since it is a community act. Jesus described prayer that was of a public, attention-drawing nature as hypocritical. The synagogue looked at indoor prayer, while the streets looked to prayer given outdoors, so there is a contrast between religious service or community prayer and general public settings (Nolland 2005, 277). The reward for such attention-seeking public prayer was whatever the person received from people. Davies and Allison (1988, 586) observe how often Jesus was described as praying in private (Mark 1:35; 6:46; 14:32–42; Luke 5:16; 6:12; 9:18, 28–29).

6:6. So one should go into the "inner room" of the house, a place of privacy, a point reinforced by the fact the door also is closed (BDAG s.v. "ταμεῖον" 2, 988; Matt. 24:26; Luke 12:3, 24). The inner storeroom might be the only room with a lockable door inside a house and often was quite small. However, some homes did not have such a room. The point was to use a vivid picture to indicate privacy. The application switches back to the second-person singular. Prayer was to take place in secret, just like the giving of alms (Matt. 6:3–4). God saw and honored such private prayer, and the petitioner would receive a reward from him. Only God's reward really counted, so one was to heed Jesus's word here. Now the point was not to act so as to receive a reward—that would be another form of self-focus—but to act in a way that honored God with the sincerity he would reward (so correctly Morris 1992, 138; Osborne 2010, 220).

There is discussion about whether God was in secret, so the stress was on his invisibility (so France 2007, 239) or God saw in secret, being in the secret place as well (Hagner 1993, 142; Nolland 2005, 276). The latter is more likely given the refrain in Matthew 6:4, 6b, 18.

6:7. Jesus gave a second negative example on prayer. This time the negative example was from the nations. Referring to "the nations" like this reflected a Jewish perspective. Disciples were not to babble on in their prayers with many words or repetitions as the nations did, thinking that the prayer commended itself and would be heard because it was long. This attacked the nature of prayer by degrading it (Stott 1978, 142). The term "babbling" sounds like what it meant and can refer to stammering speech (BDAG s.v. "βατταλογέω" 172; Betz 1995, 364–67). It may be related to the Aramaic term that means to speak idly (Betz 1995, 365, is against such a connection). It is a rare term as this is its only NT use. The later reference to praying with "many words" added to the picture (BDAG s.v. "πολυλογία" 847). This remark may have included allusions to magical incantations that also had a repetitive character. It also pointed to the habit of piling up the names of deities in prayer to make sure the right god was addressed (Keener 2009, 212). One was not to pray in a longwinded way nor in a mechanical way (Stott 1978, 145). Prayer was not to be this formulaic nor was it a session to negotiate with God.

What Jesus said also was said in Judaism. Ecclesiastes 5:2 urges that one's words to God be few while exhorting people to not be rash with their speech or hasty to speak before God (2 Bar. 48:26 speaks of praying honestly).

6:8. The reason prayers should not drone on was because God knew what a disciple needed before he or she asked. They didn't need to badger God (France 2007, 240). Disciples should not pray as the Gentiles did. They could trust God to care for them. His omniscience is at work here, as is his compassion for his own. He knows what we truly need (Betz 1995, 368–69; on the term "need," BDAG s.v. "χρεία" 1, 1088). Such ideas reflect the Old Testament, where God answers before his people call and he hears while they speak (Isa. 65:24; Dan. 10:12; Acts 10:31; Turner 2008, 185). Matthew 6:32 and Luke 12:30 are similar in force (cf. 1 Peter 5:7). Wilkins (2004, 274) makes two points about prayer in reflection on this text: (1) we should come to God in prayer without hesitation, and (2) we should know that sometimes Jesus spent entire nights in prayer, not in repetition but in a full conversation with God.

> **The OT on God Responding to Prayer**
>
> **Isaiah 65:24:** "Before they even call out, I will respond; while they are still speaking, I will hear."
>
> **Daniel 10:12:** "Then he said to me, 'Don't be afraid, Daniel, for from the very first day you applied your mind to understand and to humble yourself before your God, your words were heard. I have come in response to your words.'"

6:9. Jesus then turned to a short sample prayer. It is "not a set prayer but a model for prayer: 'When you pray, pray in this way'" (correctly, Culpepper 2021, 129). In contrast to how not to pray with many words, this was a crisp prayer. It contained affirmations about what God should do in the creation and requests of how he could help the disciples. The prayer showed how to address God. This is the "Disciples' Prayer." Again, the location of the apostrophe is important. This is not a prayer from an individual. It was and is a shared corporate expression of how to come to God as a group and pray for each other. Rather than coax God or barter with him, one could come to him confident of his care and rest in his familial goodness (Nolland 2005, 285; Ps. 55:22; Isa. 30:19).

The prayer has three affirmations reflecting submissive dependence and reverent respect for God's actions in the world, followed by three core requests that cover key areas of life. Only when we have placed ourselves in the context of God and his character are we ready to ask of him for ourselves (France 2007, 243). This was a sample prayer and was not initially intended to be a liturgical prayer, but its popularity led into it having that function.

The prayer opened with an affirmation and petition that God's name be set apart or hallowed (*Did.* 8:2). Both the affirmation and request were important here. The disciple was recognizing God's uniqueness and calling for that uniqueness to show itself as God acted in the world. Implicitly this meant the disciple also would honor God by how that person lived (Keener 2009, 219).

The term "hallowed" means "to set aside" something, often to dedicate something (BDAG s.v. "ἁγιάζω" 3, 9–10). In this context it means to consecrate or sanctify God's name, which is a way to speak of his person (Gen. 32:28–29; Exod. 3:13–14; Isa. 52:6). The reference to God's "name" is a way of saying God's name and person should be seen as distinct and be honored as one of a kind (BDAG s.v. "ὄνομα" 1dβ, 713). The prayer opened with a recognition of the respect and reverence that God was to possess from his children. God was called upon to show his uniqueness, to vindicate himself (Hagner 1993, 148). A paraphrase might be that God should magnify his name (Ezek. 36:23); literally, it is "let your name be holy." Such honor comes when God shows his character and does what he has promised. There is the presence of eschatological hope and expectation in this prayer that looked to God doing all he has promised, but it is not exclusively eschatological as the coming request for daily bread involved basic needs out of the core of current life. Jewish prayers also had such themes. The call was to lead disciples into living in a way that honored God and to have a world filled with the same.

The prayer was uttered in a familial context for those who believe (Deut. 14:1; 32:6; Ps. 103:13; Jer. 3:4; 31:9; Hos. 11:1; Wilkins 2004, 275). God was respected as unique, but the relationship was still one of love and intimacy. Disciples addressed God intimately as the Father in heaven, an emphasis in the sermon (Matt. 3:17; 5:9, 16, 45, 48; 6:1, 4, 6, 8, 14–15, 18, 26; 7:11, 21; 10:20, 29; 13:43; 23:9). This close connection to God was part of the covenantal background of God's relationship to his people. It did not apply to the world in general (Davies and Allison 1988, 601; Quarles 2011, 187; against Betz 1995, 387). God not only is the originator of life and so Father, but also maintains a kinship to people who are connected to him. God is not cold or distinct, even as he is sovereign. He cares for and draws near to his own. So those who pray to him can do so as his children who seek and depend on his care. Everything about the prayer communicates dependence on God for core dimensions of life. In making affirmations that show dependence, one makes requests for daily needs, spiritual needs in spirit of forgiveness, and for divine protection. Nevertheless, God is accessible to his children as a most loving parent (Blomberg 1992, 119).

It is often said that this note of intimacy is unique to Jesus's teaching, but the claim is exaggerated (Wis. 14:3; Sir. 23;1, 4; 51:10; 3 Macc. 6:3, 8; *m. Ber.* 5:2 show otherwise; *Ta'an.* 23b). It is better to say the address reflects a characteristic of Jesus's teaching that has an emphasis on the disciples' relationship to God.

Jewish Texts on Intimacy with God as Father

Wisdom 14:3: "But it is your providence, O Father, that steers its course, because you have given it a path in the sea, and a safe way through the waves."

Sirach 23:1, 4: "O Lord, Father and Master of my life, do not abandon me to their designs, and do not let me fall because of them! . . . O Lord, Father and God of my life, do not give me haughty eyes."

Sirach 51:10: "I cried out, 'Lord, you are my Father; do not forsake me in the days of trouble, when there is no help against the proud.'"

3 Maccabees 6:3, 8: "Look upon the descendants of Abraham, O Father, upon the children of the sainted Jacob, a people of your consecrated portion who are perishing as foreigners in a foreign land. . . . And Jonah, wasting away in the belly of a huge, sea-born monster, you, Father, watched over and restored unharmed to all his family."

6:10. Two more request-affirmations followed to round out the first three general requests about God and the world. The first was a call for God to bring his kingdom (*Did.* 8:2). This was a request for God to complete his promise and bring the consummation of the kingdom that Jesus introduced. The "kingdom" stands at the center of Jesus's teaching (BDAG s.v. "βασιλεία" 1bη, 168–69). It was announced as near by both John the Baptist and Jesus (Matt. 3:2; 4:17). With its consummation, justice and peace will come. The request was for the final vindication of the saints. God will come in his kingdom or in his day to judge the earth (Nolland 2005, 287; Pss. 96:13; 98:9). The reference in Matthew 6:33 to seek the kingdom travels in the same direction. The exact expression of the kingdom coming did not appear in Judaism, but the general idea of God's arrival in power and victory was common (Isa. 35:4; 40:9–10; Zech. 14:5; Davies and Allison 1988, 604). Part of the Jewish prayer the *Kaddish* says, "May he let his kingdom rule in your lifetime and in your days and in the lifetime of the whole house of Israel, speedily and soon. And to this say, Amen" (Quarles 2011, 196). This was the spirit of what Jesus asked for here.

The third request was actually quite similar to the second. It was that God's will be done on earth as it is in heaven (*Did.* 8:2). Heaven is always the realm of God's presence in Matthew and so there is no idea of evil there (Nolland 2005, 289; Matt. 5:34). This also expressed a desire that God's rule be demonstrated throughout his creation, not just in heaven. God's honor in the world was to be the chief concern of disciples in these first three requests (Turner 2008, 187).

6:11. The first three requests were about God's activity in the world. Now Jesus gave three more personal requests. The first was for the basic needs of life, namely the giving of daily bread. The term ἐπιούσιος is rare ("daily," BDAG s.v. "ἐπιούσιος" 376–77; Hemer 1984). Its only use in the New Testament is in this passage and its conceptual parallel in Luke 11:3. It was future looking as a reference for God to supply something for each day, including for the coming day. The request set forth the core need of sustenance each day from God, who is seen as a provider of such gifts (Pss. 104:14–15, 27–28; 107:9; 146:7; Prov. 30:8–9). This request is also rooted in trusting God (Osborne 2010, 229).

6:12. The second personal request was about forgiveness, described as forgiving debts, a common picture from the Old Testament. The term "debt" in this context referred to a moral debt and so was equal to sin (BDAG s.v. "ὀφείλημα" 2, 743; 11Qa Targum Job 34:4; Rom. 4:4—with its normal meaning of financial debt; conceptually, Luke 7:41–43). The same verb was used for both monetary and spiritual debt in Aramaic (Keener 2009, 223). The request for forgiveness was balanced by a willingness to forgive. This was also taught in Judaism as Sirach 28:2–5 has a similar idea when it reads, "Forgive your neighbor the wrong he has done, and then your sins will be pardoned when you pray. Does a man harbor anger against another, and yet seek healing from the Lord? Does he have no mercy toward a man like himself, and yet pray for his own sins? If he himself, being flesh, maintains wrath, who will make expiation for his sins?" Other Jewish texts include T. Zeb. 5:3; 8:1–2; and T. Jos. 18:2 (Davies and Allison 1988, 610; Wilkins 2004, 279). Psalm 103:10–13 shows the roots of this kind of idea, where we do not receive what we deserve but God is compassionate. This idea will be reinforced in the call to be forgiving in Matthew 6:14–15 and in the vivid parable of Matthew 18:23–35 (also Matt. 9:5–6; 12:31–32). A forgiven person should be forgiving, giving what he or she has received.

6:13. One more personal request completed the prayer. Luke 11:4 has this in a shorter form, only mentioning temptation, not deliverance from evil (*Did.* 8:2). The first part of this request was not to lead disciples into temptation, followed by a request to deliver them from evil. This was a prayer for spiritual direction and protection. The term "temptation" can refer either to a test or to a temptation depending on the context (BDAG s.v. "πειρασμός" 2b, 793). With the image of "rescue," the point was about temptation (BDAG s.v. "ῥύομαι" 908). God tests, but he does not tempt (James 1:13; Osborne 2010, 230; Stott 1978, 150). Quarles (2011, 216) adds that the term πειρασμός is consistently negative in Matthew (Matt. 4:1, 3; 16:1; 19:3; 22:18, 35; 26:41). The idea as a whole was not that God can and does lead into temptation, but that he protects one from it. The idea of rescue speaks to the deliverance God can provide. The request reflected dependent disciples who sought to be led by God and shielded by him. The idea parallels things taught in the Old Testament and in Judaism. Psalm 17:30 LXX sees God as a shield to those who take shelter in him. Sirach 33:1 teaches that the one who fears the Lord will not experience evil but will be rescued from trials. The Babylonian Talmud *Berakot* 60b reads, "Bring me not into the power of sin, and not into the power of guilt, and not into the power of temptation, and not into the power of anything shameful." First Corinthians 10:13 shows God's side of response in these circumstances. Quarles (2011, 213) argues this terminology is against reading this petition as exclusively eschatological. It covers all kinds of situations.

The reference of delivery from evil is unclear as to whether "evil" in the abstract was meant or deliverance from "the evil" one since the term πονηροῦ can be read as either a neuter or masculine. The point would be virtually the same. If one sees parallels to Matthew 13:19 and 38, then the evil one could well be meant (also Luke 22:28–32; John 17:15). Nonetheless it is not so clear the threat was this personalized in the context as temptations come in many ways, so the rendering is better seen as "from evil." Matthew 5:39 is read in this more general way. The stress was on the disciples' response to the potential for sin in general, whether from Satan, circumstances, or themselves. Avoiding sin takes turning to God because we see ourselves at risk otherwise.

The prayer probably did not end with a doxology at the end. The manuscript evidence suggests this was added later to the prayer as the result of its use in liturgy. To add such a refrain would not be surprising, given how the prayer came to be received into church liturgy. The many variations of wording in the manuscripts also point to an addition.

The Structure and Core Content of the Disciples' Prayer

Three General Requests:

God's person be honored
God's kingdom come
God's will be done

Three Personal Requests:

For daily core needs
For forgiveness
For spiritual protection and deliverance

6:14–15. Jesus drove home the importance of forgiveness for "transgressions" as he concluded his discussion on prayer (BDAG s.v. "παράπτωμα" a, 770—offenses against people). This term for sin looks at offenses committed. Mark 11:25 is close in concept to this verse. In a balanced contrast involving two third-class conditions, Jesus noted that the Father forgives those who forgive, while God will not forgive those who do not forgive. What we receive from God, we are graciously to provide for others. We are to learn from his model and behavior toward us (Matt. 5:48; Nolland 2005, 293).

The conditional clauses leave the two options about forgiveness equally on the table (note the two uses of ἐὰν—"if"). The idea of "releasing" from sin looks back to Matthew 6:12 (BDAG s.v. "αφίημι" 156). This forgiving attitude reflected an appreciation for what grace is for us. That kindness is to impact the way disciples live. Jesus made exactly the same point in a teaching-and-parable combination in Matthew 18:21–35. The repetition shows how important this idea is in Matthew and how central a gracious spirit is for the community of disciples. The gospel of grace is to impact us in a way that grace is evident (for how this works in relationship to Paul and the gospel as a gift, see France 2007, 253). Morris (1992, 149–50) says, "Jesus is saying that to fail to forgive others is to demonstrate that one has not felt the saving touch of God."

6:16. Jesus came to his third and final topic, fasting. Fasting was a regular practice in Judaism (Neh. 1:4; Dan. 9:3; Joel 1:14; 2:15; Tob. 12:8). *Didache* 8:1 says Jews fasted twice a week, on Monday and Thursday. The Day of Atonement also included fasting (Lev. 16:29–31; 23:27–32; Betz 1995, 418). Normal fasting involved abstaining from everything except water, while occasionally it would involve total abstention for a short time (Wilkins 2004, 281; see also discussion above in Matt. 4:1–2). It was to be a time of focus and reflection on God, often done in mourning or to humble oneself before God (Judg. 20:26; 2 Sam. 3:35; Esther 4:3; 9:31; Ps. 35:13–14; 2 Macc. 13:12; Keener 2009, 226). Jesus taught how not to fast. Do not draw attention to yourself as you fast, like hypocrites do (Matt. 6:2, 5). Do not be "sullen" (BDAG s.v. "σκυθρωπὸς" 933) and make your faces "unrecognizable" (BDAG s.v. "ἀφανίζω" 2, 154). Betz (1995, 420) notes that being sullen was often a critique of false religion among Greco-Roman philosophers. Often one wore sackcloth, donned ashes, and rent clothes while fasting (Dan. 9:3; Jonah 3:5; Jdt. 8:5; 1 Macc. 3:47). In this way people saw you and knew you were fasting. Those who drew such attention to themselves had their reward. This remark is like Matthew 6:2 and 6:5. God criticized an improper fast in Isaiah 58 as well (Jer. 14:12—a fast God refuses; Joel 2:12–13—a fast after repenting; Zech. 7:5–7; Sir. 34:26; T. Ash. 2:8; T. Jos. 3:4–5—to be done in secret; Davies and Allison 1988, 617). They were paid in full with the praise they got from people.

Fasting is occasionally mentioned in the New Testament (Acts 13:2–3; 14:23; 27:9). The early church work of the *Didache* also discusses fasting (*Did.* 1:3; 7:4; 8:1).

6:17–18. Instead of drawing attention to yourself, you were to anoint your head with oil (Jdt. 16:8) and wash your face—a picture of consecration—so that one could not tell you were fasting. Such anointing could point to joy (Pss. 23:5; 104:15) and was also used as a normal form of washing so that nothing special was pointed to by doing this (Keener 2009, 227). Ecclesiastes 9:7–8 (NIV1984) says, "Go, eat your food with gladness, and drink your wine with a joyful heart, for it is now that God favors what you do. Always be clothed in white, and always anoint your head with oil." Only the Father in secret was to know about the fast. Then the Father, the one who sees in secret, would give the reward. The term for "secret" refers to something hidden or unseen (BDAG s.v. "κρυφαῖος" 571). The term's only two appearances in the New Testament are in this passage, though a related term shows up in Matthew 6:4 and 6:6. Fasting that honors God was to be only between the disciple and God.

THEOLOGICAL FOCUS

The exegetical idea (Jesus urged that alms, prayer, and fasting be directed sincerely to the Father with a spirit of dependence and trust rather than before people) leads to this theological insight: Jesus seeks a sincere integrity to the worship we perform, as offered to and for God alone.

This unit is about sincere piety. Genuine worship of God (whether in almsgiving, prayer, or fasting) is done before God and to God and is not done as a show before people. We are to trust God and his ability to see our hearts by engaging in almsgiving, prayer, and fasting in secret. Religious activity is not for drawing attention to or bringing praise to ourselves. It is to be an act before God, an audience of one. Jesus emphasized that these activities and those like them are to be done in a way that acts out of a genuine heart of service. Our heart's prayer is to trust God for his name being honored, his kingdom coming, his will being done, as we also rely on him to meet our daily needs as well as to forgive and protect us. As a result of experiencing God's grace, we also are to be gracious, being willing to forgive others. To seek and accept praise from God alone is to trust in his goodness and care.

This sermon also is about character building and formation. A sensitive heart seeks to honor God's will with sincere acts of spirituality. Whether we are giving to those in need, praying, or fasting to reflect on God, we are called to do so as an act between ourselves and God. The disciple is to be generous and forgiving to those who sin. This tone of graciousness drives how disciples should live, even in the midst of a world that is full of sin and selfishness. Disciples touched by God's grace are to be different.

PREACHING AND TEACHING STRATEGIES

Exegetical and Theological Synthesis

The exegetical section describes the centrality of almsgiving, prayer, and fasting in the Christian life. Jesus assumed his followers would adopt these faith practices, modeled by Jewish predecessors and the wider world. However, like his elaboration of the law, Jesus set a high expectation for devotional practices. He wanted heartfelt engagement with the disciplines because the heavenly Father would reward them by his loving presence and approval.

Nonetheless, private disciplines must not become the high mark for spiritual devotion. Inevitably these become a source of pride—a disciple's undoing (Rom. 12:3; Gal. 6:4–5; James 4:6–10). Community keeps us grounded, humble. Jesus has already stressed the importance of elaborate love (5:21–48). James describes true religion as caring for orphans and widows (James 1:27). Paul offers nearly fifty mutual ("one another") exhortations. Sincere devotion combines a robust inner life with intentional relationships.

Preaching Idea
Sincere devotion avoids the spotlight.

Contemporary Connections

What does it mean?
What does it mean that sincere devotion avoids the spotlight? Those who practice sincere devotion take seriously Jesus's expectation to give, pray, and fast. They integrate these practices into their daily and weekly rhythms. They see giving as an opportunity to help churches and charities, boost folks in financial troubles, and encourage others with a timely gift. They pray for others without sounding pious about it. If they fast, they do not skulk about at lunchtime saying, "Boy, that sandwich looks delicious. I wish I could eat it but I'm fasting. Hopefully, my grumbling stomach won't keep you from enjoying it."

Furthermore, we should not view Jesus's three acts of devotion as exhaustive. Protestant Christians may brag about church attendance, Bible reading, community service, and evangelistic outreach. In our day it is too easy to share that we completed a Bible reading plan on the YouVersion app, gave online to World Vision, or volunteered, posting a picture with our small group in matching church tees holding rakes outside a widow's yard. We have been conditioned to share because our brains crave the reward of blue thumbs, red hearts, and numerous comments. Publicity may not prompt our devotion and service, but it certainly can corrupt it. We must beware. Our devotion is for God and so is focused on him.

Is it true?
While it is true that sincere devotion avoids the spotlight, we have just seen how easy it is to shine a spotlight on our prayers, Bible reading plans, and acts of charity. Those who created the app or platform want to make sharing easy to create a virtuous reward cycle and subtle social pressure to do good. They are strategic, not evil, but their methods certainly train us to spotlight our acts of devotion.

The question is, then, how do we share our private spiritual lives without feeding pride and the social media machine? This question is critical in our networked age. The answer comes by considering circles of intimacy. Followers of Jesus must share their spiritual lives with one another; however, not every act of devotion should be broadcast to faceless masses. As a rule, our innermost circle will be small: family members, a mentor, close friends, and accountability partners. A secondary circle may include a couple of colleagues or small group members. Because these people are "in the circle" with us, they have access, in varying degrees, to our devotional habits. There is no pretense or spotlight when we talk about praying and Bible reading, fasting and solitude, giving and service; we simply confess, commiserate, and hold one another accountable.

One other caveat: pastors, parents, and spiritual leaders have a responsibility to spotlight their devotional practices in appropriate ways. Sharing and sincerity are not mutually exclusive. Moreover, because people look to them for modeling, they should share about giving, prayer, and fasting in ways that offer helpful advice while also admitting personal struggles. Most of us learn best by real-life examples, not abstract principles. Humility is essential for public figures sharing about private practices; none of us is perfect. And yet, if no one cast light on their devotional lives, Christian history would suffer the loss of gems like Brother Lawrence's *Practicing the Presence of God,* the Puritans' *Valley of Vision,* Bonhoeffer's *Life Together,* David's psalms, and Jesus's "Disciples' Prayer." Ultimately the issue is for whom this is being done. What makes our devotion sincere is not in our reporting of it, broadcasting about it, or even others seeing it in its natural flow, but that it is directed to and for God.

Now what?

Clearly this an opportunity for the pastor to describe his rich and flourishing prayer life, rigors in fasting, and giving record, as annually reported to the IRS. This is a joke, and the humor only underscores the challenge of a public figure sharing on private acts of devotion without striking an air of superiority. Discussing practices of personal piety begins with a posture of humility and tone of grace. We must not guilt people into giving, praying, and fasting. From the outset, we must admit our struggle with secret devotion and give them the benefit of the doubt ("When you pray . . .") in their discipleship to Jesus.

After establishing a humble posture and gracious tone, we should offer practical guidance for giving, praying, and fasting. Each of these spiritual disciplines has been discussed in detail elsewhere. In fact, whole books have been written on the so-called "Lord's Prayer." What may be most helpful here is to encourage basic next steps in giving, praying, and fasting. One should focus on the actions, not on just one person's role in it.

Tips for giving could include increasing regularity (from once in a while to once a month; from monthly to weekly), amount (from 1 percent to 5 percent; from $7,000 to $8,000), and distribution (from church alone to several charities). Because almsgiving and church offerings are not direct parallels, it is wise to broaden the discussion beyond the giving to the church.

Tips for praying could include finding a specific time and place to pray. Jesus prayed early in the morning in remote places (Mark 1:35). David prayed on his bed in the night watches (Ps. 63:6). Jonah prayed from the belly of a fish (Jonah 2). When and where we talk to God is less important than that we talk together. However, our environment affects us, so finding a setting with limited distractions can help us focus. Furthermore, the Bible provides many templates for prayer, from the Psalms to Paul's epistolary prayers, to the praises of the elders in Revelation. Any of these can aid us in our times of intercession.

A Primer of Biblical Prayers

Praying with Moses: Exod. 15:1–15; 20:1–17; Deut. 6:4–6

Praying with the Psalms: Pss. 1; 8; 23; 51; 62–63; 67; 100; 103; 121; 145

Praying with Jesus: Matt. 26:39; Luke 11:2–4; 18:13; John 17

Praying with Paul: Rom. 15:13; Eph. 1:3–14; Phil. 1:9–11; Col. 1:9–12; 1 Thess. 3:11–13

Other biblical prayers: 1 Sam. 2:1–10; Neh. 9:5–38; Jer. 32:17–20; Jonah 2:2–9; Heb. 13:20–21; Rev. 5:9–13

Tips for fasting could include various forms of fasting (from skipping lunch to taking a month off from social media) and reasons for the practice. On this topic, Whitney (2014, 191–219) has compiled a list of ten forms of fasting and nine reasons, which may be worth reviewing. Fasting is countercultural; as consumers we like to satisfy our cravings quickly. But we must fight the urge to be heroic in fasting. Making small, deliberate, secretive advances will help us maintain a positive face.

Finally, Jesus's exhortation to avoid the spotlight does not preclude personal accountability. His disciples observed his prayer life; they likely saw him give and fast. As intimate allies, they were given access to his personal devotional habits. Wisdom urges us to invite a few friends into the dim light of our devotion for encouragement and accountability. Facebook may not be the platform for our stuttering prayer life, but friendship welcomes honest sharing. Devotion grows when, together, we draw close to our heavenly Father.

Creativity in Presentation

To reiterate the spotlight imagery, consider playing with the lighting during your sermon. If you have actual spotlights, ask the people running them to move the spotlight off you at certain points in the message. You might talk about loving the spotlight, so you chase after it (like a cat with a laser pointer). On cue, the spotlight could move to a different part of the stage, and you take chase. Or, admitting your need to avoid the spotlight, you could teach part of the sermon in the dark. (For some, especially those watching online, this may prove more distracting than helpful, so limiting the illustration to a few minutes would serve the purpose.) Finally, a simple adjustment is to have the words *Giving*, *Fasting*, and *Praying* on poster boards, set behind a giant work light. After discussing each word, you could extinguish the light, and say, "But God doesn't need a spotlight to see our giving/praying/fasting. He sees our sincerity without the spotlight."

The made-for-Christians film *War Room* (directed by Alex Kendrick, 2015) provides a challenging (albeit kitschy) picture of a prayer closet. A struggling marriage experiences transformation after the wife (played by Priscilla Shirer) meets Miss Clara (played by Karen Abercrombie), a congenial, elderly woman who shows Elizabeth her prayer closet, which she names her "War Room." Written on the wall are her requests to God. Karen eventually turns her lush, suburban closet into a war room. The scenes where Miss Clara reveals her war room or Elizabeth renovates her closet to accommodate praying would illustrate the need to create a place of prayer.

In a 2016 *On Being* interview with Krista Tippett, Eugene Peterson talks about his prayer life. He hesitates to begin. "It's hard to talk about," he admits. Then he begins to describe his first hour of the day with coffee and the Psalter. He lists a few of his favorites, as well as how he reads them meditatively. Then Peterson abruptly stops, pivots, and says, "I don't think it's a very good idea to give people a pattern to work with in prayer. We're all a little bit different. And I did that myself. I just figured out what seemed possible to do, and I did it. But, when I was a pastor, I would spend time with people figuring out what to do . . . helping them . . ." Tippet clarifies, "Helping them . . . find whatever their seven psalms might be or the equivalent." Peterson affirms this. This rich dialogue points to the importance of personal practices of devotion, and demonstrates how one person, finding himself pulled into the spotlight, recedes into the shadows.

To provide a bit of humor, let people know about your growing concern for declining giving trends in the church. Assure them that not everyone is guilty as charged; the church has a few star givers who are sustaining the budget. This morning you want to spotlight them. Hold up a sheet of paper (or a plaque or set of reward ribbons), as though you plan to read the list of names, and look around the room, as if trying to locate someone. Then tell them to relax—their giving records are a private act of devotion between them, God, the folks who record the offering, and their banking institution. You can point out this is how it ought to be, according to this text.

Regardless of the creative elements you adapt for your message, be sure to communicate that Jesus seeks a sincere integrity to the worship we perform as offered to and for God alone. Moreover, sincere devotion avoids the spotlight.

- Jesus offers three case studies for sincere devotion (6:1).
- God rewards sincere giving (6:2–4).
- God rewards sincere praying (6:5–8).
- Jesus offers a model prayer (6:9–15).
- God rewards sincere fasting (6:16–18).

DISCUSSION QUESTIONS

1. How do public righteousness and private devotion interact with one another?
2. What reward does God give and how does it contrast with society's rewards?
3. Why is it better to call Jesus's model prayer the "Disciples' Prayer"?
4. What roles do others (church, family, friends) play in our private devotion?
5. What are your current habits in giving, prayer, and fasting? How have they changed over the years? What would you like them to look like in the future?
6. In addition to seeking the praise of others, what are other potential dangers in personal devotional practices?

Matthew 6:19–34

EXEGETICAL IDEA

Jesus urged seeking heavenly treasure by being careful about what we see and think, avoiding the pursuit of material things over God, and trusting God to give us what we need so we avoid worrying in this life.

THEOLOGICAL FOCUS

The disciple is to live a disciplined life, focused on the inbreaking kingdom and honoring and trusting God.

PREACHING IDEA

Entrust your overwhelming cares to God's overwhelming care.

PREACHING POINTERS

As Jesus's masterful sermon continued, he moved from the disciples' private devotion to God's daily provision. More people in Jesus's day were overwhelmed by worry than wealth. Goods were limited; jealousy and greed were common. Thus, Jesus taught the need to keep one's eye and heart pure by focusing more on God's provision than their stockpile of supplies. For Matthew's audience, the rising pressures of persecution surfaced the threat of suffering and material loss. They likely needed to double down on their trust in God's provision and inbreaking kingdom.

Today consumer options abound in the West. How we shop, where we eat, what we wear, and how we customize our products to express our individuality and fit our mood seems endless. Furthermore, diverse currency and credit options remove barriers for buying homes, cars, and knee replacements. Ironically, our material prosperity has not alleviated our worries. In fact, anxiety is epidemic. We worry about the safety of our homes. We worry about the legitimacy of our warranties. We worry about the purity of our water and additives in our meat. We worry about the style of our clothes, smoothness of our skin, and future of our children. Our cares cascade into full-blown panic. This message implores us to entrust our overwhelming cares to God's overwhelming care.

SEEK THE KINGDOM AND LIVE WITHOUT WORRY (6:19–34)

LITERARY STRUCTURE AND THEMES (6:19–34)

This unit has four themes: seeking heavenly treasure (vv. 19–21), watching what comes through the eyes (vv. 22–23), not being able to serve both God and mammon (v. 24), and not worrying but trusting God (vv. 25–34). The strand that ties it all together is to focus on heaven and the pursuit of God's ways. There is an underlying call to trust God in each of these areas.

There are a few conceptual parallels to this unit. The light and body image is found in Luke 11:34–36. The God and mammon saying is paralleled in Luke 16:13, while the text on worry is like Luke 12:22–31. The distribution may show floating traditions of teaching, perhaps present in a variety of contexts as part of an itinerant teaching ministry.

The unit itself has short maxims tied to one comprehensive exhortation on not worrying but seeking kingdom things (vv. 19–21, 25–34). Sandwiched between are two warnings: be careful about what we see (vv. 22–23) and be careful not to succumb to serving money before God (v. 24). In this way it is like the previous unit, where there are parallel topics, but there some are discussed in more detail. It also follows the pattern of the sermon by saying what not to do before discussing what to do. The structure of this unit also mirrors what comes next in Matthew 7:1–12 (Davies and Allison 1988, 625–27).

A context of persecution and rejection may well be at work in this exhortation (Turner 2008, 193). Contrasts also drive the unit: earth and heaven, temporary and permanent, light and dark, service to God alongside service to things, and what Gentiles seek versus what disciples seek.

EXPOSITION (6:19–34)

In a time of pressure and persecution, the challenge was to have the right priority in life and to trust God. This involved taking in the right things and not allowing possessions to distract one's direction in life. The life of faith was existence under pressure as the sermon called for people to live distinctively in ways counter to the world. Jesus anticipated Jewish and Gentile opposition mounting against disciples, and they were feeling such pressure. So a call to prioritize the kingdom and trust God was like a compass for their souls.

Jesus urged seeking heavenly treasure by being careful about what we see and think, avoiding the pursuit of material things over God, and trusting God to give us what we need so we avoid worrying in this life.

6:19–20. Jesus exhorted disciples not to store up for themselves treasure on earth, for here the moth destroys and food is consumed. As in other sections of the sermon, he started with what not to do before pointing to what to do. The expression "for yourselves" (ὑμῖν) showed where an error resided, with selfish desires, with hoping on earthly things as the core focus.

Literally the verse says, "Do not be treasuring up treasure on earth, but treasure up treasure in heaven"—no stockpiling the things of earth (Prov. 23:4–5; Eccl. 5:8–6:7). The present imperative looks to an ongoing attitude. The term for "treasure" pointed to what one values (BDAG s.v. "θησαυρός" 2a, 456). The image of the moth is like that of James 5:2–3. This idea was rooted in the Old Testament picture of the moth or others destroying what is fragile (Job 4:19; 13:28; Isa. 33:4—locusts 50:9; 51:8; Hos. 5:12; also in Judaism, Sir. 34:5; *m. 'Abot.* 2:8; Keener 2009, 231–32, has a full survey of ancient texts). The reference to "food" or eating looked at the non-eternal nature of earthly life and probably alludes to how insects devour food (BDAG s.v. "βρῶσις" 2, 184; Isa. 51:8), showing the transitory nature of the things consumed. It was a synecdoche, for food was consumed and thus was destroyed (Nolland 2005, 298). Davies and Allison (1988, 629) prefer an allusion to a grasshopper with the word, citing Malachi 3:11 LXX A. That is conceivable. Hagner (1993, 157) prefers to render the term here "rot," while an older rendering is "rust." That certainly was the point regardless of the rendering. One can think of the impact of plagues and other types of disasters involving insects here.

Whether a reference to food or to another insect, the point was that things are not permanent on the earth. Disciples should not hoard things that are ultimately lost. Such a perspective should make us generous with what we do have (Blomberg 1992, 122). Neither was the point that material things mean nothing (Luke 8:3; 1 Tim. 4:3–5; 5:8; 6:18); they just are not to be the focus of life. The issue was the "selfish accumulation of goods," that is, excessively having things, saving, or enjoying what we do have (Stott 1978, 154–55).

On the earth, there was moral corruption, as well as the thief who broke in and stole. Literally, "breaking in" refers to "digging in" (BDAG s.v. "διορύσσω" 251; Hagner 1993, 157). The picture was of digging through mud-dried brick or under a wall. It may also allude to earthly treasure stored in strongboxes in the home or in the floor (Keener 2009, 230).

What we have can perish or be seized (Pss. 39:6; 49:16–19; Eccl. 2:20–26 all argue for how wealth perishes; France 2007, 259). The things of this life do not last and cannot be taken with us. So why focus on them? The one with the most toys ends up with nothing. Luke 12:16–21 warns directly against such greed.

OT Discussions on the Transience of Wealth

Psalm 39:6: "Surely people go through life as mere ghosts. Surely they accumulate worthless wealth without knowing who will eventually haul it away."

Psalm 49:16–17: "Do not be afraid when a man becomes rich and his wealth multiplies. For he will take nothing with him when he dies; his wealth will not follow him down into the grave."

Ecclesiastes 2:20–21: "So I began to despair about all the fruit of my labor for which I worked so hard on earth. For a man may do his work with wisdom, knowledge, and skill; however, he must hand over the fruit of his labor as an inheritance to someone else who did not work for it."

In a straight contrast, Jesus now said what to do and called for disciples to store up treasure in heaven. Here the moth does not destroy, food is not consumed, and the thief does not steal. This exhortation set up the unit's theme. It showed the poor in spirit who are rich toward God and have eternity and connection to the Eternal One to show for it (Betz 1995, 431). This was a frequent image in Judaism (Tob. 4:8–9; 2 Bar. 24:1; Ps. Sol. 9:5). Fear of the Lord was said to be such treasure in Isaiah 33:1–6. Sirach 29:10–11 says, "Lose your silver for the sake of a brother or a friend, and do not let it rust under a stone and be lost. Lay up your treasure according to the commandments of the Most High, and it will profit you more than gold" (Wilkins 2004, 293). The kind of trust and character Jesus urged fits into these pictures. The storage comes in acts of character the sermon described (Davies and Allison 1988, 632; also in generosity, Matt. 19:21, 29; 25:21, 23, 34, 46; 1 Tim.

6:7–10, 17–19 cover the handling of wealth; also 1 Peter 1:4; France 2007, 259).

Jewish Texts on Being Rich Toward God

Tobit 4:8–9: "If you have many possessions, make your gift from them in proportion; if few, do not be afraid to give according to the little you have. So you will be laying up a good treasure for yourself against the day of necessity."

Psalms of Solomon 9:5: "The one who does what is right saves up life for himself with the Lord, and the one who does what is wrong causes his own life to be destroyed; for the Lord's righteous judgments are according to the individual and the household."

2 Baruch 24:1: "For behold, the days are coming, and the books will be opened in which are written the sins of all those who have sinned, and moreover, also the treasuries in which are brought together the righteousness of all those who have proven themselves to be righteous."

6:21. To reinforce the exhortation, Jesus made the point that where one's treasure is also is where one's heart is. "Heart" here pictured the center of the person, more than emotion but what drives them (Morris 1992, 153). The remark lacks any parallels in the ancient world, unlike most of the rest of the sermon (Betz 1995, 435).

The point was to examine what one values. Does one value heavenly things and focus on those matters, or is one focused on things of the earth? The subsequent examples applied the point in a variety of ways: to what a person focuses on, to what a person owns, and to the worries of life. Colossians 3:1–9 is conceptually parallel as it is focused on the virtues required to live with a focus on the virtues that matter to God.

6:22–23. The eye as a lamp was the image Jesus used next. The eye functioned as a light or torch shining out in the Old Testament (Dan. 10:6; Zech. 4) and in Judaism (1 En. 106:2, 5; 2 En. 1:5). The teaching involved a simple contrast. If your eye is clear or uncluttered, then light gets out or in and the body functions well. The term "sound" points to a clear, moral line of sight, referring to that which is open, sincere, without guile, generous, unjaundiced (BDAG s.v. "ἁπλοῦς," 104). It would mean "healthy" here. Light was an image for internally illumined and enlightened, being and doing that which is good.

There is much discussion whether the point was about what comes in through the eye or what came out of it. Did the eye reflect or enable the person? In the ancient world, the light often comes out from the eyes (Prov. 15:30; Lam. 5:17; Tob. 10:5; eyes compared to flames—Dan 10:6; Rev 2:18; 19:12; Culpepper 2021, 141). Davies and Allison (1988, 635–37) have a long discussion arguing for a "from the eyes" emphasis. Quarles (2011, 242–46) tries to refute Davies and Allison but all he shows is that the ancient material shows pictures of light both coming in and going out from the eye. It is hard to be certain which direction was meant, but the bulk of the ancient evidence points to a direction from the inner person through the eye out. The ambiguity may mean the entire package was in view. The issue either way was what the eye reflected about the person, because in the ancient world the eye projected sight and understanding as well as taking it in (Quarles 2011, 246, correctly makes this point). The point was to have a clear and clean character. "A person's eyes are an index to his or her whole character" (so Konradt 2020, 110). In many ways, this has been the sermon's entire theme. Pay careful attention to the inner self and what you embrace.

From the Eyes

More ambiguous is Betz (1995, 439–52), as he speaks initially of the eyes being the means by which the body is illuminated, but later of the eye being a means by which an inner spark shows itself. France (2007, 260–61 n. 20) appears to have misread Betz as speaking only in one direction by not reading beyond page 251 where both directions are noted. Nolland (2005, 300–301) argues for a back-and-forth relationship but stresses what comes in through the eye.

But if the eye is evil, then there is darkness, and that darkness is great. Davies and Allison (1988, 640) argue that the background here might be the "evil eye" of Judaism (also Hagner 1993, 158; on what such an attitude can produce in terms of actions—Deut. 15:9; 28:54, 56; Prov. 23:6; 28:22; Turner 2008, 197). Two third-class conditions introduced the positive-negative contrast, so they were presented equally, but Jesus dwelt slightly longer on the darkness, when he said how great the evil is that comes with darkness.

6:24. Jesus next turned to primary loyalty and said no one can have two masters. They hate one and love the other or are devoted to one and despise the other. The term for "devoted to" can also mean cling to (BDAG s.v. "ἀντέχω" 1, 87). The context's ethical emphasis raised the issue of ultimate devotion.

The remark was laid out in a negative, positive, positive, and then negative manner. The principle was stated on both ends of the exhortation, surrounding the negative-positive movement. There was a simple balance to how this was said. A choice was laid before the reader, but the proper choice was clear: one should choose God.

The conclusion made Jesus's topic clear: one cannot serve both God and mammon. The repeated verb for "serve" is important since it is the word for the work of a slave (BDAG s.v. "δουλεύω" 2aα, 259). "Mammon" was also to be appreciated as a broad concept, referring to wealth as a whole and so including possessions and not just money (BDAG s.v. "μαμωνᾶς" 615). It is all the aspects of pursuing wealth that Jesus warned about here. Not seeking earthly treasure was clearly what was in view (Matt. 6:19). Everything said about earthly treasure in that verse also applied to this teaching. Luke 16:13 is conceptually parallel. The Gospel of Thomas 47 has a variation on this idea. The Old Testament and Judaism also have similar concerns (Exod. 20:5; 34:14; Deut. 4:23–24; 5:8–9; 6:14–15; Sir. 31:8–11; T. Jud. 18:2–6—"Love of money . . . enslave[s] him, so that he is unable to obey God"; 19:1—"Love of money leads to idolatry, because once they are led astray by money, they designate as gods those who are not gods"; 1 En. 63:10; 94:8; 96:4; 97:8; 1QS 10:18–19; 11:2; Nolland 2005, 304, n. 388; Turner 2008, 198 n. 8). Greed and covetousness were also precluded here, with those ideas also having Old Testament roots (Exod. 20:17; Deut. 5:21; Job 31:24–25; Ps. 49; Sir. 11:18–19; 1 En. 97:8–10; Wilkins 2004, 296).

Some Jewish Texts on Possessions

Sirach 11:18–19: "One becomes rich through diligence and self-denial, and the reward allotted to him is this: when he says, 'I have found rest, and now I shall feast on my goods!' he does not know how long it will be until he leaves them to others and dies."

Sirach 31:8: "Blessed is the rich person who is found blameless, and who does not go after gold."

1 Enoch 97:8–10: "Woe unto you who gain silver and gold by unjust means; you will then say, 'We have grown rich and accumulated goods, we have acquired everything that we have desired. So now let us do whatever we like; for we have gathered silver, we have filled our treasuries (with money) like water. And many are the laborers in our houses.' Your lies flow like water. For your wealth shall not endure but it shall take off from you quickly for you have acquired it all unjustly."

6:25. Jesus shifted attention to worry. The idea of worry dominates the unit (Matt. 6:25,

27–28, 31, 34 twice). He exhorted disciples not to worry about what one might eat or wear. The connection may be if one was not to be too concerned about possessions, then how would one be cared for in life? Davies and Allison (1988, 646) speak of Matthew 6:25–34 as a *gemara*, or exposition, on Matthew 6:19–24, a good point. Jesus said not to worry about what one might eat or how one was clothed. The reference to one's soul in the verse pointed to the person as a whole being, just as a physical body. Together they cover the immaterial and material parts of a person. Jesus's explanation for not worrying was that the soul is about more than food and the body is about more than clothing. The explanation comes as a rhetorical question expecting a positive reply, using οὐχὶ. There was more to life than food and clothing. Luke 12:22–34 is conceptually parallel.

This exhortation was also about how the disciple should trust God fully, even for the things of this life (Phil. 4:6; Heb. 13:5; 1 Peter 5:7). The sermon's focus on a life dependent on God continued in the set of illustrations about worry. It is among the most developed themes in the sermon. The idea has Old Testament roots (Lev. 25:18–24; Ps. 127:2—"It is vain for you to rise early, come home late, and work so hard for your food. Yes, he provides for those whom he loves even when they sleep"; Isa. 32:17). It was given with reassuring details that urged the disciple to take this step of trust. God would care for you—now here was why. Worry reflected another form of being too attached to the world and its circumstances.

6:26. The example of being fed came from the birds of the air that do not sow, reap, or gather food. Just observing nature can teach us how God cares (Job 12:10; 38:41; Pss. 104:10–15, 27–30; 147:9; Prov. 6:6–11—learn from the ant; Jer. 8:7; Pss. Sol. 5:9–10). The reverse idea was taught in the Mishnah *Qidd.* 4:14, which reads "R. Simeon b. Eleazar says: 'Have you ever seen a wild animal or a bird practicing a craft? Yet they have their sustenance without care and were they not created for nothing else but to serve me? But I was created to serve my Maker. How much more then ought not I to have my sustenance without care? But I have wrought evil, and forfeited my [right to] sustenance [without care]'" (Davies and Allison 1988, 649; France 2007, 268; Quarles 2011, 265). In the Mishnaic quotation there is no expectation God will give care if we are not righteous. Jesus's remarks went in a different direction. God cared for the birds, and even more for people. Luke 6:35–36 has God caring even for the wicked.

These birds did nothing to gather food, yet God still fed them. The term for "birds" was general and so the illustration was generic (BDAG s.v. "πετεινόον" 809). Jesus simply asked, "Are you not more than them?" This was another rhetorical question expecting a positive reply, using οὐχ. Humans are more than birds, so God will care for them. Application of this saying requires sensitivity for some situations of poverty and deprivation. The premise for the care is that humans are the crown of God's creation (Ps. 8:3–8; Wilkins 2004, 297).

6:27. Jesus added a practical observation about worry not gaining us anything. Was one able to add to one's stature/length of life by worrying? There is debate whether the reference to a "cubit" should be seen in terms of an absurd picture of adding eighteen inches to one's height by worrying or as a figure for adding length to one's life (BDAG s.v. "πῆχυς" 812 opts for height). It was more natural in thinking about food that stature was the point and that Jesus engaged in an exaggeration tied to the nourishment food gave to make his point. We either have a very vivid hyperbole about height (so Morris 1992, 159) or a reference to not being able to add length to our lives (so most). Either way, the core point is the same: worrying changes nothing, so why worry? As France (2007, 266) puts it, "Worry is the antithesis of faith."

6:28–29. Jesus next asked why one should worry about clothes. Jesus said to "observe" the lilies of the field (BDAG s.v. "καταμανθάνω" 522, an NT hapax). They neither labored nor spun to make their clothes, yet they were marvelously clothed. Not even Solomon, as the great king, was clothed as they were. Solomon was often used as the example of Israelite splendor (1 Kings 9:26–10:29; 2 Chron. 9:13–28; Eccl. 2:1–11; 1 Esd. 15; Josephus, *A.J.* 8.39–41; Davies and Allison 1988, 655). Conceptually similar is Gospel of Thomas 36: "Do not be anxious from morning to evening and from evening to morning about what you shall put on" (P.Oxy. 655 is an even longer version of what Thomas has and speaks of clothing being dispensed with).

The transitory nature of human life is often compared to flowers or grass in the Old Testament (Job 8:12; 14:1–2; Pss. 37:2; 90:5–6; 102:11; 103:15–16; Isa. 37:27; 40:6–7; also in the NT: James 1:9–11). However, here the image was of how God cared for and provided for these elements in the creation. No specific flower was named, just flora in general, but the colorful wild lilies of Israel were probably in view (Guelich 1982, 339).

Short-Lived Humanity Like Grass or Flower

Job 14:1–2: "Man, born of woman, lives but a few days, and they are full of trouble. He grows up like a flower and then withers away; he flees like a shadow, and does not remain."

Psalm 37:2: "For they will quickly dry up like grass, and wither away like plants."

Isaiah 37:27: "Their residents are powerless; they are terrified and ashamed. They are as short-lived as plants in the field or green vegetation. They are as short-lived as grass on the rooftops when it is scorched by the east wind."

6:30. Jesus finalized his point with another "how much more" argument tied to a rhetorical question: If this grass which is here today and burned up tomorrow was so clothed, then how much more will not God clothe you? This kind of "how much more" argument was common in Judaism, being one of Hillel's rules for interpretation, involving moving from the lesser to the greater.

The condition was really a statement of fact here (Osborne 2010, 252). The question expected another positive reply (οὐ). The term χόρτον now calls the flowers "grass," a way to discuss the "flowers" (κρίνον) of Matthew 6:28 as clothing for the ground (BDAG s.v. "χόρτον" 1087; s.v "κρίνον" 567). The call to faith was also made by addressing those who might doubt this with the vocative of being people of "little faith" (BDAG s.v. "ὀλιγόπιστος" 702). The verb for "dress" is also rare in the New Testament, occurring only here and in Matthew 11:8 (BDAG s.v. "ἀμφιέννυμι" 55). Matthew always used this address "of little faith" as a description of some believers and used it to rebuke them for a deficient or weak faith (Matt. 8:26; 14:31; 16:8; 17:20). They were the "little faiths." Luke's only use of the term is in the parallel (Luke 12:28). The call was to be more, to have deep faith.

6:31. Jesus began to wrap up his discussion on worry by repeating the call not to worry about what one may eat, drink, or wear. The aorist imperative was summarizing, "Do not worry." Our idiom is, "Do not be a worrywart." The verse is very much like Matthew 6:25. The idea is repeated in Matthew 6:34.

The addition of drinking here simply filled out the example areas where one should not worry about core needs of life. Sirach 29:21 says this clearly: "The necessities of life are water, bread and clothing, and also a house to assure privacy." As often in the sermon, Jesus started with what not to do before turning to what to do. The three questions were genuine deliberative questions. One was asking what to do with the day, with the subjunctives giving a note of uncertainty about the answer (Turner

2008, 200; Wallace 1996, 466). People did often ask sincerely about what they *might* eat, drink, or wear, yet Jesus said they should not have excessive concern about what might be provided.

6:32. The core things of life were things all people seek, even the Gentiles. As in Matthew 6:7, Gentiles represented those who have no trust in God and so live in an undistinguished manner. The Jewish Letter of Aristeas, 140–41, argues that those who are worshipers of the true God were distinguished from "those who are concerned with meat and drink and clothes, their whole attitude being concentrated on these concerns" (France 2007, 270 n. 21). For Gentiles, the gods were capricious and had to be placated with careful ritual (Turner 2008, 200). This may be in the background. God did not need to be bartered with in this way.

One need not worry because the heavenly Father who cares knows you need these core things in life (Bruner 2004a, 269). This verse is the application of the "how much more will God do this for you." God knows you need all these things and supplies what is needed to give them. If that was God's concern, then the disciples' concerns were to be placed elsewhere. The priority was to pursue the things of God, as the next verse argues. Luke 12:30 is similar to this verse. God's omniscience, power, and compassion combined here to be the reason why one should not worry.

6:33. The disciple was to seek first the kingdom of God and the righteousness that was a part of it. "Seeking first" referred to a priority, not merely the first thing to be done in time (Morris 1992, 161). In many ways, this was a major theme of the sermon. Life's chief concern was the pursuit of God and the connected desire for a high degree of righteousness (Matt. 5:20; Wilkins 2004, 299). One was to be perfect as the Father is perfect, and to live as a child of God reflecting his character (Matt. 5:45–48). Davies and Allison (1988, 660) argue that seeking the kingdom focuses on those things tied to the kingdom now and, as a result, one enters into its effective dynamic presence. We think there is an ethical thrust to this given the context of this remark. One should reflect the character that reflects God's presence and rule. Piety was to be done in secret between the disciple and the Father. Core integrity was the point of the long exposition in Matthew 5:21–48. One was to seek God's rule and let his way and enablement lead one into righteousness. It was a righteousness only God could give, so it was called his righteousness, as it came from him (Morris 1992, 162; Quarles 2011, 279–80, speaks correctly of a genitive of source here). God would provide the rest of what was needed.

6:34. This verse has no parallel in Luke but has many parallels in the culture (Betz 1995, 484–85). One example is the ancient Egyptian text *The Eloquent Peasant* 183: "Do not prepare for tomorrow before it is come. One knows not what evil may be in it." Most parallels have an element of fatalism in them, but Jesus was focusing on the need to trust God to help us through the trouble each day might bring. There was a recognition here that life brings trouble, even "evil," but that there was a way through it (BDAG s.v. "κακία" 3, 500).

This remark added another dimension to Jesus's exhortation. One should not worry about tomorrow. That day has its own anxieties and troubles. Proverbs 27:1 may be in the background: "Do not boast about tomorrow; for you do not know what a day may bring forth." James 4:13–14 is like it in tone. The ninth benediction of the Jewish prayer the *Amidah* says, "Whoever has a morsel in his basket and says, 'What shall I eat tomorrow?' is among those of little faith" (Keener 2009, 238). Each day is another day to entrust to God's care. Life is full of toil with worry surfacing for seemingly good reasons, but that is not the way disciples are to cope. Worry can pile up and paralyze us. Better to trust God than to be overwhelmed with life's cares.

THEOLOGICAL FOCUS

The exegetical idea (Jesus urged seeking heavenly treasure by being careful about what we see and think, avoiding the pursuit of material things over God, and trusting God to give us what we need so we avoid worrying in this life) points to this theological idea: the disciple is to live a disciplined life, focused on the inbreaking kingdom and honoring and trusting God.

The way the disciple lives is important to Jesus. Discipleship is not merely about learning; it is about trusting God. It is not merely about facts and ideas, but also about relationships. Jesus focuses on how God will care for the disciple. One need not worry about the core provisions of life, but rather can concentrate on pursuing the righteousness God enables and desires. The one who does this stores up the right kind of treasure, a heavenly one. Our character is to reflect the light that God gives us, and our service is not ultimately to be directed toward the earth but toward heaven. Where our heart is focused, that is where our treasure will be. In all of this the disciples are to trust God's knowledge of us, our needs, and his goodness.

Two foci dominate this text. One is God's knowledge and care. He sees us. He cares for us and his creation. The examples of the birds and the flowers show this. Jesus notes that God knows what we need. The fact that humanity is made as the crown of the creation means God will care for us even more than the way he provides for the creation. The intensity of God's involvement with his creation is something that secularism may blunt in terms of our appreciation. The impact of that is that we might come to trust God less than we should and take on a burden for what happens in life more than we should. Only a robust theology of God can attack the danger that worry generates for righteous living.

The second theme is the focused pursuit of righteousness and the things of heaven. These should be a priority. Only trust in God can take us there. Jesus stresses trust in this passage, even as he urges us not to let the things of earth become a distraction to us or, even worse, an attraction for our affections. Only a focus on God and his goodness will drive us to become the good people God seeks us to be for his kingdom.

Stott (1978, 165–68) notes three things the passage shows by implication. (1) Believers are not exempt from earning a living, but God has provided what they need to get there. (2) They are not exempt from responsibility to others. (3) They are not exempt from trouble. All that Scripture says makes these points. Part of the way God provides is by our fulfilling the stewardship he calls us to. Part of that stewardship is caring for others as he asks us to do. "God fulfills human needs through culture, but he does so only as long as those needs remain 'natural' and therefore ethically justifiable" (so Betz 1995, 480). Trouble comes from a fallen world. In all of it, there is the opportunity to gift others with the provision God makes possible in his creation. When we do so, we recover why God made us as he called us to have dominion over the creation in Genesis 1:26–28. We were made to manage the earth well and serve one another. The sermon points to our original and ultimate calling as human beings.

PREACHING AND TEACHING STRATEGIES

Exegetical and Theological Synthesis

The exegetical section underscores the importance of trust. Genuine faith chooses to focus on God rather than material goods, earthly comforts, or daily needs. God has a long history of providing for his people, both in the miraculous provisions of the wilderness generation (see Exod. 16; Num. 11; Deut. 8) and the regular work of harvest (Deut. 28:4–5, 8–12; Ruth 1:20–3:17). On some occasions, God even withheld material blessing from his people to return their focus on him (Deut. 28:17–18, 38–42; Hab. 3:17–19; Hag. 1:7–11). As Creator and Sustainer of life, providing for the world is his prerogative.

Knowing God's generosity, sovereignty, and care is critical for disciples who face two pernicious threats in our modern age: greed and anxiety. Jesus's prohibition against serving mammon and stockpiling goods appears more appropriate now than ever. Coupled with these commands, the apostle Paul likened greed to idolatry (Col. 3:5). Moreover, the greedy are lumped together with drunkards, thieves, and adulterers as those standing outside the kingdom of heaven (1 Cor. 6:9–10) And yet, the advertising industry inflames our restless desire for *more, better, now.* We must remind our greedy hearts that God provides for our basic needs not our bucket lists.

Likewise, anxiety has plagued the Western world. Even before the global pandemic, anxiety was becoming a mental health crisis for people across demographic lines. Our collective anxiety centers around political division, racial injustice, gender confusion, gun violence, blurry ethics, anti-religious activism, advancing secularism, nuclear weapons, environmental change, artificial intelligence, immigration laws, and nutritional information. (Just writing this made me anxious!) Moreover, anxiety is not only a learned behavior, carving grooves into the brain that reinforce anxious thinking, but it is also a chemical reaction in the brain that immediately puts a persona in flight, fright, or freeze mode. As much as we would like to say, "Just choose not to be anxious," or, "Stop! Jesus said so," the fallen condition and cultural context demands pastoral concern for our anxious congregations. Empathy matters.

Preaching Idea

Entrust your overwhelming cares to God's overwhelming care.

Contemporary Connections

What does it mean?

What does it mean that you should trust your overwhelming cares to God's overwhelming care? Few would deny their lives are filled with cares. Some cares feel overwhelming some of the time; others feel overwhelming all the time. These cares may be financial (e.g., unexpected car repairs, mounting credit card debt, a missed payment on school loans, loss of job), relational (friend and family drama, loneliness, bitterness, loss of a loved one), occupational (underpaid, meddling boss, few advancement opportunities, frustrating coworkers), and/or physical (achy joints, irritable bowels, aging, COVID-19, diabetes, dentist appointments, chemotherapy). As such, they can pile upon one another. While anxious people have the tendency to turn their worries into worst-case scenarios, it does little good to minimize or deny what overwhelms us. We all have our fair share of cares.

Nevertheless, overwhelming cares can quickly become a black hole. They rob us of joy and steal our ability to focus. Jesus encouraged his disciples to set their eyes on their generous Father in heaven who will supply their needs. God does it for birds and blades of grass, so we should expect his provision for us, as well. We are, in fact, the crown of creation (Ps. 8).

To trust God, we must know his character—generous, glorious, able, and involved—and resist the pull of self-sufficiency. Grocers, banks, clothing stores, and Amazon make it easy to provide for ourselves. With one-click shopping we can have a set of dishes or a bulk order of toilet paper delivered to our door. Who needs God, right? However, as suggested above, consumerism has only fed our anxiety. Walmart and Piggly Wiggly can fill our shopping carts; they cannot fill our hearts. Because God alone can guarantee satisfaction to our restless hearts, we must approach him as our greatest treasure.

Is it true?

Is it true that we face overwhelming cares? Absolutely. Ours is an anxious age, affecting every generation with overwhelming cares. Adolescents feel anxious about their changing bodies, education, and peer groups. Young adults feel anxious about their career options, marriage prospects, and financial security. Middle-aged people feel anxious about the world that has rapidly changed beneath their feet as they age and raise children. Empty nesters are anxious about their adult children and retirement nest egg. Seniors are anxious about declining health and rising death rates among their peers.

But can God be trusted with these overwhelming cares? Yes, and his care is truly overwhelming. Jesus's illustrations reinforced this notion, moving from lesser to greater (birds and grass to humans). Furthermore, he stressed God's intimate knowledge of us, knowing the number of hairs on our heads. (He probably knows the tint and texture, too.) Thus, 1 Peter 5:7 (ESV) implores us, "Cast all your anxieties on him, because he cares for you."

God's overwhelming care extends beyond food and clothes. His care appears in his provision of supportive communities (e.g., church, family, friendships, recovery groups), spiritual encouragement (e.g., Scripture, songs, beauty of creation, a sense of his presence), wise advice (e.g., from doctors, counselors, pastors, and parents), and common graces (e.g., laughter, exercise, a good book, a favorite drink, eight hours of uninterrupted sleep). James affirmed this, writing "Every good and perfect gift is from above, coming down from the Father of heavenly lights, who does not change like shifting shadows" (1:17 NIV).

Now what?

What should we do when our cares begin to overwhelm us? What does it look like to entrust our cares and ourselves to God's care? These are critical questions for an anxious age, and we must resist providing pat answers for distressed people. "Let go and let God" may fit the bill for a bumper sticker, but it does not provide real solutions for real struggles. Overwhelming cares are a mental health challenge. In a 2020 interview with Carey Nieuwhof, Dr. Henry Cloud describes anxiety as a "brain fart," which hijacks linear thinking and bathes the brain in adrenaline manifested in illogical thoughts. J. P. Moreland (2019, 11–33) describes the complex interactions between brain, body, and spirit when anxiety strikes. In other words, the psychological literature about anxiety should warn us against glib answers. Real caring can take time.

Nonetheless, every person is accountable to God and must steward their mind. We are commanded to "take every thought captive" (2 Cor. 10:5). We experience transformation by renewing our minds (Rom. 12:2). Choosing joy, expressing gratitude, praying, and meditating on what is good, true, noble, pure, and lovely can provide a safeguard to our minds, securing them with God's overwhelming peace (Phil. 4:4–9). Stewardship of our minds is an ongoing, deliberate practice, aided by written lists, verbal affirmations, breath prayers, journal notes, and supportive people who share our cares with us (Gal. 6:1–5). It can help to seek others who can give perspective and encourage us. We need not face our cares alone. It may even help to compile a list of our cares in one column and in an adjacent column of what is within our control or must be fully entrusted to God.

Breath Prayers

A *breath prayer* is a simple petition you can regularly repeat. It comprises an address and request. The divine name is spoken as you inhale; as you exhale, speak the request. The genius of the prayer is that it calms the body and mind while helping you focus on God's care.

- "Father, provide." (Matt. 6:25–34)
- "Jesus, hold me together." (Col. 1:17)
- "Spirit, comfort me." (John 14:16)
- "Lord, here I am." (Gen. 22:1, 11; Exod. 3:4)
- "God cares for me. He'll take care of me." (1 Peter 5:7)

Finally, because overwhelming cares can be . . . well, overwhelming . . . there are times where professional interventions may provide the greatest immediate assistance. Medication may balance the overactive wiring in the brain. Counselors may validate a disorder and provide helpful tools for coping. Support groups normalize our cares while surrounding us with people who can lift us up when panic knocks us down. Books, workshops, and webinars offer various angles to understand our anxiety. Trusting God is not at odds with using manmade tools we have crafted from his resource-rich world. In fact, God designed us to care for one another as an expression of our because he asked us love for one another.

Creativity in Presentation

In a classic sketch from *Mad TV* (2001), Bob Newhart plays a counselor who epitomizes a careless response to our overwhelming cares. His client expresses her fear about being buried alive in a box and how it affects her daily life. He validates she is claustrophobic. Then he offers his careless, two-word response: "Stop it!" You can find the short clip (2:11) on YouTube. After the laughter subsides, consider saying, "You may not be claustrophobic, but I bet you have fears. How would you like it if that was God's response to your overwhelming cares—'Stop it!'? Sometimes people who give spiritual counsel express the same uncaring tone but use religious words: 'Just trust God! Trust him! Trust him!'"

To create a shared sense of the overwhelming nature of our cares, you might invite audience participation. You could accomplish this through using a "word cloud," which invites people to text or post words that reflect their cares. Many of these are free if you search them online. Your people would have a growing awareness of the cares that hover over them. A tech-free way of accomplishing the same thing is to have people shout out their cares for a thirty-second stretch in the service. A person poised at a whiteboard may be able to record these cares. You might get them started by listing a few of your own cares: rust on the bottom of your car, melting ice caps, and that odd-shaped mole on your back.

Because Jesus talked about birds and flowers, you could easily represent his imagery by placing birdfeeders and flowerpots all around the stage. You might even put a cooler or minifridge by the feeders and a laundry basket of folded shirts by the pots. As you talk about God's overwhelming care, you then have visual aides to reinforce Jesus's message.

As with any sermon, personal stories can have a profound effect. You might find someone who has experienced the overwhelming care of God in the face of traumatic loss, major surgery, financial hardship, or relational strain. Invite them to the stage for an interview or prerecord their brief testimony. My (Tim's) wife suffers from anxiety, induced by a series of traumas—her mother's stroke, two difficult labors, her mother's death, and an adoption process fraught with hardships. In recent years, she and another couple from our church (one a trained counselor) started an anxiety support group that has not eradicated the overwhelming cares from the participants' lives, but has resulted in noticeable gains, practical tools, and shared trust in God's overwhelming care.

The creative elements should reinforce the main idea. The disciple is to live a disciplined life, focused on the kingdom and honoring and trusting God. And so we should entrust our overwhelming cares to God's overwhelming care.

- See God as greater than our material goods (6:19–24).
- Trust God as giver of our daily need (6:25–34).

DISCUSSION QUESTIONS

1. What is the connection between our focus on material goods and our feelings of anxiety? How does our consumer age feed anxiety?

2. How should we understand Jesus's statement about the eye as a lamp?

3. What Jewish exegetical strategy did Jesus make use of in this passage?

4. What truths and experiences have tested your trust in God? What has built it?

5. What overwhelming cares rob your joy and deflect your focus from God? What practical strategies do you take to cope with anxiety?

Matthew 7:1–12

EXEGETICAL IDEA

Jesus urged treating others with prayerful love and an absence of hypocritical judgment—by being honest about our own faults before helping others, regarding what is holy with care, asking for good things from a gracious God, and treating others as we wish to be treated.

THEOLOGICAL FOCUS

Treating others sensitively and seeing ourselves realistically reflects our calling and requires being spiritually discerning.

PREACHING IDEA

Train your eyes to empathize through honest self-reflection.

PREACHING POINTERS

As Jesus wrapped up the core section of the Sermon on the Mount, he closed with a series of maxims about relating to others and God. Jesus called for honesty and self-reflection rather than launching a social campaign for moral reform. Throughout the sermon, the Master Teacher reminded his disciples of the heart of the law—sincere devotion to God and elaborate love for others—as well as the heavenly Father's intimate attention to their needs. He affirmed their blessed status and missionary role in God's inbreaking kingdom. The cumulative effect of these themes should produce humility, discernment, and prayerfulness. Matthew's audience may have been prone to criticizing others, showing a lack of discretion about holy matters, and being presumptuous about God's provision due to their religious standing. Jesus's teaching provided an opportunity for earnest self-reflection.

In today's post-Christian culture, Jesus's prohibition against judgment rules the day. "Do not judge" is the banner under which people flaunt their sexual choices, justify consumer habits, defend divorce, allow for abortion, endorse vulgar speech, and excuse addictive behavior. It is claimed that judgment displays rank ignorance of cultural and chemical factors that cause people to do what they do; everyone has a story, reason, or excuse for their decisions. Moreover, judgment threatens their personal pursuit of happiness, which is the aim of life in the secular age. Although these claims may be overstated, they do underscore complex and unseen factors that feed into another person's actions. Properly understood, Jesus's call to inspect oneself before casting stones (or pearls) trains our eyes to gaze inward before glaring outward. In fact, this message compels us to train our eyes to empathize through honest self-reflection.

BE CAREFUL ABOUT JUDGING, SELF-DISCERNING, AND HOW YOU TREAT OTHERS (7:1–12)

LITERARY STRUCTURE AND THEMES (7:1–12)

This unit contains a series of four brief commands/maxims. Two commands are treated (not judging [vv. 1–6] and asking of God while treating others well [vv. 7–12], each with a second maxim following (do not give to swine [v. 6] and the Golden Rule [v. 12]). The themes of judging others (7:1–5) and asking God for good things (7:7–11) are more developed, with a principle and then supportive illustrations. We have a balanced set of imperatives: teaching-maxim-teaching-maxim. We also have a negative command (do not judge) and a second one (do not give pearls to swine) followed by two positive commands (ask and do unto others), fitting the "do not do this, but do that" pattern of the sermon.

A key theme is having an awareness of others that is honestly discerning about oneself as well as the role God has to judge and give. There also is an emphasis on respect: to treat holy things with care and respect them and to respect others. As with the rest of the sermon, the focus is on the disciple's character.

Parallels to the teaching on not judging in Matthew 7:1–5 are found in part in Luke 6:37, 41–42. Luke 6:38c has parallel imagery used in a distinct way. Luke's material also is arranged in a distinct manner and is abbreviated. Matthew 7:6 has no parallel. The teaching on asking God in Matthew 7:7–11 is paralleled in a distinct Lucan context in Luke 11:9–13, falling outside his Sermon on the Plain. The Golden Rule is paralleled in Luke 6:31, a part of Luke's sermon. We have material that is parallel in Luke both inside his equivalent Sermon on the Plain and elsewhere in Luke. What Matthew has brought together, Luke has scattered across Jesus's teaching. The difference may well reflect Jesus's itinerant ministry.

EXPOSITION (7:1–12)

Having considered how disciples were to look at themselves in their life walk, Jesus turned to how to deal with others and how to relate to God. One was not to be judgmental, but discerning about self as a way to set up interaction with others. One was to be respectful of divine things. One was to ask of God and treat others as one would wish to be treated. In a world where one looked out for the self and often was not concerned for others, these exhortations continued the call to respect God, depend upon him, and be considerate of others while being honest about one's own faults. The humility this required was a contrast to the world, which did not highly regard such humility.

Jesus urged treating others with prayerful love and an absence of hypocritical judgment by being honest about our own faults before helping others, regarding what is holy with care, asking for good things from a gracious God, and treating others as we wish to be treated.

7:1. This is one of the most misunderstood verses in the New Testament. It is used by people to argue that Jesus taught not to make spiritual assessments of others. Ethical reflection and discernment are not excluded by this verse. The entire context is necessary to see his point, not to mention his own ministry where spiritual judgments were made regularly. Stott (1978, 177) comments that the point was "not a requirement to be blind, but rather a plea to be generous."

The act of judging can refer to a variety of assessments: simple evaluation (Luke 7:43), a legal judgment (Matt. 5:40), making a reward (Matt. 19:28), or pronouncing guilt (John 7:51; Wilkins 2004, 308). In Matthew 7, when Jesus said that one is not to judge others, he meant not to reject them in a way that dismissed them. The issue here was a decisive condemnation especially when combined with hypocrisy (Nolland 2005, 318). One's final fate was in God's hands, so one should be careful how one critiqued others (Matt. 13:36–43, 47–50; Keener 2009, 239–40). Jesus went on to say that the spirit one uses about others is what will be used on the one who judges. Most importantly, Matthew 7:3–5, especially verse 5, showed that Jesus affirmed helping someone appreciate where they truly are spiritually. Assessment with discernment was to take place. Correction might be called for. However, one was to keep an eye on one's own needs and faults when engaging others about their shortcomings. We were never to judge "from an assumed superior position" (Konradt 2020, 116). Spiritual discernment was also the point in Matthew 7:6. Matthew 18:15–17 assumes making spiritual assessments. So what Jesus rejected here was a decisive critical judgment, especially one that ignored the judge's own shortcomings.

The ideas expressed here have parallels (Rom. 2:1—not to judge and be guilty yourself; 14:10—decisive judgment is God's task; 1 Cor. 4:5—final judgment is God's; 5:12—spiritual assessment is to take place within the community; James 4:11–12—who are you to judge your neighbor; 5:9—how you judge leaves one vulnerable before God; Davies and Allison 1988, 668). The context of conflict with the Pharisees in Matthew may be in play here, so that the idea was not to be judgmental as many of them were (Matt. 9:10–13; 12:1–8).

Jesus said not to judge in order that one might not be judged. What was meant is explained in what follows, as well as by the tone set by urging us to be quick to forgive in the previous chapter (Turner 2008, 203). Matthew 5:7 had stated the idea positively.

7:2. Jesus now explained his point using γάρ ("for"). The way someone judged and measured others will be the way they also are judged and measured (James 2:13). The implication here was that God would do the final judging and measuring. Watch what standard you set against yourself. The picture was of measuring grain. His standards will be right and will be rooted in how we have sought to treat others. Jesus urged us to be forgiving and gracious. This text warned about the failure to do so. The point was that we were all ultimately accountable to God for how we treat others. Rabbinic teaching also says this, as in the Talmud, *Šabb.* 127b and 151b, "He who is merciful to others, mercy is shown to him by heaven, while he who is not merciful to others, mercy is not shown to him by heaven." Other Jewish texts include Sirach 18:20 ("Before judgment comes, examine yourself; and at the time of scrutiny you will find forgiveness") and *m. 'Abot.* 1:6; 2:5. Another way to read the verse is that the measure we use will be used by others against us. This also is possible here, as the expression was ambiguous. However, the sermon's overall context focuses on our ultimate accountability to God, so that is what was most likely in view here. The call to grace made here and in other texts highlighted being gracious (Matt. 18:21–35).

Watch how you judge others. Be sure and do so with an eye to your own faults and needs. Galatians 6:1 says it in a different way: restore, but do so with an eye to one's own failings. Other NT texts also discuss making spiritual judgments, including 1 Corinthians 5:5, Philippians 3:2; Hebrews 3:13, and 1 John 4:1 (Osborne 2010, 257).

7:3–5. The illustration Jesus used was of seeing a speck in someone else's eye while ignoring the wooden beam protruding from one's own eye. The contrast is in the terms "chaff" or "a splinter" (BDAG s.v. "κάρφος" 511) and a "beam of wood" (BDAG s.v. "δοκός" 256). It was a contrast between a small piece of straw and a log. The log often was used to support a roof or function as a bar for a door. One saw little flaws in others and missed the big flaws one has in oneself. The contrast is in a rhetorical question that is designed to show how silly it was to live in this way.

The second question intended to show the audacity of speaking to your brother about his speck when you had a log in your own eye. This use of "how" reflects a question asked with disapproval (BDAG s.v. "πῶς" 1aγ, 901), even though the request to "permit" one to remove the speck is asked politely (ἄφες; BDAG s.v. "ἀφίημι" 5b, 157). Only someone with insensitivity and unwise nerve would seek to correct someone else in this way. The illustration pointed to the absurdity of doing things like this. Bruner (2004a, 274) says that it is like "a Redwood teaching a scrub to be low profile."

Next, Jesus offered advice to the hypocrite who is inclined to act in this way. The term "hypocrite" comes often in the Sermon (Matt. 6:2, 5, 16, and here). It also appears frequently elsewhere in Matthew (15:7; 22:18; 23:13, 15, 23, 25, 27, 29; 24:51; elsewhere only Mark 7:6; Luke 6:42; 12:56; 13:15). This was the only use that looks to be of a disciple versus an outsider (France 2007, 276). The juxtaposition with the term "brother" added to the insult. This was not appropriate for how to act in the community family.

Two steps were presented. First, take the log from your own eye. Second, only then would you be able to see to help with the speck in your brother's eye. The assumption was that being spiritually engaged with another is a good thing. It just needed to be done in a healthy, humble, and proper way. Our engagement with each other should have empathy for how we all can fail. It should come as an offer of sincere, reflective help and not involve a detached critical spirit. Wilkins (2004, 310) cites William Warren (1992), "After self-criticism takes place, relationships are based on redemptive empathy rather than condemning detachment." Stott (1978, 180) cites Chrysostom who speaks of correcting not as a foe or adversary, but as a physician giving medicine. Other texts also make this kind of point about seeing our own flaws (Prov. 28:13—to confess and forsake sin is to find forgiveness; John 9:41; 1 John 1:8).

7:6. In a short maxim that has no parallel in the Gospels, Jesus gave two pictures that also showed spiritual discernment. The verse served to qualify the previous passage by making it clear that spiritual discernment was to be a part of the disciple's walk (Davies and Allison 1988, 674; 2 Cor. 6:14–18). One was not to give what is holy to dogs nor cast pearls before swine. Who would ever consider doing such a thing? (Culpepper 2021, 151, notes that shock and outrage are the emotions under the imagery.) "Dogs" is a reference to a kind of unclean animal, as they often were not pets but ran wild in the ancient world and had contact with the dead and other unclean elements (BDAG s.v. "κύων" 1, 579). Dogs are not fit for that which is holy. The term often was used negatively (1 Sam. 17:43; 24:14; 2 Sam. 9:8; 16:9; Ps. 22:20; Prov. 26:11; Isa. 56:10–11). Swine also are unclean animals (BDAG s.v. "χοῖρος" 1086; Lev. 11:7; Deut. 14:8; Ps. 80:13—pigs ravage fields), not fit for that which is precious, like pearls. Pigs can be paired with dogs to picture uncleanness (1 En. 89:42—dogs, foxes, and pigs devour the sheep; 2 Peter 2:22). Pearls can illustrate wisdom because it is precious. Proverbs 23:9 (NRSV) says a similar thing this way: "Do not speak in the hearing of a fool, who will only despise the wisdom of your words" (Keener 2009, 243). Proverbs 9:8 (ESV) also shows the tone of this text, "Do not reprove a scoffer, or he will hate you; reprove a wise man, and he will love you" (Stott 1978, 180–81).

The reason one should not give the animals these things was that they would trample these precious things under their feet and turn to attack you. The trampling likely described the pig's reaction, while the attacking reflected the dog's action. If so, a chiasm is present (Turner 2008, 206). The point was that they will abuse what is offered to them. The application is to be careful with whom and how you share holy things. To think dogs referred to Gentiles is not right, given Matthew's emphasis on the gospel going to all (Matt. 28:19 and failing to complete the exchange with the Canaanite woman in Matt. 15:21–28 by ignoring how that passage resolves itself with Jesus's care in responding to her). Spiritual counsel is a precious thing; so is the gospel. Some people were hardhearted and were not prepared to be responsive. The context assumed persecution for the kingdom message (Matt. 5:10–16; 10:16–39; 13:28, 39; Hagner 1993, 171–72) and rejection of the pursuit of genuine spirituality. Disciples needed to be aware the message would cause some to react negatively. Judgment about when, how, and what to share was required. The point wasn't to prejudge how someone would respond, but that one should not force it on someone who was clearly not interested (Keener 2009, 244).

As Turner (2008, 207) says, disciples were to be neither inquisitors nor simpletons when it came to the gospel, neither censorious nor naïve. The message was not to be forced on people who had no desire at all to hear it (France 2007, 277). This kind of imagery is common in the NT. Within the gospel, Matthew 10:14 is an example (Morris 1992, 168, also cites Jesus as an example in Luke 23:9; also Mark 6:11; Luke 9:5; 10:11). Esoteric teaching was not the point, which is how the Gospel of Thomas 93 reads the image. Other readings of Matthew 7:6 are less likely.

7:7–8. Jesus turned to asking God for good things. The disciple who trusted God turned to him for what was needed in life, as Matthew 6:7–11 shows. A life of balance between worrying about needs, helping others, and deciding when not to engage was not easy. It needed judgment. Jesus called on disciples to ask, seek, and knock with the hope that what was asked for would be given and found. In this way, God opened the door. Beginning with γάρ, Matthew 7:8 points to God's generosity as the reason one should seek from God (Hagner 1993, 174). This entire sermon stresses the emphasis on God being gracious, as the following illustrations also show.

Carson (1984, 186) points to Matthew 7:1–6 as the context for these requests, while France (2007, 278) looks back to 6:25–34 and Blomberg (1992, 129) refers to the entire sermon. A choice is not required here. The prayer was for good things. It was generic (Keener 2009, 244–45). Quarles (2011, 299–301) argues the request was about entry into the kingdom. This is too narrow and underplays the sermon's context of what was said about following God. As Nolland (2005, 325) says, "The challenge is to find one's way forward in life with a clear focus on the kingdom of God and a deep trust that, as one looks to him, God will open the way ahead." Asking took the humility of dependence on God. Seeking showed initiative in seeking God's way and will. Knocking showed perseverance (Wilkins 2004, 312). The disciple was to come to God and seek the wisdom and care he offers.

The present imperative looked at iterative prayer (Wallace 1996, 722). Jesus promised God will respond so that the disciple receives, finds, and gains an open door. The root for such a request was the idea that God gives wisdom to those who seek it from him (Prov. 2:1–5; 8:17; Jer. 29:13–14a). Gospel of Thomas 94 is similar in imagery.

OT Texts on God Giving Wisdom or Listening

Proverbs 2:1–5: "My child, if you receive my words, and store up my commands inside yourself, by making your ear attentive to wisdom, and by turning your heart to understanding, indeed, if you call out for discernment—shout loudly for understanding—if you seek it like silver, and search for it like hidden treasure, then you will understand how to fear the Lord, and you will discover knowledge about God."

Proverbs 8:17: "I will love those who love me, and those who seek me diligently will find me."

Jeremiah 29:13–14a: "'When you seek me in prayer and worship, you will find me available to you. If you seek me with all your heart and soul, I will make myself available to you,' says the Lord."

The exhortation was unqualified and had no exceptions. This was what makes the saying a maxim, as something that is generally true. The point of the promise stated this way was that you will receive the good things you need. This was not a *carte blanche* to ask for whatever you want and you will get it (France 2007, 279; Quarles 2011, 297; Stott 1978, 188). The good things here were things one needs, not what one wants.

7:9–11. Jesus followed with two illustrations of how people give. These are in the form of questions about how a father gives to a son, mirroring the Father-disciple relationship. No father gives a stone to the son who asks for bread nor does he give a serpent when a fish is requested. In this second case, the gift might bite and poison the recipient (Osborne 2010, 261). The rhetorical questions in these verses were asked with μή, pointing to a negative answer. No sensitive parent would do something so heartless and cruel. The requests involved basic needs of life: bread and fish. The double illustration set up the "how much more" application to God.

Jesus closed the exhortation by focusing on God's goodness. This was a classic rabbinic lesser-to-greater argument, common in Judaism. If humans, being evil, know how to be gracious to their children, how much more will the heavenly Father give good things to those who ask him? In Luke 11, the parallel has the Holy Spirit, but in a distinct context. It also has another difference in that what is given is a snake and a scorpion. We likely are dealing with a similar image used in a fresh setting. "Good things" for Matthew is a general reference reflecting a broader application than Luke's referring to the Spirit (BDAG s.v. "ἀγαθός" 1a, 3; Davies and Allison 1988, 685). There was a triple trust called for by Jesus here: trust that God can be asked and is generous, trust that he knows what we need, and trust that God gives what is good. So, we are to come to God and ask for what is spiritually needed and for discernment in life, and know that God will respond. James 1:5–8 urges the one who asks not to doubt.

7:12. This text is well known as the Golden Rule. That title came from the Middle Ages, reflecting a tradition tied to the Roman emperor Alexander Servanus (ruled A.D. 222–235) who had this verse placed in gold on his throne room wall (Betz 1995, 509; France 2007, 284; Quarles 2011, 306). There were parallels to this idea all through the ancient world, although Jesus stated it in the most emphatic way. It was a core ethical ideal that all recognized as reflecting the best of what people should be.

Parallels to the Golden Rule

Tobit 4:15: "And what you hate, do not do to anyone."

Sirach 31:15: "Judge your neighbor's feelings by your own, and in every matter be thoughtful."

***Epistle of Aristeas* 207:** "As you wish that no evil should befall you, but to be a partaker of all good things, so you should act on the same principle towards your subjects and offenders."

Testament of Naphtali 1:6: "Nothing do to his neighbor, what he does not like for himself."

Sextus, *Sentences* 89: "As you wish your neighbors to treat you, so treat them."

Babylonian Talmud, *Šabb.* 31a: "To Hillel is attributed the following: 'What is hateful to you, do not do to your neighbor: that is the whole Torah, while the rest is commentary on it. Go and learn it.'"

In everything, treat others as you wish to be treated. The present tense imperatives spoke of a principle to be lived out on a regular basis. The passage's entire thrust called for a sensitivity to how others wished to be regarded and related to as a guide for how we should treat them. Just as we wish to be regarded and related to with sensitivity, so we should be sensitive to others. A disciple was to be "others-directed" in how they engaged.

This kind of considerate relating summarized what the law and prophets called for, namely, to be sensitive to others in how you treat them. This is what the law called "loving your neighbor" (Lev. 19:18; Matt. 22:34–40; the "royal" law of James 2:8; Hagner 1993, 176). This also pushed the exhortation back to Matthew 5:17 and showed how what was being discussed encapsulated the entire sermon and its exhortations (Turner 2008, 211).

THEOLOGICAL FOCUS

The exegetical idea (Jesus urged treating others with prayerful love and an absence of hypocritical judgment—by being honest about our own faults before helping others, regarding what is holy with care, asking for good things from a gracious God, and treating others as we wish to be treated) points to this theological focus: treating others sensitively and seeing ourselves realistically reflects our calling and requires being spiritually discerning.

As disciples, our calling is to avoid hypocritical judgment, be discerning with spiritual things, seek God's guidance for our spiritual needs, and treat others as we wish to be treated. Disciples are to live a life of balance. They are not to judge but be spiritually discerning. They are not to give what is precious to those who do not appreciate it. They are to ask God and seek the good things he will give. They are to be sensitive to others, living kindly and loving well. This is the sum of the law and the prophets, to live and love with an eye to how others wish to be treated. In all of this, there is a trust of God for what he will do in judging and guiding. The sermon's ethical thrust continues to be the key theme in this unit. Real theology is not about ideas held in abstraction but is found in how we live. Life involves a quality of discernment and dependence that is concerned not only with what God desires reflecting truth, but with others, humbly treating others with respect.

The assumption in this text was of a deep trust and dependence on God and his ways for making judgments and receiving his guidance. It assumed a respect for life as God had designed it to be lived. So genuine spiritual well-being for oneself and for others is a concern for disciples. Receiving the good things God offers by seeking him out is to be a staple of life. Treating others as you wish to be treated means that life is lived with a regard for others. A healthy relationship to God translates into treating others well and leads into a spiritual walk that also depends on God for how to get there.

PREACHING AND TEACHING STRATEGIES

Exegetical and Theological Synthesis

The exegetical section stresses the horrors of hypocrisy. John the Baptist and Jesus hammered the Pharisees for pretentious, religious performance. Whether getting baptized (Matt. 3:7–10), giving alms (6:2), washing their hands (15:7), or selecting the best seats in the synagogue (23:6), crowd appeal motivated the Pharisees. Jesus saw through their act, citing Isaiah 29:13—"This people honors me with their lips, but their heart is far from me"—indicating hypocrisy is an ancient problem (Deut. 10:16; 28:47; Ezek. 36:26).

In fact, careful attention to the heart—the locus of our affections and volition—is essential to loving God and others. Unfortunately, as Jeremiah noted, the heart is deceitful (Jer. 17:9). The apostle Paul built on the prophet's observation, making a case for the depraved nature of all humanity (Rom. 3:9–23). Religious people have no advantage over pagans; all have sinned. Religion merely masks the deceptive state of our hearts.

Fortunately, the Bible provides a roadmap for self-examination. David's penitent prayer in Psalm 51 stripped away his pretense, inviting God to cleanse his heart and restore his spirit (v. 10). He understood that a contrite heart mattered more than sacrificial performance (v. 17). Likewise, the apostle Paul viewed himself as an imperfect disciple and foremost sinner (Phil. 3:12–17; 1 Tim. 1:15). Then, in an interesting turn, both David and Paul implored fellow sinners to replace their selfish ways with godly virtues (Ps. 51:11–13; Gal. 5:17–6:10; Eph. 4:17–31; Col. 3:5–15). Their self-examination turned them into empathetic instructors. In other words, moral perfection is not a prerequisite to exhorting others, but honest self-reflection is imperative.

Preaching Idea

Train your eyes to empathize through honest self-reflection.

Contemporary Connections

What does it mean?

What does it mean to train your eyes to empathize through honest self-reflection? Honest self-reflection builds off David's "search me and know me" prayer from Psalm 139:23–24. It is what Calvin called "self-knowledge" in the opening section of his *Institutes*. He deemed "knowledge of God" and "knowledge of self" inseparable ventures in theological understanding. "Know thyself" is more than a philosophical maxim, it is a key to virtue.

Before honest self-reflection builds empathy for others, it nurtures compassion for oneself. When we train our eyes not to overlook or understate our inadequacies, failings, prejudices, defense mechanisms, emotional overreactions, pride, and selfish tendencies, but accept these faults as growth areas, our appreciation of God's lavish grace increases. We should not actively sin to make grace abound (Rom. 6:1), but awareness of sin magnifies our appreciation of grace.

True recipients of grace naturally return the favor. They have experienced the warmth of God's compassion and want to share it with others. Their empathy comes out in many ways: sponsoring a fellow addict, listening to a grieving friend, forgiving a child for repeating the family sin of anger, hearing a confession without heaping on judgment.

Is it true?

Should we train our eyes to empathize through honest self-reflection? Doesn't self-reflection breed selfishness? Isn't empathy too soft for a world bent on sin? These questions are important in our self-centered, soft-on-sin times. In *The Rise and Triumph of the Modern Self*, Carl Trueman (2020, 25, 42–52) charts the march in culture toward progressive sexual ethics. Self-expression rules our therapeutic age. But we must distinguish self-*expression* from self-*reflection*. The former is noncritical, fluid, and unbound by God's law. The latter is self-critical, focused, and governed by God's law. Self-expression says, "Take me as I am (or will be) or leave me alone." Self-reflection says, "Here I am, Lord. Mold me." Self-reflection is a timeless virtue. Self-expression is a vice of our times.

But before casting aspersions on our self-expressive age, we must recognize it as a byproduct of uncritical, evangelistic efforts. We have proffered a gospel of easy belief, devoid of daily sacrifice (Luke 9:23). We offer heaven without calling for holiness. We say, "Come as you are," and have enabled spiritual squatting. We have failed to give sinners tools for honest self-reflection and growth in sanctification (Phil. 2:12).

Contrarily, rigid moral codes and uniform standards have made holiness unattractive. Sadly, churches can breed such narrow forms of holiness that their gatherings feel like high tea parties for pharisaical elites—only those who have arrived are invited. However, an empathetic person is willing to pull up extra chairs to the table. She knows she is only there by Jesus's invitation. She wants to extend the favor and teach others the graces she continues to learn as she draws near to Jesus. Indeed, empathy is inviting, not enabling.

Now what?

How do we train our eyes to empathize? How can we practice honest self-reflection? As mentioned above, honest self-reflection begins with God. We present ourselves to him and ask him to search us (Ps. 139:23–24). We confess sin as it comes to mind (Pss. 32, 51, 103; 1 John 1:9). Moreover, we pay attention to how God has shaped us from our early days to the present moment, including our tragedies and triumphs, family and friendships, college and career, and hobbies and interests. A life map or storyboard may help visualize the arc of our lives, aiding our self-reflection. As we pray, confess, and consider our lives, we recognize God's merciful hand over every moment (Rom. 8:38–39).

A second step to self-reflection invites other voices to speak. We can ask a spouse, mentor, colleague, parent, or close friend to share with us needed growth areas. Honest criticism is hard to receive, but we must permit them to tell the truth in love (Eph. 4:15). Of course, a personality test or professional counseling offers a less risky form of reflection. We may not agree with our Enneagram results, but we're not likely to exact revenge on the test either.

As we establish empathy with ourselves through honest self-reflection, we are poised to pay it forward. We know every friend, neighbor, and stranger is a fellow sinner with a broken past, learned behaviors, and bad habits. We know everyone has a personal story and personality type that explains their choices. An empathetic person can discern between an explanation and excuse. More importantly, an empathetic person will give others the opportunity to tell their story rather than throw stones at them. Thus, it is not only our eyes we train for empathy, but also our ears (for empathetic listening) and mouths (for empathetic speech).

Creativity in Presentation

Gender identity is one of the more complicated and tense topics in our age. Christians, especially older generations, have a reputation for responding in disdain or disgust toward people with same-sex orientation or gender expressions that do not align with their biological sex. Yarhouse and Sadusky (2020) suggest a posture of "compassionate conviction." Rather than condemning someone's divergent expression of gender, they suggest saying, "It seems like I'm coming into your life seven or eight chapters into the story. Can you tell me about the previous chapters?" This comment and question could curb our judgment instinct with any issue. Remind your people, "Every life is a story in progress. Every action that triggers your inner critic has seven or eight chapters behind it. Engaging the earlier chapters will help you empathize rather than criticize." That empathy may place you in a space to be of real help and correction.

Brené Brown has become a cherished speaker and author for her work on vulnerability, bravery, and empathy. Her 2010 TED Talk "The Power of Vulnerability" remains one of the most popular in the TED library. You can find a three-minute excerpt from her work on empathy with charming illustrations (of a bear, fox, and antelope) that differentiate between "sympathy" and "empathy." She explains, "In order to connect with [someone else], I have to connect with something in myself that knows that feeling." You can search for this clip on TED.com or YouTube.

The film *Just Mercy* (directed by Destin Daniel Cretton, 2019) describes the real-life work of lawyer Bryan Stevenson (played by Michael B. Jordan), who began his work with death row inmates in Alabama in the 1990s. Stevenson began his work after meeting his first prisoner, an underrepresented black man his age. Empathy motivated his merciful work of justice. The film climaxes with Stevenson helping exonerate Walter McMillian (played by Jamie Foxx), who had been wrongfully convicted of murder. In his closing argument, Stevenson challenges a legal system that makes judgments based upon "bigotry and bias" due to skin color and socioeconomic conditions instead of hard evidence. In other words, our judgments are often superficial, unfounded, and wrong.

Personal examples of overcoming bias may prove effective. You may have had a friend whom, at first, you considered odd or unlikable, only to develop a deep bond. Often married couples started out as lopsided, romantic pursuits—she's just not that into you—later to morph into a loving communion. (From years of premarital counseling, I know several stories that follow this script.) Sadly, even my experience as a parent has made me face a bias—namely, I can be more critical toward my oldest daughter—whose personality mirrors mine—than her behavior warranted.

Finally, though the "plank" and "speck" images speak for themselves, you might have fun illustrating Jesus's concept with some props. For the speck, you could have a toothpick or pile of sawdust. For the plank, you could hold up a two-by-four or two-by-six. Moreover, you could have a large mirror on stage, facing the audience at first. Then, as you stress the importance of self-reflection, you could move in front of the mirror, casting glances at self and the audience reflected. Eventually, you might move the mirror around, setting it between you and the audience, and say, "There. Now I'm not distracted by you. I can see me. And I can see there's plenty of work to do."

As you adapt your creative ideas, stay focused on the main ideas. Treating others sensitively and seeing ourselves realistically reflects our calling and requires being spiritually discerning. Therefore, train your eyes to empathize through honest self-reflection.

- Self-reflection spares others from harsh criticism (7:1–5).
- Discernment safeguards holy truths from careless people (7:6).
- Dialogue with God keeps us dependent on him (7:7–11).
- Self-reflection ensures good treatment of others (7:12).

DISCUSSION QUESTIONS

1. What exegetical rules should guide our approach to preaching Jesus's maxims?
2. How do Jesus's maxims accord with wider Jewish and cultural teaching present in his day? How do they differ?
3. What makes "do not judge" such a powerful maxim in our culture?
4. How does honest self-reflection turn into empathy? How might empathy lead to enablement?
5. What are good examples of discernment that lead to safeguarding sacred things?
6. Why is it helpful to view Jesus's exhortation to "Ask, seek, and knock" as a maxim rather than a fixed law of prayer?

Matthew 7:13–29

EXEGETICAL IDEA

Jesus underscored the importance and consequences of a proper response to his message and authority by speaking of the narrow gate, fruit on the tree, knowing others, and the house built on a good or bad foundation.

THEOLOGICAL FOCUS

Responding by doing what Jesus says leads to fruit and wisdom in life.

PREACHING IDEA

Following Jesus leads to true flourishing.

PREACHING POINTERS

Jesus taught among many types of teachers in his day. Other rabbis trained their disciples. Groups of scribes, Pharisees, and elders instructed the Jewish populace. Even itinerant teachers stirred up crowds. A teacher's credibility, however, was not determined by the size of their audience but the soundness of their words. Matthew reminded his original audience of Jesus's profound wisdom. His vivid imagery—two gates, two trees, and two foundations—grips the imagination. The conclusion to the sermon gave a final call to its hearers to inspect their hearts and reject messianic pretenders, which was especially relevant for those facing persecution and political pressures in Matthew's day. Only Jesus's words offered wisdom for the day and confidence for the coming day of judgment.

There is no shortage of advice in our information age. It buzzes from blogs and social media sites. TV screens and newspaper columns shout it. People post their opinions, offer self-help insights, provide motivational tips, and share DIY instructions for projects ranging from "build your own changing table" to "how to bake eggplant lasagna." Anyone can become an expert these days; all they need to do is drive enough traffic to their website. Unfortunately, the wisdom of our age is not only self-focused but also fleeting. Our "best life now" may get worse tomorrow. Fortunately, Jesus's teaching has endured the ages and prepares us for eternity. We should put it to work. This message reminds us that following Jesus leads to true flourishing.

JESUS TEACHES ON THE NARROW GATE, FALSE PROPHETS, AND HEEDING HIM (7:13–29)

LITERARY STRUCTURE AND THEMES (7:13–29)

This unit involves a series of pictures and warnings that urges one to embrace what Jesus said because life itself before God was at stake. There is an exhortation (vv. 13–14), a warning (vv. 15–20), another warning (vv. 21–23), and then a summary call to listen and do (vv. 24–27), followed by a closing remark about concluding the sermon and the authority of Jesus (vv. 28–29). The unit not only emphasizes responding to Jesus but urges one to be careful who to allow to teach and guide you. So we have a call about entering by the narrow gate (vv. 13–14), while the warning about false prophets suggests a competing set of ideas that can be followed but that lead to death and destruction (vv. 15–20). Death and destruction come through missing the narrow gate and embracing the false prophets. Another set of dangers was not knowing Jesus while using his name (vv. 21–23) and not doing what he teaches (vv. 24–27). Exposure to Jesus was not the same as knowing and engaging with him. Everything about this unit stresses the need to respond to Jesus by doing what he says and embracing what he teaches. The entire gospel continues to make this point. The crowd's response of amazement closes the unit (vv. 28–29).

This series of exhortations and warnings has parallels. Matthew 7:13–14 is like Luke 13:22–30, especially 13:24–27, but the differences are great enough that these may not reflect a similar source or setting (Davies and Allison 1988, 695). Matthew 7:15–20 is like Luke 6:43–45. Matthew 7:21–23 is like Luke 6:46. Luke's form in both cases is much more abbreviated. Matthew 7:24–27 is like Luke 6:47–49. Matthew 7:28–29 is like Mark 1:21–22 and somewhat like Luke 5:15–16. Once again we see material that parallels with Luke's Sermon on the Plain and material that falls outside of it. Jesus's teaching was stitched together into one locale in Matthew, while Luke spreads it across his gospel.

EXPOSITION (7:13–29)

The presence of opposition and persecution meant that false teaching was a challenge for the new movement. Jesus was aware of the risk and taught about how to spot it. Matthew had a theme of Jesus being the only teacher, unlike the array of teaching rabbis in Judaism (Byrskog 1994). There also was the threat of internal false teachers, those who claimed Jesus's name but did not actually respond to his teaching (Matt. 7:21–23). Jesus's exhortation is broad, so all these groups are in view. His authority to possess this role was highlighted here and maintained throughout the gospel.

Jesus underscored the importance and consequences of a proper response to his message and authority by speaking of the narrow gate, fruit on the tree, knowing others, and the house built on a good or bad foundation.

7:13–14. This short passage is a simple contrast between two paths: one has a narrow gate and the other is wide. The two ways is a theme in the Old Testament (Deut. 11:26; 30:15; Pss. 1:6; 119:29–32; 139:24; Prov. 28:6, 18; Jer. 21:8) and in Judaism (T. Ash. 1:3–5; 2 En. 30:15—God showed Adam two ways; 1QS 3:13–4:26). The picture of God's gate was also common (Ps. 118:19–20—a major messianic psalm quoted in the NT; Isa. 60:11, 18). One road was traveled by few, and the other was the road most traveled but yielding less. Jesus urged that life's way was through the narrow gate that few find. It was hard to find, while many traveled the wide way to destruction. The image may be of the kingdom as a city-state and the need to enter the right municipality (Nolland 2005, 332). Nolland argues for an image of a roadway to the gate that was the choice (so also Quarles 2011, 311–14), but Wilkins (2004, 322) says the issue was the choice of what to enter and then came the way to be traveled. The fact the experience of the movement was called "the Way" may slightly favor the latter choice. Morris (1992, 176) and Hagner (1993, 179) refuse to make a choice about the images, seeing it as about the way of discipleship. In either case, the emphasis was on making the right choice about the right path.

Two-Way Texts

Deuteronomy 11:26: "Take note—I am setting before you today a blessing and a curse."

Deuteronomy 30:15: "Look! I have set before you today life and prosperity on the one hand, and death and disaster on the other."

Psalm 1:6: "Certainly the Lord guards the way of the godly, but the way of the wicked ends in destruction."

Psalm 139:24: "See if there is any idolatrous way in me, and lead me in the everlasting way."

This is the only place Matthew uses the term ἀπώλεια for "destruction" (BDAG s.v. "ἀπώλεια" 2, 127). The term τεθλιμμένη may have meant not just "narrow" but "constricted" and may allude to the pressure of persecution, given this term referred to tribulation and pointed to the presence of pressure (Nolland 2005, 333–34; BDAG s.v. "θλίβω" 2, 457).

Spirituality was about a quest, so one must find their way and make good choices. Pay attention to spiritual things, Jesus said. Even more, pay attention to what I am saying about them. In them was the way of life, that is, eternal life (1QS 4:7; Pss. Sol. 9:5; 14:10; T. Ash. 6:3).

The core exhortation was to "enter" (εἰσέλθατε) by the narrow gate (BDAG s.v. "εἰσέρχομαι" 1γ, 293–94). The emphasis on the narrow gate was made both by the exhortation at the start and by a break in the parallelism of the verse at the end. The narrow gate in the parallelism is introduced with the particle τί to bring attention to the line (BDAG s.v. "τίς" 3, 1007—untranslated but means *how* the gate . . .). This was an exclamation that can be seen to work semantically as explanatory, meaning "for" or as an exclamation drawing attention to the point, meaning in effect "how." The force of the latter option, which was likely, is "how" narrow is the gate, making the point emphatic. Understand how narrow this gate is. The option took focus to execute. The door is an image common in John's gospel (John 10:7, 9; 14:6).

Stott (1978, 194–96) speaks of the sets of two in the comparison. There was the broad and narrow gate, the constricted and broad way, there were the few and the many, and there was the way of life and of destruction.

7:15. Jesus warned of false prophets who look like sheep but actually were more like devouring wolves. The hypocrisy of a deceiving appearance was central to the image. The present imperative pointed to being on constant watch against such. These prophets looked like sheep, that is, like members of the community, but they were not (Greco-Roman examples can be found in Keener 2009, 250). The key term here is "wolf," which refers to a dangerous animal that is destructive, brings death, and so was compared to evil, destructive people (BDAG s.v. "λύκος" 2, 604; Jer. 5:6; Ezek. 22:27; Zeph. 3:3; Acts 20:29). Have nothing to do with such teachers, Jesus commanded.

Who were they? Certainly, in the context of Jesus's ministry, there would be opponents out of Judaism, but their opposition would be obvious. Yet their religious connection to Jesus's own roots might make them candidates to be heard. There were also people who would claim Jesus as a connection by calling him Lord but ignored what he said. Turner (2008, 217) sees them as libertines because of the lawlessness tied to them in Matthew 7:15–23. Jesus would be teaching in Matthew 13 about the kingdom message. There he referred to the community that included people mixed together like the wheat and tares (see also Matt. 24:11, 24). Jesus likely has in mind either group. Nolland (2005, 336) speaks of the exhortation's general nature. It is important to recall that Jesus preached from within Judaism and was calling the nation to her hope. However, these false prophets were more likely to portray themselves as inside the community, working for its interests. That form of false teaching was more subtle and difficult to spot. *Didache* 16:3–4 talks about this issue in the early church: "For in the last days the false prophets and corrupters shall be multiplied, and the sheep shall be turned into wolves, and love shall be turned into hate."

7:16. Identifying false prophets should not be difficult. Their fruit would reveal their hearts. Jewish texts already taught this kind of an idea (Sir. 27:6; 2 En. 42:14). Jesus compared the nature and fruit-bearing of trees to people's spiritual product. Thornbushes cannot yield grapes, nor can thistles bring forth figs. The question uses the emphatic μήτι and expects a negative answer ("no way"). In Israel, thornbushes and thistles were a major problem for those who farmed. False prophets would be evident by what they produced. See James 3:8–12 about speech, and Matthew 3:8, which calls for a life in line with one's intent.

7:17–18. The illustrations involving produce continued in these two verses with a simple contrast. "In the same way" (οὕτως), a healthy tree makes good fruit, while a rotten tree makes worthless/evil fruit. This was stated both positively and negatively in a mirrored manner. A rotten tree cannot bring forth good fruit, just as a healthy tree will not yield worthless fruit. The key terms are the negative ones: σαπρός and πονηρός. The first term points to that which is "rotten" or "stale" (BDAG s.v. "σαπρός" 1bα, 913; Hos. 2:4 LXX; Matt. 12:33; 13:48), while the second term can refer to "evil" in a moral context (BDAG s.v. "πονηρός" 2, 851–52). In a nonmoral context as here, it means worthless or bad fruit, but the tinge of a moral implication is not far away (Davies and Allison 1988, 710). Just as a tree showed its quality by its fruit, so did how a teacher lived showed the person's virtue or lack of it. People are what they are (Jer. 13:23). The Old Testament has similar ideas (Job 14:4; Jer. 23:9–14; France 2007, 291).

7:19. Accountability for this fruit was the next topic. Jesus noted that every tree not bearing fruit will be cut down and cast into the fire. The implication was why follow that which God will judge to be evil? Why be on the wrong side? This principle of judgment mirrored what John the Baptist said in Matthew 3:10. The image of burning alluded to the judgment in Gehenna (Matt. 5:22, 29, 30; 10:28; 18:9; 23:15, 33). The verse was a bridge to the following remarks in Matthew 7:21–23 on judgment for not doing what the Lord Jesus said.

7:20. The conclusion to this passage simply reiterates the principle that fruit reveals the nature of any prophet (Matt. 7:16a). "So" (ἄρα) one will know them by their fruit (BDAG s.v. "ἄρα" 127). This verse also links to what follows with the use of the idea to know someone. Actions revealed the heart.

7:21. Jesus's next warning dealt with the question of who enters the kingdom. Not all who say "Lord, Lord" to Jesus will enter in (Luke 6:46).

Rather, those who do the will of the heavenly Father get in. Fruit shows relationship to God through responsiveness that is at the core of faith. Jesus was challenging those who only give lip service to God's way in him. False prophets and those who make false claims of relationship to Jesus were challenged here. These were false disciples (Wilkins 2004, 324). They would not make it into God's kingdom. There was a profound difference between profession of faith and actual faith (Morris 1992, 178–79; James 2:14–26).

The term "Lord" (κύριος) was an important one for Matthew (BDAG s.v. "κύριος" 2bγב, 578). It pointed to one with authority who gives divine-like aid and echoed a name for God (Matt. 8:2, 5, 25; 9:28; 14:28, 30, 33; 15:22, 25; 17:15; 20:30, 31, 33). The link between Jesus and judgment showed his authority and parallels how Jesus would speak about the Son of Man in glory (Matt. 10:32–33; 11:27; 13:41–43; 16:27; 19:28; 24:29–31; 25:31–46, 26:64; 28:18; Turner 2008, 219). This is the first place Jesus speaks of "my Father" in Matthew (Matt. 10:32–33; 11:27; 12:50; 15:13; 16:17; 18:10, 19; 20:23; 25:34; 26:29, 39, 42, 53). In the following verses, those in this group even appeared to do things in Jesus's name, yielding a kind of pseudo-fruit, but their hearts were still not right (France 2007, 292–93). In this verse, knowing Jesus appeared tantamount to entry into the kingdom, but a surprise was coming.

7:22. This scene assumed a refusal to be welcomed on "that day," the day of judgment. The appeal of those who called Jesus "Lord" was based on their activity in his name, a reference made three times in an emphatic position in the Greek. Jesus gave three examples: prophesying, casting out demons, and performing miracles. The question "did we not" expects a positive answer (using οὐ). Acting in Jesus's name was the warrant for acceptance, in their view. It probably meant they acted in light of his authority or with his power (Davies and Allison 1988, 715–16). It is interesting to see that miracles in themselves were not automatic proof of a divine presence, as a false witness was also possible. First Corinthians 13:2 says that prophesy without love is nothing (Osborne 2010, 274). Jesus had other standards of evaluation. One was given already: the fruit of the claimant (Matt. 13:24–30, 36–43, 47–50). Another comes next: really knowing Jesus and being recognized by him as a result.

7:23. Jesus's standard was his knowing the one who made a claim to act for the Lord. Did they relate to and with him? Jesus declared as he judged them that he did not know them. The strong expression "I will confess" (ὁμολογήσω) is used here (BDAG s.v. "ὁμολογέω" 4a, 708). The key term for what was missing is ἔγνων or "knowing" (BDAG s.v. "γινώσκω" 7, 199–201). To say "I do not know you" is a repudiation formula. The verb means to "know" in the sense of recognize and be familiar with someone. Even more emphatic is adding the idea of "never" (οὐδέποτε) having known them (BDAG s.v. "οὐδέποτε" 735). Jesus did not know them as a part of the family (Matt. 25:12—picture of judgment). So "I never recognized you as one of my own" (Amos 3:2; John 10:14; 1 Cor. 8:3; 2 Tim. 2:12, 19; Davies and Allison 1988, 717; Turner 2008, 219). Their hearts were not connected to him. They were doers of lawlessness and so they were sent away (Matt. 13:41; on the language of dismissal or refusal to go God's way: Job 21:14; 22:17). The sent-away, rejection language recalls Psalm 6:10 [Eng.]. Osborne (2010, 274) notes Judas as an example. Stott (1978, 207) says their profession was verbal, not moral. It was not charismatic activity that was the issue here, but how one engaged in ministry (Hagner 1993, 188).

Jesus was seen as the judge in this text, or at least as a key, decisive figure in that judgment. Nolland (2005, 341) may understate how Jesus was portrayed here by saying he had influence in the assessment. Betz's claim (1995, 554–56) that Jesus was only an advocate here also says too little. The text leaves a stronger impression than this (Keener 2009, 253–54; Quarles 2011, 335–36; Sim 1996, 130–39; Wilkins 2004, 325, has discussion of judgment in Matthew). Jesus executed the judgment. The remark about Jesus's authority in Matthew 7:28–29 probably looked back to claims like this.

Again, as throughout the sermon, the standard was the heart. That was what got examined in the judgment. Activity without relationship was meaningless before God (Jer. 7:4–11). Faith that knows Jesus responds to him (Matt. 6:10; 12:50; 21:31; 26:42; Rom. 2:13; 3:8; 8:25; 11:22; 13:14; Gal. 5:6; Eph. 2:10; 4:17; Col. 1:23; Titus 2:7, 14; 3:8, 14; James 2:14–26). Turner (2008, 220) says the text was against any idea of cheap grace that ignored grace's product from a response of faith. Quarles (2011, 333) surveys Jesus's teaching on the Son of Man and judgment in Matthew 13:24–30, 37–43, 16:27, and 25:31–46. In the context of the sermon, the response was to Jesus and his offer of the kingdom (Wilkins 2004, 325).

7:24–25. Jesus closed the sermon with a call to respond to him in relationship by hearing and doing what he has taught. Keener (2009, 255) observes that what Jesus said about his own teaching here is what was often said about the law in Judaism. There was a compare-and-contrast antithetical parallelism in the two pictures he gave. This time Jesus started with the positive example and ended with the negative, the reverse of most of the sermon. This allowed his remarks to end with a warning about not responding. The image of standing or falling or of a good foundation was common in the Old Testament (Prov. 10:25; 12:7; 14:11; Isa. 28:16–17—an important apologetic text in the New Testament; Ezek. 13:8–16; also in Judaism: Sir. 22:16–18).

Standing, Falling, and Foundation Texts

Proverbs 10:25: "When the storm passes through, the wicked are swept away, but the righteous are an everlasting foundation."

Proverbs 12:7: "The wicked are overthrown and perish, but the righteous household will stand."

Proverbs 14:11: "The household of the wicked will be destroyed, but the tent of the upright will flourish."

Isaiah 28:16–17: "Therefore, this is what the Sovereign Lord says: 'Look, I am laying a stone in Zion, an approved stone, set in place as a precious cornerstone for the foundation. The one who maintains his faith will not panic. I will make justice the measuring line, fairness the plumb line; hail will sweep away the unreliable refuge, the floodwaters will overwhelm the hiding place.'"

The positive example was the person who heard and obeyed. Doing what Jesus said was important to him (Luke 8:21—those were his family; John 12:47–48; also Luke 6:47; James 1:25). The person should respond directly to Jesus's teaching, called "my" words. This was the wise person who built a house on a rock. In Israel, such foundations might go ten feet into the rock (Wilkins 2004, 327). It was work, but it worked. Such a foundation was able to stand the storms of life as a result (variations of this image are Matt. 16:18; 1 Cor. 3:10–15). Rain, flood, and wind could not overtake that house. A house being rooted in the rock allowed it to stand. The idea of the tempest was not so much about the tensions of this life as being able to stand up in the final judgment (Gen. 6–7; Ps. 66:10–12; Isa. 28:2; 29:6; 30:27–30; Ezek. 13:10–16; 38:22; Quarles 2011, 345–46).

7:26–27. The opposite of being wise and building a house on the rock was to be foolish and build it on the sand. Jesus often taught with contrastive pairs (Matt. 18:23–34; 21:28–31; 24:45–51; Luke 7:41–42; 12:24–26; 16:19–31; 18:9–14; Davies and Allison 1988, 723). The contrast in this picture was the person who only listened to Jesus but did not do what he taught (Ezek. 33:32). This person was foolish, which in Matthew referred to those who did not respond to Jesus and lacked good judgment (Matt. 25:2, 3, 8—opposite the wise; Hagner 1993, 191). The result was tragic, for the rain and wind came and beat against the house, tearing it down. Storms that destroyed the wicked person's home parallel Old Testament imagery (Job 8:15; Pss. 11:6; 83:15; Prov. 14:11; Isa. 28:15–18; Dan. 9:26; Turner 2008, 222). Its fall was great. The additional description at the end of the verse about the fall being great extended the description of the result, broke the parallelism, and placed a stress on the failure's significance. What a waste and loss was the feeling of the closing picture Jesus painted. The sermon ended with a thud of the failure that came from not applying what Jesus had said. Jesus had been alluding to the destructive path throughout this chapter (Matt. 7:13, 19). Here he ended the sermon with a warning that failure to embrace what he said would have a negative impact on how we lived.

7:28–29. The reference to Jesus completing his words was something Matthew uses to close all the major discourse blocks in Matthew 10, 13, 18, and 23–25 (see Matt. 11:1; 13:53; 19:1; 26:1). The teaching Jesus gave generated "amazement" (ἐξεπλήσσοντο) from the crowd (BDAG s.v. "ἐκπλήσσω" 308). That the crowd was listening when earlier Jesus had withdrawn to speak to disciples is not a real issue, as certainly some followed to hear him (Hagner 1993, 193).

The verb about being amazed has the force of being overwhelmed. The imperfect portrays the amazement as ongoing, even lingering. Jesus's teaching made a deep impression in terms of its claims. The language is like Mark 1:22, but Mark's use ties the authority to Jesus's words and deeds. In Matthew, amazement was always for Jesus's words (Matt. 13:54; 19:25; 22:33). His teaching came with a sense of "authority" (BDAG s.v. "ἐξουσία" 2, 353). This idea is developed in the following chapters (Matt. 8:9; 9:6, 8; 10:1; 28:16–20; Quarles 2011, 350). Jesus showed an independent capability with regard to the things of God. It was unlike how the scribes taught. There was no appeal to other authorities or even in many cases to God. The close connection between God's will and Jesus's pronouncements about his role in judgment were where the sense of authority surfaced. The emphasis here can be seen in the sermon's repeated refrain "But I say to you" and in Jesus's claims tied to judgment. Wilkins (2004, 328) notes that the prophets said, "This is what the Lord says." Jesus's claims are more direct.

Matthew handles this scene differently from Mark. There is no Sabbath context and no healings as in Mark. Matthew fails to note such a Sabbath context for Mark's Sabbath healings four times (Mark 1:21–34—three sets of healings; Mark 6:1–6; Oliver 2013, 53–79).

In this text, the crowd was respectful but deliberative about what Jesus was doing. They did not respond in faith but mere wonder. They were more open and neutral than the Jewish leaders.

THEOLOGICAL FOCUS

The exegetical idea (Jesus underscored the importance and consequences of a proper response to his message and authority by speaking of the narrow gate, fruit on the tree, knowing others, and the house built on a good or bad foundation) points to this theological notion: responding by doing what Jesus says leads to fruit and wisdom in life.

The focus of this unit is responding to Jesus. His way is the narrow way. It takes work, like building a good foundation for a house. It is the way of wisdom. It involves both hearing and doing. It also means recognizing the false prophets who steer one in a wrong direction and who love lawlessly in doing so. Responding to Jesus means knowing him. Knowing him means going in the direction he calls. For Jesus, there is no such thing as a mere intellectual faith. Faith acts and embraces action in the direction Jesus says to go.

Everything about this closing unit points to Jesus's authority. His words mean life. Failure to respond to them leads to destruction. He will be the judge in the end. Jesus does not allow himself to be placed alongside other religious greats. His voice gives unique access into God and his program. The kingdom message is about life and death. At its center stands Jesus's authority within that kingdom. His call is for an integrity of character and heart that expresses itself in activity that reflects a genuine allegiance to him.

Another point is that the fruit of one's character and actions reveal the nature of one's heart. So the product of a false prophet's character will show who he or she really is. Good character will hear, respond, and bear good fruit.

PREACHING AND TEACHING STRATEGIES

Exegetical and Theological Synthesis

The exegetical material presents two clear paths. Echoing imagery of wisdom literature (Deut. 11:26; 30:15; Pss. 1:6; 119:29–32; 139:24; Prov. 28:6, 18; Jer. 21:8), Jesus offered a binary: choose life or death. The additional metaphors of fruit and foundations implied a similar choice: flourishing and fortitude or corruption and crumbling. Discipleship is an all-or-nothing decision (Matt. 8:18–22; 10:11–15, 32–39; 12:30; Luke 11:23; 14:28–35). To merely marvel at Jesus's words and work is not the same as following him.

To compel a response, Jesus described future reward or punishment. The Lord did not mince words about eternal suffering, hell, or damnation. He described a place of darkness, destruction, and separation from God (Matt. 5:22, 29–30; 7:13, 19, 23; 10:15, 28; 13:40–42, 49–50; 25:41–46). For some the threat of hell was enough to cause repentance.

Others, however, responded more readily to reward. Of course, the greatest reward was to know him, which meant sharing in his glory in eternity (Matt. 7:21–23; 13:43; 25:34–40). But other rewards were stated in the Beatitudes (5:3–12) or in response to their practice of sincere devotion (6:1, 4, 6, 18). Heaven will be a storehouse of eternal treasures (6:20–21; 19:28–30). The fullness of these rewards is yet to be revealed, but even now we can enjoy assurance of salvation, confidence in our new identity as kingdom saints, and the familial bond with fellow disciples (5:3, 10; 7:24–25; 18:15–20).

Preaching Idea

Following Jesus leads to true flourishing.

Contemporary Connections

What does it mean?

Following Jesus requires more than mental assent to his teaching. The life the Master Teacher prescribed must be put into action. Genuine faith combines belief and behavior (James 2:14–26). Trust leads to obedience (Heb. 11). The Great Commission punctuates this notion, calling disciple-making disciples to "teach others obedience" (Matt. 28:19).

Thus, we learn to practice Jesus's "elaborate love," not only by avoiding bitterness toward those who have hurt us but by speaking truth even when it could result in friction at home or work. We not only acknowledge our missionary identity as salt and light, but we act on it by "being a force for good" via digital evangelism, advocacy for the poor, and volunteering in local schools or shelters. And we fight the urge to roast our enemies, but instead listen to their perspective and empathize with shared humanity even as we sometimes challenge.

Is it true?

Does following Jesus lead to true flourishing? Yes, but the flourishing he promised was eschatological. He did not preach a prosperity gospel. While we may make some gains for the gospel here and now—seeing new people come to faith and pockets of global suffering alleviated—the fullness of flourishing will greet us in the age to come. Upon his return, Jesus will vanquish evil, reward righteousness, and reconcile creation to its Creator. This hope of future flourishing provides hope against today's despair and a foretaste of the glory to come when we glimpse God's peace breaking into the present.

Indeed, future flourishing spills into the present when we spot signs of in daily life: freedom from a nagging sin; restoration of a broken parent-child bond; a sense of belonging in an age of isolation; a restoration of justice; a calling that gives meaning to our work; corporate worship that causes awe; the read, preached, or spoken word of God that shatters our autonomy and proclaims Christ's authority. This momentary flourishing comes in myriad ways, "producing for us an eternal weight of glory far beyond all comparison" (2 Cor. 4:17).

Now what?

While we should be cautious when charting a discipleship methodology, we can insist on three postures for flourishing as Jesus-followers. First, repentance is an ongoing posture. We come to Jesus as humble sinners. We are poor in spirit, open to hear God. Our knowledge is limited. Our independence often flares in us. Daily our hearts pull us toward the idols of comfort, success, security, power, and ease. Repentance says, "Jesus, you are Master; I am not. I will follow."

Discipleship Methodology

Jesus invited individual disciples and needy crowds to follow him. His invitation was not a one-time offer, but a long-term commitment to be with him, learn from him, and imitate his kingdom mission. The relationship began with a summons to "repent and believe" and then progressed through stages of growth: learning, sharing, serving, suffering, and going. Many authors (Bruce 2009; Coleman, 2010) have developed a discipleship methodology from their synthesis of the Gospels, thereby stripping the gospel authors of their unique approach to discipleship (Wilkins 1992).

Second, we maintain the mindset of a learner. Jesus, the Master Teacher, has much to say about God and Spirit, love and relationships, law and grace, health and purity, creation and self-care, heaven and hell. Willard (1997, 93–94) calls Jesus the "smartest man in the world." We must not understate the brilliance of his teachings. Of course, studying the Gospels will deepen our understanding of Jesus. But discernment allows us to see Christ at work in all areas of life: science, literature, film, history, nature, and strangers at the grocery store.

Third, obedience is our objective. We are students of Jesus, learning what he said, watching how he lived so we can imitate his ways. Jesus is more than an object of study. The gospel of Matthew is more than interesting subject material. The Sermon on the Mount is more than a rhetorically impressive speech. This is a person, story, and message to put into action. Lest we are overwhelmed by the mountain of maxims in this homily, we wisely heed one or two key exhortations that the Spirit has brought to mind to do.

Creativity in Presentation

In the original *The Karate Kid* (directed by John Avildsen, 1984), Daniel LaRusso, a teenage misfit (played by Ralph Macchio), learns karate from the enigmatic maintenance man at his apartment, Mr. Miyagi (played by Pat Morita). The unlikely pair teams up after Daniel, new to town, suffers a beating from a high school gang. Mr. Miyagi teaches Daniel karate indirectly: by painting a fence, sanding a floor, and waxing a car. At a critical point in the film, Daniel threatens to quit the lessons, unconvinced he has learned anything. His mentor offers a classic all-or-nothing response: "Either you karate do 'yes.' Or karate do 'no.' You karate do 'guess so,'"—*squash*—"just like grape." Following Jesus is not a "guess so" if we want to flourish.

Testimonials are a great means of marketing the success of a product or self-help programs. Their before-and-after shots capture the effect of following the plan. Think about advertisements for dietary supplements that led to dramatic weight loss or exercise plans that trimmed fat and produced a six-pack. Some have attributed their revitalized marriage to following advice from a counselor, doing the Love Dare, or attending a Weekend to Remember conference. Dave Ramsey's radio show and his book *Total Money Makeover* offer a six-step strategy to financial freedom (and flourishing). Daily, people call in to the show and shout over the airwaves, "I'm debt-free!" At the heart of every testimonial is someone who heeded the practical advice given to them. Following directions led to true flourishing. You might play a testimonial from the Dave Ramsey show, an infomercial, or find before-and-after pictures of someone.

Or you may infuse some humor by overlaying your face on several before-and-after images. From "bald" pastor to "coiffed" pastor. From "scrawny" pastor to "chiseled" pastor. From "poor" pastor to "*bling*" pastor. In any case, be sure to let people know Jesus offered three "before-and-after" images in his sermon.

Jesus's Three Before-and-After Images

1. "I was a wanderer, lost in the crowd. When I followed Jesus, I found the way."
2. "I was a withering tree, bereft of fruit. When I followed Jesus, I became fruitful."
3. "I was a house on the sand, ready to fall. When I followed Jesus, I moved to the rock, and now my foundation is firm."

Finally, you may appeal to the wisdom of following directions. You might hold up an impressive Lego creation and say, "My son followed the directions." You might show an image from a gourmet meal your spouse cooked and say, "She followed the directions." You might cast an image of a tree you planted in your yard and say, "When we planted this four years ago, we followed the directions (including calling 811 before we dug!)." Then you could point to a rickety piece of furniture on the stage and say, "Whoever built this didn't follow the directions. Who wants to sit here?" Your point will be clear: "If following directions in lesser things leads to true flourishing (and avoids frustration), how much more eager should we be to follow Jesus's directions?"

In any case, you want to make sure your sermon stresses that responding by doing what Jesus says leads to fruit and wisdom in life. Or, more concisely, following Jesus leads to true flourishing.

- Pay attention to your direction (7:13–14).
- Pay attention to your instructors (7:15–20).
- Pay attention to your motivation (7:21–23).
- Pay attention to your foundation (7:24–27).
- Pay homage to Jesus's authority (7:28–29).

DISCUSSION QUESTIONS

1. What does the narrow road mean? How do we stay on it?
2. How did Jesus describe coming destruction? What imagery did he use?
3. What are signs of a false teacher? How should we respond to them?
4. What flourishing can we expect in the present? What is to come? What is the problem with expecting too much flourishing now?
5. How was Jesus's authority different from that of his contemporaries?
6. Where does your following of Jesus need greater attention?

Matthew 8:1–22

EXEGETICAL IDEA

Jesus's healings and exorcisms showed his ability to cleanse and the value of faith in the fulfillment of the promise to bear our infirmities. This section highlights why discipleship under pressure is a priority.

THEOLOGICAL FOCUS

Jesus's miracles reveal his authority and lay a basis for a total faith commitment to the ways of God in discipleship.

PREACHING IDEA

Forget your comforts and follow Christ.

PREACHING POINTERS

On the heels of the Sermon on the Mount, Jesus descended the hill and began to serve. His words did not stand alone but came with deeds to show what he meant. Not only was Jesus a master teacher but also a burden-bearer and miracle worker. Matthew wove together three miracles—cleansing a leper, healing a centurion's servant, and ridding Peter's mother-in-law of a fever—that signaled Jesus's authority. Moreover, Jesus's powerful and compassionate work affected all types of people. Matthew's audience would have taken note of the inclusive nature of the Son of Man's ministry. Likewise, they would have heard the high demands Jesus placed on would-be disciples. Due to increasing social pressures in Matthew's day, these statements on the cost of discipleship were timely.

Today the cost of discipleship remains steep. In many parts of the world, the church remains underground, not afforded the comforts of public gatherings or personal confessions of faith. Even in the United States, the aggressive push of secularism and "safe places" has made it more difficult for Christians to share their convictions without facing repercussions, like getting "canceled" or publicly shamed. Followers of Jesus are no longer afforded the comforts from the days when they constituted the majority. This, however, may be a blessing in disguise. Seeking and securing comforts easily becomes selfish. Showing compassion can be costly. In fact, Jesus modeled compassion to those needing spiritual and physical comforts regardless of their social status. We should do the same. This passage encourages us to forget our comforts and follow Christ.

JESUS HEALS A LEPER, A CENTURION'S SLAVE, AND PETER'S MOTHER-IN-LAW (8:1–22)

LITERARY STRUCTURE AND THEMES (8:1–22)

This unit begins a section of Matthew where deed and word alternate as Jesus shows his power and authority as the promised Messiah. The full section of triads runs from Matthew 8:1 to 9:38. In the larger unit are three series of three miracle story accounts (Matt. 8:1–17; 8:23–9:8; 9:18–34) interspersed with teaching blocks (Matt. 8:18–22; 9:9–17; 9:35–38). So we split these units up into the triad of miracles and then teaching link. Davies and Allison (1991, 1–3) cover the array of theories that treat the structure of these chapters. So also in this specific unit there are three miracles (vv. 1–4: leper; vv. 5–13: centurion's servant; vv. 14–17: Peter's mother-in-law, closed with a common Matthean scriptural note about fulfillment) followed by a block of teaching on discipleship (vv. 18–22).

The word-deed alternating theme also fits with Matthew 5–7, as that unit highlights Jesus's teaching while this one is dominated by his acts (Davies and Allison 1991, 1). Davies and Allison also note that those healed come from the fringe of the culture: a leper, a centurion's servant, a mother-in-law of a fisherman, two demoniacs, a paralytic, an anonymous woman, an unclean woman, a little girl, two blind men, and a demoniac. The number of women involved is significant (four out of twelve).

In Matthew 8:1–4, we have a simple miracle account of a leper's cleansing. So we have the approach of the one seeking healing, the healing, and then the response to the healing. In Matthew 8:5–13, we have a miracle account mixed with a pronouncement as its turning point appears in Matthew 8:10–12. In Matthew 8:14–17, we have a short miracle account and a miracle summary statement side by side. To it is attached a common Matthean narrative note on the fulfillment of Scripture, citing Isaiah 53:4. These miracles showed Jesus's messianic authority, while the centurion's example showed the appropriate response to that authority. The remark by Jesus about who will respond is the first clear saying in Matthew that Gentiles will be responsive to Jesus in ways that exceed Israel's response, although hints of this were encased in the infancy material with the development of the magi's role at Jesus's birth. Finally, we have a double pronouncement account on discipleship (Matt. 8:18–22). In the first pronouncement we have the situation of the Son of Man's present ministry meeting rejection, while in the second we have a challenge to disciples not to let family priorities block the pursuit of discipleship. So Jesus's authority, faith, and discipleship are the themes of the unit.

Jesus's messianic authority to heal and cleanse was the context of a call to a tough discipleship. Thus, the miracles framed a disciple's appreciating that the Son of Man had no place to put his head and the disciple's call to leave behind such high commitments as family life. Jesus's acts fulfilled Scripture in promises Isaiah taught. In the middle of the unit stands by far the largest piece, the example of the centurion's faith. That miracle shows us exemplary faith with its appropriate response to Jesus's presence. Jesus may have great power to cleanse, heal, and exorcize demons, but it only does people good if they exercise faith and appreciate the priority and demand that will come from choosing to follow him.

The parallels to Matthew 8:1–4 are in Mark 1:40–44 and Luke 5:12–14. The parallel to Matthew 8:5–13 is Luke 7:1–10. Luke's version is more complicated than Matthew's since Luke indicates Jewish emissaries who spoke for the centurion, so the soldier in Luke never directly saw Jesus. Matthew presents a more condensed and simplified form of the event, with the centurion and Jesus interacting. In the culture when a representative spoke, it was as if the person commissioning them had spoken, so Matthew's version reflects this. Matthew 8:14–16 is paralleled by Mark 1:29–34 and Luke 4:38–41. It is interesting that we are moving backward with reference to Mark and Luke. This difference shows that chronological sequence was not always a priority in discussing these events. That they happened was more important than in what order. Matthew 8:17 is unique in citing Isaiah. The parallels to Matthew 8:18–22 are Luke 9:57–60 and Mark 4:35–36. As already noted, we get three miracle clusters and then a block of short teaching. Jesus's deeds framed his words and gave context for them.

EXPOSITION (8:1–22)

Jesus's ministry was about word and deed. So the sermon is followed by a section of miraculous activity and closed out with teaching. That Jesus's words and deeds matched underscored his credibility. It was a model for Matthew's readers. That this work also involved people on the fringe whom society left behind also served as a model for how the community was called to minister and how it grew. This concrete concern in action for people on the fringe was a way the community showed it was different from the world. This concern for those on the fringe served as a testimony to the work and presence of God.

Jesus's healings and exorcisms showed his ability to cleanse and the value of faith in the fulfillment of the promise to bear our infirmities. This section highlights why discipleship under pressure is a priority.

8:1. This verse is a transition from the sermon to the activity to follow. Jesus descended from the mountain (Matt. 5:1—he ascended it). The mountain was a key backdrop for many Matthean events (Matt. 4:8; 5:1; 8:1; 14:23; 15:29; 17:1, 9, 20; 21:21; 24:3, 16; 26:30; 28:16; Turner 2008, 230). The language is close to Exodus 34:29 LXX A. There Moses came down after receiving the revelation from God. Here Jesus revealed God's way and will directly. Jesus descended with a great crowd following him (Matt. 4:25–5:1 and 7:28–29 note the crowds). He was drawing attention. His miraculous activity will only intensify that interest.

8:2. This miracle account is told with great economy of space. We get very little detail besides the one seeking cleansing, his condition, and Jesus's response. We are told he bowed down before Jesus in making the request. Although this verb "to bow" can refer to bowing down to worship, in this context it was probably a reference to showing respect to a social superior from whom a request is being made (BDAG s.v. "προσκυνέω" 1b, 882, as messianic king and helper; France 2007, 307; Hagner 1993, 198). The request was presented in a third-class conditional form, leaving Jesus's response open and making no presumptions. It was a statement of implicit faith: "If you wish (and you may or may not wish), then you are able to make me clean." Jesus would honor the request made in faith. This stood in contrast to the customary Old Testament call for lepers to cry out "unclean" (Lev. 13:45–46). Something about Jesus made the leper sense that Jesus could do this. There was an implicit faith present. Davies and Allison (1991, 12) say the man was "full of faith." So Matthew tied this faith to the centurion's faith in the next healing. The leper's faith also was humble as the centurion's would be (Keener 2009, 260).

There was no request that Jesus ask God to heal. The approach to the healing was direct, involving Jesus's response alone. France (2007, 307) argues the reader is left to contemplate christological implications that Jesus was willing to heal rather than God being asked to heal (contrast Wis. 12:17–18 and Job 42:2, where God willed it and it happened; Ps. 54:1). As Eric Eve notes, most of Jesus's miracles did not make an appeal to God nor did they use some intermediate object (Eve 2002, 14–16). That direct style of power and presentation was unlike most miracles presented in a Jewish context where God received an appeal to heal or some object was used as an intermediate element in the healing.

God's Use of Power

Job 42:2: "I know that you can do all things; no purpose of yours can be thwarted."

Psalm 54:1: "O God, deliver me by your name. Vindicate me by your power."

Wisdom 12:17–18: "For you show your strength when people doubt the completeness of your power, and you rebuke any insolence among those who know it. Although you are sovereign in strength, you judge with mildness, and with great forbearance you govern us; for you have power to act whenever you choose."

The need came from a leper. This term covered an array of skin conditions from psoriasis and vitiligo to formal leprosy (Hansen's disease; Davies and Allison 1991, 11). They rendered one unclean and put one on the edge of society. Lepers were forced to live in isolation so as not to give their uncleanness to others (Lev. 13–14; Num. 5:2; 12:12; 2 Kings 5:7; 7:3–10; 2 Chron. 26:16–21; Mishnah *Neg.*). The tractate did allow lepers to sit separately at a synagogue. Lepers were healed in Numbers 12, and in 2 Kings 5:1–14 in Elisha's healing of Naaman. There are no Second Temple Jewish or pagan accounts of such healings, although they were expected to come in the messianic era (Nolland 2005, 348; Matt. 11:5).

Jesus and lepers appear in this account, Matthew 10:8; 11:5, Luke 7:22; 17:11–19, and the meal in the home of Simon, a former leper (Matt. 26:6; Mark 14:3; Simon is a former leper because if he had leprosy no one would be at a meal hosted by him). This covers an array of sources (Mark, Q, L [L material is material only in Luke]), showing how deeply rooted such accounts were in the Jesus tradition. Such healings were common for Jesus and show his commitment to those on the fringe of society.

8:3. To show his will Jesus reached out to touch the leper. Moses and Elisha did not touch the lepers they helped to heal. This act of touching would normally have rendered Jesus ritually unclean (Lev. 5:3). But in the case of Jesus, ritual cleanliness triumphed over uncleanliness as the touch with his word would lead to cleansing and healing. In this way, Jesus's word was as much or more as the washings of cleansing often undertaken in Judaism. Jesus said to him, "I will; be cleansed," and immediately the leprosy was gone and the leper was cleansed. The miracle was an audio-visual of how Jesus can transform a person's life. He was shown to have the healing power on his own terms. He was a "bearer of numinous power" (Eve 2002, 14–16), meaning his authority to cleanse was presented as a direct authority without an intermediary.

8:4. Jesus told the leper to follow the law and offer the appropriate sacrifice for a leper's cleansing (Matt. 5:17–20; Davies and Allison 1991, 9, 14). He was to "see" to it (ὅρα) that he spoke to no one else (BDAG s.v. "ὁράω" B2, 719–20; Matt. 9:30; 12:16; 16:20; 17:9 also had a command for silence). Jesus showed his commitment to the law by having the leper follow it here. The call to silence was to prevent miracles from becoming the focus of what Jesus did, as opposed to what those miracles pointed to: his ability to deliver totally.

The sacrifice was offered as a testimony for the priests. This probably indicated that those priests would be told how God had worked through Jesus. Jesus tried to keep his miracles from being the major thing people were drawn to about him, but those miracles also showed how God was working through him. The instruction to the leper simply had to do with a desire that Jesus had that his miracles not be the reason people came to him (correctly Morris 1992, 190; Turner 2008, 231; Wilkins 2004, 341). France (2007, 308) speaks in Mark of "not encouraging popular enthusiasm for a wonder-worker," but merely sees a priority in fulfilling the law in Matthew. Matthew's handling of this theme looks to be similar. However, the pressure the reaction to miracles generated is seen in Matthew 8:18, 13:2, 14:23, and 21:11, while other texts show that this attention to Jesus created hostility with some leaders (Matt. 9:32–34; 12:22–24; 15:12, 21; 16:1, 4, 6, 21). The reasons for the instruction to silence were multilayered.

The desire to have the man go to a priest meant that until the man was recognized as healed in legal terms he was not to circulate among the people. All of this fit a very Jewish setting. Even the language of showing oneself to a priest echoed Leviticus 13:49 LXX (also *m. Neg.* 3:1—only a priest can declare a leper clean or unclean). The sacrifice was either two clean birds, cedarwood, scarlet material, and hyssop (Lev. 14:4), or two male lambs without blemish, one ewe lamb, a cereal offering, and one log of oil (Lev. 14:10). This was an involved process, taking eight days and requiring a trip to Jerusalem.

The element of testimony was interesting. If God had healed through Jesus, then the priest should be responsive to Jesus because of what God was doing through him. Turner (2008, 231) says the testimony was about the kingdom's power (Matt. 10:8, 18; 11:5; 24:14). All of this also affirmed that (1) Jesus was sensitive to the law, (2) he was a force for restoring people by giving the leper back to his community, and (3) God was manifesting himself through Jesus. Interpreters debate whether the meaning here was positive or negative. Did it stand as a testimony to the priests' lack of response, or was it a testimony to Jesus's power to be appreciated? It had the capability of being both, depending on the reaction to the healing. As such it is a false choice. Some argue all that was meant is a testimony to the complete cure (France 2007, 308; Nolland 2005, 350) or to a restoration to society (Hagner 1993, 199–200), but it surely was significant that the leprosy did not just go away and did not do so over a period of time, but instantly. This was an unusual restoration tied to a healer with a message. Witness in Matthew was usually tied to the kingdom (Matt. 10:18; 24:14).

8:5. Jesus entered the village of Capernaum and encountered a centurion. The village was primarily a fishing community located on the edge of the Sea of Galilee. Its population was estimated to have been no more than a thousand.

A centurion was a Roman solider in charge of one hundred foot soldiers. Centurions served under a tribune, represented the presence of Roman sovereignty, and generally were not popular in the Jewish culture. With no Roman legion present in Israel, this would have involved some kind of auxiliary troops, probably Phoenician or Syrian, although a Roman was possible. They would have operated like police in overseeing the collection of customs. The centurion may have been the senior officer in the area (France 2007, 311). Nonetheless, there was Old Testament precedent for this kind of sensitive Gentile (Abimelech, Gen. 20–21; Rahab, Josh. 2; Ruth, Ruth 1–4; Naaman, 2 Kings 5; Davies and Allison 1991, 18). They appeared in a few spots in the New Testament (Matt. 27:54; Mark 15:39; Luke 23:47; Acts 10; 22:25–26; 24:23; 27:1, 6, 11, 31, 43; 28:16). The centurion sought Jesus's help. Miracles often were told with a simple description of the setting as was done here. This was an outsider, but one who would

Photo of statue of Emperor Augustus of Rome.

Photo of life-sized foot soldier in uniform.

have great faith. The other story parallel to this in Matthew is in Matthew 15:21–28, the Syro-Phoenician woman. The healings took place and reflect a gender balance given both men and women are seen as beneficiaries.

Matthew has a different word order for this healing than Mark, who has the leper's healing followed by the healing of the paralytic brought to Jesus as he taught. Matthew saved the paralytic's healing for later in Matthew 9:2–8. The gospel writers handled the issue of chronological sequence in different ways because sequence was less important to them than that Jesus performed these acts. Sometimes themes, like faith, determined the choices.

Another difference is with Luke 7:1–10, in that Luke has Jewish emissaries communicate with Jesus, not the centurion. This allowed Luke to highlight themes of Jewish and Gentile reconciliation in ways Matthew's account doesn't. Matthew also commonly simplified his stories, so here the encounter may be seen as direct as the emissaries in Luke were speaking for the centurion and represented him as worthy (Blomberg 1992, 140; France 2007, 309; Morris 1992, 191). John 4:46–54 was a different event as the many differences show, including the location in Cana and the general, more negative tone of the scene.

8:6. Jesus was addressed as Lord as a sign of respect. The centurion told Jesus that he had a slave who was paralyzed, lying at home. The term παῖς can mean "son" (John 4:51) or "slave" (Matt. 14:2; 12:18), but most often points to a slave, as in the LXX it often translates to the term "servant" (Gen. 9:25, 26, 27; 12:16), not "son" (BDAG s.v. "παῖς" 2a, 750). Luke 7:7 also sees the figure as a slave.

The servant was also in terrific pain, which the centurion described as "terrible torment" (δεινῶς βασανιζόμενος; BDAG s.v. "δεινῶς" 215; s.v. "βασανίζω" 2b, 168). Matthew on occasion refers to such tormenting circumstances (Matt. 8:29; 14:24; also 4:24). This indicates the situation was dire. In describing the painful and sad condition, the centurion had the faith that Jesus could heal the boy and was asking for help.

8:7. There is debate about how to punctuate this verse. Is Jesus asking a question about whether he should come and heal or is he making a statement that he will come? If one sees Jesus staying focused on his ministry within Israel, then a question becomes possible. Much of the other rationale for seeing a question here rests on how one reads parallel scenes, but that is a slim basis for making the point. The more important reason is the word order with the opening first-person pronoun in Greek. France (2007, 313) reads the question's force as "You want me to come and heal?" This means a question is possible (so also Nolland 2005, 354). Morris (1993, 193) speaks of a question given as a courtesy, which is likely if a question was present. If this was a question, then this became a test of the centurion's faith.

However, a statement with an emphatic declaration seems slightly more likely (Hagner 1993, 204; Osborne 2010, 290). Blomberg (1992, 141) notes that Luke 7:6 assumed a positive response, and that text is the parallel to this event. Jesus would come and heal. We really do not have a text where in the end Jesus refused a request to heal, although the Syro-Phoenician woman met with initial hesitation (Matt. 15:21–28). Jesus agreed that he did wish to heal the servant, so he would come to the boy. The expectation was he would go to the centurion's home until the centurion gave a surprising response. Nothing in what Jesus had said caused the centurion to doubt Jesus would act, so a statement is more likely here.

8:8–9. The centurion responded in a way that made the healing easier for Jesus. It was not a word of surprise or gratitude (but so Davies and Allison 1991, 22, if a statement was present in v. 7.). Rather this was a recognition of respect for the healer, wishing to trouble him as little as possible. It may even have been sensitivity that usually Jews would be sensitive about coming to a Gentile home because of issues of uncleanness (Acts 10:28; 11:3; Turner 2008, 232; Josephus, *B.J.* 2.150; *m. 'Ohal.* 18.7 says Gentiles homes were unclean).

The centurion simply said that Jesus need not come to the house but merely utter a word to perform the healing, because the centurion was not worthy of having Jesus under his roof. The centurion explained that he understood authority. The use of the illustration probably was not designed to make a point about Jesus's divine authority. The illustration simply showed how authority worked, even though in Matthew the Son responded to the Father later in describing his work (Matt. 11:27; 28:18). The centurion would have seen God working through Jesus in some sense, but how much he understood is unclear (Carson 2010, 239).

The centurion could command one to go, come, or do that, and it got done. So a word given with authority meant it would happen. The statement showed great faith in Jesus's word, even a word from a distance. Healing from a distance was not a normal way to portray healing in the ancient world. Keener (2009, 267) mentions only Hanina ben Dosa as a Jewish example, and Hanina was known as a man of exceptional prayer, so it was not direct authority but an invoking of God. The example of command also communicated the centurion's humility about not being worthy of Jesus making a visit. The humility paralleled that of John the Baptist (Matt. 3:11). This was a remarkable statement, even beyond a Gentile being sensitive to Jews (Wilkins 2004, 342).

8:10. Jesus praised the depth of faith the centurion showed. This was the only place in Matthew where Jesus was explicitly amazed at another's response. More common for Jesus's amazement is a text like Mark 6:6, which is negative and where Jesus marveled at unbelief. The centurion's combination of humility and trust was what was being affirmed. First, the centurion knew he had no entitlement to what Jesus could give. Second, he knew Jesus's word could work from afar. Third, he sensed Jesus's compassion. Fourth, he took initiative in approaching Jesus. All of this was what Jesus affirmed in speaking about "such" (τοσαύτην) faith (BDAG s.v. "τουσοῦτος" 3, 1012). There was a quality to this faith Jesus wished to underscore.

The declaration was made with solemnity in being introduced with "truly I say to you." Jesus also noted that such faith was not found in Israel. This allowed a transition to the idea that the response to Jesus may well come mostly from those outside the nation, something the following short proclamation (vv. 11–12) also drives home. It is significant that in addressing those who were following him, the point was made to Jews. Luke 18:8 has a contrastive idea about whether the Son of Man will find faith when he returns. Healing and faith are often tied together in Mark, but this act of faith came before any healing (Mark 2:5; 5:34, 36; 9:19, 23–24; 10:52). Davies and Allison (1991, 25) note that faith had three kinds of meaning in Matthew: intellectual assent (Matt. 24:23, 26), faith as belief in Jesus (like in Paul; Matt. 18:6; 21:25; 27:42), and faith in Jesus as one who heals (Matt. 8:13; 9:22, 28–29; 15:28—the other passage where faith of a Gentile was noted). Faith gained Jesus's response (Matt. 8:13; 9:22, 28).

8:11–12. Jesus contrasted the many from the east and west (Ps. 107:3) entering into the kingdom versus the "sons of the kingdom" being outside in outer darkness. Jesus said this to those who followed him as an example of a proper response. This is the first mention of faith in the book (Matt. 9:2, 22, 29; 15:28; 17:20; 21:21; 23:23; Hagner 1993, 205). The saying is very similar in force to Luke 13:28–29. Davies and Allison (1991, 27) argue that the background of Psalm 107 and the common use of the expression "east and west" pointed to Jews of the diaspora (Isa. 43:5; Zech. 8:7; Bar. 4:37; 5:5; Pss. Sol. 11:2. Cf. Deut. 30:4 LXX), but this idea is too harsh as it would introduce a contextual break with the link to the centurion's faith as a Gentile. It also seems to ignore the expected force of the "sons of the kingdom" expression as referring to Jews as a surprise. If the saying was about a split within Judaism, then it was disconnected to a healing event and said nothing fresh about what Jesus was doing in terms of Judaism. Nor did it picture a challenge of the Jewish lack of response. It was not unusual for Jesus to play with and alter standard Jewish themes. The contrast's stark and absolute nature pointed in a vivid way to a warning and should be seen as hyperbolic, as also was common with Jesus. It was a call to Israel to have a faith like the centurion's and not risk getting caught outside the promise. It also anticipated that many who responded would come from outside of Judaism.

East-West Texts

Isaiah 43:5: "Don't be afraid, for I am with you. From the east I will bring your descendants; from the west I will gather you."

Zechariah 8:7: "The Lord of Heaven's Armies asserts, 'I am about to save my people from the lands of the east and the west.'"

Baruch 4:37: "Look, your children are coming, whom you sent away; they are coming, gathered from east and west, at the word of the Holy One, rejoicing in the glory of God."

Psalms of Solomon 11:2: "Stand on a high place, Jerusalem, and look at your children, from the east and the west assembled together by the Lord."

The context makes it clear that Jesus was contrasting those in Israel with those from the nations. The latter will get to recline with Abraham, Isaac, and Jacob, the great patriarchs of promise in the nation. The picture was of the eschatological banquet of blessing and soteriological rest (Isa. 25:6; 65:13–14—in a contrasting note of judgment; Matt. 22:1–14; 25:10; Luke 14:15–16; Rev. 19:9). Normally the expectation was that the gathering would involve Israel (Ps. 107:3; Isa. 43:5–6; 49:12; 65:13–14; Turner 2008, 232). Reclining was the ancient way to partake in a meal, with the table present in a U shape and participants reclining with pillows and couches around and using their elbows to prop themselves up (Davies and Allison 1991, 30). Gentile response to God's promise was foretold in the Old Testament (Isa. 2:2–3; 45:6; 59:19; 60:3–4; Mic. 4:1–2; Zech. 8:20–23; Mal. 1:11).

God Holds a Banquet

Isaiah 25:6: "The Lord of Heaven's Armies will hold a banquet for all the nations on this mountain. At this banquet there will be plenty of meat and aged wine—tender meat and choicest wine."

However, the sons of the kingdom will be cast into outer darkness (1 En. 63:10—oppressive Sheol; Pss. Sol. 15:10). Keener (2009, 269) speaks of damnation, where there will be weeping and gnashing of teeth, a theme pointing to rejection (Ps. 112:10). The "sons" were a reference to the initially expected heirs of the kingdom, but now they are cast out and excluded. They end up in "outer darkness" (τὸ σκότος τὸ ἐξώτερον; on perdition as a dark place, see 2 Peter 2:17; Jude 13; Tob. 14:10; Wis. 17:20–21). This place of rejection was separated from the light that is God. Weeping and gnashing of teeth pointed to the reaction of frustration, suffering, and despair at having been rejected by God (Matt. 13:42, 50; 22:13; 24:51; 25:30). This is like the warnings of Matthew 3:7–10, warning those who think they have a bright future that they may not be headed for the blessing they think they have (Bruner 2004a, 306). The remark was not absolute, as some Jews would respond, as Jesus's own earliest disciples showed (Carson 2010, 240).

Judgment and Darkness

Psalms of Solomon 15:10: "And the inheritance of sinners is destruction and darkness, and their lawless actions shall pursue them below into Hades."

Wisdom 17:20–21: "For the whole world was illumined with brilliant light, and went about its work unhindered, while over those people alone heavy night was spread, an image of the darkness that was destined to receive them; but still heavier than darkness were they to themselves."

Tobit 14:10: "Ahikar came out into the light, but Nadab went into the eternal darkness."

8:13. Jesus announced the healing. He told the disciple that his faith had brought to pass his request. It was not a healing in proportion to any faith he possessed, nor is his faith a cause of healing, as Jesus was the cause, but his faith led to Jesus's response (Carson 2010, 241; Nolland 2005, 343). Jesus was the clear source of the healing in this scene (Matt. 8:7–8). Then there is a summary, noting that the healing took place in that very hour. The remark shows how the centurion's faith is at the center of this unit. Jesus had healed from a distance by his word, as the centurion had said.

8:14–15. These verses cover the healing of Peter's mother-in-law's fever in Capernaum. Mark 1:29–31 is the parallel. If the current site tied to Peter's home is correct (see photo at 4:12–13), then the proximity of these actions with the previous scene is transparent (Wilkins 2004, 344). Keener (2009, 271) considers the possibility the mother-in-law was now living with Peter, which implied she might be a widow. First Corinthians 9:5 also indicates Peter was married.

This is about as crisp a miracle story as one can get, even more reduced than the account in Mark. We have the note of her condition, Jesus's touch, and the evidence of the healing in her serving. She "began to serve" (taking διηκόνει as a conative imperfect; Carson 2010, 242). Mark 1:30 is the parallel and is the only other text where πυρέσσω ("to have a fever") is used in the New Testament (BDAG s.v. "πυρέσσω" 899). Unlike the previous two miracles, Jesus initiated this healing, rather than having it requested of him.

Healing by touch was echoed in Acts 28:8 (also Matt. 9:29; 20:34; another fever healing with another term is found in John 4:52 and Acts 28:8). There was no word of command here. The healing was also instantaneous.

The economy of the third miracle simply allowed Matthew to note another category of healing. We have seen leprosy, a tormenting condition, and fever healed in this unit. We also had a sequence of purity, ethnic, and gender contexts for these three miracles. All three of the beneficiaries were people who could not attend the formal temple. Jesus was working with all sorts of people, showing they had access to God. "Scruples about ritual purity, ethnic exclusivism, and gender stereotypes must not hinder this mission" (Turner 2008, 237). Seeming outsiders were welcome.

This third miracle's simplicity underscores that Jesus's authority was the point, something the summary of Matthew 8:16 and the scriptural citation of Matthew 8:17 also highlight. Other issues attached to the earlier healings, whether issues of law and purity or the emphasis on faith. With Peter's mother-in-law, we merely have Jesus healing.

8:16. This verse is a summary of Jesus's activity. He continued to exorcize demons and heal. It was unusual to refer to demonic spirits without some qualifier to point to their evil or unclean nature, but Matthew does that here.

The defeat of the devil as a sign of the new era is in the background (T. Mos. 10). Exorcism was common in Matthew (Matt. 8:28–34; 9:32–34; 12:22–24; 15:22–28; 17:14–20; Hagner 1993, 210; Osborne 2010, 299). Craig Evans has a full treatment of the role of exorcisms in Jesus's ministry (Bock and Webb 2009, 151–79; summarized in Bock 2012, 79–92). The casting out of the demons came by his word, not using the incantations or recipes for exorcism so common in the culture (Keener 2009, 272; Tob. 6:7–8, 16–17; 8:2–3; Jub. 10:10–13). Jesus's authority and compassion were the points. He also healed all the sick. Jesus can heal any malady. Mark 1:32–34 is similar, as is Luke 4:40–41. Mark tells us this was in the evening after the Sabbath.

8:17. This activity pointed to the servant of God from Isaiah 53. Other potential allusions to the book of Isaiah in Matthew include Matthew 20:28 (Isa. 53:10–12); 26:28 (Isa. 53:12); 27:12 (Isa. 53:7); 27:38 (Isa. 53:12); and 27:57 (Isa. 53:9; Hagner 1993, 210). Carson (2010, 243–44) notes the idea may well have been influenced by the entire context of the servant's work in dealing with sin. In a note of scriptural fulfillment reminiscent of his infancy material, Matthew cited Isaiah 53:4. The citation differs from the LXX and Targum. It looks like Matthew's own handling of the Hebrew (Davies and Allison 1991, 38). Jesus took on illness and disease, showing himself to be the one hoped for as bringing God's healing. He "lifts" the illnesses and "carries" the diseases (France 2007, 322; Wilkins 2004, 345). He not only would bear the effects of sin and disease by his work on the cross, he showed his qualifications for doing this by his healing work. That is probably the association that was at work here (Osborne 2010, 300; Turner 2008, 235). This work of healing became an audio-visual of his ministry. He faced down the devil and disease, stopping that which destroyed people. He showed he was God's chosen one and that the new era had come (Matt. 11:5; cf. Isa. 29:18; 32:3–4; 35:5–6; Gundry 1982, 150). Miracles were Jesus's power points.

This action is not a guarantee that one can have healing now, as some argue; rather, it was a pointer to what Jesus's entire ministry was about, the restoration of people. The action also showed Jesus serving others, an example for us not so much in the miracle as in the intent of the act. The fact that people still die today shows the imagery was directed to the kingdom's future culmination and was not focused on guaranteed healing today.

8:18. Jesus wished to take a break from the crowds, so he ordered a trip to the other side of the Sea of Galilee. Mark 4:35 is similar to this verse. This need for a break was probably indicated to the disciples. Before he reached the boat, there was one more encounter with a pair of potential disciples; one is called a scribe and the other a disciple. Jesus would challenge both of them. Matthew's placement of this scene gave it a fresh angle about discipleship. They headed over to the Gadara area, a mostly Gentile region known as the Decapolis. A fine and detailed monograph on the background to this scene and discipleship of Jesus in comparison to Jewish models is by Martin Hengel (1981), *The Charismatic Leader and His Followers.* Some of what Jesus did fits that model and other things he did uniquely.

8:19. This final subunit contains teaching about discipleship. Jesus's activity was attracting prospective followers. Jesus wanted them to know what was involved in following him. A scribe said he was ready to follow Jesus wherever he might go. The scribe was quick to promise much. Jesus's response made it clear the prospect likely did not yet understand all that this might mean. Students picked their rabbis in Judaism. The scribe was following that pattern. He was attracted to Jesus and his teaching but did not yet comprehend what following Jesus might require. Jesus wanted him to understand what was involved as the prospective disciple desired to sign on to the calling.

The term "disciple" here was probably used in a loose sense, one who was following Jesus and considering following him, as the very request indicated (Carson 2010, 246). Carson argues Matthew was not anti-scribe nor anti-Semitic, but that a response to the absolute claims of Jesus was central for the evangelist. Although most of the references to scribes or religious experts in Matthew are negative (Matt. 5:20; 23:13, 15, 23, 25, 27, 29), there are places in Matthew where Jesus had a positive response to a scribe or to what they taught (Matt. 13:52; 23:2–3, 34; Turner 2008, 239).

In most Matthean texts, the term "teacher" was not uttered by a disciple (Matt. 12:38; 19:16; 22:16, 24, 36; but see Matt. 9:11 and 17:24 where Jesus was said to be a teacher to the disciples). This teacher reference is one of the reasons for seeing the use of the term "disciple" as loose here. This was someone drawn to Jesus, listening to him, and considering following him in a next step. This person was a sympathetic seeker. He addressed and approached Jesus as he might a rabbi.

We are not told how the scribe responded, but he was warned—as was Matthew's reader—not to have a superficial response to Jesus. What Jesus represented and the kingdom he brought was too important not to realize; it contained both a challenge and an opportunity.

8:20. Jesus responded by noting foxes and birds had places of rest, but the Son of Man had nowhere to put his head. Jesus was pointing out that he would be rejected and would be moving around (Nolland 2005, 366). There was no place on earth that was home for him. His was an "urgent, homeless, wandering ministry" (Hagner 1993, 216). Discipleship would not be easy, was the point. Followers faced the same fate as the Son of Man. Disciples were sojourners or aliens in a foreign land, citizens of heaven (Phil. 3:20; 1 Peter 1:1). They needed to be aware of what following Jesus might cost. Jesus made this clear up front.

Jesus described himself as the Son of Man. This was a key title for him. This was the first use out of thirty in Matthew. In Aramaic and

Hebrew, the expression simply refers to a human being. It can be an indirect, idiomatic self-reference, as it was here. The image also appears in Daniel 7:13–14 regarding the one who was received by the Ancient of Days and received judgment authority. Because it is an idiom and has scriptural background, it is hard, especially in its initial uses, to be sure of all that the term means. At the least, it was a self-reference. Jesus used the expression in three ways: (1) to describe aspects of his present ministry as he does here ("present ministry sayings"), (2) to point to suffering as he will in the passion predictions ("suffering sayings"), or (3) to point to his authority in judgment as he does in the Olivet Discourse ("glory sayings"). Wilkins (2004, 348) speaks of the humble servant, the suffering servant, and the glorious king and judge to summarize these three categories. The latter use was clearly influenced by Daniel 7. In Matthew, thirteen uses are about Jesus's authority in judgment, ten are involved with suffering, and seven are present ministry sayings. The use here is a present ministry saying. The term, especially in its early use in Jesus's ministry before he attached a text to it, is enigmatic and also somewhat empty in content, being simply a reference to a human being. As a result, Jesus could fill it with content as he used it to be about this human being and what God was doing through him with a mix of divine authority. If the term has an exalted sense, then there is irony in how it was being used here (Davies and Allison 1991, 52). If it was simply a self-reference, as is likely, then it merely described the uncertain life he would lead in ministry, having no home. Even as a human, he would not do better than foxes and birds.

8:21. Another disciple asked if he could wait to follow until he had buried his father, a primary family responsibility in the culture that was regarded as a given to perform. The response seemed to assume Jesus made a call to him as well. This obligation was rooted in the commandment to honor one's parents (Exod. 20:12; Deut. 27:16; Sir. 38:16; Tob. 4:3; 14:10–11). Mishnah *Berakot* 3:1 reads, "He whose dead lies unburied before him is exempt from reciting the *Shema,* from saying the *Tefillah,* and from wearing phylacteries." This showed that even significant religious activity was set aside to undertake this responsibility. There was precedent for this request in 1 Kings 19:19–21 from Elisha as well.

In contrast to the scribe, this disciple wanted to push back following for a time (Carson 2010, 247). It is not clear whether the death had occurred, was imminent, or was simply down the road. It is hard to think if the father had just died, that the person would be out following Jesus. If a death had just taken place, burial likely would take place that day before sunset, a point that would mean the delay would not be long. That scenario seems unlikely, however. The request was likely to wait until his father had died, although whether he was currently sick or not is not clear. It might even have meant waiting until the weeklong period of mourning was done or until the bones were interred in an ossuary, a year after death as was the custom in the first century. This latter scenario involved an act tied to this obligation and made cultural sense (Blomberg 1992, 148). Given Jesus's reply, the exact scenario mattered little to the teaching as the prioritized requirement to bury the father was there in each of these cases.

8:22. Jesus responded by calling the disciple to follow him and insisted that the dead be left to bury their own dead. The present tense in the call to follow meant to keep following. The remark made a figure out of the dead who can bury. With no commitment to the kingdom, they were free to take care of these core earthly responsibilities. They were either the spiritually dead or Jesus used sarcasm in his reply to let the real spiritually dead bury the dead. Either way, the disciple was not to wait, and the remark was a shock culturally.

This response not only rejected the request, it showed that kingdom work was to be a priority, even more important than primary family responsibilities. It was very vivid language designed to underscore the priority that following Jesus had because it was about God's kingdom. Being a disciple comes first. The kingdom is that important. The harshness has led to much discussion to explain or tame the saying. That should not be done. One should simply appreciate the saying's rhetorical vividness as pointing to a responsibility even more important than family obligation (as in other texts: Matt. 10:34–37; 12:46–50; 19:29), making it the most important priority.

It is interesting to note that high priests and Nazirites were exempt from such responsibilities, so this kind of prioritizing had precedent as well (Lev. 21:11; Num. 6:6–7; Turner 2008, 239). Here, even what seemed as a legitimate reason for delaying discipleship was exposed by Jesus not to be a reason at all. The precedents for this might make some sense out of what seemed harsh, although it clearly was a challenging call. France (2007, 330) may make too much of a contrast here when he says Jesus's response would be incomprehensible to normal Jewish piety.

Once again we are not told how the petitioner responded. The point is for the reader to reflect on the exhortation and respond.

THEOLOGICAL FOCUS

The exegetical idea (Jesus's healings and exorcisms showed his ability to cleanse and the value of faith in fulfillment of promises to bear our infirmities, explaining why discipleship under pressure is a priority) results in this theological one: Jesus's miracles reveal his authority and lay a basis for a total faith commitment to the ways of God in discipleship.

Jesus's miraculous work provided concrete visual confirmation and divine affirmation that he could cleanse, defeat the devil, and reverse that which destroys people. Four themes dominate this section: Jesus's authority, faith, whom Jesus heals, and the priority that is at the heart of kingdom discipleship.

Jesus's authority was seen in his healing, which covers both disease and evil spirits. In Judaism the expectation was that the era of salvation would involve such acts of mercy. Jesus's authority showed the special nature of the time to which Jesus belonged and to which people should respond. The citation of Isaiah 53 points in the same direction. God is at work through Jesus, raising eschatological hope.

Faith is seen in a leper who knew Jesus can cleanse. An exemplary, exceptional faith appeared through a centurion who understood that only Jesus's word, not his visible physical presence, was necessary to heal. There was a humility in this faith that did not possess entitlement but asked for healing. Whether it was expressed in "if you wish" or as "just say the word for I am not worthy," faith asked humbly and not demanding or expecting healing. What such faith did recognize was that God is capable of healing should that be his will.

Jesus ministered to all in need—an unclean leper, a foreign soldier, a woman, and all who were brought to him. He came to minister to any who came to him. He is neither elitist nor exclusive, but leaves the door open to any who will seek him out in faith.

The openness of salvation's offer is not to be undertaken casually. Following Jesus has its demands. There is rejection one faces in following Jesus's path in ministry. He wants disciples to understand this. Discipleship also is to be a priority, more important than core family activities. Jesus wants those who would follow him to appreciate all of this about the call. To embrace Jesus and life is to embrace a challenging walk.

Behind everything in this unit is the kingdom's precious nature and its importance. Jesus's work is an audio-visual that he can cleanse, defeat the devil, and reverse that which destroys people. Following him is worth the cost. Jesus's authority rings through the entire unit. Part of the issue tied to his word is appreciating his right to issue that challenge about life and ministry. Appreciating his authority means his word should meet with faith and a humble recognition that his word and way are worth following.

PREACHING AND TEACHING STRATEGIES

Exegetical and Theological Synthesis

The exegetical section highlights the audio-visual nature of Jesus's ministry. After the Sermon on the Mount, the crowds responded in awe to his authoritative teaching. This following passage links three miracles and a summary statement of his powerful works. Jesus did not withhold his healing power from needy people but aided a diverse set of sufferers: unclean leper, Gentile soldier, elderly woman, and demon-possessed people. Jesus demonstrated gracious *inclusion* when healing people.

On the other hand, when it came to recruiting disciples, Jesus's teaching conveyed firm *exclusivity*. His sayings about foxholes and funerals underscored the costly way of discipleship leading to not having a worldly home in the deepest sense. Every would-be follower had to weigh the cost of Jesus's call. Peter, Andrew, James, and John left their nets, boats, and families (Matt. 4:18–22). Matthew left his tax booth (9:9). Moreover, disciples were asked to be perfect, deny themselves, carry their crosses, and serve others (5:48; 16:24–27; 20:24–28).

Fortunately, followers of Jesus were not reliant on their own ability and volition. The same Jesus who called them would remain with them after the resurrection. He maintained "all authority in heaven and on earth" (28:18). Thus, the same Jesus who healed the sick, calmed storms, fed thousands, and cast out demons, would remain with his disciples "always, to the end of the age" (28:20). His presence empowers us to continue the costly road of discipleship.

Preaching Idea

Forget your comforts and follow Christ.

Contemporary Connections

What does it mean?

What does it mean to forget our comforts and follow Christ? Most disciples in the developed world are surrounded by comforts—too many to count. We live in furnished homes with central air that maintains a perfect temperature. We sleep in cozy beds with memory foam pillows. We secure our money in banks. We protect our all our stuff with various forms of insurance. Pills and knee replacements mitigate our pain. Therapists help us cope with emotional discomfort. In church we choose our favorite seats, friends, and points from the sermon we want to apply. And the list of comforts goes on.

To deny these comforts exist and affect us is foolish. Their cumulative effect may cause us to be overly cautious, protective, and averse to risk. Unfortunately, these qualities are antithetical to following Christ. Bonhoeffer (1995, 89) reminds us, "When Christ calls a man, he bids him come and die." As we'll see below, that does not mean living recklessly, but it does entail calculated risk and deliberate discomfort.

Several examples will illustrate healthy ways to forget our comforts. A follower of Jesus may tell her coworker about Jesus's offer of forgiveness, knowing it could cause relational awkwardness. A church may decide to dedicate ten percent of its budget to build up local nonprofits (food bank, homeless shelter), knowing it may pinch the fund available for internal programming. A disciple may wake up an hour early to give his first, weary moments of the day to personal devotions. A long-standing small group may opt to disband so its members can pursue new, less comfortable connections.

Is it true?

Is it true we should forget our comforts and follow Christ? Absolutely. However, this concept requires some nuance, otherwise it may feed legalism or martyrdom. The Master Teacher was not a proponent of either extreme.

Instead, his invitation to discipleship first called for awe, awareness, and action. Only in some instances did he press for total abandonment (Matt. 10:27–39; 16:24–26; 19:16–26).

Likely, these tough teachings about "costly grace" (Bonhoeffer, 1995, 33–35) were meant to expose the idolatry of comfort held by the prospective follower. This idol has only become more attractive in our age. Post-COVID, some will choose the comfort of online worship over embodied gatherings. Others give only comfortable amounts of time and money to charity or church service. Many find the work of evangelism too uncomfortable, so they remain private about their faith in Jesus.

To live in perpetual discomfort was not Jesus's intention—aspiring to martyrdom and self-flagellation were errors of the early church—but he certainly did not come to make life comfortable for disciples. A disciple may enjoy a good meal, nice home, hobbies, entertainment, and savings account. She should count these goods as gifts from God, holding them loosely, sharing them freely, and stewarding them well (Matt. 6:19–24; 1 Cor. 4:2; 2 Cor. 9:6–15; Phil. 4:10–13; James 1:17).

Now what?

A follower of Jesus will express awe toward him. His power, gentleness, wisdom, and sacrifice should grip our imaginations. Certainly, his words and deeds are more impressive than our favorite comfy sweatshirt. Matthew's bundling of miracles shows that Jesus was willing and able to heal. Successive miracles will demonstrate his command over storms, demons, and food supply. Jesus is truly awe-inspiring.

Moreover, disciples should increase their awareness of the comforts that compel them. They may take the comfortable seat, comfortable job, and eat comfort foods. They may attend comfortable churches and maintain comfortable relationships. We dress comfortably and sleep in comfort-level beds. We rarely venture beyond our "comfort zones." We readily seek the "easy way out."

But as disciples draw close to Jesus, they become uncomfortable with their comforts and take action to undo them. They begin to stretch themselves: giving away more time and money; initiating more conversations; facing conflict they have avoided; studying theological topics previously considered too heavy. They may sleep a half hour less to pray a half hour more. They may admit "family time" has become an excuse to live in seclusion and decide to pursue meaningful friendships outside their living room. For each follower of Jesus, the particulars of awe, awareness, and action will be different, but collectively they opt for a more costly discipleship.

Creativity in Presentation

Every person has her comfort items. You can vividly illustrate this during the message by providing an assortment of comfort items on the stage. An email or Facebook poll could get ideas from your church in advance. Comfort items generally include lounge pants, stuffed animals, blankets, hooded sweatshirts, bulky sweaters, chunky mugs, family photos, or a variety of comfort foods and drinks. Spread these out on the stage. Slowly, happily, with sighs of pleasure, eat your comfort foods (e.g., chocolate ice cream), even offering some to people in your congregation. Explain the satisfaction that comforts bring. Then explain that greater satisfaction comes from those who take comfort in Jesus (Matt. 11:28–30).[1]

A variation on the comfort items is to talk about comfort zones. We all have comfortable environments we prefer, which includes everything from lighting to temperature to sound to seating capacity. This is true in church as well. People generally sit in the same spots next to the same people. Consider putting yellow caution tape around one or two seating areas. Let

1 Some of these creative ideas may also work with the sermon on Matthew 16:13–28.

people know (by a sign or announcement) that those seats are available for those willing to go outside their comfort zone. Draw attention to them in the message. Dare people to move to them or affirm those who chose to sit there. As an act of solidarity, you may consider changing your preaching style for this message to get out of your own comfort zone. Preach from a different spot, use a different Bible translation, opt for a different presentation software (e.g., Prezi, ProPresenter), or use a manuscript or outline only.

Stories of international missionaries are prime examples of forgetting comforts to follow Christ. You could highlight Hudson Taylor's travels to China, Jim Elliot's death in Ecuador (and his wife's continued work there), or George Mueller's prayerful work with orphanages in England. However, it may be more effective to discuss a missionary supported by your own church, noting the sacrifices they make to learn a new language and culture, establish new rhythms and relationships, and live without many of their guilty pleasures from home (reliable plumbing, hot water, central air, and peanut butter). A two-minute Zoom interview with one of them about comforts they miss from home could be very effective.

Finally, you might engage people in a mental exercise about simplifying life for the sake of Jesus. Most of us have more than we need. Let them know Jesus asks us to travel lightly, not to be encumbered by too many comforts. Liken this to carry-on luggage or a backpack designed for day hikes. You might even have such baggage on the stage. Let your people know, "Jesus is waiting. You have ten minutes to pack and limited space. This is more about mobility and flexibility than comfort. What will you bring?" Provide them with some time to think about it. To cut the tension, play the song "Leaving on a Jet Plane" at the end.

Whatever creative elements you adapt for your message, be sure to emphasize that Jesus's miracles reveal his authority and lay a basis for a total faith commitment to the ways of God in discipleship. Therefore, we should forget our comforts and follow Christ.

- Jesus's compassionate healing is awe-inspiring (8:1–17).
- Jesus's hard call to discipleship is discomforting (8:18–22).

DISCUSSION QUESTIONS

1. What do Jesus's miracles signify about his character and mission?
2. What details did Matthew feature in these miracles, and why?
3. How does the fulfillment motif continue in this passage?
4. How do these would-be disciples respond differently than the original four? Be specific.
5. When are comforts permissible? When should they be avoided?
6. What discomfort have you accepted as a follower of Christ?

Matthew 8:23–9:17

EXEGETICAL IDEA

Jesus's calming of the storm, the exorcism of the Gadarene demoniac, and the healing of the paralytic showed the fulfillment of his calling to provide forgiveness, although many would not embrace it despite the evidence God gave through him.

THEOLOGICAL FOCUS

As Jesus provides evidence that God is at work through him, people are forced with a choice to accept or reject him.

PREACHING IDEA

Let the evidence of Jesus's actions address your inner skeptic.

PREACHING POINTERS

The mighty works of Jesus begin to pile up in the next section. Matthew linked three miracles together to showcase the scope of Jesus's power and recipients of his healing touch. He stopped a storm and awed his disciples. He cast out demons and unnerved pig farmers. He forgave a paralytic and fixed his legs, which aggravated scribes. Moreover, Jesus called a despised tax collector to discipleship and dined with his unsavory friends, leading to a final conflict about his choice of company and eating habits. The original audience would have felt the tension Jesus created by the evidence of his powerful works and perplexing words. Matthew provided the evidence for them to examine and respond with faith toward this merciful, miracle-working Son of Man.

In our secular age, many people treat miracles as ancient folklore. They view Jesus's healings, exorcisms, and command of nature as unscientific accounts of preliterate cultures. While a degree of chronological snobbery exists, these people cannot be blamed. We are trained to be skeptics (Lewis 1963 is a solid discussion of miracles; Keener 2012). We know marketing promises more than any product can offer. We know politicians play politics. We know history exalts winners, silences losers, and tells only one side of the story. We know "innocent until proven guilty" does not apply equally to all ethnicities. Finally, we know no truth is absolute (except for this one), so unless it feels right or the evidence compels us, we are under no obligation to believe. In the face of such uncertainty, this passage admonishes us to let the evidence of Jesus's actions address our inner skeptic.

JESUS CALMS THE STORM, EXORCIZES DEMONS, AND HEALS A PARALYTIC (8:23–9:17)

LITERARY STRUCTURE AND THEMES (8:23–9:17)

This unit repeats the three-miracle sequence, followed by teaching structure, common to Matthew's word-and-deed units at this point of this gospel. Jesus's calming of the storm produced a reaction of amazement from disciples that Jesus could command the wind and waves (Matt. 8:23–27). It raised the question: Who is he really? Jesus's healing of the demoniacs at Gadara showed his power to transform that which the demonic had hold of, but also showed that some fear that kind of power and want nothing to do with it (Matt. 8:28–34). The healing of the paralytic showed Jesus's authority over sin, including the power to forgive it, again leading to amazement as well as skepticism about such claims of authority (Matt. 9:1–8). Jesus's call of Matthew to follow him led to a complaint about Jesus's ministry in terms of reaching out to those on the edge of society, leading Jesus to reply he had come to call the sick and minister to sinners, as an expression of God's mercy (Matt. 9:9–13). Finally, the dispute over fasting led Jesus to explain the new way he brought could not be patched onto the old way of doing things, just as fresh wine needed new wineskins (Matt. 9:14–17).

Gadara

The name of the location is part of a complex textual problem involving three different names: Gadara, Geresa, and Gergesa. That confusion of letters that could produce the result is easy to see. Gadara was a city of the Decapolis (see map in Matt. 8:18). It was located about six miles southeast of the Sea of Galilee. Geresa was another city of the Decapolis located some thirty miles southeast of the Sea of Galilee. Gergesa is traditionally located on the eastern side of the sea and was Origen's preferred locale for this event and would be included in a reference to Gadara (Wilkins 2004, 352). Gadara was often perceived to run out to the sea, as coins tied to it portray a boat (Metzger 1971, 23–24; Morris 1992, 208 n. 75; Josephus, *Vita* 9.42). Gadara is the best attested name in terms of external evidence in Matthew, while Geresa is better attested in Mark and Geresa and Gergesa are almost equally attested in Luke. It is likely we are dealing with a description of the sea as it connected with other key locales in the region. The traditions appeared to have made distinct links to cities in the area associated with the locale. Gadara is best attested for Matthew. Nolland (2005, 374) goes his own way, arguing that Geresa was original in all the Gospels as the harder reading.

This unit is the most complex of the triad set of three miracle and teaching units in Matthew 8–9. Not only are the miracles told with more detail, but the teaching section has two accounts, not just one. The first triad had three healings. Here we have three distinct miracle accounts: a nature miracle, a detailed exorcism, and a healing.

The unit builds into its theme. We move from Jesus's authority over creation and the demons—forces outside of us—to his authority over sin, where the unit lands and focuses. The healing of the paralytic leads into discussion of a ministry to sinners as an expression of God's practical mercy, which was to be a priority over sacrifice. This new era and the message of deliverance that came with it meant a new way was present that required fresh packaging in one's thinking about what God was doing, which some were open to while others resisted.

As with the previous section, we have deed and then word. Jesus showed his authority, did ministry, and then explained it. Jesus's way was about more than teaching; it was about living what was taught. The word-deed combination showed his claims were credible. The pattern and presence of both word and deed were important as a principle of effective ministry.

The parallels to the calming of the storm in Matthew 8:23–27 are Mark 4:35–41 and Luke 8:22–25. The Gadarene demoniacs healing is paralleled in Mark 5:1–21 and Luke 8:26–40, but Matthew is alone in describing the healing of two figures here, although he does it in his usual, more concise way. The parallels to the healing of the paralytic are Mark 2:1–12 and Luke 5:17–26. Matthew's call and the question about fasting is like Mark 2:13–22 and Luke 5:27–38.

It is interesting to note that Mark and Luke have a sequence of four miracles that Matthew broke up and linked distinctively. The four miracles in Mark and Luke are the calming of the storm, the healing of the demoniac, the woman with the hemorrhage, and the raising of Jairus's daughter. Matthew brought in the healing of the paralytic and delayed the last two miracles of the sequence until Matthew 12. This allowed Matthew to focus on Jesus's ministry and call as being about sin and his resultant justification of a ministry to those in need.

The core theme is the wide scope of Jesus's authority, as his power over creation, the demonic, and sin showed. That authority touched on divine power as creator and redeemer. These miracles covered the seeming domain of Satan as these demonic elements threatened humanity's well-being, the chaos of nature, the spirit world, and disease (Wilkins 2004, 350).

That power also produced a host of reactions. Amazement that called for reflection was one reaction, appearing in the first and last miracle scene. In the middle was the rejection by some, who simply wanted Jesus to go away. Other people did not like those Jesus ministered to, but this was because they neither appreciated God's mercy nor the nature of Jesus's ministry to restore the broken and fallen. Jesus came to restore those he described as sick and needing a doctor. Recovering those God desired and being sure those in need were ministered to meant things were done differently from recent tradition and religious practice, not to mention the normal reaction of human nature. New things have come. We see some drawn to Jesus, while he made others very nervous.

Another theme is that miracles did not decide things, although they could give cause for people to reflect about Jesus. The assessment was that miracles lay "in the eye of the beholder" (Davies and Allison 1991, 66). Davies and Allison (1991, 66) also note one must have eyes to see and ears to hear. As they say, "Miracles will not compel unbelief to relinquish its doubt."

EXPOSITION (8:23–9:17)

Jesus continued to show his authority to reverse that which threatened humanity and/or was rooted in demonic presence. Matthew highlighted the capability Jesus had to bring deliverance. The miracles showed Jesus's ability to deliver at a deeper level. Their presence, however, was not a guarantee of a positive response, as some rejected what they saw. The brief move into Gentile territory was a hint of things to come, but it also showed that the varied responses were not a matter of ethnicity nor religion.

Jesus's calming of the storm, the exorcism of the Gadarene demoniacs, and the healing of the paralytic showed the fulfillment of his calling to provide forgiveness, although many would not embrace it despite the evidence God gave through him.

8:23. Jesus finally headed to the other side of the sea and entered the boat with his disciples. These boats often handled between five and sixteen people. One such boat was found in 1986 and now is on display at Ginosar in Israel. It measures 26.5 feet by 7.5 feet with a height of 4.5 feet (Morris 1992, 205 n. 62; see photo of this boat at Matt. 4:18–20).

The description that the disciples "followed him" in the verse (ἠκολούθησαν) pictures the experience they were about to have as a discipleship experience (BDAG s.v. "ἀκολουθέω" 3, 36–37). That language connects to Matthew 8:19–22. The storm was about to teach them. The nature miracle was designed to be instruction about the scope of Jesus's authority.

Photo of the Sea of Galilee Terrain.

8:24–25. As they crossed, the sea began to shake. The term here is σεισμός (BDAG s.v. "σεισμός" b, 918). It would normally refer to an earthquake on the land, but here it visualized the upset of the waves tossing the boat to and fro. It is a term neither Mark nor Luke uses for this event. In other texts, it is a term used for the trials or shake-ups of life (Matt. 24:7; Mark 13:8; Luke 21:11). Those waves were overwhelming the boat. Literally the boat was "covered" by the waves (BDAG s.v. "καταλύπτω" 1, 505). The men were in great danger. These kinds of storms were not unusual, as the Sea of Galilee is surrounded by hills in most directions that can allow moisture to become trapped in certain conditions. The sea is 636 feet below sea level, while the surrounding terrain reaches up to 2,650 feet. Easterly winds often get trapped in this bowl (Wilkins 2004, 351).

That God controlled and contained the flood and seas is a major Old Testament theme (Job 38:8–11; Pss. 29:3; 65:5–8; 89:8–9; 93:4; especially 107:25–32; 124:4–5). The sea also could picture the chaos of the world (Pss. 65:5; 69:1–2; Isa. 43:2; 57:20; Dan. 7:2–3; Davies and Allison 1991, 68). This was one of several nature miracles in Matthew (14:15–21, 23–33; 15:32–38; 21:18–22; France 2007, 334). Nature miracles tend to be doubted by many scholars today, but Keener (2009, 278) is right to note this may say more about a Western Enlightenment mindset than reflecting reality. Keener also notes that unlike many ancient miracle accounts that were recorded long after its players lived, these miracle stories were recounted within the lifetime of its potential eyewitnesses.

God's Control of the Seas

Psalm 107:25–30: "He gave the order for a windstorm, and it stirred up the waves of the sea. They reached up to the sky, then dropped into the depths. The sailors' strength left them because the danger was so great. They swayed and staggered like drunks, and all their skill proved ineffective. They cried out to the Lord in their distress; he delivered them from their troubles. He calmed the storm, and the waves grew silent. The sailors rejoiced because the waves grew quiet, and he led them to the harbor they desired."

Jesus was asleep in the midst of all of this chaos. That was no accident, as sleep can picture trust and resting securely in God's care (Job 11:18–20; Ps. 3:5–6; Prov. 3:24–26; Turner 2008, 244).

The nervous disciples went to Jesus and wakened him, likely in a kind of panic. This was significant since four of the twelve were fishermen. The storm was serious enough for them to be concerned. The disciples addressed him as Lord and called to him to save them, because the waves threatened to kill them. They were perishing and so Jesus needed to act to save them. This was the first use of the term "save" since Matthew 1:21. Its use is part of what makes the miracle an historical audio-visual of Jesus's larger ministry to save.

The entire episode was a picture of Jesus's general ministry to the disciples and others. Elements of this story are like Jonah (Jonah 1:4), but Jesus showed himself to be more than Jonah (Matt. 12:41; France 2007, 336). Where Jonah appealed to God to save the sailors (Jonah 1:12–4), Jesus merely acted to stop the storm. Jesus was doing "God stuff."

8:26. Jesus issued a rebuke and calmed the storm. The order is reversed from Mark's parallel. Davies and Allison (1991, 73) claimed the order is more natural in Mark and that Matthew was focused on the lack of faith, but the distinction is not so clear. Is there really a great difference between Jesus speaking a rebuke and then calming the storm or the reverse order? Is one sequence more natural? Among ancients, sequence was sometimes less important than the fact that things happened. Each evangelist made a distinct choice here, and both points mattered.

Jesus asked the disciples why they were timid, describing them as those with little faith. They should be able to trust him. The term δειλός refers to someone who is "cowardly" or someone who is "timid," even fearful (BDAG s.v. "δειλός" 215). This is a person who lacks confidence. The disciples were anxious in ways Jesus had exhorted them not to be in Matthew 6:24–34. They had failed to trust that God would care for them.

Then Jesus rebuked the winds and the sea (see Pss. 105:9 LXX; 107:25–32). Is "rebuke" used to suggest an evil force at work, or is it merely a way of challenging the creation? It is not clear.

This rebuke was followed instantly by a great calm, amazing given that the sea had been tossing and turning. The term for "calm" only appears with this event in the New Testament (Mark 4:39; Luke 8:24; BDAG s.v. "γαλήνη" 187). Normally such power belonged to God as he had created the seas and their boundaries (Job 38:8–11; Ps. 33:7; Prov. 8:22–31; Jer. 5:22; 31:35—"He promises it as the one who stirs up the sea so that its waves roll"). Calming the sea is often an image used to picture God's victory in the end (Ps. 46; Isa. 17:12–14; 50:2–3; Davies and Allison 1991, 75). Nolland (2005, 372) contended that such a miracle has no Greco-Roman parallels, but Keener (2009, 279) notes some parallels.

8:27. The act left the disciples amazed (Matt. 7:28; 9:8, 33; 12:23). They pondered who was leading them. What sort of person was this who the winds and sea obeyed? This reaction to the question was left unanswered for the reader to ponder, although the demons' addressing of Jesus as "Son of God" in the next scene pushed in the direction of an answer (Matt. 8:29). It certainly implied Jesus was most unusual, but those who knew Psalm 107 knew that God carried such authority over the creation. Jesus made no appeal to God in prayer. He offered no incantation nor formula. He acted directly. The authority was his. The faith of the disciples was deepening. They were yet to realize they could trust one with such power. The process of their growth was only beginning here.

8:28. The next miracle in the triad was an exorcism. Exorcisms or references to demons abound in Matthew (4:24; 7:22; 8:16, 28–33; 9:32–34; 10:8; 11:18; 12:22–28; 15:22–28; 17:18; Keener 2009, 283–85, has a long excursus on demons and exorcism). This event is very abbreviated in form versus Mark 5:1–20. Matthew often has crisper versions of Mark.

This miracle took place in the region of Gadara on the Decapolis side of the Sea of Galilee; the disciples had made it to the other side

(Matt. 8:18). The exact locale is part of a textual problem. Matthew's placement in Gadara is distinct from Mark's location in Gerasa, which was a larger and more prominent location (Mark 5:1; see sidebar above on Gadara). The city of Gadara was some six miles southeast of the sea, while Gesara was thirty miles away, but the description of people among the tombs meant they were outside the city in an area associated with a cemetery and connected to both locales. So the difference was one of regional clarity where today one might face a choice between mentioning a main city versus being specific about a suburb.

Two demon-possessed men met Jesus. The parallels in Mark 5 and Luke 8 mention only one demoniac. Matthew often has double the presence in events (Matt. 9:27; 20:30; 21:7; 26:60; plus 24:40–41; 24:45–51). Mark and Luke are simplified versions of the healing, possibly highlighting the spokesperson in the group.

The men's condition was severe, as they were extremely violent and their presence meant no one could pass their way, unless they were someone like Jesus. The term used to describe them is χαλεπός. It means to be troublesome, hard or difficult to deal with, giving an implication they were "violent" and dangerous (BDAG s.v. "χαλεπός" 1075–76). The adverb λίαν ("very") adds a level of intensity in terms of the degree of threat they possessed (BDAG s.v. "λίαν" 594, bα). They were not merely troublesome but very violent to others, who found it best to avoid them.

The presence of pigs in the scene tells us we are in Gentile territory (Lev. 11:7), and along with the mention of tombs points to two elements associated with ritual uncleanness in the event (*m.* B. Qam. 7:7). The pigs were being raised for food. The area had a mixed Jewish and Gentile population (Josephus, *B.J.* 3.51–58). For a Jewish audience, Jesus and the disciples were very much in foreign soil, a place to be avoided. Pigs, tombs, and demons were here. One is reminded of the expression in the *Wizard of Oz*, "Lions and tigers and bears, oh my!"

8:29. The spirits in the demoniacs confronted Jesus, recognizing his authority as Son of God. Jesus as Son is a Matthean theme (Matt. 1:23; 2:15; 3:17; 4:3, 6; 14:33; 16:16; 17:5; 27:54; Turner 2008, 246). They were aware of who they were facing (Mark 3:11; 5:7; Luke 4:41; Acts 16:17). They wondered if Jesus was going to torment them now on earth, as they tried to suggest that there was nothing he should have to do with them. It was an attempt to get control of a situation they knew was not good for them. Naming someone was an attempt to control the situation (Osborne 2010, 319). They literally asked, "What is it to us and you?" The idiom means, "What do we have in common?" (Davies and Allison 1991, 81; Maynard 1985; in the LXX: 2 Kgdms. 16:10; 3 Kdgms. 17:18; 4 Kdgms. 3:13). It was a request to be left alone as they had nothing to do with each other. Of course, Jesus had much to do with evil. He opposed it. The reference to torment "before the time" shows an awareness that one day there would be a judgment of them, conceding they did have a connection (1 En. 12–16; 55:4; Jub. 5:6–10; 10:1–13; T. Levi 18:12; 1QS 3:24–25; 4:18–20; France 2007, 341; in the New Testament, Rev. 19:20; 20:10–14). They did not wish a preview of that day, which would yield a bad result for them.

Jewish Texts on Judgment of Evil Entities

1 Enoch 55:4: "Kings, potentates, dwellers upon the earth: You would have to see my Elect One, how he sits in the throne of glory and judges Azaz'el and all his company, and his army, in the name of the Lord of the Spirits!"

Jubilees 5:6: "And against his angels whom he had sent to the earth he was very angry. He commanded that they be uprooted from all their dominion. And he told us to bind them in the depths of the earth, and behold, they are bound in the midst of them, and they are isolated."

Jubilees 10:5: "And you know that which your Watchers, the fathers of these spirits, did in my days and also these spirits who are alive. Shut them up and take them to the place of judgment. And do not let them cause corruption among the sons of your servant, O my God, because they are cruel and were created to destroy."

Testament of Levi 18:12: "And Beliar shall be bound by him. And he shall grant to his children the authority to trample on wicked spirits."

8:30–31. Matthew now notes that there was a herd of pigs some distance from them. This was an indicator we are in Gentile territory, as pigs were unclean (Lev. 11:7; Deut. 14:8; Isa. 65:4; 66:17). It was the offer of pigs by Antiochus Epiphanes at the altar of the temple that helped to start the Maccabean War (Josephus, *A.J.* 13.243; 1 Macc. 1:47; Davies and Allison 1991, 82; on attitudes toward swine, Keener 2009, 287 n. 62).

If Jesus was going to cast them out, then the demons were content to be cast into such unclean beasts. The desire was expressed in a first-class conditional clause that showed regard for Jesus's authority. They knew he could do this. They were looking for another place to reside and might have felt safe in unclean pigs. Another instance of demons seeking a place to reside is Matthew 12:43–45. The power Jesus had just shown over creation now was being shown as extending over evil spirits.

8:32. Jesus commanded the demons to go. They ended up in the pigs, who ran down the bank into the sea. The effort to end up in the pigs failed, as the beasts drowned. All of this made clear that an exorcism had taken place. In Mark 5:9 we are told the demons' name was Legion, pointing to a multiple possession, since legion was a military term describing a group of six thousand soldiers. That the demons moved to the whole herd also showed the same thing, pointing to the size of the possession. Demons sometimes are portrayed as not always comfortable in water as in Testament of Solomon 5:11, where a demon named Asmodeus asks not to be sent into water. However, other texts show they can function in water (Davies and Allison 1991, 84). The result here was that the demons were being judged. The spirits were not dead, as the point in the verse about death involved the pigs drowning. The demonic spirits did not die but became homeless again. The spirits' continued destructiveness becomes evident in how the pigs reacted to the presence of such a power; even unclean pigs were not suitable for them and were damaged by their presence. Where demons resided was where destruction lurked. Jesus's acceptance of the demons' request gained the demons nothing (Hagner 1993, 228). The focus was on Jesus's authority to restore people in need. That should be the preferred option.

8:33. The herdsmen fled into the city and reported all that had taken place, especially what happened as a result of the exorcism. Matthew does not discuss the condition of those healed, but that is transparent. They were no longer possessed. It is likely the herdsmen sought to explain what happened to the pigs they were watching (Morris 1992, 211). The pigs were part of an economic reality for the herdsmen, so their deaths would have been disturbing and traumatic.

8:34. So the city went out to meet Jesus. In Matthew, Jesus and his authority were the message gained from the healing. In the parallels, there is a note about the status of the healed. Matthew only mentions Jesus and the city. They asked him not to stay. No reason was given in Matthew, but the parallel in Luke refers to fear. Hagner (1993, 228) and Keener (2009, 287) say they suspected him of being a magician, even a malevolent one, but there was no formula used by Jesus and his work was positive in healing the men. Of course, the herdsmen did not note that so much, since the destruction of the herd was their major concern. France (2007, 343) says they saw Jesus as a "wandering holy man." That was possible, and holy men could also scare people. Economic concern was especially transparent. In any case, the fact that a significant healing had taken place was ignored. Rather than rejoicing at the healing, the men were more concerned with the loss of income from the herd of pigs.

Miracles did not guarantee a positive response. Where the heart was determined the response. Some preferred not to engage with God's power and presence. This rejection of Jesus was spiritually blind and deaf. It raised a theme Matthew will continue to note. God's power was at work through Jesus, but many refused to see it. As Carson (2010, 258) says, the event exposed where the people were and "they preferred pigs to persons, swine to the Savior." This summary is a bit rhetorical as Jesus had not shown himself to be the Savior to the herdsmen, but he had evidenced the presence of divine power and they were not interested because they had other priorities.

9:1. Jesus returned to the western side of the Sea of Galilee and his home, Capernaum (Matt. 4:13, 24—Galilee only noted; 8:5–6). The remark sets up the transition to the paralytic's healing. Jesus alone was the figure in this event. The disciples drop from view until Matthew 9:10.

9:2. This is the last of the second triad of miracles. As was his custom, Matthew had a more concise description of this event than the parallels in Mark 2:1–12 and Luke 5:17–26. This is the only detailed healing of a paralytic in the Gospels. Other such references are found in summaries on Jesus's miracles (Matt. 15:30–31—of the lame; 21:14—of the lame; Luke 7:22; John 5:3).

The Matthean relocation in comparison to Mark and Luke may suggest a topical versus chronological arrangement here (Blomberg 1992, 153), although the sequencing with the return on the boat makes this less than certain. In many places in the Gospels, the exact chronological placement of events is not clear. Matthew has pushed this event back from its much earlier location in Mark, although Mark's sequence also was probably topical in giving a series of early controversies (for one suggestion on chronology, Carson 2010, 260–61). Many details are lacking in Matthew: there are no remarks about Jesus's teaching, the size of the crowd in a home, or the paralytic being lowered through a roof. All Matthew provides is a simple miracle account with little extra detail.

The paralytic was brought by his friends. He was lying on a mat. Jesus reacted to "their" faith, a reference to the paralytic and his friends as a group. It was this team of faith that Jesus responded to when he told the paralytic to take heart and that his sins were forgiven. Other texts where faith extended beyond the sufferer are Matthew 8:10, 13; and 15:28 (France 2007, 344). He was commending them as a group, responding to and including the care and love the paralytic's friends had shown toward their brother in need.

Jesus addressed the paralytic directly with a tender "my son." The expression "take heart" or "have courage" refers to having strength in a context of adversity (BDAG s.v. "θαρσέω" 444). The verb can mean do not fear (see the LXX, Gen. 35:17; Exod. 14:13; 20:20). Matthew 9:22 makes a similar juxtaposition of encouragement and faith.

The remark about forgiving sin is odd because the paralytic came to be healed and be able to walk, not to have his inner condition treated. One can imagine how bewildering Jesus's response was to his friends and him. However, sin and disease are often linked in the Old Testament (Lev. 26:14–33; Deut. 28:15–68; 2 Chron. 21:15–19—Jehoram's judgment) and in Judaism (4Q510; 1QS 3:20–24; 4Q242 [4QprNab]; T. Gad 5; Davies and Allison 1991, 89; Osborne 2010, 327). Yet in John 9:1–3 such an explanation was excluded as a cause in that particular case. James 5:14–16 suggests a link may sometimes exist. Theologically, it was clear that the bigger problem between sickness and sin involved sin (Hagner 1993, 232). In fact, Jesus's healings pointed to the larger issue as an audio-visual. This passage helps to show that Jesus's work is about more than physical healing.

Linking of Sin and Disease Texts

Leviticus 26:14–16: "If, however, you do not obey me and keep all these commandments—if you reject my statutes and abhor my regulations so that you do not keep all my commandments and you break my covenant—I for my part will do this to you: I will inflict horror on you, consumption and fever, which diminish eyesight and drain away the vitality of life. You will sow your seed in vain because your enemies will eat it."

Deuteronomy 28:20–22: "The Lord will send on you a curse, confusing you and opposing you in everything you undertake until you are destroyed and quickly perish because of the evil of your deeds, in that you have forsaken me. The Lord will plague you with deadly diseases until he has completely removed you from the land you are about to possess. He will afflict you with weakness, fever, inflammation, infection, sword, blight, and mildew; these will attack you until you perish."

The theme of forgiveness looks back to Matthew 1:21 and forward to Matthew 26:28. The linkage becomes important later in the event since healing is something one can see, but forgiveness is invisible, so how can one know that forgiveness has taken place? Jesus's linking allowed him to claim you could see the unseen by what you could see.

Jesus's declaration of forgiveness is a classic example of a speech act, where what is said is not merely described but accomplished. Some see the passive ("are forgiven") in the remark as a divine passive with God being the one who forgives sin here, but Matthew 9:6 says the Son of Man is performing this act (correctly Davies and Allison 1991, 89). So Jesus's claim of authority was direct. Other than this scene, only one text has Jesus directly forgive sin in his earthly ministry (Luke 7:48).

9:3. The scribes were theologians and some of them immediately reacted to Jesus's remark. There is irony here given that the observation the theologians made was entirely correct and served as a premise for what Jesus was doing. These were probably local Galilean legal officials. In Matthew, this is Jesus's first controversy with scribes or Pharisees (France 2007, 343). Controversy emerges much later in Matthew's gospel than in Mark's, as Mark 2:1–3:5 has a series of controversies early on. This antagonism grows in Matthew (12:38–39; 15:1–2; 16:21; 20:18; 21:15; 23; 26:57; 27:41). Wilkins (2004, 355–56) notes that Jesus challenged them for their ethics and interpretations in Matthew 5:17–48, about the Sabbath in Matthew 12:1–4, and on their righteousness in Matthew 5:20.

This Matthean passage also contains a second less-than-positive response to a claim by Jesus in this second triad of miracles. In Gadara it was from the populace. Here it was from theologians. Miracles did not guarantee faith. Resistance was rising.

Some scribes saw Jesus's claim as blasphemy, an insult against the person and prerogatives of God, as blasphemy was a form of slander against God (Lev. 24:10–16; *Sanh.* 6:4; 7:5; Bock 1998). This reaction to Jesus surfaces again in Matthew 26:65. We are told they thought this among or in themselves. This could be internal thinking (so Nolland 2005, 380, with many), but it would be better to think of some kind of a public exchange of ideas, as Matthew 9:4 indicates Jesus saw their reaction. Did Jesus catch their glances and the fact they were talking to each other? Making this reading more complicated are the parallels. Mark 2:6–8 speaks of them dialoguing in their hearts and Jesus knowing in his spirit that they were thinking this. Luke 5:21–22 is more ambiguous, since they were dialoguing among or in themselves, but Jesus knew their hearts. Mark does look more internal, while Luke is unclear but suggestive of the same. Making this more complicated still is yet another factor. This is that thoughts do come from within a person, even when expressed. Carson (2010, 261) and France (2007, 346) speak of whispering, while Nolland (2005, 381) sees a reading of faces. The scribes did not go public but were engaged with each other on this. Jesus still got what they were doing. So we can translate the idea of ἐν ἑαυτοις as "among themselves" but it could well read "in themselves." Even though these leaders did not believe and were antagonists in Matthew, the gospel writers often show Jesus's opponents understood the point Jesus was trying to make. That is the case here as well.

The scribes apparently understood that only God had authority to forgive sin (Isa. 43:25), although Matthew also lacks noting this specifically, unlike the parallels. The only Jewish text that raises a question about this apparently exclusive divine prerogative is 4Q242 (=4QprNab), where an exorcist is said to have forgiven sin. The key phrase there is "an exorcist forgave sin for Him." So God is mentioned in the verse, making its point less emphatic than the text here about Jesus. Jesus's remark in healing the paralytic was about his own authority, what Turner (2008, 247) calls "the most crucial aspect" of his authority and the event's central claim. The scribes got that point. Jesus was either insulting God or was revealing his own authority by forgiving sin. In this miracle, Jesus's claim of a divine prerogative is the single issue. The healing served as a visual vindication of Jesus's point.

God Forgives Sin

Isaiah 43:25: "I, I am the one who blots out your rebellious deeds for my sake; your sins I do not remember."

9:4. The text says that Jesus saw their thoughts. Even though there is a reference to thoughts twice in the verse (once as a noun and another as a verb), the fact these thoughts were seen appears to suggest the scribes were talking among themselves or that, at the least, those thoughts were somehow being read. If one sees an internal reading of thoughts, then the Holy Spirit's work may be in view (Turner 2008, 248).

So Jesus responded to their reaction about blasphemy with a question. The claim Jesus blasphemed meant they were contemplating evil in their hearts. Why were they doing this? They were missing God's presence and activity tied to Jesus. Their reaction was not God's will and reflected a spiritual dullness. They were supposed to know God, his law, and his will, but they were missing what God was about here through Jesus. This rejection yielded a malice toward Jesus that was evil (Hagner 1993, 233). They were rejecting Jesus without paying attention to what he was doing. So Jesus acted to give them another chance to reflect on what they were thinking.

9:5–7. To make his point, Jesus explained the situation with another question: "Which is easier, to say, 'Your sins are forgiven' or to say 'Stand up and walk'?" (v. 5). Now this was very much a question to contemplate. On the one hand, to tell someone their sins were forgiven was easy, as it could not be seen or tested to see if it has taken place. In one sense, talk can be cheap. However, if one told a lame person to walk, that would be a hard saying because then they needed to walk. That required a miracle. Yet, in reality, forgiving sin was harder because the authority to actually perform it was so limited ("it takes deity really to forgive sins"; Morris 1992, 216).

But Jesus was not merely raising a question to make a few points. What Jesus did was to link the two questions. He showed he could do both things. In order that they see what cannot be seen and understand that the Son of Man

(Jesus) had authority to forgive sins, Jesus told the man to arise, take his mat, and go home. The word "authority" (ἐξουσίαν) is thrown forward in the sentence for emphasis. The healing pictured and gave evidence for Jesus's authority to forgive sin. What was unseen was demonstrated by a miracle that could be seen. Jesus did the "hard" thing in order to show the "easier" thing to say (but actually harder to do). He also did a "God thing." All of this explained why Jesus first forgave sin and then healed the man. He was making it clear what kind of authority the healing was designed to picture. There was more to this miracle than the miracle.

The verse has another present-ministry, "Son of Man" saying in which no specific Scripture is invoked. So the crowd heard, "That you might know that this human has authority on earth to forgive sins . . ." Jesus again used the title about himself but did not indicate a scriptural context for his use of the idiom. The idea of "this" human was bound up in the consistent expression "the" Son of Man. The fact that judgment authority over sin was at work may imply Daniel 7:13–14 was in the background since sin and judgment are related, but that is at most an inference. Keener (2009, 290) speaks of a subtle allusion. It is clear that an earthly but personal authority was at work given what Jesus was about to do, but divine power was also being exercised. The juxtaposition of human and divine was intended here. Did the act assume the Son of Man was heavenly and had a heavenly authority as well (so Morris 1992, 217)? Or is the point Jesus's divine judgment authority at the end of time was now also at work on earth in the present (so Hill 1972, 172)? Which of these options was present is not clear, given they assume an inference that is not expressly stated. The clearer assumption in the remark is that this divine prerogative is one God was sharing with the Son of Man. The healing vindicated the claim about the divine-like authority to forgive sin.

There is real discussion about whether this remark about the Son of Man is a narrative comment or a saying of Jesus. Much can be said for a narrative aside (Davies and Allison 1991, 93–94, have six arguments). However, the most important feature is that Son of Man sayings come only on Jesus's lips in the Gospels (France 2007, 347 n. 48). The evangelists did not use it as a title independently of him elsewhere. That would suggest Jesus is portrayed as the speaker here.

The miracle was evident when the paralytic got up and headed home. If one views the action as rooted in what God was doing, then Jesus's healing, tied to the claim in his remark, pointed to support for his claim to forgive sin and perform God stuff.

9:8. The crowd's reaction was a combination of fear and joy. This is the first mention of the crowd in Matthew's version, unlike in Mark, who introduces them earlier.

The crowd was afraid. Fear here should be seen in terms of awe and respect, a reverential fear, a mix of terror and awe (Matt. 14:30; 17:6; 27:54; Blomberg 1992, 154; Turner 2008, 249). God was acting. He was doing so through a human in an unusual way. The crowd did not perceive Jesus's uniqueness, so their perception was that God was working through humans in this new way. They were half-right. God was at work, but so was the Son of Man. This was not an allusion to absolution in the church, against what Davies and Allison (1991, 96) suggest. Neither were the disciples meant, as they had not done any healing yet. The passage is thoroughly christological, rather than about the church (Carson 2010, 262). France's (2007, 348) alternative is that the crowd's reaction referred to such authority being given to any human at all, which though possible, is not really reflected by the plural "men," which he calls a generalizing plural (one out of many). The plural here is really plural (many). It is better to see the crowd in an assessing position and not quite in tune with what exactly was happening. The crowd failed to appreciate Jesus as the *unique*, representative man, the Son of Man, who had this authority (Wilkins 2004, 356). The authority Jesus had does not extend to all people. He alone was able to reverse the presence of sin in humanity. So the healing clearly made a deep impression. The people recognized that authority and Jesus were linked and that God was at work in a special way, but they failed to see how unique this authority was, an issue still with us today when people think about Jesus.

9:9. With the second triad of miracles now completed, the sequence of teaching pronouncements follows in two parts. First, we have the call of Matthew and then the discussion of fasting. Both show Jesus taking his own route on religious matters. He brought a new way but in a manner that honors what had been (Matt. 9:17). The unit also allows Jesus to show what his mission was about: it was to call the sick and reach out to those who knew they needed God's help. So Jesus spent time with those who lived in need of such help from God. This move parallels his earlier dealing with lepers, centurions, and women in the first triad of miracles.

The call of Matthew is told in extremely simple terms. Jesus came to the city and saw Matthew seated at a tax collection booth, located either on the lake's edge or along the Via Maris, a major trade road described as a trade route that runs by the sea (McNeile 1915, 117; Osborne 2010, 335). In the parallels from Mark 2:14 and Luke 5:27, the tax collector was Levi, but this was likely nothing more than a second name for the same person, just as Simon-Peter and Saul-Paul had two names. "It is very improbable that the evangelist would have gotten away with the substitution of Matthew for Levi were they not in reality the same person" (so correctly Hagner 1993, 238). Culpepper (2021, 263) engages with Bauckham's skepticism about the two-names approach to this difference and finds the dual-name explanation as the most plausible way to see this text. The name "Matthew" either means "gift of God" (= Mattaniah—1 Chron. 9:15) or "the faithful" (from the Hebrew *ʾemet*; Carson 2010, 262–63). As a tax collector, Matthew would have been literate in Aramaic and Greek, making him a good candidate for writing a gospel (on tax collection, Donahue 1971).

These taxes would have functioned much like customs do today. The tax collectors were gathering up funds owed to Herod Antipas for commerce in Galilee. Matthew would have been but one of many such tax collectors in the city, as the banquet he hosted later showed. Their role was not appreciated by most citizens, so they were treated like sinners as they were often suspected of being morally corrupt (France 2007, 351). Keener (2009, 292–93) has many texts noting how tax collectors were seen and about their reputation for corruption (Philo, *Spec.* 3.30; *De Legat.* 199). This set an important tone to what Jesus was doing when he called such a figure. Jesus was fraternizing with the despised, even someone whose morality could be questioned.

Jesus called Matthew to follow him (Matt. 4:20; 8:19, 22), and the tax collector did. Unlike students who chose their rabbis, Jesus as teacher issued his call to follow. All of this simply set the stage for the controversy account to follow when Jesus dined with more tax collectors and sinners.

9:10. Jesus went to a home and had a meal with a host of tax collectors and sinners. These sinners would have been people who were connected with wickedness. The idea of reclining, which many translations render as sitting, was the standard way to have a major ancient meal, a banquet, or other kind of special meal (Hagner 1993, 238). Luke 5:29 speaks of a great banquet. One reclined on the floor leaning on one's elbows on couches or pillows and facing the food. Sharing such a meal communicated a form of acceptance at a cultural level. Jesus's associations with such people were a marker of his ministry. It was one of the controversial acts that created a reaction against him (Blomberg 2005, 2009a, and 2009b; Bock 2012, 48–59; Davies and Allison 1991, 101, call it a prophetic symbol; on how sages handled such meals, Keener 2009, 296–97).

So where was this meal held? Matthew, in his typical abbreviating style, did not clearly indicate who was the host of the meal, as the home was not specified in terms of whose home this was. Luke 5:29 resolves the question, indicating the home was Levi's (i.e., Matthew's home). France (2007, 353) notes the home of such a figure would likely have been larger, reflecting an affluence that could host such a grand event. For sure Matthew was responsible for the guest list. The complaint of the Pharisees was unlikely to have been at the meal (as they would not attend such a meal with such a guest list). Upon hearing about it, they complained to the disciples.

9:11. Jesus's seeming association with and acceptance of these lowly regarded reprobates produced a question from Pharisees about why Jesus would have done this. In effect, the objectors were asking: How could a man of God associate with such people? Did this not endorse all those sinners represented? In the earlier controversy, the scribes were circumspect about their criticism of Jesus's claim to forgive sins, but here the Pharisees were more direct and asked the disciples about their rabbi's practice. This was really a complaint. The key premise was that the righteous do not associate with sinners, not because of the association as such but because of the risk of becoming like them, giving the appearance of endorsing their actions, or their doing the righteous harm by compromising moral standards. The teaching had much precedent (Ps. 1:1; Prov. 13:20; 14:7; 28:7; Sirach 12:13–18; 13:1; *Ep. Arist.* 130; *m. 'Abot.* 1:6–7; 2:9; Keener 2009, 297). The question is presented with "tax collectors" and "sinners" being moved forward in the Greek to signal emphasis. Jesus should not have been associating with such people.

On Associating with Sinners

Psalm 1:1: "How blessed is the one who does not follow the advice of the wicked, or stand in the pathway with sinners, or sit in the assembly of scoffers."

Proverbs 13:20: "The one who associates with the wise grows wise, but a companion of fools suffers harm."

Proverbs 14:7: "Walk abreast with a foolish person, and you do not understand wise counsel."

Proverbs 28:7: "The one who keeps the law is a discerning child, but a companion of gluttons brings shame to his parents."

Sirach 12:14–15: "So no one pities a person who associates with a sinner and becomes involved in the other's sins. He stands by you for a while, but if you falter, he will not be there."

Letter of Aristeas 130: "'You observe,' he said, 'the important matter raised by modes of life and relationships, inasmuch as through bad relationships men become perverted, and are miserable their whole life long; if, however, they mix with wise and prudent companions, they rise above ignorance and achieve progress in life.'"

9:12–13. The complaint generated Jesus's response and explanation. He used the picture of a physician. A physician treated the sick. The proverb was common in the Greco-Roman world (Plato, *Resp.* 4.444E; Menander, fragment 591K; Diogenes Laertius 6:1:1; Davies and Allison 1991, 103; Keener 2009, 298). The sick also sought a doctor when they recognized that they needed help. Jesus's mission was to deal with the sick and to exemplify God's mercy. Interestingly, Jesus accepted that he was with sinners, but was with them deliberately, urging the Pharisees to engage them in a different way (Nolland 2005, 386). One can associate with sinners in a way that honors righteousness and reflects the opportunity for God's mercy, keeping the door open for a response and change in the person. So we must not overapply calls not to associate with sinners.

This led Jesus to cite an Old Testament text (Hos. 6:6), where God said he desired mercy, not sacrifice. The term for mercy was rooted in the Hebrew concept Hosea uses of *ḥesed*, or covenantal love. This was a call for the priority of treating others justly. The rhetorical pattern "do A, but not B" meant to prioritize what was said. Such justice meant reaching out to those in need. So Jesus did not focus on calling the righteous but the sinners. To worship with sacrifices and not pursue justice was not real worship. To meticulously follow law but not be gracious was not God's desire. The right thing done in the wrong way was still wrong. The Pharisees had their relational priorities exactly the reverse of what they should have been (Turner 2008, 253). Relationships can be a way to bridge to the truth. Matthew 22:34–40 will elaborate on this theme.

The introductory remark to go and learn was a call to contemplate anew the importance of the passage often used by the rabbis (Hagner 1993, 239; SB 1:499). It was a rebuke of sorts for those who thought they knew the law and prophets. So the reference to the righteous had the ironic and sarcastic force of referring to the self-righteous who would not sense their need for what Jesus offered. The Pharisees may have seen themselves as righteous, and Jesus's remark accepted that at a rhetorical level, but their lack of awareness of their own need was blinding them to what really was needed, as the citation and physician illustration show.

When Jesus said that he came to call the sick, he gave a mission statement. This was the call he had in the world. He could be in no other place and do no other thing. Calling sinners back to God and making them healthy was why he was sent. Luke 5:32 speaks of calling people to repentance.

Jesus's offense seemed to have been these associations with sinners, not because he sought their repentance, as that would be the hope of all, but in the associating way he did it. Where the Pharisees would have challenged such folks from a distance, Jesus engaged them directly and intimately in relationship (Osborne 2010, 336 n. 12). He received and then challenged, versus waiting for the challenge to be received. Jesus's call to turn to him after such an initial reception was reflective of the kingdom and grace (Nolland 2005, 386), so he did not stress the Pharisees' more common way to pursue such restitution. The New Testament makes this point about Jesus's mission in other places (Luke 19:10; 1 Tim. 1:5; in the early church: Barnabas 5:9; 2 Clem. 2; Justin, *1 Apol.* 15:8; Davies and Allison 1991, 106). Jesus was no resolute separatist. He engaged and pursued the unrighteous, associating with others in ways that caused the more scrupulous to complain. Maintaining his own righteousness, Jesus, as a physician, sought to draw the unrighteous to a new, more healthy way of life.

Blomberg (1992, 157) rightly says, "We do well to consider substantially increasing our spiritual, evangelistic, and social outreach to minorities, the homeless, prostitutes, addicts and pushers, gays and lesbians, AIDS victims, and the like, as well as to the more hidden outcasts such as divorcees, single parents, the elderly, white-collar alcoholics, and so on. We must get to know them as intimately as Jesus did—only close and trusted friends shared table fellowship over meals. We dare not join with sinners in their sinning, but we may well have to go places with them and encounter the world's wickedness in ways that the contemporary Pharisees in our churches will decry."

9:14. Not just in his relationships but in pietistic actions, Jesus's style was different. So the disciples of John the Baptist asked him why the disciples of the Pharisees and John fasted, but his disciples did not. Apparently it was a widespread concern that provoked the question. Mark 2:18 has people ask this question, while Luke 5:33 has Pharisees make the query (Osborne 2010, 341).

John's disciples appear here and there in Matthew (Matt. 11:2; 14:12, also John 4:1–2; Acts 18:25; 19:3). According to *Didache* 8:1, very pious Jews fasted twice a week on Mondays and Thursdays (also Luke 18:12). This was not a Torah-required fast tied to Atonement (Lev. 16:34; Num. 29:7–11) but was voluntary. It may well be it was these voluntary fasts that were in view. Jesus's disciples apparently were known for not fasting at all. The difference seemed significant, as fasting pointed to humility and repentance. It did not seem his disciples were pious enough. Jesus's lifestyle was another difference between John the Baptist and him (Matt. 11:19). The teacher was held responsible for the difference (Daube 1972). Put this difference alongside Jesus's association with tax collectors and sinners, and Jesus's way appeared morally and socially lax to some.

The sequence in Matthew of these two events being placed side by side matches Mark 2:13–22. Both events involved food, feasting, and fasting. Once again Matthew's version is shorter. He lacks the reference to disciples of the Pharisees here, so we have three distinct groups in the last three events: scribes, Pharisees, and now John's disciples.

9:15. Jesus replied with three illustrations. The last two were similar in emphasis but looked at what was happening from slightly different angles (Gospel of Thomas 47 has a similar saying). The first illustration is unique to Matthew.

Jesus began by picturing a wedding. His presence was like that event. With Jesus present, the hope of promise and the kingdom were present. Groomsmen or guests did not mourn while the groom was present. The guests or groomsmen were called very literally "sons of the wedding hall," although Osborne (2010, 342) prefers a reference to all the wedding guests on the premise. All disciples were meant. Ancient weddings often went on for several days of celebration (France 2007, 356; Tob. 11:19 has a week of celebrating). Mourning was not a part of the celebrating, as even religious duties were suspended during such celebrations (Ber. 2:5).

The question is asked with the particle μή and expects a negative reply. There was no mourning when the groom was there (1 Macc. 9:39). Jesus then noted that a time was coming when the groom would not be present. He would be taken from them. Then fasting would take place.

The remark about being taken from them is suggestive. Is this an allusion to Isaiah 53:8b? At most it is a conceptual allusion as there is no terminological link. The arrest of John may have impacted Jesus here to see his fate as similar when rejection comes (Matt. 4:12; 11:2). The remark shows Jesus was aware of the rising opposition that Matthew has been describing as present. He would suffer and be removed. Nolland (2005, 391) limits this to the arrest and crucifixion period, but that seems unlikely narrow, given the disciples did not fast in the few days between Jesus's death and resurrection. They did after his death (Acts 9:9; 13:3; 14:23; 27:9; Morris 1992, 225). Although the period between Jesus's resurrection and return was seen as one of Jesus being present and one of joy for his still being alive, it also was seen as a period of a lack of consummation, where all was not what it could be. Creation groaned for the completion of the promise (Rom. 8:18–24), and the full kingdom would come only after tribulation (Acts 14:22).

This is the first note of an awareness of his coming death in Matthew. There also will be hard times for the disciples. Then they will fast and look to God for the way through the difficulties. The groom's presence and the hope of the promise for now gave reason to celebrate. Matthew 25:1–12 has a similar image about being ready for Jesus's return, as does Matthew 22:1–14.

The images of marriage and the people of God are present in the Old Testament with the book of Hosea as the prime example (especially Hos. 2:6–23; also Isa. 54:5–6; 62:4–5). The image of celebration also appears for eschatological hope (Isa. 25:6–10). John 3:29 has similar groom imagery. It is interesting that God is the groom in these Old Testament texts, so Jesus's presence and God's are linked. The remark was implicitly christological.

Celebratory Marriage Imagery

Isaiah 54:5–6: "For your husband is the one who made you—the Lord of Heaven's Armies is his name. He is your Protector, the Holy One of Israel. He is called 'God of the entire earth.' 'Indeed, the Lord will call you back like a wife who has been abandoned and suffers from depression, like a young wife when she has been rejected,' says your God."

Isaiah 62:4–5: "You will no longer be called 'Abandoned,' and your land will no longer be called 'Desolate.' Indeed, you will be called 'My Delight is in Her,' and your land 'Married.' For the Lord will take delight in you, and your land will be married to him. As a young man marries a young woman, so your sons will marry you. As a bridegroom rejoices over a bride, so your God will rejoice over you."

Hosea 2:16: "'At that time,' declares the Lord, 'you will call, "My husband"; you will never again call me, "My master."'"

9:16. The second illustration was of placing new, unshrunk cloth to patch an old, worn spot on clothes. The term ἄγναφος refers to "unshrunk, new" cloth (BDAG s.v. "ἄγναφος" 12). The word ῥάκος pictures a rag or "tattered" cloth (BDAG s.v "ῥάκος" 2, 903). Here the word πλήρωμα means a supplement, so in this particular case, a "patch" (BDAG s.v. "πλήρωμα" 1b, 829). The problem was that when the new patch shrank, it strained and stretched the immovable old piece of cloth, a wonderful metaphor for what was happening with Jesus's coming and ministry in the face of old traditions and ways. If you tried to wed the two, there would be a tear and the patch would not work. In fact, the tear would become worse.

Wilkins (2004, 369) says that what was offered was not a patch on traditional Judaism but a fresh move into righteousness and the new era. This was where the promise of Judaism was always headed and supposed to go. The picture of salvation to come brought a new era and creation (Isa. 65–66).

9:17. So the third illustration was about what was coming. New wine went into new wineskins. This way both the wine and the skins survived the fresh fermentation that would take place. If new wine were placed in old wineskins, the fermentation would tear the brittle old leather wineskins so that both the wine and skins would be lost. Just like the new patch made the old tear on the cloths worse in the previous verse, so the old wineskins would not work with new wine. Such wineskins were made of animal skins (Keener 2009, 301). To preserve the wine and the skins, the new wine needed new wineskins. In this image of newness, everything was preserved.

The new wine and the wineskins, both old and new, were preserved (with Davies and Allison 1991, 112, 115; Wilkins 2004, 369, and Nolland 2005, 391–92, versus Hagner 1993, 244, and France 2007, 357, who only see the new preserved). This remark is unique to Matthew and has brought much comment. Jesus brought fresh ways for fresh ways of engaging. However, was it in ways that the old was still sometimes preserved or does only the new remain? In answering the question, it is important to recall that fasting will return in the church down the road, so we do not have complete replacement here. These remarks defended a limited discontinuity in what Jesus brought, a theme seemingly distinct from notes of ethical continuity declared in the Sermon on the Mount. However, to see that contrast as absolute would be superficial. In the sermon, Jesus presented a fresh way with his "but I say to you" remarks, yet Jesus was continuous in accomplishing and fulfilling what the law called for. So Jesus did it in ways that did not allow forms of old brittleness to remain. The new era has a newness about it, a fresh focus on the heart, that people must learn to embrace, where what is new preserves where the old was headed (old and new: Rom. 7:6; Eph. 4:22; Col. 3:9–10; Heb. 8:13).

THEOLOGICAL FOCUS

The exegetical idea (Jesus's calming of the storm, the exorcism of the Gadarene demoniacs, and the healing of the paralytic showed the fulfillment of his calling to provide forgiveness, although many would not embrace it despite the evidence God gave through him) leads to this theological insight: As Jesus provides evidence that God is at work through him, people are forced with a choice to accept or reject him.

The theological focus is on Jesus's authority for what he brought in five distinct ways. Jesus brought (1) peace as seen in the calm of the storm, (2) victory over evil as seen in the exorcism, (3) forgiveness of sins in the paralytic, (4) mercy as seen in his associations, and (5) a new era and way as seen in his lack of fasting. Jesus is the hub of kingdom presence and activity. Despite all the power Jesus showed and divine attestation that came with it, many still do not embrace him. That storyline was surprising, tragic, and revealing. One would think people would flock to such opportunity. It is sad to see what many are missing. However, the heart's condition that will not seek the cure God graciously offers shows how deep the real need for God is. The heart's eyes need to be opened and changed to embrace what God offers. Faith involves a humility, seeing that what we need we cannot supply for ourselves. God needs to give to us on his terms.

The unit, though large, has a triad of themes that Matthew brings together. They are Jesus's authority, the new era, and the mercy with compassion that comes with this new time. Also important is the varied reaction to that combination of gifts.

The scope of Jesus's authority appears in his ability to calm creation, exorcize demons, and heal the paralytic. All of these show a power that points to transcendent presence, since God is the creator. Demons are forces of evil only God can stop. Assessing and forgiving sin is a prerogative of God. So the authority in view is extensive and comprehensive. Creation and redemption are addressed.

That such authority resided in a representative human showed the newness of the era and the comprehensiveness of what it was designed to treat. The forgiveness of sins meant there is a mission to those in need with its hope of an era of joy and celebration.

The call to mercy is an extension of God's care and character. Jesus associated with tax collectors and sinners, those often disdained by the self-righteous. He saw his mission in terms of a doctor seeking to cure the sick. His ways may have seemed new, but they were designed to preserve what was best from God. Some of the old brittle styles would not work in this new era that came with new promise and enablement. The new ways needed embracing.

Sadly, despite all of this being offered, many were questioning or rejecting what was being offered. The Gadarene crowd asked Jesus to go. The scribes questioned Jesus's right to forgive sin. The Pharisees saw Jesus's associations as offensive. John's disciples were not sure about Jesus's lack of common religious practices. The new ways were causing people to reflect on how they followed God. Some were not willing to follow in the new ways that validated where

Jesus was going. Matthew will continue to chronicle this amazing lack of response as his gospel continues.

PREACHING AND TEACHING STRATEGIES

Exegetical and Theological Synthesis

The exegetical section explains the scope of Jesus's power, describing not only what he does—stopping a storm, casting out demons, and healing a paralytic—but for whom he does it—his disciples, two Gentiles, and a long-suffering Jew. Furthermore, what stands out are the responses of the benefactors and bystanders, ranging from awe to outright skepticism. Matthew has begun to raise the volume on the theme of opposition.

One of Jesus's key opponents, perhaps the driving force of all opposition in the gospel, is the devil and his demonic brigade. Jesus's wilderness test (Matt. 4:1–11) introduced spiritual warfare, which surfaced again in the final petition of the Disciple's Prayer—"deliver us from evil" (6:13). Matthew often lists exorcisms in summary statements (4:24; 8:16), but he also provides detailed accounts (9:32–34; 12:22–29; 15:21–28; 17:14–21). Demons oppressed people with physical, mental, and social ailments, which Jesus and his disciples healed as a sign of God's inbreaking kingdom (10:7–8; 12:28).

The audio-visual nature of Jesus's ministry provided ample evidence not only of his power but also his mercy. He embraced the outcast, healed the oppressed, and invited sinners to feast with him (9:9–17). Whereas Satan steals, kills, and destroys, Jesus came to offer fullness of life (John 10:10; cf. Matt. 13:19). He offers new garments, new wine, and new beginnings for those who follow him.

Preaching Idea

Let the evidence of Jesus's actions address your inner skeptic.

Contemporary Connections

What does it mean?

What does it mean that the evidence of Jesus's actions should address our inner skeptic? From the outset, we must acknowledge the inborn skepticism many of us inherit in the Western world. Two factors feed this skepticism. First, the scientific method has trained us to question anything that cannot be tested, examined, and reproduced in a laboratory. Miracles, by definition, break natural law. They defy the senses and avoid the examination table. Therefore, they cannot be trusted.

Second, postmodernism has trained us to question history. It is told by winners, the argument goes, suppressing the voices of the marginalized. This accounts for the rise in popularity of gnostic gospels and various methods of biblical criticism. Although many Christians may not read authors from these streams, that thinking has crept into popular culture through books such as Dan Brown's *The Da Vinci Code* and Elaine Pagels's *The Gnostic Gospels*. Once put into the mainstream, these ideas cannot help but feed our skepticism.

Fortunately, classical apologists (e.g., C. S. Lewis) and current biblical scholars (e.g., Craig Keener) have argued for the authenticity of miracles. In a two-volume work on miracles, Keener (2012) accounts for thousands of examples of supernatural intervention. Furthermore, according to McDowell (2017), miracles are not the only "evidence that demands a verdict" concerning Jesus Christ. Prophetic fulfillment, personal testimonies of change, extrabiblical material about his life, and the fact of the empty tomb make a strong case for the inner critic to consider.

Is it true?

Is it true that we should let the evidence of Jesus's actions address our inner skeptic? Indeed, but the inner skeptic persists with probing questions. How can I be sure? Why do the gospel accounts differ? Isn't the Bible biased? What should I make of outdated traditions like head coverings or insensitive teaching about divorce and sexual promiscuity? We must not let these questions harden our skepticism, but they should direct our quest for truth.

As mentioned above, we are trained to doubt. However, this is not all bad. In fact, Keller (2008, xvii–iii) nudges Christians to take a "leap of doubt," because honest inquiry works like an influenza vaccine. Putting a little skepticism into our faith inoculates us against extreme skepticism. Researchers at the Fuller Youth Institute make a similar claim, finding that making room for doubt and discovery results in "sticky faith" (Powell and Clark 2011, 33).

Therefore, as pastors, parents, teachers, and friends, we not only wrestle with our own questions but also direct others through theirs. A pastor must not cringe when someone from his church shares doubts about the reliability of the gospel accounts. He might simply invite the person to read the Gospels with him. A mother must not overreact when her teenage daughter says the hypocrisy of the church has "made this whole Jesus thing seem unbelievable." Instead, the mother may listen to her daughter's lament and then prayerfully invite her to take Jesus on his own terms, not the misrepresentations of others. The antidote is graciousness toward others. The same approach applies to skeptical friends and coworkers, inviting them to see the evidence of Jesus's actions with their own eyes by reading his story together.

Now what?

What should we do about our inner skeptic? How should we approach the evidence of Jesus's actions? Reiterating what was written above, we cannot overstate the reality of our inner skeptic. By virtue of living in a secular age, we breathe skepticism every day. We must first admit most of us are more skeptical than we perceive ourselves to be. We must also note the forces that feed skepticism: scientific method, postmodernism, historical deconstructionism, critical theory, pop culture, and personal experience.

While we cannot silence the inner skeptic, we can affirm its existence and redirect its focus. We do so by sharing our doubts with trusted family, friends, and spiritual mentors. In addition to airing out our doubts, we must pursue honest inquiry with them. This begins by looking at the evidence of Jesus's actions (and words) provided to us by the Gospels. We read them prayerfully, attentively, and critically. We make observations, ask questions, and research with tools available to us (dictionaries, commentaries, and study Bible notes). We engage with those who think differently than we do and show a different way to go. If the inner skeptic remains resistant, we may add to our inquiry writings by apologists or biblical scholars who validate the reliability of the Gospels. If it is our skepticism that needs treatment, a dose of faith is recommended. If it is the skepticism of another, then drawing near and engaging honestly but respectfully is what is needed.

Finally, we must expand the evidence of Jesus's actions beyond the Gospels and Bible itself to church history and personal narratives. The sacrificial faith of the early church in the face of a deadly plague in A.D. 250 gives evidence of Jesus's actions (Sittser 2019, 146–47). The boldness of Bible translators and Reformers in the face of martyrdom gives evidence of Jesus's actions. The courage of missionaries and underground churches in the face of persecution gives evidence of Jesus's actions. Even the generosity of the Christian business owner and transformation of the former prostitute gives evidence of Jesus's actions. Evidence of his work abounds.

Creativity in Presentation

The need for compelling evidence conjures up scenes of a courtroom. Whether the famous glove in the O. J. Simpson trial ("If it doesn't fit, acquit") or the dispatch report from the Delta 191 crash, strong evidence persuades an undecided jury. Evidence includes audio or visual recordings, DNA, fingerprints, physical objects (e.g., knife), eyewitness testimony, personal confession, and other documentation (e.g., email). Consider referring to a famous court case where evidence made a difference in the decision.[1]

Borrowing from the courtroom motif, you may frame your message as a legal drama. At the beginning, address your congregation as members of the jury. Ask them to set aside their biases and listen to four pieces of evidence about Jesus with an open mind. Let them know at the end you will ask them to make an informed decision.

Evidence 1: A comparison of weather maps. The first map shows the Sea of Galilee at 10:22 P.M. Galilee Standard Time (GST) during monsoon conditions. According to the disciples, shortly after 11:00 P.M. (GST), Jesus awoke, rebuked the storm, and it immediately ceased. The second map shows a cloudless sky over the Sea of Galilee at 11:06 P.M. (GST).

Evidence 2: A personal testimony. A pig herder from Gadarenes reports seeing two demonized men freed from their oppression and thousands of pigs dive into the sea. He comments, "I can't explain it. All I know is that as soon as Jesus showed up, those crazy men got right in the head, and our little piggies went bonkers."

Evidence 3: A bed mat. The object belongs to a former paralytic. Prior to his encounter with Jesus, the subject could not walk. His friends carried him to Jesus, who fixed his legs and forgave his sins. The mat reminds the man of Jesus's authority.

Evidence 4: A picture of Jesus at a party. The photo was taken at Matthew's home. Jesus reclined at a table covered with food and drink, engaging guests in meaningful conversation with an unlikely crew of tax collectors. It was taken by one of John the Baptist's hungry disciples.

After presenting each piece of evidence during the sermon, be sure to make a closing statement that highlights Jesus's authority over nature, demons, sin, and social norms.

You may want to acknowledge how skepticism is a natural byproduct of our secular age. It is the air we breathe. We want empirical evidence, scientific proof, data, and case studies to support our beliefs. Meanwhile, unanswered prayers, widespread suffering, and the absence of miracles may feed our skepticism. Thus, it is not uncommon for Christians to battle some skepticism. However, not all skepticism is the same. Use the chart below to help people identify the skeptic from Scripture that best represents their inner skeptic.

Finally, many skeptics have turned to Jesus after considering his words and deeds. Many Christian apologists were once skeptics. Ironically, their effort to disprove the Christian faith resulted in their converting. Notable examples include C. S. Lewis, Josh McDowell, Lee Strobel, Nancy Pearcey, and J. Warner Wallace.

Asssessing Your Inner Skeptic: A Biblical-Emoji Taxonomy					
Closed Caiaphas	**Cynical Iscariot**	**Noncommittal Nicodemus**	**Tactile Thomas**	**Self-protective Sarai**	**Passionate Peter**

1 UMKC Schol of Law has compiled a hundred historic cases on their website: https://www.famous-trials.com/.

The Case for Christ begins with the Lee Strobel's early life as a skeptic. Strobel (2016, 13) writes, "For much of my life I was a skeptic. In fact, I considered myself an atheist. To me, there was far too much evidence that God was merely a product of wishful thinking, of ancient mythology, of primitive superstition . . . I had read enough philosophy and history to find support for my skepticism . . . As far as I was concerned, the case was closed. There was enough proof for me to rest easy with the conclusion that the divinity of Jesus was nothing more than the fanciful invention of superstitious people. Or so I thought."

Likewise, Josh McDowell's quest to undercut Christianity left him sleepless many nights. Despite amassing tomes of evidence, McDowell (2009, 65) recalls, "The evidences did not bring me to Christ. The evidences got my attention, but it was God's love that drew me in." As Jesus himself predicted in John 13:35, a loving community of Christ followers is compelling evidence for the Christian faith.

As you deliver this message, clearly communicate that as Jesus provides evidence that God is at work through him, people are forced with a choice which some will accept, and others will reject. Thus, we must let the evidence of Jesus's actions address our inner skeptic.

- Miraculous works give evidence that Jesus is Messiah (8:23–9:8).
- Surprising welcome gives evidence that Jesus is Messiah (9:9–17).

DISCUSSION QUESTIONS

1. How did Matthew's arrangement of this triad of miracles differ from Mark and Luke? What does this suggest about Matthew's focus?
2. Think through the responses of all of the witnesses of Jesus's miracles and mercy in this section. How does this range of responses fit those who encounter Jesus today?
3. Why does Jesus call his disciples cowardly? Have you ever responded like them?
4. What do we say to modern skeptics of the miracle accounts in the gospels?
5. Can skepticism ever be a gift? Explain.
6. What compelled you to follow Jesus?

Matthew 9:18–38

EXEGETICAL IDEA
Jesus's works of healing as Son of David brought the Pharisees' negative reaction that he healed by demonic power, even as Jesus issued a call to pray for more harvest laborers.

THEOLOGICAL FOCUS
Jesus's show of kingdom authority often meets with opposition, even as he asks for prayer for more laborers.

PREACHING IDEA
Jesus's compassion deserves a positive reaction.

PREACHING POINTERS
Jesus continued to display miraculous powers in the next passage. For the third time, Matthew bundled a triad of miracles (one is a double miracle), followed by a short teaching. Though his description is brief, the narrative showcases Jesus's compassion and rising fame. He healed an unclean woman, resuscitated a girl, restored sight to two blind men, and cast out a demon. Jesus did not discriminate in exercising his power; however, he did manifest caution, aware that too much attention to his charismatic gifts might incite mixed reactions. The Pharisees validated this concern; their hard hearts prohibited them from holding a positive view of Jesus. Instead, they accused him of colluding with the prince of demons. Matthew wanted his audience to consider Jesus's compassion and respond positively. He wanted them to prayerfully join Jesus the Messiah in proclaiming God's kingdom.

The compassion of Jesus remains a compelling characteristic in our day. It is a heartfelt, measured response toward others as he sees their suffering. Our compassion often discriminates and easily burns out. On one hand, group polarization has hardened us. We hesitate to cross political, religious, gender, or racial lines; we do not want to be polluted by their propaganda. Compassion is too soft a word for our polarized world, so it meets with a worldly skepticism. Nevertheless, it is a virtue Jesus valued. On the other hand, the constant stream of sad stories and suffering fatigues us. We see images and read stories of hurricane destruction, Afghan refugees, race riots, lost jobs, dead pets, and loneliness. Compassion is too great a need for our groaning world. Fortunately, what we lack in compassion, Jesus fully embodies. This passage reminds us that Jesus's compassion deserves a positive reaction.

JESUS HEALS A WOMAN, A DAUGHTER, TWO BLIND MEN, AND A MUTE MAN (9:18–38)

LITERARY STRUCTURE AND THEMES (9:18–38)

This unit has a sequence of three events that reflect four miracles (vv. 18–26: a hemorrhaging woman and Jairus's raised daughter; vv. 27–31: two blind men; and vv. 32–34: one mute). Paralleling the earlier two units, a concluding teaching follows the three miracles (vv. 35–38). This final triad of miracles in the sequence of three triads includes the only intertwined miracle story in the Synoptics: the healing of the woman with a hemorrhage and the raising of Jairus's daughter (Matt. 9:18–26). Both of the people seeking healing in the first story had a faith that Jesus could do it. In addition, two blind men calling out to the Son of David were healed (Matt. 9:27–31), as well as a demon-possessed man who was dumb (Matt. 9:32–34). The two blind men also showed extraordinary faith and insight into the power of the one from the line of David. Once again the miracles did not persuade some, as the Pharisees made the assessment that Jesus's power was demonic, even though the crowds saw that what Jesus was doing was without precedent. Rejection was now intensifying despite the evidence of Jesus's activity. Following the deed-word sequence of these units, Matthew closes it with a healing summary and teaching from Jesus about praying for workers of the harvest to come forward (Matt. 9:35–38). This remark sets up the transition to the mission of Matthew 10.

The unit highlights the continued working of Jesus's power, healing, exorcism, and giving sight to the blind and speaking to the dumb, including raising one from the dead. These acts of extraordinary compassion picture the arrival of the new era of deliverance (Isa. 35:5–6; Wilkins 2004, 370). The crowds and others spread the word and observed that what Jesus was doing had not been seen before. Jesus's work continued to evoke an array of responses, but the religious leaders were less than impressed. Their opposition was rising as they connected Jesus to malevolent powers, even though his healings reversed the normally perceived actions of such hostile figures.

Parallels to the bleeding woman and Jairus's daughter appear in Mark 5:21–43 and Luke 8:40–56. The healing of the two blind men is like Mark 10:46–52 and Luke 18:35–43, only Matthew has two blind men healed, not just one as in the supposed parallels. In addition, Matthew has a healing of two blind men as Jesus approached Jerusalem (Matt. 20:29–34), so the event in Matthew 9 is not, strictly speaking, a parallel. It is best to see this as independent tradition of a distinct event (Carson 2010, 271; France 2007, 365; and Osborne 2010, 353, versus Nolland 2005, 399–400). The doubling of who was healed in the accounts both here and in Matthew 20 mirrors what took place with the Gadarene demonic account, where Matthew alone has two demoniacs healed. Matthew also has this event much earlier than the parallels, pointing to his more topical structure versus strict chronology. The healing of the dumb man reflects Luke 11:14–20. Here also Matthew has reduced the account to its most central elements. The saying about praying for more laborers has a parallel in Luke 10:2, while the sheep without a shepherd saying is also in Mark 6:34. In the three miracles, five people were healed.

The three miracle accounts cover an array of maladies and types of people. Jesus healed the bleeding unclean, the dead, the blind, and the dumb. Men and women were the beneficiaries. The first event was an intertwined miracle, where the first miracle story is interrupted by a second healing. Matthew's version of this healing has parallels, and he significantly reduced the details as was his custom. Each healing got a reaction. In the first healing, reports about Jesus went out. In the second, those healed made the report. In the third, the reaction of the crowd was that this was unprecedented. The Pharisees' negative reaction that Jesus healed by demonic power closes out the miracle sequence. The telling of multiple miracles accounts over several chapters pictures the consistent character of Jesus's ministry, yet it has not persuaded them. Hard hearts are hard to break. Some hearts are too hard to soften. Still Jesus's mission went on, so after a healing summary, Jesus told the disciples to pray for more laborers. The mission went forward even in the face of continued and rising opposition.

EXPOSITION (9:18–38)

Jesus's consistent ministry of miracle working continued to underscore that God was at work. Despite its variety and consistency, the activity did not produce a response that changed the minds of those opposed to Jesus. The opposition to him and his movement arose despite the work of compassion he had engaged in and the evidence of a divine heart of caring it revealed. The inconsistency of this is something Matthew is pointing out as the sequence of miraculous activity continues. The opposition to Jesus made no sense.

Jesus's works of healing as Son of David brought the Pharisees' negative reaction that he healed by demonic power, even as Jesus issued a call to pray for more harvest laborers.

9:18–19. As Jesus ministered and taught about the new way of the new era, a religious ruler approached and bowed before him. He was probably a synagogue ruler who also was a civic leader. Mark 5:22 and Luke 8:41 give his name as Jairus. His responsibility was to oversee worship at the synagogue. Some Jews were being drawn to Jesus.

As in Matthew 8:6, this man sought healing for another. He announced that his daughter had died. He also declared with significant faith that Jesus could heal his daughter just by touching her dead body. Normally this act would have rendered one unclean, but not in Jesus's case where his power overcame uncleanness. The same dynamic was a part of the healing of the woman with a flow of blood. Precedent for such healing was found in the Old Testament (1 Kings 17:17–24—Elijah; 2 Kings 4:32–37—Elisha).

This scene in Matthew is condensed from its parallels in Mark and Luke. The lack of any messenger in the reduction meant the death must be moved to the start (Davies and Allison 1991, 126). In the other two synoptic gospels, the daughter died as Jesus was interacting with the woman who had a flow of blood. Matthew simplified the account and simply had her dead from the start, since the issue was her condition when Jesus finally got to her. It also allowed for the ruler's faith to be evident. Since in the longer parallel version he did not give up on Jesus healing his daughter, his faith was summarized here as a request to raise her. Jesus and the disciples followed him to his house. The result of Matthew's simplification of the account meant that some of the drama of the delay was lost. The focus was only on the opportunity to raise someone from the dead.

9:20–21. Along the way, an unclean woman touched Jesus. She had lived with the pain and estrangement of a twelve-year flow of blood. This was a potentially embarrassing uterine condition. According to likely practice, she rendered those she touched unclean and therefore should let people know of her condition. Nolland (2005, 395) notes with care that informing others was not clearly required at the time. Still, this condition was socially restricting (Keener 2009, 301–3). However, she also had faith that if she could just touch the tassels of Jesus's garment (Num. 15:37–38; Deut. 22:12), she would be healed. Her faith was not as bold as the ruler's, for he sought Jesus in public while she tried to conceal her action. In her heart, she had some level of faith. It was even stated as a third-class condition, which leaves the results open. The force was, "If I might only touch the hem of his garment." The ambivalence could reflect either a touch of uncertainty or a lack of presumption on her part. Her hesitation to go public may have been the result of a sensitivity about her condition that caused her to cover her act publicly and/or of such supreme confidence that she felt she need not disclose it. Even though her situation rendered her unclean, she thought Jesus could reverse the entire situation (Lev. 15:25; Ezek. 36:17; CD 4:12–5:17; 11QTa 48:15–17; the entire Mishnaic tractate of *Mid.* as well *as m. Zabim* 4:1).

Texts on Uncleanness

Leviticus 15:25: "When a woman's discharge of blood flows many days not at the time of her menstruation, or if it flows beyond the time of her menstruation, all the days of her discharge of impurity will be like the days of her menstruation—she is unclean."

Ezekiel 36:17: "Son of man, when the house of Israel was living on their own land, they defiled it by their behavior and their deeds. In my sight their behavior was like the uncleanness of a woman having her monthly period."

There is nothing negative about her attitude in how she is described. Her faith and Jesus's authority dominate the event. The cleanliness Jesus brought overcame any sense of uncleanness. Her action interrupted Jesus's journey to the ruler's house and added some drama to the scene. The touch was enough to work a healing and got his attention (Acts 19:12). The verb for success of the deliverance of the healing is σώζω ("to deliver/save"), pointing to a deeper picture of deliverance portrayed in what the healing represented (BDAG s.v. "σώζω" 1c, 982). Jesus could deliver one from any form of uncleanness (France 2007, 361).

9:22. The scene is significantly reduced from the version in Mark 5:30–34a. There Jesus felt power going from him and asked who had touched him. Matthew has a no-frills version of the event. He was summarizing. In Matthew, Jesus simply addressed her desire to be healed.

Jesus cheered up the woman from her suffering. He addressed her tenderly as daughter (Ruth 2:8; 3:10–11) and told her to be of good cheer, echoing the language of deliverance (σώζω) in verse 21. The address as "daughter" may suggest she was relatively young. To call her "daughter" parallels the earlier address of the paralytic as "son" in Matthew 9:2.

Jesus noted that the woman's faith had saved her (that faith delivers is a synoptic theme—Mark 10:52; Luke 7:50; 17:19; 18:42). Her openness to the kingdom and Jesus's power had served her well (Nolland 2005, 397). God healed through Jesus, but faith had opened up its possible presence and the chance of something even more than she had intended. This was no act of magic; it was God's work, reflective of the program Jesus represented. From the hour Jesus spoke, the woman was delivered. The touch was effective because of God's grace honoring faith. Rather than Jesus becoming unclean, she was cleansed with what Blomberg (2005) has called contagious holiness.

9:23–24. Matthew instantly moves from the first miracle to the healing of the ruler's daughter. At the house, Jesus dismissed the flute or clarinet players and the disorderly crowd. These would have been reed pipe players gathered as mourners according to Jewish custom because the girl had died (2 Chron. 35:25; Eccl. 12:5; Jer. 9:17–22; Ezek. 24:17, 22; Hos. 9:4; Amos 5:16; Josephus, *B.J.* 3.437). Mishnah *Ketuboth* 4:4 notes a custom that even the poorest were to have two clarinets and one wailing woman for the death of a woman (also Matt. 11:17 portrayed mourning with music; Turner 2008, 259). Since this man was a ruler, we should think of a larger group of mourners. Some of them may have been paid to perform this role. Burial among Jews usually took place within twenty-four hours without embalming the body. This was because the body was seen as unclean (Num. 19:11), so burial was to take place as soon as was possible. They mourned and sang dirges in honor of the dead. It would have been noisy and tumultuous. Jesus dismissed them because death was not going to linger. He would perform a resuscitation.

The girl, he announced, was not dead but was sleeping. Sleep was a metaphor for death (Dan. 12:2; John 11:11–12; 1 Thess. 4:13). Jesus's statement was rhetorical and not a remark that said they were mistaken having thought the girl was dead. The mourners were there because of her death. The summary of Jesus's work in Matthew 11:5 will speak of Jesus raising people from the dead, of which this present scene is the only example in Matthew (France 2007, 364). Knowing they were there because the girl was dead, the mourners laughed at Jesus. The term here is καταγελάω, which can mean to "laugh at" or "ridicule" (BDAG s.v. "καταγελάω" 515). Thinking death was the end of the girl's story, they mocked him. In Genesis, another had laughed, thinking something was not possible, only to find God could do the unusual (Sarah in Gen. 18:13).

The intertwined miracles may suggest something else beyond the authority in the healings. We had a probably isolated and poor woman healed of a flow of blood and a wealthy man whose daughter was brought back to life (Keener 2009, 305). So these healings covered a wide social spectrum. Its involvement of women also showed the scope of Jesus's ministry.

9:25. After the crowd was cast out, the miracle is depicted with an everyday feel that defies what took place. The miracle's private nature has parallels in 1 Kings 17:19; 2 Kings 4:4, 33; and Acts 9:40 (Davies and Allison 1991, 132, note other extrabiblical texts with a similar theme). The idea here is simply that mourners were no longer required for the girl.

Jesus took the hand of the girl and raised her, much like he was helping her rise from a slumber. Being raised from the dead became more like awakening from a nap. Jesus's power over death was that simple. There was no uncleanness contracted by Jesus, for his power to bring life reversed any of that. Matthew lacks any address to her, omitting the Aramaic call for the girl to arise as in Mark 5:41. There is no hint of any magic or use of a formula in how Matthew narrates the event. Only Jesus's acting was required.

9:26. The healing drew attention. The "report" (φήμη) of what took place went out to the entire land (BDAG s.v, "φήμη" 1053, a term from which we get our word "fame"). The reference here is to the district around the healing's locale of Capernaum. McNeile (1915, 126) shows a narrow use of the term γῆ in this way for "district" (Matt. 2:6; 4:15; 9:31; 10:15; 11:24; BDAG s.v. "γῆ" 3, 196). Only Matthew uses this word this way. We are told nothing of the girl or the family, despite the fact this account combines two major life themes: parental love and power in the face of death (Turner 2008, 260). The issue is simply how the event pointed to Jesus. He is the light under which everything is placed.

9:27. Jesus was now on the move. As he left the home, two blind men followed him. They were appealing for his help, crying to the Son of David for mercy. This was normally a regal term and would have pointed to the hoped-for promise of a regal deliverer (2 Sam. 7:12–16; Pss. Sol. 17:21–25). Here another hope was at work. The request, appealing to the term ἐλεέω ("to have mercy"), was for an act of compassion (BDAG s.v. "ἐλεέω" 315; Matt. 9:13). The insight of the blind men is stunning, for they recognized that Jesus as Son of David had such a capability. The association of the Son of David with healing is somewhat common and has produced discussion about whether this connection was made distinct from a recognition of Jesus as Messiah (Berger 1973; Chae 2006; Chilton 1982; Davies and Allison 1991, 136; Duling 1975, 1978; especially Novakovic 2003). For all that can be said for this idea, the only reason to connect Jesus to David is to make a regal-messianic point, so one idea (David) came with the other (deliverer-healer), especially when healing was tied to the new era (Hagner 1993, 253). Josephus does note that Solomon had such a reputation (*A.J.* 8.42–49), but this connection shows these blind men saw a link between Jesus's position and all he was able to do and had been doing. Though physically blind, they could see thigs spiritually quite clearly. David's son healed frequently in this gospel (Matt. 12:23; 15:22; 20:30–31). This role as David's son is important to Matthew later in his gospel (Matt. 12:3; 21:9, 15; 22:41–43, 45). He uses the phrase far more than Mark or Luke, but Luke makes such associations in distinct ways (Luke 1:31–33; 2:11; also see Acts 2:29–36; 13:22–23; Rom. 1:3; 2 Tim. 2:8). Josephus also discussed David's ability to heal (*A.J.* 6:166–68).

Davidic Hope

2 Samuel 7:12–16: "When the time comes for you to die, I will raise up your descendant, one of your own sons, to succeed you, and I will establish his kingdom. He will build a house for my name, and I will make his dynasty permanent. I will become his father and he will become my son. When he sins, I will correct him with the rod of men and with wounds inflicted by human beings. But my loyal love will not be removed from him as I removed it from Saul, whom I removed from before you. Your house and your kingdom will stand before me permanently; your dynasty will be permanent."

Psalms of Solomon 17:21–25: "See, Lord, and raise up for them their king, the son of David, to rule over your servant Israel in the time known to you, O God. Undergird him with the strength to destroy the unrighteous rulers, to purge Jerusalem from Gentiles who trample her to destruction; in wisdom and in righteousness to drive out the sinners from the inheritance; to smash the arrogance of sinners like a potter's jar; To shatter all their substance with an iron rod; to destroy the unlawful nations with the word of his mouth; At his warning the nations will flee from his presence; and he will condemn sinners by the thoughts of their hearts."

Blindness was not only a handicap; it could also have religious implications, leading to restrictions in what one could do in worship in terms of offering a sacrifice (Lev. 21:20). We see the blind defiling the holy city in 11Q19 45:12–14 (Temple scroll). To heal the blind pointed to the new era (Isa. 29:18; 35:5; 42:7). There were no healings of the blind in the Old Testament, but early Jewish tradition had a few, although they did not involve an intermediary performing the healing (Tob. 2:10; 3:16–17; Ep. Arist. 316). Greco-Roman sources had one famous example later involving Vespasian (Tacitus, *Hist.* 4:81).

9:28. Once he entered the house, Jesus pulled the blind men aside and asked if they thought he was able to perform this rare kind of healing. Such faith had been assumed in other healings (Matt. 8:2; 9:18, 21). Their reply was affirmative. They had faith in Jesus. They addressed him respectfully as Lord, an expression of the awareness that Jesus had this power. This is the only place in Matthew where such a question about faith was explicitly presented with a healing. We are not told whose house we are in. It could be Peter's or the one Jesus lived in. The only concern is the question, can this Son of David heal?

Davidite Healers and Exorcisms

Josephus, *Antiquities* 6.166–68: "So Samuel, when he had given him these admonitions, went away. But the Divine Power departed from Saul, and removed to David, who upon this removal of the Divine Spirit to him, began to prophesy; but as for Saul, some strange and demoniacal disorders came upon him, and brought upon him such suffocations as were ready to choke him; for which the physicians could find no other remedy but this, That if any person could charm those passions by singing, and playing upon the harp, they advised them to inquire for such a one, and to observe when these demons came upon him and disturbed him, and to take care that such a person might stand over him, and play upon the harp, and recite hymns to him. Accordingly Saul did not delay, but commanded them to seek out such a man; and when a certain stander-by said that he had seen in the city of Bethlehem a son of Jesse, who was yet no more than a child in age, but comely and beautiful, and in other respects one that was deserving of great regard, who was skillful in playing on the harp, and in singing of hymns [and an excellent soldier in war], he sent to Jesse, and desired him to take David away from the flocks, and send him to him, for he had a mind to see him, as having heard an advantageous character of his comeliness and his valor. So Jesse sent his son, and gave him presents to carry to Saul; and when he was come, Saul was pleased with him, and made him his armor bearer, and had him in very great esteem; for he charmed his passion, and was the only physician against the trouble he had from the demons, whensoever it was that it came upon him, and this by reciting of hymns, and playing upon the harp, and bringing Saul to his right mind again."

Josephus, *Antiquities* 8.45–46a: "God also enabled him [Solomon] to learn that skill which expels demons, which is a science useful and sanative to men. He composed such incantations also by which distempers are alleviated. And he left behind him the manner of using exorcisms, by which they drive away demons, so that they never return, and this method of cure is of great force unto this day."

9:29. Jesus touched their eyes (touch: Matt. 8:3, 15; 9:25; 14:36; 20:34) and declared them healed. The touching was a vivid reinforcement that blind people were being healed by the healer, showing the blind men how it was done (Matt. 20:34; Mark 8:23, 25; John 9:6; France 2007, 367). The touch would have signaled a positive response from Jesus to the blind men. He could have spoken an order, but this touch made it more personal. There was a concrete affirmation of their faith that served as a basis for Jesus responding to their request (Matt. 8:10, 13; 9:2, 22; 15:28). His power honored faith. Bruner (2004a, 349) says, "You believe; you have it." Faith connected one to God.

9:30. The touch opened the eyes of the pair to see. The healing is depicted with simplicity. There was a touch and immediate healing. Jesus sternly warned them not to tell anyone (Matt. 12:16; 16:20; 17:9). The term ἐμβριμάομαι meant "to insist on something" (BDAG s.v. "ἐμβριμάομαι" 1, 322; Mark 1:43; 14:5; emotionally moved in grief—John 11:33, 38). It can mean to scold in certain contexts. This is the only place Matthew uses this verb. As rare as healing of the blind was, in Matthew it is common (Matt. 9:27–31; 12:22–23; 15:30–31; 20:30–34; 21:14–15; Wilkins 2004, 372).

Jesus was hesitant that he become known primarily for his miraculous activity (Turner 2008, 261; Wilkins 2004, 373). He wanted to limit how much was said about what he was doing. His miracles were not the point of his ministry. What they pointed to was the issue he wanted people to see. Although this call to silence is often claimed to support the idea of the messianic secret as a theological creation of the evangelists, there is little compelling evidence that this was what was going on. The confession of Jesus as the Messiah was so deeply rooted in the earliest life of the early church that it was unlikely this was a post-Easter creation.

9:31. The two blind men could not contain themselves (Hagner 1993, 254). Despite Jesus's warning, they went out and spread the news about what Jesus had done. Matthew says that they reported his fame to the entire land or region (Matt. 4:24; 9:26). Despite Jesus's best efforts, the story of his miraculous works circulated widely. Miracles did not lead to obedience.

9:32–33. The final miracle of the third triad is told just as crisply as the others. Here, a demon-possessed man who could not speak was brought to Jesus. Given the term is κωφός, he could have been deaf and dumb, a likely possibility given Matthew 11:5 (BDAG s.v. "κωφός" 1, 580). The miracle is much like Matthew 12:22–23. Jesus simply cast out the demon so the man could speak. There is a note of compassion here. Despite the risk of the news of Jesus's work spreading even more, just as it had with the blind men, Jesus healed.

The stress on this healing is not on Jesus's ability to heal, but the reaction. The crowd was amazed. What Jesus was doing had not been seen before in Israel. It was unprecedented. The remark was surely about the aggregate of what Jesus had been doing (contra Morris 1992, 236, who seems to limit the remark to this single healing). What Jesus had been doing was so widely reported people were bringing the sick to him. Something must be going on, at least that was the impression Matthew wanted the reader to draw. It is the last and climactic note to the series of miracles Matthew has told in the last two chapters. However, not all reactions reflected amazement or were positive.

9:34. Despite all the good that Jesus was accomplishing, the judgment by the Pharisees was that this power was demonic. It was by the power of the ruler of the demons that the demons were cast out. The claim, at one level, made no sense. Why would the devil block his own work? However, the alternative conclusion—that God was at work—would force a positive evaluation of Jesus and the need to respond to him. That kind of accountability was a place these religious leaders did not want to go. The direction things were headed in was becoming clear. Many leaders were not going to be responsive to what God was doing through Jesus. This initial judgment set the tone for the rising opposition to Jesus. The rejection of Jesus by many Jewish leaders is a theme all of Matthew has and will be traced further by him, just as it is highlighted in these sequences of miraculous triads (Matt. 2:7–10; 8:10–12; 9:3–4, 11, 14; 10:17, 21–23, 25; 11:2, 20–24; 12:14, 22–24; 22:15; Osborne 2010, 360).

These remarks also set up things Matthew will say in Matthew 10:25 and 12:24, 27. The ruler of the demons is known today as Satan, but he had many names then, including Beelzebul (T. Sol. 3:1–6). The crowd saw what Jesus was doing as unprecedented, but the leaders did not want him to receive any positive credit and tried to block any perception of Jesus that would draw people to him. It is important to see that the leaders did not deny that Jesus was performing great works. The roots of the transcendent source was all that was being debated. The option that he was only a respectable leader was not on the table. This is a popular view of Jesus today, but the text will not permit one to land there. The leaders were not challenging that these miracles were happening, a point of some significance for evaluating whether they took place. The detail is an argument for the authenticity of these events.

9:35. This verse is a ministry summary on Jesus's work in all the towns and villages he was visiting. His was an itinerant ministry. Surely he repeated himself in these locales. These words and deeds showed that God cared. Jesus was teaching, preaching, and healing. Word and deed went together. He was present in the synagogues, teaching the kingdom, and healing all who were brought to him. Sometimes the presence of miracles gets in the way of seeing what Jesus was doing that was most basic: he was caring for and serving people. It is an example for ministry. Our actions are to reflect and enhance our words. That amplification happens when word and deed match. The juxtaposition of this verse to the previous one gives a sense that this was hardly the devil's work.

This verse's theme and wording is like Matthew 4:23 and the verse here forms brackets with that passage. Matthew 5–7 shows Jesus's word about the kingdom, while Matthew 8–9 highlights Jesus's work for the kingdom (Wilkins 2004, 374).

The verse begins a transition to the theme of mission that also becomes the focus in Matthew 10 (France 2007, 371). Jesus had shown himself to be well qualified to lead the mission of the kingdom, despite the hesitating and negative judgment of some. This passage could just as well be seen as the beginning of Matthew 10:1–42 as well as concluding this unit. But given the pattern of miracle triad and then word in Matthew 8–9, we have left it to conclude this earlier piece of Matthew.

9:36. What motivated Jesus was a deep compassion for the crowds (Matt. 14:14; 15:32; 20:34). Their needs were not only for healing and physical concerns; they had deep spiritual deficits as well. As he looked at the people, he sensed they were sheep without a shepherd (Matthew also uses shepherd imagery in Matt. 25:32; 26:31). The image of the shepherd could have messianic implications and has rich historical roots, beginning with the picture of how Joshua stepped into Moses's shoes (Num. 27:17–18; 1 Kings 22:17; Jer. 3:15; 23:4; Ezek. 34:23–24; 37:24; Zech. 10:2; 13:7; Davies and Allison 1991, 148; France 2007, 372). Micah 5:2 is especially important here, as the shepherd came to deliver the nation, having been born in Bethlehem, a point Matthew 2:6 makes (Osborne 2010, 365). God watched over his people like a shepherd with sheep (Ps. 23; Isa. 40:10–11). This text in Matthew 9 echoes in contrast to Ezekiel 34 and the prophet's complaint against Israel's leaders as not being good shepherds. Jesus was supplying what the nation lacked and what Ezekiel had promised would come. The people were at great risk, just as sheep roaming the fields would be if there were no protection. This indictment of the leadership reaches its height in Matthew 23.

Ezekiel on the Davidic Hope

Ezekiel 34:23–24: "'I will set one shepherd over them, and he will feed them—namely, my servant David. He will feed them and will be their shepherd. I, the Lord, will be their God, and my servant David will be prince among them; I, the Lord, have spoken!'"

Ezekiel 37:24: "My servant David will be king over them; there will be one shepherd for all of them. They will follow my regulations and carefully observe my statutes."

Jesus's acts of compassion showed God's desire to fill this leadership gap. The "compassion" (σπλαγχνίζομαι) was for a people who were harassed, helpless, and beaten down by a lack of direction (BDAG s.v. "σπλαγχνίζομαι" 938). "Compassion" refers to an empathy or sympathy felt for someone going through a difficult time. It is a strong term, referring very much to a gut reaction to what is taking place, as the term alludes to the inside of a person and the reaction from within. The people were lost, so Jesus was responding to their need.

The description of their condition is also vivid. The term σκύλλω means "to be weary," "harassed," or "troubled" (BDAG s.v. "σκύλλω" 1, 933), while ῥίπτω literally means "to throw something down," so for a person it means "to be beaten down" or "overwhelmed" (BDAG s.v. "ῥίπτω" 906). These were a people in need, being overtaken by predators like exposed sheep. The lack of discernment about God's will had left the people in deep pain and need. God was moving to resolve the dilemma through Jesus if the leaders and people would see it.

9:37–38. The concluding pronouncement speaks of opportunity and need. There was a great harvest, as many were ready to respond to God's kingdom offer, but the workers were few. God needed to cast out workers into the harvest. Jesus said meeting this need was a matter for prayer. Of the twenty-two times the Greek term for "to pray" is used in the New Testament, this is the one use in Matthew (BDAG s.v. "δέομαι" 218; Morris 1992, 240 n. 91). In effect, Jesus was calling disciples to pray for additional workers to help them in the task. The call to pray shows the importance of the effort. This was ultimately God's work. What the work needed was not so much a look at techniques but faithful laborers.

Prayer was given to the Lord of the harvest, a description of God pointing to his sovereignty over the entire program. A challenge led those who trusted God to turn to him in prayer. There was an urgency to the kingdom task that made it worthy of prayer (Garland 1995, 109). The labor would not be easy, as Matthew 10 also shows. The verb "cast out" (ἐκβάλλω) is an intense term as it is also used of driving out demons (BDAG s.v. "ἐκβάλλω" 2, 299; Matt. 7:22; 8:16; 10:1). The Gospel of Thomas 73 has a similar saying.

In the Old Testament, the harvest is usually associated with judgment (Isa. 18:4; 63:1–6; Jer. 51:33; Hos. 6:11; Joel 3:13). It also appears this way with John the Baptist (Matt. 3:12). Here the figure is positive, looking to the gathering of the saved and is tied to the present. *Mishnah 'Abot.* 2:15 has an image close to this, speaking of the day being short, the task being great, and laborers being idle (Davies and Allison 1991, 149). This also has precedent in the Old Testament (Jer. 2:3; Isa. 27:12–13; France 2007, 373; Hengel 1981, 75). In Matthew 13:24–30, 36–43, both elements of gathering and judgment are present. The rising opposition shows people were dividing over Jesus, and God would render a verdict one day, vindicating those who had chosen God's way. The presence of kingdom gathering was another indication the new era arrived with Jesus.

THEOLOGICAL FOCUS

The exegetical idea (Jesus's works of healing as Son of David brought the Pharisees' negative reaction that he healed by demonic power, even as Jesus issued a call to pray for more harvest laborers) points to this theological one: Jesus's show of kingdom authority often meets with opposition, even as he asks for prayer for more laborers.

Jesus's authority and compassion though various miracles was leading to the spread of the word about him and the encouragement of faith in those who responded positively, as well as reaction against him by those who doubted the source of his effective ministry. This reality created a need to pray for more laborers for the harvest.

Jesus's ministry was gathering attention and dividing people into those who responded and those who rejected. The miracles in this triad point to faith. Whether we think of the shy faith of the woman with a flow of blood, the bold faith of the ruler who knew Jesus could raise people from the dead, or the sight the blind men had that the Son of David could heal, faith is highlighted as that which God rewards.

However, miracles were no guarantee of faith. The reaction of people around Jesus was mixed. Some said he healed by the power of the prince of demons. Others saw what he was doing as unprecedented but still were processing what was taking place. The report and fame of Jesus was spreading with an array of views about what his activity meant. Matthew is clear in showing this ministry of word and deed meant the arrival of the new era, even vindication by God, but some saw it and others did not. Which side will Matthew's audience fall on?

The people were in deep need, like sheep left exposed without a shepherd. There was a harvest that was ready, but laborers were few. The Lord of the harvest had to be approached to provide more laborers. Along with labor, there was a prayer for the mission. The mission would follow. All of this expressed God's deep love and compassion to care for the lost. Bring your burden to him; he seeks to bear it in the right and needed way.

The stress in this unit is on God's response to faith. He honors it with grace. The power of Jesus so evident throughout Matthew 8–9 continues in this unit but now the response to him is what receives more attention. Those who embrace Jesus by faith receive reward, but others are keeping a distance from him, whether in rejection or mere reflection. Neither rejection nor reflection alone represents a good place to be. Yet the mission will go on and expand to include workers besides Jesus and his earliest disciples. A harvest is there to be collected. In the face of an array of responses, God's kingdom program proceeds. The only question is whether some will watch it go by or have a share in it. Faith brings one through the door.

This is all rooted in God's care and compassion. He is ready, willing, and able to bear our burdens. In fact, he is the only one capable of doing so. Jesus's miracles and ministry of compassion show this care. Word and deed show God at work.

PREACHING AND TEACHING STRATEGIES

Exegetical and Theological Synthesis

The exegetical section emphasizes the mixed reactions to Jesus's miracles ministry. Some expressed wonder, gratitude, and joy; these were faith reactions. Some viewed Jesus with curiosity and uncertainty; these were crowd reactions. The Pharisees doubted and maligned Jesus's work; this was oppositional reaction. Matthew captured not only the range of reactions but also Jesus's growing popularity in Galilee.

More importantly, Matthew accounted for Jesus's reaction to individuals and crowds. To the suffering, Jesus slowed down, drew near, listened, and healed. He spoke words of comfort to a grieving father and desperate woman. He touched the eyes of two blind men who cried out for healing. Neither a demon-possessed man nor Jesus's name-calling opponents repelled him. Even the "harassed and helpless" crowd evoked his empathy. Indeed, Jesus embodied compassion.

Meanwhile, Jesus's disciples were silent bystanders, bookending the passage. They traveled with Jesus to Jairus's home (Matt. 9:19); they received Jesus's exhortation to pray for harvest workers (9:37). Matthew does not mention them in the intervening miracles, but their silence is not an indictment. Before the disciples work, they must watch and pray. They learn not only Jesus's kingdom words but also his compassionate ways. If they intend to imitate Jesus, earnest prayer to the Lord of the harvest is an appropriate entry point.

Preaching Idea

Jesus's compassion deserves a positive reaction.

Contemporary Connections

What does it mean?

What does it mean that Jesus's compassion deserves a positive reaction? This preaching idea recognizes not everyone will react positively to Jesus's compassion. During his earthly ministry, the Pharisees viewed his compassion either as a threat because of the popularity it produced or as an offense because he ignored purity laws in some of his healings. Even the disciples occasionally pushed back against his empathetic responses to hungry crowds and harmless children. Compassion interrupted Jesus, and the disciples did not like it.

Acts of compassion continue today in Jesus's name. Not all are well received. Many people resist faith-based programs in their communities. Some people oppose homeless shelters and halfway houses for fear that they will "disrupt" their peaceful neighborhoods. Some church folks resist using their building for daycare or AA meetings because those using it will "destroy" or "disregard" the property. Other people exempt themselves from various acts of compassion—giving money, providing food, opening their home—by claiming such deeds lead to enablement.

Rather than looking for loopholes or exemptions from extending Jesus's compassion, disciples of Jesus should celebrate compassionate acts done in his name. They shine forth the heart of God. The sheep and goats parable encourages ministries of mercy: feeding the hungry, welcoming the stranger, clothing the naked, attending the sick, and visiting prisoners (Matt. 25:31–46). Certainly, this list of compassionate acts is not exhaustive. Clearly, Jesus's response betrays a delight in compassionate deeds done in his name.

Is it true?

Is it true that Jesus's compassion deserves a positive reaction? Absolutely! Unfortunately, neither Jesus nor his disciples get the reaction they deserve. As mentioned above, often our efforts at loving the "least of these" and "lost" comes with a cost. Longtime church members can mimic the older brother from the prodigal son parable, acting entitled to their father's attention and material rewards (Luke 15:11–32). They may grumble when the church gives more financial resources to outreach programs than children's ministries. They may fuss when church leadership decides to change music styles to appeal to seekers, rather than keeping a steady diet of hymns to please those who love tradition.

Moreover, the compassion of Jesus shows up in individual acts of mercy to people in need: the family that welcomes a drifter into their home; the counselor who provides *pro bono* sessions to a depressed divorcee; the lawyer who represents underrepresented criminals on death row. These are real examples of Christlike compassion that *deserve* a positive reaction, but sadly are often met with resistance, skepticism, and unsolicited criticism. If we are on the receiving end of these negative reactions, we can take comfort in the fact that Jesus experienced the same pushback from his opponents.

Now what?

What is a proper response to Jesus's compassion and the reactions it elicits? First, we should take notice of Jesus's compassion. It was central to his character. Matthew, who is notably sparce in his details, made a point to describe Jesus's compassion. His compassion crossed social, ethnic, gender, and religious boundaries. His compassion allowed for interruptions. His compassion refused to view the crowds as a public menace but valued them as a hurting people. Moreover, his compassion saw suffering individuals as image-bearers, not as ministry obstacles or opportunities to advance his fame. This loving, life-giving, dignifying, and transformative compassion deserves our notice.

Second, we should imitate Jesus's compassion. Though we cannot readily apply Jesus's healing power, we can demonstrate his careful attention to others' needs and serve them. We should become more open to interruption, willing to stop, look, listen, and lend a hand when opportunity arises to show compassion. This could include holding a door open for someone, helping a person change brakes on their vehicle, buying groceries for a single parent, or sitting with a friend after a surgery. Churches or Christian organizations should identify compassion ministries they can launch or support through partnerships. These may include working with pregnancy centers, shelters for abused women, addiction recovery groups, or various efforts to alleviate global poverty and illness.

Third, we must pursue our ministries of compassion with a sensitivity to others. Not everyone wants help. Forcing acts of mercy on someone may only push them away; it certainly does not grant them dignity. Jesus's acts of compassion often followed a request from the person in need. Corbett and Fikkert (2014) make a compelling case for partnering with those in need to improve their lot rather than rushing to their rescue.

Finally, we must understand the limits of our acts of compassion. God tasked Jesus, not us, with redeeming the world. Jesus, not us, holds all things together. Jesus, not us, will bring heaven and earth and all that is within to its glorious end. We do good as we can, without developing a messiah complex. Moreover, our good deeds should go hand in hand with gospel proclamation (Matt. 5:13–16; Phil. 2:14–18). Compassionate acts help us point to Christ; our work is part of our witness. When we lose sight of the evangelistic aim of compassion, we simply become social (justice) workers who may eventually flame out from compassion fatigue. We are, in fact, harvest workers, who prayerfully join Jesus in proclaiming the kingdom in word and deed (Matt. 9:35–10:8).

Creativity in Presentation

Social media and reality TV have trained us to post our reactions. We can call in or text our vote to elevate a star performer on primetime television shows. We choose one of many emojis to respond to Facebook posts. Even when we buy products on Amazon or listen to podcasts on iTunes, we express our review with stars. Because these reactions are so prevalent, consider printing off sets of responses to have people raise in the air at different points in the sermon. To keep it simple, you might use an 8"x11" sheet of paper, printing opposite reactions on either side:

After describing each miracle, you could ask people to post their reaction by holding up an image. Or, to vary the exercise, you could assemble a panel of judges to sit on the stage during the sermon and show their reactions after you describe each compassionate act. Some form of this activity will engage your listeners.

Specific examples of negative reactions to compassion ministries may help people better understand Jesus's experience. For example, the early church won over many critics for its care of corpses and children exposed to the elements. As an act of compassion, Christians buried the dead during early plagues, even as it risked their own health, and they adopted babies despite limited resources. In early American history, Christians who fought for abolition of slavery did not get a positive reaction. The same could be said of early advocates for American civil rights. Martin Luther King Jr. had a great many opponents among white Protestants during his day. Likewise, it has become fashionable to deem modern missionary efforts, whether to unreached tribes or nations steeped in other religions, a waste of time, misuse of money, or abuse of power. The legal work of Bryan Stevenson in representing death-row inmates, depicted in the 2019 film *Just Mercy*, provides a recent example of compassionate work that had many critics. Finally, I (Tim) know of local efforts to ban a faith-based homeless shelter and rehab facility from entering our community. Apparently, some people think compassionate acts breed undesirable people. However, compassion can lift up people and change them.

On the other hand, the sermon may benefit from specific examples of Christlike compassion that earned positive reactions. Consider spotlighting historical figures of faith whose compassion emulated Jesus. George Mueller oversaw the care and education of thousands of orphans during his ministry. Famously, he never raised funds but earnestly prayed for God's provision and gratefully received financial gifts. His model of compassion and prayer has encouraged Christians for more than a century. Cast an image of such figures and list career highlights. Mother Teresa won the Nobel Peace Prize in 1979; her treatment of the sick and dying in Calcutta was remarkable. Other historical figures include Nelson Mandela and others.

However, emphasizing local people may prove more effective. In fact, you may consider giving out Compassion Awards to a few shining examples in your congregation: for the woman who always has a dinner ready to share with someone after recovering from surgery; for the college student who tutors kids with learning disabilities; for the man who mows laws and plows driveways for widows in your congregation. Their compassion in Jesus's name deserves a positive response.

As you integrate creative elements into your message, be sure to communicate that Jesus's show of kingdom authority often meets with opposition, even as he asks for prayer for more laborers. Or, more simply, Jesus's compassion deserves a positive reaction.

- Faith evokes Jesus's compassion (9:18–31).
- Fame provokes Jesus's opposition (9:32–34).
- Jesus invokes prayerful participation (9:35–38).

DISCUSSION QUESTIONS

1. What is the significance of Matthew's word for healing?
2. What is the relationship between faith and healing?
3. How did Jesus demonstrate his compassion?
4. How are people around you "harassed and helpless" today? What spiritual deficits do they face?
5. What causes you compassion fatigue?

Matthew 10:1–11:1

EXEGETICAL IDEA

As Jesus called his disciples to trust in a priority mission for the kingdom to Israel, he predicted opposition alongside enablement from God, who knew what was taking place.

THEOLOGICAL FOCUS

God oversees the word-and-deed mission Jesus's disciples undertake even though there is opposition to it.

PREACHING IDEA

Go public and don't panic: God's got your back.

PREACHING POINTERS

Matthew recorded Jesus's second sermon, a summons to mission. Calling the twelve disciples by name, Jesus prepared them for entering villages and encountering fellow Israelites with news of the inbreaking kingdom of God. As with Jesus, wonderful works would validate their words. Like Jesus, they would face opposition—religious, political, and familial. To help his disciples overcome this opposition, Jesus promised the Spirit's empowerment and Father's protection. For Matthew's audience, this message offered assurance of God's care in the face of rising political tensions. Moreover, the sermon served as a fresh summons to proclaim Jesus's kingdom message until his return.

Opposition toward Jesus and his message persists today. In numerous countries the church remains underground; persecution is aggressive and overt. In the West, animosity toward believers continues to rise. We are flagged for our political views, moral standards, and theological positions about gender, creation, and eternal judgment, to name a few. Moreover, faith in the West primarily remains a private matter. People may vote their beliefs at the polls or share them on social media, but rare is the follower of Jesus who deliberately, personally, and articulately shares his or her faith. Indeed, most disciples keep quiet, afraid they might sound pushy, awkward, hateful, or inarticulate in proclaiming Jesus. This passage confronts such fear head-on with a personal call to join Jesus's mission. He still says, "Go public and don't panic: God's got your back."

JESUS SENDS THE DISCIPLES ON A MISSION TO ISRAEL (10:1–11:1)

LITERARY STRUCTURE AND THEMES (10:1–11:1)

The unit is the second of five Matthean discourses. It contains a series of instructions on an initial mission for ministry that was undertaken into Israel. It contains exhortations to stand firm in the face of opposition, with a trust that God was present in their midst and giving them enablement through the Spirit. The first fifteen verses cover how they were to minister, while the rest of the discourse is about what they could expect.

Jesus called out the Twelve and gave them authority for mission, including the ability to cast out demons and heal (Matt. 10:1–4). He gave them a series of instructions about how to go to Israel and proclaim the gospel using the combination of word and deed of his own ministry (Matt. 10:5–15). He warned them the mission would be dangerous, including persecution, but that the Spirit would be with them (Matt. 10:16–23). They were to beware of persecution, yet not be anxious, while still being prepared to flee if persecution became intense (Matt. 10:17, 19, 23). Their situation as disciples did not differ from the opposition the teacher had faced (Matt. 10:24–25). They were not to fear, for God knew what was taking place and Jesus would acknowledge those who acknowledge him (Matt. 10:26–31). The call not to fear appears three times (Matt. 10:26, 28, 31), following Matthew's love of triads. In many ways, this is the center of the discourse. There also would be those who respond (Matt. 10:11, 40). There was an exhortation to acknowledge Jesus in the face of opposition and coming accountability to God (Matt. 10:32–33). Jesus created a division among people, but those who placed Jesus before family and took up the cross found life (Matt. 10:34–39). People who received those Jesus sent would have a reward (Matt. 10:40–42). Jesus's discourse on mission ended as he also engaged in mission (Matt. 11:1).

A presentation of this structure follows the discussion and topic outline of Davies and Allison (1991, 160–62) but does not embrace their chiasm as convincing. There are instructions (Matt. 10:5–15), warnings about divisions (Matt. 10:16–23), notes that they will be tied to Beelzebul (Matt. 10:24–25), the centerpiece on consolation and encouragement (Matt. 10:26–31), the call to acknowledge Jesus (Matt. 10:32–33), warnings about tribulation and family division (Matt. 10:34–39), and a call to receive the missionaries and be rewarded (Matt. 10:40–42).

The unit is a combination of material shared with Mark and Luke. In some cases, the parallels are in all three synoptic gospels, while in others the material is shared only with Luke. The sequencing is not in the order of those other gospels, as one can see.

The call and naming, respectively, of the Twelve in Matthew 10:1–4 has parallels in Mark 6:7 and 3:13–19, as well as Luke 9:1; 6:14–16; and Acts 1:13. Matthew 10:1 is a commissioning statement. The remark about the ministry being for the lost sheep of Israel is unique to Matthew 10:5–6. The preaching of the nearness of the kingdom and the right to heal in Matthew 10:7–14 is like Luke 9:2 and 10:9, while their traveling light is like Mark 6:8–11 and Luke 9:3–11; 10:4–11. The doubling of parallels with Luke reflects the third gospel's telling of a mission of the Twelve and of the seventy(-two), which mirror each other. The warning to cities about being worse than Sodom and Gomorrah in Matthew 10:15 is like Luke 10:12. How to respond to persecution in Matthew 10:17–22 is paralleled in Mark 13:9–13 and Luke 21:12–19. The remark that they will not finish going through all the towns before the Son of Man returns is unique to Matthew. The saying about what happens to disciples is like what happens to the teacher in Matthew 10:24–25 also appears in Luke 6:40, although the Beelzebul remark appears in a completely distinct context of Luke 11:15. The call not to fear in Matthew 10:26–33 is like Luke 12:2–9, except that Matthew's triad of "do not fear" is unique to him. The idea of division pictured as bringing a sword in Matthew 10:33 is similar to Mark 8:38 and Luke 9:26, though Mark and Luke lack the sword imagery. The remarks on division in Matthew 10:34–36 is like Luke 12:51–53, as well as Mark 13:12 and Luke 21:12 though Luke 21 does not mention family. The teaching on disciples' priorities over family and life while taking up their own cross in Matthew 10:37–39 is like Mark 8:34–35 and Luke 9:23–24; 14:26–27; and 17:33. The theme of rewards for accepting those sent by Jesus in Matthew 10:40–42 is like Mark 9:37, and Luke 9:48 and 10:16 (also Matt. 18:5; John 13:20). The final image of giving a cup to one who ministers for Jesus is like Mark 9:41.

A look at the whole of these parallels showed how stitched together this material is in terms of where it falls in the other tradition strands. This was either its own distinct discourse of themes Jesus also discussed elsewhere in a variety of settings or it was an anthological combination on the theme of what Jesus taught about mission as he sent his disciples out over time (Morris 1992, 241).

Key themes are enablement from God, how to deal with opposition, a call to understand the mission's demand, and the ability to trust God in the midst of this pressure. The Spirit would give them what to say. The demand of mission made it a priority, greater than family or life. They needed to realize God was aware of what would happen to them and would reward those who embraced what Jesus represented. The division that Jesus brought has already been shown in Matthew 8–9 as his miraculous activity had not brought universal approval. Tension and opposition were no surprise. The disciples' experience would mirror what the teacher had seen. Jesus prepared them for it by what he taught here. Jesus did not pretend that following him was easy or without tension.

EXPOSITION (10:1–11:1)

Jesus empowered his disciples for a special mission to Israel. They were to declare the approach of the promised kingdom. With Jesus giving instruction about how to carry on the mission and what to expect, the disciples were being prepared for the opposition they would face and their need to trust God in the midst of it. Some of the instructions here were tied to the special circumstances of this specific mission, as Jesus altered such instructions later (Luke 22:35–36).

As Jesus called his disciples to trust in a priority mission for the kingdom to Israel, he predicted opposition alongside enablement from God, who would know what was taking place.

10:1. The move into mission began with the call of the Twelve. Mark 3:13–19 and 6:7 have the call of the Twelve and the mission separated, but Matthew has these together, showing again his tendency to edit and simplify the gospel tradition. Up to this point, five disciples had been named (Matt. 4:18–22—Peter; Andrew; the sons of Zebedee, James and John; 9:9—Matthew). Matthew paired the names after an Old Testament pattern about witnesses (Deut. 19:15; Blomberg 1992, 167).

This group represented the restoration of Israel and pointed to Jesus's call to bring the new era (Bock 2012, 39–47; McKnight in Bock and Webb 2009, 181–214, Num. 1:1–16; Matt. 19:28). They were given authority to cast out demons and to heal, to picture the arrival of the new era as Jesus's ministry had done. The verb for casting out unclean spirits matches the verb of the previous scene for casting out laborers for the harvest. The description of healing is like Matthew 4:23 and 9:35, which was said of Jesus. He now mediated a larger work that mirrored his own work. The Twelve are mentioned now and again in Matthew (Matt. 10:2, 5; 11:1; 20:17; 26:14, 20, 47), but only in Matthew 10:2 are they called apostles. Jesus had authority over disease and demons, but also over Israel.

10:2–4. The Twelve were called the apostles. This is the only verse where Matthew uses this term. This is the "sent man" of Judaism (Davies and Allison 1991, 153–54; Ber. 5:5). The Twelve are listed in pairs and this likely reflects that they were sent out two by two (Mark 6:7) to guarantee trustworthy witnesses (Deut. 19:15). Simon (Peter) always starts these lists. Judas is always last in the lists in the Synoptic Gospels (Mark 3:16–19; Luke 6:14–16). The lists can be seen as three groups of four, with the same name starting each group and the same four names in each grouping, though not always in the same order (Morris 1992, 243).

"The Agent Is Like the Sender" Text

Mishnah, Berakot 5:5: "One who prays and errs—it is a bad sign for him. And if he is a communal agent, [who prays on behalf of the whole congregation], it is a bad sign for them that appointed him. [This is on the principle that] a man's agent is like [the man] himself."

Peter, Andrew, James, and John are always the first four, but not always in the same order. Simon came to be known as Peter as Matthew 16:16–18 shows. The call of these first four is told in Matthew 4:18–22 (Mark 1:16–20). Peter, James, and John are sometimes singled out as present at events, such as the transfiguration (Matt. 17:1), the raising of Jairus's daughter (Mark 5:37–40), and at the Olivet Discourse (Mark 13:3 with Andrew). James was martyred by Herod Agrippa I (Acts 12:2). John lived a long life and ended up in Ephesus (Carson 2010, 278). The four were fishermen. In John 21, Nathaniel and Thomas join them in fishing.

Philip is only named in the Synoptics but appears in a few spots in John (John 1:43–51; 6:5; 12:20–22; 14:8). The Philip of Acts 6 and 8 who is a deacon and evangelist is not the same figure as the apostle mentioned here in Matthew. The daughters of Philip in Acts 21:8–9 belong to the deacon Philip. Bartholomew is only mentioned in these lists. The fact that some figures have no prominence outside the naming, yet are part of a consistent list, points to the authenticity of their role. One would have expected made-up figures to have more prominence.

Photo of St. Thomas, life-size figure in Chennai, India at a church commemorating his commission by Jesus and his ministry in India.

Thomas also appears in John (also called Didymus, the Aramaic for "twin," in John 11:16; 14:5; 20:24–29; 21:2). He is famous in John's gospel for his doubting the resurrection until he saw the raised Jesus. He is said to have taken the gospel to India according to tradition (Schnabel 2004, 1:880–895).

Matthew the tax collector is the only apostle whose occupation was named outside of the first four, who are fishermen. Matthew's vocation is noted within the listing. That is unique. His vocation would have been controversial, as was noted in the discussion of Matthew 9:9, and he was probably also known as Levi.

Nothing else is known about James of Alphaeus nor about Thaddaeus. James was named with his father to distinguish him from James the brother of Jesus and James, son of Zebedee. He might be Levi/Matthew's brother (Matthew is called a son of Alphaeus in Mark 2:14). Thaddaeus may be the same figure as Judas, son of James, in Luke 6:16 and Acts 1:13, assuming he had two names as others did.

Simon the Canaanite is Simon the Zealot of Luke 6:15, as that was the meaning of the name. This connection also allowed him to be distinguished from Simon Peter. If he was a political zealot, then to have him in a group with Matthew, who collected taxes, would be revealing. That a zealot Simon and Matthew could be in the same group showed the breadth of Jesus's impact across the social-political spectrum.

Judas was the one who betrayed Jesus (Matt. 10:4; 26:14–16, 20–25, 47–56; 27:3–10). Matthew 26:14–16 and 27:3–10 give us unique details about this defection in comparison with Mark's gospel.

10:5–6. The discourse proper begins with a call not to go to the Gentiles, nor to the Samaritans, but to the lost sheep of Israel. This remark is unique to Matthew. This shows that Jesus's focus initially was on the nation. This was something Matthew 15:24 also emphasizes with the same description of Israel as lost sheep, but in a context where Jesus would minister to a Gentile (the Syro-Phoenician woman), showing the issue was one of sequence and initial priority, but not an absolute or timeless limitation. His call to Israel was one of restoration as he announced the new era, something the preaching that followed also highlighted. The picture of Israel as sheep recalls Matthew 9:36, where the image of sheep also appears. Jeremiah 50:6 and Ezekiel 34 place significant responsibility for the people's lost condition on the leaders (also Isa. 53:6—of all the people wandering; Jer. 23:2–3). Covenantal faithfulness directed Jesus at this point, as God sought to reclaim all his people (Hagner 1993, 271). The genitive in the phrase the "lost sheep of Israel" (τὰ πρόβατα τὰ ἀπολωλότα οἴκου Ἰσραήλ) should be seen as explication, the lost sheep who are Israel, not partitive, the lost sheep out of Israel (the latter would suggest some did not have a need; Wilkins 2004, 389). Jesus may have been laying groundwork through a remnant to develop the new program (Scott, 1990).

The Lost Condition of the Nation

Isaiah 53:6: "All of us had wandered off like sheep; each of us had strayed off on his own path, but the Lord caused the sin of all of us to attack him."

Jeremiah 23:2: "So the Lord God of Israel has this to say about the leaders who are ruling over his people: 'You have caused my people to be dispersed and driven into exile. You have not taken care of them. So I will punish you for the evil that you have done. I, the Lord, affirm it!'"

Jesus extended his ministry of compassion to others by his mission here. Matthew 10:7–8a shows this would be a ministry of word and deed, one reinforcing the other. In fact, the ministry did not really work without both elements, as the actions of care and compassion backed up the message and gave it credibility as genuine.

The reference to the "way of the Gentiles" (ὁδὸν ἐθνῶν) probably describes taking roads that head to their cities, something the parallel reference to a "city of the Samaritans" (πόλιν Σαμαριτῶν) also suggests. Gentiles would be a part of the mission later as Matthew 28:16–20 makes clear, but for now it was to the Jew first (Acts 13:46; 18:6; 19:9; 28:25–28; Rom. 1:16–17; Bruner 2004a, 372). Matthew suggests as much about Gentile mission throughout his gospel (Matt. 2:1–12; 4:15, 24–25; 8:11, 28–34; 10:18; 21:43; 22:9; 24:14). Turner (2008, 268–69) also develops how the priority of Israel in God's plan worked theologically.

This is Matthew's only note about Samaritans, in contrast to Luke 9:51–56; 10:30–37; 17:11–19; and John 4, which picture at least some time spent ministering to them. Matthew is focused on Israel as the initial, primary point for Jesus's attention. In making this remark, Matthew appears to suggest that Samaritans were not truly Jewish, a point that also reflected the perspective of pious Jews (Sir. 50:25–26), since the Samaritans were a people of mixed racial background and religious practice (Josephus, *A.J.* 9:277–91; *m. Qidd.* 4:3). Acts 8 shows the early church making a conscious outreach to them as a part of her mission, with actions that showed their hybrid status in relation to Israel.

10:7. As they went in mission, the message the disciples had was one of hope and encouragement. They were to preach that the kingdom of heaven was at hand. The language recalls Matthew 3:2 and 4:17. The present imperative for "preach" points to the ongoing character of this early mission. They were now on a preaching mission about the kingdom that would continue. The key phrase here is ἤγγικεν ("at hand/is near/arriving"; BDAG s.v. "ἐγγίζω" 2, 270). The stress was on the nearness of the kingdom. Something long looked for was now dawning.

The exact force of the expression "is near" has been debated. Does it mean the kingdom approaches as to be close ("near") or that, in effect, it is "arriving/dawning"? In one sense the signs that follow point to the answer, since in prophetic hope these kinds of healings pointed to the presence of God's promise and power, a point Jesus made later in response to a query from John the Baptist's messengers (Matt. 11:2–6; cf. Isa. 29:18; 35:5–6; 42:6–7—of the servant; 26:19; 61:1–3—of his power; see also Luke 4:18–19). The kingdom was either present or so close that response to its coming was urgent. The kingdom was not in the distant future. This was not about a kingdom offer to be taken back or delayed, if refused. Instead that offer would go to others who would receive it, as this discourse also indicated. It was about God's program beginning to unfold, the start of something to which one had access that would end in God's total rule of peace and righteousness. Jesus's ministry and the kingdom's arrival coincided. It was the front end of the program and its arrival that was being preached. Everything about this discourse pointed to a mission carried out with urgency and an awareness of the accountability to God it raised.

OT Texts on Actions That Point to Deliverance and the Arrival of Salvation

Isaiah 26:19: "Your dead will come back to life; your corpses will rise up. Wake up and shout joyfully, you who live in the ground! For you will grow like plants drenched with the morning dew, and the earth will bring forth its dead spirits."

Isaiah 29:18: "At that time the deaf will be able to hear words read from a scroll, and the eyes of the blind will be able to see through deep darkness."

Isaiah 35:5–6: "Then blind eyes will open, deaf ears will hear. Then the lame will leap like a deer, the mute tongue will shout for joy; for water will burst forth in the wilderness, streams in the arid rift valley."

Isaiah 42:6–7: "'I, the Lord, officially commission you; I take hold of your hand. I protect you and make you a covenant mediator for people, and a light to the nations, to open blind eyes, to release prisoners from dungeons, those who live in darkness from prisons."

Isaiah 61:1–3: "The Spirit of the Sovereign Lord is upon me, because the Lord has chosen me. He has commissioned me to encourage the poor, to help the brokenhearted, to decree the release of captives, and the freeing of prisoners, to announce the year when the Lord will show his favor, the day when our God will seek vengeance, to console all who mourn, to strengthen those who mourn in Zion, by giving them a turban, instead of ashes, oil symbolizing joy, instead of mourning, a garment symbolizing praise, instead of discouragement. They will be called oaks of righteousness, trees planted by the Lord to reveal his splendor."

10:8. Beyond the message, there was the ministry activity to support it. Jesus told his disciples to heal the sick, raise the dead, cleanse lepers, cast out demons, and receive and give gifts. This mirrored what Jesus had been doing in Matthew 4 and 8–9 (Matt. 4:23–24; 8:1–4, 17, 28–34; 9:18–26, 32–34). It showed the arrival of the new era (Matt. 11:4–5; OT texts noted in the chart above). The combination of word and deed was crucial to the ministry's character. It was not word only, nor was it deed only. There was engagement to show that the declaration of the word was matched by the activity of those who preached it. What was done pointed to the divine program that underwrote it. Keeping the connection was crucial to both sides. There was no specific account of the healing of a leper by the disciples, but we do see engagement with the sick (Acts 3:1–10; 8:13; 9:32–35; 14:8–10), the raising of the dead (Acts 9:36–42—Peter; 20:9–12—Paul), and reports of exorcisms (Mark 6:13; Luke 10:17–20; Acts 8:7; 16:18; 19:13–16).

The idea of receiving and giving gifts pointed to acts of grace that mirrored how God had blessed them. Judaism also had this idea that the teaching of God came without charge (Ber. 29a: "Just as you received it [Torah] without payment, so teach it without payment"; *m. 'Abot.* 1:3, 13). Hagner (1993, 272) notes the gospel was not for sale nor for purchase (Acts 8:20). Everything about how ministry was conducted was to picture what God was offering and how God acted. There would be both offers of grace and statements of accountability to God.

10:9–10. Jesus also instructed his disciples to travel very light. They were to depend on God for their supplemental provisions in the mission. Those who received them were to meet their needs (Matt. 10:11–13, 40–42).

There was to be no acquiring of gold, silver, or copper in their money bags. The verb here, "acquire," looks primarily to acquisition of things, although it can mean "to possess" (BDAG s.v. "κτάομαι" 1, 572). Mark 6:8 speaks of not starting out with money. The term for "money bag" refers to a belt or girdle (BDAG s.v. "ζώνη" 431). Gold, silver, and copper refer to all levels of coin, those of the rich, middle class, or poor. The disciples were not in this to acquire wealth. Neither was there to be a travel bag, an extra tunic, sandals, or staff. The noted "leather pouch," "travel bag," or "knapsack" could be used as a beggar's bag (BDAG s.v. "πήρα" 811). A knapsack was most likely intended here. A staff often functioned for protection against attack from robbers or beasts (Keener 2009, 318).

These items were normally things a traveler would take (*m. Ber.* 9:5), with the equivalent today being to take a suitcase and proper funds. But the disciples' ministry was not tied to this world nor was it a ministry for financial gain (Bruner 2004a, 375–76). Their lifestyle was basic and humble. In this it was like the Cynics who ministered and had a humble lifestyle (Davies and Allison 1991, 172; Diogenes Laertius 6:13; Downing 1984). One difference was that the philosophers charged fees for their work and carried a travel bag to collect their fees and gifts (France 2007, 384–85). There also was a real question how well Cynics would have been known in Galilee.

The list differs some from Mark 6:8, both in terms of the order of the mention of materials and the list itself. Only Matthew 10:8–9 notes the giving of and receiving of gifts, gold, and silver. In Matthew the disciples need not worry about provision or payment for lodging. Mark mentions bread, which Matthew lacks. Where Matthew says sandals and a staff were permitted, Mark says they were prohibited. It is hard to imagine traveling a lot without sandals (France 2007, 384), so the idea in Mark was very likely to mean extra sandals or an extra staff; that is, Mark was referring to extra provision beyond what one would normally carry. Matthew states what would be normally the case, one travels with sandals and a staff. It is likely a differing perspective has produced this difference. For this, Morris (1992, 248) notes that in Matthew 10:14 they were told to shake the dust from their feet, something that more likely assumed sandals. Another possibility is that the account in Matthew was a composite of a variety of missions and the instructions here matched the sending out of the seventy(-two) in Luke 10:2 and 7b, which was a distinct mission and may have had slightly different instructions (Blomberg 1992, 172; Osborne 2010, 379).

The point with either wording is the same: they were to travel as light as possible and as unencumbered as possible. To lack sandals would have indicated poverty (Deut. 25:10; Luke 15:22). The ministry without financial gain is a theme in the New Testament (Acts 3:6; 4:32–5:11; 8:18–20; 18:1–3; 20:33–35; 1 Cor. 9:18; 2 Cor. 11:7; 12:14–18; Phil. 4:10–18; Turner 2008, 269).

The explanation (γὰρ) was that a worker is worthy of his hire (Luke 10:7; 1 Cor. 9:14, 17–18; 1 Tim. 5:18; also suggested in the Old Testament: Lev. 19:13; Num. 18:31; Deut. 24:15; 25:4). Turner (2008, 271) notes the early church saw such hospitality as a sacred duty (*Did.* 11–13). The mission was rooted in dependence on God and a facility to move from place to place as needed (Matt. 6:25–34).

10:11. Jesus next gave instructions about what to do when they arrived in a city or village. The reference to city or village looks back to Matthew 9:35. They were to go around as Jesus had done. The remarks are very much like Mark 6:10–11 and Luke 10:5–8, 10–11.

The disciples were to find someone worthy, someone responsive as a host and thus deserving. The disciples were to stay there until they left. They were entering new territory, which was why they must find someone open to what they were doing, possibly people who already had heard about Jesus (France 2007, 386). The verb for their quest means "to enquire" or carefully to look at something (BDAG s.v. "ἐξετάζω" 1, 349, where the term can have legal overtones of an examination). Matthew liked to use the word "worthy" to discuss the suitability of someone, seven of his nine uses in this chapter appearing here (BDAG s.v. "ἄξιος" 2a, 93–94; Matt. 10:37–38; 22:8: Luke 15:19; Rom. 16:2–3; 3 John 6; *Did.* 13:1; Turner 2008, 272 n. 1). The following verses define the meaning of the term "worthy." It was not a moral term in an abstract sense but had to do with welcoming the messenger and the message, someone open to what God was doing. Staying in one place was efficient, reflecting the urgency of the mission. Hospitality was considered a virtue in the culture, so the search for a host was not unnatural (Keener 2009, 319; Gen. 19:3; Judg. 19:20; Tob. 5:1–5; 7:8–9). One would not host someone who was seen as a false teacher (Sir. 11:29, 34; *Did.* 11–12).

10:12–13. When they arrived at a home, they were to give it a greeting. The greeting was one of *šālôm*, or of the offer of peace, good wishes, and well-being from God (Judg. 6:23; Luke 10:5).

The greeting would have been "peace be to you." They were "wish prayers" for others (Keener 2009, 320; Osborne 2010, 380). However, in this case the greeting came with the offer of the promise of the new era, an important detail of why the disciples were making the visit.

If it was worthy, that is, if the people in the home were receptive, then the word of peace was to remain on that home. Matthew 10:40–42 elaborates on the benefits of being receptive, as does Matthew 25:31–46. If it was not worthy, then the greeting of peace was to be taken back. This rise of rejection became the concern of the core of the discourse. The task and accountability of the kingdom cause was so important that peace from God was impacted (Matt. 10:32–39). One either was allied to what God was doing in promise and wished to receive it or was not. In rejecting those God had sent, one was rejecting the offer of a gift of peace God brought (Isa. 9:6; 52:7; Mic. 5:5; Nah. 1:5). Davies and Allison (1991, 176) note rejection of the messengers hurt not only the proclaimers but the prospective recipients. France (2007, 387) compares the refusal of the greeting to an uncashed check. For the greeting to be effective, the disciples' presence must be embraced.

10:14. Rejection of the message brought a prophetic symbolic act of renunciation. Some see a movement to more intense opposition as we proceed through the discourse from Matthew 10:11–14 (Osborne 2010, 381), moving from welcome to rejection. This is less than clear. The disciples might meet with an array of reactions, but they had to be particularly prepared for rejection that would come.

As they left the city where there has been rejection, they were to shake the dust from their feet (also Mark 6:11; Luke 9:5; Acts 13:51). Luke 10:10b–11 has a proclamation that was to be made as they departed, "Even the dust of your town that clings to our feet we wipe off against you. Nevertheless, know this: The kingdom has come." This was a way of signaling that nothing from the city clung to them. The village or city was on their own before God for having rejected the kingdom. The point of the act was to say that they were accountable to God whether they recognized it or not. Similar acts involving clothing appeared in Nehemiah 5:13 and Acts 18:6. These prophets had done their job. They had offered what God had made available and the city had made its choice.

10:15. There also was a warning. The locale that rejected the kingdom message was vulnerable to severe judgment, a judgment more severe than that of Sodom and Gomorrah, figures for the most sinful of cities, along with Tyre and Sidon (Gen. 18–19; Deut. 29:23; Isa. 1:9; 13:19; Jer. 49:18; Ezek. 16:46–56; Amos 4:11; Jub. 16:5; Matt. 11:22, 24—of Tyre and Sidon; Luke 10:14—of Tyre and Sidon; 2 Peter 2:6; Jude 7; Davies and Allison 1991, 179). This was a way of saying that the greater the blessing rejected the more severe the judgment. Matthew stresses the accountability one will have before God at the judgment (Matt. 8:12; 11:22, 24; 12:36; 13:42, 50; 18:9; 22:13; 23:15, 33; 24:51; 25:30; Osborne 2010, 381).

10:16. So the reality of rejection and persecution lay before the disciples. Opposition would not merely be passive; it might be aggressive. Jesus now elaborated on this theme. The landscape was full of danger. The disciples were like sheep placed in the midst of wolves (Luke 10:3; Gospel of Thomas 39; Ignatius, *Pol.* 2:2). Wolves pointed to danger for sheep (John 10:12; Acts 20:29). In Matthew 7:15 wolves represented false teachers, but here the meaning is a broad reference to danger from those who would reject them. The picture of sheep had already been introduced (Matt. 9:36; 10:6). Bruner (2004a, 380) notes that sheep had a timidity to them—they were not to be fighters, haters, or users of invectives. This idea fit with the image of doves later in the verse.

What this hostile environment required was being wise as serpents, but innocent as doves. Being discerning but gentle and righteous were necessities. Jesus spoke generically of what all future mission would entail. Tone mattered and so being like a dove meant being winsome. Serpents had a reputation for being clever, pictured by how they escaped and hid when trouble appeared or how they hid and then struck (Gen. 3:1). They were not frontal attackers. The term φρόνιμος means "to be prudent," sensible, or wise (BDAG s.v. "φρόνιμος" 1066). The word ἀκέραιος means "pure" or "innocent," unmixed with evil, having a "purity of intention" (so Blomberg 1992, 174; BDAG s.v. "ἀκέραιος" 35). The reference was to a simplicity and lack of hypocrisy (Rom. 16:19; Phil. 2:15). What you saw is what you got, but there was both wisdom in how to proceed and engage as well as ethics in how it was done. There also was a gentleness in how this took place. Jesus would model this as he headed to the cross. France (2007, 391) says, "They need the cunning of snakes without the venom." He also notes that evil was to be overcome with good (Rom. 12:17–21). Nolland (2005, 423) speaks of a consistent integrity. Carson (2010, 287) sees innocence as not being so cautious that it degenerates into fear or elusiveness.

The image has traditional Jewish roots of what it meant to be a Jew among rulers who fail to guide (Ezek. 22:27; Turner 2008, 275). In other texts, sheep among wolves also had pictured Jews among the Gentiles (Osborne 2010, 387; 1 En. 89:55; 90:6–17; 4 Ezra 5:18). More generically in a later Jewish text, it refers to those who were innocent like doves with God but cunning like serpents with the nations (Midrash on Canticles 2:14; Nolland 2005, 423). Carson (2010, 286–87) notes the midrash was late and goes in the opposite direction, seeing Jesus calling the disciples to be prudent and innocent to outsiders before God. The dust may be seen as unclean on the analogy with how dust in a Gentile context might confer uncleanness (Morris 1992, 250 n. 27; SB 1:571; *'Ohol.* 2:3). Regardless of the exact background, now the tables were turned as the Jewish people who are rejecting the message were now seen in a hostile light, being compared to wolves. It was not just the leaders who had responsibility before God; citizens did as well.

Some see Matthew as speaking only into the disciples' immediate ministry of the Twelve to Israel and to the exclusion of the church's earliest mission. In contrast, Davies and Allison (1991, 179) speak of the passage going "beyond the historical situation of the twelve." The references to governors, kings, and Gentiles in Matthew 10:18 point in this broader direction for them, as does the family opposition noted later in the discourse. There also is a shift to future tense verbs. Since this short-term ministry was limited to Israel (Matt. 10:5), the reference to Gentiles anticipated a longer time range. However, this claim can go too far and can fail to appreciate that once Jesus saw and sensed there would be opposition, he recognized this situation would remain so for the variety of circumstances disciples would face (Osborne 2010, 385–86; Wilkins 2004, 392). The deadly precedent of John the Baptist's martyrdom set the stage for seeing this kind of situation and warning about it. So these remarks do extend beyond the initial mission, but not to any exclusion of what was being instructed here. The opposition to Jesus that was forming now began to extend to the disciples, and it would only grow. France (2007, 389–90) highlights how the opposition was "on account of" Jesus (Matt. 10:16, 18, 22–23).

10:17–18. Jesus warned them to beware constantly of people, since persecution and opposition were inevitable due to the challenge Jesus's message brought. The present imperative for "beware" (προσέχετε) looks to an ongoing problem.

Disciples were going to be handed over to councils and flogged in the synagogues.

Flogging is commanded in the Old Testament for certain community offenses (Deut. 25:1–3; *m. Mak.*). This could have included up to thirty-nine lashes with a calf-leather whip that had thongs attached to it. The one convicted of a crime requiring this punishment had his hands bound to a pillar so his body would be stretched out to flog both front and back in turn or he would be required to lie on the ground for the beating (Keener 2009, 322–23). The New Testament also gives evidence of flogging, showing that outreach to Jews was still taking place (Acts 5:40; 22:19; 2 Cor. 11:25; note also Matt. 23:34). These punishments also suggest disciples still were connecting themselves to the synagogues and their authority. Nonetheless, there was a tension here as the verse does refer to "their" synagogues, so a division of identity was emerging (Wilkins 2004, 392).

The word for "council" is where we get the word "Sanhedrin" (BDAG s.v. "συνέδριον" 1a, 967). It is plural here and refers to local councils of elders who made civil and religious decisions for a city or area. *Sanhedrin* 1:1–6 shows that by A.D. 200 these could have up to twenty-three members to decide major cases that might theoretically involve death. Rome kept the power to execute to herself, but the Jews had rules for when they had such authority (France 2007, 391). Keener (2009, 322) speaks of an average of seven elders in a council like this (Josephus, *B.J.* 2.251; *A.J.* 4.214; 4.287). Tribunals involved in a judgment for flogging consisted of three members (*m. Sanh.* 1:2). The picture here is of intense persecution. Disciples would be taken to rulers and kings as they would be handed over to them for civil judgment. They would be handed over "on account of me" (Jesus; ἕνεκεν ἐμου). It was Jesus and his message that were opposed.

However, the experience was an opportunity to be a witness to those who handed them over to the Gentiles and others. Paul's attitude in Philippians 1:12–18 showed an application of this point (Blomberg 1992, 175). The gospel could spread even in the midst of being in custody or through persecution, something the book of Acts shows (Acts 4:1–22; 5:27; 6:12; 7:51, 55; 13:9–12; 18:12–17; 25:23; 27:24), as do the prison and pastoral epistles of Paul. Acts had events before governors (Acts 13:6–12; 18:12–17; 23:23–25:12) and kings (Acts 12:1–4; 25:13–26:32; France 2007, 392), those in Israel (Acts 12:1–4; 21:27–23:11) and those of the Roman world (Acts 14:5; 16:19–34; 17:1–9; 18:12–17; 23:24–26:32; 28:17–31; Wilkins 2004, 393). The experience went as high up as Nero, who was the unnamed Caesar of Acts 28. Nolland (2005, 424) speaks ironically of Paul having a "captive" audience. Of course, this opposition and persecution extended into the rest of the church's early history.

The emphasis in these next several verses is very much like Mark 13:9–13 and Luke 21:12–19. The observation is important, because those texts deal with the disciples' mission up to the return of Jesus. It means this initial mission was part of a much larger, more long-term effort that involved bringing the message but also delivered with it tribulation. Jesus was preparing his disciples for all of this. The pushback of the world should not be surprising.

10:19–20. Despite their plight, the disciples were not to worry about what to say. The words echo the call to trust God in Matthew 6:25–33. The Spirit that would indwell them would give them what to say, speaking through them. This was a divine passive as God gave them ("will be given") the Spirit and enablement. There is the hint of the indwelling Spirit here (note the explanatory γάρ in verse 20). There is a declaration about the empowerment for mission we see repeatedly in Acts (Acts 4:8; 5:32; and Stephen's speech in Acts 7; cf. John 14:26; 1 Peter 4:12–17). First Peter 3:14–16 describes the attitude that prepares one for this kind of a defense of the faith. Still, this is the only place in Matthew that the Spirit is noted as being in believers, though he is promised in Matthew 3:11. Everything about the instruction assumed a lack of any form of armed or hostile resistance. Their message was their only response. This did not mean they were not to be prepared themselves, but simply that God would be working through them.

Still, they were to be assured God was with them and would enable them. The theme of God helping his own speak has Old Testament roots (Exod. 4:12—to Moses; Ps. 119:41–46; Jer. 1:6–10 (Davies and Allison 1991, 185).

God Helps His Own Speak

Exodus 4:12: "So now go, and I will be with your mouth and will teach you what you must say."

Psalm 119:41–42: "May I experience your loyal love, O Lord, and your deliverance, as you promised. Then I will have a reply for the one who insults me, for I trust in your word."

Jeremiah 1:6–7: "I answered, 'Oh, Sovereign Lord, Really I do not know how to speak well enough for that, for I am too young.' The Lord said to me, 'Do not say, "I am too young." But go to whomever I send you and say whatever I tell you.'"

10:21. Jesus predicted division coming for families. Brothers would hand over brothers for death; so also fathers would hand over children and vice versa. The scene here extended well into the future, as martyrs came after this particular mission. The two actions were described as "handing one over" (BDAG s.v. "παραδίδωμι" 1b, 761–62) and "rising up in rebellion" (BDAG s.v. "ἐπανίστημι" 359) to give one over to death. Given the family was a core unit, this showed how deep the opposition would run. Even kinship meant nothing. The mention of rebellion pointed to sin and a violation of core commandments.

The remark echoes Micah 7:6, which is also cited in Matthew 10:35–36. However, the reference here was more intense, since in Micah all we have is enmity, not family members being handed over to death. In the Old Testament and in Judaism, sometimes the period of eschatological tribulation is portrayed as dividing families (1 En. 100:1–3; *m. Soṭah* 9:15, which expresses an idea similar to this, also cites Micah 7:6; also Isa. 19:2). The warning was painful, as family meant a lot, but there also was the prospect of having a new family with God as Father (Matt. 10:20; 12:46–50; 23:8–11; Turner 2008, 276).

The opposition in these verses is intense. We have religious leaders, civic leaders, and even family members who would oppose what Jesus represented. The kingdom message of hope was a great one, but its exclusiveness was a challenge that many would react to with hostility.

10:22. In a hyperbole, Jesus noted they would be hated by all on account of his name (Hagner 1993, 278). Matthew had already discussed persecution in Matthew 5:10–12. The hyperbole was a way of saying opposition would be widespread. The rejection's cause was also explicit. It was on account of their association with Jesus. The reference to Jesus's name was a way of speaking about what Jesus represented and the message he brought. To speak for Jesus in his name also meant suffering rejection (Wilkins 2004, 393; 2 Tim. 3:12; 1 Peter 4:13–14). Judaism had anticipated that the Messiah's coming would meet with negative reaction, speaking of the period as the "messianic woes" (Osborne 2010, 389; Dan. 9:20–27; 12:1–4; 1 En. 80:2–8; 98:4–9; 4 2 Bar. 25–27; Ezra 5:11–13; 7:10–35; Sib. Or. 3.538–44;).

The exhortation was to remain faithful. The one who remained steadfast to the end would be saved (Matt. 24:13; Mark 13:13). "To be steadfast" refers to staying the course or enduring (BDAG s.v. "ὑπομένω" 2, 1039; Heb. 10:32–33; James 5:11). Salvation was through faith in Jesus. Since martyrdom had already been referred to, salvation here must be spiritual deliverance (Blomberg 1992, 175). Matthew often pointed to endurance (Matt. 7:21,

24; 13:21; 24:13). The end here was probably a reference to the end of the program or mission, until justice came, since the point was a generic one. Yet for an individual it meant until their time in mission was done.

10:23. This verse is unique to Matthew. Jesus said if persecution came in one location, they were to flee to another (Matt. 23:34). It was appropriate to seek to preserve one's life. As Davies and Allison (1991, 190) note, "There is no eagerness for martyrdom" (*Mart. Pol.* 4). The prospect of martyrdom became real under Nero and remained so as the later examinations of Christians in the time of Trajan show (Tacitus, *Ann.* 15.44; Pliny, *Ep.* 10.96–97; France 2007, 394). Even as early as the reign of Herod Agrippa I in the 40s, some were dying, as did Stephen even earlier (Acts 7—Stephen; 12:1–4—James).

Yet the job was to get done and victory would come. For they would not "finish" going through (τελέσητε) all the towns of Israel before the Son of Man came. It is an open question whether this reference to cities of Israel included the diaspora. In other words, was the phrase geographical or ethnic? Another interpretive dilemma contextually is whether "finish" referred to going through all the towns and thus was about the mission, or referred to fleeing and so was about the duration of persecution. Either makes sense, as the return of the Son of Man would end both, being the arrival of justice and vindication. Both ideas also are contextually proximate. It is hard to be certain which is meant here, especially since opposition was what came to a head at the end. The ambiguity may well be intentional. What was clear is that Matthew did not see the mission to Israel as complete (Evans 2012, 224).

Regardless, the mission would succeed. God would bring the salvation they announced and the kingdom they proclaimed. The issue that surrounds the verse and its meaning was the timing of the Son of Man's coming. Many short-term alternatives have been proposed, such as the return of the disciples from this mission, the resurrection, Pentecost, the destruction of Jerusalem, or the raising of the issue of salvation (Osborne 2010, 390–91; Turner 2008, 277, notes seven options). Seeing a reference to an ongoing mission to Israel as long as mission was necessary is not insuperable difficulty. Even more, in Matthew, it is the Son of Man's future coming that will bring the kingdom in its fullness and the vindication that reverses the unrighteousness of the current persecution (Matt. 13:41; 16:27–28; 24:27–44; 25:31; 26:64). Accountability to God in the end was part of the discourse (Matt. 10:26). Also, the discourse about this mission in Matthew 10 was left open in terms of how far into the future it extended, clearly describing issues that went beyond what the Twelve faced in this short-term excursion in Galilee. A longer term of persecution was in view. It did not stop with the destruction of Jerusalem, as the persecutions of Trajan and Diocletian showed, and the context suggests that salvation would come with its end. A reference to the return in the Son of Man's coming is more likely here.

Now this can appear to suggest Jesus got this prophecy wrong, since the Son of Man seemingly did not appear before the end of the mission to Israel; but as Davies and Allison (1991, 190) note the mission to Israel was still ongoing for Matthew. It was not yet complete, even when he was writing (McDermott 1984). When one appreciates how this missionary discourse extended the church's mission until the proclamation of the kingdom was done, then one can see that the time frame for what was said here is broad. Even in the Great Commission (Matt. 28:19), the call was to go to all nations, and that includes Israel as a people. The point of the verse was that its mission to Israel was to continue until the return, no matter how difficult it would be (Davies and Allison 1991, 192; Nolland 2005, 428).

10:24–25. Jesus used the analogies of teacher-disciple and master-slave to make two points.

First, a disciple or a slave was not more than their teacher or master (Luke 6:40; John 13:16; especially 15:20). The best that could be hoped for was that they would be compared to each other. That led to the second point: if the teacher and master was called Beelzebul, those who followed would be seen in the same light. Beelzebul was another name for Satan, likely a variation on the name for Baal, the Canaanite god, pointing to him as the Baal of the Exalted Abode or Master of the House, so there was a play on words here (Carson 2010, 294; Davies and Allison 1991, 195; MacLaurin 1978; Nolland 2005, 434; Wilkins 2004, 395; T. Sol. 3:6; 6:1–2—the origin of these Jewish texts is disputed, seen as perhaps being Christian additions). The verse recalls Matthew 9:34 and the charge that Jesus cast out demons by the demon ruler's power. It anticipates Matthew 12:24, 27, where the Pharisees made this specific charge. If Jesus as teacher and master was rejected and tied to evil, the disciples could expect the same.

A "how much more" argument was common in Judaism and that is what Jesus used here. If they picked on the leader, so also especially the underlings. Such opposition was not to be sought (1 Tim. 3:7; 1 Peter 2:12; 3:15–16); it simply emerged from the reaction of others to the message and should not catch one by surprise.

Photo of Caesarea Maritima where Paul is said to have initially been examined by leaders as he appealed to be heard by Caesar in Rome.

The comparison of disciples with slaves obviously struck a chord among believers. Paul referred to himself this way and called believers "slaves of righteousness" (Rom. 1:1; 6:18; 1 Cor. 7:22; Phil. 1:1).

10:26. They were not to fear those who persecuted them, because in the end accountability did not fall to them (1 Peter 3:14; Rev. 2:10). The aorist imperative "not to fear" is a summary exhortation of a general attitude. The reference to Beelzebul in the last verse meant the Jewish leaders were primarily in mind, but the entire discourse's description of the opposition also pointed to rulers and even family.

There was nothing hidden or secret that will not be revealed or made known. This point conceals a divine passive. God will reveal the truth one day about what they had proclaimed. The gospel may seem hidden, but one day it will be clear what it is. God will make all clear, including those who are his and those who opposed him. So the one to fear was God, because all will be accountable to him. It is discussed whether this reference is to God's judgment, as that which will be revealed, or to the proclamation of the gospel, now hidden but then to be made manifest. The choice is a false one. Both proclamation (Matt. 10:27) and divine judgment (Matt. 10:28) were in view. How one responds to God is the issue of the judgment, which implicitly also brought in the gospel. So both ideas are intertwined here as suggested above.

The beginning of wisdom is to fear God (Prov. 1:7). That is true even in the face of deep opposition. Fear him above all. Recognize he will bring justice one day, reveal all, and declare all. Part of the joy of the eschaton coming in fullness involves the arrival of justice and vindication for God's people. The word was designed to encourage and comfort, even in the midst of raising the prospect of suffering. The remarks in these verses are like Luke 12:2–7.

The point was one Jesus emphasized. Jesus told them not to fear two more times in the next few verses (Matt. 10:28, 31). He gave three reasons to fear God and not be afraid of the opponents. God's justice pointed to two such reasons, for it assured them of vindication and meant their future was secure. In the following verses, God's care and awareness of what was happening to them also should give them comfort (Wilkins 2004, 395–96).

This remark set up the next verse in which they were told to preach the gospel openly. They could do so without fear.

10:27. Jesus turned to discuss their preaching directly. What Jesus had revealed to them in the dark or privately, they were now to proclaim openly. The time frame and contrast in view here is not pre-Easter (privately) versus post-Easter (openly), but time for instruction versus time for mission, which was commencing now (Osborne 2010, 397). Still, it is the case that some things were made clearer as a result of the resurrection.

As he did often in the discourse, Jesus gave two examples in parallel. There were no mysteries in the Christian faith. What was said in private about what the faith proclaimed was to be declared in public. The very public nature of the preaching appeared in the picture of preaching from the rooftops. The roof was a flat area and often one could speak to people on the street from it (Josephus, *B.J.* 2.611). There was also the point that their message came from him. It was not something for them to create.

In a distinct context, Luke 12:3 has a statement about what was said in the dark. This was about behavior, not mission. Gospel of Thomas 33 has a saying closer to Matthew's version.

10:28. They were to preach without fear of those they faced. They should not fear the ones who can only kill the body (Prov. 29:25), but the one to fear was the one who can destroy soul and body and cast it into Gehenna, a biblical term for hell. Luke 12:4–5 is similar. Fourth Maccabees 13:14 says, "Let us not fear him who thinks he kills," showing the idea also existed in Judaism (see also Wis. 16:13–14; 2 Macc. 6:30—of a martyr's testimony; Turner 2008, 278).

Whom to Fear

Wisdom 16:13–14: "For you have power over life and death; you lead mortals down to the gates of Hades and back again. A person in wickedness kills another, but cannot bring back the departed spirit, or set free the imprisoned soul."

2 Maccabees 6:30: "When he was about to die under the blows, he groaned aloud and said: 'It is clear to the Lord in his holy knowledge that, though I might have been saved from death, I am enduring terrible sufferings in my body under this beating, but in my soul I am glad to suffer these things because I fear him.'"

The key here is the reference to the soul, made twice in the verse. The soul was seen as the spiritual part of the person in this verse, that which survived death and connected the person to real life extending beyond mere physical presence (Luke 23:43; 2 Cor. 5:1–10; Phil. 1:23–24). They were to fear God, who had the power over soul and body in an ultimate sense, as he decided if one resided in Gehenna where real destruction existed (BDAG s.v. "γέεννα" 190–91). The sentiment is like Hebrews 10:31 or James 4:12. Revelation 20:14–15 speaks of hades in the same way. "Hades" was the common Jewish term for this locale (Dan. 3:88 LXX; Tob. 13:2; Wis. 16:13; 17:14; Sir. 21:10; 51:5–6), which was related to the Old Testament concept of Sheol, where the dead awaited the judgment and then were either accepted or rejected by God (Pss. 15:10 LXX; 88:49 LXX). The name "Gehenna" came from a ravine in Jerusalem where later Jewish expectation says judgment would take place (2 Esd. 2:29). It was a place where terrible sacrificial burnings of humans had taken place

(2 Kings 23:10; 2 Chron. 28:3; 33:6; Jer. 7:31; 19:4; 32:35). So Gehenna had a negative reputation. Matthew mentions it in other passages (Matt. 5:22, 29–30; 18:8; 23:33; 25:41). Destruction here was not annihilation in the afterlife but that which ended a rich life (Morris 1992, 263; Osborne 2010, 397; Matt. 18:8; 25:41, 46; Rev. 14:11; 19:3; 20:10).

10:29–31. Jesus reassured his disciples with an illustration involving sparrows. This illustration also appears in Luke 12:6–7, although there five sparrows were sold for two coins. As throughout, Matthew and Luke are slightly different, but also are in distinct contexts.

Jesus noted how inexpensive, and thus seemingly insignificant, a sparrow was. They were sold for one copper coin for two in the market as the cheapest food available (Keener 2009, 327). They were equal to the cost of a loaf of bread (Luz 2001, 103 n. 45). An assarion (ἀσσάριον) was one-sixteenth of a denarius, about thirty minutes of an average worker's wage. A denarius was a small denomination of currency, about a day's wage for a worker.

A sparrow was worth next to nothing, yet nothing happened to it without the Father's knowing. The Father saw all, knew all, and his will was engaged, aware of what was taking place. Exactly how this worked, Jesus did not specify. Was God merely present? Was he passively permitting this? Was it his active will at work? All the text says is that this did not happen "without" the Father (BDAG s.v. "ἄνευ" a, 78, rendered the contextual force as "without the knowledge and consent of"). Jesus did not answer such specific questions here and simply observed God was quite aware of what happened to the sparrow. They were to know God would see their faithfulness and any injustice. Nolland (2005, 435) says, "Nothing escapes detection." What Jesus went on to say in verse 31 was that if God cared and was aware of what happens to a nearly worthless sparrow, then how much more would he be aware of what happened to you. Also significant is that it was God as "your Father" who saw what happened to the sparrow (Hagner 1993, 286). This was not a distant God. He watched over his children.

Beyond the sparrows, God even knew the number of hairs on someone's head (Luke 12:7). The pronoun "you" in the verse is thrown forward for emphasis. Jesus now discussed how this also applied to the disciples.

That nothing happened to even a hair on one's head is an Old Testament idea about God's care (1 Sam. 14:45; 2 Sam. 14:11; 1 Kings 1:52). Another image is that of sin or enemies being greater than the number of hairs on one's head (Pss. 40:12; 69:4). Jesus was highlighting that God knew every detail in his creation. The Old Testament and Jewish wisdom materials have the idea that God can count what we cannot (Ezra 4:7; Job 39:2; Sir. 1:2, 4; 1 En. 93:14). To know the count of something this small showed the presence of careful attention. God's sovereignty extended to details (Carson 2010, 296). The point was not about a guarantee of protection from harm, as in this context it was clear some would be persecuted, beaten, and even die. It was rather that they could trust God for whatever happened (Garland 1995, 118). He knew what was happening to them. No harm in an ultimate sense would come to them, whatever happened now (see Matt. 10:32, which begins with a "therefore," οὖν). So they should fear, trust, and proclaim him.

This was the third call to fear God in the passage (Matt. 10:26, 31—not to fear humans, 28). The disciples could be assured they were more valuable than the sparrows. Matthew 12:12 says the same about people being more valuable than sheep. God knew and would care for them. In this, Jesus's remarks recall Matthew 6:31–34.

10:32–33. We now lose imperatives, as there are no more commands in the discourse. Instead, we have a backdrop for why one should fear God by a look at three settings: at the judgment where one should acknowledge Jesus (Matt. 10:32–33), in relationship to family and Jesus's mission so that one takes up one's cross (Matt. 10:34–39), and the relationship between those who preached Jesus and those welcoming them (Matt. 10:40–42).

The issue of embracing Jesus and his message was so important that those who acknowledged or confessed Jesus before men will be acknowledged before the Father. In the same way, those who denied him will be denied by him (Matt. 25:31–46; Mark 8:38; Luke 9:26; 12:8–9; Rev. 3:5). Once again, Matthew used parallelism. This time the parallel contained a contrast. The picture was of Jesus as judge, and the conceptual background is Daniel 7:13 (Davies and Allison 1991, 214–15; France 2007, 405). There was no other Son of Man figure than Jesus (Carson 2010, 297, against the idea that in Mark 8:38 there is another who is Son of Man). What Mark 8 has as the Son of Man acknowledging in the end, Matthew put in the first person ("in me") to make the connection clear. Those who were allied to Jesus identified with him in the face of rejection. God knew the heart and the allegiance; so did Jesus. Note how closely they were connected as Jesus speaks of "my" Father in these verses.

The term for describing the allegiance is ὁμολογέω, which pointed to one "confessing" allegiance before people (BDAG s.v. "ὁμολογέω" 4b, 708–9; John 9:22; Rom. 10:9). Denial would distance oneself from him. Jesus was the issue, not just his message (Davies and Allison 1991, 215). He was at the center of the kingdom message he brought. This was set up by things Jesus had already said in Matthew 10:18 ("for my sake") and in Matthew 10:22 ("for my name's sake"). In Matthew 10:24–25 we saw a connection between Jesus and his followers described as a teacher-disciple, master-slave relationship.

Jesus also functioned in the end as a judge (Matt. 7:21–23). France (2007, 406) observes that the example of Peter's denials showed we were dealing with a course of life, not a specific moment. There was a high christology present. What was said here is echoed later in John 14:6, where Jesus said he was the way, the truth, and the life, with no one coming to the Father but through him (Blomberg 1992, 179).

The word was designed to encourage. The point was not the present but the justice of God in the end. Because of the acceptance that confession of Christ yielded in the end, disciples could be courageous now and confess him in public. This should lead to allegiance to God over family (Matt. 10:34–39) and to welcoming those who represented Jesus (Matt. 10:40–42).

10:34–36. Jesus came and brought division within families. Jesus would not bring peace, but a sword, a picture of conflict and division as the following verses show. Luke 12:51, 53 is similar. Matthew again has a shorter version, as is his style. It is shorter than Luke's version and uses only one of the verbs that Micah 7:6 uses ("divide," BDAG s.v. "διχάζω" 252). The image is of a rift or a separation. In fact, that is what Luke 12:51 says explicitly. The version in the Gospel of Thomas 16 is more like that of Luke.

Jesus brought a sword. In fact, the text says he "casts" it (BDAG s.v. "βαλεῖν" 4, 163–64). The text literally says he has not come to cast peace but to cast a sword. Jesus threw a sword into the mix of life. The sword referred to is a "short sword," but it was the imagery of a divider—not the size of the sword—that is the point (BDAG s.v. "μάχαιρα" 2b, 622). This was a figure for God's judgment (Isa. 66:16; Wis. 5:20; Sir. 39:30; En. 62:12; 63:11; 90:19; 91:11–12; 2 Bar. 27:5; 40:1; Jub. 9:15; 1; Pss. Sol. 15:7). Davies and Allison (1991, 218–19) correctly note that all forms of triumphalism about Jesus that minimize tribulation and rejection in this age fail to deal with this teaching. What Jesus was saying was that he brought accountability to God and that accountability produces a separation, a division (Wilkins 2004, 397). Garland (1995, 118) and Bruner (2004a, 488–89) call it a sword of decision, the result of a call to take the narrow way (Matt. 7:13–14). Peace with God was not automatic, nor was it an entitlement. It was rooted in response to him and the program tied to Jesus. Jesus's coming resulted in a purging, something the kingdom parables of Matthew 13 also teach as they look to a separation between the righteous and wicked.

The image of the sword was illustrated by how families would divide over claims of accountability to God. Three oppositions are noted and then a summary. A man is against his father, the daughter against a mother, and a daughter-in-law against the mother-in law. This moves from young to old, but the summary in verse 36 shows the point is the division, not youthful rebellion (France 2007, 409). The words recall Micah 7:6, especially in the LXX in terms of who is named, but the LXX speaks of shaming and rebelling. A daughter-in-law was noted because the woman moved into her husband's home. The theme is in several Jewish texts about eschatological woe, which emerged because the world was seen in conflict with God's ways (1 En. 56:7; 100:1–2; 2 Bar. 70:3; 4 Ezra 5:9; 6:24; Jub. 23:16, 19). All of this background was in play in these verses. The reaction to Jesus showed the nature of people's hearts; he was a litmus test. Some came to him; others reacted against him.

Second Temple Jewish Texts on Family Division to Come

Jubilees 23:16: "And in this generation children will reproach their parents and their elders on account of sin, and on account of injustice, and on account of the words of their mouth, and on account of great evil which they will do, and on account of their forsaking the covenant which the Lord made between them and himself so that they might be careful and observe all of his commandments and his ordinances and all of his law without turning aside to the right or left."

Jubilees 23:19: "Some of these will strive with others, youths with old men and old men with youths, the poor with the rich, the lowly with the great, and the beggar with the judge concerning the Law and the Covenant because they have forgotten the commandments and covenant and festivals and months and sabbaths and jubilees and all of the judgments."

1 Enoch 56:7: "But the city of my righteous ones will become an obstacle to their horses. And they shall begin to fight among themselves; and (by) their own right hands they shall prevail against themselves. A man shall not recognize his brother, nor a son his mother, until there shall be a (significant) number of corpses from among them. Their punishment is (indeed) not in vain."

The result was that a person's enemy was in that person's own home. This verse is unique to Matthew. This was a shocking mission statement, especially for those who thought the Messiah was only about peace. What it recognized was the varied reactions Jesus generated. Jesus had said that peacemakers were blessed in Matthew 5:9. So he was dealing with the reaction his ministry would bring, because of the claims it made and how some would react to them. Jesus sought peace with people, but some would refuse to embrace it, leaving division as its result. A person's failing to come in faith would be worse for then all would be lost, but Jesus's coming meant people had a choice, with some choosing to opt out and resist changing to embrace God. Matthew 10:12–15 shows the pattern as disciples entered into a city in hopes of peace but then might well be forced to move on because of the negative reaction. Some people embraced Jesus and others were hostile to him.

Matthew has several mission statements in his gospel (Matt. 5:17; 20:28; and a God-calling statement is in Matt. 9:13). This statement is the harshest of the group. The following verses also play into the theme, showing that the priority is to follow God, not appease family who may be going in a different direction. Osborne (2010, 405) observes how in Greco-Roman homes families shared in the worship of the cult in the house, with children pouring the libations offered daily to their household gods. A split in a family made this impossible to do as a family.

10:37–38. The cost of discipleship was Jesus's next topic. Who was worthy of Jesus? France (2007, 410) suggests the point about worthiness here meant the equivalent of "having what it takes" to be a disciple, but one cannot exclude the sense of doing what is appropriate given who was involved. Wilkins (2004, 397) points to Deuteronomy 33:9–10 as making a similar point about faithfulness to God (Hill 1972, 194–95). The one who loved father, mother, son, or daughter more than Jesus was not worthy of him. Only an implication about being transcendent could mean one had more value than the family. As Bruner (2004a, 490) notes, if Jesus was not who he claimed to be, we would rightfully ask, who does he think he is crashing into history and demanding this of our lives? Carson (2010, 299) observes this was a saying of "the Messiah or a maniac."

There was a practical background to this remark. If love and acceptance by the family meant more to someone than responding to Jesus, they would not respond to Jesus. Jesus's point was that he deserves a primary allegiance. What he represented, commissioned by God, was more important than anything else, including something as important as family. Luke 14:26 also spoke rhetorically of hating father or mother (Matt. 16:24; Mark 8:34; Luke 9:23).

Beyond how one related to family, there was how one related to oneself. One had to be willing to suffer shame, something pictured by taking up a cross. At the time, before the cross developed its Christian association and reputation, this would have been a shocking idea. Crucifixion was a well-known punishment with a horrid reputation. It was reserved for the worst crimes. This fact meant that one need not see the expression here by Jesus as an anachronistic, post-cross saying of the church (correctly McNeile 1915, 148; Osborne 2010, 405, versus Hagner 1993, 292). To bear a cross was to be crucified, die for sedition, and suffer the shame of the public humiliation of carrying the horizontal part of the cross to your execution (Hengel 1977; Turner 2008, 282; Josephus, *B.J.* 5.449–51; Tacitus, *Ann.* 15.44.4). The rejection by the state meant social rejection. This was the language of self-denial for a cause one saw as worth it. As Epictetus says, "One must value the good higher than any kinship" (*Diatr.* 3.3.6; Luz 2001, 112).

The entire discourse had made clear that with a response to Jesus came the shame of rejection. One had to be to be prepared to go there. Receiving such a judgment from a world that also misjudged Jesus came with the territory. To consider what Jesus was offering and receive grace from him, and then be unwilling to travel the same road as Jesus, showed one was not worthy of what Jesus represented.

10:39. This verse showed that the last three verses were about being too concerned with self-preservation. If a person tried to preserve his own life and was not willing to travel the road of rejection Jesus was on, then he would not respond to Jesus and would lose his life (Matt. 16:25; Mark 8:35; Luke 9:24; 17:33; John 12:25). But if someone was willing to lose his life on account of Jesus, then life and vindication would come. He would gain his soul. As throughout the discourse, the issue is whether one was willing to suffer on account of an identification with Jesus. In fact, in many ways, this verse summarizes the entire discourse.

10:40–42. Those who allied with those Jesus sent were also seen by God and rewarded. The principle was set at the start. Those who received the messenger Jesus sent received both Jesus and the one who sent Jesus, a clear reference to God (Mark 9:37; Luke 9:48; 10:16; John 12:44, 48–49;

20:21; McNiele 1915, 149). As throughout this discourse, Jesus tightly linked his work to God's call, plan, and authority (1 Clem. 42:1–2). So those he sent are called prophets, the righteous, and disciples. This is the first direct mention by Jesus in Matthew that he was sent by God (Nolland 2005, 444).

Gospel > Apostles < > Christ < > God

1 Clement 42:1–2: "The apostles received the gospel for us from the Lord Jesus Christ; Jesus the Christ was sent forth from God. So then Christ is from God, and the apostles are from Christ. Both, therefore, came of the will of God in good order."

There also was a solidarity between those Jesus sent and Jesus himself. To receive them was to receive him. Luke 10:16 and John 13:20 say the same thing in a distinct way. This is illustrated in detail in Matthew 25:31–46. The one Jesus sent reflected his message and represented his presence. This was rooted in the idea of the "sent one," an apostle or emissary (Luz 2001, 120, calls this an emissary law). *Mishnah Berakot* 5:5 says, "A man's emissary or agent is like the man himself" (Hill 1972, 195). To see the emissary was to be in contact with the one who commissioned him. It is appropriate that a commissioning mission ends on this note.

Those who welcomed God's messengers would be rewarded. This note about reward for the welcoming of messengers is one we only see in Matthew. The hosts would be rewarded with honors that befit those who accepted the prophets and righteous. In fact, it was like accepting Jesus, since they were his representatives. The solidarity between Jesus and his messengers now extended to those who welcomed them. France (2007, 414) speaks of receiving life for accepting that which Jesus represented (Matt. 10:39; also Blomberg 1992, 182). The phrase εἰς ὄνομα means "in the name of" and points to accepting the messenger as representing the righteous one (BDAG s.v. "ὄνομα" 3, 711–14). The idea of the name was that this was who the person was seen to be connected to and so who he represented. As with other elements in this discourse we have parallelism: what was said of prophets was said of the righteous (also linked in Matt. 13:17; 23:29). These men were called prophets because they proclaimed and revealed the message of God's kingdom with a direct commission from Jesus (Morris 1992, 270). They also were righteous for responding to this call.

This term "prophet" probably was used in its most generic sense, as one commissioned with Jesus's message. Jesus generalized this commission and brought all followers of him under it in Matthew 28:16–20. It meant this discourse served as a guide for mission to the community in terms of how to face opposition and also noted the benefits of responding as long as there was a commission (Luz 2001, 120). To the extent one delivered the Jesus-apostolic message to others, they shared in the authority Jesus discussed here (Bruner 2004a, 494).

A third element pictured giving a cup of cold drink to a disciple. It completed the illustration with Matthew's penchant for triads. Mark 9:41 is similar. Several terms appear three times (those who receive, reward, in the name, prophet, righteous). Jesus called the offered drink "cold," which referred to a refreshing cup of water (BDAG s.v. "ψυχρός" 1b, 1100), an act of kindness and compassion. The picture drew on the value of hospitality in the culture, saying God would see this and reward it (Keener 2009, 332; a cultural example is in Josephus, *A.J.* 18.193–94; Garland 1995, 119). The picture also drew on the kind of experience Elijah and Elisha had in terms of hospitality, with the result of a reward (1 Kings 17:9–24; 2 Kings 4:9–37; Turner 2008, 283). A simple cup of water portrayed a modest example of acceptance and gained a great reward.

In the context, the fact such hospitality was rewarded in the face of severe opposition showed the level of tension Jesus anticipated and the value he placed on those who sided with those he sent. The setting was balanced by calling the disciples "little ones" showing God's tender care and concern for his own (Matt. 11:25; 18:5–6). The assurance about reward was emphasized with an amen ("truly"), something Matthew often did for this theme of reward or judgment (Matt. 5:26; 6:2, 5, 16; 19:28; 23:36; Davies and Allison 1991, 229). People who received those sent lent their important support to the mission. Where Matthew 10:1–39 was directed to the one sent in mission, these final verses addressed anyone responding to the mission, something already suggested in Matthew 10:11–13 but now noted directly.

11:1. As with the Sermon on the Mount, and as will be the case in subsequent discourses, Matthew marked the end of this message with a note about concluding and a transition back into ministry (Matt. 7:28–29; 13:53; 19:1; 26:1). Jesus completed his teaching and then preached and taught in the cities of the region. Teaching was highlighted in this summary as there was nothing said of healing, but that action appears in the next passage in the response to John the Baptist. Unlike Luke, nothing is said about the result of this mission, but that may be because the mission discourse covered more than this initial stage. The result of the mission was well known to those reading Matthew, both in terms of reception and rejection.

THEOLOGICAL FOCUS

The exegetical idea (as Jesus called his disciples to trust in a priority mission for the kingdom to Israel, he predicted opposition alongside enablement from God, who knew what was taking place) leads to this theological statement: God oversees the word-and-deed mission Jesus's disciples undertake even though there is opposition to it.

This discourse is about the mission God has given to those who follow Jesus. It looks at both the short-term effort of Jesus's twelve disciples and a longer term look at mission in general. It is a study in realism and makes it clear that any sense of triumphalism about the mission is mistaken.

Jesus was sent by God, but that does not mean the world would embrace his message or that his disciples would have it easy. Jesus sent the Twelve out with an urgency to preach to Israel. They were to travel light and trust in those who welcomed them. They were to stay in one place and not linger in locales where they were not wanted. They were to anticipate being accepted by some and rejected by others. That rejection was harsh, involving arrests, beatings, and in some cases even death. That rejection came from everywhere, even within the family. Jesus forces choices, and not everyone chooses well. Jesus taught that the decisions his mission generates will bring division.

Disciples are to have faith in the God who calls them to mission. He will provide the Spirit to give them what to say when they are challenged. He will provide hosts who will welcome them and give them the provisions they need. They are to trust that God sees how people treat them and that all will be made known one day at the judgment seat. They are to fear God, who is able to judge not only in the taking of earthly life but in the decision about what happens to the soul. They are to be discerning as serpents and innocent as doves, judging well how to function as sheep among wolves and having an integrity that shows who they are. They are to represent Christ faithfully, but this also means doing so in a way that does not result in a battle over power but involves an engagement that proclaims and invites. They are to remind people that the one who holds people accountable is God. They are to appreciate that in representing Jesus and God, they have a solid position that is in solidarity with true life's design and direction. They are to know that those who receive them also share in this solidarity. They travel the path of their teacher and can expect to receive what he receives. They are to trust God, his providence, and timing. They can rest in the authority he has.

The goal of followers is mission—mission in a needy and even hostile world. Jesus prepared his disciples for what they would face. Many Christians engage the world in ways that do represent God well. Some do so with expectations of immediate victory over the world, while others reflect a hostility that hardly communicates God's love. Both of these orientations fail to get at what mission involves. The tension in carrying out mission involves a combination of challenge and invitation. All challenge and no invitation does not portray God's will and actually never gets to the gospel of good news. In contrast, all invitation and no challenge fails to reflect his calling to recognize our need for him and his provision. Graciousness in the midst of conviction reflects the balance.

True mission requires a faithfulness that understands that when rejection comes, a choice must be made to follow God at all costs. A faithful disciple will be regarded as his teacher was. Nothing in Scripture tells us to expect a world that will embrace Jesus without question. It is through many tribulations that we come into the kingdom of God (Acts 14:22). Jesus wants his disciples to get this from the very start of the mission they undertake. It means it will often be the case that they will be operating from the position of a minority under social pressure. Wise discipleship and faithful mission involve appreciating how to live well and represent God faithfully in a context of such intense social tension. Mission is not about a program; it is about a way of living that understands that the acceptance that counts comes from God. Bold witness involves living in a manner pleasing to God and sharing about that life with others. It can expect to meet with rejection, but our allegiance to God and our union with Christ draw on what God provides in faith. That faith enables us to rest in his will, pursue his calling, and honor God, leaving the results to the one who one day will make the final assessment. All the while, the disciple recognizes that some will be drawn to the message and share in what is offered. So the disciple pursues mission, taking up his cross and understanding that when he or she lost his or her soul to God, what was gained was a life that is a living beyond this life.

PREACHING AND TEACHING STRATEGIES

Exegetical and Theological Synthesis

The exegetical section explains Jesus's summons to mission. Jesus called, prepared, and empowered the Twelve to join him on mission. It was a risky proposition to put the keys of the kingdom in the hands of men, but God has a history of entrusting humans with carrying forth his plans. In the beginning, he tasked man and woman with ruling over creation as his image-bearers. The creation mandate (Gen. 1:26–28) was the initial summons to mission. Later, God summoned Noah, Abram, Moses, David, and the prophets to join him on mission in their diverse roles. He called the liberated nation of Israel to live as a "royal priesthood" (Exod. 19:5–6). He expected his exiled people to be a "light to the nations" (Isa. 42:6; 49:6). Both are missionary titles. Then he sent his Son as the missionary "par excellence" (Heb. 3:1–6).

God's mission has always had its rivals. Noah's generation jeered while he built the ark. The Philistines mocked and oppressed the holy nation of Israel. Assyria and Babylon exiled the people of God who had spent decades turning a deaf ear toward their own prophets. For Jesus and the early church, adversity came from scribes and Pharisees, synagogue officials and Sanhedrin, politicians and Zealots. Most of the Twelve died for joining Jesus's mission. Living on mission is also risky proposition for people of faith.

Fortunately, Jesus and the apostles insisted on God's sustaining power in the face of opposition. He provides people of peace, timely words, supernatural courage, and spiritual community to fight our lingering fears or rising panic. Ironically, while warning of the pressures we face on mission, the discourse takes the pressure off us. Salvation is God's work, not ours. Our wit and wisdom will not win people to Jesus, but a compassionate work or word of hope may do wonders (1 Peter 3:15–16). Our job is to show up and speak up for Jesus, not to sidestep or silence opposition.

Preaching Idea

Go public and don't panic: God's got your back.

Contemporary Connections

What does it mean?

What does it mean to go public and not panic? How does God have our back? Jesus called the Twelve to proclaim the message of God's inbreaking kingdom through the ministry of Jesus Christ. They were to share about Messiah in word and deed. He wanted specific people to go to specific places and make their presence known. By extension, Matthew's audience and modern disciples are given the same task: to show and tell about Jesus.

Going public for Jesus today includes casual conversation with family and coworkers about Jesus's teachings, posting verses from the Gospels on social media, participating in community service with the church to show Jesus's compassion, or explaining the gospel or plan of salvation to a spiritual seeker. Ultimately, going public means one's Christian faith is evident for others to hear and see.

As we go public for Jesus, we reduce our panic by remembering our task is to share our faith, not save others. We are representatives, not redeemers. Thus, if a conversation goes sideways or the message is rejected, we need not worry. Jesus predicted people would reject us and our message, like they rejected him.

Moreover, when we go public, we never go alone. God the Father oversees our efforts; God's Spirit empowers us. He may give confidence and calm in a hostile classroom. He may give wisdom and clarity when questioned about our convictions. He may help us recall a faith experience or Bible verse that addresses others' doubts. He may prompt us to avoid fruitless discussions with skeptics and find a person of peace whose hunger for God is apparent in his eagerness to talk.

Is it true?

Is it true that we should go public and not panic? Indeed, Jesus's message of the inbreaking kingdom is good news for all. Although his first commission focused on the "lost sheep of Israel" (Matt. 10:6) the Great Commission embraced "all nations" (Matt. 28:19). The gospel is public domain; it has no copyright claim. Jesus tasked his disciples with showing and telling about him.

Then again, Jesus also provided cautions. He warned of persecution and division. He admonished shrewdness. Using the language of vipers, courts, and swords, he clearly outlined the cost of going public. In our day and age, going public about one's faith could cost you a promotion. Going public about your traditional view of gender and sexuality could get your business or church "canceled." Going public about your religious convictions on many political issues could result in strained relationships.

Not only should we realize the cost of going public, we also should monitor our tone and volume. Christians have a reputation for being merciless, hateful, and extreme. Tone matters. Though our public message is bound to be rejected by many, we do not help our cause by sounding loud, angry, or alarmist. Nor must we go public about Jesus at every street corner, in every coffee shop, or on every social media platform we encounter. Sometimes the best way to go public is by remaining quiet until someone asks us to share the reason for our hope (1 Peter 3:15). Then by all means, do so gently, respectfully, and fearlessly.

Now what?

Like the Twelve, we are called to go public today. Though the marching orders Jesus gave to them had specific application to their times, the simple principles and fearless nature remain relevant. First, we should precede our going public with prayer. We may view Matthew 9:38 as a mandate to ask God for harvest workers. This prayer, which could be spoken daily at 9:38, will sensitize us to the needs of our harassed and helpless world and mobilize us to meet these needs in the name of Jesus.

Second, we should make a simple plan to go public. Drawing from Jesus's short-term commission (Matt. 10:5–15), we should find a place to establish our presence, make a connection with a "worthy" person who welcomes our presence, and share about Jesus through word and deed. Simply put, going public entails our going, staying, connecting, and sharing. More specifically, we might establish a presence at a local coffee shop, gym, or service group. A worthy person could be a coworker, neighbor, another parent in the PTO, or the cashier we see every week at the grocery store. This is someone we connect with frequently and who demonstrates openness to conversation. And our sharing may include God-talk, invitations to church, references to prayer, questions about their beliefs, or direct testimony of Jesus's work in our lives.

Third, when we go public, we should expect some pushback. Often people react awkwardly to spiritual conversations. They squirm, change the subject, or act defensively. We must prepare for negative reactions but avoid the temptation to argue. Pushy Christians are repulsive. Apologetics and debate rarely win people to Jesus. Barna's 2019 *Reviving Evangelism* report confirms this:

- 7 percent of non-Christians want to talk with someone who "has all the answers to questions about faith";
- 9 percent find it winsome when someone can point out inconsistencies in other faiths;
- Meanwhile, 50 percent prefer talking with someone who "does not force a conclusion";
- 62 percent want to talk with someone who "listens without judgement."[1]

Our willingness to walk away from an uninterested party is a modern form of shaking the dust off our feet and moving on. Where this becomes difficult is in friendships or family relationships where our evangelistic efforts have borne no fruit. Perhaps, in these cases, we resolve to pray for them and love them but limit our verbal witness, trusting God to grow the gospel seeds we have already planted.

Creativity in Presentation

"Don't panic" is an iconic phrase in Douglas Adams's Hitchhiker's Guide to the Galaxy series. The first book begins with the destruction of Earth. Before its annihilation, Arthur Dent, the bumbling protagonist, is plucked from the planet and commissioned for service. To navigate the complex world of intergalactic travel, Dent is given a complicated guidebook with the words "Don't Panic" etched on the front. The simple phrase is pure irony, considering the guide has countless, pointless, and outdated entries about businesses (e.g., Sirius Cybernetics Corporation), aliens (e.g., Vogons), sex, and personal crises (e.g., what to do if you're stuck in a crack in the ground with no hope of escape) but no instructions of real value.[2] Consider comparing Jesus's simple instructions for itinerant mission to Adams's complicated manual for

1 Accessed digitally through Barna Access website: https://barna.gloo.us/reports/reviving-evangelism.

2 For more specific "Entries" from the Guide, see https://en.wikipedia.org/wiki/The_Hitchhiker%27s_Guide_to_the_Galaxy_(fictional) or https://sites.google.com/site/h2g2theguide/Index/allentries. Moreover, "Don't Panic" icons are easy to find online.

intergalactic travel. Assure people, "Either way, 'Don't panic' is good advice."

A visual illustration may demonstrate how God's got our backs. Collect travel items from Jesus's list in Matthew 10:9–10. These may be modern versions: a wallet or purse, a satchel, a walking stick, a knife, a coat, a pair of sandals, a lunchbox. One by one, remove the items from the display table. You might say, "I may not have my wallet, but God's still got my back. I may not have my pepper spray, but God's still got my back." On a separate table, you may present a pillow, blanket, cup of water, and loaf of bread. Point to these items and reassure your people, "For the Twelve, God provided people to greet, a place to sleep, and food to eat. He had their back."

Help your congregation consider the damage caused by panicking. Describe a few scenarios where preparation may save lives, whereas panicking may result in fatalities.

- A fire breaks out in a movie theater. Prepared people know where the exits are and calmly exit. Panicked people trample one another on the way out.
- A tornado signal goes off in the town. Prepared people move to the basement and huddle in a corner. Panicked people run outside to look at the funnel clouds.
- A global pandemic hits the country. Prepared people purchase sufficient supplies, avoid large gatherings, and wash their hands regularly. Panicked people stockpile toilet paper, move underground, get their news from Facebook, and believe conspiracy theories.
- A bear appears in the woods near the hiking trail. Prepared people stop, speak calmly, and back away slowly. Panicked people scream, turn, and dash away, hoping to outrun the wild beast.

Scenarios like these underscore the folly of panic. Of course, sometimes we cannot control the panic response in our brain—flight, fight, freeze, or faint—since it is a built-in biological mechanism to protect ourselves. We can, however, train our brain to believe "God's got our back," by repeating this refrain on a regular basis.

Ultimately, you want your sermon to communicate that God oversees the word-and-deed mission Jesus's disciples undertake even though there is opposition to it. Therefore, we should go public and not panic: God's got our backs.

- Going public responds to a personal summons (10:1–4).
- Going public relies on a simple strategy (10:5–15).
- Going public results in predictable opposition (10:16–24, 34–39).
- Going public resolves not to panic (10:25–33, 40–42).

DISCUSSION QUESTIONS

1. How do you explain the exclusive focus (lost sheep of Israel; no Samaria) Jesus set at the beginning of the discourse? How did this shift as the sermon continued?
2. What was the purpose of Jesus's simple instructions? How does this apply today?
3. How does the Spirit help disciples who go public?
4. How does this passage further the opposition theme described in Matthew?
5. What are the main excuses Christians give for not going public?

Matthew 11:2–30

EXEGETICAL IDEA

The special nature of the current time, shown by John's relationship to Jesus, made the rejection by Israel's cities an act worthy of judgment but also offered opportunity for spiritual rest to those who embraced Jesus.

THEOLOGICAL FOCUS

The way in which John the Baptist's ministry mirrors Jesus's and the new era's presence offers a choice between judgment and spiritual rest.

PREACHNG IDEA

Only Jesus can recharge our spiritual batteries.

PREACHING POINTERS

Spiritual giants and sinful cities have something in common: their response to Jesus is paramount to their future hope. John the Baptist, whom Jesus acknowledged as a spiritual giant, began to question his understanding of Jesus during his imprisonment. His initial fervor waned as Jesus failed to meet his expectations of Messiah. Jesus sent word through John's disciples that God indeed was doing something new through him. The cities of Chorazin and Bethsaida took John's uncertainty a step further by rejecting Jesus and sealing their condemnation. On the other hand, children depicted those who received Jesus's embrace. They embodied the trust and reliance desired of disciples who take up Jesus on his offer of rest. For Matthew's original audience, this section continued to reveal Jesus's nature and mission, as well as the benefits of embracing him. To those burdened by sin, self-reliance, and religious duty, he would give lasting relief.

Life wears us down. It is fast-paced with constant inputs and endless obligations. Media and entertainment mask our problem. Multitasking, time management, and medication only take us so far. We need more than sleep and mindfulness techniques. Our souls need rest. Fortunately, Jesus's invitation to rest remains available to those willing to embrace him. Unfortunately, this is more difficult than it may seem. Our doubts keep Jesus at a distance. Our sin pushes him away. The lack of embrace leads to languishing energy. This sermon reminds us that only Jesus can recharge our spiritual batteries.

JESUS'S MINISTRY SHOWS ITSELF TO BE FROM GOD (11:2–30)

LITERARY STRUCTURE AND THEMES (11:2–30)

This unit is about the nature of the times, despite appearances, and what that meant for how people responded both positively and negatively to Jesus. It has three core parts: discussion of John the Baptist (vv. 2–19), a reproach of Galilean cities (vv. 20–24), and a call to faith and rest with thanksgiving to God for those who are humble and come like children (vv. 25–30).

First, we see an exchange between John the Baptist and Jesus (Matt. 11:2–6). Jesus was not quite the style of Messiah many anticipated. This led John to ask if Jesus was the coming one. Jesus responded by allowing his deeds to speak for who he was. The various works Jesus performed were things God had promised in Isaiah and would belong to the new era.

Jesus underscored the current time's special nature by discussing John as the greatest figure of the old era, yet who was nothing compared with what was coming for anyone in the kingdom (Matt. 11:7–15). John was the messenger of God who prepared the way for the promised salvation of God. He was Elijah to come. Those who benefited from what Jesus brought belonged to a far greater era.

But opposition reigned. It did not matter if God's messenger came as an ascetic like John or engaged like Jesus (Matt. 11:16–19). It was not good enough to be culturally engaged. This reality led Jesus to warn the cities of their culpability before God (Matt. 11:20–24). The judgment on Chorazin, Bethsaida, and Capernaum would be harder than on some of the most despicable of Old Testament cities because what was rejected was so much greater.

Still Jesus rejoiced because in God's plan it was not the wise and understanding who came (Matt. 11:25–27). Jesus embraced those whom the Father had brought to him. Some were responding. So Jesus issued an invitation to those weary and beaten up by life to come and find spiritual rest in him (Matt. 11:28–30). In the contrast between John and Jesus, in the confrontation with Israel's cities, and in Jesus's prayer, the unit stresses the special nature of the times Jesus brought and the choice people faced: judgment or rest.

Most of what we see in this unit has parallels in the other gospels. The focus is Jesus discussing the nature of the times. The catalyst was John's question, which had both a private response back to him and an elaboration by Jesus about John. A demarcation in the kingdom program resulted from Jesus's presence and the special nature of the time he brought.

Matthew 11:2–6 has a parallel in Luke 7:18–23. Matthew 11:7–11 is like Luke 7:24–28. Matthew 11:12–16 has unique material about John being Elijah, but also has material like Luke 16:16 with the saying about those entering the kingdom. Matthew 11:16–19 can be compared to Luke 7:31–35. Portions of Matthew 11:20–24 overlap with Luke 10:13–15, as well as 10:12. Matthew's sequence has a reference to Sodom at the end of the remarks in contrast to Luke, who starts there. Jesus's prayer and the remarks about his authority in Matthew 11:25–27 are mirrored in Luke 10:21–22. Matthew 11:28–30 is unique to Matthew's gospel. So much of what we have here reflects Q, the teaching material of Jesus that Matthew and Luke shared. There is no overlap with Mark.

There are a variety of scenes that make up this unit. We have a short dialogue between the disciples of John the Baptist and Jesus. We have Jesus's commentary on John's ministry, a discussion of who John was, and what that showed. We also have a commentary on the reactions to John and Jesus, despite their differing styles. We have a warning of coming judgment to Israel for her lack of response. We see Jesus pray, revealing the approach of God's program. We close with an invitation to benefit from what Jesus had to offer.

Key themes are a focus on John as the preparer for Jesus and what the presence of the two indicated. Jesus's actions and works showed he was the one to come. John pointed the way to him and represented a transition from the old era to the new. The greatness and arrival of the new era is the key theme around which everything else in this unit rotates (Matt. 11:2–15). The unit ends with a call to hear but is followed by declarations about a failure to hear, pointing to the very opposition Jesus had just discussed in Matthew 10.

As great as the opportunity was, Israel's response had been disappointing at one level, because the complaint about John and Jesus was that they did not play the way Israel expected, even though John and Jesus had very different styles (Matt. 11:16–19). This left the nation seriously at risk of severe judgment before God (Matt. 11:20–24). Still, this was no surprise, as Jesus's prayer showed (Matt. 11:25–27). God planned all along to call children to faith, not the wise, by which Jesus meant those who would trust God as a child did a parent. Jesus had in mind those whom the Father and Son had brought into the fold. In a sense, the unit is about Jesus's work in relationship to John (Matt. 11:2–19), failure (Matt. 11:16–24), and success (Matt. 11:25–30). Note how the theme of opposition overlaps the first and second emphases. Jesus was concerned to explain the rejection he was facing.

The unit concludes with a positive theme built around Jesus's prayer and invitation. The new era's arrival opened up opportunity to come to Jesus and find true spiritual rest. With the privilege of the kingdom came a great opportunity that had one responsibility: to accept what Jesus offered as a gift. Allying oneself to Jesus meant refreshment from God. These verses are divided into a thanksgiving through prayer (Matt. 11:25–26), a revelation about God's ways (Matt. 11:27), followed by a call to share in what Jesus offered (Matt. 11:28–30).

EXPOSITION (11:2–30)

The surprise of Jesus's style of messianic ministry and his contrast to John the Baptist raised questions even for his forerunner. Jesus responded by telling John to look at the fact that he was performing the activity tied to the new era. Jesus showed who he was as much as talking about it. He also noted that despite their difference in ministry style, Israel's leaders were not embracing either message. They were rejecting both the Elijah who had come and the one he pointed to that brought the deliverance of God. This led to a warning about accountability to God. So this section deals with the unusual style of Jesus's ministry in contrast to previous expectations. All of this was no surprise to God. He was calling people who sought to be dependent on him by faith, like children who trust a parent. It was to such as these that he offered his invitation into rest.

The special nature of the current time, shown by John's relationship to Jesus, made the rejection by Israel's cities an act worthy of judgment but also offered opportunity for spiritual rest to those who embraced Jesus.

11:2–3. The nature of Jesus's ministry and the rising opposition ended up causing John the Baptist to send a pair of emissaries to ask Jesus if he was the one to come. Was he the Messiah or not? Should they look for another?

The address of "you" (σύ) was thrown forward in the question for emphasis. The subjunctive προσδοκῶμεω looks at genuine deliberation. (Turner 2008, 290; Wallace 1996, 465–67; BDAG s.v. "προσδοκάω" a, 877). Should they "contemplate" another as Messiah?

John was in prison (Matt. 4:12), probably in Herod Antipas's fortress at Machaerus, east of the Dead Sea, not quite twenty miles from Jerusalem (Josephus, *A.J.* 18.119). The journey would have been about one hundred miles by foot or a three-to-four-day trip (Wilkins 2004, 412). Matthew 14:1–12 explains more about that imprisonment, as does Luke 3:19–20.

Photo of Machaerus.

The kind of powerful Messiah who was going to vindicate the saints had not yet appeared with Jesus. Jesus as a wonder worker also did not fit in with messianic expectation, France (2007, 423 n. 17 and 424 n. 20) observes that 2 Baruch 73:1–2 and 4Q521 2:1–12 suggest a Messiah-miracles connection. Nolland (2005, 450) notes that the stress in the 4Q521 text was one of God fulfilling these expectations. John had proclaimed the hope of a powerful Messiah in Matthew 3:13–17. The term "Messiah" had not appeared in Matthew since Matthew 1:16–18 and the generic question about the figure in Matthew 2:4. The messianic idea is not used again until Matthew 16:16.

Messiah and Healing

2 Baruch 73:1–2: "And it will happen that after he has brought down everything which is in the world, and has sat down in eternal peace on the throne of the kingdom, then joy will be revealed and rest will appear. And then health will descend in dew, and illness will vanish, and fear and tribulation and lamentation will pass away from among men, and joy will encompass the earth."

4Q521 2:12: "For He shall heal the critically wounded, He shall revive the dead, He shall send good news to the afflicted."

This combination of conflicting ideas was probably what drove John to ask his question, a reflection of a note of doubt, bewilderment, or uncertainty, and probably also was reflective of the thoughts of others. The question was not hostile but simply reflected uncertainty (France 2007, 422). Konradt (2020, 172) argues that this text is about John the Baptist as a character and not the historical John since it implies John did not "get" Jesus and so his messianic expectation was misguided. But this objection says too much. What John was wrestling with is why messianic power and full victory were not in evidence in Jesus's ministry. Jesus, Matthew, and the gospel tradition contended that was yet to come. There was a step all who anticipated the Messiah were missing and that was that he would be rejected and suffer first. Peter would have a similar reaction later in Matthew 16.

Contextually, in the narrative the question also made sense. How could a Messiah who brought God's promise be a bringer of opposition and division among God's people in Israel? Why was Jesus "out in the sticks of Galilee" and not challenging the structures of Israel and the power of Rome (Bruner 2004a, 505–6)? Jesus's response was the answer to that question. The unit as a whole through Matthew 11:6 is telling us what kind of Messiah Jesus was in contrast to such expectations rooted only in power.

Despite some who have trouble accepting that John could ask such a question of doubt, the question seemed to be a genuine inquiry from John, not a query asked for the sake of others (Wilkins 2004, 413). Faith can sometimes be shaken (Bruner 2004a, 506). Keener (2009, 334–35) notes the examples of Elijah (1 Kings 19:4), David (1 Sam. 25:21–35), Jeremiah (Jer. 20:14–18), and the psalmist of Psalm 89:38–51. John asked about "the one who comes" (ὁ ἐρχόμενος), an expression that may have alluded to Psalm 118:26, where a king who led in battle came to the temple for blessing and was welcomed as the one who comes in the name of the Lord. The coming one also alludes back to Matthew 3:11, where John spoke of one "coming after me" (Osborne 2010, 414).

One should consider what Matthew calls the "deeds of the Christ" (τὰ ἔργα του Χριστοῦ). This Matthean narrative note sets the stage for the question and the reply in Matthew 11:5 in terms of actions. It also echoes what has already been recorded in Matthew 5–9, since teaching the gospel to the poor and Jesus's actions are covered in those chapters through a word-and-deed ministry. Matthew's narrative remark frames John's question in the next verse and makes clear John was asking about messianic hope. The tension was between the great things Jesus was doing and the lack of response that work was generating, alongside Jesus's humble style and lack of an exercise of power against Rome. Jesus was working from a ministry grounded in service versus mere demonstrations of power, and that power was not yet directed in judgment but in service and compassion. In many ways, the question and scene serve to summarize what Matthew has presented up to this point in his gospel, making it a significant text.

11:4–6. Jesus did not answer the question yes or no. He told the emissaries to tell John what was happening, what God was doing through him. The list of that activity followed, using the language of Isaiah. These passages described what the new era of hope would bring. It was not Jesus's words that were to convince, but his deeds. In Matthew the messengers were to proclaim what they heard and saw. Luke has it in the reverse order: saw and heard.

It is interesting that the text says John asked Jesus, even though the question was delivered through the emissaries. This fits beautifully the emissary principle: the one who speaks is not the emissary, but the one who sent him (like the emissaries who spoke for the centurion in Luke 7:1–10).

The list is a review of Jesus's activity, much of which was seen in Matthew 8–9, along with the words about preaching to the poor, which reflected Matthew 5–7. It is paralleled in Luke 7:22. Some of these actions will also come later in Matthew. The list also appeals to actions described from Isaiah about how God would save: so the deaf hear (Matt. 9:32–33; 12:22; 15:30–31) and the blind see from Isaiah 29:18 and 35:5–6 (Matt. 9:27–31; 12:22; 20:30; 21:14), the blind see in Isaiah 42:6–7, the lame leap from Isaiah 35:6 (Matt. 9:1–8; 15:30–31; 21:14), the dead are raised in Isaiah 26:19 (Matt. 9:18–26; 10:8), and the poor are preached to in Isaiah 61:1 (Matt. 4:17, 23; 5:3; 9:35; 10:7; Culpepper 2021, 213, has nice charts summarizing this use of Isaiah). Only a leper cleansed (Matt. 8:1–8; 10:8) was not connected to an OT text, although 2 Kings 5 does show a healing like this. Jesus responded positively to the question, but did so not with words spoken or titles claimed, but by an appeal to his activity. God's promises about the new era were being fulfilled (See Chart on OT Texts on Actions That Point to Deliverance and the Arrival of Salvation located after Matthew 10:7 on page 315)

The passages in Isaiah also all took place in a context of judgment. Jesus's response pointed to implications about accountability that came with the new era (Carson 2010, 304). This led to his final word to John.

That word affirmed a blessing on those who were not offended by Jesus (Luke 7:23). His style should not have put people off. The remark was a warning and a challenge, a warning not to reject Jesus and a challenge to stay committed to the faith (Wilkins 2004, 414). The key expression here is "to not being offended," a response that was tied to sin (BDAG s.v. "σκανδαλίζω" 1b, 926). This was an appeal to believe in what Jesus was doing and how he was doing it.

Note again the tight link between the new era and Jesus (Matt. 10:32–33; 12:38–42). They were inseparable. This argued against any claim that Jesus preached the kingdom but not himself. For the authenticity of Jesus's response is that previously the Messiah was, for the most part, not seen as a wonder-worker but as a powerful conqueror. The connection to make the point about who Jesus was looks like something formulated by Jesus and his ministry's activity, not an idea made up later to convince people. Without the activity such a question would never have been raised after the fact, because this activity was a twist on the normal expectation about Messiah (Davies and Allison 1991, 245). There did exist an occasional note in this direction like 4Q521. However, the 4Q text looked to the future, not the present as Jesus did here (France 2007, 424 n. 20; Novakovic 2003, 169–79). This text from Qumran referred to Messiah's care for the poor, his causing the blind to see, raising the downtrodden, healing the sick, and resurrecting the dead (Garland 1995, 125; see chart with 11:2–3 for a part of that text).

11:7–8. Jesus turned to describe who John was to the crowds. He began with a question repeated three times, about what people went into the desert to see when they went to see John and his ministry. Had they simply gone out to observe desert scenery? Did they go out to see a reed shaken by the wind (Luke 7:24)? The implied answer was no. If taken literally, the meaning of the reed was that they went out to see desert scenery (Nolland 2005, 454–55). However, many see a metaphorical sense about John being portrayed as weak and waffling, but that was not his reputation; so if this were the sense, which might have been possible, the remark would have been sarcastic (Turner 2008, 293). They went out to see something more, as verse 9 shows. Jesus's question set up a compliment to and commendation about John.

The second question asked if they went out to see someone dressed in fine clothes (Luke 7:25). The Greek term μαλακός refers to "soft" clothes of the wealthy (BDAG s.v. "μαλακός" 1, 613). Again, the answer was no. John was an ascetic. Such finely clothed people were found in the palaces of kings. Although some palaces existed in the desert, people did not go out to see the rich and powerful when they came to see John.

11:9–10. What they journeyed out to see was a prophet (Matt. 14:5; 21:26). Indeed, he was not just any prophet, but more than a prophet (Luke 7:26). He was a prophet of the eschaton, preparing the way for the people as verse 10 shows, which cites a combination text of Exodus 23:20 and Malachi 3:1 (Mark 1:2; Luke 7:27). Turner (2008, 293) calls him a "superprophet," a way of describing the effect of Matthew's using the superlative "most," a superlative used as a comparative (BDAG s.v. "περισσότερος" b, 806). The Exodus text looks at the angel who guided the people as they prepared to enter the promised land, while Malachi looks to a figure who is said to prepare for the new era, the coming Elijah (Mal. 4:5–6). The Matthean text speaks about the Messiah bringing the kingdom and God's salvation (Matt. 11:11–12) for whom John prepared the way, in language that previously had been used of God (Bruner 2004a, 510–11; Morris 1992, 279). The connection between God and his Messiah was tight. In Matthew 11:14, Jesus made John's connection to Elijah explicit.

11:11–12. Jesus discussed the new era. It was a period that came with conflict and that involved God's promise. The elevation and distinction between the eras surfaced in the fact that Jesus called John the greatest person born of a woman, but John was a member of the old era, and even the one who was least in the kingdom of heaven was greater than he (Luke 7:28 has "kingdom of God" in the parallel; Gospel of Thomas 46 has a variation and expanded form of this saying).

The demarcation in time came after John. The separation point was the kingdom Jesus offered. It brought such blessing, long promised, that it elevated the status of anyone who shared in it (2 Cor. 3:7–18). John was great but was nothing compared to what the kingdom made of people. There is an issue as to whether John was seen as in the kingdom or not. One view says Jesus referred to those who were in the kingdom in the second half of the saying, including John. However, the remark emphasized the kingdom's value and was rhetorical, looking at the kingdom through the eyes of the passage of time in sequence, as the discussion through verse 13 shows. John was placed for rhetorical reasons in the old period in terms of what he announced and what was available when he preached. He preached the transition but did not offer it himself. That was why John was described as a forerunner and was a foil to those who came after him. John's ultimate status was not in view in these remarks but the period of preaching to which he belonged (Nolland 2005, 457, speaks of a salvation-historical perspective; Turner 2008, 293). The text assumes that the kingdom arrives inaugurally with Jesus. The kingdom's arrival breaks the calendar into a new era.

The kingdom began to appear when John announced its approach. The "from" (ἀπὸ) here in "from the days of John the Baptist" is inclusive. The reaction had been hostile. John was in prison. Jesus had faced opposition. From the days of John, the kingdom and its approach came as part of a struggle where the kingdom suffered violence, and violent people tried to take away what it offered by force. The key terms here are "to inflict violence" (BDAG s.v. "βιάζω" 2 and 3, 175) and its cognate noun, "violent" (BDAG s.v. "βιαστής" 176). Both terms describe intense hostility. This all added to the theme of tension and opposition the kingdom's presence brought. It also pointed to the eschatological war the kingdom's announcement produced. The kingdoms' arrival produced a spiritual battle. This meaning gives another reason Jesus's coming divided, as Matthew 10:34–36 teaches. How this relates to the supposed Luke 16:16 parallel is discussed. For those who identify the two passages as part of the same event and setting, battle imagery prevails. For those who see Luke 16:16 as a separate context, an alternative reading of Luke is sometimes suggested that prefers an invitation image versus a battle rendering (See chart below).

Alternative Reading of Luke 16:16 Parallel

Luke 16:16 (emphasis added to show the options): "The law and the prophets were in force until John; since then, the good news of the kingdom of God has been proclaimed, and everyone is *urged to enter it/enters it violently*."

11:13–15. All that was taking place had been announced. The prophets and the law prophesied until John. They had announced what was to come. The law was seen as containing promise, a common idea in the New Testament (Gal. 3). They also announced an Elijah to come. Jesus said that this Elijah was John, if they would accept it (Matt. 17:12–13). John 1:21 showed John himself rejected this association. Nevertheless, this call to accept was not expressing uncertainty, but was an appeal for faith. They were to believe this was the role God had given to John, as verse 15 also indicated. Jesus can say that in part because of the text he cited in Matthew 11:10, for Malachi 3:1 and 4:5–6 announced such a figure, as did Sirach 48:10. These texts described a figure that would help peple prepare for the coming day of the Lord that brought in the new era, by purging the people and bringing reconciliation

(Garland 1995, 128). It was a look at the beginning of the vindication of God's people. John called the people to repent and prepare for the kingdom as Malachi promised (Luke 1:17). This was his role, and it may well be typological in that it had more than one realization, as the idea of an Elijah figure before Jesus's return is something the book of Revelation may suggest in the motif of the two witnesses (Rev. 11:3). John was a transition figure, living in the old era but pointing to the approach of the new. His presence represented the dawn of a new age, even though he only pointed ahead to the new era and did not proclaim directly what it offered. He anticipated and prepared for what came (Matt. 11:10).

Efforts to suggest John was not Elijah (but only potentially so) because Israel did not respond, fail. Making the kingdom's arrival contingent on Israel's response does not deal with Luke's similar identification with no qualification and the idea that Jesus said Elijah had already come in Matthew 17:12, just as Jesus also said here (against Toussaint 1980, 153). The Matthew 17 text came after the nation's rejection had set in (Matt. 13). In the Gospels, the kingdom came, whether Israel responded or not. It simply came in stages and was offered to others instead, both believing Jews and Gentiles, when the rejection had set in. Why would Jesus tell people to pay attention as he did in Matthew 11:15, if Matthew's portrayal would only reverse it all in a few chapters?

The one with ears was to pay attention to the points Jesus was making about the kingdom's arrival, the nature of John's ministry, and the opportunity the kingdom gave to elevate a person's stature. The call to hear appears in the Gospels in various locations to highlight a saying (Matt. 13:43; Mark 4:9, 23; Luke 8:8; 14:35). One might say it was a call to use your ears and actually reflect on what was heard. In this case, everything said here pointed to John's ministry as turning a key corner in God's plan. It was the beginning of the arrival of what the prophets had promised. Luke 16:16 says a similar thing.

11:16–17. Jesus now told a parable about the response to John and Jesus that illustrated the opposition he had just described (Luke 7:31–35). It is the parable of the complaining children, or what could be called the parable of the brats. Its authenticity is suggested by the fact that Christians were unlikely to make up a story where Jesus was called a glutton and that John and Jesus were simply compared with no ranking between them (Davies and Allison 1991, 260). The evocation of this generation was likely negative, equal to "evil" generation as in the Old Testament (Matt. 12:39, 45; 16:4; 17:17 are explicit; Deut. 1:35; 32:5, 20; Josephus, *A.J.* 5.442; Davies and Allison 1991, 261). This was a complaint much like the prophets made about Israel's lack of response to a divine initiative.

The parable assumed a real complaint from many about John and Jesus during the time they ministered because the two divinely sent messengers failed to respond to the group's desires. The scene involved marketplaces where one group of children was playing and wanted others to join in on their terms, depending on what tune they played. The plural of "marketplaces" may suggest this was not merely a single reaction but took place again and again. The complaint was when music was piped there was no dancing, and when a dirge was played there was no mourning. Those playing the tune wanted the others to dance to their tune, meeting their expectations. John and Jesus did not meet those expectations, so the others complained. John and Jesus did not dance or mourn to the tune the generation set. This is the opposite of how this text is often read (France 2007, 433), as in most interpretations the call or tunes were said to come from Jesus and John, and the failure was in the response of the generation (so the following verses which register a complaint about what Jesus and John did). However, the order does not match (although one might appeal to a chiasm to make that work). More importantly, the comparison seemed to make this generation the main actors in the parable and not merely responders (correctly in our view, Davies and Allison 1991, 261–62, and Keener 2009, 341). Either way, the point was the lack of response to Jesus and John and the opposition it represented.

11:18–19. The application to John and Jesus followed. John was an ascetic who fasted and lived in the desert, so he neither ate nor drank, not in a full literal sense but in a more rhetorical sense (Matt. 3:4; 9:14—of John's disciples, not just John, and the Pharisees; Luke 1:15). This was hyperbole. He did not enjoy the normal elements of life in the desert. Nevertheless, this generation complained that he had a devil (Luke 7:33). His unusual lifestyle made some think that he was possessed. In doing so, they missed that he was a prophet and the preparer of the way.

The Son of Man was a reference to Jesus. He came eating and drinking, the exact opposite of John. He was engaging and associating with people where they lived, even people who others kept some distance from in terms of hospitality. The charges against him were multiple. He was a glutton, a drunkard, and a friend of tax collectors and sinners (Luke 7:34). The charges of glutton and drunkard echoed the picture of the rebellious son of Deuteronomy 21:20 (Keener 2009, 342). Jesus's associations were a topic of controversy earlier in Matthew 9:10–11. In this way, by dismissing Jesus as nonspiritual because of the way he lived, critics missed the one who brought the kingdom.

The Rebellious Son

Deuteronomy 21:20: "They must declare to the elders of his city, 'Our son is stubborn and rebellious and pays no attention to what we say—he is a glutton and drunkard.'"

Putting both figures together, it made no matter where on the spectrum God's messenger was in terms of lifestyle; there was still an objection to what they were doing. This negative reaction to John and Jesus for opposite reasons was what made the complaint that this generation wanted John and Jesus to play by their rules and dance to their tune. Wilkins (2004, 419) says, "It is the way of those with hardened hearts to try to rationalize their decision to reject the message by falsely accusing the messenger."

Jesus's response to this was short: wisdom was vindicated by her deeds. Luke 7:35 speaks of wisdom being vindicated by all of her children. The idea is the same. Wisdom showed itself in what took place and vindicated herself in the process. We probably should equate the works of wisdom in part with the works of the Messiah in Matthew 11:2 and 5 and see a link here. Jesus's activity and personified wisdom were related, but not in an exclusive way. John's ministry was also in view (France 2007, 435; Nolland 2005, 464). The revelation of God's program was seen in both of them. Thus, the response should have been positive to both of them, but it had not been. Despite the reaction, God's way showed itself to be right. John and Jesus lived "justifiable" lives (Osborne 2010, 428).

11:20. A new unit involves the reproach of three Galilean cities: Chorazin, Bethsaida, and Capernaum. This verse is the narrative introduction of the sayings to the cities. Keener (2009, 344) speaks of a judgment oracle here. Interestingly, Capernaum was a headquarters city for Jesus's ministry in Galilee, but Chorazin is otherwise unmentioned in the Gospels as it appears only here and in the parallel in Luke 10:13 (BDAG s.v. "Χοραζίν" 1086; the locale may be the current ruins of Kerâzeh, a half-hour's walk north of Tell Hum). The obscurity of this city points to an authentic saying, since it received no development anywhere else. The mention is not here for any clear reason that reflects a later significance.

One can think of how Matthew 9:35–10:42 described the negative reactions to Jesus to see why he said what he did here. The reaction there was more of indifference than outright rejection, but it was not a positive response. This lack of response was surprising given what was being offered and demonstrated through the miracles. The danger of indifference always is that it can grow into outright rejection. Jesus had warned of opposition, now he discussed the consequences of it. Matthew 12 and beyond will show how it arose to the level that led to the cross.

These cities pictured the failure to respond, for Jesus had done many mighty acts among them but they had not repented (John 12:37). Matthew 4:17 shows the call to repent. Jesus warned them of the consequences of their lack of response. In doing so, Jesus showed his authority by declaring what rejection of him and his message meant in terms of judgment. The key term here is "to reproach" or reprimand (BDAG s.v. "ὀνειδίζω" 2, 710). The rebuke was like the fuller condemnation coming in Matthew 23. It was a "woe" as the following verses indicate, showing the accountability one had to respond to God and the dire consequences for failing to do so.

11:21–22. The first two Galilean locations Jesus rebuked were in the region of Capernaum: Chorazin and Bethsaida. Bethsaida appears in a few texts as the home of Philip and the original home of Andrew and Peter in John 1:44 (BDAG s.v. "Βηθσαϊδά(ν)" 1, 175), although Matthew 8:14 has Peter in Capernaum as his current hometown (Bethsaida—Mark 6:45; 8:22; Luke 9:10; John 12:21; Bethsaida with Chorazin—Luke 10:13). Chorazin was two miles from Capernaum and may be located in ruins at a locale also called Khirbet Kerâzeh, while Bethsaida was near the northern apex of the Sea of Galilee tied to ruins associated with et-Tell, about three miles from Capernaum (Arav in Charlesworth 2006, 145–66; Pixner 1985; Yeivin 1987). Matthew does not mention these cities again.

Jesus made two points as he issued his woes. The first was that if the miracles they had experienced had been done for Tyre and Sidon, then those ancient cities would have repented. The images of sackcloth and ashes pointed to actions that accompany repentance or mourning (Esther 4:1–3; Isa. 37:1–2; 58:5; Dan. 9:3; Jonah 3:5). Sackcloth was rough attire of goat's hair and was worn alone when repenting. Jesus's remark was a stinging rebuke because it said that even Gentiles would have responded to what they had rejected. Tyre and Sidon were key cities on the Mediterranean coast and were the topics of Old Testament prophetic rebuke (Isa. 23; Jer. 47:4; Ezek. 28; Joel 3:4). The second point was that as a result, the judgment would be more bearable for Tyre and Sidon than for Chorazin and Bethsaida. With greater opportunity came greater responsibility and accountability. The key term for the degree of judgment is a word meaning "bearable" or able to be endured (BDAG s.v. "ἀνεκτός" 76). The idea of a more severe judgment for these Jewish cities really served to underscore how serious this lack of response was.

11:23–24. In many ways the woe to Capernaum parallels the other two cities. This city was more well known than the other two, being a headquarters for Jesus's ministry (Matt. 4:13–17; 9:1–13; Mark 1:22–38; Luke 4:31–44). Osborne (2010, 433) says its population was about 1,500. Here the query was whether Capernaum would be lifted up (Luke 10:15). The allusion was to the self-exalting pride of the king of Babylon in Isaiah 14:13 (Davies and Allison 1991, 268). The answer was no. She would be brought down to hades. "Hades" was the equivalent Greek term for the Hebrew Sheol and referred to the underworld, or even more explicitly Gehenna, as the place of the wicked. The corporate judgment did not mean that no one from this city responded, as some of Jesus's disciples were from Capernaum. However, the bulk of the community did not respond. The reason repeated the idea of the previous woe. Had the works done in Capernaum been done in Sodom, then Sodom would not have been judged and would have remained until the present. Sodom would have responded to what Jesus was doing. Sodom had a reputation as a very sinful city (Gen. 18:20–19:28; Deut. 29:23; 32:32; Isa. 1:9–10; 13:19; Jer. 23:14; 49:18; 50:40; Ezek. 16:46–56; Amos 4:11; Matt. 10:15; 2 Peter 2:6; Jude 7; Turner 2008, 300 n. 4). The charge for a second time was that even the Gentile city with the worst of reputations would have been more responsive than Capernaum had been. It would be more bearable for Sodom on judgment day than for Capernaum. The term for "bearable" is the same as in the previous woe. Konradt (2020, 180) rightly notes that this was not a condemnation on all Israel, but is more selective of those in Israel who reject Jesus. This observation is correct because the text shows Jesus moving on to other Israelite towns and cities. Invitations to faith to those in Israel follow after Matthew 11:20–24. There is a call to decision and also a warning, and yet the door to enter in is always open.

Photo of Ruins at Capernaum.

These rebukes indicated the responsibility Israel had to respond to Jesus and the severe cost of refusal. There was a covenant violation in play in not being faithful in responding to God's program, so judgment followed. These were the strongest words Jesus had uttered up to this point in Matthew. In the narrative, things were becoming quite serious in light of Israel's growing rejection. More woes in Matthew followed along later (Matt. 18:7; 23:1–39—multiple woes; 24:19; 26:24).

11:25–26. Jesus now offered a prayer of praise and thanksgiving to the Father for the divine program's nature and direction (Luke 10:21). Contrary to what often is said, "Father" was a title that sometimes showed up in Judaism for God (Sir. 51:10). Jesus's praise for God's work covered all the elements of Matthew 11:25–30. The reference to the Lord of heaven and earth opened the theme of God's sovereignty over the plan. Acts 17:24 is the only place in the New Testament where heaven and earth are so juxtaposed other than in this passage and its parallel (Tob. 7:17; but Acts 7:49 and Rev. 10:6; 14:7 are conceptually close). Intimacy and majesty are an important combination in New Testament texts. Think of the opening line of the Lord's Prayer ("Our Father, who is in heaven"). This linkage stands in contrast to approaches to God that emphasize only one element or the other for the way God relates to the creation. He is sovereign yet caring. In Judaism, Sirach 51:1–10 works with a similar juxtaposition.

Majesty and Intimacy of God

Sirach 51:1–2a, 10: " I give you thanks, O Lord and King, and praise you, O God my Savior. I give thanks to your name, for you have been my protector and helper and have delivered me from destruction and from the trap laid by a slanderous tongue, from lips that fabricate lies. . . . I cried out, 'Lord, you are my Father; do not forsake me in the days of trouble, when there is no help against the proud.'"

God had revealed himself to the humble, the little ones, and not to the wise or understanding. The point was about a dependent spirit that made one responsive to God because it sensed one's need and was not blinded by thinking one was self-sufficient. This dependence was a picture of the righteous (Pss. 19:7–11; 116:2; 119:130–135; Prov. 1:2–6). The prayer opens with a note of praise using the term "to confess" or to acknowledge something before someone, but in a context where God is invoked, means "to praise" (BDAG s.v. "ἐξομολογέω" 4, 351). The word "innocent" points to those unspoiled by a learning that can make one proud (BDAG s.v. "νήπιος" 1bβ, 671). It pleased God to reveal himself in this way, while these things were hidden to those who are wise. This kind of move with the humble was something God did, sometimes through wisdom (Pss. 16:11; 19:7; 25:4; Dan. 1:17; Wis. 10:21; Sir. 3:19—it is the meek who reveal God's secrets). He also blocked those who thought they were wise (Job 5:13; Isa. 5:21; 29:14; Jer. 8:8; 9:23–24; 1 Cor. 1:19). The kingdom and its hope dawned for those open to acknowledging their need for it (Matt. 9:13).

There was a knowledge, a wisdom, that functioned above and was separate from any so-called knowledge of real life. There was a wisdom in the world that did not lead into wise living but prevented one from gaining it (1 Cor. 8:1). The "wise" in this verse were the worldly wise, or wise in a sense the world affirmed but were not wise in a more profound sense that was connected to God. Jesus was working with common themes from Old Testament wisdom literature and in Jewish religious thought. Only those wise enough to be open to see their need and what God was doing received the things Jesus was teaching. Jesus's teaching and the response to it was a litmus test for the heart. Did one sense a need for God or not? Did one think one could stand on one's own before God or not need what God provided? First Corinthians 1:18–30 is very close to this verse in perspective.

11:27. Jesus then turned to how this revelation took place. It was a joint work of the Father and Son (Luke 10:22). All things were given over to the Son (Matt. 28:18; John 3:35). The Son and Father had a unique joint understanding and experiential knowledge of each other (John 5:19–20; 6:46; 7:16, 28–29; 8:27–29, 54–55; 10:15; Osborne 2010, 440). That knowledge was only shared with those to whom the Son wished to reveal it. The verb here for "knowing" is the more intensive form of the term for having knowledge of something (BDAG s.v. "ἐπιγινώσκω" 1b, 369). It speaks of a thorough knowledge. The language is like what some Old Testament and Jewish texts say about wisdom (Job 28:12–27; Wis. 8:4; 9:1–18; 10:10; Sir. 1:6–9; Bar. 3:32; Davies and Allison 1991, 272). Interestingly, Sirach 51:25–26 also has wisdom make a call to take up her yoke, which is a theme of the following passage. The background also has parallels with God's interaction with Moses (Exod. 33:12–14; Davies and Allison 1991, 272).

Wisdom as Yoke

Sirach 51:25–26: "I opened my mouth and said, 'Acquire wisdom for yourselves without money. Put your neck under her yoke, and let your souls receive instruction; it is to be found close by.'"

The text proclaimed that knowledge of God the Father came only through the Son (John 1:18). In spirit, the text is like John 14:6, where Jesus said he is the way, the truth, and the life and that no one comes to the Father but through him. It was a claim that put Jesus right at the center of God's program. Those who received it did so by embracing the Son (John 1:12). The reference to the Son without qualification is not that frequent in the New Testament (Matt. 28:19; Mark 13:32; 1 Cor. 15:28; Heb. 1:8). Matthew has several "Son of God" texts (Matt. 3:17; 8:29; 14:33; 16:16; 17:5; 27:54). The remarks here show why it is appropriate to speak of the son as "the" Son. Jesus is a Son of God in ways unique from all others (France 2007, 445–46; Morris 1992, 294). This text represents a high point in Matthew's presentation of Jesus (Wilkins 2004, 421–22). Jesus was the "Revelator" of God (Bock 2002, 646–48).

This kingdom program proceeded by God's sovereign direction through the Son. This was yet another text in Matthew where Jesus stood at the hub of God's program. More than that, the unique intimate relationship between the Father and Son was affirmed. The text brings the Father and Son so close to one another that the verse has been called a "bolt from the Johannine blue" because it sounded so much like the explicit thrust of that gospel. It showed such sayings from Jesus were embedded and attested multiple times across the Gospels' sayings traditions and pointed to the saying's authenticity (Hagner 1993, 317–18; Keener 2009, 346–47).

11:28. Jesus offered rest to the weary in light of his close association with the Father. Those whom life was wearing down were invited to the benefits Jesus offered. Jesus would enable them to bear their burdens. This was like what God said to Moses in Exodus 33:14, where he offered Moses rest (also Deut. 12:10; 25:19 as peace in the land). Wisdom also invited one to come in texts like Sirach 6:23–31; 24:19; and especially 51:23–27 (see also Sir. 24:19). In Psalm 34:5 one came to God. The roots of this idea appeared in the teaching of Proverbs 8:1–21, 32–36; 9:4–6, with personified wisdom's invitation to come to her (Deutsch 1987; Turner 2008, 305). There was a familiarity with what Jesus said, except God or his wisdom was not being named as the source of rest; Jesus was. There was no intermediary. So he stepped into a divine-like role. Jesus brought such benefits and blessing directly.

The question was, what did the burden involve? Was it the pressure of the Pharisees (Oliver 2013, 85) or of life and sin in general? A concern about the Pharisees, though not excluded, seems too specific, especially since the opposition to Jesus in this context was not stated in such focused terms. More importantly, the theme of rest and the general eschatological context point to rest as equivalent to the peace salvation was to bring (Heb. 4:9; 4 Ezra 7:36–38; 8:52; 2 Clem. 5:5; Davies and Allison 1991, 289; Hagner 1993, 324). This burden dealt with all of life, though it included the burdensome teaching of the Pharisees.

The invitation does contrast, however, with what is said later about the burdens the Pharisees placed on others (Matt. 23:4) and has been compared to the picture of being freed from political oppression (Exod. 6:6–8; Lev. 26:13; Isa. 14:25; Ezek. 34:27; Wilkins 2004, 423).

11:29. They were invited to take up the yoke Jesus offered. They were to learn from the way he walked with God. The humility of his trust of God was in view. This was what Jesus's meekness and gentleness pointed to: his responsiveness to God. Moses also was described this way (Num. 12:3; Sir. 45:4). Reflecting on God was the source of rest. The one who came to Jesus accepted his easing yoke and learned from him how to bear his light load. This was the way of discipleship.

Moses's Humility

Numbers 12:3: "Now the man Moses was very humble, more so than anyone else on the face of the earth."

Sirach 45:4: "For his faithfulness and meekness he consecrated him, choosing him out of all humankind."

There was a play on the idea that the Torah or wisdom had a yoke to be taken up (Sir. 6:30; 55:2—of wisdom; 2 Bar. 41:3—of law; Pss. Sol. 7:9; 17:30—of the yoke of Messiah). The metaphor was clearly seen in Mishnah *'Aboth* 3:5, which reads, "He who takes upon himself the yoke of the Torah, from him shall be taken away the yoke of the kingdom and the yoke of worldly care; he who throws off the yoke of the Torah, on him will be laid the yoke of the kingdom and the yoke of worldly care" (see France 2007, 448 n. 29). A yoke was a wooden clamp placed on the neck of two animals to allow them to work together or involved a plank placed on a person to allow them to bear heavy materials (Jer. 27:2). The image was about being able to bear an additional load as an individual. It was often used to signify submission to another's rule. Scripture argues that we all labor under a yoke in life, the question was which one we would serve (Rom. 6:12–23). Kingdom in the Mishnah citation was about the kingdom of the world. A contrast was present. By serving God, we would learn how not to be a slave to the world and burdened by it, where the world was seen as a flawed and difficult place to live. Jesus's remark was yet another significant claim, and the contrast added to this common image with an alternative question. What the law or wisdom claimed to do, Jesus now provided. He made bearable the loads that inevitably came in life.

The idea of finding rest for the soul reflects the language of Jeremiah 6:16, where taking God's path in facing life's choices brought rest (similar is Isa. 28:12). Grace was liberating (Gal. 5:1) and the commandments were not a burden to those who love God (1 John 5:3).

11:30. The yoke Jesus gave in the leaning on God was easy, and the burden one bore from him was light. The Gospel of Thomas 90 has a similar saying but speaks of Jesus's lordship being gentle. Josephus retold an account from 2 Chronicles 10:4 of the people's request to Rehoboam to lighten the burden of labor from his father Solomon and make it easier than the previous heavy yoke (*A.J.* 8.213). Josephus mentions an "easier" yoke (χρηστότερον), like Matthew's use of χρηστός here (BDAG s.v. "χρηστός" 1, 1090; Oliver 2013, 85). There is irony here, given that normally yokes were not light. Jesus reversed what was normal about life. Real life as God designed it to be lived, though lived in a context of opposition and pressure, led to a life connected to God yielding peace with the one who counted. There likely was an allusion here to the Spirit's enablement that gave one the strength to perform the task.

THEOLOGICAL FOCUS

The exegetical idea (the special nature of the current time, shown by John's relationship to Jesus, made the rejection by Israel's cities an act worthy of judgment but also offered opportunity for spiritual rest to those who embraced Jesus) leads to this theological truth: the way in which John the Baptist's ministry mirrors Jesus's and the new era's presence offers a choice between judgment and spiritual rest.

The divinely sent ministries of John the Baptist and Jesus left people with a choice and an accountability before God. The presence of divine power in Jesus attested to the new era, even in the face of a growing rejection that desired a Jesus in its own image rather than seeing what God was doing.

This unit is about the special new time that John the Baptist introduced and Jesus brought. Two key ideas control the section: (1) this was the arrival of the long-promised time of God, and inseparable from the arrival of that time was (2) the central role of Jesus in it all. Those two facts meant a choice of the highest significance lay before all. The kingdom came into a world where people would fight its coming, but its presence was evident in what Jesus was doing. Those who could hear should pay attention.

However, the reaction of many was not good. Their response was like children who do not get their way. John and Jesus did not come in the way they expected and so they would not play along. This led Jesus to issue his first remarks about judgment. Chorazin, Bethsaida, and Capernaum would have it worse in the judgment than Tyre, Sidon, and Sodom, because what was offered was so great.

The choice is either to be "self-wise" and miss what Jesus offers or be open and responsive like a child and receive what God offers. This is how God designed it. Those who think they have no need for God do not come to him. Those who sense their need come.

Jesus offers an invitation to take up his light yoke and find rest. The unit is about the choice the new era requires all of us to make. At its center is Jesus. No one comes to the Father but the one to whom the Son reveals him. As one used to come to the law and wisdom, one now comes to him. The nature of the time demands the choice and urges that the right choice be made. To find God and rest, one must take up the yoke Jesus offers like a child trusts a good parent.

In the end, this unit is about the demand the gospel makes for a good response to what God has done in and through Jesus. John and Jesus are part of a program God revealed long ago. Opposition is a part of how many will react. But the greatness of the kingdom offer means it makes all of us accountable to the creator God and his plan. Also important is how central Jesus is to that plan. One cannot share in what God offers without recognizing the need Jesus shows we all have to come to God on the terms his program sets. What is at stake? Just about everything life offers. The difference between the judged fate of the Galilean cities and the offer of rest shows the difference. The options are judgment for rejecting God's grace or rest. Such rest resides in the peace that comes with salvation and being reconnected to the living God.

The text shows that what causes people to reject Jesus is not recognizing what God was doing through Jesus. Such rejection arises from expectations that ask God to save us on our terms, not his. In contrast is the heart that comes to what God offers and, like a child with a parent, trusts in and is dependent upon the Father's provisions. The call of the unit is to use your ears and eyes to see and hear what God is doing—and have the wisdom to make the right decision. Come to Jesus because God has shown him to embody God's wisdom and way.

PREACHING AND TEACHING STRATEGIES

Exegetical and Theological Synthesis

The exegetical section describes our need to respond to Jesus as revealed by God. His messianic role and unique connection to the Father become clearer in this pericope. Likewise, his gracious nature surfaces in his invitation to rest. Jesus's desire to sustain and restore souls through rest was not novel. This reflects the heart of Yahweh in his command for Sabbath (Exod. 16:5; 20:8–11; Deut. 5:12–15). Although we will deal with Sabbath in greater detail in the following preaching unit (Matt. 12:1–21), it is worth noting that God built rest into creation (Gen. 2:2–3) before weaving it into Israel's calendar. God values rest and extends it graciously through Jesus (Heb. 4).

Not only does God offer physical rest—to people, land, and animals—but also spiritual rest. While the Sabbath provides time to worship, build community and enjoy creation, the rest Jesus offers transcended the Sabbath day. His rest frees us from the burden of our sin, self-reliance, and religious duty. Sadly, we often find meaning in accomplishing goals and impressing others. We measure our worth in our bank accounts, appearance, career achievements, and social media following. But these cannot satisfy because they are unstable, insatiable, and idolatrous. Idols exhaust us. Jesus restores us.

Preaching Idea

Only Jesus can recharge our spiritual batteries.

Contemporary Connections

What does it mean?

Humans do not have an inexhaustible reserve of energy. Our bodies get tired. Our spirits grow weary. Both aspects of our nature—physical and spiritual—need recharging like cell phone batteries. Recharging the body comes from sleep, hydration, nutrition, and healthy movement. We go to bed or the gym when our bodies need refreshment. Recharging the spirit comes from coherence, purpose, identity, and love. We go to Jesus and his church when our spirits need recharging.

What makes the spirit weary is its ongoing work of thinking, wanting, choosing, emoting, and relating. My body may tell me I am hungry; my spirit weighs its dining options. My face may blush when I trip in public; my spirit processes the shame. My spirit manages sexual drives and bitter feelings. My spirit reaches out to God and others for connection. Its work never ends.

Thus, we need Jesus to recharge us. Self-care will only take us so far. Eventually, all efforts to maximize our energy, control our calendar, perfect our diet, master sleep, and "always look on the bright side" become a spirit-sapping, self-made religion. Jesus recharges us with his message of grace, model of gentleness, and ongoing presence.

Is it true?

It is true that only Jesus can recharge our spiritual batteries. However, God created us as psychosomatic creatures. Body and spirit interact as a complex whole. This means caring for our bodies can positively affect our spirits. When an overweight person loses twenty pounds, he may see an increase in confidence. When a college student gets serious about her sleep schedule, she may experience more focus in her prayer life. When a parent identifies an allergy in her child, she may see an immediate improvement in behavior. When an anxious person exercises, he may feel his stress diminish. Caring for the body often benefits the spirit.

However, self-care cannot fully charge our spiritual batteries. Worse yet, self-care can become an idol. Instead of relying on personal techniques to stay refreshed, followers of Jesus should respond to his invitation to come to him, learn from him, and walk with him. Jesus's metaphor in John's gospel is apt: we abide in him and his love (John 15). This is a way of life. Going to church, reading a devotional, and saying some prayers may temporarily boost our battery life. An abiding relationship with Jesus sustains our spiritual battery life.

Now what?

If only Jesus can recharge our spiritual batteries, then we must establish regular ways of connecting with Jesus. We need to learn to abide. However, a critical first step is an assessment of our battery health. Just as our phone or computer will tell us what apps or features are bleeding our batteries dry, we need to take inventory of what drains our spiritual batteries. Thus, a fundamental question would be, "What is spiritually draining me?" Answers may include busyness, legalism, loose boundaries with others, bad theology, sinful habits, and unaddressed mental health struggles.

After assessing what drains your spiritual batteries, receive Jesus's invitation to come to him, learn from him, and walk with him. Rest is a byproduct of a relationship with Jesus. This invitation lingers and deserves careful consideration. In fact, without trying to sound too mystical, the initial response to the invitation should be to meditate on it. Read it aloud. Memorize it. Make it personal. Let Jesus's words in Matthew 11:28–30 consume your thoughts, comfort you, and compel you to receive his invitation.

Finally, after receiving Jesus's invitation to recharge your spiritual batteries, mimic his patterns of renewal taught and modeled in the Gospels. Jesus practiced solitude, silence, and prayer to recharge his spiritual batteries. So should we. Jesus enjoyed table fellowship, feasts, and corporate worship to recharge his spiritual batteries. So should we. Jesus thought deeply about Scripture and integrated it into his daily life to recharge his spiritual batteries. So should we. Jesus relied on the Father's direction and Spirit's empowerment to keep his spiritual batteries charged. So should we. These practices should not become a new law; rather, they are part of the easy burden and yoke Jesus carries with us.

Creativity in Presentation

Each of us has experienced the inconvenience of a depleted battery.

- A cell phone dies on a road trip.
- A TV remote control stops working during a football game.
- A camera will not take any more pictures.
- A laptop shuts down in the middle of a study session.
- An electric car warns it has less than ten miles left on its latest charge.

Unless our batteries are recharged, the devices they energize may die inconveniently. Low-battery notifications cause distress, leading to a modern phenomenon called "low-battery anxiety."[1] Share a story about a low-battery anxiety—what happened and how you responded—showing this image as you talk.

Of course, the metaphor of batteries lends itself to using a prop. Consider showing several types of batteries—AAA, AA, C- and D-cell batteries; lithium batteries; bulky car batteries. Discuss how to recharge different types of batteries. Draw people's attention to the proliferation of "charging stations" at libraries, conference centers, and airports. You can use the icon below or hold up a docking station and tangle of charging chords.

The important thing to stress is that recharging batteries requires a faithful power supply. A car battery needs an alternator. Rechargeable cell or lithium batteries need a plug. Our spiritual batteries need Jesus.

Another way of illustrating recharging is to show a Gatorade commercial. Gatorade sells its ability to refuel the body. The commercial documenting its origin story at the University of Florida demonstrates the need for the body to get recharged.

For rich devotional reflections on Jesus's invitation to rest, consider the opening chapters of *The Spirit of the Disciplines* (Willard 1991, 1–10) and *Gentle and Lowly* (Ortlund 2020, 17–24). The following quotes come from these works:

> And in this truth lies the secret of the easy yoke: the secret involves living as [Jesus] lived in the entirety of his life—adopting his overall life-style. Following "in his steps" cannot be equated with behaving as he did when he was "on the spot." To live as Christ lived is to live as he did *all* his life. (Willard 1991, 5; italics original)

> You don't need to unburden yourself and then come to Jesus. Your very burden is what qualifies you to come. (Ortlund 2020, 20)

> His rest is gift, not transaction. . . . Jesus Christ's desire that you find rest, that you come in out of the storm, outstrips even your own. (Ortlund 2020, 21)

> All Christian toil flows from fellowship with a living Christ whose transcending, defining reality is: gentle and lowly. He astounds and

1 Consider the article by Emma Gray Ellis, "Diagnosing (and Dealing with) Your Low-battery Anxiety," *Wired Magazine*, May 6, 2019, https://www.wired.com/story/diagnosing-and-dealing-with-your-low-battery-anxiety.

sustains us with his endless kindness. Only as we walk ever deeper into his tender kindness can we live the Christian life as the New Testament calls us. (Ortlund 2020, 22)

Finally, the television series *The Chosen* features Jesus's invitation in season 3, episode 8.

Ultimately, you want your sermon to teach the way in which John the Baptist's ministry mirrors Jesus's and the new era's presence offers a choice between judgment and spiritual rest. And only Jesus can recharge our spiritual batteries.

- Jesus reveals a new era of God's work (11:2–19).
- Jesus rebukes those who reject him (11:20–24).
- Jesus invites us to find and receive him (11:25–30).

DISCUSSION QUESTIONS

1. How did John the Baptist change between his first appearance in the gospel and this one? What can we learn from his doubts?
2. What are key distinctions between John the Baptist's old era and Jesus's new era?
3. What are modern ways we make Messiah (or Jesus) in our own image?
4. What makes children a powerful metaphor for faith?
5. Describe the state of "weariness" in your life and church. What are the causes and effects? Be specific.
6. How have you experienced the "recharge" that Jesus alone offers?

Matthew 12:1–21

EXEGETICAL IDEA

Jesus's response to Sabbath controversies, including acts of healing, showed him to be the promised Servant and Lord of the Sabbath, despite the objections of some.

THEOLOGICAL FOCUS

Jesus shows himself to be Lord of the Sabbath and the fulfillment of a long-awaited promise.

PREACHING IDEA

Serving others matters more than saving time.

PREACHING POINTERS

Controversy with the Pharisees continued to escalate. In consecutive scenes, Jesus tested conventional teaching about the Sabbath. First, he allowed his hungry disciples to graze on the Sabbath, defended them against accusation, and declared himself Lord of the Sabbath. Second, he healed a man in the synagogue with a hand deformity, appealed to rabbinic logic, and made a case for doing good on the Sabbath. For his original readers, Matthew linked these stories to Isaiah's portrait of the Suffering Servant. He described Jesus as the prophetic embodiment of these ancient promises. Matthew presented Jesus as Suffering Servant and Lord of Sabbath, granting him authority to subvert traditional Sabbath practice for the good of others.

Time is our greatest asset in the age of efficiency. Although we have equal amounts of it, the best of us makes the most of our time. We don't want to waste time or lose it. We're willing to bank time or borrow it. Saving time is a virtue. We hallow it, hedge it, and hate to get interrupted or delayed. Consider the collective sigh at the airport when they announce your flight will depart an hour late! Our protectiveness of time parallels the Pharisaic practice of Sabbath, which was riddled with restrictions. Time is a gift. It should free us to feast, enjoy fellowship, and serve others. Knowing Jesus is the master of time means we are not enslaved by it. This sermon reminds us that serving others matters more than saving time.

THE SABBATH ACTS POINT TO JESUS'S AUTHORITY (12:1–21)

LITERARY STRUCTURE AND THEMES (12:1–21)

This unit begins to trace the rise of more official opposition to Jesus with two Sabbath controversies (12:1–14) followed by a scriptural commentary on these events (12:15–21). The first incident was the disciples' plucking of grain on a Sabbath (Matt. 12:1–8). The second was the healing of a man with a withered hand in the synagogue (Matt. 12:9–14). Both acts raised a complaint, the first after the act and the second before with a question from the synagogue attenders about what should be done. The fact that no judgment came and the healing took place showed that no Sabbath violation took place as God had supported Jesus's action. It was believed God did not help sinners or sinful acts on the Sabbath (John 9:16b). A healing summary follows with a citation of Isaiah 42:1–4 as an indication that the promise of Isaiah was being fulfilled (Matt. 12:15–21).

The juxtaposition of opposition followed by passages in support of what Jesus was doing set up the same kind of contrast and choice for the reader as Matthew 11:2–30. The dispute was about the authority behind Jesus's actions and what that authority meant. Was he a violator of the law or did he possess divine authority to do what he was doing? The citation of fulfillment was Matthew's answer to the question.

It was Jesus's authority that was highlighted at the end of the first controversy. He was Lord of the Sabbath. His actions also showed there was no Sabbath violation as examples in David, the priests, and the prophetic declaration about mercy over sacrifice indicated. The fact God would heal through him on a Sabbath showed that the doing of good was permitted on the Sabbath and that Jesus did not violate the law. Oliver (2013, 80–99, 114–24) argues there is no abrogation of Sabbath here, but an alternative Jewish reading of it. In the end, there also is an appeal to Jesus's authority for such a reading.

Jesus was the promised Servant in whom God was pleased and through whom God worked. The Spirit of God was at work through Jesus. He humbly brought victory and justice. It was in his name the nations should hope. The use of Scripture supplied another reply to the charge of unfaithfulness and legal violation. God's chosen one was at work. The response should be to respond to what God was accomplishing through him.

We have four elements in the unit. It opens with two Sabbath controversies in Matthew 12:1–8 and 12:9–14. The parallels are in Mark 2:23–28 and Luke 6:1–5, followed by Mark 3:1–6 and Luke 6:6–11. Matthew is running in Marcan sequence here. The healing summary comes next in Matthew 12:15–16. This passage has parallels in Mark 3:7–12, which is a much more detailed form of this summary, and Luke 6:17–19, which is closer in length to Matthew. The appeal to scriptural fulfillment of Isaiah 42:1–4 is the fourth element of the unit and is unique to Matthew, containing his narrative fulfillment formula like we saw so often in Matthew 1–2 (Matt. 1:22; 2:5, 15, 17, 23). It is important to note that Matthew had delayed the grain-plucking incident in terms of both Mark and Luke. These two Sabbath controversies are part of five consecutive controversies in Mark and Luke. Matthew has isolated them to make them key and somewhat distinct evidence for the rising official opposition to Jesus.

The narrative started chronicling the rising opposition to Jesus anticipated by the remarks in Matthew 10–11. What Mark 2:1–3:5 and Luke 5:12–6:11 place all together in a series of controversies Matthew has spread across Matthew 8–12. The difference reflects a different narrative construction allowing for a gradual building up of opposition (Matthew) versus presenting the controversies in one locale (Mark, Luke). Differences like this show the distinct ways the evangelists chose to arrange their material.

The juxtaposition of controversy and Scripture is a key literary feature for this unit. The Scripture served as divine commentary on the events. It showed that the opposition rejected the divine program. The structure is like Matthew 8:1–17, which has two healings and then a summary with a citation.

Some key themes are tied to the Sabbath. Mercy, more than sacrifice, is the principle. Whether one thinks of the disciples merely plucking grain to have a meal or Jesus giving a word to heal on the Sabbath, both acts are not to be seen as Sabbath violations. It may be no accident that the issue of Sabbath law came up after Jesus mentioned the offer of rest and the picture of a different kind of yoke than the law (Turner 2008, 309; Verseput 1986, 153–206).

Christology is also important, for Jesus presented himself as Lord of the Sabbath. In this he showed authority over a most sacred Jewish day that was a part of the creation story as well as one of the Ten Commandments (Yang 1997). It is crucial to appreciate how important this day was to Jews in order to appreciate the claim's scope. Doering (1999) treats the day in detail, working through all the various sects and key works in the Second Temple period. To be Lord of the Sabbath was to claim authority over one of the most distinctive elements of the law and divine calendar. This claim came right after the previous unit's claims about Jesus as the Son who uniquely knows the Father and Jesus's substitution of himself in the role the law and personified wisdom played in the Hebrew Scripture. Add to this the thrust of the citation from Isaiah and we connect the image of the Servant of God to all of these claims. Matthew highlighted how God's program was tied to the key person who brought that program.

The miracles served as audio-visuals of the time, pointing to Jesus's unique work in bringing justice and victory. He served as God's figure of hope for the nations.

EXPOSITION (12:1–21)

So how did Jesus stack up to sacred times of piety like the Sabbath? What did God think about what Jesus was doing on such days? Answering that question is the burden of this unit. God was at work through Jesus. Not only did Scripture show what the Sabbath was designed to be about, but it pointed to Jesus as Lord of the Sabbath. What his opponents objected to and saw as a lack of piety was actually a demonstration of divine support for Jesus and reflected his authority. If God did not approve of sinful actions on the holy day of the week, then how can one explain Jesus's ability to heal on that day and his claim that he was Lord of the Sabbath? The only option that remained was that Jesus was who he claimed to be. He was a servant with authority to serve and explain God's ways.

Jesus's response to Sabbath controversies, including acts of healing, showed him to be the promised Servant and Lord of the Sabbath, despite the objections of some.

12:1–2. As Jesus moved along during a Sabbath, his disciples were hungry and so plucked grain on the Sabbath and ate. Even though Sabbath is grammatically plural, such an expression can have a singular meaning (1 Macc. 2:38). The detail about hunger pointed to a core human need as the action's cause. If *Mishnah Šabb.* 7.2 is a guide (see chart below), then the plucking of the grain and the winnowing required to eat it would have been seen as violations of the

Sabbath (also Philo, TMos. 2.22). The roots of the day's importance and uniqueness came from the Hebrew Scripture (Exod. 20:10; 34:21; Deut. 5:14; cf. Jub. 2:16–18; 50:12). So the Pharisees, when seeing this, inquired of Jesus how the disciples could violate the Sabbath. The question was quite explicit that the disciples did "what is not permitted" (ὅ οὐκ ἔξεστιν) on the Sabbath (BDAG s.v. "ἔξεστιν" 1a, 349). The issue was not taking grain from a field, as that was permitted (Lev. 19:9–10; Deut. 23:24–25). The issue was performing this activity on the Sabbath and whether the sacred character of the day permitted any exceptions (Davies and Allison 1991, 307–8). A walk of up to two thousand cubits was also permitted on the Sabbath (*m. Soṭah* 5.3)

Mishnah on Sabbath Violations: The Forty Less One

(numbering added to show the 39 things listed)

Šabbat 7.2: "The generative categories of acts of labor [prohibited on the Sabbath] are forty less one: (1) he who sows, (2) ploughs, (3) reaps, (4) binds sheaves, (5) threshes, (6) winnows, (7) selects [fit from unfit produce or crops], (8) grinds, (9) sifts, (10) kneads, (11) bakes; (12) he who shears wool, (13) washes it, (14) beats it, (15) dyes it; (16) spins, (17) weaves, (18) makes two loops, (19) weaves two threads, (20) separates two threads; (21) ties, (22) unties, (23) sews two stitches, (24) tears in order to sew two stitches; (25) he who traps a deer, (26) slaughters it, (27) flays it, (28) salts it, (29) cures its hide, (30) scrapes it, and (31) cuts it up; (32) he who writes two letters, (33) erases two letters in order to write two letters; (34) he who builds, (35) tears down; (36) he who puts out a fire, (37) kindles a fire; (38) he who hits with a hammer; (39) he who transports an object from one domain to another—lo, these are the forty generative acts of labor less one."

E. P. Sanders (1983, 20) has a famous objection to this event that the Pharisees did not patrol the fields to check for Sabbath violations, but Davies and Allison (1991, 304–5) note that all we may have here was a literary compression of a more complex process of discovery about the event. They present full arguments for the scene's historicity. Wilkins (2004, 439) observes that once Jesus began to come on the Pharisees' radar, they might have paid more careful attention to what he did or what they heard about what he did (see also Yang 1997, 168–69). A major reason in support of historicity is that the defense of this activity was not really aimed at defending or reflecting a general Sabbath problem in the church about which Matthew wrote. By then, Sabbath observance was no longer an issue for the church. Jesus's reply about David was rooted in focusing on compassion; it was not a defense of a change in the day of the week or a refutation to the church's need for strict Sabbath observance.

Following Sabbath practice was an important Jewish distinctive, so the issue here was not only about keeping the law, but a perceived issue of faithfulness that marked out distinctive Jewish piety and identity. Just how important this was to pious Jews can be seen in 1 Maccabees 2:31–38, where the Maccabees allowed themselves to be killed in a battle on the Sabbath versus fighting back. Also, Pompey put up earthworks for a siege of Jerusalem, including on Sabbath days without being disturbed by Jews on those days (Josephus, *A.J.* 14.63).

12:3–4. Jesus's reply in Matthew 12:3–8 set forth four examples. The first and fourth have parallels in Mark 2:23–28 and Luke 6:1–5. Matthew's treatment is the most detailed, filled with halakic argumentation common in Jewish study.

The first example was David and his men eating the temple showbread that was reserved for priests (1 Sam. 21:1–6; cf. Lev. 24:5–9). Jesus was just as explicit as the Pharisees had been about the fact this was a violation of the law's letter, using the phrase "which is not permitted" (ὅ οὐκ ἔξον) to point it out (BDAG s.v.

"ἔξεστιν" 1d, 348–49). The example was not explicitly on a Sabbath but was a situation (tied to issues of hunger) that was a violation of a law that involved bread limited to priestly consumption. Apparently the fact there was no judgment from God for doing this meant that Jesus raised a haggadic (life) example to raise the halakic (legal Torah) question about whether this could be done without being seen as a violation (Hagner 1993, 328). A question not answered was whether David's position as king was in play here or whether the response was rooted in a general remark about compassion having precedent, so as to question certain kinds of stricter oral tradition. It might even be the case that both of these concerns were at work.

12:5–6. The second example was the priestly activity in the temple on the Sabbath. Jesus's illustration was vivid. Debate exists over whether this is a Matthean addition. He asked the Pharisees to recall what was read, which spoke directly to a law, not oral tradition. He spoke of David and his men "desecrating" (βεβηλοῦσιν) the temple and yet still being innocent (BDAG s.v. "βεβηλόω" 173). The word "desecrate" means to make something common as opposed to being set apart as holy. The background for verse 5 is Numbers 28:9–10, which commanded the priests to offer Sabbath sacrifices (Lev. 24:8; 11Q19 13.17 [Temple Scroll]). Two principles were at work here. First, the example showed a clear exception to the rule of Sabbath rest. *Mishnah Pesaḥ* 6:2 recognizes the presence of such exceptions. Second, if the temple practice was more important than the Sabbath, then anything more important than the temple also had precedent. This is why Jesus went on to claim that something more important than the temple was present. Did his presence equal another expression of divine presence to which the temple pointed? That may be an implication here (France 2007, 460–61). At the least, the remark set up the Lord of the Sabbath remark that serves as the final argument Jesus made. However, France's description of Jesus's view of the temple being negative confuses critique about how temple practice was carried out versus Jesus's feelings about the temple itself. The claim was like Jesus saying he was greater than Jonah or Solomon in Matthew 12:41–42, but here we are dealing with the institution representing God's presence, so the claim was greater than those other examples because God himself and his honor were in view.

Sabbath Exceptions

***Mishnah Pesaḥ* 6:2a:** "Said R. Eliezer, 'Now is it not logical [that these too should override the prohibitions of the Sabbath]? Now if slaughtering, which is prohibited under the category of labor, overrides [the prohibitions of] the Sabbath, these, which are [prohibited only] by reason of Sabbath rest [relying not upon the scriptural prohibition of actual labor]—should they not override [the prohibitions of] the Sabbath?' Said to him R. Joshua, 'A festival day will prove [to the contrary. On festival days it is permitted to prepare necessary food, Ex. 12:16]. For they permitted work to be done on that day which is normally prohibited by reason of labor, but it is prohibited to do on that day [other actions] which are prohibited [merely] by reason of Sabbath rest.'"

The temple was a special place, but Jesus made a common Jewish "how much more" argument. He declared that something "greater" than the temple was present (note the neuter μεῖζόν; BDAG s.v. "μέγας" 4a, 624). Some argue that something other than Jesus is alluded to here like the kingdom, love, or compassion, but the connection to verse 8 would be against this. Jesus has to be in view in some way (as Hagner 1993, 330; and Osborne 2010, 453 n. 23 [both said it is about Jesus and his ministry]; Nolland 2005, 484 n. 16). The confident assertion was developed and explained even more in Matthew 12:8, when Jesus claimed the Son of Man is Lord of the Sabbath. The use of γάρ in that verse made it an explanation for what preceded it and so was the point of what was being said here. Jesus was referring primarily to himself here, as the conclusion to the four-part argument showed. It was not that the kingdom is excluded here, but it was not considered in the abstract without Jesus being in it (Morris 1992, 303). Jesus with the kingdom was likely intended here.

12:7. The third response appealed to Hosea 6:6. This is the second time Matthew has cited this text (Matt. 9:13). God desired mercy, not sacrifice. The term for "mercy" (ἔλεος) is thrown forward in the remark for emphasis (BDAG s.v. "ἔλεος" a, 316). If they had understood the priority of mercy over sacrifice, then the Pharisees would not have condemned the innocent. The contrary-to-fact condition showed they did not work sufficiently with this prioritization. "If they had understood, but they do not" is the force of this construction. Eating to address hunger needs on the Sabbath was not a violation. Repeating the idea of being "innocent" (ἀναίτιος) twice in these few verses was another way to say the disciples did not engage in a violation (BDAG s.v. "ἀναίτιος" 64). It is the central role of the appeal to mercy that Doering (1999, 434–36) sees as the key argument in the passage contending for a lesser-to-greater move, as Matthew proceeds through the examples.

These first three arguments were theological and stated the examples and principles involved in making the judgment that a violation had not taken place. There was a logic to the sequence and the appeal involved the law, prophets, and writings—that is, the three sections of the Hebrew Scripture (Keener 2009, 357). David's example with his men showed exceptions existed. The temple example pointed to another precedent where Sabbath had a second place. It also introduced Jesus's importance and what he represented in the situation. The appeal to mercy was focused on the disciples' right to eat by itself. Jesus was covering every angle, and the full argument was that there wasn't an either/or choice here (either Jesus had precedent over Sabbath or compassion permitted this), but a both/and argument, where both sets of premises were at work (Osborne 2010, 453; Verseput 1986, 166–68). The argument in this verse parallels what is said in Matthew 12:12, where one can do good on the Sabbath. Everything up to this point made biblical-theological points in a very halakic manner. The final of the four arguments found in verse 8 was of a different order and upped the stakes in Jesus's reaction to this challenge about the Sabbath and the law.

12:8. The final argument was the decisive one. It also helped explain what was going on. It was that the Son of Man was Lord of the Sabbath. It explained one part of Jesus's previous claims. There was something present that was greater than the temple. The title "Son of Man" was a self-reference to Jesus. The term "Lord" (κύριος) was also thrown forward in this remark for emphasis. This was a claim to be in charge of the Sabbath (BDAG s.v. "κύριος" 1a, 577). Jesus had authority over this sacred day, to be able to make the judgment about what was a violation for this sacred part of the calendar. Just as the temple could take precedence over the Sabbath, so could the Son of Man. One could discuss whether this kind of activity was allowed on the Sabbath, but in the end *and* in addition, Jesus had the right to make the final call! This was a radical claim to have authority over something God had set up and saw as "his" day (Gen. 2:3; Exod. 31:13; Lev. 19:3, 30; France 2007, 463). Jesus was not rejecting the Sabbath here, but was putting it in its proper place in relationship to him. The Lord's day was his day!

Sabbath as a Set Apart Day

Genesis 2:3: "God blessed the seventh day and made it holy because on it he ceased all the work that he had been doing in creation."

Exodus 31:13: "Tell the Israelites, 'Surely you must keep my Sabbaths, for it is a sign between me and you throughout your generations, that you may know that I am the Lord who sanctifies you.'"

Leviticus 19:3: "'Each of you must respect his mother and his father, and you must keep my Sabbaths. I am the Lord your God.'"

Leviticus 19:30: "'You must keep my Sabbaths and fear my sanctuary. I am the Lord.'"

The claim that this verse was Mark's creative editorial addition to the argument that Matthew simply follows struggles with the fact that Jesus was the consistent speaker in Son of Man sayings (but so Nolland 2005, 485). Jesus is making a key self claim here; it is not the word's of the evangelist. "Son of Man" was not a title used in narrative frames.

12:9–10. The scene shifts to a synagogue. The fact the synagogue is described as "theirs" may show a growing rift with Judaism by Jesus-followers. This narrative remark may reflect Matthew's attitude toward the Jews who rejected Jesus versus one at the time of the event, as Jesus often went to the synagogue to worship with his people. Morris (1992, 305) contends "their" synagogue was simply a reference to the locals in a town that was not that of Jesus, which is a possibility but does seem overly subtle as the synagogue was a home for Jews whether local or traveling.

Present in the service was a man with a withered hand. The term ξηρός means "to be dried up" and so the hand is portrayed as shriveled (BDAG s.v. "ξηρός" 2, 685; 1 Kings 13:4; Zech. 11:17). Luke 6:6 tells us it was the right hand. Obviously, this limited what the man was able to do for a living. Some in the synagogue asked Jesus if it was permitted to heal on the Sabbath. However, the rise of opposition was clear in Matthew's narrative framing, for Matthew went on to note that the question was asked so they could accuse him. They expected a positive answer, that Jesus would heal on the Sabbath. They saw this response as a Sabbath violation. Jesus was supposed to wait a day to heal. They saw such an act as disrespectful of God.

We know that the Essenes would have had the view that one was not to heal on the Sabbath (Jub. 2, 50; CD 11:9–11). Others had the view that only in the case where life was threatened could one undertake to heal. This situation in the synagogue was not life-threatening. *Mishnah Yoma* 8:6 allows one to save a life on the Sabbath, including treating a sore throat that might be seen as life-threatening, but that was not this situation. Oliver (2013, 118–19) notes that Matthew's emphasis was simply on doing good, not a life-threatening situation, shedding Mark's allusion to saving a life (also Saldarini 1994, 132). Davies and Allison (1991, 318) note a few other exceptions in later texts (Eccl. Rab. 9:7—show mercy to a leper on the Sabbath). *M. Šabb.* 14:4 and 22:6 allow for healing if nothing special was done. So if one washed someone normally or dipped food in something normally and they were healed, that was fine; but one was not to set a bone on the Sabbath, showing the tension. *M. Šabb.* 18:3 allows for assisting in childbirth. *M. Šabb.* 6:2 advises against wearing an amulet on the Sabbath but does not make it a sin. The list of prohibited Sabbath actions in *m. Šabb.* 7:2 does not mention healing as prohibited. The majority opinion appears to be against doing such healings in any active way.

The historicity of the scene is defensible in part because there is no evidence that healing on the Sabbath was an issue debated in the church and thus no reason for it to be the subject of a created story (Hagner in Bock and Webb 2009, 263–66, whose entire discussion works from the Marcan account; Bock 2012, 73–74).

12:11–12. Jesus replied with an example of a sheep that fell into a ditch on the Sabbath. Matthew simplified the account in comparison to

Mark and Luke, who have Jesus stand with the man as he responds. Again, Matthew often told his events in the simplest form.

Jesus asked if they would not pull the sheep out in such a circumstance. The scene may assume this was the one beast the person owned (Luz 2001, 187; Osborne 2010, 459), but the text does not seem that specific. It may simply be just that one sheep had gotten into trouble (Carson 2010, 328). Luz notes the Aramaic and Greek "one" can function like an indefinite article. All that was going on here was that someone had the risk of lost property and productivity. If this was a poor man's single sheep, then the need to rescue the animal did become more important. Keener (2009, 358) notes how some hunters camouflaged pits to catch prey, so that animals sometimes ended up trapped. Josephus in *Jewish Antiquities* 4.283–84 explains how wells were to be built so as to prevent people from falling into them and notes that if an animal fell in and died, then they were to pay for the loss (Exod. 21:33–34).

The question was asked with οὐχί, so it expects a positive reply. This was something they would do. Caring for one's animal was a biblical idea (Deut. 22:4; Prov. 12:10). Jewish materials differ on this possibility, with some groups being very strict about it. CD 11:13–14 prohibits such an action (also 4Q265; Keener 2009, 357; Yang 1997, 201–3). Later rabbinic materials allow one to feed the animal or throw things in to help the beast extract himself, but one could not actively extract him (*Šabb.* 128b; also t. *Šabb.* 14.3; France 2007, 464–65; Oliver 2013, 120). What was less clear was what the average person would have done. Jesus seemed to assume most would have rescued the sheep. Jesus's point was that if one could rescue an animal, perhaps to prevent economic loss or further damage to the animal that might occur by waiting, then how much more could one do to relieve human suffering?

Helping an Animal Prohibited on the Sabbath

CD 11:13–14: "No one should help an animal give birth on the Sabbath; and if it falls into a well or a pit, he may not lift it out on the Sabbath."

4Q265: "Let no one raise up an animal which has fallen into the water on a Sabbath day."

Jesus stated the point in two steps. First, a person was more valuable than a sheep (Matt. 6:26; 10:31). In another "how much more" argument, Jesus was saying if one could rescue a sheep on the Sabbath, one could do good to a person. The second step stated the principle. It was permitted to do good on the Sabbath. To do good was love for one's neighbor (Luz 2001, 188). Mark 3:4 uses a rhetorical question to make the point. Jesus as Son of Man was again asserting his ability to interpret what the Sabbath was about. In addition, Jesus was challenging how the Sabbath was interpreted in the oral law, not challenging the Sabbath itself, since specific activities violating rest were not named in the Scripture. Jesus argued this was an acceptable act on the Sabbath, especially since it only involved him telling the man to move his hand.

12:13. Jesus's "labor" consisted of a command to the man to stretch out his hand. This was distinct from other healings where there was at least a touch (Matt. 8:3, 15; 9:25). As the man did so, his hand was restored to health like the other hand (OT and Jewish examples: 1 Kings 13:1–10; T. Sim. 2:11–14). An unexpressed issue here was that God was not believed to help those who violated the Sabbath, nor would he support a sinner, so the healing should have given pause (John 9:16, 31). If God opposed such activity, how in heaven's name did it take place? In terms of form, we have more of a pronouncement controversy account than a miracle, although technically the two are combined here (France 2007, 465). The text's emphasis is on the Sabbath controversy for which the miracle was the context. The healing made evident Jesus's authority, but the demonstration did not guarantee acceptance by those who saw it.

12:14. The Pharisees' reaction was revealing. The miracle and its positive result were ignored. Instead, they took counsel to stop Jesus, to destroy him (Matt. 22:15; Mark 3:6; John 5:18). The term συμβούλιον means "to form a plan" (BDAG s.v. "συμβούλιον" 3, 957). The key term in the verse is ἀπόλλυμι, which means "to destroy" someone (BDAG s.v. "ἀπόλλυμι" 1aα, 115). This might not mean to eliminate Jesus physically at this point, but stopping his influence was in view at the least. Matthew focused on the Pharisees' reaction; he lacks the reference to the Herodians from Mark 3:14.

This set of Sabbath controversies was seen as a significant reason the opposition to Jesus intensified and solidified. The leaders may have thought they were acting in response to Exodus 31:14 or were protecting the nation from a Roman reaction (Turner 2008, 314). This sacred day was seen as too important and distinctive to have someone challenge the way it was viewed. The authority challenge Jesus issued was simply too great to ignore.

12:15–16. Jesus withdrew, but his ministry continued. Matthew presents a healing summary here followed by a citation of Scripture, as he did in 8:16–17. In both cases the Scripture involved Isaiah's Servant.

Jesus continued to draw many who followed him and healed all who were brought to him. These crowds continued to be present later in Matthew (Matt. 15:30; 19:2). Matthew does not mention exorcisms here that are present in Mark 3:11–12.

Jesus did not want excessive attention on his healing, so he commanded the crowd not to make him known. This was something Jesus consistently did (Matt. 9:30; 16:20; 17:9). Jesus's primary work was not about miracles. It was about the coming of kingdom hope. The risk was Jesus would be approached only for his healing ability. Nolland (2005, 491) speaks of Jesus avoiding publicity stunts for self-promotion. The service Jesus performed was to be linked to his reason for coming, bringing the kingdom. The following citation made that point. In addition, Blomberg (1992, 200) argues that Jesus did not want to create so much reaction that he might be arrested too early. Jesus set the time to confront the leadership when he eventually went to Jerusalem and forced their hand to decide about him. Wilkins (2004, 444) argues the goal was not to create false expectations about seeking to overthrow Rome. The text here does not give the reason for the call to silence, but each of these suggestions may be a part of the explanation.

12:17. Matthew now appends his explanatory text from Isaiah 42:1–4. This verse has an introductory formula about what had been spoken by someone, just as we saw frequently in the infancy material. Such formulae appear ten times in the gospel (Matt. 1:22–23; 2:15, 17–18, 23; also 4:14–16; 8:17; 13:35; 21:4–5; 27:9–10). This is the longest citation of the Old Testament in Matthew. These events showed Jesus was God's chosen one and Servant. The double mention of Gentiles pointed to the beginning of a turn in terms of audience (Yang 1997, 219). Many in Israel might have rejected the Messiah, but God's promised program involving Gentiles moved forward just as Isaiah predicted, even as outreach to Jews continued. Victory and justice would come from the one who ministered without trying to make a stir. Jesus simply did what God called him to do, bringing justice with victory.

12:18. The citation makes several points. First, it is rendered in a form independent of both the Hebrew and the Greek, although it has the feel of a rendering tied to the Hebrew (Hagner 1993, 336–37; the discussion in Davies and Allison has details involving one line of the text at a time). Only Matthew 12:21 looks like it was impacted by the LXX rendering, so the text has the character of a targumic rendering (Davies and Allison 1991, 323).

Jesus was the Servant that God had chosen. This language echoes the voice from heaven at Jesus's baptism (Matt. 3:17; also 17:5 at the transfiguration). This was the one God loved and delighted in, having shown his Spirit was on him (Matt. 3:16). Jesus's mission was to proclaim justice to the nations (for the themes in the entire citation, Beaton 1999; Neyrey 1982). The note of hope in verse 21 pointed to the meaning of justice in the sense of righteousness here versus the bringing of judgment (France 2007, 472; Nolland 2005, 493; also Isa. 49:6). This theme is like the citation from Isaiah 61:1 in Luke 4:16, yet another text that rang out with Servant song themes. The picture was of a humble Servant who did what God asked (Bruner 2004a, 453).

Keener (2009, 360) points out that excluding the later Targum, few Jewish texts see the Servant as Messiah, preferring a reference to Israel. He points to texts like Isaiah 41:8–10; 44:1, 21; 45:4; and 49:3. He goes on to argue that reading the figure as Israel fails to deal with how in Isaiah Israel had come up short in being what God had called her to be. Such a reading also ignored how God came to focus on an individual in solidarity with the nation to accomplish what the nation had failed to do (Isa. 42:6–7—an individual chosen; 42:18–19—the problem; 49:5–7—the answer as the one who restores is distinct from the nation and remnant; 52:13–53:12—also an individual; on Isaiah 53 and the Servant Songs, see Glaser and Bock 2012).

Texts on the Need for a New Servant to Serve Israel

Isaiah 42:6–7: "I, the Lord, officially commission you [singular]; I take hold of your hand. I protect you and make you a covenant mediator for people, and a light to the nations, to open blind eyes, to release prisoners from dungeons, those who live in darkness from prisons."

Isaiah 42:18–19: "Listen, you deaf ones! Take notice, you blind ones! My servant is truly blind, my messenger is truly deaf. My covenant partner, the servant of the Lord, is truly blind."

Isaiah 49:5–6: "So now the Lord says, the one who formed me from birth to be his servant—he did this to restore Jacob to himself, so that Israel might be gathered to him; and I will be honored in the Lord's sight, for my God is my source of strength—he says, 'Is it too insignificant a task for you to be my servant, to reestablish the tribes of Jacob, and restore the remnant of Israel? I will make you a light to the nations, so you can bring my deliverance to the remote regions of the earth.'"

12:19–20. Jesus had a humble ministry in terms of how he went about his mission. He did not quarrel or complain by crying out for aid, as the reference to crying out was probably more about the response to opposition. We just saw this approach with his opponents when he withdrew upon their becoming hostile. Nor did he raise his voice in the streets, as we saw when he told those he healed not to make him known. He simply ministered. The remark is very similar to Isaiah 53:7 (also 1 Peter 2:23; Osborne 2010, 466).

He did not break a reed or put out a light. A broken reed was next to worthless, as was a smoldering wick that was running out of the ability to burn. All the wick did was produce smoke versus light; it was no longer very useful. Jesus was so gentle; he would not harm even things like these. He would minister until justice turned into victory. The broken reed and smoldering wick probably alluded to those on the fringe whom Jesus helped, those who were viewed as of no value to society or were invisible to that society. "He will handle the weak" (Turner 2008, 316). These were Matthew's tax collectors, sinners, and poor (Matt. 9:10–13, 36; 11:28; 12:1–14, 28; Nolland 2005, 494).

It was a note of hope that Isaiah described, with a style of ministry that was less about exercising power to force a response than service. He would bring justice one day. With justice came victory, but the style did not involve the exercise of raw power that many had anticipated. Here was the "gentle Servant Messiah" (Wilkins 2004, 445). Matthew folded Isaiah 42:3–4 into verses 20b–21, using 42:3c and 4b. Matthew reduced the citation to the themes of victory and hope among the nations.

12:21. The ministry's result was hope. Hope came especially in his name to the Gentiles. In the MT, it was the coastlands that hoped, but the point was the same. Here was where Matthew started to point to a turn in Jesus's ministry. The impact Jesus had would be felt among the nations. This was something that parts of the Hebrew Scripture and promise had anticipated. This was a part of God's program tied to the Servant. Gentile inclusion was not a new plan written up because Israel did not respond. Their inclusion was something promised as a part of the work of the planned kingdom's arrival.

So in this text we see (1) an explanation of the character of Jesus's ministry in reaching out to those in need while not seeking to draw undue attention or conflict in terms of intent (of course, the actions with outsiders brought some pushback and so controversy with opposition); (2) a pointer to Gentile inclusion; (3) evidence that the roots for all of this involved a work of the Spirit in the Anointed One (Turner 2008, 316–17). There would come a time when his presentation of himself would yield intense controversy (when he entered Jerusalem), but his ministry style was simply to do what God willed through him. How people reacted to that approach was something between God and them. Even in that setting, when the tension became high, Jesus did not resort to violence or self-defense. He simply declared who he was (Matt. 26:52–56, 62–63; 27:12–14; France 2007, 472).

THEOLOGICAL FOCUS

The exegetical idea (Jesus's response to Sabbath controversies, including acts of healing, showed him to be the promised Servant and Lord of the Sabbath, despite the objections of some) points to this theological insight: Jesus shows himself to be Lord of the Sabbath and the fulfillment of a long-awaited promise.

The unit focuses on the kind of ministry Jesus had by God's direction. He knew that God's will on the Sabbath did not prohibit needs such as eating a meal or performing a healing. Jesus's ministry and his Sabbath work portrayed living a life that reflected mercy and the doing of good, rescuing the one found in the pit. He did not act in a contentious way; he simply lived out the principles God had called him to reflect. Even though he had the authority to be Lord of the Sabbath, he lived as one who came to serve people, even down to those the society regarded as on the fringe. Genuine Sabbath-keeping meant being able to recognize the one who was Lord of the Sabbath, especially given how God was working through him. To do less was not only to reject Jesus, but to reject the God who had promised to send him and the Spirit who was working through him. Israel was leaving herself in a very serious place of covenantal violation. Even that potential rejection would not stop the plan, as God knew the Servant also would be a blessing to the nations.

We see the heightening of opposition to Jesus. A cause of this reaction was Jesus's unconventional handling of the Sabbath. He explained his rationale for his acts in valuing mercy over sacrifice and sensing a call to do good on the Sabbath. Above all, he claimed authority over the Sabbath as its Lord. This meant that what seemed unconventional was what should have been all along. Even though God vindicated Jesus by performing a healing through him on the Sabbath, the opposition escalated to the point of seeking to destroy Jesus. Here is a picture of hard-heartedness and spiritual blindness, good deeds going condemned, and people opposed to the act and its message even to the point of seeking the elimination of the one performing that good deed.

Yet this was still God's plan. He promised a Servant figure who would be Spirit-anointed and would conduct himself not with the exercise of overwhelming power, but by the mere presence and demonstration of mercy and service. Even though people fell short then and fall short now in their reaction, Scripture still speaks and points the way to Jesus as one who embodies God's plan and program. He is an example to be followed.

PREACHING AND TEACHING STRATEGIES

Exegetical and Theological Synthesis

The exegetical section describes Jesus's mastery over holy days, human traditions, and health issues. At all times, over all things, Jesus is supreme (Col. 1:15–20). This fits God's sovereign plan, which he patiently unfolded from the garden of Eden (Gen. 3:15) to Abram's call (Gen. 12:1–3) to the Davidic covenant (2 Sam. 7:8–14) to Isaiah's anointed Servant to the nations (Isa. 41:8–10; 42:6–7, 18–19; 44:1, 21; 45:4; 49:3, 5–7; 52:13–53:12). At the right time, God sent his Son (Gal. 4:4), who would fulfill many long-awaited promises (1 Peter 1:10–12). This commentary has repeatedly highlighted Matthew's use of prophetic fulfillment; however, here the stress is on God's timing.

Sadly, we find it difficult to deal with time. Some of us ignore or erase the past, resulting in "the dominant script of amnesia" (Brueggemann 2006, 9–12). Forgetfulness leads us to repeat old sins or doubt God's faithfulness. Others elevate the past, which leads to "nostalgia" (Peterson 1989, 117). Of course, the "good old days" were not good for everyone; nostalgia glosses over past inequalities and personal wounds. Our struggles with time include the times to come. Those who rarely consider the future can feel hopeless. Those who obsess about the future can feel anxious. Those who have tried to predict or control the future only to see it elude them can suffer despair.

The biblical corrective to our trouble with time is to understand the times (1 Chron. 12:32), number our days (Ps. 90:12), and redeem the moment (Eph. 5:16). This includes setting aside time for personal devotion (Matt. 6:1–18; Mark 1:35) and corporate worship (Acts 2:42–47; 1 Cor. 16:2; Heb. 10:25). However, we must guard against turning our spiritual practices into new restrictions (Col. 2:16–23). In Jesus's economy, every day and good deed can be used for his glory (1 Cor. 10:31; Col. 3:17).

Preaching Idea

Serving others matters more than saving time.

Contemporary Connections

What does it mean?

Serving others comprises many acts of kindness. We may serve others informally:

listening to a coworker's problems, helping a widow change the oil in her minivan, hanging drywall for a friend, offering to babysit for a single parent, or mowing a neighbor's lawn. We may serve others formally: volunteering with a tutoring program at the local elementary school, ushering at the community theater, mentoring a youth group student, or joining the greeting team at church. Service opportunities are endless.

More importantly, service is a way of life for Christians. Service was mission-critical for Jesus (Matt. 20:28; Mark 10:45); he deliberately embodied the role of Isaiah's Suffering Servant and implored his disciples to do likewise (Matt. 20:20–28). True servants do not post hours when they will be available to serve; they are at the mercy of others when needs arise. Servants get interrupted, distracted, and pulled aside to change diapers, run errands, take emergency calls, and troubleshoot computer problems. To serve is to lose time for the sake of others.

Is it true?

In God's economy, serving others is more important than saving time. As mentioned above, service is the way of Jesus. We were designed to serve God and others. We were not, however, called to enable others or be enslaved to them. Balance is needed.

Moreover, we are called to make the most of the time God has given to us. We do not redeem our time by stockpiling flex hours or vacation days. Nor do we redeem our time by working more, sleeping less, and multitasking. Sadly, all the time-saving devices and hacks have only made our lives more frenetic. In aiming to master time, we have lost our call to service. Serving others comes most naturally when we have established healthy rhythms of work and rest.

Now what?

This passage invites you to assess your relationship with time and your heart for service. First, you should take a careful look at your schedule. You should ask the following questions: *How do I rate my level of busyness? When do I feel rushed? When do I feel interrupted? When do I rest? Where am I guilty of overworking? Where am I most often wasting time? If I had an extra hour each day, what would I do with it? If I lost an hour each day, what would I have to give up?* After assessing your schedule, consider one change to make in the coming week.

Second, you should assess your heart for service. Review service opportunities that were available to you in recent weeks. Consider the following questions: *What formal and informal opportunities to serve arose? Which did I prefer and why? What compelled me to serve? What held me back from serving? How did I feel during and after serving? What needs to change in my heart to respond more gladly to serve others?* After your assessment, pray for God to provide opportunities to serve in the coming week.

Finally, if saving time is an idol, consider "wasting" a block of time in the coming week. Schedule an extended lunch, nap, or afternoon walk. Ride a bike to work or take a longer route home. Choose the checkout line at the grocery store with several other shoppers. Get lost in the woods. Practice Sabbath. As you meander, reflect on Jesus's way of service. Who knows, he may provide an informal opportunity for you to help someone along the way.

Creativity in Presentation

All our time-saving tools and techniques have not resulted in unhurried lives. If anything, our ability to save time has cost us time. You will be able to illustrate this in your sermon by presenting several of these tools and techniques and their failure to fulfill their promise.

The following examples can get you started:

Tool or Technique	Its Failure to Save Time
Smartphone	Instead of getting a quick response to a simple question, a notification leads you down a social media rabbit hole. Ten minutes later you emerge, forgetting your initial question.
Email	Instead of quick communication, you spend ten minutes trying to draft the perfectly worded message.
Air Travel	Instead of a two-hour flight to Florida, your departure gets delayed twice, rerouted, and your baggage is lost along the way.
Universal Remote Control	Instead of having one remote that easily controls five devices (TV, cable, speakers, DVD player, Xbox), you have one remote that is too complicated to control a single device before the game starts.
Talk-to-text	Instead of composing a text with your slow thumbs, you speak your text into your phone, which does a pathetic job translating, so you end up editing it and it takes twice as long to send.
Self-checkout	Instead of a quick checkout process, you need an attendant's help several times, but she is not available because she is helping three other customers in adjacent self-checkout lines.

One of the clearest ways our devices encourage us to save time is by showing us the quickest option when traveling. Choose a departure and destination, input them in Google Maps, and take a screenshot of the different options. (For example, there are three routes from Columbus, Ohio, to Sarasota, Florida. They range from sixteen hours and seven minutes to seventeen hours and seven minutes. Which would you take?)

The analog (and digital) clock is a recent innovation that revolutionized how we experience time. Whereas humans used to align their lives with sunlight and circadian rhythms, now we measure time by *ticks* and *blips*. While this has increased productivity in factories, punctuality in Amazon deliveries, and precision in travel, it has not resulted in human flourishing. In fact, while saving time we are losing our souls. The following research may compel your congregation to reconsider our idols of speed and efficiency:

- Americans are sleep deprived. We ignore the natural rhythms of our bodies and sun, so we can work, watch TV, and play games late into the night. Poor sleep negatively affects physical and mental health (Comer 2019, 31–32).
- Americans are busy. Our time-saving devices have made some work easier, resulting in more time for work or leisure. We tend to fill our extra time with extracurricular activities—sports, camping, or house projects (Comer 2019, 33).
- Americans are distracted. Our attention span has dwindled to eight seconds, eroded by the constant distractions and notifications on our phones. Most people spend more than three hours on their phone, touching their screen more than 2,500 times a day (Comer 2019, 37; Hari 2023, 20).
- Americans are deceived. Multitasking is a myth. Our brains cannot complete

two tasks at once. Rather, they switch back and forth between tasks, which reduces our ability to think deeply or extensively (Hari 2023, 37–44). Moreover, our time-saving devices have only added more responsibilities to our lives. For example, the advent of laundry machines means we wash our clothes more often (Honore 2004, 31).

- Americans suffer "time-sickness." This disease is existential. People fill their lives with activity that lacks meaning (Honore 2004, 33–34). The rush leaves people restless. Many feel something akin to an addict's crash after a high.
- Americans are out of balance. Technology provides "effortless power," granting a sense of accomplishment with minimal effort. According to Andy Crouch (2022, 40–59), these "superpowers" diminish our humanity: we think, move, and relate with others less than previous generations.

The emphasis on Sabbath in this text allows for reflection on Sabbath practice. In recent years, there has been a resurgence in teaching on Sabbath.

Books on Sabbath

Ruth Haley Barton, *Embracing Rhythms of Work and Rest* (2022)
Mark Buchanan, *The Rest of God* (2007)
John Mark Comer, *The Ruthless Elimination of Hurry* (2019)
A. J. Swoboda, *Subversive Sabbath* (2018)
Lauren Winner, *Mudhouse Sabbath* (2007)

Following in the footsteps of Eugene Peterson (2011, 218–22), my wife and I (Tim) have made a practice of "Sabbath walks." Every Friday we unplug from our devices, set aside our ministry responsibilities, and spend a day away from the hustle. Our Sabbath practice includes prayer, a long walk in the woods, tasty food, an episode or two of a favorite sitcom, pleasure reading, and a nap. This day of rest recharges us for the coming week where we seek to live as servants.

You may also consider the last two creative examples about "service over status" and "sacrificial service" described in the Preaching and Teaching Strategies of Matthew 20:17–28.

In the end, you want your sermon to communicate that Jesus shows himself to be Lord of the Sabbath and the fulfillment of a long-awaited promise—and that serving others matters more than saving time.

- Jesus restores the Sabbath for us (12:1–8).
- Jesus restores us for the Sabbath (12:9–14).
- Jesus faithfully serves us (12:15–21).

DISCUSSION QUESTIONS

1. How did Pharisaic traditions about Sabbath expand on Old Testament laws?
2. What do these two healing stories illustrate about Jesus "from the ground up"?
3. What do you make of the modern resurgence in Sabbath practices?
4. Which Sabbath practices have you found most helpful? Why?
5. Reread Isaiah 42:1–4. What are the specific ways in which Jesus serves?
6. How can you and your church grow as servants? Be specific.

Matthew 12:22–50

EXEGETICAL IDEA
In the face of choices about Jesus and the good, Jesus urged his audience to see that his presence pointed to the kingdom's arrival and doing God's will.

THEOLOGICAL FOCUS
Jesus defends the nature of activity coming from him as coming from above and warns of the serious consequences of rejection.

PREACHING IDEA
Pick Jesus's side when people are polarized.

PREACHING POINTERS
Opposition against Jesus continued to intensify. Religious teachers contested his words and deeds at every turn. They accused him of collusion with the devil. They requested signs to authenticate his identity. Even his family members betrayed disbelief in his messianic identity. Jesus was a polarizing figure. Nonetheless, he did not entertain their criticisms but responded with wisdom and prophetic rebuke. He came to reveal God's kingdom and redeem God's people. Matthew's sequence of stories stressed the gravity of rejecting Jesus. His words and deeds spoke for themselves. The demand for additional evidence or desire to remain neutral were subtle forms of denying him.

Polarization plagues our age. Partisanship has turned politics into a circus. Churches and denominations have divided over sexual ethics, theological disagreements, and musical styles. Many friends and families have experienced the loss of relationship following miscommunication or a difference of opinion. In an age of polarization, neutral ground vanishes and people on opposite sides of an issue become enemies. Jesus and his disciples were not strangers to such strife. Their strong stance for God provoked strong opposition. Those who stand for Jesus today feel similar stress. Thus, this sermon reminds us to pick Jesus's side when people are polarized.

A WARNING ABOUT NOT DOING GOD'S WILL (12:22–50)

LITERARY STRUCTURE AND THEMES (12:22–50)

This unit presents five scenes that continued to urge the proper response to Jesus because of who he was. The first engaged the question of whether Jesus cast out demons by the power of Beelzebul (Matt. 12:22–32). The scene ends with a warning that blasphemy against the Spirit would not be forgiven. This is the first of several remarks in this unit raising the issue of accountability to God for one's response to Jesus. Jesus's work pointed to the kingdom's arrival in God's power, a reality not to be bypassed.

The second scene made the point that the response revealed the heart, just as a good tree produced good fruit and a rotten tree produced bad fruit (Matt. 12:33–37). Jesus noted for a second time the accountability one would face on judgment day for the good and bad they have done. The remark served as commentary on the hard-hearted rejection of the previous scene, since the judgment of words was a rejection of what God was doing through Jesus.

The third scene was a controversy account that dealt with the issue of whether Jesus would give a specific sign to show who he was (Matt. 12:38–42). Jesus said no other sign was to be given other than that of Jonah, with his call to repent and his three days in the belly of the whale. Jesus made the point that one greater than Jonah and Solomon was present; therefore, the Ninevites and the Queen of the South will rise up and judge those who do not respond, yet a third note of accountability before God.

The fourth scene warned that when a person was cleansed of an unclean spirit and did nothing with the opportunity for a fresh start, then the demon would come back with seven more demons, and the new situation would be worse than the first (Matt. 12:43–45). Jesus warned it would be so for this evil generation. Here was the real danger of not responding to Jesus. One did not remain in a neutral position but fell back into a worse state.

The fifth scene of the unit had Jesus state that his family was made up of those who did the Father's will (Matt. 12:46–50). Implied was a call to respond and do his will.

The unit is about proper response to Jesus and the kingdom's arrival. There are serious consequences of rejection that Jesus highlighted. In effect Matthew was saying, "don't go there."

The narrative has several parallels. Matthew 12:22–24 is like Mark 3:22 and Luke 11:14–15, while 12:25–30 has Mark 3:23–27 and Luke 11:17–23 as parallels. Matthew 12:31–32 is echoed in Mark 3:28–29 and Luke 12:10. Matthew 12:33–35 is like Matthew 7:16–18 and Luke 6:43–45. The plethora of other parallels point to imagery Jesus used repeatedly, as these are genuine conceptual parallels, some set in the same and others in differing contexts. Matthew 12:38–39 is like Luke 11:16, 29, and Mark 8:11–12. Matthew 12:40–42 recalls Luke 11:30–32, while Matthew 12:43–45 is like Luke 11:24–26. Finally, Matthew 12:46–50 has Mark 3:31–35 and Luke 8:19–21 as parallels. The mix and reordering of the parallels point to a unit stitched together where the shared theme was more important than rendering things in chronological sequence.

The unit is a collection of a mixed variety of forms. The first scene is a very short miracle story and then a controversy account where the various reactions to the miracle make up the points. It's a reversal of a normal miracle account in that the reaction is the most developed point, unlike most miracle accounts. Usually the reaction is told briefly, if at all, and there is more detail about the miracle. This shows that the point is about how Jesus performed his miracles, making this an important miracle summary. The key points are Jesus's claim to bring the kingdom and the warning about blasphemy against God's Spirit. The second scene develops a proverb about a tree being known by its fruit and closes with a note of accountability for what we produce. The third scene is a developed pronouncement as Jesus refused to give any signs other than the one of Jonah. The unit ends with a note about accountability to God. The fourth unit tells the story of unclean spirits seeking a home as a metaphor for the danger of a lack of response. Those who refused Jesus were like those possessed by a host of evil spirits. By not seeking that which cleansed, they ended up unclean. The last scene is also a pronouncement on who Jesus's real family was. It was not a matter of biology, but a function of sharing in being responsive to the Father's will.

EXPOSITION (12:22–50)

This is a crucial section of Matthew's gospel as he recorded how rejection of Jesus intensified as the Servant-Messiah continued to heal people. Matthew also underscored that the responsibility for that choice lay with those who made the decision not to embrace what God was doing. There is a warning that when God acts to bring cleansing and that is not heeded, the result would be worse than where one started. Jesus also described his family as those who do God's will. This combination of invitation and warning reflected how the new community brought its message about the coming kingdom. Tracing how the separation occurred and the accountability it produced was one of Matthew's core goals in his gospel.

In the face of choices about Jesus and the good, Jesus urged his audience to see that his presence pointed to the kingdom's arrival and doing God's will.

12:22. In an exceptionally brief miracle account, the entire healing was told in two simple moves. A blind, dumb, and demon-possessed man appeared before Jesus and Matthew simply notes that Jesus healed him so that the man could speak and see. What normally is told with detail over several verses is here reduced to a mere description. The emphasis in the account focuses on the reactions. Demon possession has been in a few earlier Matthean texts (Matt. 4:24; 8:16; 9:32) and also appears again later (Matt. 15:21–28; 17:14–20). Healing the blind is also a common Matthean scene (Matt. 9:27–31; 15:30–31; 20:30–34; 21:14–15).

12:23. The first reaction came from the crowd. They asked if this "might be" the Son of David. The question, asked with μήτι, assumes a negative answer, so it was presented with hesitation. That he could not really occupy this role was the force of their statement. Still, the fact it was even raised shows a potential openness that would contrast with the Pharisees' far more negative reaction. It might seem odd that David was tied to healing, since he only performed one miracle (1 Sam. 16:14–23—an exorcism). However, Solomon, as David's son, had a reputation as a miracle worker and so this idea seems to have become tied to the hope of the Davidic son to come (Duling 1975 and 1978; see earlier discussion in Matt. 9:27).

12:24. The Pharisees had a decidedly different view. They did not deny that Jesus was doing unusual works. They simply attributed that power to Beelzebul, the ruler of the demons (this figure had various names: 1 En. 10:4—Azaz'el; Jub. 48:15—Mastema; 1QM 17:5–6—prince of demons; Apoc. Ab. 13:6–7—Azazel; T. Levi 18:12—Beliar; T. Dan 5:6—Satan; see earlier discussions on Matt. 9:34 and 10:25). The claim was that a malevolent power was at work, even though the outcome was a good one. The hostility was shown in not even naming Jesus, simply calling him "this one" (οὗτος). The remark was a reply to the crowd's opinion as the leaders were responding to what "they" had said. The negative reaction here had been building for several chapters in the gospel (since Matt. 9:32–34). Jesus's warnings had gone nowhere. The view probably meant the Pharisees saw Jesus leading Israel astray, as Deuteronomy 13:1–5 discusses. The text from Deuteronomy points to a false prophet and is alluded to in *m. Sanh.* 7:4 as the tradition considered as to what made someone subject to stoning (France 2007, 475). The charge lived on into the second century (see Justin Martyr, *Dial.* 69). The account reflected an authentic dispute as the church was unlikely to invent such a charge, and the Jewish tradition afterward seems to show that this line of thinking went back to an early Jewish response (Keener 2009, 361–62). Ironically, it acknowledged Jesus was doing unusual things and did not deny those things were taking place.

Some New Testament and Jewish Names for Satan (Jewish texts noted with *)

*Mastema
Prince of the Demons
Beelzebul
The Devil
Satan
The Tempter
*Azazel/Azaz'el
*Beliar

12:25–27. Jesus's recognition about the Pharisees' view ("when Jesus realized what they were thinking ") led into a full-orbed response (Matt. 9:4; Luke 11:17). The first part of the response raised a series of questions before making an important observation.

The first set of questions was designed to reveal a fallacy in making the claim that Jesus did his work through Beelzebul. It was that a kingdom, city, or house that worked against itself could not stand. He stated the point three ways to drive it home and worked from the largest kind of collective to the most basic social level. Satan was not in the business of exorcisms; he was in the business of taking possession of people. He had a kingdom he was attempting to sustain, and this kind of internal civil war was not the way to do it (4Q286 10 ii.1–13; 4Qamrambar fragment 2; T. Dan 6:1–4; Davies and Allison 1991, 336).

A second question asked: If Jesus procured an exorcism by malevolent power, then how did their sons perform exorcisms? The reference to "your" sons may look at the Pharisees' sons in particular or to Jewish sons in general (1 Sam. 16:14–23; Tob. 8:1–3; 1QapGen ar 20.29; Mark 9:38; Acts 19:13–14). Did they make the same attribution for them when *they* performed exorcisms? Where was the consistency in that response?

This remark has been understood in one of two ways (Nolland 2005, 499). One view is that the reference was to Jewish exorcists, and the point was the hypocrisy of accepting one kind of exorcism from them but not the ones that Jesus performed. In that case the concluding statement was that these exorcists would be judges of those who reject Jesus. The remark is rhetorical more than literal, probably seeing the exorcists as witnesses against them at the judgment as it is not clear how other Jewish exorcists could be judges in the end unless they had become believers. This is the most common reading, but the reference to these exorcists' judging others is problematic unless it was mere rhetoric. The other view sees the exorcists specifically as Jesus's disciples who as Jews also did exorcisms. Then the point is that the evidence that God was at work went beyond him alone. In this case, the remark about these exorcists being judges of those who reject Jesus was a proclamation of something to come that underscored accountability to God. That is a theme repeated multiple times in this unit. Though not as common, this reading seems quite likely. The first-class conditions of verses 26–28 simply present the various options about Jesus side by side in equal terms.

12:28. Jesus now presented the alternative that he was contending for as true. He followed it with an illustration in verse 29 and then a summary claim in verse 30. Its authenticity has been generally accepted (Davies and Allison 1991, 339; Dunn 1975, 47–49).

A truly key saying followed the statement about judges. If Jesus cast out demons by the Spirit of God, then the kingdom has overtaken them (Luke 11:20). Luke has the casting-out done by the finger of God. Exodus 8:19 is the echo for Luke's text. What Jesus did was like the power of the plagues that delivered Israel. Matthew's rendering personified Luke's anthropomorphism of "finger," identifying the source of the power as the Spirit. It is an interesting difference because Luke normally did not hesitate to mention God's Spirit. In both versions, Jesus was focusing on the fact that it was he who cast out the demons by the Spirit and brought the kingdom of God. Note how Jesus said "if *I* cast out demons" here. In the previous verse, Jesus was simply noting that exorcisms were something the Jewish leaders normally accepted as coming from God. This remark in verse 28 made a key observation and upped the ante. The allusion here was likely to the scope of Jesus's activity against Satan (France 2007, 480). So Jesus's reply was much like the one to John the Baptist in Matthew 11:4–5, and also was suggested by the citation of Isaiah 42:1 in Matthew 12:18, which in turn looked back to Matthew 3:16.

The key term here is ἔφθασεν, which as an aorist looks at something that has taken place (Kümmel 1957, 105–9). Everything in this context was saying to read the exorcisms as the demonstration of what God had done and is doing through Jesus. There was no idea pointing to the future here (Nolland 2005, 501). Jesus declared the kingdom's arrival with his work. The verb φθάνω means "to come upon" or "arrive" (BDAG s.v. "φθάνω" 2, 1053). The presence of God's victorious power as seen in these healings meant that God's rule had shown itself. Matthew used "kingdom of God" here, but there was no distinction for him between the kingdom of God and the kingdom of heaven (Turner 2008, 37–39). It was simply two ways to refer to the same thing. The kingdom of Satan almost demanded a counter-reference to the kingdom of God to make the parallelism. Where earlier texts spoke of the kingdom's approach (Matt. 3:2; 4:17; 10:7), the signs of Jesus overtaking Satan were evidence of its breaking in, an inauguration of its presence, and a vindication of what Jesus represented. This process of obtaining victory over evil will continue until the victory becomes complete and peace is totally established at the completion of all the kingdom is. This is the beginning of a long journey that culminates in what Jesus has yet to do when he returns.

12:29. The illustration or short parable was of someone overtaking another's house and plundering his goods. The house pictured Satan and his presence in the world. He is the strong man who is bound by one stronger, so his house can be defeated. The illustration then reinforced the idea that Jesus's exorcisms were an act against Satan, overturning what the devil was doing versus being an act in association with the devil. This version of the image is like Mark 3:27 and the version in the Gospel of Thomas 35. Luke 11:21–22 has slightly distinct imagery of overcoming a palace. The core point is the same. This saying is also seen as authentic by many because usually the image of victory in the church was placed at the cross or at the end, so if the church had created the saying that would more likely have been the reference point for victory (Davies and Allison 1991, 342). The image of overtaking a house through strength appears here and there (Isa. 49:24–25; Pss. Sol. 5:3–4). The picture of binding is something Jewish texts discuss in relationship to what God does with malevolent figures (1 En. 10:4; 11–13; 13:1; 69:28; T. Levi 18:12). The theme of the binding and victory's timing had already–not yet dimensions to it, as did the theme of the kingdom (already—see John 12:31; 16:11; Acts 26:18; Eph. 2:1–6; Col. 1:13; not yet—Rev. 20–22; Keener 2009, 365; Turner 2008, 322). Binding in the present was not an absolute image claiming Satan had no power but was an eschatological image saying Satan could no longer stop what was in the process of coming (Nolland 2005, 502). This was the beginning of Jesus's release of the captives (Luke 4:18). The picture of total victory over Satan is in Jewish texts as well (1 En. 10:4–7; 54:4–6; T. Mos. 10:1; T. Zeb. 9:8b).

Jewish Texts Where God Binds or Has Victory over Satan

1 Enoch 10:4: "And secondly the Lord said to Raphael, 'Bind Azaz'el hand and foot (and) throw him into the darkness!'"

Testament of Levi 18:12: "And Beliar shall be bound by him. And he shall grant to his children the authority to trample on wicked spirits."

Testament of Moses 10:1: "Then his kingdom will appear throughout his whole creation. Then the devil will have an end. Yea, sorrow will be led away with him."

Testament of Zebulun 9:8b: "He will liberate every captive of the sons of men from Beliar, and every spirit of error will be trampled down."

12:30. The principle was that anyone who was not with Jesus was against him (Luke 11:23). This was because anyone who did not align with Jesus did not share in the important cause Jesus represented. Another way to say it was that the ones who did not gather with Jesus scattered. They did not contribute to bringing people closer to the rule of God that Jesus's ministry reflected. The picture was either of gathering sheep (Matt. 25:32; 40:11; gather and scatter—Ezek. 34:13, 21; Zech. 13:7–9) because of scattered sheep or sheep without a shepherd (Matt. 26:31; Isa. 13:14; Ezek. 34:5). Jesus is thinking of people gained for God, or of the gathering for harvest (Matt. 3:12; 13:28–30; cf. Job 39:12) and so of salvation. Most likely the image was one of gathering sheep. That image spoke about the relational mission Jesus had to procure a community for God, a family where his children responded positively to his rule. However, either meaning fits the context. There was no such thing as a neutral position when it came to Jesus and the kingdom. There was no fence one could sit on to simply watch what he was doing. His claims were too comprehensive; they force a decision.

12:31–32. Jesus now turned to discuss the implications of the Pharisees' judgment about him. He contrasted what was said about forgiveness of all sin and blasphemy against the Son of Man with blasphemy against the Holy Spirit. The first was forgivable, while the second was not. By mentioning the Spirit twice, Jesus focused on the consequences of misreading what God was doing by the power of the Spirit working through Jesus. These words were warnings about what lay ahead if one did not embrace what God was accomplishing through Jesus. The outcome of rejection or indifference was judgment.

Every sin a person committed could find forgiveness except for blaspheming the Spirit (Luke 12:10; *Did.* 11:7). Gospel of Thomas 44 has a variation that allowed forgiveness of blasphemy against the Father and the Son but not the Spirit. This difference in the Thomas saying went too far by including God as one spoken against, as that would clearly be blasphemous. The reaction in Matthew is more focused, being against what was being said about Jesus, with God's activity in him specifically as the point.

Blasphemy was about slander against God or misusing his name (Lev. 24:16; Bock 1998) or not giving someone due honor. What was in view here was the rejection of what God was doing through Jesus as a set decision, not a mere one-time remark as in Peter's denials. When the Pharisees claimed Jesus was casting out demons by Beelzebul's power, they were decisively denying what God was doing through Jesus, who in turn was working by the Spirit. They failed to see what God was testifying to by the Spirit through these actions. A word against the Son of Man is a remark made in a moment or perhaps over a period of time as Peter's denials were (Morris 1992, 318), but a word against the Spirit was a decision made that was not reversed, such as the way the Pharisees were reacting to Jesus's miracles. It was a mind closed to what the Spirit was doing. The distinction between a word against the Son of Man and blasphemy against the Spirit was one of duration. To speak against the Son of Man involved a remark, while the other reflected a set decision. In this case, it was the decision that not only was the Spirit not at work, but that Satan was (France 2007, 482). Blomberg calls it "the unrelenting rejection of his [Jesus's] advances" (Blomberg 1992, 204). The Pharisees could not have been more incorrect, and Jesus could not have been more emphatic about the consequences. Not only was this an unforgiveable sin but it was so for all time, as that absence of forgiveness applied to both this age and the one to come. It was seen as a "high-handed" sin that could not be forgiven (Num. 15:30–31; Deut. 29:19–20; Jub. 15:34; CD 8.8). Wilkins (2004, 448–49) notes it was the testimony of the Spirit that was at work in the gospel message (John 16:8). It was a sin that only unbelievers commit when they refuse to believe.

This was yet another way to show how important Jesus is. No other decision about creation and reality was more important. Forgiveness could be found for everything except for refusing the way God wished us to acknowledge our need for forgiveness. To say God need not forgive me on his terms was to refuse forgiveness. This was not a post-conversion sin because the context was applying the text to people who had never embraced what Jesus did. It was the failure to respond at all that was in view.

12:33. The principle that was at work in this judgment about Jesus was about the heart. Jesus compared the heart to a tree and its fruit (Matt. 7:17; Luke 6:43). A good tree had good fruit, while a rotten tree had bad fruit. The term σαπρός means "rotten" or "spoiled" and refers here to false speech (BDAG s.v. "σαπρός" 1bα, 913). The implied call came in a rhetorical statement to make the tree a good one by its having good fruit. In this context, the point was to make the proper judgment about what God was doing and come to the right decision about it. What the tree was emerged as the tree produced its fruit (Matt. 7:20; Luke 6:44; Ignatius, *Eph.* 14:2). Where the person was spiritually surfaced by how they responded to what God was doing. The words showed where the heart was, as the context was about speech and judgment concerning the person and work of Jesus. Jesus's good deeds showed his roots, but the judgment that Jesus's good activity was demonic reflected a rotten judgment from a flawed core (Osborne 2010, 478).

12:34–35. Jesus directly challenged the Pharisees' conclusion about him. He called them a brood of vipers, as John had done (Matt. 3:7; also 23:33). Jesus's critique was often harshest on those who should have known better. Then he asked how they could speak good, being evil. Since one spoke from what the heart was, they spoke evil (Sir. 27:6). What was said reflected the heart (Matt. 15:18; Luke 6:45; James 3:12). For the good person spoke good things out of a good heart, just as the evil person spoke evil things from an evil heart. What Jesus called the "treasury" was the storehouse of the heart (Matt. 6:21; Gospel of Thomas 45).

Fruit and Speech

Sirach 27:6: "Its fruit discloses the cultivation of a tree; so a person's speech discloses the cultivation of his mind."

12:36–37. One day there will be accountability for what was said. Jesus noted that every idle word would be judged in the accounting that comes on the day of judgment (Matt. 15:11; Luke 19:22). The key term here is ἀποδίδωμι, which means "to pay back" and looks to an accounting that reckoned what one had done (BDAG s.v. "ἀποδίδωμι" 2c, 109–10). That accounting extended down to every "idle" or "empty" word (BDAG s.v. "ἀργός" 3, 128). The point was not that what was said is insignificant, but that it was valueless because it was not true (France 2007, 486). One's word would either be justified or condemned at that judgment (1 En. 100:9; Hagner 1993, 350; Keener 2009, 366). Justification looked to vindication and being accepted, while condemnation looked to rejection. It is an example of contrastive parallelism that is common in Matthew. Jesus referred to the judgment day regularly in Matthew (Matt. 10:15; 11:22, 24; 12:41–42).

12:38. The scribes and Pharisees asked Jesus for a sign (Matt. 16:1–4; John 6:30). Here scribes and Pharisees act together for the first time in Matthew (Konradt 2020, 197). The opposition is coalescing. This was an odd question in a way, since Jesus was doing all kinds of activity that had a clear transcendent quality to it. Apparently, the request involved some type of specific request, perhaps a heavenly portent of some kind as Matthew 16:1–4 suggests. The sign was designed to authenticate what Jesus was doing, as if authentication was currently lacking. Pharaoh had done the same with Moses (Exod. 7:9). In fact, the request was a demand to operate on their terms that recalls the parable of the brats (Matt. 11:16–19).

12:39–40. Jesus's reply had several elements. There was a rebuke, the example of Jonah, and the lesson of the Queen of the South (Luke 11:29–32).

Jesus made it clear that only an evil and adulterous generation asked for a sign. The language was about the wilderness generation (Deut. 32:5, 20). In the background likely was the fact that divine power was already evident. To ask for a specific sign was an affront to what already had been shown. It was evidence of desiring a response on their own terms, much as Jesus's parable in Matthew 11:16–19 indicated.

The only sign to be given was the sign of Jonah. The lesson of the prophet should have taught them. This sign had two elements: Jonah's three days and nights in the belly of the whale and his preaching to Gentiles. The text cited Jonah 2:1 LXX (Jonah 1:17) to make the point about Jonah. The term Matthew uses refers to a "sea monster" (BDAG s.v. "κῆτος" 544). Jesus noted first that the Son of Man would be in the heart of the earth three days and nights. Jesus began to point to his death and vindication by God as the key sign of who he was, since his time in the heart of the earth was limited (with Blomberg 1992, 206; contra Nolland 2005, 511, who does not see a reference to resurrection here but only to Jesus as a preacher of judgment). The remark was like the "lifted up" sayings in John (Osborne 2010, 486; John 3:14; 8:28; 12:32). This was another allusion to Jesus's coming death in Matthew (earlier Matt. 9:15).

The reference to three day and three nights was to be counted inclusively, so any part of the day or night counted as the whole of both (Gundry 1982, 244; Keener 2009, 367 n. 86; Gen. 42:17–18; 1 Sam. 30:12–13; 1 Kings 20:29; Esther 4:16; 5:1). The point about counting needs to be made as some challenge how this time frame could cover from Friday to Sunday when nights are noted and given the saying applied to Jesus's death and resurrection. Keener also notes the Ninevites never saw the sign Jonah experienced, so part of the point could be they repented without seeing a sign, while those currently seeking a sign were missing all Jesus was doing.

12:41–42. Jesus now declared that the judgment would involve condemnation by the Ninevites (Jonah 3:2–5) and the Queen of the South (1 Kings 10:1–13; 2 Chron. 9:1–12; Josephus, *A.J.* 8.165–73), for they responded to God's initiatives, while these Jewish leaders have not. Luke 11:31–32 reverses the order of these two examples. The Ninevites and the Queen would rise up at the judgment and condemn them because these two examples knew better than to not respond.

This saying is like the earlier warning to the Galilean cities in Matthew 11:20–24, where Tyre, Sidon, Sodom, and Gomorrah were said to experience less judgment because of the greatness of what was now being rejected, something these cities would have been open to had it come in their time (Osborne 2010, 486). A key here was that Gentiles were responsive to that which Jewish leaders were not. In the case of Nineveh and the Queen of the South, we had two Gentile experiences where responses took place, so they would serve as witnesses against those being judged. The Queen of the South was the Queen of Sheba in southwest Arabia, in what is Yemen today. This kind of cross-ethnic rebuke from within the Jewish circle also occurred later in Judaism, as in *Mekilta* on Exodus 12:1 (Pisha 1:81–82) also appeals to the example of Jonah (Davies and Allison 1991, 358; Keener 2009, 368).

Jesus noted that a reason for this judgment was that one greater than Jonah and greater than Solomon was here. This was like Jesus's remark about being greater than the temple in Matthew 12:6, except here the message's wisdom is in view. Jesus was referring to himself and the time of kingdom fulfillment as the greater things, including the power to overcome spiritual forces. In the flow of Matthew, Jesus had argued that he was greater than the temple, greater than a prophet (Jonah), and greater than a wise king (Solomon; France 2007, 493). Solomon's wisdom included power over spirits in Judaism (Josephus, *A.J.* 8.44–48; Wis. 7:7, 17–22; much of the T. Sol.). This may well have been in view here given the context of confrontation with spiritual forces (Perkins 1998). Jesus's remarks reminded one yet again of accountability before God because of who Jesus was and is.

Solomon's Power, Including over Spirits
(see also chart on Matt. 9:28 for Josephus, *A.J.* 8)

Wisdom 7:7, 17–22: "Therefore I prayed, and understanding was given me; I called on God, and the spirit of wisdom came to me. . . . For it is he who gave me unerring knowledge of what exists, to know the structure of the world and the activity of the elements; the beginning and end and middle of times, the alternations of the solstices and the changes of the seasons, the cycles of the year and the constellations of the stars, the natures of animals and the tempers of wild animals, the powers of spirits and the thoughts of human beings, the varieties of plants and the virtues of roots; I learned both what is secret and what is manifest, for wisdom, the fashioner of all things, taught me."

12:43–45. Jesus now warned with a picture of what would happen when an opportunity for cleansing came from the extraction of an unclean spirit, and nothing was done to stay clean afterward (Luke 11:24–26).

The image also pictured the consequences from a lack of response. Indifference as well as rejection were in view. The image opened with the unclean spirit looking for a waterless place to reside. Demons were often associated with dry places like the desert (Tob. 8:3; 1 En. 10:4). The need for spirits to be outside the water was evident in the healing in Matthew 8:28–34. Finding none, the spirit decided to return to the house he left. That there existed a belief that a demon could return to indwell is something Mark 9:25 also indicates (Josephus, *A.J.* 8.47). After finding it unoccupied, the demon took seven other spirits and now the home had eight spirits dwelling within as opposed to the one that started out there. Seven was a number pointing to completeness. The demon returned to stay with all of his helpers (Wilkins 2004, 453). Do the additional demons represent the effect of the opponents and their false rejection of Jesus that now resides in those who will not respond, solidifying one's rejection (so Konradt 2020, 199)? Apparently if nothing filled the void, then the demons could return. They settled in for a long stay as κατοικέω ("to dwell/reside") is a more intensive way to speak of living somewhere and pointed to a long stay (BDAG s.v. "κατοικέω" 1b, 534).

The consequences were tragic because of the lost opportunity. The result was even dire. There was no such thing as neutrality when it came to Jesus (Morris 1992, 328). It was dangerous to be spiritually empty. Something always would fill such a void. The house would not remain empty or neutral for long.

Jesus concluded that the last state was worse than the first and compared that result to where this evil generation was headed. When people kept God distant, the presence of evil lurked, ready to strike. In an irony, Jesus reversed the charge that he cast out demons by Beelzebul's power and said that the danger of rejecting him left one in the grip of the demons (Matt. 12:22–24; Keener 2009, 369). The picture's point was that an opportunity to keep the house clean existed after a past where the need for cleansing was evident. It may be that what was in view here was responding to Jesus and gaining access to God's Spirit, which in effect blocked the possibility of repossession. "Ownership by the devil must be replaced with ownership by Christ" (Blomberg 1992, 207). By failing to respond to that opportunity, things got worse. Evil would keep its grip on the nation that failed to embrace God's way out.

This final remark about it being so for the evil generation has no parallel. Matthew intensified the challenge and warning by pointing to this result should things not change. A generation that rejected Jesus let themselves open to more false teaching, descended deeper into being misdirected, and showed themselves to be evil.

12:46–48. Jesus was speaking when his mother and brothers approached (Mark 3:31–32a; Luke 8:19–20). When he became aware of this, he asked who his mother and brothers were. There is a textual issue that raises a fair question about whether verse 47 was originally in Matthew as testified to in many of the manuscripts as a whole. The earliest manuscripts, including original א and B, lack it, so it may not be original to Matthew. The verse only moved the event along by making a note that "your mother and brothers are outside wishing to speak with you." In the end, deciding on exclusion or inclusion does not alter the passage in any significant way.

The opening verse has Jesus addressing the crowds. The controversies with the leaders have passed. Jesus used the opportunity of his family's visit to make a point about response to God. He asked them to consider who his family was. It may be significant that other texts showed that not all of Jesus's family had embraced his mission (Mark 3:21 possibly; John 7:5), but Matthew gave no motive for the visit, unlike the context in Mark where the family had some concerns about the hostile reactions to his claims (Mark 3:21). It is hard to make much of this difference since Matthew so often abbreviated his telling of events. Matthew was simply focused on the teaching about doing God's will.

12:49–50. Jesus declared his family to be those who did the will of his Father (Mark 3:34–35; Luke 8:21; 2 Clem. 9:11). Gospel of

Thomas 99 has an addition about entering the kingdom. Jesus signaled the priority of his mission in this remark. He also made it clear that responding to him was paramount. The privilege that resulted was that God formed a new family around the one God sent to bring the kingdom. The more important family for Jesus was the one that connected to God. The additional mention of "sister" also showed that women were consciously included, a key point to make in an ancient world where women often did not count as fully independent beings (France 2007, 498; Hagner 1993, 360; Aristotle, *Pol.* I.V.1–2—discussing husband and wife). This view of God's priority does have some Old Testament precedent as the remarks of Levi in Deuteronomy 33:9 suggest with the acknowledgment of keeping covenant being greater than family in the face of events tied to the golden calf. The Essenes at Qumran and Josephus also took this view about the priority of the relationship with God and his people (1QS 1–9; Josephus, *B.J.* 2.120–58; Davies and Allison 1991, 364). The remark is very much like Matthew 7:21; 8:21–22; and 10:37. Keener (2009, 369) argues against the scene being invented by the church or Matthew since the remark implied a distance from James and even his mother, who was treated positively in Matthew 1:18–25.

THEOLOGICAL FOCUS

The exegetical idea (in the face of choices about Jesus and the good, Jesus urged his audience to see that his presence pointed to the kingdom's arrival and doing God's will) points to this theological focus: Jesus defends the nature of activity coming from him as coming from above and warns of the serious consequences of rejection.

Jesus's ministry led to a choice, either to becoming a member of Jesus's family in recognition that he brought the kingdom or to rejecting that offer based on an absence of logic and ignoring signs that he already evidenced in his ministry.

The focus of the unit points to the two options that one has when it comes to Jesus. The scenes build around a classical literary contrast. One can opt for rejecting Jesus, as the leadership had. However, that fits no logic for what Jesus was doing, and, if that judgment is wrong, then one is accountable for denying the core work Jesus was doing for God's program. It is to commit blasphemy of the Spirit to reject what the Spirit was showing God was doing. The other option is to respond to Jesus as the one God has sent. This shows a good and responsive heart. It means to have a place in the family Jesus forms. Some may think there is a third possibility, to remain neutral, but that is another position of non-reception and leaves one still exposed to being overtaken by evil. Jesus is either from above or from below. The one option that does not exist is that he is merely a good teacher, because that is not a choice he permits.

Since Matthew focuses on the digging in of opposition, the unit also shows how stubborn rejection of Jesus is. It makes no sense and yet it continues. It has great risk, and yet it remains. Even after warnings and repeated acts, the opposition remains. It is why spiritual opposition to Jesus is portrayed as being blind or dull-hearted.

Matthew was developing in this passage the rising opposition to Jesus. Despite his acts of compassion and power, many had decided that Jesus's activity was rooted in the power of Beelzebul. Jesus's response was that this would be Satan fighting against himself. A kingdom operating that way could not stand and made no sense. The alternative was that it was by the Spirit of God that Jesus acted, showing the arrival of God's kingdom. The dispute was such that Matthew was declaring what the miracles as a group showed: Jesus acted by God's power and presence.

This means that how people respond to Jesus shows the condition of the heart and that there is accountability for rejecting Jesus, whether one recognizes that reality or not. A good tree has a good heart and responds to what God is doing. A good heart sees that one greater than Jonah or Solomon is present. A good heart need not ask for a sign to determine what Jesus is doing, but sees God is in Jesus's healings. There is no neutral position to take when it comes to Jesus. The kingdom's importance forces a choice. To be neutral is to leave oneself exposed to evil's grip. Jesus offered such arguments to challenge the decision the Pharisees had made. Matthew's readers, both then and now, are reassured about Jesus and the role he has. It is an invitation to remain loyal. The member of the family tied to Jesus is the one who does the Father's will and embraces him through Jesus.

PREACHING AND TEACHING STRATEGIES

Exegetical and Theological Synthesis

The exegetical section highlights the controversy that surrounds Jesus. As Matthew's gospel progresses, the controversy swells. Jesus is unflappable in the face of controversy, but the Pharisees, disciples, family members, and crowds have different responses.

Social tensions offer a testing ground for the strength of our faith and theology. It is easy to profess faith when no one presses us for it. However, as we begin to experience criticism, isolation, family conflict, or persecution, the depth of our faith becomes clear. People-pleasers wither; God-fearers show resiliency.

Sadly, following his arrest, Jesus's disciples proved timid. Most of them fled; Peter denied knowing Jesus. Faith is not without its moments of weakness. However, faith that cannot withstand social tensions tacitly rejects Jesus. He clearly warned his disciples that they must endure opposition, accusation, and persecution (Matt. 5:10–12; 10:16–39). Jesus has always been a polarizing figure. His followers are guilty by association. Fortunately, our troubles will end since he has overcome the world (John 16:33).

Preaching Idea

Pick Jesus's side when people are polarized.

Contemporary Connections

What does it mean?

First, we should clarify the type of polarization we are talking about. We are not talking about matters of personal preference. Jesus does not have a favorite sports team, fast-food restaurant, or retirement locale. He does not side with Pepsi over Coke or Hulu over Netflix. We understand this principle intuitively when it comes to personal preference. Choosing sides in personal preference is more playful than polarizing.

Similarly, we are not talking about personal convictions. This principle is less intuitive because we tend to baptize our convictions. For example, we associate Jesus with our political party, brand of Christianity, and expressions of piety. Personal convictions become polarizing when we force them on others. We should be humble enough to admit that faithful Christians vote for various political parties, constitute many denominations, and experience a range of spiritual gifts and practices. There is no "Jesus" party, "Jesus" church, or "Jesus" spirituality. Fighting about personal convictions polarizes people who should be united in Christ.

To pick Jesus's side is to uphold Jesus's values and emulate Jesus's virtues. We choose to speak with Christlike charity in heated conversations. We choose to show Christlike resolve when falsely accused. We choose the way of service rather than self-promotion, submission rather than autonomy, accountability rather than privacy. Siding with Jesus is a commitment to the blessed life he embodied as God's anointed servant.

Is it true?

We certainly want to pick Jesus's side when people are polarized. However, two cautions are worth stating. First, we must beware of "weaponizing our beliefs" (Muehlhoff and Langer

2020, 66–67) against other believers. According to Muehlhoff and Langer, a conviction turns lethal when it becomes "too powerful" and is applied too broadly. For example, convictions about divorce and remarriage, Sabbath practice, musical styles, and gender roles can get "amplified" to the category of core doctrine. Some might claim "Jesus had female disciples; he would have no qualms about a female pastor." Others would say, "Jesus's inner circle was exclusively male; he viewed men as the primary leaders." Both parties put their words in Jesus's mouth but refuse to hear Jesus in their opponents' arguments. Sadly, such disagreements often become divisive in the church.

Second, we must guard against an "us versus them" mentality toward unbelievers. Although Jesus's own teaching acknowledged the opposition believers will have in the world (Matt. 5:10–12; 10:16–39; John 15:18–25; 16:33), he persisted in love for the lost (Matt. 9:13; 20:28; Mark 10:35; Luke 19:10; John 3:16). More remarkably, Jesus exhorted his followers to love their enemies (Matt. 5:43–47). Such an admonition subverts the "us versus them" mentality that has pervaded our polarized culture, especially given that "us" was once "them" before God redirected us by his grace. If we appreciate where we came from and how God moved us, we will care for people who need the grace we have received.

Now what?

The passage invites us to commit to Jesus, clarify our convictions, and show charity toward our opponents. First, we must acknowledge that commitment to Jesus is not a one-time decision. We reconfirm our commitment to Jesus every day by walking in his footsteps. With every major decision or crisis, our commitment solidifies or softens based upon our levels of trust and obedience. As commitment grows, we often experience greater appreciation for Jesus and our place in his family.

Second, we must clarify our convictions to guard against division in the church. Jesus wanted a united church (John 17), and Paul echoed this desire (Eph. 4:1–8; Phil. 1:27–2:5; Col. 3:12–14). Of course, unity does not mean every person in the church thinks exactly the same about every theological or practical topic. Rather, the goal is to hold core doctrines (e.g., Jesus is God) firmly while allowing for healthy disagreement in personal convictions (e.g., playing *Dungeons & Dragons* is a sin). This requires room in the church for people to articulate their convictions without weaponizing them.

Finally, we must show charity toward our opponents. Whether we face polarization within the church or from those outside, charity begins with granting dignity to those who disagree with us. We must resist the tendency to villainize others; they are image-bearers, not enemies. Moreover, we should practice active listening. Asking clarifying questions may help us learn something about the other person and their beliefs. And listening may grant us an opportunity to challenge their thinking and share our convictions. Even if a charitable interchange does not change our opponents' minds, it may affect their hearts or plant a seed that will grow later. Love is the most winsome apologetic.

Creativity in Presentation

We do not need to look far to illustrate how polarization has plagued life in the West. Certain topics quickly divide people into camps. To keep things light for your church, you can let them know you are going to rearrange seating at the beginning of the sermon. Much like we divide wedding guests into two sides to represent the bride and groom, announce you will have two sections. However, be clear you have not decided if you wanted to divide into the following groups:

- Republicans on the right; Democrats on the left

- Android users on the right; Apple users on the left
- Hunters on the right; gatherers on the left
- Hymn lovers on the right; contemporary worship lovers on the left
- Coke drinkers on the right; Pepsi drinkers on the left
- Uber riders on the right; Lyft riders on the left
- Giants fans on the right; Eagles fans on the left (or whatever teams would apply)

You might note this will allow you to address these distinct groups in light of their distinct needs. You can turn to each distinct group as you address them specifically! If you get some laughter, you might let them know this exercise would quickly become more heated if you divided along different lines, such as: gay-affirming versus traditional marriage; egalitarians versus complementarians; theistic evolutionist, versus young-earth creationists. At the end of this exercise, assure your congregation you will retain open seating because you do not want to divide God's household.

A childhood memory many of us remember is dividing into teams for gym class, recess, or camp. Two captains would take turns selecting teammates. They would typically choose players by their skill or popularity level. The captains picked with hopes of winning. This familiar scenario can serve as an analogy to contests in everyday life. If we are the captain, we always want Jesus on our side. Pick him first. If Jesus is the captain, we wave our hands in the air, jump up and down, and shout "Pick me! Pick me!" We always want to be on his side.

For disturbing examples of political polarization in modern US politics, consider David French's book *Divided We Fall* (2020). [1]French maps the geographic division of political thought (blue on the coasts and urban centers; red in the midwestern and southern states) and describes the shrinking "Overton window." This latter term "refers to the range of acceptable political discourse on any given topic" (French 2020, 93). Over the years this window has shifted to reflect those in power at the time. Once gay marriage was outside the window. Now the window has no room for traditional views of gender and sexuality.

According to French (2020, 95), "negative polarization" in our culture has become so toxic that instead of a shared window of discourse, we have two windows, resulting in an inability for any productive conversation with people across the political aisle. Toward the end of his book, French envisions two scenarios where America divides: (1) *Calexit* (California secedes, with gun control at the core), and (2) *Texit* (Texas secedes, with abortion at the core).

National division, of course, has precedent. In fact, Abraham Lincoln used Jesus's clever comment about a divided house in his famed speech at the Illinois Republican State Convention on June 16, 1858.[2] It should be noted that Lincoln's speech quoted Jesus and made a plea for standing firm in unity. Thus, he took Jesus's side when the nation was polarized.

Ultimately, you want your sermon to communicate that Jesus defends the nature of activity coming from him as coming from above and warns of the serious consequences of rejection. In response we should pick Jesus's side when people are polarized.

---

1 An interview and transcript about the book can be found on Biola University's *Think Biblically* podcast, hosted by professors Sean McDowell and Scott Rae.

2 The full transcript of that speech can be located here: https://www.nps.gov/liho/learn/historyculture/housedivided.htm.

- Jesus's power provokes mixed reviews (12:22–32).
- People are accountable for their lives (12:33–37).
- Jesus's power speaks for itself (12:38–42).
- People are spiritually vulnerable (12:43–45).
- Jesus's family is a faithful crew (12:46–50).

DISCUSSION QUESTIONS

1. How would you explain "blasphemy of the Spirit"? What would you say to someone who is concerned they have "lost their salvation"?
2. What aspects of spiritual warfare need more clarification for your congregation?
3. What are some personal convictions you treat as core doctrines?
4. What topics do you tend to avoid because you know they lead to polarization?
5. How does the idea of "no neutrality" mesh with giving people time and space to make an informed decision about Jesus?

KINGDOM, PROVISION–ACCEPTANCE–CALL, AND REJECTION BY ISRAEL (13:1–20:28)

After introducing the extremely important explanation of the kingdom program through numerous parables, Jesus continued to minister to increasing opposition. He began to reveal his coming suffering and prepared the disciples for a ministry that also would meet with resistance. Peter's confession that Jesus was the Christ met with Jesus's affirmation that he had been taught by God. Jesus revealed more detail about his coming suffering, while God gave some disciples a glimpse of Jesus's coming glory. Jesus also taught the disciples about the accountability they must have to one another in a community that also was rooted in a forgiveness that appreciated how much they had been forgiven. They were to have a stewardship before God that understood how God had been gracious to them all. His own example of service was to guide how they also led and served. Jesus was set on the path that would take him to his work in Jerusalem. He also was preparing them for life after his suffering.

This section contains sixteen preaching units and covers two of the five discourse units of Matthew. The mixture of word and deed continues even in the face of continued opposition. The opportunity to turn back to God remained, but the unit concentrates on developing faithful disciples.

Matthew 13:1–23

EXEGETICAL IDEA
As one of the kingdom's mysteries revealed to the disciples, Jesus's parable of the soils showed the different reactions people have to the kingdom's offer and explained the obstacles that get in the way of responding.

THEOLOGICAL FOCUS
The parables extend Jesus's teaching to disciples who have access to the mysteries tied to God's kingdom with its call for receptive hearts.

PREACHING IDEA
When God speaks, be a good listener.

PREACHING POINTERS
After rebuking religious leaders and redefining family as those who did God's will, Jesus returned to the seashore for his third discourse. This teaching comprised a series of parables, explanations, and intimate instructions to his disciples about the dynamics of the kingdom of God. The first parable used agricultural imagery—seed, soils, and fruit—to illustrate good and bad responses to Jesus's message. When pressed by his disciples for clarity, Jesus quoted Isaiah 6:9–10 to explain his purpose of revealing truth to receptive people while concealing it from those with hardened hearts. Neutrality toward Jesus was not an option. For the original audience, Jesus's invitation to discipleship lingered, while judgment for rejecting him loomed ever larger.

The parables of Jesus have maintained their simplicity, mystery, and ability to captivate listeners. The parable of the soils is no exception; it presses modern hearers to reflect on their level of receptivity to Jesus. Despite our ready access to Bibles, commentaries, sermons, devotionals, Christian literature, and podcasts, we can be poor listeners. Rather than putting Jesus's teaching into practice, we doubt it, forget it, or get too busy to do what we hear him say. We must learn to fight deception, danger, and distractions that keep us from responding to Jesus's invitation to discipleship. This passage says, "When God speaks, be a good listener!"

ON THE KINGDOM AND ITS MYSTERIES, PART 1 (13:1–23)

LITERARY STRUCTURE AND THEMES (13:1–23)

We have split the Kingdom Parables Discourse into two parts, even though it is presented as one speech. This was simply because there is too much here to cover in one message. The split first worked through the core of the discourse, the parable of the soils—or better, Responses to the Word as Seen in the Soils. That parable was the topic of the bulk of the discourse's beginning.

This overall discourse comes in three core parts, all of which introduce Jesus's larger kingdom parable teaching (Matt. 13:1–52), the third discourse block of Matthew's gospel. This larger unit is best divided into three parts: (1) Matthew 13:1–23 with the parable of the soils; (2) 13:24–43 with the parables of the Tares, Mustard Seed, and Leaven, along with a citation of Scripture; and (3) 13:44–52 with the parables of the Treasure, Pearl, Net, and the remark about the scribe (Davies and Allison 1991, 370–72). Some propose a break at Matthew 13:35 because the parables were told to the public and then Jesus spoke to the disciples (Turner 2008, 335), but he was also speaking to disciples alone in Matthew 13:10–23. Our discussion will divide all of this into two distinct teaching and preaching sections with the second portion adding a non-parabolic scene at the end.

In this initial section, after a short introduction of the setting (Matt. 13:1–2), Jesus told the parable of the soils (Matt. 13:3–9). Jesus then explained the point of parables, both for those who had not responded and for the disciples (Matt. 13:10–17). He then interpreted the parable for the disciples (Matt. 13:18–23).

This is the core parable of the discourse and is presented with more detail than most of the parables in the full chapter. Its importance is evident in that it also appears in Mark and Luke as the leading kingdom parable. It explained mostly rejection and treated three categories of factors that caused people not to respond: Satan, persecution, and the cares of life. It also suggested that Jesus taught in parables in part as a judgment against those who were not responding, while the parables also provided deeper understanding for those who embraced Jesus. Disciples should make the effort to appreciate what the parables taught. Jesus also noted how special the time was in which his disciples lived, for kings and prophets had longed to see and hear what his disciples were experiencing.

The parable discussed response not in terms of where a person was in a given moment, but across the full journey of life. This was why some believed for a time but did not endure. The parable answered why some rejected the message and what caused them to be drawn away. Only the ones who heard and understood the word bore fruit. One not only was to listen to the message but receive it. The call was to give special attention to what Jesus said here.

The imagery was important. A person planted seed for it to bear fruit. Otherwise the planting was a failure. From this perspective, three of the soils were tragic in their results (Blomberg 1992, 214). Only one reached the sower's goal. There was no effort by Jesus to offer comfort for the first three soils. The call to embrace and believe the word was what Matthew had been pleading for in the last several chapters as he has highlighted the rising opposition to Jesus. Natural questions arose about why so many in Israel were not responding (France 2007, 499). Here Matthew illustrated the consequences and causes of such choices. It is important to note that Jesus still preached the word of the kingdom, and some did bear the fruit intended from its sowing. This positive response was yet another way to show the kingdom and its impact.

The telling of the parable has parallels in Mark 4:1–9 and Luke 8:4–8 (also Gospel of Thomas 9). In Mark it is present in the first of only two Marcan discourse units. In the discourse itself, Mark has fewer kingdom parables than Matthew 13 has. Luke has only this parable in this location and lacks a discourse with kingdom parables. Luke has other kingdom parables in other locales.

The citation of Isaiah 6:9–10 has parallels in Mark 4:10–12 and Luke 8:9–10. The idea of the special nature of the revelation in Matthew 13:16–17—to be blessed to see what they see—is like Luke 10:23–24. Mark does not have such a remark about the revelation's special nature.

The explanation of this parable also appears in Mark 4:13–20 and Luke 8:11–15. The key differences in the wording between these versions are covered in the exposition.

Thus, the unit is comprised of (1) a parable, (2) an explanation about parables in general with a call to appreciate the mystery and time they contain, and then (3) an explanation of the parable. The core subunit concludes with a call to hear the parable.

The key themes involve the reasons people do not respond to the sown word, as well as what does bring fruitfulness. Understanding or the lack of it is a topic and becomes a fresh focus for Matthew (Konradt 2020, 201). This is why it is better to call the parable the parable of the Responses (as seen in the soils) versus the parable of the Sower or of the Seed. The bulk of the explanation treated the responses. The seed (= the word about the kingdom) did not change in the parable, but the response depicted in the soils determined the results.

Another theme is the idea that sometimes revelation is missed because a heart has become dull and is not able to respond (Matt. 13:15). This theme is set up by the depiction of opposition in the last few chapters.

A final major note is the privilege of what the disciples have gained access to by participating in the events tied to Jesus. Kings and prophets longed for these days. The opportunity was great, but so was the tragedy of what got in the way of response.

A prominent chiasm appears in Matthew 13:10–17. It has seven elements with eyes closed and eyes perceiving as the center (Carson 2010, 352). It suggests that 13:16–17 belongs to this unit and is not a distinct idea.

EXPOSITION (13:1–23)

The kingdom that Jesus brought was distinct from what many had expected to come. The anticipation was of a powerful, delivering Messiah who would deliver and judge all at once. Jesus taught these parables to make it clear that the kingdom program was not going involve an instantaneous exercise of power as many had expected. The mystery of the kingdom involved a prolonged program in which the kingdom would occupy space in the world, with the righteous and unrighteous living side by side for some time. The kingdom made a claim on all humanity, but the reckoning of judgment was to come later. In the meantime, the kingdom would be offered in a context where threats to its acceptance existed. The tension about God's way in this mixed world was something disciples needed to grasp. The rest of the world lacked such understanding because they did not grasp the mysteries of the kingdom as they were revealed in these parables and their disclosure was a work of God. The kingdom space was sacred, and people were invited into it to experience the benefits and power of the kingdom that did not yield fruit without the embrace of the word about the kingdom. The kingdom existed in the midst of a pluralistic world and made a claim on all of it, but only those who responded with a receptive ear fully benefited from its presence. God was most active in showing his ways within that community of people who came to be connected to him. The way of the kingdom was best seen by being in it and receiving its benefits. That took a receptive heart, what we often call faith in God and his kingdom work through Jesus.

As one of the kingdom's mysteries revealed to the disciples, Jesus's parable of the Soils showed the different reactions people have to the kingdom's offer and explained the obstacles that get in the way of responding.

13:1–2. On the same day as the dispute with the leaders, Jesus went to the sea, that is, the Sea of Galilee. Only Matthew made this link with the dispute, showing a connection to what had just taken place. We are not told where this was, but Capernaum is possible (France 2007, 502).

A great crowd followed, so he taught by getting into a boat, and sitting and teaching from there as the crowd stood on the shore (Mark 4:1). The Sea of Galilee had a variety of outlooks from its edge. Many areas of the sea

Photo of the View from Arbel to the Sea of Galilee.

have a shoreline that ascends from the coastline making its acoustics theater-like. Jesus also sat to teach in Matthew 5:1 and 24:3, and sometimes taught sitting in a boat.

Photo of Sea of Galilee Coastline.

What followed was a series of parables about the kingdom and how people would respond to it. Questions abounded: What was it like, how would it come to pass, and what was the accountability that came with it?

13:3. Matthew mentions the term "parable" here for the first time. It refers to the Hebrew literary form of the *māshāl*, which can be a proverb, riddle, or a longer story. It was used of a story that required some reflection, like figuring out a puzzle (on parables, see Keener 2009, 371–75). Of Matthew's sixteen uses of this term, eleven take place in this chapter. Carter (2004, 282) observes that Solomon (1 Kings 4:32; Sir. 47:15–17), David (2 Kgdms. 23:3 LXX), and God (Ezek. 17:2) all spoke in parables.

Jesus's parable was rooted in everyday life (Ps. 126:6; Isa. 55:1–11). Sometimes such activity pictured spiritual realities in Judaism (the slightly later 4 Ezra 3:20; 8:41; 9:31–32; also 2 Bar. 32:1). In this case the parable pictured a sower tossing seed into the field. At that time, the seed usually came from a bag slung over the shoulder (1 Clem. 24:5). Farming was a core occupation in the region, so Jesus used a common activity to describe the kingdom. A common question sometimes raised about the image was whether one should assume plowing had taken place or that such activity would have followed the sowing. In fact, both orders were attested in the ancient world (before: Isa. 28:25; Jer. 4:3; after Jub. 11:11; *m. Šabb.* 7.2), and the decision makes no difference to the telling of the parable as the key issue was where the seed landed when it was cast out (Payne 1978, 123–29). The Gospel of Thomas also has a version of this parable.

Contrasting Sequence of Seed and Plow

Before—Isaiah 28:25: "Once he has leveled its surface, does he not scatter the seed of the caraway plant, sow the seed of the cumin plant, and plant the wheat, barley, and grain in their designated places?"

After—Jubilees 11:11: "And Prince Mastema sent crows and birds so that they might eat the seed which was being sown in the earth in order to spoil the earth so that they might rob mankind of their labors. Before they plowed in the seed, the crows picked it off the surface of the earth."

13:4. The first seed Jesus mentioned was sown on the road and never took root in any form (Mark 4:4; Luke 8:5). That was because the birds came and devoured the seed. The road here was a footpath, which could mark the field's edge (*m. Pe'ah* 2.1) or was a path running through a larger field.

13:5–6. The second seed fell among the shallow ground (Mark 4:5–6; Luke 8:6). Its fate in producing no fruit was tied to the soil's lack of depth. It sprang forth with the initial budding of fruit, but the sun scorched it (James 1:11) and it died after a time because there was no depth to its root system.

13:7. The third group of seed fell among the thorns (Mark 4:7; Luke 8:7). The thorns choked out this seed. This implied some initial growth and potential, but the seed eventually died out. As with the first two groups, there was no fruit. However, with each successive seed we get closer to making the goal.

13:8. The last group of seed fell in good soil (Mark 4:8; Luke 8:8). It produced a variety of yields: hundredfold, sixtyfold, and thirtyfold. The imperfect verb ἐδίδου is either ingressive, so the seed "began" to produce fruit in varying yields (Osborne 2010, 507), or is ongoing ("kept producing"; so Hagner 1993, 369). Matthew speaks of fruit in the plural, while Mark has the singular. Matthew also has a reversed order of yield from Mark. None of this materially impacts the point and the reason for the differences is not clear. All of these were good yields, some of them were even outstanding. Davies and Allison (1991, 385) and Carter (2004, 282–83) cite the ancient author Varro (*Rust.* 1.44.2) and others (Pliny, *Nat.* 18.21.95) to note yields ran from tenfold to a hundredfold in the area (Gen. 26:12; Jub. 24:15; also Keener 2009, 378; Luz 2001, 241–42; McIver 1994; Payne, 1980, 182–86). Bailey (1998a, 183) notes a citation of Pliny the Elder, *Natural History* 5.249, where the yield in Africa was four hundredfold, while in other regions it was a hundredfold. It is debated whether or not the high yields were exaggerated (McIver, yes; Payne, no). Either way, the yield was outstanding. This was the seed that reached its goal and produced a great deal, though to varying degrees. There was a lot of failure to reach the goal, but the success that came from good soil was quite impressive. Of course, the difference in yields pointed to the fact that some disciples were more fruitful than others.

13:9. Jesus issued his call to hear. Those with ears were to hear. This meant they were to reflect on what the parable taught. They were to see that the key issue in fruitfulness was good soil, that is, a faithful, responsive heart. Disciples were not to be indifferent to the word of the kingdom, because such apathy could point to a subtle form of rejection and hostility. What follows in Matthew 13:10–17 helps explain why people should pay attention. These parables contained the secrets of the kingdom. Only those whose spiritual antenna were up would benefit.

13:10. This intensification of a new type of discourse led the disciples to ask Jesus why he was teaching in parables (Mark 4:10). Mark 4:13 and Luke 8:9 asked about this parable specifically. It was probably the less explicit, enigmatic style of the parables that prompted the question. The query led Jesus to respond with the benefit followers had and the risk of thinking you had something spiritually when you did not. Jesus had shared parables before (Matt. 7:24–27; 9:15–17; 11:16–19), but now he was doing so more frequently.

13:11. God's sovereign program had led the disciples into the secrets or "mysteries" (μυστήρια) of the kingdom, while those outside did not get such access and understanding (BDAG s.v. "μυστήριον" 1a, 662; Mark 4:11–12; Luke 8:10). The plural "mysteries" pointed to the array of details in God's plan (Hannan 2006, 105). Mark has the singular to point to the program as a whole. The passive ("has been given") pointed to God as the giver.

They were beneficiaries of a grace-gift, which opened their eyes. The reference "to you [all]" (ὑμῖν) is in the emphatic position in the Greek. The idea of the *rāz*, mysteries, secrets, or insight into the depths of God's program, is a theme in the Old Testament and in Judaism (Keener 2009, 378–79; Osborne 2010, 509; Dan. 2:27–28; 1QS 9:17; 1QH 1:21; 1 En. 68:3–5—fate previously concealed now revealed; 2 Bar. 81:4 4; Ezra 10:38; 12:36–37; Brown 1968). Revelation contained such treasure and God controlled its release (Wilkins 2004, 476; Deut. 29:29; Ps. 25:14; Prov. 3:32; Amos 3:7). Access to these divine internal ideas came to those to whom it was given and who received it in a way that they also got more. The issue was not availability, but responsiveness and receptivity (Mark 4:22; 2 Bar. 51:4; Davies and Allison 1991, 390; France 2007, 511). As Carter (2004, 284) observes, Jesus had been quite public about declaring these things.

Keener (2009, 378) notes how Greek philosophers like Plato or Pythagoras often gave more time to teaching insiders. So the disciples get an inside look at these kingdom issues.

Texts on Mystery and God's Plan

Daniel 2:27–28: "Daniel replied to the king, 'The mystery that the king is asking about is such that no wise men, astrologers, magicians, or diviners can possibly disclose it to the king. However, there is a God in heaven who reveals mysteries, and he has made known to King Nebuchadnezzar what will happen in the times to come.'"

4 Ezra 10:38: "He answered me and said, 'Listen to me and I will inform you, and tell you about the things which you fear, for the Most High has revealed many secrets to you.'"

4 Ezra 12:36–37: "And you alone were worthy to learn this secret of the Most High. Therefore write all these things that you have seen in a book, and put it in a hidden place."

2 Baruch 81:4b: "And the Mighty One did according to the multitude of his grace, and the Most High according to the magnitude of his mercy, and he revealed to me a word that I might be comforted, and showed me visions that I might not be again sorrowful, and made known to me the mysteries of the times, and showed me the coming of the periods."

The remark parallels Matthew 11:25–26 about those God had chosen to reveal these things to, that is, to babes (Nolland 2005, 533). Those not open and responsive to what God was doing risked ending up with nothing. It was a heart's openness to reception that made the difference. This was why Jesus called on people to hear. This access had to do with people truly grasping, appreciating, and appropriating what Jesus had said. They might understand what he was saying but might not have accepted it as worth paying attention to and embracing. To understand in this way required response, as the final part of the citation of Isaiah 6:9–10 in Matthew 11:15 showed. This also explained why neutrality was really not a good place to be. It led to having nothing.

As subsequent exposition made clear, the kingdom came in stages, growing to greatness, not all at once. The place of judgment tied to it came later. The kingdom came, but not with "irresistible power" (Blomberg 1992, 215). There were many obstacles to its acceptance. There was no kingdom postponement here. It came, and things about its coming across a period of time were revealed to those inside (Turner 2008, 339). This is the only way to read the parables about the kingdom starting out small and becoming big. The anticipation had been that the kingdom would be big from the start. So this was a surprise and part of the mystery to grasp.

While this verse stressed sovereignty, the next one addressed responsibility. How the two precisely interacted in God's sovereign design was a mystery in itself.

13:12. Jesus presented a contrast between those who got it and those who did not. The contrast drove home the point about the need to respond. To the one who had, more was given, even in abundance (Mark 4:25; in another context: Matt. 25:29; Luke 19:26). To be open to God was to get more and more from him. But for those who lacked, even what they had was taken away. This was a kind of new math, where the person with nothing ended up with less than nothing. The point was a rhetorical way to stress that this person ended up with no spiritual benefits. Luke 8:18 speaks of what one "seems to have" (also Gospel of Thomas 41). What they currently were on the edge of access to, they would have no access to if they did not respond.

13:13. Because of this divine design, Jesus spoke in parables, because they saw and heard but did not really see and understand (Mark 4:11–12; 8:18). Carter (2004, 284) observes that nine chapters of ministry and rejection have preceded this remark (also Luz 2001, 246; Osborne 2010, 510). That was the background for this challenging response from Jesus. Matthew has taken Mark's "in order that" in Mark 4:12 and made it into a "because." France (2007, 513) notes the difference is not as great as some claim in saying Matthew highlighted human responsibility, as Matthew still has sovereignty in the context. The interaction between sovereignty, which Mark stresses, and responsibility, which Matthew notes, is complex and involves the presence of both elements (Bruner 2004b, 11–12; Carson 2010, 355–56, has a full discussion; Hagner 1993, 375).

There is a play on words here involving seeing and hearing, because Jesus had restored sight (Matt. 9:27–31; 12:22), speech (Matt. 9:32–34), and hearing (the parallel to Matt 9:32–34, which is Mark 7:31–37), as well as speaking of sight and hearing in Matthew 11:5.

13:14–15. Jesus then noted that this rejection fulfilled the pattern of declaration from Isaiah 6:9–10. Unlike most of Matthew's citations, which were narrative remarks, this one was made by Jesus directly. The text is like the LXX in making a statement versus the command of the MT, but the point is the same. The citation follows the LXX exactly except it lacks one reference to "their" from Isaiah 6:10b. People would not respond. Acts 28:26–27 matches how this Isaiah text was cited (also noted in Mark 4:12; Luke 8:10b; John 12:39–40). The text was so traditional, it was likely available to Matthew in its traditional form. Its presence in Mark 4:12 made it likely that Matthew also would cite the text but may have elongated it to show its full force.

The fulfillment was expressed most emphatically, because the introductory formula uses ἀναπληρόω, which refers to a "complete fulfillment," being the intensive form of the word "fulfilled" (BDAG s.v. "ἀναπληρόω" 2, 70). The term appears first in the formula. This is Matthew's only use of this word. In Isaiah, the prophet was told he would preach God's message, but the people would not respond. Isaiah's ministry became a confrontation with a nation slow to respond because it was hardhearted, leading to the possibility of more judgment. Israel's behavior here with Jesus mirrored that experience and fulfilled that pattern of action.

The text shows how people listened and looked but did not understand nor comprehend. They had, and have, plenty of opportunity to see and respond, but fail to embrace the offer. Why? Because their hearts were dull (Deut. 32:15). The term here speaks of a "fat" heart (BDAG s.v. "παχύνω" 2, 790). Their ears were hard of hearing, literally "heavy" (BDAG s.v. "βαρέως" 167). Their eyes were shut because they did not see what was happening right in front of them. Jeremiah 5:21–23 makes a similar point (Hagner 1993, 373). That had been Matthew's point for several chapters. By refusing to pay careful attention and observe all that Jesus was doing (especially in his signs), they did not see nor hear nor understand with their eyes, ears, and heart. The whole person was in view here. Osborne (2010, 511) speaks of a "spiritual heart attack." Had they done so, they would have turned and been healed. A future verb rather than a subjunctive is present, but the point was that a potential situation had gone awry (Nolland 2005, 536). There was no turning, so there was no healing (2 Thess. 2:11). Was this God's intent or their responsibility? It was both. There came a point by divine design when rejection yielded judgment. How that all worked in combination was an inscrutable mystery rooted in God's character which was good, just, and righteous.

13:16–17. Jesus issued a blessing for those who had responded (Luke 10:23). Disciples could understand, if they heeded Jesus (Osborne 2010, 510). They were blessed for seeing and hearing what the prophets and righteous had longed to see and hear. The remark looked back to Matthew 13:13–15. Those who responded to the gospel were linked to hopes of the prophets and righteous. Their response represented the true completion of the old promise. Matthew was teaching continuity with kingdom hope here.

Again the use of "you [all]" (ὑμῶν) at the start of the verse made that term emphatic. Those greats of old desired to hear it and did not. Jesus was saying that these were special days, despite the opposition. The explanation of the role of parables ended on a positive note. The emphasis for those who responded was on the privilege of being beneficiaries of God's grace and selection (Bruner 2004b, 14–15). The text also made clear that Israel was divided. Still, some within the nation did respond and received what many greats of the past in the nation had longed to obtain. Psalms of Solomon 17:50 and 18:6 express hope for a day like this (Davies and Allison 1991, 394). The New Testament also highlights this idea (Matt. 11:11–13; John 8:56; Eph. 3:4–5; Heb. 11:13, 39–40; 1 Peter 1:10–12; Turner 2008, 340).

As Wilkins (2004, 478–79) notes, the parables did two things at once. (1) The parables tested the listener's heart. They required a concern to hear and a concentration to receive what was said. (2) The parables instructed the responsive and took them into a deeper understanding and appreciation of God's program. As Morris (1992, 341) says, the word of God either yielded enlightenment or judgment.

13:18. So Jesus turned to explain the parable of the soils to the disciples. The "you" at the start is slightly emphatic. The disciples were to get this. Here was how people reacted to the word about the kingdom. The parable has been called the parable of the Sower to echo the opening words of the account, a common way to identify a story in the ancient world. God's work triggered everything, but the thrust of the parable is made clear by what it discussed, so to call it the parable of the soils or the parable of the Responses to the Kingdom is to describe what the parable concentrated on as key. France (2007, 517–19) had a defense of the authenticity of the explanation, as well as Payne (1980) and Keener (2009, 381–82).

13:19. The seed was about the kingdom of heaven, what was called the "word of the kingdom." Luke 8:11 speaks of the word of God. In fact, often in many texts in the NT the word of God is about the word of the kingdom or the gospel. In Judaism, this could be about the law, and similar imagery of varied response also existed (Culpepper 2021, 254; 4 Ezra 8:41—varied responses; 4 Ezra 9:41—of the law as sown seed). The sower was not named here, but in Matthew 13:37 he was the Son of Man, a reference to Jesus. That word was sown in the heart (καρδίᾳ) of people, but how would the person respond? Some of those who did not understand had the seed taken from their heart by the evil one (Mark 4:15; Luke 8:12). They did not react to the message at all. The same word for "seizing" (ἁρπάζω) appears in Matthew 11:12 for violent people snatching the kingdom (BDAG s.v. "ἁρπάζω" 2a, 134). The kingdom came with a spiritual battle.

The association of birds with evil sometimes shows up in Judaism (Davies and Allison 1991, 400; Jub. 11:11—birds sent to devour seed [see chart at 13:3]; Apoc. Ab. 13—Azazel in the form of an unclean bird). The absence of understanding looked back at the previous verses. Here was the person who never even really responded at all. What God had put in their heart about him was taken away before it even had a chance to produce. This was unlike the next two soils where some initial reaction did take place.

13:20–21. The second soil was the rocky ground (Mark 4:16–17; Luke 8:13). Here there was an initial excited response of joy. However, with no root, there was no long-term belief. Luke has "believe for a time"; Matthew has "temporary." When tribulation and persecution came (Matt. 5:11–12; 10:16–25; 23:34–36; 24:9–13), there was a falling away. The key term here is σκανδαλίζεται, which refers to a "fall" or a "stumble" into sin (BDAG s.v. "σκανδαλίζω" 1a, 926). The context made it clear that the faith was short-lived and that there was no fruit, so Jesus was describing a falling away (France 2007, 521). Matthew described these categories in the singular to emphasize the individualized application (Nolland 2005, 540).

13:22. The third soil was the seed among the thorns. Here the obstacles to fruitfulness were the cares of this age and the deceit of riches. Here it was the world, the comfort of acceptance, and being desirous to function in society as an accepted person that prevented growth to fruition (Matt. 6:19–34; Jub. 23:21). The term μέριμνα refers to "worries" or the "cares" of life (BDAG s.v. "μέριμνα" 632). Riches are described with ἀπάτη, which points to being "deceived" or "misled" about what riches can do (BDAG s.v. "ἀπάτη" 1, 99). This is Matthew's only use of the word. Since a sinister result was in view, "deceit" is appropriate (Eph. 4:22; Col. 2:8; 2 Thess. 2:10; Heb. 3:13; 2 Peter 2:13).

The explanation was clear that no fruit was the result. This also is Matthew's only use of the word that means "unfruitful" (ἄκαρπος). The remark reminds one of the rich ruler (Matt. 19:16–22).

Jubilees on Deceptiveness of Callous Wealth

Jubilees 23:21: "And those who escape will not be turned back from their evils to the way of righteousness because they will lift themselves up for deceit and wealth so that one shall take everything of his neighbor; and they will pronounce the great name but not in truth or righteousness. And they will pollute the holy of holies with their pollution and with the corruption of their contamination."

The key obstacles to faith were Satan, persecution, the desire for comfort with secular concerns, and greed (Turner 2008, 342). Self-protection was what drove the categories that failed. Such people lost their soul to gain this life (Matt. 10:39). It was a bad trade.

13:23. The final soil reached the goal. This soil represented those who heard and understood (Matt. 3:8–10; 7:16–20; 12:33; 21:19, 34, 41, 43). This was the only soil said to understand. All the other soils fell short. Fruit was the result in distinct yields of a hundred, sixty, and thirty. There were a variety of yields, but the point was that there was produce from the seed. This was the only commendable soil. Disciples who got it had different levels of production, but all reached the goal. Fruit is a major image in the New Testament (John 15:1–8; Rom. 1:13; 1 Cor. 12; Gal. 5:22–23; Col. 1:10; 1 John 3:9; Wilkins 2004, 481).

As noted, these evaluations covered the span of life, not a specific moment. There was the passing of time that allowed either a failure to yield fruit or a product. It was a parable about one's spiritual career of response. One should not make percentages out of this parable (e.g., only one in four accept; but so Bruner 2004b, 19). The point was to discuss types of soils and responses, not to say the percentage between them was equal. The parable did likely indicate that many would not respond, as the current context of Matthew also indicated, which was in part why the parable was told.

THEOLOGICAL FOCUS

The exegetical idea (as one of the kingdom's mysteries revealed to the disciples, Jesus's parable of the soils showed the different reactions people have to the kingdom's offer and explained the obstacles that get in the way of responding) leads to this theological one: the parables extend Jesus's teaching to disciples who have access to the mysteries tied to God's kingdom with its call for receptive hearts.

Jesus revealed the obstacles to the effective reception of the kingdom word as he taught the disciples about the mysteries of the kingdom. Those obstacles were Satan, persecution, and the cares of life, but good hearts received the word and yielded fruit in varying degrees.

Matthew continued to explain how people rejected the great opportunity Jesus placed before them, as well as the blessing that came for those who did respond. The parable calls for reflection about where the heart is and identifies that which can stunt or even kill genuine response. The call is to be aware of what can stop fruitfulness, and that rejection often comes because other things take priority over God. The greatest commandment is to love the creator-redeemer God with all one's being. These obstacles show things that get in the way of that most basic allegiance. Good soil gets the priority right. The good heart listens and responds when God speaks. Blessing and fruitfulness come to those who embrace what Jesus offers and turn their backs on the things that get in the way.

The parable also yields understanding about how to engage in the mission that lies ahead. One should be patient and not overly triumphalistic, understanding that reactions pro and con will come (Bailey 1998a, 185–86). God is still effectively at work in his own way and time. We sow. The responsibility for results lies elsewhere. Our call is to be faithful in the sowing.

The opening of the parable discourse focuses on two issues: how people respond and the inscrutable, mysterious nature of the interaction between God's design and human responsibility.

There is an array of obstacles to a positive, fruit-bearing response. Many people have an opportunity to sense God being present, but not all act on it with some not even giving it a chance. For others, the pressure of tribulation or persecution prevents fruitfulness. That pressure of rejection causes one drawn to faith ultimately to step away from it. Still others are overwhelmed with the concerns of life or with the pursuit of wealth. Mammon becomes a god, and life is managed and manipulated without God being present. Here also there is no fruit.

What leads to fruitfulness is faith. Faith as genuine trust understands and responds. In other words, faith works; it works fruit to show that faith is present. In fact, trust without response is not actual trust. This is why Jesus often spoke of hearing *and* doing God's word as being what makes one a member of his family. Often in the church we oppose faith and works, but this opposition is only correct when works are seen to earn one salvation on one's own merit and obligate God. When works are seen as the natural extension of faith, they are put in their proper place as a response to grace. Such faith-that-works does not gain merit but evidences the change God has brought to the heart and an authentic response to grace. The New Testament clearly teaches this sequencing in key passages about grace (Eph. 2:8–10; Titus 2:11–14; James 2:14–26).

Jesus's juxtaposition of divine design and human responsibility is simply an area where Scripture affirms both are present. Yet another theme is that the telling of parables obscures truth to the skeptical because they had been exhibiting dull hearts. God in his design comes to a point where that rejection is made firm. How exactly that works, we are not told. God permits prodigals to go their own way by their own choice, even as he keeps the opportunity of response in front of them and urges them to turn. The freedom to leave has with it the opportunity to return when one senses the need that going one's own way ironically has come up empty. God is working to change the heart in this effort to keep the hope in front of people. Some change; others do not. The change will never come without God's initiative. The moral choice to go one's own way comes at great risk unless one sees the danger and returns. The opportunity to change always exists, as Jesus's teaching is always urging people to respond.

PREACHING AND TEACHING STRATEGIES

Exegetical and Theological Synthesis

The greatest obstacle to hearing God is a hard heart. Jesus recognized this theological reality. He envisioned his ministry in the vein of the prophet Isaiah, whose call to preach to Israel would be met by rejection (Isa. 6:1–13). Calloused hearts were the cause of the rejection (Isa. 6:9–13). Isaiah was not the lone prophet to rebuke hard-heartedness; Moses, Jeremiah, Ezekiel, Hosea, and Zechariah each called out God's people for their wandering, deceitful, and stony hearts (Deut. 29:18; Jer. 17:9; Ezek. 36:26; Hos. 10:2; Zech. 7:12). For Jesus, the heart could be equally irresponsive to God (Matt. 5:28; 9:4; 12:34; 13:15; 15:8, 18–19; 19:8).

On the other hand, prophets also acknowledged the heart could be a locus of repentance, renewal, and responsiveness to God (Deut. 30:6; Jer. 31:33; Ezek. 36:26; Joel 2:12–13). The heart was the center of one's will and emotional reasoning. Thus, God's people were expected to love him with all their hearts (Deut. 6:5; 10:12; 11:13). According to Jesus, this was the greatest command (Matt. 22:37). Moreover, receptive hearts could entertain pure thoughts (5:8), treasure heavenly things (6:21), and forgive others (18:35). Nurturing a heart receptive to God is paramount to faithful and fruitful living in God's kingdom.

Unfortunately, the opportunity for a receptive heart has its obstacles. The parable lists three: deception, danger, and distraction. Concerning deception, the father of lies (John 8:44) has flooded the world with untruths about God, humans, sin, salvation, and the good life. False narratives about gender identity, sexual fulfillment, blindness to injustice, and financial security top the list. Concerning danger, the secular age has denied God and described his people as hateful, hypocritical bigots. The fear of offending others, losing friends, or getting canceled can uproot our fear of God. And concerning distractions, the pursuit of wealth, pleasure, or social standing can squelch good intentions to hear from God. Phone notifications, social media feeds, streaming platforms, house projects, and job demands never rest. Constantly responding to these distractions drains us. Less deception, danger, and distraction is best for our hearts to remain receptive to God.

Preaching Idea

When God speaks, be a good listener.

Contemporary Connections

What does it mean?

First, we must recognize that God still speaks. He speaks through his Word, creation, our circumstances, conscience, and other people. Both general and special revelation remind us that our God speaks. He is a personal God who enjoys communicating with his people. According to 2 Timothy 3:16, God speaks to teach, rebuke, correct, and train us to be like Jesus. We must tune our ears to hear him.

Second, we must be good listeners, who train our ears to hear God. We will do so by spending quality time in his Word. We may listen to the audio Bible on our commute to work or read it early in the morning. We will focus during sermons. We will look for encouragement, affirmation, or guidance from God in conversations with others. We pay attention to how the Spirit of God nudges our conscience. A good listener is attuned to God and receives what he says.

Moreover, good listeners obey God. According to James 1:22–25, the best listeners do what God says. Their faith is more than auditory; it is active. If God tells them to be more honest, they live more honestly. If God asks them to hold back criticism of others, they zip their lips. If they hear God's refrain of enduring love, they trust that love is real.

Is it true?

It is true that God speaks, but we must beware of divine counterfeits. Too often, we make God say what we want to hear. Some of us hear promises that God never made about health, wealth, and the universal embrace of heaven. Others hear God accuse and condemn in a voice that is not his. Whatever we think we hear from God must be tested against Scripture. On matters that are not part of direct revelation, such as what college we should attend or when to purchase a new vehicle, God expects us to use wisdom.

Now what?

A good listener does three things. He clears distractions, pays attention, and takes action. Distractions include internal and external triggers. We may be distracted by our thoughts: a busy schedule, to-do list, favorite sports team, or how our coupon for Subway expired. As these thoughts cycle through our heads, we cannot pay attention to God. External triggers include a buzzing phone, a barking dog, running water, or a stain on our shirt. These triggers pull us from paying attention to God. Although we will never cancel all the noise in our lives, we can work to eliminate distractions by finding ideal times and places to listen to God, with our phones stowed away. Good listeners know the devil loves distraction.

A good listener pays attention. Paying attention means tuning our ears to God's voice. He knows God wants to speak to us. He speaks through Scripture, prayer, creation, circumstances, conscience, and other people. A good listener pays attention to *how* God speaks—gently, quietly, seriously—and *what* he says—words of comfort, conviction, and encouragement. Thus, as we read the Bible, hear sermons, pray, work, and interact with others, good listeners are always searching for divine undertones. Good listeners know God may speak at any moment.

Finally, good listeners take action. As mentioned above, good listeners have a predisposition to say "yes" to Jesus. They do not merely hear God but also do what he says (James 1:22–25). Thus, if God says through his Word to stop coveting, a good listener will fight his covetous impulses. If God speaks a hopeful word through a friend, a good listener will take it to heart. Good listeners also read their circumstances and heed their conscience in response to God's guidance. Good listeners know God's voice should direct their lives.

Creativity in Presentation

To illustrate Jesus's rationale for teaching in parables, you can show the Gospel Project's five-minute video on parables. Search for this video or something similar. The video does not focus only on parables from Matthew 13 but offers an overview on how the parables "revealed" the kingdom of God and "concealed" it from crowds. This video could also work for the sermon on the next passage, Matthew 13:24–58.

To visualize the parable of the soils, consider signifying four soils at four different locations on the stage. For the first station, set out sidewalk pavers with fake birds beside them. For the second station, spread a small pile of rocks. For the third station, gather a tangle of weeds or thorns. For the fourth station, set up a large planter with a plant growing in it. In your hand, have a small bucket filled with seeds. Have someone else read the parable as you act it out (or someone else can be the sower while you read).

A simple way to encourage the preaching idea (be a good, receptive listener) is to point repeatedly to your ear and your heart. For dramatic effect, you can turn your head sidewise, lean toward the seats, and cup your ear while saying, "Be a good listener." To indicate "hard hearts," you may pound your fist against your chest and say, "Hard hearts."

We probably all remember what good listeners look like from our days in school. They sit straight in their chairs. They keep their phones tucked away. They have their pens in hand and notebooks open. If they have a question, they raise their hands for the instructor to call on them. Conversely, bad listeners slouch in their seats, keep their heads down, play with their phones, and perhaps fall asleep. Consider setting a chair and desk on the stage and demonstrating the differences between good and bad listeners.

Distractions divert our attention. The include internal and external noise. Define both kinds of noise and how they disrupt the communication process (see image).

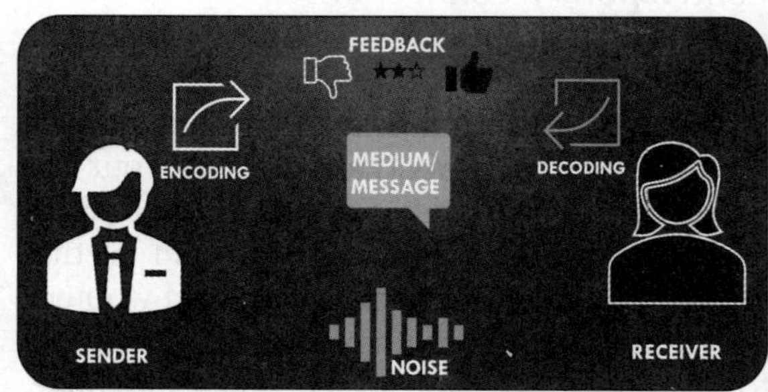

Figure of the Communication Process.

Let the church know you are going to provide a minute to take a noise inventory. Encourage everyone to write down all the internal and external noise they hear. After the exercise, cite a few examples of external (e.g., baby crying, pens scratching, heater) and internal noise (*Has it been a minute yet? What's for lunch? I need to text Joe back.*) that likely appeared in people's inventories. Exhort them to tone down the noise to be better listeners.

Ultimately, the sermon should teach that parables extend Jesus's teaching to disciples who have access to the mysteries tied to God's kingdom, with its call for a receptive heart. Or, more simply: when God speaks, be a good listener.

- Jesus invites crowds to listen to stories (13:1–9).
- Hearing is hard when our hearts are impaired (13:10–17).
- Jesus explains his stories to disciples (13:18–23).

DISCUSSION QUESTIONS

1. Which title do you prefer, "parable of the Sower" or "parable of the Soils"?
2. According to the parable, what prevents people from listening to Jesus?
3. What was the "mystery" of the kingdom? Why did the disciples get access to it?
4. How does Matthew typically present the crowds?
5. Review the ways God still speaks. Through which of these media has he recently spoken to you? What did he say and how did your respond?
6. What would show up in your "noise audit"? What tends to distract you?

Matthew 13:24–58

EXEGETICAL IDEA

Jesus's kingdom parables showed that the kingdom would start small and end up large, involved a judgment coming at the end, and was so precious that one should give up all to get it, all in a context where many still rejected him because of spiritual blindness.

THEOLOGICAL FOCUS

Despite all that the kingdom offers and the certainty that it will be universal in scope one day, people still reject the offer of God's grace.

PREACHING IDEA

Stay tuned: God's plan is full of surprises!

PREACHING POINTERS

Jesus's teaching on the mysteries of the kingdom continued. Following the parable of the soils and his private explanation to the disciples, Jesus rattled off six more stories, pictured through key metaphors: wheat and tares, mustard seed and leaven, treasure and pearl, and a massive catch of fish. The parables, ripe with Old Testament allusions, pointed to God's slow and steady growth of his kingdom. This work is inclusive and pervasive but not universally accepted because of the sacrifice involved in those who receive it. In fact, Jesus's subsequent rejection in Nazareth underscored for Matthew's audience the need to listen, watch, and respond to Jesus's subversive and surprising ministry as Son of God.

God continues to move in mysterious ways. He follows his own timeline. He works at his own pace. He includes unlikely people in his plan and leverages unfortunate events for our good. In short, God is full of surprises. Our task is to trust and stay attuned to his activity. We get to watch and see him work deathbed conversions. We get to watch and see him grow the underground church in Communist countries. We get to watch and see him turn selfish people into sacrificial disciples. And we get to watch and see him crush unresolved evil with unwavering justice. Someday his kingdom will indeed arrive in full. Thus, this sermon teaches us to stay tuned: God's plan is full of surprises.

ON THE KINGDOM AND ITS MYSTERIES, PART 2 (13:24–58)

LITERARY STRUCTURE AND THEMES (13:24–58)

This section has a series of parables, with some having additional explanation for the disciples (Matt. 13:24–52; directly only to the disciples—Matt. 13:36). The unit ends with a scene of Jesus preaching in the synagogue (Matt. 13:53–58), where the crowd considered who he was only to reject his claim to bring anything special. In a sense the unit serves as a summary of all that had taken place up to this point in Matthew. Jesus offered kingdom benefits to those who would respond, but many did not accept his offer.

In sum, there are six parables about kingdom truth plus one summary image about the disciple of the kingdom, the kingdom scribe (13:24–30—wheat and tares, with interpretation in 13:36–43; 13:31–32—mustard seed; 13:33–35—leaven with a citation of Psalm 78:2; 13:44—treasure in a field; 13:45–46—pearl of great price; 13:47–48—great catch of fish, with interpretation in 13:49–50; 13:51–52—treasure with things old and new). The first three parables are introduced as such in Matthew 13:24, 31, and 33, while the next three all begin with "the kingdom of heaven is like" (Matt. 13:44, 45, 47). The last image is a summary of what the disciple has uncovered in terms of kingdom truth. This wave of teaching, plus more in the synagogue, did yield discussion about Jesus, but in the end there was still rejection of him.

First, the parables made it clear that the kingdom entered the world and was mixed up in it until the end when the "sorting out" of judgment would take place. Good and evil existed side by side in the world in this early phase of kingdom work. The old fallen world now was faced with a counterbalance from God that was Spirit indwelt. The parable was not about internal church conditions of good and evil (Carson 2010, 363). Weeds were removed from the world before the harvest, in contrast to Matthew 18:15–20 where the church exercised discipline and excommunication to keep it internally pure (Davies and Allison 1991, 409; Hill 1972, 232). Second, these parables also made clear that the kingdom started out as small, and unexpectedly so, but it would eventually cover everything. Third, so important was what Jesus offered that one should give up all one had to obtain it. The contrast between what the kingdom was worth and the rejection that closes the unit is tragic. Failure to embrace the message was not because people lacked opportunity to respond to God.

Although Jesus was teaching new and mysterious things about the kingdom here (Bailey 1998a, 176), the connection to fulfillment with Old Testament texts in this section and the previous one showed that there was a continuity with the kingdom program of the past (Matt. 13:14–15, 35). There were things old and new in the program (Matt. 13:52). These events contained mysteries, but there was no withdrawal of the kingdom offer. It continued to come. Those who responded were a part of it. The sorting out of it all awaited the judgment.

Jesus instructed the crowds from Matthew 13:24–35. This was unclear at first, since Matthew 13:10–23 was with the disciples, but Matthew 13:36 makes it clear that Jesus had been with the crowds up to this point when he was telling the new parables. A similar ambiguity reappears at Matthew 13:44–52. This ambiguity is not so clearly resolved. However, on the pattern of telling parables to the crowds, these also should be seen as being given to all. The question-and-answer exchange in Matthew 13:51–52 showed the listeners as very confident, even too confident, that they understand. The discourse ends with Matthew's usual marker in Matthew 13:53a, and we move immediately into the synagogue scene. It was there that we see that the crowd was still not getting it. They did not embrace Jesus with faith.

The key themes treat the kingdom's character. It started small and would become overwhelming, filling everything. It had a mixed character of good and evil present around it until the end. It was in the world and sown in the world but was distinct from it. There would be an accountability of all at the end, at the harvest, a picture of final judgment. The kingdom was worth giving up everything to have. It contained promises and elements both old and new. So what Jesus described as the kingdom was expected in part and not expected in part. The kingdom mysteries had revelatory elements in them. It was not merely a repeat of past revelation. Yet it still connected to and completed old promises. It came despite rejection. It did not come in power all at once. It would be sorted out at the harvest. Justice would come at the end.

Most of this kingdom parable material is unique to Matthew. The synagogue scene is paralleled in Mark 6:1–6a. Luke 4:16–30 is a longer version of the scene that Luke has moved forward to show its paradigmatic character. Interestingly, the scene has the same function in Matthew even though Matthew has it more centrally located in the Galilean ministry section of his gospel. Matthew and Luke were doing the same thing in different literary ways.

The two kingdom parables that do have parallels are those regarding the mustard seed and leaven. The mustard seed appears in Mark 4:30–32, as well as in a later Lucan scene in Luke 13:18–19. The parable of the Leaven appears in Luke 13:20–21 in a sequence that matches Matthew's but is distinct from Luke's telling of the parable of the soils in Luke 8:1–15. That Jesus was said to have spoken in parables recalls Mark 4:33–34. Interestingly, Matthew lacks the parable of Mark 4:26–29. It is not clear why, although Nolland (2005, 543) suggests that the parable of the Wheat and Tares functioned similarly for Matthew.

The Gospel of Thomas 57 is similar to the parable of the Wheat and Tares (Davies and Allison 1991, 415, see the version as secondary and compressed). This may well suggest the parable was a part of circulating tradition about Jesus's teaching. For authenticity is its character in not looking to the creation of a new entity but the picture of the arrival of a promised entity with old ties (Carson 2010, 362; Davies and Allison 1991, 410–11, of the wheat and tares).

This overview of parallels shows that most of this unit is unique to Matthew. At a narrative level, the crowd was still not responding to Jesus despite all his efforts to make clear how important the kingdom was. That kingdom was both like and unlike what they had expected. It may well be that some of these unanticipated elements were what was giving the crowds pause. The parables were affirming this was all a part of the divine design, as Jesus now disclosed many kingdom mysteries.

EXPOSITION (13:24–58)

Jesus continued to unfold what was both new and old about the kingdom program he was called to bring. Good and evil would exist side by side in the world until the judgment. The effective presence of God's power would exist in the believing community. However, God's kingdom claim existed for all people whether or not they accepted it. Eventually the kingdom would cover the entire world, making it worth everything to belong. The discourse is designed to show Jesus brought a kingdom promise that was anticipated on the one hand, while having some surprises on the other.

Jesus's kingdom parables showed that the kingdom would start small and end up large, involved a judgment coming at the end, and was so precious that one should give up all to get it, all in a context where many still rejected him because of spiritual blindness.

13:24. The opening of the parable of the Wheat and Tares (Weeds) came in three parts. The parable is unique to Matthew. First, a man sowed good seed in his field. The phrase "the kingdom of heaven is like" is in most of the parables of this unit in one form or another (Matt. 13:24, 31, 33, 44, 45, 47; also 18:23; 20:1; 22:2; with a slight variation, 25:1). The imagery of seed for people is not uncommon in Jewish texts (Hos. 2:23; 4 Ezra 8:41–45; Nolland 2005, 547).

As already noted, the return to address disciples in Matthew 13:36 indicated Jesus spoke to the crowds here, although no such note is explicitly present in introducing this parable. Matthew 13:34 assumes the crowd as the audience as well.

13:25–26. Second, as people slept, an enemy came and sowed weeds in the same field. The result was the third element in the story. The ζιζάνιον are "harmful weeds" (BDAG s.v. "ζιζάνιον" 429). It is a kind of ryegrass with poisonous fungus in its grain that wrecks a crop (Bailey 1998b, 270; France 2007, 525). Most suggest *Lolium temulentum* was referred to here (Keener 2009, 386). The word only appears in this chapter in the New Testament. It is a rare term, as it also does not appear in the LXX.

The devil was in view here (Matt. 13:39). His being called "the enemy" is also common in Judaism (Adam and Eve *(Greek)* 2:4; 7:2; 25:4; 28:3; 2 Bar. 13:2; T. Dan 6:3; T. Job 47:10; Nolland 2005, 547 n. 76). The devil sowed as Jesus did, but the result was very different. When the crop finally grew, wheat and weeds were present, mixed together. The good and bad were together in the field, which very importantly was described as "the world" in Matthew 13:38. The kingdom made a claim in the world, not just in the church. Yet it also created a sacred space in the world among those who responded and were connected to each other by the Spirit of God. The gospel invited people into that space and the Spirit enabled people to live as God called them to live. That did not happen with seed sown by the devil. Such acts of mixed sowing took place in everyday life. They were viewed so negatively that later legal codes outlawed them (Kerr 1997, who cites the later legal code of the *Digest* 9.2.27.14).

13:27–28a. This mixed crop result led the slaves to ask if indeed the owner had sown only good seed, for they thought that was what had been done. The parable pictured a wealthy landowner with a set of slaves. The question about sowing good seed was asked expecting a positive answer (οὐχι). The question assumed the owner should be concerned about the quality of the seed he appeared to be sowing. The reply came that an enemy had done this. The enemy was described literally as a "hostile" man, as the meaning of ἐχθρός is "enemy" (BDAG s.v. "ἐχθρός" 2a, 419).

13:28b–30. This led the slaves to ask if they should gather the weeds. The owner replied no, because then the risk was that wheat would be lost with the pulling of the weeds. All was to be left until harvest time. The image appears to be that the weeds were so prevalent that to tear them up with their roots also would damage the productive crop, so better to leave it alone for now. The mixed character of things would remain until the harvest, which pictures judgment (Isa. 63:1–6; Jer. 25:30–31; Joel 3:13; Mic. 4:11–13). At the time of the harvest, reapers will be told to gather the weed into bundles so they can be burned up, while the wheat will be gathered into the barn. The idea here is like Matthew 3:12 and Luke 3:17. Vindication will come. The kingdom will be pure one day. Full justice will wait until then. The judgment tied to the kingdom's arrival in the mind of many of Jesus's listeners actually would come later. There was one difference between these OT texts and the use Jesus made of the image here. In the OT the prominent image was of defeat of the nations. In Jesus's use, it was all evil that would be judged along with anyone, Jew or Gentile, who rejected God's way, being accountable to God whether or not they recognized it. That difference may be part of the mystery Jesus was revealing.

Harvest Imagery for Judgment

Isaiah 63:3–4: "I have stomped grapes in the winepress all by myself; no one from the nations joined me. I stomped on them in my anger; I trampled them down in my rage. Their juice splashed on my garments, and stained all my clothes. For I looked forward to the day of vengeance, and then payback time arrived."

Jeremiah 25:30: "Then, Jeremiah, make the following prophecy against them: 'Like a lion about to attack, the Lord will roar from the heights of heaven; from his holy dwelling on high he will roar loudly. He will roar mightily against his land. He will shout in triumph, like those stomping juice from the grapes, against all those who live on the earth.'"

Joel 3:13: "Rush forth with the sickle, for the harvest is ripe! Come, stomp the grapes, for the winepress is full! The vats overflow. Indeed, their evil is great!"

Micah 4:12: "But they do not know what the Lord is planning; they do not understand his strategy. He has gathered them like stalks of grain to be threshed at the threshing floor."

13:31–32. The parable of the Mustard Seed is the first of two growth parables that Jesus told next (Mark 4:30–32; Luke 8:18–21; Gospel of Thomas 20; Davies and Allison 1991, 421, discuss this Thomas gospel parallel as likely secondary). This small seed was sown in a field and grew into a "garden herb" (λαχάνων) that was described as a tree in whose branches birds lived (BDAG s.v. "λαχάνων" 587). It was likely the *Sinapis nigra* (Sproule 1980, 40). The seed was rhetorically described as the smallest of seeds because of its stature among garden plants in Israel (*m. Nid.* 5.2; Bailey 1998c, 453; Sproule 1980, 40–41; *TDNT* 7:286–90—Greek term for mustard). The expression should be read as a comparative with superlative force, not elative, "smallest of all seeds," but it was not an erroneous reference given the region it was describing and the remark's populist nature (Wallace 1996, 301). These plants can be eight to twelve feet high, but it is unusual for birds to dwell in a bush, so the result is in one sense unexpected given the start.

"Birds" likely referred to Gentiles (Ezek. 17; Dan. 4; other tree, bird, or nesting in branches texts: Judg. 9:15; Ezek. 31:3–14). Ezekiel 17:22–23 is the likely background for the image here (Isa. 11:1–2). France (2007, 527) suggests a contrast to the temporary kingdom of Babylon from Dan. 4:7–23, which God's kingdom replaced. It pictured the rebuilding of the Davidic house which did connect to Jesus. The parable made him a messianic claimant. Jewish imagery on the messianic community can also connect to this imagery (Pss. Sol. 14:2–3; 1QH 6:14–16; 8:4–8; Davies and Allison 1991, 420).

Imagery of the Tree, Kingdom, and Hope of a Good Rule

Isaiah 11:1–2: "A shoot will grow out of Jesse's root stock, a bud will sprout from his roots. The Lord's Spirit will rest on him—a Spirit that gives extraordinary wisdom, a Spirit that provides the ability to execute plans, a Spirit that produces absolute loyalty to the Lord."

Ezekiel 17:22–23: "This is what the Sovereign Lord says: 'I will take a sprig from the lofty top of the cedar and plant it. I will pluck from the top one of its tender twigs; I myself will plant it on a high and lofty mountain. I will plant it on a high mountain of Israel, and it will raise branches and produce fruit and become a beautiful cedar. Every bird will live under it; Every winged creature will live in the shade of its branches.'"

The parable is not so much about gradual growth as about the kingdom starting out small and ending up as a place where creatures would dwell. This alluded to the fact the kingdom did not start off as large, as many had anticipated, making it another mystery element in Jesus's teaching. However, disappointment is not the final point; growth and success gave a note of encouragement (Bailey 1998c, 450–51). The seed sown was positive and the end of the parable was positive, portraying the growth of God's rule, not Satan's. The parable is not ultimately about evil in its result (Turner 2008, 344–46). In the end, the kingdom, despite starting out small, will cover the earth.

13:33. The second growth parable was the parable of the Leaven (Luke 13:20–21; Gospel of Thomas 96; Davies and Allison 1991, 424, discuss the Thomas text as secondary). Here the movement was again small to large. A woman took yeast and placed it in three measures, or seahs, of flour. This was about forty "liters," or almost fifteen gallons of flour or a full bushel, a major baking operation (BDAG s.v. "σάτον" 917—Greek is transliterated from Aramaic; Turner 2008, 344). It would have weighed around fifty pounds and could feed a hundred and fifty people, no small meal (France 2007, 528). The size was not unusual in biblical texts (Gen. 18:6; Judg. 6:19; 1 Sam. 1:24). In the end, the yeast filled the entirety of the flour. Though yeast was normally a negative image, in this context it was a positive image (Lev. 23:17 is also positive), giving encouragement and explanation (Lev. 7:13–14; 23:17; Morris 1992, 353). The previous parable explained that growth would take place. Here the picture was how, with imagery of growth and ferment (Bailey 1999a, 62). God was at work in kingdom growth. The world would be impacted. Encouragement yielding confidence was the point yet again (Bruner 2004b, 34; Nolland 2005, 552). Note also how this event has a woman while the previous one involved a man.

In both cases, the picture was how the kingdom, though starting small, would fill the earth. Nothing would escape its presence. It would house many. There was an implicit call for patience in how all of this would develop (France 2007, 526).

13:34–35. The idea that Jesus was speaking mysteries was repeated, just as it was declared in Matthew 13:11. Jesus spoke in parables and revealed what had been hidden from before the foundation of the world. This remark about the constant teaching of parables is like Mark 4:33–34. The citation of Psalm 78:2 is in a form like the LXX in the first line and more paraphrastic in the second and like the MT. The citation is unique to Matthew. In Jesus's parables was the opportunity to understand what God had made known and what was new in what Jesus is doing. Mysteries were being revealed that gave new detail about the kingdom program. The verb in the second line is vivid, ἐρεύγομαι. Given the word literally means "to belch," the very vivid idea is "to pour forth" hidden things (BDAG s.v. "ἐρεύγομαι" 391). The psalm looked at a fresh disclosure of a known history, looking at it from a new angle. That is the point of this citation as well. Jesus was revealing a fresh look at an old promise (Carson 2010, 368; Turner 2008, 346–47, discusses Ps. 78 in some detail; this psalm also is quoted in John 6:31).

The citation makes a good transition to Jesus's explanation to the disciples. They got to understand what Jesus was teaching. The context shows that Matthew's point was not about hiding revelation but disclosing things that required understanding and reflection. Among the new things were the ways in which the kingdom grew from small to large, that judgment would include any who reject, and that judgment would come later as initially the kingdom was mixed in with the world.

13:36. As Jesus headed back to the house (Matt. 13:1), the disciples asked him to explain the parable of the Wheat and Tares, as they did in Matthew 13:10 after the Soils parable. At least they showed a desire to know and understand. Once again, Matthew gave a short title that was less than the whole of the parable. It simply identified what he was discussing. The parable stressed the present age's mixed character and the nature of the judgment, and served as a climactic note (Matt. 13:43).

13:37–39. Jesus first identified the parable's associations. The list was straightforward, involving seven elements.

The sower of good seed was the Son of Man (Matt. 13:24). This was Jesus's favorite way to refer to himself (see Matt. 8:20 discussion).

The field was the world (John 4:35—world as a harvest field). This is very important. It was not the church, nor is the parable about the church only. The kingdom of God came into the world and made a claim on every individual. Everyone was and is accountable to the kingdom's presence. The church is the community of those who believe. The kingdom is bigger than the church. However, the kingdom is effective in and through the church. The kingdom benefits are visible in the church, but the kingdom makes a claim on everyone, even though not everyone will end up in the kingdom at the end.

The good seed were the people of the kingdom, not the word of the kingdom as earlier in the parable of the soils in Matthew 13:3–8. "Sons of the kingdom" did not have the same meaning as in Matthew 8:12, where "sons of the kingdom" described Israel as in line for the kingdom but excluded because of a lack of faith (Davies and Allison 1991, 428). In Matthew 13 the sons were those who did respond and were blessed as a result (Matt. 13:43). These were hearts God had sown into and brought to himself. The presence of good in the world was the work of God in the hearts of people drawn to him.

The weeds were the people of the evil one (Matt. 5:37; 6:13). The two groups coexist in the world. There was and is no neutral place, no third option, and no secular place to dwell.

The enemy sowing the weeds was the devil. There is a spiritual battle on the earth until the end. One is in the hands of one spiritual force or another. Satan is seen as a spoiler of that which is good (France 2007, 535). As Blomberg (1992, 222) notes, in this chapter refusal to believe has three reasons: God's sovereign design, human rebellion, and Satan's work.

The harvest was the end of the age (Matt. 3:12; 9:37 for judgment; end of the age: Matt. 13:40, 49; 24:3; 28:20; only in Matthew in the Gospels, elsewhere in the NT only in Heb. 9:26). The image is common in Jewish literature (1 En 16:1; 2 Bar. 13:3—of Baruch; 19:5; 21:8; 27:15; 4 Ezra 7:113; As. Mos. 12:4; T. Levi 10:2; T. Benj. 11:3; Davies and Allison 1991, 429). Judgment would sort it all out. Harvest is also a common image (Isa. 17:5; Jer. 51:33; Joel 3:13; 4 Ezra 4:30–32). All would be involved.

End of the Age Texts

1 Enoch 16:1: "From the days of the slaughter and destruction, and the death of the giants and the spiritual beings of the spirit, and the flesh, from which they have proceeded forth, which will corrupt without incurring judgment, they will corrupt until the day of the great conclusion, until the great age is consummated, until everything is concluded (upon) the Watchers and the wicked ones."

Testament of Levi 10:2: "See, I am free of responsibility for your impiety or for any transgression which you may commit until the consummation of the ages, in leading Israel astray and in fomenting in it great evils against the Lord."

2 Baruch 13:3: "Because you have been astonished at that which has befallen Zion, you will surely be preserved until the end of times to be for a testimony."

The reapers were the angels (Matt. 13:41; 16:27; 24:31; 25:31). This also is a common image in Judaism (1 En. 46:5; 54:6; 63:1). They would not be those who judge but those who gather the judged.

With the players in place, Jesus explained the parable.

13:40–42. These verses focus on the judgment at the end. The point of the comparison is what happened to weeds when they were burned. Just as weeds were cast aside and served no more role by being burned, so those things that caused "stumbling" (i.e., sin; BDAG s.v. "σκάνδαλον" 3, 926) and those who do "lawless" things were thrown into the fire and burned (Ps. 140:9b LXX; Nolland 2005, 560; literally, "those who practice lawlessness," ποιοῦντας τὴν ἀνομίαν; BDAG s.v. "ἀνομία" 2, 85, "lawless deed"). Zephaniah 1:3 may be in the background (Osborne 2010, 534). The imagery of Daniel 3:6 was reversed. All evil and that which caused it were extinguished from the kingdom. Righteousness was vindicated. The idea of being burned up is a common image for judgment (1 En. 54:6; 98:3; 4 Ezra 7:36). There would be weeping and gnashing of teeth (Matt. 8:12), a picture of the torment about the people who have been rejected by God because of their previous rejection of his ways.

Judgment and Burning

1 Enoch 54:6: "Then Michael, Raphael, Gabriel, and Phanuel themselves shall seize them on that great day of judgment and cast them into the furnace (of fire) that is burning that day, so that the Lord of the Spirits may take vengeance on them on account of their oppressive deeds which (they performed) as messengers of Satan, leading astray those who dwell upon the earth."

1 Enoch 98:3: "For this reason, they are devoid of knowledge and wisdom, so they shall perish thereby together with their goods and together with all their glory and honor. Then in dishonor, in slaughter, and in great misery, their spirits shall be cast away."

4 Ezra 7:36: "Then the pit of torment shall appear, and opposite it shall be the place of rest; and the furnace of Hell shall be disclosed, and opposite it the Paradise of delight."

The description of the angels as "his" and belonging to the Son of Man made him the judge (Matt. 16:27; 24:30–31; 25:31–33; Hagner 1993, 393–94). This reflected a high Christology and alludes to Daniel 7:13–14.

13:43a. In contrast were "the righteous" (οἱ δίκαιοι; BDAG s.v. "δίκαιος" 246, 1aα). They were going to shine as the sun. In the judgment we have the picture of two very different kinds of light: fire that lays waste (Isa. 10:17) and a light that shines. The image of the shining light pointed to the glorious state of being raised and made immortal (Dan. 12:3; 1 En. 104:2; Col. 3:4; 2 Thess. 1:10;). The righteous will reside and belong in the kingdom of their Father.

13:43b. Jesus closed the explanation with his typical call to hear (see Matt. 11:15; 13:9). He was saying, pay attention to this.

13:44. Jesus turned now to two short parables that pointed out the kingdom's value followed by a third parable that came with explanation like the parable of the soils and the wheat and tares.

The first parable was about treasure found and then reburied. This parable of the Treasure is unique to Matthew in the four Gospels, but a secondary and expanded version also appears in the Gospel of Thomas 109 as it has a person discovering the treasure of a field sold to him with the treasure in it that the original owner did not know was there (Davies and Allison 1991, 437).

Discovery of the exposed treasure led the man to rebury it in the field and sell everything to buy that field. Contracts in that time contained a clause about owning the contents of the real estate sold (B. Bat. 4.9; Wilkins 2004, 487 n. 36). Before there were banks and safe-deposit boxes one might hide treasure like this to protect access to it (3Q15 is a list of such places Qumran knew existed; Matthew 25:25; Davies and Allison 1991, 436; on hidden treasure in ancient stories, Keener 2009, 391). Joy was the driving emotion at having found that treasure. This image of wisdom like the treasure of wealth appears often (Prov. 2:1–4; Sir. 20:30). That combination of wisdom's value and joy was Jesus's point. The kingdom was worth everything. It was a joy to have access to it. Earlier, Matthew had expressed a note about the blessing it was to experience what others had longed to see (Matt. 13:16–17). An awareness of how precious the gospel was, along with joy, should be the attitudes one had toward the kingdom.

The stumbling over treasure only to procure, hide, and buy the land in which it was present has given some pause about the haphazard way the man worked by finding treasure and then burying it in a place he did not own and then buying the land, but we should not give a parable too much analysis for being vivid (Blomberg 1992, 223; Morris 1992, 359). It may well be that the original person who had placed or lost the treasure originally in the field was long gone, but the parable did not seek to answer such questions. Certainly, the person who sold the land in the parable was not aware the treasure was there (Keener 2009, 391).

The idea of discovering this treasure in a context of treasure being hidden also made the point that not everyone would find the kingdom. That fit the chapter nicely in terms of the kingdom not being appreciated by all for what it is.

13:45–46. The second parable on the kingdom's value was like the first. This parable is also unique to Matthew among the four Gospels but appears in the Gospel of Thomas 76 in a secondary form, where a merchant finds goods and a pearl. In that version, he sells the goods and buys the pearl (Davies and Allison 1991, 339–40).

Matthew's version pictures finding a pearl of great price. The difference between this parable and the previous one is that here the searching person was seeking what was found while in the last parable the person stumbled upon it. This tie of pearls and something of value is another image often tied to wisdom (Job 28:18; Prov. 3:15; 8:11). A merchant appreciated the value of this pearl and so sold everything to buy it. The kingdom was so valuable that it was worth that high price (Matt. 6:33; Phil. 3:8). This kind of sacrifice was something Matthew portrayed about discipleship (Matt. 4:20, 22; 9:9; 16:25–26; 19:21–22, 27–29; Turner 2008, 353).

Bailey (1999b, 176) notes five parallels between these last two parables: finding, something of value, hiding, going to sell all he has, and buying. Joy is unique to the first parable, as is hiding the treasure again. The parable taught that the kingdom was worth a total sacrifice and yields joy.

13:47–48. The parable of the Dragnet was a mirror to the parable of the Wheat and Tares, except the dragnet had no mention of the enemy. This parable was about the mixed nature of what the net brings in and the judgment that followed. This parable is unique to Matthew among the four Gospels, but the Gospel of Thomas 8 has a version of this parable with one large and many small fish, with the fisherman keeping the one large fish. Davies and Allison (1991, 443) argue the Thomas version is secondary, especially in light of only one fish being kept.

Matthew's image is simple. There was a catch of fish in a "large net" (dragnet) that had weights tied to its bottom and floaters on the top (BDAG s.v. "σαγήνη" 910). This net could hold hundreds of fish and took several men to operate. John 21:6–8 describes such a scene. France (2007, 542) notes there were more than twenty kinds of fish in the Sea of Galilee; Keener (2009, 392) puts the number at twenty-four. The net was often pulled between two boats or pulled to shore after boats dropped it into the sea. Wilkins (2004, 489) puts the dimensions at 750 to 1,000 feet in length and a depth of up to twenty-five feet high in the middle and five feet at the ends. This is the only use of the word in the NT. The men gathered the catch of all kinds of fish on the shore and separated the good from the bad. Bad fish might have included unclean eels as well as other unclean fish or those that were too small (Lev. 11:9–12). The nature of the catch shows all nations of people were in view (Hagner 1993, 396). The kingdom program was shifting to all people (Bailey 1999c, 283).

13:49–50. Jesus said it will be like this at the end of the age, when the evil are separated from the righteous. The evil will be cast into the fiery furnace. Fish were not normally burned up, but this explanation was focused on what happens at the end of the age, not on the picture of the fish. There will be weeping and gnashing of teeth. This was the picture of the torment of rejection. The parable focuses strictly on the judgment of those who are evil, as in Matthew 13:41–42, and anticipates the judgment of sheep and goats in Matthew 25:31–46. Here is the sad end of those who reject Jesus. The parable's wording has vocabulary very much like Matthew elsewhere.

13:51. Jesus asked the audience of disciples (Matt. 13:36) if they understood what he had said. They confidently replied that they did. This contrasted with their recognition of not understanding earlier in the chapter (Matt. 13:10, 36). It was likely the disciples were further along, but there were still things for them to learn as their reaction to certain things indicated, such as Jesus's coming predictions about his suffering (Matt. 16:21–23; also 15:16; 16:5–12; France 2007, 544). This exchange is unique to Matthew's gospel. Understanding what was taking place has been a major idea in this discourse (Matt. 13:11–14, 16–17, 19, 23).

13:52. Then Jesus noted that the scribe of the kingdom—that is, the teacher of these things—had things new and old to present. Note how the new preceded the old because it gave the old its frame. The reference to the scribe was the idea of a trained teacher. That is part of what this chapter has been about: to inform the disciples of God's program, especially the new things in it. The teaching had been about the kingdom program, especially what has been unexpected: small to large, judgment deferred, the kingdom in the midst of the world for a time, the judgment involving all people and not just the nations, and containing things old and new that were worth everything.

This was the eighth parable and it used the "is like" formula common to parables. Jesus was commending the disciples as teachers of the kingdom and reminded them that what they taught was a mix of new and old things. Likely in view was the idea of being a scribe teaching eschatological truth about the promise (Osborne 2010, 544).

Kingdom Parables of Matthew 13 and Kingdom Scribe

Soils	The Different Responses to the Kingdom
Wheat and Tares	The Mixed Character of the Kingdom Until the End
Mustard Seed	Kingdom Starts Small, but Ends Up a Dwelling Place
Leaven	Kingdom Starts Small, but Ends Up Filling the Whole
Hidden Treasure	Kingdom Worth Selling All with Joy
Pearl of Great Price	Kingdom Worth Selling All
Dragnet	Kingdom's Mixed Character Purged of Evil at the End
Kingdom Scribe	Teaches Things New and Old

Orton (2004) traces the theme of the scribe in full with its eschatological significance. The "new" things were not so much completely new. Rather what was new was the presentation that the kingdom was always coming in stages and with a move from small to large. That had not been anticipated, although on review one could see it in the old program (Pss. 2:1–2; 118:22–26; Isa. 52:13–53:12). The scribe was like a rich landowner who had a treasure of wonderful things. The picture of treasure reinforced the parables of the Hidden Treasure and the Pearl of Great Price (Matt. 13:44–46). These old and new things were the gifts he cast out in his teaching. These were not ideas to hoard but to distribute (Wilkins 2004, 490). This was like what was said of wisdom (Prov. 3:14–15; 8:1–36; Wis. 7:8–14; 8:5; Sir. 41:14; Keener 2009, 393).

13:53. Jesus completed the discourse. Matthew used the same summary he did to end the Sermon on the Mount and the Mission Discourse (Matt. 7:28; 11:1; also 19:1 and 26:1). From there, Jesus resumed his ministry. In the next scene we are in Nazareth.

13:54. This scene is also in Mark 6:1–6 and in Luke 4:16–30. The Lucan account has much more detail. The scene had probably been moved forward by Luke, given Luke has a visit to Capernaum after this scene (Luke 4:31–44) and yet the previous scene of Luke 4:16–30 refers to Jesus doing what he had done in Capernaum. In Luke, Jesus had not yet been to Capernaum until that following scene. So, the scene in Luke was paradigmatic of the entire ministry in Galilee. It also was paradigmatic here in Matthew as it capped off the kingdom discourse. Again, the evangelists sometimes said the same thing in different ways, making different literary choices.

Jesus went to the hometown synagogue and taught on the Sabbath. "Their" synagogue probably reflected the fact that Nazareth was no longer Jesus's home. The crowd was amazed by what he said and did (Matt. 7:28; 8:27; 9:33; 15:31; 22:22, 33; 27:14). Two things impacted them: his wisdom (Matt. 11:19; 12:42) and his miracles. What we see expressed here reflected what Matthew had shown about Jesus's ministry. There was word and deed, a call that God loved people undergirded by evidence of that love. Ministry is more effective when both are present. Jesus modeled it here. France (2007, 548) notes that this was the second time Galilean cities were shown as having rejected Jesus (Matt. 11:20–24)

13:55–56. A series of reflective questions followed. They were asked with the interrogative οὐκ, expecting positive answers. Was not Jesus the son of the one who works with wood (John 6:42)? A τέκτων described the vocation of Jesus's father. It refers to "a builder" or one who constructs, so it could include working with stone or metal (BDAG s.v. "τέκτων" 995; Turner 2008, 360; 1 Sam. 13:19 [=1 Kgdms. LXX]). Did we not know his mother Mary and his brothers: James, Joseph, Simon, and Judas? Were not his sisters with us? The fact Jesus had a family was noted in Matthew 12:47. Here we see some specific names. James became the leader of the church in Jerusalem (Acts 1:14; 15:13; 1 Cor. 9:5; Gal. 1:19; 2:9). Jude is associated with one New Testament letter. The underlying question that fueled their astonishment was, so where does this wisdom come from? Jesus was not a formally trained teacher (John 7:15). The crowd had trouble combining their familiarity with Jesus and his family with the apparent authority he claimed and demonstrated.

13:57. The crowd took offense at Jesus (Mark 6:3). This meant they rejected him, as the next verse also makes clear. The key term here is ϵσκανδαλίζοντο ("they were offended"; BDAG s.v. "σκανδαλίζω" 1b, 926). The imperfect speaks to an ongoing, settled response. Jesus had urged people not to be offended by him by calling those blessed who were not offended (Matt. 11:6; cf. the Pharisees in Matt. 15:12). The result was failed soil.

Jesus's response declared that a prophet had honor everywhere except in his hometown (Luke 4:24; John 4:44). Gospel of Thomas 31 adds the note that a physician did not heal those he knew (P. Oxy. 1). Sayings like this were common among the Greeks (Davies and Allison 1991, 459–60; e.g., Epictetus, *Diatr.* 3.16.11). Mark 6:4 has a longer form of this saying and mentions family as well. Matthew does mention his house, which may be an allusion to the family or the city. Normally this would have referred to family, so Matthew was saying what Mark was in a distinct way. So other people saw who Jesus might be, but not those closest to him. Other prophets, such as Isaiah and Jeremiah, experienced this (Isa. 6:9–10; Jer. 11:21–22; 12:6).

13:58. The result was that Jesus did not perform many miracles there, because of the "unbelief" (ἀπιστία; BDAG s.v. "ἀπιστία" 1, 103; Mark 6:5). Offense and rejection went together. Offense reflected an absence of faith.

Matthew did not say Jesus was unable to heal, as in the language in Mark, but focused on the impact of the lack of faith. Jesus did not act like a magician by simply showing his capability but called for faith (Keener 2009, 396). This is another text highlighting the fact that moving toward rejection can cut off the possibility of benefiting from what God was doing. Jesus had warned of the consequences of moving toward rejection. Here we see it. So there was much at stake in this response. Mark 6:6a has Jesus marvel at the unbelief around him. The disciples were sometimes rebuked for having little faith (Matt. 6:30), but here there was nothing to work with and no place to go.

THEOLOGICAL FOCUS

The exegetical idea (Jesus's kingdom parables showed that the kingdom would start small and end up large, involved a judgment coming at the end, and was so precious that one should give up all to get it, all in a context where many still rejected him because of spiritual blindness) points to this theological focus: Despite all that the kingdom offers and the certainty that it will be universal in scope one day, people still reject the offer of God's grace.

The nature of the kingdom is that it starts out surprisingly small but eventually will cover all, is worth everything, and has things old and new. The mix of good and evil in the world will not be sorted out until the judgment of the end, a kingdom ministry Jesus's own hometown struggled to accept. That judgment was deferred until the end.

God had a promise he was keeping. The kingdom Jesus brought was entering the world. It started off hardly noticeable, tucked away in a corner of the Roman Empire far from its center. Still God was at work in Israel for the world. The kingdom would coexist with evil for a time. There was a battle between Satan and God for the hearts and souls of people. Jesus continued to show who he was by what he did. Some saw his claims and pondered them, but in the end found it hard to believe that such a humble start could be the beginning of a cosmic program. Matthew was teaching this is a tragic misjudgment. This kingdom is worth selling everything to obtain. It is hope and life, a precious treasure, a pearl of great price. Do not miss what God offers because of wrong expectations about how God will work.

Jesus revealed much about the kingdom in this series of parables. The Wheat and the Tares showed the kingdom will be a mix as it makes claims on the world. Good and evil will not be sorted out until the end. Satan is at work mixing in evil as good seed is sown. The parables of the Mustard Seed and Leaven showed how the kingdom starts small but ends up large, a place where many can dwell. The Hidden Treasure and Pearl of Great Price indicated that gaining the kingdom is worth selling everything. The Dragnet indicated also that the kingdom is mixed until all is sorted out in the end. The one who teaches about the kingdom has things new and things old to share. This was why listening was required.

All this was lost on those in Nazareth. Like those in other Galilean cities, they did not respond. Their reasons for rejection were more intimate than other locales. They knew Jesus's family and struggled to believe his authority could be genuine, even though they recognized the power of his acts and claims. It was another kind of spiritual blindness. They were too close to Jesus to see. Sometimes those most exposed to Jesus failed to see him correctly.

God has a program and a plan. The kingdom does not come all at once with only power. It gradually emerges. That is a part of the program. It will exist in a world filled with evil for a time. This is why the right choice about what is around us is so important. To look for the wrong kind of kingdom is to risk missing it.

PREACHING AND TEACHING STRATEGIES

Exegetical and Theological Synthesis

The exegetical section describes the inevitability of God's kingdom. It would come—eventually and mysteriously—as John the Baptist predicted, and Jesus preached. The coming kingdom was inevitable. What Jesus's parables clarified was the small start, slow timing, and wide reach of the kingdom. God controlled its pace. God controlled its scope. Among the recurring fallacies in Jesus's day and ours is the notion that humans can usher in the kingdom by their own efforts. Political, educational, and economic reform will not bring it. Military force, evangelistic efforts, or social programming will not bring it. No, the kingdom will grow as God deems fit (Mark 4:28).

Although God controls the pace and scope of his coming kingdom, believers are not exempt from laboring on God's behalf. In the Sermon on the Mount, Jesus taught his disciples to pray for the kingdom's arrival (Matt. 6:10). Later, he sent his disciples to declare the coming kingdom in word and deed (Matt. 10:7–8). Now the treasure and pearl parables (Matt. 13:44–46, 52) compelled believers to make sacrifices on behalf of God's kingdom. Prayer, witness, and sacrificial living constitute the human response to the heavenly kingdom. We do not simply watch and wait for it; we join God in his work.

Preaching Idea

Stay tuned: God's plan is full of surprises!

Contemporary Connections

What does it mean?

God's plan is packed with plot twists. Scripture pulses with surprises. The biblical story opens with God's surprising creation: orderly, rhythmic, diverse, and intimate. It answers the tragic fall of humanity with surprising stories of divine rescue: from Noah's flood to the exodus to Nehemiah's rebuilding of the wall. And it brings surprising figures—Moses, Rahab, David, Naaman, Josiah, Jeremiah—into the spotlight. God admits his own genius in Isaiah 55:8: "For my thoughts are not your thoughts."

These surprises continue today, inviting us to stay tuned, pay attention, and be amazed when God does something unlikely. For example, God may bump us to first class on a flight. He may draw our crankiest coworker to Jesus. He may provide an unexpected financial gift to cover our monthly mortgage payment. He may bring renewal on college campuses following a humdrum chapel service (e.g., Asbury). The more we pay attention, the more surprises we see.

Is it true?

God's plan is undoubtedly brimming with surprises. However, two points of clarification are worth noting. First, not all surprises are happy ones. God sometimes allows sin to advance his plans. Biblical history records God's surprising use of evil figures like Satan, Pharoah, Jezebel, and Nebuchadnezzar. He used surprising events like flood, exile, and crucifixion to secure salvation. And he allowed personal suffering to afflict faithful people, as evident in stories of Job, Joseph, Naomi, and Paul. Such unhappy surprises continue today. God's plan does not spare us from parental abandonment, financial crises, abuse, allergies, or loneliness. Although we would not write such suffering into our own stories, many can testify how God has used unhappy surprises for their good (Rom. 8:18–30; 2 Cor. 4:7–18; 12:7–10). These surprises may deepen faith, open doors, or redirect us.

Second, God often works in ordinary ways. Creation is governed by natural laws. Actions have consequences. Much of the wisdom in Proverbs relies on how God has designed a predictable world. We reap what we sow (Gal. 6:8). Hard work precedes success. This is not surprising. Good listening makes better friendships. This is not surprising. Faithful, prayerful witness to Jesus makes new disciples. This is not surprising. Greed and comparison lead to a joyless life. This is not surprising.

Now what?

Staying tuned is about paying attention to God.[1] First, we focus on God, tuning out distractions (e.g., social media, news) so we can see him at work. We must remember that God works in both mysterious and ordinary ways. Sometimes his work is slow; other times his interventions are immediate. As the Wheat and Tares parable illustrates, the presence of wickedness is not the absence of God. So, our paying attention requires prayerful discernment. As we pray for God's kingdom to come on earth as it is in heaven, we keep our eyes open to glimpses of justice, peace, provision, blessing, courage, and transformation. Often, evidence of his work appears among faithful believers committed to bearing witness to him in word and deed.

Second, our focus on God grows into a fixation on God. We keep an eye on his Word and an eye on the world, connecting what he *has done* with what he *is doing*. Scripture shapes a theological imagination, helping us see the world pulsing with divine activity. As the poet Gerard Manley Hopkins observes, we see the world "charged with the grandeur of God" who "plays in ten thousand places." Seeing God everywhere is not New Age mysticism or panentheistic sentiment but deep belief in the promise of Jesus who is "with [us] to the end of the age" (Matt. 28:20).

Finally, our attention should turn toward action. God's work moves through his people. We are not bystanders in his redemptive mission but sacrificial agents. Thus, we are not only looking for God but also looking for opportunities to show God to others in word and deed.

1 Note: This is an extension of the previous sermon. However, instead of paying attention with our ears ("Listen up!"), we are paying attention with our eyes ("Watch!").

When God shows us a friend in crisis, we accompany them. When God shows us a lost soul, we share Christ. When God shows us an injustice, we look for constructive ways to confront it with the love, mercy, and truth of Scripture.

Creativity in Presentation

"Stay tuned" was a phrase when TV and radio broadcasts ruled the day and wanted to keep their audiences engaged. Radio hosts would encourage their listeners to "stay tuned" for next week's episode. TV news reporters would encourage those watching to "stay tuned for updates at eleven." A more memorable tactic was used on children during Saturday morning cartoons. At the commercial break, animated clay figures would dance and sing: "After these messages, we'll be right back." The message underscores our tendency to tune out or change the channel.

For a variation on the idea of "staying tuned," consider having an analog radio on stage. Start with a station cued in. Then slowly turn the dial. Make sure people can hear the sound of static. Work your way toward another clear signal. And discuss the slow, precise, patient work of staying tuned. (Note: You could achieve a similar effect by having someone from the worship band tune his guitar while you talk about the importance of staying in tune.)

Stereograms are 3D pictures buried beneath 2D patterns. These were popularized in the 1990s, printed in "Magic Eyes" books or posters (see magiceye.com). The key to spotting the magic image is "staying tuned" (i.e., staring at it) long enough from a close distance (two inches). From the blurry pattern emerges an unexpected icon. A web search of "stereograms" will produce many results. You can even generate your own to show to the congregation. Just note that these "surprise" images that require you to "stay tuned" are best seen on paper, not screens. Also beware of the frustration for those whose eyes are unable to see the image!

This sermon invites us to appeal to our love for surprises. Of course, not everyone loves a surprise party. But most of us can relate to the happy surprise of finding our lost wallet in the trunk of our car, having someone unexpectedly buy us a Starbucks drink, or news of a pregnancy after years of infertility. In addition to a personal story about a happy surprise, consider something more basic and iconic. Have a box of cereal or Cracker Jack with the prize at the bottom. Or fill several buckets with rice or sand and let people know you've hidden a gift card in each one. Invite a couple of people to dig for their prize.

For those who love surprise endings, you could mention TV shows, movies, or books with unexpected plot twists (see the sidebar). We all like a good surprise ending. However, be sure not to spoil the ending; just let people know they will be surprised.

Movies with Surprise Endings

Planet of the Apes (1968)
The Crying Game (1992)
The Shawshank Redemption (1994)
The Usual Suspects (1995)
Sixth Sense (1999), and most M. Night Shyamalan movies
Oceans Eleven (2001), as well as most sequels, heist movies, and anything else directed by Steven Soderbergh
The Prestige (2006)
Now You See Me (2013)
Gone Girl (2014)
Arrival (2016)
Coco (2017)
Game Night (2018)

As you describe a favorite plot twist in a TV show, book, or movie, remind people that the biblical story has more surprises than Hollywood or Penguin Books could muster. God gave an old man and barren woman a promised child. He made an enslaved people into a holy priesthood. He selected a ruddy, lastborn son to lead a chosen nation. He put a harlot in the Messiah's genealogy. He called outcasts to be disciples. He used a Roman cross to secure our salvation. And he views sinners as saints because of the work of his Son.

Here are two final ways to illustrate our response to surprises: First, have a jack-in-the-box up front. Slowly turn the crank. Watch your people as it pops out. "Surprise!" Second, do a simple card or coin trick. If you cannot make a quarter disappear or force a card on someone, then find a person from your church capable of a little magic. "Surprise!"

Ultimately, you want your sermon to show that despite all that the process of kingdom arrival offers and the certainty it will be universal in scope one day, people still reject the offer of God's grace. Therefore, we should stay tuned: God's plan is full of surprises.

- Kingdom growth is not straightforward (13:24–30, 37–43, 47–52).
- Kingdom growth is slow and steady (13:31–36).
- Kingdom growth requires sacrifice (13:44–46).
- Lack of faith slows kingdom growth (13:53–58).

DISCUSSION QUESTIONS

1. What does the parable of the Wheat and Tares tell us about God and evil?
2. How has the church grown since its inception? How does this fit the parables of the Mustard Seed and Leaven?
3. When have you been surprised by God? What did he do to surprise you?
4. Why is it important to distinguish between spiritual growth, church growth, and kingdom growth based on these parables?
5. What prevents you and your people from staying focused and fixed on God?

Matthew 14:1–12

EXEGETICAL IDEA
Herod's execution of John the Baptist led him to think Jesus was working with powers from a raised John.

THEOLOGICAL FOCUS
Some are perplexed about who Jesus is and are struggling to explain his power.

PREACHING IDEA
Exposing corruption may leave you exposed.

PREACHING POINTERS
Matthew briefly shifts the spotlight from Jesus to John the Baptist. Both figures spoke against corrupted power, religious hypocrisy, and marital infidelity; their preaching packed a punch and impressed crowds. Thus, Jesus and John the Baptist became a threat to Herod Antipas, the political icon of the region. Matthew recounts the personal tension between John the Baptist and Herod Antipas stemming from the prophet's confrontation of the king about his unlawful marriage to his sister-in-law. Herod imprisoned John and eventually executed him at the public request of his stepdaughter at a party. For the original audience, both Herod's cowardice and corruption of power were obvious. Sadly, this served as one more story of how godless authority figures oppose godly truthtellers.

Corruption of power is a timeless problem. From persecutions by Herod the Great and Nero to papal abuses near the Reformation to mass murders by Stalin, Hitler, and Pol Pot to the modern misconduct of Watergate, Enron, #MeToo abusers, and rogue police officers, stories of corruption are readily available. These examples illustrate Lord Acton's famous insight: "Power corrupts. Absolute power corrupts absolutely." Sadly, anyone with power may go to great lengths to preserve it, including a spouse, parent, pastor, or boss. Worse, those who push back against abuse of power often suffer more abuse. This is no reason to remain silent in the face of injustice. It is, however, a reality check: exposing corruption may leave you exposed.

HEROD STRUGGLES TO FIGURE OUT WHO JESUS IS AND SLAYS JOHN THE BAPTIST (14:1–12)

LITERARY STRUCTURE AND THEMES (14:1–12)

This unit contains two parts: the opinion of Herod about Jesus (Matt. 14:1–2) and the story of Herod ordering John's beheading (Matt. 14:3–12). As such, it is a straightforward historical report, explaining John's death and how it disturbed Herod.

Opposition to God's kingdom program had become serious. Not only was Jesus opposed, but John the Baptist was martyred by Herod Antipas. This unit tells that story. It also shows an ironic touch of guilt from Herod. For he had heard about Jesus and had concluded that Jesus's power came from a raised John the Baptist. This was an interesting mix of right and wrong conclusions. Yes, Jesus like John was working with power from God. Yes, they were connected to each other in God's plan. However, Jesus was not simply another John. Jesus was not merely a prophet. Yes, Jesus's power was from God, not from Satan as the religious leaders claimed. However, Jesus's story was not just about miracles; it was about God's kingdom program. No, Jesus was not John. He was far more. So the mix of ideas ultimately was quite wrong.

Matthew told this story to show how deep the opposition to Jesus had become, as well as how confusing things were for those trying to assess things on their own. Some were unwilling to allow God's own revelation to speak to what was happening. The result was a mix of ideas, some of which contained an inkling about what was going on, but the bottom line was that there was not a real recognition of what was taking place.

This scene complements the previous scene in Nazareth (Matt. 13:53–58). While that scene showed how common people were reacting to Jesus, here we see a cultural elite who rejected and underestimated Jesus. What we see here is also like Matthew 11:18–19.

The parallels to this event are in Mark 6:14–29 and Luke 9:7–9. Luke does not relate how John was slain. He only has a presentation of what Herod thought of Jesus, as one of the prophets or John raised from the dead. Mark parallels the whole scene and notes that the idea of Jesus being one of the prophets was a popular idea (also Matt. 16:14), while Herod thought Jesus was John. As is typical, Matthew's version is much shorter than Mark's.

The story of John's death explained Herod's view of Jesus as John the Baptist raised from the dead. It indicates an awareness that God was not done with Herod. Herod had a sense of concern about what he had done to John. Unfortunately, having a concern and acting right about it are not the same thing. So Herod was exposed as having a moral need as others did. The message of God's work in John and Jesus came to call people like Herod to turn back to God, just as it had come for more common people.

The unit's themes are focused on the scope of the rise of opposition, reaching even to the rulers of the land as well as involving martyrdom in death. It shows Herod's insensitivity to the moral challenge John had raised, because the Baptist's righteous complaint led to his arrest and death. Here we have caught a despot at work. We also see the confusion that Jesus caused for those trying to guess who he was. It was better to listen to what was being revealed about him. This showed the fog that resulted when one stepped back or away from revelation. In the end there was rejection and even the potential for violence and death. The text ironically shows the link between John and Jesus, while also showing that some saw that connection but could not explain it clearly. Jesus, having seen this result, could also begin to sense where opposition to his work might lead (Matt. 17:10–13). It could lead to death.

EXPOSITION (14:1–12)

This text is about an abuse of power from an earthly ruler. It also shows the kind of danger that emerges if one stands up for the truth and righteousness. Herod's high governmental position did not exempt him from scrutiny before God and his standards. John the Baptist made that clear and eventually lost his life for saying so. He spoke truth to power and paid for it, but he did what was right. Conflict with the world and its ways can take one there.

Herod's execution of John the Baptist led him to think Jesus was working with powers from a raised John.

14:1–2. The scene opens with Herod receiving reports about Jesus (Mark 6:14–16; Luke 9:7–9). It is clear from what follows that Jesus's miracles were included in what Herod was hearing. Herod's response and association of Jesus with John indicate he was nervous about how he slew John (Matt. 14:9).

Antipas ruled Galilee and Perea from 4 B.C. to A.D. 39. He was one of Herod the Great's three sons to share his rule after the patriarch died (on Herod and the historicity of this scene, Hoehner 1972). Herod's capital city, Tiberias, was only eight-and-a-half miles from Capernaum, Jesus's headquarters (Wilkins 2004, 511). So it was quite likely he had heard about Jesus's activities. Herod had been married to the daughter of the king of Nabatea (Petra) for fifteen years before falling in love with Herodias. His treatment of his first wife and Herodias's insistence he divorce her led to tension with the Nabatean king (Josephus, *A.J.* 18.109–19, also notes John's arrest; Webb 1991, 368). The title "tetrarch" was of a lesser status than being called a "king," as it referred to a ruler with a limited realm and authority (Morris 1992, 369). This is Matthew's only mention of this ruler.

Josephus on Herod Antipas

***Jewish Antiquities* 18.109–11, 116–17:** "About this time Aretas (the king of Arabia Petrea) and Herod had a quarrel, on the account following: Herod the tetrarch had married the daughter of Aretas, and had lived with her a great while; but when he was once at Rome, he lodged with Herod, who was his brother indeed, but not by the same mother; for this Herod was the son of the high priest Simon's daughter. However, he fell in love with Herodias, this last Herod's wife, who was the daughter of Aristobulus their brother, and the sister of Agrippa the Great. This man ventured to talk to her about a marriage between them; which address when she admitted, an agreement was made for her to change her habitation, and come to him as soon as he should return from Rome; one article of this marriage also was this, that he should divorce Aretas' daughter. So Antipas, when he had made this agreement, sailed to Rome; but when he had done there the business he went about, and was returned again, his wife having discovered the agreement he had made with Herodias, and having learned it before he had notice of her knowledge of the whole design, she desired him to send her to Macherus, which is a place on the borders of the dominions of Aretas and Herod, without informing him of any of her intentions. . . . Now, some of the Jews thought that the destruction of Herod's army came from God, and that very justly, as a punishment of what he did against John, that was called the Baptist; for Herod slew him, who was a good man, and commanded the Jews to exercise virtue, both as to righteousness towards one another, and piety towards God, and so to come to baptism; for that the washing [with water] would be acceptable to him, if they made use of it, not in order to the putting away [or the remission] of some sins [only], but for the purification of the body; supposing still that the soul was thoroughly purified beforehand by righteousness."

Herod's conclusion about the report on Jesus was expressed to his servants. Joanna, the wife of Herod's steward, was a believer; so here was a potential source (Luke 8:1–3). Herod believed that Jesus was John the Baptist raised from the dead. Mark 6:14 has the people expressing this view. It is hard to be sure exactly what was meant by John's resurrection, since Jews believed in a general resurrection at the end of history. Was this spirit of John in Jesus seen as a form of popular superstition (Davies and Allison 1991, 468; 2 Kings 2:9–15; Luke 1:17)? What also was odd was that John the Baptist was known as a prophet but did not work miracles, yet Herod thought Jesus's miracles were wrought by a raised John the Baptist. A prophetic connection seemed at work in that conclusion.

14:3–5. There was a note of possible guilt in what Herod said, since Matthew reports that John had been arrested and ultimately executed because he repeatedly challenged Herod's marriage to Herodias. She originally was the wife of Herod's half-brother, probably known as Herod Philip, and Herod divorced his first wife to marry her. Josephus, *Antiquities* 18.136–37, said she flouted the ways of the fathers by confounding the nation's laws. Herod Philip was a distinct figure from Philip the tetrarch (Carter 2004, 303; Morris 1992, 370). Hoehner (1972, 125–36, 170–71) has this arrest taking place in A.D. 30 or 31 with execution a year later. John expressed that the marriage was not "lawful" (ἔξεστιν), incurring Herod's use of power to stop him from speaking about this (BDAG s.v. "ἔξεστιν" 349). The verb here (ἔλεγεν, "was saying") is imperfect, pointing to John's repeated charge of Herod's immorality. Here was an abuse of power in the face of a moral challenge, as John feared God more than political leaders and spoke up (Matt. 10:26–31; Davies and Allison 1991, 470). There not only were multiple divorces but the marriage involving a brother's spouse (Lev. 18:16; 20:21), as well as her being his niece, which was not against the law (Webb 1991, 366–67).

Josephus on Herodias and Salome

***Jewish Antiquities* 18.136–137:** "Herodias, their sister, was married to Herod [Philip], the son of Herod the Great, who was born of Mariamne, the daughter of Simon the high priest, who had a daughter, Salome; after whose birth Herodias took upon her to confound the laws of our country, and divorce herself from her husband while he was alive, and was married to Herod [Antipas], her husband's brother by the father's side; he was tetrarch of Galilee; but her daughter Salome was married to Philip, the son of Herod, and tetrarch of Trachonitis; and, as he died childless, Aristobulus, the son of Herod, the brother of Agrippa, married her; they had three sons, Herod, Agrippa, and Aristobulus."

John was brought to Machaerus, a fortress east of the Dead Sea, thirteen miles southeast from another key Herodian place, the Herodium (Josephus, *B.J.* 7.163–209; for photo of Machaerus, see Matt. 11:2–3 above). Josephus gives another reason for John's arrest (*A.J.* 18.118–19; see chart with 14:1–2). It was sedition, but this may be nothing more than an interpretation of the effect of John's challenge (Hoehner 1972, 136–46, defends the scene's historicity). As Hagner (1995, 412) says, "Any form of opposition from an apocalyptic preacher could easily been regarded as seditious."

Matthew is clear about Herod's desire to kill John but specifies that his fear over John's popularity with the crowds caused him to hesitate. This is best described as one impulse among many Herod had about John, as Matthew 14:9

shows. There Herod was hesitant to slay John. The people saw him as a prophet (Matt. 21:26; said by Jesus, Matt. 11:9; of his popularity, Matt. 3:5–6). So Herod held John in prison. Mark 6:19–20 sees Herodias as the cause for this desire to kill John, while Herod feared John's righteous character giving him pause to act. They both had reason to see John removed, but Herod was sensitive to the consequences of such an act (Morris 1992, 371).

14:6–7. Herod's birthday was the turning point in these events. Mark 6:21–22 tells us the scene was a banquet for Herod's officers and Galilee's leading men. Matthew has a very shortened version, as is his stylistic custom.

The daughter of Herodias danced for Herod and the crowd celebrating on that occasion. The verb ὀρχέομαι simply means "to dance" and does not indicate the style of the display (BDAG s.v. "ὀρχέομαι" 725). There are no parallels for this kind of activity by a princess or family member, but neither should one assume it was not possible nor should one presume the kind of dance this was (Davies and Allison 1991, 472). She is described as a "little" girl, using the diminutive κοράσιον in verse 11 (BDAG s.v. "κοράσιον" 559; Hoehner 1972, 154–56; Turner 2008, 364). Even at her young, tender age, she was shown the head after the execution. Her age of around twelve or so made it possible that this dance was not erotic (Nolland 2005, 584), although the reputation of Herod's parties and the kind of dancing normally done by courtesans may leave room for this idea (Blomberg 1992, 230; Luz 2001, 307; Osborne 2010, 558; Wilkins 2004, 512). Better to think of Herod reacting in part because they all were in a very celebratory mood with much drink common to such parties. Stories of questionable morality could accompany rulers. Josephus (*A.J.* 12.187–89) has an account of a Jewish ruler, Joseph the Tobiad, falling in love with a foreign dancer, only to have a brother's daughter provided to him at night to prevent him marrying the foreigner (see also Babrius 80.1–2). Keener (2009, 399) notes the low reputation of Herod's brother Archelaus in Josephus, *Jewish War* 2.29. Carter (2004, 303–4) also regards the scene to have the feel of low morality. Whatever the ultimate character of the dance was, it was entertaining to the men and pleased Herod. Neither Matthew nor Mark name her, but she is often identified as Salome (Josephus, *A.J.* 18.136–37; see chart above in 14:3–5). The verb "to dance" appears in the NT only here and in the parallel in Mark 6:22, and in Matthew 11:17 and its parallel in Luke 7:32.

Herod was pleased and swore with an oath in public that he would give her whatever she might ask to have. Matthew summarizes what Mark 6:22d–23 has Herod say directly to her, not only giving an oath but offering her half his kingdom, an allusion to Esther 5:3, 6, and 7:2, where Esther pleads on behalf of her people, the Jews, to Xerxes the king and he permits her to asks for up to half the kingdom.

14:8–11. So the daughter, given this opportunity, was prodded by Herodias to ask for John the Baptist's head on a platter (Mark 6:24–25). The verb here is προβιβάζω, which means "to be pushed ahead in something" (BDAG s.v. "προβιβάζω" 866). This is the verb's only use in the NT. It means her mother urged her to do this; probably its force indicates that Herodias "coached" or instructed the daughter to do this. The remark shows Matthew and Mark in agreement that John's death came in the decisive moment from Herodias (Morris 1992, 373; see Mark 6:19). It would not be unusual in this cultural context to place some blame on a woman for a morally deficient action of a man.

This request grieved the king, either because his oaths committed him to act or because he really did not want to do this at this time. The syntax here is not clear, but in the end it makes little difference. Herod is portrayed as being backed into acting either way; he had committed himself to grant her request. The idea of oaths in the plural contrasts with the singular use of the term in Matthew 14:7. It may well be his promise came in parts or was given with reassurances, as Mark 6:22–23 speaks of Herod's offering up to half his kingdom, repeating the commitment already made.

Herod had made an oath in public. He had no wiggle room. So he went ahead and ordered John decapitated (Mark 6:26–27). The head was "a trophy of death" and a particularly gruesome choice to end up displayed on a platter at a banquet (Davies and Allison 1991, 473; Josephus, *A.J.* 18.116—mentioned the slaying, see chart in 14:1–2; in Jewish contexts, 2 Sam. 16:9; 2 Kings 6:30–33; slaying at a banquet, Josephus, *A.J.* 13.380; Nolland 2005, 584). So once Herod committed himself, he followed through with gusto, executing John without any trial. This would have been seen as a shameful way to die (Sanh. 7.3). This action may explain why Herod felt "haunted" by Jesus and saw Jesus as John (Matt. 14:2). Blomberg (1992, 230) observes that Herod was called king when he acted in the least kingly manner. His uncertain state of mind was like what we will see with Pilate in Matthew 27:11–31.

On Beheading as Disgusting

Mishnah, *Sanhedrin* 7:3: "The religious requirement of decapitation [is carried out as follows]: They would cut off his head with a sword, just as the government does. R. Judah says, 'This is disgusting. But they put his head on a block and chop it off with an ax.' They said to him, 'There is no form of death more disgusting than this one.'"

Josephus on Alexander's Earlier "Barbarous" Slaying of Eight Hundred at a Banquet

***Jewish Antiquities* 13.380:** "And when he had shut up the most powerful of them in the city Bethome, he besieged them therein; and when he had taken the city, and gotten the men into his power, he brought them to Jerusalem, and did one of the most barbarous actions in the world to them; for as he was feasting with his concubines, in the sight of all the city, he ordered about eight hundred of them to be crucified; and while they were living, he ordered the throats of their children and wives to be cut before their eyes."

The verb saying Herod beheaded John is causative. It does not indicate Herod did the beheading, merely that he ordered or caused it. So the head showed up on a platter for the young girl (Mark 6:28–29). She took it to her mother. Herodias had her revenge.

14:12. The disciples of John honored their leader. They had appeared twice before in the gospel (Matt. 9:14; 11:2). Joseph of Arimathea would do the same for Jesus (Matt. 27:57–61). Caring for the dead was a value in Judaism (Tob. 1:16–20; 2:3–9; 4:3–4; 12:12–14; 14:10–12; Turner 2008, 365). They collected the body and buried him. Then they went to tell Jesus what had taken place. John became a lesson in what could happen if someone stood up and spoke about what God was doing and what God required, even of governmental leaders.

The idea of respecting governmental leaders does not exempt them from moral responsibility, nor from accountability for their actions. Character mattered, especially for leaders—something recognized even outside of ancient religious circles (Aristotle, *Pol.* 3.5.11; 5.9.4–7—on tyrants; Cicero, *Off.* 2.11–12—where character is tied to justice; Plato, *Resp.* 1.353–54). John knew this, spoke up, and paid the price for it. The prophets paid a similar price. But overlooking character comes at a deeper cost to society.

THEOLOGICAL FOCUS

The exegetical idea (Herod's execution of John the Baptist led him to think Jesus was working with powers from a raised John) points to this theological focus: some are perplexed about who Jesus is and are struggling to explain his power.

John the Baptist's theological faithfulness in confronting sin had led to a hostile rejection and John's unjust death, showing how some react negatively to being called to repent. Even rulers were not exempted from God's call to be moral, even if they held public power.

This was a tragic scene that involved an abuse of power. A prophet speaking of righteousness was arrested and executed on the whim of a woman seeking revenge and her reputation-seeking husband. Here was what could happen when someone stood up and spoke righteously. Those in power might try to snuff them out. It was a preview of what would happen to Jesus. The event was a reason Jesus could have sensed what might be coming for him. Unrighteousness had no patience for righteousness. The lesson was that in a fallen world the righteous might well face severe persecution and death. The opposition Jesus had been describing showed its worst face here.

A lesson emerging from this unit points to the depth of sin. Herod had power and abused it, counter to John's admonition about misappropriating power in Luke 3:14. Herod's confrontation with John the Baptist's call to change led to hostility and violence. John did nothing wrong and died for speaking the truth. Jesus would face a similar fate. In a fallen world, righteousness can have a tough time (1 Peter 3:14–17).

PREACHING AND TEACHING STRATEGIES

Exegetical and Theological Synthesis

A biblical prophet cannot stay silent when witnessing injustice and idolatry. Moses shattered the tablets of stone when he discovered Israel worshiping a golden calf (Exod. 32). Jeremiah poetically expressed his inner turmoil: his heart was aflame; his bones burned (Jer. 20:9). Amos enumerated the many sins of Israel and Judah, giving special attention to the abuse of power by the rich (Amos 2–4). John the Baptist followed in the footsteps of his Old Testament predecessors, exposing the abuses of tax collectors and soldiers (Luke 3:7–14) and immorality of Herod Antipas (Matt. 14:1–12).

Unfortunately, prophetic correction often comes at a cost. Jezebel killed many prophets who opposed Baal (1 Kings 18:4). Luke mentions other prophets who suffered a similar fate (Luke 11:47–51). John the Baptist faced a similar end. But even prophets who did not lose their lives suffered loss. Ezekiel lost his wife. Enemies of Jeremiah threw him in a pit. Those who stood for righteousness, Jesus warned, would experience persecution (Matt. 5:10–12). He was hated; his followers would be as well (Matt. 10:16–25; John 15:18–25). Although standing for righteousness in a godless world leaves us exposed, we may take comfort in the help of God's Spirit, support of God's people, and certainty of God's justice.

Preaching Idea

Exposing corruption may leave you exposed.

Contemporary Connections

What does it mean?

Corruption is a real problem in our world. No one in power is exempt. Pastors abuse the pulpit to shame people. That is corrupt. Politicians line their pockets rather than represent the people. That is corrupt. CEOs skim from the company earnings without reporting. That is corrupt. A mother may hit her son to control his behavior. That is corrupt. A husband may gaslight his wife to get his way. That is corrupt.

Identifying corruption is only the beginning. Exposing it is the necessary next step. As the saying goes: if we see something, we should say something. However, exposing corruption is risky, especially when power dynamics exist, or evidence is lacking. Exposure may increase corruption before eradicating it. For example,

- When a boss gets accused of sexual harassment, he may deny it, turn up the charm, or attempt to silence the accuser.

- When a father hears his child has spoken of abuse, he may admit he has "a bit" of a temper, but his kid "has a wild imagination." Then his child is likely to experience his temper in verbal or physical pain.
- On a less personal level, when masses march in protest of police brutality, the crowd may be subject to rubber bullets or pepper spray if the march turns aggressive.

Those who expose corruption may pay a price before those in power lose their authority.

Is it true?

It is true that exposing corruption may leave us exposed. We do not think fondly of "narcs," tattletales, rats, or whistleblowers. These pejorative terms betray our distaste for people who expose others' sins. In Mafia movies and political thrillers, those who try to bring corruption to light end up dead. In real life, they get trolled on X (Twitter), banned from Facebook, ghosted by extended family, and fired from their jobs.

These, of course, are worst-case scenarios. Sometimes rumors of corruption are met with incredulity. Without evidence, we struggle to look beyond appearances. No one wants to believe the meek pastor is a bully, the decorated coach is a pedophile, or the skilled physician is a predator. Gladwell (2019) offers several haunting case studies where the bias toward trusting authority figures resulted in gross betrayal.

Other times, we normalize corruption. We expect bad behavior among powerful people and thus feel little compulsion to expose it. We all know wealthy people cheat the IRS. We all know politicians cater to lobbyists. We all know the police take bribes. In many cases, we no longer expose the obvious, not out of fear that it will hurt us but because we have little hope it will result in justice.

Now what?

Corruption is a problem. Exposing it can lead to more problems—threats, violence, and financial loss—than resolution. We live in a fallen world with sinful people and broken systems. This should give us pause. Our efforts at exposing corruption may come back to haunt us. However, this is no reason to remain silent. We must proceed with caution. Or, as Jesus said, we must match our gentleness with shrewdness (Matt. 10:16).

First, prayer should precede exposure. Jesus taught his disciples to pray for God's will to be done "on earth as it is in heaven" (Matt. 6:10). The earth is still not perfectly aligned with heaven. Corruption persists. The urgency of this prayer remains.

Second, we must live with integrity. Jesus called his disciples the "salt of the earth" and "light of the world" (Matt. 5:13–16). These metaphors picture the church as a vanguard of virtue. Jesus wanted our love to undermine hate, goodness to overshadow evil, and righteousness to overthrow corruption. The better we embody Jesus's ethic, the more credibility we have in calling out corruption.

Third, we must address corruption in the church as intensely as we expose it outside the church. Recent abuses of power or sexual misconduct in the church are egregious. We are all too familiar with aggressive tactics of pastors, including Mark Driscoll, Bill Hybels, and James MacDonald. Moreover, the stunning report of sexual abuse and cover-up in the SBC churches was horrifying. Such corruption calls for public confession and stronger policies for protecting children, women, and staff members at churches. McKnight and Barringer (2020, ch. 9) offer practical suggestions in leading public lament, so the church becomes a place that names pain and prays for God's healing.

Finally, we must prepare ourselves for backlash when addressing corruption. People in the church do not like it when a pastor outs a favorite politician. Managers do not like being accused of mistreatment. Abusive parents or spouses are likely to manipulate when confronted. Backlash will come. And to be abundantly clear, when a significant disparity in power exists between the accuser and her subject, she should not expose the corruption without a support network (e.g., a counselor, elder, friend, or HR representative).

Creativity in Presentation

Protests, riots, and mass movements against corruption provide memorable imagery of how exposing power can expose you. Consider showing imagery of a few such incidents, giving people fair warning that they may be disturbing. The following pictures would be effective:

- The famous image of a student standing in front of a tank in Tiananmen Square (1989)
- A photograph from the Civil Rights march from Selma to Montgomery, where police violently opposed those marching across the bridge (1965)
- A snapshot from the Kent State protest where university students opposed the government sending additional soldiers into the Vietnam War (1970)

After displaying and describing each image, you can say, "Exposing misuse of power left these people exposed."

A variation of this tragic but creative element could be images of various devices used to execute people who attempted to expose corrupt political leaders. These could include a hangman's rope (e.g., Dietrich Bonhoeffer), a guillotine (e.g., Robespierre), blade for disembowelment (e.g., William Wallace), stake (e.g., Joan of Arc), and, of course, a crucifix (e.g., Jesus).

Many films feature how exposing power leaves people exposed. The Bourne series (directed by Doug Liman, Tony Gilroy, and Paul Greengrass, 2002–16) features the efforts of rogue agent Jason Bourne (played by Matt Damon) to expose corruption in the CIA. Corrupt leaders send many assassins to eliminate Bourne to keep him from exposing the agency's illicit programs. Virtually all legal dramas based upon John Grisham books (e.g., *The Firm*, *The Pelican Brief*, *Runaway Jury*, *The Rainmaker*) feature corrupt lawyers, judges, governmental agencies, or companies who get exposed and then ruthlessly pursue their exposers. Finally, *Snowden* (directed by Oliver Stone, 2016) is based on the life of Edward Snowden (played by Joseph Gordon-Levitt), who exposed immoral data-tracking by the NSA. Consider referencing one of these familiar stories to illustrate the preaching idea for your audience.

Consider illustrating the idea of exposure by contrasting light and darkness. Consider dimming the auditorium or stage. Describe something in the darkness that no one wants to see: a stain, monster, rat, or cockroach. Then add something like, "What is worse than seeing these things is letting them linger in the dark. Darkness gives them power. Darkness increases our fear. We need to dispel the darkness." Then turn on the lights or shine a bright flashlight into a corner of the stage and say, "You've been exposed."

A variation on this illustration could be describing the old way of processing film. When cameras held rolls of 35mm film, it was important not to overexpose the film. Too much light would wash out the image. However, the ambient, reddish glow in the darkroom, plus the proper mix of chemicals, would turn the original image into a vivid picture. Your point here is that the methods of exposure produced different results.

Finally, a personal story may be effective here. You may have confronted a bully, bad boss, or renegade leader at your church for misbehavior. Their initial response may have been a dismissal ("No one will believe you") or threat ("If you tell anyone, I'll make you pay"). If you cannot recall a personal story, or it is too sensitive, there are many stories to draw from in recent years. Testimonies from the #MeToo and #ChurchToo movements abound. Likewise, the podcast *The Rise and Fall of Mars Hill* and *A Church Called Tov* (McKnight and Barringer, 2020) have many stories of pastoral abuse.

A word of caution is needed here. It has become common to exploit others' sins for our entertainment. I (Tim) recently heard this described as "failure porn." We expose sin only to foster justice, not to feel better about ourselves in comparison to others' bad behavior.

Ultimately, you want your sermon to communicate that some are perplexed about who Jesus is and are struggling to explain his power. Moreover, exposing corruption may leave us exposed.

- Spiritual power perplexed Herod (14:1–2).
- Political power crushed John (14:3–12).

DISCUSSION QUESTIONS

1. What was the Jewish understanding of resurrection in the first century A.D.?
2. How did Herod's actions echo those of Xerxes from Esther?
3. In Jesus's day, what were some ways of demonstrating power?
4. What are a few good rules for exposing corruption, so that you are able to mitigate backlash?
5. How can you assure your congregation that leadership at your church takes measures to avoid abuse of power?

Matthew 14:13–36

EXEGETICAL IDEA
Jesus's miracles around the lake showed that he could prevail over nature as well as provide for and direct those who turn to him.

THEOLOGICAL FOCUS
Jesus's actions show the comprehensive scope of his power.

PREACHING IDEA
Whatever we need, Jesus can exceed it.

PREACHING POINTERS
Jesus's control over nature contrasted with Herod Antipas's political might. Herod used his power to hurt others; Jesus used his power to help others. Jesus fed five thousand hungry travelers in the wilderness, rescued his disciples in a sea storm, and healed many with illnesses. Whereas self-protection marked the way of Herod, compassion defined the way of Jesus. He expected his disciples both to experience his power and to extend it, as evident in their distribution of bread and Peter's walking on water. Matthew here continues to describe Jesus's unique identity (Bock 2020b). His original audience would have seen him as the Son of God and Messiah who met their needs.

Meeting our needs comes easy today. We satisfy our need for food at grocery stores, fast-food, and whatever snacks we can find in the kitchen. We satisfy our need for protection through savings accounts, insurance policies, and protective headgear. We satisfy our need for physical health through exercise, surgery, rest, and a healthy diet. Modern methods in food production, finances, and medicine can make us feel like masters of the natural world. This, of course, is an illusion. We can predict the weather but cannot control it. We can treat cancer but cannot prevent it. We can mass-produce food but cannot distribute it to the masses. We are limited in our ability to meet needs. Jesus is not. This passage shows that whatever we need, Jesus can exceed it.

JESUS FEEDS 5,000 AND CALMS THE STORM (14:13–36)

LITERARY STRUCTURE AND THEMES (14:13–36)

This unit has two miracle scenes and a summary of miraculous activity. The two miracles were nature miracles. The first was a gift miracle, where the provision was the point (Matt. 14:13–21; Hagner 1995, 416); the second was a rule miracle, where authority was the point (Matt. 14:22–33). His walking on the water can also be seen as a sea rescue miracle and an epiphany (Davies and Allison 1991, 498). One provided, while the other showed Jesus's power. The provision was one greater than the one Elisha made for the hundred in 2 Kings 4:42–44. The summary involved healings (Matt. 14:34–36).

In contrast to the violence of the ruler Herod, Jesus continued to work a series of miracles that showed his unique power and authority. Jesus had authority of a different kind from governmental rulers and used it in a different way. God's Son reconfigured how power was used as an example to all.

The three scenes occurred around the lake. He fed the five thousand and walked on water, showing such power that the disciples confessed him as Son of God. In a summary on his continued work, Jesus continued to heal despite all the opposition around him. The opposition did not stop Jesus from serving or ministering even to those who opposed him. God's grace abounds. Jesus showed love for his enemies. The contrast with Herod is obvious. One decapitated his enemies, while Jesus sought to draw them to God by serving them.

Jesus revealed his power over nature in two ways: providing food as God did manna for the nation, and in walking on the water and enabling Peter to do the same for a time. The exercise of power over nature recalled God's authority as declared in Psalm 107:28–29. This led the disciples to see Jesus's unique connection to God. In the provision of the food, they saw how God could work through them, as the food became a picture of divine provision and spiritual food. Jesus's feeding the needy also pictured what God does, while refusing to do so leads to God's rebuke (Job 22:5–11; Ps. 22:26; Isa. 58:6–7; Ezek. 18:5–9; 34:2–4; Carter 2004, 305). It was how God sustained Israel in the desert with manna (Exod. 16). Matthew's later readers might also have thought of the Eucharist, but that was hardly the point in the original scene because no one at the original event could have made that connection (France 2007, 559).

The feeding of the five thousand is the one miracle that appears in all four Gospels (Mark 6:30–44; Luke 9:10b–17; John 6:1–13). Matthew continues in the order of Mark's gospel here. The scene anticipates the messianic banquet (Isa. 25:6; 2 Bar. 29:1–8; 4 Ezra 6:52; Osborne 2010, 564), as people shared a meal of *šālôm* that God through Jesus supplied. As was his custom, Matthew again has a condensed version of the story in comparison to Mark.

Jesus's walking on the water is also another parallel miracle (Mark 6:45–52; John 6:16–21). This miracle combination is one of the few places Mark and John overlap together with Matthew. The healing summary is like Mark 6:53–56. This unit continues to parallel Mark in sequence.

The issues of Jesus's provision, power, and authority dominate this unit. His continuing to minister with compassion in the face of rising opposition showed God's continued grace. Jesus as the provider is being consistently highlighted. The world, seen in Herod, was violent, but Jesus was one sent by God to meet core human needs of food and protection. The disciples learned that they could be a source of sustenance and could accomplish unusual things if they would trust Jesus. The key theme is a call to have great faith in what Jesus can do, even in this context of rising opposition. Jesus can provide out of little or nothing. Some were responsive and would receive ministry. So the call to serve continued.

EXPOSITION (14:13–36)

Two themes are present here. First, there is a contrast with the violent ways of the world toward enemies that continues from the previous scene. Jesus was a different kind of ruler, bringing a different kind of kingdom with a different way of reacting to people in the world. Those opposed to him were not crushed but loved. Judgment for poor choices would come later; now was a time of invitation. Second, Jesus's divine power would be on display by how things in the creation like bread and storms were handled. The power on display meant one could rest in the different way of life Jesus was calling disciples to reflect.

Jesus's miracles around the lake showed that he could prevail over nature, as well as provide for and direct those who turn to him.

14:13. The news about John caused Jesus to withdraw and seek some privacy. It was not a time for confrontation, so he left the scene of potential tension. This is another hinge verse in Matthew. It looks back and moves events forward at the same time. One could well link it as the end of the previous event as well as allow it to begin this miracle. Luke 9:10 puts this event near Bethsaida on the northeast shore of the Sea of Galilee. It is unclear whether the allusion to a report was about John the Baptist's death (Hagner 1995, 417)—in which case we are still in a sequence that has been temporally relocated, as the death took place earlier—or whether the passage describes the report about what Herod believed about Jesus from Matthew 14:2 (so Carson 2010, 389–90). Whatever the reason for withdrawal, the crowds would not permit it.

When they heard where he had gone, they came out to him. This would have been a trip of a few miles on foot.

14:14. Jesus saw the crowd, and as earlier (Matt. 9:36) he had compassion on them (also Matt. 15:30–32). Mark 6:34 speaks of the people being like sheep without a shepherd, a remark Matthew has at Matthew 9:36. Jesus healed those who were sick. The term for "sick" (ἄρρωστος) is used by Matthew only here (BDAG s.v. "ἄρρωστος" 135; Mark 6:5, 13; 16:18 are other NT uses). This summary brackets the events to follow with a healing summary presented on the other end of this unit (Matt. 14:34–36). An earlier healing summary is in Matthew 4:23–24; a later one appears at Matthew 19:2.

14:15. The disciples were concerned that the day was late and there was no food where they were. It was a straightforward request borne out of legitimate concern. They urged Jesus to release the crowd so they could travel home and eat (John 6:5). It is not clear whether the small size of the villages around the location could have handled the number of people, but nothing could happen out here as far as the disciples were concerned. To act is the "best of difficult options" (Osborne 2010, 565).

This notice of a lack needing to be filled before a gift miracle is common (Davies and Allison 1991, 487; 1 Kings 17:12; 2 Kings 4:2; John 2:3). The expression involving the "hour has passed" was referring to the fact that mealtime had passed and so the hour was late (BDAG s.v. "παρέρχομαι" 2, 775–76, "to pass by").

14:16. Jesus chose not to release the multitudes and instead challenged the disciples themselves to give the crowd something to eat (Mark 6:37; Luke 9:13). In Jesus's view, the crowd had no need to go—a remark only Matthew has. It is clear that something unusual was about to take place. The idea of giving them something to eat alludes to 2 Kings 4:42–43, where Elisha fed a hundred people. Jesus commanded the disciples to feed the crowd. They were able to care for the crowd. They were to have faith that Jesus knew how to care for them (Keener 2009, 404).

14:17–18. The disciples' inventory of food was five loaves and two fish. Mark 6:36–37 has more detail about how the count was made, as does John 6:9, telling us the food came from a boy. The amount of bread and fish were not even close to being enough to feed the crowd. There is nothing symbolic in these numbers. It just indicated how little food there was. Jesus told them to bring him the food.

14:19–21. Jesus had the crowd recline on the grass (Ps. 23:2). Mark 6:39–40 has more detail as the crowd sat in groups of a hundred or fifty. Matthew is his usual crisp self in narrating this event. Jesus took the food and prayed a blessing (Matt. 26:26), looking up to heaven. He then gave the food to the disciples to distribute to the crowd (Mark 6:41). And he just kept giving out the food! The crowd had a full meal, plus leftovers (John 6:11–12). The disciples collected twelve baskets full of broken pieces (Mark 6:43)—was there one full basket for each disciple? Regardless of how the leftovers were distributed, Jesus had supplied what the crowd needed and cared compassionately for them, even beyond what they could enjoy. He could provide—a hope sometimes tied to Messiah (Blomberg 1992, 233; Hagner 1995, 418). The disciples needed to appreciate this and note that Jesus could serve through them (Wilkins 2004, 515). Efforts to explain this miracle on naturalistic terms, such as that Jesus's teaching on compassion moved people to give their food to others around them, reads into the text things that are not there and fails to appreciate how all the scenes in this unit point to a miraculous work by Jesus, as we are in a section about Jesus's miraculous, divine-like authority over creation. It is fascinating to see Konradt (2020, 227) try to grapple with the miracle here—what he calls a mythic account—and leave something of value even as he notes Matthew himself saw more than a myth in it. He ends up seeing a call to be willing to share as Jesus does here, so that needs could be met.

This was not a small crowd. Matthew estimated it was about five thousand excluding women and children (Mark 6:44). Only Matthew notes that the count did not include women and children. So the actual number was much more. Jesus could provide bread for life (John 6, esp. v. 48).

14:22–23. This next scene of Jesus walking on the water has a parallel in Mark 6:45–52 (also John 6:16–21), but Peter's walking on the water is unique to Matthew. In the miracle, God's power was seen (Job 9:8; Ps. 77:19; Isa. 43:16; Hab. 3:15; France 2007, 566; Keener 2009, 406). Jesus could manage the creation. This is clearly presented as a miracle that is not to be rationalized into something else; as Morris (1992, 380) says, such rationalized readings reflected the "presuppositions of the expositor." There are no Jewish examples of such a miracle (Nolland 2005, 597).

Jesus sent the disciples by boat to the other side of the lake (Mark 6:45). In fact, he demanded it, because ἠνάγκασεν meant "made" or "compelled" them to take the boat (BDAG s.v. "ἀναγκάζω" 2, 60). Mark has them headed to Bethsaida.

Jesus did not go with them. Instead, he headed in private to a mountain to pray (Mark 6:46). John 6:15 alone notes that it was the crowd's desire to make Jesus king that drove him away. At evening time, he was still alone in prayer. This is one of only three texts in Matthew where Jesus prayed (see also Matt. 11:25–26; 26:36–44); Luke has several more such texts

(Luke 5:16; 6:12; 9:18, 28–29; 11:1; Turner 2008, 372; Jesus prayed alone in Mark 1:35; France 2007, 569). Jesus showed himself as one in communion with God.

14:24. The setup for the miracle was a headwind against the boat (Mark 6:47–48; John 6:18). It produced waves that beat up the boat when it was several stadia from the shore. A stadia is one-eighth of a mile, or 192 meters (BDAG s.v. "στάδιον" 1, 940). John has them three to four miles out. This is the second scene with such a storm in Matthew (Matt. 8:23–27). God alone rescued from the sea in Jewish texts (Exod. 14:10–15:21; Pss. 69:1–3, 13–15; esp. 107:23–32; Jonah 1:1–16; 1QH 6:22–25; T. Naph. 6:1–10—Levi calmed a storm through prayer; Davies and Allison 1991, 503).

God Rescues on the Seas

Psalm 107:23–29: "Some traveled on the sea in ships, and carried cargo over the vast waters. They witnessed the acts of the Lord, his amazing feats on the deep water. He gave the order for a windstorm, and it stirred up the waves of the sea. They reached up to the sky, then dropped into the depths. The sailors' strength left them because the danger was so great. They swayed and staggered like drunks, and all their skill proved ineffective. They cried out to the Lord in their distress; he delivered them from their troubles. He calmed the storm, and the waves grew silent."

14:25–26. Jesus showed up walking on the water late in the night, as the fourth watch was the last evening watch by Roman reckoning (Mark 6:48; John 6:19; on God and the sea: Job 9:8; Ps. 77:19; Isa. 43:16; Hab. 3:15; Sir. 24:5–6—of wisdom; Nolland 2005, 600). God's power was showing itself as present in Jesus. This miracle was a second overcoming of creation in this miracle sequence after the provision of food. It was the last three hours of the evening. The text says it in a very matter-of-fact manner. There are at least three miracles here: Jesus knowing what they were doing, the walk on the water, and the calming of the storm (Osborne 2010, 574). Actually, there is a fourth, as Jesus enabled Peter to walk on the water as well. The account countered common claims that emperors were rulers of "land, seas, and nations" (Juvenal, *Sat.* 4.83–84; Carter 2004, 310; so later of Domitian). Luz (2001, 319–20) in numerous texts notes how this was seen as a divine or a divine-human skill. The scene pushes the limits of who Jesus was and is. Jesus was doing God stuff.

Needless to say, the disciples were shocked, even terrified, being caught off guard by the numinous display of a figure on the water (Mark 6:49–50). So they cried out from fear that they saw a "ghost" (BDAG s.v. "φάντασμά" 1049; Ps. 77:16). This could have been understood to have been an angel (Josephus, *A.J.* 1.331–33; 5.213; Turner 2008, 372), a demon (Ignatius, *Smyrn.* 3.2), or the spirit of a dead person (1 Sam. 28; Job 20:8 LXX). Two distinct expressions for fear showed how disturbed they were ("were terrified," BDAG s.v. "ταράσσω" 2, 900; "from fear," BDAG s.v. "φόβος" 2, 1062).

14:27. Jesus calmed the nervous disciples. He told them to have courage (Matt. 9:2, 22; Acts 23:11; Mark 10:49—not by Jesus). He identified himself with the expression "I am," which also could allude to the divine name (Mark 6:50; John 6:20; cf. Exod. 3:14; Isa. 41:4; 43:10; 47:8, 10; 51:12; Davies and Allison 1991, 506, who says the Son is revealing the Father). At the very least it was an expression of self-identification. He reassured them telling them not to fear (Matt. 17:7; 28:5, 10; Luke 1:13, 30; 2:10; Rev. 1:17). There was nothing to be afraid of in this numinous appearance.

14:28–29. Peter urged Jesus to bid him to come. This exchange between Peter and Jesus has no parallel in the other gospels. Matthew has several texts on Peter not present in the other gospels (Matt. 15:15; 16:17–19; 17:24–27; 18:21;

Blomberg 1992, 235). It is debated if this was a test or was real faith. Matthew's use of the first-class condition presents the scene as if Peter was assuming that it was Jesus who was present. It may well be a combination of the two, a test and an example of an initial faith, given what Peter was requesting. If Jesus was present, then Peter would step out in faith. Peter often was the representative for the disciples in Matthew (Matt. 15:15; 16:16; 17:4; 18:21; 19:27; 26:33, 35; Turner 2008, 373). It was an expression of faith in an important way. He understood that Jesus was capable of making him able to do things he otherwise could never consider doing, but he would do it only at Jesus's command. Peter had gained some understanding from the feeding of the five thousand (Osborne 2010, 575). He was imitating Christ while depending on him (Davies and Allison 1991, 507). Jesus accepted the request. So, Peter emerged from the boat and began to come to Jesus. Jesus was sharing his power. It worked, but only for a time.

14:30–31. Peter noticed a strong wind and began to fear, so he began to sink. He cried out for help and asked Jesus to rescue him (Ps. 69:1–3, 14–15; Luz 2001, 321). In a great wordplay, Ephrem the Syrian says Peter began to sink like a rock, echoing a name Peter would receive in Matthew 16:18 (Davies and Allison 1991, 508). Peter cried out for the Lord to save him, using the exact words the disciples had in the earlier storm miracle (Matt. 8:25). Matthew clearly intended the two miracles to mirror each other.

Jesus stretched out his arm and grabbed Peter (Ps. 18:15–16—of God's reach to rescue from the waters; 2 Sam. 22:17; Ps. 144:7). This makes it clear Peter got close to Jesus before being distracted. Jesus addressed Peter's little faith and asked why Peter doubted. Having just a little faith that needed to become more consistent is a common Matthean theme (Matt. 6:30; 8:26; 16:8; 28:17). The lesson was that Jesus's presence was bigger than the circumstances Peter faced. Peter's faith needed staying power (Wilkins 2004, 517). Peter was being pressed to have a more consistent faith in the face of danger, exactly what would be needed in a hostile world. Jesus still saved "despite inadequate faith" (Davies and Allison 1991, 509). Jesus had power he used graciously. The verb διστάζω means to have second thoughts, lack trust, being double-minded, and so here "to doubt" (BDAG s.v. "διστάζω" 1, 252; only here and Matt. 28:17 in the NT; Osborne 2010, 576).

14:32–33. As Jesus got in the boat, the winds ceased and the storm died (Mark 6:51). "The forces of nature know their master" (Nolland 2005, 602). The wind is simply said "to have ceased" or "rested" (BDAG s.v. "κοπάζω" 558; only here and in Mark 4:39 and 6:51 in the NT). The control Jesus had shown over the creation led the disciples to worship Jesus as Son of God (Matt. 28:17). In an earlier miracle involving a stilling of a storm, they asked a question (Matt. 8:27). Here, they answer it. They recognized that it was God who controlled the wind and waves (Job 9:8; 26:11–12; 38:16; Pss. 65:6–7; 89:9–10; 107:29; Jonah 1:15; 2:2, 7–9; Sir. 43:23; 4Q381 15.4; Turner 2008, 373). They recognized Jesus's act as revealing something profound about him as well. He had a unique and special connection to God. This was the first clear confession of Jesus as Son by the disciples. They had heard Jesus speak of the Father (Matt. 7:21; 10:32–33; 12:50; especially 11:25–27). Here they recognized Jesus's unique connection to the Father, something that also would be developed for them in the ministry to come (France 2007, 571). They still had things to learn (Matt. 15:16; 16:9). They were grasping Jesus from the earth up, so that it was dawning on them all of who he was and is. They were gaining insight into Jesus's power but did not yet get his suffering (Blomberg 1992, 236). With Jesus they had all they needed. Matthew loves to speak about Jesus as the Son (Matt. 2:15; 3:17; 4:3, 6; 8:29; 11:27; 16:16; 17:5; 24:36; 26:63; 27:40, 43, 54; 28:19). Jesus shared power and authority with the Father. He could do what the Father did. Osborne (2010, 577) speaks of a "vaguely messianic sense" present here, yet there was an acknowledgment through worship of a unique figure (Carson 2010, 394). This confession will be linked explicitly to messianic hope in Matthew 16:16.

God Calms the Waves

Psalm 65:6–7: "You created the mountains by your power, and demonstrated your strength. You calmed the raging seas and their roaring waves, as well as the commotion made by the nations."

Psalm 89:9: "You rule over the proud sea. When its waves surge, you calm them."

Sirach 43:23: "By his plan he stilled the deep and planted islands in it."

Rescues from the dangers of the seas end up in praise or worship elsewhere in Scripture (Exod. 14:31; Ps. 107:30–32; Jonah 1:16; on this miracle as a whole, Heil 1981).

The end here is very different than Mark 6:51–52. There the disciples did not get what was taking place because of a hardness of heart. Mark is often more critical of the disciples than the other evangelists. The difference also likely has a temporal element in play. Mark was covering why they did not get what was happening from the start, while Matthew told his readers where the event took the disciples in the end. The disciples did grow from the event. Events have depth and can possess such diverse dimensions when we consider what it would have been like to go through them and what one might realize as a result of having gone through them. The last two events showed Jesus with authority over the creation, pointing to his stature as Son of God.

14:34–36. The last few verses of this unit are a healing summary, one of several in Matthew (Matt. 4:23–25; 8:16; 9:35; 14:14; 15:30–31). Mark 6:53–56 is the parallel. Jesus crossed over to Gennesaret, another name for the plain south of Capernaum (BDAG s.v. "Γεννησαρέτ" 194; Josephus, *B.J.* 3.516–21; also known as Ginnesar/Ginosar/Gennesar, where a first-century fishing boat was found in 1986; see picture at 4:18–20). The Sea of Galilee also used this name. Mark 6:45 had them headed to Bethsaida, but they may have been pushed here by the storm.

Those present in the region discovered Jesus was present and came out to have their sick healed by him. Their hope was such that merely touching the edge of his garment would lead to their being healed (Matt. 9:20–21; Acts 5:15; 19:12 are similar in spirit). Jesus was gracious about such tiny faith. As many as touched the garment were healed. Despite the opposition Jesus was facing, he was healing those who sought him out (Hill 1972, 249; Morris 1992, 385). His ministry of compassion continued even in the face of opposition. How different was his response to challenge than that of Herod Antipas.

THEOLOGICAL FOCUS

The exegetical idea (Jesus's miracles around the lake showed that he can prevail over nature as well as provide for and direct those who turn to him) leads to this theological focus: Jesus's actions show the comprehensive scope of his power.

The unit serves to enhance the picture of Jesus as he showed control over the forces of nature. It also serves to develop how the disciples were able to do amazing things if they trusted Jesus. God was working through Jesus. Jesus could provide sustenance. He could overcome threats. The miracles picture more profound kinds of provision. Jesus could deliver. Jesus was aware of what was happening to those around him. Jesus could heal and restore those in need.

Two miracles and a healing summary show Jesus's care for those around him. Jesus acted with compassion, even in the context of intense opposition. The disciples were as much the audience for these miracles as anyone. In the feeding of the five thousand, they learned that Jesus was the great provider. They could serve amazingly through him. His compassion could extend through them.

In the walking on the water, the disciples saw Jesus doing what God does, control the seas and wind. Peter saw for a time that he could do unusual things because of Jesus. His was a wavering faith that needed consistency. So Jesus called him to not let circumstances distract his trust. The result was that the disciples came to see Jesus as Son of God in some initial sense. There was more for them to learn, but they were on the right track.

The summary shows Jesus's continued compassion. Jesus continued to have a reputation as a healer. Jesus's word continued to be supported by his actions. God was underwriting what he was doing. Word and deed continued together with consistency to show the heart of God in the kingdom program Jesus was bringing.

PREACHING AND TEACHING STRATEGIES

Exegetical and Theological Synthesis

Fear is an impediment to faith. In these stories, the disciples wrestle with different types of fear. In the miraculous feeding story, their concern is for the crowd. The remote location, late hour, and lack of bread distressed them. They asked Jesus to send the people away. Instead, he invited them to participate in a miraculous feeding. Fear restricted their vision. Whereas the disciples were overwhelmed by the needs of the crowd, Jesus felt compassion and fed them.

Similarly, the disciples endured a long night on a stormy sea. When Jesus walked across the water to them, their response was fear, not relief. Fear made their imaginations run wild. However, Peter fought his fear and stepped onto the waters. His unlikely journey quickly ended after taking his eyes off Jesus. Fear of the water stole his focus, and he began to sink.

Few of us will chide the disciples for their reactions. Fear is a natural response to food shortages, raging storms, ghostly figures, and sinking at sea. However, these stories remind us that faith is supernatural because its focus is the God who controls all things.

Preaching Idea

Whatever we need, Jesus can exceed it.

Contemporary Connections

What does it mean?

We all have needs. According to Maslow's pyramid, our most basic needs comprise nourishment, shelter, and rest. When these needs are met, we want to climb the pyramid, finding a community of people and our purpose in life. At every age and stage of life, these needs will persist. We are all needy people.

The good news is that Jesus meets our needs. During his earthly ministry, Jesus readily ministered to others' needs. He gave food to the hungry. He protected his disciples at sea. He healed people with sickness and disabilities. He restored a demonized man to his right mind. He integrated outsiders into spiritual community. Moreover, his teaching matched his actions. He encouraged people not to worry because his heavenly Father would take care of their daily need for food and clothing (Matt. 6:25–34). He taught his disciples to meet the needs of others (Matt. 25:31–46). Jesus resassures us that God will provide for his people.

Not only does Jesus meet our needs, but he also may exceed them. Instead of giving a taste of bread and fish to the five thousand, he provided a feast. Instead of providing his disciples a basic career boost, he gave them the Great Commission. His bounty continues today. Jesus has provided for many of us access to grocery stores and medical providers, opportunities to travel and learn, furnished homes and indoor plumbing, printed copies of the Bible and multigenerational churches. These exceed our needs.

Is it true?

It is certainly true that Jesus can exceed our needs. However, two clarifications are important. First, just because Jesus can exceed our needs does not mean he will. His ability to do something does not oblige him to do it. He is not obliged to cure someone of cancer, answer prayers for fertility, or erase our credit card debt.

Second, we often confuse wants with needs. Living in a consumer age has malformed us. We are easily dissatisfied. We want more. We want better. We want new and shiny things or opportunities. For example, we all *need* sleep, but some people *want* eight hours on a king-sized memory-foam mattress with matching memory-foam pillow. We all need food, but some people want food with style, a story, and made from scratch. Jesus can exceed our needs without catering to our insatiable menu of wants.

Now what?

Knowing that Jesus can exceed our needs should provoke three responses. First, we should distinguish between *needs* and *wants*. A fair question to ask when praying for or purchasing something is, "Do I really *need* this?" In general, unmet *needs* lead to legitimate stress; unfulfilled *wants* lead to ingratitude, envy, and entitlement. No one needs to eat at a restaurant, play golf, or subscribe to a plethora of streaming services. These are luxuries. Jesus is not opposed to luxuries, but he makes no promise to provide them.

Second, we should view unmet needs as an invitation to pray. Not knowing if you will be able to pay rent, schedule a surgery, feed your children, or last another month at your job causes anxiety. Jesus admonishes us to pray for daily bread and give our worries to God. Paul echoes this sentiment, encouraging believers to share their needs with God (Phil. 4:6–8). Petition is a gateway to God's peace.

Finally, Jesus's faithfulness in meeting needs gives us reason to give thanks. Gratitude recognizes the thousand good and perfect gifts God provides daily for us (James 1:17). The more we thank Jesus for his provision, the more our lives are marked by satisfaction rather than want. Contentment comes from knowing God provides enough and exceeds our needs through Christ who strengthens us (Phil. 4:10–13).

Creativity in Presentation

This sermon offers a chance to distinguish between "wants versus needs." The movie *The Jerk* (directed by Carl Reiner, 1979) tells the rags-to-riches-and-back-to-rags story of Navin Johnson (played by Steve Martin). After moving from his farm to the city, finding his name in the phone book, and creating a new kind of eyeglass frame, Navin strikes it rich. However, the frames cause people to become cross-eyed, leading to a ten-million-dollar lawsuit. At the end of the movie, as Navin writes dozens of checks to winners of the lawsuit for $1.09, he admits, "I don't need any of this. I don't need this stuff. I don't need anything. Except this . . ." He picks up an ashtray and starts walking out. Then he notices a few other "needs": a paddle game, remote control, matches, a lamp, magazine, chair, and dog. Before picking up each new item, Navin declares, "All I need is this." The scene ends with him dragging all his items down the street. The clip is easy to find on YouTube.

Another way to illustrate "wants versus needs" is to hold up a few different advertisements that show up in the mail: for example, a grocery store ad, clothing store ad, and holiday gift catalogue. My (Tim's) family will often circle the grocery story items we want. However, what we want (e.g., ice cream, steak, pretzel bites) is not necessarily what we need (e.g., vegetables, milk, and bread). My children have always been eager to circle what they want in the holiday gift catalogues. One year my son circled every item. I've had to remind the children, "These are things we want, not things we need."

This sermon also provides a chance to reflect on joy that comes from Jesus exceeding our needs. We can help people see that everyday life is bursting with abundance. Joy is our ability to taste and see it. You might say:

- Jesus exceeds our need for food; he allows us to enjoy the smell of coffee, sweetness of honey, and savory taste of steak.

- Jesus exceeds our need for clothes; he allows us to enjoy the comfort of our favorite jeans, warmth of a wool sweater, and confidence of looking good.

- Jesus exceeds our need for shelter; he allows us to have bedrooms with mattresses, two-ply toilet paper, working utilities, and locks on the doors.

- Jesus exceeds our needs for relationships; he allows us to enjoy the support of family, laughter of friends, counsel of mentors, and solidarity of church.

You could, of course, add to or modify these reflections. Likewise, if your context allows it, you could invite people to participate, shouting out joys they experience in daily life.

In 2012, my friend and his wife heard a sermon about Jesus's miraculous feeding. God then provoked him to sports ministry to underprivileged kids. Eleven years later, AGAITAS has invested in the lives of nearly 3,800 kids through free sports camps. Every time my friend talks about AGAITAS, he describes God's ability to multiply our efforts to meet others' needs. I can recount similar stories of God magnifying efforts to meet needs in my life and church. He provided $40,000 from grants and fundraisers so my wife and I could adopt internationally. He provided $5,000 through an anonymous donor for legal fees, for a church member securing permanent guardianship. He provided a home for a family through Habitat. And he provided thousands for medical assistance for a surgery through Samaritan Ministries. These stories should surface examples of God's generous provision for your church members when they really needed it. Share those stories or invite those individuals to share.

Ultimately, you want your sermon to stress that Jesus's actions show the comprehensive scope of his power. Moreover, whatever we need, Jesus can exceed it.

- Jesus meets our need for sustenance (14:13–21).

- Jesus meets our needs for safety (14:22–33).

- Jesus meets our needs for healing (14:34–36).

DISCUSSION QUESTIONS

1. How does this narrative demonstrate Jesus's identity from the earth up?

2. How does Matthew describe the emotional range of Jesus in these stories?

3. What do you say to someone whose needs have not been exceeded by Jesus?

4. How does Matthew portray Peter in the miracle on the water? At this point in the gospel, how would you rate the disciples' level of understanding about Jesus?

5. When have you seen Jesus exceed your needs? What are some current needs?

Matthew 15:1–20

EXEGETICAL IDEA

In a dispute with the Pharisees and scribes over handwashing purity issues, Jesus charged his opponents with hypocrisy and taught that real defilement came out of the heart, when it perverted relationships.

THEOLOGICAL FOCUS

Jesus teaches that real defilement is not a matter of legal practice but of heart relations.

PREACHING IDEA

More laws don't lead to better lives.

PREACHING POINTERS

The Pharisees return to the scene. They arrive from Jerusalem, armed with a fresh point of contention: Jesus's disregard for purity laws. His response was equally charged, accusing them of elevating tradition over Torah and lip service over love. The offensive interchange led to a follow-up explanation with his confused disciples about getting to the root of impurity. The heart, not the hands, was the source of sin. Matthew's audience would have been familiar with oral customs added to the written Torah, as well as the weight they carried. Moreover, purity laws were a chief distinctive of the Jewish people. Jesus's dismissal of handwashing would have been a surprising claim of divine authority.

Too many people approach the Bible as a moral blueprint or game plan for their lives. They highlight the commands and underline the prohibitions, hoping that following the rules will lead to God's favor (or, at least, protect them from harm). This kind of thinking exposes an unhealthy view of the law as a guarantee of the good life. The logic extends: more laws mean a better life for more people. Families have household rules that build upon the Bible. (*Always pray before you eat!*) Churches develop corporate practices that build upon the Bible. (*Stand and sing three hymns. Then sit for a three-point sermon.*) Christian institutions design conduct policies that build upon the Bible. (*Students will refrain from dancing or drinking alcohol.*) And while these efforts may be well-meaning, too often our so-called biblical rules become more sacred than Scripture. Meanwhile, in an effort to manage behavior, we fail to address our defiled hearts. This passage reminds us that more laws don't lead to better lives.

JESUS DISCUSSES DEFILEMENT AND PURITY AS A MATTER OF THE HEART (15:1–20)

LITERARY STRUCTURE AND THEMES (15:1–20)

This unit is a controversy account that comes in two parts. First there is the challenge of the Pharisees and scribes about the failure of the disciples to wash hands for purity. Their protest led Jesus to rebuke them (Matt. 15:1–9). That is followed by Jesus's commentary on the dispute that produced a rebuke of the Pharisees and a pronouncement that what defiled was not what was put into the body but what came out of the heart and damaged human relationships (Matt. 15:10–20). The general pronouncement about defilement was made to all (Matt. 15:10–11), but the disciples received a more detailed explanation (Matt. 15:12–20).

The unit does three things. First, it shows how Jesus and the Jewish leadership were in tension on the relationship of God's commands and tradition, even tradition that treated themes of Torah. Second, it shows Jesus's ethical priorities were aimed at relationships. Third, it challenges the reader to follow the right teachers, as Jesus called the Pharisees "blind guides." Mark 7:19b alone notes the full implications of what Jesus said. The implication was that Jesus declared all food clean. That lesson did not really sink in for the new community until Acts 10 and Peter's vision tied to God's call to share with Gentiles. We can observe these priorities in the ways Jesus handled issues like touching a corpse, being touched by a woman with a discharge, eating with tax collectors and sinners, as well as moving through Gentile unclean territories.

France (2007, 574) observes that this was one of the last major scenes in Galilee before Jesus began to move to Caesarea Philippi and then on to Jerusalem. The fact that the Pharisees had sent a delegation from Jerusalem also showed how things were heating up.

The unit really has two literary parts in terms of form. The first portion is a controversy account. The bulk of it involves Jesus's rebuke of the Pharisees for hypocrisy. They were so committed to issues of purity that they ignored relational commitments. Being right was more important than how one was to be right. Jesus was stressing that tone matters, and so do relationships. Truth alone can still be wrong if done in the wrong way. The second portion gives Jesus's commentary in three parts. First was the principle that what came out of the mouth was what defiled. Then Jesus charged the Pharisees as being blind guides. Finally came the climactic pronouncement about true defilement coming out of the heart. Note how we move from the mouth to the heart in the unit. Also important is the relational focus on what defiled. We honor God with real purity when we treat others well.

A key theme is that what matters ethically before God is how we treat others in word and deed. The rebuke came because the charge against the disciples represented a kind of unjust slander against them. Note how slander is the last thing in the list in Matthew 15:19. Hypocrisy is also presented in the passage as having an excessive concern for matters of law while forgetting how to relate well to others.

The scene also traces one of the factors that led to the opposition Jesus faced. He not only had a distinct view of how to deal with purity and tradition, but he confronted the scribes and Pharisees about it.

The parallel to this text appears in Mark 7:1–23. Matthew continues to track with Mark in this section of his gospel. Following Matthew's custom, his version of the events is much shorter than the parallels. The image of the blind leading the blind we see in Luke 6:39.

The sequence of confrontation and then instruction is like other sequences where we had Jesus with the crowds and then teaching the disciples, as in Matthew 13. Here there are three steps, as first there was the confrontation (Matt. 15:1–9), then a short remark to the crowds (Matt. 5:10–11), and then instruction to the disciples (Matt. 15:12–20). The event had historical roots as it was not a dispute we see as being associated with later church practice.

EXPOSITION (15:1–20)

There was a distinct ethical tone in the new community Jesus was forming and in what he taught about the law. This unit showed that difference in emphasis. The Pharisees in their desire to be faithful and orthodox cared about the practice of the law in the way they saw it. They equated their reading of the law with the way the law was designed to function. Their priorities risked canceling out the relational dimension of one's walk with God. They had defined defilement so narrowly that they missed major evidence for the presence of defilement: how someone treated one's neighbors. Jesus moved to correct this grave misalignment in priorities. Matthew made sure his readers saw and understood the difference. The kingdom would always push for character in all its relationships. Relational virtue was never to be sacrificed at the altar of law or truth.

In a dispute with the Pharisees and scribes over handwashing purity issues, Jesus charged his opponents with hypocrisy and taught that real defilement came out of the heart, when it perverted relationships.

15:1–2. This scene opens with a query from the scribes and Pharisees who had come up from Jerusalem to observe Jesus. The Pharisees and scribes reappeared in Matthew for the first time since Matthew 12:38. This was the first note that the opponents were from Jerusalem.

They observed that Jesus's disciples did not keep to the handwashing requirements of the tradition when they ate bread, a reference simply to eating (Mark 7:1–4; Luke 11:38). They transgressed those practices. The key term here is παραβαίνω, which means "to transgress" or "break" a commandment (BDAG s.v. "παραβαίνω" 2a, 758). This was not a matter of hygiene. This involved issues of ritual cleanliness. The tradition had extended some laws on purity intended for the temple to eating in the home by equating the need for purity in general to the need for purity at meals, while also claiming that the home was a place like the temple. Various causes of impurity tied to touch included dead carcasses or anything such a carcass touches, certain animals, seminal emissions, and menstruation. Purity was not always about sin but about ceremonial cleanliness.

Numerous Jewish texts describe and discuss this issue, including an entire tractate in the Mishnah (*m. Yad.*; *m. Ḥag.* 2.5; Ep. Arist. 305–6; and Jdt. 12:7). Discussions in Mishnah *Yadayim* include how much water to use to accomplish the washing, what vessels counted as requiring a washing, what kind of water could be used, and how far up the hand cleanliness extended after a washing. Running water had to be poured up to the wrist. *Mishnah Ḥagigah* covered when to wash hands: for unconsecrated food, tithes, heave offerings, and eating food having the status of holy things. Being careful not to become unclean had led to a series of rules about the washing of hands before meals (France 2007, 576–77). The concern was that uncleanness would move from hands (often made unclean in the practices of life and seen as distinct from the person) to food and then to the person, a progression the careful worshiper would wish to avoid. Consuming unclean food was seen to make one unclean (Lev. 11:39–40;

17:15). Washing was seen to remove the uncleanness from the hands and thus protect the hands from ritually contaminating the food before it entered the body. Oliver (2013, 257) speaks of six assumptions about purity tied to the scene: (1) impure hands can cause impurity and thus (2) can defile kosher food, and (3) impure kosher food ingested defiles the body, so (4) handwashing would be required before any meal, which (5) the Pharisees did and (6) expected of other Jews. Oliver goes on to note that unwashed hands were defiled only at a second-degree level so that they did not pass on their uncleanness to food, since only first-degree defilement could do that. However, if liquid contact occurred with the food, then defilement of food could result as that involved first degree impurity (Oliver 2013, 260–61).

The Mishnah

Many of the rules we interact with to understand the thinking here come from the Mishnah. The Mishnah was compiled in about A.D. 200 by Rabbi Judah ha-Nasi and was the written codification of such oral tradition, much of which was practiced earlier than when it was written down in that work. Three centuries later a commentary on the Mishnah led to the creation of the Babylonian Talmud. These sources became the core of rabbinic Judaism. What scholars often debate is how much of this practice was in place in the first century. Some practices seem to have been in play before the texts were written, even if we cannot be sure if all of the Mishnaic instruction was old.

Texts on Uncleanness

Leviticus 11:29–32: "Now this is what is unclean to you among the swarming things that swarm on the land: the rat, the mouse, the large lizard of any kind, the Mediterranean gecko, the spotted lizard, the wall gecko, the skink, and the chameleon. These are the ones that are unclean to you among all the swarming things. Anyone who touches these creatures when they die will be unclean until evening. Also, anything they fall on when they die will become unclean—any wood vessel or garment or article of leather or sackcloth. Any such vessel with which work is done must be immersed in water and will be unclean until the evening. Then it will become clean."

Leviticus 11:39–40: "Now if an animal that you may eat dies, whoever touches its carcass will be unclean until the evening. One who eats from its carcass must wash his clothes and be unclean until the evening, and whoever carries its carcass must wash his clothes and be unclean until the evening."

Mishnah *Ḥagigah* 2:5: "They wash the hands for eating unconsecrated food, tithe, and heave offering and for eating food in the status of Holy Things they immerse; and as to [the preparation of] purification water [through the burning of the red cow], if one's hands are made unclean, his entire body is deemed to be unclean as well."

The Jewish leaders' question was posed explicitly as the disciples violating the tradition of the elders. They saw this tradition as a natural extension of the commands of God from Torah. *Mishnah 'Abot.* 1.1–3 teaches this oral stream came from Moses then on to Joshua to the elders then on to the prophets and then finally to the great synagogue apparently in the time of Ezra (Nolland 2005, 611–15). They believed they were to "make a fence around Torah." This authoritative role for oral tradition was part of what Jesus challenged in his response. The Pharisees have asked for more than God required, reflecting the human tendency to extend the command of God beyond what he demands.

Why the leaders challenged the disciples and not Jesus's practice is not clear, since in Luke 11:38 Jesus was also said not to observe these traditions. Regardless, Jesus would have been seen as responsible for the disciples' practice.

It is important to note that in the Torah, handwashing is much more limited and does not apply to meals at home (Exod. 30:17–21—for priests at the tabernacle; Lev. 15:11—after a discharge; Deut. 21:1–9—touching a dead body; see Lev. 11:39–40 text in chart above; Turner 2008, 378–79). Certain traditions had extended this to meals for all people. So the dispute was about a tradition, not a Mosaic stipulation.

Jewish Text on the Source of Tradition

***Mishnah 'Abot.* 1.1–3:** "Moses received the Torah at Sinai and transmitted it to Joshua, Joshua to the elders, and the elders to the prophets, and the prophets to the Men of the Great Assembly. They said three things: Be patient in [the administration of] justice, raise many disciples and make a fence round the Torah."

Handwashing Laws

Exodus 30:18–21: "You are also to make a large bronze basin with a bronze stand for washing. You are to put it between the tent of meeting and the altar and put water in it, and Aaron and his sons must wash their hands and their feet from it. When they enter the tent of meeting, they must wash with water so that they do not die. Also, when they approach the altar to minister by burning incense as an offering made by fire to the Lord, they must wash their hands and their feet so that they do not die. And this will be a perpetual ordinance for them and for their descendants throughout their generations."

Leviticus 15:11: "Anyone whom the man with the discharge touches without having rinsed his hands in water must wash his clothes, bathe in water, and be unclean until evening."

Matthew's account is much shorter than Mark's. Mark 7:1–4 explains the practice to his non-Jewish audience as something all the Jews do, a remark that was likely rhetorical in saying this was a common Jewish practice.

Matthew presents another text on the direction of such distinctive practice for the disciples in 9:14–17, where Jesus's disciples did not fast as John the Baptist's disciples and the Pharisees did (Nolland 2005, 608). It was a signal that Jesus's way might be slightly different from other Jewish pietistic environments. New wineskins were at work. This was part of the old/new and continuity/discontinuity tensions Matthew worked with in that Jesus went where the law intended to take people, but not in the way many were used to doing it. The challenge of Matthew 12:2 also fits in here. There it is the Sabbath that is being handled in a distinct way. This distinctive practice emphasis is not unique in terms of the ethos of Jesus's ministry.

15:3. Jesus responded directly not to handwashing, but to the principle involved in having traditions. He asked why they transgressed the command of God for the sake of the tradition (Mark 7:9). Jesus demoted the Pharisees' tradition "of the elders" to simply "your tradition." He differentiated that category from God's commands. Jesus's response laid out a different approach to such questions.

Jesus used the same verb of breaking a command that they had used in asking him their question. Jesus distinguished between what God had commanded and what the tradition taught. This was part of the major difference between the two groups. Keeping God's commands was a theme in Judaism (2 Chron. 24:20; Tob. 4:5; Jub. 23:19–21; T. Levi 14:4; T. Ash. 7:5—possibly a Christian interpolation). Other Jewish groups challenged keeping traditions in this detailed a manner since the Sadducees did not follow such traditions (Josephus, *A.J.* 13.297). The Pharisees also were critiqued by the Qumranians in 1QH 4:14–15 as teachers of "smooth things" (Davies and Allison 1991, 520). The kind of challenge Jesus made here was not his alone, and he was not directly challenging explicit Torah teaching by not washing hands. But his claim to legislate the Torah was significant. He made no appeal to other teaching authorities, as would be common in Judaism, in doing this. The authority was his alone.

15:4–6. Jesus illustrated his claim with a specific example. He pointed to the hypocrisy of having the command to honor one's parents but failing to do so (Mark 7:10–13). Where Mark has Moses giving these commands, Matthew has God doing so. That move was making explicit what was implicit in citing the law. Matthew cites the commandment to honor one's father and mother (Exod. 20:12; Deut. 5:16), while noting the penalty of death for dishonoring a parent (Exod. 21:17; Lev. 20:9). The serious penalty showed how important the failure to obey was (also Prov. 28:24). The illustration that follows showed that honoring parents meant caring for them as they grow old (France 2007, 580; 1 Tim. 5:8 shows this value).

The means of such failure involved an oath known as the "Korban" (Josephus, *A.J.* 4.73; *C. Ap.* 1.167). "Korban" means "gift devoted to God" (BDAG s.v. "κορβᾶν" 559, used in Mark 7:11 but not here). It allowed someone to say something was dedicated to God for the temple treasury at one's death and so prevented using the dedicated object to help the parents (Baumgarten 1984; Sanders 1990, 53–57). Such dedicated items could be used by the person but by no one else. Later texts may have allowed one to cancel such a commitment, including concerns dealing with parents (*m. Ned.* 9.1), but Jesus's scenario is that the oath became a pretext for not helping the parents. In *Mishnah Nedarim* 9.1, although the view was disputed by the sages, Rabbi Eliezar allowed a vow to be unloosed or no longer valid to honor a father and mother. No doubt the sages' views were rooted in Numbers 30:2, where one was not to break a vow (Deut. 23:23; Keener 2009, 410–11; Nolland 2005, 617). The way this is discussed in the Mishnaic passage shows this difference of opinion was the subject of significant dispute. The Mishnah (*m. Ned.* 4.7–8) gives other circumstances where such a vow could be set aside. Matthew has presented the example very briefly in comparison to Mark, indicating his audience likely knew what this involved. The argument is that here one of the Ten Commandments was violated, while the above concern was on a tradition tied to purity (Oliver 2013, 268).

Unloosing a Vow Because of Parents

Mishnah *Nedarim* 9:1: "R. Eliezer says, 'They unloose a vow for a person by [reference to] the honor of his father or mother.' And sages prohibit. Said R. Sadoq, 'Before they unloose a vow for him by [reference to] the honor of his father or mother, let them unloose his vow by reference to the honor of the Omnipresent.' If so, there will be no vows! But sages concede to R. Eliezer that, in a matter which is between him and his mother or father, they unloose his vow by [reference to] the honor of his father or mother."

In this case, one did not honor their father (Mark 7:12). This result was stated emphatically with οὐ μὴ. So Jesus said this outcome was voiding God's word by "your" tradition (Mark 7:13). The term here is ἀκυρόω, which refers to "nullifying" something (BDAG s.v. "ἀκυρόω" 40). God's word was canceled out and disobeyed. Using God to prevent commanded service to others was not honoring to God (Davies and Allison 1991, 525).

15:7–9. So Jesus called them hypocrites and cited Isaiah 29:13 to make the point (Mark 7:6–7). Matthew notes this charge elsewhere (on hypocrites, see Matt. 6:2; also used in 22:18; 23:13–15, 23, 25, 27, 29). That text declared that the people honor God with their lips but that their heart was some distance away. This made their worship empty, in vain. For they taught with the teachings of men, not God. The use of Isaiah 29:13 applied the text to the current time as prophecy, probably as a typological fulfillment. As it was in Isaiah's time, so it also was the case now (France 2007, 581). Isaiah speaks of "these people" when speaking of those whose heart was far from God as they followed human teaching (Hatina 2006). It is like the use of Isaiah 6:9–10 by Paul in Acts 28:25–27 (Davies and Allison 1991, 525). Romans 9:20, 11:8, and 1 Corinthians 1:19 also appeal to Isaiah 29. The citation is more like the LXX than the MT, in the direct appeal to vain worship, but the idea is similar. The MT says, "Their fear of me is a commandment of men that has been taught." The spirit of this rebuke is like Isaiah 1:12–17, Micah 6:6–8, or Amos 5:4–13, where worship was empty and not well received by God if others were not treated correctly. Such a rebuke was a way of saying this was a serious violation of what God desired. Genuine worship of God followed through on commandments about caring for people versus caring for oneself. It did not allow for a tradition that canceled out proper care for others at the expense of self-interest.

15:10–11. Jesus made a brief remark to the crowds that started his commentary on the controversy. It was really the principle that drove his reaction. He told the crowd to hear and understand. It was a call to pay attention (Mark 7:14). Jesus rebuked the Pharisees, not all Jews, with these remarks.

The point Jesus made was that it was not what goes into the body that defiled but what comes out of the mouth, what comes from the person relationally in the interaction with others (Mark 7:15; Gospel of Thomas 14). It is not clear that Matthew's lack of a reference to "nothing" coming from the outside may defile, as Mark 7:15 has, meant or assumed contaminated or prohibited food was not in view (but so Oliver 2013, 272, versus the overexpression, as we shall contend in Matt. 15:12 below, of France 2007, 583, who argues for a total negation of food laws here). Both of these options may make too much of the difference, which is simply a stylistic simplification much like Matthew's style to shorten. A shift of emphasis emerged over time in seeing the implications about practice. This is not an outright denial of Jewish practice as much as in how absolute it was seen to be for all who believed and for an array of situations (see 15:12).

Here was Jesus's emphasis: what came out of people's mouths showed what was in their hearts. By saying this, Jesus connected the call to honor God with the way others were treated. Real defiling had to do with worship and people. What came from a person's mouth in speech had to do with how they engaged God and others (Luke 3:8–14). Jesus connected, in effect, the two parts of the Ten Commandments in saying this and also pushed toward what would become the great commandment. What Jesus taught fit what the Old Testament and Judaism also taught (Exod. 20:17; 2 Chron. 30:18–20; Pss. 24:3–4; 51:2–3, 6, 10, 16–17; 78:37; 1QS 3.6–9; 5.13–14; Josephus, *A.J.* 18.117; *m. 'Abot.* 2.9; Philo, *Spec.* 3.209; Turner 2008, 381; Greco-Roman examples: Menander, Fragment 540; Sextus, *Sentences* 110; Davies and Allison 1991, 526).

Defiling through food was rare in the Old Testament. It usually involved eating an animal that had died (Lev. 11:40–44; 17:15). The scenario here was contracting uncleanness through unwashed hands touching the food, something the Old Testament did not address.

Davies and Allison (1991, 529–31) raise the issue of this saying going back to Jesus since it implied the end of food laws. A position arguing for a saying tied to the early church says the later controversies did not make sense if Jesus uttered a prohibition here (see Acts 10). However, as they note, one may well see Jesus prioritizing here with an implication that later indicated a contrast. In this way the remark was like saying God desired mercy, not sacrifice, and so what really mattered was mercy (Hos. 6:6). It was also like God saying, "Your worship means nothing to me if you do not pursue justice" (see Mic.

6:6–8). Jesus was saying the stress was in the wrong place. In the relativizing, there were the genuine seeds for the later relegating to insignificance of issues tied to food laws, especially in mixed cultural contexts as we see in Romans 14–15. Matthew is like Mark in this point, but Mark is more explicit about the implications for food laws present in what Jesus was saying. The difference may reflect the fact that Mark was concerned mostly with Gentiles, while Matthew had Jewish believers primarily in view. In contrast, France (2007, 583) argues for a full negation by Jesus, but this says too much and would be hard to see in light of Acts 10 and Peter's initial hesitation to eat unclean food. Nothing in what Jesus said here nor in what Jesus showed as he lived with the disciples disabused Peter of his approach to food until his vision in Acts 10. Blomberg (1992, 239) credibly speaks of implications emerging from the saying. Either way, it is clear that the full force of this saying was realized later and not when Jesus said it. As Osborne (2010, 588) says, the crowd and disciples "hardly caught all of this." It also is important to note that the statement of declaring all foods clean is a narrative remark by Mark, so it is likely a view that emerged over time about what Jesus did say here, reflecting an implication of his teaching

15:12. Next, Jesus discussed matters with the disciples (Matt. 15:12–20). This was his pattern in Matthew, to instruct the disciples in detail, giving them more information than the crowds. Matthew 15:12–14 is unique to Matthew.

The disciples were concerned that his challenge of the Pharisees had offended these leaders (Mark 7:17). It is hard to see this objection emerging if the problem were only as Oliver had said it above (in the discussion of 15:10–11), as that position argued that Jesus hardly said anything too controversial in terms of overall halakah. What Jesus had said had to be unusual enough in terms of its application to be disturbing and a little surprising. The disciples also may be concerned that they were popular (Josephus, *A.J.* 18.17; Keener 2009, 413). It was not clear if the Pharisees said something to the disciples (so Morris 1992, 396) or they just deduced this. The term σκανδαλίζω means "to give offense" to someone, to repel them by what has been said (BDAG s.v. "σκανδαλίζω" 2, 926). The rest of Jesus's response was his explanation for why he had challenged and rebuked them. The disciples and Matthew's readers were to learn from Jesus's reply.

On the Sadducees Bowing to the Pharisees' Popularity

Josephus, *Jewish Antiquities* 19.17: "This doctrine [of the Sadducees] is received but by a few, yet by those still of the greatest dignity; but they are able to do almost nothing of themselves; for when they become magistrates, as they are unwillingly and by force sometimes obliged to be, they addict themselves to the notions of the Pharisees, because the multitude would not otherwise bear them."

15:13. Jesus made two distinct points in his response. The first was that every plant not planted by God would be uprooted. Jesus spoke as one who knew where judgment was headed. The reference to "my" (μου) Father here underscored that point. There was an intimacy about relationship that fed into reading about the judgment.

This picture of judgment was a variation on the idea of the parable of the fig tree where there was no fruit and so it was uprooted (Isa. 5:7; Jer. 1:10; 11:17; 45:4; Matt. 3:10; 21:33–44; Luke 7:6; 13:6–9; Gospel of Thomas 40). The image also was a reversal of Isaiah 60:21 and 61:3, where God spoke of planting a shoot or tree. The image was actually quite common across Judaism (Jer. 32:41; 1 En. 10.16; 84.6; 93.2, 5, 10; Jub. 1.16; 7.34; 1QS 8.5; 11.8; CD 1.7; 1QH 6.15; Pss. Sol. 14:2–3; Mart. Ascen. Isa. 4.3; Davies and Allison 1991, 532; Turner 2008, 381). In part what was at work in this critique was the refusal of Jewish leaders to recognize the arrival of the promise with Jesus.

15:14. The second point gave an explanation and exhortation. Jesus told his disciples to leave this kind of teaching. The reason was that the Pharisees were blind guides (Isa. 6:10; Matt. 23:16, 24; Luke 6:39–40, but about disciples, showing the same imagery can have distinct applications and settings). This was irony since they may have thought that the Pharisees guided the blind (Rom. 2:19) and this was the opposite of that perceived calling (Isa. 42:6–7). They only led others into the pit. This way of spirituality did not direct others into light nor into spiritual benefit. Their teaching was not to be followed, for it led to damage and disaster.

15:15. Peter asked for an explanation of this parable, speaking for all as he often did in Matthew (Matt. 16:16, 22; 17:4, 24–25; 18:21; 19:27). Mark 7:17 mentioned the disciples asking Jesus in the house. The parable really was only a comparison, and so he wanted Jesus to elaborate on the error he was rebuking. It is hard to be sure if Peter was asking about the statement of verses 13–14 or what he had said to the crowds as well. Jesus's answer looked to the entire rebuke and harkened back to verse 11.

15:16. Jesus rebuked the disciples for still not understanding, for being foolish after all this time (Mark 7:18). The rare adverb ἀκμήν means "even still" (BDAG s.v. "ἀκμήν" 36). This is its only use in the New Testament (Heb. 5:13 has it as a variant reading). Jesus was complaining that they still did not get it after having heard him teach over time, especially since they were benefiting from private discussion like that in Matthew 13:11–15 and teachings like those in Matthew 5:21–48 (Wilkins 2004, 538).

15:17. Jesus first explained that what goes into the mouth proceeds to the stomach before being disposed of through waste elimination into the "latrine" (Mark 7:19a; BDAG s.v. "ἀφεδρών" 155). In the ancient world, the latrine would normally have been either a bucket (which then was tossed into a sewer), a dung heap, or a place to sit (Blomberg 1992, 241; Morris 1992, 398). That refuse did not defile because it did not remain. It was not what you ate that made you who you were (France 2007, 586: Rom. 14:14, 17; 1 Cor. 8:8; Heb. 9:10). Jesus was expounding Matthew 15:11a. He asked it as a "do you not know" question. The question expected a positive reply (οὐ). They should have known better.

Matthew eliminated Mark's narrative remark that all food was made clean. It is debated why the omission exists. Some think Mark's expanded remark about all food being unclean was too harsh for Matthew (Davies and Allison 1991, 535). However, Matthew did live within a church that had moved away from such concern for Gentiles. He has the "new wineskins" saying. It is more likely that since this understanding of the saying's implications came later, he simply left it out.

15:18–19. What defiled a person was what came out of the mouth, from the heart (Mark 7:20–23). On the mouth as damaging, one can think of James 3:6. That was what made a person common and showed they were not set apart. "Defiling" referred to someone not living as they were set apart to do—to live well—no longer being in a state appropriate for God and worship. This remark was about Matthew 15:11b.

Jesus's vice list is mostly relational in its thrust. Vice lists were common in the ancient world (Aristotle, *Eth. Eud.* 2.3.4, 1220b–21; Epictetus, *Discourses* 2.8.23; Plato, Leg. 1.649D; Wis. 14:25–26; 1QS 4:9–11; Rom. 1:29–31; 1 Cor. 6:9–10; Gal. 5:19–20; Eph. 5:3–4; 1 Tim. 1:9–10; 2 Tim. 3:2–5; Titus 3:3; 1 Peter 4:3; Keener 2009, 414). Keener (2009, 414) also notes Matthew raised these categories in his gospel: "evil reasonings (Matt. 9:4; 16:7; 21:25), murders (Matt. 2:16; 5:21–26; 14:10; 23:34–35; 27:24–25), adulteries (Matt. 5:27–32; 14:3–6), sexual immoralities (Matt. 5:32; 12:39; 21:31; contrast 1:25), theft (Matt. 27:64), false witness (Matt. 26:59–61), and slander or blasphemy (Matthew 12:31–32)." Matthew's vice list has seven items while Mark 7:21–22 has thirteen. Matthew again has written a briefer account. Matthew's list focuses on the second part of the Ten Commandments: murder (6), adultery (7), stealing (8), false witness (9). Evil reasonings and blasphemies are the only two parts not mentioned directly in the Decalogue, but blasphemy is implied by the first part of the Decalogue and evil is a general heading for all that followed in Jesus's list.

15:20. Jesus restated the principle of Matthew 15:11 yet again. What came from the heart defiled, not food that was touched by unwashed hands. Jesus's attitude here helped to explain how the church moved in a direction that came to disregard issues tied to the ceremonial law and to diet issues that could separate Jewish and Gentile believers (Osborne 2010, 591). How we related to each other was where Jesus placed his ethical focus, versus trying to make the home like a temple in terms of ritual purity.

THEOLOGICAL FOCUS

The exegetical idea (in a dispute with the Pharisees and scribes over handwashing purity issues, Jesus charged his opponents with hypocrisy and taught that real defilement came out of the heart, when it perverted relationships) leads to this theological idea: Jesus teaches that real defilement is not a matter of legal practice but of heart relations.

Jesus's declaration that real defilement came from the heart and out of the mouth challenged some Jewish leaders' definition of spirituality, which adopted external practice traditions that canceled out the relational will of God.

Jesus distanced himself from Jewish traditions in this text. His ethical focus was on the heart and relational matters, not so much on issues tied to ritual purity. He rejected the development of rules in this area. God cared more about the heart. The danger was that in the pursuit of such rules, relating would take a back seat. Jesus accused the Pharisees of being hypocrites in caring about hands but failing to honor parents. Defilement that reflected God's desires cared about the heart and others. The fact that Jesus's vice list focused on the Ten Commandments and those parts where people were in view showed where his focus was.

Like the antitheses in the Sermon on the Mount, Jesus said that God looked at the heart of people as a measure of spiritual well-being. How we treat others and keep our commitments comes in for focused affirmation. Building a fence around the law often ends up building a hedge around the heart and produces division among people. Jesus was against those kinds of additional rules. Making the Bible do too much is as much a problem as making it do too little. Jesus rebuked the Pharisees because in trying to make the home like a temple, they had risked making rules more important than people. Worship should not draw you away from people and caring for them, but toward them. Jesus asks his audience to look at their hearts and warns that teaching like that of the Pharisees will not take one to a place of caring for others. It is understanding that defilement is about the heart that gives one the proper trajectory on spiritual engagement.

PREACHING AND TEACHING STRATEGIES

Exegetical and Theological Synthesis

External acts of obedience can disguise our internal rejection of God. Again and again, Jesus exposed this tendency in the Pharisees. He called them hypocrites, pretenders, and whitewashed tombs (Matt. 6:2; 22:18; 23:13–32; 24:51). Pharisees followed manmade rules but failed in human relationships. They spent more time in creating, debating, and enforcing the oral traditions than practicing the written Torah. Jesus called their bluff.

Of course, religious hypocrisy was nothing new. In his indictment of the Pharisees, Jesus cited the prophet Isaiah's rebuke of his ancestors. Ancient Israel had a long history of hypocrisy. Israelites offered sacrifices with unclean hands and impure motives (1 Sam. 15:22; Isa. 1:11–15; Mal. 2:13–14). They attended festivals while exploiting neighbors (Amos 5:21–24). They praised God and practiced injustice. God regularly used the Jewish prophets to condemn wicked hearts and call for repentance from within the nation (Jer. 3:1–25; Hos. 5:4; 14:1; Joel 2:13). God's people were accountable and were to be self-critical. Jesus preached with the same passion, imploring God's people to purity of heart and hands.

As the writings to the early church indicate, the creep toward religious custom persisted. The Jerusalem Council tried to unburden Gentile believers from too many laws (Acts 15:20, 28–29). Paul regularly challenged legalism in the church (Gal. 3:1–5; 5:1–12; Titus 1:10–16), insisting on the centrality of love (Rom. 13:8; Gal. 5:13–14) and freedom of conscience (Rom. 14). An increase in religious customs only burdens God's people. Purity of heart comes from God's Spirit, not our good works.

Preaching Idea

More laws don't lead to better lives.

Contemporary Connections

What does it mean?

What does it mean that more laws don't lead to better lives? First, we must understand the role of biblical law. It was given to reduce chaos and restrain sin. Laws give boundaries to keep us from harming ourselves and others. Their aim is to decrease damage, not increase virtue. In other words, laws do not make us better but help us from becoming worse. Laws tutor us in our shortcomings and point us toward Jesus (Gal. 3:19–25).

Second, we all tend to add to God's law our own rules for better living. These moral guidelines may be practical, well intended, and in alignment with Scripture, but their ability to make us better is limited. Bedtimes may give us better sleep, but they cannot make us better people. Dietary restrictions may give us better health, but they cannot make us better people. Corporate standards for social media use may give us better efficiency at work, but policies do not make us better people. Self-improvement hacks and codes of conduct only produce better behavior (or reduce worse behavior!).

Third, the better life described in the Bible starts with a change of heart. Better behavior may follow, but it is the byproduct of keeping in step with the Holy Spirit, not of keeping the law. Changed hearts regularly say "no" to selfish desires. Instead, the greatest commandment—to love God and others—compels followers to better living (Matt. 22:34–40; 2 Cor. 5:14; Gal. 5:16–26; Titus 2:13–14).

Is it true?

Is it true that more laws don't lead to better lives? The answer is not straightforward. Laws can be helpful. For example, traffic laws provide protection for drivers, passengers, and pedestrians. A church's bylaws ensure consistency in function and clarity in roles of its members. And any game or athletic competition without rules can become chaotic. Thus, rules, laws, and guidelines can play a positive role.

When it comes to religious rules or moral laws, better lives do not necessarily follow. As mentioned above, law can affect behavior without changing hearts. Laws are more performative than transformative. As laws increase, personal freedom decreases and bland uniformity results.

Worse yet, more laws may cause complexes. Those who excel at obeying the law may develop superiority complexes. Such people are prone to strutting, assuming grace is unnecessary, and criticizing others. Experts of the law make lame friends. Those who struggle to keep the law may develop inferiority complexes. Such people are prone to groveling, assuming grace is out of reach, and comparing themselves to others. Serial transgressors make bad company. Thus, more laws do not lead to better lives but less freedom and diversity or more comparisons and shame.

Now what?

Now that we have established that more laws do not lead to better lives, should we jettison law, flaunt our freedom, and claim our best life now? No. Getting the right laws is not the most central issue; getting our hearts right must be our main concern. This is especially relevant in our secular age, where the heart has become the guide to moral truth. In fact, if one law rules the day in the secular West, it would be this: *You do you*. Sadly, this law is based upon a faulty premise, namely that our hearts are trustworthy guides. Jeremiah, Jesus, and Paul assure us they are not (Jer. 17:9; Matt. 15:18–20; Rom. 1:21–24). Thus, we must ask God to search, test, and renew our hearts (Pss. 51; 139:23–24; 2 Cor. 4:16).

Additionally, we should view the law with Jesus's perspective. Rather than abolishing it, he looked beneath it. In the Sermon on the Mount, he elaborated on six oral traditions, seeing each one as an opportunity to show elaborate love to God and others (Matt. 5:17–48). Later, he summarized the law in the bidirectional command to love (22:34–40). Thus, it may be more accurate to say we need less law and more love. And a better measure of our spiritual maturity is not church attendance, Bible reading, alcohol intake, or tithing, but our growing affection for others. Am I showing greater patience to my family? Can I see the *imago Dei* in my coworkers? Are my prayers and praise authentic? For the most accurate measure, I should test the level of my love over time.

Finally, we may need to let go of some laws we have learned or imposed over the years. Consider laws that feed an inferiority or superiority complex in your life. Look at laws that mask a selfish heart. Think about the reason for the law and how keeping it could be an opportunity to love God and others. You may find that some laws, rules, traditions, and customs encourage better living.

Creativity in Presentation

This sermon will allow you to make light of strange laws that are in place. The game Beyond Balderdash includes a category of "Laughable Laws." The card provides the beginning of a strange law that players must complete. On the back of the card is the correct answer. A few examples include:

- In Little Rock, Arkansas, it is against the law to blindfold . . . [a cow.]
- In Mesquite, Texas, it is considered a crime for kids to have . . . [outrageous haircuts.]
- In Atlanta, Georgia, you are forbidden to tie . . . [a giraffe to a telephone pole.]
- In Chicago, Illinios, you are forbidden to fish while wearing . . . [your pajamas.]
- In Lexington, Kentucky, it is against the law to use a lizard . . . [in a religious ceremony.]

If you cannot secure a copy of the game, you can search "ridiculous laws" on Google or your preferred search engine to compile your own list.

Continuing on the theme of strange or outdated laws, consider highlighting blue laws. Although few blue laws remain—such as alcohol and car sales prohibited on Sundays—a survey of former blue laws might interest the congregation. Given the size and interactive nature of your congregation, you could even ask people to provide answers to Balderdash questions or share school rules from their days.

Rules in schools have changed over the years. Codes of conduct for students have certainly loosened, giving them more opportunities to express themselves. Consider interviewing a couple of older members about rules their schools had. Then interview current high school students about whether they would want those rules applied to them.

Rules have likewise changed for teachers. A great example of retro rules comes from the We Are Teachers website, entitled "The Retro Rules." See https://www.weareteachers.com/retro-school-rules for glimpses of rule changes in the past 150 years.

Highlighting unwritten rules could be humorous. Surely every church or household has them. Consider creating a "Ten (Unspoken) Commandments" of your church or home. For example, "Mom is always right"; "Dad gets the remote"; "If you're not five minutes early, you're late"; "Children should neither be heard nor seen"; "No running in church". My (Tim's) father's favorite rule was never written but often spoken. He said, "3.5 or you don't drive," which was a threat to take away our driving privileges if we did not keep our grades up. After reading these rules, encourage people to take stock of their own unwritten rules.

Ultimately, you want your sermon to communicate that Jesus teaches real defilement is not a matter of legal practice but of heart relations. Or, more concisely, more laws don't lead to better lives.

- More laws lead to more loopholes (15:1–9).
- More laws lead to more missteps (15:10–14).
- More laws mask a defiled heart (15:15–20).

DISCUSSION QUESTIONS

1. When did the handwashing tradition develop? What motivated it?
2. How did Jesus handle the Torah? What place did the Ten Commandments have in his preaching?
3. Where have you been guilty of looking for loopholes?
4. What traditions in your church get treated as laws?
5. How can you cultivate a pure heart toward God and others?

Matthew 15:21–39

EXEGETICAL IDEA

The continuing and expanding compassion of Jesus in the face of opposition showed itself in his exorcism of the Canaanite woman's daughter, his healing of the crowds, and his feeding of the four thousand–plus.

THEOLOGICAL FOCUS

Jesus extends a ministry of God's compassion to new groups even in the face of opposition, while a woman shows an exemplary faith of humble non-entitlement.

PREACHING IDEA

Desperation draws Jesus to us.

PREACHING POINTERS

As opposition toward Jesus continued to escalate, he again withdrew. This pattern repeats throughout Matthew's gospel. In his current retreat, Jesus and his disciples first migrated to Gentile territory and encountered a desperate Canaanite woman with a demonized child. Her bold faith persuaded Jesus to heal her child. Jesus interacted with and responded to one who many would have regarded with disdain, even as the enemy—a Gentile woman. After returning to an unnamed mountain in Galilee, Jesus healed many needy people before feeding a hungry crowd. The scene pulses with Old Testament imagery foreshadowing the messianic age. For Matthew's readers, these stories and summaries narrated the deep compassion of Jesus and wide reach of his ministry. Rising opposition would not suppress his expansive love to desperate people.

There is no shortage of needy people today. Despite the promises of late modernity to overcome human suffering through education, economics, medication, and technology, global suffering remains. Child trafficking, dirty water, ethnic persecution, gender inequality, and war plague our world. Citizens of the United States are not exempt from suffering. Despite priding ourselves on liberty, equality, and opportunity, signs of desperation are evident: increasing rates of single-parent homes, obesity, drug abuse, and suicide, mental health crises, the vanishing middle class, rising crime and houseless populations in cities. We live in desperate times, and our diversions, distractions, and digital solutions cannot save us. Fortunately, this sermon reminds us that desperation draws Jesus to us.

JESUS HEALS AND CARES FOR PEOPLE, INCLUDING A GENTILE WOMAN (15:21–39)

LITERARY STRUCTURE AND THEMES (15:21–39)

This unit has a healing (vv. 21–28), a healing summary (vv. 29–31), and a nature miracle (vv. 32–38), and closes with a travel note (v. 39). The narrative has been highlighting the rising opposition to Jesus, yet he still ministered. Three scenes dominate this section: the exorcism of a Gentile woman's daughter (Matt. 15:21–28), a healing summary (Matt. 15:29–31), and the feeding of the four thousand (Matt. 15:32–38). Jesus then traveled to Magadan (Matt. 15:39).

Each scene shows Jesus's compassion. The first scene shows that although Jesus was called to Israel, he would minister to anyone seeking him. This woman's lack of any sense of entitlement and appeal to Jesus's mercy met with commendation for having a great faith. This pairs nicely with the faith of the centurion, another Gentile whose faith was commended as exemplary (Matt. 8:5–13).

Jesus continued to heal an array of maladies. The lame, blind, crippled, and mute had their needs met. This had a similar thrust to a passage in Luke 14:7–24 esp. vv. 13, 21. Jesus continued to show God's care for those others opposed or for those on the fringe. No one was invisible to Jesus.

The feeding of the four thousand mirrors the earlier feeding of the five thousand, except here Jesus took the initiative to feed the crowd. Jesus was able to meet needs again and again.

The unit showed that despite the rejection of many in Israel, Jesus still reached out to care for those he was calling to respond to God. He was loving his enemies.

The exorcism of the woman's daughter has a parallel in Mark 7:24–30. The healing summary is a reduced version of Mark 7:31–37. The feeding of the four thousand follows Mark 8:1–10. So once again Matthew is following along with Mark.

The key character in the unit is the Canaanite woman. Culturally she had two strikes against her as a Gentile and a woman. The nature of the feelings against Canaanites can be seen in Jubilees 22:20–22 (Keener 2009, 414). That text argues that they were seed to be rooted out from the earth because of Ham's sin, with no chance of being saved. Jesus treated the issue of her ethnicity by initially refusing to help because she was not from Israel. However, her humble claim was that she was not due mercy, but that benefits could graciously come to those who did not sit at the table. Such humility led Jesus to help her as he pointed out that her faith was amazing. It was one of very few places where Jesus commended a response. Those who recall Tamar and Ruth from the genealogy of Matthew 1:3, 5 will not be completely surprised by this ethnic development. The evidence of Jesus's work with the centurion and the Gadarene demoniacs in Matthew 8:11–12, 28–34 also shows Gentiles could be included in blessing (Turner 2008, 386). The movement of the gospel was slowly expanding.

EXPOSITION (15:21–39)

Jesus had spent a great deal of his ministry time focused on Israel. Here there was a glimpse of what was coming: ministry to Gentiles. A woman of exemplary faith asked Jesus to heal her daughter. Jesus responded to the example, pointing out that her appeal to God's mercy and lack of demand about blessing presented a lesson about faith. Yet ministry to Israel also continued, even in the face of continued rising opposition. The offer of gospel hope continued despite the failure of many to respond. Matthew was showing how to continue to love others who might not appreciate your faith.

The continuing and expanding compassion of Jesus in the face of opposition showed itself in his exorcism of the Canaanite woman's daughter, his healing of the crowds, and his feeding of the four thousand plus.

15:21. Jesus crossed over into Gentile territory as he traveled to the region of Tyre and Sidon (Mark 7:24a; on these cities, see Matt. 11:21–22). These Phoenician cities are now in Lebanon and Syria. Sidon was around twenty-five miles north of Tyre. They were thirty- and fifty-plus miles from Galilee's northern edge (Osborne 2010, 597). It was not a short trip.

This was the sixth time in Matthew that there was a withdrawal because of opposition, and the fourth time that Jesus himself had withdrawn (Matt. 2:12–14, 22—Joseph; 4:12; 12:15; 14:13). The trip into unclean territory was significant after a dispute about food. Things were changing, as the next event showed, but Jesus did not come here to minister as his initial reaction to the woman indicated. Only an exemplary response changed that intent.

15:22. A Gentile woman had a daughter who was severely demon-possessed (Mark 7:25–26). The remark was made in a way to show the daughter was not with her. She had gone out of her way meet Jesus. She understood his authority meant all he had to do was speak and it would be done. Mark describes her as a Syro-Phoenician woman, while Matthew speaks of a Canaanite woman. She was clearly a foreigner and outsider. Davies and Allison (1991, 547) suggests the change was because Canaanites were historic enemies, adding to the event's significance. In the normal Jewish view, these were wicked, unclean people. If she were served, then we have a "potent symbol to Jewish readers of the universality of the gospel" (so France 2007, 592). This is the first of only a few scenes involving a conversation with a woman in Matthew (Matt. 20:20–21; also, women are noted in 8:14–15; 9:20–22; 14:21). Women are more prominent in Luke.

She cried out for mercy to Jesus as Lord, Son of David. The cry for mercy is unique to Matthew's version. She showed not only respect to Jesus but some kind of recognition of his person, perhaps even a sense that he was a messianic claimant. Here was a Gentile asking for the help of a Jewish deliverer. There was a kind of reconciliation built into the request that acknowledged him. "Son of David" is an important title in Matthew (Matt. 1:1, 20; 9:27; 12:23; 20:30–31; 21:9, 15; 22:42). She made no claim to have the right to have her daughter healed. She simply asked that Jesus extend his kindness to her. Her desperation was clear from her ongoing crying out for help, something the use of the imperfect ἔκραζεν ("keeps on crying out") suggests (BDAG s.v. "κράζω" 2a, 563). Her respect for Jesus was consistently communicated by her repeated use of the term "Lord."

15:23. Jesus initially said nothing. The disciples took this as a rejection and asked him to dismiss her as they were seemingly annoyed by her presence and outcries. Interpreters discuss if they wanted him to heal her quickly or simply dismiss her without doing anything. Where the disciples were with regard to the healing is not clear. Jesus spoke to them in the next verse that he was called to Israel. This may well suggest the disciples did want Jesus to heal her daughter so she would just go away (Morris 1992, 403). Nolland (2005, 633) sees Jesus speaking to the woman in verse 24 and assumed the disciples had no interest in her daughter being healed, an analogy with a negative reading of Matthew 14:15. However, it is not clear that Matthew 14:15 was a negative idea. On the other hand, Jesus's focus on Israel might have triggered a rejection of help to a Gentile by the disciples and the disciples' complaint appears to be negative (Osborne 2010, 598). The woman's plea following also suggests a negative perception about what the remark meant for the possibility of healing, as she appeared nervous that she was being rejected. Either way, Jesus was interested in more than merely healing, so he drew out the event.

15:24. Jesus probably replied to the disciples since the woman approached again in verse 25. He told them that his calling was to the lost sheep of Israel. He seemed to want to rein in any expectation that he would heal the daughter. He likely said it so she also could hear. It appeared he was going to dismiss her request, but the event as a whole gives the sense of his probing her faith. The remark about only going to the lost sheep of Israel mirrors the mission of Matthew 10:6 which also was limited to Israel, whose lost state needed attention by one sent to aid them (Isa. 53:3; Jer. 50:6).

Servant Rejected by People and the People Lost

Isaiah 53:3: "He was despised and rejected by people, one who experienced pain and was acquainted with illness; people hid their faces from him; he was despised, and we considered him insignificant."

Jeremiah 50:6: "My people have been lost sheep. Their shepherds have allowed them to go astray. They have wandered around in the mountains. They have roamed from one mountain and hill to another. They have forgotten their resting place."

15:25–27. The core of this scene is the following exchange between the woman and Jesus (Mark 7:27–28). She repeated her request for help, addressing Jesus respectfully a second time as Lord and bowing before him. This was an act indicating submission, not worship. She was demanding nothing, only seeking his mercy and grace.

Jesus responded by noting that it was not right to give the children's bread to the dogs. He is vivid in saying this, as the bread was "tossed" or "thrown" (βαλεῖν) to the dogs (BDAG s.v. "βάλλω" 1b, 163). Jesus's point was that the promise was for Israel at this time. They were in line as the recipients of the messianic promise (Gen. 12:1–3; Deut. 14:2; Hos. 11:1). The remark about dogs was figurative and rhetorical in light of a redemptive-historical priority (John 4:22; Rom. 1:16–17; 11:17; Turner 2008, 388).

Israel as the People of God

Genesis 12:1–3: "Now the Lord said to Abram, 'Go out from your country, your relatives, and your father's household to the land that I will show you. Then I will make you into a great nation, and I will bless you, and I will make your name great, so that you will exemplify divine blessing. I will bless those who bless you, but the one who treats you lightly I must curse, so that all the families of the earth may receive blessing through you.'"

Deuteronomy 14:2: "For you are a people holy to the Lord your God. He has chosen you to be his people, prized above all others on the face of the earth."

Hosea 11:1: "When Israel was a young man, I loved him like a son, and I summoned my son out of Egypt."

Jesus's remark did not put off the woman. Her reply had a "yes, but" feel of rebuttal in it. For a third time she called him Lord. She was making no claims on Israel's benefits. She simply recognized that grace could spill beyond those for whom it was initially targeted. She asked for the crumbs falling from the table, not the loaf. She noted that even dogs get the crumbs from the table. She knew that Jesus's ministry was focused on Israel, but that did not mean a conversation could not be had about what was possible. This exhibited deep faith, for it made clear that there was no sense of entitlement or rights to this request. She accepted the picture of the "dog" and yet used it to make her request. She was simply appealing for God's mercy.

The term for "dog" is important here. It is κυνάριον (BDAG s.v. "κυνάριον" 575). This is the diminutive form of the word for dog. It pictures a lap dog, not a wild dog of the street. It is discussed if this kind of detail was possible in Aramaic (Davies and Allison 1991, 553–54), but it may well be the canine image was made clear by the context of a meal in the home. This was a dog of the house, but likely a working dog or a watchdog, not a pet in modern terms (Keener 2009, 416–17; Nolland 2005, 634, including n. 203; Wilkins 2004, 540; Job 30:1; Tob. 6:2; 11:4; Jos. Asen. 10:13. France (2007, 595) still sees the remark as derogatory, given that even house dogs were unclean and such references were usually negative (1 Sam. 17:43; 2 Sam. 16:9; Ps. 22:17, 21 LXX; Prov. 26:11; Phil. 3:2, but none of these is in the diminutive). The remark was striking and challenging, but not as much as it would have been if a wild dog were portrayed. Domestic dogs got leftovers (Philostratus, *Vit. Apoll.* 1.19; Konradt 2020, 241). In other biblical terms, this was the one who was far away from the promise versus others who were near. Still, some access was possible (Isa. 57:19; Eph. 2:11–13).

15:28. Jesus commended the faith of this woman, much as he did the faith of another Gentile earlier (the centurion in Matt. 8:10; also 9:22, 29). Her faith was great, because it was humble, understood where she fit, and did not presume, as well as had tenacity. Morris (1992, 405) for some odd reason distinguishes these traits as not about her faith. Matthew alone mentions her great faith. Jesus granted her request (Mark 7:29). Her daughter was healed at that very hour (Mark 7:30). The scene underscores the value and quality of a great faith. Only healings involving Gentiles, both here and in Matthew 8, took place from a distance (France 2007, 596). The space pictured the reality of Gentile inclusion. They operated from a distance relative to Israel's proximity.

The emotion of Jesus's reaction was marked by his address to her as "O" (ὦ) woman, a vocative used rarely and often with emotion (BDAG s.v. "ὦ" 1a, 1101; Acts 1:1; Rom. 2:1, 3; 9:20; 1 Tim. 6:11, 20; James 2:20). He had compassion for her.

15:29–31. The structure of this healing summary parallels Matthew 14:13–21 with a sequence of healing then feeding (Turner 2008, 390). However, Matthew 15:30–31 is more detailed in its healing summary than Matthew 14:14. It also is distinct from Mark 7:31–8:10 because Mark has a specific healing of the deaf and dumb man versus a healing summary before the four thousand are fed.

Jesus returned to Galilee and came to an unspecified mountain by the Sea of Galilee. This is one of several Matthean texts that have Jesus teaching from a mountain (Matt. 5:1–2; 24:3). Might the mountain picture a place of gathering and healing, while the audience suggested Isaiah 35:5–6? Davies and Allison (1991, 566) make this argument. They see a Mount Zion image of the eschatological gathering of God's people who were then fed. Ezekiel 34:14 may be at work here with this theme since Jesus can be seen as the anticipated Ezekiel 34 leader for the people. In Ezekiel 34 Israel's leaders had been rebuked for not being the leaders they should have been, so another must come. Jesus is portrayed in Matthew as that leader.

Complicating matters is that we may still be in a Gentile setting as the praise of the God of Israel may make more sense as a response from Gentiles, but we cannot be sure of this level of detail (but so Blomberg 1992, 245; Carson

2010, 407; France 2007, 597; Hagner 1995, 446; Osborne 2010, 601; Wilkins 2004, 541). An option not entertained, but also quite possible in a Decapolis setting, is a mixed audience, given the locale's proximate location to both groups. This might explain why ethnicity is not noted. A mixed audience was a given in this locale. The audience would parallel that of the Sermon on the Mount (Matt. 4:24–25). If Gentiles were present to a degree, then the meal mirrored the care Jesus gave to Israel. This could make sense, indicating where Matthew was headed ultimately in including the nations (Isa. 25:6; see Donaldson 1985, whose Mount Zion thesis is variously assessed with Davies and Allison 1991, 567, for it and Luz 2001, 344, against it). If the audience was predominantly Jewish, then we simply are seeing the continued service and acts of mercy extended to the children of Israel. Multiple feeding miracles are tied to Moses, Elijah, and Elisha (Exod. 16; Num. 11:4–9; 2 Kings 4:1–7; 42–44). A mixed audience also might explain why we get a second feeding. Jesus performed the miracle again for a broadening expansion of blessing, pointing to where things were headed.

Konradt (2020, 243 and 245) sees a correction by Matthew of Mark 7:31 in placing Jesus at the Sea of Galilee, by which Matthew means the Galilean side of the lake as at Matthew 4:18 and 13:1, but the remark is not that specific, so we do not know if Jesus is back in Israel or on the edge of the Decapolis. Jesus had been in the Decapolis before (Matt. 8:28–34), so the idea he could be here at this point is not implausible, though we actually do not know where he was exactly other than on the fringe of both regions. It is possible that Jesus was now beginning to reopen the option of Gentile inclusion, even as Israel remained a focus.

Jesus continued to minister with compassion. The crowd brought him many who had maladies of one kind or another. Jesus treated and healed the lame, maimed, blind, dumb and many others. Interestingly when the list is repeated a verse later, it is in a different order: people saw the dumb speaking, the maimed whole, the lame walking, and the blind seeing. Jesus's work continued. Only the maimed have not been mentioned before in healing accounts (Matt. 9:27–28—blind; 9:32–33—deaf or dumb; 11:5—blind, deaf, lame; 12:22—blind, deaf; noted later in Matthew as well: 20:30—blind; 21:14—blind, lame). Healing blindness was without an example from the Old Testament. His service to needy people went on, despite the opposition and doubt surrounding him. The healing encouraged people.

The service led to the God of Israel being glorified by an amazed crowd (amazement: Matt. 8:27; 9:33; 27:14). His ministry of compassion gave pause about what God was doing. The text was like Matthew 11:5 in force and seemingly alludes to Isaiah 35:5–6, suggesting evidence the eschaton was present as it foresees God delivering in such a manner at that time. So Jesus could not be a disastrous shepherd to be rejected, for such a shepherd did not care for the maimed nor did he nourish the healthy (Zech. 11:16; Nolland 2005, 639–40). Jesus was the opposite of a disastrous shepherd. Opposition to him did not reflect the reality of who Jesus was and is; although some might think such rejection meant he was not the leader he claimed to be. He was a good shepherd. His actions showed his character. There may be a complex set of allusions at work here from Ezekiel 34 (shepherds), Isaiah 25 (judgment) and 35 (healing), and Zechariah 11 (shepherds and judgment).

The expression "God of Israel" is common in the Old Testament and is not at all only present in a Gentile context. It often appears in a mixed setting to address more than Israel (Exod. 5:1—mixed; 1 Kings 1:48; 1 Chron. 16:36; Pss. 41:13; 59:5; 68:35—mixed; 69:6; 72:18—mixed; 106:48; Isa. 29:23; Cousland 1999, who showed this most often was an expression of praise for Israel's salvation program; Davies and Allison 1991, 569). The expression often appears with notes of deliverance. That may be its thrust here.

15:32. The fact that this miracle was so much like the feeding of the five thousand in Matthew 14 has led some to doubt this event and see it as a doublet (Hagner 1995, 449–50). However, this seems most unlikely (Blomberg 1987, 146–48). Carson (2010, 407–8) points to the differences between the two accounts, noting the number fed, locale, different starting amount of food, and different number of leftovers. The writers wrote within the lifetime of some witnesses, so why invent such a repeated event and risk losing credibility? Both Mark 8:17–21 and Matthew 16:9–11 appear to recognize two events. The rationale for the repetition has been noted, especially if this audience was different and broader in ethnic scope than the first feeding.

Jesus sought to care for a crowd that had been with him for three days and needed food (Mark 8:2). The text notes specifically that compassion moved Jesus to feed the crowd. Whatever had been brought, the crowds were now out of food. If they were not fed, then they would faint (Mark 8:3). Here Jesus initiated the effort to feed the crowd and did express it in a manner that looked like he would feed them there. He was unwilling to send them away hungry. The disciples did not get this at first.

15:33–34. The disciples did not contemplate another miracle, but asked where in this desert place enough food could be found (Mark 8:4). The expression in "this desert place" is thrown forward in the Greek for emphasis. Jesus, playing to their concern, asked for an inventory. The numbers were not encouraging: seven loaves of bread and some fish, not nearly enough. Mark 8:5 refers only to the bread, but Mark 8:7 refers to fish, so Matthew combined those references. The fish were not big, as the term ἰχθύδιον, the diminutive form, is used (BDAG s.v. "ἰχθύς" 485). They only had "little fish" to distribute. These fish were likely dried, since the people were traveling.

Some commentators comment on how odd it was that the disciples did not respond, in light of the previous miracle. However, this assumes the disciples thought of the earlier event as a kind of automatic thing. Osborne (2010, 608) notes we often struggle with unbelief. Keener (2009, 419) suggests they see Jesus so much in his humanness that "they do not expect miracles from him all the time." They responded in more normal terms. Jesus must deepen their appreciation of what he could do—and how regularly.

15:35–38. Matthew presents the miracle itself with simplicity. It mirrors the miracle that is told in Matthew 14:19–21 and parallels the miracle of Mark 8:6–8. Jesus had the crowd sit on the ground, took the food, gave thanks, and handed it to the disciples who distributed it to the crowd. The people ate their fill, so much so that seven baskets were left over. There is no clear point to the number seven other than to describe what was collected, although some have suggested the idea of perfection or completion was present (Hagner 1995, 451–52). The term for "basket" here is σπυρίς (BDAG s.v. "σπυρίς" 940), different from what is used in Matthew 14, which is κόφινος (BDAG s.v. "κόφινος" 563). The first term can refer to a large container like a hamper. In fact, the first term is used to refer to a container large enough to carry Paul to escape persecution at Damascus in Acts 9:25. So these baskets could be quite large. The second term also can refer to baskets of various sizes, so it is not completely clear if a size distinction is in view. The term used here refers to non-wicker baskets of hemp or rushes, while the earlier term involves wicker (Morris 1992, 410 n. 86; Osborne 2010, 608, who argues wicker baskets were smaller and usually used for provisions). Some see the first term as more appropriate for Gentiles (Blomberg 1992, 246), but we may simply be dealing with stylistic variation in telling a similar event (so Nolland 2005, 645).

Once again Jesus has supplied the crowd's core needs. The event showed Jesus's compassion for the crowd and pictured him as one who was able to provide. The crowd was sizable, being four thousand men apart from women and children (Mark 8:9).

15:39. Jesus now moved across the sea again. He arrived at Magadan. The exact location is only cited here in the New Testament and is uncertain. Some connect it to Magdala, near Tiberias on the sea, as do some manuscript variants. The same uncertainty applies to the parallel locale in Mark 8:10 of Dalmanutha.

THEOLOGICAL FOCUS

The exegetical idea (the continuing and expanding compassion of Jesus in the face of opposition showed itself in his exorcism of the Canaanite woman's daughter, his healing of the crowds, and his feeding the four thousand–plus) leads to this theological idea: Jesus extends a ministry of God's compassion to new groups even in the face of opposition, while a woman shows an exemplary faith of humble non-entitlement.

Jesus's continued ministry of compassion to a humble Gentile woman of exemplary faith and a needy crowd showed that his compassion would extend broadly to anyone who humbly approached him with faith. This exemplary faith did not have a sense of entitlement but embraced divine mercy and grace.

Matthew's narrative shows how God continued to reach out to bring people to himself through Jesus. None of the previous tension stopped Jesus from ministering. Even when his mission was focused in a different direction and had a specific audience, he reached out to those who cried out for help from him, as with this Canaanite woman.

Her faith also provided an important theological lesson. Her humility and persistence were important core attributes of the trust she had that Jesus could and would provide. He honored all of that and commended her when her faith stood firm. Matthew was calling his readers to have a similar trust.

Jesus continued to show compassion by healing and feeding, even when pressed by a Gentile woman to do so. This tension in the exchange with the Gentile woman allows the unit not only to highlight Jesus's continued ministry in the face of rising opposition, but also to focus again on the value Jesus placed on faith. Faith that Jesus commended was humble, had no sense of entitlement, but regarded Jesus's act as an expression of his mercy. God owes us nothing. We benefit from his kindness to us. The woman accepted her place with humility in God's program. Still, God was gracious to her as Jesus acted to affirm her faith.

The repeated provision of food underscored Jesus's continual ability to provide. It is hard to be sure if this second feeding miracle was primarily for Gentiles; although it is likely some if not many Gentiles were present, given the location. What the event did show is God's continuing work of grace pictured in compassionate provision.

PREACHING AND TEACHING STRATEGIES

Exegetical and Theological Synthesis

The exegetical section illustrates the Canaanite woman's humble faith and Jesus's profound compassion. Her love for her daughter motivated her. She pled with Jesus repeatedly. She would not take no for an answer. Her persistence mirrors that of the widow in Jesus's parable in Luke 18:1–8, who wears down an unjust judge with her cries for mercy. A widow in need of justice is desperate. A mother whose child is in peril is desperate. Our desperation humbles us and drives us to God for help.

We see a similar pattern in the psalms. The psalmist repeatedly cried out to God to rescue him from death, shame, war, or opposition. For the person of faith, desperate times do not call for desperate measures but deliverance. Thus, the person in need says, "Help me. Save me. Be my shelter. Crush my enemies." Although few of us want crises, challenges, or trying circumstances, desperation breaks us of self-reliance. When life is easy, we take God for granted; he is invisible. When hardships arise, he enters our minds; he is available.

Preaching Idea

Desperation draws Jesus to us.

Contemporary Connections

What does it mean?

First, we could just as easily say that "desperation drives us to Jesus." As mentioned in the section above, suffering has that effect. It exposes the deception of self-reliance and pushes us toward Jesus. However, these two stories give more attention to Jesus's compassion than to human faith. Jesus is the focus. And those times of great need, anxiety, or personal crisis when we cry out to him are desperate times.

Second, Jesus responded indiscriminately to needy people. He helped men and women, young and old, Jews and Gentiles, individuals and crowds. The common characteristic of those whom he helped was their humble recognition that they could not help themselves. Sometimes this recognition was through intercession: a parent for a child (Matt. 17:14–16), a centurion for his servant (Matt. 8:6), or a group for their friend (Mark 2:1–5). In today's world, needy people abound. They include drug addicts, inmates, children of divorce, people living in war-torn countries, caregivers, cancer patients, and the gender-dysphoric.

Third, our needs are not a burden to Jesus. In the Gospels, he was drawn to desperate people. This remains true today. When Jesus finds us weak, weeping, or worried, he is drawn to us. When he sees us in pain, in peril, or oppressed, he is drawn to us. When he hears our cries, laments, and rants, he is drawn to us. This could be on the edge of a highway where we ran out of gas, during a final exam when our grade hangs in the balance, or in our basement where we huddle for protection during a tornado warning.

Is it true?

It is true that Jesus is drawn to us in our desperation. As discussed above, desperation comes in many forms. At some point in life, we are all needy. And the good news is that Jesus finds our neediness attractive. Indeed, he is our empathetic high priest who gives mercy and grace in our times of need (Heb. 4:15–16).

However, just because desperation draws Jesus to us does not mean we should live in a perpetual state of desperation. He also sends the Spirit to guide, help, and empower us to live a resilient life amid adversity. He has overcome the world and given us resources to walk in his victory (John 16:33; 1 John 4:4). We do not have to rely on our own strength. God has provided biblical insight, wisdom, and other people to help us navigate the vagaries of life. Some desperation is avoidable by living responsibly.

Finally, we must clarify that Jesus's affection for us does not guarantee deliverance from desperate situations. For reasons we may never know, Jesus may not cure a disease, mend a broken relationship, or remove a thorn. Sometimes suffering lingers and desperation gets drawn out. Although we may not like trials, they shape character (Rom. 5:1–5; James 1:2–4). Whether or not Jesus answers our desperate cries, we can be sure that he abides with us in the crisis. He promised to be with us until the end (Matt. 28:20).

Now what?

First, the preaching idea invites us to be honest about our desperation. Rather than denying our troubles, we should express them. Rather than remaining self-reliant, we should surrender. We see Jesus model this in Gethsemane. He prays for deliverance ("take this cup from me") before praying surrender ("not my will but yours be done"). Instead of relying on our wisdom, wealth, or physical strength, we should admit our weakness to God. "God, this diagnosis scares me." "God, the tension at work is killing me." "God, I don't know what to do to help my depressed daughter." "God, I feel crippled by my loneliness." Praying our desperation diminishes our self-reliance.

Second, we may intercede and intervene for those in desperate situations. This is what the Canaanite woman did for her daughter. Similarly, a group of friends carried their crippled peer to Jesus for healing since his own legs would not take him there. Like Jesus, they were moved with compassion by others' desperation. Intercession and intervention are means through which we imitate Jesus today. God designed the body of Christ to bear one another's burdens (Gal. 6:1–4). When we comfort the hurting, care for orphans, feed the hungry, and advocate for the oppressed, we manifest Jesus to desperate people.

Finally, this passage invites us to marvel in the compassionate presence of Jesus. His love is deep, wide, and tangible. He heals, frees, and humanizes hurting people. He does not discriminate in showing care. We often believe the lie that Jesus loves us most when we are at our best. At our worst, we expect him to treat us like a stray dog, shooing or shouting us away. This is not true. He is a reservoir of compassion that never runs dry. Meditate on his compassion. Envision him sitting with you. Marvel at his love.

Creativity in Presentation

When our loved ones' lives are on the line, we often turn toward Jesus. These are desperate times. We see this in the movie *Heaven Is for Real* (directed by Randall Wallace 2014), where pastor Todd Burpo (played by Greg Kinnear) makes a desperate plea to God to heal his dying son. This brief prayer in the hospital chapel provides a modern parallel of the Canaanite woman's desperation.

Another film that depicts a desperate person to whom Jesus is drawn is the Christmas classic *It's a Wonderful Life* (directed by Frank Capra, 1946). After his uncle accidentally hands thousands of dollars to the greedy Mr. Potter (played by Lionel Barrymore), George Bailey (played by Jimmy Stewart) faces arrest. In desperation, first he runs to Mr. Potter for help, but Potter calls the police. Then George goes to the bar and prays. "Dear Father in heaven, I'm not a praying man, but if you're up there and you can hear me . . . show me the way. I'm at the end of my rope. Show me the way, God." This is desperation at its cinematic finest. God responds by sending the angel Clarence (played by Henry Travers) to keep George from suicide.

If you prefer visual aids, you might illustrate desperation by assembling a few props on the stage. The following items signify various types of desperation:

- An empty milk jug (especially when you need it for cereal)
- An empty roll of toilet paper (especially when you're in a public bathroom stall)
- A flat tire (especially when you're on the side of the highway)
- An empty wallet (especially when you're trying to pay at a "cash only" line)
- A "past due" notice (especially when you're pinched for cash)
- A report card (especially when you're failing English class)

These visual aids should not require much explanation. They can combine silly and serious forms of desperation. You want to stress with each one how it may cause you to feel desperate and cry out to Jesus.

On a more serious note, we often provide signals for first responders when we encounter desperate situations. Stranded people shoot flares or send S-O-S calls. Injured people shout "Help!" or call 9-1-1. A child in need on the playground waves his arms. Describe how first responders are drawn to these signals of desparation. Remind them Jesus was the ultimate first responder.

One final iconic image may help illustrate Jesus's response to our desperation: the Bat-Signal. In the Batman universe, the Bat-Signal is a powerful spotlight used by to summon Batman to help citizens of Gotham City. The signal projects a colossal silhouette of a bat on Gotham's skyline. Whenever Batman sees it, he comes rushing to the rescue. In this way, the Dark Knight is a type of King Jesus who comes to seek, save, and serve the desperate. Our crises and cries for help are similar to the Bat-Signal. Help is on the way!

In the end, you want your sermon to stress that Jesus extends a ministry of God's compassion to new groups even in the face of opposition, while a woman shows an exemplary faith of humble non-entitlement. Or, simply: desperation draws Jesus to us.

- Dogged persistence appeals to Jesus (15:21–28).
- Diverse needs appeal to Jesus (15:29–31).
- Compassion compels Jesus to serve the masses (15:32–39).

DISCUSSION QUESTIONS

1. What provoked Jesus's latest withdrawal?
2. In your own words, describe Jesus's conversation with the Canaanite woman.
3. How does Matthew present the disciples in both stories? What does this suggest about their development?
4. Explain the differences between the feeding miracles.
5. When have you experienced desperation? What is the difference between "Desperation drives us to Jesus" and "Desperation draws Jesus to us"?
6. Does greater faith guarantee Jesus will fix our desperate situations? Explain.

Matthew 16:1–12

EXEGETICAL IDEA
The result of Jesus's confrontation with Jewish leaders was a call to recognize the divine vindication of him by the sign of Jonah and the destructive teaching of the leaders.

THEOLOGICAL FOCUS
Jesus contrasts what is at stake in the choice between the Jewish leaders and himself.

PREACHING IDEA
Sharpen your spiritual dullness.

PREACHING POINTERS
Matthew combines two conversations to stress the importance of thinking clearly about Jesus. First, the Sadducees and Pharisees requested a sign from Jesus. Their inquiry was a test. Jesus knew it and replied with a rebuke and a veiled reference to Jonah. Next, Jesus warned his disciples against letting the religious teachers corrupt their thinking. The disciples slowly caught Jesus's meaning because his reference to yeast provoked a tangential discussion about their lack of bread. He spoke harshly of their weak faith before explaining his comment about the Sadducees and Pharisees. For Matthew's original audience, these conversations stressed the importance of clear thinking about Jesus. His words and deeds provided sufficient evidence of his identity and authority.

Discernment is essential for navigating today's complex world. We have more access to more information than at any moment in history. However, the deluge of data has not made us more loving, wise, or faithful followers of Jesus. Sadly, our learning has led many away from Jesus. Consider the explosion of faith deconstruction stories—tales of people who have rejected historic Christianity and biblical authority for a feeble faith in a reconstructed Jesus or hollow faith in humanity. While every faith deconstruction story is different, each one is affected by the yeast of secular, postmodern thinking. Secular people may not search for signs, but they look for patterns, meaning, and coherence. Truthfully, they are looking for God—we all are—but spiritual dullness prevents them from admitting it. This sermon encourages us to sharpen our spiritual dullness.

JESUS CONTRASTS THE RESULTS OF HIS MINISTRY WITH THOSE OF THE JEWISH LEADERS (16:1–12)

LITERARY STRUCTURE AND THEMES (16:1–12)

This unit involves a rebuke (vv. 1–4) that expands into an explanatory teaching about the Pharisees and Sadducees (vv. 5–12). This text advances the narrative by showing the rising tension between Jesus and the two Jewish groups, the Pharisees and Sadducees. The confrontation generates a warning from Jesus to his disciples about the Jewish leaders' teaching, even as the disciples were still struggling to appreciate the symbolism of Jesus's remarks and actions. Both the leaders and the disciples were seen as spiritually dull. The leaders could read the weather but failed to read what God was doing through Jesus. The disciples failed to see that when Jesus spoke of leaven, he was not speaking of real food. It is hard in this context to know if the sign of Jonah was his call to repent, the sign of the resurrection, or a combination. Either way, God was behind what Jesus was doing. Meanwhile the Jewish leadership with their teaching brought leaven, a picture of spiritual corruption. The disciples were slow to learn and had little faith, but the leaders were hostile and were said to be part of a wicked generation. Readers were to appreciate the choice that difference made. Faith needed to see clearly and to be spiritually discerning. Spiritual discernment need not seek signs, but rather observe how God is working.

The scene where a heavenly sign was requested has parallels in Mark 8:11–13 and has some similarities with Luke 11:29–32 without the request for a sign. Jonah as one pointing to Jesus is also noted in Matthew 12:38–40. The exchange over the yeast of the Pharisees and Sadducees mirrors Mark 8:14–21. Jesus stood in contrast to the leaders and the nature of the disciples' dullness. The leaders' rejection should not be taken seriously.

The first scene is a controversy pronouncement account, as the leaders' testing question led Jesus into a rebuke of the generation seeking a sign. No sign was to be given but what Jonah could teach us. In the second scene, the disciples' failure to bring bread led Jesus into a teaching pronouncement and his remarks about avoiding the yeast of the Pharisees and Sadducees. This was misunderstood and taken literally by the disciples, leading Jesus to press the disciples to be discerning and appreciate that he was speaking of the Jewish leaders' teaching. Having good theological judgment and being discerning of teaching in theology is important.

There are different kinds of spiritual insensitivity. One comes out of hostility like that of the leaders. That was rebuked. Another comes out of a lack of application of faith. Jesus exhorted the disciples not to remain in that place but to become discerning. This contrast provides the unit's main theme. Jesus reinforced the idea God was at work through him and not through the leadership.

EXPOSITION (16:1–12)

The result of Jesus's confrontation with Jewish leaders was a call to recognize the divine vindication of him by the sign of Jonah and the destructive teaching of the leaders.

16:1. Some members of both the Pharisees and Sadducees came to test Jesus (Mark 8:11). The note about testing made it clear that their question was hostile. The last person to test Jesus was the devil (Matt. 4:1). Opposition was rising. This was the second recent challenge as in Matthew 15:1 the Pharisees asked about handwashing (Turner 2008, 396). Here two groups banded together to make their test. It was not common to see these two groups acting together, as they held to distinct views of the Jewish faith. The combination appears only in this scene and in Matthew 3:7 (Matt. 16:6, 11–12). Mark 8 does not mention the Sadducees. In both instances in Matthew, they were checking out ministries of others (John the Baptist in Matt. 3). The Sadducees tended to be in Jerusalem. This was one of only two scenes where they were outside of Jerusalem in Matthew (Matt. 3:7 was the other). The detail shows that Jesus had the attention of those in Jerusalem. Carson (2010, 410–11) defended the reference to the Sadducees here as historically accurate in the face of some who doubted they would be in Galilee.

The request was for a sign from heaven. This built from an earlier request for a sign (Matt. 12:38). In one way this was an amazing request, given all Jesus had already done. He had given plenty of signs. Matthew had just summarized healings and other miracles, but apparently the request was for something specific from heaven, like making the sun or moon dark (on such signs: Gibson, 1990; Keener 2009, 421). The request for some type of specific heavenly sign had made them oblivious to all Jesus was doing. As Turner (2008, 397) says, "Seeing is not always believing."

16:2–4. Jesus's response to a request for a sign was a rebuke about spiritual dullness (Mark 8:12). Jesus noted that they could predict the weather. If the sky was red in the evening, they knew the weather would be good (Luke 12:54). If it was red and dark in the morning, they knew it would be stormy. This reflected weather conditions dictated by the Mediterranean Sea. This they saw clearly.

The scene is built around contrasts: (1) Jesus with the leaders and (2) the nature of the disciples' dullness with the leaders' rejection of Jesus. The crowd could read signs in the sky for weather. What they were able to do was "discern" weather (BDAG s.v. "διακρίνω" 3a, 231).

However, they were not able to discern the signs of the times, even though those signs had been performed again and again in their midst (Luke 12:56). The verb is unstated and is picked up from the previous example. Note Jesus's claims in Matthew 9:6–8 and 12:28. Hearts that were not open could not see what might well be happening before their eyes. They would object or seek another line of proof, as was happening here. The Lucan parallel is sufficiently different in wording and context that it is clear that Matthew and Luke were not following each other's version (Gospel of Thomas 91 is also quite distinct from Matthew; Davies and Allison 1991, 582).

Jesus went on to deliver a more severe rebuke. He called them a wicked and adulterous generation (Matt. 12:39, 41–42, 45; 17:17; 23:36). This was a charge that spoke to a hardness of heart and a rejection of what God was doing. The rebuke was for unfaithfulness. It recalled the generation of the wilderness (Deut. 1:35; 32:5, 20; Isa. 57:3–9—because of idolatry; Jer. 3:9–10—because of idolatry; Osborne 2010, 613). They sought to demand from God a particular sign. That was not coming. The only thing coming was the sign of Jonah. The wording is very much like Matthew 12:39. This sign could either be the resurrection to come, only alluded to here (so most), or it could be the message of Jonah to repent, or a combination of the two seen as a package. Both ideas were tied to Jonah in Jesus's gospel teaching, best seen in Luke 11:29–32. Matthew 12:40 discusses the image of Jonah in the belly of the whale; yet Matthew 12:41 also alludes to Jonah's call to repent. Wilkins (2004, 555) sees the message of repentance now and the resurrection later as the sign (also Osborne 2010, 613). Such a call to repent was exactly what Jesus had been doing to draw people to the kingdom. So that could well be Jesus's point. Carter (2004, 330) sees death as the point and notes the irony that Jesus's death was the sign even as the leaders were planning for it. The point is valid but lacks an explicit connection to the resurrection, which was the point of the image of three days in the whale in Matthew 12:38–40. His effort to limit the point to Jesus's suffering is too narrow.

A Wicked Generation

Deuteronomy 1:35: "Not a single person of this evil generation will see the good land that I promised to give to your ancestors!"

Deuteronomy 32:5: "His people have been unfaithful to him; they have not acted like his children—this is their sin. They are a perverse and deceitful generation."

Deuteronomy 32:20: "He said, 'I will reject them. I will see what will happen to them; for they are a perverse generation, children who show no loyalty.'"

When Jesus said this, he departed (Mark 8:13). He ended up in another lake scene with another very large crowd.

16:5–7. The disciples were dealing with the fact they had forgotten to bring bread for their next journey. Mark 8:14–15 has the conversation on the boat as they traveled on the lake. Again, Matthew has a shorter, more compact version of events (with France 2007, 608, against Luz 2001, 447). Jesus was not traveling separately from them. The issue was important because they were coming to a new location.

Jesus responded by telling them to beware of the "yeast" (ζύμη) of the Pharisees and Sadducees (BDAG s.v. "ζύμη" 2, 429). Mark 8:15 mentions the Pharisees and Herod. The present tense infinitive (προσέχετε) called them to be on constant alert, "constantly beware" (BDAG s.v. "προσέχω" 1, 879). Leaven was seen as an alien element in ancient bread-making. Passover bread was unleavened (Exod. 12:14–20; Osborne 2010, 618). First Corinthians 5:6 and Galatians 5:9 show its force with this meaning. Jesus was speaking of the damage the teaching of the Jewish leaders did. The real danger of leaven was that it spread and took over the whole loaf. Used negatively, it pictured the spread of that which invades or spoils. Luke 12:1 and Matthew 23 added to this objection the picture of yeast pointing to hypocrisy as dangerous. In Matthew 13:33 the image was positive for how God's kingdom would invade and eventually spread across the world.

As the rest of the passage makes clear, the disciples did not get what Jesus was saying (Mark 8:16). They were fixed on the fact they did not have physical bread, and perhaps that Jesus was noting their failure to adequately plan and provide. They went on discussing (so the imperfect tense) their lack of bread. The force of the verb is either "they began discussing" or "were discussing." They were so occupied with everyday matters that spiritual realities were passing them by. They missed not only the lesson of the two feedings Jesus was about to mention, but also his warning about the Pharisees recorded in Matthew 15:13–14 (Turner 2008, 400). The disciples had a spiritual dullness Jesus would now address. It was most likely that what was addressed here was that the disciples were missing the leaders' opposition to Jesus and the pressure that put on the community and its ministry, as shown by Matthew 16:1–4 (France 2007, 609; Keener 2009, 422, speaks of their "toxic cynicism"; Wilkins 2004, 556).

16:8–11. Jesus moved into his rebuke for the disciples' spiritual dullness. He described them, as he often did, as having little faith (Matt. 6:30; 8:26; 14:31; 17:20). They were not to be "little faiths," but people with a big faith. He challenged them about their arguing over literal bread. Then he recalled the two feedings of the five and four thousand. He reminded them there were leftovers in both cases. They could trust God to direct and provide.

Mark 8:17–21 is more detailed. There, the disciples recounted what had been left over. Jeremiah 5:21 also is cited there. Matthew lacks Mark's direct charge that the disciples' hearts were hardened. Mark is often harsher on the disciples. Matthew has simplified the account.

From here on Matthew is unique. Jesus asked somewhat incredulously how they could think he was speaking about real bread. No, it was about the yeast of the Pharisees and Sadducees. They were to be constantly beware of that threat.

16:12. The rebuke struck home. Now the disciples understood what Jesus was saying. The teaching of the Pharisees and Sadducees was what should not influence them nor should that teaching be what others should follow. They had to stay vigilant against teaching that failed to recognize what Jesus was doing and who he was. They learned from the rebuke, unlike the Pharisees and Sadducees of the previous scene. Part of the point in Matthew's gospel as a whole was to make this warning to those believers of Jewish background.

THEOLOGICAL FOCUS

The exegetical idea (the result of Jesus's confrontation with Jewish leaders involved a call for spiritual discernment for the divine vindication of him by the sign of Jonah, versus the leaven of the leaders' destructive teaching) leads to this theological focus: Jesus contrasts what is at stake in the choice between the Jewish leaders and himself.

Spiritual dullness during Jesus's ministry came in two sizes: hostility and dullness. Instead of openness to God, some reacted negatively with rejection and hostility. That rejection led to destruction, while the dullness involved a lack of discernment about what was going on spiritually by being overwhelmed by life's concerns. Such dullness also led to immaturity.

There was a lack of openness to God that was destructive. Matthew was chronicling such a reaction to Jesus. The Jewish leadership reflected this spiritual hardness. Whatever Jesus did, it was not enough. People were capable of being truly discerning about what happened in the world for things like the weather. However, without an open heart, they would miss what God was doing in his creation.

Then there is a spiritual dullness that results when the cares of this world gain our full attention. That is when we miss what might be really damaging to us spiritually. The disciples were learning that lesson. Jesus's rebuke sought to shake them out of their doldrums. It did. They were early in the process of learning to be spiritually sensitive. As they learned, they became more able to reflect about what God was doing.

There are two types of spiritual insensitivity to Jesus: skepticism and getting too distracted from spiritual things by life. One is to not appreciate who he is and approach all he does with skepticism. The Jewish leadership's request for a sign from heaven failed here. Such dullness takes one nowhere. The second is getting so focused on the details of life that spiritual discernment falls to the side. That was the disciples' problem. This was correctable because their hearts were open to learn. Jesus pushed them to be more sensitive. This openness is something that is to be continual. Disciples continue to grow as they walk with Jesus. That is as it should be.

PREACHING AND TEACHING STRATEGIES

Exegetical and Theological Synthesis

The exegetical section describes two forms of spiritual dullness. The religious teachers embodied dullness that came from hostility toward Jesus. They were skeptics. The disciples represented dullness that came from immaturity. They were anxious. Both forms of dullness obscured a clear understanding of Jesus. Therefore, Jesus responded to both groups firmly.

For the skeptics, Jesus strung them out. He did not entertain their questions, knowing that it would only lead to further questioning. His treatment of them illustrated his earlier teaching about not throwing pearls before swine (Matt. 7:6). During his final week in Jerusalem, Jesus would continue to sidestep the cynical traps of the religious leaders by responding to their questions with questions (Matt. 22) or parables (Matt. 25).

For the anxious disciples, Jesus allowed them to ramble about bread before rebuking them. Their fear was an ongoing impediment to faith. Their want for material goods (Matt. 6:30) or need for safety (Matt. 8:26; 14:31) provoked earlier rebukes of their "little faith." Jesus would address their "little faith" again regarding their impotent prayers (Matt. 14:31; 17:20). Although Jesus's reproof of anxiety sounds harsh, especially to the sensitive ears of our therapeutic age, it is important to name anxiety as a cognitive distortion. Unless we name them, the worries of the world will hold us captive. Fear clouds our thinking unless we address it. Fear leads to relational mistakes. Anxious disciples may need a firm challenge to reject fear and choose faith.

Preaching Idea

Sharpen your spiritual dullness.

Contemporary Connections

What does it mean?

According to this passage, spiritual dullness comes in two subforms: disbelief and distraction. The religious leaders represent the skeptics. They demand signs from Jesus; his words and deeds are not enough to convince them. In Jesus's day skeptics were steeped in their religious traditions. In our day, skeptics may be influenced by personal experience or ideology. For example, if someone had a negative interaction with judgmental Christians or abusive church leaders, they may be skeptical, even rightfully so. However, they should not stay in that more negative space. Move on. Moreover, if philosophical materialism governs a person's belief system, that person may be skeptical of Jesus's miraculous ministry or the Bible's divine origin. Disbelief dulls us to Jesus's words and deeds.

In this passage, the disciples represent those dulled by distraction. They got obsessed with power, anxious about weather, and concerned with the crowds. The tyranny of the urgent negatively impacted their spiritual sensibilities. In our day, distractions comprise internal and external noise. Internally, we wrestle with busy schedules, to-do lists, intrusive thoughts, traumatic memories, fears, and catchy song lyrics. Externally, we must sift through phone notifications, traffic delays, medical bills, work memos, our neighbor's lawnmower, and television. Distraction dulls us to Jesus's words and deeds.

Sharpening our spiritual dullness means using discernment when we deal with disbelief and distractions. Discernment helps us face doubt without deconstructing our faith. It helps us separate biblical truth from church tradition. When we sharpen our minds against skepticism, we can guard our faith against materialism, secularism, and other ideologies. We can move on to what we should be focused on and draw nearer to God. Moreover, discernment focuses our minds, so that both internal and external noise do not distract us. As we become spiritually sharp, we discern how to limit our screen time, manage our schedules, and handle our stress. We see and respond to our mission in why God called us.

Is it true?

Spiritual discernment is an ongoing, essential task of disciples. We are bombarded daily with distractions. It is hard to argue that too much time on social media, streaming movies, or listening to podcasts weakens our ability to focus or think clearly. We become addicted to distraction and submerged in noise. Sadly, many of us prefer distractions to the internal noise of our self-criticism, shame, and our need to move on in a positive way.

Moreover, our distractions often undermine biblical faith. They are driven by a secular worldview, which elevates the virtues of self-indulgence, self-reliance, and self-expression. When we are spiritually dull, secularism drives our behavior. For example, greed exceeds generosity; sexual sin exceeds purity; bitterness exceeds forgiveness; and force exceeds gentleness. We can counter spiritual dullness by practicing discernment.

Now what?

The passage calls for three responses. First, we may need to name our skepticism. Are there areas where you doubt the Bible's ability to speak truth? For example, you might not trust the Bible as an accurate guide to human origins in God, gender roles in ministry, final judgment, or God's love. Additionally, you may think Jesus's teaching on marriage, loving enemies, and forgiveness is too soft. You may be skeptical toward church leaders amid recent abuse stories or toward believers who claim certain gifts of the Holy Spirit. Skepticism may guard us from deception, but it also blocks us from trusting God and others. Naming skepticism softens our hearts and sharpens our faith.

Second, we may need to identify our anxieties. Are you consumed by the cares of this world? Do your scarcity mindset, desire for safety, or people-pleasing tendencies draw you away from Jesus and turn you inward? Although anxiety can signal danger, it can also become dangerous by dulling our thinking. Fear lies. It tells us God does not care, does not act, or cannot help. Identifying our anxieties robs fear of its power and sharpens our faith.

Finally, we must learn to discern. Part of discernment is rooting out cynicism and anxiety from our minds. After we have confessed these faulty thought patterns, we can enter the focused work of discernment. To discern is to hear God amid the noise of everyday life. He speaks through his Word, Spirit, other people, and our circumstances. God personally prompts, guides, affirms, and redirects us, especially when we create time and space for listening to him. Discernment helps us know what is best, what comes next, or how to understand the moment. For example, discerning people may sense God pushing them to change jobs, pursue adoption, resign from the worship team, or delay surgery for an alternative treatment plan. Learning to discern opens our ears and sharpens our faith.

Creativity in Presentation

The imagery of sharpening lends itself to using a dull knife as a prompt. The key is to find a blade large enough for people to see it. You want to illustrate the difficulty of cutting with the dull blade. Then, as you discuss the process of sharpening the blade, use your sharpener to improve the blade's quality. Note: If you do not have a sharpening device, you can purchase one, but they get pricey. For the sake of this illustration, the standard iron rod will make your point. Just like a dull knife is no good for cutting food, a dull mind is no good for discerning truth. For a variation on this idea, you may discuss sharpening an axe with a coarse stone or lawnmower blades using a file.

"Sharpening the Saw" is the name of one of Stephen Covey's famed *7 Habits of Highly Effective People*. This habit is the seventh, culminating habit. According to Covey (2020, 341–43), it holds the other six habits together, ensuring the person is renewed in mind, body, spirit, and social life. Covey insists this habit is the "single most powerful investment we can ever make in life" because it keeps us refreshed, engaged, and prepared for life's challenges. Although Covey's writing focuses more on personal development than service to Jesus, his principle applies to the preaching idea. Personal renewal will keep us from becoming spiritually dull.

To illustrate spiritual dullness, share a deconstruction story. Sadly, your church likely has several to choose from; however, it may be wiser to talk about someone outside your congregation. I (Tim) have friends from high school and college who have deconstructed their faith. While each deconstruction story is personal, there are common themes (Keller 2016, 30): lack of empirical evidence for faith or God, the problem of evil, the existence of good and happy atheists in contrast with mean and miserable believers, and "coming out" as an atheist felt freeing. Despite its "powerful storyline," deconstruction is not a feat of rationalism but a fruit of spiritual dullness.

Photography can be an effective way to contrast sharpness with dullness. Take a series of pictures of the same subject. You may capture an image of a face, pet, flower, or national monument. As you snap the shot, adjust the lens so the images become more or less clear. (If this is too technical, you can take a single picture and use filters to blur the image.) As you display the picture, begin with the blurriest one. Ask people to identify it. Advance to the next images, becoming more and more focused as the images proceed. Because this invites participation from your audience, you may want to show several images to increase engagement. Wrap up the illustration by saying, "Faith brings Jesus into focus. We need to sharpen our eyes to see him."

Finally, to demonstrate how distractions make us dull, you could assemble a pile of props that serve as common distractions: cell phone, laptop, calendar, whiteboard with to-do list items, grocery bag, dog leash, alarm clock, and golf clubs. Point to each item and describe how they interrupt your flow, hijack your brain, and turn you into a distracted mess. You might even display a "monkey brain" GIF (there are many to choose from), which will distract your audience as you speak. After going through the distractions, you might say, "What was I talking about? Oh yeah—distractions make us spiritually dull."

In the end, you want your sermon to focus on the fact that Jesus contrasts what is at stake in the choice between the Jewish leaders and himself. Therefore, we must sharpen our spiritual dullness.

- Cynicism makes us spiritually dull (16:1–4).
- Distractions make us spiritually dull (16:5–12).

DISCUSSION QUESTIONS

1. What is significant about the Sadducees joining the Pharisees in this story?
2. What evidence had Jesus already provided about his messianic identity? What is the meaning of the allusion to Jonah?
3. Where have you seen cynicism in your life? In your church?
4. What feeds cynicism in our culture? Be specific.
5. How can you help people identify and eradicate their distractions? Be specific.

Matthew 16:13–28

EXEGETICAL IDEA

Peter's confession of Jesus as the Christ led to the revelation of a suffering Messiah in whose way the disciples were to follow, even as the church shared in his prevailing authority.

THEOLOGICAL FOCUS

Jesus affirms the disciples' confession of Jesus as the Christ, and yet tells them that he—and they—will suffer.

PREACHING IDEA

A true confession comes at a cost.

PREACHING POINTERS

Jesus withdrew from Galilee with his disciples. This excursion allowed him space to question his disciples. He asked them about others' perceptions of him: others called him a prophet. He asked them about their own perception of him: Peter called him the Christ. This confession revealed Peter's understanding; however, his picture of Messiah was incomplete. Thus, Jesus filled in the detail about suffering, an experience each disciple would share by following in his footsteps. From the outset of his gospel, Matthew has provided hints of Jesus's messianic mission. This pericope clarifies that mission by predicting Jesus's suffering, death, and resurrection. The original audience would have heard Jesus's suffering as a summons to self-denial.

In the secular age, self-denial is a sin. Self-indulgence and self-expression are virtues. Digital media allows for nonstop streaming and shopping. The consumer is king! Social media allows for unlimited posting and scrolling of our overstated lives. Influencers are modern-day royalty! Sadly, secularism has dethroned Jesus and installed the self in his place. In this tragic reversal, Jesus exists to serve us and meet our desire for happiness. To resist self-rule, we must see Jesus for who he really is: Messiah, Son of David, and Suffering Servant. Jesus is not merely one religious great among others. He is unique in the purposes of God. This sermon reminds us that a true confession comes at a cost.

PETER CONFESSES JESUS AS THE CHRIST (16:13–28)

LITERARY STRUCTURE AND THEMES (16:13–28)

This unit comes in three parts and represents a turning point in Matthew. First is the confession that Jesus was the Christ, the Son of God. Peter's remark showed that the disciples understood the major role of Jesus as the central figure in God's program (Matt. 16:13–20). Their confession stood in contrast to the populace's evaluation of Jesus as some kind of a prophet. The difference was crucial. Jesus demanded more than mere respect as a great religious man. He was unique with a distinctive role. The Old Testament backdrop to the confession was the idea that Messiah is as a Son to God (2 Sam. 7:4–16; 1 Chron. 17:3–15; Ps. 89:27–29). The parallels only mention Peter's confession of Jesus as the Christ, so it was the key point in the confession. The picture of the keys of the kingdom is from Isaiah 22:22. The images are regal and Davidic. That is where the stress is on this scene, but Jesus would build off that understanding and develop how he was the Son, even alluding to it here by calling God "my" Father in heaven. Peter's confession caused Jesus to promise to build a new community on the kind of confession Peter made—something Peter had understood because God had revealed it to him. Peter himself had a key role in that work, so Jesus's reply concentrated on him.

This is the first and one of the few mentions of the church in this gospel, the only gospel to use the term. Matthew had been setting up the messianic confession since Matthew 1:1, 16–18, 2:4, with references to the Son of David in Matthew 12:23, the disciples' reaction in Matthew 14:33, and requests for signs that pointed to a sent figure of the eschaton in Matthew 12:38 and 16:1 (France 2007, 612).

Second, the confession also led Jesus to predict his suffering, something Peter was not yet ready to accept, leading Jesus to rebuke the idea that suffering could be avoided—an idea that came from Satan (Matt. 16:21–23).

Third, there is teaching on following in the way, not accomplished by power but through suffering (Matt. 16:24–28). Jesus prevented any sense of triumphalism about what was ahead. Disciples would have to deny themselves and take up the cross's shame of experiencing rejection. To gain the soul, one would have to lose it. The Son of Man would come in glory but first there was suffering, along with a preview of glory for some.

This unit overviews the program of Jesus. He was not the strictly powerful Messiah many had anticipated, but a figure who first must bear the pain of sin before the glory to come. It was a lesson the disciples were slow to learn and that the Jews did not expect. But the Lord worked in mysterious ways, ways he also revealed to those whose hearts were open to let God speak.

Peter's confession in Matthew 16:13–20 has parallels in Mark 8:27–30 and Luke 9:18–21. Matthew is still following with Mark here as he has for several units. However, Matthew has skipped Mark 8:22–26, which he never uses. He also has additional detail from Mark, which is not his common practice. Matthew had access to additional material or knowledge here. The passion prediction of Matthew 16:21–23 is like Mark 8:31–33 and Luke 9:22. The discipleship teaching mirrors Mark 8:34–9:1 and Luke 9:23–27. Other elements are like Matthew 10:38–39, Luke 14:27 and 17:33, and John 12:25.

This unit focuses narratively on developing the disciples' understanding of God's program and affirming their confession of Jesus as the central figure in it. Dominant are exhortations about what God was doing through Jesus and what he called those who follow him to be.

The first scene of the confession is a dialogue pronouncement, where Jesus affirmed what Peter declared. The middle unit is the first passion prediction of three in Matthew. The third unit is a series of maxims on discipleship. Jesus made it clear that following him would be demanding. The program also would end in the glory of the Son of Man. That was a reason discipleship was worth it.

There are numerous important themes. The Christology of this scene is most central. Jesus was not one player among many in God's plan. He was the Messiah, the Son of God. Exactly what "Son" meant Matthew will develop, but what Jesus affirmed from Peter's remark was the central and distinctive role Jesus had as Messiah in God's program. His central role was and is the basis for a new community and judgment about what was pleasing to God. No one else before or since has stood in such a place as Jesus had.

We watch the disciples struggle to get this in the rest of the gospel. They thought of a Messiah of power; one of suffering was hard to swallow. Jesus would repeat himself on this over and over, yet it was not clear to them until the end.

Part of this road was that it was not for Jesus alone. Disciples would walk the same path. The world treats the students as the teacher, the followers as the pathfinder. Discipleship was a way of self-denial, because the understanding was that gaining life required giving up life. It also involved looking at Jesus's life as an example, to clear the way. To learn from Jesus and be a disciple was to follow him in his way. Jesus was always making it clear that disciples received everything as a gift and were asked to give everything as a response. God is worthy of nothing less. Pushback from the world should come as no surprise.

For a full defense of the historicity of this scene, one can look at the essay by Wilkins (Bock and Webb 2009, 293–381) or the discussion of Davies and Allison (1991, 604–15). The discussion of Wilkins is summarized in Bock (2012, 93–106).

EXPOSITION (16:13–28)

This unit makes clear the dividing line between the new movement Jesus brought and the Jewish leadership that opposed him. Jesus *was* that dividing line (Luke 2:34). Did God actually send Jesus, showing him to be at the center of the divine program of deliverance, or not? The confession of Peter showed that it was on that understanding about Jesus that God was doing his long-promised work. It was not that this was a new teaching set apart from a long-established Jewish hope and expectation, but rather that Jesus was the source to realize that hope. Part of what Jesus was doing, however, was a surprise. It was that this promised Messiah would suffer. This also was embedded in the hope as Scripture laid it out, but that point had been missed (Ps. 118:22; Isa. 52:13–53:12). Jesus redirected attention to this aspect of his work after gaining the core confession, because that example laid out the path before his disciples as well.

Peter's confession of Jesus as the Christ led to the revelation of a suffering Messiah in whose way the disciples were to follow, even as the church shared in his prevailing authority.

16:13. Caesarea Philippi was a region known for its worship of many pagan gods (Josephus, *A.J.* 15.263–64; *B.J.* 1.404–6; 2.168; 3.509–15; BDAG s.v. "Καισάρεια" 1, 499). It was about twenty-five miles north of the Sea of Galilee, about a day's journey from Jesus's normal ministry locale near the source of the Jordan River. Its other name was Panias, named after the Greek god Pan. A shrine to that god existed there. It was a grotto cut into a rock cliff. This may explain some of the imagery Jesus used later in the scene. The name Caesarea came from Philip the tetrarch, honoring Augustus. The sub-name Philippi distinguished it from

Photo of Grotto Area of Caesarea Philippi. Note the big grotto area and other niches where pagan temples had been, as the site was also called "Panias" after the god Pan.

Caesarea Maritima, located on the Mediterranean coast. It was a very Hellenistic area.

Somewhere around the locale (note the reference to this region), Jesus began a conversation with his disciples about who he was as Son of Man (Mark 8:27). Mark has Jesus and his disciples headed there. This difference is like other places where Matthew simplifies the account (e.g., Matt. 14:34). Jesus asked, "Who do people say the Son of Man is?" and then followed it with a question about who the disciples thought he was. Mark 8:27 has Jesus ask, "Who do the people say I am?" as does Luke 9:18. So was Matthew responsible for highlighting this title (so most), or did Mark and Luke simplify the identification? The answer to that question is not clear. Since Jesus used "Son of Man" to refer to himself, the question in either form asked for the same thing. Given how Jesus had referred to himself, the questions in this event were about who the crowd thought he was versus who the disciples thought he was. Given that the title Son of Man normally was confined to Jesus's own speaking, it may well be that Matthew gives us the original wording, while Mark and Luke make the referent for the title clear by linking it to Jesus. They make the implication in Jesus's normal use of the title explicit.

16:14. The disciples said the crowds thought the Son of Man was one of the prophets: John the Baptist, Elijah, Jeremiah, or one of the other prophets (Mark 8:28). Of those named, one could think of a coming proclaimer of the kingdom (John), someone who pointed to the kingdom and worked miracles (Elijah), or someone who called the nation to account (Jeremiah). In a certain way, each option made some sense, but it was not the entire picture. Herod had already made the John the Baptist connection in Matthew 14:2. Elijah was associated with the end in Malachi 4:5 and Sirach 48:10. Jesus tied Elijah to John the Baptist in Matthew 11:14, and did so again in Matthew 17:10–12. Luke 9:19 notes John the Baptist, Elijah, and one of the prophets, omitting reference to Jeremiah. In fact, only Matthew notes Jeremiah. Konradt (2020, 250) has a full explanation of what this mention means to Matthew). Jeremiah was critical of Israel and noted the coming fall of Jerusalem.

Sirach on the Forerunner Elijah

Sirach 48:10 (said about Elijah): "At the appointed time, it is written, you are destined to calm the wrath of God before it breaks out in fury, to turn the hearts of parents to their children, and to restore the tribes of Jacob."

16:15. Jesus turned to ask who the disciples thought Jesus was (Mark 8:29a; Luke 9:20a).

The pronoun "you all" (ὑμεῖς) is in the emphatic position in Greek. The contrast that the question probed for was whether the disciples had an appreciation of Jesus that went beyond the limits the public had. As is often the case in Matthew, Peter stepped forward to represent the disciples (Matt. 15:15; 19:27).

16:16. Peter answered the question confessing Jesus to be the Christ, the Son of the living God. The reply contained an ambiguity. Given where Matthew's community was, they rightly would have heard a full sense in "the Son of God," a claim of a close divine relationship. However, Mark 8:29b has "You are the Christ." Luke 9:20b has "the Christ of God." Given that the king can be the "son" as 2 Samuel 7:7–17, Psalm 89:27–29, and 1 Chronicles 17:3–15 indicate, the confession could be seen to stress the messianic side of Jesus's role as Son with that being capable by further explanation to be developed for all "Son of God" can mean (also Ps. 2:6–8). John 1:49 makes a similar juxtaposition. Nolland (2005, 662–65) gives an overview of this term, while Bateman, Johnston, and Bock (2012) work through the individual kingship and messianic texts in detail. This "regal and more" idea may be part of what Jesus meant when he said he would build off Peter's confession. If Jesus was Messiah, the question became what kind of Messiah he was. The point then was that Jesus was more than a prophet and stood at the center of God's program. The issue was that the confession showed Jesus was at the center of the kingdom story. One could not have the kingdom without the king in the middle of it all. This was clearly the emphasis in Mark and Luke. It is likely Matthew was going down a similar path. After this use of the title, it is not seen in Matthew for a while, then it reappears several times almost as a refrain for Jesus (Matt. 22:42; 23:8, 10; 24:5, 23; 26:63, 68; 27:17, 22). The same happened with the idea of sonship (Matt. 26:63; 27:40, 43, 54; 28:19). The next scene about the Son of Man's suffering shows Peter still had some things to learn. His confession was not perfect in knowledge, but on target with its major recognition (France 2007, 618; Morris 1992, 423).

16:17. The next three verses are only in Matthew. Jesus emphasized that Peter's perception was not merely self-generated. Peter was blessed because God had revealed this to him (Matt. 11:25–27; 13:11). Jesus's description of the heavenly Father did emphasize the unique position Jesus had to the Father ("my Father in heaven"). It underscored and pushed the confession to its limits. It also showed how God was at work in changing and opening hearts.

16:18. Peter continued to be addressed as an individual. In a wordplay, Peter was named "the rock." His confession or his representative response as a person reflected the rock on which the church would be built. Peter was affirmed for his recognition of Jesus.

This text has been the center of controversy between Roman Catholics and Protestants. Catholics see Peter himself as the Rock and the keys being given to him to pass on to other rulers. Nothing in the text actually speaks of a passing on of this authority in this way, as France (2007, 622) and Konradt (2020, 255) correctly note. It is also uncertain if Jesus was saying he would build on Peter as the core image present (so Roman Catholics, as well as Blomberg 1992, 252; Davies and Allison 1991, 627; France 2007, 622; Turner 2008, 405; and Wilkins 2004, 563) or on what Peter believes, namely, his confession. It actually is hard to separate the two here (with Morris 1992, 423; and Nolland 2005, 669). It is the confession that counts most here, as it is what Jesus was driving at in asking the question. Because the confession means life and forms the content of what brings one into the church, Hades cannot stand against it. The church was built on this confession, not on Peter, though one could say the church was built on confessions like Peter's of other people. Yet the wordplay does bring Peter personally into this saying, since it distinguishes him from everyone else present or future as the first such confessor. Peter became the exemplar for the confessing believer. Davies and Allison (1991, 624) argue that Peter was given a new name, as Abraham was, to show a fresh forging of God's people, with Isaiah 51:1–2 in the background. Ephesians 2:20–22 may reflect the complicated nature of this imagery (also Rev. 21:14). If a formed people were in view, then it refers to the first generation on which the church was built. The church was also pictured as a sacred place, a temple. Hades was the Sheol of the Old Testament (Isa. 28:15–19; 38:9–10). Nothing would stop the church from delivering her promise even in the face of a full onslaught (Davies and Allison 1991, 632–33).

The Rock Image as an Ancestor Base

Isaiah 51:1–2: "Listen to me, you who pursue godliness, who seek the Lord. Look at the rock from which you were chiseled, at the quarry from which you were dug. Look at Abraham, your father, and Sarah, who gave you birth. When I summoned him, he was a lone individual, but I blessed him and gave him numerous descendants."

"Church" is not a common word in the Gospels. A church was a *qāhāl*, an assembly (Blomberg 1992, 252; Deut. 31:30 LXX). In the Gospels, the term only appears in this passage and in Matthew 18:17. Peter's role might be important in that church because he helped establish this confession after Jesus's death as one rooted in apostolic experience and truth. It was Peter the Rock who spoke boldly at Pentecost in Acts 2. The man and message belonged together, and as the first confessor he had a unique place. Matthew loves to focus on Peter as the leader and spokesperson for the Twelve. Matthew refers to Peter twenty-three times total, but twenty-one of those come from Matthew 14 on. So Peter emerges as the Matthean narrative advances. Culpepper (2021, 312–13) probably makes too much of the Pauline versus Petrine tension in the church to explain this. Peter himself kept the focus on Jesus in using this imagery in 1 Peter 2:4–8, which also points to a temple.

In sum, Jesus made three points. Peter was seen as a rock by his confession. The church that Jesus would build was tied to the solid base Peter represented. Nothing would prevail against the hope that Peter's understanding of Jesus as the Christ brought.

16:19. Jesus now underscored the church's authority, with Peter as a representative of its core belief. He gave the keys of the kingdom to Peter. The picture is of authority, unlocking the way to God in the kingdom (Isa. 22:22; Luke 11:52; Rev. 1:18; 3:7; also 3 Bar. 11:22; 3 En. 18:18). The power was of binding and loosing. The kingdom was bigger than the church since it had the mix of the world in it (Matt. 13:24–30, 36–43), but access to its benefits is what was in view.

Image of the Keys

Isaiah 22:22: "I will place the key to the house of David on his shoulder. When he opens the door, no one can close it; when he closes the door, no one can open it."

Perfect passive participles are used for heaven's relationship to what Peter bound and loosed. Their force is debated. Is what Peter binds and loosens "shall have been" bound or loosed in heaven (looking to the past) or "will be bound and loosed" (looking to the future) on analogy with uses in the LXX and NT (Isa. 8:17; Heb. 2:13)? This line points to the cooperative authority that Peter acts with in connection to what God has willed. The debate is which way the influence goes. Those who look to the near context of verse 18 contend for a future response of heaven ratifying what the church does (Turner 2008, 405; Davies and Allison 1991, 638, note Matt. 5:7; 6:14–15; 10:32–33 as places where heaven responded to earth). This sequence gives the idea that nothing prevails against the church. In addition, in Matthew 18:18, the sequence is that the church prays and heaven endorses. Those who think about God's sovereignty being preferred see a look back. Seen in this light, it is divine guidance that was promised (so France 2007, 627; Wilkins 2004, 568). Blomberg (1992, 255) argues for a generic use where there is a state of being bound and loosed so there was no sequence intended, just a relationship. What is bound on earth has the same result in heaven at the same time. Nolland (2005, 681) argues similarly and sees community forgiveness in view in a way that hints at church discipline for behavior. Whichever way one takes binding and loosing, and it is not clear, that judgment is based on something consistent with what Peter had confessed. The response to the gospel message is that which provides access to or denies access to the kingdom and to such authority (Blomberg 1992, 254; Nolland 2005, 676; Luke 11:52; John 20:23).

Is there more pictured in this authority? Many things have been suggested: exorcism, salvation, doctrinal teaching, or church discipline (Turner 2008, 405). Teaching is likely, given the negative example of the Jewish leaders in texts like Matthew 21:43, 23:13, and Luke 11:52, as well as the near context of Matthew 16:5–12 where teaching was the concern. The near context had sought a connection between teaching and life, so issues of behavior were possibly in view. France (2007, 626) and Wilkins (2004, 566) opt for community regulation and administrative oversight of gospel expansion, something possible because of Matthew 18:18 and rooted in Peter's role of the inclusion of Gentiles and others in Acts 2, 8, and 10. The uniqueness of the application to Peter favors this option as tied to entry to the gospel and community purity. Morris (1992, 426) cites Acts 8:20–23 as an example of this purity category. The keys dealt with access, while binding and loosing treated conduct and teaching. Morris (1992, 427) notes that the options here are so numerous and complex that one should be careful about being too dogmatic.

16:20. Jesus next told his disciples not to tell anyone that he was the Christ (Mark 8:30). Two reasons for this are likely, one of which surfaced in the next event. First, the people have only an expectation of a Messiah of power (Osborne 2010, 630). To declare Jesus as Messiah would raise the wrong kind of expectations. It might even have prematurely involved Rome in a reaction if the popular response were to be intense. Second, Jesus's sharing of his suffering, which he did next, was not yet appreciated by the disciples, as Peter's response to it showed. Before they shared that Jesus was the Christ, the disciples needed to appreciate what kind of Messiah Jesus was (Keener 2009, 430). That was what Jesus was going to teach them. Jesus himself did not use the title much in public in Matthew. Only in Matthew 22:42 did he raise it in a generic discussion about who the Messiah was (France 2007, 627).

Once the disciples understood the kind of Messiah Jesus would be, they became free to discuss it. Matthew 17:9 says that would be after the resurrection. The emphasis on Messiah showed itself consistently in the early church, even to the point that Jesus became known as Jesus Christ in all layers of the tradition.

The call to be silent touches on what has been called the messianic secret. This idea argues that the church created this confession of Jesus as a messianic figure and retrojected it back into Jesus's ministry, even though Jesus himself did not harbor messianic expectations. They covered up the move by this call to be silent.

The claim of a later secret retrojected back has major problems. First, it is clear that the confession of Jesus as Christ came very early in the church as it was at every level of the extant tradition, even to the point of being tied to Jesus's name. Second, it is not clear why being the Messiah would have been made up by the church had Jesus not taken them there already, especially if he had no such expectation. A resurrection would not cause them to go there because there was no expectation in Judaism that Messiah would be raised. Also, the claim would have placed the community at risk with Rome, so one would not go there unless there was a real reason to do so. It is far more likely this focus on Jesus as Messiah came from his own ministry and teaching than that it came later after a non-messianic ministry.

16:21. Now Jesus turned to discuss the character of his messianic calling (Mark 8:31; Luke 9:22). There were surprises coming for the disciples. Matthew notes that Jesus began to tell the disciples about what was to come. There was a divine "must" (δεῖ) in what he revealed (Matt. 26:24; BDAG s.v. "δεῖ" 1, 213–14). France (2007, 631) contends that Matthew 20:28, with its mission statement, began to show why this was a necessity (also Matt. 26:28). Texts looking to vindication may be at work (Pss. 110:1; 118:22–26; Isa. 52:13–53:12; Dan. 7:9–14; Davies and Allison 1991, 656). Jesus was headed for Jerusalem. He would suffer at the hands of the elders, chief priests, and scribes there. The Sanhedrin might be in view (Morris 1992, 428). The one Greek article groups these parties all together as unified opponents. Jesus would be killed, but on the third day he would be raised by God. These days were counted inclusively. Jesus had hinted about a possible death in Matthew 9:15 and 10:38, while Matthew noted the leaders' plot in 12:14. Jesus would continue to mention suffering or the vindication to follow it (Matt. 17:9, 12, 22–23; 20:18–19, 28; 21:38–39; 26:2). This was the first of four specific predictions for Matthew (Matt. 17:22–23; 20:17–19; 26:2).

This is another historically disputed part of Jesus's teaching. It is said the predictions do not fit the surprise the disciples had at Jesus's resurrection. However, the text indicates that the disciples wrestled with believing and understanding these sayings in the sense of how they could possibly work. Peter's reaction here at this first announcement shows the hurdle Jesus faced in making these claims. The disciples were simply slow to accept this idea.

16:22–23. In an exchange partly unique to Matthew, Peter was horrified at Jesus's prediction. Peter responded, "God forbid!" There is an idiom here for the remark is "May God be merciful to you" for saying such a thing. In this context, it rejected that God would do this, with a force rendered in the LXX as either "far be it" (Gen 44:7) or "may it never be" (1 Sam. 14:45; Turner 2008, 410 n. 2). Peter then followed it up with a remark that this would never happen to Jesus. It is stated most emphatically with the use of οὐ μή. Peter could not conceive of Jesus as a suffering Messiah being killed. Peter's attitude was like that which caused John the Baptist to have questions earlier in Matthew 11:2–3.

Apparently, they were talking side by side, or Jesus had his back to Peter, so Jesus turned to address Peter. In Mark 8:32–33, Jesus addressed Peter in front of the disciples. Mark also uniquely says that Jesus spoke plainly to introduce it. Luke does not record any of this exchange.

Jesus's remark was not so much to Peter as to what Peter's remark represented. Matthew lacks the use of the verb "rebuke" in Mark 8:32, but the remarks were clearly that. Jesus said, "Get behind me, Satan." The response was like Matthew 4:10. Peter's idea of no suffering was not God's way. Peter was so focused on suffering that the word about resurrection seemed not to have registered. There was no need for such a path in Peter's view. Yet Peter's belief represented an attempt to undercut all Jesus was doing. The idea of no suffering was from Satan. Peter was not possessed by Satan, he was simply thinking as Satan would (Davies and Allison 1991, 663). His thinking was "in league" with the devil (Keener 2009, 434). It was a "stumbling block" (σκάνδαλον) to the program of God (BDAG s.v. "σκάνδαλον" 2, 926). In a very short time, the "rock" had become the "stumbling block." Ironically, Paul would call the cross a stumbling block for others (1 Cor. 1:23; Gal. 5:11). The avoidance of suffering for Jesus did not reflect God's thoughts but those of men. Jesus would not be deterred.

This was a remark so strong that the idea that this scene would have been made up later by the church is most unlikely. This was not how to portray a leader like Peter. The only explanation for its presence was that it happened.

16:24. In light of the suffering Jesus would undergo, he turned his attention to the path others would follow as a result. The cross had a future for his disciples beyond Jesus. Jesus talked about a discipleship that required an "all-in" commitment. He was discussing potential martyrdom and intense self-denial before the world (see vv. 25–26). To follow Jesus would require self-denial, taking up the cross and following in his way of suffering. Mark 8:34 notes that Jesus said this to the multitudes as well. Matthew focuses on the disciples who were really to get what discipleship would involve. The first two imperatives are aorist, looking to an orientation, while the third verb is in the present tense, pointing to a constant response. One was to deny oneself as a matter of orientation, then take up the cross in a similar way. Only then was one ready to follow Jesus day to day.

Denial is a form of disowning, like the time Peter denied Jesus in the Passion account. Only here we are speaking of denying the self, not defending oneself. The image of taking up the cross probably alluded to taking up the cross beam for one's own crucifixion, where its joining to an already erect vertical post awaited. Matthew 10:38 had already said this. Luke 9:23 speaks of taking up the cross daily. It is an act pointing to rejection and shame, as crucifixion was a most feared and horrific form of death (Chapman 2000; Hengel 1977). In choosing to trust Jesus, this was where disciples were headed in terms of the world. Jesus wanted his disciples to understand this. As far as their relationship to the world was concerned, their old life had died; their values now came from elsewhere (2 Cor. 5:17–18; Davies and Allison 1991, 671). Spoken of positively, it was part of being born again or born anew. One's life had moved from being aligned to the world to being aligned with God. The world would react. Nolland (2005, 691) says it meant "to put your head in the noose" or "on the chopping block," taking up the risk of rejection in pursuit of the "greater good" tied to Jesus. Taking this path was what it meant to follow Jesus daily.

16:25–26. Jesus gave a rationale for his remarks. This parallels Matthew 10:39 (also Mark 8:35–37; Luke 9:24–25). To protect one's life by seeking the world's approval and fearing its rejection would lead to losing one's soul. To lose one's life for Jesus's sake was to gain life. Jesus was that central and important to real life, as he was its source. Kingdom benefits were tied to how one responded to him. This set some context for what was said about doing works in Matthew 16:27.

There was no profit in gaining the world and losing one's life. Gaining the world meant acceptance from the world on its terms and gaining its possessions. One could have all that and lose life. Tragically, there was nothing one could give in exchange for one's life. Once it was lost, one had nothing. The two rhetorical questions in the verse made the points that (1) it profited nothing to gain the world and lose the life, and (2) nothing could be given in exchange for the soul (Ps. 49:7–8; Nolland 2005, 693). The idea here is like Luke 12:13–21 and the parable of the Rich Fool, whose soul was required of him after he thought he had everything. The reverse of what is said in the Lucan parable is found in Galatians 2:20, where real life came through being crucified (Davies and Allison 1991, 671). That is a nice commentary on Jesus's remark in Matthew 16:25–26.

16:27. Beyond the practical rationale Jesus gave, there also was an eschatological rationale that undergirded it. In fact, Jesus could not say what he did in Matthew 16:25–26 unless what was said here was the case. Life, described as ψυχή or "soul," would be assessed by the Creator at the judgment (BDAG s.v. "ψυχή" 2e, 1098–99). The Son of Man would do that work. He would come with his angels and the glory of the Father and render accounts. Jesus's authority was seen in his unique relationship to the Father and the fact the angels were said to be his. Daniel 7:9–14 appears to be in the background, also Zechariah 14:5. The Son of Man, that is Jesus, had the right to judge. In a remark unique to Matthew, each person would be repaid according to what they had done (Prov. 24:12). In this context, what they have done regarding Jesus was central to that evaluation (see v. 25; Matt. 25:31–46; Rom. 2:6; 1 Cor. 3:10–15; 2 Cor. 5:10; 2 Tim. 4:14; Rev. 2:23; 22:12). The New Testament sees a connection between responding to Jesus in genuine faith and what one does as a result. The latter shows the former. The fact that "work" is singular points to the product of the life as a unit. France (2007, 640) speaks of "their commitment to Jesus in the face of hostility." Note also 2 Thessalonians 1:7–8. A tie to Jesus, the word of the kingdom, and fruit recall Matthew 13:8 and 13:23. Matthew lacks anything like Mark 8:38 here.

16:28. So important was Jesus that he issued a promise that some would not die before they saw the Son of Man coming in his kingdom. This promise is much discussed. Was Jesus saying the kingdom in power would come soon, with an implication that Jesus was wrong? Or was he promising a preview of his kingdom glory for some—something realized at the transfiguration (Blomberg 1992, 261; Toussaint 1980, 209) or at the cross and what follows (Nolland 2005, 695), with resurrection (Davies and Allison 1991, 679; Konradt 2020, 261, with transfiguration as proleptic to this event), with the Spirit at Pentecost (McNeile 1915, 248), at the judgment of A.D. 70 (Hagner 1995, 486–87), or at the end (Culpepper 2021, 322)? Of these, the proximity of the transfiguration seems to speak for it as the best option, especially since only a few of the disciples experienced it versus the other options where most did (2 Peter 1:16–18) or would, as in the case of A.D. 70 or the end. It is preferable to see the transfiguration as a preview of the judgment authority Jesus would possess.

THEOLOGICAL FOCUS

The exegetical idea (Peter's confession of Jesus as the Christ led to the revelation of a suffering Messiah in whose way the disciples were to follow, even as the church shared in his prevailing authority) leads to this theological idea: Jesus affirms the disciples' confession of Jesus as the Christ, and yet tells them that he—and they—will suffer.

Peter's confession of Jesus led into instruction that the Messiah would suffer. Discipleship would require the same path, something that the judgment would examine.

The key theme of this unit is christological. Jesus was more than a prophet. He was Messiah, Son of God. This placed him at the hub of God's kingdom program. Jesus was not just one religious great among many. He was unique. However, he was not merely a Messiah of power and glory, though that would come one day. He would suffer, as would those who follow him. The disciples struggled to understand this. Only the death and resurrection made it clear to them. But they were faithful in having the boldness to stand up for Jesus and challenge the world after he was raised. They denied themselves, took up their cross, and followed him. They became examples to us of those who were faithful. They had their failures, but they represented their Messiah well in the end.

There also is some initial ecclesiology in this passage. The confession of Jesus as the Christ, Son of God, was the basis for this new community Jesus was forming. It has a message that even hades cannot defeat. It is a message of life. The church is the place where God has placed his presence in a special way. He works through it and its message. Peter as the apostle who confessed Jesus was given a singular and unique place in getting the church off the ground after Jesus's death. Peter preached at Pentecost (Acts 2), checked on the word of the kingdom as it came to the Samaritans (Acts 8), and was the figure present to preach to Cornelius (Acts 10). He was the first one through whom the Gentiles were included. The keys he received unlocked the gospel to those beyond Israel.

We see a community growing and deepening in its understanding of who Jesus is and how that frames how we follow him. Discipleship is demanding. It requires a form of self-denial many will not choose to undertake. Disciples need to be willing to face rejection. Those who seek to protect their honor in the world will not join. Those who lose their lives for Jesus's sake gain life as it was designed to be lived.

The judgment was and is about Jesus. He leads it. How one responds to him is a predictor of its outcome for everyone who will face judgment. We tend to live today ignoring eschatology, but Jesus says the accountability and hope that are a part of eschatology help to drive us in the right direction in terms of responding to him. It reminds us we are accountable to the living God, our Creator. We are not independent franchises when it comes to life. Giving an account means we have to watch how we invest in the choices we make in life, especially the choice tied to who Jesus is. Keeping that most central question in front of us is Matthew's burden in this unit.

PREACHING AND TEACHING STRATEGIES

Exegetical and Theological Synthesis

Discipleship entails more than right doctrine. A confession of faith must be matched with a posture of surrender. Orthodoxy and obedience go together. Peter's interchange with Jesus illustrates the point. Turner (2008, 244) notes Peter's "quick shift from blessed confessor to rebuked adversary," insisting on his agenda over Jesus's messianic mission. As the poster child of discipleship, Peter demonstrated our persistent grasp for control. The ploy is as old as Eden, where Adam and Eve chose self-rule over God's rule when tempted by the serpent (Gen. 3:1–6). The true test of our confession is not what we say, but our commitment to applying Jesus's words (Matt. 7:24–27; 28:20).

The opposite of self-rule is self-denial. This is also the hallmark of Christian discipleship. Jesus combined stark images of dying and crucifixion to explain the cost of discipleship. These built upon earlier call narratives (Matt. 4:18–22; 8:18–22; 9:9), his discourse on mission (10:1–42), and teaching about persecution (5:10–12, 43–47). Followers of Jesus may lose family, sleep, and their lives. Followers of Jesus are guaranteed conflict rather than comfort. However, self-denial is less a set of masochistic behaviors—never watch TV, avoid sugar, self-flagellation—than a commitment to say, "Not my will, but God's be done."

Preaching Idea

A true confession comes at a cost.

Contemporary Connections

What does it mean?

What does it mean that a true confession comes at a cost? There is a general principle here: confessions have consequences. A man can confess his love to a woman, but true love costs: time with friends, emotional energy, bouquets of flowers, and an engagement ring. A friend may confess to hating big social gatherings, but it may cost him future invitations. An employee may confess to expertise in an area of work, but it may cost her leading a project or putting in extra hours of labor. A confession of love, preference, or skill shapes expectations.

When it comes to a confession of faith, the expectation is obedience. Words are cheap. Even Jesus recognized that many could call him "Lord, Lord" but did not know him (Matt. 7:21–23). Similarly, the prophet Isaiah rebuked Israel for calling on God but not obeying him—an echo in Jesus's conflict with the Pharisees (Isa. 29:13; Matt. 15:8–9). Calling Jesus "Lord" should result in a lifestyle of self-denial. Although self-denial will look different for each disciple, the cost of obedience includes surrendering our rights, our will to rule, and our personal comforts.

Is it true?

Does a true confession come with a cost? It certainly does. The cost of self-denial varies from person to person, but it tends to fall in the categories mentioned above: loss of rights, self-rule, and personal comforts.

The loss of personal comforts may result from time given to church activities, money given to charity, a week of vacation given to volunteer at a youth camp, or opening one's home to foster children. A true commitment to Jesus manifests itself in these kinds of sacrifices. The loss of self-rule may include one's willingness to set aside an agenda to help a friend in need, commitment to sexual abstinence while single, a pattern of praying for God's direction rather than relying on one's impulses, the humility to confess sins and seek counsel from spiritual companions, and trust in God's Word as the way to live. Obedience is evidence of a true confession.

The loss of rights may include the inability to speak about Jesus without losing a job, friends, or social media followers. In places where the church is persecuted, true confessions may result in a church being burned, a pastor imprisoned, or its members killed. In the United States, many of the privileges afforded the church—tax-exempt status, housing allowances, public service opportunities—may not last. Those who truly confess Jesus appreciate their privileges but see themselves as citizens of heavens (Phil. 3:20).

Now what?

First, this sermon should invite us to check our vision of Jesus. Have we reduced him to a prophet? A moral teacher? Have we divorced him from his humanity and focused solely on his divinity? The question Jesus asked Peter ("Who do you say I am?") not only remains relevant, but it is the most important question we can answer. We want to be sure our vision of Jesus matches the gospel portrait. He is Messiah, Son of God, Son of Man, Savior of the world, Suffering Servant, rabbi, and friend of sinners. Clarity about Jesus is central to our confession as his disciples.

Second, we should consider the cost of discipleship. Our confession may cost us rights, self-rule, and our comforts. For example, God may call us to leave the comfort of home to do global mission work. He may urge us to initiate tense conversations with family members. He may ask us to remain quiet in the face of false accusations. He may ask us to give more, serve more, pray longer, and sin less. The cost of discipleship is real.

Finally, disciples must learn to say "yes" to Jesus. Our default response should be to go where Jesus says, do what Jesus asks, and avoid what Jesus condemns. Obedience is the evidence that we love him, trust him, and abide in his word (John 15:9–17; 1 John 5:3). Moreover, obedience leads to a full and stable life (Matt. 7:24–25).

Creativity in Presentation

In real life, certain confessions come at a cost.[1] People will hold us to our word. You can illustrate this with three examples. First, if you confess to a police officer who pulls you over that you know you were speeding, it may cost you a

1 Some of the creative ideas from Matthew 8:1–22 may work here as well.

speeding ticket. Second, if you confess to your boss amazing skill with budgeting, it may cost you hours serving on the budgeting committee. Third, if you confess your love to a dating partner, it may cost you an engagement ring. Confessions come with a cost.

As consumers, we have an innate sense of counting the cost. Whether we are planning for a vacation, budgeting for college, or purchasing a new vehicle, any savvy spender knows how to add up the costs. Consider walking your congregation through one of these costly scenarios:

> Price of travel (airfare, car rental, gas) + price of lodging (including taxes and cleaning fees) + price of food (groceries, restaurants, drinks, and dessert) + price of souvenirs + price of excursions = a *costly* vacation!
>
> Price of enrollment + price of tuition + price of books + price of room/board + price of laptop + price of dorm décor + price of parking fees + price of late-night Taco Bell runs + price of antacids x 4 years = a *costly* collegiate experience!
>
> Base price of car + price of upgrades (self-parking, heated seats, cameras, 5G) + price of sales tax + price of warranty + price of insurance = a *costly* new car!

Because this passage centers on the imagery of a cross, consider having a giant cross on the stage. You could also get an eight-foot landscaping timber to represent the cross beam. As you talk about carrying the cross, lift the timber on your shoulders. Describe the weight of the beam, the pressure on your shoulders, and shameful ties to crucifixion.

Christian history records the death of many martyrs. Those who have died for their faith illustrate the cost of confession. Remarkable stories of the earliest martyrs can be found in *Foxe's Book of Martyrs*. More modern examples of martyrs are captured in the magazine *The Voice of the Martyrs*. Consider selecting one or two of these stories to illustrate the ultimate cost of confession.

Famous Christian Martyrs

Apostles: James, Peter, and Paul
Patristic Period: Polycarp, Justin Martyr, Perpetua, Cyprian
Middle Ages: Thomas Becket, Joan of Arc
Reformation: William Tyndale, Thomas Cranmer
Post-Enlightenment: Dietrich Bonhoeffer, Jim Elliot, Nate Saint[2]

Ultimately, the sermon should stress that Jesus affirms the disciples' confession of Jesus as the Christ and yet are told that the Christ and they will suffer. Indeed, a true confession comes at a cost.

- Misperceptions of Jesus are common (16:13–14).
- True confession builds community (16:15–20).
- True confession comes at a cost (16:21–28).

2 For a comprehensive list, see: https://en.wikipedia.org/wiki/List_of_Christian_martyrs.

DISCUSSION QUESTIONS

1. Why did the religious leaders and crowds think Jesus was Elijah or a prophet?

2. How do you make sense of Peter's dramatic shift from Spirit-filled confessor to Satan-inspired denier of Jesus?

3. What does it mean to "bind and loose"? Was that authority delegated only to the early church? If not, what does it look like to bind and loose today?

4. In addition to martyrdom, what are other costs believers may incur for their faith?

5. Who has modeled a costly faith for you? Be specific.

Matthew 17:1–20

EXEGETICAL IDEA

Jesus's preview of glory, the promise of suffering, and the failure of the disciples to heal the demon-possessed boy showed their need for a deeper faith as Jesus's destiny approached.

THEOLOGICAL FOCUS

The nature of who Jesus is requires disciples to pay closer attention to him and their faith.

PREACHING IDEA

Learning from Jesus is a lifelong journey.

PREACHING POINTERS

Matthew combines two stories, both featuring the disciples' immaturity. First, God revealed Jesus's identity in sight—radiant face, white robes, beside Moses and Elijah—and sound—"This is my beloved Son. Listen to him!" During the transfiguration, Peter made a foolish comment, proving he had more to learn about Jesus's uniqueness and redemptive mission. Second, Jesus encountered a distressed father who begged for help with his ailing son after the disciples had failed to heal him. Jesus rebuked the unbelieving crowd, the destructive demon, and his ineffective disciples. For the original audience, the combination of stories would have provoked an increase in faith by listening more closely to Jesus and trusting his power at work in them.

To be a disciple is to be a learner; it is implied in the name. This was true in Jesus's day and is true in ours. We all have room to grow in our knowledge. Not only do we have gaps in our knowledge, but we are also prone to cognitive bias and fallacious thinking. Our brains like shortcuts. Thus we oversimplify, stereotype, cherry-pick data, and outsource our research to the first page of results on any Google search. Perhaps these mental tricks work when we are trying to learn about the ten-day forecast, date for Easter in 2027, or filmography of Tom Hanks. However, when trying to learn about Jesus—a subject of inexhaustible and glorious nature—we are all novices. This sermon teaches that learning from Jesus is a lifelong journey.

THE TRANSFIGURATION AND THE DISCIPLES' FAILURE TO HEAL A YOUNG BOY (17:1–20)

LITERARY STRUCTURE AND THEMES (17:1–20)

This unit is built around a contrast, the glory of the divine voice confessing Jesus, reinforcing what Peter confessed (Matt. 17:1–8) and the failure of the disciples to heal a demon-possessed boy who Jesus then came and healed (Matt. 17:14–20). The painter Raphael made the scene famous in a memorable canvas that hangs in the Vatican Museum in Rome. It was the thrill of victory and the agony of those needing more instruction. The disciples had much more to learn. That was always the case. In between, Jesus told those who saw the transfiguration to keep silent, affirmed Elijah had already come, and repeated his prediction of suffering, pointing to the example of John the Baptist (Matt. 17:9–13). From glory their attention needed to turn to a season of suffering.

At the core of the scene is the affirmation of the heavenly voice that repeated what had been said to Jesus at his baptism. Now the voice went more public with one point added, "Hear him!" Jesus was different than what many, including the disciples, had expected. To understand Jesus they would have to listen to him. That was why they needed to be silent for now, because they still had much to learn. One thing they needed to learn was that Elijah had come in John the Baptist. Another thing they needed to learn was that even a little faith could accomplish much, so they needed to apply the faith they had.

Matthew 17:1–8 is paralleled in Mark 9:2–8 and Luke 9:28–36. Matthew 17:9–13 is paralleled by Mark 9:9–13. Matthew 17:14–18 is like Mark 9:14–27 and Luke 9:37–42. Matthew 17:19–21 mirrors Mark 9:28–29 and Luke 17:6. The saying on faith is also like Matthew 21:21 and Mark 11:22–23. Matthew is still tracking alongside Mark in this unit.

Reactions to Jesus drive the first scene of the transfiguration. The heavenly affirmation of Jesus is central to the event. Peter thought Jesus should be honored alongside Moses and Elijah, but the voice stressed Jesus's uniqueness, a second text after Peter's confession to argue Jesus was more than a prophet. Jesus took the initiative in discussing Elijah and John the Baptist and in reacting to the disciples' failure to heal, taking the opportunity to challenge their faith. We continue to see the disciples needing to grow as Matthew develops their character as a group.

The first scene is a direct supernatural encounter miracle account, since we have the divine voice in the passage and Jesus's transformation (Matt. 17:1–8). It is an epiphany (Osborne 2010, 644). It also is a type of pronouncement story, but here the pronouncement came from the heavenly voice, not Jesus. The pronouncement carries the passage's theological weight and direction alongside the portrait of Jesus's physical transformation. Jesus called for silence until the Son of Man was raised (Matt. 17:9; also 16:20). One should be careful about how one presented the Messiah. So once again there was instruction not to share all they knew, for they still had much to learn. With this instruction Jesus shared a time limit on their silence. When the Son of Man was raised, they might speak. Then they would understand better exactly what to say about who Jesus was.

Jesus announced that Elijah was John the Baptist in another pronouncement that was a disclosure (Matt. 17:10–13). The remark helped confirm the eschatological calendar. On the discussion about the historicity of the scene, Davies and Allison (1991, 689–93) and France (2007, 644) defend a historical core.

These announcements about the divine program stand in contrast to the disciples' failure in healing (Matt. 17:14–20). This was a complex miracle account, since the failure became an obstacle before Jesus healed the boy. The healing also led to a pronouncement that was a call to exercise faith. We have a mix of Christology, eschatology, and discipleship in this passage. The entire text served to reassure that Jesus was who he claimed to be. Heaven was now speaking up about him, in the midst of the conflict on earth.

EXPOSITION (17:1–20)

This unit shows how disciples always remain disciples, needing to keep learning. There is always more to learn about Jesus and the ways of God. Once we turn off listening to God and try to live by cruise control, we go backward. The earliest disciples also had to learn this lesson after gaining the affirmation of their recognition of Jesus. They also needed reaffirmation of that confession in light of the disputes swirling around Jesus. God picked this moment to give some disciples a glimpse of what was to come through a glorified Jesus. What Jesus was asking for by his disciples continuing to be teachable had heavenly endorsement. When the church and disciples stop learning and changing, they not only stop growing, they often go backward. Matthew showed it always pays dividends to keep listening to Jesus.

Jesus's preview of glory, the promise of suffering, and the failure of the disciples to heal the demon-possessed boy showed the need disciples had for a deeper faith, as Jesus's destiny approached.

17:1. Six days after the prediction in Matthew 16:28 Jesus took a few of the disciples—Peter, James, and his brother John—up a high mountain (Mark 9:2; Luke 9:28). These three were also separated out at Gethsemane (Matt. 26:37). The mountain's description has led to speculation about which mountain was meant: Carmel (1 Kings 18), Tabor (Origen), Meron as Galilee's highest peak (Blomberg 1992, 263), and Hermon (Culpepper 2021, 324; Wilkins 2004, 590) are the most often mentioned candidates (Davies and Allison 1991, 695). Hermon is often viewed as being too far away. Any one of the other three is possible. The exact location is not clear (Osborne 2010, 645). Luke 9:28 has this event after "about eight days."

17:2–3. Jesus was transformed into a glorified, heavenly form, indicated by brightness of the sun and light (Mark 9:3–4; Luke 9:29–31). The verb here is μεταμορφόω and means to have one's appearance change, "to be transformed" (BDAG s.v. "μεταμορφόω" 1, 639; 2 Cor. 3:18). The passive voice suggests an outside act. God was doing the transforming. Jesus's face was changed to shine like the sun. This detail is unique to Matthew. This reflection recalls Moses in the wilderness or descriptions of angels (Exod. 34:29–35; Dan. 10:6; Philo, *Mos.* 1.70). God is also described in this way (Ps. 104:2). The scene echoes Exodus 24 with its six days, three followers, glory, a cloud of presence, a voice, fear from the scene, and a mountain (Turner 2008, 419). If so, Jesus was a second, greater Moses. Jesus was a greater Moses because this is a different glory, as Moses's glory faded and reflected his presence with God (2 Cor. 3:7–18; Keener 2009, 438). This was something more innate to Jesus (John 1:14, 18; 2 Peter 1:16–18). The form of appearance was like what was said will happen to believers one day (Dan. 12:3; 4 Ezra 7:97; Rev. 3:4–5). This was inner glory shining forth. The picture of white clothes is not like Exodus 24 but is common for shining glorified beings (Dan. 7:9—the Ancient of Days; 12:3—the wise; 1 En. 62:15–16; Matt. 28:3; Mark 16:5; Luke 24:4; just shining–Rev. 1:16; 10:1).

Moses's Face Shines and the Glory of the Wise

Exodus 34:29: "Now when Moses came down from Mount Sinai with the two tablets of the testimony in his hand—when he came down from the mountain, Moses did not know that the skin of his face shone while he talked with him."

Daniel 12:3: "But the wise will shine like the brightness of the heavenly expanse. And those bringing many to righteousness will be like the stars forever and ever."

Moses and Elijah were talking with Jesus. Moses and Elijah likely represented the law and the hope of eschatological renewal from the prophets (Nolland 2005, 701). Previous mentions of Elijah pointed to eschatological elements. This eschatological theme also reappears in Matthew 17:10–13. Malachi 4:4–6 mentions them together in such an eschatological context. Both also had mountain experiences (Exod. 19:20; 1 Kings 19:8–14). They were talking. Luke 9:31 tells us it was about Jesus's upcoming exodus. All of this was designed to reassure the disciples, given what Jesus had said about suffering. The divine program would reach its goals through Jesus.

17:4. In another move showing why the disciples needed to learn, Peter excitedly spoke of his building three booths to honor Moses, Elijah, and Jesus. Peter again dove in, as he often did in Matthew (Matt. 14:28–31; 15:15; 16:16–19; 17:24–27; 18:21; Wilkins 2004, 591). Did he simply want to give his heavenly visitors hospitality? Mark 9:5 has a plural here, so Peter expected help but would lead the effort. There seemed to be more than hospitality in view with the mention of tents, as that pointed to the Feast of Tabernacles. This mirroring of Tabernacles suggested an equality between the three figures, what Turner (2008, 418) calls "damning Jesus with faint praise." This feast, known as *Sukkot*, celebrated the harvest but also was connected to eschatological harvest and the judgment (Nolland 2005, 702; Turner 2008, 417; Hos. 12:9; Zech. 14:16–20). Peter was still in a power mode when it came to leadership. In his view, the kingdom was coming soon to crush. It did not reflect an appropriate positioning of Jesus nor an understanding of the tone of Jesus's current ministry goals. Peter still needed instruction about Jesus's uniqueness and the emphasis on outreach in the current phase of Jesus's work. Mark 9:5 is similar, while Mark 9:6 says they spoke out of fear and Peter did not know what to say. Matthew presented yet again a more condensed version. Luke 9:33 says the remark came as they started to leave and, like Mark's version, that Peter did not know what he was saying. Luke 9:32 also notes uniquely that they had been sleepy when the two men appeared, jarring them awake.

It is also interesting that Peter's address to Jesus with the proposal differs: Matthew—Lord; Mark—Rabbi; Luke—Master. These variations, all communicating respect, show the variation with which ancient stories were told while the gist remained the same.

17:5. At this point a bright cloud that represented the divine *Shekinah* appeared and overshadowed them (Mark 9:7; Luke 9:34; cf. Exod. 13:21–22; 33:9–10; 40:35; 1 Kings 8:10–11; Ezek. 1:4; Rev. 14:14). Second Maccabees 2:7–8 looked forward to a return of the cloud in the days of Messiah (Blomberg 1992, 264). Was this experience the heavenly sign given to some disciples that the Jewish leaders had been denied?

In the midst of the cloud's enveloping them, a voice spoke. It repeated the words of the divine voice at the baptism (Matt. 3:17) with one addition: the call to listen to Jesus. Mark's rendering also repeats, with the additional call to listen, the words of Mark's version of the baptism plus one more change: the shift from "you" at the baptism to "this" here, as now the voice has gone more public. Luke 9:35 describes Jesus as "the elect one" as well as Son. There was a progress of divine disclosure taking place. Jesus was the beloved Son in whom God was pleased (2 Peter 1:17). Jesus's role was superior to Moses and Elijah, who pointed to him. This language combines Psalm 2:7 and Isaiah 42:1. The first person and scriptural allusions make it clear that God was speaking. The call to listen to him comes from Deuteronomy 18:15. Jesus was the leader-saving prophet like Moses (Acts 3:22; 7:37), but as Son he was greater than Moses was, even though both were described as servants of God (Exod. 14:31; Num. 12:7–8; Heb. 3–4; Carson 2010, 438–39; Davies and Allison 1991, 702). The voice gave the passage's central pronouncement. The disciples were to be assured Jesus possessed unique glory and authority to bring God's program. The just announced suffering would not stop the program; it was in the plan. So was the glory that they had expected. The Father gave "the seal of approval" upon the Son (Morris 1992, 440).

17:6–8. The disciples were overwhelmed with fear (Exod. 20:18–21; France 2007, 650). Out of respect, they fell to their faces, in effect bowing down. Tobit 12:16 shows the tone of this act, as Tobit and Tobias fell as they encountered the angel Raphael, a response also seen in Daniel 8:17 in response to an angel (Nolland 2005, 704). They sensed the moment's uniqueness. Jesus told them to get up and not be afraid. It was a moment of profound revelation, but there was no danger. This set of details is unique to Matthew.

When the disciples arose, only Jesus remained (Öhler 1999; Mark 9:8; Luke 9:36a). Did the cloud take Moses and Elijah away? Josephus has a text about Moses that has a similar move (*A.J.* 4.325–26; Davies and Allison 1991, 704). Jesus was now the lone voice (Turner 2008, 419). Looking forward, Jesus's unique glory had been seen, but there also had appeared a preview of heavenly glory in general that awaited all. Looking back, there was a note of hope from the Hebrew Scriptures in the figures of Moses and Elijah, along with an independent declaration from God. God's program was moving ahead, with the disciples' needing to pay attention as Jesus prepared them for what was ahead and for his departure. What was coming, they did not expect. What was coming meant they would follow in Jesus's path. There was much to learn as registration for class was over and fresh schooling began (Penner, 1995).

Moses and Others before a Cloud

Josephus, *Antiquities* 4.325–26: "Now as soon as they were come to the mountain called Abarim (which is a very high mountain, situated over against Jericho and one that affords, to such as are upon it, a prospect of the greatest part of the excellent land of Canaan), he dismissed the senate; and as he [Moses] was going to embrace Eleazar and Joshua, and was still discoursing with them, a cloud stood over him on the sudden, and he disappeared in a certain valley, although he wrote in the holy books that he died, which was done out of fear, lest they should venture to say that, because of his extraordinary virtue, he went to God."

17:9. Jesus brought them down from the mountain and told them not to share the vision with anyone until the Son of Man was raised (Mark 9:9). The term ὅραμα, often translated "vision," can also simply mean "something seen," which is its more likely force here, since several people were involved (BDAG s.v. "ὅραμα" 1, 718). This was not a privatized vision but more like an appearance. After the resurrection, all of what was happening would make better sense (France 2007, 652). It makes sense this was the last time Matthew notes a call to silence, as also had been called for in Matthew 16:20 (also Matt. 8:4 and 9:30 for people other than the Twelve). They were gaining an appreciation for how God was working. Once they got it, they could speak. In the meantime, they were to listen and learn. Luke 9:36 does not mention Jesus's instruction, only that the disciples were silent and did not tell anyone what they had seen. In this Luke follows Mark 9:10.

17:10. The disciples now turned to discuss Elijah. His presence at the transfiguration was likely a reason for the question arising. They asked Jesus why the scribes taught that Elijah must come first. By mentioning "first," they introduced the topic of the eschaton, as that was what was being alluded to here. Malachi 3:1 and 4:5–6, as well as Sirach 48:10, were probably in view as Elijah was to bring in the era of hope (see chart at 16:14; Davies and Allison 1991, 715). The question showed the disciples had yet to appreciate all Jesus had said in Matthew 11:10–14 about John introducing the new era of hope, especially 11:14 (Turner 2008, 420).

17:11–12. Jesus responded in three parts. First, Elijah was coming and would restore all things (Mark 9:12). These verbs are in the present and future tenses. There would be an era of restoration (Matt. 19:28; Acts 1:6; 3:21). In one sense, nothing had changed in terms of ultimate expectation.

Second, in contrast, Jesus went on to say that Elijah had already come (Mark 9:13). It is very much discussed whether Jesus was saying John was Elijah so that there was nothing more left to this prophecy (France 2007, 654; Keener 2009, 440; Osborne 2010, 649) or whether John was a type of Elijah with Elijah still to come (so Wilkins 2004, 594; Blomberg 1992, 266, and Nolland 2005, 708, are uncertain). John 1:21 has John refuse to be called Elijah, and Luke 1:17 speaks of him ministering in the spirit of Elijah. These remarks suggest a type, as does Elijah-like imagery described in Revelation 11:3–6. John prepared Jesus's way as the use of Isaiah 40:3 in the Synoptics says. What made John like Elijah was his introducing the eschaton and calling for repentance, leading to restoration, but that restoration was and is Messiah's work, not Elijah's. And there was more to come in that restoration than what Jesus was doing now. The Elijah-type figure of John the Baptist initiated the sequence (Wilkins 2004, 593–94).

Third, however, Jesus said that they did not recognize John as Elijah and did to him as they wished. This pointed to John being rejected by the leadership and to his suffering and death. The path John walked was now going to be the path of the Son of Man. Jesus's remarks concluded by noting so also the Son of Man was about to suffer by the same hands that did in John. "The same hands" referred to those who were rejecting God's messengers. This was Matthew's first suffering Son of Man saying. Mark 9:12 has this earlier in sequence, posed as a question. The point is the same.

17:13. The disciples now understood that Jesus was referring to John the Baptist. He had opened up the era of the eschaton. He had suffered. Now it was left for the Son of Man to suffer. Jesus continued to reinforce the idea that he was traveling down a road bound for suffering.

17:14–16. Matthew's version of this scene describing a healing that met with trouble is much shorter than Mark's version, as is common with Matthew. Mark 9:14–29 has sixteen verses, while Matthew 17:14–20 has seven. Luke 9:37–42 also is shorter. This scene depicts our last miracle until the healing at Jericho in Matthew 20:29–34 (France 2007, 658). The focus in this healing is entirely on the disciples and their need for faith. The disciples' failure of faith was distinct from that of the leadership (contra Nolland 2005, 710) because it was not out of malice but simply immaturity.

While a transcendent moment took place in the transfiguration, the other disciples were struggling. On his return, Jesus encountered in the crowd a man who knelt in respect before him and asked for mercy (Mark 9:14–18; Luke 9:37–40). The respect was shown in his addressing Jesus as Lord, a remark that simply placed Jesus in a position of authority (Matt. 15:22; 20:31–32). This request involved a son who suffered terribly with seizures that took control over him and led him to fall repeatedly either into fire or water. He may have had epilepsy, although France (2007, 659–60) notes that that term does not appear anywhere in the text. The term σεληνιάζομαι refers "to being moonstuck," describing epileptic-like seizures as impacted by the powers of the moon (BDAG s.v. "σεληνιάζομαι" 919). The fire normally is tied to scenes where cooking or perhaps the burning of vegetation was taking place. Matthew 17:18 tells us the boy was possessed. This is an important detail because we never get an example of a demon-possessed person asking for their own healing (France 2007, 659). The stress is on the condition's serious nature with an emphasis on the possession's relationship to a disease, as disease and possession could be combined.

The man had asked the disciples to heal his son, but they were not able to do so. Such requests for healing are common in Matthew (Matt. 8:5–13; 9:18–26; 15:21–28). This is a rare example of a failure by the disciples to heal, like the failure of Elisha's disciple to heal in 2 Kings 4. The disciples have more to learn, as Matthew 17:20 shows. The failure was surprising given the commission of Matthew 10:1, where they could perform exorcisms.

17:17–18. Jesus rebuked the generation for its failure of faith, calling it wicked and perverse (Deut. 32:5, 20; Matt. 12:39; Luke 9:41; Mark 9:19 speaks only of being faithless). Carter (2000, 354) thinks it was only the disciples who were rebuked. This is unlikely given the broad remark about the generation. Two other options remain. Was Jesus addressing the crowd (Hagner 1995, 504; Turner 2008, 424; Wilkins 2004, 597) or the crowd and the disciples (Blomberg 1992, 267; Carson 2010, 443; Davies and Allison 1991, 724; France 2007, 661; Nolland 2005, 712)? It is not entirely clear which view is present, because usually such rebukes were to outsiders and the disciples had some faith, as Matthew 17:20 shows. That would exclude the disciples from the rebuke. On the other hand, it was the disciples' failure that triggered this outburst. It does seem likely that part of what triggered Jesus's response was that the disciples were also struggling to understand and go as far as they needed to in reacting to Jesus. An inclusion of them in this rebuke is more likely. Either way, Jesus was displeased and expressed himself clearly on the point about the current generation in general. Jesus asked how long he would have to bear with and endure them, like God's observation about the generation of Israel in the wilderness (Num. 14:27). He would bear with them as long as he had to in order to achieve his mission, but it was very much an uphill climb. It may be the issue was that people were drawn to Jesus as a healer versus responding to his message and mission, as well as the disciples' failure to draw on what Jesus provided. People came to his disciples for those needs, but not for all Jesus and his disciples had to share. Hill (1972, 270) speaks of "prophetic exasperation" here, while Hagner (1995, 554) describes it as a prophetic lament. In many ways it was both.

God Bearing with Israel

Numbers 14:27: "How long must I bear with this evil congregation that murmurs against me? I have heard the complaints of the Israelites that they murmured against me."

Jesus asked for the boy to be brought to him. Despite his complaint, Jesus still acted with compassion, mercy, and grace (Luke 9:42). Jesus rebuked the boy but was calling to the demon in the boy. This led to the boy's healing. Clearly, Matthew and Luke's version encapsulated in a verse is a much simpler and shortened description of the miracle than that of Mark 9:20–27 with all of its details. What the disciples failed to do, Jesus did.

17:19–20. Jesus's success caused the disciples to ask why they had failed to cast out the demon

(Mark 9:28). Once again there was private instruction in Matthew (Matt. 13:10; 15:15). Luke lacks this discussion.

Jesus explained that they had a lack of faith, a "little faith" as in Matthew 14:31 and 16:8. Mark 9:29 speaks only of needing prayer, with some manuscripts of Mark adding fasting. Most see Matthew 17:21 as a later addition to Matthew because of this agreement with Mark and the addition. This little faith was probably a weak or wavering faith that needed some bolstering (James 1:5–8; Hagner 1995, 505). Osborne (2010, 657) speaks of a "vacillating, struggling faith." Jesus encouraged them in their weak faith. Even a little faith truly applied like a mustard seed could do the impossible. As Wilkins (2004, 597) says, it was not the size of the faith but its focus that was the point. Such faith exercised can call for a mountain to move and it will (Mark 11:23; Luke 17:6; Gospel of Thomas 84, 106). The remark was rhetorical. Faith makes everything possible, rendering people able to do the kingdom's work of amazing compassion, which was the topic in the context and thus defined the scope of the application (Carson 2010, 444). Hagner (1995, 505) correctly speaks of the passage's limit to the signs of the kingdom. God's power can be triggered by the smallest faith that genuinely trusts God can and will act (Blomberg 1992, 268). The rhetorical expression of moving mountains for doing great things was a common one (Isa. 54:10; Matt. 21:21; 1 Cor. 13:2; Josephus, *A.J.* 2.333).

Josephus on Moving Mountains as a Figure of Speech

***Jewish Antiquities* 2.333:** "Depend, therefore, upon such a protector as is able to make small things great, and to show that this mighty force against you is nothing but weakness, and be not affrighted at the Egyptian army, nor do you despair of being preserved, because the sea before, and the mountains behind, afford you no opportunity for flying; for even these mountains, if God so please, may be made plain ground for you, and the sea become dry land."

THEOLOGICAL FOCUS

The exegetical idea (Jesus's preview of glory, the promise of suffering, and the failure of the disciples to heal the demon-possessed boy showed the need the disciples had for a deeper faith as Jesus's destiny approached) points to this theological one: the nature of who Jesus is requires disciples pay closer attention to him and their faith.

Various events, including especially the divine voice at the preview of Jesus's glory and the disciples' failure to heal a demon-possessed boy, showed that the disciples needed to grow in their faith as the beginning of the kingdom era came with John functioning as Elijah.

At the core of this unit is the divine affirmation of Jesus as the beloved Son. This remark in the midst of the opposition to Jesus reassured Matthew's readers about God's kingdom program. It makes an important theological point: God the Creator is about rescuing his creation through what Jesus is doing. In ancient times, one could choose among many gods or worship as many as one wished. It was a diverse culture. Yet this text's point is that there is only one Son. Even when Jesus is surrounded by prophets like Moses and Elijah, there should be no mistake in equating him with others. Who he is and what he brings is unique. That is also an important point in our own day, when people wish to make all religions the same and desire to make all the roads to salvation converge. Jesus's message and the call to learn from him are not about mere self-discovery coming from a mere spiritual guide. It is about seeing what is unique in the salvation Jesus offers. This section of Matthew's gospel has stressed the need to learn from Jesus. Such is required even from those who already are allied to him and believe. Those who believe already understand that God has saved them because they are unable to save themselves. They understand that forgiveness is not something we earn, but is a gift from God. They appreciate that for a broken world to get fixed, God must fix what we cannot. To get there one must sit at Jesus's feet and learn what he has to teach about life, the walk with God, and even the path of suffering.

The remark about John being Elijah tells us, as the kingdom parables did, that the kingdom comes in stages and has already begun to mark its place in the world. Having argued that Elijah is a type figure and that John is the initial Elijah figure, it also suggests there is more to come from the kingdom. One day there will be an accounting and a time when God assesses how we have responded to the program, whether we recognize that or not. This also matches the kingdom parables like the Wheat and the Tares and the Dragnet. We may think we have the option of taking Jesus seriously or not, but Matthew makes the point that to miss who John and Jesus are is to miss blessing.

The way in involves an ongoing faith, not merely an initial faith of belief. It is a faith that walks through life to experience what God can bring. That living faith takes us into a deeper appreciation for who God is. The disciples were beginning that journey and were tripping up along the way. Still, Jesus encouraged them that even with a small faith they could tap into God's great power that could make amazing things take place within the kingdom. It is on this note of hope and, amazingly, out of failure that spiritual growth can take place, because the goal is to learn and grow as we listen to him.

PREACHING AND TEACHING STRATEGIES

Exegetical and Theological Synthesis

The exegetical section stresses the importance of continual growth for followers of Jesus. Disciples are works in progress. Their initial confession of faith lays a foundation upon which they build a life of obedience, service, and mission. But the original disciples' progress remained slow. They repeatedly sounded confused, looked fearful, and got chided for their "little faith" (Matt. 6:30; 8:26; 14:31; 16:8). These two stories reiterate that theme.

Growth requires more than biblical knowledge. Throughout Matthew's gospel, the Pharisees illustrate the limits of a cognitive faith. Even when their interpretations of the Hebrew Scriptures were spot on, their hypocritical hearts plagued them (Matt. 23). And even though Jesus's disciples heard public sermons (Matt. 5–7; 13; 18) and private instruction (Matt. 13:10; 15:15), immaturity plagued them.

What stimulates continual growth for disciples is the combination of biblical knowledge with a trusting heart and lifestyle of obedience. The Christian life begins with a summons to repent and believe (Matt. 4:17). The Sermon on the Mount culminates with a call to obedience (Matt. 7:24–27). Jesus expected trust and obedience when he sent his disciples on mission (Matt. 10). Finally, the Great Commission included an exhortation to teach new disciples to obey everything Jesus commanded (Matt. 28:19). Trust and obedience are threads that run throughout Matthew's gospel. Growth happens when knowledge, obedience, and trust collide.

Preaching Idea

Learning from Jesus is a lifelong journey.

Contemporary Connections

What does it mean?

Learning never ends in our pursuit of Jesus. Because Jesus is an infinite subject, we can always learn more *about* him. Because life circumstances constantly change, we can always learn more *from* him. Jesus is our consummate teacher. Each new personal challenge, relational role, or work assignment affords fresh opportunities to learn. When we face mounting medical bills, we learn to depend on God's provision. When we begin our marriage, we learn the dance of mutual submission and loving sacrifice. When we manage an unmotivated team at work, we learn the skills of encouragement and candor.

The disciples' curriculum is Christlikeness. We want to learn from Jesus how to think like him, serve like him, love like him, and order our inner world like he does. Through reading and reflecting on the Gospels, we absorb Jesus's vision of God's kingdom, elaborate love, and spiritual authority. From Jesus we learn to stop and listen to children, welcome outcasts to our table, heed cries for help, and allow ourselves to be interrupted when a service opportunity arises. He is our model for loving others. Surely, we all have room to grow in our love for our political opponents, noisy neighbors, callous coworkers, obnoxious in-laws, and unreciprocating friends. Jesus teaches us patience, forgiveness, honesty, mercy, and tolerance. Finally, from Jesus we learn to be still and prayerful, to find our identity in God not crowds, to rely on the Spirit's power in us, and to surrender our will to God's perfect plan. Christlikeness takes a lifetime to learn.

Is it true?

It is true that learning is a lifelong journey. Any educational specialist or psychologist will confirm this. They have noted common stages of growth: from infancy to maturity, from discovery to mastery, from concrete to abstract thinking.

Books About Adult Development and Discipleship

J. Robert Clinton. 2012. *The Making of a Leader: Recognizing the Lessons and Stages of Leadership Development*. 2nd ed. Colorado Springs: Nav Press. Clinton's five stages and transition points are foundational to successive books about leadership development.

Neil Cole. 2011. *Journeys to Significance: Charting a Leadership Course from the Life of Paul*. San Francisco: Jossey-Bass. From each of Paul's missionary journeys, Cole draws lessons about growth in faith and leadership.

Janet O. Hagberg and Robert A. Guelich. 2005. *The Critical Journey: Stages in the Life of Faith*. Salem, WI: Sheffield Publishing. In their developmental theory, the authors describe six stages, the final two separated by "The Wall" that few climb over to reach a life of outgoing love.

Randy Reese and Rob Loane. 2014. *Deep Mentoring: Guiding Others on Their Spiritual Journey*. Downers Grove, IL: IVP. The authors encourage using a life map to chart evolving chapters of a believer's spiritual journey.

Gordon T. Smith. 2011. *Courage and Calling: Embracing Your God-Given Potential*. Downers Grove, IL: IVP. Smith articulates different mindsets, strengths, and opportunities from early adulthood to senior years.

What generally applies to child and adult education also applies to discipleship. Jesus developed disciples through a process. He used public teaching, private instruction, observation, participation, and empowerment to mature them. They advanced from new "converts" to disciple-making missionaries. Even after his ascension, he sent his Spirit to continue to teach them (John 15). Contemporary disciples experience a similar journey, learning from the Spirit, Scripture, and other believers along the way.

A critical part of the learning is reframing failure. A lifelong learner sees mistakes as growth opportunities, not setbacks. A botched sales pitch or Spanish exam may teach us to prepare better. Getting cut from a sports team may teach us to find another sport or hobby. An angry overreaction to our child's misbehavior may teach us the need to pause, breathe deeply, and respond with patience. A bad investment may teach us to seek out financial counsel with our extra income. Our failures can be a source of discouragement or development. Jesus, our gracious teacher, wants us to grow, not languish in guilt and regret. We must learn from him: His yoke is easy and his burden light (Matt. 11:30).

Now what?

To fully appreciate this lifelong journey of discipleship, it is important to know the stages along the way. A basic breakdown of these stages includes childhood, adolescence, midlife, and elder (Smith 2011).

In the *childhood stage* of your faith journey, everything is new and exciting. You know little but your desire to learn is insatiable. You ask loads of questions. You are eager and energetic, wanting to get involved in faith activities and discover your spiritual gifts.

In the *adolescent stage* of your faith journey, your questions change. You begin to make your faith your own. You rely less on authority figures and more on your ability to think, research, and analyze. Tensions in your belief system emerge that you begin to wrestle with. Personal shortcomings surface, which result in a deeper self-reflection. Restlessness grows.

In the *midlife stage* of your faith journey, you begin to slow down. The frantic energy of adolescence eases. Changes in your body, social life, and family roles affect you. You move from reflecting on your past to embracing it. Contentment seems within reach as appreciation has begun to replace ambition. You are beginning to accept yourself as God's favored child.

In the *elder stage* of your faith journey, you have perspective. Changes do not faze you. Fads do not entice you. However, you battle nostalgia and fear for the younger generation. As losses in your life compile, your longing for heaven swells. Although you often feel unseen or unwanted, you recognize your role as a mentor. Death looms, compelling you to consider your legacy.

Knowing these stages allows us to appreciate lessons and opportunities in our current or past stage. Moreover, we can anticipate lessons and opportunities in future stages. In other words, the adolescent who is wrestling with questions of purpose can rest assured she will find some rhythm in years to come. Likewise, the elder who has stepped out of formal leadership at his church can offer perspective to the younger generation on their journey.

Creativity in Presentation

Today's educational system is primed to help students of varying potential and abilities to achieve success. For those with ambition to pursue marine biology, many public high schools have career tracks that push them toward that goal. For students with special learning needs, they receive Individual Education Plans (IEPs), which account for a learning disability or emotional need and set realistic goals for these students. You might ask a parent, public educator, or school counselor at your church to describe the importance of an IEP. Likewise, a high school or college student could provide a testimonial about the significance of her career track. The point to emphasize here is that all good learning has a "track" or "plan." Perhaps we should be as vigilant about developing "discipleship tracks" or "Individualized Discipleship Plans." These, of course, last a lifetime.

Because many of your listeners respond to visual cues, you might consider displaying a picture or chart of adult developmental stages. Clinton's timeline of six stages is easy to find online. Psychologist Erik Erikson envisioned eight stages of development from infancy to late adulthood, which is also easy to find online.

However you present the stages, you can ask your people:

- What stage are you in now?
- What stages have you come through? What did you learn there?
- What stage are you headed to next? What do you expect to learn?

A variation of this creative element could be a life map. Reese and Loane (2014, 50–72) provide step-by-step guidance in creating a "story framework" that attractively showcases God's work in our lives.[1]

Another effective way to illustrate the lifelong journey of learning from Jesus is to interview people in your church from different generations. Have a teenager, young adult, middle-aged adult, and late adult share the stage. Ask each of them two questions:

- What life stage are you in?
- What is something you have recently learned from Jesus?

With so many people on stage, you will want to be sure they come with brief answers already prepared. Moreover, you will want to coach them in the life stage terms you are using in your sermon, so your messaging remains consistent.

In the end, your sermon should highlight that Jesus's nature requires disciples pay closer attention to him and their faith. Or, more simply, learning from Jesus is a lifelong journey.

- Jesus is a transcendent Son (17:1–8).
- Jesus is a suffering Son (17:9–13).
- Disciples are in development (17:14–20).

DISCUSSION QUESTIONS

1. What are the various connections between Jesus's baptism and transfiguration? What do these connections mean?
2. What role did Moses and Elijah play in the transfiguration? In Matthew's gospel?
3. How does this second passion prediction differ from Jesus's first one in Matthew 16:21?
4. Why does Jesus accuse his disciples of "little faith"? What does "little faith" look like today? How much spiritual authority do disciples have today?
5. What life stage are you in? What are you currently learning from Jesus? What lessons do you anticipate in the next stage?

1 Loane's nonprofit VantagePoint3 explains the discipleship process on their website: https://vantagepoint3.org/vp3-pathway/the-journey.

Matthew 17:22–27

EXEGETICAL IDEA

After predicting his death and resurrection, Jesus explained and performed a miracle to show that although children of the kingdom were exempt from paying the temple tax, they would pay it.

THEOLOGICAL FOCUS

Despite being separated from the world, disciples will participate in earthly life.

PREACHING IDEA

Engage your world as long as you live in it.

PREACHING POINTERS

Jesus predicted his death and resurrection a third time. His fate in Jerusalem loomed, but not before another stop in Capernaum to give further instructions to his disciples. Back in his hometown, Peter encountered a tax collector, who inquired about Jesus's payment of the temple tax. This led to a private conversation between Jesus and his disciples about their heavenly status and earthly responsibilities. This tension between heavenly and earthly citizenship, as well as exemption and engagement, would have resonated with Matthew's audience. Although their Jewish roots and Christian loyalties pulled them in different directions, this passage reminded them that religious freedom does not give them the right to withdraw.

From the outset of Jesus's earthly ministry, his followers have had to manage tensions of their dual citizenship. As heavenly citizens, we pledge loyalty to Jesus alone, obey the laws of God, and find our identity in Christ, not in ethnic, gender, or socioeconomic markers. As earthly citizens, we pay taxes, volunteer in our towns, follow federal laws, and vote for national leaders. Unfortunately, managing these tensions has proven challenging. At times we have become overzealous in trying to bring the kingdom of God to earth through proselytizing indigenous people, legislating morality, or launching bloody crusades. On other occasions, Christians have withdrawn, crossing oceans to establish religious freedom or creating subcultures replete with schools, camps, clothes, candles, and media. Jesus's calling finds a happy medium between withdrawal and culture war—engagement. Indeed, this sermon implores us to engage our world as long as we live in it.

JESUS PREDICTS HIS SUFFERING AND REMINDS DISCIPLES OF THEIR OBLIGATIONS (17:22–27)

LITERARY STRUCTURE AND THEMES (17:22–27)

This unit has two parts. First, Jesus predicted the betrayal, death, and resurrection that lay in the Son of Man's future (Matt. 17:22–23). Matthew had already made it clear that the Son of Man was Jesus. This was a prediction of his upcoming suffering, a continuing theme as Jesus drew ever nearer to Jerusalem and his mission's goal. Jesus was very aware of where he was headed and that he would not be with the disciples much longer. Headed to Jerusalem, his teaching in this section also was preparing the disciples for when they would carry the baton of the kingdom and preach the message. The disciples really did not yet understand how all of this worked. They heard and understood what Jesus was saying, but they did not comprehend how it exactly fit together in God's plan. The announcement of his upcoming death so saddened them that it seemed the word about resurrection was lost to them. And of course, without the resurrection, Jesus's death made no sense. Only when these events took place did they finally get it.

Second, as disciples, they still had to live in the world, even as members of the kingdom. Matthew told of paying the temple tax as a way to show that earthly obligations were still to be met, even though the disciples were free people whose core relationship was no longer tied to the world but instead was linked to the kingdom as God's children (Matt. 17:24–27). The disciples were to be so heavenly minded that they *were* earthly good. The promise of the miraculous catch to pay the temple tax shows that Jesus intended his disciples to function in and contribute to the world, even though God also had freed them up to be his in his distinct kingdom. Matthew does not narrate the fulfillment of this miracle, only that Jesus predicted it.

The challenge of this short unit is a seeming lack of connection between these two elements. But Jesus's program and departure, even the world's hostility to him and those who followed him, did not cancel out the need to be good citizens, faithful to contribute even to some things that no longer seemed quite so relevant or important. Just because Jesus's coming would change how one saw the temple did not mean one should withdraw from supporting it. Jesus's coming did change how one saw the world, but that did not mean one was to withdraw completely from its structures. Being present and representing God faithfully in the world was far better than withdrawing from it.

The passion predictions were simply pronouncements by Jesus. They also served to show what was ahead. Jesus accepted his mission and knew what God was calling him to do. He passed on to the disciples how they could prepare for the same path.

The temple tax discussion presents a complex text. It was a pronouncement by Jesus coming after a query about Jesus's support of the temple. The reply showed Jesus declaring both an independence from Jewish ties and a support of it at the same time. It was a correction of Peter's reply in terms of the rationale for participation. The scene also anticipates a gift miracle. The assumption is that Peter caught the fish and paid the tax with the funds that God had provided, as Jesus predicted. This scene is about a discipleship that stayed engaged in the world, even as one had taken up spiritual commitments. Disciples were not to go out of their way to offend with regard to activities in the world. They should support the temple, as this was an activity that was not offensive in its intent.

The parallels to the passion prediction are Mark 9:30–32 and Luke 9:43b–45. The key characterization points to the disciples' continued lack of perception and perplexity. There was even pain because of their lack of understanding. It shows the need for continuing instruction.

The scene involving the temple tax question is unique to Matthew. It was an issue that fit only a gospel written for a Jewish context. There are two parts: the exchange between tax collectors and Peter and then the exchange between Jesus and Peter. Jesus's response reflected ambivalence about support for the temple, but one that was resolved in the direction of contributing to its maintenance. The narration here focuses on an issue of discipleship and the relationship between the believer and the world from which he or she has become free. Interestingly, here freedom does not mean asserting one's independence, but showing care and concern for that which had been left behind, something that only continued participation could demonstrate.

EXPOSITION (17:22–27)

Suffering for the Messiah was certain, but this did not mean withdrawal from the obligations of earthly life. The disciples were still to be good and participating citizens. Jesus did not call people to cloister themselves from the world. Discipleship meant engagement, not isolation.

After predicting his death and resurrection, Jesus explained and performed a miracle to show that although children of the kingdom were exempt from paying the temple tax, they would pay it.

17:22–23. In Galilee, Jesus now predicted his suffering a third time, just as he had after Peter's confession in Matthew 16:21–23. There also is a mention of suffering in Matthew 17:12. This prediction has more detail than the earlier ones (Mark 9:30–32; Luke 9:43–45). The Son of Man would be given over, a reference to the betrayal by Judas (Matt. 10:4; 26:2). Davies and Allison (1991, 734) and Nolland (2005, 720) argue that God and the divine plan perform the handing over here, since it was into the hands of men that Jesus was sent. Nolland appeals to Daniel 7:25 as background, while Morris (1992, 450) cites Romans 8:32. However, it is more likely, given how consistently παραδίδωμι is used of Judas later in similar sayings, that Jesus was merely describing how Judas would give Jesus over to those who sought to harm him (BDAG s.v. "παραδίδωμι" 1b, 761–62; Matt. 26:2, 21, 23, 24, 25, 45, 46, 48). This was still all a part of a divine plan. Carson (2010, 445) speaks of ambiguity and takes allusions to God and Judas as present, which makes contextual sense. Judas was distinct from the people into whose hands Jesus was given. Those who took Jesus would kill him, but on the third day God would raise him from the dead. The passive verb "will be raised" attributes the raising to God. Of course, this was all part of a divine plan.

It is clear the disciples understood the meaning of the words and all they seemed to hear was about the upcoming death, for they were distressed. They reacted the same way when Jesus pointed out the betrayal at the Last Supper (Matt. 26:22). However, they did not get how it would all work. Only the events themselves would take them there (with Hill 1972, 271, and Osborne 2010, 662, versus Davies and Allison 1991, 735, who say the disciples got it). Mark 8:32 said they were ignorant about the saying and feared to ask him. The ignorance here was about knowing how it all fit together. If they had understood the remarks about resurrection, and heard it as vindication, then it was unlikely they would have been sad.

17:24–25a. When the disciples came back to Capernaum, the collectors of the temple tax wanted to know if Jesus would pay the half-shekel temple tax. These tax collectors worked for the priests in Jerusalem. The discussion is unique to Matthew's gospel. Mark 9:33 has the next scene of Matthew 18:1 in Capernaum. The prediction of a catch of fish in the lake at the end of the scene means the conversation likely took place at a locale near the sea. A toll booth was there (Matt. 9:1 with 9:9). The query was probably probing how faithful Jesus was to Jewish concerns and worship, and could have been potentially hostile in intent.

This is called the "two-drachma" tax (τὰ δίδραχμα; BDAG s.v. "δίδραχμον" 241–42). It was an average worker's two-day wage and equaled a half-shekel. Exodus 30:11–16 was at its base, for this was a census tax that was to be used to help administer the tabernacle. Exodus 30:12 notes that the tax was paid in place of serving at the temple as a ransom. France (2007, 668) presents details on the tax. Horbury (1984) treats the scene in detail and defends its historicity. Osborne (2010, 662) correctly defends the idea this was the temple tax, not a Roman census tax. Carter (2000, 356–57) defends a Roman tax and makes the message political, but this scene was more about Jewish concerns than Roman ones. That one-time tax had now become an annual payment (Exod. 38:25–26). Nehemiah 10:32–33 notes an annual levy (Josephus, *A.J.* 18.312). The Mishnah speaks of an annual tax paid by men twenty and older in the month of Adar, or February–March; although other texts show a one-time payment and debate over whether priests had to pay (*m. Šheq.* 1.1–4; 2.1; 4Q159:6–7 (Ordinancesa); Davies and Allison 1991, 743; Luz 2001, 414–15). It was paid with special Tyrian currency, which was one reason the temple had money changers. It could be paid during Passover in Jerusalem or was collected locally a month before that holiday elsewhere. Rabbis could be exempt, and there was discussion about exemptions as others simply did not pay it (Nolland 2005, 724). Sadducees saw it as voluntary. So maybe "the teacher" thought he need not pay.

Temple Tax

Exodus 30:11–16: "The Lord spoke to Moses, 'When you take a census of the Israelites according to their number, then each man is to pay a ransom for his life to the Lord when you number them, so that there will be no plague among them when you number them. Everyone who crosses over to those who are numbered is to pay this: a half shekel according to the shekel of the sanctuary (a shekel weighs twenty gerahs). The half shekel is to be an offering to the Lord. Everyone who crosses over to those numbered, from twenty years old and up, is to pay an offering to the Lord. The rich are not to pay more and the poor are not to pay less than the half shekel when giving the offering of the Lord, to make atonement for your lives. You are to receive the atonement money from the Israelites and give it for the service of the tent of meeting. It will be a memorial for the Israelites before the Lord, to make atonement for your lives.'"

The tax collectors asked Peter. Nothing to this point in Matthew helps us understand why this might have been a question. Jewish sensitivities likely explained the reason for the query. Peter simply replied positively in line with the positive expectation the question had (οὐ). Jesus is portrayed in all the Gospels as active in Jewish worship. The answer was no real surprise, though it could have been asked with the possibility that Jesus was turning his disciples away from Jewish pious practices.

17:25b–27. Jesus then engaged Peter privately, as it is common in Matthew to follow a public exchange with more private reflection (Matt. 13:10; 15:15; 17:19). How Jesus heard of it or whether he was correcting Peter is not clear. Jesus asked who pays "customs duties" (BDAG s.v. "τέλος" 5, 998–99) and "poll taxes" (BDAG s.v. "κῆνσος" 542), or indirect and direct taxes. This did open up the application and topic to all such taxes. The illustration argued that it was not the king's children but the others who bore responsibility for family obligations. Children were free from such obligations, at least normally. The analogy suggests Jesus was speaking of taxes in general, but that included especially the temple tax. Since the temple pictured the worship of the God of Israel, Jesus was relating the kingdom with God as King to worship at the temple. Could the temple and kingdom coexist? At one level, Jesus said there was no obligation. The plural speaking of "sons" certainly looked both to him as Son and to the disciples as sons (Carson 2010, 447; Hagner 1995, 512). It may well have included Jews, since they could be seen as having a corporate covenant relationship to God as well (Davies and Allison 1991, 745; Luz 2001, 417; Matt. 8:12; 17:27). Nolland (2005, 726–27) sees Jesus speaking of Jews and Matthew of disciples, but such a shift of referents is unlikely. A kingdom context pointed to the disciples, not Israel. The remark may imply that the disciples would no longer need to sacrifice animals in light of what Jesus would bring (Wilkins 2004, 600). A broad remark about Israel was unlikely, given the remark about not causing offense. If Jesus's point was to revamp the temple tax, which was what that broader application to Jews would imply, then he would not have gone this route and advocated for paying the tax. The text shows that entry into the kingdom changed some past ways of looking at things. Yet what one should do was bigger than merely what one had the right to do. Other considerations tied to serving applied, so that the issue of personal rights was not the only thing to take into account.

What was allowed was not necessarily what was to be done. Jesus raised the issue of offense to others. This referred to the misunderstanding others may have had about an action disciples might perform, a principle Paul will use in 1 Corinthians 9–10. Creating such a misunderstanding was not to be done in such a sensitive corporate activity that involved approaching the true God. Jesus did respect the temple and its sanctity, as his activity there in John's gospel and in the Passion Week showed (Morris 1992, 454). Jesus told Peter to go and fish. The first fish he caught would have a "stater" coin, worth four drachmas, to pay the tax for Jesus and Peter (BDAG s.v. "στατήρ" 940). No note is made of this being fulfilled, but given Jesus's past record, the assumption is that it took place. Jesus and his disciples remained participants in Israel's worship and contributed to it, even in the face of continuing opposition as he had just predicted. This was the case despite the fact that they belonged to a kingdom that the nation en masse had not joined. The New Testament urges the payment of taxes elsewhere as well, including those involving Rome (Matt. 22:15–22; Rom. 13:1–7; 1 Peter 2:13–17). These other texts were likely an application of these remarks.

THEOLOGICAL FOCUS

The exegetical idea (after predicting his death and resurrection, Jesus explained that although kingdom sons were free from paying the temple tax they would pay it, and Jesus performed a miracle to pay it) leads to this theological focus: despite being separated from the world, disciples will participate in earthly life.

In the face of predicting his suffering, the resurrection, and the freedom of being kingdom members, Jesus's disciples should continue to participate in the worship at the temple, so as to not bring offense.

This is a complex passage once we get past the predictions of Jesus's suffering. As familiar as the themes of Jesus's betrayal, death, and resurrection are to us, the passage on the temple tax is more enigmatic. Jesus declared that the disciples had a freedom that they were not to use. Jesus as Son, and the disciples as sons, need not pay the temple tax as they were free to engage God and would have no need of a sacrifice after Jesus's death. But having rights and using them were two different things. Jesus did not desire to communicate a separation from the God of the kingdom, who also was God of Israel. As a result, the disciples were to pay the tax, even though they were free not to do so. This kind of restriction showed sensitivity to others. The principle reappears in the area of meat offered to idols discussed by Paul in 1 Corinthians 8–10 and in Paul's command to pay taxes to Rome in Romans 13:1–7. It reflects a core ethical awareness of how certain actions might be misunderstood. One was careful not to cause offense for the sake of the gospel, as long as the act did not confuse a person about the gospel.

PREACHING AND TEACHING STRATEGIES

Exegetical and Theological Synthesis

The exegetical section addresses our dual citizenship. Followers of Jesus live *in* the world but are not *of* the world (Phil. 3:20). They should not adhere to the world's values. They should not adopt the world's beliefs. Their behavior should contrast with the indulgent, self-focused ways of the world. We are in the world to win the world to Jesus. Thus, he prays for our ongoing unity, purity, and love as his sent ones (John 17).

As missionaries and disciple-makers, we are called to engage our neighbors and the nations (Matt. 28:18–20; Acts 1:8). The work of missionaries is tenuous because they must translate the gospel in diverse contexts. The book of Acts illustrates Paul's strategic framing of the gospel to different groups of people: Jews, Gentiles, Athenian polytheists, Roman politicians, and Asian pagans. While the gospel never changed, Paul's presentation of Jesus did. He explained his philosophy of ministry in 1 Corinthians 9: he became all things to all people to win them to Jesus. This accorded with the Jerusalem Council's verdict that evangelism should ease the religious burden on unbelievers (Acts 15:24–29).

At the same time, Paul wielded his missionary freedom sensitively. In 1 Corinthians 8, he admitted to forgoing certain foods if eating them would cause a stumbling block to new believers. He viewed his rights as secondary to others' growth. This principle, known as Christian liberty, applies to any mature believer (Rom. 14). How we handle our freedom in Christ affects others. Thus, Jesus's law of love remains our north star (John 13:34–35; 15:13; Rom. 12:10; 13:8; Gal. 5:13; 1 Thess. 4:9; James 2:8; 1 John 3:10–11).

Preaching Idea

Engage your world as long as you live in it.

Contemporary Connections

What does it mean?

First, what this passage does not advocate for is withdrawing from the world. Followers are discouraged from creating their own Christian enclaves. While withdrawal may be wise where believers are targeted for persecution, as a rule hiding from the world reduces the influence believers have on those around them. Engagement starts with knowing God has placed us in particular times and places to do his work.

Second, engagement does not mean indiscriminately participating in the patterns and activities of the world. We do not have to watch every show, play every sport, consume all the news, wear trendy clothes, and purchase the latest iPhone to engage our world. If anything, this so-called engagement does not bolster our witness but deforms our soul. Engagement becomes a front for indulgence. This is not Jesus's dream for his disciples.

Third, engagement *does* mean identifying our spheres of influence—the places we live, work, serve, play—and showing the love of Jesus there. Our primary sphere of influence comprises people in our family, neighbors, schools, local stores, the YMCA, workplaces, and church. They are part of our daily life. A secondary sphere of influence includes our loose connections: social media circles, extended family, childhood friends, acquaintances, and former colleagues. We connect with them regularly. A tertiary sphere of influence describes the impersonal forces that shape the world in which we live. These include politics, media, entertainment, education, finance, and retail.

Finally, regardless of the sphere, to engage is to give something of ourselves: time, money, attention, advice, and/or care. Engaging the first two spheres of influence involves personal interaction. We throw parties. We coach teams. We unload moving trucks. We have conversations. Engaging the third sphere is almost entirely transactional. We purchase a product. We cast a vote. We watch a show. We pay our mortgage.

Is it true?

Jesus's call to engage the world is clear. We are salt and light. We bear witness to him in word and deed. This requires intentional engagement wherever he has placed us. And this is an important clarification. We engage *our* world—where we live, work, and play—not *the* world. Globalization and technology have deceived us into thinking our sphere of influence comprises eight billion people on our planet. This task is too massive for any of us. We can, however, engage our next-door neighbor, the local food pantry, a waitress at our favorite restaurant, and the members of our gardening club. Our most profound engagements often occur in our personal and proximate worlds.

Moreover, as we age our spheres of influence expand and opportunities for engagement increase due to education, work experience, and relational networks. Three-year-olds live within tiny circles; thirty-somethings have broader spheres. Then, as we reach our final years, limitations to our health, finances, and mobility may shrink our world. We engage when we can, how we can, as long as we can.

Now what?

This passage invites three responses. First, disciples are called to be honest citizens. We pay taxes and report them honestly. We respect our governing authorities by obeying laws—from permanent speed limits to temporary mandates during a pandemic—unless they directly oppose biblical ethics. We clean up after our dogs when they do business in our neighbors' yards. We educate ourselves on important local issues and legislation to vote. Citizenship is an important form of engagement.

Second, disciples are expected to be public servants. Jesus set this model for us (Matt. 20:28; Phil. 2:6–8). Formal public service opportunities abound: first responder, ESL instructor, library page, hospital chaplain, tutor, usher, and Little League coach. These are often overseen by schools, hospitals, churches, and nonprofit organizations. Also, informal opportunities to serve surface daily. Public servants may help a friend move furniture, pick up trash in the park, reunite a stray dog with its owners, and return a shopping cart to a store. Public service is an important form of engagement.

Finally, disciples are expected to be good neighbors. For Jesus, loving our neighbor is the second most important command, trailing only loving God (Matt. 22:37–40). We show love for neighbors in the simple act of knowing their names, greeting them, and engaging them in conversation. Good neighbors keep an eye on the neighborhood to ensure others' safety. They avoid being a nuisance to their neighbors by not being too noisy or nosy. Of course, the definition of "neighbor" extends beyond the people who live in your building, on your block, or in your subdivision. A neighbor is anyone we cross paths with during our day. To engage them well is to see their humanity, grant them dignity, and extend them grace. This is an important form of engagement.

Creativity in Presentation

You can easily illustrate the idea of a sphere of influence with a variety of rubber playground balls or dodgeballs. Different colors and sizes would signal the different spheres of influence represented in the church. Hold the ball and say, "This is more than a ball. It is a sphere. It represents your network of connections and opportunities.

It is the place you live, work, and play. You have a sphere of influence. Engage it." You can purchase hundreds of tiny plastic spheres used in ball pits at little cost. Consider buying some as take-home reminders for your church members.

At this point, you may also consider describing the seven spheres in which Christians dutifully engage. These include family, religion, education, media, entertainment, business, and government.

However, you want to be clear that engaging these seven spheres is not driven by "dominion theology" or Christian nationalism; rather, it is a holistic approach to living as salt and light in our worlds.

Invite your congregation into a brief game of "Engaged or Disengaged?" The rules are simple. You will display a series of pictures that capture people (or creatures) that are engaged or disengaged. After showing the picture, you will ask, "Engaged or disengaged?" and give the audience a chance to shout their answers. Five to ten pictures would be adequate. The following list will get you started:

- A teen staring at her phone (disengaged)
- A mother playing with her child (engaged)
- A man proposing marriage to a woman (engaged)
- An ostrich with its head buried in the sand (disengaged)
- A city block full of people walking with their heads down (disengaged)
- A nurse caring for a patient (engaged)
- An athlete sitting on the bench looking despondent (disengaged)
- A teacher tutoring a small group of students (engaged)

Schools often end their academic year with an awards ceremony. Teachers honor students for their academic achievements, leadership, resilience, and citizenship. This final award stands out because it highlights a student's overall positive engagement at school. Good citizens followed the teacher's instructions. Good citizens respected school property. Good citizens helped their classmates. Good citizens modeled kindness, honesty, inclusivity, and sportsmanship. Consider making a few "Citizenship Awards" to give out during your sermon to church members who engage their world.

Finally, you can weave into your message profiles of public servants. These could be historical figures or people from your church. You want to name them, share highlights from their lives, and clearly state how these people "engaged their world as long as they lived in it." The sidebar will get you started.

Profiles of Public Servants

Florence Nightingale: A British nurse and statistician who responded to God's call, intervened during the Crimean War to save wounded soldiers from premature death, and helped reform sanitary practices in hospitals, which drastically reduced death rates

Dorothy Day: A political activist and Catholic whose writing in the *Catholic Worker* advocated for the poor, women's rights, and pacificism. Although Day's socialist sympathies were controversial, her work for the oppressed was laudable. Brooks (2015, 74–104) offers a concise biography.

Timothy Keller: Prior to his recent death from cancer, Keller served as a trusted evangelical voice, author, and public intellectual. His decades at Redeemer Presbyterian in New York City afforded him opportunities to plant churches, develop leaders, and converse with secular leaders. Redeemer was a model church in its outreach, arts, and apologetics.

Dr. Paul Brand: A missionary kid, doctor, and author whose medical career focused on those with leprosy, a neurological disease that leads to physical damage and social ostracism. He worked in India before joining a research center in Louisiana focused on patients with leprosy. Yancey (2003, 61–86) provides a wonderful overview of Brand's life.

For a variation on the creative element above, consider profiles of honest citizens and good neighbors and feature people from your church. You may honor a public school teacher, CPA, first responder, caregiver of an aging spouse or parent, or teenager who does landscaping for widows in the church.

What you want your sermon to emphasize are these truths: Despite being separated from the world, disciples will participate in earthly life. Therefore, you must engage your world as long as you live in it.

- Jesus would not escape death (17:22–23).
- Christians should not evade taxes (17:24–27).

DISCUSSION QUESTIONS

1. How does the current passion prediction tie into earlier ones?
2. What kind of taxes were the disciples being questioned about? How do we know?
3. In addition to paying taxes, what are other ways Christians should engage their world? Are there areas where Christians should disengage?
4. What spheres of influence are people in your church most/least engaged in? Why?

Matthew 18:1–20

EXEGETICAL IDEA

After proclaiming that humility and trust defined greatness, Jesus urged accountability for holiness by warning the one who causes stumbling, urging the regaining of the wayward believer, and introducing a process for dealing with and disciplining stubborn, sinful believers.

THEOLOGICAL FOCUS

Jesus teaches on community relations, balancing accountability with forgiveness.

PREACHING IDEA

Messy people need more structure to shape up.

PREACHING POINTERS

Matthew introduces Jesus's fourth discourse. In this block of teaching, Jesus focused on the role of humility, accountability, and forgiveness in shaping a healthy community. The discourse is packed with surprising imagery—millstones, dismemberment, and wandering sheep—as well as terms of endearment: children, little ones, brothers. Sadly, shaping a healthy community is no easy task. Obstacles to community abound. For Matthew's original audience, the discourse identified pride, stumbling blocks, and persistent sin. Such obstacles undermine the community's shared pursuit of holiness. Thus, Jesus spoke firmly about pursuing childlike faith, purging sin, and confronting persistent sinners with a deliberative process that would keep the community pure.

Jesus's message remains relevant for today's church. Christian communities are messy. At every level—from denominations to local churches to elder boards to small groups—we struggle with pride, stumbling blocks, and persistent sin. Look no further than the last few years of pastoral scandals, pandemic policies, or denominational spats about female leaders. Our dysfunction disrupts spiritual health. According to Jesus, the key to developing healthy communities is confronting our messes, not covering them up. Healthy communities create structures where candor is welcomed, feedback is expected, and accountability is ingrained. Although external structures cannot change a stubborn heart, they can mitigate messes in a spiritual community. This passage emphasizes that messy people need more structure to shape up.

JESUS TEACHES ABOUT COMMUNITY, ACCOUNTABILITY, AND FORGIVENESS, PART 1 (18:1–20)

LITERARY STRUCTURE AND THEMES (18:1–20)

This unit is in four parts: on humility (vv. 1–5), on not being a cause of stumbling (vv. 6–10), a community parable about lost sheep (vv. 12–14), and a discussion of community accountability (vv. 15–20). Matthew 18:11, which has a mission saying about the Son of Man, is likely not original to Matthew.

Matthew 18:1–5 treats humility and responding like a child as a sign of greatness. Receiving a person, like receiving a child, without social status is also urged. In this example, the definition of greatness is flipped upside down. It is a pronouncement that uses the child as a visual parable.

Matthew 18:6–10 urges one not to cause kingdom people to stumble. There is a woe for the person who causes serious sin because God is watching over the community. One is to remove from oneself what causes one to fail. This is a warning pronouncement.

Matthew 18:11 about the Son of Man coming to seek and save the lost is likely not original to Matthew. It is missing in our best early manuscripts and exists in varying forms in many other textual witnesses.

Matthew 18:12–14 urges through a parable the recovery of lost sheep from within the community. This is a different use of the lost sheep metaphor than Luke 15, where seeking those outside the community is in view. Here it is restoration in a context of accountability. Matthew was not using Luke 15. This was from a distinct event and source.

Matthew 18:15–20 closes the emphasis on community accountability by discussing how one should correct or exclude a straying member in the clearest passage on community discipline in the Gospels. Matthew 18:15 is like Luke 17:3. This is a piece of community instruction, a kind of community rule, though not through the administration of church leaders or of rigid regulations but as a matter of the actions of individuals (Carson 2010, 448–49). France (2007, 673–74) also defends its historical setting in Jesus's ministry.

This discourse involves the movement through several topics and covers all of Matthew 18. Linking words like "little ones" (Matt. 18:1–5 with 18:10–14) tie some passage parts to other parts. It is quite possible to divide this material at Matthew 18:15 on the basis that parables end each unit (Matt. 18:10–14 and 18:23–35; Turner 2008, 432). Matthew 18:15–20 is a hinge, as a reference to brothers also makes a tie to the parable to follow in Matthew 18:35. However, one could divide the subunit at Matthew 18:20–21 because of the parable at the end of the chapter and its previous teaching on forgiveness in 18:21–22. The break is important to balance the community accountability established in Matthew 18:1–20. We divide the material for content reasons versus structural ones at Matthew 18:20.

This discourse on corporate relationships is best divided in half because of its balanced themes. Besides Jesus's remark at Peter's confession, it is the only place where the term for "church" (ἐκκλησία) appears in any gospel. The first half treats humility and accountability in the pursuit of holiness with a goal of restoration. The second half (the next unit) treats forgiveness to make sure that the pursuit of accountability does not become oppressive. Forgiveness and humility also connect well in such a context. These two virtues bracket the entire chapter and set a frame for accountability. The framing and balancing themes are why we split the unit at Matthew 18:20–21, along with the fact that two questions can be seen to drive the chapter, with the second appearing in Matthew 18:21.

An initial reading of this discourse might suggest a detached message with miscellaneous emphases, but there is more unity in the move from humility to a warning about offense, to a call to restore the brother, and instruction about rebuking than one might initially see. Seeing the whole context means that each piece of the discourse belongs in community relations.

The passage shows a more complex combination of relationships to the other Synoptics than most passages in Matthew. It also displays an array of forms.

In the discussion of greatness and the use of a child to point to humility, Matthew 18:1–5 is paralleled in Mark 9:33–37. Matthew's version is somewhat shorter and simplified, as Mark 9:35–36 and the latter part of 9:37 are not reflected in Matthew, while Matthew 18:3–4 is not found in Mark's version.

Matthew 18:6–9 has parallels in Mark 9:42 for verse 6, parallels in Mark 9:43 and 45 for verse 8, and Mark 9:47 for verse 9. Matthew 18:7 is like Luke 17:1–2. The unit shows a mix of sources. These texts are all maxims. The same presence of maxims is true of Matthew 18:15–20, which also reflects an ecclesial rule.

Matthew 18:10, and 12–20 lack any real synoptic parallels, although Luke 17:3–4 is close to Matthew 18:15 and 18:21–22.

Major themes of the section involve defining greatness in terms of humility rather than social status or power, the call to avoid being a cause of sin as a way into themes of accountability, an encouragement to seek to restore those who stray, and a procedure for how to deal with a person who has strayed and is not responsive. All of this shows a seriousness about pursuing community holiness and accountability. To keep the accountability from being overbearing, Jesus closed the discourse with a teaching and then a detailed parable about being forgiving, something that along with humility sets a context for how accountability can function (Matt. 18:21–35). Humility and a forgiving spirit are at the core of all relationships.

EXPOSITION (18:1–20)

The combination of holding people spiritually accountable while also showing grace and being forgiving is not an easy balance. One can err in one of two ways: (1) be so forgiving there is no accountability nor growth to maturity, or (2) make the environment so accountable that it becomes stifling and harsh. Jesus's teaching aims for the balance. The stress on being quick to forgive that comes in the next unit balances the call for spiritual accountability here. Galatians 6:1–5 expresses in an epistle and church context much of what is presented here.

After a call for humility and trust as defining greatness, Jesus urged accountability for holiness by warning the one who causes stumbling, by urging the regaining of the wayward believer, and by introducing a process for dealing with and disciplining stubborn, sinful believers.

18:1. Matthew presents his fourth discourse, covering issues of community relationships. This is not just about leadership and offices, but about how the entire community relates to itself. Each member is in view. The starting point is humility (Culpepper 2021, 339).

The first discussion was triggered by a question asked in Capernaum (Mark 9:33–34; Luke 9:46). Who was the "greatest" in the kingdom? A comparative (μείζων) is used with superlative force here (BDAG s.v. "μέγας" 4a, 623–24). Both Mark and Luke note that this question was triggered by a discussion involving the disciples. It is not evident why it had become a topic, although Peter's recent prominence in Matthew is often suggested as a cause (Matt. 10:2—Peter first in the list as in all such lists of the Twelve; 16:17–19; 17:1, 24–27). This is likely, or the fact Jesus only took a few disciples with him up the Mount of Transfiguration, suggesting a kind of ranking of them (Blomberg 1992, 273). The disciples were still in a learning mode, since Jesus had been speaking much about suffering and nothing about greatness (Hagner 1995, 517; Turner 2008, 435). The topic will come back (Matt. 20:20–28; 23:11–12; Luke 22:24–27). Old ways of seeing rank and status die hard.

18:2. Jesus's reply began with his having a child placed in their midst. He called to the child, who was old enough to respond. Unlike our culture, children had no status until they became useful (Hobbs, 1990; Wilkins 2004, 612–13). *Mishnah 'Abot.* 3.10 speaks in negative tones about speaking with children (Turner 2008, 436). It was not worth the time. That cultural viewpoint is important to the background of what Jesus said. He was making an example of one who normally would not have served such a function (Keener 2009, 448; Morris 1992, 458).

A Mishnaic View on Children

***Mishnah 'Abot.* 3.10:** "He would say, 'Anyone from whom people take pleasure—the Omnipresent takes pleasure. And anyone from whom people do not take pleasure, the Omnipresent does not take pleasure.' R. Dosa b. Harkinas says, '(1) Sleeping late in the morning, (2) drinking wine at noon, (3) chatting with children, and (4) attending the synagogues of the ignorant drive a man out of the world.'"

18:3–5. Jesus's response pointed to the child and made three points. The first was that one needed to have the humility of a child in order to enter the kingdom (Mark 10:15; Luke 18:17; the Gospel of Thomas 22 and 46 have variations on this saying, especially in saying 22 with an expanded discussion). Such humility was not concerned about rank. The reversal Jesus made here pushed back on the intent behind the question. Heaven and knowing God were not about status but about presence. The point was made most emphatically that one would "absolutely not" (οὐ μή) enter the kingdom without such a humble heart. This emphasis on ethical responsibility and entering the kingdom is common in Matthew (Matt. 5:20; 7:21; Osborne 2010, 669). Humility was at the core of faith, for it said, "I trust God to do what I cannot do for myself," and understood that salvation was a divine act of mercy. One recalls the examples of the centurion seeking his son's healing and the Canaanite woman (Matt. 8:5–13; 15:21–28). The centurion was not worthy of his request and the woman compared herself to a dog that received crumbs from the table. There was no entitlement in their faith. The practice of lowliness is a theme of this entire discourse: accepting the lowly (v. 5), accepting the wayward returned (vv. 11–14), and being forgiving (vv. 21–35). Humility that expressed itself in consideration of others and not oneself appears in other texts as well: loving the neighbor (Matt. 19:16–21), renouncing honor (Matt. 23:8–10), and serving (Matt. 20:26–28; 23:11). Osborne (2010, 670) notes Jesus showed this quality in Matthew 11:28–29, 12:17–21, and 21:5. Humility was not considered a virtue in the Greco-Roman world (e.g., in Aristotle there is no mention of this character trait [so MacIntyre 1988, 163]). This was a culturally distinctive emphasis in Jesus's teaching.

The second point was that humility led to greatness in the kingdom (Matt. 5:5; 23:12; Phil. 2:5–11; James 4:10; 1 Peter 5:6; Hagner 1995, 518). Entry into the kingdom was not on the basis of merit nor was greatness earned. Appreciating grace meant understanding it was the Lord's work, not the disciples'. Just as children were humble and relied on parents, so the disciples should rely on God.

The third point was that receiving a child in the Lord's name was like receiving him (Mark 9:37; Matt. 10:40–42; John 13:20). Where Mark speaks of children, Matthew highlights receiving "one such child" in this manner. This elevated the status of a person who normally had no status. It was a way of saying all were important. The focus was on disciples, as the chapter makes clear (Carson 2010, 451), but the picture of a child showed the way. The example is found in Matthew 19:13–15. In an honor-and-shame culture like the Greco-Roman world, where social status and power meant much, this was really a challenge to be different. People were precious. Jesus was saying that we show our appreciation for God best by being sensitive to people who have less status, not more. As Keener (2009, 449) says, "Jesus is modeled best among the most powerless, not among the powerful." Matthew 25:35–40 elaborates on the point made here (Nolland 2005, 734). France (2007, 679) points to James 2:1–4 as an application.

Jesus was lifting up service here to a high level. Those who cared for people in Jesus's name, especially people with no status, were doing a work just as good as if they were caring for Jesus.

This was about more than hospitality; it was about how others were treated. Romans 14:1–15:13 and 1 Corinthians 8–10 are examples of deferring rights for others, just as was discussed in paying the temple tax. That was part of being welcoming and receptive of others. It was about the practice of humility (Bruner 2004b, 211–12).

The next exhortation will say this was explicitly the case for those in the community. Treat the little ones correctly and do not lead them astray. This verse is a hinge into that one, so some place it with the next section of Matthew 18:6–9 (Osborne 2010, 674). We left it here because Jesus still used the child as a picture.

18:6. This subunit has two parts. First there is the woe in Matthew 18:6–7 on those who cause stumbling. Then there is the responsibility for avoiding stumbling in Matthew 18:8–9. Next Jesus issues a warning about those who cause believers to stumble (Mark 9:42; Luke 17:1–2). The key term in this unit is σκανδαλίζω and its related noun, σκανδαλον (BDAG s.v. "σκανδαλίζω" 1a, 926, and "σκανδαλον" 2, 926). They appear six times in verses 6–9. Ezekiel 14:3, 7 uses the concept this way (John 6:61; also Sir. 9:5; 25:21; Jub. 1:9, where idolatry and living like Gentiles are in view; Keener 2009, 449). It is "causing someone to fall away" from the Christ as well as from the core teaching and behavior of the faith (Carter 2000, 364; Davies and Allison 1991, 761–62; Matthew 11:6; 13:21; 24:10). Blomberg (1992, 274) notes it was not about a single act, but a style of teaching that took someone away from faith. France (2007, 680) speaks of causing those to fall out of the faith entirely. Bruner (2004b, 214) names false teaching and living. The pressure Matthew's community was getting from Jews might be in view. Matthew 13:41 has a similar image in a parable where evil was sown in the world.

Figure of Stumbling

Sirach 9:5: "Do not look intently at a virgin, or you may stumble and incur penalties for her."

To lead such a precious little one astray was serious before God. Jesus said a better fate was drowning in the sea with a millstone around the neck. This was regarded as one of the worst forms of death (Keener 2009, 449). Jeremiah 51:63–64 shows the image of what a rock can do. This was worse, since the millstone was a heavy stone that could be several feet in diameter and was pulled by a beast of burden to grind grain. Such a death was better than what happens to those who lead people away from Christ.

18:7. Jesus then pronounced a woe on the world for its role with such stumbling blocks, telling us the opposition was coming from outside the real community. The woe pointed to judgment from God. The world suffered and caused suffering when people were drawn away from God's program. Jesus noted such stumbling blocks would come, but the one who brought it was the object of the woe. God would judge such dangerous instruction. The person who caused this was really bringing "trouble for himself" (Morris 1992, 462).

18:8–9. Jesus gave a series of examples about separating oneself from whatever caused the stumbling (Mark 9:43, 47–48). In both cases he used the first-class condition εἰ (if) to introduce the condition. Interestingly, Mark 9:43 uses a third-class ἐάν (if) in the same locations. Wallace (1996, 685) notes how usage of the conditional can overlap in force between first class and third class. These conditional clause classifications point to how reality was portrayed rhetorically versus being a statement about reality by the author.

Jesus used pictures of self-mutilation, which would have been shocking to a Jewish audience, so this imagery was quite vivid. It was designed to get attention. Here the issue was how to respond to this pressure to go astray. If the hand caused sin, cut it off. If a foot caused stumbling, cut it off. If an eye caused stumbling, pluck it out. These were all rhetorical images of separating oneself from that which led into such serious sin. Jesus concluded it was better to live life maimed in each case than to burn in eternal fire of hell. Jesus was calling and reassuring that the good choices for life were better than courting relationships that led one astray. Hands and feet looked to action, while the eyes looked to how we saw things and took a direction. Disengagement with that which caused sin was the point.

It is debated who was addressed here (Osborne 2010, 675–76). Was it the person sinning or the one who caused the sinning, seeing a causative force in the verbs for offending? The move to the second person points directly to an application to the audience and favors including taking personal responsibility for stumbling for whoever listened to the false teaching. Nolland (2005, 738) argues against a causative force here. However, there may be room for the ambiguity. Serious sin was to be avoided whether causing or succumbing to it. The point was that one was not to cause it nor respond to the temptation to go there. The verse highlighted personal responsibility either way. The remarks set up the discussion of church discipline to come.

The threat here was serious. It showed how eschatology was important, especially maintaining a sense that we were ultimately accountable to God. Failure to sense this and thinking we operated independently could lead to going astray. Bruner (2004b, 215) notes that Jesus, as one who loved the most, discussed hell as a reality. For accountability to be real, it had to have a cost.

18:10. In another transition verse, Jesus talked about not looking down on these little ones, a picture of the disciples of the community who were the topic of the chapter. This was the opposite of welcoming in Matthew 18:5 and did not reflect the humility Jesus had just advocated. This theme of being sensitive to others is repeated in the New Testament (Rom. 14:3, 10, 15; 1 Cor. 11:22; 1 Tim. 4:12; Turner 2008, 439). He then mentioned how angels watch over them (Pss. 34:7; 91:11–12; Heb. 1:14). The note was not about a single guardian angel for each person but how heaven as a whole watched what was taking place with believers (Nolland 2005, 741; on the topic, Davies and Allison 1991, 771–72, who see a guardian angel, as does Keener 2009, 450). There are texts that give the sense of an angel tied to a person or nation, but the point here is broader (Gen. 48:16; Dan. 10:13; Rev. 1:20; Morris 1992, 464). The angels had access to the Father, pointing to the Father's care.

[18:11]. The rationale for Matthew 18:11 not being original to Matthew is noted above.

18:12–14. Jesus took up restoring a brother or sister. The picture of the lost sheep has roots in the Old Testament (Ps. 119:176; Isa. 53:6—all we like sheep have gone astray; Jer. 50:6; Ezek. 34:15–16). The imagery in Matthew matches Luke 15:1–7 and the parable of the Lost Sheep. However, that Lucan context was why Jesus spent time with tax collectors and sinners. Here we have bringing back a brother or sister from sin in the context of community accountability. This is a distinct use of the imagery in a fresh context. This distinct context raised questions about the reading of Davies and Allison (1991, 773) that the shepherd here was Jesus, although Jesus did serve as an example for community behavior. The picture of the shepherd was anyone in the community who moved to restore a wayward brother.

The image is well known. A shepherd left ninety-nine sheep to find one who was lost (Gospel of Thomas 107 has an expanded version that likely is secondary; Davies and Allison 1991, 776). The expectation, with the use of οὐχί, is that the shepherd would make this move, as the particle expected a positive response to the scenario. The issue of leaving the sheep unprotected makes too much of the parable, which was only stressing pursuing rescue. It often was the case that shepherds worked in pairs or more, so the issue is not really relevant anyway (Keener 2009, 452; Wilkins 2004, 616). When the shepherd found the lost sheep, there would be more rejoicing than over the ninety-nine who remained behind. The application is in verse 14. Here God was said to respond in the same way to a brother or sister who was lost. The call was for recovering the disciple and not losing him or her. Restoration from backsliding was an important task for the community.

18:15. Jesus now shifted to what to do with someone in the community who needed restoration. Most of this after Matthew 18:15a is unique to Matthew, although Luke 17:3–4 combines Matthew 18:15 and 18:21–22. Starting in this verse, we meet nine "if" (ἐάν) clauses through verse 19. Matthew had been alternating condition terms up to this point in the chapter, with ἐάν used in verses 13 and 14, while εἰ appears in verses 8 and 9.

Jesus gave various steps. One only went through the options if there was failure with the previous step. So, the first step was to go to the person privately (Lev. 19:17–18). The attitude while giving reproof is covered in Galatians 6:1. The wording of the verse is disputed. There was a sin against the person who started the process. If this phrase "against you" is not read, then sin is one that one became aware of leading to the confrontation. Either way, this confrontation had to be done with assurance that there was sin; it was to be raised with care and utilized a principle of minimum exposure (i.e., no gossip about it), only disclosing to more people as refusal set in. The first challenge involved a private rebuke between the two involved. This was not about gossip nor was gossip supposed to drive the process (Prov. 25:9–10). Those with direct involvement were to be those who engaged in it. If he or she responded, then the brother or sister had been gained (James 5:19–20). "Listening" throughout this instruction was about responding to the critique in a positive way. To not listen meant there was a failure to respond. That the response will be positive is the hope and the goal.

18:16. If there was a refusal to respond, then the second step was to take two or three witnesses and confront the brother or sister again. Taking two or three was rooted in the Old Testament teaching about the value of two or three witnesses (Deut. 19:15). The expression "two or three" may mean more than two (Davies and Allison 1991, 784). The point was to have multiple witnesses, but not in an overwhelming way. This was to assure fairness and also to set up testimony to the church if the effort failed. Interestingly, there was no hierarchy involved here nor any insistence that this involved church leaders

(France 2007, 693). This was the body caring for itself naturally and not through leadership structures.

18:17. If there was another refusal to respond, then the third step was to go to the church, meaning the local community. The assumption was that the church community, or whoever acted in its name, regarded the offense as real. It shows that Jesus was not discussing personal grievances but a real wrong (France 2007, 693). The person being challenged had been given every opportunity to respond to a critique that was seen by the growing group to be valid. There is a great deal of patience in this effort to get a response, not a rush to judgment (Konradt 2020, 280–81).

If there was still refusal to respond, the result was the offended party separating from the person in question. The "you" here is singular, but that should not be read too narrowly or else the point of community rebuke seems empty.

The offender was to be treated like "the" Gentile or "the" tax collector. Jesus's point in using the definite article (ὁ) in each case is that he was speaking of a class of people within the Gentiles and tax collectors, of a certain type of person to be kept at a distance (Wallace 1996, 228). This didn't necessarily mean a total withdrawal, but it did mean the absence of community support to prevent the community from appearing indifferent to what had been done (Garland 1995, 192; Turner 2008, 445). The instruction anticipates a form of excommunication in that the person was not given full rights in the community and there was some form of separation from them (2 Thess. 3:14; 1 Tim. 1:20; Titus 1:13; 3:10–11). In a later church context, it probably meant not participating in the Lord's Table, table fellowship, or in certain community activities and service (France 2007, 694, speaks especially of table fellowship). This meant that it would become an act of church discipline. The goal of the separation was that the shame of some form of isolation would mean enough to cause the person to engender a different response (1 Cor. 5:1–5; 2 Cor. 2:5–11). A key assumption behind church discipline is that the community and its opinion mean enough to someone to give them pause and lead them into responding. It also assumes other communities will support what a given community has done (Blomberg 1992, 280).

18:18. This power to discipline was something heaven supported. The imagery of binding and loosing recalls Matthew 16:19. Loosing was what happened with repentance, while binding pictured the act of disciplining. Here the church had this power, while in Matthew 16 it was Peter. What judgment they made as a community would be supported in heaven, whether the choice was to bind or loose.

18:19–20. The idea of agreement in the church by two or three is contextually tied to this judgment about discipline (Blomberg 1992, 281; but for the view a broad promise has been brought into a narrower context, see France 2007, 697, or Morris 1992, 469, who see it as a completely independent teaching). The start of verse 19 says, "Again I tell you the truth," looking back to verse 18; and the "two or three" looks back to verse 16, showing the context remains (Keener 2009, 455; Osborne 2010, 687). The linkage and mention of agreement before God show how important this was. If two or three agreed and asked for anything in this regard, the Father would do it. For where two and three were gathered, Jesus was in the midst of them. It may be that the two were a part of a three-member panel or council, which pointed to a majority or plurality sensing the need to act (Hagner 1995, 533; Turner 2008, 446; Matt. 5:22; *m. Sanh.* 1.1 shows Jews had a three-member panel, so Jesus may be working with an analogy here). Such actions were serious enough that they should be conducted seeking the Lord's direction.

This remark carries some potentially high Christology, for it affirmed a presence

Jesus had in the community wherever it was gathered. It was a claim of divine-like or divinely rooted authority (Ezek. 43:7; Joel 2:27; Zech. 2:10–11; Turner 2008, 446). What was said here of Jesus was said by later rabbis of God as a divine presence in the midst of two speaking the Law (*m. 'Abot.* 3.2–3, 6; Davies and Allison 1991, 790). The church was truly representative of Christ's presence, which was why Paul called it Christ's body. The idea of spiritual presence in the midst of physical absence was something Paul also could claim in 1 Corinthians 5:3–5; so the idea Jesus could say this in the context of his earthly ministry is possible. More than that, he had anticipated and predicted his vindication by God when he faced death (Matt. 16:21; 17:9, 23), so he could promise he would be with them. Jesus is "God with us" (Matt. 1:23; 28:20; Blomberg 1992, 281).

This process was a serious one that needed to be executed with much care and compassion, aiming at restoration. However, if it led to a refusal to respond, then the pursuit of community holiness called for actions that sanctioned the behavior in some way that limited the offender and served as a rebuke for poor behavior.

THEOLOGICAL FOCUS

The exegetical idea (after proclaiming that humility and trust defined greatness, Jesus urged accountability for holiness by warning the one who causes stumbling, urging the regaining of the wayward believer, and introducing a process for dealing with and disciplining stubborn, sinful believers) leads to this theological idea: Jesus teaches on community relations, balancing accountability with forgiveness.

In a context of humility that was not concerned about rank, Jesus urged mutual accountability for holiness that warned of judgment for those who led others astray, encouraged the seeking of restoration for a wayward disciple, and gave a procedure for rebuke sanctioned by God.

Four ideas dominated this unit. The first involved a humility that sought neither greatness nor status but to welcome others and was open in its recognition of the need for grace. This reversed the normal cultural norms where status and honor were important. The image for this surprising comparison was a child who had no status. Jesus said disciples needed to be like children, even to the point of welcoming people who lacked such status.

Second was a warning. Those who caused disciples to fall away would be judged. Jesus also urged all to be responsible to separate from that which could cause sin and straying. The warning set a context for God's judgment and explained why the pursuit of holiness was a community goal. Jesus underscored the exhortation by noting that angels watched over what was taking place.

Third was the note of how heaven rejoiced when a straying disciple was brought back to the fold. Here the joy was like recovering a lost sheep. God rejoices at one restored. Everything in this discourse is pushing for spiritual health and mutual accountability in the community in the hopes it will remain theologically and morally sound.

Fourth came a process that was a means of community self-regulation. Confrontation for sin was appropriate and needed to take place in measured stages. First it was between the individuals, then with two or three, and finally with the church. If there was a refusal, there was a sanction against fellowship and community support. The process as a whole sought (1) to make a statement about faithful holiness in the community, as well as (2) to regain the one rebuked. Such discipline had divine sanction. It was not undertaken merely by leadership but by mutually accountable members. All of this showed how serious community integrity was to Jesus. To keep the environment from being overbearing, there was much said about the goal as restoration. In addition, the rest of the discourse in the following unit is going to highlight the need to be forgiving, so that a return can bring genuine restoration and the community environment has the right tone.

PREACHING AND TEACHING STRATEGIES

Exegetical and Theological Synthesis

God created humans to flourish in the context of community. From the opening pages of Scripture, he envisioned a growing population of image-bearers doing good in the world. We were meant to rule, subdue, tend, and care for God's creation (Gen. 1:26–28; 2:4; Ps. 8). We would do this in the context of family, since it was not good for man to be alone (Gen. 2:18–24). Sadly, as quickly as the Bible depicts the good aims of family, it describes the unraveling of human relationships. Adam and Eve fail to communicate and shift blame (Gen. 3). Cain kills his brother Abel (Gen. 4). Lamech marries two women and boasts of murder (Gen 4:19–23). From Eden to the Babylonian exile, this pattern of messy human relationships carries throughout the Hebrew Scriptures.

Similar struggles arise in Jesus's day and the emerging church. James and John jockey for status (Mark 10:35–45). Paul and Barnabas fight over the inclusion of John Mark in their second missionary journey after he abandoned them during their first (Acts 15:36–41). Euodia and Syntyche squabble about personal issues (Phil. 4:2). And the Corinthian church plays favorites with their leaders (1 Cor. 1, 3), while letting sexual sin corrupt them from within. Church people are messy.

Nonetheless, messiness does not excuse people from living in spiritual community. Discipleship is inherently communal. Jesus called disciples into a family faith (Matt. 12:48–50). He established the church for accountability (Matt. 18:18) and shared authority in his disciple-making mission (Matt. 16:16; 28:18–20). The first believers gathered regularly for teaching, fellowship, worship, prayer, and service (Acts 2:42–47; 1 Cor. 11:17–34; Heb. 10:19–25). Leadership provided oversight (Acts 15; 20:24–36; 1 Thess. 5:12; 1 Tim. 3; Titus 1:5–9; Heb. 13:17; 1 Peter 5:1–5). Every member of the body heeded a call to mutual service and personal holiness (e.g., 1 Cor. 12–14; Eph. 4–5). The liturgy, leadership, call to holiness, commitment to service, and regularity of gatherings provided a structure to mitigate messes in the church.

Preaching Idea

Messy people need more structure to shape up.

Contemporary Connections

What does it mean?

What does it mean that messy people need more structure to shape up? To be clear, messiness is synonymous with sinfulness. Scripture clearly brands us as sinful (Gen. 6:5; Eccl. 7:20; Jer. 17:9; Rom. 3:23). However, the sin addressed in this text is a particularly stubborn, insistent, or careless type of sinning. The depraved spiral into deeper patterns of sinfulness described in Romans 1 captures human messiness at its worst. Ingratitude leads to doubt to indulgence to outright rejection of God. He lets us sink deeper into our sin. Unchecked sin always festers like a tumor.

The structure needed to help people shape up is not religious systems. Romans 2 illustrates that Jewish law merely masked Jewish immorality. More religion does not change a stubborn heart. Nor is structure a set of personal disciplines, life hacks, or sticks and carrots to change habits. Behavior modification does not change a stubborn heart.

The structure envisioned by this passage is a humble community committed to corporate holiness. Accountability is how the community will achieve heart change and holiness. The local church was designed for this purpose. In fact, a key metric of a church's effectiveness is how well its liturgy, leadership, ministries, and small groups hold its people accountable. Clear and consistent teaching from the Bible adds structure. A robust assimilation process and membership pathway add structure. Small groups designed for authentic, life-on-life exposure add structure. Service opportunities with clear goals, strong leadership, and honest feedback add structure. And when stubborn, insistent, and careless sin becomes apparent, church discipline practices add structure.

Is it true?

Messy people will not shape up without some relational structure. Alcoholics Anonymous provides an example of the power of structure in helping people shape up. The twelve-step recovery program combines regular meetings, personal confessions, accountability partners (i.e., sponsors), and sobriety plans to help recovering alcoholics stay clean. Such programs have countless success stories, even when occasional relapses occur, because the structure moves them out of their mess. Similarly, counseling provides a more intimate structure for people to deal with their messiness.

Throughout its history the church has experimented with various accountability structures to help its people shape up. The early church used extensive catechism practices. John Wesley, the founder of Methodism, developed levels of accountability through smaller circles of relationships (societies, schools, bands). Modern churches offer accountability in myriad forms: discipleship groups, life transformation groups, missional communities, Fight Clubs, and mentorship programs.

The effectiveness of these groups (or any accountability structure) in helping messy people shape up is tied to the level of trust and commitment of its members. A personal trainer cannot help a cynical, half-hearted client lose weight. A career coach cannot magically make an undedicated manager an overnight success story. A pastor cannot exhort an addicted disciple out of viewing porn without him first admitting he wants to break free. Healthy relationships and a commitment to change make structures work.

Now what?

Two responses flow from the preaching idea. First, we must confess our messiness. Whether we are guilty of pride, causing others to stumble, straying from God, or offending others, we are all guilty of making messes. Hopefully, the longer we walk with Jesus, the fewer messes we make. However, we all continue in stubborn, insistent, and careless sin. Making confession part of our daily practice and corporate worship services is a good structure to help us shape up. Fortunately, God graciously forgives (1 John 1:9).

Second, we must carefully design structures in our churches that move us from sin to holiness. In fact, we need two types of structures: formative and corrective. Most churches already have formative structures, which were mentioned above: liturgy, leadership, ministries, and small groups. On a personal level, the formative structures would include one's devotional habits or spiritual disciplines (e.g., prayer, fasting, study, silence, giving; see Matt. 6:1–18). Collectively, these practices are known as a "rule of life," which provide a deliberate and holistic way of growth in love for God and others (Ortberg, 2002, 200).

Corrective structures in the church and spiritual life are different. They surface when a messy situation arises requiring intervention. When a personal confrontation does not curb another's sin, corrective structures help bring church leaders into the confrontation. Every church should have a written church discipline policy that outlines the offenses and process by which corrective actions will be taken. This is not the place to prescribe a discipline policy, but anyone preparing for a sermon on this text would benefit from reviewing their church's bylaws and policies on the topic. This sermon gives an opportunity to refresh the congregation on the details of your policy.

Creativity in Presentation

Messes and messy people are not hard to find. Consider illustrating messy people by displaying pictures of messy people. A list of potential candidates includes Pig Pen from Peanuts, Harold with his purple crayon writing on the wall, two people in a mud-wrestling match, a toddler in a high chair surrounded by a food explosion, or a painter in his splotchy uniform. After each picture, you might say, "That is a messy person." A second grouping of candidates would illustrate the mess of sin: an image of an alcoholic holding an empty bottle, a picture of a teenager vandalizing a public building, a shot of a raging father yelling at his children, or an image of a celebrity recently caught in a scandal. You could say, "These are messy people, too."

The Berenstain Bears and the Messy Room (Berenstain and Berenstain, 1983) provides an example of how structure can help messy people shape up. In the book, Mama Bear cannot handle another day of her cubs' disastrous room. After tripping over toys and getting crushed by falling objects in an overstuffed closet, she demands a change. Mama Bear conscripts Papa Bear to construct shelves and storage bins to keep their mess contained. The moral of the story is clear: messy cubs make life miserable for everyone, but structure helps them shape up. If you cannot procure a copy of the book, images from it are easy to find online.

Physical structures are helpful for bringing shape. The following objects could serve as effective visual aids: braces make crooked teeth straight, a trellis helps vines climb, a support cage helps a tomato plant grow tall and strong, a cast helps a broken arm heal cleanly, a back brace keeps a spine aligned, and a bundt pan gives a cake its form.

When it comes to discussing church discipline, you might have to address faulty images. You could use object lessons, with a touch of humor, to make your point. Bring a belt, paddle, wooden spoon, stopwatch, and a box on stage. Discuss how discipline methods have changed over the ages. "Discipline used to be straightforward. We showed kids who was the boss and scared them into submission. We used the belt, paddle, or wooden spoon to shame you." Hold up each item as you name it. "Then we tried timeouts to tame you." Hold up the stopwatch. "Now we take away privileges like your video games or vehicle to bore you." Hold up a box. Then ask, "Which method worked best: shaming, taming, or boring you?" After giving people a few seconds to ponder the question, say: "We're considering an update of our church discipline policy, and we can't decide which method to use. Should we shame [hold up paddle], tame [hold up stopwatch], or bore [hold up box] the messy people in this church?" (Note: You know the sensitivities of your congregation. If corporal punishment is a polarizing topic, adapt or ignore this suggestion.)

Finally, case studies of church discipline could be very effective in this message. You will not want to draw from recent or well-known examples in your own congregation, but you could build cases from your reading, conversations with other pastors, or combining details from different scenarios you have encountered. Here are three generic examples:

- A student in the youth group confides to you that her mother, a member of the church and volunteer of the First Impressions Team, has an addiction to pain medicine. She confronted her mother several times but without effect. What should you do about this mess?

- The VBS coordinator has run the annual outreach event for years. What used to be a hallmark event for the church has been dwindling. Getting and keeping volunteers has become a challenge. You have gleaned from former volunteers that the coordinator "gets heated." No one wants to confront him. What should you do about this mess?

- A married man from the church has been spotted with a single woman from the church at a coffee shop and park. When one of the men from his small group asks him about it, the man demurs. "She's just really struggling right now and needs a friend. There's nothing to it." Weeks later, another guy from the small group sees the married man and single woman holding hands. He gathers the other men from the small group for a confrontation. Again, the married man denies any wrong-doing. What should you do about this mess?

These creative ideas can make the message more memorable. Ultimately, you want your sermon to communicate that Jesus teaches on community relations, balancing accountability with forgiveness. And messy people need more structure to shape up.

- Messy people make too much of themselves (18:1–5).
- Messy people make others stumble (18:6–10).
- Messy people get God's attention (18:12–14).
- Messy people need correction (18:15–20).

DISCUSSION QUESTIONS

1. What is the difference between formative and corrective church discipline?
2. How should we understand Jesus's bold imagery: millstones and self-mutilation?
3. When have you seen the principles of Matthew 18 work effectively? When have you seen them applied poorly?
4. What makes church discipline so challenging in modern times? Be specific.
5. What other structures aid the spiritual growth and maturity of your church?

Matthew 18:21–35

EXEGETICAL IDEA

God's forgiveness of us makes forgiving others imperative, something Jesus emphasized by calling for repeated forgiveness through a saying and a parable.

THEOLOGICAL FOCUS

The example of God's forgiveness of us should make us forgiving.

PREACHING IDEA

Messy people need more grace.

PREACHING POINTERS

Jesus's teaching about accountability provoked a question about forgiveness. Peter spoke for the group, asking if forgiving seven offenses extended enough grace. Jesus dwarfed Peter's number with an absurd figure: seventy-seven acts of forgiveness. Then he told a story about a Gentile king's absurd accounting as an illustration of God's abundant grace. The parable concluded with a warning: God's grace endured for those who extended it to others. For Matthew's original audience, the message of forgiveness replaced their right to revenge. Jesus repeatedly subverted the law of retribution with a call to mercy.

We live in a messy moment. Political parties are polarized. Voices on social media convey mean and hateful comments. Disagreement in the church leads to division. Even friends and family members quickly sever ties at misunderstandings and petty offenses. In this combative age, the need for mercy, grace, and forgiveness is undeniable. Sadly, people today are quicker to practice self-protection, social distancing, and ghosting than to show grace to someone who hurt them. We need a fresh hearing of Jesus's radical call to forgiveness. This sermon reminds us that messy people need more grace.

JESUS TEACHES ABOUT COMMUNITY, ACCOUNTABILITY, AND FORGIVENESS, PART 2 (18:21–35)

LITERARY STRUCTURE AND THEMES (18:21–35)

This unit's structure is fairly straightforward. There is a short pronouncement about the readiness to forgive many times over (Matt. 18:21–22). This is followed by the parable of the Unforgiving Servant, whose example was not to be followed (Matt. 18:23–35). The parable stresses accountability before God if disciples did not forgive each other. At the root of the parable is the recognition that God has forgiven us a huge debt in forgiving sin, so we should be ready and able to forgive others their much smaller debts in their acts against us.

By urging a community that was quick to forgive, Jesus pushed the emphasis in the direction of restoration that was humble and as compassionate as God was with those who recognized their debt to the Almighty. An emphasis on accountability alone might make the community oppressive. The recognition that forgiveness should be readily available makes the unit not about control but restored relationship as the ultimate aim. This attitude is what preaching should highlight, as well as sow a deep appreciation for God's grace. How much he has forgiven us is to be a driving force in how we relate to others.

Jesus's pronouncement to forgive was triggered by Peter's question about forgiving up to seven times, a generous request given that three times was the rule in some Jewish contexts. Jesus's reply to forgive up to seventy-seven times was really a reply to forgive always, since one would not keep such a high count. Jesus put a premium on forgiveness as the immediately following parable of the Unforgiving Servant also showed.

The parable itself had three movements and then the application. First, there was the king forgiving his servant the large debt (Matt. 18:23–27). Second, there was the servant's failure to forgive his debtor his little debt (Matt. 18:28–30). Third, there was the crowd's reaction with its report to the king, who rebuked the servant and placed him in prison, making him repay the debt, something that actually would be impossible (Matt. 18:31–34). The application was that the Father would do the same in punishing disciples who were not forgiving (Matt. 18:35). This is the point of the parable. We are to be forgiving because God has been so very forgiving to us. Those who are not forgiving may not truly appreciate being forgiven themselves and are accountable to God as a result. It was a passage designed to challenge and shake up the reader.

Matthew 18:21–22 has a conceptual parallel in Luke 17:4, where Jesus said to forgive a brother seven times in a day. It is a related teaching, but not strictly a parallel (France 2007, 700). The parable of the Unforgiving Servant is unique to Matthew.

EXPOSITION (18:21–35)

To maintain community holiness and health requires a challenging balance. Spiritual accountability to each other can lead to confrontation, so the balance is a healthy compassion. This part of the discourse underscores the importance and necessity of a forgiving environment so that accountability does not poison that community. To ignore accountability will damage holiness, but to ignore the need to be forgiving will choke the community and destroy its well-being.

The example of what God has done through Jesus in forgiving our great debt of sin made being forgiving imperative, something Jesus emphasized by calling for repeated forgiveness through a saying and a parable.

18:21. Peter asked Jesus how often he should forgive a brother who sinned against him. This was the fifth time he had stepped forward (Matt. 14:28; 16:16, 22; 17:24) with one more to come (Matt. 26:33–35). Jesus had discussed the theme in several texts in Matthew (Matt. 6:12, 14; 9:2, 6; 12:31–32; one text is yet to come in 26:28). To Peter's credit, he asked if seven times was enough. This was a large number given that in later Judaism three times often was seen as sufficient for premeditated sin (*'Abot. R. Nat.* 40A; *b. Yoma* 86b, 87a). Testament of Gad 6:3 also speaks of being forgiving when forgiveness was sought (Blomberg 1992, 281; Keener 2009, 456). *Mishnah Yoma* 8.9 only allows such a request provided the victimized person accepted it. Old Testament roots may exist for this number (Job 33:29–30; Amos 1:3; 2:6; Wilkins 2004, 622). Seven appears to reverse claims of vengeance as well (Gen. 4:15, 24; Lev. 26:18) or reflect perfection (Luz 2001, 465; Lev. 16:19; 2 Sam. 12:6 LXX).

The Mishnah on Forgiveness

Yoma 8:9e: "For transgressions between man and man, the Day of Atonement atones, only if the man will regain the good will of his friend."

18:22. Jesus's reply stressed the need to be forgiving. Jesus spoke of forgiving seventy-seven times, as that reading is more likely for ἑβδομηκοντάκις ἑπτά than seventy times seven (France 2007, 701 n. 1; Turner 2008, 449). This reflects the Hebrew of Genesis 4:24 LXX, which is mirrored here. Seventy times seven is the number in early versions. That reading takes the number in its most hyperbolic form. Either way, Jesus was saying do not count, just be forgiving. The mood was to be generous as the Father in heaven was generous to those who seek forgiveness.

Jesus's reply completely revamped that seven-times standard with seventy-seven, a number that reversed the revenge declared in Genesis 4:24 LXX. That vengeance had already been checked by the eye-for-eye standard of the Torah which limited revenge. Where vengeance had been carried out without limit, now mercy and forgiveness were carried out without limit (Davies and Allison 1991, 793). Disciples were to err on the side of mercy. This reinforced what Jesus said in Matthew 5:43–47.

18:23–25. Jesus backed up the call to forgive with a powerful parable going in a fresh direction, focusing on the importance of forgiveness and what motivated it.

The parable is about a king settling accounts. He brought in a slave who owed a massive amount of money, "ten thousand talents" (μυρίων ταλάντων). This slave was probably one of his assistants, a minister, since he had access to such a large amount of money. Matthew 18:27 calls this debt a loan, so perhaps it was a business venture that failed. This was a big, billionaire-sized debt. A talent was a silver coin worth six thousand drachmas, so this was sixty million drachmas or ten million weeks of work for an average worker! It was about three hundred tons of silver (France 2007, 706). The value comprised 193,000 years of labor on a six-day work week (Turner 2008, 450). It was a hyperbolic number to portray incredible debt. By comparison the entire tax collected for all of Galilee and Perea in a year was two hundred talents and all of the area of Israel was eight thousand talents (Josephus, *A.J.* 12.175; 17.318;

France 2007, 706; Morris 1992, 473). It was a debt no slave could repay. To put whatever chink in the amount he could, the king ordered the selling of the highly indebted slave, his wife, children, and all he had (Diogenes Laertius, *Life* 4:46–58; Exod. 22:3; Isa. 50:1; Amos 2:6). The slave would be left with nothing.

Davies and Allison (1991, 795–96) as well Nolland (2005, 756) argue Matthew had inflated a much lower original number from Jesus, either ten thousand denarii or ten talents. This is speculative. Jesus's parables have enough surprising elements, and the depth of divine forgiveness is so deep that one should be slow to think the high and decidedly hyperbolic number is out of line. There was a sense in which Jesus was saying the nature of divine forgiveness was beyond this world in every sense. Davies and Allison (1991, 797) also argue that the parable was originally about merchants and his slaves, not a king and his servants, but this ignores the way in which kings also pursued business and wealth, so the distinction is not necessary.

18:26–27. The desperate slave fell to his knees and implored the king to have the patience to allow him to pay his debt. He promised to pay back what he would never be able to pay back. This really was a plea for mercy.

The king, in a surprisingly gracious move that came out of "compassion" (BDAG s.v. "σπλαγχνίζομαι," 938), released the servant and canceled the "debt," which is what the word δάνειον meant (BDAG s.v. "δάνειον" 212). By the king's grace and kindness, the servant no longer owed anything. The debtor was now a free man, having received much more than he pled for, an act like the way the father handled the prodigal in Luke 15:11–32. Of course, all of this pictures God's grace in forgiving sin and restoring us as full children of God when we seek his forgiveness. The Father was the subject of the parable, as the application of the parable was made to him in Matthew 18:35.

18:28–30. The second part of the parable repeated the first sequence almost exactly with the now-forgiven servant and one of his debtors. There were three big differences. First, the amount of debt was not great. One hundred denarii, which equaled one hundred drachmas, was one hundred days of work, about four months of labor. This was far less than the hundreds of thousands of years the forgiven servant owed. His debt was six hundred thousand times greater (Luz 2001, 473; Osborne 2010, 696). Turner (2008, 451) says the difference is "zillions versus peanuts." Second, the forgiven servant refused to show mercy and forgive the servant who owed him money. His response was the exact opposite of the king's compassion. Even the way the debtor's request to the forgiven servant was made indicated just how parallel the scenes were. It matched exactly how the forgiven servant had asked the king for patience. There was one difference. This debtor's request was reasonable as it could be done, unlike that of the forgiven servant whose request was unreachable. Third, there also was the violence with which the demand to pay was made. The forgiven servant grabbed his debtor by the throat. Nothing of the compassion or mercy of the king had made it into the heart of the forgiven servant. The debtor was thrown into prison until the debt was paid. The forgiven servant had violated Matthew 7:12. He had not treated others as he wished to be treated.

A Comparison of the Two Debts in the Parable of the Unforgiving Servant

Servant to king	10,000 talents	= 193,000 years of labor
Servant to forgiven servant	100 denarii/drachmas	= 4 months of labor

18:31–34. The lack of forgiveness shocked and distressed the other servants, who told the king what had taken place. They correctly read the act as hypocritical. They reflect a community that appreciates forgiveness and reacts when it is not offered (Konradt 2020, 283). This report caused the king to confront the forgiven servant. Addressing him as "wicked" (πονρέ), the king reminded the debtor of how he had forgiven him when that request was made (BDAG s.v. "πονηρός" 1, 851). The king then asked a rhetorical question that expected a positive answer (οὐκ). Did not that regal act make it necessary for him to be forgiving and show mercy as well? Should his response not be in line with what he had experienced? The term ἔδει points to a moral obligation to show mercy (BDAG s.v. "δεῖ" 2b, 214). "Was it not necessary" to show mercy? The question was really a rebuke at the lack of impact the king's kind act had on the forgiven servant. It pictured the response to be like that of the Father (Matt. 5:48; Luke 6:36).

So, in anger, the king reversed his earlier decision, changed course, and tossed the previously forgiven but unforgiving servant in jail. The king required the now unforgiven servant to pay the debt. The term for those with whom the rebuked servant now resided is quite descriptive. Those prison officers (βασανισταῖς) were called "oppressors" or "tormentors," not jailers (BDAG s.v. "βασανιστής" 168). They were torturers (France 2007, 708). This was the only use of this word in the New Testament. The violence the servant had shown on his debtor was now coming back on him. He could never repay the debt owed from here.

The parable reflects the idea that the measure by which one measures others God will measure back in judgment (Matt. 7:2; Nolland 2005, 760). Since the forgiven servant had been unforgiving, he now experienced a lack of forgiveness, as he did not really respond to what the king had done for him. One who was genuinely impacted by what God has done should treat others in a similar way (Matt. 6:14–15). The forgiveness obtained by the servant had been exercised "under false pretenses," since it had no effect on subsequent behavior (Turner 2008, 451–52).

18:35. Jesus applied the parable to the Father. He warned that God would do as the king did, in "the same manner" (οὕτως), unless each one forgave a brother from their hearts (BDAG s.v. "οὕτω" 1b, 742). Forgiveness was to be sincere and deep. The intermix of singular and plural (each one/their hearts) applied the remark corporately and individually. This was a community standard that also was to be applied individually.

Grace was designed to yield more grace. Failure to do so meant that grace had not been embraced with a faith that appreciated what it was and what it was teaching (Wilkins 2004, 625; Matt. 12:33–37; 13:8, 23; 15:17–20). With this ending, the parable became another "odd man out" parable where someone who appeared "in" ended up "out" (Bruner 2004b, 241; Blomberg 1992, 285, says the scene pictured is not purgatory but hell). Matthew 6:14 makes the same point in reverse (Matt. 7:21–23; Luke 6:36; Eph. 4:31–5:2; James 2:13; 1 John 4:11). Those forgiven a great debt by God were to be forgiving to others.

THEOLOGICAL FOCUS

The exegetical idea (God's forgivness to us made being forgiving to others imperative, something Jesus emphasized by calling for repeated forgiveness through a saying and a parable) turns into this theological one: the example of God's forgiveness of us should make us forgiving.

Being forgiving is imperative, and forgiveness should be readily provided to others, given what God has done for us.

Jesus could hardly be clearer or stronger here. Forgiveness is a given response in life for those God forgives. The debt God has forgiven us is so great that what others ask of us is nothing in comparison. So how he has treated us should model and impact how we treat others. Yet again we see in this text how a proper relating to God and his impact on us should define how we relate to and treat others.

The community Jesus formed is to be a forgiving community. It is to pursue holiness with accountability, as Matthew 18:1–20 showed. Yet its environment is not to become oppressive. That is because a context of restoration and forgiveness is to be a priority.

Another key idea here is that a real understanding of grace makes us gracious in turn. Those who seek God's mercy but are not merciful themselves have not experienced God's mercy. Forgiveness is not merely something I receive by intellectual request and assent. Forgiveness and grace impact the soul and make us into a new people with a fresh take on how we are to relate to others. This is why the fruit of the Spirit in Galatians 5 is so loaded with relational terms. This is why the Spirit is said to give us a new life and we are born anew (John 3:1–15). Grace has an impact. This parable explored that idea through a negative example.

The reversal of the king can disturb people. Does God take back what he gives? That is to make too much of the parable's image. The point pictured in this challenging imagery is that when we are genuinely impacted by what God has done and embrace it with a trust that is appreciative of what God has done, we are changed and so is our behavior. Failure to be impacted is really a failure to possess grace and be impacted by its presence. That idea is what the parable teaches. The community of the forgiven, whose existence is rooted in forgiveness, is to be forgiving because that is the very essence of what makes them God's community.

The parable is one of a series Jesus tells of the "odd man out." These are figures who look like they are within the story of the parable and are recipients of the opportunities for blessing but in the end are outside. Their heart shows no renewal by grace. It was so with the stewards of the vineyard who beat up the sent servants (Matt. 21:33–41). It was so with the steward who beat the servants he was left in charge of (Matt. 24:49). It was so with the man who did nothing with the talents the steward gave him (Matt. 25:24–28). In each case, those parabolic figures ended up with nothing, just as this servant figure ended up with nothing but being tortured. Jesus is serious that grace makes an impact. His parables show it. One great impact grace is designed to have is that it is to make us forgiving souls, because God has forgiven us.

PREACHING AND TEACHING STRATEGIES

Exegetical and Theological Synthesis

Jesus's story surfaced the chasm between our reception of God's grace and our willingness to extend it to our offenders. The absurd accounting underscores the king's massive loss in releasing his servant from debt. Jesus understood his heavenly Father as extravagant in grace (Matt. 6:12, 14; 9:1–8; 20:1–16; 26:28), a concept embedded in the Hebrew Scriptures (Exod. 34:6–8; Pss. 103; 145:8; Mic. 7:18–20).

However, grace is not free. The servant's debt does not simply disappear; it is absorbed by the compassionate king willing to bear 193,000 years' worth of labor. Similarly, the debt of sin does not vanish; rather, Jesus pays the wages of sin on the cross (Rom. 3:23). His earlier passion predictions (Matt. 16:21; 17:22–23) hinted at his vicarious death. Not until his final meal with the disciples does Jesus explicitly tie his suffering to the remission of sin (Matt. 26:26–29). His death will be the ultimate act of grace.

Not only does grace have a cost—wages lost and death on a cross—but it assumes a response. Those saved by grace will live as grace-givers and faithful workers. As mentioned above, grace changes people. Dead people come alive. Rebels become saints. Strangers become members of the household of God. The apostle Paul summarizes this transformation in

Ephesians 2, where our response to grace is evident in a changed life. We become God's workmanship, doing good and extending grace in the world (Eph. 2:10). As mentioned above, such a response to grace does not earn it but provides evidence that we have truly "possessed" God's grace.

Preaching Idea

Messy people need more grace.

Contemporary Connections

What does it mean?

In the previous chapter we described "messy people" as those committing stubborn, insistent, and careless sin. That we all sin is clearly stated in Scripture. However, persistent sin leaves hurt and broken relationships in our wake. Whether we are the offender or the offended, making up requires grace. And more hurt requires more grace. Peter may have felt generous in suggesting seven acts of forgiveness, but Jesus countered with an absurd number and a story illustrating God's grace.

Herein lies the secret in becoming more gracious: contemplating God's grace. Before anyone can suffer another hurt from a spouse, slight from a friend, offense from a boss, or attack from a parent, they should consider their own spiritual bankruptcy. Apart from the Spirit's help and Jesus's strength, our messiness in the flesh endures (John 15:5; Rom. 6:5–14; Gal. 5:16–26; Eph. 4:17–32; Col. 3:5–14). With the Spirit's help and Jesus's strength, we can grow in grace (Titus 2:11–14; 2 Peter 3:18).

Over time, a more profound appreciation for God's grace toward us should translate to extending grace toward others. More grace does not mean every broken relationship will be reconciled or old hurts will be forgotten. Rather, more grace results in less bitterness, more understanding toward the offender, a willingness to forgive sins, and the ability to live at peace with messy people (Rom. 12:18).

Is it true?

It is certainly true that messy people need more grace. God is lavish with grace. We should follow his example. However, it is neither realistic nor wise to assume every messy relationship will make up. Reconciliation requires two messy parties to meet in the middle. This only works if both parties are humble, honest, open to correction, and willing to work on the relationship.

Sadly, these virtues are absent in many broken marriages, abusive homes, divided churches, or toxic workplaces. Serial offenders make excuses for their harsh words and mean behavior. Abusive people create hostile environments where relationships languish. Narcissists fail to heed correction or hear others' perspectives. Relationships affected by serial offenders, abusive people, and narcissism are not congenial to reconciliation. In these cases, separation may be more gracious than saying, "I forgive you" for the seventh time in a day (Luke 17:4).

In fact, it is important to nuance forgiveness. To forgive does not mean forgetting an offense, acting as if nothing happened, or keeping a relationship intact. According to Anderson (1990, 192), forgiveness is "resolving to live with the consequences of another person's sin" by not holding it over them. It is an act of mercy and grace, not a feeling. Forgiveness mimics Jesus's suffering on our behalf (Mark 10:45; 1 John 2:2). Finally, forgiveness does not guarantee restored relationships, but it accelerates personal healing.

Now what?

Taking account of God's grace is a better starting point for healing than tallying others' sins against us. Until we admit the mess of our own sin and overwhelming grace of God, we will live bitter, petty, and easily offended lives. Thus, the first step in applying this passage is to meditate on God's grace. Jesus's story highlights God's abundant, elaborate, and absurd grace. He has forgiven an eternal lifetime of debts. We should revel in this amazing grace.

When it comes to extending this grace to others, we should take or encourage appropriate steps toward forgiveness. It should be noted that physical and emotional safety are prerequisites for reconciliation. In the meantime, an offended person can deal with hurt, bitterness, and longing for healing. Counseling, trusted friends, support groups, or journaling are effective methods for moving toward forgiveness. Neil Anderson has a list of twelve steps to forgiveness that are helpful in moving toward forgiving others (1990, 192–95).

At some point, it is important to say "I forgive you" to an offender. Ideally, forgiveness follows an apology; however, this is not always possible (in case of death, distance, or danger). Verbalizing an apology and forgiveness brings hurt and healing into the open. There is power in words. In some cases, the best way to extend grace is to write a letter of forgiveness, which may or may not be read to the offending person.

Creativity in Presentation

While seven acts of forgiveness can sound generous, you can illustrate to your congregation how quickly seven offenses pile up. Consider adapting the following examples of seven misdeeds by a parent, friend, and boss.

To keep people engaged, after reading each offense, have them count from one to seven. After you finish listing the offenses of each person, say, "One more offense, and you owe them no more grace."

Research on forgiveness in the last few decades has identified many of the positive effects. Consider using some highlights from positive psychology literature (McMinn 2017, 46–55), which include lower blood pressure, better sleep, reduced back pain, and decreases in heart disease, cholesterol levels, anxiety, and depression.[1] You might work through some of the health conditions forgiveness can help, one symptom at a time, asking church members:

- Would you like relief from back pain?
- Would you like to lower your blood pressure and cholesterol?
- Would you like better sleep?
- Would you like to reduce anxiety and depression?
- Would you like to decrease your chances of heart disease and cancer?

Let the questions sink in. Then tell them you have an unlikely cure for their ailing body: forgiveness. "It can heal your physical body and bring healing in the body of Christ." (Note: You do not want to overpromise the cure of forgiveness. You are simply illustrating the God-given scope of forgiveness in overall health.)

Historic stories of forgiveness are impactful. Consider Desmond Tutu's willingness to forgive his jailers and political opponents when he stood against apartheid in South Africa. Another powerful example of forgiveness is that of three witnesses in the case against Dylann Roof, who in 2015 murdered nine people from Emanuel African Methodist Episcopal Church in Charleston, South Carolina. Racism drove the offender to execute his heinous act. During his trial, three of the surviving members verbally forgave Roof. Their extension of grace was covered by every major media outlet. Another nationally televised act of forgiveness was Brandt Jean's gracious embrace of Amber Guyger, the police officer who killed his older brother, Botham. You might have a more local or personal story of forgiveness that would connect with your congregation.

1 An article from the Johns Hopkins Medicine website summarizes these findings. See https://www.hopkinsmedicine.org/health/wellness-and-prevention/forgiveness-your-health-depends-on-it#:~:text=The%20good%20news%3A%20Studies%20have,of%20anxiety%2C%20depression%20and%20stress. Accessed 9/5/23.

7 Misdeeds by a Parent, Friend, and Boss		
7 Offenses of a Parent	**7 Offenses of a Friend**	**7 Offenses of a Boss**
1. Broke a promise to come to my Little League game 2. Called me a little brat 3. Got drunk at my birthday party 4. Gave me the silent treatment 5. Cussed at the TV 6. Ate my peanut M&Ms 7. Told me to lie to the telemarketer	1. Betrayed a confidence 2. Talked about me behind my back 3. Said she couldn't hang out because she had family plans but I saw pictures of her at a friend's pool party 4. Didn't return my text 5. Never paid me back for coffee 6. Called me a narcissist 7. Took my costume idea for Halloween and claimed it as her own	1. Offers an endless stream of criticism 2. Reneged on promise of an extended weekend 3. Deflects blame about poor performance 4. Gave my promotion to her nephew. 5. Took credit for an employee's idea 6. Intimidated a coworker 7. Doesn't follow company policy about social media use

Finally, this sermon may provide an opportunity to illustrate the breadth of God's grace toward our mess of sin. On one side of the stage construct a heaping pile of boxes, giant stack of paper, or huge collection of coins. The pile must be obviously large. Let the congregation know the massive mess represents our sins against God. You can point to the mess and name various sins: lust, pride, greed, cursing, deception, and envy. On the other side of the stage, have one box, a few pieces of paper, or a couple of coins. The smaller mess represents others' sins against us. You might say, "If God can forgive my big mess [pointing toward the massive pile], I should be willing to extend grace to this lesser offense [pointing toward the small pile]."

Ultimately, you want your sermon to communicate that the example of God's forgiveness of us should make us forgiving. In other words, messy people need more grace.

- Messy people cause many offenses (18:21–22).
- Messy people need massive amounts of grace (18:23–27).
- Messy people share meager portions of grace (18:28–34).
- Messy people need more grace (18:35).

DISCUSSION QUESTIONS

1. What was significant about Peter's number of seven regarding forgiveness? What about Jesus's counter-number: seventy-seven?
2. How does our willingness to forgive factor into our receiving divine forgiveness?
3. What are the conditions or complexities regarding forgiving serial offenders?
4. How does the practice of confession help us receive and extend God's grace?
5. What is preventing you or your people from forgiving others?

Matthew 19:1–12

EXEGETICAL IDEA

Jesus affirmed marriage as a lifelong bond between a man and a woman, while divorce was the result of hardness of heart and was only permissible for immorality. This led the disciples to say it might be better not to marry. Jesus acknowledged that only some were able to live that way.

THEOLOGICAL FOCUS

The design of marriage was to be a permanent bond before God between a man and woman, making divorce a violation of that promise.

PREACHING IDEA

Marriage maximalists strive for God's design.

PREACHING POINTERS

After concluding his fourth discourse, Jesus changed locations and entertained another challenge from the Pharisees. In their latest encounter, Jesus responded to questions about divorce. Two schools of thinking dominated the debate—a strict camp (i.e., Shammai) and a looser group (i.e., Hillel). The Pharisees wanted to trap Jesus by mapping his marital ethic into the controversial topic. However, Jesus transcended the debate by taking them back to God's original design for marriage in Genesis. Marriage had a good and beautiful beginning; it was a sacred bond, neither meant to be broken nor promised to all people. Matthew's original audience would be familiar with disagreements about marriage, divorce, and singleness. Moreover, they would again see Jesus's respect for God's law and exceeding righteousness on display.

Marriage ethics have tanked in the last half century and we have strayed from God's design. Upon closer scrutiny, Western sentiments toward marriage appear lukewarm, evident in delayed marriages, decreases in marriages, and increases in sexual expression and identity. We are marriage minimalists. Not only is God's standard for marriage countercultural, it is viewed by our age as outdated and oppressive. Sadly, our pursuit of sexual happiness at the expense of sexual holiness has led to brokenness within and outside of the church.[1] Being marriage minimalists is less beneficial than we think. This passage reminds us that marriage maximalists strive for God's design.

1 Those who have been through a divorce already know how painful it is and that it has consequences. It is usually others, who have not been through it, who need the help. A preacher will have to work hard to balance biblical standards and truth with pastoral awareness of the havoc divorces cause. Solid theological and exegetical treatments of this passage and of the issue in general are Blomberg 1990; Instone-Brewer, 2002; and Instone-Brewer 2003.

JESUS DISCUSSES THE DESIGN OF MARRIAGE AND THE IMPACT OF DIVORCE (19:1–12)

LITERARY STRUCTURE AND THEMES (19:1–12)

This unit has two parts. First, there is the dialogue about marriage and divorce between the Pharisees and Jesus (Matt. 19:1–9). Second, there is the reaction of the disciples to the standard Jesus has set. That led to a discussion of eunuchs and the choice to be single (Matt. 19:10–12). The rooting of marriage in Genesis 2 showed this societal structure was deeply connected to God's basic ordering of life in the world. A volume dedicated to all the aspects of marriage and its theology is Hamner, et al. (2018).

The introductory verse has a parallel in Mark 10:1. The marriage and divorce discussion parallels Mark 10:2–12. Two key differences exist between the parallels. The first is that Mark notes no exceptions. Mark may have chosen to highlight what Jesus was emphasizing, that marriage should be a lifelong commitment. The second difference is that Mark has no parallel to the eunuch discussion. Despite these differences, Matthew continues to parallel Mark's sequence of events at this point in his gospel.

The setting of the discussion on marriage includes a move to Judea and a short healing summary (Matt. 19:1–2).

Jesus's discussion with the Pharisees is more of a controversy dialogue than a pronouncement account. It is a controversy account because the initial question was called a test. Jesus turned the question about when divorce was permitted into a focus on what marriage was intended by God to be. Jesus often took a minimalist question and turned it into reflection about the standard God set for an area of life. That was what Jesus did here. The disciples' shock at the standard Jesus affirmed was not because Jesus set a standard with no exceptions, or else we never would have gotten the kind of discussion Paul had about unbeliever desertion in 1 Corinthians 7, since Paul knew what Jesus said on this topic, as he indicated there (Blomberg 1992, 292; 1 Cor. 7:12). Rather, the standard was very high in comparison with options that were discussed in the culture, which included allowing divorce if one found a more beautiful woman or was dealing with a woman who had fixed a poor meal!

The theme of the unit is how God was involved in matrimony. In marriage, God made a new societal unit out of the couple and was present with them. He made the two into one. This was why a divorce was like ripping something apart that had been made into a unit.

The second key theme is about being a eunuch for the kingdom. The disciples sensed how high the standard for marriage was. Jesus noted here that only some accept such a calling to be singly focused on the kingdom, a point Paul also will make in 1 Corinthians 7.

EXPOSITION (19:1–12)

So what were Jesus's ethical standards like? The discussion about marriage and divorce allowed Matthew to show the high ethical standards Jesus set. Jesus did not think about the minimum that was required, but about what God had intended for marriage and was insistent that such vows were important to keep, given that marriage was not just an act about two people but a commitment made before God. Given the views that existed in Judaism at the time, Jesus's response showed how seriously he took marriage vows. He also exposed how easy it was to fall into sin by not taking that commitment seriously. God's standards were high, and Jesus affirmed them by focusing on what God intended in marriage.

Jesus affirmed marriage as a lifelong bond between a man and a woman, while divorce was the result of hardness of heart and was only permissible for immorality. This led the disciples to say it might be better not to marry. Jesus acknowledged that only some were able to live that way.

19:1–2. As with the end of other Matthean discourses (Matt. 7:28; 11:1; 13:53; 26:1), the idea of Jesus completing his words makes the transition to a new scene and the end of the discourse.

Jesus then headed from Galilee and entered Judea on the other side of the Jordan (Mark 10:1). This was a trip of some fifty miles. The mention of the other (eastern) side of the Jordan may suggest they traveled south by way of Perea and did not go into Samaria on this trip. Their location in Jericho in Matthew 20:29 favors seeing this as the route. In Matthew, this was Jesus's one trip south. In John, Jesus had been there several times (John 2:1–13; 4:1–5:47; 7:1–52; 10:22–42; Osborne 2010, 702).

Jesus was traveling to Jerusalem, moving ever closer to completing his mission. Luke 9:51–18:34 makes much more of this period of travel. In Matthew, Jesus did not come back to Galilee until after his resurrection (Matt. 28:7, 16). In Judea, Jesus continued to minister and heal people in the crowd. The setting of the marriage controversy includes a short healing summary (Matt. 4:23–25; 9:35; 12:15; 14:14; 15:30–31). The note about healing here is unique to Matthew, as Mark 10:1 speaks only of teaching. Jesus continued to show compassion despite opposition. He did so in Judea as well as in Galilee.

19:3. The Pharisees asked if divorce was permitted for any cause. "For any cause" is broad and leaves open that there could be many reasons for a divorce. The question may assume the more open approach of Hillel noted below. Only Matthew has the detail about the question involving divorce for any cause. Mark 10:2 speaks only of divorce. It was a question about the law, a halakic question (France 2007, 715). Two schools of approach existed in Judaism (grounds present in *m. Giṭ.* 9.10; *m. Ketub.* 7.6—see sidebar and chart just below; Josephus, *A.J.* 4.253). *Mishnah Giṭṭin* is later developed in the Talmud in *Giṭṭin* 90a. There could be divorce for unchastity (school of Shammai) or there could be divorce for any cause (school of Hillel), including finding another woman or being unhappy with a meal. The view of Hillel was the more common. Here is the *Mishnah Giṭṭin* 9.10 text that presents the views of both schools: "The House of Shammai say, 'A man should divorce his wife only because he has found grounds for it in unchastity, since it is said, "Because he has found in her indecency in anything"' (Deut. 24:1). And the House of Hillel say, "Even if she spoiled his dish, since it is said, 'Because he has found in her indecency in anything.'" Rabbi Aqiba said, "Even if he found someone else prettier than she, since it is said, 'And it shall be if she find no favor in his eyes' (Deut. 24:1)'" (*m. Giṭ.* 9.10). Josephus divorced his wife because "he was not pleased with her behavior" (*Vita* 426). At Qumran, CD 4:19–21 upheld monogamy and appealed to Genesis 1:27 (Davies and Allison 1997, 10). Ezra forced divorces for having foreign wives (Ezra 10:3; Nolland 2005, 768). The exclusively male context of the question reflected a patriarchal society in both the Jewish and non-Jewish contexts. Carter (2000, 378–79) notes women also could divorce, but the two cases he mentions were of elitist women whose actions were criticized (Josephus, *A.J.* 18.136; 20.142–47—of Herodias and Drusilla). One other case was where a wife was falsely accused of not being faithful, then she was permitted to leave her husband (Philo, *Spec.* 3.81–82).

Philo on a Woman's Reputation

***On the Special Laws* 3.81–82:** "For in such a case, not only are their daughters themselves in danger, as to their reputation as having preserved the chastity of their bodies, but their guardians are likewise imperiled, not only because they have not kept them safe till the important period of their marriageable age, but because they have given in marriage as virgins those who have been defiled by others, deceiving and imposing upon those who have taken them to wife. Then if they appear to have justice on their side, let the judges impose a pecuniary fine on those who have invented these false accusations, and let them also sentence those who have assaulted them to corporeal punishment, and let them also pronounce, what to those men will be the most unpleasant of all things, a confirmation of their marriage, if their wives will still endure to cohabit with them; for the law permits them at their own choice to remain with them or to abandon them, and will not allow the husbands any option either way, on account of the false accusations which they have brought."

There was some hostility in the Pharisees' question, as it was posed as a test for Jesus, the first such test since Matthew 16:1. There would be a few more (Matt. 22:18, 35). He was being asked where he fell on the issues noted from Deuteronomy 24:1. Was he more like Shammai or Hillel? Would he challenge Moses? What had taken place with John the Baptist because he discussed Herod Antipas's marriage and divorce showed how dangerous this discussion could be (Matt. 14:3–12). John's insistence on marital faithfulness had led to his beheading.

19:4–6. Jesus went behind the question to a more fundamental level. He appealed to their reading of Scripture and began at the start in Genesis, not in Deuteronomy. His question about reading assumed they knew the texts he would cite as the question expected a positive reply (using οὐκ). He opened with marriage, monogamy, and the sacred union God made when a marriage took place (Mark 10:3–9). He did not discuss divorce, but marriage.

Next Jesus went to Genesis 1:27 on people being created male and female, and to Genesis 2:24 to define marriage (also cited in Jub. 3:7). He placed the two passages side by side to make the point. Jesus was affirming what Judaism already taught in light of the Hebrew Scripture. The appeal to Genesis, being earlier, argued for an earlier precedent than Moses (Osborne 2010, 703). Carson (2010, 466) speaks of the principle, "the more original, the weightier." Jesus went back to the beginning. He had divine design in mind. Marriage involved a man and a woman. God created the genders to complement each other. Marriage consisted of forming a fresh family unit in three steps. It meant (1) leaving one's family, (2) a man cleaving to his wife, and (3) the two becoming one flesh (Gen. 5:2; 1 Cor. 6:16; Eph. 5:31). In fact, God had joined this couple together to make them a unit. He had melded them into one. The verb κολλάω for "cleaving" means to bind together or attach (BDAG s.v. "κολλάω" 655). Marriage was about three, not two. It was about being made one, forming a family unit before God. So what God brought together, people were not to separate (Mark 10:8). The term συζεύγνυμι means "to yoke together" (BDAG s.v. "συζεύγνυμι" 954). God had fused the couple together.

Marriage was not about social convention nor was it a social construct; it was a sacred bond. What God brought together was not to be separated as that was a mutilation of the bond (Nolland 2005, 773). This emphasis on God making the union was the positive way to say what Malachi 2:16 teaches, namely, that God hated divorce. Later R. Judah in an ironic twist said about Malachi, "If you have hated her, put her away" (Osburn, 1981, 196; *Giṭ.* 90a [trans. Neusner]). In contrast, R. Yohanan said, "He who puts his wife away is hated" (*Giṭ.* 90a [trans. Neusner]). There was debate about divorce in

Judaism. However, the consistent view on marriage was that it was intended to be permanent. That was the starting point for any discussion. This idea was supposed to have priority over any other consideration. Starting here, Jesus stood alone in his view because he was stressing not what was allowed but what should be done.

Put Her Away

In sum, various grounds existed with an array of options beyond those noted, namely unchastity, a poorly cooked meal, or a prettier woman. These were not unanimously recognized but were among reasons given. In the Mishnah, views argued a wife could be put away for feeding a husband food not tithed, having sex while menstruating, not cutting off her dough offering, failing to carry out a vow, leaving the house with hair flowing loose, spinning in the marketplace, talking with just anybody, cursing a husband's family in his presence, or being a loudmouth, which meant talking in the house loud enough the neighbors could hear (*m. Ketub.* 7.6). Adultery or a serious rumor of it could be grounds for divorce (*m. Soṭah.* 6.1). Disobedience also could be grounds for divorce (Sir. 25:26). A man with a serious blemish could be forced to put away a wife (*m. Ned.* 7.10). Remarriage was generally not permitted to a former wife who had married someone else after but now was divorced or widowed, a sister-in-law who had been renounced in levirate marriage earlier or a relative to such a woman (*m. Yebam.* 4.12).

Another Mishnaic Text on Grounds for Divorce

Mishnah *Ketuboth* 7.6: "And those women go forth without the payment of the marriage contract at all:

She who transgresses against the law of Moses and Jewish law.

And what is the law of Moses [which she has transgressed]? [If] (1) she feeds him food which has not been tithed, or (2) has sexual relations with him while she is menstruating, or [if] (3) she does not cut off her dough offering, or (4) [if] she vows and does not carry out her vow.

And what is the Jewish law? If (1) she goes out with her hair flowing loose, or (2) she spins in the marketplace, or (3) she talks with just anybody,

Abba Saul says, 'Also: if she curses his parents in his presence.'

R. Tarfon says, 'Also: if she is a loudmouth.'

What is a loudmouth? When she talks in her own house, her neighbors can hear her voice."

For Jesus, the following discussion of divorce from Deuteronomy 24:1 was framed by this starting point. In Matthew's version, the discussion of hardness of heart found in Mark 10:3–5 comes later in response to a direct question, while Mark starts there with Jesus asking about Deuteronomy and then moving to Genesis. Matthew has discussed the texts in their logical and biblically sequential order, an editorial choice (France 2007, 716). Jesus's core point was that if the intent of marriage were followed, there would be no need for divorce. The need for the question about cause already suggested that there was a problem.

19:7. The Pharisees may think they have caught Jesus in a denial of Moses, so they ask why Moses commanded the issuing of a certificate of dismissal and permitted divorce. Such certificates stated the divorced person had the right to remarry. One got a divorce to procure this right (*m. Giṭ.* 9.1; see chart at Matthew 5:31).

19:8–9. Jesus replied that it was "hardness of heart" that allowed for the permitting of divorce (BDAG s.v. "σκλληροκαρδία" 930; Deut. 10:16; Prov. 17:20; Jer. 4:4; Ezek. 3:7; Mark 10:5). It is a term that describes sin. Moses did not command divorce. Divorce reflected moral weakness, not a clear desire of God. This was a concession, nothing more. Thus, the verb ἐπέτρεψεν, "he allowed" (BDAG s.v. "ἐπιτρέπω" 1, 384–85). This certificate did accomplish three things:

(1) it protected the relationship for "indecent" defiling; (2) it protected the woman from being sent away without cause; and (3) it documented her status as legitimately divorced (Morris 1992, 483; Wilkins 2004, 643).

Mark 10:3–5 handles this question differently. Jesus asked what Moses had commanded. They answered that Moses permitted the writing of the certificate. Then Jesus said that Moses had permitted this because of people's hardness of heart, which still explained it all as a concession. The core point is the same.

In the beginning, the goal was what Jesus had already emphasized, to stay married (Mark 10:6). In Matthew uniquely, Jesus went on to note that anyone who received a divorce, except for sexual immorality, and married another committed adultery. Mark 10:11 has the emphasis on not divorcing and notes no exception. Jesus made this point about divorce as a violation because the couple had torn apart the sworn union of the original marriage (Blomberg 1992, 293, who notes this was not continuous adultery; defended in detail by Osburn, 1981, 193–203, who argues that the present indicative here does not demand an "in progress" or "continuous" repeated force, as an indicative requires contextual evaluation versus having a fixed meaning with a simple descriptive present being more common than a continuous present). The remark also showed that any marriage, not just one with a formerly married person, resulted in adultery. This expanded the way this had been normally viewed in Judaism, making the impact even more extensive (Davies and Allison 1997, 16).

Jesus spoke of remarriage because an assumption in getting a divorce was that one was freed up to remarry. There was likely an assumption about an "innocent" party here as well when adultery was in view. The non-adulterous partner was free to make the choice whether or not to divorce. As Turner (2008, 462) notes, if divorce did not convey the right to remarry "it is essentially meaningless." The divorce decree came with the statement that the spouse had the right to remarry (*m. Giṭ.* 9.1–3).

The Divorce Writ in Judaism

Mishnah *Giṭṭin* 9:3: "A. The text of the writ of divorce [is as follows]:

"B. 'Lo, you are permitted to any man.'

"C. R. Judah says, '[In Aramaic]: Let this be from me your writ of divorce, letter of dismissal, and deed of liberation, that you may marry anyone you want.'

"D. The text of a writ of emancipation [is as follows]:

"E. 'Lo, you are a free girl, lo, you are your own [possession]' [cf. Dt. 21:14]."

The exception was much discussed, as was noted in Matthew 5:31–32. The term πορνεία is broad, referring to "various kinds of 'unsanctioned sexual intercourse,'" so sexual unfaithfulness in the context of a marriage union (BDAG s.v. "πορνεία" overview and 1, 854). This case appeared to exempt only the non-adulterous person getting the divorce for another's infidelity. The position seems similar to that of the school of Shammai, except that Jesus had started in a different place with an emphasis on marriage's permanence in terms of its original design (France 2007, 721). This meant he had a different emphasis than the school of Shammai. One should seek to keep the marriage together and not look for exceptions. Unfortunately, sin often made that goal a hard one to maintain, so exceptions to the standard existed, just not as many as Hillel affirmed. Mark 10:11 has no exception and was expressed only to the disciples. Matthew has no equivalent to the woman's situation expressed in Mark 10:12. Blomberg (1992, 292), Keener (2009, 467), and Morris (1992, 484) argue Mark and Luke assumed this exception for adultery as it was a given in the culture already and adultery was seen to have already broken the union. This could be right, but it was also likely that Mark and Luke merely stressed what Jesus emphasized as the priority, that marriage was designed to be permanent with divorce reflecting a breakdown of that commitment.

19:10. The disciples saw this standard as demanding, especially in light of how lax things were then. They observed that it was better to stay single than to risk such a moral violation.

19:11–12. Jesus replied not by challenging that conclusion directly, but by noting that not everyone could accept such a limitation. There is a question as to what the "matter" is that Jesus referred to in this response. Is it verse 6 (being one flesh), verse 9 (on committing adultery), or verse 10 (being single)? In one sense it makes little difference between these options, for the force of each is the same: not all could live with such a standard for marriage, that is, that marriage was for life. Still, it is more likely Jesus was responding to the disciples' remarks about being single, for the other views in any form meant Jesus gave away what he had just affirmed, which is very unlikely. If Jesus was referring back to Matthew 19:10, his point was that celibacy required a giftedness. He was not making a law here, but an observation about pursuing singleness.

The disciples' conclusion was not exactly right. It worked only in certain circumstances. Jesus observed there were three kinds of eunuchs. (1) Some were eunuchs from the womb, from birth. (2) Others were made eunuchs, such as some who served royalty, especially to be made safe for the royal harem. These were made eunuchs by others for their roles in society (perhaps like the Ethiopian eunuch of Acts 8; Nolland 2005, 777–78, also covers the issue of castration). (3) Then there were those who made themselves eunuchs, figuratively, for the sake of the kingdom. They chose not to be married. They could accept such a limitation, and the choice was commendable.

Nolland (2005, 779–80) discusses Jewish and Greco-Roman views toward abstention, which could be positive in certain contexts. However, the common Jewish view was that one should marry and not abstain from sex, even called the "duty" of marriage (*m. Ketub.* 5.6; *m. Yebam.* 6:6 in *order* to obey the command to be fruitful and multiply; in the later Talmud, to avoid immorality, Qidd. 29b–30a; Sanh. 76a–b). Purity issues were reasons to abstain (Exod. 19:15—when Israel received the law; Lev. 15:18–26, 33—emission or menstruation; 22:4; Deut. 23:9–11—holy war). Some Essenes were an exception to this preference for marriage and pursued chastity (Josephus, *A.J.* 18.21).

The thrust of Jesus's remark about being single was like Paul's in 1 Corinthians 7. This role was not made mandatory but was part of choosing such a role for the sake of the kingdom. Examples abound: John the Baptist, Jesus, Paul, and Philip's four daughters (1 Cor. 7:32–38; 9:5; Acts 21:9; Turner 2008, 463). Part of accepting such a role consisted in the ability to live this way. Paul notes that those who burned should not stay single but marry. This "gift" or ability was not for everyone. There is a value to being single and in living that way for the kingdom that needs to be more appreciated and affirmed in the church.

THEOLOGICAL FOCUS

The exegetical idea (Jesus affirmed marriage as a lifelong bond between a man and a woman, while divorce was the result of hardness of heart and was only permissible for immorality, leading the disciples to say it might be better not to marry and Jesus to note that only some were able to live that way) morphs into this theological focus: the design of marriage was to be a permanent bond before God between a man and woman, making divorce a violation of that promise.

Returning to the picture of the creation, Jesus affirmed marriage to involve a man and a woman with an intention of God forming a permanent union. The exception for divorce was permitted but not required in cases of sexual immorality. Singleness was preferable only for those who were able and gifted to bear it.

Marriage is a sacred bond, intended for a man and a woman, intended to be for life. Jesus was clear on all of these points. Divorce represents a failure to reach that ideal. It is permitted in very limited cases because of hardness of heart. Sexual immorality allows an injured partner to have the right to divorce, but even then it is not required. This is what Matthew affirms through what Jesus taught. This standard was high enough that the disciples sensed it was better to be single. Jesus noted that such a choice was only for some who could accept it.

What has made this Matthean text so discussed is how it relates to Mark and Luke where no exceptions appeared. That combined with Jesus's declaration that an inappropriate remarriage was adultery has made divorce and remarriage a controversial topic in a church attempting to affirm and reflect the high moral standard Jesus affirmed.

In general, two paths have been taken. (1) One can regard the Matthean exception as very limited in a cultural sense, referring to a rarely attained limitation, such as some sort of premarital state during the engagement period. Or (2), one can see Matthew as giving the full teaching in detail, while Mark and Luke stressed marriage's sanctity, which was Jesus's emphasis. The general nature of πορνεία (sexual immorality) favors the second approach. Moreover, Paul's appeal in 1 Corinthians 7:12–16 to the Lord's teaching while seeing unbeliever desertion as also permitted showed Jesus did not have a view that had no exceptions at all. The biblical standards are high. The church should seek to maintain them. The question is how to do so in a world with so much divorce and remarriage, as well as how to pursue restoration for those who have failed to meet such standards.

Here it is important to recall that sins are forgivable. Sin also may come with consequences. So many communities rightly accept people into their communities to hear the gospel message with an eye to forgiving their past failures when acknowledged, but may choose to limit how someone serves, at least for a time, if not on a more permanent basis in certain church roles where the moral example is to be paramount. This allows both forgiveness and a standard of holiness to be affirmed simultaneously. It may be the wisest way to balance the ethical concerns a passage such as this raises.

PREACHING AND TEACHING STRATEGIES

Exegetical and Theological Synthesis

God's ideal has not changed. His intention for marriage between one biological male and one biological female in a lifelong covenant finds its origin story in Genesis 1–2. Mosaic law affirmed the ideal (Exod. 20:14; Lev. 18, 20; Deut. 24:1–4). Prophetic preaching and wisdom literature affirmed the ideal (Prov. 5; all of Song; Jer. 7:9; Hos. 4:2). Jesus and Paul affirmed the ideal (Matt. 19; 1 Cor. 7). Every affirmation of monogamous, heterosexual marriage points back to Genesis 1–2. The ideal is firmly established in Scripture.

Sadly, deviations from the marriage ideal abound, including fornication, adultery, polygamy, rape, and of course, divorce. Each transgression misses God's mark, which is true of all sin; however, sexual sin has different effects and consequences. In the Old Testament, sexual sin is often tied to idolatry. A case in point was Solomon's hoarding of foreign brides, which led his heart from pure worship of God (1 Kings 11). Other kings followed similar syncretic paths. In the New Testament, sexual sin breaks the exclusive bond intended between husband and wife. Both Paul and Jesus condemned sexual sin for this very reason (Matt. 19:5–6; 1 Cor. 6:15–16).

Fortunately, sexual sin is not outside the scope of God's forgiveness. Despite the sordid past of the Corinthians, Paul acknowledged that they were no longer defined by their sexual misdeeds but washed, sanctified, and justified in Jesus (1 Cor. 6:9–11). In a contested account because of textual uncertainty (John 8:1–11), Jesus forgave a woman caught in adultery, ordering her to "Go and sin no more." This response betrays his perfect blend of truth and grace. Even his maximalist standard for marriage makes an allowance for divorce due to infidelity. The exception clause betrays God's grace. When hard hearts and sexual sin put the ideal out of reach, divorce may be an escape hatch for the hurting partner. Though not the ideal option, it is permitted.

Preaching Idea

Marriage maximalists strive for God's design.

Contemporary Connections

What does it mean?

Marriage maximalists do not have perfect marriages. Every marriage suffers from poor communication, lapses in intimacy, conflict, and seasons of busyness. Moreover, every marriage comprises two imperfect people with sinful tendencies, family baggage, and personal quirks that cause tension in the relationship. To be a marriage maximalist is not to be without struggles.

What sets marriage maximalists apart is their willingness to bear with one another's sin, selfishness, and peculiarities. Maximalists forgive rather than hold grudges. They prioritize the relationship rather than letting their friendship drift. They honor one another rather than criticizing their partner. They direct their sexual energy toward pleasing their spouse (1 Cor. 7:1–5). Maximalists view marriage as more than a right or privilege; it is a symbol of Christ's profound commitment to and sacrifice for his church (Eph. 5:25–32).

Is it true?

Marriage maximalists certainly strive for God's design. They make marriage a priority. They cultivate love and respect for one another. They serve, defend, and enjoy one another. For the marriage maximalist, the relationship is a locus of spiritual formation.

Of course, marriage is not required for spiritual formation or flourishing. Single people fit into God's design. Singleness may be a lifelong calling or stage of life. According to Paul, it frees people to serve God's kingdom with undivided attention (1 Cor. 7:32–35). It also leads to people feeling left out in churches overly focused on families. Singleness should not make people feel like second-class citizens or third wheels in the church. He designed the church to be inclusive, which means there is room at the table for singles.

Part of God's design for marriage in Genesis 1–2 was procreation. Husband and wife were intended to be fruitful, multiply, and fill the world with image-bearers. Sadly, following the curse of Genesis 3, childbirth is fraught with complications. Some children do not survive the pregnancy. Some women cannot get pregnant. Some men are infertile. Childbirth is not guaranteed. Couples who make childbearing part of the marriage ideal, only to see their hopes dashed, suffer greatly.

Finally, some marriages will not last. Contemporary reasons for divorce exceed the two biblical exceptions: adultery and abandonment.[2] Today people divorce because they are unhappy, unfulfilled, and tired of fighting. These reasons reduce God's marriage ideal to

2 Certainly, wisdom would suggest separating from an abusive spouse. Personal safety and protecting children are high priorities.

a means of personal fulfillment. Even those who subscribe to God's ideal for marriage may deal with sexual sin and neglect. Some of these couples may not entertain the biblical exceptions to divorce but pursue counseling, accountability, and reconciliation.

This is a long, hard road. Other couples may end their marriage. This, too, is a painful decision. Those who choose divorce should not be branded with a "Scarlet D." They need support, not shame. Preaching through this text requires pastoral sensitivity to the pain resulting from divorce. For thoughtful, biblical treatment of this text and topic, see Blomberg (1990), Instone-Brewer (2002), and Instone-Brewer (2003).

Now what?

Striving for God's design as marriage maximalists requires us first to review our concepts of marriage, divorce, and singleness. Have we given in to the world's version of marriage as a means of securing personal happiness? Or do we view marriage as a covenant aimed at cultivating holiness? When it comes to divorce, are we magnifying, multiplying, or manufacturing exceptions? Or do we approach divorce as a last resort? Concerning singleness, do we view it as a sorry condition for those who cannot commit or find love? Or do we see singleness as a gift, calling, and opportunity for believers to give undivided attention to serving God's kingdom? Reviewing our concepts of marriage, divorce, and singleness helps us avoid slipping into a worldly view of these topics. If we have traded God's maximal standard for a lesser one, we must repent and return to the ideal.

Second, churches that strive for God's design as marriage maximalists will develop robust teaching and programming to nurture healthy marriages. Ministry to married people need not be original; churches may promote and partner with nationally recognized marriage-enrichment ministries, such as A Weekend to Remember, Prepare/Enrich, MarriageRestored, or RightNow Media's *Marriage Night*. Additionally, churches may resource their people with premarital counseling, marriage mentor programs, or audio/visual resources on healthy marriages. Finally, church leaders should model healthy marriages, including appropriate disclosure of how they work through struggles.

Reading Resources for Marriage, Divorce, and Singleness

Sam Allberry, *7 Myths about Singleness* (2019)
Barry Danylak, *Redeeming Singleness* (2010)
Emerson Eggerichs, *Love & Respect* (2004)
John M. Gottman, *The Seven Principles for Making Marriage* Work (2015)
Willard Harley Jr., *His Needs, Her Needs* (2022)
Les and Leslie Parrott, *Saving Your Marriage Before It Starts* (2015)
Lysa TerKeurst, *Good Boundaries and Goodbyes* (2022)
Gary Thomas, *Sacred Marriage* (2000)
Danielle Treweek, *The Meaning of Singleness* (2023)
Leslie Vernick, *The Emotionally Destructive Marriage* (2013)

Third, while celebrating the ideal of biblical marriage, churches should also minister to single and divorced people. Marriage maximalists are not exempt from the call to compassion and inclusion. Outreach to divorced people may include recovery groups, childcare for single parents, and counseling. Ministry to single people may include events that are not family-centric, small groups, teaching illustrations involving single people, and service teams. Ultimately, churches must avoid stigmatizing divorce and singleness because it does not fit the ideal of biblical marriage.

Finally, we must call all people, regardless of their marriage status, to holiness.

Married people should strive for joyful, selfless, God-honoring care for their partner. Single people should strive for joyful, self-controlled, God-honoring service in his kingdom. Divorced people should strive for joyful, gracious, God-given healing from their past. Maximalists strive for God's holy standard in all of life circumstances.

Creativity in Presentation

Debates about divorce date back to before Jesus's day. As the exegetical section illustrated, two rabbinic schools dominated the discussion. Consider staging a debate between the liberal Rabbi Hillel and conservative Rabbi Shammai for your congregation, so they can hear the contrast between the two camps. Using excerpts from the extrabiblical sources cited above, you could reenact the conversation using the script below.

> R. SHAMMAI: Hillel, you're looking very relaxed today.
> R. HILLEL: Well, Shammai, that's because I wasn't expecting to see you.
> R. SHAMMAI: I hear your sarcasm and raise you three, yea, verily, four.
> R. HILLEL: So it begins. And what's today's debate? Loincloths? Handwashing? How many bathroom breaks you're allowed to take on the Sabbath?
> R. SHAMMAI: No. Those are softball topics. Let's talk divorce.
> R. HILLEL: This could be a long discussion.
> R. SHAMMAI: Doesn't have to be. Not if you read Moses. You do read Moses, right, Hillel?
> R. HILLEL: I do read him right, Shammai. It's you who don't. Moses made allowances for divorce. You make him sound like a stickler.
> R. SHAMMAI: Moses said, "If a wife is indecent, her husband may write a writ of divorce." *Only* in cases of indecency. That means impure, adulterous, unchaste.
> R. HILLEL: Shammai, you stuffy old brute, that's not what Moses said. He wrote, "If a husband finds *any* indecency, he can write the divorce certificate and send her away. It's not only indecency, it's any.
> R. SHAMMAI: Hillel, you silly liberal scholar, it's *only*, not *any*.
> R. HILLEL: Any.
> R. SHAMMAI: Only.
> R. HILLEL: Any.
> R. SHAMMAI: Only.
> R. HILLEL: Let me spell this out for you, Rabbi Stoggypants. If the wife has spoiled a dish, he can divorce her. If she has a bad hair day, puts on too much weight, or talks too loudly, he can divorce her. If she breaks a promise or talks bad about the in-laws, he can divorce her.
> R. SHAMMAI: How does a woman survive a marriage in these conditions, Hillel?
> R. HILLEL: She doesn't. If she wants to stay married, Moses says, she has to remain in her husband's good graces.
> R. SHAMMAI: I think you're misreading Moses. He wanted to protect marriage, not make it easily ended.
> R. SHAMMAI: It's really not that complicated. All a wife has to do is keep her husband happy all the time.
> R. SHAMMAI: All the time?
> R. HILLEL: All the time!
> R. SHAMMAI: Without exceptions?
> R. HILLEL: Without exceptions!
> R. SHAMMAI: Hmmm. That's funny. Suddenly, the liberal Rabbi Hillel sounds like the legalist.
> R. HILLEL: Ha. Well played, Shammai.

Another way to illustrate the preaching idea is to contrast maximalists and minimalists in other areas of life. The following examples may serve as starting points for contrasts that could be most relevant to your church context.

Contrasting Maximalists and Minimalists		
Topic	**Maximalist**	**Minimalist**
Academics	• Schedules time for homework • Completes all required reading • Studies for all quizzes and tests • Researches, writes, edits, and reviews papers and projects • Earns an A+	• Procrastinates • Skims • Studies a bit • Turns stuff in • Earns a passing grade
Athletics	• Completes off-season training • Gives strong effort in practice • Learns playbook and executes • Takes correction and improves • Stays rested and hydrated • Recovers well from injury • Demonstrates teamwork and a winning attitude	• Shows up to practice • Completes most workouts • Learns fundamentals • Doesn't quit
Finances	• Develops a working budget • Designates money for giving, saving, and investing • Automates bill payments • Works with a financial advisor • Pays off debt early • Establishes a diverse portfolio	• Pays most bills mostly on time • Spends less than is made • Saves and gives some money
Marriage	• Gives unconditional love and respect • Keeps the marriage bed pure • Delight in one another sexually • Love, forgive, forbear, serve, and encourage one another • For better or worse, in sickness and in health, faithful unto death	• Limits conflict • Doesn't sleep around • Tolerate each other • Stays married

A more personal approach would include interviews or testimonies from people within the church describing how they maximize their marital status. These interviews could be live or recorded. Church members would benefit from hearing from a long-term married couple, faithful single person, and someone who has found grace following divorce. Use pastoral sensitivity when selecting the subjects and questions. Consider these:

Questions for Married Couples: How long have you been married? What hardships have you faced together as a couple? What have you learned about conflict management over the years? What is one piece of advice you would give to a newly married couple?

Questions for Single Person: What are some of the challenges of singleness in today's culture? Where have you seen benefits of being single? How can the church strengthen its ministry to single adults? What is something to avoid saying to a single adult?

Questions for Divorced Person: What challenges have you faced as a divorced person? How is God helping you heal from your divorce? What are some practical things the church can do to minister to divorced people?

Lastly, to communicate the importance of having a design for a better final product, consider displaying different types of designs and their end products. Show a picture of a blueprint, followed by an image of the house constructed from it. Show a picture of a football playbook, followed by a video clip of that play executed by a team. Show a brownie recipe, followed by a tray of brownies. Show a costume design pattern, followed by the actual costume. (Note: A humorous spin on this exercise is to compare the blueprint, play, recipe, or pattern to a product where the design was not followed—instead of a sturdy home, a condemned property; instead of an effective football play, a fumble; a mound of brownie sludge instead of brownies; a tangle of clothes instead of a costume.)

In the end, you want your sermon to stress that the design of marriage was to be a permanent bond before God between a man and woman, making divorce a violation of that promise. Marriage maximalists strive for God's design.

- God set a high standard for marriage (19:1–9).

- We have a low view of singleness (19:10–12).

DISCUSSION QUESTIONS

1. How do the first-century debates about marriage and divorce compare to contemporary discussions around marriage and divorce?

2. What does Jesus's appeal to Genesis 1–2 teach us about marriage and sexuality?

3. What comfort does a passage like this provide for those who have experienced divorce? How does it help us rethink singleness?

4. How does your church resource marriages? Divorced people? Adult singles?

5. What are the biblical exceptions to divorce?

6. How can the church be more consistent in its teaching and practice on sexual sin?

Matthew 19:13–30

EXEGETICAL IDEA

After noting that the kingdom belonged to people who are like children, and while asking that one leave all behind and follow him, Jesus observed that wealth often blocked one from coming to the kingdom and following him.

THEOLOGICAL FOCUS

Jesus discusses humility and then has a conversation with a rich man that shows how wealth can be an obstacle to the pursuit of God.

PREACHING IDEA

Wealth is worthless if it keeps us from Jesus.

PREACHING POINTERS

Jesus did not subscribe to the value system of his day. He preferred humility to honor, sacrifice to status, allegiance to wealth. These insights emerged from controversies with his disciples and a rich young man about eternal life. Misunderstandings about wealth, status, and God's favor were common among Matthew's readers. The original audience lived during a time when wealth was not widely distributed and often mistaken as a sign of divine reward. By extension, poverty was a punishment. Jesus's teaching countered these misconceptions and assured them of future reward for those who followed him.

In our day, wealth is power, privilege, and opportunity. Wealth can buy elections. Wealth provides purchasing power to secure a home in a safe cul-de-sac and lease a reliable car for daily commutes to work. Wealth can jump-start a child's academic and athletic journeys. Wealth is wonderful for those who have it. Except for this fact: one's wealth is never enough. As Rockefeller famously said, "A little bit more" would satisfy him. To paraphrase The Beatles: money can't buy you love. And most importantly, Jesus told us that eternal life has no sticker price. Thus, this sermon teaches that wealth is worthless if it keeps us from Jesus.

JESUS DISCUSSES CHILDLIKE FAITH AND THE CHALLENGE OF WEALTH (19:13–30)

LITERARY STRUCTURE AND THEMES (19:13–30)

This unit has two core parts. There is Jesus's point about receiving the kingdom like a child (Matt. 19:13–15). Then there is a much longer discussion with the rich man and the disciples' reaction (Matt. 19:16–30). The first scene produces a pronouncement about faith. The second is a kind of controversy dialogue.

The two scenes here are both controversy stories, following one in Matthew 19:1–12 (Blomberg 1992, 296). In each case the controversy was started by a different source: the disciples and the rich man. Jesus's teaching was challenging everyone.

Matthew 19:13–15 parallels Mark 10:13–16 and Luke 18:15–17. With this event Matthew picks up with the latter section of Luke's journey to Jerusalem, as well as continuing to follow Mark, as Matthew has been doing for a while.

Matthew 19:16–30 has parallels in Mark 10:17–31 and Luke 18:18–23. So again, Matthew is tracking with both Synoptics here. This is one of the few places where Matthew is more detailed than either Mark or Luke in a parallel passage.

The scene with the children is a short pronouncement scene, designed to equate disciples with the humble status and dependence of a child. It is an important, contrastive point in light of the sense of independence the rich man has in the scene that followed.

The longer scene with the rich man is initially a running dialogue (Matt. 19:16–22), one of the few in Matthew. The first part of it ends with the man walking away (Matt. 19:22). The man had rejected Jesus's instruction that concluded with a call to follow Jesus after promising the man treasure in heaven if he obeyed. This led into a pronouncement about the rich, which then made a transition into the disciples' reaction. The reaction introduces part two of this scene, the interaction with the disciples about what just took place. The rich man's departure led them to ask who could be saved (Matt. 19:23–30). This second portion is split into two parts itself. First, there is the shock about a wealthy person not being saved (Matt. 19:23–26); then, there is Peter's appeal about what the disciples have done (Matt. 19:27–30). With God all things were possible. When Peter asked if they had followed, he was querying if they had done what Jesus had asked the rich man to do. Jesus affirmed and assured them in his climactic pronouncement by noting that they would share in his rule, receive many more things, and gain eternal life. He concluded with his note that the first shall be last and the last first.

The key themes here focus on how one responded to the kingdom. On the one hand, a disciple was like a child, being humble and dependent. In addition, a person should come to Jesus with nothing to claim for himself, having no status other than what was received from God.

The scene with the rich man pictured a person who wanted to keep one hand on what he has in this world and who did not think he had spiritual needs because he thought he was obeying all of God's commands. The rich man denied a need for God by walking away from Jesus's instruction. The scene shows that without God's help, people do not come to God on the terms he has set. It also indicates that wealth, its security, and its breeding of independence can keep someone from following Jesus. In fact, in terms of expectations, the children of the previous scene should have been ignored and this rich man should have been honored (France 2007, 729). The reversal was startling to the disciples. Jesus had spoken about wealth and trust in the Sermon on the Mount (Davies and Allison 1997, 39–40; Matt. 6:19–21 on treasure on heaven; 6:22–24 on generosity; 6:25–34 on trusting God). Matthew 19 develops those ideas. Luke's gospel has much more to say about money and wealth (Luke 1:53; 6:20–26; 12:13–21; 16:1–13, 19–31; 18:18–30). Still, what Jesus asked for was not impossible. The disciples showed that. Jesus affirmed that the disciples would participate in his future rule and gain eternal life. They had left all and had come to him, knowing only he could give eternal life. That life was found nowhere else and in nothing else.

EXPOSITION (19:13–30)

This passage is built around a contrast between a childlike faith that trusted Jesus and a warning about how difficult it was for the rich to come to God. Wealth could lead to such independence and attachment to the world that it could damage recognizing one's need for God. The way of God called for focused allegiance, something the disciples had given and would be rewarded for possessing. The dependent nature of genuine faith, contrasted with what could get in the way of such faith, is what Matthew highlights here.

After noting that the kingdom belonged to people who are like children and asking that one leave all behind and follow him, Jesus observed that wealth often blocked one from coming to the kingdom and following him.

19:13–15. In a passage very much like Matthew 18:1–5, children are brought for Jesus to pray over and bless, a point made by speaking of laying on of hands (Mark 10:13; Luke 18:15). Jesus had cared for children beyond Matthew 18 (Matt. 9:18–26; 15:21–28; 17:14–21). The laying on of hands was for blessing (Gen. 48:14–15; Num. 27:18; Deut. 34:9). Thinking this was a poor use of Jesus's time, the disciples tried to stop this and rebuked those who were bringing their children.

Jesus challenged the disciples' thinking, as again the disciples must learn about status and people (Mark 10:14; Luke 18:16; Davies and Allison 1997, 34, notes that the expanded saying in the Gospel of Thomas 22 is secondary). Jesus gave a command, then a prohibition, before giving an explanation. The children were to be left alone. They were not to be prevented from seeing Jesus, because the kingdom of heaven was made up of people like these. Jesus was affirming the value of children whose status was not highly regarded in the culture (see Matt. 18:2 discussion). Keener (2009, 473) says, "Children were low-status dependents; they had to trust adults and receive what they provided." Jesus was associating a child's lack of position with the seeming lack of social importance in the world for disciples who were in the kingdom. They too were seen as weak and irrelevant by many. The children's humility, lack of status, and dependence were likely all in view in this comparison (Wilkins 2004, 646–47). By saying the children were important enough to have his attention, he elevated the status of disciples as well. There were no unimportant people.

Jesus received the children and then departed (Mark 10:16). There was no point being made here about infant baptism, as the text was using children as a picture for believers (Turner 2008, 465).

19:16–17. Someone in the crowd asked Jesus what good he must do to inherit eternal life. Luke 18:18 describes him as a ruler, indicating also that he had social status. Later Matthew 19:22 tells us he was rich. The assumption in the question was that one must earn eternal life.

Jesus examined and exposed this premise in his long and developed answer.

Matthew touches on this topic elsewhere (Matt. 7:14; 18:8–9; 19:29; 25:34–46). This was a question about being saved. Mark 10:17 and Luke 18:18 have Jesus addressed as "good teacher" and report the man asking only what he must do, not what good he must do, to inherit internal life.

Jesus began by issuing a rebuke to put the questioner on notice. Jesus started with challenging an assumption about the good thing to do as he made his response. Mark 10:18 and Luke 18:19 have Jesus ask, "Why do you call me good?" in line with the address in Mark and Luke of Jesus as good teacher; those gospels have the added remark that no one is good but God (Osborne 2010, 716, covers the differences well). Matthew's rebuke was about the good in line with the question Matthew had about the good thing one must do. Only one is good. This is an allusion to God (Deut. 6:4), so Matthew overlaps with Mark and Luke here, but does so in a way that did not bring Jesus into the picture as in Mark and Luke.

Jesus focused the man on God, not anywhere else (Nolland 2005, 789). The rebuke assumed that people were not good and thus innate goodness was not the basis for qualifying for heaven. God was the source of that which was good (Ps. 16:2). Then Jesus said if the man wanted to enter life, that he should keep the commandments (Mark 10:19; Luke 18:20). This was not to earn salvation but reflected a humble response of childlike faith and dependence in following the Father, a quality Jesus had just noted in the previous event (Wilkins 2004, 648). The man should be focused on God's goodness or on the commandments that came from him that lead into goodness (Lev. 18:5). Jesus was still developing his full answer to the question.

19:18–19. There was still an issue as the man asked which commandments he should keep, as if one could sort out what one obeyed from God from what could be ignored. There are 613 commands in the Torah, so in one sense the question made sense. Were there commands one should really note? This question is unique to Matthew as he gives more details to this event than the parallels, given its nature as a Jewish legal issue.

Nonetheless, Jesus answered focusing on five parts of the Ten Commandments that deal with how we relate to others (Mark 10:19; Luke 18:20, but they lack mention of defrauding). They all come from the second part of the Ten Commandments. One's relationship to God gets translated into how we treat others made in his image. The only one of those commandments Jesus omitted was covetousness, but stealing and defrauding have to do with how money or possessions are handled. He goes from the sixth to the ninth and then back to the fifth commandment (Exod. 20:12–16; Deut. 5:16–20). Jesus ended with the summary command to love your neighbor as yourself (Lev. 19:18). Only Matthew cites Leviticus here. Gospel of Thomas 25 is close to this in wording but only presents Leviticus by itself as a maxim with no context for the citation. This Leviticus text was quite popular in Judaism (Turner 2008, 469; CD 6:18–20; 1QS 5.25; Sir. 13:15; Jub. 7:20; 20:2; 36:4; T. Reu. 6:9; T. Iss. 5:2; T. Gad 4:2; T. Benj. 3:3–4). This ethical Leviticus passage is the most cited text from the Pentateuch in the New Testament (Davies and Allison 1997, 44). Elsewhere Matthew notes Jesus's use of it in 5:43 and 22:39. Responding to God meant others were treated well. Calvin said right action was proof of right religion (*Institutes* 2.8.52–53; Davies and Allison 1997, 43).

Use of Leviticus 19:18 in Judaism

Sirach 13:15: "Every creature loves its like, and every person the neighbor."

Jubilees 7:20: "And in the twenty-eighth jubilee Noah began to command his grandsons with ordinances and commandments and all of the judgments which he knew. And he bore witness to his sons so that they might do justice and cover the shame of their flesh and bless the one who created them and honor father and mother, and each one love his neighbor and preserve themselves from fornication and pollution and from all injustice."

Jubilees 20:2: "And he commanded them (a) that they should guard the way of the Lord so that they might do righteousness and each one might love his neighbor, and (b) that it should be thus among all men so that each one might proceed to act justly and rightly toward them upon the earth, and (c) that they should circumcise their sons in the covenant which he made with them, and (d) that they should not cross over either to the right or left from all of the ways which the Lord commanded us, and (e) that we should keep ourselves from all fornication and pollution, and (f) that we should set aside from among us all fornication and pollution."

Jubilees 36:4: "And among yourselves, my sons, be loving of your brothers as a man loves himself, with each man seeking for his brother what is good for him, and acting together on the earth, and loving each other as themselves."

Testament of Reuben 6:9: "I call to witness the God of heaven that you do the truth, each to his neighbor, and that you show love, each to his brother."

Testament of Issachar 5:2: "Love the Lord and your neighbor; be compassionate toward poverty and sickness."

Testament of Gad 4:2: "Hatred does not want to hear repeated his commands concerning love of neighbor, and thus it sins against God."

Testament of Benjamin 3:3–4: "Fear the Lord and love your neighbor. Even if the spirits of Beliar seek to derange you with all sorts of wicked oppression, they will not dominate you, any more than they dominated Joseph, my brother. How many men wanted to destroy him, and God looked out for him! For the person who fears God and loves his neighbor cannot be plagued by the spirit of Beliar since he is sheltered by the fear of God."

19:20. The man said he had kept all of these commandments (Mark 10:20; Luke 18:21). Luke 18 adds from his youth he had done this. He was (over)confident that he had no need before God on this score. The statement was like that by Paul before he saw his need for Jesus (Rom. 7:7–8; Phil. 3:6). The inquiring man still wanted to know what he lacked, a detail only Matthew gives us. Either he had a sense he still was not there or else with confidence he wanted Jesus to assure him of blessing. Who knows which is present here?

19:21. Jesus replied with a series of challenges, five commands linked together (Culpepper 2021, 364: go, sell, give, come, and follow me; Mark 10:21; Luke 18:22). If he wanted to be perfect (Matt. 6:48)—that is, complete with a full maturity that showed his heart—then he was to sell all his possessions and give the money to the poor (Tob. 4:5–11; Luke 12:33). Jesus promised him that this would give him treasure in heaven. In effect Jesus asked the man to concretely love his neighbor with a full sacrifice and know that God would see it (Osborne 2010, 718). Jesus was not done. The rich man was then to come and follow Jesus. The present imperative for "follow" speaks of a continuous following. In the end in answering the initial question and in speaking of what it took to gain life, Jesus asked the man to follow him. That is where the request for eternal life begins and ends. Without this last step, the rest was trivial. However, the two parts are also linked, since the way to gain the ability to keep the commandments is to respond to Jesus and receive the divinely enabled grace God gives in the new covenant (i.e., the law on the heart). Jesus was checking to see if God and his way to the kingdom through Jesus was really first. The man needed to appreciate that what Jesus offered took one to the relational goals God had for his people. This linkage to life and its tie to relationships is why the two-part Great Commandment to love God and neighbor is great. It is a landing point for all of this. Just as the Sermon on the Mount dealt with the heart before God, so does Jesus's reply here. Caring for people with our resources is a part of this new way. Tobit 4:7–9 speaks of such generosity that lays up treasure in heaven.

19:22. The man departed, sad. His wealth meant too much to him (Mark 10:22; Luke 18:23). Konradt (2020, 293) says he "clings to his property." It was "property uber alles." Jesus had exposed the focus of the man's heart. It had become an obstacle to treasure in heaven. It is important to note this response was for this man and his need (Turner 2008, 471). The teaching reflected what Jesus had taught earlier in Matthew 13:44–46, that the kingdom was worth everything. There those who found what the kingdom contained were willing to sell what they had to obtain it. It also reprised the question what good was it to gain the world but lose the soul (Matt. 16:24–26). This man coveted possessions more than God (Matt. 6:24; also 6:33). Zacchaeus in Luke 19:1–10 was not asked to sell all; half was good enough because Zacchaeus's heart was in the right place as he responded to Jesus in making restitution for his wrong. As a result, Zacchaeus was commended by Jesus in Luke's gospel. That affirmation came in a gospel that said more about wealth than the other three gospels. First Timothy 6:17–19 shows how the rich should handle what God gives to them.

Our inability to give all in our own strength and our inability to earn salvation is in part why we need to turn to God. God can make it possible (Matt. 19:26–30). This wealthy man needed to become like a child and depend on God (Wilkins 2004, 649; Matt. 18:1–4; 19:13–15).

19:23–24. Jesus addressed the disciples, noting how hard it was for a rich person to enter the kingdom (Mark 10:23, 25; Luke 18:24–25). Mark 10:24 was not picked up by either Matthew or Luke. The term δυσκόλως means something takes place "with difficulty" (BDAG s.v. "δυσκόλως" 265). In fact, it was easier for a camel to go through the eye of a needle than for a rich person to enter the kingdom on their own. Jesus was indicating it was impossible on human terms, as his response in Matthew 19:26 showed. Although other meanings have been suggested to make the image less striking, they ignore this verse and the disciples' astonishment in the next.

19:25. Because it was believed rich people who were righteous were blessed (Prov. 3:9–10; 8:18–21; 22:4), the disciples were amazed (Mark 10:26; Luke 18:26). However, wealth was not an automatic sign of blessing and could lead to God judging the rich who took advantage of others (Prov. 22:16, 22–23; 1 Tim. 6:10).

Wealth in Proverbs

Proverbs 3:9–10: "Honor the Lord from your wealth and from the firstfruits of all your crops; then your barns will be filled completely, and your vats will overflow with new wine."

Proverbs 8:18–21: "Riches and honor are with me, long-lasting wealth and righteousness. My fruit is better than the purest gold, and my harvest is better than choice silver. I walk in the path of righteousness, in the pathway of justice, that I may cause those who love me to inherit wealth, and that I may fill their treasuries."

Proverbs 22:4: "The reward for humility and fearing the Lord is riches and honor and life."

Proverbs 22:16: "The one who oppresses the poor to increase his own gain and the one who gives to the rich—both end up only in poverty."

Proverbs 22:22–23: "Do not exploit a poor person because he is poor and do not crush the needy in court, for the Lord will plead their case and will rob the life of those who are robbing them."

The term ἐκπλήσσω ("astonished") in the Gospels usually refers to how people react in amazement to the force of Jesus's teaching or the power of his miracles (BDAG s.v. "ἐκπλήσσω" 308; Matt. 13:54; Mark 6:2: 7:37; Luke 2:48). The disciples asked, "Who then can be saved?" If a rich person could not get into the kingdom, then who could? The question at one level seems odd, because Jesus had affirmed the poor as recipients in Matthew 5:3. It was a question asked from shock because riches were commonly tied to blessing.

A variety of terms were overlapping to describe things associated with salvation in this text: eternal life (Matt. 19:16, 29), perfect (Matt. 19:21), saved (Matt. 19:25), kingdom of God (Matt. 19:24–25), and kingdom of heaven (Matt. 19:23). The terms showed the connection between the kingdom and salvation, between responding to Jesus and eternal life (Turner 2008, 473). They also showed that "kingdom of God" and "kingdom of heaven" meant the same thing (see the interchange of the phrases between vv. 23–24).

19:26. Jesus closed this part of the discussion by noting that what man could not do, God was able to accomplish (Mark 10:27; Luke 18:27). God could move and change hearts. To value God and place him first required God's inner work in the heart. Salvation was a gift from God (Eph. 2:8–10). Then it was possible, not just for the rich, but for anyone to respond to God. Divine work and human response were both affirmed in the text, but God must move to open and cleanse the heart. Zacchaeus (Luke 19:1–10), Joseph of Arimathea (Matt. 27:57), and Barnabas (Acts 4:36–37) were positive examples of rich people who had been responsive to God.

19:27. The last sequence in this discussion on eternal life came when Peter asked a final question. First, Peter affirmed that the Twelve had left everything to follow Jesus. He was looking for assurance that they had responded well (although Osborne 2010, 720, reads the remark negatively as "a delusion of grandeur"). Jesus's lack of rebuke for the premise spoke either to a genuine querying or the remark's positive force.

Peter asked what they would receive as a result. Peter had possibly noted that Jesus had spoken of reward and now wanted to know what might be coming (Matt. 5:3–10; 10:41–42; 16:27). Mark 10:28 only has the statement about leaving everything. Luke 18:28 follows Mark and adds they had left "our own things." Jesus first affirmed that reward was coming, but he also would warn in Matthew 25:14–30 that the reward was related to faithfulness. There was no room to be smug.

19:28–30. Jesus affirmed the disciples by noting what would come in the new era, what was called the "regeneration" (BDAG s.v. "παλιγγενεσία" 1b, 752). This reference to the new era alluded to Isaiah 65:17 and 66:22. The regeneration referred to the full blessing to come. That is where salvation will take things because it is about the restoration or new birth that returns us to what creation was designed to be. It is not a stoic hope, as Keener (2009, 480) correctly shows. The allusion to twelve thrones judging twelve tribes looks to a rule over Israel. In Acts 1:6–8, the Twelve were still asking about when this role for Israel would occur, even after Jesus had taught them after his resurrection. They discussed the hope in Acts 3:21. The regeneration involved the restoration of all things into righteousness about which the Hebrew prophets spoke. Israel was involved in what was to come and the Twelve would have a key role in that time of rule. Turner (2008, 476) notes that to see this as referring to the church judging the nations is to make an anachronistic point and dismiss why Israel was specifically noted here (but so read many, including Blomberg 1992, 301; France 2007, 744; Nolland 2005, 801; Osborne 2010, 722). With Turner in seeing a future for Israel is Davies and Allison (1997, 56–58), who also defend the saying about restoration as going back to Jesus. Peter proclaimed a future that was described in detail by the prophets of the Hebrew Scripture and that had a role for the nation of Israel. The New Testament also speaks of believers ruling in a general sense (1 Cor. 4:8; 6:2; Eph. 2:6—but as a present authority of spiritual access; Rev. 1:6; 3:21; 20:4–6).

Restoration

Davies and Allison (1997) see the restoration as a reference to a new age of messianic rule, but say Matthew did not really engage the detail of whether this was an earthly kingdom or a renewed earth (Nolland 2005, 799, sees a new earth claiming a mix of Stoic and Jewish background; contrast the more circumspect remarks of Morris 1992, 495–96, about the lack of details here, saying only this is about cosmic renewal and a judging in which the apostles will have a role. Nolland appealed to Matthew 5:18 and 24:35 to support his reading). Jesus did see a renewal of the earth, a new earth, but it is not clear at all that this was all he saw in the future. Much of how one reads this text turns on how one sees Luke's teaching about a future for Israel that is tied to Jesus and the apostles, as well as how one reads Revelation 20:4–6 and the teaching on millennium (for these issues, see Bock [2013] on Luke–Acts and Bock [1999] on issues tied to the millennium debate). Jesus may well be pointing to a time of real rule and judging over Israel in the era to come, including a millennium before a period involving the new earth. There would be irony in this and vindication for Jesus and the apostles, given the current rejection by so many in Israel and the casting out that the disciples had experienced. Matthew was documenting that what was then going on would be reversed, as also was noted with the blessing in the Beatitudes.

Jesus noted in passing that Peter and his company were said to have done what was required, even though Peter still had his home and boat (France 2007, 742) and even though they were described as leaving their nets behind (Matt. 4:20, 22). The issue with the rich man involved a probe of his heart that was not in the same place as the hearts of the disciples like Peter.

Except for the transition into the reply, everything said in Matthew 19:28 is unique to Matthew. The direct promise of rule over Israel in the era to come (Luke 22:30; Rev. 21:12) and when the Son of Man would show his authority was a direct answer to Peter about the Twelve. The mention of the Son of Man with others sharing in that rule may also look to Daniel 7:9–27. Such a rule Judaism also expected for the Messiah (Pss. Sol. 17:28). Davies and Allison (1997, 54) also note that Matthew alone in the New Testament speaks of a throne for the Son of Man, leading Davies and Allison to ask if Matthew might have known of 1 Enoch 37–71 (on this 1 Enoch text and its use in Matthew and availability to Jesus, see Bock and Charlesworth 2013). Davies and Allison (1997, 55–56) argue that this judgment was not a condemnation of Israel but related to governing, as Daniel 7:9–27 suggests (also Luke 22:28–30). France (2007, 744) holds out for an alternative, speaking of announcing judgment to Israel and arguing that the verb "to judge" nowhere meant rule (also Luz 2001, 517). However, rule is seen in the imagery about seating on a throne or a sending from heaven (Matt. 13:41–43; Rev. 3:21; 20:6), not in the verb alone (Wilkins 2004, 651–52). The passage does not exclude judging as that is a part of ruling (Matt. 16:27; 25:31–32), but the authority was broader than judgment. Wilkins (2004, 652) is right to see a future for Israel and hope of rule here. This fit with what Luke–Acts teaches from Jesus and the apostles, especially in several "until" texts where judgment on Israel for rejection is temporary and anticipates a turning back of the nation to her Messiah (Bock 2013; Luke 13:34–35; 21:24; Acts 1:6–8; 3:18–21).

Psalms of Solomon on the Kingdom

Psalms of Solomon 17:21–32: "See, Lord, and raise up for them their king, the son of David, to rule over your servant Israel in the time known to you, O God. Undergird him with the strength to destroy the unrighteous rulers, to purge Jerusalem from Gentiles who trample her to destruction; in wisdom and in righteousness to drive out the sinners from the inheritance; to smash the arrogance of sinners like a potter's jar; To shatter all their substance with an iron rod; to destroy the unlawful nations with the word of his mouth; At his warning the nations will flee from his presence; and he will condemn sinners by the thoughts of their hearts. He will gather a holy people whom he will lead in righteousness; and he will judge the tribes of the people that have been made holy by the Lord their God. He will not tolerate unrighteousness (even) to pause among them, and any person who knows wickedness shall not live with them. For he shall know them that they are all children of their God. He will distribute them upon the land according to their tribes; the alien and the foreigner will no longer live near them. He will judge peoples and nations in the wisdom of his righteousness. And he will have Gentile nations serving him under his yoke, and he will glorify the Lord in (a place) prominent (above) the whole earth. And he will purge Jerusalem (and make it) holy as it was even from the beginning, (for) nations to come from the ends of the earth to see his glory, to bring as gifts her children who had been driven out, and to see the glory of the Lord with which God has glorified her. And he will be a righteous king over them, taught by God. There will be no unrighteousness among them in his days, for all shall be holy, and their king shall be the Lord Messiah."

Jesus then addressed what all would receive (Mark 10:29–31; Luke 18:29–30). Matthew and Mark share the final remark about eschatological reversal that Luke lacks. Jesus promised that anyone who left family or labor for the sake of his name would gain one hundred times more and eternal life in the new era. Mark speaks of receiving things like more family in the present time. Matthew looks to the end as the time when one would be recompensed. Luke has the time of recompense as involving both the present and the future, family now and eternal life to come. In sum, the family of God will be big. God's provision will be huge. The quality of life with God will never end. The passage ends where it started in verse 16, with eternal life as the topic. Those who came to Jesus and connected to his name would have eternal life. What was lost then was nothing compared to what would be gained later.

The responsibility this entails was noted in the parable that followed in Matthew 20:1–16, which also ends with the remark about the last being first and the first last. One could very easily place that parable in this section and view the chapter break here as unfortunate, since no fresh setting was given to introduce the parable in Matthew 20:1. However, to treat the parable as distinct but related to these remarks also makes sense, for there the issue has shifted to appreciating the grace one gets as a recipient of God's goodness. In sum, these verses form a transition into the next parable. The remarks looked back and forward.

In the era to come, there will be reversal, where many who have it well here will not then. Many who lack now will be first then. This reversal theme is noted elsewhere in the New Testament (Matt. 5:3–10; 20:16; Mark 9:35; Luke 1:52–54; 6:20–26; 13:30). Davies and Allison (1997, 61) speak of this entire reply as offering congratulations, an apt description as Jesus reaffirmed what these disciples have done.

THEOLOGICAL FOCUS

The exegetical idea (after noting that the kingdom belonged to people who are like children, and while asking that one leave all behind and follow him, Jesus observed that wealth often blocked one from coming to the kingdom and following him) leads to this theological focus: Jesus discusses humility and then has a conversation with a rich man that shows how wealth can be an obstacle to the pursuit of God.

Warning about how riches make response difficult, Jesus showed how eternal life is tied to following him and giving God first place, something that reaps rich reward and eternal life.

This passage—with its mixture of keeping the commandments, the call to sell all, and the discussion of wealth and following Jesus, as well as themes of eschatology—is one of the most complex texts in Matthew. The text is clear that following Jesus involves a divine work in the heart to change the way we naturally see things and how we respond to others. The passage challenges what we tend to be drawn to in gaining security in life. The rich man's failure shows who we are without a focus on God. We seek for, and cling to, what we possess. Treasure in heaven does not come from clinging to what we have. It comes from turning to the living God and trusting what he provides through Jesus, a heavenly treasure named at the end of the passage that includes a big, new family. That treasure also gives us possession of the greatest thing of all, eternal life in the presence of God. To go there, one must be humble, trusting, and dependent as a child. One can also be assured that whatever lack of status a believer has in the world, they have full status with God. Jesus welcomed the children to show that all have stature before God. It is no accident that Matthew has the remark about being like a child before he works through this more complex scene with the rich man. As the parable of the soils showed, riches can be a distraction from approaching God. This scene shows why.

In the end, the question about eternal life was resolved in Jesus's call to follow him. Those who do so for his name's sake are rewarded by God, so what they lose now is nothing compared to what they will gain later. This was said to reassure Peter and the disciples that God honored their choice to leave all and follow Jesus. The same is true of disciples today.

One day the apostles will share in Jesus's rule. They will help to preside over righteousness. Matthew does not give details here about how that will work or even of the exact time frames. Other New Testament texts in Luke, Acts, and Revelation help us with those ideas. Israel will be involved. The Twelve will have authority over all people, and Israel will be present.

The stress of the text is not on those eschatological details, but merely the fact that one can follow Jesus, know God, and become a citizen of heaven who sees one's life on earth as a sojourn of one who is an alien in a different land and yet cares and serves. Such an allegiance is what the disciples were experiencing. Jesus was grateful for it (Luke 22:28–30). As believers turn to him, not only are they rewarded with life but they are given the capability to live as God would have people live so others are loved and cared for, the very things called for in Jesus's opening reply to the rich man. Salvation is not earned by our works or by keeping the commandments. Rather, the one who trusts God walks in ways that please him as a result of salvation and are led to do what God desires and commands. Works are not a cause of salvation but a product of God's saving presence in our lives.

PREACHING AND TEACHING STRATEGIES

Exegetical and Theological Synthesis

Wealth is a common theme in Jesus's teaching. Jesus never treated money as evil; however, he understood its idolatrous pull (Matt. 6:24; cf.

1 Tim. 6:10). In his first sermon, he encouraged almsgiving (Matt. 6:2–6), prayed for daily bread (6:11), and warned against trusting in material goods (6:19–34). Moreover, as an itinerant preacher, he learned to rely on God and others' hospitality.

The call to discipleship required Jesus's followers to forsake self-reliance and adopt lives of simplicity (Matt. 4:18–22; 8:18–22; 10:9–15). As mentioned in the exegetical section, Jesus did not require all disciples to liquidate their wealth. In fact, many stewarded their wealth well. Female disciples financially supported Jesus's ministry (Luke 8:1–3). The rich Joseph of Arimathea funded Jesus's tomb (Matt. 27:57). Later, the early church pooled its resources to serve the poor in Jerusalem (Acts 4:32–37; cf. 2 Cor. 8–9). Although wealth is a terrible master, the Bible illustrates how it can effectively serve kingdom purposes.

The willingness to sacrifice money to serve Jesus is a genuine mark of a disciple. Discipleship is costly (Matt. 16:24–27). However, as Jesus assured Peter, the rewards outweigh the costs. Earthly sacrifices will result in heavenly rewards (19:28–30). Again, no one can pay his way to heaven. Giving, serving, and sacrificing are an outworking of God's grace, not a way of earning it.

Preaching Idea

Wealth is worthless if it keeps us from Jesus.

Contemporary Connections

What does it mean?

Saying wealth is worthless means we cannot purchase good standing with God or buy our way to heaven. We are talking about worldly wealth—money, personal assets, and material goods. God is not impressed with our retirement portfolios, charitable giving records, or savvy use of coupons. He does not rank us by the number of properties we own, cars we drive, or vacations we take.

Conversely, such wealth may grieve God because it becomes a barrier to our loyalty, love, and service for him. Our golf membership limits our attendance in church. Upkeep of our elaborate home keeps us from practicing hospitality. The energy we give to investing, online shopping, and negotiating a deal makes us fixate on securing our money rather than on our security in God.

Is it true?

It is true that wealth is worthless if it keeps us from Jesus. However, as noted above, there were wealthy disciples. According to Paul, the secret to following Jesus while managing wealth was contentment (Phil. 4:11–13). Moreover, gratitude and generosity help wealthy disciples set Jesus above mammon (1 Tim. 6:6–10). The richest people see every good gift as coming from the heavenly Father (James 1:17).

It is also worth noting that wealth has positive uses. In fact, in a surprising parable, Jesus described how wealth could be used to make friends (Luke 16:1–9). In another parable, Jesus illustrated how stewardship of wealth could demonstrate faithfulness (Matt. 25:14–30). Wealth could also provide for needy people and pay workers (Matt. 20:1–16; James 1:27). Businesses that fail to compensate their employees out of greed may need to hear the rebuke of James 5:1–6. The call is to be generous with what God gives us and hold what we have with loose hands.

Finally, we should be cautious of going to the other extreme and lionizing poverty. Poor people are not inherently more virtuous than the wealthy. Poverty is not a direct path to discipleship. Poverty can provoke anxiety, bitterness, entitlement, or envy. Those in dire situations may be tempted to steal, take advantage of others, or cheat systems. While wealth obscures our desperation, poverty can explode it. The poor may not see God because they are so fixated on finding their daily bread.

Now what?

Wealthy people are not barred from the kingdom of God; however, wealth makes drawing close to Jesus difficult. To keep their money from becoming an obstacle to discipleship, they should develop the following practices: gratitude, generosity, and simplicity.

Gratitude views wealth, opportunity, and privilege as a gift. A grateful person recognizes that wealth is not simply earned but inherited or received. One regularly thanks God for the thousands of little gifts encountered daily: a warm bed, indoor plumbing, clean socks, a favorite podcast, an income, groceries, close friends, a worn Bible, candlelight, and a familiar hymn at church. Cultivating gratitude helps fight entitlement.

Generosity keeps wealth from piling up for no purpose other than personal security. Generous people believe Jesus's quotation that giving is better than receiving (Acts 20:35). They view their wealth as a resource for enriching others. In addition to giving money, they give time, energy, and emotional support. Generous people give regularly, freely, and joyfully. Practicing generosity helps them stifle greed.

Simplicity is a choice to put limits on our lives. The person who practices simplicity does not spend too much money or overextend his time. He prefers constraints to excess, a few options to hundreds. In our indulgent age, with endless distractions and countless ways to waste money, the simple person says "no" often because he has predetermined a better "yes." Simplicity affects bedtimes, wardrobe, diet, entertainment, social media consumption, and spending. Living simply helps us resist indulgence.

Creativity in Presentation

Movies and literature have provided some memorable misers. These characters embody the power of greed:

- King Midas from the "the Midas (golden) touch" myth
- Ebenezer Scrooge from Dickens's *A Christmas Carol*
- Scrooge McDuck from Disney's *DuckTales*
- Shylock in Shakespeare's *The Merchant of Venice*
- Mr. Potter from the film *It's a Wonderful Life*

Pictures of these characters and a sentence summarizing how their wealth turned them inward could be effective.

Sadly, real-life misers may also illustrate the corruptive influence of money. Kellen Perry lists eleven historic misers—from a husband who starved his wife to a boss who fired his employee over a wasted paperclip.[1]

Charitable giving remains low among Americans. According to Greer and Horst (2018, 62), for nearly fifty years the figure has peaked at 2 percent of the GDP. This figure falls well below the 10 percent that is often associated with a tithe. In other words, there is room to grow in our generosity. Greer and Horst (2018, 118–20), who fundraise for HOPE International, have an unusual practice: they "give away their platform" and publicly recommend other charitable organizations. They do this on Giving Tuesday, which follows Black Friday and feeds into the end-of-the-year giving frenzy. What drives them is a theology of abundance—God gives more than enough to spread the wealth. This sermon gives you a chance to challenge generosity. Consider displaying the two-percent (2%) figure in large bold lettering. Then, following Greer and Horst's model, reference five charitable causes beyond the church and encourage people to give. These could include a local shelter for houseless people or abuse victims, food pantry, reputable orphan care ministry, mobile medical clinic, or mentoring

1 See https://www.ranker.com/list/famous-misers/kellen-perry (accessed July 24, 2024).

program. Let your people know that "wealth is worth more when you share it."

This sermon could induce audience participation. Play a game called "Need It or Not?" Gather a pile of items we often spend money on. Hold them up or display them on a screen, one at a time, and ask, "Need it or not?" Encourage people to respond with a single word, and wait for a reply. For example:

- A tenth pair of shoes. Need it or not?
- A venti soy, no whip, peppermint mocha latte. Need it or not?
- A stylish yoga mat. Need it or not?
- The Lord of the Rings extended version DVD boxed set. Need it or not?
- Any DVD. Need it or not?
- A fifty-dollar gift card to Amazon. Need it or not?
- Another book by James Patterson. Need it or not?
- Any book by James Patterson. Need it or not?

The exercise illustrates how much unnecessary stuff we have. Surely we could spend less, give more, and simplify our lives.

Finally, check out ilikegiving.com for a library of delightful, well-produced videos on generosity. "I Like Car" shows a woman named Catherine give away her entire savings to help a widow. "I cannot give what I do not have," Catherine said, "so I gave what I had." At the end of the video, her generosity is rewarded. The I Like Giving website, founded by Brad Formsma, identifies seven ways to live generously—thoughts, words, time, money, influence, attention, and belongings—and offers other great resources.

Ultimately, you want your sermon to show how Jesus discusses humility and then has a conversation with a rich man that shows how wealth can be an obstacle to the pursuit of God. Indeed, wealth is worthless if it keeps us from Jesus.

- Humility opens us to Jesus (19:13–15).
- Wealth closes us off to Jesus (19:16–26).
- Temporary losses open us to eternal gains (19:27–30).

DISCUSSION QUESTIONS

1. How does this teaching on children relate to Matthew 18:1–5?
2. What is the significance of the commandments Jesus cited to the young man?
3. What makes wealth such a powerful obstacle to discipleship? Be specific.
4. How can you encourage sacrificial living and giving in your congregation?

Matthew 20:1–16

EXEGETICAL IDEA

Jesus's parable of the hired workers showed God's grace by highlighting that all who come receive the same benefits no matter when they come—something all were to appreciate about grace.

THEOLOGICAL FOCUS

Grace gives the same access to God's benefits, no matter when we come to him.

PREACHING IDEA

There's plenty of grace for last place.

PREACHING POINTERS

Matthew recounted another parable of Jesus. The story of the generous manager is unique to Matthew. It described a manager hiring groups of laborers from dawn to the end of the day but paying them an equal wage. His generosity surprised the earliest group of workers, who expected a greater amount for their longer shift. Their reaction exposed a faulty understanding of grace as merited rather than received. For the original audience, benefaction and grace were built into everyday economics (Keener 2009, 481–83). Moreover, the caution against envy would have challenged their desire for greater reward at the expense of others. Again, Jesus illustrated his heavenly Father's inclusive and extravagant nature.

God's grace is an inexhaustible resource. This is good news. And it is good news for all people, since God's grace extends to anyone willing to receive it. Those born into Christian families in Midwestern suburbs can receive grace. Those who unexpectedly encounter Christ in a liberal university can receive grace. Those who first meet Christ through a dream and break from their Muslim upbringing can receive grace. And those who respond to a chaplain's gospel presentation within hours of their death can receive God's grace. We neither earn nor inherit grace. God mercifully extends it up to the eleventh hour. This sermon communicates that there's plenty of grace for last place.

JESUS TELLS THE PARABLE OF THE HIRED WORKERS (20:1–16)

LITERARY STRUCTURE AND THEMES (20:1–16)

This unit is built around a single parable that has the sequence of hiring (Matt. 20:1–7) followed by the doling out of wages (Matt. 20:8–16). Despite being unique, the parable does belong in a group of parables where God is a landowner and oversees workers (Matt. 10:25; 13:27; 21:33–46; 24:42–51; 25:14–30; Luke 12:35–38; 13:6–9). These parables fit the agrarian background of the people Jesus taught and emphasized the accountability people have to God as owner or master.

The parable was built around five rounds of trips to hire workers during a day: in the morning, at nine, noon, three, and five. For day laborers, the custom was that they would gather in the city square or marketplace and be hired out for a proper day's wage. Here the vineyard owner agreed to pay the first group a denarius for the day and then continued to add workers throughout the day for "whatever is right." The rub was that at the end of the day, when all are paid, the first and last groups hired all got the same wage. The complaint was that this was not fair. The reply was that the wages those hired earliest had received had already been negotiated. The owner reserved the right to pay those who came later what he wished. There was no need to envy generosity. The last were first and the first last. The use of this final saying matches Matthew 19:30 and connects this unit to that one. The use of the expression here is distinct. In the earlier use the point was about eschatological reversal, while here the point is that there is no first and last in rank in God's grace (with Davies and Allison 1997, 68, while defending its roots in Jesus's teaching; contra Turner 2008, 477, who sees the saying as a bracket for the parable meaning the same thing in each place). All received the same benefits. Grace left no room for boasting or pride.

A few themes appear in the story. God is gracious to those he brings into his presence to labor with him (France 2007, 749). There is no room for envy for those who are all given grace in the same manner. The community consists of people all of whom have what they have because God is good and kind. No matter when one comes or how long they have labored, they are full members of the community.

EXPOSITION (20:1–16)

Grace is not ultimately about reward, although God does honor his own. What believers have access to is shared among them, because they all receive what God graciously gives no matter when they enter into God's blessing. This should prevent any jealousy or envy. Sharing the same blessing should tighten the bonds between believers as they labor together in the calling God has given them. This equal share in God's grace probably served as a contrast to the pursuit of merit or honor in both the Jewish and Greco-Roman cultures. We serve because God has graciously provided for us and brought us into his work. Our labor is a product of being the beneficiaries of grace and promise, not something to be earned or competed for through length of service.

Jesus's parable of the hired workers showed God's grace by highlighting that all who come receive the same benefits no matter when they come, something all were to appreciate about grace.

20:1–2. Jesus told a parable about a landowner needing workers for his vineyard. He hired them daily. The landowner went to the marketplace early in the morning (probably 6 a.m.) and found some there who were ready to work for the day. He told them he would pay them a denarius a day, a standard day's wage (Tob. 5:15; Tacitus, *Ann.* 1.17; Nolland 2005, 806 n. 145). A denarius is the Roman coin name for the drachma in Greek. The workers agreed and went to work in the vineyard. In the Old Testament, Israel is the vineyard (Isa. 5:1–7). Culpepper (2021, 371–72) nicely overviews the general economic situation in Galilee. Agriculture and fishing were key economic drivers, but the region also had pottery work, weaving, oil pressing, and flour milling. Many agricultural workers were illiterate and worked on a daily basis in the fields. Elites would hire them, or they might get picked up to help on a small plot of land. Culpepper also notes that the wage earned could buy about ten days' worth of wheat. So it was a typical but very basic wage. Here the vineyard pictured the kingdom and labor for it.

Denarius/Drachma a Day

Tobit 5:15: "Then he added, 'I will pay you a drachma a day as wages, as well as expenses for yourself and my son.'"

20:3–5a. At the third hour, which was measured from sunrise, the owner returned to do the same thing. It was now nine o'clock. He promised to pay them "whatever is right" (BDAG s.v. "δίκαιος" 2, 246–47). They went to work.

20:5b–7. The owner repeated the process at noon and at three o'clock. Finally, at five, he went one last time for the final hour of labor. He asked why those present in the marketplace were not working. They responded that they had not been hired. There is no note whether this was true or whether the men not hired were lazy. The owner simply generously gave them all work. Everything about the scene pointed to the urgency of a harvesttime labor (although Nolland 2005, 806, disagrees, since nothing was said of the point). Such hiring for harvest would need no mention. The very repetition of hiring during the day makes this meaning likely. It was no accident that Jesus was discussing labor as a picture for kingdom harvest. The image pointed to work for the kingdom, or fruit.

20:8–9. The owner now paid the workers as he instructed his "manager" to pay them last to first (BDAG 38 s.v. "ἐπιτρόπος" 1, 385; of Chuza in Luke 8:3). The language of "last and first" looks back to Matthew 19:30 and forward to Matthew 20:16. The idea of paying promptly is an Old Testament teaching (Lev. 19:13; Deut. 24:15; Josephus, *A.J.* 20.220). The last hired "eleventh-hour" workers were paid a denarius, a day's wage. France (2007, 750) suggests they were paid out of a sensitivity for their need, not pure reward for labor (also Morris 1992, 501).

On Paying Wages Quickly

Leviticus 19:13: "You must not oppress your neighbor or commit robbery against your neighbor. You must not withhold the wages of the hired laborer overnight until morning."

Deuteronomy 24:15: "You must pay his wage that very day before the sun sets, for he is poor and his life depends on it. Otherwise he will cry out to the Lord against you, and you will be guilty of sin."

Josephus, ***Antiquities*** **2.220:** "While they were unwilling to keep them by their treasuries that were there deposited, out of fear of [their being carried away by] the Romans; and while they had a regard to the making provision for the workmen, they had a mind to expend those treasures upon them; for if any one of them did but labor for a single hour, he received his pay immediately; so they persuaded him to rebuild the eastern cloisters."

20:10–12. Those who worked all day thought they would get paid more. Perhaps because they worked twelve times as long, they expected twelve times the wage (Turner 2008, 479). However, they were paid one denarius as well. The payment led them to complain to the landowner about injustice. The imperfect tense for grumbling pictured an ongoing discontent that began when they got less than they expected ("They began to complain"). The term sounds like what it is (BDAG s.v. "γογγύζω" 1, 204). This lingering complaint seemed to be pictured as well in a movement from complaining to the manager when they were paid and the owner was not present to the owner then being present to deal with the complaint directly in verse 13.

Here was the complaint: the eleventh-hour workers only labored for an hour and avoided the bulk of the work as well as the heat of the day. Yet they have been treated equally. That was not right. In a sense, one can feel the power of the criticism and sense of injustice in the reaction. However, the reply said that something more profound was taking place.

20:13–15. The owner responded with two points to an individual who represented the entire group. The address as "friend" was a mild but respectful rebuke in this setting (BDAG s.v. "ἑταῖρος" 398; Blomberg 1992, 304). Those complaining were thinking about themselves alone and not others (Wilkins 2004, 665). No one had received more than another. All had received what they were promised. All had needs met.

First, there was nothing unfair in paying what was agreed would be the wage for the labor (Matt. 20:2). This was asked as a question that expects a positive reply (οὐχί). "Didn't you agree with me to work for the standard wage?" Yes, they had. He told them to take what was theirs and go. Legally in terms of what had been agreed, no violation had taken place. No one was cheated out of what had been decided. Yet there was more than what was legal going on here. The owner dismissed the complaining worker and told him to go but added one more word.

The owner then expressed his desire to pay the last laborers the same as the first. This will connect to what will be said in Matthew 20:16. The owner desired to be gracious to the others, and he had that right as well. So he asked if he was not permitted to do what he wished with what belonged to him. Again, a positive reply was expected (οὐκ). He then asked if "their eye was evil" because the owner was good to others. He was accusing them of being covetous or ungrateful. He implied they were selfish. In this context, an evil eye was a jealous, resentful eye. Matthew 6:23 also has the evil eye image, noting what it indicated about a person. The owner was defending his action as good, kind, and gracious. When wages were given to all who had nothing before they were hired, then who should complain if a fair, set, and predetermined wage was paid to all and some are given more grace? The owner had been just *and* merciful; just to the original workers and merciful to those who came later. The theme echoes in the story of the acceptance of the prodigal as well, where there was a similar cry of injustice from the complaining brother (Luke 15:11–32).

20:16. The scene closes by noting the last were first and the first last. In this context it meant that they had been treated equally in terms of benefits. The remark looks back to Matthew 20:12 and the accusation of having made the later workers equal to the earlier ones. It transformed the claim of the complaint by the workers into a sign of generosity by the owner, not injustice. It was reinforced by Matthew 20:14 and the desire the owner had to give his laborers the same wage. Of course, the picture is that all are saved with the same gracious benefit of life; some are not "more saved" than others (France 2007, 751). The parable's conclusion is open-ended, since there was no picture of how things were resolved nor how those who complained had reacted (Nolland 2005, 812). It was there for Matthew's readers to ponder. They should appreciate that God is gracious to all he gathers to share in his labor. We should rejoice for all who are included (Wilkins 2004, 666).

THEOLOGICAL FOCUS

The exegetical idea (Jesus's parable of the hired workers showed God's grace by highlighting that all who come receive the same benefits no matter when they come—something all were to appreciate about grace) leads to this theological focus: grace gives the same access to God's benefits, no matter when we come to him.

The equality of what God gives in salvation should not lead to jealousy but joy because God is gracious to all.

God is good and gracious. That is the point of this parable where everyone receives the same wage for the work in the field. He gives what he promises to those who come early. He gives more than expected to those who come late. All have their needs met. Whether one labors long and hard for God or one receives grace near the end of life, God welcomes all as his children. We should not begrudge what happens with others but be grateful for what God has given to each of us, especially since what we receive we gain by his grace and the product of his mercy. That is this parable's simple message.

The reading of this idea, especially of first and last, has caused many to draw implications from this simple image. Those extensions of the parable also have merit, even though they are not the image's explicit intent. In the time of Jesus one can contrast the pious responder as the first, while the tax collector or sinner as the last. Yet both get in. One can contrast the Jewish believer as first and the Gentile believer as later. Yet both get in. In life, one can think of a person who believes as a child as first and a deathbed conversion as last. Yet both get in. All of these ways of thinking about how the parable works do reflect its point. God's grace extends in such a way that whether we connect to his mission early or late, we are in and share in the same benefits. God's way is rooted in grace, because all of us need what he provides regardless of whether we get it early or late. Disciples are simply to rejoice that they are in, and to be encouraged by all others who receive grace from God.

PREACHING AND TEACHING STRATEGIES

Exegetical and Theological Synthesis

The kingdom of God turned the social world of Jesus's day upside down. Jesus showed incredible affection for the lower class, outcast, and misfit. He demonstrated this in his repeated embrace of children (Matt. 18:1–5; 19:13–14), inclusion of female followers (Luke 8:1–3), a motley crew of disciples (Matt. 10:1–4), and interaction with tax collectors and sinners (9:9–13). Moreover, he advocated for ministry to those in the margins, the so-called "least of these" (25:31–46).

Of course, this welcome of tax collectors, sinners, and social misfits upset the religious elite of his day. This led to the three-part parable of lost things (Luke 15). In the famed "lost son" story, the older brother sounds similar to the grumbling workers who were hired first in the story of the generous landowner (Matt. 20:1–16). God's grace extends to all people willing to accept it.

Sadly, sometimes religious performance dulls our felt need for grace. In his sobering description of human depravity, Paul showed how people rejected God in pursuit of pleasure and destructive behavior (Rom. 1:18–32). It is too easy to read this story of sinful descent as a tale for godless, worldly pagans. However, Romans 2 turns the tables; even law-abiding, churchgoing, religiously active people need grace. Hays (1996, 389) calls this a "theological sting operation," also known as a "gotcha" moment. Religion's greatest trick is convincing people they have evolved beyond the need for grace. Sin struggles remain throughout life, leaving a prevailing need for grace (Rom. 3:23–24).

Preaching Idea

There's plenty of grace for last place.

Contemporary Connections

What does it mean?

God does not reserve grace for the religious elite, A+ Christians or try-hards of the faith. He offers it to all people. His grace is a gift, his invitation to eternal life and everlasting favor. It reflects his overwhelming generosity, not our outstanding performance. It is not based upon effort, rank, status, or personal accomplishment. Thus, even those who stumble along in life, struggling to pay their bills, read their Bibles, tame their tongues, and show up at church have God's grace available to them.

Is it true?

It is true that grace is available for last place. Indeed, there's plenty of it. Grace is an inexhaustible resource because it flows from a rich God who gives lavishly (Eph. 1:6–8). Not only does he give grace, but mercy and love (Ps. 145:8; Eph. 2:4). The gift of his beloved Son Jesus, who gave his life for our sins, was the ultimate gesture of his generosity (John 3:16; 15:13).

Unfortunately, the manifold gift of grace is difficult to believe when most of society is merit-based. The top students earn the best scholarships. The star athletes earn blockbuster contracts. Even the early bird gets the worm. Therefore, few worms, contracts, and scholarships remain for late risers, latecomers, late bloomers, and those at the back of the line.

Now what?

The parable offers three principles of application: work hard, be grateful, and quit keeping score. First, faithful people work. Paul and James agreed on this. Paul encouraged believers to work out their salvation earnestly (Phil. 2:12–13). He called believers "God's workmanship" and insisted we had good works to do (Eph. 2:10). Moreover, the apostle modeled a life of hard work and intense labor (1 Cor. 15:10; 2 Cor. 11:23; Col. 1:29–2:1; 1 Thess. 2:9). To be clear, this effort was evidence of faith, not an attempt to earn God's grace.

Second, gratitude is the appropriate response to God's abundant grace. He is the great benefactor; we are the humble beneficiaries. He rewards; we receive. Grace is a gift given by a generous God to undeserving rebels, selfish sinners, and eleventh-hour laborers. We cannot forget that before responding to God's gracious calling, each of us was dead in sin (Eph. 2:1–3). Or, to borrow from the parable of the Generous Manager, before God recruited us to his cause, we were waiting on a street corner with no money, no job, and no way of securing our future. Remembering where we came from provokes gratitude.

Third, we should quit keeping score. Paul wrote that "love keeps no record of wrongs" (1 Cor. 13:5 NIV). Neither should it keep a record of "rights." God is not impressed with our scorecard of moral victories, religious triumphs, and physical feats. Perfect attendance at small group does not make us better than the members who regularly miss. A better grasp of the Bible will not earn us a bigger mansion in heaven. Conversely, God gives no less grace to those who never experienced a mission trip, rarely share their faith, and struggle with addiction. Performance, rank, and status only obscure our universal need for grace.

Creativity in Presentation

For years I (Tim) have coached cross-country. Practices can be grueling, but races are rewarding. Runners have an opportunity to prove themselves on the course. One of the unique aspects of cross-country is that every athlete does the same thing. There are no positions or roles—everyone runs the same race. Spectators typically congregate at the start and finish lines to cheer on runners. Here's an interesting observation: the front-runners and last-place finisher get the loudest cheers. In fact, on numerous occasions, I have watched teammates surround the last-place runner on the final 100 meters of the race. They cheer. The crowd cheers. It's a lovely picture of grace for last place.

This message will give you a chance to expose how prevalent meritocracy is in our culture. Let the congregation know you want them to participate by finishing a few phrases.

- The early bird . . . gets the worm.
- Second place is the . . . first loser.
- You get what you . . . deserve.
- Fail to prepare . . . prepare to fail.
- No guts . . . no glory.
- No pain . . . no gain.
- Early to bed, early to rise, makes us . . . healthy, wealthy, and wise.
- If you dream it, you can . . . achieve it.

You should note these phrases betray simple logic and reflect common grace, but when applied to our life with God, they distort our understanding of saving grace.

A cafeteria, wedding banquet, or church carry-in provides a picture of plenty. Help your people imagine the last time they attended such an event. Even if they came into the cafeteria in the closing minutes or sat at the last table dismissed for food at the banquet, they realized there was plenty of food. In fact, whenever calls for "seconds" or "thirds" sounded, it reiterated the point: there's plenty for all. (I experienced this every summer of my childhood at summer camp, where tables were called by a lottery system. The longer my table waited, the more anxious I felt. Inevitably, we were called. Inevitably, there was enough food.)

Finally, collect enough coins or candy to distribute during your sermon. Have a bucket (or several) filled with items to give away. As you or a few others walk around the auditorium, remind the people in the back rows that there will be plenty for them. Just like grace does not run out, your supply of coins (or Jolly Ranchers) will be sufficient. (Note: There may be an opportunity to make a joke about the choice seats being the back row, and the front row functioning as the only seats available for latecomers.)

For this sermon, your goal is to clearly show that grace gives the same access to God's benefits, no matter when we come to him. Hence, there's plenty of grace for last place.

- There are plenty of opportunities to work (20:1–7).
- There is plenty of reward for working (20:8–16).

DISCUSSION QUESTIONS

1. How does this parable relate to others about work and reward?
2. What kind of work were the day laborers doing? Is this detail significant?
3. How can you explain the difference between working *for* our salvation and working *from* our salvation?
4. What is evidence of meritocracy in our culture? How does it rob us of gratitude?
5. Where have you seen God's grace on display in your life and church?

Matthew 20:17–28

EXEGETICAL IDEA

Announcing his coming suffering, Jesus issued a call to be a servant for those asking about kingdom rank, with the example being his death as a ransom.

THEOLOGICAL FOCUS

Jesus reconfigures how rank in the world should work by pointing to the example of being a servant.

PREACHING IDEA

Service over status is the way of Jesus.

PREACHING POINTERS

Matthew records Jesus's third and most detailed passion prediction. His arrival in Jerusalem will upset the social order and will lead to his gruesome death. News of Jesus's death and resurrection does not penetrate his disciples' delusions of grandeur. In fact, the mother of James and John requests seats of honor for her sons. Rather than a crown, Jesus warned they would share his call to service and cup of suffering. For the original audience, these themes remained relevant. In a culture obsessed with honor, the status of a servant forced them to rethink their lust for status.

The drive for status is timeless. Although today's status symbols may differ from Jesus's era, the want for power, prestige, rank, and honor remain. In the modern era, status shows up in the size of one's popularity or platform. Influencers have status. We rank people based upon their beauty, athleticism, or physical strength. Athletes and celebrities have status. We herald successful CEOs, entrepreneurs, and politicians. The rich have status. Meanwhile, those who keep houses, care for the elderly, teach children, wait tables, and work retail rarely make headlines. Service is not a status symbol in our culture. This sermon comes as a corrective. Service over status is the way of Jesus.

JESUS PREDICTS HIS SUFFERING AND PRESENTS HIS SERVICE AS AN EXAMPLE (20:17–28)

LITERARY STRUCTURE AND THEMES (20:17–28)

This unit is set in three parts. Jesus's passion prediction comes first (Matt. 20:17–19). Then comes the request for the sons of Zebedee to sit with Jesus in power (Matt. 20:20–23). This leads Jesus to teach about servant-leaders and how not to think about rank and power (Matt. 20:24–28).

The prediction had more detail than previous predictions. It includes chief priests and scribes. It predicted the handing over to Gentiles. It spoke of mocking and flogging. Jesus was clear that he was going to die by crucifixion and be vindicated in resurrection. The following request about rank showed that the disciples still were not appreciating the importance of, and modeling in, Jesus's suffering and the fact that this was the way disciples also must be prepared to go.

This query about being seated at Jesus's left and right is a pronouncement account. The pronouncement came in response to a question from the mother of the sons of Zebedee (Matt. 20:20–23). The scene is a dialogue concluded by the pronouncement. The mother's question to Jesus reflected the typical human desire for power. However, the kingdom's work was not about rank tied to power but was to be focused on service. It was about faithfully living out God's call and reflecting his character. Jesus was still trying to get the disciples to grasp this. Jesus began his point with the cup he would drink that the disciples would share. Disciples must be prepared for such suffering. Everything about these final chapters in Matthew stressed servanthood in the midst of the world's pushback to this gospel's readers.

The final unit in this section is another place where Jesus taught the disciples alone. It also is a pronouncement account (Matt. 20:24–28). Jesus contrasted the way of Gentile rulers who focused on their power and lorded it over others with the way of service as a means for greatness. The example was the coming ransom of the Son of Man. His sacrifice would show the way. The path to greatness was not a throne, but a bent knee and caring hands.

The parallels to Matthew 20:17–19 are Mark 10:32–34 and Luke 18:31–33. Matthew returns to tracking with Mark's gospel here. The parallel to Matthew 20:20–23 is Mark 10:35–40. Luke lacks this request. The parallels to Matthew 20:24–28 are Mark 10:41–45 and Luke 22:24–27. Luke places teaching about being a servant not on the way to Jerusalem but as part of Jesus's remarks at the Last Supper. In Luke, this is a distinct event appealing to the same theme, so it is not a strict parallel.

EXPOSITION (20:17–28)

As Jesus's suffering drew near, he worked to prepare the disciples for how they must live and advance the kingdom cause when he no longer was physically present with them. That way contrasted with how power is held in the world. That new way was about service, not rank. This exchange made that difference clear. The distinctive way of kingdom life was one of the ways the community would show God was at work. It stood out in a world where many only look out for themselves.

Announcing his coming suffering, Jesus issued a call to be a servant for those asking about kingdom rank, with the example being his death as a ransom.

20:17–19. As Jesus and the disciples traveled to Jerusalem, he revealed what is often called the third, but is better called the fourth, passion prediction in Matthew (Matt. 16:21; 17:12; 22–23; parallels: Mark 10:32–34; Luke 18:31–33; Morris 1992, 506). This is private teaching as he takes them to the side. Jesus knew where he was headed and what he would be facing. It had several fresh details, and it was the longest such prediction we have in Matthew, yet still was condensed in comparison to Mark 10:32–34 (Matt. 16:21; 17:22–23). Chief priests and scribes, mentioned in Matthew 16:21 with elders, have a major role. Matthew 17:22–23 had added the note about betrayal. Now there was more. The Jewish leadership will condemn Jesus. There will be mocking (Matt. 27:29, 31, 41), scourging (Matt. 27:26), and a death by crucifixion (Matt. 27:35). Gentiles will be involved in the handover (Matt. 27:1–2), so the opposition will come from all quarters. Jesus did predict both crucifixion and resurrection (Matt. 26:32; 27:63; 28:6). This prediction is so full it forms a summary of what is to come in the narrative (Culpepper 2021, 377). Matthew alluded to or discussed crucifixion often, but here is its first mention in a passion prediction (Matt. 10:38; 16:24; 23:34; 26:2; 27:22–23, 26, 31–32, 35, 38, 40, 42; 28:5).

Comparison of Passion Predictions in Matthew (emphasis added)

Matthew 16:21: "From that time on Jesus began to show his disciples that he must go *to Jerusalem* and *suffer* many things at the *hands* of the elders, *chief priests*, and *experts* in the law, and *be killed*, and *on the third day be raised*."

Matthew 17:12b: "In the same way, the *Son of Man* will *suffer* at their *hands*."

Matthew 17:22–23: "When they gathered together in Galilee, Jesus told them, 'The *Son of Man* is going to be betrayed into the *hands* of men. They *will kill him*, and on *the third day he will be raised*.' And they became greatly distressed."

Matthew 20:18–19: "Look, we are going up *to Jerusalem*, and the *Son of Man* will be *handed over* to the *chief priests* and the *experts* in the law. They will condemn him to death and will turn him over to the Gentiles to be mocked and flogged severely and crucified. Yet on the third day, he *will be raised*."

Crucifixion was a horrid form of death reserved by the Romans for noncitizens and for acts of sedition (Hengel 1977). It took place in public as a deterrent for others contemplating such acts of betrayal against Rome. Such a death was seen as a curse (Deut. 21:23; Gal. 3:13). There was no glorious martyrdom here (Davies and Allison 1997, 81). What Jesus predicted was not pleasant. The vindication to come, so central in early church preaching, was not even noticed because of the horror of what preceded its mention (Turner 2008, 82; Acts 2:24–36; 3:15; 4:10; 5:30; 10:40; 13:30, 33–37; 1 Cor. 15:4–28).

Curse of One Who Dies on a Tree

Deuteronomy 21:23: "His body must not remain all night on the tree; instead you must make certain you bury him that same day, for the one who is left exposed on a tree is cursed by God. You must not defile your land that the Lord your God is giving you as an inheritance."

As the next scene shows, all the disciples could think about was their role in kingdom power and rule. What Jesus was saying about suffering and rejection had not yet registered.

20:20–21. The mother of James and John, the sons of Zebedee, knelt before Jesus to make a request (Matt. 4:21; 10:2; 17:1; 26:37; 27:56). She may be Salome, a sister of Mary the mother of Jesus, making her Jesus's aunt and the request one made within the family (Morris 1992, 508 n. 33; Matt. 27:55–56; Mark 15:40 with John 19:25 as Mary's sister). She wanted her sons at Jesus's immediate side in the kingdom. Mark 10:35–37 was longer, as was typical for him. In Mark, the sons made the request, but their presence here may indicate they were behind this request or at least supported it. She may well represent them, as Jesus's direct address to James and John in Matthew 20:23 showed (France 2007, 756). The fact the other disciples were angry with the sons for this query also suggested their involvement (Matt. 20:24). It is not the case that Matthew was softening a criticism of the boys by having the mother ask the question. They were there and were actively participating in Matthew.

She wanted them to sit at his right and left hand, places of the highest honor (1 Kings 2:19 LXX; Neh. 8:4; T Ab. 12:8; Josephus, *A.J.* 6.235; Davies and Allison 1997, 88). Perhaps she had heard of Jesus's promise to the Twelve to rule as reflected in Matthew 19:28. She wanted her sons to have the most prominent place in his kingdom. It was a natural request for a mother to make for her children and it was all about rank and power (like Bathsheba for Solomon in 1 Kings 1:15–21). Nolland (2005, 819) notes that if this came to pass, then she shared in their status. It is a question that is off course and out of line with all Jesus was saying about upcoming suffering and constant service. It ignored not only these predictions, but also what Jesus had already taught, even recently (Matt. 5:5; 18:1–4; 19:30; 20:16). Jesus had noted the last would be first. But to this mother, being first at the first mattered most. As France (2007, 755) observes, such basic human desires had to be unlearned by disciples (Matt. 20:26—not so among you).

20:22–23. Jesus's response moved to correct not only a misguided question but to establish what lay ahead, making it the example for disciples to pursue. Before one considered glory and power to come, one needed to focus on what was required before that time (Davies and Allison 1997, 84). This service was the disciples' immediate calling.

Jesus asked the sons if they were able to drink the cup he was about to drink (Mark 10:38). This was an allusion to his approaching suffering, as the remark about the ransom of the Son of Man in Matthew 20:28 and the context of the last passion prediction showed (Matt. 26:39; John 18:11; on the cup as punishment or suffering, Ps. 75:8; Isa. 51:17, 22; Jer. 25:15–17; Ezek. 23:33—"cup of horror and desolation"; Lam. 4:21; Hab. 2:16; Pss. Sol. 8:14–15; 1QpHab. 11:14; 4QpNah. 4:6; Davies and Allison 1997, 89). It was the cup of judgment and eschatological sorrow Jesus would bear for others.

They claimed they were ready (Mark 10:39). One wonders if they even understood what Jesus was asking, given how unfocused they were on his coming rejection. Matthew 26:56 suggests their lack of focus because when the next time came to stand up for Jesus, they fled. Their response was reversed by the time of Acts 12:2 with martyrdom for James the apostle and in Revelation 1:9 with exile for John (France 2007, 758; Morris 1992, 510). Davies and Allison (1997, 90–91) defend the saying's authenticity, as well as noting John died late in life during Trajan's rule as Irenaeus notes in *Against Heresies* 2.22.5. So eventually they did respond. Eusebius in *Ecclesiastical History,* Book 3, 1–2, briefly notes Peter's martyrdom, reporting how Linus became bishop of Rome after Peter and Paul were martyred. There is included the observation that Peter was crucified upside down. First Clement 5 also mentions the martyrdom of Peter and Paul. Suffering was to be the destiny for many who followed Jesus.

Jesus responded that they will drink his cup. They will suffer rejection. James will be martyred (Acts 12:2) and John exiled. Their role in the kingdom was not in Jesus's hands; it was the Father's business, just as was the time of Israel's restoration (Acts 1:6–7). Jesus could not grant their request. This kind of limitation shows some things involved the Father's authority (Matt. 24:36). The idea of prepared events points to divine planning (Matt. 25:34, 41; John 14:2; 1 Cor. 2:9; Rev. 21:2; Culpepper 2021, 381).

Martyrdom or Death of the Apostles and Others

Acts 12:2: "He [King Herod] had James, the brother of John, executed with a sword."

Josephus, *Antiquities* 20.200: "When, therefore, Ananus was of this disposition, he thought he had now a proper opportunity [to exercise his authority]. Festus was now dead, and Albinus was but upon the road; so he assembled the sanhedrin of judges, and brought before them the brother of Jesus, who was called Christ, whose name was James, and some others, [or, some of his companions]; and when he had formed an accusation against them as breakers of the law, he delivered them to be stoned."

1 Clement 5: "But to pass from the examples of ancient times, let us come to those champions who lived nearest to our time. Let us consider the noble examples that belong to our own generation. Because of jealousy and envy the greatest and most righteous pillars were persecuted and fought to the death. Let us set before our eyes the good apostles.

"There was Peter, who because of unrighteous jealousy endured not one or two but many trials, and thus having given his testimony went to his appointed place of glory.

"Because of jealousy and strife Paul showed the way to the prize for patient endurance. After he had been seven times in chains, had been driven into exile, had been stoned, and had preached in the east and in the west, he won the genuine glory for his faith, having taught righteousness to the whole world and having reached the farthest limits of the west. Finally, when he had given his testimony before the rulers, he thus departed from the world and went to the holy place, having become an outstanding example of patient endurance."

Irenaeus, *Against Heresies* 2.22.5: "Now Jesus was, as it were, beginning to be thirty years old," when He came to receive baptism); and, [according to these men,] He preached only one year reckoning from His baptism. On completing His thirtieth year He suffered, being in fact still a young man, and who had by no means attained to advanced age. Now, that the first stage of early life embraces thirty years, and that this extends onwards to the fortieth year, every one will admit; but from the fortieth and fiftieth year a man begins to decline towards old age, which our Lord possessed while He still fulfilled the office of a Teacher, even as the Gospel and all the elders testify; those who were conversant in Asia with John, the disciple of the Lord, [affirming] that John conveyed to them that information. And he [John] remained among them up to the times of Trajan. Some of them, moreover, saw not only John, but the other apostles also, and heard the very same account from them, and bear testimony as to the [validity of] the statement."

Eusebius, *Ecclesiastical History* Book 3, 1.2: "Peter appears to have preached in Pontus, Galatia, Bithynia, Cappadocia, and Asia to the Jews of the dispersion. And at last, having come to Rome, he was crucified head-downwards; for he had requested that he might suffer in this way."

20:24. The query got a reaction from the other ten (Mark 10:41). They were angry about the request. Jesus came in to set it all straight. He would return to the image of humility, a teaching that had yet to register with the disciples (Matt. 18:1–14; 23:11–12).

20:25–28. Jesus's reply came in stages. The teaching was for all the disciples. Jesus's goal was to avoid the building up of any jealousy. Mark 10:41–45 is very similar. He started with power in the world. Gentile rulers and the powerful lord it over others (Luke 22:25). For rulers of the world the emphasis was on honor through status and power. The world valued and presented greatness in this way. This was not to be the path for Jesus's disciples. He was clear that the world's way and how it rated greatness was not to be the example for the disciples (Luke 22:26). Greatness was defined by service and by being slaves. The key terms here are διάκονος and δοῦλος, "servant" and "slave" (BDAG s.v. "διάκονος" 2, 230–31, and "δοῦλος" 2bα, 259–60). A servant worked for a wage to maintain an owner's house, often waiting tables. A slave was one step lower, as he was not a free man (Wilkins 2004, 699). This would have been a shock in a culture where slaves were not models. Philo in *Rewards and Punishments* 137 says, "To free born people slavery is a most intolerable evil, to avoid it wise men are even willing to die, resisting in a gallant spirit which despises all danger the attacks of those who seek to inflict upon them the domination of a master." Carter (2000, 404) describes the slave as "a marginal person, physically alive, but socially dead."

The surprising call of Jesus was to be a servant of others (Matt. 23:11; Luke 22:27). The picture was the slave who serves another. The issue was not what you could do for me, but what I could do for you. In *The Shepherd of Hermas*, bishops are described as hospitable, welcoming slaves into their homes and providing shelter to those in need and for widows (T. Sim. 104:1–2)

Jesus left an example that also was a mission statement, since it explained why Jesus came (other mission statements: Matt. 5:17; 9:13; 10:34–35; Luke 19:10; John 9:39; 10:10; 12:46–47). The Son of Man was about to give his life as a "ransom" for many (BDAG s.v. "λύτρον" 606; Mark 10:45). This term only appears here and in the parallel in Mark 10:45 in the NT (1 Tim. 2:6 has ἀντίλυτρον; 1 Peter 1:18 has the verb). Redemption was the more common idea related to the idea of shed blood (Matt. 26:28; Rom. 3:24; Gal. 4:5; Eph. 1:7, 14; Col. 1:14; Heb. 9:7–14; France 2007, 761). The imagery here is of sacrifice, and the language alludes to Isaiah 53:5–6, 12 or, less likely, 43:3–4 (Rom. 5:15, 19). A ransom involved deliverance produced through the payment of something else in its place (Exod. 21:30; 30:12). Carter (2000, 406) defines the way the many are liberated as an act that "frees those who live in the sinful world of imperial control" or a "'moral confrontation' with Gentile power." This link misses a real point of Jesus's battle: the need for internal redemption for sin and the spiritual battle for what drives the inside of people. Biblical ethics does address what happens in the world and its abuses, but it does so from the inside out. Power is best dealt with not only by confronting its abuse around us but by making sure that such a challenge comes from a serving heart. In the New Testament there is no time spent answering to whom the payment was made. The stress is on the deliverance that is the result and the need to be redeemed for one's own sin. Perhaps the idea is that a debt to death and justice has been paid, since that is what sin yields. A debt paid is the result for one who responds to Jesus's work, a life that is established as righteous by God's grace.

Jesus's Mission Statements in Matthew

Matthew 5:17: "Do not think that I have come to abolish the law or the prophets. I have not come to abolish these things but to fulfill them."

Matthew 9:13: "Go and learn what this saying means: *'I want mercy and not sacrifice.'* For I did not come to call the righteous, but sinners."

Matthew 10:34: "Do not think that I have come to bring peace to the earth. I have not come to bring peace but a sword."

Matthew 20:28: "The Son of Man did not come to be served but to serve, and to give his life as a ransom for many."

Jesus did not come to be served but to serve, despite the power and position he had. Rank is not the question, nor are thrones, but faithfully serving those around you. Jesus showed the way (Phil. 2:5–11). Scripture reconfigures how roles are to be seen versus the world, a point often ignored when the discussion of leadership roles, whether in the church or in marriage, appears in debates today. We tend to default to the way the world looks at these categories, with power and rank coming before service.

THEOLOGICAL FOCUS

The exegetical idea (announcing his coming suffering, Jesus issued a call to be a servant for those asking about kingdom rank, with the example being his death as a ransom) points to this theological focus: Jesus reconfigures how rank in the world should work by pointing to the example of being a servant.

This unit is about serving, having an approach to others that is rooted in humility and selflessness. This attitude does not worry about status but majors in how to minister to others. It gladly takes on the place of a servant or a slave. Matthew sees Jesus's own death for sin on behalf of others as the example to follow. This idea is celebrated by Paul in Philippians 2:5–11. There Jesus is the model for all having the same humble mind in the community. The idea is not hard to contemplate, even though it is completely countercultural. The difficulty is in its application, as it means stepping aside from normal ambition, something this scene also shows when Jesus rejected the request of two of his disciples to sit by his side when he rules. This kind of intense self-renunciation is part of what Jesus has taught about the disciple who is willing to lose his life so as to gain it. The way to greatness is not found by sitting on a throne but with a bended knee and a towel, with serving hands and a caring heart. Jesus's washing of the disciples' feet in John 13 pictures what is meant.

PREACHING AND TEACHING STRATEGIES

Exegetical and Theological Synthesis

Life boils down to a question of service. Will we serve God or mammon? The Lord or the idols of our age? The risen Christ or our wounded egos? As much as we would like to declare our unwavering loyalty to God, we know better. Adam and Eve chose self-rule over service to God (Gen. 3). The people in Babel wanted to expand their fame instead of exalting God (Gen. 11). Ancient Israel regularly worshiped neighboring gods rather than exclusively serving Yahweh. Thus, Joshua's memorable plea to "choose . . . this day whom you will serve" functions as a challenge to all generations (Josh. 24:15 NIV).

Similarly, New Testament authors war against divided loyalties. Jesus assured his disciples that service to him would be costly (Matt. 8:20; 16:24). We cannot secure our comfort and serve Jesus. Paul taught that saints were to walk in the Spirit not the flesh (Gal. 5:16–24). We cannot indulge our desires and serve Jesus. Peter reminded his readers that service to Jesus required submission to Caesar (1 Peter 2:13–17; cf. Rom. 13:1–4). We cannot grasp for autonomy and serve Jesus.

Fortunately, Jesus redeemed the image of servitude. It was his preferred self-description (Matt. 20:28). And Jesus came by service honestly. He learned servitude from his mother (Luke 1:38). He heard it lauded in Isaiah's poetry (Isa. 42:1–4; 52:13–53:12) and David's psalms (Pss. 19:11; 27:9; 78:70; 86:4, 16). Many Hebrew prophets were referred to as servants (Isa. 20:35; Dan. 9:17; Amos 3:7; Zech. 1:6). For Jesus service was a mark of honor, not shame. His sacrificial service earned him praise from the early church (Phil. 2:5–11). We should approach service with similar joy.

Preaching Idea

Service over status is the way of Jesus.

Contemporary Connections

What does it mean?

Service over status describes rival mindsets. The status lens is self-focused. It craves attention, influence, and fame. Status is both earned and inherited. For some, status centers on one's family name, zip code, and financial bracket. Kingston Everly Jr. of Beverly Hills likely has more inherited status than Ryder Jones of Dallas Center, Iowa.

A status-hungry person wants to climb the corporate ladder, receive honors at school, or get recognition for athletic prowess. Additionally, in our social media culture, status-seeking people obsess about looking good, sounding witty, and amassing a following.

Contrarily, the service mindset is self-forgetful and others-oriented. Those with a service mindset do not simply look for random acts of service; they live as servants. They see a need and meet it without thinking about how to exploit the moment to boost their image. Servants are eager to help others in small ways: opening doors, carrying bags, lending money, listening carefully, or letting others step in front in the grocery store line when they have only a few items. Like Jesus, servants eschew the spotlight. Success for a servant is not whether others saw them serve, but whether they saw opportunities to serve and seized them.

Is it true?

Service is more Christlike than status. However, this does not mean that Christians should avoid status at all costs. Fame does not negate faith. Popularity does not corrupt spiritual impact. In fact, some followers of Jesus should hold office, make money, leverage social media, and influence crowds. Giftedness in these areas may be God-given. Moreover, throughout history God has used politicians, business leaders, and celebrities to spread the gospel. Nonetheless, those with status should proceed with caution. Status can undermine service when protecting one's reputation becomes more important than helping others.

It is also worth noting that not all service emulates the way of Jesus. Plenty of service lacks the self-giving, self-denying, sacrificial ethos Jesus modeled. Too much service in the church is mechanical, compulsory, and tainted by complaints. Likewise, extra effort at school and work can be motivated more by a desire to impress than a heart of service. Even charitable service may lack the compassion of Jesus. Whereas he viewed needy people as sheep without a shepherd, we may view them as irresponsible citizens looking for a handout or helpless victims of a broken system. In either case, we reduce others to problems to be solved, not people to be loved. Service devoid of love is not Christlike.

Now what?

The call to service is clear in this passage. However, it is a particular kind of service. It is sacrificial service that imitates the way of Jesus. Similarly, the Christ Hymn (Phil. 2:6–11) presents the mindset of Christ, our ideal servant and exalted Lord.

First, service in the way of Jesus is humble. In *Mere Christianity*, C. S. Lewis (1996a, 114) teaches that humility is not thinking less of ourselves, but thinking of ourselves less. In other words, humility does not gaze inward. Disparaging ourselves—negative self-talk, announcing our flaws and failures—is false humility because it keeps the spotlight on us. Truly humble people can appreciate their history, gifts, strengths, and opportunities, but view them as gifts from God. Humility is grateful, not grandiose.

Second, humility looks outward. A humble woman sees others' needs and meets them through a kind word, calming presence, or helping hand. She does more than random acts of service; rather, she lives as a servant. In her service, she is not keeping track, patting herself on the back, or hoping for favors in return. She serves sacrificially, yes, but also joyfully.

Finally, Christlike service advances Christ's status. This should be the motivation of our service. Status-seeking people want to make a name for themselves. Status-giving people want to exalt the Lord. Individually, we must fight the urge to turn our service gigs into social media posts. When a good deed is broadcast, it deflects glory onto us. The same danger applies to churches whose community service morphs into an attempt to boost attendance or the congregation's image in the community. While it is appropriate to celebrate opportunities to serve, our focus must return to Christ.

Creativity in Presentation

To exploit how status crazed our culture has become, find examples of this in everyday life. For example:

- Compare similar items from Amazon with different ratings. Ask church members if they would prefer the 4.8-star product or 3.7-star product?
- Ask, "When you choose a movie, do you prefer the Rotten Tomatoes 100% "Fresh" scale, the IMDb 10-point ranking system, Amazon's 5-star review, or Ebert's 2-thumb review?"
- Describe two recent posts to social media, one which had many responses, and another which had few. Show them the posts and ask which one was better.

Additionally, you might consider some of your favorite ranking tools or review sources, including but not limited to Yelp, Google reviews, Angi, Ranker, Reddit, and Consumer Reports. Our obsession with ranking even appears in annual magazine issues that list "America's Sexiest People" or "Best Businesses in 2024."

The PBS television series *Downton Abbey* (created by Julian Fellowes, 2010–2015) captured the radical distinction between the servant class and those with status. The show centered on the Crawley family and their army of butlers, maids, cooks, and drivers. The show illustrated the vapid lives of those with status, whose days were filled with preening, socializing, and dining. Servants experienced much more excitement, drama, and struggle. Familiarity with the show is not necessary to illustrate the point that status is a bottomless pit, whereas service offers more excitement. A similar contrast between classes is evident in the epic film *Titanic* (directed by James Cameron, 1997), where those with status come across as self-serving, but the servant class can enjoy a dance.

Speaking of movies, no character better embodies the role of a servant than Westley (played by Cary Elwes) in the classic comedy *The Princess Bride* (directed by Rob Reiner, 1987). Westley faithfully serves Buttercup (played by Robin Wright), who does not realize his love for him. For every request—fetch water, feed the horses, trim the hedges—Westley replies, "As you wish." Those seeking status think, "I wish . . ." Those set on serving say, "As you wish."

For a humorous illustration, consider staging several photo ops during the week, where you are "caught doing good." Of course, these pictures would be best if they clearly show you doing little more than posing, while others are doing the real work in the background. Make a montage of these activities. For example:

- Smiling while holding one clean plate, while your spouse in the background is carrying a stack of dirty dishes
- Smiling while folding one clean shirt, while your spouse is in the background surrounded by a pile of laundry
- Smiling while holding a rake in front of a tiny pile of leaves, while your children amass giant piles in the background
- Smiling while stacking two chairs together, while others from the church manage stacks that are eight chairs high

As you set up the montage, sell the fact that you did some good this week and wanted to celebrate. You might add, "Serving is a good feeling and great look!"

When I (Tim) was growing up, my parents modeled service in many ways. In addition to the regular domestic duties, they spent years driving me and my siblings around town to participate in clubs, sports, and theater. In retrospect, each of these activities helped build our status as children. Through their humble service, my parents elevated their children. Think about similar examples from your childhood or church, where the sacrifices of others elevated those around them.

In the end, your sermon should clearly articulate that Jesus reconfigures how rank in the world should work by pointing to the example of being a servant. Service over status is the way of Jesus.

- Jesus predicts his suffering (20:17–19).
- Jesus rebukes our ambition (20:20–23).
- Jesus redefines status (20:24–28).

DISCUSSION QUESTIONS

1. Despite Jesus's early predictions of his death and resurrection, the disciples could not make sense of it. Why was this?
2. Only in Matthew's account of the story does the mother of James and John make the request for her sons' status. How do you harmonize this with other accounts?
3. How did they mark status in Jesus's day? How do we mark it in our day?
4. What is the difference between random acts of service and living as a servant?

REJECTION AND VINDICATION OF THE MESSIAH-SON IN JERUSALEM (20:29–28:20)

Matthew's final section deals with events occurring over a period that has been called the Passion Week. Jesus now entered Jerusalem and faced the leadership in a series of events and challenges that were designed to force their hand to decide about him. The action in the temple, which the leadership had responsibility for, meant the leadership had to act, for Jesus was claiming the right to assess the way in which worship proceeded. This was but the start of a series of disputes that sought to raise questions about authority and who was best placed to show the way of God. The challenge is summarized in a series of woes about the scribes and Pharisees. The eschatological discourse made the point that judgment was coming on the nation for covenantal unfaithfulness and that vindication would come to the righteous with the Son of Man's return to complete the promise that meant the end of the age. After holding a meal where he reconfigured Passover imagery to point to his own death and the disciples' deliverance, Jesus faced his arrest, trials, and crucifixion. The beginning of vindication came when God's vote in the dispute was made through his resurrecting Jesus. That act led to appearances by Jesus in Galilee and a call to make disciples in all the world, teaching them to obey all Jesus had commanded. In a sense, Matthew's gospel sought to record and contribute to the carrying out of that call.

This unit is comprised of fifteen preaching units. Jesus presented himself to the city, making his claim as king. He cleansed the temple to challenge the leadership. A series of confrontations show Jesus repelling all the efforts to question his claims. Then at a final meal, he prepared the disciples for his death. All that is left is his sacrifice, a death produced as the Jewish leadership persuaded Pilate to crucify Jesus for sedition, as they saw him as a blasphemer. Claiming God would exalt and vindicate him, Jesus went to his death trusting God would deliver him. An empty tomb generated by God's raising him from the dead was God's vote in the dispute, as it pointed to the vindication of Jesus and served to add substantiation to his claims to be the way of God. Now his cause would be assumed by his followers taking the kingdom message of life into the world.

Matthew 20:29–21:11

EXEGETICAL IDEA
The healing of two blind men in Jericho who cried out to the Son of David illustrated Jesus's messianic authority, something that Jesus's entry into Jerusalem also declared.

THEOLOGICAL FOCUS
Jesus's actions point to him as the promised king of eschatological hope, something his power to heal underscores.

PREACHING IDEA
Don't overlook Jesus's public service announcement.

PREACHING POINTERS
As he headed from Jericho to Jerusalem, Jesus enacted his penultimate healings. Two blind men cried out for mercy, calling him the Son of David. Although the crowds rebuked the men, Jesus restored their sight. When his march to Jerusalem continued, Jesus enlisted his disciples to procure a donkey and colt for his entrance to the city (Zech. 9:9). The scene is packed with messianic imagery. A band of travelers cheered him along, waving branches, tossing coats, and shouting "Hosanna" (Ps. 118). The original readers would have noticed Jesus's change of strategy. He went public. In Jerusalem, he would claim his messianic identity, confront religious hypocrisy, and suffer Roman brutality. Matthew's audience observed the return of Israel's king. With his return, tensions would rise.

Many Westerners consider faith a private matter. They value it so long as it does not infringe on them. They want to keep church and state separate. They want to keep Christ out of Christmas. They are comfortable with "prayers and wishes" when crises arrive; however, they cringe when they see teams huddle in prayer before a football game or families bow to bless their food in a restaurant. Public announcements of Christian faith cause tension. They expose cultural beliefs and values at odds with God's kingdom (e.g., might vs. meekness, dominance vs. service). To make a public announcement of faith is to pledge allegiance to King Jesus, not political parties and consumer brands. This sermon encourages us not to overlook Jesus's public service announcement.

JESUS PERFORMS A HEALING AND PRESENTS HIMSELF TO JERUSALEM (20:29–21:11)

LITERARY STRUCTURE AND THEMES (20:29–21:11)

This unit opens the gospel's final section as Jesus approached Jerusalem as Davidic king, Son of David. Jesus has decided to go very public in his claims, forcing the leaders to act. The climactic crucifixion and resurrection resulted from Jesus's earthly ministry. The Jericho miracle is paired with the entry because the theme of kingship ties them together. The miracle at Jericho authenticated all Jesus was about to do, showing God was still working through him as he approached his destiny.

> **The Amidah, Benediction 14, and a Prayer of Hope for Jerusalem**
>
> **14th Benediction:** "And Jerusalem, Your city, return in mercy, and dwell therein as You have spoken; rebuild it soon in our days as an everlasting building, and speedily set up therein the throne of David. Blessed art thou, O L-rd, who rebuilds Jerusalem."

Two scenes are present. There is a miracle account and call to discipleship involved healing two blind men (Matt. 20:29–34). It is followed by the entry into Jerusalem (Matt. 21:1–11).

The Jericho miracle event frames the entry into the capital. Mark's version (Mark 10:46–52) is more about discipleship, while Matthew's simplified version is mostly about the miracle (Davies and Allison 1997, 105). The entire set of actions rotates around the idea that Jesus responded as Son of David. Jesus's work of compassion, even to those who did not socially count, continued as he prepared to face his fate. Such work was important, showing his heart and establishing his credibility.

The second scene culturally was a common triumphal entry scene for a cultural luminary. Yet it took place in reverse, since Jesus was not welcomed as such a dignitary even as he was presented as one. He entered only with his disciples. The crowd's closing confession of Jesus as a prophet came up short about who he was and is (Matt. 21:1–11; Kinman in Bock and Webb 2009, 383–427, who appropriately calls it atriumphal; Bock 2012, 107–21; Davies and Allison 1997, 112–13, who call it anti-parousia, as such entries were seen as "comings"; 1 Kings 1:32–40; 1 Macc. 5:45–54; Plutarch, *Ant.* 24). Such scenes normally were reserved for political dignitaries like Pilate. In such scenes, the entire city would go out to welcome the dignitary as a show of support. That did not happen here.

Jesus was going public. He accepted public praise as Son of David. However, he only was accepted as a prophet by many in the crowd at the end of the scene (v. 8 with v. 11). The public had learned nothing since the time of Peter's confession in Matthew 16:13–14. Interestingly, the outright rejection of the leaders in the gospel parallels is not noted by Matthew. He preferred to save that rejection for the challenges to come and only portrayed that those around Jesus did not appreciate fully who he was. The failure to appreciate who Jesus really is, even in the midst of praise and respect, drives these final chapters of Matthew's account. The tension between who Jesus is and the failure to recognize him as such is central to the rest of Matthew's gospel. Eventually hostility to

Jesus will produce his death. Only God's vindication of him dramatically changes the narrative and the history of what is taking place.

The parallels to the healing of the blind men are Mark 10:46–52 and Luke 18:35–43. They each only note one blind person being healed. Matthew 9:27–31 notes another healing of a blind person. The Matthew 9 account is not a doublet to this event, but represents a separate healing event (Turner 2008, 490, against Luz 2001, 548–49).

The entry into Jerusalem is told in all four Gospels: Mark 11:1–10, Luke 19:28–38, and John 12:12–15. John 12:16 notes that some of the significance of this event, including the relevance of Zechariah 9:9, was not appreciated until after Jesus had been raised.

EXPOSITION (20:29–21:11)

Matthew frames the opening of the final section of his gospel with an emphasis that Jesus was the promised Son of David. Here is the claim that Matthew was debating and defending in the face of the current Jewish opposition. This entire final section is his summary of all he had been contending for in the gospel. Jesus was acting as Son of David even as he arrived to meet his calling and fate on a cross in Jerusalem. The presence of divine support was with him and his acts of compassion. As he entered Jerusalem presenting himself to be a different kind of humble king, many in the city only saw a prophet. Stronger opposition lingered as well, as Matthew will show later in the section. The battle for who Jesus was and is, as well as whether God was behind him, has arrived at its climactic moments. Matthew desired that his readers grasp what truly took place and that they sense that God was behind the one who entered Jerusalem.

The healing of two blind men in Jericho who cried out to the Son of David illustrated Jesus's messianic authority, something that Jesus's entry into Jerusalem also declared.

20:29. The setting for this miracle was Jericho, an indication that Jesus and his followers were getting closer to Jerusalem, only about sixteen miles away to the southwest. It was a 3,500-foot uphill climb, which was why people spoke of "going up" to Jerusalem. Matthew has them departing Jericho, while Luke 18:35 has them near Jericho and seemingly approaching it, since the Zacchaeus incident in Luke 19:1–10 is in Jericho. Jericho has three locations: modern, ancient, and New Testament, but it is not clear if this played into the issues of the differences of where this took place, though it does complicate the conversation (Davies and Allison 1997, 106; Morris 1992, 513–14, Osborne 2010, 747, and Wilkins 2004, 671, see the two locales as the source of the confusion about location, which is possible; Josephus, *B.J.* 4.459). New Testament Jericho was about a mile south of the original site (Wilkins 2004, 671). Mark 10:46 has them departing after entering the city. Both Mark and Luke note only one blind man. Mark gives his name as Bartimaeus. Mark's account is, as usual, much more detailed, while Luke's version is more detailed than Matthew's but less detailed than Mark's. Culpepper (2021, 387–88) notes how often Matthew uses the number two (Matt. 8:28; 9:27–31; 18:16, 19–20; 20:21, 24; 21:1, 2, 7) and how these two men contrast with the just-made request for the two sons of Zebedee.

20:30. As Jesus departed Jericho, two seated blind men cried out to him as Son of David, asking for mercy (Mark 10:47; Luke 18:38). The request for mercy is common in Matthew (Matt. 9:27; 15:22; 17:15; 18:33). The "Son of David" title pointed to a regal and messianic view of Jesus (Matt. 1:1, 20; 9:27; 12:23; 15:22; 21:9, 15; 22:41–46). It is the title that dominates this unit, as it also is the title of Jesus's entry into Jerusalem (Matt. 21:9). The fact these men were seated by the road likely indicated they were there begging. Mark 10:46 says as much. Most people would have ignored them.

20:31. The crowd sought to stop the blind men from appealing to Jesus (Mark 10:48a; Luke 18:39a). They told the men to be silent. It is the first time in Matthew that the crowd was on a different wavelength from Jesus and was opposed to something he would do. Others had been resistant to Jesus's efforts before only to be reversed by him (Matt. 15:23; 19:13). The blind men's marginal social status made their appeal irrelevant to the crowds. The crowd's view was that surely Jesus had more important concerns. This opposition did not stop the two men. They repeated their cry for help in exactly the same words, "Lord, have mercy on us, Son of David!" (Mark 10:48b and Luke 18:39b—one person crying out).

20:32–34. Jesus stopped and asked what they wished for him to do (Mark 10:51a; Luke 18:41a). Matthew lacks most of Mark 10:49–50 and the conversation leading into the miracle. In Matthew, the men simply asked for their eyes to be opened. They wanted to be able to see (Mark 10:51b; Luke 18:41b). They had faith Jesus could do this. Their trust in Jesus was deep not only in Jesus but in resisting the crowd's negative view of their request. Jesus had compassion on them—a common Matthean theme (Matt. 9:36; 14:14; 15:32; 20:34). He touched their eyes and immediately they were healed. Touching also is common in Matthew (Matt. 8:3, 15; 9:29–30; 14:36—of others healed as they touched Jesus). Mark 10:52 and Luke 18:42 have Jesus merely send the one man on his way, healed (Mark 10:52b; Luke 18:43a). This is a simple miracle account, very similar to Matthew 9:27–30. The miracle confirmed Jesus's authority and position as Son of David (Isa. 35:5; Osborne 2010, 748). He was the "messianic restorer" (Nolland 2005, 829). The mirroring of the earlier miracle shows little had changed about Jesus's outreach to people, even as opposition had risen (Wilkins 2004, 671). God still was at work through him. Jesus loved despite the opposition to him. The miracle was another point about Jesus. Healing the blind is another important Matthean theme (Matt. 9:27–31; 11:5; 12:22; 15:30–31; 21:14). It pictured how Jesus as Son of David brought light (Matt. 4:16; cf. Isa. 9:2).

Isaiah Pictures the Time of Deliverance

Isaiah 35:5–6: "Then blind eyes will open, deaf ears will hear. Then the lame will leap like a deer, the mute tongue will shout for joy; for water will burst forth in the wilderness, streams in the arid rift valley."

21:1–3. Jesus and his disciples were on the other side of the Mount of Olives from Jerusalem in Bethphage. The exact location of Bethphage, which means "house of unripe figs," is not known. They were near Bethany. Jesus had predicted he would come to Jerusalem (Matt. 16:21; 20:18–19). The Mount of Olives was associated with the eschaton (Ezek. 11:23; Zech. 14:4). He sent two disciples to procure a donkey and colt for his entry into the city (Mark 11:1–3; Luke 19:29–31). If they were asked about what they were doing, they were simply to say the Lord had need. This was an appeal to the *angaria*, the rights of a dignitary to use resources (Derrett 1971). Jesus was aware of what was going on and was in control of events. To ride an animal when one was expected to walk to a feast made an intentional statement by not doing what was normal (*m. Ḥag.* 1.1—those unable to walk are not required to make an appearance before the Lord; France 2007, 776).

Mount of Olives and Deliverance

Ezekiel 11:23: "The glory of the Lord rose up from within the city and stopped over the mountain east of it."

Zechariah 14:4: "On that day his feet will stand on the Mount of Olives that lies to the east of Jerusalem, and the Mount of Olives will be split in half from east to west, leaving a great valley.

Half the mountain will move northward and the other half southward."

21:4–5. This event took place in light of Scripture, as Matthew presents an edited version of Zechariah 9:9 (John 12:14–15). Matthew inserted the text as a narrative note, much as he did with Scripture in his infancy material. The opening wording drew from Isaiah 62:11 ("Tell the daughter of Zion"). Some associated the Zechariah passage with Genesis 49:10–11, which had messianic significance in the first century (4Q252 V:6 [4QPBlessing/CommGen A]; also later among the rabbis: Gen. Rab. 98.9; Sanh. 98a, 99a; Qoh. Rab. 1.9; Blomberg 1992, 311). It speaks of a lion of Judah who tethered his donkey and colt. The reference to the daughter of Zion was to the city of Jerusalem (2 Kings 19:21; Isa. 16:1; Zeph. 3:14). Here was the humble king, riding on a donkey, presenting himself to the city (1 Kings 1:33, 38). The emphasis was on humility, as reference to being vindicated and saved was omitted. That work comes later. John 12:16 tells us the disciples did not put all of this together until after Jesus was glorified. Matthew's scriptural narrative note is reflective on the event versus being about what they understood at the time. Mark and Luke lack this citation. The point was that God was coming in deliverance to Zion through her messianic king. The choice of a donkey and not a warhorse is distinctive and significant. France (2007, 777) says the presentation saw him as "victorious yet meek" with his triumph "received rather than won," presenting a kingdom "of peace rather than coercion." Jesus was going public for the first time with his messianic claim and was changing the common imagery to make a point.

Two animals were present. This is likely because the donkey ridden was a young and inexperienced colt that could not be left to itself (Blomberg 1992, 312; Gundry 1982, 410; Osborne 2010, 755; Wilkins 2004, 687). The pairing of animals suggests Jesus rode an animal not previously ridden, something Mark 11:2 says explicitly (Davies and Allison 1997, 120–23).

21:6–7. The disciples did as they were told and collected the animals. Matthew's description is much shorter than those in Mark 11:4–7 and Luke 19:32–34. The disciples placed their garments on the animals to show honor to Jesus. The scene parallels what David did for Solomon (1 Kings 1:32–40) and Jehu's later entry (2 Kings 9:13). The plural reference to garments on the horses and Jesus sitting on them leaves an impression to some commentators of Jesus sitting on both animals, but this says too much. Jesus was seated on garments that were previously together and now were placed on both animals (Morris 1992, 522; Turner 2008, 496). The spreading of branches reflected respect, a kind of ancient red carpet. Palms were not meaningless in this culture. They were associated with victory and pictured Jewish nationalism (1 Macc. 13:51; 2 Macc. 10:7; Wilkins 2004, 687). They even appeared on coins, a symbol of national celebration on the famous Judea Capta coin and on another during the later Bar Kochba rebellion, and are also described in some ancient texts tied to the Maccabean revolt.

Palms as a Symbol of Nationalism

1 Maccabees 13:51 [on reentering the city during the Maccabean War]: "On the twenty-third day of the second month, in the one hundred seventy-first year, the Jews entered it with praise and palm branches, and with harps and cymbals and stringed instruments, and with hymns and songs, because a great enemy had been crushed and removed from Israel."

2 Maccabees 10:7 [celebrating the regaining of the temple in the Maccabean War]: "Therefore, carrying ivy-wreathed wands and beautiful branches and also fronds of palm, they offered hymns of thanksgiving to him who had given success to the purifying of his own holy place."

Photo of a Roman Judea Capta Coin Replica.
Old display at the Antonia Fortress in Jerusalem.

21:8–9. The crowd also spread their garments and branches before Jesus (Mark 11:8–10; Luke 19:36–38). Following in front and behind, they were crying out in praise to the Son of David, announcing him as coming in the Lord's name. Most of the language is from Psalm 118:26. The "crying out" is in Matthew's common imperfect tense. It is pictured as ongoing praise. The exclamation "Hosanna" means "to save" (BDAG s.v. "ὡσαννά" 1106). The cry could be read as asking for deliverance by the Son of David. However, the phrase had become idiomatic for praise and that was its possible use here. The recognition of the Son of David by those who offered praise does give an eschatological tinge to the scene. The expression of "the one who comes" raises another common Matthean theme (Matt. 3:11; 11:3; 23:39). Those praising Jesus were affirming that this one was sent from God. "Hosanna in the highest" reflects Psalm 148:1. The cited Psalm 118 is one of the Hallel psalms recited at feasts such as Passover, Tabernacles, and Hanukkah (*'Arak.* 10a; Turner 2008, 496). Matthew uses Psalm 118 a few times more after this (Matt. 21:42; 23:39). Psalm 118 is one of the most underappreciated of the messianic texts of the New Testament, as it points to acceptance of the Messiah from Psalm 118:26 and in its other use treats the theme of rejection/exaltation from Psalm 118:22. In fact, in the Gospels it is used for the theme of rejection as much or more than Isaiah 53. Although Mark does not refer to Jesus as the Son of David here, he does mention the praise for David's coming kingdom, so the difference here is not great and should not be pressed (Mark 11:10).

The reference to Son of David echoed the insightful cry of the blind men from Matthew 20:30–31 (on that title or concept: Matt. 1:1; 9:27; 12:23; 15:22; 22:41–46). These events were framed by Matthew at a literary level as being about a Jesus who was descended from David. It is the story of a king offering a kingdom to the people. The roots of this title go back to 2 Samuel 7:12–16. Jesus rode in with the hope of Davidic promise on his back. Some, like Jesus's closest disciples, raised this note consciously as Jesus entered. Others may simply have joined in because of the general note of hope that came with such a feast. Luke 19:37 says it was a crowd of his disciples who offered this praise.

21:10–11. The act drew the city's attention and those in it asked who this was. This was another indication that the praise came from disciples and pilgrims, not the citizens of Jerusalem. The population of Jerusalem has been estimated at various levels, with Osborne (2010, 756) contending for a base population of seventy thousand or so. At festival season he saw its size almost quadrupling to a quarter million. Estimates vary up and down from this figure with numbers as small as twenty-five thousand and as large as a hundred thousand for the base population. Festivals would cause the city to swell in size up to three or four times. Interaction between citizens and pilgrims was inevitable.

The response was that this was the prophet Jesus from Nazareth of Galilee. Though some appeal to a prophet like Moses (Davies and Allison 1997, 127), this is less than clear from what was said here. The response was short of all who Jesus was, even as he presented himself as king to the city. The idea of Jesus as prophet was popular but did not reflect an appreciation of all that he was (Matt. 16:13–16; Nolland 2005, 840). Jesus's entry was not completely grasped (but for a view that this was a good and adequate answer, just giving additional information about Jesus, Davies and Allison 1997, 127). France (2007, 781) argues that a prophet from Galilee would not be a good thing to those Judeans thinking about Rome. There was a risk from Rome for Jews from having this kind of regal claimant in the city. Rome had political power, and to foster such a ruler could bring a negative reaction from those powers. Wilkins (2004, 689) suggests the welcome was of a crowd mostly desiring political, not spiritual, deliverance, noting that Jesus entered the city having wept for it, as Luke 19:42–44 shows. That pain was from their not recognizing all of who he was and that judgment would come for the city as a result (Matt. 24–25).

The event had layers in that the praise of Jesus as king likely initially came from disciples, as Luke 19:37 says the whole crowd of disciples offered praise. Others in the crowd probably observed what was taking place and tried to make sense of it, just as the residents of Jerusalem were trying to do. At the end of the Matthean scene, it seems people were trying to sort out what was taking place and coming up with an explanation that way underestimated what was happening. Perhaps the humility of the entry kept people from getting the point, as normally kings entered with much more pomp, using a greater animal and having an impressive entourage.

The endings to this scene differ in each gospel. In Mark 11:11, Jesus went to Bethany after going to the temple as it was late in the day. In Luke 19:39–40 the Pharisees protested about the demonstration's content. Jesus responded that if the disciples did not speak, the stones would cry out. John 12:12–16 simply describes the entry, ending with a citation of Zechariah 9:9. So Matthew's description of the city's response is unique to him and lacks the protest of the leadership. The city is simply left to ponder what was taking place.

Some have questioned whether Jesus could have survived such an event without a Roman or Sadducean response by arrest. However, the size and tumult of the large crowds streaming in from the Mount of Olives for the feast when observed from the Temple Mount meant that the event need not have garnered a great deal of concerned attention since there was no violence or anything like an army present (correctly Keener 2009, 493). The crowd's judgment that Jesus was merely a prophet also would have meant a political threat was minimized in the understanding of some. Yet some were bothered by what was being said, if we note Luke's account. They sought to warn Jesus, rather than react immediately. Festival times were potentially politically sensitive, so actions needed to be measured with care. That is what the accounts reflect. The entry should be considered "atriumphal" because the city did not welcome Jesus as a dignitary, but only tried to figure out what was going on.

THEOLOGICAL FOCUS

The exegetical idea (the healing of two blind men in Jericho who cry out to the Son of David illustrated Jesus's messianic authority, something that Jesus's act of entry into Jerusalem also declared as one who comes in the name of the Lord) leads to this theological focus: Jesus's actions point to him as the promised king of eschatological hope, something his power to heal underscores.

Jesus showed himself to be Son of David in two ways: (1) by healing, and (2) through a humble entry into Jerusalem that fulfilled Scripture. The significance of these actions was not entirely appreciated.

Jesus arrived at the city where he fulfilled his mission to serve and to give his life a ransom for many (Matt. 20:28). He did so as Son of David. Both in healing the two blind men and in humbly riding a donkey, he showed that he came to deliver and to bring peace. Jesus was going public and making a key claim. He was forcing the Jewish leadership to deal with him one way or another, to accept or reject him.

The crowd, at least some of them, sensed the moment and praised God for the Son of David and the one who came in the Lord's name. They perceived that Jesus was offering himself as king. Others were still trying to sort out who Jesus was. The question circulating through the city was yielding a less-than-Messiah answer: Jesus was a prophet. He pointed the way to God but himself was not the story. That, for Matthew, was inadequate. The king and the kingdom belonged together. You could not have one without the other. The Son of David healed as a sign that the eschaton had come. He entered the city making the same claim. The questions of the narrative were: What would the city do with it, and what would Matthew's readers do with such a claim? Was Jesus the one who came in the name of the Lord in fulfillment of what Scripture had long promised? To understand Jesus as a prophet was not good enough. To appreciate that he was the Messiah at the center of God's program of deliverance meant one could begin to comprehend what God was and is and will be doing.

PREACHING AND TEACHING STRATEGIES

Exegetical and Theological Synthesis

The exegetical section stresses the importance of seeing Jesus's true identity and swearing loyalty to him. In an earlier critical conversation with his disciples, he asked directly, "Who do you say that I am?" (Matt. 16:15). Despite his correct answer, Peter's lack of understanding showed when he rebuked Jesus for revealing the plan to die in Jerusalem. Peter was not the only disciple to waver in his faith. Even after the resurrection, some disciples doubted (Matt. 28:17). Faith does not erase all uncertainty.

However, certainty is not necessary for loyalty. Faith is dynamic. It wavers. It ebbs and flows. It makes bids for Jesus's comfort, healing, guidance, and intervention. When Jesus responds to those bids, faith increases. When he delays or denies our bids, uncertainty may creep in. For the blind men whose sight was restored, Jesus responded to their plea for mercy and request for sight. That "they followed him" speaks to their newfound loyalty (Matt. 20:34).

Sadly, not all acts of loyalty result in a lifetime of discipleship. Jesus watched crowds scatter and dissolve when he said hard things (John 6:60–66). Moreover, of those who sang "Hosanna" upon Jesus's arrival in Jerusalem, many likely shouted "Crucify him!" a few days later. This underscores the need to test our loyalty to Jesus daily. We cannot let the fluctuating conditions of our lives and moods dictate our loyalty. Were he merely a prophet, president, CEO, or quarterback of our favorite team, we could shift loyalties. He is not. He is the royal Son of David, Suffering Servant, Messiah. We owe him our lives.

Preaching Idea

Don't overlook Jesus's public service announcement.

Contemporary Connections

What does it mean?

Jesus made a public statement when riding into Jerusalem on a donkey. His actions, albeit meek, were clearly messianic. His arrival in the city to a modest chorus of "Hosannas" alerted his disciples, pilgrims, and anyone watching that his campaign to serve as Israel's king was no longer a secret. From now on, no one could ignore him.

Just as people in Jerusalem needed to reckon with Jesus's true identity, people today must take a careful look at his actions and claims. The Gospels are public records of Jesus's public life. They describe how he came to serve, suffer, and save the lost. They constitute the most important public service announcement in history.

Typically, public service announcements warn listeners of a danger and prompt us to respond: inclement weather, disease, gambling problems, or sexual harassment. Radio, TV, social media, and posters broadcast them. They are common in public places, such as college campuses, high schools, libraries, and subways. Although they are difficult to avoid, they are easy to ignore. So it goes with Jesus.

Is it true?

We must not overlook Jesus's public service announcement. Jesus's teaching provided plenty of warnings; he often referred to hell and judgment. The danger may not feel imminent, but it is eternal. Denying Jesus as Savior, Lord, and Messiah leaves us cut off from God's presence forever. We suffer the wages of sin—outer darkness, death, and destruction. A threat of such eternal weight must be announced!

However, we should mimic Jesus's approach to public service announcements. In my (Tim's) lifetime, evangelistic efforts have relied too heavily on scare tactics or bait-and-switch methods. We pretend to take surveys, only to crack the door open for preaching. We describe the horrors of hell to frighten people into heaven. Even if billboards (e.g., "You think it's hot down there?"—God) and gospel tracts (e.g., *Heaven Is No Trick and Hell Is No Treat*) that provide public warnings intend well, they do not echo Jesus's winsome tone. His public service announcement invited people to follow him and experience rest, purpose, community, and fullness of life.[1]

Now what?

All public service announcements compel a response. They may encourage better handwashing techniques to fight germs or greater vigilance in spotting sexual predators. In the case of Jesus's public service announcement, the response required is binary: overlook him or be loyal to him. Reject him or accept him. We must choose. So consider these questions:

- Do we take Jesus at his word?
- Do we believe his claim to kingship?
- Do we give our lives to him in loyalty?

If not, then we have rejected Jesus's public service announcement. There is no third way.

The good news—and it's public news!—is that until we die and face judgment, Jesus's public service announcement remains. On any given day the opportunity to repent, believe, and accept King Jesus is available to us. We can still respond wisely. We can take Jesus at his word, believe his claims to kingship, and give our lives to him in loyalty.

Once we have responded openly to Jesus's announcement, he sends us to spread the message. Disciples are expected to carry forth his announcement of the coming kingdom, which encompasses the overthrow of Satan, forgiveness of sin, defeat of death, and restoration of life. Disciples become disciple-makers (Matt. 28:18–20). Followers of Jesus become ambassadors of Christ (2 Cor. 5:20). We do the work of evangelists (2 Tim. 4:1–5). We join Jesus's triumphal procession and sustain the "Hosanna" refrain: "God saves. The King of kings has come."

Creativity in Presentation

The (a)triumphal entry lends itself to a reenactment. While it may be difficult to secure a donkey and colt for the scene, you may certainly collect coats and find palm branches to wave in the air. To capture the energy of the story, recruit a small group of people who are willing to march

1 The bulk of Jesus's public ministry focused on the coming kingdom of heaven. It was a message of anticipation not escapism. He publicly announced the coming kingdom through teaching, healing, exorcism, and calls for repentance. This does not deny times where Jesus spoke harshly and warned of hell. However, he mostly reserved those public service announcements for hypocritical religious leaders and unbelieving groups of people. Jesus knew his audience and could masterfully tailor his message to provoke a response. What makes the gospel good news is what the gospel offers people in terms of a new life with God.

from the back of the auditorium to the front stage with Jesus at the center. The louder they cry "Hosanna!" the better. Bundles of palm leaves are available on the Oriental Trading Company website. You may even opt to use a hobby horse for Jesus to ride on. Once the processional reaches the stage, you or the person playing the part of Jesus should face the audience and say, "Ladies and gentlemen, King Jesus has arrived."

To illustrate how common public service announcements are, you could gather several posters, images, or ads to share. Collect a variety, showing the range of these announcements covering everything from washing hands to sexual assault to gun violence to alcohol abuse to piracy. A simple Google search will provide numerous options; the DEA.gov website has many.

Public Service Announcement Phrases

"See something, say something."—about suspicious people and terrorism
"No means No."—about sexual abuse
"Don't text and drive."—about safe driving
"Stop the swerve."—about driving without being intoxicated
"Talk: They hear you."—about intentional parenting

A key to making these public service announcements effective is helping people realize how often we overlook them. When they are on TV or radio, we tune them out. When they are on bathroom walls and bulletin boards, we overlook them. Sadly, we do the same with Jesus's public service announcement. The consequences are eternal!

You can find a humorous example of a public service announcement from the TV series *Parks & Recreation* (created by Greg Daniels and Michael Shur, 2009–15). In season four, episode eleven, "The Comeback Kid," Leslie Knope relaunches her campaign for town council at a local ice rink. It is three minutes of hilarity. They make an atriumphal entry, slipping and falling across the ice. The soundtrack glitches; "Get on Your Feet" by Gloria Estefan loops awkwardly. Leslie cannot mount the podium and her note cards get disordered, making for a discombobulated speech. Her announcement to be a public servant is certainly memorable.

Whatever creative elements you adopt or adapt, be sure your sermon shows that Jesus's actions point to him as the promised king of eschatological hope, something his power to heal underscores. Therefore, don't overlook Jesus's public service announcement.

- We see Jesus's mercy and power on display (20:29–34).
- We see Jesus's humble authority on display (21:1–11).

DISCUSSION QUESTIONS

1. How is Matthew's version of the healing of the blind men different from Mark's?
2. The title "Son of David" ties these stories together. What does the title mean?
3. What is the messianic meaning in Psalm 118?
4. What makes this story anticlimactic? What kept Roman soldiers from quelling it?
5. Why is public faith more troublesome than private faith? How have Christians in the West settled for a faith that is either too private or too political?

Matthew 21:12–22

EXEGETICAL IDEA
By cleansing the temple and cursing the fig tree, Jesus symbolically purged the nation and warned them of judgment.

THEOLOGICAL FOCUS
Jesus shows his authority by challenging the nation's worship and spiritual state.

PREACHING IDEA
Purity is priority when we gather to worship God.

PREACHING POINTERS
The population in Jerusalem swelled for Passover. Pilgrims came from all directions to worship at the temple. Jesus was among them; however, when he found the outer court of the complex littered with merchants selling sacrificial animals to travelers for profit, he responded indignantly. He overturned tables, rebuked religious leaders, and quoted prophets in protest. Then tension built as Jesus healed crowds, received praise, and cursed a fig tree in subsequent scenes. For Matthew's audience, Jesus's actions showed his authority over nature and religious leaders. He could curse a fig tree and condemn priests who failed to perform their God-given tasks. Jesus's public opposition was profoundly offensive to Jerusalem's brass. This scene precipitated his coming crucifixion.

For too many churches, contemporary worship gatherings have become performances. They are timed and designed for efficiency and entertainment. The countdown clock ticks off seconds before the show begins. Video announcements run like commercials. The worship band blasts music for a crowd shrouded in darkness. The preacher dashes out during a slick bumper video and delivers an inspiring talk with a few practical takeaways. After a closing prayer, people vacate their seats, shuffle through the doors, and exit the building until next week's service. We act more like consumers than worshipers. The formative elements of church life—prayer, confession, fellowship, communion, giving, service—get sacrificed on the altar of performance. Unfortunately, high production value does not translate to holiness. Precision does not make us pure. This sermon renews Jesus's vision for corporate worship: exalting God. Purity is priority when we gather to worship God.

JESUS PURGES THE TEMPLE AND CURSES A FIG TREE (21:12–22)

LITERARY STRUCTURE AND THEMES (21:12–22)

This unit has three parts. First, Jesus cleansed the temple (Matt. 21:12–13). The event is much discussed because there is a significant debate whether Jesus was purging the temple for a future work or predicting a decisive judgment on Israel with the temple's permanent end. The difference for the action's meaning and its theology is important, even though the text is very brief.

Second, there is a healing summary that also produced indignation from the chief priests and scribes (Matt. 21:14–17). Here is where Matthew shows the official reaction to Jesus's claim on Jerusalem, as opposed to at the entry itself as the other Synoptics did. This portion of the text is unique to Matthew. It is close in tone to the Pharisees' reaction to Jesus's entry in Luke 19:39–40. The passage shows that the leadership was not open to accepting Jesus, despite the good he was doing.

Third, Matthew describes the cursing of the fig tree (Matt. 21:18–22). This was certainly a warning about judgment for the nation. The question is whether it was a prediction of a temporary or a more permanent judgment.

The temple cleaning was a messianic declaration, a symbolic parable and claim to authority. It reflected an expectation of an act the Messiah was expected to perform for the city in the eschaton by purging the city of sin (Pss. Sol. 17:26–31; see chart at Matt. 19:28–30).

The reaction of the leadership against Jesus and his work of healing simply played out the rising narrative tension between Jesus and the leadership. His actions were forcing their hand. Jesus was acting intentionally and quite publicly now. In fact, there could hardly have been a more public action than this one, at what Jews regarded as earth's most sacred spot.

The cursing of the fig tree also was an enacted parable. It is told in two parts. Matthew 21:18–19 is a curse manifested as a miracle, while the disciples' reaction and a pronouncement follow (Matt. 21:20–22). It was a rare case of a miracle of judgment from Jesus, with the only other example involving Jesus being the destruction of pigs with the Gadarene demoniacs (Matt. 8:28–34; there are other examples in Acts 13:11 and 19:16, both involving Paul; Nolland 2005, 850, briefly defends its historicity). The cursing of the fig tree pictured judgment on Israel, something the Olivet Discourse would develop and that Jesus's rebuke of the leaders justified (Matt. 23). A key issue is deciding if that judgment was permanent for Israel or only for a time. The lesson, however, was a call to faith as seen in the pronouncement. Jesus was urging the disciples to have faith in the mission, even in the face of such seemingly significant opposition.

The parallels to the temple cleaning are Mark 11:15, 17 and Luke 19:45–46. As is common in Matthew, his version is condensed. The connection of the parallel in John 2:13–22 is much discussed because of the cleansing's location early in John's gospel and its differences with the Synoptics. Are there two cleansings or one? It is hard to be sure. Turner (2008, 502) prefers two cleansings. There are differences of placement and detail that make this possible, but it being one event that John moved is also likely, as it was very unlikely Jesus would get away with such a cleansing twice nor would an initial cleansing lead only to questions, while the second would lead to hostility (Snodgrass 2009, 445–47). The action was so provocative that a full reaction initially would be inevitable. For John to make such a move for literary purposes shows what Jesus's ministry entailed. This kind of a move does not distort the event nor take away from the fact that it took place. In fact, the paradigmatic relocation shows its significance.

The healing summary of Matthew 21:14–17 has no parallel. The cursing of the fig tree is also in Mark 11:12–14 with a conversation unique to Mark in Mark 11:20–25. Luke does not have this event. The differences in timing between Mark and Matthew also produce much discussion that the exposition will cover.

Everything about these events escalated the tension that led into Jesus's arrest and death. Despite Jesus's good deeds and the divine authentication they represented, he was not being accepted by those who led the nation. Nothing could persuade them God was acting through Jesus.

EXPOSITION (21:12–22)

Israel was in sad spiritual shape, consistently rejecting Jesus's overtures for faith. Those who opposed Jesus needed to appreciate what was at stake, while those who had come to faith in Jesus needed to be reassured they had done the right thing. Matthew recounts some of the events that led to the division within Judaism and Israel over Jesus. With an eschatological and regal claim of the right to purge the nation, Jesus cleansed the temple and cursed a fig tree as a warning to the nation. God was still at work through Jesus in the midst of these challenges, as his healing work continued. God was showing that Jesus had the right to make the claims he was making and perform the acts he was doing, even as the leadership continued to reject his challenges.

By cleansing the temple and cursing the fig tree, Jesus symbolically purged the nation and warned it of judgment.

21:12–13. The temple was a huge area, the size of thirty-five football fields (Bahat in Charlesworth 2006, 300–308; Turner 2008, 499). It also was seen as the most sacred spot on earth by Jews because it was the location of the one temple dedicated to the one God. Josephus described Solomon's construction of it in great detail (*A.J.* 8.63–98; *B.J.* 5.184–227, and compared it to a shiny and snow-clad mountain when the sun shined on it in 5.222–24). It was the center of the world for a Jew (Davies and Allison 1997, 133). The money changers were likely present near the southern portico and the Court of the Gentiles. They may have recently been moved into the temple precinct (Eppstein 1964).

Josephus on the Appearance of the Temple

Josephus, Jewish War 5.222–24: "Now the outward façe of the temple in its front wanted nothing that was likely to surprise either men's minds or their eyes, for it was covered all over [with] plates of gold of great weight, and, at the first rising of the sun, reflected back a very fiery splendor, and made those who forced themselves to look upon it to turn their eyes away, just as they would have done at the sun's own rays. But this temple appeared to strangers, when they were at a distance, like a mountain covered with snow; for, as to those parts of it that were not gilt, they were exceeding white. On its top it had spikes with sharp points, to prevent any pollution of it by birds sitting upon it. Of its stones, some of them were forty-five cubits in length, five in height, and six in breadth."

Jesus cleansed the temple in a messianic act (Mark 11:15, 17; Luke 19:45–46). This event was much discussed in treatments about Jesus (Snodgrass in Bock and Webb 2009, 429–80, with a full discussion of issues tied to historicity; Bock 2012, 122–36; Davies and Allison 1997, 135–37; Evans 1989a; Keener 2009, 495–96; Turner 2008, 501–2). Snodgrass works through seven options for how this event was seen and opts for a "prophetic protest that pointed to future eschatological hope" (Snodgrass 2009, 471). Many see elements of predicting temple destruction and cleansing in the scene, as well as complaints about corruption, which was why there was a need for cleaning. Numerous Jewish texts point to eschatological cleansing of the temple as God draws near to save (4Q174; 11QTa 29:8–10; Tob. 13:16–17; 1 En. 90:28–29; Jub. 1:15–17; Benediction 14 of the Shemoneh Esreh [Amidah]—see chart at the beginning of the section on Matt. 20:29–21:11 before t). The eschatological cleansing looked to an ideal temple. Zechariah 14:21 was also in the background.

Temple and Eschatology

4Q174 1.5–6a: "[His glory shall] be revealed for[ev]er; it shall appear over it perpetually. And strangers will lay it waste no more, as they formerly laid waste the sanctua[ry of I]srael because of their sin."

11QTa 29:8b–10: "And I will consecrate my [te] mple by my glory (the temple) on which I settle my glory, until the day of blessing on which I will create my temple and establish it for myself for all times, according to the covenant which I have made with Jacob at Bethel."

1 Enoch 90:28–29: "Then I stood still, looking at that ancient house being transformed: All the pillars and all the columns were pulled out; and the ornaments of that house were packed and taken out together with them and abandoned in a certain place in the South of the land. I went on seeing until the Lord of the sheep brought about a new house, greater and loftier than the first one, and set it up in the first location which had been covered up—all its pillars were new, the columns new; and the ornaments new as well as greater than those of the first, (that is) the old (house) which was gone. All the sheep were within it."

Tobit 13:16–17: "For Jerusalem will be built as his house for all ages. How happy I will be if a remnant of my descendants should survive to see your glory and acknowledge the King of heaven. The gates of Jerusalem will be built with sapphire and emerald, and all your walls with precious stones. The towers of Jerusalem will be built with gold, and their battlements with pure gold. The streets of Jerusalem will be paved with ruby and with stones of Ophir. The gates of Jerusalem will sing hymns of joy, and all her houses will cry, 'Hallelujah! Blessed be the God of Israel!' and the blessed will bless the holy name forever and ever."

Jubilees 1:15–17: "And afterward they will turn to me from among the nations with all their heart and with all their soul and with all their might. And I shall gather them from the midst of all the nations. And they will seek me so that I might be found by them. When they seek me with all their heart and with all their soul, I shall reveal to them an abundance of peace in righteousness. And with all my heart and with all my soul I shall transplant them as a righteous plant. And they will be a blessing and not a curse. And they will be the head and not the tail. And I shall build my sanctuary in their midst, and I shall dwell with them. And I shall be their God and they will be my people truly and rightly."

Jesus's action came after his messianic entry and also was a messianic act. He claimed authority over the temple by turning over the money changers' tables and the seats of those who sold pigeons. These services did make some sense, in that the law required spotless sacrifices and because the temple tax was paid in a specific Tyrian currency (Exod. 13:12–13; Lev. 5:7, 11; esp. 5:15; 12:6, 8; 14:10–11, 22; Deut. 15:21; *Šheq.* 1.3, 6; 5.6). It was easier to get the sacrifice at the temple than to haul it almost one hundred miles from Galilee. Something about the way this was done, and possibly where, was the problem, as the site seems to have been in the portico area on the southern side of the temple. *Mishnah Keritot* 1.7 is a complaint against high prices at the temple.

A Spotless Offering

Leviticus 5:15: "When a person commits a trespass and sins by straying unintentionally from the regulations about the Lord's holy things, then he must bring his penalty for guilt to the Lord, a flawless ram from the flock, convertible into silver shekels according to the standard of the sanctuary shekel, for a guilt offering."

Leviticus 14:10–11: "On the eighth day he must take two flawless male lambs, one flawless yearling female lamb, three-tenths of an ephah of choice wheat flour as a grain offering mixed with olive oil, and one log of olive oil, and the priest who pronounces him clean will have the man who is being cleansed stand along with these offerings before the Lord at the entrance of the Meeting Tent."

Deuteronomy 15:21: "If one of them has any kind of blemish—lameness, blindness, or anything else—you may not offer it as a sacrifice to the Lord your God."

Jesus cited Scripture as the tables were overturned. This probably took place in the southern portico area of the Temple Mount alongside the outer court. Jesus's rebuke combined Isaiah 56:7 and Jeremiah 7:11. In these texts, the nation was instructed in how to worship (Isaiah) and was being rebuked for poor temple worship (Jeremiah). The house of prayer had become a den for "robbers," a bandit or insurrectionist's cave (BDAG s.v. "λῃστής" 1, 594). They were on the Jeremiah side of the worship scale and that was not good. The complaint was of a bazaar in the house of God where people were taken advantage of in the sales that took place. The table-turning event was more symbolic than grand in scale, as it was a one-man protest that probably involved a few tables (France 2007, 786; Keener 2009, 498). It was small enough that neither temple police nor Roman police responded to it. It was designed to picture a point: the temple was a corrupt place that needed renewal (Evans 2012, 361).

Photo of replica of first-century Temple Mount and temple, making clear the location of the southern portico (the roofed area to the left of the temple)

This action also raised points about Jesus's authority. Who had the authority to challenge the temple leadership so directly and mess with the most sacred space in the world? There was a culturally rooted challenge in what Jesus did. He was claiming total rights over the temple. He did so having just entered the city as a regal claimant. Those two acts reflected on each other. Who was doing the purging was as important as the symbolic purge itself. Worship before God was to be done in ways that honored him. Jesus had every right to point that out.

21:14. Matthew 21:14–17 is unique to the gospel. Jesus healed the blind and the lame (Matt. 11:5; 15:30–31). This short summary was more important for the reaction it generated. Jesus still showed compassion in the midst of heightened opposition. It is the final healing note in Matthew. Davies and Allison (1997, 140) observe that in contrast, Mark has no healing in Jerusalem. The effect of Jesus's healing was that those disqualified from being in the temple proper could now be full participants (Lev. 21:18–19). It was a picture of what Jesus's overall work meant. He restored connection to God.

21:15–16a. Jesus received praise as Son of David from children. Little ones were what believers are to be like (Matt. 10:42; 11:25; 18:1–6; 19:14; 25:40, 45). Even the young recognized that God was at work in the hope of promise. Wisdom 10:21 is similar in tone: "Wisdom . . . made the tongues of infants speak clearly" (Davies and Allison 1997, 142). This echoed the praise of the entry (Matt. 21:9) and the cry of the two blind men (Matt. 20:29–31). It continued Matthew's framing of these acts as coming from the regal Son of David. It was kings who cleansed the temple (Josiah in 2 Kings 22–23; Hezekiah in 2 Chron. 29:3–11; Judas Maccabeus in 1 Macc. 4; 2 Macc. 10).

The praise and actions made the leadership of the chief priests and scribes indignant. They did not appreciate the healing and restoration nor consider what it might point to; rather, the note of praise and acceptance of Jesus disturbed them. There also was a rebuke in this observation: children saw better what was happening than the leaders. The term ἀγανακτέω is a strong one, speaking of "intense anger" or displeasure, thus "indignation." (BDAG s.v. "ἀγανακτέω" 5; Matt. 20:24). They asked him to stop the praise by complaining about what the people were saying.

21:16b. Jesus refused, citing Psalm 8:2 (Ps. 8:3 LXX), showing this was something God accepted. The language is closer to the Greek than the MT, but what was praised in the original psalm was the strength of God in the face of enemies. God's strength and power pointed to a reason to praise God (Exod. 15:2; Davies and Allison 1997, 142). France (2007, 789) notes how in the psalm God was being defended, and here it was acts tied to Jesus's entry that were being defended as an expression of God's program. The citation called what the children were doing "prepared praise" (BDAG s.v. "καταρτίζω" 2b, 526—to prepare, and s.v. "αἶνος" 27—praise). What was taking place was right. Nothing needed to be done to stop it. Jesus again was challenging the leaders' understanding of what was taking place.

21:17. Jesus returned to stay the night in Bethany. The verb points to a place of temporary "lodging" (BDAG s.v. "αὐλίζομαι" 150). Jesus had come as a pilgrim along with other worshipers, but he was not merely a pilgrim.

21:18–19. Jesus came into the city the next morning and was hungry. Mark says it was not the season for figs. On the other hand, leaves being present on a fig tree normally meant it did have some initial buds of fruit (Osborne 2010, 769). Keener (2009, 504) speaks of early figs that were less than ideally palatable but eaten on occasion in cases of hunger. Despite the promise of the leaves, the tree lacked any fruit.

Photo of a Fig Tree.

Upon seeing a fig tree only with leaves and having no fruit, he cursed it by commanding that it never yield fruit again. That tree withered immediately. Mark 11:12–14 is the parallel.

Mark also develops the event in Mark 11:20–25 with the observation that on the next day the disciples saw the fig tree had withered. In the Markan discussion, Jesus issued his call to pray with faith and be forgiving. Wilkins (2004, 693) observes in Mark we were on Monday and Tuesday of the last week. This difference is a classic case of what happens when Matthew presents his account more concisely. Turner (2008, 503) speaks of Matthew telescoping the account of Mark, which has the entire fig tree incident split over two days, since Jesus cursed the fig tree one day and the withered tree and discussion followed the next. With Matthew's shorter account, certain details of timing were omitted. Matthew was more interested in giving the core teaching and less concerned about details on the timing.

The withered tree was another enacted parable and pictured judgment on the current generation of Israel's leadership. Konradt (2020, 314) limits the point to the power of faith and sees no allusion to judgment on the nation. However, this entire section is an indictment of the leadership, so it is not the nation as such that is in view but where the leadership is taking the nation. So there is a primary target to the remark but the effects will spread across the nation. Matthew 23 will finish the indictment.

Even though there was destruction in this miracle, the tree was not a person and so was simply used as a prop for the imagery. Such prophetic acts are common in the Old Testament (Isa. 8:1–4; 20:1–6; Jer. 13; 19; 27–28; Ezek. 3:1–3; 4:1–5:17; Hos. 1:2–9; Turner 2008, 504). Fruitless fig trees pictured judgment, often of Israel or Judah (Isa. 34:4 of nations; Jer. 8:13 of Israel; 24:1–10; Hos. 2:12; Joel 1:7). Temple leaders were the object of judgment here (Davies and Allison 1997, 148, 151–52) versus Israel as a whole, at least in a permanent sense (but France 2007, 794, calls it "terminal"). But is more than the leadership somewhat in view?

Hagner (1995, 603–4) and Osborne (2010, 770) appeal to the parable of the Wicked Tenants as the backdrop, but that text was only against the leadership as Mark 12:12 showed. Such background alone would not point to an expanded application beyond the leadership to Israel as a whole. However, that is not the only context to consider. The issue of a future for Israel is not a theme Matthew developed, but Luke and Paul held to it—this judgment was unlikely to be totally terminal for the nation, but the text does suggest a more corporate dimension or implication than the leadership alone, even though the leadership is seen as the core cause for this evaluation by Jesus. Luke 13:34–35 speaks of "until" Israel recognizes Jesus, with the nation as a whole in view in a temporally limited national judgment. Luke 21:24 speaks of "until" the times of the Gentiles are fulfilled, implying a restoration of Israel on the other end. This would fit with Acts 1:6–11, which does not reject the premise of the question about the kingdom restored to Israel but only says that is the Father's business. Acts 3:18–22 also anticipates the fulfillment of the expression of OT prophetic hope as realized in Jesus's return, a hope that included a blessed place for national Israel. Romans 11:17–36 looks to a regrafting of Israel as the natural branches placed back into blessing in the end. Any judgment extending to the nation beyond the leadership, which is likely in view here, was not permanent nor total, but tied to the length of the lack of national response to her Messiah. The Olivet Discourse would look to more than the leadership being impacted by the coming overrunning of the temple. This text is more like Luke 13:34–35 than is normally noted.

Fruitless Fig Tree as Israel

Jeremiah 8:13: "I will take away their harvests, says the Lord. There will be no grapes on their vines. There will be no figs on their fig trees. Even the leaves on their trees will wither. The crops that I gave them will be taken away."

Jeremiah 24:8–10: "I, the Lord, also solemnly assert: 'King Zedekiah of Judah, his officials, and the people who remain in Jerusalem or who have gone to live in Egypt are like those bad figs. I consider them to be just like those bad figs that are so bad they cannot be eaten. I will bring such disaster on them that all the kingdoms of the earth will be horrified. I will make them an object of reproach, a proverbial example of disaster. I will make them an object of ridicule, an example to be used in curses. That is how they will be remembered wherever I banish them. I will bring war, starvation, and disease on them until they are completely destroyed from the land I gave them and their ancestors.'"

Hosea 2:12: "I will destroy her vines and fig trees, about which she said, 'These are my wages for prostitution that my lovers gave to me!' I will turn her cultivated vines and fig trees into an uncultivated thicket, so that wild animals will devour them."

Joel 1:7: "They [the nation of locusts] have destroyed my vines; they have turned my fig trees into mere splinters. They have completely stripped off the bark and thrown it aside; the twigs are stripped bare."

What Ezekiel 34 had warned about had now taken place. God was providing new shepherds for the sheep to replace those who had failed. There had been plenty of time for fruit and for a response to what God was doing through Jesus, but none had appeared. So a judgment will follow. The Olivet Discourse in Matthew 24–25 will expand on this note of judgment, and the rationale for it will come in Jesus's condemnation of the leadership in Matthew 23. The opposition to Jesus was reaping its consequences.

21:20–22. The withering of the fig tree amazed the disciples, and they asked how this could have happened. This was yet another Matthean scene where an act led to private teaching for the disciples. The disciples were more impressed by what Jesus had done than with understanding why he did it.

Jesus highlighted faith without doubt (Mark 11:20–24). He noted that such faith not only could accomplish unusual things like the withering of the fig tree, but it could move mountains as well (Matt. 17:19–20; Luke 17:6; James 1:6). The remark spoke of asking anything, but the context framed the scope of that request. Matthew specifically says, discuss "this" (τούτῳ) mountain. So what is in view here? Some see the Mount of Olives and Zechariah 14:4–5 in view (Nolland 2005, 854). However, the Mount of Olives does not go to the sea in the Zechariah text. It only will split in two. Also, the disciples and their prayers do not trigger such a future event. The best that can be said is that an eschatological time is present, with judgment on the temple drawing near. A reference to the Temple Mount is also possible with this sense. But faith and prayer are the main topics, as well as the unusual things prayer can accomplish, so debate about what the precise example was may miss the emphasis (Culpepper 2021, 402).

Keener (2009, 505) prefers to see Zechariah 4:6–9 in the background, which is possible. It teaches that amazing things happen by the Spirit of God to bring about God's presence and rule. The faith in view is contextually focused on God's power and capability. France (2007, 795) observes the plural verbs throughout were looking at corporate prayer. Blomberg (1992, 319) limits the application in prayer to things tied to God's program, which was in view in this scene (also Nolland 2005, 855). Wilkins (2004, 694) sees the point as saying yes to God's will in the context of work emerging from his power. Morris (1992, 532) notes that the call for faith precludes selfish requests and is related to Christian service. Osborne (2010, 771) speaks of prayer in Jesus's name, appealing to John 14:12–14. The picture of moving mountains is a metaphor for being able to accomplish things one might not think possible with reference to the plan of God. The pronouncement closes with the word that one who prays with belief will receive (especially Matt. 7:7–11; also Matt. 6:8; 18:19). Matthew lacks the mention of forgiveness that Mark 11:25 presents.

Jesus entered Jerusalem with three symbolic acts: the entry on the donkey, the temple cleansing, and the fig tree curse. He was the Messiah who purged the city, but the city's lack of response made her accountable.

THEOLOGICAL FOCUS

The exegetical idea (by cleansing the temple and cursing the fig tree, Jesus symbolically purged the nation and warned them of judgment) points to this theological focus: Jesus shows his authority by challenging the nation's worship and spiritual state.

In a call to reform and an act of messianic cleansing, Jesus called Israel to make the temple a house of prayer, while the cursing of the fig tree pictured judgment on the nation's leadership with coming national impact. The cursing also led to a call to faith for the disciples.

Jesus's challenge to Israel continued. His prophetic act warned the leadership about judgment, a judgment that would certainly occur if those in the nation followed the example of their leaders. Events were coming to a head. To reject Jesus and not respond to him was to be left accountable to God. That was what the cursing of the fig tree represented. Other biblical passages speak of a role and restoration for Israel one day when she recognizes Jesus as the one who comes in the name of the Lord. Matthew did not discuss this. His concern was for the current accountability Israel had before God. Yet the widespread early church expectation of such a hope meant it was likely in the background.

A second theme is the importance of faith and prayer. Faith with prayer could accomplish amazing things when it was removed from doubt and pursued God's program and will. Jesus encouraged such faith, even in the midst of the opposition now surfacing to him and the disciples. The juxtaposition of opposition, call to faith, and a reminder of accountability before God was no accident. Sometimes opposition can cause doubt and lead us to forget where our ultimate accountability lies. The tyranny of the urgent blocks our way, keeping our eye from seeing what is really important. As a result, Jesus issued a renewed call for faith while noting God would bring justice and hold those who did not respond to him accountable. Freedom from God and his way meant accountability and judgment. Not all freedom is good.

PREACHING AND TEACHING STRATEGIES

Exegetical and Theological Synthesis

The exegetical section describes Jesus's emotional intensity. He overturned tables, healed the disabled, and cursed a fig tree. These actions show his zeal for God, advocacy for the hurting, and frustration with corruption. These stories become case studies in Jesus's emotional life: his anger stands opposite his compassion. Jesus was not "behaving badly" (Strauss 2015) but boldly. Now that he had made his public service announcement, Jesus would pull no punches. He would not go down without a fight, challenging the religious complex with a combination of sharp words and prophetic actions.

The role of prophets is a lonely one. Much of their ministry is dedicated to exposing sin. They speak with heat in their voices. They call out arrogant leaders, greedy businessmen, unjust institutions, and idolators. Their righteous indignation runs like a thread through the Old Testament prophets. Jesus echoed it, especially upon arriving in Jerusalem. Like the prophets of old, his zeal led to him being ostracized. And he warned his disciples they would suffer a similar fate (Matt. 5:10–12).

Preaching Idea

Purity is priority when we gather to worship God.

Contemporary Connections

What does it mean?

First, we must clarify what we mean by "when we gather to worship God." A worship gathering happens at a set time with other people to honor God. In Jesus's day, worship gatherings included shared hours of prayer, weekly sabbath meetings at the synagogue, and annual feasts like Passover and Tabernacles. For the contemporary church, worship gatherings include but are not limited to Sunday morning services, annual conferences, and occasional times of prayer and praise. Additionally, special events such as a baptism service, wedding, or Communion celebration constitute worship gatherings.

Second, the purity of the participants matters. Those who come to worship should attend with pure motives, not simply to socialize. They should come with pure hearts, not deceitfulness, bitterness, or divided loyalties. They should come with pure thoughts, not the arrogant belief that they are better than others.

Third, the purity of our worship practices matters. Although the New Testament does not prescribe every detail for weekly gatherings, it describes an ethos and essentials for the church. Prayer, teaching, fellowship, worship, and service are nonnegotiables (Acts 2:42–47). Gatherings should be purposeful, orderly, well led, and inclusive (1 Cor. 14). Ordinances should be observed faithfully (1 Cor. 11:23–34). Worship services should happen regularly, spur others toward love, and equip one another for service (Eph. 4:11–16; Heb. 10:24–25). God does not delight in haphazard worship services.

Is it true?

It is certainly true that purity is priority when we gather to worship. However, two clarifications are needed. First, extenuating circumstances may disrupt when and how we gather. The COVID pandemic was a recent study in reconfiguring weekly worship. Many complained that online church did not constitute a pure gathering. However, due to safety precautions and government mandates, most churches had to find creative ways to worship. In places where the church is persecuted, a similar tension exists. (And a case could be made for the pilgrims who waited until arriving in Jerusalem to purchase their sacrifices in order to keep their luggage light!) Sometimes the purity of the gathering is at the mercy of external factors.

Second, the purity of the participants in worship is the ideal but rarely the reality. Every church is a mixed bag of sinners and saints. Worship services are not holiness clubs, where bouncers take confessions at the doorway. Rather, corporate worship provides time and space for confessing sin and receiving God's forgiveness. We may "come as we are" with the hopes that we leave purer than when we came. This does not mean worship gatherings become a moral free-for-all or platform for self-expression. We must remember that the goal of worship gatherings is to elevate God, not to lower standards.

Now what?

Jesus's righteous indignation forces us to take an honest look at our own corporate worship. Every church has room for growth in purity—both for its participants and its practices. Indeed, this passage invites us to assess, confess, and address the priority we place on purity when we gather to worship God.

First, we assess areas of impurity. What kind of worship environment do we create? How do we talk about God? What aspects of our services are confusing, distracting, or focused more on human needs than God's glory? Are we creating spaces where people can reflect, pray, confess, and praise? Asking these and similar questions will start our assessment process. Assessment moves us toward purity.

Second, we confess areas of impurity. Psalms 15 and 24 provide a call to worship where purity of heart and hands matter for the worshiper. These may be used in a service to help people confess. Likewise, Psalms 32 and 51 are classic confessions that may help worshipers confess their sins during a worship service. More succinctly, 1 John 1:9 reminds us that forgiveness follows confession. More liturgical churches have a time of confession built into their worship services. For those who do not regularly integrate confession, it would be wise to provide moments early in the gathering to invite God to search people's hearts, expose any area of impurity, and extend forgiveness (Pss. 19:14; 139:23–24). Confession purifies us.

Third, we address areas of impurity. If our worship services have become performances, we address the issue by shifting the focus to God. This may mean lowering the volume, having the worship leader talk less, or selecting songs better suited for congregational singing. If our gatherings are plagued by distractions, we address the issue by eliminating the distractions. This may mean we dim the lights, fix the flickering projector, dismiss the children earlier, or simplify the stage decorations. If our worship services offer no time for self-examination and confession, we address the issue by inserting time for these activities. This moment may be tied into the worship set or following the service in a designated prayer room. Addressing impurity helps us remain pure.

Creativity in Presentation

Consider building ideas from the sermon into the beginning of the worship service. As you greet people, let them know you will be talking about the priority of purity in worship and you want to help them succeed from the start. Thus, you will be giving an opportunity for self-examination and confession. You can read Psalms 15, 24, 139:23–24, or 1 John 1:9 to prompt them. If you want to add a touch of humor, you could hold up a bottle of hand sanitizer and say, "We'll be passing this around. We need clean hands and a pure heart to enter God's presence."

The story of Jesus's overturning tables lends itself to an illustration. Several examples are available on YouTube. However, you might set up a table on the stage with several items that signify how the temple had become a marketplace. Since live animals would be too complicated, you could gather stuffed animals or pet cages to represent the offerings. You could also add items typically sold in contemporary churches: books, concessions, church swag, concert tickets, and items from school fundraisers. If you want to be dramatic, you could literally flip the table over. If you want to maintain your cool, simply point to the items and ask, "Has our church become a marketplace?"

You can easily illustrate how we take purity for granted. Hold up a clear bottle of water. Talk about the refreshing, thirst-quenching experience of drinking clean water. Ask your congregation if they would drink water filled with bacteria or pollutants. After they respond, you can say, "Purity is priority in drinking water." You could follow this example with others: comparing a pure diamond (4Cs: cut, color, clarity, carat) to a flawed diamond; a personal love letter to an AI-generated love letter; unleaded, premium gasoline to gas mixed with oil; or a juicy, Grade-A angus beef burger to the infamous "mystery meat" in the school cafeteria.

We have all encountered "purists" of one form or another. A purist is "a person who advocates the strictest application of the principles or standards in any field, or who insists on purity of language, style, etc."[1] These people appreciate their trade, hobby, or field, but can come across as sticklers. Consider describing some modern-day purists before turning the discussion toward worship.

Examples of Modern-day Purists

- The person who drinks home-roasted, fair-trade coffee black.

1 See https://www.dictionary.com/browse/purists (accessed July 24, 2024).

- The person who insists on proper grammar, applying the rules to whomever she meets!
- The person who laments the pitch timer in baseball because changes have ruined the game.
- The person who runs meetings with Robert's Rules of Order.
- The person who grows their own vegetables.
- The people who cling to hymns and organ music as the way to worship at church.

Purity does not always have a positive connotation. Purity culture has become scrutinized in recent years. Since Joshua Harris deconstructed his faith and disavowed his popular book *I Kissed Dating Goodbye* (1997), countless voices have echoed his criticism of purity culture, which focused exclusively on sexual purity and caused excessive guilt to young people for sexual desires. Purity culture put tremendous pressure on young women to dress modestly lest they "cause their brother to stumble." While purity culture was not all bad, it certainly revealed the danger of limiting purity to one area: sexuality. Consider addressing purity holistically. Let your people know God wants "clean hands and a pure heart." You might work through several areas of life where purity should be priority, making your way toward worship gatherings. "Purity is priority in our homes, in our beds, on our phones. Purity is priority while working, watching TV, and washing the dishes. Purity is priority in our thoughts, motives, actions, and prayers. Purity is priority in our family, friendships, and dating relationships. Purity is priority when we gather to worship."

Ultimately, you want your sermon to teach that Jesus shows his authority by challenging the nation's worship and spiritual state. Therefore, purity is priority when we gather to worship God.

- Impure worship angers Jesus (21:12–13).
- Illness moves Jesus to compassion (21:14–17).
- An impotent fig tree angers Jesus (21:18–22).

DISCUSSION QUESTIONS

1. What made the sale of sacrifices in Jerusalem so infuriating to Jesus?
2. How did the cleansing of the temple factor into the rest of Jesus's passion week?
3. What are parallels between impure worship practices in Jesus's day and our day?
4. When have you seen confession practiced well in corporate worship settings?
5. How can the call to purity be abused? Be specific.

Matthew 21:23–46

EXEGETICAL IDEA

In a series of controversies and parables that were leading the leadership to seek to arrest him, Jesus emphasized the value of obeying God and showed how the kingdom program was being passed on to others because his authority came from God.

THEOLOGICAL FOCUS

The authority of Jesus and the danger of opposition to him are shown in final controversies tied to Jesus's presence in Jerusalem.

PREACHING IDEA

There's no higher authority than heaven.

PREACHING POINTERS

Tensions in Jerusalem continued to rise during Jesus's final week. After Jesus cleared the temple, religious leaders confronted him, demanding an explanation for his bold actions. Jesus responded with a question and two stories that exposed their rejection of heavenly authority. The parable of the Two Sons illustrated God's desire for obedience over lip service. The parable of the Wicked Tenants illustrated the religious leaders' preference for self-rule over submission to God. Matthew tethered these three narratives together to highlight how Jerusalem's elite could not accept Jesus's authority. For the original audience, their rejection of Jesus justified God's shifting focus to tax collectors, sinners, and Gentiles who would respond in faith.

Respect for heavenly authority remains low today. Since the Enlightenment, humans have steadily replaced God with mammon, technology, medicine, and politics. These tools provide for us the illusion that we are masters of our own fate and rulers of our private domains. We can reassign sex through surgery. We can control birth dates and euthanize the elderly. We can harness nuclear energy and produce food with 3D-printers. We no longer think the sky is the limit. We have no limits. This, of course, is the myth of progress. It is bound to fail because human striving will never replace God's strength. This sermon reminds us that there's no higher authority than heaven.

DISPUTES AND PARABLES SHOW JESUS'S AUTHORITY AND WARN THE OPPOSITION (21:23–46)

LITERARY STRUCTURE AND THEMES (21:23–46)

This unit has three parts: the dispute over where Jesus's authority came from (Matt. 21:23–27), the parable of the Two Sons (Matt. 21:28–32), and the parable of the Wicked Tenants (Matt. 21:33–46). This final parable is a detailed picture of Israel's history and a rebuke of the leadership's response as fitting a pattern in the nation's history. Matthew continues the pattern of threes that has been common in his gospel since Matthew 8–9.

Fortunately, the parables are not complex. They juxtapose the importance of a proper response to God's kingdom program with the picture of official disobedience placed alongside a critique of what the leadership was failing to do. John the Baptist, another representative of God whom the leadership did not embrace, is the foil for the theme. Other foils are the tax collectors and harlots who have responded in contrast to the leaders, reminding us that God often saves in surprising ways and from surprising places. The parable of the Wicked Tenants is a clear allegorical parable about Israel's history in failing to respond to God's prophets and now to the Son. In it is a warning to the leadership that their actions will not stop God's program, nor will they escape accountability. Leadership will go to others who respond. It is a reminder that we are all accountable for how we respond to God's program in Jesus. We are all called to respond well.

The parallels to the discussion of Jesus's authority in Matthew 21:23–27 are Mark 11:27–33 and Luke 20:1–8. Matthew still is tracking with the Marcan sequence and presents a more concise form of the event.

The parable of the Two Sons is unique to Matthew. The key theme focuses on who had responded to John the Baptist (Matt. 21:32 with 21:25).

The parable of the Wicked Tenants has parallels in Mark 12:1–12 and Luke 20:9–19. In this case, Matthew's length is like that of Mark and Luke. The Gospel of Thomas 65 also has a version of this parable that is close in form to Luke's (Nolland 2005, 867–68). Davies and Allison (1997, 187) see evidence of independent tradition at work here in this version from Thomas.

The first scene on the source of Jesus's authority is a controversy account, a conflict story, presented in a short dialogue. The dispute was about where Jesus received the authority to do what he was doing. The hidden premise was that the leaders did not give him that authority. The key theme emerging from this unit was that the leaders were shown to have not responded to the lead of heaven. Their deliberations also showed that they were not really interested in the real answer to the question, but simply how they would appear to others if they answered Jesus's query.

The second scene involves a simple parable where the contrast is between what one said and what one did. It also has a note of controversy because it challenged the leaders' lack of response. What one did was more important than what one said would be done. So, the son who said he would obey but did nothing was worse than the son who said he would not obey but eventually did respond. The emphasis, as the end of the parable shows, was on repenting, seeing the need to respond, and engaging in a change of direction that God called for in order to share in the kingdom.

The third scene is a complex parable that is an allegory. The vineyard looked to God's promise and the hope that resided currently in Israel. That hope was tied to the production of fruit. The owner was God. The servants were the prophets. The son was Jesus. The workers were the leadership. In a real lack of logic showing the blindness of sin, the workers beat and slew not only the servants but the son as well. Judgment came on those workers. They should not have rejected the stone God had sent. The kingdom was being given to others who would be fruit bearing. The result of this controversy was that the leaders decided they must stop Jesus.

EXPOSITION (21:23–46)

The fate of Jesus is firming up as the challenges continue. The leaders challenged where Jesus had received his authority, since he did not get it from them. John the Baptist was his answer as the authority for John came from God and not the leaders. Jesus did not answer the question directly but left the example for them to ponder. Jesus followed up with a couple of parables. Jesus emphasized the value of obeying God and showed how the kingdom program was being passed on to others because his authority came from God. Jesus warned that it is not those who say they will obey God but those who do obey him with whom the Father is pleased. This was immediately followed by a parable that contended that the nation's leadership had consistently disobeyed God and now was at risk of doing it again with the Son. The oversight of blessing was going to be given to others as a result. This was all too much, so the leaders resolved to get rid of Jesus. Warnings unheeded had led to disobedience, and now the consequences would result in the cross and in God's judgment on the nation. Matthew made clear the dangers of rejecting Jesus and reassured Jesus's followers that they were in the right place despite the pressure of rejection some were throwing at them. The presence of the kingdom program meant there were consequences for not obeying God. So he should be obeyed as participation in the kingdom will be passed on to those who respond.

21:23. From here until Matthew 22:40, the evangelist presents a series of controversies that showed Jesus as qualified to lead the people, while the leaders were not so qualified. We get three parables and then three controversies. A probing question in Matthew 22:41–46 closes the series of controversies. Then Jesus condemned the leaders in Matthew 23. The continued opposition within the narrative was building to fresh heights and was approaching final resolution.

Jesus's activities have caused the chief priests and elders to confront him (Mark 11:27; Luke 20:1). The chief priests were Jesus's key opponents in Jerusalem (Nolland 2005, 856–57). On a Tuesday, Jesus was in the temple courts, in the Court of the Gentiles, teaching as was his custom. Jesus's presence and teaching were disturbing to the leadership. They asked him by what authority was he doing these things (Mark 11:28; Luke 20:2). Jesus's authority served as a consistent issue in Matthew (Matt. 9:1–8; 12:6, 8, 28, 38, 41–42; 15:1–12; 16:1). The plural "these things" (ταῦτα) looks back at events, making it clear that more than the temple cleansing was in view (BDAG s.v. "οὗτος" 740–41, 1bα). A premise in the question was that the leadership had not commissioned him to act on their behalf. It was a question about control and power. It implied the leaders' discontent with Jesus's independence from them. It also was a trap question. It was designed to get him to make public claims and open the door for Roman reaction in terms of sedition, which would mean death (Davies and Allison 1997, 159).

21:24–25a. Jesus's response was to ask a question in return (Mark 11:29–30; Luke 20:3–4). Using a counterquestion was common in rabbinic-like debates (Keener 2009, 506; Wilkins 2004, 695). Jesus's question was about John the Baptist, who became a major topic in much of the rest of this unit. John also acted outside of the leadership's direction. Was his ministry from men or from heaven? Heaven was a circumlocution for God (Matt. 3:17; 16:1, 19; 18:18). To attribute the ministry to men was to declare it was not directed by God. Of course, in Matthew, John pointed to Jesus and was sent from God (Matt. 3:2, 11–16; 4:17; 11:2–6, 16–19). To answer about John was to answer about Jesus. The leaders publicly could make the call.

The counterquestion put the onus back on the leaders. An answer tied to God suggests God's protection of Jesus no matter what comes. How would they respond?

21:25b–27a. The leadership contemplated their options (Mark 11:31–33a; Luke 20:5–7). They were not good. The trappers had become the trapped. The deliberation showed a calculating mindset that was not interested in answering the question but in how the answer would be perceived. The issue became saving face. This was part of Matthew's characterization of the leadership as calculating versus spiritually sensitive. If they were to respond with "from heaven," then they would be challenged for not having believed John. If they were to respond with "from men," then the crowd would react, for they saw John as a prophet (Matt. 14:5; Josephus, *A.J.* 18.118). So they claimed they did not know. The response was not honest, but strictly for public play. They also showed "blindness to the obvious" (Davies and Allison 1997, 162).

Josephus on John the Baptist

***Antiquities* 18.118:** "Now, some of the Jews thought that the destruction of Herod's army came from God, and that very justly, as a punishment of what he did against John, that was called the Baptist; for Herod slew him, who was a good man, and commanded the Jews to exercise virtue, both as to righteousness towards one another, and piety towards God, and so to come to baptism; for that the washing [with water] would be acceptable to him, if they made use of it, not in order to the putting away [or the remission] of some sins [only], but for the purification of the body; supposing still that the soul was thoroughly purified beforehand by righteousness. Now, when [many] others came in crowds about him, for they were greatly moved [or pleased] by hearing his words, Herod, who feared lest the great influence John had over the people might put it into his power and inclination to raise a rebellion (for they seemed ready to do anything he should advise), thought it best, by putting him to death, to prevent any mischief he might cause, and not bring himself into difficulties, by sparing a man who might make him repent of it when it should be too late."

21:27b. Jesus replied that he would not answer either (Mark 11:33b; Luke 20:8). This is a passage where what was done in the passage is the opposite of what the passage accomplishes in the narrative (Davies and Allison 1997, 162). There is irony here. By Jesus simply raising the question about John, he answered the query. Just as God was behind John, and the leadership had nothing to do with it, so he was also with Jesus. The next parable of the Two Sons made the point more explicitly and placed responsibility squarely on the leadership.

21:28–30. The initial parable in this unit is unique to Matthew and is about two sons. It is the first of three parables in a row. All picture the leadership's rejection that would lead to exclusion from the kingdom (Matt. 21:28–32—two sons; Matt. 21:33–44—wicked tenants; Matt. 22:1–14—wedding banquet). There is the parable proper in Matthew 21:28–30, and then the explanation in Matthew 21:31–32. Each subunit has a question to start.

The parable, although unique to Matthew, is conceptually like Luke 15:11–32 (two sons) and 7:41–43 (two levels of response), as well as Luke 7:29–30 (also two kinds of response), so this kind of thematic contrast is multiply attested in sources and forms in the Jesus tradition, with unique material tied to Matthew and unique material tied to Luke. That scope of traditional usage points to its historical authenticity.

The landowner asked the sons one at a time to work in the vineyard. This had the look of a small family farm, since the sons worked it. The first son refused to work but then went to work in the vineyard after a "change of mind" (BDAG s.v. "μεταμέλομαι" 2, 639). The initial refusal would be a shock culturally, as sons obeyed their fathers. However, Jesus's parables often had such twists that were part of what made the story captivating. The second son said he would go work, but did not.

21:31–32. Jesus then asked, "Which did the father's will?" The leaders respond correctly: the first. It was not what was said, but what was done that showed who obeyed the father. In responding this way, the leaders fell into Jesus's trap as the second son pictured them and their ultimate disobedience, despite their claims of doing God's work. One of the effects of the narrative was to portray who was really qualified to lead Israel. Jesus had a far better grasp of things than the leadership, as he constantly instructed them.

Jesus declared that tax collectors and prostitutes would go before the leaders into the kingdom. This would have placed ahead of the leaders people from whom the leaders would have distanced themselves, making Jesus's remark a challenge to them at several levels. Those whom they rejected would have "shown the way" (France 2007, 805). The parable was about those within Israel and their differing responses to Jesus.

Jesus explained that John the Baptist went the way of righteousness, and the leaders did not believe, but the tax collectors and prostitutes did respond (Matt. 9:10–11; 11:19). When they saw this reaction from those previously on the fringe, the leaders did not have a change of heart but remained resolute in their unbelief. The repentance of others had taught them nothing. There can be no misunderstanding about how to read this parable and who it critiqued. It is important to note that the obedience that was the "work" in the passage was the repentance that accepted the father's will. It is not a picture that it was works that saved, but that those doing the work showed where their heart allegiance was (Osborne 2010, 782). Faith responds concretely to God and his will.

Once again John the Baptist pictured God's way and will, as in Matthew 21:25. The pronouncement closed the parable and again showed that the leaders were outside the promise. The key to relating to the Father was not in a claim of obedience, but in what one actually did (Osborne 2010, 781; Matthew 7:24–27; John 14:15, 21, 23). This is not a parable about Jews and Gentiles, as some teach. It is about the leadership and more common people: one group claiming to be pious but actually disobedient, another with a checkered past who responded in repentance and believed (Davies and Allison 1997, 171–72; Turner 2008, 510).

21:33. Jesus began the next parable by speaking of the planting of a vineyard on an owner's land (Mark 12:1; Luke 20:9). The building on the land showed this was either new land or a new section of land being developed. Isaiah 5:1–2 is in the background, but Matthew changed the order of the description. Isaiah spoke of a loved one (Israel) who built a vineyard. Matthew had

Israel as the vineyard built by God, with it being leased to tenants to tend it so it would have fruit. The owner took much care in building the vineyard, as he added a fence, placed a winepress there, and had a watchtower to protect it. The fence and tower protected the land, while the winepress was where the fruit was extracted from the produce. It would have been two basins, one higher than the other and connected by a channel so the juice could flow down and be collected (Morris 1992, 540). Then he leased it and went on a long journey, expecting the tenants to care for it so it would be fruitful. It would have taken time for the vineyard to yield usable fruit, at least four years (Keener 2009, 509–10; Lev. 19:23–25).

Israel as a Vineyard

Leviticus 19:23–25: "When you enter the land and plant any fruit tree, you must consider its fruit to be forbidden. Three years it will be forbidden to you; it must not be eaten. In the fourth year all its fruit will be holy, praise offerings to the Lord. Then in the fifth year you may eat its fruit to add its produce to your harvest. I am the Lord your God."

Isaiah 5:1–2: "I will sing to my love—a song to my lover about his vineyard. My love had a vineyard on a fertile hill. He built a hedge around it, removed its stones, and planted a vine. He built a tower in the middle of it, and constructed a winepress. He waited for it to produce edible grapes, but it produced sour ones instead."

The scene from everyday Galilean agriculture pictured Israel's history. The landowner was God. The vineyard was Israel (Isa. 5:1–7), seen as the place of promise, covenant relationship, and blessing. In Isaiah 5 the vineyard had produced bad fruit, and the nation was facing exile because of the sin that pictured. Jesus's version of the image added a layer to the picture involving the leaders' failure.

The coming request for fruit showed this was the point. The parable is very much an allegory with its multiple points of representation of Israel's history. The one major difference between Isaiah 5 and this parable involves the presence of tenants, highlighting the leaders' failed stewardship. The image's development is like the Targum to Isaiah 5 (Turner 2008, 514).

21:34–36. The parable told of two waves of many slaves sent to collect fruit. In each case, they met with violence. They were beaten, killed, and stoned in both waves. The stoning of prophets appears in 2 Chronicles 24:21 and is associated with Jeremiah in Lives of the Prophets 2.1 (France 2007, 813). Mark 12:2–5a has three slaves who were beaten, struck on the head, and killed. A second wave of slaves were sent, some were beaten, and others killed. Luke 20:10–12 has three slaves sent, with the first beaten, the second beaten, and the third wounded. This violence portrayed the prophets sent and the past leaders' covenantal unfaithfulness from whom spiritual fruit had been expected (1 Kings 18:4; Neh. 9:26–30; Jer. 7:25–26; 20:1–2; Matt. 3:8–10; 7:16; 13:23, 37–39; 21:19; 23:29–37). What was happening now was part of a long pattern of unfaithfulness.

21:37–39. So the owner sent his son, expecting the tenants to respect the heir. Illogically, and showing the blindness of sin, the tenants planned to kill the son so they could inherit the vineyard. The language here mirrors Genesis 37:20 and the Joseph episode (Davies and Allison 1997, 183). France (2007, 813) calls it "an ill-conceived impulse." They cast out the son and killed him. They had made him a cursed one, who was to die outside the camp (Lev. 24:13–14, 23). This part of the parable pictured Jesus's approaching crucifixion. He was the Son functioning as a sent one, a point John's gospel highlights (Matt. 10:40; 15:24; John 4:34; 12:24–25; 13:20; 14:24; 17:3, 8). Mark 12:5b–8 has the son sent for the same reason (to collect fruit), but he was then killed and tossed out of the vineyard. Luke 20:13–15a has the same sequence as Matthew, with the son thrown out of the vineyard and killed.

Cursed Is the One Who Dies Outside the Camp

Leviticus 24:13–14, 23: "Then the Lord spoke to Moses: 'Bring the one who cursed outside the camp, and all who heard him are to lay their hands on his head, and the whole congregation is to stone him to death.' . . . Then Moses spoke to the Israelites and they brought the one who cursed outside the camp and stoned him with stones. So the Israelites did just as the Lord had commanded Moses."

21:40–41. With the parable completed, Jesus asked what the owner would do to the tenants. The leaders responded honestly with two points. First, the owner would destroy the evil men. Second, he would lease the vineyard to others to tend. Their response was exactly correct. Their answer showed their own guilt, as in the previous scene (Matt. 21:31). Unfortunately, they did not see it and would not learn from the example. This detail of Jesus's question and the response is not in Mark or Luke, as Mark 12:9 and Luke 20:16 have Jesus pronouncing the outcome, matching Matthew 21:43.

What was in view here in terms of the time frame? Two options put forward are the return of the Lord or the destruction of the temple in A.D. 70 (Davies and Allison 1997, 183–84, mention both and opt for the latter, as does Osborne 2010, 789). But the remark that looked to giving the vineyard to others was already at work, so it may be that one specific event was not in view at all, but a process of transfer tied already to Jesus's presence and coming. Davies and Allison (1997, 186) speak of the death and resurrection as a point also involved, but this also may be too specific. Jesus's ministry as a whole was in view. The idea of destroying the current leadership in Matthew 21:41 anticipated a judgment for covenantal unfaithfulness just as is described in the Olivet Discourse of Matthew 24–25 and in the image of Matthew 22:7. However, the entire response, though including it, involved more than that event.

21:42–44. Jesus's own response had three parts. First, he cited the Scripture and asked the leaders if they had not read Psalm 118:22–23 (= Ps. 117:22–23 LXX; Mark 12:10–11; Luke 20:17). Jesus often asked a "have you not read" question when he was critiquing the religious leaders (Matt. 12:3; 19:4; 21:16). Psalm 118 is one of the Hallel psalms used during feasts, so they had read and known the text. In fact, they celebrated it in anticipation of such a wondrous day when God's people would be delivered. It declared that the stone the builders rejected had become a keystone. The consistent New Testament use points to a cornerstone versus a capstone.

The point was, the rejected stone became a stone honored by God. Mark 12 lacks this detail. There may be an Aramaic wordplay with "son" and "stone" that showed the tradition was old (*bēn* and *eben*; Nolland 2005, 877). The rejection pointed to Jesus's death, while the lifted-up position pointed to God's vindication that followed in resurrection. The psalm said that this act came from God and was a marvelous sight. In the psalm, it was the one who comes in the name of the Lord who was so honored (Ps. 118:26), a passage used elsewhere (Matt. 21:9, 15; Acts 4:11; 1 Peter 2:7). In the original context of the psalm, it was about a king or representative of Israel welcomed into the temple (France 2007, 815). Jesus saw himself described by this imagery. He applied the psalm as a type or pattern prophecy, where a near event mirrored one coming later as the ultimate fulfillment.

Second, Jesus gave a verdict that mirrored what the leaders said would happen to the tenants. This was not Israel as a whole (but so Osborne 2010, 790 and 792, claiming they represented Israel as whole). The disciples were from Israel as well, and so all the nation could not be the point. In addition, Matthew 21:45 says the leaders saw themselves as the parable's subject.

The kingdom was taken from them and was given to a "people" (ἔθνει) who would bear fruit. In the discussion of this term, BDAG (s.v. "ἔθνος" 1, 276) notes that Gentiles were not meant here, but other leaders distinct from the current leaders. The detail about bearing fruit is unique to Matthew. Kingdom people were fruitful people through faith, the regenerative work of God, and the Holy Spirit (Wilkins 2004, 699). Mark 12:9b and Luke 20:16 discuss the taking of the kingdom from the leaders and giving it to others. Jesus started with the Twelve to make this move, as their future judging of Israel showed (Matt. 19:28; Nolland 2005, 879; Turner 2008, 516–19). The term "nation" could be used of Israel (Gen. 12:2; Exod. 19:6; Isa. 1:4). The eschatological remnant was where the new stewardship started. Even if the term about new people eventually pointed to the church made up of Jew and Gentile (Blomberg 1992, 325), which is probable, the passage did not address the ultimate fate of Israel as a nation, since the current leadership were who was excluded here (correctly Davies and Allison 1997, 189–90; Keener 2009, 511Wilkins 2004, 699).

Third, to come against the stone in any way was to be destroyed (Luke 20:18). The background here was the imagery of Isaiah 8:14, 28:16, and Daniel 2:34–35, 44–45. In Isaiah 8:14, the stone over which one stumbled was God, while here it was Jesus, showing how tightly they are seen to act together. The stone that falls and crushes looks to Daniel 2:34–35, 44–45. The result was the same whether one fell on the stone and was shattered or whether the stone fell on someone so he was crushed. It was judgment authority that was in view here. Opposition to the Son was deadly.

21:45–46. The chief priests and Pharisees knew that Jesus had told the parables against them. Mark 12:12 is vague, speaking only of "they." Luke 20:19 has "experts in the law" or "scribes," not "Pharisees," but scribes were mostly Pharisees so there is no real difference. In Matthew, the pairing of these two Jewish groups occurs only here and in Matthew 27:62. The parable was not against Israel as a whole, as Konradt (2020, 324) and Plummer (1910, 296) rightly note. Rather, it was focused on the lack of shepherding that Jesus would now replace. Since they would not repent and Jesus was challenging their authority, the leaders decided that Jesus had to be stopped.

The irony here was that they plotted what the parable showed, an action they had already acknowledged was an evil act. They plotted to kill the Son, because they failed to see him as the Son despite all he had said, warned about, and shown them. They wanted to arrest him, furthering opposition already noted in Matthew 12:14. Jesus's popularity with the crowds, who saw him as a prophet, complicated matters. This meant they had to be careful not to provoke a popular reaction. The narrative remark says that they feared the crowds. The remark recalls a previous concern about popular reaction tied to John the Baptist in Matthew 21:26. An arrest with a crowd reaction could induce a Roman response. The leadership needed to be careful. Judas led them out of that dilemma. What was clear here was that Jesus's challenge had only hardened their resistance. Of course, a key part of the crowd would turn by the end of the week and also reject Jesus (Matt. 27:20).

THEOLOGICAL FOCUS

The exegetical idea (in a series of controversies and parables that were leading the leadership to seek to arrest him, Jesus emphasized the value of obeying God and showed how the kingdom program was being passed on to others because his authority came from God) points to this theological notion: the authority of Jesus and the danger of opposition to him are shown in final controversies tied to Jesus's presence in Jerusalem.

This passage stresses several ideas and juxtaposes them. First, Jesus is the Son whose work comes from heaven, just as John the Baptist pointed the way to him. Second, God desires sons who, despite claiming disobedience, in the end do obey versus those who claim to obey but do not. Actions count for more than words. Third, all will be held accountable to the Son, who is the stone God exalts. Fourth, the current leaders' failure matched Israel's history. They were consistent in spurning God's messengers. Fifth, God would vindicate his Son and hold those accountable who reject him. All these ideas interact with each other in this unit.

The concluding parable puts the leadership on notice that what they are doing is offensive to God and will produce judgment. The kingdom hope, which has been in their hands, will go to those who respond to God and the sent one. The kingdom is coming and those who respond in faith will bear fruit. They are its representatives versus those who claim to obey God but ignore his promise. Yes, the Messiah faces predicted rejection, but God will vindicate him. To come against the vindicated stone is to face a shattering result.

The narrative is driving toward its ultimate conflict and the opposition that will lead to Jesus's death. The plot to arrest Jesus is being formed. These parables point out a need to repent. Yet the opportunity has been rejected even though the points in the story are evident. By failing to connect the dots and see Jesus is the Son, the leaders will do what the parables warn should not be done. When the leaders remove the Son, they seal their fate, as the kingdom will be taken from them. God's vindication comes to the Son while the kingdom goes to those whose faith is responsive to God. Matthew is noting that those with Jesus are on the right side of this divide.

PREACHING AND TEACHING STRATEGIES

Exegetical and Theological Synthesis

The exegetical section describes the religious leaders' failed attempt to undercut Jesus's authority. They perceived him as a threat to their influence and Jerusalem's tenuous peace under Rome. Their question to Jesus backfired when he responded with his own question; they were trapped. Then Jesus's two parables added insult to injury. The religious leaders could not outsmart him.

Attempts to outsmart divine authority are as old as Eden. Believing they could "become like God," Adam and Eve ate from the Tree of Knowledge of Good and Evil. After realizing his mistake, Adam hid, covered himself, and blamed God for giving him a wife who led him astray (Gen. 3). Cain could not conceal his brother's body from his Creator (Gen. 4). The people of Babel thought they could build their way to heaven and make a name for themselves (Gen. 11). Since our primitive history, humans have grasped to define good and evil on their own terms, shift blame, dodge consequences, and make a name for themselves. In Romans 1:18–32, Paul narrates this ageless attempt at autonomy. All have sinned and fallen short of heaven (Rom. 3:23). Every attempt to outmaneuver God fails.

Preaching Idea

There's no higher authority than heaven.

Contemporary Connections

What does it mean?

Heaven is the circumlocution for God. It describes the place where God dwells. Moreover, he rules the world from heaven. There Jesus is seated at the Father's right hand (Heb. 1:3). The earth is God's footstool (Isa. 66:1). Here history unfolds. Nations rage. Kings rise and fall. Societies form. Populations increase and decline. People work and play, gather and scatter, love and hate. God oversees all these happenings; he holds the world together in Christ (Col. 1:17). Nothing happens outside of his will (Isa. 46:10).

As the Creator and King of heaven, God is the ultimate authority. But he is not the only authority. As his image-bearers (Gen. 1:26–28), humans reflect God's right to rule. Authority is the exercise of power, which may be inherited or earned, and should be stewarded for the good of others. Parents have authority over their children. Elders have authority over their communities, tribes, and congregations. Kings have authority over their nations. Teachers have authority over their classrooms. God delegated his authority to establish order, reduce chaos, and reflect his character in the world.

Is it true?

The Scriptures are uncontested in their claim about God's ultimate authority. He reigns and has no rivals. His authority is ultimate. He shares *all* authority with his Son and delegates *some* authority to humans (e.g., parents, kings, elders) and our institutions (e.g., government, church). All human authority derives from him.

When stewarded well, delegated authority reflects God's design. When abused, delegated authority reflects our Edenic grasp for power. In the West, suspicion about power has recently exploded. Debates about critical race theory have manifested in most schools, with real issues tied to justice sometimes being lost in the process. However, cries for police reform, stories of pastoral abuse, and the #MeToo movement have respectively exposed misuse of force, betrayal of spiritual authority, and sexual predation. We should seek to correct abuses of power. When human authority goes wrong, heaven is not to blame. We are. Manipulation, intimidation, and coercion are perversions of heavenly authority.

Now what?

We do not want to follow in the footsteps of the religious leaders. To deny heaven's authority and misuse human authority is a grave error. Thus, we are wise to resist autonomy, submit to God, and steward our authority well.

First, we must resist autonomy. This is, of course, much easier said than done. Not only have we inherited a natural bent toward self-rule, but we live in a society dedicated to autonomy. In the West, we are repeatedly told we can be or do anything we set our minds to. We are told our bodies belong to us, and we may (mis) treat them however we please. Authenticity and self-expression have become key virtues. We take up two parking spaces, exceed the number of items allowed in the self-checkout line, and text while we drive. Autonomous people know there are rules but always see themselves as exceptions. We must resist this mindset. It is spoiled, entitled, and godless. It places privilege in the wrong place.

Second, we must submit to God. He is the ultimate authority. The chain of command does not get higher than heaven. Submission first recognizes his authority then responds to it. When God gives an order, we should obey. We must heed Jesus's teaching in the Sermon on the Mount (Matt. 5–7). When he calls us, we should come. When he sends us, we should go. When he orders us to carry a cross, we should hoist it on our shoulders and march. True submission to God shows in daily obedience.

Third, we must steward our authority well. It is critical to identify where God has granted authority to us. As image-bearers, all of us have some delegated authority. We may have influence among our teammates, coworkers, or friends. We may have a leadership role in our family, workplace, or church. Good stewardship is less about the size of our responsibility and more about character and integrity. Jesus set an example of using his power to help, heal, and serve people. He was gentle and humble. He only used force where demonic powers or religious leaders misused their authority. We are to follow his lead.

Creativity in Presentation

Most people in your congregation will understand the idea of a "chain of command." Every institution (e.g., family, military, company) has a key person in charge who provides the "marching orders." Beneath the key leader may be several levels of authority that execute the plan. Consider showing some different chains of command (see sidebar). Let people know that regardless of the institution, there always seems to be another level higher. Ultimately, all authority is derived from heaven.

Various Chains of Command (from lowest to highest)

Family	Company	Elder-led Church
Youngest child Oldest child Mom/Dad Dad/Mom Patriarch/matriarch	Employee Shift supervisor Department manager Store manager District manager CEO Board of directors	Attendee Church member Pastor Elder board

Dr. Seuss wrote and illustrated a cautionary tale about grasping for power. *Yertle the Turtle* (1950) chronicles the rise and fall of an ordinary turtle whose ambition gets the best of him. Yertle orders all turtles in his pond to pile up, making a turtle stack that reaches to the heavens. Yertle sits atop the precarious pile, wanting to rise higher than the heavens. He wants to rule over all creation. However, when a plain turtle named Mack at the bottom of the stack lets loose a burp, Yertle's throne comes crashing down. Neither turtle nor tyrant will be able to rise higher than heaven's authority. Consider reading a couple pages from this story and sharing an image or two from the text.

In 1954, President Dwight Eisenhower signed a bill that augmented the Pledge of Allegiance to include the words "under God" after "one nation" and before "indivisible." The original pledge, published in 1892, did not reference God. The amendment came in response to the fear of Communism and its godless ideology sweeping across the nation.[1] What is important about this historical illustration is that even the U.S. president recognized heaven as a higher authority than the Oval Office.

Finally, you might compare the heights of heaven to high points people in your church have visited. Work your way up to higher heights to build your point. Often, the higher we go, the more powerful we feel (e.g., Gen. 11:1–9; Matt. 4:8–9). You might say, "We want to see what kinds of heights people have achieved from our church. You can respond by throwing your hand in the air. Raise it high!"

- Climbed an oak tree? (15 ft.)
- Stood on your roof? (30 ft.)

1 Your rationale in revisiting American history is not to lament how far we have come from our Christian origins. Nor are you calling people to Christian nationalism. Rather, you are simply sharing appreciation for our predecessors who respected heavenly authority. For a summary, see https://www.history.com/news/pledge-allegiance-under-god-schools (accessed July 24, 2024).

- Stayed on the twentieth floor of a hotel? (200 ft.)
- Went to the top of the Statue of Liberty? Washington Memorial? Empire State Building? Willis Tower? (111–1,450 ft.)
- Climbed a peak in the Smoky Mountains? Appalachian Mountains? Rocky Mountains? (6,600–14,500 ft.)
- Flew on an airplane? (33,000–40,000 ft.)

After working through some heights, you might conclude with, "No matter how high we may climb, we'll never reach heaven. Its authority and altitude remain out of reach."

In the end, you want your sermon to communicate that the authority of Jesus and the danger of opposition to him are shown in final controversies tied to Jesus's presence in Jerusalem. Moreover, there's no higher authority than heaven.

- Jesus's authority came from heaven, not men (21:23–27).
- God wants obedience, not lip service (21:28–32).
- Rejecting Jesus has grave consequences (21:33–46).

DISCUSSION QUESTIONS

1. What tactics did Jesus employ in responding to the religious leaders? Be specific.
2. How does Jesus's teaching about obedience differ from "works righteousness"?
3. Did Jesus's condemnation apply only to the religious leaders? Explain.
4. Where do you see heaven's authority being jettisoned in our day?
5. How do you resist the urge toward autonomy?
6. Where do you have God-given authority? How can you exercise it for good?

Matthew 22:1–14

EXEGETICAL IDEA

The refusal of some to attend the son's wedding, and of others not to be appropriately responsive, meant that many of the first to be invited would be excluded, while others would be brought into blessing.

THEOLOGICAL FOCUS

Jesus tells yet another parable about the consequences of rejection that also shows the program will go forward with others.

PREACHING IDEA

Honor your RSVP to be with King Jesus.

PREACHING POINTERS

Jesus continued to give the religious leaders in Jerusalem reason to fear him. His parable of the Wedding Feast completed a series of three that illustrated good and bad responses to God's kingdom program. In this story, the king's original guests had backed out; however, since the tables had been set and food had been prepared, the king would not let all the expenses go to waste. He extended the invitation to anyone who would respond. Many came, but one stood out for his filthy dress. He was banished from the banquet. The parable illustrates three different responses to Jesus: outright rejection (i.e., original guests), uncommitted interest (i.e., poorly dressed guest), and true allegiance (i.e., those who came dressed for the party). For the original audience, these three types of responses gave a warning (Davies and Allison 1997, 188–89; Turner 2008, 521), coaxing them to reflect and reaffirm their response to Jesus.

We live in an age averse to commitment. Despite our loaded schedules, we are always looking for better options. Opportunities abound. We can choose between sports and school events, work and family obligations, social and religious gatherings. Deciding can be exhausting. Worse, making a commitment does not alleviate the fear of missing out (FOMO). Saying "yes" to one invitation necessarily means "no" to another. So we keep our options open, wait until the last minute to commit, and look for an "easy out" of an obligation. While our half-hearted responses may pass for family dinners and pickup basketball games, they do not bode well for discipleship to Jesus. Rather, this text teaches we should honor our RSVP to be with King Jesus.

THE PARABLE OF THE WEDDING BANQUET (22:1–14)

LITERARY STRUCTURE AND THEMES (22:1–14)

This unit is composed of one parable leading into an application. The parable has a conceptual parallel in Luke 14:16–24. There are important differences, as Luke elaborates on the reasons for refusal and lacks any remarks about harming the slaves. Luke has a banquet, while Matthew has a king who holds a wedding banquet for his son. Matthew has two waves of slaves sent to encourage the original invitees to come. That may picture John the Baptist and the disciples, respectively, pointing to Jesus. Luke also lacks any mention of an attendee inappropriately dressed; that detail, and section of the parable, is unique to Matthew. Matthew's section adds another dimension and theme to the account, the odd man out, namely, one who looked to be in but ended up outside. These parables also appear in very distinct settings, since in Luke Jesus was traveling to Jerusalem. What we likely have are two fairly similar parables told on distinct occasions and told with some variation (Davies and Allison 1997, 194, speak of M as the source, indicating a difference; France 2007, 821; Turner 2008, 521).

The Gospel of Thomas 64 also has a seemingly independent version of this parable. Thomas's version is closer to Luke's in structure and adds a fourth figure who rejected versus Luke's three (Davies and Allison 1997, 195–96). He also lacks Matthew's two waves of servants sent out.

This parable was told in five parts. First, the core parable was the refusal to attend in Matthew 22:1–6. Second, there was the reaction, a judgment in Matthew 22:7. Third, there came a new set of invitees in Matthew 22:8–10. Those who received the new wave of invitations were said to be both good and bad. The hall was now filled. Fourth, one guest gained special attention, the one not appropriately dressed in Matthew 22:11–13. He was cast out and placed in outer darkness as the parable moved from its imagery into its application. Fifth, Matthew 22:14 stated the principle: many are called, but few are chosen.

The key theme treated the various responses to the arriving kingdom. It was important to note that the wedding banquet was not postponed; it was held as scheduled. Others who desired to come were invited. This detail pictured the kingdom's arrival as preached and promised. There was opportunity to participate in fellowship with the Son who had announced its coming and represented its presence. Two types of refusals received special attention: (1) those who came to see other things as more important and thus did not respond when the notification of the wedding was received, and (2) those who came but on the wrong terms, not responding appropriately. Nonetheless, the hall was filled. So opportunity to come to the wedding was spread with a wide net, but only some took advantage of it and enjoyed the celebration.

EXPOSITION (22:1–14)

Matthew warned about two types of people who end up outside the kingdom. One group was clear, the other less so. Those who refused Jesus's invitation would miss the kingdom celebration they had been in line to enjoy. This was a reference to many who rejected the call to come. A second group was associated with the new movement but really did not put on "its clothes." They lacked the trust that reflected a new birth. They ended up excluded from the celebration as well. They were left to outer darkness. To hear the word of the kingdom early on did not mean automatic entry. Nor did flirting with the faith by being close to it match a response of faith. Matthew was issuing a warning to both groups. Only the few who respond appropriately make it in and show that they have been chosen.

The refusal of some to attend the son's wedding and of others not to be appropriately responsive meant that many of the first to be invited would be excluded, while others would be brought into blessing.

22:1–2. Jesus told a third parable in succession. The parables have moved in focus from John to Jesus to the church (Matt. 21:32, 37, 42; 22:10–14). This thread reflects Matthew's preference for telling things in groups of three, as we saw especially in Matthew 8–9. This parable was about a king giving a wedding banquet for his son. The introduction speaks of comparing the kingdom to something. Such a remark was common with parables (Matt. 13:24, 31, 33, 44, 45, 52; 18:23).

The cultural background added to the drama of this scene. To plan an ancient wedding, one must know how many were planning to come. There was no way to refrigerate what had been prepared. Invitations to attend would have gone out before and would have been responded to before the call to come to the wedding ever took place (Culpepper 2021, 415–16; Esther 5:8; 6:14). Keener (2009, 519–20) discusses this background in detail (sample invitations: P. Oxy. 112, 1214, 1485, 1487, 2147). This meant the original invitees would have told the wedding party that they had planned to come long before the event.

22:3–6. The king sent out the slaves to announce the time had come to attend the wedding. The celebration pictured the kingdom (Isa. 25:6; Matt. 8:10–12; 9:15; 15:26–27; 26:26–29; Luke 13:29; Rev. 19:6–9; 2 Bar. 29:3–8; Osborne 2010, 798). This action culturally assumed a previous note had gone out regarding the approaching wedding. It had been responded to positively. But those previously invited to the banquet decided not to come when the time of the event was announced. To go back on what had been promised was like what the one son did in Matthew 21:30. Culturally, this would have been seen as a severe insult to the king and son. Culpepper (2021, 416) says "the host is snubbed."

Banquet or Plenty as a Picture of the Kingdom

Isaiah 25:6: "The Lord of Heaven's Armies will hold a banquet for all the nations on this mountain. At this banquet there will be plenty of meat and aged wine—tender meat and choicest wine."

2 Baruch 29:3–8: "And it will happen that when all that which should come to pass in these parts has been accomplished, the Anointed One will begin to be revealed. And Behemoth will reveal itself from its place, and Leviathan will come from the sea, the two great monsters which I created on the fifth day of creation and which I shall have kept until that time. And they will be nourishment for all who are left. The earth will also yield fruits ten thousandfold. And on one vine will be a thousand branches, and one branch will produce a thousand clusters, and one cluster will produce a thousand grapes, and one grape will produce a cor of wine. And those who are hungry will enjoy themselves and they will, moreover, see marvels every day. For winds will go out in front of me every morning to bring the fragrance of aromatic fruits and clouds at the end of the day to distill the dew of health. And it will happen at that time that the treasury of manna will come down again from on high, and they will eat of it in those years because these are they who will have arrived at the consummation of time."

The king sent out a second wave of slaves with details to try to persuade the invited guests to come. It was to stress that their promise to come had led to full preparations. The slaves noted that the feast was ready. The slaying of the oxen and fatted calf, no cheap menu, had taken place. Everything was ready and lavishly prepared so they should come. The text described the invited guests as "being indifferent" or "unconcerned" (BDAG s.v. "ἀμελέω" 52). They did not come. Instead, one went to his field and another to his business. They resumed their normal lives. It was as if they had never been invited and accepted the invitation. Others reacted with more hostile intent. They "abused" or "mistreated" the slaves and killed them (BDAG s.v. "ὑβρίζω" 1022). This pictured rebellion and rejection of the kingdom message. The invitation pictured the announcement of the kingdom's arrival (Matt. 3:2; 4:17; 10:7; 12:28), while the hostility reflected their consistent rejection involving the prophets and Jesus (Matt. 5:12; 21:35, 39; 23:29–36). The second sending to ask the invited portrayed Jesus's message through his followers.

The two kinds of response—indifference and hostility—pictured the variety of reactions Jesus's ministry had produced. Not all rejections were the same, but both were serious.

22:7. This refusal angered the king. He sent his soldiers out to those who murdered the slaves and rendered justice to them, an eye for an eye, one death for another. He burned their city. The association of judgment with fire has OT roots (Isa. 5:24–25). This detail in the parable clearly foreshadowed the destruction of Jerusalem in A.D. 70 and is unique to Matthew (Matt. 22:41–45; 24:2, 15; Luke 21:20). Jerusalem was burned by the Romans (Davies and Allison 1997, 201; Josephus, *B.J.* 6.353–63, 406–8). This was not necessarily prophecy after the fact with A.D. 70 in the rearview mirror. All one needed to know was how Rome conquered by siege. This was their standard way to overrun a location. One also could infer a total destruction of a city by a foreigner on analogy with Old Testament judgments for unfaithfulness and in light of instruction about the consequences of covenantal disobedience in Deuteronomy (Deut. 28–32; Judg. 1:8; 2 Kings 25:9; 2 Chron. 36:19; Isa. 5:24–25; Bar. 1:2; 1 Macc. 5:28; T. Jud. 5:1–5; Blomberg 1992, 327; Nolland 2005, 887–88). The nation would pay for her covenantal unfaithfulness. If one sensed judgment was on the way, this is how it would come. Even in the face of many warnings and much evidence, she had foolishly rejected the one God had sent. This rejection of the invitation insulted the king and the son, who represented God and the sent one.

Judgment by Burning

2 Kings 25:9: "He [Nebuchadnezzar] burned down the Lord's temple, the royal palace, and all the houses in Jerusalem, including every large house."

2 Chronicles 36:19: "They [Babylonians] burned down God's temple and tore down the wall of Jerusalem. They burned all its fortified buildings and destroyed all its valuable items."

Isaiah 5:24–25: "Therefore, as flaming fire devours straw, and dry grass disintegrates in the flames, so their root will rot, and their flower will blow away like dust. For they have rejected the law of the Lord of Heaven's Armies, they have spurned the commands of the Holy One of Israel. So the Lord is furious with his people; he lifts his hand and strikes them. The mountains shake, and corpses lie like manure in the middle of the streets. Despite all this, his anger does not subside, and his hand is ready to strike again."

1 Maccabees 5:28: "Then Judas and his army quickly turned back by the wilderness road to Bozrah; and he took the town, and killed every male by the edge of the sword; then he seized all its spoils and burned it with fire."

Baruch 1:2: "In the fifth year, on the seventh day of the month, at the time when the Chaldeans took Jerusalem and burned it with fire."

22:8–10. In the king's eyes, the original invitees who refused to attend were not worthy of participating in the wedding (worthy: Matt. 10:10–11, 37–38). Their refusal showed their decision not to be a part. Nonetheless, the celebration proceeded. The wedding was ready. Guests would be present. Slaves were sent into the main thoroughfares of the city to invite all who would come. They went and gathered a crowd that filled the hall. People of all sorts, evil and good, were there. This mix is a theme in Matthew (Matt. 7:15–27; 13:20–23, 25–26, 41–42, 49–50). The picture was about the kingdom message offered to all. There was no postponement here. Access to blessing remained for those who came. The kingdom had been announced as near and now was coming with Jesus's approaching work. The perspective calling those responding as good or evil was based on their past lives, applying a relative scale to them and the society's evaluation of their status. Nolland (2005, 888) speaks of "riffraff" and "people of quality." Thus, people were included whom the more pious likely would have rejected as being acceptable. The acceptance of the kingdom message changed everyone's status in the eyes of God. Those now present at the banquet were depicted as "reclining," the expected posture at an ancient meal that pointed to welcome and celebration.

22:11–13. The king surveyed the gathered guests and saw one present not dressed appropriately for wedding. This was another sign of disrespect for the occasion. The host asked the man how he came to a wedding and did not dress for it. The man had no answer and was silent. There was no good reason not to appreciate the occasion.[1] The king expelled the guest. He had the servants not only toss him out but expel the man, bound up and placed as far away as possible. By switching to language about outer darkness and gnashing of teeth, the parable moved toward its application and pictured complete rejection. The use of space as imagery showed a person far away from the celebration, while the gnashing of teeth pictured the reaction at being on the outside looking in with a glimpse of what had been missed (Matt. 8:11–12; 13:40–42; 24:51; 25:30; 1 En. 10:4–5—of Azaz'el; Turner 2008, 524). The man stood for a class of people (Davies and Allison 1997, 203).

Tossed into Darkness

1 Enoch 10:4–5: "And secondly the Lord said to Raphael, 'Bind Azaz'el hand and foot (and) throw him into the darkness!' And he made a hole in the desert which was in Duda'el and cast him there; he threw on top of him rugged and sharp rocks. And he covered his face in order that he may not see light."

1 The prime example of this kind of a figure in the gospels was Judas. These texts are especially problematic for people who hold to a once-saved-always-saved idea and place the emphasis on a moment of profession of faith. Preaching texts like this must be carefully explained. The one truly responding in faith trusts God, at least to some degree, so that the faith shows itself (Eph. 2:10; James 2:14–26). That person will have fruit, as the last parable already suggested. That disciple responds and comes prepared to fellowship appropriately. In other words, faith works. Others show up but really have not responded with faith. They hang around but do not engage God on his terms. That type of figure is warned at the end of this parable. They are harder to spot than the people who walk away and do not respond to the invitation at all. Jesus told several parables that went this direction. Matthew 8:5–13 is the first such indication of the last being first and the first being last, with an original invitee left outside. Matthew 24:45–51 is another text that belongs in the same grouping. Not everyone who thinks he or she is in line with the kingdom is in. Jesus's parable warned such figures even as it taught that some did not respond to begin with, while others entered in from surprising places.

This figure was different from the earlier unworthy attendees in that there was a response and a presence, an attraction to the event the king was putting on. The first invitees never entered the room, but this figure did come. Still, he did not come respecting where he was going. There is debate whether the king supplies such clothing, or whether the man should have dressed appropriately on his own (Morris 1992, 552). That point of detail is not clear in the text, but either way the man was more an observer than a participant sharing actively in the event's aura. He also was not worthy of attending because he lacked a real appreciative response to what the king offered, a theme that echoes back to Matthew 18:23–35.

This "odd man out" pictured a person who got close to Jesus and his program but did not respond with an open heart of faith that meant being clothed with engagement and participation in the kingdom banquet. Matthew was warning his listeners. Jesus taught that mere presence in a believing community was not enough. What was needed was a faith that recognized what was going on and responded. Turner (2008, 525) sees false teachers and the lawless one addressed here (Matt. 7:15–23; 13:41–42), while Blomberg (1992, 330) and Keener (2009, 522) refer to professing Christians. Nolland (2005, 891) speaks of those who come to God on their own terms. Debate exists about what the garment represents: works of righteousness (France 2007, 827) or a resurrection body (Davies and Allison 1997, 204, opt for a resurrection garment, appealing to Matt. 13:43). There is no reason to choose between a reference to repentance and a reference to righteous conduct, as one leads to the other (Osborne 2010, 803; Wilkins 2004, 717; James 2:14–26). To have faith in God is to be trusting and responsive to him. Faith is not about just a moment but includes an orientation to God. The themes of Matthew likely point to a fruitful response, but with the proviso that such exist because there has been a response of faith (Matt. 3:8). The parables of Matthew 13 also point in a similar direction to explain why the righteous shine.

Odd Man/Woman Out Parables in Matthew

- Matthew 18:21–35: Parable of the Unforgiving Servant
- Matthew 22:1–14: Parable of The Wedding Banquet
- Matthew 25:1–13: Parable of the Ten Virgins
- Matthew 25:14–30: Parable of the Talents

22:14. The parable ends with the application, "Many are called, but few are chosen." Opportunity to enter the kingdom was widespread, but only a few heard and responded to the call. The kingdom would be full of all sorts of people coming from all sorts of backgrounds, having lived a wide variety of styles of living, good and bad, but not all who came or heard the message really got it and responded. Faith that was real responded to God's leading. That response would vary in degree and fruit would be yielded up in differing amounts, but there was some level of response in all who genuinely came in faith. Those who heard the call as the chosen did respond to the calling with an embracing faith. Election was not by default nor ethnicity; it was reflected in response.

THEOLOGICAL FOCUS

The exegetical idea (the refusal of some to attend the son's wedding, and of others not to be appropriately responsive, meant that many of the first to be invited would be excluded, while others would be brought into blessing) leads to this theological notion: Jesus tells yet another parable about the consequences of rejection that also shows the program will go forward with others.

This parable is about response. Transparent is the rejection some give to Jesus. People walk away from what is offered. They take other events in life to be more compelling. Others may react with hostility. Both responses are rejections of God, serious offenses before the Creator. The accountability that resulted in Jesus's day meant judgment on the nation, at least for a time. The leaders may seem to have stopped the Jesus movement and thought that they still had control of the faith with its promise, but God's judgment would show otherwise, as would his coming vindication of the Son.

The rejection of Jesus by others is subtler. There is a seeming interest in being present with him. There is a connection to his community, but something is missing. The response is not appropriate to the occasion. This is a person who flirts with Jesus without coming to him on his terms. That type of person ends up just as rejected as those who refuse to come. Jesus is not to be flirted with; he is to be embraced in faith with all that he offers. The parable not only challenges those who have never come to Jesus; it also challenges anyone to be sure he or she has come to him with a faith that is on Jesus's terms.

PREACHING AND TEACHING STRATEGIES

Exegetical and Theological Synthesis

The exegetical section highlights God's grace, mercy, and severity. He provides both invitations and warnings. Some people respond in faith, others reject him, and a third group will flirt with God. They get close enough to see if his program will serve their self-interest. What distinguishes the faithful from the flirtatious is the fruit of their lives. Those truly committed to Jesus abide in his love, walk with his Spirit, and evidence his character in growing measure. They experience transformation. Those who flirt with Jesus and feign commitment rely on their own strength, avoid sacrifice, and lack love. They remain unchanged because the Spirit of God is not in them.

As mentioned in the exegetical section and throughout this commentary, we neither earn our salvation nor author our sanctification. Both are gifts from God. However, spiritual growth is not automatic for Christians. We work out our salvation with fear and trembling, relying on God's power to sustain us (Phil. 2:12–13). Indeed, sanctification is a collaborative exercise between God and us. He provides the Spirit; we crucify the flesh (Gal. 5:16–26). He renews us; we take off the old man (Eph. 4:17–32). He gives us everything we need for a godly life; we adorn ourselves with Christlike virtues (2 Peter 1:3–11). Salvation comes with a whole new wardrobe—Christ's righteousness for our filthy rags—our response is to wear the garments God has given.

Preaching Idea

Honor your RSVP to be with King Jesus.

Contemporary Connections

What does it mean?

God has invited us into a relationship with him. King Jesus opened the way for anyone to respond to God's gracious offer. As with any party or wedding invitation, two responses are appropriate: yes or no. RSVPs do not have a checkbox for "maybe" or "if nothing better shows up." Saying "yes" helps the party planners prepare to receive you. Saying "yes" obliges you to show up, bring your gift, and claim your seat. Saying "yes" also means you have said "no" to any other option for that time. We need to honor our yeses.

Saying "yes" to God is comprehensive. We are promising him our time, attention, and resources. We are committing to his agenda, not ours. His will, not ours. His ways, not ours. Every "yes," in fact, has a built-in "no." Saying "yes" to God means we sacrifice our agenda, will, and need for control to God's calling. He may call us to move, change careers, stay single, serve the elderly, or give up our liberty to sip bourbon in order to help a friend stay sober. Thus, honoring our RSVP to be with King Jesus may come at a cost, but the eternal joy of the heavenly banquet—being with Jesus, worshiping with others, freedom from sin, and feasting—will be worth it.

Is it true?

It is true that we should honor our RSVP to be with King Jesus. If we have professed faith, we should live faithfully. If we call ourselves Christians, we should live like Christ. Of course, becoming like Jesus grows out of being with Jesus. Intimacy with him feeds imitation of him. Fortunately, his gracious invitation to be with him and learn from him remains for every disciple today (Matt. 11:28–30). Therefore, a critical part of honoring our "yes" to Jesus is to prioritize time with him in his Word, prayer, corporate worship, mission, and community service.

There is one caveat: if our initial response to Jesus is "no," there is always time to change our minds. Until our final breath, the invitation to repent and believe lingers. The previous parable about the two sons illustrated this point (Matt. 21:28–31). A rebellious teenager can give her life to Jesus when she hits rock bottom in her mid-thirties. A felon can become a man of faith when he learns of Jesus while in jail. An atheist may make an earnest profession of faith on his deathbed. God will honor yeses that come later in life.

Now what?

To honor our RSVP to King Jesus implies that we have made a response to him. It never hurts to double-check our stated commitment. Therefore, before we take the next steps, we want to make sure we have made a profession of faith. This typically means we have confessed our sins, accepted God's forgiveness in Jesus, and committed to following him. With this initial response to Jesus comes two responsibilities: clearing our schedules and getting clothed in Christlikeness. We will consider each briefly below.

First, we need to clear our schedules. Honoring our RSVP to King Jesus means we make time for him. This RSVP, of course, envisions our eternal banquet with him, but it also comprises spending time with Jesus each day. We talk with him. We read his Word. We experience his presence when we gather with other people. King Jesus wants more than a one-time response; he desires an ongoing responsiveness to him. In other words, we will not avoid or ignore him when life is tough, work is busy, or the television is on.

Second, we need to get clothed in Christlikeness. Honoring our RSVP to King Jesus means we reflect his holy character. True belief in Jesus leads to becoming like Jesus. We take off our greed and put on his generosity. We strip off our pride and wrap ourselves in his humility. We mortify our flesh and manifest fruit of the Spirit. The genuineness of our response shows in how we work out our salvation: we put on Christ's righteousness.

Creativity in Presentation

Jesus's parable sets up nicely for treating the Sunday morning service like a wedding. Consider preaching with a suit and tie. Open the service with a formal greeting or language adapted from the Book of Common Prayer. Set a banquet table on the stage. Provide people with a generic wedding invitation at the door with a line that clearly asks for an RSVP. (You could also send these out a week before this sermon to seed the idea before Sunday.)

In the film *Finding Neverland* (directed by Marc Forster, 2004), J. M. Barrie (played by Johnny Depp) invites a group of orphans to his early viewing of Peter Pan because he is concerned that the typical audience will not respond to the story. Orphans, of course, are not expected guests at the theater. The owner (played by Dustin Hoffman) is shocked to see them arriving at the "last call." Although they are dressed for the occasion, members of the crowd give them strange looks as they take their seats. However, as the play begins, the children respond better than other ticket holders. They laugh aloud and appreciate the whimsical story. Consider showing the two-minute clip of unlikely guests arriving at the "last call." You can find online by searching for *Finding Neverland* and "seats for orphans." At the conclusion of the clip, you might say, "Sometimes the least likely guests are the most responsive and appreciative of an invitation."

Finally, you might consider contemporary examples of when RSVPs are not honored, and the cost incurred.

- Overbooked flights do not honor all the tickets sold for that flight. This results in people getting bumped or airlines giving out credits.
- Busy restaurants do not honor the timing of all their reservations. This results in grumpy guests and people leaving.
- A small percentage of guests who RSVP to a wedding do not show up. This results in extra food. (Although, some who failed to RSVP may show up and eat the extras. Hopefully, they're dressed for the occasion!)
- Not every student who enrolls in college makes it to campus. This results in the loss of their deposit and rearranging of dorm space for student life staff.
- Some movie tickets purchased online are never claimed. This results in empty seats for the theater and a missed opportunity for the ticket owner.

These scenarios are too common. Choose a personal example of how dishonoring an RSVP negatively affected you.

Ultimately, you want your sermon to show how Jesus tells yet another parable about the consequences of rejection that also shows the program will go forward with others. In response, you should honor your RSVP to be with King Jesus.

- Many will refuse God's gracious invitation (22:1–7).
- God extends his gracious invitation to many more (22:8–10).
- God's guests must dress for the occasion (22:11–14).

DISCUSSION QUESTIONS

1. How were ancient weddings different from contemporary ones?
2. How does this parable fit with the two previous ones from Matthew 21?
3. What are the various forms of refusal? What do these look like today?
4. Diagnose the problem with the "odd man out." What has he done wrong?
5. How do you explain the imagery of "darkness," "weeping," and "gnashing teeth"? What would you say to someone who finds this offensive or too harsh?

Matthew 22:15–46

EXEGETICAL IDEA
A series of controversies showed a very competent Jesus who was not a revolutionary, believed in resurrection as taught in Torah, taught loving God and neighbor as the Great Commandment, and challenged the leaders to understand why the Messiah was called Lord by David.

THEOLOGICAL FOCUS
Though rejected, Jesus shows himself fully qualified to lead God's program through his understanding of hope, ethics, and the promise of God.

PREACHING IDEA
Jesus passes every quality control test imaginable.

PREACHING POINTERS
Jesus provoked opposition from several fronts in Jerusalem. In a series of oral tests, Jesus responded to questions from Herodians, Sadducees, and Pharisees before posing a question of his own. The first group tried to surface his zealous motives with a question about taxes; the second group challenged his treatment of the law; and the final opponent asked Jesus about ethics. While each controversy stands alone, they collectively illustrate Jesus's competency as Messiah. Matthew's audience would have marveled at Jesus's understanding of Scripture, wisdom, and ability to sidestep rhetorical traps.

In the age of Big Data, we test everything. We do medical testing: DNA, white blood counts, and cholesterol. We do academic testing: ACT, SAT, MCAT. We test personalities: Myers-Briggs, DISC, and various internet inventories (e.g., Which Hogwarts House would you be in?). We test our water for chemicals, our basements for mold, and our vehicles for carbon emissions. With our endless need to rank, rate, understand, and make improvements, there is no shortage of testing. This compulsion to test applies to Jesus. People still test his words, deeds, and the biblical claims about him. Fortunately, his reputation as a teacher, ethicist, and debater stands the test of time. This sermon reminds us that Jesus passes every quality control test imaginable.

FACING CHALLENGES DEALING WITH POLITICS, THEOLOGY, AND ETHICS (22:15–46)

LITERARY STRUCTURE AND THEMES (22:15–46)

This unit has three controversies (Matt. 22:15–40) and then a challenge from Jesus (Matt. 22:41–46).

The first controversy was political, about whether one should pay taxes to Caesar (Matt. 22:15–22). It was either an attempt to get Jesus to refuse payment, getting him in trouble with Rome, or to say they should pay taxes, getting him in trouble with the crowds seeking revolution. Jesus avoided the trap, opting for taxes *and* honoring God but not revolution. He turns the either-or question into a both-and.

The second controversy involved theology, as Sadducees, who did not believe in resurrection, tried to show the weakness of holding that view (Matt. 22:23–33). Jesus defended resurrection by pointing to Torah texts that the Sadducees would respect and by noting that the afterlife would not be like this life.

The third issue was ethical and involved asking Jesus to name the greatest commandment (Matt. 22:34–40). We are told the question was a test. It may have been to see if Jesus would somehow challenge God's unique centrality. His reply was that one should love God completely and one's neighbor as oneself. The combination was important, as Jesus had shown that loving God should lead one to a respect of others. How we live is important, not just what we believe.

Jesus's challenge came last (Matt. 22:41–46). Here Jesus raised for reflection a question from Psalm 110:1 about Messiah, son of David. He did not answer the question. Rather, it set up an issue that became central when Jesus was examined by the leadership in Matthew 26:57–68. The answer would come there. The issue was how could the ancestor David call his son, a descendant, "Lord," when the respect was to go to the elder? Jesus was not denying that the Messiah was a son of David here; rather, he was focusing on why this figure would be called "Lord" by the founder of the dynastic line. The dilemma posed went unanswered for now. It was to be pondered as it was a core question about who the deliverer would be.

The series of challenges left no one wanting to confront Jesus anymore with questions. Who would the reader rather have in charge of leading God's program, the stumped leaders or a competent Jesus? That is the conclusion the unit drives the reader to see. It is in this conclusion that the passage has its unity. Whether the challenge was political, theological, ethical, or messianic, Jesus is competent. In other words, he is fully qualified to be at the center of God's kingdom.

Most of these texts have parallels. The dispute over taxes to Caesar is also in Mark 12:13–17 and Luke 20:20–26, as well as in a much shorter, likely secondary form in the Gospel of Thomas 100 (Davies and Allison 1997, 219). Herodians would have supported such taxes. Pharisees were probably ambivalent about it. They wanted to know which side Jesus would take. It took three rounds of exchange to resolve the issue.

The resurrection controversy is in Mark 12:18–27 and in Luke 20:27–40. The discussion of the greatest commandment is in Mark 12:28–34. Mark's version is expanded as there was an additional exchange from a scribe about God being one and about these commandments being more important than sacrifices that Matthew lacks. Luke does not have this scene.

The discussion of David and Psalm 110:1 is in Mark 12:35–37 and Luke 20:41–44. Mark 12:38–40 and Luke 20:45–47 follow with a short rebuke of the scribes, while Matthew 23 will devote a whole chapter to this critique. Mark 12:41–44 and Luke 21:1–4 then share about a poor widow's mite, something Matthew lacks.

As is often the case, Matthew's story line parallels Mark's most closely. The link here is a topical examination of a series of disputes covering a diverse range of areas.

The passage contains four consecutive controversies and continues the contentious tone that has been a part of the last several scenes. The opponents differ in each case: Pharisees and Herodians, then Sadducees, and finally a scribe. Jesus was being tested in turn by the whole Jewish leadership establishment. He got the better of them all. The themes beyond establishing Jesus's credibility are tied to the issues raised.

Jesus was no advocate of governmental revolt. He was not a Zealot. Caesar had his administrative realm, and God, who had set government in place, had his realm. Government had the right to exist and be supported; yet, at the same time, God should be honored. This was not so much about an argument of separation of church and state as about their coexistence, with both spheres being respected. This was why one could be a believer and still be a good citizen (Rom. 13:1–7; 1 Tim. 2:2; 1 Peter 2:13–17; Osborne 2010, 805).

Resurrection would not be like this life. Relationships like marriage would be altered. However, God's promises made to the patriarchs showed that they too participated in the promise, a statement that assumed resurrection and its roots in Torah teaching.

Jesus's ethical call was to love God and one's neighbor. This twofold structure mirrored the Ten Commandments with a table of commands about God and a section about people. There was to be a link between how we love God and how we treat people. If one lives and loves well, one does what the law and prophets have called for in life.

Finally, the Messiah had so much respect that even the patriarch David called him "Lord." More than that, God asked Messiah to sit with him in heaven. The significance of that position is something Matthew saved to develop until later in his gospel. This position for Jesus will become a core claim that discloses his full identity.

EXPOSITION (22:15–46)

This gospel has been about two views of how the promise of the Hebrew Scripture applied to the world. There was the position of a long-established faith that rejected the teaching of a messianic claimant who called for national repentance and a return to God. Then there was a new movement, under pressure from that more established group. Who had it right? This unit was Matthew's last attempt to argue that Jesus's way was the better path. In these controversies, Jesus covered the scope of life from taxes to death to ethics. He closed with a question to ponder: If the dynastic founder David gave honor to his messianic descendant, then who did that mean that descendant was? If God should vindicate Jesus and give him a place of honor, what should that mean about our response? The question was posed here. God answered it later with an empty tomb.

A series of controversies showed a very competent Jesus who was not a revolutionary, believed in resurrection as taught in Torah, taught loving God and neighbor as the great commandment, and challenged the leaders to understand why the Messiah was called Lord by David.

22:15–17. The Pharisees and Herodians now sought to entrap Jesus (Mark 12:13–15a; Luke 20:20–22). The term "Herodians" only appears in New Testament texts (Mark 3:6; 12:13). They tended to support Rome, as Herod Antipas was a client king in Galilee, although the last Herodian ruler in Jerusalem (Archaelaus) had been deposed for some time, so maybe they longed for a return to shared power (France 2007, 832). The word for "entrap" is a New Testament hapax (BDAG s.v. "παγιδεύω" 747). It is a hunting term. The noun refers to an animal trap. The effort to get Jesus was not new (Matt. 12:14; 16:1; 19:3; one more trap to come–22:35). The trap involved politics—sensitive and controversial relationships with Rome. Should people pay taxes to those foreign overlords? The taxes were not light, and people were not rich. The reference is likely to the census or head tax (Josephus, *B.J.* 1.154; 2.188, 403–5, 433; Tacitus, *Ann.* 2.42). A positive answer might upset the crowds longing for freedom. A negative reply would allow Jesus to be charged with sedition, a crime that meant death.

After some flattery about Jesus teaching the truth, which those asking did not really believe, they asked if it was right if one should pay taxes. Taxes were estimated to have run anywhere from 35 to 50 percent, with some taxes going to the temple along with a tithe that had nothing to do with Rome (Wilkins 2004, 720, notes the high-end number). The question was a halakic query: What did the law permit? Should one support a pagan ruler, maybe even an oppressor (Blomberg 1992, 331)? The flattery was not only hypocritical but ironic, as it was true in contrast to how it was being said. The remark about not caring what others thought might have been baiting Jesus to challenge Rome (Deut. 10:17—of God; 28:50—of the nation; Acts 10:34). The image "to look on the faces of people" here is very vivid: one looked on someone's face and then responded (BDAG s.v. "βλέπω" 4, 179—not caring what one might think). The flattery was calling Jesus impartial.

22:18–20. Jesus knew they were seeking to trap him (Mark 12:15a; Luke 20:23). He had dealt with them long enough to know. The flattery may have given them away as seeking to trap him. Before answering, he asked why they were testing him and called them hypocrites (Matt. 6:2, 5, 16; 7:5; 15:7; 23:13, 15, 23, 25, 27, 29; 24:51). Davies and Allison (1997, 215) speak of seeing "the daggers in the men's smiles." Ironically, the response proved the point. He was responding because he knew their motive versus their social position.

He asked to see the coin that paid the tax (Mark 12:15b–16a; Luke 20:24a). It was a denarius, a Roman coin. The denarius was used to pay a toll or census text. In showing him the coin, they already were indicating that they participated in and benefited from the economy of which taxes were a part, since another tax was an indirect consumption or sales tax (Osborne 2010, 809). Jesus asked whose image and inscription it bore, for a Roman coin not only often pictured the emperor but named him on its face. In this case, we were likely looking at a silver imperial coin with the image of Tiberius and an inscription identifying him as Caesar Son of Augustus, since it was required for the poll tax (Keener 2009, 525; Turner 2008, 528 n. 3).

22:21. Jesus's response to the presence of Caesar's image on the coin was to argue that the things of Caesar belonged to him, just as the things of God belonged to the deity (Mark 12:17a; Luke 20:25). Sextus in *Sentences* 20 says a similar thing of the world and of God (Davies and Allison 1997, 216). Pay back to Caesar what is his and to God what is God's. This is not separation of church and state, as much as it represents a recognition of the side-by-side existence of two realms, with God having sovereignly set up government to manage our corporate affairs (Dan. 2:21, 37–38; Bruner 2004b, 784–87; Wilkins 2004, 722). Government had things for which it was responsible. People could be good citizens (Rom. 13:1–7; 1 Peter 2:13–17), but were also responsible to God at the same time. They could be good worshipers. Jesus said each was to get its due. What was asked as an either-or question Jesus turned into a both-and response. The assumption in the answer was that what the government had asked its citizens to do was not unethical (an unethical request applied in a religious context in Acts 4:19; 5:29 so that disobedience is a result).

Sextus on the Things of the World

***Sentences* 20:** "Be careful to pay back to the world what is of the world, and to God what is of God."

22:22. The questioners were amazed by the reply (Mark 12:17b; Luke 20:26). The trap had been avoided. God was honored; the government was respected. They departed.

22:23–28. Next, some Sadducees stepped up to the plate. Most of the priests and elders in Jerusalem were Sadducees. Their group did not believe in angels nor in the resurrection (Josephus, *A.J.* 18.16–17; *B.J.* 2.162–66). They were far more naturalistic in their theology. They posed a question to Jesus to try to show how silly resurrection belief was. The question was built off of levirate marriage (Gen. 38:8; Deut. 25:5–6; the entire *m. Yebam.*), which said if a brother died without leaving descendants, then his brother must marry the widow to leave a family line for the deceased brother (Mark 12:18–22; Luke 20:27–33). A *levir* was the surviving brother of a childless brother.

Josephus on the Sadducees and Pharisees

***Antiquities* 18.12–17:** "Now, for the Pharisees, they live meanly [cheaply], and despise delicacies in diet; and they follow the conduct of reason; and what that prescribes to them as good for them, they do; and they think they ought earnestly to strive to observe reason's dictates for practice. They also pay a respect to such as are in years; nor are they so bold as to contradict them in anything which they have introduced; and, when they determine that all things are done by fate, they do not take away the freedom from men of acting as they think fit; since their notion is, that it hath pleased God to make a temperament, whereby what he wills is done, but so that the will of men can act virtuously or viciously. They also believe that souls have an immortal vigor in them, and that under the earth there will be rewards or punishments, according as they have lived virtuously or viciously in this life; and the latter are to be detained in an everlasting prison, but that the former shall have power to revive and live again; on account of which doctrines, they are able greatly to persuade the body of the people; and whatsoever they do about divine worship, prayers, and sacrifices, they perform them according to their direction; insomuch that the cities gave great attestations to them on account of their entire virtuous conduct, both in the actions of their lives and their discourses also.

But the doctrine of the Sadducees is this: That souls die with the bodies; nor do they regard the observation of anything besides what the law enjoins them; for they think it an instance of virtue to dispute with those teachers of philosophy whom they frequent; but this doctrine is received but by a few, yet by those still of the greatest dignity; but they are able to do almost nothing of themselves; for when they become magistrates, as they are unwillingly and by force sometimes obliged to be, they addict themselves to the notions of the Pharisees, because the multitude would not otherwise bear them."

The story began with a wife and a deceased brother; the husband died while the family was childless. He had seven brothers. The widowed wife next married brother number two. He died childless. Brother three was next. And so it went. The tone is humorous to belittle resurrection, for by the time she got to brother number three, the rest of the brothers must have been getting nervous. She was truly a widow of death. The query proceeded until the woman had worked her way childless through the entire list of brothers. She had become like the plague. Finally, mercifully, she died.

The question was: In the afterlife whose wife would she be, since she had seven husbands? The picture was of an overburdened woman committed for eternity with many men sharing her as one wife. The scene was supposed to show how ridiculous resurrection was because it resulted in an absurd situation. Even though the Sadducees doubted resurrection, many Jews believed in it (Job 19:25–27; Isa. 26:19; Dan. 12:2; 2 Macc. 7:9–11, showing a physical dimension to resurrection as the one being executed offers his hands and tongue to be destroyed knowing God will give them back to him one day; 1 En. 103:4; *m. Sanh.* 10.1; Turner 2008, 531). The Sadducees' question implied it was better not to believe in resurrection.

Belief in Resurrection

Daniel 12:2: "Many of those who sleep in the dusty ground will awake—some to everlasting life, and others to shame and everlasting abhorrence."

2 Maccabees 7:9–11: "And when he was at his last breath, he said, 'You accursed wretch, you dismiss us from this present life, but the King of the universe will raise us up to an everlasting renewal of life, because we have died for his laws.' After him, the third was the victim of their sport. When it was demanded, he quickly put out his tongue and courageously stretched forth his hands, and said nobly, 'I got these from Heaven, and because of his laws I disdain them, and from him I hope to get them back again.'"

1 Enoch 103:4: "The spirits of those who died in righteousness shall live and rejoice; their spirits shall not perish, nor their memorial from before the face of the Great One unto all the generations of the world. Therefore, do not worry about their humiliation."

Mishnah, *Sanhedrin* 10:1: "All Israelites have a share in the world to come, as it is said, 'Your people also shall be all righteous, they shall inherit the land forever; the branch of my planting, the work of my hands, that I may be glorified (Is. 60:21).'"

22:29–30. Jesus responded in two parts, with two points. The first response was about the afterlife. The remark came with a rebuke. The Sadducees were deceived. They did not understand the Scripture nor the power of God (Mark 12:24). Jesus took up these two points in reverse order, moving from God's transforming power to the Scriptures (Nolland 2005, 904). The implication was that they did not understand resurrection because of these errors. Point one was that the afterlife was not like this life (Hagner 1995, 641). God transformed people into a form of existence that differed from this life. There was no marriage. They neither married (men) nor were given in marriage (women). They lived like angels with glorified bodies (2 Bar. 51:10; Philo, Sacr. 1.5; T. Isaac 4:45–47; 1QSb [1Q28b] 4:24–26; Keener 2009, 527–28; Nolland 2005, 905 n. 89). The mention of being like angels likely was another challenge to Sadducean views, since they did not believe in angels (Blomberg 1992, 333). Davies and Allison (1997, 227) hold it was unlikely that Sadducees denied the existence of angels since they believed the Torah, but as naturalists, the Sadducees may not have accepted everything in the Torah but embraced its prescriptive teaching.

Afterlife Like Angels in Judaism

2 Baruch 51:10: "For they will live in the heights of that world and they will be like the angels and be equal to the stars. And they will be changed into any shape which they wished, from beauty to loveliness, and from light to the splendor of glory."

Philo, *On the Sacrifices of Abel and Cain* 1.5: "for Abraham also, leaving mortal things, 'is added to the people of God' (Gen 25:8), having received immortality, and having become equal to the angels; for angels are the host of God, being incorporeal and happy souls."

Testament of Isaac 4:45–47: "Then they will be engaged in holy, angelic service by reason of purity. They will be presented before the Lord and his angels because of their pure offerings and their angelic service. For their earthly conduct will be reflected in heaven, and the angels will be their friends because of their perfect faith and purity."

Jesus was not saying people would become angels but would have an existence like them (correctly noted by Wilkins 2004, 724). Relationships would be newly and more deeply present in heaven. As important as marriage and sex within it were on earth, all of that would be transcended in heaven.

Mark 12:25 makes the same two points about Scripture and God's power. Luke 20:34–36 makes the same points with more detail, speaking of the resurrected as being sons of God. Those observations negate the scenario's core premise. One need not worry about the woman or which brother (or brothers) is married to her. One does not have spouses in heaven. Procreation and the need for families in a state that is eternal will no longer be necessary (1 En. 15:6–7). France (2007, 839) notes love will continue to be present but not marriage.

22:31–32. However, what shows resurrection itself was to be believed? Here is Jesus's second point. Jesus asked if they had not read the standard phrase where God described himself and named the patriarchs, "I am the God of Abraham, the God of Isaac, and the God of Jacob" (BDAG s.v. "Ἀβραάμ" 2; "Ἰσαάκ" 480; "Ἰακώβ" 1, 464). Matthew explicitly included the present-tense verb εἰμι ("I am") to help make the point. Jesus did not say God "was" their God. The LXX has the verb, while the MT lacks it, though one should supply the idea. God's name was repeated and tied to each one of the patriarchs individually to make the point emphatically. The argument is not merely one of tense but is tied to God's covenant commitments made to the patriarchs (Keener 2009, 529). God made commitments to the patriarchs he would keep and they would experience. Despite their death, he is still their God. Jesus also focused on the address to the Sadducees of this promise when he asked, "have you not read what was spoken to you by God . . . ?" They were supposed to have grasped that this text taught them this.

Of course, they had read this text. The question expected a positive reply (οὐκ). The expression cited Exodus 3:6. They should have understood this point. Jesus observed that God is the God of the living and not the dead. Mark 12:26–27 makes the same arguments and adds they were badly mistaken. Luke 20:37 explicitly notes that Moses showed the idea that all live before God. The argument proceeded along the following lines. Now if God could speak of the patriarchs in the present tense in addressing Moses, and he is the God of the living, then the patriarchs must be raised from the dead. Long seemingly dead, they still live (4 Macc. 7:19; 13:17; 16:25; Turner 2008, 532). The argument may actually have had steps, since there was a belief in an intermediate state until the resurrection, with one gathered to the patriarchs to await that resurrection. The holding of the people until the resurrection and judgment meant that one state pointed to the other (2 Macc. 7:9; 36; 1 En. 22:l–14; 60:8; 62:15; 4 Ezra 7; Josephus, *B.J.* 3:374; Davies and Allison 1997, 231). Evans (2012, 384) discusses similar kinds of arguments out of Second Temple texts.

Jewish Texts on Resurrection, with the Forefathers Gathered to Await Judgment

4 Maccabees 7:19: "Believing that to God they do not die, as our patriarchs Abraham, Isaac, and Jacob died not, but live to God."

4 Maccabees 13:17: "After our death in this fashion Abraham and Isaac and Jacob will receive us, and all our forefathers will praise us."

4 Maccabees 16:25: "And they knew full well themselves that those who die for the sake of God live unto God, as do Abraham and Isaac and Jacob and all the patriarchs."

1 Enoch 22:3–4: "At that moment, Rufael, one of the holy angels, who was with me, responded to me; and he said to me, 'These beautiful corners (are here) in order that the spirits of the souls of the dead should assemble into them—they are created so that the souls of the children of the people should gather here. They prepared these places in order to put them [i.e., the souls of the people] there until the day of their judgment and the appointed time of the great judgment upon them.'"

Jesus's argument came from the Torah, the portion of Scripture the Sadducees most respected. The argument by inference challenged their rejection of the resurrection. Jesus's second point was that the Torah taught resurrection by implication.

Resurrection is a key element of Christian teaching since it affirms a life after death and an ongoing accountability to God. It was defended by Paul (1 Cor. 15; note especially verse 43 on the power of God) and in some expressions of Judaism (Wis. 3:1–8; 1 En. 103:1–4—see chart above at 22:23–28; Davies and Allison 1997, 226 n. 36). It is rooted in God's presence and power.

Jewish Text on Hope of Resurrection

Wisdom 3:1–8: "But the souls of the righteous are in the hand of God, and no torment will ever touch them. In the eyes of the foolish they seemed to have died, and their departure was thought to be a disaster, and their going from us to be their destruction; but they are at peace. For though in the sight of others they were punished, their hope is full of immortality. Having been disciplined a little, they will receive great good, because God tested them and found them worthy of himself; like gold in the furnace he tried them, and like a sacrificial burnt offering he accepted them. In the time of their visitation they will shine forth, and will run like sparks through the stubble. They will govern nations and rule over peoples, and the Lord will reign over them forever."

22:33. Only Matthew notes the public reaction to this exchange. The crowds were said to be amazed at his teaching (Matt. 7:28). Jesus had stumped the Sadducees and had avoided the theological trap with an appeal to the very portion of Scripture Sadducees embraced. He had responded to them on their own terms. Mark has no public response, while Luke 20:39–40 has some scribes praise Jesus's answer, saying he had spoken well. Luke also caps off his sequence of controversies initiated by the Jews by noting they no longer asked Jesus anything.

22:34. The Pharisees heard that Jesus had silenced the Sadducees and joined them in considering what to do about him. They must deal with Jesus. The fact this verse precedes the next question suggests that that question was not the act of merely one person, but that the scribe made the probe representing them all. An allusion to gathering together to oppose God and his anointed may be present (Ps. 2:2; Acts 4:26).

22:35–36. A scribe now tested Jesus with a question. Mark 12:28 has the scribe ask which commandment was "first of all." He wanted to know what Jesus thought the greatest commandment was. It is unclear where the test lay in this question, especially when Jesus answered it in a simple and direct way. Discussions like this did appear in later Jewish texts (*m. Mak.* 3.16; *m. 'Abot.* 6.11; Turner 2008, 535–36; ; 23b-24a). Still, the expectation behind the question might have been that Jesus would nullify something in Torah and expose himself to critique (Davies and Allison 1997, 239). Rabbis did make a distinction between heavy and light commands that opened the door for such priority thinking about commandments. The Ten Commandments and idolatry often were at the top of the list (Keener 2009, 530). Later texts that show this included the Babylonian Talmud, *Qiddushin* 40a and Palestinian Talmud, *Nedarim* 3.9 § 3.

22:37–40. Jesus answered in three steps (Mark 12:29–31). He cited two commands and then summarized.

First was the call to love God with all one's heart, soul, and mind. The threefold combination looked to loving with the entire person, with the innermost person and the understanding. Mark 12:30 mentions the heart, soul, mind, and strength, as does Luke 10:27. Deuteronomy 6:5 is the cited passage (Jub. 1:15–16). It immediately follows the Shema confession of the one God of Israel, which pious Jews uttered twice daily and was a central text in Jewish worship. This command was placed on doorposts and phylacteries (France 2007, 845). It was a common starting point for the answer. Jesus called this the greatest and first commandment, a remark only Matthew has.

Second, Jesus cited the call to love one's neighbor as oneself (Matt. 5:43; 7:12; 19:19; the law of love—John 13:34–35; Rom. 13:8–10; Gal. 5:14; James 2:8; 1 John 4:20–21). This citation is from Leviticus 19:18 (*m. 'Abot.* 1.12; CD 6.20–21; Philo, *Spec.* 2.15, 63; Josephus, *B.J.* 2.119). It allowed Jesus to link how we interact with God to how we interact with others, just as the Ten Commandments do (France 2007, 843; Turner 2008, 537). Rabbi Akiba called this verse a "great principle in Torah" (Wilkins 2004, 725; Gen. Rab. 24.7—Akiba said it was a greater principle than the existence of the book of the descendants of Adam, that is, of human existence).

The expression "as yourself" has generated its own debate. Is a kind of self-love in view here or not? It would be better to think of self-regard and a concern for well-being and self-preservation here as opposed to a self-love that might turn into a kind of selfishness where life becomes all about me and my desires. That kind of self-focus is excluded by all Jesus taught about care for others, service, and sacrifice.

Jesus called the second command "like the first." This distinction is another Matthean distinctive in this scene. Jesus was not saying this is a less important idea but that this is the second part of his answer to the question, linking to it to the call to love God fully. Both were necessary, as appreciation for God led to appreciation of those created in his image. Loving those created by God showed respect for the lives God created. Love here was not seen so much as an emotion as an attitude expressing itself in concrete actions. As Wilkins (2004, 726) says, "Love is an unconditional commitment to an imperfect person in which one gives oneself to another to bring the relationship to God's intended purposes." It was a moving toward another person versus moving against or withdrawing from them.

Jesus summarized that on these two things all the law and prophets hung (Donaldson 1995). Only Matthew says this among the Synoptics. Jesus was saying the efficacy of scriptural teaching was dependent on this kind of love. A reference to the law and prophets pointed to the whole of the Hebrew Scripture. Jesus's combination of Deuteronomy 6:5 with Leviticus 19:18 here is unique, but others had placed these ideas in proximity to each other (similar kinds of juxtapositions: T. Dan 5:3;

T. Iss. 5:2; 7:6; Philo, *Abr.* 208; France 2007, 843). Mark 12:31 says there is no other command greater than these. Mark 12:32–34 continues the exchange, providing details Matthew lacks. The scribe went on to speak of God as one, an allusion to Deuteronomy 4:35. Mark also added that to love God and one's neighbor was more important than offerings and sacrifices. Mark 12:33 treats the two commands as a unified command in this comparison. In Mark, Jesus responded to the scribe that he was not far from the kingdom in thinking these things. With that close, Mark now noted no one dared to ask Jesus any more questions.

Deuteronomy 6 and Leviticus 19 in Jewish Texts

Testament of Dan 5:3: "Throughout all your life love the Lord, and one another with a true heart.

Testament of Issachar 5:2: "Love the Lord and your neighbor; be compassionate toward poverty and sickness."

Testament of Issachar 7:6: "I acted in piety and truth all my days. The Lord I loved with all my strength; likewise, I loved every human being as I love my children."

22:41–42. Now it was Jesus's turn to ask a question. When the Pharisees gathered, Jesus began a conversation with them about the Messiah. The first round of questions asked what they thought about who the Messiah was and whose son he was. The Pharisees replied quite naturally: "The son of David." Numerous texts, starting with 2 Samuel 7:12–14, noted this phrase (1 Chron. 17:11–14; Ps. 89; Isa. 11:1, 10; Jer. 23:5–6; 33:15; Ezek. 34:23–24; 37:24; Sir. 47:11; 48:15; 4 Ezra 12:32; Pss. Sol. 17:21–43; 18:7–9; 4QFlorilegium [4Q174] 1.10–14; Bateman, Johnston, and Bock 2012). This led Jesus to probe further. The Son of David had been a topic for Matthew in these final scenes (Matt. 20:30–31; 21:9, 15; earlier in 9:27; 12:23; 15:22; Culpepper 2021, 435–36). This is the last mention of this title in Matthew.

22:43–45. Jesus now brought a second round of questions and asked how the Spirit prompted David to call his promised descendant "Lord." Mark 12:35–37a has Jesus teaching this in the temple courts and lacks the opening exchange, going directly to Jesus's remarks on Psalm 110:1. Luke 20:41–44 also only has the questions about the psalm. This is unlike the normal pattern where Matthew has the more condensed version of a parallel.

In a patriarchal society where honor went to elders, this was a surprising declaration. Jesus wanted to know why David would do this. The point came from Psalm 110:1, which Jesus cited in a form very close to the LXX but which also reflects an oral reading of the Hebrew text. Here Yahweh addressed David's son as "my Lord," using *ʾădōnî*, which means "Lord." In Greek we get *kyrios*, meaning "Lord," twice, probably because God's name was not to be pronounced and "Lord" became the substitute for the name of God that opened the psalm. The opening to the psalm in the Hebrew, translated literally, says, "Yahweh said to my Lord," but with the substitution we got "The Lord said to my Lord." The assumption was that David had written the psalm or was the speaker of the initial words as is seen in the reference to the Spirit. The dilemma surfaced in the total respect the ancestor David showed to the descendant.

This scene has historical authenticity and went back to Jesus (Bock 1987, 128–32, discussing the Lucan parallel; Bock 1998, 209–33, of the use of Psalm 110:1 in Mark 14:62; contra the position of Davies and Allison 1997, 250–51, who argue that even if the saying went back to Jesus, we cannot know what he meant in using it). There is an underlying cultural logic here that drove the query. Without it, the question made no sense.

So Jesus asked: If David called the son "Lord," then how was the Messiah David's son? The question is asked as a first-class condition (εἰ), assuming in the presentation that the premise was so. The question was asked in an open way that was to be contemplated. Matthew presents Jesus throughout his gospel as a transcendent Son (Matt. 1:23; 2:15; 3:17; 4:3, 6; 7:21; 8:29; 11:25–27; 16:16; 17:5; 21:37–39; 22:2; 24:36; 26:29, 39, 42, 53, 63; 27:40, 43, 54; 28:19; Turner 2008, 541). He is one seated at God's right hand. This exalted role is more significant than seeing him as only David's son (on David's son: Matt. 1:1, 16–17, 20). There are suggestions in this direction from the Old Testament beyond Psalm 110:1 (Ps. 45:6–7; Isa. 9:6; 11:1, 10; Jer. 23:5–6; 33:15–16; Zech. 12:10; 13:7). Matthew has also pointed in this direction (Osborne 2010, 829; Matt. 10:32–33, 40; 11:27; 14:33; 16:16).

The question was raised most indirectly and was simply presented as a dilemma about messianic teaching. There was no direct connection to Jesus. This indirect use is part of what makes the scene look authentic. If the church had created the scene, one would expect the pointing to Jesus would be made more explicitly (Keener 2009, 532). Many commentators argue Jesus was correcting a militaristic and political view of the Messiah from the Jews (Morris 1992, 566–67), but that is not so clear by what Jesus raised here. It was Jesus's position, not the form of his messiahship, that this question surfaced. There was nothing about suffering here. It was all about his exalted status. The remark raised the question, "What does it say about that figure that one can sit with God in heaven?" (Bock 1998).

This psalm and its point left an impact and is cited in numerous New Testament texts. They include Psalm 110:1 cited in Matthew 26:64 = Mark 14:62 = Luke 22:69; Acts 2:34–35; and Hebrews 1:13. Psalm 110:4 appears in Hebrews 5:6; 7:17–21. Possible allusions to Psalm 110:1 appear in Romans 8:34; 1 Corinthians 15:25; Ephesians 1:20; Colossians 3:1; Hebrews 1:3; 8:1; 10:12–13; 12:2; and Revelation 3:21. Possible allusions to Psalm 110:4 occur in John 12:34; Romans 11:29; and Hebrews 5:10; 6:20; 7:3, 11, 15. Romans 2:5 may allude to Psalm 110:5. This text had left its mark on the early church. Its claim of authority for the Messiah in a position next to God was what was the most common point of reference.

Jews debated what this text meant. Hay (1973, 22–33) treats the details on the variety of Jewish readings and argues a messianic reading was contemporary to Jesus's time (also Bateman, Johnston, and Bock 2012). Job, Abraham, the Messiah, and David were among the candidates seen as fulfilling the text in Jewish readings. One text at Qumran has two messiahs, one political and another priestly (1QS 9:11); 11QMelchizedek shows an eschatological reading of this text. Nolland (2005, 915) notes later Jewish messianic readings (in Gen. Rab. 85:9—where a reference in Ps. 11:2 is said to allude to the staff of the royal Messiah; Num. Rab. 18:23—where the staff of Aaron is said to become the staff of the royal Messiah also citing Ps. 110:2; *Midr. on the Psalms* 110.4—where the Messiah will sit at the right hand and read Torah). The original text was a royal psalm but was applied ultimately to the Messiah as part of the dynastic line the text mentions. It expressed what the king was to be in ideal terms, something the Messiah would fulfill. That the text was about Messiah is assumed in Jesus's reading.

22:46. There was no answer from the Pharisees. The Psalm 110:1 passage was reintroduced at the Jewish examination of Jesus where the answer to this question would emerge (Matt. 26:64 = Mark 14:62 = Luke 22:69). In the meantime, no one dared ask Jesus any more questions. The challenges to him were over. Jesus showed how qualified he was and is to lead God's people. Mark 12:37b says the crowd listened with delight, while Luke has no concluding comment on any reaction.

THEOLOGICAL FOCUS

The exegetical idea (a series of controversies showed a very competent Jesus who was not a revolutionary, believed in resurrection as taught in Torah, taught loving God and neighbor as the Great Commandment, and challenged the leaders to understand why the Messiah was called Lord by David) results in this theological focus: Though rejected, Jesus shows himself fully qualified to lead God's program through his understanding of hope, ethics, and the promise of God.

The final controversies involving Jesus and the Jewish leaders showed he was competent to lead God's people and pointed to an anticipated messianic role at God's side, as he showed he was not a revolutionary, affirmed resurrection, demonstrated a love for God, and issued a call to love one's neighbor. However, these controversies also raised other issues that are theologically and practically important.

The first is the believer's relationship to government. Generally speaking, Christians are not revolutionaries in terms of the rights of governments to exist and function. Here, Jesus affirmed the right of Rome to tax. He articulated a side-by-side relationship between government and spiritual priorities. The assumption here is that as long as the government does not violate core religious and ethical rights, it should be followed. A different kind of tension will surface in Revelation, where the world government, now totally pagan and hostile, faces an accountability and judgment from God. Governments do not get moral carte blanche. Numerous NT texts call for a respectful regard for government, even a government as corrupt as Rome (Rom. 13:1–7; 1 Peter 2:13–17). However, that does not place them beyond critique, as the prophets showed. This tension of how government functions in a fallen world is always with us until Christ returns to establish righteousness. Christians are to appreciate the limits of what politics can achieve. Real change comes from a change of heart before God, which is where the gospel takes us. Respect is not the same thing as agreement, nor are we to have moral indifference to what goes on around us.

Jesus also affirmed resurrection without qualification in a dispute with the Sadducees. This formed the backbone of his own mission and message in terms of expected vindication from God for his upcoming death. Resurrection extends to all who will each face the Son of Man and Creator God one day (Matt. 24–25). Everyone will be accountable to God one day whether they recognize it or not. Those who respond to God in faith will receive the blessing of eternal life with God. The centrality of this teaching appears in most detail in 1 Corinthians 15, but also is suggested in texts like Colossians 1:15–23.

Jesus affirmed the core ethic of Scripture as completely loving God and loving one's neighbor as oneself. On this the law and prophets were said to depend. Nothing about what Jesus was doing undercut the core relational calling of God. In fact, Jesus reinforced what God desired by what he taught and how he taught it.

Finally, Jesus raised a question that anticipated the Messiah would sit with God in heaven and share in heavenly authority. This not only anticipated a coming vindication, but also a coming role in judgment. The authority is comprehensive, and the seating indicates a level of equality with God that the church clarified over the next few centuries, resulting in affirmations about the Trinity. Exactly how this works is something Jesus's handling of Psalm 110:1 at the examination by the Jewish leadership developed (Matt. 26:57–68). It is best to wait for that passage before detailing how Psalm 110:1 contributed to a high regard for the personal uniqueness of Jesus that became core Christian teaching on Christology.

PREACHING AND TEACHING STRATEGIES

Exegetical and Theological Synthesis

The exegetical section describes Jesus's mastery in navigating theological and ethical landmines. He sidestepped traps set by the religious leaders while providing theological and ethical correctives. His rhetorical strategy has merit: clarifying questions can be more persuasive than direct answers. When questioned about taxes and resurrection, Jesus responded with a question. Moreover, he concluded the series of tests with a question of his own about Messiah. In controversial conversations, responding to a question with a question forces the other person to clarify their position and possibly admit a faulty premise. Koukl (2009) has built an apologetic strategy reflective of Jesus's method.

Not only did Jesus employ a brilliant rhetorical strategy, but he also spoke with clarity about ethics. He placed love at the core of the law, tying divine and human love together. While Jesus's call to love was not original, the intersection of love for God and others and the weight he gave them reshaped ethics for the early church. NT writers regularly appealed to the centrality of love (Rom. 13:8; 1 Cor. 13; Gal. 5:14; James 2:8). Jesus considered love the defining feature of disciples (John 13:35). John saw it as the surest fruit of faith (1 John 3–4). Indeed, we are called to elaborate love (Matt. 5:21–48).

Preaching Idea

Jesus passes every quality control test imaginable.

Contemporary Connections

What does it mean?

What does it mean that Jesus passes every quality control test imaginable? First, it means that anyone who questions his intellect, authority, or understanding of God's plan will find themselves on the losing side of an argument. Of course, Jesus does not orally debate people today! However, we can revisit the Gospels to remember his brilliance. His masterful handling of the Herodians, Sadducees, and Pharisees testifies to his rhetorical skill. His forthcoming interactions with Pilate and the chief priests will reinforce this perspective. Willard (1997, 93–94) calls Jesus the "smartest man who ever lived." The praise is merited.

Second, anyone who applies Jesus's teaching on citizenship, hope, and ethics can be confident. Jesus is a master teacher and qualified source on these matters. We are wise to pay our taxes, vote in elections, respect governing authorities, and use civil means of protesting injustice rather than violent methods. Moreover, we should anticipate the glories of resurrection without too much speculation about the dimensions of heaven. Finally, we should make love of God and others our primary pursuit. This contrasts with our world, which prioritizes the pursuit of happiness, freedom, and financial gain.

Is it true?

It is true that Jesus passes every quality control test. His teaching on citizenship, hope, and ethics is better than today's sages. However, two caveats are needed. First, Jesus is right, but his responses are not always received by others. Despite his qualified answers to questions about citizenship, hope, and ethics, the religious leaders of his time were not persuaded. Similarly, we may give right answers about sexual ethics, heeding governmental mandates, and handling abuse, but this competent response may not be received. Opponents outside the church may consider them old-fashioned, bigoted, or hateful. Opponents inside the church may consider them soft, progressive, or prudish. When we can separate the quality of Jesus's teaching from its reception by others, we can be certain it passes the test.

When we "lose" the argument in the public square, how we deal with losing becomes important. The ends do not justify the means. We should engage in ways that are in contrast with how the world contests ideas. When we fight like the world, we lose our distinctiveness and sometimes cede moral ground, making us look hypocritical. We become more like those we contend with and lose the appeal and example of being different than the world.

So Jesus is right, but views like his are not instantly rewarded. His teaching on citizenship, hope, and ethics takes time to transform the world. We might prefer loud protests or messianic presidential figures to the slow work of paying taxes and community service. We likely prefer conditional love to unconditional love because it costs less, hurts less, and takes less time. Likewise, our love for God is partial; we give pieces of our heart and mind but reserve our bodies for work and pleasure, which feel more rewarding than praying on our knees or memorizing Scripture. When we can separate the quality of Jesus's teaching from immediate reward, we can be certain it passes the test.

Now what?

Knowing that Jesus passes every quality control should give his followers a feeling of confidence. Our Messiah is a master teacher. We serve a competent King. His quality is unquestionable. So our first response to this passage is to appreciate the genius of Jesus.

Second, we should apply his teaching. We can study citizenship, hope, and ethics all day long, but until we practice public service, patient waiting, and unconditional love, we can only claim partial knowledge.

Applying Jesus's Teaching

Citizenship Test: Do I pray for my governing authorities? Do I honestly report my taxes? Where do I serve my community (e.g., school, food bank, church)? Do I honor my leaders? How do I protest?

Hope Test: Do I believe in a physical resurrection? Do I believe in heaven and hell? What kind of judgment and reward do I expect in the end times? Does my understanding of end times fuel more fear, speculation, or hope?

Ethics Test: What parts of my life am I withholding from God? How has my love of God grown over the years? What do I love more than God? For whom does unconditional love come naturally? For whom is unconditional love difficult? What are the conditions?

The more we do what Jesus says, the better we know what he means. Moreover, we realize, as stated above, that the quality of Jesus's teaching is not always received or immediately rewarded. We press on nonetheless, trusting his teaching has passed the test of time.

Finally, we may take a page from Jesus's debate book. We should be ready to give a reason for our hope when asked (1 Peter 3:15). We do it with courtesy and respect, as 1 Peter 3:16 notes. Christian faith is rational. It is based upon the life and teaching of history's most qualified leader. However, having an answer does not demand we give it. Nor are answers to be forced on someone. Each person is accountable to God for how they respond to choices in life. In Jesus's model of debate over politics, eschatology, and ethics, he sometimes deferred. He turned the question back on his opponents. He did not feel compelled to get the last word but wanted to expose his opponents to the weaknesses of their own beliefs. This apologetic method is readily applied by modern apologists (Geisler and Turek 2004; Keller 2016, 29–54; Koukl 2009, 42–103).

Creativity in Presentation

As you describe Jesus as a master of intellect, great debater, and rhetorical genius, you can give your church a live demonstration of his methodology.

- You may plant a question with a staff member or elder.
- You may use an online platform (e.g., Slido) to aggregate questions.

- You should clarify that you want to answer substantive questions, not trivial ones.
- You are allowed (and even encouraged) to use your Bible in your response.
- Most importantly, you should graciously turn the question back on the one asking. In other words, answer the question with a question.

This exercise has the potential to go sidewise if someone asks something deeply personal (e.g., "Will I see my stillborn baby in heaven?"), so a planted question or aggregated ones may be best. For a brilliant example of how this style of debate can work against Christians, see apologist Sean McDowell interact with questions from high school students while pretending to be an atheist; search "Atheist Encounter" on YouTube.

Anyone who has cooked for others has probably experienced "quality control" moments in the kitchen. When I (Tim) was a kid, my parents used to offer a "tester" pancake before our Saturday morning feast. Not only did the "tester" appease the hungry children; it assured my parents that their batter passed the quality test. I have continued this tradition with my family. In fact, before most of our meals, my son crowds the kitchen, peering over our shoulders as my wife and I cook. When he first comes in with his rapacious eyes, we say, "Here comes quality control!"

In the world of manufacturing—from vehicles to replacement knees—quality control plays an important role in assuring a safe and reliable product for end users. It also protects companies from losses and lawsuits. Quality controllers may take samples, run tests, or verify contents.[1] Consider choosing an industry where you have benefited from or been hurt by their "quality control" process.[2]

Testing plays a prominent role in education. From early reading tests to college placement tests to post-graduate exams, testing proves the quality of students and their educators. Often the pressure to pass a test overshadows the value of a quality education. Consider interviewing a student and teacher who understand the true value of a quality education.

Sample Interview Questions About Testing

Questions for a Model Student

- How do you handle the stress of taking tests? What study hacks or rituals do you use?
- What are some major exams you have had to take in your academic career?
- What has test-taking proven about your character?

Questions for a Model Teacher

- How many tests do you give in a year?
- In addition to quizzes and exams, what are other ways you "test" your students?
- What are the key ingredients to a quality education?

In the end, be sure your sermon stresses that, Though rejected, Jesus shows himself fully qualified to lead God's program through his understanding of hope, ethics, and the promise of God. Clearly, Jesus passes every quality control test imaginable.

- Jesus passes the citizenship test (22:15–22).
- Jesus passes the hope test (22:23–33).
- Jesus passes the ethics test (22:34–40).

---

1 For an overview on quality control, see https://www.simplilearn.com/what-is-quality-control-article.
2 For ideas, check the latest recalled product list at https://www.cpsc.gov/Recalls (accessed July 24, 2024).

- Jesus administers his own test (22:41–46).

DISCUSSION QUESTIONS

1. When you add in Romans 13, 1 Peter 2, and the prophets, what are some key principles on citizenship that apply to the church today?
2. In what ways were Sadducees different from Pharisees? How were they similar?
3. What was the Jewish expectation of resurrection in Jesus's day?
4. What does holistic love for God look like? Be specific.
5. What does unconditional love for neighbors look like? Be specific.
6. If love is the key metric to Christian maturity, what is a good way to measure it?

Matthew 23:1–39

EXEGETICAL IDEA

After denouncing the scribes and Pharisees for hypocrisy, pride, blocking the way to blessing, misuse of oaths, neglecting mercy, and working against what the prophets represented, Jesus pronounced judgment against Israel until she recognized the one who comes in the Lord's name.

THEOLOGICAL FOCUS

Jesus issues a full indictment of the nation's leadership for spiritual failure and announces judgment against the nation until she recognizes who God has sent.

PREACHING IDEA

Shallow religion needs a sharp rebuke.

PREACHING POINTERS

After responding to a series of tests, Jesus preached his final public message—and it was not a pleasant one. Summoning his inner prophet, Jesus lambasted the religious leaders for their pride, hypocrisy, and poor direction of God's people. With a series of woes, Jesus made his case for reform in Jerusalem. He preached passionately; as a faithful Jew, he lamented the shallow spirituality of his own people. Matthew's audience would have understood Jesus's zeal for religious integrity—honesty, mercy, and covenant faithfulness. They would have sensed the seed of hope buried in his rebuke—namely, that those who followed Messiah's leadership would escape the trap of bad religion.

Shallow religion is an age-old problem. Worse yet, throughout history religion has been weaponized. It has sparked tribal feuds, justified witch trials, silenced victims of abuse, and preyed on desperate people hoping to find healing by funding televised preachers. All religions are prone to hypocrisy, scams, and crowd control. As Marx opined, "Religion is . . . the opium of the people." Christianity is not immune. One of the favorite labels critics throw at Christians is "hypocritical" (Kinnaman and Lyons 2012, 27). Clergy scandals in recent years have only bolstered these claims. Fortunately, Jesus's tough talk to religious leaders encourages all of us to take a close look at our religious commitment. Indeed, shallow religion needs a sharp rebuke.

JESUS ISSUES AN INDICTMENT OF WOES AGAINST THE SCRIBES AND PHARISEES (23:1–39)

LITERARY STRUCTURE AND THEMES (23:1–39)

This unit contains a series of seven prophetic woes (Matt. 23:13–36) that come with an opening introduction (Matt. 23:1–12) and closes with a summary prophetic declaration of judgment (Matt. 23:37–39). The passage is built around these seven woes.

Matthew 23 is a bridge passage. It concludes the controversies of Matthew 21:15–22:46 with a prophetic indictment by Jesus. It also sets up the Olivet Discourse, which includes remarks about the coming judgment upon Jerusalem that would take place in A.D. 70. Most importantly, it concludes with a note of proclaimed judgment to close out the controversies. This shows its most important link is to behavior. We call it part of a discourse block because it is immediately followed by the Olivet Discourse and its parables in Matthew 24–25, even though that discourse is a distinct event. This block presents the only sequence of discourses in Matthew and is the fifth discourse block in Matthew (Matt. 5–7; 10; 13; 16–18 are the others).

After a general introduction about hypocrisy and pride (Matt. 23:1–12), Jesus followed with seven woes. The first was about blocking access to heaven (Matt. 23:13). Matthew 23:14 is not well attested as an original part of Matthew, so it does not belong in the listing. It is not in the best manuscripts and much of the content repeats some of verses 12–13. The second was about producing a false kind of discipleship that did not save (Matt. 23:15). The third was about oaths that misled (Matt. 23:16–22). The fourth was about neglecting mercy, justice, and faith (Matt. 23:23–24). The fifth was about being corrupt on the inside (Matt. 23:25–26). The sixth was about religiosity hiding spiritual death (Matt. 23:27–28). The seventh was about a hypocritical life that showed why the prophets had been killed even as their tombs were celebrated (Matt. 23:29–36). This led into Jesus's judgment. God longed to call the Jewish leaders to himself, but that was something they did not respond to nor desire (Matt. 23:37–39). In this final description, we see that judgment was something that reflected a choice not to come God's way. In judgment, those denounced receive what they have asked for, walking in a way independent of God, but experiencing the accountability that this choice brought with it.

The chapter does two things at once: (1) it shows the spiritual condition of those who reject Jesus; and (2) it teaches by negative example what the spiritual should not look like. Jesus's followers were not to be like them, for God was not pleased with this kind of walk with him (Keener 2009, 537).

There is a major conceptual parallel to Matthew 23 in Luke 11:37–54. This is not strictly a parallel because the setting differs and the woes are in a completely different order (Davies and Allison 1997, 283–84, has details). Matthew has seven woes plus two other complaints in the following order: burdens, seats-greetings, woe1-key, woe2-proselytes, woe3-oaths, woe4-tithes, woe5-cup, woe6-tomb, and woe7-murder. Luke has seven of these nine topics in a different order and with a different woe listing and only one complaint without a woe: cup, woe1-tithes, woe2-seat and greetings, woe3-tombs, woe4-burdens, woe5-murder, and woe6-key. Luke lacks crossing the sea for proselytes and swearing false oaths. Following Luke's order, Luke shares clean the outside of the cup (but Luke lacks a woe here), tithe the mint, seats and greetings, prophet's tombs, do not take up burdens, murder the prophets, and the key to the kingdom. One other difference is worth noting. Luke indicates that Jesus spoke to Pharisees first and then turned to rebuke the scribes in a succession of three woes each. Matthew has Jesus addressing all seven woes against both groups together. However, worth noting is that the scribe who caused the audience shift in Luke said to Jesus that by rebuking the Pharisees, he was rebuking "us" (the scribes). Jesus thus accepted that premise and redirected his remarks without arguing for a hard distinction. Luke 11 took place on the way to Jerusalem at a dinner held by a Pharisee. Six woes followed, with three against the Pharisees and three against the scribes. Matthew 23 has a two-three-two pattern to his seven woes (Konradt 2020, 345). The core charges are basically the same, but the differing order and location look to a distinct event where Jesus issued a similar critique. An itinerant ministry can yield such similarity. Mark 12:38–40 and Luke 20:45–47 have a singular denunciation in the narrative place where Matthew 23 sits.

Themes are mostly negative in showing the leaders' deep spiritual flaws. These deficiencies included hypocrisy and pride, as well as neglecting mercy, justice, and faith. Their modeling made the same kind of flawed disciples. Despite claiming to lead people to God, they actually led people away from him, into uncleanness and death. Their form of worship and instruction had destructive results, earning Jesus's rebuke.

The concluding judgment was severe but temporary. Israel's house would be desolate until she recognized the one God had sent (Luke 13:34–35). The desolate house reflected the language of exilic-like judgment from the prophet Jeremiah. The spirit of Jesus's remarks echoed the condemnation of Jeremiah in Jeremiah 7 and 12. It was full of pain, not revenge. That pain responded to their choice not to draw near to God. The leadership was held accountable before God for their lack of spirituality. The nation they led paid the price. Forgiveness was available, but avoiding judgment would require a national turn to the one sent in the name of the Lord.

EXPOSITION (23:1–39)

The tension of rejection now led Jesus to speak with a prophetic voice about the consequences for the nation. He had claimed his right as king to purge the city, and the leaders had refused to respond, not seeing their need to turn to God. Jesus laid out the spiritual case against them and announced the consequences of their actions. What had been warned about over and over was now going to come to pass. This judgment was what rejection of Messiah produced as a response from God. Disciples were to note the nature of the spiritual failure and not repeat the shortcomings Jesus recounted.

After denouncing the scribes and Pharisees for hypocrisy, pride, blocking the way to blessing, misuse of oaths, neglecting mercy, and working against what the prophets represented, Jesus pronounced judgment against Israel until she recognized the one who comes in the Lord's name.

23:1. Jesus addressed the crowds and disciples about the spiritual flaws of the Pharisees and scribes. Crowds were last noted in Matthew 22:33. It was still Tuesday of Jesus's last week. The condemnation in the chapter was not aimed at all of Israel but at these spiritual leaders. Still the impact was transferred to the nation at the end of the chapter. The focused address to scribes and Pharisees shows itself in Matthew 23:13, 15, 23, 25, 27, and 29. These link back to the complaint Jesus starts with in Matthew 23:2–3. It was important the crowds and his own disciples understood the risk of being spiritually misdirected by the teachers they chose to follow.

23:2–3. Despite sitting in Moses's seat, the Pharisees and scribes were not to be followed in their practice, only in their teaching. This was because they did not practice what they preached. This was the general indictment on the leaders: hypocrisy. The remark is unique to Matthew. Details for the charge followed.

Jesus's challenge made sense because the Pharisees and scribes were heavily influential among Jews (Josephus, *A.J.* 13.298; 18.15, 17—see chart at Matt. 22:23–28). In some ways, they were the most logical next option if one did not embrace Jesus. Their approach needed to be challenged, especially because of the buildup of tradition that fed their approach to issues and sought unsuccessfully to "build a fence around the Torah" (*m. 'Abot.* 1.1). The result was a failed leadership that also was missing what God was doing now in Jesus.

Josephus on Pharisees' Influence

***Antiquities* 13:298a:** "And concerning these things it is that great disputes and differences have arisen among them, while the Sadducees are able to persuade none but the rich, and have not the populace obsequious to them, but the Pharisees have the multitude of their side."

Moses's seat was either, at the least, a metaphor for being the interpreters of Torah or referred to a specific chair picturing such authority (Davies and Allison 1997, 268; Turner 2008, 546). After Jesus's time, in the third and fourth centuries, synagogues appeared to have had such singular seats, but it is not clear how far back the practice went (France 2007, 859; Levine 2000, 323–27). It does seem that some such locale tied to worship existed (Wilkins 2004, 745). The verb that speaks to those who "sit" (ἐκάθισαν) in this seat is likely gnomic in force (Osborne 2010, 835; BDAG s.v. "καθίζω" 3, 491–92). This was a claim to expound Moses. Jesus recognized the Torah's authority such leaders taught, but challenged how they modeled what they instructed. Some read this as ironic sarcasm (Carson 2010, 531–32; France 2007, 860), but it is hard to see a real hint of this given the rest of the speech (Blomberg 1992, 341, has a balanced discussion; Hagner 1995, 654). What Jesus respected was the source of the teaching's content in biblical texts, not those who taught it or how they did it (Nolland 2005, 923). Romans 2:21–24 has a similar contrast.

23:4–7. The first specific was that they made great spiritual burdens for others but did not lift a finger with regard to them. These were the burdens of traditions like those debated in Matthew 12:1–14 (on the Sabbath) or 15:1–20 (on defiling; Acts 15:10, 28; 1 John 5:3). They contrasted with Jesus's earlier claim that his burden was light (Matt. 11:30). Unclear is whether the charge was that they did not lift a finger to help others succeed or simply that they did not bear the same burdens themselves, looking back to verse 3b. It seems the idea was that they were slow to help others beyond their own hypocrisy. The lack of engagement contrasted with Jesus's active ministry of compassion. It also fit what followed. The leaders loved to be the object of attention.

Second, they loved to bring attention to their own spiritual acts, so they made large phylacteries for their heads and prayer tassels for their garments. Phylacteries were little boxes that had Scripture in them. They were attached to the head or left forearm to show one bore the commandments (Exod. 13:9, 16; Deut. 6:8; 11:18; Ep. Arist. 159; Josephus, *A.J.* 4.213). Some of these were found at Qumran and were an inch long for the head and a third of an inch for the forearm (Wilkins 2004, 747). Tassels on the side of the garment were for prayer (Num. 15:38–39; Deut. 22:12), functioning like prayer beads do for others today. The Jewish leaders loved the first seats whether at the banquet or in the synagogue. At a banquet, the seating was shaped in a U, and the chief seats usually were at the center of the base of the U (Morris 1992, 575). In an honor-and-shame culture, first seats were badges of recognition. Davies and Allison (1997, 274) note several ancient examples, among them Josephus, *Jewish War* 2.25, 1QS 2:14–20, and Suetonius, *Augustus* 44. They loved the honor of being greeted in the market and enjoyed being hailed as rabbi. Rabbi means "my master," so Jesus returned to this role in what he said next (BDAG s.v. "ῥαββί" 902). The term came to be regarded as synonymous with being someone's teacher. Jesus challenged this kind of self-attention in whatever form it took (Matt. 6:1–6, 16–18).

On Phylacteries

Josephus, *Antiquities* 4.213: "They are also to inscribe the principal blessings they have received from God upon their doors, and show the same remembrance of them upon their arms; as also they are to bear on their forehead and their arm those wonders which declare the power of God, and his good will towards them, that God's readiness to bless them may appear everywhere conspicuous about them."

Letter of Aristeas 159: "He also strictly commands that the sign shall be worn on our hands, clearly indicating that it is our duty to fulfill every activity with justice, having in mind our own condition, and above all the fear of God."

23:8–10. Jesus now engaged in the correction. He used three examples: rabbi, father, and teacher. The context indicates he was dealing with religious teachers in all the examples (Jesus affirms earthly fathers in Matt. 15:4; 19:19; see Exod. 20:12; Deut. 5:16; Morris 1992, 577; Wilkins 2004, 748).

First, there were to be no rabbis. There was one teacher (John 13:13) and a recognition all were brothers. The point about one teacher appears twice in these verses for emphasis (Ignatius, *Mag.* 9:1l; *Eph.* 15:1). Jesus's emphasis was about status that honored some more than others.

Second, one was not to have a father on earth, for there is one Father: the one in heaven. This was about ultimate loyalty and respect. No teacher should be called by this title as a matter of rank. Second Kings 2:12 did use the term to communicate respect. Sometimes teachers in Judaism were called "the Fathers" (*m. 'Abot*; France 2007, 863). Of course, the term "patriarch" meant this as well in referring an ancestor of Israel. One could be a "father" without being addressed as such in a way that was too deferential and communicated superiority (1 Cor. 4:15; Philem. 10; even Jesus in Matt. 13:52; Osborne 2010, 838). An improper commending of status was the point here, not the mere use of words.

Third, one was to avoid being called "teacher." The hapax NT term here refers to an academic leader, a "tutor" (BDAG s.v. "καθηγητής" 490; Winter 1991, 152–57). There was only one from whom doctrine and teaching came, the Christ. Those who taught only mediated what came from God through the Christ. The result was an egalitarianism that worked within and alongside elements of hierarchy (Turner 2008, 548). This attitude promoted humility and mutuality (Davies and Allison 1997, 275; Eph. 5:15–21). Disciples were to avoid the use of titles that blurred where the real direction came from for the church.

23:11. Jesus then reiterated this leveling of status by noting that the greatest among them was the servant of all. This reinforced points already made in Matthew 20:24–28 (also 18:4; said in a distinct way: 19:30; 20:16). Leadership was not about power or rank, but service.

23:12. So the one who exalted himself, like the leaders did in Matthew 23:5–7, would be humbled. Those who humbled themselves would be exalted. The example here would be Jesus, who chose death in serving others and whom God would then exalt. Much of the ground summarized here was prepared for in what Jesus taught the disciples earlier in Matthew 18:4 and 20:24–28.

23:13. In the introduction in Matthew 23:1–12, Jesus discussed the Pharisees and scribes with the crowds and disciples. Now he addressed them directly, whether through his remarks or because they were present. The language was strong as he called them hypocrites, blind guides, and snakes who disrespected the prophets and led others into death. France (2007, 867) notes this text had as much invective as any text from Jesus, with the possible exception of John 8.

The woes Jesus spoke began with a general charge that the leaders' approach locked people out of heaven. Woes reflected prophetic laments, an interjection of pain or displeasure (Culpepper 2021, 446; BDAG s.v. "οὐαί" 1, 734). Those who thought they led people to God were doing the exact opposite. The core hypocrisy reflected charges like Isaiah 5:8–23 with its six woes, Jeremiah 23:2, and Ezekiel 34:2–8. The crime was not one of malicious intent, but of being self-deceived (France 2007, 869). They were poor shepherds just like the leaders of Ezekiel's time. They shut the door to entry into the kingdom, another way to speak of preventing salvation (Matt. 5:20; 7:21; 18:3; 19:23–24). Their keys did not unlock the kingdom but barred the door. Peter was given such keys in Matthew 16:19. The Gospel of Thomas 39 has a similar sounding rebuke about not possessing the key to knowledge that is more like Luke 11:52.

As Turner (2008, 550) notes, these woes combined many emotions that we also see in the prophets: anger, grief, and alarm. A woe was a declaration of judgment for an action. An example is Deuteronomy 27:15, which issued a curse for a covenant violation. The anger spoke for God against acts of sin. Grief resulted from the painful consequences of the act. Those who knew the prophets understood this kind of prophetic challenge. In Matthew, we have had woes over Israeli towns (Matt. 11:21) and the world (Matt. 18:7). Now it was time to challenge those who directed God's people. We will see other woes against Judas (Matt. 26:24) and against those who are unfortunate enough to be caught in the chaos described in Matthew 24 (see verse 19; Nolland 2005, 932).

The first six woes came in pairs. The first two treated the failure to bring entry into the kingdom. The middle two dealt with specifics. The last two returned to the theme of hypocrisy, since what was outside did not match what was inside. The seventh woe stood alone and summarized.

As was noted above, Matthew 23:14 on hypocrisy, devouring widows' property, and long prayers is unlikely to be original to Matthew. It is like Mark 12:40 and Luke 20:47 that appear in this equivalent location in those respective gospels and looks like an effort to harmonize with them by supplying what is lacking in Matthew. Most early key manuscripts lack it (א, B, D, L, Θ, f1, and old Italic, Syriac, and Coptic translations), so most modern translations do not include it as original in Matthew.

23:15. This woe and the next have no parallel in the Luke 11 scene. The second woe said that all of their effort to gain converts in fact produced someone who was more destined for hell. The disciple was like the teacher, only worse.

What is not clear is whether they were seeking converts to Pharisaism, seeking out God-fearing Gentiles to become full, circumcised proselytes, or to Judaism in general. The problem was neither labor nor zeal—as they traveled land and sea to do this—but an unproductive end. The allusion to a journey most likely refers to the encouragement of making Gentile proselytes full converts (Josephus, *B.J.* 2.560–61; *A.J.* 20.24–48; McKnight 1991; Keener 2009, 548–49, argues for more such activity than McKnight). Konradt (2020, 346) sees a push to make God-fearers into full proselytes as there is less evidence of a mission directly to Gentiles with no contact with Judaism. In other words, their discipleship took people backward. Sometimes followers have a zeal that goes beyond those who converted them (Morris 1992, 580). This may be what the "twice as much" refers to in the verse. Their conversion certainly did not lead to the Messiah. It led to Gehenna, another way that said it resulted in destruction (on Gehenna, see discussion of Matt. 5:22). Jesus was not preventing Gentiles from coming to the God of Israel, but was challenging how Pharisees did this (Wilkins 2004, 752).

23:16–19. The third woe was against oaths that made distinctions. It also introduced three woes that raised questions about how these leaders understood Torah (vv. 16–26; Konradt 2020, 346). The charge of being blind guides repeated Matthew 15:14. It was repeated here three times for emphasis (vv. 16, 17, 19). In the tradition, oaths based on the temple had no merit, but those that evoked the gold were to be fulfilled. The distinction may have to do with the *korban*, things dedicated to the temple. To declare something as *korban* would make the oath rooted in a dedicated sacred item and thus bound to that holy context (Davies and Allison 1979, 291; Garland 1997, 134–35; Osborne 2010, 849; esp. Matt. 15:5–6). If such an item were dedicated to the temple, then it couldn't go to anything else. Jesus was against such distinctions that weighed against integrity. Jesus had said as much in Matthew 5:33–37. Now Jesus asked what was greater: the gold, or the temple that made the gold sacred and set apart? The question showed the silliness of the distinction. How could the temple oath be denied value? The gold mentioned here was either gold utensils or gold given to honor the temple.

Jesus then cited another distinction. If one swore by the altar, that meant nothing. But if one swore by the gift on it, then one was bound. Another question challenges the distinction. What is greater, the gift or the altar that made it sacred and set apart? How could the altar oath be worthless? These kinds of distinctions showed the shallowness of the spirituality that allowed for such distinctions. The process of swearing reversed the values as things were more valuable than the sacred contexts and the worship tied to those locations. These were examples of blind guidance that went the wrong way. We have no outside contemporary evidence for these distinctions, but one is hard pressed to see Matthew note them unless something like this existed. Šebu'ot discusses oaths. *Mishnah* Šebu'ot 4.13 covers terms tied to oaths (Lieberman 1942; Nolland 2005, 935). A later text has this kind of thing with a vow by the Torah not being binding, while one appealing to its contents is (Ned. 14b). Vows involved not using something, while an oath dealt with undertaking certain acts. Part of the complaint here was that there were ways to swear that compromised the integrity of the normal use of things. In addition, an oath that was not binding showed that what was uttered was not intended, pointing to a hypocrisy where what appeared to be intended was not the case.

Mishnah and Talmud on Oaths

***Mishnah Šebu'ot* 4.13:** "(1) 'I impose an oath on you,' (2) 'I command you,' (3) 'I bind you,'—lo, these are liable. 'By heaven and earth,' lo, these are exempt.

"(1) 'By [the name of] Alef-dalet [Adonai]' or (2) 'Yud-he [Yahweh],' (3) 'By the Almighty,' (4) 'By Hosts,' (5) 'By him who is merciful and gracious,' (6) 'By him who is long-suffering and abundant in mercy,' or by any other euphemism—lo, these are liable.

"'He who curses making use of any one of these is liable,' the words of R. Meir. And sages exempt. "'He who curses his father or his mother with any one of them is liable,' the words of R. Meir. And sages exempt.

"He who curses himself and his friend with any one of them transgresses a negative

[If he said,] (1) 'May God smite you,' (2) 'So may God smite you,' this is [language for] an adjuration [conforming to] which is written in the Torah (Lev. 5:1). (3) "'May he not smite you,' (4) 'may he bless you,' (5) 'may he do good to you'—R. Meir declares liable [for a false oath taken with such a formula].

"And sages exempt."

***Mishnah Nedarim* 1.3:** "He who says, 'Not-unconsecrated produce shall I not eat with you,' 'Not-valid [food],' and, 'Not pure,' '[Not] clean [for the altar],' or 'Unclean,' or 'Remnant,' or 'Refuse'—is bound.

"[If he said, 'May it be to me] like the lamb [of the daily whole offering],' 'Like the [temple] sheds,' 'Like the wood,' 'Like the fire,' 'Like the altar,' 'Like the sanctuary,' 'Like Jerusalem'—[if] he vowed by the name of one of any of the utensils used for the altar, even though he has not used the word qorban—lo, this one has vowed [in a binding way as if he had vowed] by qorban.

"R. Judah says, 'He who says, "Jerusalem," has said nothing.'"

***Mishnah Nedarim* 14b:** "It is taught in a *baraita*: One who takes a vow by associating an item with a Torah scroll has not said anything, and the vow does not take effect. However, he associates the item with what is written in the Torah scroll, his statement is upheld. Since the name of God is written in the Torah, he has invoked God's name in his vow. If he associates the item with it and with what is written in it, his statement is upheld."

Jesus next noted that the altar or temple makes what was on it sacred. The distinction made actually reversed what was important and blinded those who shared in such acts.

23:20–22. Jesus now made his final point about oaths. Whether one swore by the altar, the temple, or heaven, distinctions did not work. A reference to the altar included what was on it. Exodus 29:37 says what touched the altar was made holy. To Jews, God was seen to indwell the temple with his presence. The reference to the temple included who dwelt in it (Ps. 135:21). The reference to heaven included the one who sat on its throne (Isa. 66:1). In the Mishnah, *Šebu'ot* 4.13 an oath by earth or heaven was not binding, but one who appealed to the first two letters of the divine names Adonai or Yahweh were bound (Morris 1992, 581; see chart above on oaths). Jesus did not accept such differentiations. It was all sacred, all binding. "Let your yes be yes and your no, no" (Matt. 5:37). It was a matter of the integrity of one's word for it was before God and to God one made an oath. One's word before God mattered, no matter what was invoked.

23:23–24. Jesus's next woe, the fourth, was about majoring in the wrong things (Luke 11:42). To tithe herbs but ignore the relational dimensions of justice, mercy, and faith was to ignore and neglect the "weightier" elements of the law (Matt. 7:12; 22:34–40). One generally tithed a tenth of what they had, but the total combination of tithes meant as much as twenty percent ended up being collected (Num. 18:27–28; Sanders 1990, 43–47). To tithe the small herbs required being meticulous. Justice referred to righteous acts. Mercy pointed to a key relational attitude. Faithfulness or faith concerned a relational trustworthiness before God that also impacted others (Prov. 28:20). This is like sayings about God's desiring mercy and not sacrifice, that worship without relational integrity means nothing, or that love for others expresses a key command as a linked reflection to loving God. Jesus had addressed this in Matthew 5:21–26. In some ways these woes are a reversal of the values in his Sermon on the Mount. The sermon involved what to do, while these condemned acts described what not to do.

The tithing of produce was an Old Testament command with elaboration in the Mishnah (Lev. 27:30; Deut. 14:22–23; *m. Šeb.* 9.1; *m. 'Abot.* 1.16; *m. Ma'aś.* 4.5; *m. Demai* 2.1; Davies and Allison 1997, 294). Tithing was important because it sustained the temple and priesthood, but also how people related was important, as the Ten Commandments show. *Mishnah Demai* discusses some agricultural thing being *demai* or dubious because it was not clear if it had been properly tithed. So the tractate discusses how to make things right. There was much detail in tithing correctly. The themes of justice recall the prophets as well. Micah 6:8 speaks of doing justice and walking humbly with God (Isa. 1:16–18; Jer. 22:3; Hos. 6:6; Amos 5:14–15; Mic. 6:1–8; Zech. 7:9–10; Matt. 9:13; 12:7).

Mishnah on Tithes

***Mishnah Shevi'it* 9.1:** "Rue, goosefoot, wild coriander, water parsley, and eruca of the field are exempt from [separation of] tithes and may be bought from anyone during the Sabbatical year, because produce of their type is not cultivated [but grows wild].

"R. Judah says, 'Aftergrowths of mustard are permitted [may be bought during the Sabbatical year], "because transgressors are not suspect concerning them [they are not suspected of cultivating mustard and then claiming that it is an aftergrowth]."'

"R. Simeon says, 'All aftergrowths are permitted, except aftergrowths of "because produce of this type does not [grow uncultivated] among wild vegetables.'"

"And sages say, 'All aftergrowths are forbidden.'"

***Mishnah 'Abot.* 1.16:** "Rabban Gamaliel says, (1) 'Set up a master for yourself.' (2) 'Avoid doubt.' (3) 'Don't tithe by too much guesswork.'"

***Mishnah Ma'aserot* 4.5:** "One who husks barley removes the husks [from the kernels] one by one, and eats [without tithing]. But if he husked [a few kernels] and placed [them] in his hand, he is required [to tithe].

"One who husks parched kernels of wheat sifts [the kernels] from hand to hand, and eats [without tithing]. But if he sifted [the kernels] and placed [them] inside his shirt, he is required [to tithe].

"Coriander which [the farmer] sowed [in order to harvest its] seed [for future sowing]—its leaves are exempt [from the removal of tithes if they are eaten]

"[If he] sowed it [in order to harvest its] leaves [for use as an herb]—[both] the seeds and the leaves are subject to the law of tithes.

"R. Eliezer says, 'Dill is subject to the law of tithes [in regard to its] seeds, leaves and pods.'

"But Sages say, 'Nothing is subject to the law of tithes [in regard to both its] seeds and leaves save cress and field rocket alone.'"

***Mishnah Demai* 2.1:** "These items are tithed as demai produce in every place [viz., both in and outside the Land of Israel]—(1) pressed figs, and (2) dates, and (3) carobs, and (4) rice, and (5) cumin.

"Rice which is [grown] outside of the Land-all who make use of it are exempt [from tithing]."

The following illustration pictured the point and is unique to Matthew: to tithe, yet ignore the relational dimensions of law, was to strain at the gnat and swallow the camel. It missed the big thing that should be done. In saying this, Jesus said to make sure both were done, especially justice, mercy, and faith. References to mercy are rare in Matthew (9:13; 12:7—both citations of Hos. 6:6). Mercy often refers in the LXX to a translation of the Hebrew term for lovingkindness (*ḥesed*; Culpepper 2021, 452). The picture may be ironic, since gnats and camels were unclean (Lev. 11:4, 41; Turner 2008, 556). There may be a wordplay in Aramaic since camel (*gamlā*) and gnat (*gālmā*) involved words with related sounds (Blomberg 1992, 346).

23:25–26. Jesus's fifth woe accused the Pharisees and scribes of hypocrisy. They had clean appearances on the outside like a clean cup, but inside was a heart that robbed and was self-indulgent (Luke 11:39–41; Gospel of Thomas 89, which is closer to Luke's than Matthew's version; Davies and Allison 1997, 297). The term ἁρπαγή refers to robbing or pillaging and suggests "greed" (BDAG s.v. "ἁρπαγή" 2, 133; Morris 1992, 584). The charge may be parallel to Mark 12:40 and Luke 20:47, where the Pharisees were charged with "devouring widow's houses." The term ἀκρασία points to "self-indulgence" or "self-control" (BDAG s.v. "ἀκρασία" 38). This charge was made by other Jewish writers of the self-proclaimed pious (As. Mos. 7:6–10; Pss. Sol. 4:1–5; Turner 2008, 556). Jesus repeated this accusation of hypocrisy several times in verses 25–28, as well as in the opening complaint. It was a central indictment by Jesus. As France (2007, 875) says, "Ritual purity without moral cleanness is a sham." The leaders were too focused on themselves, rather than others.

Jewish Charges Against Jewish Leaders for Self-Indulgence

Assumption of Moses 7:6–10: "But really they consume the goods of the (poor), saying their acts are according to justice, (while in fact they are simply) exterminators, deceitfully seeking to conceal themselves so that they will not be known as completely godless because of their criminal deeds (committed) all the day long, saying, 'We shall have feasts, even luxurious winings and dinings. Indeed, we shall behave ourselves as princes.' They, with hand and mind, will touch impure things, yet their mouths will speak enormous things, and they will even say, 'Do not touch me, lest you pollute me in the position I occupy.'"

Psalms of Solomon 4:1–5: "Why are you sitting in the council of the devout, you profaner? And your heart is far from the Lord, provoking the God of Israel by lawbreaking; Excessive in words, excessive in appearance above everyone, he who is harsh in words in condemning sinners at judgment. And his hand is the first one against him as if in zeal, yet he himself is guilty of a variety of sins and intemperance. His eyes are on every woman indiscriminately, his tongue lies when swearing a contract. At night and in hiding he sins as if no one saw. With his eyes he speaks to every woman of illicit affairs; he is quick to enter graciously every house as though innocent."

Jesus exhorted a representative Pharisee (note the singular) to clean the inside, so the outside could be as well. It was what was inside that made the outside truly clean. Gospel of Thomas 22 had Jesus declare that when the inner was as the outer, one would enter the kingdom. This was the fifth and final time he called Pharisees blind in the indictment.

23:27–28. Jesus's sixth woe also spoke of hypocrisy. Here the picture was of a washed tombstone that looked great on the outside, but the inside was full of death and uncleanness, specifically full of hypocrisy and sin (Luke 11:47–48). Those rebuked had this mixed, inconsistent quality. The picture was of uncleanness caused by the dead (Num. 19:11–14; Josephus, *A.J.* 18.38; *m. Kelim* 1–4 ranks the severity of the uncleanness, with death the most severe; Keener 2009, 553). Culpepper (2021, 453) notes there was even debate if one cleaned the outside first or if the order did not matter (Shammai—makes no difference; Hillel—the inner part first). Jesus just focused on the inconsistency of action and heart. Here Jesus referred to real death, not merely spiritual uncleanness. Ezekiel 13:10–12 has a similar use of the image of the whitewash as a cleansing that was not real. Similar also is Ezekiel 22:28 (France 2007, 876). Tombs were kept clean and visible, especially at Passover, so as to avoid people walking over them and contacting uncleanness (*m. Ma'aś Š* 5.1; *m. Šheq.* 1.1; Davies and Allison 1997, 300–302). This is implied here while Luke says it explicitly in Luke 11:44. The result was the opposite of the intent.

Mishnah on Uncleanness

A Zab is a sufferer from a discharge that made one unclean. The Kelim text noted the causes of uncleanness, whether direct or by contact, with the dead as the most severe type of uncleanness. The passage notes twenty such items, which the Neusner translation lists.

***Mishnah Kelim* 1.1–4:** "The Fathers of Uncleannesses [are] (1) the creeping thing, and (2) semen [of an adult Israelite], and (3) one who has contracted corpse uncleanness, and (4) the leper in the days of his counting, and (5) sin offering water of insufficient quantity to be sprinkled.

"Lo, these render man and vessels unclean by contact, and earthenware vessels by [presence within the vessels' contained] airspace.

"But they do not render unclean by carrying.

"Above them: (6) carrion, and (7) sin offering water of sufficient quantity to be sprinkled.

"For they render man unclean through carrying, to make [his] clothing unclean.

"But clothing is not made unclean through contact.

"Above them: (8) he who has intercourse with a menstruating woman, for he conveys uncleanness to what lies [far] beneath him [in like degree as he conveys uncleanness to what lies] above.

"Above them: (9) the flux of the Zab, and (10) his spittle and (11) his semen and (12) his urine, and (13) the blood of the menstruating woman, for they render unclean through contact and carrying.

"Above them: (14) the saddle, for it [the saddle] is unclean under a heavy stone.

"Above the saddle: (15) the couch, for touching it is equivalent to carrying it.

"Above the couch: (16) the Zab, for the Zab conveys uncleanness to the couch, but the couch does not [convey equivalent uncleanness to] the couch.

"Above the Zab: (17) the Zabah, for she renders him that has intercourse with her unclean [for seven days].

"Above the Zabah: (18) the leper, for he renders unclean by his coming [into a house].

"Above the leper: (19) a bone about the size of a barley corn, for it renders unclean for a seven [days'] uncleanness.

"Weightiest of them all: (20) the corpse, for it renders unclean by overshadowing [a mode of rendering uncleanness by] which none of the rest conveys uncleanness."

Avoiding Graves

***Mishnah Ma'aser Sheni* 5.1:** "And [an area] of graves [they mark off] with lime which they dissolve in water and pour out [along the boundary]."

***Mishnah Šheqallim* 1.1:** "And they mark off the graves."

This indictment of hypocrisy in the last few verses pointed to a selfishness that impacted relationships. It repeated a point Jesus made earlier in Matthew 15:1, 10–20. It reflected the tension that some of his disputes with Pharisees raised in Matthew 9:1–13 or 15:1–20 (Wilkins 2004, 754, speaking of the previous woe).

23:29–31. Jesus's last and seventh woe said the Pharisees were like their fathers who killed the prophets (Luke 11:47–48). The woe came despite their practice of building tombs in honor of the prophets, adorning the monuments of the righteous, and making them look nice. Only Matthew notes the monuments of the righteous. It set up the reference to the blood of the righteous coming later in Jesus's remarks in Matthew 23:35. Such building was becoming common in this period to honor those of the past (1 Macc. 13:27–30; Josephus, *A.J.* 16.182; *B.J.* 4.531–32; 5.506; Liv. Pro. 1:9–12; 3:3–4; France 2007, 876; Wilkins 2004, 755).

Examples of Building Monuments to Honor Others

1 Maccabees 13:27–30: "And Simon built a monument over the tomb of his father and his brothers; he made it high so that it might be seen, with polished stone at the front and back. He also erected seven pyramids, opposite one another, for his father and mother and four brothers. For the pyramids he devised an elaborate setting, erecting about them great columns, and on the columns he put suits of armor for a permanent memorial, and beside the suits of armor he carved ships, so that they could be seen by all who sail the sea. This is the tomb that he built in Modein; it remains to this day."

Josephus, *Jewish War* 4.531–32: "They also relate that it had been the habitation of Abram, the progenitor of the Jews, after he had removed out of Mesopotamia; and they say that his posterity descended from thence into Egypt, whose monuments are to this very time shown in that small city; the fabric of which monuments are of the most excellent marble, and wrought after the most elegant manner."

Lives of the Prophets 1:9–12: "His [Isaiah's] tomb is near the tomb of the kings, west of the tomb of the priests in the southern part of the city. For Solomon made the tombs, in accordance with David's design, east of Zion, which has an entrance from Gabaon, twenty stadia distant from the city. And he made a secret construction with winding passages; and it is to this day unknown to most. There the king kept the gold from Ethiopia and the spices."

Lives of the Prophets 3:3–4: "And they buried him [Ezekiel] in the field of Maour in the grave of Shem and Arpachshad, ancestors of Abraham, and the tomb is a double cave, for Abraham also made Sarah's tomb in Hebron like it. It is called 'double' because there is a twisting passage and an upper room which is hidden from the ground floor, and it is hung over the ground level in the cliff."

The woe was set forth even though the current leaders claimed had they lived in their fathers' day, they would not have shed the prophets' blood as their forefathers had done. This conditional clause is presented as a second-class (contrary to fact) condition, since they did not live in those days (Wallace 1996, 695–96). Jesus said that ironically in honoring the prophets' burial they showed their support for their death. This misdirected witness that they did not even understand testified against them and showed them to be sons in their actions of those who killed the prophets. This is a dative of disadvantage and pointed to testimony against themselves (Wallace 1996, 142–43). Of course, Jesus said this because they were missing the ones God had sent as prophets now, namely John the Baptist and himself (Nolland 2005, 942). The remark dripped with sarcasm and was intended to shock them into a realization of their error by showing the inconsistency of their action with their claim.

23:32–33. So Jesus mocked them telling them to fill up what they lacked from the measure of their fathers. They were to finish what their fathers had started. They were to "complete their dirty work" (Blomberg 1992, 348). They were a "chip off the old block" (Turner 2008, 557). This was an ironic call to continue to walk in the same wrong direction (Isa. 6:9; Jer. 7:21; Amos 4:4–5). He addressed them as snakes and vipers (Matt. 3:7; 12:34) and warned them that they would not flee the judgment coming from God and thus leading to Gehenna. The image of snakes pointed to the poison they carried (Isa. 14:29). Once they had poured out that measure in full, showing their character, God would act. Jesus was moving toward concluding his indictment and the consequences of their behavior.

23:34–35. Jesus now predicted how the Pharisees and scribes would show where they stood before God (Luke 11:49–51). Where Luke has Jesus portrayed as wisdom speaking, here Jesus spoke directly for himself. In reality there was no difference, as Jesus revealed the will and way of God.

God would send more prophets, wise men, and scribes to them (Jer. 7:25–26; 25:4; Matt. 10:16–33; esp. v. 23; 21:41; much of the book of Acts; on Christian scribes, Matt. 13:52, who were teachers of the kingdom). They would kill and crucify them. They would beat and persecute them (Matt. 10:17, 23; 2 Cor. 11:21–27; 1 Thess. 2:14–16). The sequence of kill, crucify, and scourge recalls the passion prediction of Matthew 20:18–19 (Osborne 2010, 856). They would have no recognition that these sent ones were from God. They would be decisively rejected. This looked to the ministry of the period of the apostles and others sent to Israel by Jesus. As these sent figures represented all the promises and hopes of God, those who rejected them became responsible for all the blood of the righteous, from Abel (Gen. 4:8–10) to Zechariah, probably the figure of 2 Chronicles 24:21 who was stoned to death. Zechariah 1:1 described Zechariah as a prophet. Blomberg (1992, 349) sees the OT prophet as the one described here, but that Zechariah seems to be too late for the event described, and we have no record he was martyred (see Turner 2008, 558, and especially Wilkins 2004, 757 n. 40). The 2 Chronicles Zechariah cried out for vengeance upon his death (2 Chron. 24:22). In noting the sequence of righteous martyrs from first to last in the order of the Hebrew Bible, there is the implication that all the righteous of history will be vindicated.

Rejecting God's messengers put one in a place of accountability before God. The theme is an old one from the Hebrew Scripture, in what is called the Deuteronomistic strand of the text (Neh. 9:26; Jer. 2:30). Israel had always rejected her prophets. Stephen's speech in Acts 7 also went in this direction. God would avenge the innocent and justice would be done (Gen. 4:10–11). The theme surfaces again in Matthew 27:3–4 (of Judas) and 27:24–26 (of Pilate and the nation; Davies and Allison 1997, 317; France 2007, 880).

23:36. This generation in Israel now faced judgment. This remark likely alluded to the destruction of Jerusalem in A.D. 70, as Jerusalem was mentioned in the next verse. "This generation" may also be an allusion to this generation as a wicked one, since it was judgment that was in view (Matt. 11:16; 12:39–45; 16:4; 24:34). As Davies and Allison (1997, 314) note, "Salvation-history has become condemnation-history" because of the failed response.

23:37–39. Jesus closed the indictment with a prophetic summary (Luke 13:34–35). It was judgment mixed with lament. It was the last public word Jesus spoke in Matthew.

The double vocative "O Jerusalem" pointed to high emotion as the city was a beloved place (Ps. 137:5–6; Morris 1992, 590). Jesus spoke in the first person, representing God's long-held desire to gather and protect the nation as a hen gathered and protected chicks under her wings (Pss. 17:8; 36:7; 57:1; 61:4; 63:7; 91:1–4; Isa. 31:5; 4 Ezra 1:30). Such opportunity to be protected also had been a regular part of Jesus's call to the nation in his ministry. The call to repent had been a call to enter into spiritual restoration and protection. The city, as represented by its leaders, did not wish for it to be (Isa. 30:15–16). The result was that the nation now received what she had asked for: an absence of divine protection and independence from God. Jesus declared forsaken and desolate the house of Israel, as pictured in the capital Jerusalem. The conceptual language mirrors Jeremiah 12:7, 10–11, and 22:5 (also Isa. 64:10; Hag. 1:9). It was an exilic-like judgment rooted in the warning of 1 Kings 9:6–9. The reference to the house could be to the temple alone, but the entire context pointed to a broader judgment that the abandonment and judgment on the temple so central to national life would suppose (again Isa. 64:10–11).

The judgment would last, however, only for a time. This view contrasts to that of Konradt (2020, 354), who sees Israel's fate as sealed, and of the psalm simply being an acknowledgment of Jesus's universally seen lordship, appealing to Philippians 2:10–11. There will come a time when they recognize him and say, "Blessed is he who comes in the name of the Lord," a citation from Psalm 118:26. That text looked to the welcome of the king to the temple on behalf of the nation. It is a positive text, not a negative one. Today it is used at Jewish weddings, as the home is seen as a picture of a people. The expression says, "I recognize you are sent by God." Jesus held out hope that one day Israel would respond this way. What those in Matthew 23:34–35 failed to do, one day Israel en masse would do. Then the judgment on her would be lifted. The key term in deciding between options is "until," as it limits the judgment.

The only reason for mentioning the hope of the nation's future through a temporal limit, noted by the term "until," was with the expectation that the reversal into faith would happen. Verses like this one show Jesus held out hope ultimately for Israel. It matches texts like Luke 13:34–35; 21:23–24; Acts 1:6–11; 3:18–22; and Romans 9–11. Those texts all deal with ethnic Israel and look to a day of response (Davies and Allison 1997, 324). The judgment on Israel was temporary. France (2007, 882) states this with an uncertainty referring to the judgment remaining "unless" they acknowledged him, but Jesus said "until" here. France (2007, 884) also says this was only a condition, not a prediction, but then why mention it in a prophetic context unless there was the hope and anticipation of response, especially given how the Hebrew Scripture included Israel in the promise of ultimate redemption? Surely France has said too little as has Konradt (Keener 2009, 559). Such a conditional view of this theme is common among interpreters but is surprising given that Jesus raised the possibility of judgment being lifted. If it were permanent, then why raise the possibility at all in a context that is national in focus and not about individual response? Jesus mentioned it because he expected it one day to take place for the bulk of the nation (Nolland 2005, 953).

This passage was not and is not anti-Semitic. It was an in-house rebuke, much like the prophets gave elsewhere in the Hebrew Scripture (Turner 2008, 562–63). Israel's prophets took her position and defection seriously and did not mince words when challenging the nation. This discourse and its harsh tone were a reflection of deep loyalty to the people and nation. These prophets urged them to be self-critical. Jesus was trying to shock them into thinking differently. A patriotism or loyalty that cannot be self-critical is not a real patriotism nor loyalty about what is best for a people. It abandons them where they need it most. Jesus followed in the footsteps of the prophets here, even down to the directness of his tone. God is often hardest on the people who should know better.

THEOLOGICAL FOCUS

The exegetical idea (after denouncing the scribes and Pharisees for hypocrisy, pride, blocking the way to blessing, misuse of oaths, neglecting mercy, and working against what the prophets represented, Jesus pronounced judgment against Israel until she recognized who comes in the Lord's name) points to this theological focus: Jesus issues a full indictment of the nation's leadership for spiritual failure and announces judgment against the nation until she recognizes who God has sent.

After condemning the Pharisees and scribes for hypocrisy and neglect of key issues like justice, mercy, and faith, Jesus issued a judgment on the nation that would not be reversed until she turned to recognize him.

The key to this passage is to see it as Jesus's culminating remarks about the leaders' rejection of him. Much like a prophet, he indicted the nation for her hypocrisy and lack of response to God. High on this list was her rejection of those God had sent and continued to send to her. This direct prophetic charge with its implied warning had already been expressed in the parable of the Wicked Tenants (Matt. 21:33–46).

There were consequences for such covenantal unfaithfulness. God would respond in judgment on this generation. Next Jesus predicted the destruction of the temple and the city in which it resided. It was not a permanent judgment, for Jesus held out the prospect that one day they would see him and say, "Blessed is the one who comes in the Lord's name."

Israel's people and leaders were held accountable for how what they taught impacted the people they served. We see God bringing vengeance for the righteous. We see how not to walk with God, as hypocrisy, lack of integrity, resisting God's message, as well as avoiding justice, mercy, and faith are condemned. We also see God's pain in judging. People who opt to go without God get what they ask for, but it is a tragic and painful choice that causes God to lament. It is a far better thing to turn to him.

Yet God made commitments to Israel and she is not out of God's sight or story. One day Jesus will return and many in the nation will acknowledge him. God is faithful to his people, even when they are not faithful to him. Long before Jesus's time, Hosea had depicted the same reality. God's faithfulness will call them back to him. Yet at the individual level, each needs to respond to benefit from his faithfulness. Matthew was telling a bigger story, one that led Jesus to the cross at the leaders' instigation. For that and many other sins over a long period of time, the nation will pay for a time.

PREACHING AND TEACHING STRATEGIES

Exegetical and Theological Synthesis

The exegetical section systematically diagnoses the shallow religion of the scribes and Pharisees. Jesus did not mince words. He exposed their hypocrisy, named their sin, and pronounced judgment with seven "woes." Interestingly, the scribes and Pharisees were not Jesus's primary audience for this discourse. He directed the speech to the crowds and his disciples. Because these popular teachers influenced the masses, Jesus issued a public rebuke that served as a general warning.

Given today's media platforms, religious leaders can reach a global audience. They publish books, host podcasts, post videos, and stream their sermons. Religious content is ubiquitous. The character of these content developers is not so easily discerned. Good teachers coexist with bad ones. We must beware of the religious voices we let influence us. Unless we heed the warning, we may inherit the woes Jesus pronounced on bad teachers.

Preaching Idea

Shallow religion needs a sharp rebuke.

Contemporary Connections

What does it mean?

What is shallow religion? Based upon Jesus's discourse, shallow religion is hypocrisy. Shallow religion puts on a show, does not practice what it preaches, focuses on behavior rather than heart, and turns minor issues into major issues. Jesus rebuked these expressions of hypocrisy, citing examples from the Pharisees (e.g., hypocritical oaths and tithes). Modern forms of hypocrisy in the church include making corporate worship feel like a rock concert, shouting at gay couples while remaining silent about promiscuity in the pews, outright condemnation of dancing and drinking, and arguments over the age of the earth.

Unfortunately, shallowness in the church does great damage. It breeds distrust in leadership. It delays spiritual growth, bypassing the development of discernment in matters of conscience. It portrays God as a demanding despot whose main concern is following rules. It shames people for not fitting into a community standard. It turns people into moral police rather than agents of mercy. In short, shallow religion prevents people from seeing true righteousness at work in the world.

Is it true?

Indeed, shallow religion needs a sharp rebuke. Jesus regularly made such proclamations. However, Jesus also knew when to speak graciously. He challenged religious leaders, rebellious cities, stubborn crowds, and his own disciples. He extended remarkable grace to sinners, foreigners, outcasts, and people in crisis. We should follow his example, preferring mercy over judgment, but bringing the gavel when the audience calls for it.

A second caveat is needed: sharp rebukes are not always public rebukes. Typically, we should first opt for personal confrontation. This may not always be realistic. If there is a power dynamic (e.g., confronting a pastor or professor) or the shallow religion comes from a remote figure (e.g., deployed missionary or state politician), personal contact is not easy. Second, we may not be the right person for the rebuke. We may not have the position or platform to make the rebuke. Worse yet, we may be complicit in similar sins. Honest self-reflection is a prerequisite to doling out sharp rebukes.

Now what?

First, we must look in the mirror. Before we criticize others for hypocrisy, we must ask God's Spirit to expose it in us. Ask the Spirit to reveal where you have settled for shallow religion. The following questions, drawn from the seven "woes," may be helpful:

- Spirit, where have I been more concerned with others' behavior than mine?
- Spirit, where have I been dishonest with others?
- Spirit, where have I been withholding of my time, money, and talents?
- Spirit, where have I missed opportunities to show mercy and live justly?
- Spirit, where have I been overly concerned with what others think of me?
- Spirit, where have I been inconsistent and hypocritical?

Self-assessment opens the door for confession and repentance. Perfection is not required to rebuke others—only Jesus could claim perfection—but the pursuit of integrity matters.

Second, we should follow Jesus's instruction on righteousness. The Sermon on the Mount proactively countered this discourse. Jesus outlined nine "blessings" (Matt. 5:1–12), elaborate righteousness (Matt. 5:17–48), and sincere devotion (Matt. 6:1–18). Jesus assured his disciples that applying his teaching would lead to flourishing (Matt. 7:13–29). Jesus is the Master Teacher. Any religious leader, authority figure, or instructor who strays from his curriculum is not worth following.

Finally, we should challenge shallow religion when appropriate. As mentioned above, we should prioritize personal confrontation over public rebuke. We should pay attention to power dynamics. This includes the use of the sermon as a shaming tool. Pastors must guard against employing the Bible to control behavior. For example, we should avoid preaching while angry and resist building applications around personal information we are privy to. We preach the truth in love; the Spirit of God reaches people's hearts.

Creativity in Presentation

Jesus's vivid language lends itself to visual aids. Working through the woes in this passage, consider projecting an image of a camel next to a gnat or a bar of gold beside a sprig of mint. For a contemporary comparison, you might hold a slice of bread in one hand and paperwork from a retirement portfolio in another. Finally, you could hold up a serving bowl that has food stains on the inside. Be sure to point out the pristine exterior surface before tipping it to show its soiled interior.

In his famous "Letter from a Birmingham Jail," Rev. Martin Luther King Jr. penned a historic rebuke to Jewish and Christian leaders who cautioned his "unwise and untimely" fight for civil rights. While King's letter claims a "patient and reasonable" answer to their criticisms of his nonviolent protests, his graphic description of inequality comes across in two key rebukes. First, he rebukes passive politics. He cites "white moderates" and "negative peace" as greater threats to integration than the KKK. He deems such a response "shallow" and "lukewarm." Second, he rebukes hypocritical church leaders. He views them as "more cautious than courageous," standing on the sideline mouthing "pious irrelevancies and sanctimonious trivialities." The letter, a six-page rebuke, intentionally echoes eerily Jesus's discourse.[1]

Coaches are known for their sharp rebukes. They call out their players' discipline and dedication to winning. Some great film examples include Norman Dale's (played by Gene Hackman) speech after benching Rade in *Hoosiers* (directed by David Anspaugh, 1986). Coach Dale declares, "What I say when it comes to this basketball team is the law. Absolutely and without discussion." Another sharp rebuke comes at the beginning of *Glory Road* (directed by James Gartner, 2006), where Coach Don Haskins (played by Josh Lucas) sets the standards for his team: no booze, boobs, or late nights. "You play basketball my way. My way is hard," says Haskins. These speeches are easy to access on YouTube; however, you may opt to share a personal story of how a tough-loving coach or parent inspired you to greater discipline and dedication.

Ultimately, you want your sermon to show that Jesus issues a full indictment of the nation's leadership for spiritual failure and announces judgment against the nation until she recognizes who God has sent. Therefore, shallow religion needs a sharp rebuke.

- Beware of shallow religion (23:1–12).
- Heed seven sharp rebukes (23:13–36).
- Shallow religion may someday deepen (23:37–39).

1 See https://www.csuchico.edu/iege/_assets/documents/susi-letter-from-birmingham-jail.pdf (accessed July 24, 2024).

DISCUSSION QUESTIONS

1. Concerning the religious leaders, Jesus essentially said, "Do what they say, not what they do." What are some principles they teach that should be obeyed?
2. Why did Jesus discourage the crowd from calling others "father" or "teacher"?
3. How do the seven "woes" fit together? How do they relate to the Beatitudes?
4. Where do you see shallow religion in our day? Be specific.
5. When is a public rebuke preferred to a private one?

Matthew 24:1–35

EXEGETICAL IDEA

Jesus proclaimed judgment on the temple and discussed the signs that would accompany the return of the Son of Man for judgment and vindication of the righteous.

THEOLOGICAL FOCUS

Jesus depicts signs that show the nation's coming judgment and portend the return of the Son of Man.

PREACHING IDEA

Assurance of God's plan builds endurance to the end.

PREACHING POINTERS

In his final discourse, Jesus provided a map of things to come. This sermon drew from Old Testament prophets, apocalyptic images, and Jesus's concern that his followers remain committed to God in the face of oncoming chaos. Surely Jesus's disciples listened with rapt attention as he assured their vindication and doubled down on God's program. Although Jesus did not provide date and times, the sequence of events and hyperbolic language combined to describe events both in days to come and the last days (i.e., typological-prophetic). Matthew's audience would have heard Jesus's predications, especially the destruction of the temple in A.D. 70, as key puzzle pieces in God's big picture. They would have anticipated the fulfillment of these events and endured in faith awaiting Jesus's climatic return.

Jesus's dramatic and cryptic discourse has given the church much to speculate about concerning end times, timelines, and headlines. Views about the rapture and return of Christ are manifold. Efforts to predict precise dates are pointless. Even Jesus punted when it came to telling the time. However, disciples can rest in this fact: God's plan continues to unfold. War between nations in our time do not thwart God's plan. Contested elections in the United States or economic instability across the globe have not thwarted God's plan. God will complete the puzzle. He will execute his plan. He will bring the end. Until then, we watch, wait, and remain faithful in our chaotic times as his witnesses. This sermon insists that assurance of God's plan builds endurance to the end.

JESUS DESCRIBES THE SIGNS THAT POINT TO THE NATION'S JUDGMENT (24:1–35)

LITERARY STRUCTURE AND THEMES (24:1–35)

This unit begins the Olivet Discourse, which is much longer in Matthew than in its parallels in Mark 13:1–37 and Luke 21:5–36 (Matt 24:1–25:46; 97 verses total). The discourse predicted the destruction of the temple. It also worked through signs leading to that destruction as well as to the (later) return of the Son of Man (Matt. 24:1–31). There was the lead-up to the temple's desecration (Matt. 24:1–14). Jesus then treated the intense time of suffering that would be a part of it all (Matt. 24:15–26). Then followed a description of the return of the Son of Man (Matt. 24:27–31). Finally, there was assurance this would take place (Matt. 24:32–35). Having treated these core themes, Jesus would go on to elaborate, mostly through parables (24:36–25:46).

How the return was later and distinct from the initial temple destruction is not something the discourse itself made clear, but something that is seen by reflection on it. The discourse's goal was to assure the disciples God had a program for the vindication of their commitment to Jesus. Jesus also taught how the nation was headed to judgment, something that linked this speech to the previous indictment of the nation. There would be a period of intense persecution and chaos, both political and natural upheaval. Many would claim to be the Christ but would not be. The Spirit would enable the disciples to know how to respond. The temple would be desecrated, and the tribulation severe. When the Son of Man returned, the righteous would be gathered. This is an event of vindication. It is not about fixing a calendar of events. It is about understanding that God has a program with disciples called to be faithful until it unfolds (Keener 2009, 560–62, discusses the authenticity of this discourse).

This scene is an apocalyptic discourse, treating the signs leading to judgment and the return of the Son of Man. The discourse emerged because Jesus predicted the destruction of the temple as the disciples admired its splendor (Matt. 24:1–2). This led the disciples to ask what the signs of this catastrophic event would be, as well as the indication of Jesus's return at the end of the age (Matt. 24:3). Jesus's response came in parts. First, he covered a series of things that would take place as the start of birth pangs: the presence of messianic claimants, war, famine, and earthquakes (Matt. 24:4–8). A period of intense persecution, apostasy, tribulation, and false teaching would follow, before the end (Matt. 24:9–14). The abomination of desolation and the great, even unprecedented, suffering tied to that specific time showed how difficult things would get (Matt. 24:15–22). It is here that we get the mix of type and antitype as the destruction of the temple in A.D. 70 also pictured the end. Many claiming to be the Christ were not to be followed (Matt. 24:23–28). Davies and Allison (1997, 326) speak of the beginning of woes (Matt. 24:3–8), the intensification of the woes (Matt. 24:9–14), and the climax of the woes (Matt. 24:15–28). Then would come the Son of Man on the clouds to gather the elect (Matt. 24:29–31). There is movement from the world (vv. 3–8) to the church (vv. 9–14) to Judea (vv. 15–28). The fig tree teaches us when it buds that harvest time is near (Matt. 24:32–33). This all would come to pass (Matt. 24:34–35).

The key themes involved assurance about what lay ahead, not so much to be able to chart what was going to happen as to say that God had a program and the righteous would be vindicated. When things seemed out of control, God would still be present with a program. The Son of Man would return and gather the righteous, even though hard times of intense persecution and false teaching would precede that return. The appropriate response was to be alert and faithful as one served God (Turner 2008, 566). Jesus prepared his disciples for suffering and noted how evil in the world did not mean the end of the hope for good. One should stay responsive and watchful.

Jesus had treated some of these themes already, but here he wove them into a more coherent narrative. He has noted false teachers (Matt. 7:15–23), persecution (Matt. 10:21–39), the coming of the Son of Man (Matt. 16:27), and angels gathering the righteous (Matt. 13:49).

There are three basic approaches to the discourse: preterist, future, and typological (Blaising 2012, 138 n. 8). The preterist sees the discourse as mostly about A.D. 70 and the prediction of the temple's destruction at that time (France 2007, 890, at least to verse 35). The futurist sees the discourse as about the future of the end itself tied to Jesus's second coming. The typological says the speech covers both events as a pattern prophecy, with one event mirroring the other. This last approach deals with the discourse the best. Davies and Allison (1997, 328–33) note the Antiochene idea of the *theoria*, two things at once, and the Jewish examples from 4 Ezra and 2 Baruch (also Wilkins 2004, 771–72). Matthew 24:6–13, 21–22, and 27–31 discuss events of the end and look beyond A.D. 70. Matthew 24:14–22 may well point to both times at once. The entire speech was about the entire period of the end, not so much in a sequence as what would present within the period. The discourse is somewhat out of character for Matthew, as his version is longer than the parallels. All of Matthew 25 is unique to Matthew. He was going out of his way to reassure his readers that God had a program in the midst of seemingly emerging chaos and rejection from much of Israel.

Approaches to the Olivet Discourse

Preterist	Stresses fulfillment in A.D. 70
Futurist	Stresses fulfillment about the second coming
Typological	Sees both timings present, as one event patterns the other

The book of Daniel is a major source of background, being alluded to in the ideas of the temple destroyed, the time of the end, rumors of war, persecution, abomination, tribulation, and the coming of the Son of Man (Dan. 9:26; 12:6–7; 9:26 goes with 11:44; 7:25 with 11:33; 8:13 with 9:27 with 11:31; 12:1, 6–7, 13; Davies and Allison 1997, 332).

The parallels to the opening core of the discourse come in Mark 13:1–31 and Luke 21:5–33. Luke 17:22–37 also has material that connects to the themes of the discourse, especially Luke 17:23–24 and 37 to Matthew 24:26–28. Unique to Matthew are Matthew 24:10–12, 30a–b, and 31. *Didache* 16:3–6 is like these verses, showing we are likely dealing with traditional material (Davies and Allison 1997, 327).

EXPOSITION (24:1–35)

So, what lay ahead for the world, the nation of Israel, and those who allied themselves to Jesus? Matthew went there next. The long anticipated, powerful Messiah of judgment as vindicator of the righteous lay in the future for the world and the righteous. The returning Son of Man would bring what had been expected of the Messiah now. Jesus was turning to suffer now before his exaltation soon and his return that lay in the future beyond that. Israel would experience judgment for the current rejection of that Messiah, rooted in the charges Jesus had just laid out in Matthew 23. Even the temple would not be spared. The righteous would suffer now but be vindicated later. God's program meant there was a call now for disciples to persevere in faith and live in faithfulness to their commitment to the Messiah. Full vindication would come sometime in the future when the Son of Man gathered the saints to be with God and him.

Jesus proclaimed judgment on the temple and discussed the signs that would accompany the return of the Son of Man for judgment and vindication of the righteous.

24:1–2. Jesus moved from the temple to the Mount of Olives (see Matt. 24:3). It was late Tuesday (Wilkins 2004, 770). The disciples pointed out to him the temple buildings. Mark 13:1 simply has one disciple make this point. The parallels make it clear they were admiring the buildings of the Temple Mount, an area Herod was in the process of expanding (Mark 13:1; Luke 21:5; Josephus, *B.J.* 5.184–226, and *A.J.* 15.391–402; Tacitus, *Hist.* 5.8). The remark led Jesus to predict that the temple would be torn down completely, a point made by saying not one stone would be left on another (Luke 19:44; fulfilled in A.D. 70, Josephus describes it in *B.J.* 7.1). This was a prophetic announcement of judgment. The nation was headed to hard times. Others had foreseen such times for Jerusalem because of unfaithfulness in the past (Jer. 7:8–15; Mic. 3:12).

Josephus on the Temple Mount

***Antiquities* 15.391–93:** "So Herod took away the old foundations, and laid others, and erected the temple upon them, being in length a hundred cubits, and in height twenty additional cubits, which [twenty], upon the sinking of their foundations, fell down: and this part it was that we resolved to raise again in the days of Nero. Now the temple was built of stones that were white and strong, and each of their length was twenty-five cubits, their height was eight, and their breadth about twelve; and the whole structure, as also the structure of the royal cloister, was on each side much lower, but the middle was much higher, till they were visible to those that dwelt in the country for a great many furlongs, but chiefly to such as lived over against them and those that approached to them."

***Jewish War* 5.222–23:** "Now the outward face of the temple in its front wanted nothing that was likely to surprise either men's minds or their eyes, for it was covered all over the plates of gold of great weight, and, at the first rising of the sun, reflected back a very fiery splendor, and made those who forced themselves to look upon it to turn their eyes away, just as they would have done at the sun's own rays. But this temple appeared to strangers, when they were at a distance, like a mountain covered with snow; for, as to those parts of it that were not gilt, they were exceeding white."

24:3. At the Mount of Olives, the disciples privately responded with a set of questions. The Mount was a place already filled with eschatological overtones (Zech. 14:4). Their questions were: When will these things be? What will be the sign of Jesus's coming and the end of the age? These were two questions as the coming and end of the age were linked together as one topic. The term "coming" refers to a public arrival (BDAG s.v. "παρουσία" 780–81, 2bα). The question differs slightly from its parallels, as Mark 13:4 and Luke 21:5 ask, "When will these things be and what is the sign these things are about to take place (Luke) or be completed (Mark)?" The difference is important. Matthew explicitly connected the questions to events of the end, something the discourse in the parallels will do later, but Matthew has it right up front. Matthew also personalized the event in terms of Jesus's coming, probably a reflection on the original question as expressed in Mark and Luke since the disciples were not yet thinking about Jesus's return as they were still gaining understanding about his coming death. Turner

(2008, 569) notes the question was not anachronistic, as Nolland (2005, 961) claims. Rather, it reflected understanding implicit in how Mark and Luke present the question. Matthew is presenting what the disciples were really asking Jesus by their question, making explicit the time frame and topic that was in view in the original question. The Matthean force emerged as they reflected on their query later as what was entailed in what had been asked. It was a question about the end and Jesus's return. In their mind, to mention the temple under threat was to point to the end. Matthew simply clarified the question's ultimate force and placed the emphasis on the end and Jesus's future return.

24:4–6. Jesus then presented a series of events that all would precede his return. He began with a warning not to be deceived (Mark 13:5–7; Luke 21:8–9). Many will claim to be the Christ in Jesus's name and deceive many in the process. Jewish texts also make such a point about the end (CD 5:20—pictured by the time of Moses; 7:18–8:3; 2 Bar. 48:34; T. Levi 10:2; T. Mos. 7:4). The coming in Jesus's name was probably not a claim to be tied to Jesus but a declaration to take his place or be the event tied to his return (Blomberg 1992, 353); Jesus will expand this idea in Matthew 24:23–27. One could think of the second-century Bar Kokhba as an example, but Josephus mentions several such claimants just after Jesus's time, mostly in the sixties (*A.J.* 18.85–87, 97–99, 102, 160–61, 167–72, 188; France 2007, 902). The presence of such figures was socially and politically destabilizing. The examples France mentions became part of the lead-up to the Roman invasion that led to the temple's destruction in A.D. 70.

Jewish Texts on the End

CD 5.20: "In the time of destruction of the land the Boundary-Shifters appeared and led Israel astray."

CD 7:18b–8:3: "The star is the Interpreter of the Law who comes to Damascus, as it is written, 'A star has left Jacob, a staff has risen from Israel' (Numbers 24:17). The latter is the Leader of the whole nation; when he appears, 'he will shatter all the sons of Sheth' (Numbers 24:17). They escaped in the first period of God's judgment, but those who held back were handed over to the sword. And such is the verdict on all members of the covenant who do not hold firm to these laws: they are condemned to destruction by Belial. That is the day on which God shall judge (4Q266 adds: as He has said), 'The princes of Judah were those (B: like Boundary-Shifters) on whom I shall pour out wrath (B adds: like water)' (Hosea 5:10)."

Testament of Moses 7:4b: "Or they will be deceitful men, pleasing only themselves, false in every way imaginable, (such as) loving feasts at any hour of the day—devouring, gluttonous."

2 Baruch 48:34: "And there will be many tidings and not a few rumors, and the works of the phantoms will be visible, and not a few promises will be told, some idle and others affirmed."

Testament of Levi 10:2: "See, I am free of responsibility for your impiety or for any transgression which you may commit until the consummation of the ages, [against Christ, the Savior of the world] in leading Israel astray and in fomenting in it great evils against the Lord."

There will also be wars and rumors of wars. This also has some parallels in Judaism and the Old Testament (Jer. 51:46; Dan. 9:26; 11:44; 2 Bar. 48:34—see chart above; Davies and Allison 1997, 339). The book of Revelation portrays the end as a period of intense international disturbance. The disciples should not be alarmed (2 Thess. 2:2); it was necessary that these things take place, but it was not yet the end. The period before the end will be one of turmoil and chaos. As the discourse proceeded,

Jesus gave little markers that the movement to the end involved a sequence of events, some of which only were a precursor to the end but that showed God had planned the sequence and his program was advancing despite the chaos. Messianic pretenders and political instability were the first two of those signs. However, Jesus noted the end was still to come after these things and not be immediate. This was but the start of indicators about the coming destruction of the temple and the end.

24:7. A third indicator involved political tension and natural disasters (Mark 13:8; Luke 21:10–11). Nations will rise up against other nations, along with famines and earthquakes. These are also very common eschatological themes (both: 2 Bar. 70:8; earthquakes: 1 En. 1.6–7; 102:2; 2 Bar. 27:7; 70:8; 4 Ezra 6:13–16; 9:3; L.A.B. 3:9; Sib. Or. 3:714; Apoc. Ab. 30:6, 8; T. Levi 4.l; T. Mos. 10:4 famines: 2 Bar. 27:6; 70:8; 4 Ezra 6:22; Apoc. Ab. 30:6; L.A.B. 3:9; Davies and Allison 1997, 340 n. 86). Osborne (2010, 874) notes there were five earthquakes that we have recorded from A.D. 37–67. These are "day of the Lord" motifs (Blaising 2012, 139).

24:8. Having noted in Matthew 24:6 that the end had not yet come, these events were now called the beginning of birth pangs. This was merely the start. Birth pangs are a common eschatological image (Isa. 13:8; 26:17; 66:7–8; Jer. 4:31; 6:24; 22:23; 30:5–6; 48:41; Hos. 13:13; Mic. 4:9–10; 5:3; 1 En. 62:4; 4 Ezra 4:42; Targum on Ps. 18:14; Turner 2008, 573; Blaising 2012, 139–40). Creation was seen as groaning until the end (Rom. 8:19–22).

Birthpangs

1 Enoch 62:4: "Then pain shall come upon them as on a woman in travail with birth pangs—when she is giving birth (the child) enters the mouth of the womb and she suffers from childbearing."

4 Ezra 4:42: "For just as a woman who is in travail makes haste to escape the pangs of birth, so also do these places hasten to give back those things that were committed to them from the beginning."

24:9. Attention turned to how believers will be treated in this interim period before the end (Mark 13:9, 12; Luke 21:12). Much of this was noted in Matthew 10:17–22 in the mission to Israel. Here it was extended into the future. There will be persecution, even martyrdom for the faith. Nations will hate them because of Jesus's name. Another factor will be the opposition they will face, something Matthew has already highlighted (Matt. 10:17–23, 28; 13:21, 25, 32–33, 38; 21:35; 22:6; 23:34). They were to pay careful attention to themselves because of the danger, according to Mark 13:9. Luke alone tells us that what was noted here comes *before* what had already been mentioned. In other words, we end up leaping back in time, not forward, at this point of the discourse to recover a period that stretched back to the current time of Jesus's ministry and the aftermath in the earliest church.

24:10–12. There will be false teaching (Matt. 7:15) and betrayal as many will be led into sin (Luke 21:16–17). Apostasy was in view here (Matt. 13:21; 18:6–9; also at the end: 2 Thess. 2:3). There will be hatred, lawlessness, and deception (Dan. 12:4; Mark 13:12–13a). Love will grow cold. People will abandon each other. It will be a difficult time.

Before we get to the mention of the abomination of desolation, we have the following things listed as taking place: (1) false christs, (2) war and rumors of wars, (3) political tension of nation against nation, (4) famines, (5) earthquakes, (6) persecution and martyrdom of believers, (7) false teaching, (8) lawlessness, (9) deception, and (10) love grown cold. If the Lucan time indicators are in view, then items 6–10 in the list include a period before items

1–5 or move alongside them. This group of disciples' forthcoming experiences was included in the coming events with this list. Jesus was preparing them for it. Blomberg (1992, 357) observes that all of these signs were fulfilled before the temple's destruction and saw in this a realization of Jesus's remarks about the signs in Matthew 24:34. Blaising (2012, 140–41) opts for a partial past realization of this in view also of 24:34–36, because the coming can be tied to the entirety of the "day of the Lord" imagery present that fills the whole discourse and is described as labor pains (Matt. 24:8). Blaising argues the day can be seen as a whole or as referring strictly to the arrival at the end. One needs to pay attention to the difference, because a reference to the coming might be to either possibility depending on the specific context. He contends that Matthew 24:27 is about the arrival of Jesus's appearing like lightening as part of Jesus's second coming, and that 24:36 looks to that arrival as the culmination of whole process ending in the day and hour of the return. Yet labor pains and signs show the Day of the Lord throughout the discourse with some fulfillment tied to the past destruction of the temple and more to come with the return. This is typical of biblical pattern fulfillment where a near and far realization overlap and mirror each other. To experience the package of things referred to here as part of the coming was to also guarantee that the coming at the end will follow.

24:13. The call was to endure until the end (Mark 13:13b). Luke 21:19 says by endurance one gains his life. They were to persevere in being faithful (Matt. 10:22; 1 Thess. 5:9; 2 Tim. 2:10; 1 Peter 1:5, 9; 2 Peter 1:10–11). Salvation was by faith, not denial. Genuine faith believed and did not commit apostasy.

24:14. The gospel of the kingdom was to go out into the entire world. It would be a testimony to the nations. No longer were believers limited to preaching to Israel. With this all behind them, the end would come. These signs covered the period from Jesus's speech until the end. They also reflected what would happen in the lead up to Jerusalem's destruction in A.D. 70, a defeat and judgment that engulfed the temple (Blomberg 1992, 356–57; Hagner 1995, 693–94). Turner (2008, 575) notes parallels to Revelation 6:1–11 in the chaos described here. France (2007, 910–11) only has the destruction of A.D. 70 in view, but this undervalues the language about unprecedented suffering and cutting the days short for the elect that come later, as Wilkins (2004, 780) correctly notes. The declaration here is not preterist only. There is a future dimension to it.

The picture of the gospel in all the world perhaps should not be pressed, as Paul said this had taken place in his time (Rom. 16:26; Col. 1:6). The point is that there would be faithful people in the midst of all of this chaos as the gospel spread.

24:15. Everything said up to this point discussed the environment in the world; with Matthew 24:15, the scene shifts to focus on what was happening in Judea (Konradt 2020, 359). However, we disagree with Konradt that Matthew was looking back from here and separating the desolation of abomination Matthew mentioned in 24:15 from the end. The typological reading of pattern events is present throughout the discourse. The lack of any mention that this was past and fulfilled what Jesus had said, given the time frame Matthew gave to the discourse as rooted in Jesus's time frame, is surprising if Matthew was writing after the event and was referring only backward here. It is better to see a prediction here with events like A.D. 70 and the end mirroring each other. More than that, the exhortation to flee in verses 16–20 also makes little sense if this time has passed and was done with in Matthew's view. Culpepper (2021, 471–73) also takes the view that Matthew 24:15–28 is looking back, but also notes how some details do not match A.D. 70, which should raise questions about a reading that is exclusively tied to that event.

The abomination of desolation Daniel 9:27 mentions is the antichrist standing in the holy place, desecrating it (Blaising 2012, 138–39). Matthew alone explicitly notes the book of Daniel as the point of reference. Mark 13:14a has the expression "abomination of desolation" but does not name Daniel. Mark says simply, "Let the reader understand." Luke 21:20, broadening the reference, and looking more short-term, simply speaks of "its [Jerusalem's] desolation." These little differences between the gospels show what each evangelist is highlighting within the pattern typology, the far- versus near-term.

The precursor pointing to the type or pattern involved here is Antiochus Epiphanes in his desecrating the temple in 167 B.C. (Dan. 8:13; 11:31; 12:11; 1 Macc. 1:54, 59; 6:7; 2 Macc. 6:1–5; Josephus, *A.J.* 12.253). Keener (2009, 573–75) discusses the development of the tradition of the Antichrist rooted in the experience of Antiochus. Nebuchadnezzar had acted similarly in 597 B.C. Judaism also saw such a future figure (2 Bar. 40:1–2). Pompey was seen as such a pre-type as well (Pss. Sol. 2:2; 17:7, 11–14). Titus in A.D. 70 may well have been seen as this figure initially, but also was a type. The assumption is of a time in which Jerusalem would be overrun and the temple occupied. The conquering leader would show up in the temple. Such an act was predicted for the end (2 Thess. 2:4; Rev. 13:11–18; *Did.* 16). This sign was a key turning point. Jesus gave a multilayered, ultimate answer to the initial questions, pointing to past events as a guide for coming events.

On Antiochus and Pompey as Temple Desecrators

Antiochus

1 Maccabees 1:54: "Now on the fifteenth day of Chislev, in the one hundred forty-fifth year, they erected a desolating sacrilege on the altar of burnt offering. They also built altars in the surrounding towns of Judah."

2 Maccabees 6:1–2: "Not long after this, the king sent an Athenian senator to compel the Jews to forsake the laws of their ancestors and no longer to live by the laws of God; also to pollute the temple in Jerusalem and to call it the temple of Olympian Zeus, and to call the one in Gerizim the temple of Zeus-the-Friend-of-Strangers, as did the people who lived in that place."

Josephus, *Antiquities* 12.253: "And when the king had built an idol altar upon God's Altar, he slew swine upon it, and so offered a sacrifice neither according to the law, nor the Jewish religious worship in that country. He also compelled them to forsake the worship which they paid their own God, and to adore those whom he took to be gods; and made them build temples, and raise idol altars, in every city and village, and offer swine upon them every day."

Pompey

Psalms of Solomon 2:2: "Gentile foreigners went up to your place of sacrifice; they arrogantly trampled (it) with their sandals."

As just noted, Luke 21:20 speaks of the city's desolation and does not mention Daniel or the holy place. The difference shows Luke was interested in the near fulfillment of the temple's destruction in A.D. 70. Luke also lacks any mention of the unprecedented nature of the suffering. The pre-type before the end also showed God's program was moving ahead and pointed to guarantee the end. France (2007, 912–13) notes that three events suggested as fulfillment in the short term do not exactly match Daniel, another clue that the ultimate realization was long term. Those events are Gaius's command that a statue honoring him be placed in the temple in A.D. 40, the Zealot takeover of the temple in A.D. 67/68, and the placement of Roman standards in the temple when the city was overrun. France opts for seeing a vague prophetic allusion to A.D. 70 events, but this is not persuasive. The ruler in the temple is the point. That this short-term temple destruction is a type did not become clear until it took place without a return of the Christ and without the full fulfillment Jesus had predicted. Hagner (1995, 702–3) notes the language in Matthew here and at verses 21–22 is hyperbolic for A.D. 70 to show the depth of that suffering but literal for the eschatological end, yet another pointer to pre-type and then a foreshadowing of ultimate realization.

When Rome approached Jerusalem before the city was overrun in A.D. 70, many Jewish Christians apparently did flee to Pella in Jordan, a trip of about sixty-five miles (Eusebius, *Hist. Eccl.* 3.5.3; Turner 2008, 578; Davies and Allison 1997, 347, note some doubt if this took place as Eusebius claims, as does Morris 1992, 604).

24:16–20. It will be an intense time. Jesus gave a series of images that indicated this (Mark 13:15–18; Luke 21:21, 23). The proper response when one sees this gathering storm will be to flee. There is precedent for this kind of a response (Gen. 19:15–22; Exod. 2:15; Judg. 6:2; 1 Sam. 21:10; Osborne 2010, 884). Four indications of the intensity appear in Matthew 24:16–20, while a summary point in Matthew 24:21 drives the point home. (1) Those in Judea should flee to the mountains. (2) The one on the roof should not take time to gather any possession, nor should the person in the field take time to pick up a cloak. This had precedent in the war of the Maccabees (1 Macc. 2:28). Many ancient homes had a flat clay roof reached by a ladder. (3) Those who were pregnant and nursing children would have a difficult time. This is indicated by the woe, which here is not one of condemnation but of sympathy, for the suffering it would entail (France 2007, 914; BDAG s.v. "οὐαί" 1a, 734). (4) The prayer was that the event not take place in winter nor on a Sabbath, as this would make fleeing difficult. Mark 13 does not mention the Sabbath. The note about the Sabbath probably looked to Jewish Christians who still were sensitive to Jewish practice and would have practiced resting on the Sabbath which would mean not being able to flee, as traveling on the Sabbath was not seen as rest (Oliver 2013, 179; Osborne 2010, 885). Luke 21 calls these events "days of vengeance" that fulfilled what is written. The nation will be under intense pressure. The descriptions point to an intense siege of the city, so that a quick escape would be the best way to survive.

24:21–22. It will be a period of unprecedented tribulation, never seen before nor again (Mark 13:19). This is stated most emphatically with a pile of negatives in verse 21 (οὐδ᾽ οὐ μή). This description of unprecedented suffering is part of what tells us we ultimately are picturing the end. It is an allusion to Daniel 12:1, the period of great tribulation. Some Jewish texts anticipate such a time (1QM 1:11–12; 15:1; 2 Bar. 25:3–4; T. Mos. 8:1; Davies and Allison 1997, 350; Keener 2009, 581). The time of the Maccabees was a model for this kind of expression (1 Macc. 9:27). Luke's more short-term focus speaks uniquely of Jerusalem being trampled down by the Gentiles until the times of the Gentiles are fulfilled in a time of great distress (Luke 21:23–24). There is judgment in the short term, but redemption is coming eventually.

Intense End-Time Tribulation in Jewish Texts

2 Baruch 25:3–4: "When horror seizes the inhabitants of earth, and they fall into many tribulations and further, they fall into great torments. And it will happen that they will say in their thoughts because of their great tribulations, 'The Mighty One does not anymore remember the earth'; It will happen when they lose hope, that the time will awake."

Testament of Moses 8:1: "'And there will come upon them [. . .]' punishment and wrath such as has never happened to them from the creation till that time when he stirs up against them a king of the kings of the earth who, having supreme authority, will crucify those who confess their circumcision."

Next the note is made that had these days not been cut short for the sake of the elect, no one would have been saved (Mark 13:20). This adds to the sense that this ultimately is a later unprecedented time of suffering. Jewish texts also express such an idea (4Q385 fragment 3; L.A.B. 19:13; 4 Ezra 2:13). The end of judgment will be a time of mercy for those who believe, as the suffering will end and vindication will follow. This is about more than the Jewish war with Rome (Evans 2012, 407).

Carson (2010, 564) refers these verses to the entire church period until the return. This seems unlikely, given the force of this language about how unprecedented this period is. It is hard to see how being cut short applies to a period as long as this. There is an intensity in what is described here that is part of a more specified period (Osborne 2010, 886). It should be said, however, that the end period mirrors the earlier period, as the return to referring to false prophets shows (Matt. 24:4–5, 10–12, with 23–26). So one could see the description as applied in the front (or short-term) end of the pattern in the events tied to Jerusalem's fall in A.D. 70 and yet reserve full fulfillment for the end with Jesus's return. This is actually how typological-prophetic fulfillment works. The failure of the near event to exhaust the passage's description leads to an expectation of an event that completes the pattern. Matthew simply notes that the end will be a particularly and uniquely intensive period of suffering. The verses ultimately are about the end, but that end will be like a period in the beginning of birth pangs. A pattern prophecy is present.

24:23–26. Given the deception and false claims of Christ being present, Jesus noted that one should not pay attention should such messianic claims surface (Mark 13:21–23; Luke 17:23). Such claims will be made and even be accompanied with signs and wonders. The test for a prophet is tied to his message and divine confirmation, since not only good people can do amazing works (Exod. 7:11; Deut. 13:1–5; 1 John 4:1; of the end-time figure—2 Thess. 2:9; 2 Peter 2:1; Rev. 13:3; 19:20; Turner 2008, 578). False prophets lead one into idolatry or turn people away from Jesus and God's program through him. The disciples were not to follow those who make such claims.

Jesus told them all these things to underscore he had warned them not to be deceived. This remark likely covered all of what Jesus said, since he was turning to the climactic moment of the return. It makes the point that one should pay attention to what is being revealed.

Whether the messianic claim came in the wilderness or in inner rooms, they were not to believe such claims. The contrast pictures messianic expectations like those at Qumran. That Dead Sea community waited for Messiah in the wilderness, portraying an inner-room community filled with people who might have hoped to limit their knowledge only to an elite (Carson 2010, 565, notes the inner-room view; Morris 1992, 607). If the inner room does not allude to a hidden messiah for an elite, then a disclosure in a house was the point (Osborne 2010, 888). Regardless of how it came to them, the disciples were not to respond to such claims. This last exhortation about false prophets in the wilderness and in inner rooms is unique to Matthew. It sets up the contrast to the clear and visible appearing of the Son of Man in verse 27. Jesus now addressed ultimate fulfillment and the final part of the disciples' original question.

24:27–30. The Son of Man's return is about Jesus's coming to vindicate the saints. It will be obvious like lightning (Luke 17:24). The image may also suggest suddenness, but here visibility is the point, in contrast to the hidden gathering of a false messiah revealing where to find him. Mark 13 does not have this image.

This is followed by the mention of vultures gathering where the corpse is (Deut. 28:26; 1 Sam. 17:44; Job 39:27–30; Ps. 79:2; Ezek. 32:4; 39:17; Hab. 1:8; Keener 2009, 582; Osborne 2010, 888). This pictures death associated with the return, as it is a return to judge. The image is much discussed with various interpretations offered, but one of judgment seems most likely (Davies and Allison 1997, 355–57, note eight options, but choose one of judgment). The background of Daniel 7:13–14 speaks of judgment authority for the Son of Man who rides the clouds, an image Matthew 24:30 uses. Daniel 7:27 notes the saints are tied to the Son of Man image and the vindication in that scene.

This is Jesus's return, not any earlier event (but for a vigorous argument to the contrary, France 2007, 919–22, including how the portents are metaphorical). The various descriptions of these events in terms of an unprecedented intensity point beyond anything A.D. 70 offered. Especially problematic is how the angels gather the elect in Matthew 24:31, which France (2007, 928) simply calls a "new beginning," when it is really vindication and redemption being consummated that is in view.

Alongside the suffering of those days will come a series of cosmic signs: the sun being darkened, the moon not giving light, stars falling, and the powers of heaven shaken (Mark 13:24–25). The mention of "immediately" in relationship to the suffering and followed by these cosmic signs is unique to Matthew. These events are earth-shaking and heaven-disturbing. The allusion is to texts like Isaiah 13:10—stars, sun and moon; 34:4 (LXX)—stars; Ezekiel 32:7; and Joel 2:10. The picture is of the day of the Lord (Blaising 2012, 139). The allusion to the day is another indication judgment is coming. The heavenly portents are a way to say how traumatic the events will be. It will be very dark. Jewish sources also taught about these kinds of portents (1 En. 102:2–3; 4 Ezra 5:4–5; 7:38–42; Sib. Or. 1:200–202; 3.82, 800–804; 5:512–31; 8.190–93, 204–5; T. Mos. 10:5). Keener (2009, 584) notes sometimes these terms are used of normal events, making understanding their exact force a topic of discussion (Ps. 68:8; Jer. 4:20–28). In fact, the day itself is a pattern term as the imagery refers to a variety of catastrophic judgment events. An apocalyptic discussion of signs points to real heavenly portents, at least to a degree (Isa. 24:21, 23; Joel 2:10; Amos 5:20; 8:9; Zeph. 1:15; Osborne 2010, 893). Wilkins (2004, 783) speaks of a mix of metaphor and literal here. Blomberg (1992, 362) speaks of a metaphor for "earth-shaking" developments.

Cosmic Signs in Jewish Texts

1 Enoch 102:2–3: "All the luminaries shall faint with great fear; the whole earth shall faint and tremble and panic. All the angels shall fulfill their orders. The children of the earth will seek to hide themselves from the presence of the Great Glory, trembling and confounded. You, sinners, you are accursed forever; there is no peace for you!"

4 Ezra 5:4–5: "But if the Most High grants that you live, you shall see it thrown into confusion after the third period; and the sun shall suddenly shine forth at night, and the moon during the day. Blood shall drip from wood, and the stone shall utter its voice; the peoples shall be troubled, and the stars shall fall."

Testament of Moses 10:5: "The sun will not give light. And in darkness the horns of the moon will flee. Yea, they will be broken in pieces. It will be turned wholly into blood. Yea, even the circle of the stars will be thrown into disarray."

Next the Son of Man will appear from heaven and the tribes of the earth will mourn. Only Matthew notes the reaction of the tribes of the nations as mourning and explicitly mentions the "sign" of the Son of Man. The language is like Zechariah 12:8–14, except it is not Israel that mourns here, but the nations. Although the term "tribes" (φυλαί) is unusual for such a broad meaning and normally refers to the tribes of Israel, here the reference is to tribes of the earth as they observe the judgment's scope. In Zechariah, the event was about the nations coming against a Jerusalem in pain from the pressure coming from those nations. Blomberg (1992, 362) argues for a reference just to Israel here, but then mourning would be hard to defend, as the return should be a cause for rejoicing for an Israel that had longed for a Messiah, which is who this returning Messiah would be. France (2007, 925) says they recognize Jesus too late, but a reference only to Israel here ultimately in the negative does not seem to fit Zechariah, where vindication *and* purging of the nation followed in Zechariah 13. Zechariah is mourning out of regret and because of pressure against Israel from the nations, but in Matthew it is only out of fear of judgment. The reference to mourning is actually a figure, as the term means "to beat oneself," so the picture is of beating one's breast (BDAG s.v. "κόπτω" 2, 559). Luke 21:25–26a speaks of the nations being in distress over the roaring sea and surging waves, as well as people fainting from fear. The scope is broad.

The nations will see the Son of Man arriving on the clouds of heaven (Dan. 7:13–14) with power and great glory (Mark 13:26; Luke 21:27). The Daniel image also points to one coming to judge. Acts 1:6–11 has Jesus return to earth the same way he departed at the ascension. Second Thessalonians 1:7, Revelation 1:7, and 19:11–16 also discuss this return. This is about a coming to earth that the nations observe and is not a scene of going to heaven as the Daniel 7 passage describes, even though Daniel 7 is alluded to here. It gives the aftermath of what happens after the Son of Man receives judgment authority from the Ancient of Days. He comes to earth to exercise that authority and bring that vindication.

With a great trumpet blast, the angels will gather the elect from the four winds and the heavens (Mark 13:27). The analogies are texts that speak of Israel's gathering (Deut. 30:3–4; Isa. 43:6). Only Matthew mentions the trumpet blast. The trumpet may be the call that pictures a decisive moment like a call to battle (1QM 8:9–12; 4 Ezra 6:23–25). The trumpet is tied to Jesus's return in 1 Corinthians 15:52 and 1 Thessalonians 4:15–16, as judgment comes after Jesus returns (Rev. 20:11–15). The elect will be vindicated and gathered for salvation (Isa. 26:19; Dan. 12:1–3, 13). What is judgment for those on the outside means salvation for the elect. Angels gather as the judgment arrives (Matt. 13:41, 49; 16:27; 25:31–32).

24:32–33. Jesus used the picture of a budding fig tree to address the issue of timing (Mark 13:28–29; Luke 21:29–31). The picture is that when one sees the fig tree bud in late spring, one can know summer is near. The idea of the nearness of judgment is a refrain in the Old Testament (Isa. 13:6; Ezek. 30:3; Joel 1:15; 2:1; Zeph. 1:7, 14; in the NT: Phil. 4:5; James 5:8; Rev. 1:3; 22:10; Turner 2008, 585). As these things are all unfolding, one can know he is near and at the door (4 Ezra 8:63–9:2). This was said to reassure the disciples about what Jesus was teaching. They were called to keep watch and be discerning about what was taking place, even though much disruption was to come.

The understanding of "near" is important here. Near can mean next in the program. Jesus will indicate in Matthew 24:36 he does not know the exact time of the return, so thinking of the end as being next in the program is a good way to read the verse. Other texts also show this tension between near and enough delay that some may no longer have faith. Luke 18:8 speaks of a vindication that comes quickly but delays long enough that some will no longer believe. That is said in the space of one verse! Jesus wanted his disciples to know there was a program and the return would follow a planned sequence of things. However, there was still a need to watch and wait with a patient and faithful eye.

24:34. Then Jesus said that this generation would not pass away until all these things have taken place (Mark 13:30; Luke 21:32). This verse has produced no lack of discussion.

The issues are, what does "this generation" (γενεά) mean, and what are "all these things" (BDAG s.v. "γενεά" 2, 191–92)? Does "generation" refer to a specific generation of Jesus's time; of the time of the end; or is the term ethical in force, meaning this "evil" generation and looking to make it clear justice will be done? A reference to the generation of Jesus's time means either Jesus was referring to the destruction of the temple in A.D. 70, was referring only to portents before the destruction (so Konradt 2020, 363), or was wrong in his prediction. This last option fails because it is something the assurance of the next verse denies. What Jesus said will come to pass. A reference to the generation of the end would say that once these signs start in the final realization, it will unfold within that generation. If the reference is ethical (Gundry 1982, 491), then the point is that God will deal with the evil generation and bring justice. Konradt (2020, 363) sees this as a possible option. If the reference is to the early portents, then the point is that the start of the coming means the ultimate coming will take place. Blaising (2012, 140–41) contends that the birth pangs metaphor linking the entire package of day of the Lord events allows such a link to the front of the pattern that introduced the whole sequence as guaranteed. Davies and Allison (1997, 366–67) note seven options for "generation" and opt for the generation of the disciples, so that Jesus erred in the timing. France (2007, 930) applies the whole to the temple's destruction in A.D. 70. Neither of these last two options is likely. Any of the first three are possible.

Options for Meaning of "This Generation"

1. Specific generation in Jesus's time
   A. So Jesus erred
   B. Of portents before A.D. 70, so there is no error
2. Specific generation at the time of the return
   A. When the final events of the end arrive, they will happen quickly.
3. Ethical force ("this evil generation")
   A. Justice and righteousness will come as God's people are vindicated.

If "all these things" refers to everything Jesus had said, then the remarks do not make sense since the return is included in them (Nolland 2005, 987; Turner 2008, 586). In addition, in Matthew 24:36, Jesus says he does not know the time of the return, so the idea that here he is specifying when it would come is unlikely (Morris 1992, 612). If "all these things" refers just to the signs immediately leading to the end, then the verse could mean that all the events tied just to the ultimate end, not those tied to A.D. 70, will happen within a generation, or it could point to the start of the sequence in the near term as a guarantee of the whole. If "all these things" refers to the precursor signs tied to A.D. 70, then "this generation" refers to the apostles' generation, and the reference is that all the early precursors in the package happen before the temple is destroyed. The normal meaning for "generation" in Matthew is that of contemporaries (Matt. 11:16; 12:39, 41–42, 45; 16:4; 17:17; 23:36). If this is the sense, then the early precursors mean that all these things (i.e., the signs) will happen to the disciples and one can know the end will follow, without a time frame being given as to when the end itself will be (so Blomberg 1992, 363–64). This makes good sense of the remark and uses "generation" in a common way for Matthew, but the meaning is hardly certain and some of the other options could also explain the force of the cryptic saying.

As one can see, there are plenty of options. "Generation" either means this evil generation (part of the generation of the end) will see all the events unfold, or that the apostles' generation sees the events that point to the end. "All these things" must be limited to things that set up the end, otherwise the statement does not make sense. Wilkins (2004, 787) combines the typology and argues the reference is to both the generation that sees the temple's destruction and that of the end (so also apparently Morris 1992, 612). Both groups see the signs in their lifetime; the second also sees the end. Any of these combinations means Jesus does not err here. An ethical sense of "evil" generation is another option, though relying on a less common but possible sense for the term "generation," assuming an ellipse. A typology seeing a double referent is also possible. In that case the temple's destruction is a generation away and the events that bring the ultimate end will also fall within a generation.

24:35. What Jesus said will be the case. Heaven and earth may pass away, but what Jesus said will not pass away (Mark 13:31; Luke 21:33). Jesus already said this about Torah (Matt. 5:18). He said this of the signs most emphatically, using οὐ μή to make the point that his words would not pass away. This matches the οὐ μή of Matthew 24:34 that this generation would not pass away before these things have taken place. The Old Testament often uses such a formula to reassure (Isa. 51:6; 54:10; Jer. 31:35–36; 33:20–21, 25–26). What Jesus predicted will happen.

THEOLOGICAL FOCUS

The exegetical idea (Jesus proclaimed judgment on the temple, and discussed the signs that would accompany the return of the Son of Man for judgment and vindication of the righteous) indicates this theological focus: Jesus depicts signs that show the nation's coming judgment and portend the return of the Son of Man.

Using the destruction of the temple as a type, Jesus highlighted how chaotic the period before the end would be. It would be filled with tension, sin, deception, and persecution, and he calls for a watchful, faithful eye to know God has a plan to vindicate his saints.

Jesus gives signs in this text not so much to draw up a calendar of events, but to assure his disciples that God has a program that will vindicate them and the saints. The period between now and the end will be difficult. It will be full of tension, deceptions, sin, false claims, wars, catastrophes, and persecution. These together point to the Son of Man's arrival to judge. He will bring righteousness to the earth as the elect are gathered and wicked are judged. Chaos does not mean things are out of control. These events point to the nearness of the end as the next thing on God's calendar.

Still, people wish to know how the sequencing works. Sorting that out takes far more than the treatment of this passage, this discourse, or even this gospel. Several issues have caused a variety of positions to result from an effort to bring synthesis to all of this, including: What does one do with the mix of heavenly and earthly imagery about the end that Scripture presents? What does one make of a text like Revelation 20 and its presentation of a millennium with the noting of events before and after it? How does one assess the appearance of such a detailed event in Revelation 20 in a genre of apocalyptic passages where the point is that God has a specified calendar of events that will deal with evil? What impact does that text have on how earlier texts are read? Does Paul's teaching add anything to the portrait of the end that Jesus reveals? This last question raises the possibility of a progress of revelation about details tied to the end that comes after Jesus's own teaching.

These questions are important because Jesus had a very simple outline for events leading to the end. There is a return, a gathering, and a judgment in the midst of chaos. Paul speaks of things like a catching-up in the air for believers, an idea not expressed elsewhere in the NT (1 Thess. 4:15–17). John in Revelation 20 has the only text discussing by name a millennium, though the imagery appears to connect to kingdom hope and language found in the Old Testament, where many nations gathered around Jerusalem to share in worship with the nation of Israel and/or with the kingdom's king-deliverer providing specific vindication. Many eschatological texts have an earthly and heavenly mix, while others have one or the other. This has led to a variety of syntheses. Bock (1999) has a full presentation of three key views on the millennium.

Some see a return tied to events of A.D. 70. This view is known as preterism. Others hold to the end as still future, but in a variety of scenarios. Others argue for a return and then the new heavens and new earth. This view is called amillennialism. Still others see a return, an earthly kingdom for a thousand years, and then a new heavens and new earth. This is called premillennialism. In terms of Jesus's return, premillennials have three positions. Some see Jesus initially coming for the church before his return to earth and before the most intense period of chaos; this is called pretribulationism. Others see Jesus returning to gather the church in the midst of the chaos but before its worst phase, as a protection for them; this is midtribulationism, sometimes called the "pre-wrath" view. Others see him returning at the end of the chaos; this is posttribulationism. All tribulational views are premillennial views as well.

Eschatological Views

Preterism	Language fulfilled in A.D. 70
Amillennialism	Language means return and then a new heaven and earth
Premillennialism	Language means return, 1,000-year earthly rule, then new heaven and earth
Pretribulationism	Jesus raptures the church before the tribulation
Midtribulationism	Jesus raptures the church in the middle of the tribulation
Posttribulationism	Jesus simply returns at the end of the tribulation

Most agree that Jesus does not teach any of this detail. The synthesis for these models works with elements from texts outside the Gospels. All hold to a physical return but discuss the array of sequences noted. The key questions are: (1) whether there is an interim kingdom that fulfills promises made about peace on *this* earth in *this* history, including commitments made to ethnic Israel, and (2) whether the church is promised deliverance from the whole of the worst period of the chaos, as the sequence of events in 1 Thessalonians 4–5 suggests. A positive answer to both of these questions yields a pretribulational premillennialism. Hultberg (2010) has a three-views book on issues tied to the question of the rapture. The question of the biblical theology of the end is much bigger than this passage alone or even Jesus's teaching alone. More was revealed about the end as more Scripture was composed and more revelation was given.

This discourse is one piece of a much larger puzzle. What it affirms clearly is the certainty of an intense period of global chaos for believers before the end. It expresses certainty about Jesus's return. It uses the destruction of A.D. 70 as a picture and type of what that chaos will look like. It calls believers to watch with an expectant eye for the visible return of the Son of Man in power to judge and bring vindication to them and all the saints. However long it takes, we are called to be faithful. That is what the following section of Matthew's Olivet Discourse covers in a series of parables, mostly unique to Matthew.

PREACHING AND TEACHING STRATEGIES

Exegetical and Theological Synthesis

The exegetical section describes the complexity of this typological-prophetic passage. The various end-times views and interpretation of apocalyptic imagery lends itself to confusion or speculation. However, we must not let this important question obscure Jesus's summons to endure to the end. In fact, it is fair to call into question faith that is not faithful to the end. In his earlier parable about the soils, Jesus noted that many responses to the gospel do not result in long-term fruitfulness (Matt. 13:1–9). This observation aligns with other tough teachings about discipleship (Matt. 8; 10; 22). A faithful disciple chooses Jesus over all other loyalties: fishing and farming, land and family, Caesar and self.

As followers of Jesus, sooner or later, our faithfulness will be tested. Jesus himself was tested by Satan (Matt. 4:1–11) and the religious leaders (Matt. 22:15–33). He endured. Many New Testament writers emphasized the theme of testing (Rom. 5:1–5; 2 Tim. 3:10–17; Heb. 12:1–13; 1 Peter 4; Rev. 2–3, 13). Seeing themselves in the "last days," they knew believers would suffer for their faith. In a unified voice, these authors encouraged followers of Jesus to band together, press on, endure hardship, trust God, keep watch, and await their reward at Jesus's return. True faith endures (James 1:2–4).

Preaching Idea

Assurance of God's plan builds endurance to the end.

Contemporary Connections

What does it mean?

Assurance of God's plan means knowing he is wise, sovereign, and wants our good. He controls the future of the world and our individual lives. We do not need to know every detail of his plan (e.g., dates, times, and people) to have assurance. In fact, if God disclosed every detail of his massive plan to our limited minds, it would more likely overwhelm than assure us. This would be akin to a parent responding to his child's question, "Are we there yet?" with a mile-by-mile breakdown of the remaining drive to Daytona Beach. Thus, assurance comes from knowing God knows the plan, not our knowing it.

Is it true?

Assurance does build endurance to the end; however, we are not easily assured. In fact, we often need reassurance. The story of Gideon resonates. During his summons to battle he asked for several signs, each one to reassure him he was the "mighty warrior" intended to lead his people (Judg. 7–8). Likewise, for every excuse Moses made about leading the exodus, God offered reassurance (Exod. 4). When God includes us in his plan, we want to be sure we hear him correctly. Wanting reassurance, many have likely asked questions like:

- Does God really want us to adopt?
- Has God really called me into full-time ministry?
- I know God wants me to give. Does he really want me to give $15,000?
- If I accept God's call to singleness, will he really give me a spiritual family?

These questions are less a sign of doubt than a search for assurance. Uncertainty, trials, and troubles can serve as training ground for assurance that builds endurance. This is important because endurance stems from training. A marathon runner can endure to the end because he has spent months training on open roads prior to the race. College students can endure finals because every reading assignment, reflection paper, and lecture have trained them in the course. Throughout life, God uses trials to train us (James 1:2–4). As we experience his strength, provision, and presence in hardship, our trust in him grows. This combination of training and trust compounds in assurance that leads to endurance.

Now what?

First, we should *seek the right signs.* It is more important to seek signs of God's faithfulness than signs of the future. The former foster assurance in faith; the latter fuel speculation. Paying attention to how God provides, answers prayer, empowers, heals, enables, and teaches us through his Word is constructive. Reading headlines for signs of end times (e.g., "Russia Breeding Red Horses for War") is not. Please note this is not a plea for ignorance about eschatology. Jesus taught about the end, so we should be aware of it. End-times teaching should nurture hopeful expectation, not fearful speculation. Thus, emphasizing signs of God's faithfulness keeps our focus in the right direction.

Second, we should *see the end through the past.* We know what God will do based on what God has done. He is the God who called Abram, heard Hagar, delivered Israel, spoke to Moses, empowered Gideon, provided for Ruth, forgave David, judged the nations, exiled his people, sent his Son, and raised the dead. Indeed, God used unlikely people and unexpected means to accomplish his purposes. He is able, faithful, good, and just. Thus, whether mulling over a terminal illness, threats of war, or the second coming of Jesus, we must see these various ends through the annals of God's past work.

Finally, we should *undergo endurance training.* God has numbered our days but does not share the number (Ps. 90:7–12). Each day we move toward our end, and toward *the* end. Each day we endure. Our days are not without trial, trouble, or groaning. The struggle prepares us for a glorious end (Rom. 8:28–30; 2 Cor. 4:17; Phil. 3:21; 1 Peter 1:3–9). The first part of endurance training is this shift of mindset: seeing trials as training (Rom. 5:1–5; James 1:2–4). A second aspect of endurance training is deliberate work in spiritual formation (Phil. 2:12–13). We meditate on Scripture, pray, worship, give thanks, serve, and gather regularly with other believers for encouragement, mutual ministry, and remembering Jesus through communion. We endure best when we train with others.

Creativity in Presentation

Road trips provide a good illustration about endurance and looking forward to the end. Long days of travel tire out children. More so, parents grow exhausted of answering the "Are we there yet?" question. What can help is a look at the road atlas or GPS that shows how much longer the trip will last, as well as the expected arrival time. Consider showing a map (or screen shot of the GPS) from a recent road trip. Or, if you do not have a road trip to draw from, use the starting point of your church and a common destination spot (Daytona Beach, Myrtle Beach, San Diego). Explain how knowing the end of the trip (e.g., rest, relaxation, and recreation!) helps us endure the drive.

Knowing the end helps endurance athletes perform. As a cross-country coach, I (Tim) often have my athletes visualize different portions of the race in their preparation. I encourage them to "start strong" and "finish fast." Along the way, I implore them to "stay focused." Races that last between two and five miles are exhausting. However, when athletes can see the finish line and hear fans cheering them to completion, it builds assurance they will make it. If you have your own racing stories to draw from, feel free to personalize your experience.

Engage your congregation in a creative exercise. Have them imagine they are visited by an angel. This messenger has vital information: their death date. The angel tells them the exact day and hour their life will end. Then ask the congregation a series of questions: Did you want this information about your end? Why or why not? What will you do with this information? How do you expect to live differently, knowing when your life will end?

One area where people want assurance is medical needs. Not only do they want to find the right treatment, but they also want to avoid crippling debt. A company like Aflac, with its iconic duck mascot, provides supplemental insurance, also known as "assurance"—to help "close the gap" between expenses and traditional insurance. You may show a brief Aflac commercial and mention how important "assurance" is in the face of crises. And then you want to stress that the assurance Jesus provides dwarfs what any assurance company can offer.

Prolific authors Stephen King and J. K. Rowling know the importance of strong endings. King authored the Dark Tower series; Rowling wrote the Harry Potter series; both span many books and cover thousands of pages. And each author has confessed to having a vision of the end of their series from its beginning. Readers, however, have a different experience. They must march through the series page by page, book by book until they arrive at the end. Then the story is over. In the author's note to his series, King (2004, 1048–49) addresses his "Constant Readers" about the conclusion. He admits, "I wasn't exactly crazy about the ending, either, if you want to know the truth, but it's the right ending. The only ending, in fact. You have to remember that I don't make these things up, not exactly; I only write down what I see."

In some sense, we are all Constant Readers. Every page, step, and day is an act of endurance in a great story God has written. We shall someday come to the end.

However you choose to illustrate the homiletical idea, be sure your sermon teaches that Jesus depicts signs that show the nation's coming judgment and that portend the return of the Son of Man. Thus, assurance of God's plan builds endurance to the end.

- The end of an era is near (24:1–14).
- The end will be bitter (24:15–26).
- The Son will return soon (24:27–31).
- The Son speaks the truth (24:32–35).

DISCUSSION QUESTIONS

1. What are the four different end-times views referenced in this chapter? Which do you find most compelling, and why?
2. What does "typological-prophetic" mean? What are other examples of this interpretive method?
3. How will you handle the predictive elements of this chapter without getting sidetracked by specifics (e.g., dates, places, times)?
4. What are some great endings in movies or literature? What are some terrible endings? How does an ending affect your appreciation for the overall storyline?
5. Describe parts of the end of God's plan that you look forward to. Are there parts of the end that worry you? If so, what are they?

Matthew 24:36–25:30

EXEGETICAL IDEA

Jesus called for a faithful and alert walk until he returns, stressing the accountability that would come with his return and noting the uncertainty of when that would be.

THEOLOGICAL FOCUS

Jesus issues a call to be alert for the end and to be faithful in the meantime.

PREACHING IDEA

Get ready. Stay ready. Christ is coming soon.

PREACHING POINTERS

Jesus's final discourse concluded with a series of parables focusing on staying watchful and faithful until his return. These stories emphasized the uncertainty of the timing (e.g., "like a thief in the night") and functioned as a warning to his audience. Simply being among the crowd of disciples was no guarantee of eternal reward. Rather, these memorable parables—of servants, maidens, and stewards—described two types of responses to Jesus: faithful or listless. For Matthew's audience, this theme of separation resounded. Listeners would not want to be caught unprepared, resulting in judgment and rejection. Instead, as they waited for Jesus's return, they would have remained faithful.

Predictions of disaster have become background noise in our day. Threats of inclement weather sound on the radio. News reporters cover the latest outbreak of the newest virus. We hear stories of increasing gun violence, pollution, and fraud. With each prediction of disaster, we receive directions on how to prepare. Readiness is our best defense when trouble looms. This principle applies to the spiritual life. Though we cannot predict suffering, persecution, or the day of Jesus's return, we can prepare for it. And we should, because it is inevitable. This sermon challenges us to get ready and stay ready, for Christ is coming soon.

JESUS TELLS PARABLES ABOUT THE END-TIME JUDGMENT (24:36–25:30)

LITERARY STRUCTURE AND THEMES (24:36–25:30)

This unit is simply a sequence of five parables, regarding the unknown hour (Matt. 24:36–42), the thief in the night (Matt. 24:43–44), the faithful and unfaithful servants (Matt. 24:45–51), the ten maidens (Matt. 25:1–13), and the talents (Matt. 25:14–30). The first two are developed images, while the latter three are more developed analogies. Being ready was stressed in the first four parables, while being accountable was a point in the last three. Exclusion after potential access to blessing was also present in the last three parables. The second parable noted the danger of not being ready by comparing it to someone stealing your possessions because you were not ready for the thief at night. The point is to stay ready and remain faithful.

The parallel to the unknown hour or day is Luke 17:26–30. The thief in the night is like Luke 17:34–36, as well as conceptually like the emphasis in Mark 13:32–37, which has distinct imagery. The parallel to the faithful and unfaithful servants is Luke 12:41–48. The parable of the ten maidens is unique to Matthew. The parable of the talents has a similar but distinct parable in Luke 19:11–27.

These parables applied the points made in the core discourse of Matthew 24:1–35. The parable of the unknown hour or day not only compared the return to the days of Noah but added the picture of the end being like a thief's coming in the night. The stress was on the suddenness of the coming. The remaining three parables stressed the accountability one has to the master, who gave a stewardship to be exercised or a responsibility to be performed. Watching and being faithful were the key ideas. The possibility of one appearing in but really being out was also present in the parables where judgment was made, and one was excluded at the end.

When one puts the entire discourse together, Matthew closed it with seven parables. Five are covered in this unit, because they are thematically related. The fig tree of Matthew 24:32 tells us we can know the end is coming. These five parables called for preparedness in light of accountability. In the next part, the final parable of the Sheep and Goats (Matt. 25:31–46), that accountability is detailed.

EXPOSITION (24:36–25:30)

Faithfulness was important to Matthew, especially given the tensions the community was facing. It was too easy to let that outside pressure and coming and existing chaos overcome faith. That tension could involve coming to doubt if Jesus would return or coming to question whether Jesus would bring the judgment and vindication God had promised believers. These parables sought to assure the community a return was coming, even if the exact time was not known. They also underscored the accountability Jesus's own would have for how they applied the calling and gifts God had given to them. These themes dominate the rest of the discourse as Jesus urged his disciples to remain faithful, keep watch, and be ready for a return that could come at any moment.

Jesus called for a faithful and alert walk until he returns, stressing the accountability that would come with his return and noting the uncertainty of when that would be.

24:36. Jesus highlighted the idea that no one except the Father knew the time of the return (Mark 13:32; Acts 1:6–7). He underscored this by naming the angels and the Son as not knowing. The issue of the time was in the Father's sovereignty. The theme of eschatological ignorance of the exact time of the end has Jewish precedent (*Mekilta* on Exod. 16:32; 2 Bar. 21:8; 48:3; 54:1; 4 Ezra 4:52; Pss. Sol. 17:21; also NT: 1 Peter 1:12; Davies and Allison 1997, 378; Turner 2008, 588 n. 2). Jesus's lack of knowledge was a function of some limitations he undertook in his humanity and his subordination to the Father (Turner 2008, 589). Davies and Allison (1997, 378–79) trace how the early fathers handled the text while defending its authenticity.

Ignorance of the Time of the End

Psalms of Solomon 17:21: "See, Lord, and raise up for them their king, the son of David, to rule over your servant Israel in the time known to you, O God."

2 Baruch 21:8: "You are the one who causes the rain to fall on earth with a specific number of raindrops. You alone know the end of times before it has arrived. Hear my prayer."

2 Baruch 54:1: "And I asked the Mighty One and said: 'You alone, O Lord, knew the heights of the world beforehand and that which will happen in the times which you bring about by your word. And against the works of the inhabitants of the earth you hasten the beginnings of the times. And the ends of the periods you alone know.'"

4 Ezra 4:52: "He answered me and said, 'Concerning the signs about which you ask me, I can tell you in part; but I was not sent to tell you concerning your life, for I do not know.'"

***Mekilta* on Exodus 16:32:** "No one knows when the Kingdom of David will be restored to its former position, nor when this wicked kingdom will be uprooted."

This text was against any specific predictions about the time of the return. If the Son did not know, we cannot figure it out. This was a reason to keep alert and be ready (1 Thess. 5:1–6).

24:37. The end will come suddenly, as judgment did in the time of Noah (Luke 17:26; cf. Gen. 6:5–7:24; Isa. 54:9; 2 Peter 2:5; 3:6). Unexpectedness points to the need to stay alert and be ready. The judgment will come in the normal flow of life. Note how this verse opens with an explanatory γάρ ("for"). It explains what the implications are of not knowing the time of the return. The judgment will come as quickly and as surprisingly as the flood of Noah's day. So be alert. The scope of Noah's event was also at work here. Noah's flood was a comprehensive judgment. The event tied to the Son of Man will be similar.

24:38–41. Jesus described the situation in Noah's time. Luke 17:26–30 has a shorter form of this imagery and goes on to add a reference to the days of Lot. There is some parallelism between Matthew 24:37 and 24:38–39 as the latter elaborates on the former (note in both passages "for just as in the days of Noah . . . so also the coming"). Luke lacks the elaboration.

People were living life: eating, drinking, marrying, and being married. Life was proceeding normally. People were not concerned with God (Wilkins 2004, 801). Then Noah went into the ark (Gen. 7:7; Luke 17:27). The others had no clue until the flood swept them away. The picture of the day of the Son of Man portrayed sudden judgment and accountability to the living God through the one he had sent to execute his justice. The parallel to Noah's time also likely assumed the people of the current era were like those of Noah's time, so they are suggested to possess a negative reputation as sinners (Gen. 6:11–12; Sir. 16:7; 3 Macc. 2:4; 1 En. 67:10; Jub. 20:5–6; Josephus, *A.J.* 1.72–76; Turner 2008, 589). This is why judgment will come, and it will be comprehensive, like in the time of Noah.

The coming of the Son of Man will be like that time (Luke 17:30). Jesus pictured two kinds of separation, one involving men and the other women (Luke 17:34–35). Two men will be in the field and one will be taken and the other left. Two women will be grinding at the mill, and one will be taken and the other left. The grinding would have involved a stone hand mill that broke down the grain, which two people sitting opposite each other pulled in turn (Osborne 2010, 905). It is not clear who is taken for what and who is left for what, raising other issues about how to take the imagery.

Photo of a Grinding Mill

There is discussion about what is described here. Is this a hint of a rapture (Davies and Allison 1997, 383, discuss a taking up in the air)? This is unlikely. Paul does seemingly distinguish between the rapture and the return, but he calls what he reveals a mystery, pointing to new revelation (1 Thess. 4:13–18; 2 Thess. 1:6–10). In this discourse we seem to have only a separation of the righteous and unrighteous. The analogy of the flood has the judged swept away. Noah remains, but is he pictured as gathered/taken into the ark or left behind on earth? Matthew 13:41–42 has tares gathered to be burned, so they were taken away for judgment. On the other hand, one can argue that the gathering looks to be the one taken for salvation, and the one left was where the vultures gathered, if the earlier part of the discourse is a clue (Matt. 24:28, 31). This means that the direction of the separation was not clear, and there is no consistent application of the imagery in Matthew, making developing a key doctrinal point hard to establish (Turner 2008, 590). The real point of emphasis is seen in the fact of separation that points to accountability. That accountability leads to the exhortations that close the parable in Matthew 24:42, 44, with their call to keep alert and be ready.

24:42. The application is to watch because we do not know on what day the Son of Man comes. The present imperative looks at keeping a constant watch. This becomes a theme for the final sections of the discourse (Matt. 24:43; 25:13; 26:38, 40–41, 43–46; *Did.* 16:1). The New Testament also says this repeatedly (1 Cor. 16:13; 1 Thess. 5:6; 1 Peter 5:8; Rev. 3:2–3; 16:15).

24:43–44. Another short picture drives the point home. One should treat this as a distinct parable, but the call to know develops what has been said in the Noah imagery with a fresh image. If the house master had known when the thief was coming in the watches of the night, he would have kept watch and prevented his home from being broken into (Luke 12:39–40; Gospel of Thomas 21 and 103—of cosmic powers as the thief, not Jesus). The watches of the night were divided either into blocks of three hours for Jews or blocks of four hours for Romans (BDAG s.v. "φυλακή" 4, 1067–68). It is not clear which is meant here, nor does it really matter since the issue is one did not know when the thief was coming. When will the thief come? No one knows. Jesus coming like a thief is a refrain in the New Testament (1 Thess. 5:2, 4; 2 Peter 3:10; Rev. 3:3; 16:15). One is to be ready to prevent any dire consequences.

The thief image is used for other teaching contexts besides the end as well (Matt. 6:19–20—of temporary nature of wealth; Matt. 12:29—victory in the current era over evil forces; Mark 13:35–36 speaks of not knowing when the master of the house will return, a distinct but related image about the end). There is a contrast here (rightly noted by Culpepper 2021, 482). One watches for a thief to stop them breaking into a house, but the coming of the Son of Man cannot be stopped, so it is best to be ready for it and be on the right side of his coming by being alert and responsive to the Son of Man.

Jesus presented the application. The exhortation now was to be ready because you did not know at what hour the Son of Man comes (Matt. 24:36, 39, 42; 25:13). It could be at any hour. The uncertainty of when the Son comes and the accountability that comes with him means keeping watch and being ready. The present imperative looks to a constant readiness. That readiness means trusting God and walking faithfully until the Son of Man returns, as we keep looking for the vindication that will come with him (Col. 3:4; 1 John 3:1–3—called a purifying hope).

24:45–47. Jesus now moved to the parable of the faithful and unfaithful steward. A longer version of this parable is in Luke 12:42–49. Jesus began by asking who the wise and faithful steward was whom a master put in charge of the household to care for the other servants. Blessing would come to the steward who did what the master asked. That steward would be given the responsibility over the master's possessions. This was a way of affirming what the servant had done, honoring the steward's faithfulness. The connection showed the link between accountability and the end.

24:48–51. Jesus spent more time on the unfaithful steward. This servant is described only in Matthew as "bad" or "evil" (BDAG s.v. "κακός" 1a, 501). His attitude showed his evil heart. He saw his master was delayed in his return. This is obviously an allusion to a sense of the return not being as soon as one might hope. It may picture the frustration that justice and vindication have not yet come. It was important to remember that Jesus as Messiah did not bring the immediate justice many had expected of the anointed one. This evil servant mistakenly thought his time was his own. So he beat his fellow servants (Matt. 18:28–33) rather than caring for them, and went out to drink with drunkards (Luke 21:34). He did the opposite of what the master had asked.

The result was devastating and quite vivid. When the master unexpectedly returned at an hour the servant did not know (Luke 12:46), that servant was "cut in two" (διχοτομήσει) and placed with the hypocrites, where there was weeping and gnashing of teeth. Jeremiah 34:18 may be in the background (Wilkins 2004, 803; Exod. 29:17). The lexicon says it is "dismemberment of a condemned person" (BDAG s.v. "διχοτομέω" 253). Luke 12:46 has this judged figure placed with the unfaithful, but Matthew describes him as placed with the hypocrites. The picture is of severe punishment, an exclusion from blessing. Weeping and gnashing of teeth is consistently a Matthean term for the reaction to finding out about total rejection (Matt. 8:12; 13:42, 50; 22:13; 25:30). He was the "odd man out." "Merely belonging to the disciple community is not in itself a guarantee of ultimate salvation" (France 2007, 946). His attitude showed no faith in the master or responsiveness to him. His actions showed his heart. This is the first of four severe judgments in the discourse (Matt. 25:10–12, 30, 41, 46; Osborne 2010, 911).

The parable pictured what happened to the person who ignored accountability and the return's reality. The picture might look to leaders, since a stewardship was involved (Turner 2008, 592). However, the picture of the servant might simply be a reference to any disciple who claimed to pursue a connection to Jesus. Davies and Allison (1997, 386) say the passage was particularly but not exclusively applicable to leaders. That makes good sense of the imagery. Blomberg (1992, 368) apparently does not see Christians in view at all but people slow to come to terms with God in Christ, but this appears to ignore the internal context of Jesus speaking to his disciples. At the least, they appear to be believers. What complicates matters is that these were probably people associated with the community, but technically they had not actually embraced Jesus, making them "insiders" and "outsiders" simultaneously. They were Christians only in appearance, not in reality. Such people needed to be shocked into understanding what was going on and needed to care about their walk with God. This was an internal warning about profession of a faith that was not really a response of faith, since faith at its core is relational and responds with an open heart to God. One who actually trusts God responds to God. This person in the parable was depicted as not caring about his or her walk, and so was rejected in the judgment. The test was to stay alert and be faithful. Do not think you can do what you want because the master is failing to return, whether you think that return is not soon nor never coming at all. Those who had become complacent but had faith would be sensitive to and heed such a warning. Those who did not care showed where they stood by ignoring it.

25:1–2. Jesus now told a parable underscoring readiness. This parable is unique to Matthew. It opens with the common "the kingdom of heaven is like" introduction (Matt. 13:24, 31, 33, 44, 45, 47, 52; 18:23; 20:1), but this example has a future tense. This is what the kingdom "will be" like, since we are looking forward to the return and judgment.

The parable involved ten "maidens" or "virgins" (BDAG s.v. "παρθένος" a, 777). Very young women were in view in modern terms, likely between twelve and eighteen as the normal age of women marrying at the time (Osborne 2010, 914). In a world where the average life expectancy was in the forties, all of life was compressed. There was no emphasis on their sexual status in this context (Nolland 2005, 1003). The image was simply part of supporting the wedding imagery.

Five were foolish and five were wise. The stress was on the foolish who failed to prepare. They were named as the first group of five and the parable ended by looking at them. Such maidens had the responsibility of attending to the bride as she transferred her home to the groom's residence. They awaited his arrival, sometimes meeting him halfway, as perhaps here. Since they did not know exactly when he would show up, they had to wait for him. Another possibility was that they awaited the couple's arrival after the wedding to celebrate the feast (Song 3:11; 1 Macc. 9:37–42 describes such a procession; Josephus, *A.J.* 13.20). Then they celebrated the marriage in the walk to the feast with the groom at his home, highlighting him on the way. Nolland (2005, 1004) sees them simply welcoming the groom. Wilkins (2004, 805) sees them going from the ceremony to the evening feast, as was commonly the case. To miss that meeting was to miss what they were there to celebrate (France 2007, 947). This celebratory detail is the key to the parable.

Examples of a Wedding Procession

1 Maccabees 9:37: "After these things it was reported to Jonathan and his brother Simon, 'The family of Jambri are celebrating a great wedding, and are conducting the bride, a daughter of one of the great nobles of Canaan, from Nadabath with a large escort.'"

Josephus, *Antiquities* 13:20: "As soon as they saw them conducting the virgin and the bridegroom, and such a great company of their friends with them as was to be expected at his wedding."

This is clearly an allegorical parable. An allegory is a story that really symbolizes another narrative or point. This is different from allegorizing as an interpretive method, for the intended comparison is built into the parable's design and meaning. The virgins are associated with the believing community. The groom's arrival pictures Jesus's return. The late and uncertain arrival pictures the unknown time of the return. The banquet pictures the blessing of salvation (like Matt. 22:1–14, only there those who end up outside picture Jewish people who have not responded, not those associated with Jesus, as here). The rejection of the foolish maidens reflects the judgment of those not ready.

25:3–4. The foolish took their lamps but did not take any oil in case there was a delay in the groom's arrival. The wise took flasks of oil and so were prepared. Given the Greek term used, the "lamps" were likely torches or sticks with oil-soaked rags, although clay lamps with wicks were also possible (BDAG s.v. "λαμπάς" 2, 585, noted a wedding torch as likely). Such a torch light was normal for outdoors. Davies and Allison (1997, 395–96) discuss the possibility that lamps might still be intended, given how long the lights seem to have burned in Matthew 25:7. Torch lamps could remain lit for about a quarter hour per soaking (France 2007, 949), while Culpepper (2021, 487) says the limit was about two hours. In either case it was not much time. An oil lamp burned for a longer time. Oil was unlikely to refer to good deeds or the Spirit, as neither "run down." It is best to see this detail simply as evidence for preparedness within the parable.

25:5–9. The groom was delayed. Some had considered this possibility; others had not. The point is probably the result of Jesus not yet having returned. The groom being delayed pictures that gap. Given what Jesus had been teaching in the entire discourse about not knowing the time of the return, there was no reason not to be prepared for its seeming delay.

The groom took so much time that the maidens fell asleep as they were waiting. Then at midnight there was a loud cry that awoke them. The groom was coming. It was time to prepare to meet him. In terms of the wedding scenario, they were preparing to go with the bride to the groom's house to celebrate. Probably startled, all awoke to prepare their lights. They either dipped the rags for the torches into oil or placed oil in the lamps to light the wicks. One group was ready. The other was not. They had been given time to prepare and be ready, but when the moment came there was no time to recover from the mistake of not being prepared. They had assumed they knew when the groom would come and expected him to fit their expectations.

The unprepared asked for help, as their lamps were about to run out of oil (Prov. 13:9; Job 18:5). Those who were prepared realized if the oil was shared then the procession would go dark. The unprepared were told to go and get their own oil. The remark raised the question whether shops would be open at that hour. It may be that the celebration meant some supplies were made available. Still, they would have had to leave the group and return, at least to their home, to get the oil.

25:10. The groom collected the maidens who were prepared, and they went to the feast. The door to the celebration was shut. This detail represents that there is a time to respond and be ready for Jesus's return or else it is too late.

25:11–12. The remaining maidens arrived late and asked for entry. They were refused entrance, as the groom said he did not know them. Knowing God is important in New Testament texts (Gal. 4:8–9; 2 Tim. 2:19; especially John 17:3). It is a key idea here. Association with God is not the same as knowing him. Apparently to miss the procession and arrive late was not acceptable, as it shamed the wedding party (Keener 2009, 599). This was not so much a reflection of custom as it is the parable's move toward application (Morris 1992, 625). Jesus's parables often had a point of surprise that contained their point. When the time for response comes, one is to be ready. One is ready if one has known and prepared for the master. The imagery of entry refused recalls Matthew 7:21–23 and 22:11–14 (Luke 13:25; Ps. 1:6, respectively). Here is a key to the parable's application. There was no real connection between Jesus and these disciples. It was a way of pointing to their lack of faith. They were the "odd women out." As Davies and Allison (1997, 400) say, "External membership does not bring salvation."

25:13. The application was that disciples were to keep watch (Matt. 24:3, 36, 39, 42–44; Mark 13:35; 1 Thess. 5:2–6). That meant being prepared, being ready for the groom when he comes. One was to be faithful until the Lord returned. This readiness was a test of faith and an indication of an ongoing relationship. The parable served as a warning to the church for those not prepared to face a delay in the Lord's return (Luke 12:35–40).

25:14–15. Jesus told a new parable, the parable of the Talents. A variation of this parable appears in Luke 19:12–27 in the third gospel's parable of the minas. In Luke, ten slaves were each given pounds of silver, called ten minas. The instructions in Luke 19:13 were explicit that they should earn from the money given. Luke's parable is distinct from Matthew's, but both parables call for faithfulness in exercising responsibility (Morris 1992, 626). Mark 13:34 simply has a generic picture of slaves being told to stay alert.

In Matthew, the focus is on the servant who failed by doing nothing with his opportunity to serve. As Garland says (1995, 241), "When Christ returns, he will not ask if one had the right date for the return but 'What have you been doing?'" Differences between the parables in Matthew and Luke likely mean they are similar but distinct parables making the same point, perhaps reflecting distinct versions in the larger traditional material about Jesus.

In Matthew's version three servants were charged with responsibility for varying degrees of assets while the owner traveled. The amounts were five, two, and one talent. A talent was a large amount of currency, about six thousand denarii (BDAG s.v. "τάλαντον" 988—"not small change"). That was six thousand days of labor for an average worker, more than nineteen years of work (Turner 2008, 600). The distribution was said to be according to the ability of each. It pictured God's great gifts. There is no reason to get more specific by distinguishing between faith, the Holy Spirit, or Jesus, as the giftedness is about what all people received in the role they had (Davies and Allison 1997, 405). Then the master left on his trip.

We have another allegorical parable. The master is Jesus. The slaves are disciples connected to the church. The talents are the responsibilities (not natural endowments of talent) by which the disciples serve God (France 2007, 951–52). There are different levels of responsibility for disciples. The master's departure looks to Jesus's resurrection to heaven. His return to receive an account of what the servants had done looks to Jesus's return and judgment. In the subsequent assessment, some ended up in and one was out. Third Baruch 12–16 has a story of angels bringing three baskets: one full, one half full, and the last empty. The third group was punished. That story is like this one (Davies and Allison 1997, 404, note a few other examples as well from later Jewish materials where the issue of responsibilities is told as a story; *Mek.* on Exod. 20:2—on some being trusted with little, pictured with straw, and others more, pictured with silver and gold, because the one with little could not be trusted with more; *Šabb.* 152b—treating the responsibilities as precious and to be cared for; Cant. Rab. 7:14.1—representing keeping religious precepts and good deeds). Jesus's parable raised common Jewish themes about accountability to God.

25:16–18. The servant with five talents immediately went to work and earned five talents more. This servant was faithful to the assignment. The servant with two talents was also faithful, earning two more talents. Each had a 100 percent gain. In Luke 19:16–19, the first servant earned ten minas from his ten minas and was put over ten cities, while the second servant earned five minas and was placed over five cities. The third servant dug a hole and hid his money (Luke 19:20). Later Jewish texts advised against this for various reasons (2 En. J 51:1–2—Do not hide your silver in the earth. Help a believer in affliction; Babylonian Talmud, *Šabb.* 102b—do not dig a hole to hide money on the Sabbath), while others contended for it, at least to a degree (Babylonian Talmud, B. Mesi'a 42a—in urging one not to invest all one's money but to safeguard some of it). In Jesus's parable, the third steward did nothing with his talent. His opportunity met with no effort to apply it. There was no response to the instruction.

Do Not Hide Your Money

2 Enoch 51:1–2 |J|: "Stretch out your hands to the needy in accordance with your strength. Do not hide your silver in the earth. Help a believer in affliction, and then affliction will not find you, in your treasuries and in the time of your work."

Talmud, *Šhabbat* 102b: "The Gemara asks: With regard to any small amount of building, for what use is it suited? Rabbi Yirmeya said: As a poor person digs a hole in the floor of his house in which to hide his coins."

25:19–23. The master returned to settle accounts after a long delay (Matt. 24:48; 25:5). This is the third picture of return in the passage (Matt. 24:50; 25:6). For both the faithful servants the response was exactly the same. When each responded that he earned five and two talents respectively, they were each rewarded with a commendation of being a good and faithful servant as well as being put in charge of many things (Matt. 24:47; 25:28–29; cf. Isa. 40:10; 62:11; Rev. 22:12; Osborne 2010, 925). They were told to enter into the joy of their master. Both were commended in exactly the same way and welcomed. God sees our fruit no matter how big or small.

25:24–25. The third slave explained why he did nothing with the talent (Luke 19:20–21). He claimed the master was a hard man, harvesting what he did not sow and gathering where he did not scatter. The term for "hard" can mean harsh or cruel (BDAG s.v. "σκληρός" 4a, 930—"strict, harsh, cruel, merciless"). The master was a tough guy to deal with in the slave's view. The language is like Micah 6:15 and was a rebuke of the master (Davies and Allison 1997, 409). This third servant was afraid and hid the talent in the ground. He gave the master back his one talent with nothing else earned. This response pictures a lack of respect and relationship to the master. Inaction was disobedience and was what led the master to call the slave lazy. The slave had claimed the master was to blame for his inaction, but the master saw it otherwise. This slave was no victim, as the master's treating of the other slaves plainly showed. He did reward them so there was nothing harsh in the master's response. The blame and responsibility were the servant's alone. He blew the opportunity. He tried to place the blame elsewhere and deflect his own responsibility for what had taken place.

25:26–27. This failure was the response the parable focused on, giving it far more space. The parable served as a warning.

The master responded angrily (Luke 19:22–23). He called the slave evil and lazy, the opposite of good and faithful for the first two slaves. Being lazy is rebuked in Scripture (Prov. 6:6–9). The term "lazy" points to one who holds back, one who is hesitant (BDAG s.v. "ὀκνηρός" 1, 702—"shrinking from something . . . hesitant"). If what the slave said were true, then the slave should have done something. Note how the master did not repeat the idea that he was a "hard" man. Responsibilities were to be carried out, not ignored. If what the servant had claimed about the master were so, then why did he not place the money in the bank so he could at least earn the interest? The remark was not so much accepting the slave's evaluation as it was really a sarcastic rebuke (Blomberg 1992, 374). The reference was to moneychangers as loaners, not banks in a modern sense (Wilkins 2004, 807–8). Was there fear at work or was it simply misjudgment and laziness? No matter what the motive, and it could have been any of these, the fault was not the master's but the slave's. His grave misreading of the master yielded its consequences. This is where Jesus's warning in the parable about accountability resides.

25:28–30. So now the master acted (Luke 19:24, 26). The master took the talent from the man and gave it to the slave who had earned ten. The principle is stated next (Gospel of Thomas 41). The one who has is given more (Prov. 9:9; Matt. 13:12; Mark 4:25; Luke 19:26). He will have more than enough. The one who has not, even what he has had is taken away. The strange way this was said was emphatic. Someone with nothing loses what they seemingly had. This means they absolutely end up with nothing. Matthew lacks any crowd reactions unlike Luke 19:25, where the crowd responded when the first servant with ten minas was given the one the third servant had.

The worthless slave was cast into outer darkness where there was weeping and gnashing of teeth (Matt. 8:12; 13:42, 50; 22:13; 25:30; Luke 13:28). The term for "worthless" assessed what the slave showed himself to be in light of his inaction (BDAG s.v. "ἀχρεῖος" 1, 160). It was normally an economic term and meant useless, being of no value. Although rejection is implied in Luke's version, the third gospel does not spell out the third slave's punishment as Matthew does. This is another "odd man out" parable.

The parable shows responsibilities before God are to be carried out, as we are accountable for them. Those whose response is nothing get nothing, even losing what they never really had. So the parables together argue we should be alert for the return of the Lord, as all will be responsible for their stewardship, stewardship that either shows faith or shows its absence.

THEOLOGICAL FOCUS

The exegetical idea (Jesus called for a faithful and alert walk until he returns, stressing the accountability that would come with his return and noting the uncertainty of when that would be) leads to this theological focus: Jesus issues a call to be alert for the end and to be faithful in the meantime.

The parables in this unit focused on the person who takes the return's uncertainty as an excuse either not to be ready or to ignore their accountability to God and Jesus. The parables emphasized the time of the return is unknown with the timing of the return appearing to be longer than anticipated. This was no excuse to be irresponsible, disobedient, or indifferent. The call was to be faithful and ready, alert to the possibility that a return can come at any time.

The repeated negative fate of those who were not ready show that this series of parables contains serious warnings. We see repeated figures who were odd people out. They were involved and seemingly close to Jesus, engaged with him in a way, but in the end they were out. The references to outer darkness as well as weeping and gnashing of teeth left no doubt about this conclusion. Those who trusted God and drew near to him responded to him. They took advantage of what enablement God had given. Those who did not trust God failed to respond to him. Both groups were accountable to God, who weighs hearts along with the acts that come out of them.

PREACHING AND TEACHING STRATEGIES

Exegetical and Theological Synthesis

The exegetical section identifies the related themes of readiness and faithfulness. These are not original to Jesus but find their origin in the Old Testament prophets (Isa. 52:8; 62:6; Jer. 6:17; Ezek. 3:17; Hos. 9:8; Hab. 2:1; Zech. 9:9). God appointed his prophets as watchmen. They pronounced coming judgement; they proclaimed God's appearing. Their words were meant to prepare God's people for the future. In the early church, pastoral leaders kept watch over their people to guard them from outside threats or their own sin (Acts 20:28; 1 Peter 5:2). Likewise, God expected religious leaders to watch their lives and doctrines carefully, ensuring they remained models of godliness (1 Tim. 4:16).

Before the gospel of Matthew ends, Jesus made one more appeal to keep watch. When he invited his inner circle of disciples to pray with him in Gethsemane as he prepared for his death, he commanded them to "watch and pray" (Matt. 26:41). Although we will cover this content in coming pages (watch and see!), I mention it here because one of the best ways to get ready for future trials is watchful prayer. Indeed, prayer prepares our souls to persevere in the face of looming peril.

Preaching Idea

Get ready. Stay ready. Christ is coming soon.

Contemporary Connections

What does it mean?

What does it mean to get ready and stay ready because Christ is coming soon? First, we must reiterate an insight from the exegesis of the previous section: God's program continues forward. What is "near" is coming "next." What is "soon" is sequential. Thus, when we subject "soon" to our experience of time, we miss the point. We become squirrely kids in the backseat of a car on a long road trip asking, "Are we there yet?" When the parent says, "Not yet, but we will be soon," she doesn't mean "in five minutes," but that it's the next important marker on the itinerary. Similarly, the next major marker on God's timeline is Jesus's return.

Second, we should distinguish between getting ready and staying ready. To get ready means to prepare in advance. A student gets ready for a test by reading the assignments, paying attention to lectures, and studying for the exam. She is prepared for a pop quiz or final test. However, she may sabotage her preparation by not staying ready. If she wastes her final weeks of the semester with late night Netflix binges or sorority parties, her initial preparations will lose their impact. She must keep reading, attending classes, and studying until the term ends. The same logic applies to soldiers preparing for combat, police officers preparing for service, pilots preparing for flight, or pastors preparing for ministry. Initial training prepares them; ongoing activity keeps them ready.

Is it true?

Is it true that we should get ready and stay ready because Christ is coming soon? Absolutely. However, we must not measure "soon" in minutes and seconds, lest we get weary of waiting. Jesus is near (Phil. 4:5). His coming is next in God's program. *When* that happens is uncertain. *That* it will happen is certain.

Moreover, getting ready and staying ready are essential to lifelong faithfulness. According to Jesus's parables, the call to discipleship is a call to steward our gifts and opportunities. God has determined the parameters of our lives, he has distributed talents to us. He expects us to make the most of them. We steward our lives until our last breath or Jesus's return. This is staying ready. It is evident in a widow who keeps praying until she meets Jesus, an elderly husband who keeps caring for his wife through dementia, empty nesters who keep their home open for hospitality, and a middle-aged pastor who keeps serving faithfully while preparing for his faithful successor.

Now what?

Jesus's parables invite a threefold response. First, we need to quit speculating about when the end will come. All we need to know for certain is that Jesus's return is the next part of God's program. Predicting dates of the rapture or antichrist figures has always proven foolish. If the Son of God did not know the hour, we should humbly accept our ignorance. Jesus asked us to be prepared, not to make predictions.

Second, we should make initial preparations. This is akin to teachers leading their class through a fire drill: *Don't panic. Stay quiet. Line up. Move quickly. Exit the building. Go to your designated meeting spot.* Initial preparations warn us that disasters are unavoidable and ready us regarding what to do when they arrive. For followers of Jesus, initial preparations may look like this: *Repent. Believe. Pray. Hear and do what Jesus says. Do it together.*

Third, we should plan for lifelong development. As mentioned above, many professions require ongoing development. Software engineers learn new coding methods. Doctors stay abreast of medical advances. Educators get trained in new literacy techniques. Professional development keeps professionals prepared. Followers of Jesus are not exempt from lifelong learning. As cultural conditions change, or we enter new seasons of life, former evangelistic tactics or ways of praying may need updating. To be specific, disciples who want to stay ready and faithful in this late modern age must wrestle with secular humanism, sexual identity, consumerism, AI, euthanasia, and nationalism.

Creativity in Presentation

Various professions require rigorous training. These include pilots, doctors, lawyers, teachers, veterinarians, musicians, and soldiers. Certainly, in your congregation several of these professions are represented. Consider asking a couple of members to describe how they got ready for their career.

- What is your job/career?
- Briefly describe your training. What? Where? How long?
- What did you do to get prepared?
- What do you do to stay prepared?
- Why is preparation important to your field?

You may also describe how you got ready for your pastoral vocation or another area of competency.

No one wants to get caught unaware by natural disasters. Thus, from an early age we learn the importance of being prepared. Whether it's "stop, drop, and roll," to put out a fire or "see something; say something" to identify terrorist threats, we have been given many tools to get prepared. In fact, the government has dedicated resources to emergency preparedness at www.ready.gov. They have plans for a dozens of categories, including aging, pets, weather, technology, fires, and pandemics. You might even distribute copies of the emergency supply list and dedicate a table on the stage to the various items—which were likely in your parents' basement prior to Y2K!

Emergency Supply Kit (from www.ready.gov)

Water, nonperishable food, battery-powered radio, flashlight, first aid kit, extra batteries, whistle, dust mask, plastic sheeting, duct tape, handwipes, garbage bags, toolkit, can opener, maps, cell phone with charger, soap, prescriptions and medication, glasses, contact solution, baby formula, pet food, cash, sleeping bag and blankets, extra clothes, fire extinguisher, books, matches, games, paper, pencil

To visualize Jesus's story about the maidens, you might collect ten lights to set up on the stage. They could be oil lamps, flashlights, or table lamps. You want to make sure that five of them work and five do not. As you read the parable, you can light five of the lamps and show that the other five do not work. Later in the sermon, when you talk about "staying prepared," you can show the congregation that you brought extra supplies to get the other lamps/lights to work. Be sure to have extra batteries for the flashlights, bulbs for the table lamps, or kerosene for the oil lamps.

Finally, you could post one or two watchmen during your sermon. If you already have a safety team at your church, you might even recruit people from this team. Have them sit on the edge of the stage throughout the sermon. If you want to add drama, they could have an earpiece and sunglasses to look like secret service agents. At one point during the sermon, you could have the safety person leave his post and make a sweep of the auditorium. You could also have a second watchman relieve him halfway through.

Whatever creative elements you adopt or adapt, you want to communicate that Jesus issues a call to be alert for the end and to be faithful in the meantime. Get ready. Stay ready. Jesus is coming soon.

- Beware: Jesus is coming back (24:36–44).
- Be faithful until Jesus comes back (24:45–51).
- Be ready when Jesus comes back (25:1–13).
- Be active until Jesus comes back (25:14–30).

DISCUSSION QUESTIONS

1. What cautions should you observe about predicting the timing of Jesus's return?
2. What is the best way to interpret the "left behind" imagery in these illustrations?
3. How do these stories advance the "odd man out" motif?
4. When you consider preparing for change, crises, or emergencies, what do you find more difficult: getting ready or staying ready? Explain.
5. What have you set in place to stay alert, active, and developing as a believer?

Matthew 25:31–46

EXEGETICAL IDEA

In the parable of the Sheep and the Goats, Jesus showed that part of what will be assessed in the judgment is how one responded to those tied to Jesus.

THEOLOGICAL FOCUS

Jesus shows the tie between faith, ethics, and the treatment of his own.

PREACHING IDEA

Care for our kin is care for the King.

PREACHING POINTERS

In the concluding illustration from the Olivet Discourse, Jesus declared his reign, described his judgment, and divided people into two groups: sheep and goats. These iconic categories represented those who respond to Jesus's authority in compassionate acts to other Christ-followers (i.e., sheep), and those who failed to care for others (i.e., goats). In his explanation, Jesus provided six examples of caring for downtrodden Christians. Not only was this care commended for its benefit to other believers, but it also affected Jesus, who felt solidarity with his spiritual siblings. For Matthew's audience, this teaching reached a group of people under pressure for their faith convictions. They not only needed assurance that King Jesus would vindicate their faithfulness but also the compassionate care of other Christ-followers to sustain their faith.

Despite its prominent place in history, the church has no shortage of enemies today. In the West, opponents scrutinize its beliefs, criticize its hypocrisy, and blame it for myriad inequalities. In communist states, the church is targeted for its teaching and is forced underground. In Islamic nations, churches suffer loss of liberty, land, and life. Jesus feels these attacks; our pain is his pain. However, these critical times are a proving ground for the body of Christ to care for its own. The church does not need local government, foreign aid, or philanthropic organizations to sustain it. Jesus commissioned the church to be a community of care; our aid is his aid. This sermon shows that care for our kin is care for the King.

THE PARABLE OF THE SHEEP AND GOATS (25:31–46)

LITERARY STRUCTURE AND THEMES (25:31–46)

This unit presents a climactic parable. This parable and its explanation of the judgment are unique to Matthew. It gives a snapshot of the accountability tied to the judgment. It develops earlier Matthean images (Matt. 7:13–27; 8:11–12; 10:32–33; 13:40–43, 49–50; 16:25–26), as well as capping the discourse. It is built around the contrast of the sheep and goats. It is built on contrastive parallelism in two core steps. First, there is the explanation of the evaluation. Then, in response to a question, it details the basis of that evaluation. It shows that faith has a product as response led to action.

The passage's core structure involves a simple contrast presented with complete symmetry (Davies and Allison 1997, 416–17; Hagner 1995, 740–41). Everything said of the saved sheep was the opposite of the rejected goats. The basis of judgment was how those allied to Jesus were treated. This reflected not only how Jesus was respected, but how one viewed the kingdom program. This was about actions, not merely claims. As is the case throughout Matthew, faith reflected an active trust resulting in a response with a product.

The key theme is accountability. The Son of Man returned as judge and vindicator of the righteous. The coming kingdom would not only establish peace but also bring justice. The judgment was not merely about ideas but ideas that lead into responsiveness and action. Genuine relational faith showed sensitivity to those who belong to Jesus. The call is to be responsive and faithful to those who are his. The passage is a development of Matthew 10:40–42 and helps to explain the rationale for the gathering of the righteous in Matthew 24:29–31 (Turner 2008, 603).

Another important theme is the union or solidarity between Jesus and those who are his. To the extent one acted to care for a disciple, that person cared for Jesus. One is reminded of the Pauline picture of union with Christ, the Johannine teaching of the union of Jesus with those who are his, and how Saul's persecution of the disciples is seen as an attack on Jesus (1 Cor. 12; John 17; Acts 9, respectively). This solidarity is the basis for the call to compassion this passage reflects. God is watching how the world treats his children. They will be vindicated in the judgment.

The text is the object of much discussion about who is helped. Is this a reference to believers only or to all? The treatment of verses will handle this question, but an important observation can be made here. In Galatians 6:10, Paul gives the exhortation to do good to all people, especially those of the family of faith. This teaches that how we treat people is to be the same. It should certainly happen among fellow believers, but it also is to happen to others. This is what love for enemies looks like, a call of Jesus that is to make disciples distinctive (Matt. 5:43–48; Luke 6:27–36).

EXPOSITION (25:31–46)

God cares about his own. This parable is designed to show it. He will vindicate his own one day. How people are treated matters to God. This is especially true of his own. Part of being ready for the Lord's return is to understand how God will evaluate how people in the judgment. Loving your neighbor matters, especially if they are among the people of God. Injustice will be reversed and compassion toward them will be honored. What this shows about those in the faith also models how people should be treated in general.

In the parable of the Sheep and the Goats, Jesus showed that part of what will be assessed in the judgment is how one responded to those tied to Jesus.

25:31–33. The exposition is about what happens when the Son of Man returns. Daniel 7:13–14 is certainly in the background. Matthew 24:30 cites Daniel. The Son of Man comes with his angels (Zech. 14:5; Matt. 13:41, 49; 16:27; 24:31; 2 Thess. 1:7; Jude 14). He will sit on a glorious throne (Matt. 19:28). Davies and Allison (1997, 421) have a discussion arguing this throne for the Son of Man is distinct from God's throne as in other places in Matthew (Matt. 19:28; 20:21), but in Matthew that is a distinction, though legitimate, without a difference since other texts place Jesus at God's right hand sharing in rule by appealing to Psalm 110:1 (Matt. 22:44; 26:64). We have a picture not so much of distinct thrones, but roles, functions, and authority that are parallel. Humans do share in judgment in Jewish texts (Abel in T. Ab. A 12:4–13:4; Melchizedek in 11QMelch 2:13; Messiah in 2 Bar. 72:2–6; and Pss. Sol. 17; Davies and Allison 1997, 421). However, in Matthew the position of the Son of God made the authority in view here more than one exercised by a human (Matt. 10:32; John 5:27). To have him be king in *the* kingdom says as much; since in a Jewish final kingdom context, God is the one king (Keener 2009, 602). The combination of throne and angels is like 1 Enoch (1 En. 1:9; 61:8—a very close parallel to this verse; 62:1–5; 69:27–29; 90:20–36; on 1 Enoch and Matthew, see Bock and Charlesworth, 2013).

Two Examples of Sharing in Judgment

2 Baruch 72:2–6: "After the signs have come of which I have spoken to you before, when the nations are moved and the time of my Anointed One comes, he will call all nations, and some of them he will spare, and others he will kill. These things will befall the nations which will be spared by him. Every nation which has not known Israel and which has not trodden down the seed of Jacob will live. And this is because some from all the nations have been subjected to your people. All those, now, who have ruled over you or have known you, will be delivered up to the sword."

11QMelchizedek 2:13: "Therefore Melchizedek will thoroughly prosecute the vengeance required by Go[d's] statutes. [In that day he will de] liv[er them from the power] of Belial, and from the power of all the sp[irits predestined to him]."

The nations were gathered (especially noted in Joel 3:1–12 = 4:1–12 in Hebrew and LXX; Isa. 66:18). The king separated them into sheep and goats, just as a shepherd did. It is here that the small parable appeared in Matthew 25:32b–33. Sheep were more valuable than goats because of their wool (Blomberg 1992, 377). The rest of this passage involves exposition of the Last Judgment with a resurrection of people presupposed. The sheep ended up on his right and the goats on his left, representing honor (1 Kings 2:19) and shame (similar imagery is in Plato, *Resp.* 10:614c; Virgil, *Aen.* 6:540–43; T. Ab. A 12:12; 13:9; Davies and Allison 1997, 424). This is a judgment of all as the Old Testament and Jewish texts promised (Isa. 43:9; 44:11; 45:20–21; 66:18; Joel 3:2, 11–12; Zeph. 3:8; Zech. 14:2; 2 Bar. 72:2; 4 Ezra 7:37; T. Benj. 9:2; Turner 2008, 608). Nations are made up of people who are judged, but interestingly it includes Jews and non-Jews in a gospel that had been focused on Israel. The Great Commission says to make disciples of all nations, which is a way to say people from every nation (Culpepper 2021, 496; Matt.

28:18–20). So this judgment is a look at a comprehensive verdict over all people. The separation of sheep looks like Ezekiel 34:17–22.

25:34–36. The king invited the sheep into the kingdom. The scene portrays the Son of Man as a king, which fits the passage's kingdom picture. Here we see the consummation of the kingdom and the final decisive point at which entry will be affirmed. It is a kingdom prepared from before the foundation of the world. The kingdom is the one long promised, now coming to be fully realized. The sheep will be invited to enter into their inheritance of the kingdom (Matt. 5:5; 19:29). They themselves will share in kingdom blessing and authority (France 2007, 963; 1 Cor. 4:8; Eph. 2:6, even now; Rev. 1:6; 20:6; 22:5). Vindication for the righteous, a core theme of kingdom hope, now comes.

The basis of the commendation was their treatment of the king. This is a rare case of Jesus alluding to himself as "king" in Matthew (Matt. 21:5 does so in an action; Wilkins 2004, 810). How these people served the king received explanation later when those who served him were perplexed about when they did this. They did six things for him. These are presented in three pairs. (1) They fed him and gave him drink (Ps. 146:7; Matt. 10:42; 14:16). (2) They invited him in and clothed him (Gen. 18:1–8; Job 31:32). (3) They cared for him (Ps. 69:33; Isa. 58:7) and visited him in prison. The Old Testament speaks to such care (Job 22:7; Ezek. 18:6–9, 15–17), as do later Jewish texts (T. Jos. 1:5–7; T. Jac. 2:23). As we will see, there is a solidarity and union between Jesus and those who are his. As they did it to one of his, they did it for him. Such acts are rooted in a good heart (Matt. 7:18; 23:26; Heb. 13:2–3). This is faith working through love (Gal. 5:6; Davies and Allison 1997, 427; Morris 1992, 637).

It is this explanation that shows we are not dealing with corporate nations, but individual acts of kindness that were now commended and rewarded (Wilkins 2004, 809). To say the nations were gathered was to highlight that people from all nations were gathered, but the standards of judgment were the same. So by extension it was the case that what individuals did in treating people was how nations should treat people, as the prophets often showed in their ethical call to the nations when the issue of judgment was raised (e.g., the example of judgment of Tyre for proud, arrogant wealth in Ezek. 27–28 or the picture of the judgment of nations in Isa. 25:1–5). Interestingly, the treatment of God's people in an abusive manner was a part of this condemnation, even at the national level.

Judgment on an Arrogant Nation(s)

Isaiah 25:1–5 (of nations): "O Lord, you are my God! I will exalt you in praise, I will extol your fame. For you have done extraordinary things, and executed plans made long ago exactly as you decreed. Indeed, you have made the city into a heap of rubble, the fortified town into a heap of ruins; the fortress of foreigners is no longer a city, it will never be rebuilt. So a strong nation will extol you; the towns of powerful nations will fear you. For you are a protector for the poor, a protector for the needy in their distress, a shelter from the rainstorm, a shade from the heat. Though the breath of tyrants is like a winter rainstorm, like heat in a dry land, you humble the boasting foreigners. Just as the shadow of a cloud causes the heat to subside, so he causes the song of tyrants to cease."

Ezekiel 28:17–18 (of Tyre): "Your heart was proud because of your beauty; you corrupted your wisdom on account of your splendor. I threw you down to the ground; I placed you before kings, that they might see you. By the multitude of your iniquities, through the sinfulness of your trade, you desecrated your sanctuaries. So I drew fire out from within you; it consumed you, and I turned you to ashes on the earth before the eyes of all who saw you."

25:37–39. The righteous were surprised they had served the king, asking when they cared for him. They work back through the king's list of six items, asking when they fed, gave drink, took in, clothed, cared for, and visited him. Nothing in this text suggests that there are "anonymous Christians" here or that those benefited consist of everyone (contra Davies and Allison 1997, 428). That claim negates the entire premise of Jesus's coming, that all humanity has a need for what he supplies, and it is the righteous who gain vindication. However, the discussion over the scope of this passage is tied to the imagery to come (see 25:40). The servants' surprise was not that their work was motivated by Jesus, but that he had not been in their minds as the object of their actions (Blomberg 1992, 377).

25:40. The king responded that as they did it for the least of the king's brothers, they did it for him. There are three common options as who "the least" here are: (1) everyone who has a need, (2) disciples, or (3) new community leaders. The last two options have solid support from Matthew 10:40–42. "Brothers" in Matthew is most often meant spiritually, when it is not a reference to biological family (Matt. 11:11; especially 12:48–50; 18:6, 10, 14; 28:10; France 2007, 964; Nolland 2005, 1032).[1] The reference to the "least" of these points to needy, perhaps even persecuted, disciples, given the reference to prison (Wilkins 2004, 811). While it is certainly true all who have need are to be cared for (Gal. 6:10 as an expression of the law of love), here the issue focused on compassion toward and vindication of those mistreated for their spiritual position, those headed for vindication and gathering. The background of Daniel 7:13–14 also fits into such a narrow reference to God's people.

Here we see the solidarity the kin has with his community. Proverbs 19:17 says the one who cares for the poor lends to the Lord. To care for one of them in need was to care for the king. This union and shared identity is like the way Paul addressed Philemon about the slave Onesimus. Paul asked Philemon to treat his runaway slave as if the slave were Paul the apostle himself. That the community was under pressure is clear from texts in Acts, as well as from 1 Corinthians 4:8–13, 2 Corinthians 6:1–10, or 11:23–27.

25:41–43. Next the king turned to the goats on his left. He condemned them and told them to depart to the eternal fire reserved for the devil and his angels. The fate of the devil is seen in Revelation 19:20, 20:10, 14–15, and 21:8. The king explained that they had failed to feed him or give him drink. They had not taken him in, clothed him, cared for, or visited him. These were sins of omission involving a lack of compassion. Their response was the mirror opposite of the righteous and so was their destiny. The idea of judgment for a lack of compassion and as vindication for the righteous has Old Testament roots (Ps. 6:8; Isa. 30:33). The image of eternal fire is common in Matthew (Matt. 3:12; 13:42, 50; 18:8–9).

25:44. As the righteous had asked the king when this had taken place, so the rejected also asked. There is one contrast to the earlier verse 37 and the query of the righteous, where those who asked are called "the righteous." In verse 44, the judged are simply called "they." They have no moral identity. One is reminded of T. S. Eliot's "hollow men." They asked, "When did we see you in hungry, thirsty, a stranger, naked, sick, or in prison?"

1 Efforts to broaden the application to any person fail to appreciate the reference to brothers and sisters in the text, which has a narrow meaning for Matthew (Matt. 5:22–24, 47; 7:3–5; 12:49; 18:15, 21, 35; 19:29; 23:8; 28:10; Blomberg 1992, 377–78; France 2007, 958; Keener 2009, 605–6).

25:45–46. The king answered the same way with the opposite observation. To the extent they did not do it to one of the least of these, they did not do it for the king. So, the solidarity declared for the acts of the righteous also applied to the failure of the unrighteous to act.

The passage closes with a summarizing contrast of the results. Those who failed to act were sent into eternal punishment (Dan. 12:2; John 5:28–29; 2 Bar. 51:6). The righteous ended up with eternal life. How those who belong to the king were treated mattered. Faith showed itself in action. Jesus presented the punishment as everlasting, not temporal or limited in duration, just as salvation is eternal (but for such a limit see France 2007, 966–67; correctly Blomberg 1992, 379). Morris (1992, 641) notes much was at stake in denying eternality to the punishment by saying, "To eliminate eternal punishment is to extract the teeth of the Law and its presentation of a holy God. The blessing of the gospel can be retained only if the Law is seen as the completely serious will of the holy God, to whom sin is grievous rebellion, requiring his punishment if it is not forgiven." He goes on to say the punishment is not "some small experience that would be but for a moment."

Jesus will be the judge of the world (Acts 10:42–43). All were and are accountable to him whether they recognize it or not. How believers are treated matters as well. God sees how we care for people, especially his own. To care for them is to care for the Savior. This response shows respect for Jesus and for his own.

The timing of the judgment belongs with the return. More detail is not given, so debates are not in view as to whether it precedes or follows a millennium, about which only Revelation 19–20 gives us any detail. The parable summarizes what will happen when this judgment comes at a time after Jesus's return. God will take a close look at all of us, especially for how we treated those who are his.

THEOLOGICAL FOCUS

The exegetical idea (in the parable of the sheep and the goats, Jesus showed that part of what will be assessed in the judgment is how one responded to those tied to Jesus) leads to this theological one: Jesus shows the tie between faith, ethics, and the treatment of his own.

The sheep and goats picture a judgment to life or condemnation. This judgment measures the heart through acts of compassion to disciples in need. Those disciples represent the king's presence.

This conclusion to the Olivet Discourse points to a need to show special concern for those who belong to Jesus. They were and are to be cared for, so they may not hunger, thirst, or be in need, and are to be comforted in persecution. The solidarity with the king means they are special objects of God's concern.

Acts of compassion matter, especially those directed toward God's own people. Throughout Matthew, the call to faith expresses itself in actions. The issue is the heart's character. As early as the Sermon on the Mount, this has been a concern of this gospel (Matt. 5:21–48). The call to love was seen as the height of the law (Matt. 22:34–40). So to love God and have faith in him is to be translated into how we respond from the heart and treat others. Nothing shows this as clearly as how those who belong to God are treated. Jesus called these his brothers and sisters (Matt. 10:40–42; 12:48–50). The judgment will look at how one treated these special people. The judgment honors compassion for them, while ignoring them does not receive such honor.

Also important to this text is the Son of Man's authority. That has been stressed throughout the discourse by a consistent showing of accountability that everyone owes to the one God has sent. This sent one is the King, and we see him render accounts that lead to life or to condemnation. The judgment is universal, so all owe him the respect due to the one who will declare the destiny of every soul. Humanity ultimately is divided into two camps. There is no purgatory nor a second chance. Response and responsibility come from this life. This passage gives us one of the best glimpses of how judgment works in the New Testament. It exposits the theme as do texts in the book of Revelation. Revelation 20:12 treats this theme, where the dead are judged on the basis of works as recorded in the Book of Life. Revelation 21:7 calls the saved "those who conquer," a description of those whose faith in Jesus showed a responsiveness to God by taking the water of the Spirit he offered in the kingdom through Jesus (John 4:6–10; 7:37–39). They are those whose robes are washed (Rev. 22:14). In contrast are those who are judged (Rev. 21:8; 22:15). The picture there is of two types of people, just as we have here. All of this teaches that we should be responsive to our accountability to God by being responsive to God's offer of forgiveness and life through Jesus. Such faith also will care about how God's people are treated.

PREACHING AND TEACHING STRATEGIES

Exegetical and Theological Synthesis

The exegetical section stresses the solidarity Jesus has with his people. Our hurts are his hurts; our joys are his joys. He was the sinless Man of Sorrows who secured for us right standing with God (Isa. 53; 2 Cor. 5:21; Phil. 3:10). This is solidarity at its finest. And Jesus's intimate connection with his people did not end at the cross; rather, from his seat in heaven he still empathizes with our weaknesses and intercedes in our times of need (Rom. 8:34; Heb. 4:14–16). Jesus cares deeply for his people.

This care, however, is not an abstract, theological principle. It is a personal and practical way of showing love to others. Christian love is an extension of Jesus's care. According to Jesus, extending care to others is evidence of our discipleship (John 13:35). According to Paul, this care should be patient, kind, long-suffering, and forgiving (1 Cor. 13). Love binds the body of Christ together (1 Cor. 12–14) and compels us to bear one another's burdens (Gal. 6:1–4). Paul urges us not to grow weary caring for our spiritual kin (Gal. 6:9–10). Sadly, when selfishness, rivalry, or empathetic fatigue surface in the family of God, our ability to care for one another suffers. And we all suffer for it. Yet, if everyone in the body of Christ cared for someone in the body of Christ, we would all be stronger.

Preaching Idea

Care for our kin is care for the King.

Contemporary Connections

What does it mean?

Jesus redefined family. It does not exclude biological kin but prioritizes spiritual siblings. Church is family (Matt. 18:15–35). As discussed earlier (Matt. 10:21, 37; 12:46–50), this preference for spiritual kin over blood relatives challenged a core value of Jesus's day. However, Jesus consistently elevated the forged family of faith. We are his kin.

To live Jesus's vision of caretaking in the spiritual family, Christian communities must serve their needy and hurting members. To offer babysitting for the single parent is to care for Jesus. To sit with a bereaved widow is to care for Jesus. To provide free labor or financial assistance to an unemployed member of the church is to care for Jesus. To encourage an exhausted pastor is to care for Jesus. Ways to show care for our kin abound.

Is it true?

It is true that to care for our kin is caring for the King. Jesus clearly taught this. He reiterated the inverse of this idea as well: harm toward Christians is harm toward Christ. Paul learned he was persecuting Jesus when he imprisoned his followers (Acts 9:4). As our brother and empathetic high priest, Jesus shows profound solidarity with his spiritual siblings (Heb. 2:9–18;

4:14–16). He cares deeply for us and wants the same from us.

While this care should not exclude those outside the church—our good deeds do, in fact, point others to God's glory (Matt. 5:14–16)—this parable focuses on care for those within the body of Christ. More specifically, we should focus this care on those in need. These needs may be circumstantial, such as the loss of a job, birth of a child, death in the family, or recent injury; or they may comprise enduring problems, such as care for those with mental health challenges, physical disabilities, or generational poverty. Enduring problems are more complex and may lead to compassion fatigue; churches would be wise to create systems, plans, or networks to care for these types of needs.

Now what?

Jesus's compelling story provokes three responses. First, we should see our kin. When we gather for worship on Sunday morning, we sing, pray, and learn with our spiritual kin. When we join our church for small groups, outreach, or service projects, we work with our kin. This kinship extends beyond our local church to comprise brothers and sisters in Christ across the globe. Many of them serve King Jesus in difficult places. When we pray for the persecuted church, we pray for spiritual siblings who are suffering. All Christians are kin; Jesus wants us to see this.

Second, we should serve our kin. As described above, this service is not only tangible but also translates to Jesus. When we drive an elderly believer to a hospital appointment, we serve Jesus. When we help a troubled kid from the youth group get a job, we serve Jesus. When we volunteer for nursery duty at the church, we serve Jesus. Serving one another is essential to life in God's household (Gal. 5:13; cf. Rom. 12; 1 Cor. 12).

Finally, we must fear our King. Jesus deserves our respect. His wisdom and authority are notable. His care for his kin is unquestionable. If these facts do not provoke a healthy respect (i.e., fear) of Jesus, then we must not forget what consistently provoked his ire: uncaring religion. He turned over tables and pronounced woe over those who cared more about their status and comfort than others' needs. He warned his listeners that fake kin permeated the crowd. Their selfish actions betrayed a false faith. They will not see heaven but be separated from God. This warning echoes throughout Matthew's gospel and should inspire healthy fear of King Jesus.

Creativity in Presentation

For a simple illustration of the parable, consider dividing a small group of people from the congregation into two teams: Team Sheep and Team Goats. You can have them on either side of the stage or sitting in two different rows at the front of the sanctuary. For dramatic effect, you can point to someone from Team Sheep and say, "Good job. You saw me limping and provided me support." Then point to another and say, "Good job, you knew I hadn't eaten for a day and brought me a sandwich." Come up with as many examples as people on Team Sheep. Verbally validate each one. Once you're finished, say, "Well done, Team Sheep. You saw your kin and served your King. Join me in heaven."

After commending Team Sheep, turn to Team Goats and lament their omissions. Shake your head, make a sad face, and say, "Too bad. I limped right past you and you didn't support me." "Too bad. My stomach growled while I was beside you and you didn't share your sandwich." Proceed through all the same service opportunities as you mentioned for Team Sheep but point out their omission. At the end say, "Too bad, Team Goats. You overlooked your kin and did not care for your King. Eternal gloom awaits you."

Many faith-based organizations help provide networks of care for church people in tough circumstances. Consider highlighting one of the ministries listed below by featuring resources from its website or personal testimony from someone in your church who has served with them or benefited from their ministry. If your church has other programs to care for those in need, you might simply share a story of benevolence.

Faith-based Care Ministries

Stephen Ministries (https://www.stephenministries.org) trains people in the church to minister to others in crisis through prayer, counsel, and empathetic presence.

Hands of Hope Care Communities (https://handsofhopein.org/care-communities) surrounds foster parents with a network of caregivers who encourage them by prayer, providing food, and regular check-ins.

Habitat for Humanity (www.habitat.org) builds "decent, affordable homes" around the world. Habitat is a "hand-up," not a "hand-out," meaning the people served have skin in the game. They do construction, pay their mortgage, and undergo financial and (in some locations) spiritual counseling with a mentor.

As a special encouragement to your congregation, consider celebrating recent moments where you caught people serving. (Note: Elementary school teachers use this tactic to reinforce good behavior with their kids. Why not try it at church?) While you do not want to come across as cheesy or as though you are performing surveillance on your church, do not be shy about praising positive examples of care. If you have a picture of the person caring, the illustration will be more effective. You could even hand out "Caring Sheep Certificates."

Congratulations!
We caught you doing good!

CARING SHEEP AWARD
for kin and King

Finally, do not forget Keith Green's classic song "The Sheep and the Goats." It may be too long to fit into your sermon, but as a bonus feature to older Christians in your congregation, they may appreciate the reference. You can quickly find this on YouTube, Spotify, or iTunes.

In the end, be sure your sermon stresses that Jesus shows the tie between faith, ethics, and the treatment of his own. Indeed, care for our kin is care for the King.

- King Jesus puts people in their place (25:31–33).
- King Jesus commends those who cared (25:34–40).
- King Jesus condemns those who did not care (25:41–46).

DISCUSSION QUESTIONS

1. How do the images of sheep and goats fit into the larger biblical narrative?
2. Why did Jesus focus on care for the faith community rather than all humanity?
3. Can this passage support greater humanitarian efforts? Explain.
4. How does it help for us to know that Jesus has solidarity with us? Be specific.
5. What does it look like to balance personal care with communal care? Moreover, why is it important to care as a community, rather than relying on individuals?
6. How does your church excel at caring for its own? How do you celebrate this?

Matthew 26:1–35

EXEGETICAL IDEA

Prepared for death by an anointing and explaining that his sacrificial death was inaugurating a covenant dealing with sin and forgiveness, Jesus predicted betrayal and denial.

THEOLOGICAL FOCUS

Jesus prepares his disciples for his death by explaining what it means.

PREACHING IDEA

Godless plots cannot stop God's plan.

PREACHING POINTERS

On the heels of his final discourse, Jesus predicted his death again. In a dramatic series of stories, Matthew detailed the religious leaders' secret plot to kill Jesus, Jesus's anointing with oil by a woman in Bethany, Judas's betrayal, the inaugural communion meal, and Peter's bold claim of faith followed by Jesus's prediction of repeated denial. These responses to Jesus displayed a range of responses to Jesus likely common in Matthew's day—from faithful to confused to fed up to opposed. Even more central to the narrative than how people responded to Jesus was what he taught about salvation. In a novel interpretation of the Passover meal, he set his death—broken body and poured-out blood—as pivotal to the new covenant promise of forgiveness. Matthew's audience would have appreciated the symbolism of the Lord's Table and weight of Jesus's sacrifice.

God's plans are not relegated to days long past. He controls yesterday, today, and tomorrow. His purposes will prevail. His redemptive aims will not be waylaid by global threats like AI, political forces, economic upheaval, or rival religions. Nor will our pathetic grasping for autonomy ever overthrow God. All efforts to redefine morality, identity, and reality are "plots that will fail" (Ps. 2:1). Fortunately, God's plan included provision for our godless plots. Jesus gave his life—his broken body and blood poured out—to secure our forgiveness. This sermon reminds us that godless plots cannot stop God's plan.

JESUS PREDICTS BETRAYAL AND DENIAL (26:1–35)

LITERARY STRUCTURE AND THEMES (26:1–35)

This unit involves several distinct scenes. It begins with a series of events two days before Passover. First is the framing of the meal to come, by the leadership's desire to kill Jesus (Matt. 26:1–5). Matthew has more detail than Mark 14:1–2. His addition is the note about the plot from Caiaphas's home. There was no opening to arrest Jesus yet. But one was about to come. Then there was a woman's anointing of Jesus, an act not appreciated by the disciples (Matt. 26:6–13). The act led to Judas's betrayal (Matt. 26:14–16). When Passover itself approached, Jesus told the disciples to prepare for the Passover meal, at which he announced the coming betrayal, a betrayal Judas denied (Matt. 26:17–25). The symbolism of Jesus's death in the Last Supper came next (Matt. 26:26–30). This was followed by a prediction of scattering and denials as they moved to the Mount of Olives, a prediction Peter and the disciples challenged (Matt. 26:31–35). The pressure of coming events was mounting. The disciples had no clue about the pressure that lay ahead.

There is extensive overlap in this material with Mark 14:1–31 and Luke 22:1–38. Slight variations in the passage will be noted in the exposition.

The unit contains various pronouncements of Jesus tied to symbolic events. Two symbolic events are most prominent: the woman's anointing of Jesus and the meal's bread and wine. Both pointed to Jesus's coming death, showing the unit's central theme. In each case, explanations served as commentary on the events and the meaning they would possess.

Another tension in the unit involves the leaders' desire to kill Jesus without them having a way to get there, because of his popularity. That situation was resolved by Judas's betrayal. Now not only did the leadership have a way forward but there was a buffer on who would be to blame. The catalyst for the arrest now was one of Jesus's own, giving them a way to say they had simply been responding to issues raised for them. Before the opportunity opened for this option, they simply planned carefully, not wanting to cause a riot. Jesus knew his days were numbered. The unit's opening scene is built around this contrast.

The third key theme has to do with what the disciples lacked in terms of understanding and courage. They were not prepared for what was coming, thinking their support of Jesus was solid when it was not yet there. Peter pictured this theme most of all. By the time Jesus went to his death, Jesus was all alone.

The unit is mostly built on an alternation between what Jesus was doing and what those opposed to him were planning (Jesus: Matt. 26:1–2, 6–13, 17–19, 26–46; Enemies: Matt. 26:3–5, 14–16, 20–25).

EXPOSITION (26:1–35)

We enter the events of the Passion more directly with this scene. Few things are as important to the identity and foundation of the church as Jesus's death. Matthew works through these events with care and some detail. The unit is full of contrasts: the woman's sensitivity compared with the betrayal of Judas and Peter's false confidence. Several passages are unique to Matthew in these final chapters that go through the crucifixion and resurrection (Matt. 27:3–10, 19, 24–25, 43, 51b–53, 62–66; Culpepper 2021, 502, for the entire section). These events fulfill Scripture even as he dies shedding innocent blood (Matt. 26:54, 56; 27:4, 6–8, 19, 24–25). However, nothing is as important as the meaning of Jesus's death and his own comments about its approach. This is a sacrifice for sin that will open the door to forgiveness and establish the arrival of the new covenant with its benefit of forgiveness (Matt. 26:26–29). Jesus also shows his authority by taking an event tied to Passover and changing all of its core imagery to look toward a new foundational event. Even as Jesus headed for death, his authority is prominent. Christological implications reside in this explanatory act, for who has the authority to take a divinely sanctioned liturgy and develop it in fresh ways? The move shows his qualification to be the offering that will open up covenant promises and be the source of blessing to those who embrace what he has done.

Prepared for death by an anointing, and then explaining that his sacrificial death was inaugurating a covenant dealing with sin and forgiveness, Jesus predicted betrayal and denial.

26:1–2. According to his custom, Matthew noted the completion of the discourse, "When Jesus had finished saying all these things" (Matt. 7:28; 11:1; 13:53; 19:1). Matthew moved into the final events of the Passion Week. There might be an allusion to Deuteronomy 32:45 here in speaking of completing his words, picturing Jesus as a second Moses (Osborne 2010, 944).

Jesus now announced his coming betrayal two days before the Passover (Mark 14:1–2; Luke 22:1; 1 Cor. 5:7). Lambs were slaughtered on 14 Nisan and the meal was consumed on 15 Nisan with days reckoned from sundown to sundown, if Jewish patterns were followed. He had predicted the Son of Man would be handed over to be crucified (Matt. 16:21; 17:22–23; 20:18–19). Now he states this in the present tense (παραδίδοται). Jesus is being handed over to be crucified. There was no remark about vindication in resurrection here. Matthew is focused on Jesus's approaching death.

Passover and Unleavened Bread were celebrated together, with the entire feast being known as Passover (Exod. 12:1–27, 42; Lev. 23:5–6; note the juxtaposition in Num. 28:16–17). This celebrated the freeing of Israel from Egypt. We were still on Tuesday here, except for the repositioned event of Jesus's anointing (see Matt. 26:6–7). Jesus was announcing he knew what lay just ahead.

Passover Tied to the Seven-Day Feast That Follows (Unleavened Bread)

Numbers 28:16–17: "On the fourteenth day of the first month is the Lord's Passover. And on the fifteenth day of this month is the festival. For seven days bread made without yeast must be eaten."

26:3–5. These verses have details that Mark 14:1–2 and Luke 22:1–2 lack. They place the plan to get Jesus in the high priest's courtyard. There had been a desire to get Jesus for some time (Matt. 12:14; 22:15), but recent events, like the temple cleansing, had forced matters to a more serious level. The leaders were plotting to arrest Jesus secretly and kill him. The plot is characterized as rooted in stealth and deceit (BDAG s.v. "δόλος" 256). This might suggest an unpardonable act, making the charge serious (Exod. 21:14; Culpepper 2021, 504). Chief priests and elders are noted but not the Pharisees. This was the same group that challenged Jesus in Matthew 21:23. Pharisees are only noted one more time, in Matthew 27:62. It was now the religious aristocracy that was in charge.

The juxtaposition with Matthew 26:1–2 showed that Jesus knew what was coming, while the leaders did not. Jesus's murder was planned at the house of the highest Jewish religious leader, Caiaphas, who had been high priest from A.D. 18 and would serve until A.D. 36 (Josephus, *A.J.* 18.35, 95). Pilate appointed him high priest every year he ruled for Rome over Judea. Caiaphas served longer than any other high priest of the century (France 2007, 971). The language of being gathered against Jesus echoes Psalm 2:2 (Acts 4:24–28), while the plotting may look to Psalm 31:13 and the complaint of the righteous sufferer (Osborne 2010, 946). Caiaphas's ossuary was discovered in 1990 and is on display at the Shrine of the Book in Jerusalem (Davies and Allison 1997, 439).

The current obstacle was the feast time as an arrest might provoke the crowd's reaction. The leaders wished to avoid a riot scenario, which might have triggered a Roman reaction. Matthew 27:24 has Pilate also concerned about a possible riot. The betrayal by Judas allowed them to act and go in a fresh direction (Matt. 26:14–16, 47–56). There is irony that during the feast time celebrating the nation's freedom, the leaders contemplated slaying the one God had sent to complete that freedom.

26:6–7. Jesus was staying in Bethany for the feast. Bethany was two miles east of Jerusalem on the other side of the Mount of Olives, where many festal pilgrims would stay. Jerusalem's population would triple or even quadruple during feast time to around 200,000. John 12:1–8 places the event on the previous Saturday night. Matthew has moved it here topically to tie it to the final meal to come (Blomberg 1992, 384).

Jesus was at the home of Simon the leper, yet another indication of Jesus spending time with those on society's fringe. Simon would have been healed of that disease by now or else association would not have been possible.

During the meal, a woman came with an expensive, long necked alabaster jar carrying expensive perfume. She anointed Jesus's head. The act triggered a reaction from the disciples. It was common to anoint a guest with oil at special occasions to add a positive sense of smell to the banquet, but her use of expensive perfume from a jar that once opened then required its use was far more than what would normally take place (Keener 2009, 618). Mark 14:3 and John 12:3 tell us this was nard. Mark 14:5 notes that the perfume cost three hundred denarii, or a year's wage (Wilkins 2004, 829). The act involved special recognition of Jesus. Was it intended as a regal anointing (1 Sam. 9:16; 2 Kings 9:6)? It is possible, but the text does not put it in those terms.

This event is like one described in Luke 7:36–50, but this was not the same event, because that Lucan one was tied to the home of a Pharisee and took place outside of Jerusalem (Evans 2012, 425). Luke's anointing involved the feet and not the head. Luke's theme was forgiveness for the woman, not Jesus's burial. The parallels to this event are Mark 14:3–9 and John 12:1–8; the latter tells us the woman's name was Mary, sister of Martha and Lazarus (John 12:3). John also places the meal in Bethany, where Lazarus lived. John notes that Jesus came to Bethany six days before the Passover (John 12:1), so he collapsed the time frame by moving directly to the meal that came a few days later (John 12:2). How or if Lazarus was related to Simon is not stated. Had John simply noted the most prominent member of those who attended?

26:8–9. The disciples complained that this was a waste of resources. They were indignant (BDAG s.v. "ἀγανακτέω" 5). The perfume could have been sold, and the money could have helped the poor (Mark 14:4b–5a). Alms for the poor at Passover was common *(m. Pesaḥ.* 10:1).

Public Charity on the Passover

Mishnah, *Pesaḥim* 10:1: "On the eve of Passover from just before the afternoon's daily whole offering, a person should not eat, until it gets dark. And even the poorest Israelite should not eat until he reclines at his table. And they should provide him with no fewer than four cups of wine, and even if [the funds] come from public charity."

26:10–13. Jesus heard of the disciples' complaint and responded with commendation for the woman's action. John 12:4–6 has Judas lead the complaining. Mark 14:5 has them speaking harshly to the woman. Jesus asked why they were troubling the woman. Her act was one of good service to Jesus. The poor would always be around and should be helped (Deut. 15:11), but Jesus was about to depart (Mark 14:7). The allusion to Deuteronomy is important, for the context there makes it clear the poor should be taken care of; Jesus was not indifferently stating that the poor would always be with us.

She had acted in this special moment. She was anointing him for burial (Mark 14:8). What she had done would be recalled and acknowledged wherever the gospel was preached (Mark 14:9). Interestingly, Matthew does not mention several women who went to Jesus's tomb to anoint him, unlike Mark 16:1 (Matthew's list plus Salome) or Luke 24:10 (Matthew's list plus Joanna and several other women), referring only to Mary Magdalene and the other Mary who came only to visit the tomb.

This was the first of many scenes in the last week where the women are seen as more sensitive than the male disciples (Keener 2009, 617; Matt. 26:7; 27:61; 28:1). This woman's act stands in stark contrast to the betrayal of Judas to follow. She sacrificed much for Jesus, while Judas accepted a small sum to betray him.

The disciples would slip up repeatedly in these final moments as we have Judas's act, Peter's failure, the disciples sleeping at Gethsemane, and their scattering on Jesus's arrest. However, Judas's act was by far the worst of the responses. Judas's act was similar to Peter's denials, but with one big difference. Judas had a failure of heart, while Peter's was a failure only of nerve.

26:14–16. Judas was obviously displeased with Jesus's act of allowing the woman to anoint him (Mark 14:10–11; Luke 22:3–6; especially John 12:4–6). He went to the chief priests and offered to hand Jesus over, to betray him. He asked what their price was. Thirty pieces of silver were set out. One piece of silver was four denarii, so this was 120 denarii, equal to about four to five months of labor as it was twenty weeks of work. Mention of the amount of money is only in Matthew, as is the remark that Judas asked for money. Also, the apparent giving of the money at this point or sometime just thereafter is a unique note of Matthew's. It is somewhat unusual for Matthew to have more detail, but in the recording of the last week this becomes more common. The other gospels mention only that money was involved. Thirty shekels was the price for a slave who was gored by an ox (Exod. 21:32) and was spoken of with sarcasm by Zechariah 11:12–13 as the price for God, with the money tossed at the potter in the temple (Turner 2008, 621). Jesus was worth no more than a slave, as he died at a price that was tied to the price for God's rejected shepherd in Zechariah 11:4–14 (Davies and Allison 1997, 452; France 2007, 978). Later in Zechariah this one is referred to as one who was looked upon and pierced. This Zechariah passage describes the nation's unfaithful treatment of God and is presented as tragic, like one lamenting for an only son (Zech. 12:10). Zechariah 13:7 is cited in Matthew 26:31 of Jesus. With Psalm 118:22 and Isaiah 53, this sequence of chapters in Zechariah is another set of key texts about the suffering of God and his chosen one. Matthew was stacking up prophetic texts that pointed to God's plan.

It was interesting that Matthew has details about the money. This was a concern that fit the gospel writer's background as a tax collector.

Judas now looked for the opportune moment to betray Jesus. This allowed the leaders to move against Jesus during the feast and gave them a reason to suggest that the initiative for this effort came from one of Jesus's own followers. What else Judas may have told the authorities about Jesus is not specified, but it is likely other things were said as an assessment was made about the offer being genuine.

Culpepper (2021, 509) identifies three things Judas could do for the leadership: (1) give a time and place to get him, (2) identify Jesus, and (3) give them information they could use against him. In Matthew, Judas had only been named previously in 10:4.

No one knows the exact reason for Judas's turn, but he may have become dismayed with a Jesus who would suffer rather than bring immediate victory in political and military terms. France (2007, 977–78) suggests this. If so, then the irony would be that the main factor leading to Jesus's death was Judas's rejection of the key element of Jesus's suffering as unworthy of the Messiah. That which Judas apparently rejected, he facilitated. He also rejected what made the deliverance brought by the Messiah possible. Here is a picture of how deep sin can be in deceiving and bringing spiritual blindness. Luke 22:3 and John 13:2 speak of Satan moving Judas to act. John 6:70–71 calls him of the devil. John 12:6 notes Judas stole from the treasury and so shares Matthew's view of Judas's greed. The act was completed in Matthew 26:47–50. Judas's later regret led him to suicide (Matt. 27:3–10; Acts 1:18–19).

26:17–19. Now on the first day of the Feast of Unleavened Bread, the disciples wanted to know where they would hold the festival meal. In contrast to Judas, they did seek to serve Jesus. Jesus pointed them to a man they would encounter. They were to tell him that the Teacher desired to hold the Passover meal there. The remark that the time was near is another detail unique to Matthew. The remark about time probably alluded to Jesus's approaching death, not just to the time of the feast, as the point about the feast would be obvious (Osborne 2010, 863–64).

The Passover preceded the weeklong Feast of Unleavened Bread (Exod. 12:1–27; Deut. 16:1–8). The week could be referred to as Passover (Josephus, *A.J.* especially 18.29; also 2.317; 17.213; 20.106; *B.J.* 5.99). Exodus 12:18 treats the feast as a unit without naming it (Nolland 2005, 1062). The Feast of Unleavened Bread involved the use of bread with no leaven in it (Num. 9:11). The Passover meal opened the week. Normally it was family that celebrated the meal together. Here Jesus met with his extended family (Matt. 12:48–50).

Josephus on the Feast Week of Passover–Unleavened Bread

***Antiquities* 2.317:** "Whence it is that, in memory of the want we were then in, we keep a feast for eight days, which is called the feast of unleavened bread."

***Antiquities* 17.213:** "Now, upon the approach of that feast of unleavened bread which the law of their fathers had appointed for the Jews at this time, which feast is called the Passover, and is a memorial of their deliverance out of Egypt (when they offer sacrifices with great alacrity); and when they are required to slay more sacrifices in number than at any other festival."

***Antiquities* 18.29b:** "As the Jews were celebrating the feast of unleavened bread, which we call the Passover, it was customary for the priests to open the temple gates just after midnight."

***Antiquities* 20.106:** "When that feast which is called the Passover was at hand, at which time our custom is to use unleavened bread, and a great multitude was gathered together from all parts to that feast."

The Synoptics portray the meal as a Passover meal (Matt. 26:18–19; Mark 14:12, 14; Luke 22:7, 8, 11, 13, 15). Scholars discuss the nature of the meal, because in John 18:28 at Pilate's trial, the Jewish leaders are said not to want to enter Pilate's palace for fear of being defiled for the eating of the Passover meal. In addition, John 19:14 has Jesus presented on the day of preparation for the Passover, leaving an impression that the Synoptics have Jesus eat the meal before the actual feast day. John 13:1 also speaks of the time just before the Passover and then turns to the Last Supper. Some writers speak of an error one way or the other here and then choose either the Synoptics or John as correct. However, this type of resolution is not a given, since other options exist (Osborne 2010, 861–62). The options include:

(1) A general reference to Passover season may be all that is meant (an option noted in Davies and Allison 1997, 457; accepted by Wilkins 2004, 832). One had to stay clean for the entire week, so that was the concern and the entire period operated in the shadow of Passover. The reference to the meal then is simply a way to speak of being pure for the week, pointing to the start of the entire period. John's concern about the poor in John 13:29 looked to the time of alms which is given in relationship to Passover mealtime. In addition, the day of preparation may well have referred only to the special Sabbath tied to the Passover week with its requirements for cleanliness. Other solutions exist.

(2) Another view involves differing calendars (noted by Wilkins 2004, 832). The difference is a solar calendar base, as in Jubilees and used at Qumran versus the normal Jewish Judean calendar. This view is detailed in and accepted by Hoehner (1977). Morris (1992, 653–54) also prefers this option. The differing reckoning allows for an earlier start for the meal. There are questions about how widespread the use of this alternate calendar was and whether Jesus would have used it. A variation on this idea of an early meal is that the period for slaughter was extended to cover all the lambs that had to be slain on that day, so the slaughtering of lambs extended across two days as did meals associated with the Passover. If 125,000 to 200,000 worshipers were present and a lamb could feed up to twenty people, then at least 6,250 to 10,000 lambs were required for slaughter. Keener (2009, 624) suggests how many people a lamb could feed. If the number of people a lamb could feed was lower, the number of lambs needed went up and more slaughter would be required, taking more time. The number of Passover pilgrims in Jerusalem involves estimates ranging from 125,000 to 200,000. This view with the variation on the size of the event is noted in Marshall's treatment of the Last Supper and his discussion of the chronological issues tied to the event (Casey, 1997; Instone-Brewer 2001; Marshall 2009, 541–60, especially 556–57). If this general option is taken, it is this specific form of it that seems best (Bock 2012, 143–47).

(3) Another option is a Passover meal taken early or an earlier preparatory meal that was not formally a Passover but associated with it (McKnight 2005, 259–73). France (2007, 980–85) sees an early meal and also notes that movement into the evening and new day may also be in play in the difference. Keener (2009, 622–23) also sees an early meal as possible but prefers the choice that John associated the death with the Passover season, a variation of view 1.

Evidence for a Passover meal includes the mention of various characteristics, in details from the Gospels. The Passover has elements in the Synoptics that John's gospel also notes in places: a meal in Jerusalem (all Gospels), at night (Matt. 26:20; Mark 14:17; Luke 22:7, 14; John 13:2), a reclining meal that pointed to a special occasion (John 13:12), singing of hymns pointing to the Hallel psalms (Pss. 113–118) after the meal (Matt. 26:30), the presence of interpretation of elements (Synoptics), and remarks tied to giving to the poor (Matt. 26:9; John 13:29; Hagner 1995, 772–73; Osborne 2010, 961). The meal would have involved reclining on one's left elbow with head toward the table and feet back. Keener (2009, 625–26) has other Passover meal details.

Any of these numbered options might be right. Most likely is the first, a general reference to the week (with Osborne 2010, 862). We are now late into Thursday of the week. The year was either A.D. 33 or A.D. 30 (on chronological issues of what year, see Hoehner 1977, who prefers A.D. 33).

The disciples did as Jesus said. The meal was ready. This scene is told with less detail than in Mark 14:12–16 and Luke 22:7–12. In Luke, Peter and John set up the meal. Mark simply notes two were sent without naming them. They would have procured the room and prepared the bitter herbs along with the bread and wine tied to the meal. They also likely roasted the lamb.

26:20–21. Jesus showed he was aware of the plot involving Judas. On Thursday evening, Jesus reclined at the evening Passover meal with the Twelve and announced the betrayal that was to come from within their ranks. A low-lying table was placed in the middle of guests who formed a U. The key guests were at the base in the middle of the U and others reclined around the table, with the hosts usually at the key guests' right side. Such formal dining was known as the *triclinium*, which was named after the three couches known as the *triclinia*. This was a room configuration where all three couches had seating (thus the name; Osborne 2010, 964; Wilkins 2004, 834). Matthew focused on the meal with the Twelve. Whether others of the Galilean contingent were present was not said.

If the later liturgy helps us here, then the meal would have had eight steps: (1) a blessing with a first cup of wine, (2) food brought in (unleavened bread, herbs, greens, stewed fruit, and roasted lamb), (3) the question about this night being different from all others coming from a son, with the family head telling the exodus and giving praise for past and future redemption along with Hallel psalms (Pss. 113, 114, and perhaps 115), (4) a second cup of wine, (5) unleavened bread with herbs and fruit as the head of the house explained the meaning, (6) the meal proper completed before midnight, (7) a third cup of wine and the second set of Hallel psalms (perhaps Ps. 115, then Pss. 116, 117), and (8) a fourth cup of wine, which concluded the meal (with Ps. 118 sung at the conclusion; later reflected in a formalized form in *Pesaḥ.* 10—see charts at 26:22–23 and 26:29–30, below; Osborne 2010, 964; for the full array of issues tied to this feast, including discussion of the dates of these liturgical traditions, Bock and Glaser 2017).

Depiction of a U-Shaped Meal Setup.

26:22–23. The betrayal announcement deeply disturbed the disciples. The use of the verb λυπέω point to "grief" or "distress" (BDAG s.v. "λυπέω" b, 2604). They were grieved and found it hard to believe. Then two balanced exchanges took place: first with the disciples, then with Judas. One is honest, the other full of deceit (Davies and Allison 1997, 459). Mark 14:17–21 lacks an explicit conversation with Judas. Luke 22:21–23 has an even shorter summary of this exchange without naming Judas. Luke also has the exchange appear after the discussion of the elements rather than before as Matthew has it.

This betrayal announcement was not only personally troubling but a setback to their hopes. Each disciple began to deny that he would do this. Matthew used a Greek particle (μήτι) pointing to a negative reply, "Surely not I." They also replied with respect for the "Lord" (κύριε; BDAG s.v. "II. κύριος" 2bγ, 577). Jesus responded by noting someone who dipped his hand in the bowl with Jesus would betray him (John 13:26; m. *Pesaḥ.* 10.3—after dipping the lettuce in the vinegar, then came the bread). This action alluded to table fellowship and sharing bread with Jesus as a friend, but Matthew lacks the allusion to Psalm 41:9 that Mark 14:18 has. It also is Jesus's first clear signal that the betrayal was an inside job, although Matthew 10:4 had said this already as a narrator's comment. However, Jesus said it in a way that likely could point to any of them. Jesus knew who was betraying him and so did the betrayer. The rest were in the dark. As Morris (1992, 656) says, Judas had "covered his tracks."

Mishnah on the Early Portion of the Passover Meal and Dipping the Bread

***Mishnah Pesaḥim* 10:1–5** [haroset is the paste of fruit and nuts; dipping bread is in 10:3]: "10:1 On the eve of Passover from just before the afternoon's daily whole offering, a person should not eat, until it gets dark. And even the poorest Israelite should not eat until he reclines at his table. And they should provide him with no fewer than four cups of wine, and even if [the funds] come from public charity. 10:2 When they have mixed the first cup of wine—the House of Shammai say, "He says a blessing over the day, and afterward he says a blessing over the wine." And the House of Hillel say, "He says a blessing over the wine, and afterward he says a blessing over the day." 10:3 [When] they bring him [the food], he dips the lettuce [in vinegar] before he comes to the breaking of the bread. They brought him unleavened bread, lettuce, and haroset and two dishes—even though haroset is not a religious obligation. R. Eleazar b. R. Sadoq says, 'It is a religious obligation.' And in the time of the Temple they would bring before him the carcass of the Passover offering." 10:4 "They mixed for him a second cup of wine. And here the son asks his father [questions]. But if the son has not got the intelligence to do so, the father teaches him [to ask by pointing out:] 'How different is this night from all other nights! For on all other nights we eat leavened or unleavened bread. But this night all of the bread is unleavened. For on all other nights we eat diverse vegetables, but on this night, only bitter herbs. For on all other nights we eat meat which is roasted, stewed, or boiled. But this night all of the meat is roasted. For on all other nights we dip our food one time, but on this night, two times.' In accord with the intelligence of the son the father instructs him. He begins [answering the questions] with disgrace and concludes with glory, and explains [the Scriptures from], A wandering Aramean was my father." (Dt. 26:5ff) until he completes the entire section. 10:5 "Rabban Gamaliel did state, 'Whoever has not referred to these three matters connected to the Passover has not fulfilled his obligation, and these are they: Passover, unleavened bread, and bitter herbs.' Passover—because the Omnipresent passed over the houses of our forefathers in Egypt. Unleavened bread—because our forefathers were redeemed in Egypt. Bitter herbs—because the Egyptians embittered the lives of our forefathers in Egypt.' In every generation a person is duty-bound to regard himself as if he personally has gone forth from Egypt, since it is said, And you shall tell your son in that day saying, it is because of that which the Lord did for me when I came forth out of Egypt (Ex. 13:8). Therefore we are duty-bound to thank, praise, glorify, honor, exalt, extol, and bless him who did for our forefathers and for us all these miracles. He brought us forth from slavery to freedom, anguish to joy, mourning to festival, darkness to great light, subjugation to redemption, so we should say before him, Hallelujah."

26:24–25. Jesus issued a frightening woe, more frightening than the earlier woes in Matthew (Matt. 11:21; 18:7; 23:13, 15–16; 23, 25, 27, 29). He noted that the death of the Son of Man was predicted, written in the Scripture, but woe to that man who betrayed him. It would have been better for that man not to have been born (Job 3:3–26; Jer. 20:14–18; Sir. 23:14; 1 En. 38:2; Nolland 2005, 1067–68). In this context, this was a figure about judgment mixed with tragic deep regret (see chart below on Better Not Being Born). The reference to "that" man appeared on curses and bans (Lev. 17:4, 9; 20:3–5; Deut. 17:5; Davies and Allison 1997, 463). When one recalls that the Son of Man will be the judge of the world at the end, then to have betrayed him is serious business indeed. This should have been terrifying for Judas to hear, but he attempted to blunt the remark with a denial and thus go undiscovered. Jesus was probably alluding to suffering of the Servant from Isaiah 42 and 53 or to words about the rejected shepherd in Zechariah 11–14. In Jesus's remark we encounter side by side both the divine plan and the human act for which one was personally responsible.

Figure of Better Not Being Born

Sirach 23:14: "Remember your father and mother when you sit among the great, or you may forget yourself in their presence, and behave like a fool through bad habit; then you will wish that you had never been born, and you will curse the day of your birth."

1 Enoch 38:2: "When the Righteous One shall appear before the face of the righteous, those elect ones, their deeds are hung upon the Lord of the Spirits, he shall reveal light to the righteous and the elect who dwell upon the earth, where will the dwelling of the sinners be, and where the resting place of those who denied the name of the Lord of the Spirits? It would have been better for them not to have been born."

Judas was the last disciple to speak in an exchange unique to Matthew. Imagine his shock as he heard Jesus declare he knew of a betrayal. Judas issued his denial that mirrored what the other disciples had said. Matthew has Judas use the same Greek particle (μήτι) for his response of denial. There is one difference. Judas called Jesus "rabbi," not "Lord." Only Judas called Jesus "rabbi" in Matthew. Jesus responded to Judas's denial rhetorically. He simply said, "You have said it yourself." This looks like an acknowledgment of his denial and could have been heard that way. It actually is a rhetorical recognition of his deceit. Its force is, "You have said this, but. . ." The idiom reappears in Matthew 26:64 and 27:11 at Jesus's examinations by Caiaphas and Pilate. This little unit ends with that response. The comment immediately preceded the presentation of the elements of the Last Supper about Jesus's coming sacrifice. The juxtaposition was intentional and ironic. It also is powerful narration. Even though Jesus was betrayed, God's program and victory would emerge from its ashes. John 13:26–30 alone has Judas depart after the exchange, something implied by Matthew 26:47 as Judas later was in the group that arrested Jesus (Blomberg 1992, 390). Jesus went to his death knowing who was responsible for betraying him.

26:26–28. Jesus took the unleavened bread and a cup of wine. In sequence he issued a blessing and handed these elements to the Twelve. These already had symbolism in commemorating the Passover and the release from Egypt (Exod. 12:21–27; *m. Pesaḥ.* 10.4–5). The opening blessing praised God as king of the world, who gives bread to the earth. It was seen as the bread of affliction (Exod. 34:18; Deut. 16:3; Osborne 2010, 966). Jesus changed that liturgy. In each case he explained the symbolism of what was being done in relationship to what his death would involve, pulling his future sacrifice into the space of divine deliverance. In the Mishnah from the late second century A.D. there was a three-part meal: unleavened bread, bitter herbs, and the lamb, accompanied throughout by four cups of wine (Wilkins 2004, 836). We could be looking at the meal's start for the bread and the third cup for the wine, if the practice in the first century was like the slightly later Jewish tradition. Given the time gap, however, we cannot be certain of where the elements in Jesus's acts fit with the traditional meal (for details, see Bock and Glaser 2017, esp. 67–98).

The bread, long an allusion to the exodus event, now represented Jesus's body, offered in death. Jesus gave the bread for them to partake and share in. They identified with Jesus's death by the act and were to sense their connection to it. Luke 22:19 and 1 Corinthians 11:24 add "for you," making the substitution idea explicit. John 6 may allude to this act with the "I am the bread of life" discourse.

There also was a blessing with the wine. This was preceded by a prayer that thanked God, king of the world, for the fruit of the vine. It formerly looked to the blood of the lamb placed on the doorpost that allowed the tenth plague to pass over the house and the redeeming of Israel (Exod. 12:7, 13, 22–23; also Lev. 23:4–8; Num. 9:1–14; Deut. 16:1–8). With Jesus, the wine now also pictured the blood which inaugurated a covenant for the forgiveness of sins, a clear allusion to the new covenant (Isa. 53:4, 10, 12; Jer. 31:31–34; Ezek. 36:24–27; Matt. 1:21; 20:28). Culpepper's (2021, 516) suggestion that Matthew did not see a new covenant here but simply a sacrifice for sin is most unlikely. Jesus was talking about a sacrifice that would change things, as the addition of new liturgy tied to the Passover shows and the preaching of the promised kingdom arriving shows. Matthew was writing after the break this brought. Jesus was bringing a completion that itself was tied to the new covenant. So we have continuity and discontinuity together here. Matthew 9:15–17 speaks of new spiritual realities Jesus brought. This was for Israel but it also was something new as part of that new era of restoration that would extend itself to all.

Blood pictured life (Lev. 17:14) and poured out blood looked to an offering for sin (Lev. 4:7, 18, 25; 9:9; 17:11–14; Osborne 2010, 968). The reference to the many is an allusion to Isaiah 53:12, where the Servant bore sin for the many (on the significance of Isaiah 53, see Bock and Glaser 2012). The tie to forgiveness of sins in the symbolism of the wine is unique to Matthew and also may include a look back to Isaiah 53:5–6, 8, 10–12. Mark 14:24, which normally parallels Matthew, does not have this detail. Besides Isaiah 53, there is precedent for the idea of substitution through the death of the righteous in 4 Maccabees 6:28–29, where it was the death of several that was the ransom (also several in 4 Macc. 17:21–22; Nolland 2005, 1078). Jesus's death was about forgiveness and inaugurating a new era. The disciples shared Jesus's cup, showing their oneness. This also was different from the meal where each had their own cup. Linked to his coming death, they went forth together in newness of a restored spiritual life.

Substitution in Death in 4 Maccabees

4 Maccabees 6:28–29: "Be merciful to your people and let our punishment be a satisfaction on their behalf. Make my blood their purification and take my life as a ransom for theirs."

4 Maccabees 17:21–22: "The tyrant was punished and our land purified, since they became, as it were, a ransom for the sin of our nation. Through the blood of these righteous ones and through the propitiation of their death the divine providence rescued Israel, which had been shamefully treated."

This form of the presentation of the elements Matthew shares with Mark 14:22–24. The presentation of the elements in Luke 22:19–20 and 1 Corinthians 11:23–26 is slightly different, including an explicit mention of the new covenant (Jer. 31:31–34; Heb. 9:15–22; 10:29; 13:20; on the new covenant and forgiveness: Rom. 11:26–27; Heb. 10:16–19). Isaiah's covenant promises may also be alluded to here from Isaiah 42:6; 49:8–10; and 55:3 (Davies and Allison 1997, 473). Jesus's changing of the motifs for a commanded meal showed his authority. Who had such authority to change official Torah liturgy in terms of its core content, and what did that say about Jesus? The move was a bold one. The first picture of salvation from the exodus now was linked to the second salvation that Jesus brought for the kingdom. The phrase "blood of the covenant" looked at Exodus 24:8 and the establishment of the first covenant (also Zech. 9:11). No wonder the Last Supper became the basis for the Lord's Table.

Huge debates have set in over how to take the "is" in sayings about the elements. Is it about identity, association, or representation? Nothing here tells us the answer to that question, except that the nature of the Passover parallels points to some level of symbolic representation, not identification. Keener (2009, 630) discusses the historical roots of this tradition tied to Jesus (also in much detail: Marshall 2009, 562–76).

26:29–30. Jesus then predicted he would not drink of wine again until all was fulfilled in the kingdom of his Father (Mark 14:25; Luke 22:18—except said before the elements were distributed). The detail is important as it promised and affirmed a sure vindication after Jesus was crucified (Matt. 8:11; 22:2; 25:10; Rev. 19:7–9). It looked ahead to after the sacrifice. This is part of the reason the Lord's Supper looks to Jesus's return as it now anticipates a later meal and time to come. The Supper in the church does not fulfill this idea but looks forward to it ("proclaim the Lord's death until he comes" in 1 Cor. 11:26b). The meal looked to the vindication his death would activate. This promise is not about the Lord's Table but to what that church commemoration points to, the banquet image of the consummation, plenty, and the drinking of wine at that time (Gen. 49:11–12; Isa. 25:6; 55:1–2; Joel 2:24; 3:18; Amos 9:13; 1 En. 10:19; 2 Bar. 29:5–8; Davies and Allison 1997, 476).

Jewish Texts on the Plenty of the End Era

1 Enoch 10:19: "And they shall plant pleasant trees upon her vines. And he who plants a vine upon her will produce wine for plenitude. And every seed that is sown on her, one measure will yield a thousand (measures) and one measure of olives will yield ten measures of presses of oil."

2 Baruch 29:5–8: "The earth will also yield fruits ten thousandfold. And on one vine will be a thousand branches, and one branch will produce a thousand clusters, and one cluster will produce a thousand grapes, and one grape will produce a cor of wine. And those who are hungry will enjoy themselves and they will, moreover, see marvels every day. For winds will go out in front of me every morning to bring the fragrance of aromatic fruits and clouds at the end of the day to distill the dew of health. And it will happen at that time that the treasury of manna will come down again from on high, and they will eat of it in those years because these are they who will have arrived at the consummation of time."

They departed singing hymns. The Hallel psalms (Pss. 113–118) were normally sung in association with this meal (in the liturgy the singing was split into two portions). Psalm 113 was sung over the meal by all, while Psalm 114 was sung by some then as well. The remainder were sung at the end (*m. Pesaḥ.* 10.6–7; France 2007, 996). This reflected traditional practice in singing the latter part of the Hallel. Jesus and his disciples came to the Mount of Olives. This is another example of a Matthean transition verse; it looks back and forward at one time. There may be an allusion to 2 Samuel 15:30, where David wept on the Mount of Olives at the opposition to him from Ahithophel (Nolland 2005, 1088).

Singing the Hallel and the Rest of the Passover

Mishnah, *Pesaḥim* 10:6–9 [Hallel in 10:6–7]: "10:6 To what point does one say [Hallel]? The House of Shammai say, 'To A joyful mother of children (Ps. 113:9).' And the House of Hillel say, 'To A flint-stone into a springing well (Ps. 114:8).' And he concludes with [a formula of] Redemption. R. Tarfon says, '" . . . who redeemed us and redeemed our forefathers from Egypt." "And he did not say a concluding benediction."' R. Aqiba says, '". . . So, Lord, our God, and God of our fathers, bring us in peace to other appointed times and festivals, rejoicing in the rebuilding of your city and joyful in your Temple worship, where may we eat of the animal sacrifices and Passover offerings,'" etc., up to, "'Blessed are you, Lord, who has redeemed Israel."' 10:7 They mixed the third cup for him. He says a blessing for his food. And at the fourth cup, he completes the Hallel-Psalms and after it he says the grace of song. Between these several cups of wine, if he wants to drink more wine, he may do so. But between the third and the fourth cup of wine, he may not drink more wine. 10:8 And after the Passover meal they do not conclude with dainties. If some of those present fell asleep, they may eat again. But if all fell asleep, they may not eat again. R. Yose says, 'If they merely drowsed, they may eat again, but if they fell into a deep sleep, they may not eat again.' 10:9 The Passover offering after midnight [when it may not be eaten any longer] imparts uncleanness to hands. That which has been made refuse or remnant impart uncleanness to the hands. 'If one has said the blessing for the Passover offering, he renders unnecessary a blessing over any other animal sacrifice that he may eat. If he said a blessing over any other animal sacrifice that he ate, he has not made unnecessary a blessing over the Passover offering,' the words of R. Ishmael. R. Aqiba says, 'This one doesn't render that unnecessary, and that one doesn't render this unnecessary.'"

26:31–32. Jesus now predicted the disciples' defection from the pressure of the approaching death (Mark 14:27–31; Luke 22:40). He said they will all stumble or fall because of him. The scene compared with Judas's failure in that it was similar but less severe (Blomberg 1992, 392–93). The disciples will have a failure of nerve, not one of heart like Judas. Peter's turning back to serve Jesus after the denials showed where his heart was.

The verb σκανδαλίζω is used to picture a temporary defection or lack of faith (BDAG s.v. "σκανδαλίζω" 1b, 926; Matt. 11:6). They will "stumble." Jesus cited Zechariah 13:7 in a form closer to the Hebrew. The shepherd will be struck and the sheep will be scattered. An imperative "to strike" in Zechariah is now a future tense to point to the prediction. In Zechariah, the person who struck the shepherd was God as he exercised a judgment, so here the plan of God was proceeding as Jesus would be judged for them, as the Supper pointed out, but its initial effect on the disciples would cause them to flee (Nolland 2005, 1089). In Zechariah the shepherd was struck and the sheep scattered. The one struck was likely a Davidic king there (Davies and Allison 1997, 485 n. 18). Qumran read the text eschatologically, much like Jesus alluded to it here (CD 19.5–9; Keener 2009, 635). The Zechariah text is part of a longer passage picturing the rejection of God and his message. This section of Zechariah 9–14 is one of the key set of texts about rejection the New Testament uses to discuss Jesus's suffering. Matthew especially appeals to this material (Matt. 21:4–5 uses Zech. 9:9–10; Matt. 24:30 uses Zech. 12:10–14; Matt. 27:3–10 uses Zech. 11:12–13; France 2007, 998). Jesus said the scattering of described in the Zechariah 13:7 text was about to take place.

The disciples would cower at the pressure of persecution for a brief time, but all was not lost. Learning from failure can breed success. Jesus predicted his vindication again, noting he would be raised. He instructed them to go to Galilee to meet him there. Jesus's remark showed that their scattering, as well as their failure, would be temporary. Restoration would follow. This direction was repeated by angels in Matthew 28:7 and by Jesus in Matthew 28:10. The appearance is noted in Matthew 28:16–20, the closing scene of the gospel. Luke has appearances in Jerusalem and has the disciples staying there. Given they had traveled down as pilgrims not intending to stay, a trip back to Galilee to get more personal materials for a longer stay in Judea is not surprising.

26:33–35. Peter then had an exchange with Jesus about his fidelity that led all the disciples to declare they would not abandon Jesus. It was Peter's first word since Matthew 19:27 about leaving all to follow Jesus. Once again Jesus was portrayed as knowing events better than those around him. The disciples' false confidence would be exposed by the pressure of the events. Peter denied he would ever deny Jesus using an emphatic οὐδέποτε. The others might stumble, but he would not. The force is "no way" would he fail Jesus. The verb used here is one for defection (BDAG s.v. "σκανδαλίζω" 926). Peter declared he would not defect; he would remain loyal.

Jesus responded that there would be a denial before morning, before the cock crowed to note the dawn (Mark 14:30; Luke 22:34; John 13:38). Such crowing could start in the late evening after midnight and become heightened with dawn. The Roman watch from 3 a.m. to dawn was called "cockcrow" (Osborne 2010, 977). Keener (2009, 635) details the cultural background, noting by morning was most likely the point (3 Macc. 5:23). In fact, three times Peter would deny Jesus by morning. Mark 14:30 has the cock crowing twice as a part of Jesus's prediction.

Peter denied the prediction. He was "crowing like a proud cock" (Davies and Allison 1997, 487). He said he would even be ready to die with Jesus and that he absolutely would not deny him (Mark 14:31; Luke 22:33; John 13:37). Again there was an emphatic denial using οὐ μή. Interestingly, Peter had gone from denying that Jesus would suffer after the confession near Caesarea Philippi to saying he would suffer to the end with Jesus. He was wrong on both counts, though Peter came to be right on the second point later in his life. He would learn from his failure. The initial failure was so stark and embarrassing that it is unlikely to have been made up by the church. The unusual honesty of the account shows the scene's historical character.

The disciples repeated the same claim. They still had much to learn about what they were capable of if they went their own way and did not depend on God. Jesus knew better than they did where they were. This was a tough lesson the disciples had to learn so they would be more dependent on God and not assume they would do well on their own.

Jesus's awareness of events was highlighted as he had predicted the betrayal of Judas and that was fulfilled in Matthew 26:14–16 and 26:47–50 (Osborne 2010, 975–76). He had said the Twelve would scatter and that was realized in Matthew 26:56. He had said Peter would deny him and that took place in Matthew 26:69–75. Jesus suffered alone at God's direction. He knew where he was headed. He went alone, but he went for many.

THEOLOGICAL FOCUS

The exegetical idea (prepared for death by an anointing and explaining that his sacrificial death was inaugurating a covenant dealing with sin and forgiveness, Jesus predicted betrayal and denial) leads to this theological focus: Jesus prepares his disciples for his death by explaining what it means.

Amid several scenes pointing to his death, Jesus noted the disciples would abandon him, even as he went to die on their behalf after a betrayal by one of his own.

The passion began by noting the resolution of a narrative tension in Matthew. The opposition of the Jewish leaders resulted in their resolve to kill Jesus. He knew this was coming very soon. At a meal where a woman anointed him, he told the disciples that she was anointing him for his approaching death. God's program was moving forward with Jesus aware of each step. He faced death knowing what it meant.

The life of Jesus caused Judas to betray Jesus. He arranged to hand Jesus over and began to look for a good time to do it. Meanwhile, the Passover approached and Jesus told the disciples to prepare for that special meal. Little did they realize it would be their last time together during this phase of Jesus's ministry. Jesus announced the coming betrayal at the meal. All denied involvement, including Judas. Then Jesus explained that the death that betrayal precipitated would also be an offering for the many, a shedding of blood for the covenant and forgiveness of sins. Allusions to Isaiah 53 were present in the mention of the many. The new covenant was coming. Jesus would not celebrate again with wine until all was completed.

Despite all the remarks about the approaching death, the disciples were still not prepared for it. When Jesus predicted that the shepherd would be struck and the sheep scattered, Peter claimed he would never forsake Jesus. Jesus predicted his denials, but Peter insisted that he was willing to die with Jesus. The disciples echoed his remarks. Jesus knew better. When Jesus faced arrest, they would all scatter or deny Jesus.

This juxtaposition of God's plan, Jesus's awareness, and the disciples' shortcomings dominate this unit. The disciples had much to learn as they sought to overcome the pressure Jesus's rejection placed on them. They assumed they would do well. They needed to realize how tough it would be and to depend more on God's strength. It is a lesson they would learn after the resurrection, courtesy of the Spirit Jesus would supply to them, as the book of Acts shows. No longer cowering in the face of opposition, they boldly would declare who Jesus was in the face of rejection (Acts 2–4, esp. 4:23–31).

The second key theological theme is the meaning of Jesus's death vividly portrayed in the change of Passover imagery from God delivering Israel from Egypt into imagery about Jesus's act to save. The very act shows the depth of Jesus's authority. Who has the right to change such core symbolism? By doing so, Jesus gave commentary to his death as a sacrifice opening up the new covenant and forgiveness of sins. In taking the penalty and opening a new era, salvation now comes. That salvation was promised long ago. The rejection of the shepherd was seen in Zechariah 13. God will judge the shepherd, but he is doing it for the sake of delivering many. If Jesus can die for us, then surely his disciples should be faithful to him. In many ways, that is the message of the rest of the New Testament. Come to the one God has provided forgiveness through, and with a dependent faith, be faithful to him.

PREACHING AND TEACHING STRATEGIES

Exegetical and Theological Synthesis

The exegetical section highlights the tragic nature of God's plan. Jesus will die. He will die for the sins of the world. God determined the timing of this death. From the opening pericope in his gospel, Matthew emphasized God's sovereignty. Jesus's virgin birth fulfilled prophecy. Likewise, his escape from Herod's deadly plot showed God's providential hand. His family plans would not be thwarted. Jesus would live to die in God's time to pay for our sins. God's plan prevails.

What this passage contributes to Matthew's narrative is a series of contrasting responses to God's surprising salvation plan. They include scheming, anointing, betraying, debating, and bold claims of loyalty. Each response invites readers of Matthew's gospel to ask: "How do I respond to God's plan, especially when it entails suffering?" Even though Jesus's symbolic meal and ensuing sacrifice stand at the center of this section, they prompt us to reflect on the purity of our faith and the need for God's forgiveness.

Preaching Idea

Godless plots cannot stop God's plan.

Contemporary Connections

What does it mean?

"Godless plots" is shorthand for any negative response to God's sovereignty. Such plots are manifold. They are evident in outright rejection of God's moral authority. We saw this in the garden of Eden when Adam and Eve took from the Tree of Knowledge of Good and Evil (Gen. 3). We saw it in Babel when builders wanted to make a tower to heaven and a name for themselves (Gen. 11). We see examples of this today in our rampant consumerism, expressive individualism, racial violence, injustice, greed, and sexual indulgence.

However, godless plots also include the more subtle ways we edge God out of our lives. We make big decisions without praying. We plan our schedule around vacation, sports, and home improvements. We view church involvement as extracurricular to our lives. If we are honest, much of our plotting revolves around personal comfort, not God's plan.

Finally, God's plan includes what he prescribes (i.e., moral will) and his purposes (i.e., ultimate will). And yet, sometimes God's plan makes provisions for godless plots. The death of Jesus was a case in point. Although the Father did not delight in Jesus's death, he allowed the godless plots leading to his execution happen. In fact, godless plots were central to the God's plan. This is not evidence of God's two "wills" in conflict—for God cannot be divided (Deut. 6:4); rather, God mysteriously weaves suffering into his plan (Acts 3:17–18; Rom. 5:1–5; 2 Cor. 4:17).

Is it true?

It is true that godless plots cannot stop God's plan. Stories in the Old Testament abound. God used Joseph's brothers' godless plot to save many (Gen. 50:20). Yahweh delivered Israel from Pharoah's godless rule (Exod. 1–15). Other foreign powers—Assyria, Babylon, and Persia—became props in God's plan to punish Israel. God's plan prevails over wicked human intent.

More importantly, God's plan is good. He promised peace and prosperity to Israel even while they were exiled in Babylon (Jer. 29:10–11). Even if this plan applied specifically to the nation of Israel, it reflected the character of God's heart. His plans are suffused with grace to overcome godless plots and bring his people to glory (Rom. 8:28–30).

In modern times, God can work good from many godless plots:

- A profound mother-daughter bond may arise following the parents' divorce.
- A gruesome injury may end a dream of professional sports but open a door into higher education.
- Personal experiences of racism may lead to a thriving ministry of justice.
- Years resisting unhealthy relationships may draw a lost soul to Jesus.

These examples illustrate how God's plans triumph over godless plots in this present evil age. Although we do not always see glorious resolution to godless circumstances, we cannot deny clear biblical teaching about God's sovereignty amid suffering.

Now what?

First, this passage invites us to trust God's plan. No amount of godless plotting can subvert his sovereign will. His plan will prevail. A critical element of his plan was making provision for sin through Jesus's sacrifice. We must remember this when nations rage, creation groans, and sin abounds. Sin does not get the final word. Jesus already said, "It is finished." John the apostle reminded us that "the one who is in you is greater than the one who is in the world" (1 John 4:4). We can trust bold proclamation when we confess our godless plots.

Second, we not only confess our godless plots but also renounce them. Rather than plot in vain, we should walk in obedience. In the short run, godless plots may get us fame, fortune, and the taste of satisfaction. This, however, is fleeting. In the long run, godless plots only drive us into the grave and eternally away from God. Therefore, we should quit trying to live by our own moral standards, worldly wisdom, and physical strength. Living without the input of other believers or power of prayer is godless. Such plotting is vain.

Finally, we should endure to the end. Our present struggles are not the last word of God's redemptive story. The end is coming. Jesus will return and bring justice. God will make all things new. In the meantime, we will encounter godless plots resulting in personal suffering. Both David and Jesus lamented and prayed in the face of suffering to help them endure. We should follow their example. Endurance grows from trust in God who remains in control when we cannot see it and whose plan outlasts every godless plot.

Creativity in Presentation

Because this text focuses on the Lord's Table, you could set up a reenactment of the scene with a table, pillows, food, and place settings. As you describe the meal, hold up the bread and cup, and then stress that despite the drama around the table, God's plan was to provide forgiveness of sins. If you prefer a video version of this meal, the LUMO Project has a tasteful, three-minute rendition of the reading of Matthew 26:17–30 from the ESV you can search for it online.

Anyone who studies stories knows that the best ones have a compelling narrative arc. The same applies to our lives. As the plot unfolds—the many rises and falls—the story develops. However, we do not see the overall plan until we reach the end of the story. In her TED Talk, Nancy Duart illustrates the way a good story works.[1] The most helpful part of her talk is the illustration of a story structure: rising and falling between "what is" and "what could be." Consider displaying her image and describing the valleys as "godless plots" and peaks as "God's plan." Two sample pictures are provided.

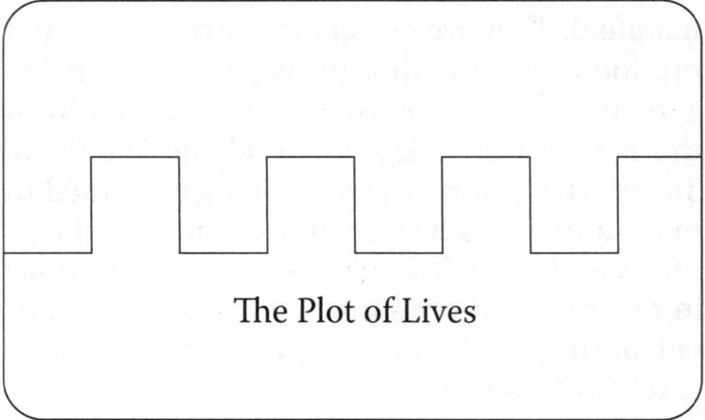

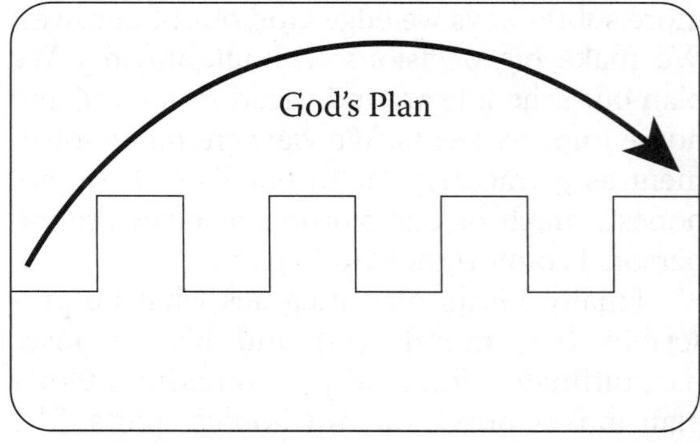

Perhaps you could share well-known stories of God's use of suffering from your life, church history, or the library of tales in your church. Keller (2015) ends every chapter in the opening section of his book about this topic with personal

1 See https://www.ted.com/talks/nancy_duarte_the_secret_structure_of_great_talks/transcript (accessed July 24, 2024).

testimonies from people he knows. They are powerful illustrations of God bringing beauty from the ashes of sickness, divorce, and physical pain. Even Keller's recurring battle with cancer became a stage for God's grace. He shared his story in a 2021 article, "Growing My Faith in the Face of Death," in *The Atlantic*.

Finally, you may return to the quotation from C. S. Lewis's *The Horse and His Boy*, cited in the creative section of Matthew 2:1–23. The climactic dialogue between Shasta and Aslan illustrates the interplay between godless plots and God's plan. In fact, you could even reference Aslan's plan in *The Silver Chair*. At the beginning of the book, he gives Jill Pole "four signs" she must remember to carry forth his plan in Narnia: (1) Eustace will meet an old friend and must greet him, (2) they must go north from Narnia and find the place of giants, (3) they must obey the writing on the stone in the ruined city, and (4) the lost prince will reveal himself by referring to the name of Aslan. Their success hinges on heeding Aslan's plan. The plot thickens when they forget Aslan's plan. We must stick to God's plan!

Regardless of your creative choices, be sure your sermon shows that Jesus prepares his disciples for his death by explaining what it means. Moreover, godless plots cannot stop God's plan.

- Jesus's opponents hatch a godless plot (26:1–5).
- A poor woman shows a costly act of love (26:6–13).
- Judas joins the godless plot against Jesus (26:14–16).
- Tensions rise around the Lord's Table (26:17–25).
- Forgiveness flows at the Lord's Table (26:26–30).
- Peter poorly predicts his future (26:31–35).

DISCUSSION QUESTIONS

1. What caused Judas to turn against Jesus? Why was he perfectly positioned to aid the religious leaders' godless plot to kill Jesus?

2. Who anointed Jesus's head with oil? What did this act mean? How does it differ from the other anointing in Luke's gospel?

3. What does the debate around the table about betrayal suggest about the disciples?

4. How did Jesus bring new meaning into the imagery of the Passover meal? How does your church observe Communion? Can you integrate it into this sermon?

5. Of the various characters and their responses to Jesus in this text, which one do you most relate to? Why?

6. How have you suffered from godless plots? Where have you been guilty of godless plotting? How have you seen God's grace transform godless plots? Be specific.

Matthew 26:36–56

EXEGETICAL IDEA

As a result of Judas's betrayal and after committing himself to God's will to accept his death, Jesus refused to fight and was arrested as a common criminal in fulfillment of Scripture.

THEOLOGICAL FOCUS

God's plan leads to Jesus's arrest and his accepting the way of God in suffering for others.

PREACHING IDEA

The higher the pressure, the harder we pray.

PREACHING POINTERS

Jesus and his disciples left the comfort of the upper room for the crucible of Gethsemane, where his predictions of suffering, betrayal, and scattered disciples would be fulfilled. He invited Peter, James, and John to join him in prayer, but they repeatedly fell asleep. In this emotionally laden scene, Matthew captures Jesus in a poignant moment of human pathos. God's "cup" brimmed with suffering; Jesus desired a different drink. Thus, he prayed, and by praying he surrendered his will to his Father's plan. Moments later, Judas arrived with an armed mob to betray Jesus. Rather than resisting arrest or calling an army of angels to his side, Jesus accepted his divine appointment to suffer while his disciples fled in the night. For the original audience, this passage underscored the contrast between Jesus's steady, surrendered life and the disciples' flighty faith.

Prayer has never lost its power or importance for God's people. Through prayer God brings healing, provides clarity, breaks strongholds, changes hearts, builds confidence, and moves the proverbial mountain. Prayer is effective. Sadly, we often take prayer for granted. We remain in a prayerless slumber until a crisis rouses us. We receive a letter from a collections agency and start praying. We wait for results from a blood test and keep praying. We watch our adult child get deployed to an unnamed location in the Middle East and intercede with intensity. Prayer not only seeks God's aid, but it also surrenders our will. This sermon teaches that the higher the pressure, the harder we pray.

JESUS IS ARRESTED AS A COMMON CRIMINAL AND DOES NOT FIGHT BACK (26:36–56)

LITERARY STRUCTURE AND THEMES (26:36–56)

This unit comes in two core parts: Jesus's prayer at Gethsemane, where he submitted to God's will to be crucified for others (Matt. 26:36–46); and the arrest of Jesus, where he went without making or permitting any trouble, showing his submission to the plan (Matt. 26:47–56).

The Gethsemane scene has three cycles. These surface at Matthew 26:39, 42, and 44. Jesus prayed each time. The disciples slept. Then there was instruction from Jesus for their failure. The threefold scheme parallels the failure of Peter's three denials (France 2007, 1002).

The arrest scene showed that Jesus and his movement were not zealots in any sense. He did nothing hostile to cause the arrest and did not fight. He even stopped his disciples from fighting and refused to call on the Father's help for rescue.

The key characterization comes in Jesus's dependence and the disciples' failure to appreciate the moment and what it required. Turner calls the disciples' response their "drowsy oblivion" (Turner 2008, 630). Jesus was ready for what was coming, but the disciples were not. Jesus looked to God in the dangerous moment, while the disciples were overcome with fatigue. Both continued a pattern of portrayal that ran through the passion events. In fact, the arrest scene ended with the disciples fleeing. They had failed to pray or be ready for the pressure when the time arose.

We observe Jesus in dependence and prayer. These are examples about how to face the rejection that often comes with going God's way. The disciples' lack of focus is the passage's negative lesson. We also see Jesus's refusal to battle for his rights.

Jesus had accepted his calling. There was no violence and no effort at a defense. This also would be a pattern in these final events. Another note in the arrest was that what was taking place fulfilled Scripture. This idea was highlighted when Jesus said it both to the disciples and then to the crowd. He said it to the crowd as he pointed out that he need not be arrested as a criminal. He had taught them daily in the temple with no violence or violation of law.

The parallels to this event appear in Mark 14:32–50 and Luke 22:39–53. The scenes are historical narratives of two key passion events: Jesus's prayer to the Father and his arrest. There are no other special forms at work.

EXPOSITION (26:36–56)

Matthew continued his narration of events leading to the cross. He contrasted how Jesus faced his calling with the failure of the disciples to grasp the moment. Jesus turned to God in prayer and dependence as he faced the moment. The disciples were too weary to pay attention. Besides narrating the events, Matthew's goal was to show how to face such a challenge. There was no defensiveness from Jesus, just trust in God.

As a result of Judas's betrayal and after committing himself to God's will to accept his death, Jesus refused to fight and was arrested as a common criminal in fulfillment of Scripture.

26:36–38. Jesus came to Gethsemane to pray (Mark 14:32). The name of the locale meant "oil press." The locale was an olive orchard. Luke

22:39 speaks only of the Mount of Olives. John 18:1 notes a garden near the Kidron Valley. We do not have any more detail as to the exact locale, so that one cannot be certain if either of the traditional locales are correct. The locale was likely close to those locations in feel, since olives grow better lower down the slope and fit being within greater Jerusalem (Wilkins 2004, 840). Jesus told the disciples to sit while he went and prayed. He took Peter and James and John with him. These were the same three who went up the mountain for the transfiguration in Matthew 17:1–13 and were witnesses to the raising of Jairus's daughter (Mark 5:37, though Matthew does not note that). Having witnessed his glory, now they were to see his suffering (Culpepper 2021, 521). The sons of Zebedee are paired in Matthew 4:18–22 and 20:20–28. Here, Jesus's distress became visible, and he discussed his state of mind with the three disciples. He described his soul as deeply grieved to the point of death. The language is from Psalm 42:6, 12 MT (= 42:11 Eng.). This is a lament psalm of a suffering righteous person. Jesus fit in that category. He asked them to remain while he went to pray. They were to stay awake.

The three terms used for Jesus's emotion are vivid (Mark 14:33–34). The first term is from the verb λύπεω, which refers to "sorrow" or "grief" (BDAG s.v. "λύπεω" 2b, 604). The second verb, ἀδημονέω, refers to "anxiety" or "distress" (BDAG s.v. "ἀδημονέω" 19). It is a rare word in the NT, appearing only here, in the parallel Mark 14:33, and then in Philippians 2:26. The third word contains an allusion to Psalm 42. It is the adjective περίλυπος, which referred to "deep sadness" or "grief" (BDAG s.v. "περίλυπος" 802). The multiplicity of terms shows how deep Jesus's pain was at this time. Besides 9:36, this is the only mention of emotion from Jesus in Matthew. Nolland (2005, 1097) notes that Matthew lacks reference to emotion where Mark has it in Mark 1:41–43 and 10:21; it is omitted in the parallels in Matthew 8:3 and 19:20.

Photo of the Traditional Site of Gethsemane, an Olive Grove.

26:39. Jesus went a little distance away. Luke 22:41 speaks of a stone's throw away. This means he was probably close enough for the three disciples to hear an outcry of anguished prayer as long as they were awake.

Opening with a sense of intimacy by calling out to God as "my Father," Jesus's prayer was in two parts: a request to let this cup pass if possible, and an acceptance to do God's will instead of his own (Mark 14:36; Luke 22:42). The prayer was simple and clear. Jesus asked if there was another way, but would accept the Father's will as he always had.

The only interpretive issue is what was referred to by the cup. Is it suffering, wrath, or both? The key texts point to a cup of wrath (Pss. 11:6; 75:8; Isa. 51:17, 22; Jer. 25:15; 49:12; Rev. 14:10; 16:19; Turner 2008, 631). It is about bearing sin and its consequences. Suffering and wrath are combined because suffering is linked to sin (Davies and Allison 1997, 497; Morris 1992, 668).

26:40–41. Jesus returned to find his three guardians asleep (Mark 14:37–38; Luke 22:45–46). In a mild rebuke, Jesus asked Peter how they could not have the strength to stay awake for an hour. The remark may well give a clue for how long Jesus prayed. At the least, it referred to a short period of time, but long enough to fail at keeping watch. It indicated Matthew was giving us a summary of the prayer's content (Osborne 2010, 980).

Jesus then told them to stay awake and pray that they did not fall into temptation. The temptation was to not be prepared to stand with Jesus (Wilkins 2004, 842), not merely about their inability to stay awake (but so Morris 1992, 670, although he allows for a broader reference). The point of keeping watch also was about standing with Jesus. Jesus knew what was coming would be difficult. He also noted that the pressure wore on the flesh and emotions. He noted how the human spirit was willing, but the flesh was weak. This, with Mark's parallel, is the only such contrast in the Synoptics. We have no reply from Peter. Jesus's remark stands alone for reflection.

26:42–43. Jesus again went to pray a second time. His prayer accepted the Father's will, noting that if the cup could not be taken away, then God's will must be done. There is a first-class condition. It presents the bypassing of the cup as not being God's will (Blomberg 1992, 396). This prayer represents an advance on the previous prayer. It showed Jesus's faithfulness in trial. Mark 14:39 simply says he prayed the same thing, while Luke does not have any mention of this second request or of the third one to come. The prayer explains the readiness to be arrested. We see Jesus's openness in prayer, even a request that was denied. Jesus engaged honestly with God, including the level of emotional distress he shared with his disciples (Blomberg 1992, 395). We also see how he obeyed (Heb. 5:7–10).

Jesus returned to find his three disciples asleep again. Their eyes were too heavy from exhaustion to stay awake. The perfect participle for their eyes being heavy pictures a condition with lingering effect, which means they were very tired. Mark 14:40 also notes they did not know how to answer him.

26:44–46. Jesus departed a third time to pray (Mark 14:41–42). Mark implies a third cycle of prayer, while Matthew is explicit about it. Jesus repeated his commitment to follow God's will, as Matthew reports he prayed the same thing again, alluding back to Matthew 26:42.

On his return, the disciples were asleep yet again. He again asked if they still were sleeping and resting. The question here parallels the question in Matthew 26:40. It was ironic. But now the time was up. The hour of betrayal was near. The Son of Man was being betrayed into the hands of sinners. Those who sought to kill Jesus were not righteous. Matthew 17:12, 22; 20:18; 26:2, 24 are earlier predictions of the Son of Man's fate. Matthew uses the verb for "betray" ten times in this chapter (Morris 1992, 671). There is pathos in this observation and in the repetition. Jesus told them to get up, so they could go and join the others. The betrayer approached. The time for the cup had come.

26:47–50a. Judas arrived with a crowd to arrest Jesus as he was speaking (Mark 14:43; Luke 22:47a). Judas knew where the disciples rested when they were in the city for feasts (Osborne 2010, 982; Matt. 26:6; John 18:2). Matthew notes again Judas was one of the Twelve to underscore the act of betrayal. With him was a large crowd sent by the chief priests and elders. These were probably the Levite temple guard and the armed auxiliary police who worked with them (Keener 2009, 640). John 18:3 and 12 refer to a cohort, which may be a way of referring to some detachment of Roman soldiers in the mix, though some see only Jews and auxiliaries in view. France (2007, 1011) says even John 18 does not refer to Roman troops. They carried swords and clubs in case there was trouble (Josephus, *B.J.* 2.176, 326). Though some object that such weapons would not be carried on the Passover, the example of suspending Sabbath rules in special circumstances also likely applied here (Keener 2009, 640; 1 Macc. 2:40–41). Given there was an attempt to surprise, these weapons were probably hidden on arrival. Still, the crowd of people probably signaled something was going on.

Breaking the Sabbath for Self-Defense

1 Maccabees 2:40–41: "And all said to their neighbors: 'If we all do as our kindred have done and refuse to fight with the Gentiles for our lives and for our ordinances, they will quickly destroy us from the earth.' So they made this decision that day: 'Let us fight against anyone who comes to attack us on the sabbath day; let us not all die as our kindred died in their hiding places.'"

Judas had told them the man he kissed would be the one to be arrested (Mark 14:44). The plan was to arrest only Jesus. Luke 22:47a simply summarizes here, saying Judas drew near to kiss him. Luke also adds uniquely Jesus's response to the approaching kiss, asking if Judas would betray the Son of Man this way. The act was necessary at night with moonlight alone and trees obscuring even that light. It was important to be quick, given they were uncertain about what would happen.

In Matthew, Judas went up to Jesus and gave the rabbi a kiss of betrayal. Mark 14:45 has Judas address Jesus as "Master." Jesus accepted the kiss, addressing Judas as friend and telling Judas to do what he was there to do, a remark unique to Matthew, as the idiom simply reads, "that for which you are here" (BDAG s.v. "ὅς" 725–26, 1bα). One supplies the verb to get the idea. Three major options are suggested: a question (why are you here?), a statement (I know why you are here), or a command (do what you have come for). A statement or command are both possible. The command is closest to the idiom (Nolland 2005, 1110; Osborne 2010, 983, opts for a statement; similar in a distinct context is John 13:27b; Blomberg 1992, 398; Culpepper 2021, 527, gives five options and opts for the question). Jesus was accepting being taken to his death and, regardless of the exact rendering, knew why Judas had come.

26:50b–54. The crowd came and laid hands on Jesus to arrest him. The act caused one of the disciples to react. Mark 14:47 has a disciple cut off the ear of the high priest's slave. Luke 22:49–51 has a disciple strike a slave of the high priest with Jesus telling them to stop and healing the ear of the wounded slave. Luke 22:36 earlier has Jesus tell the disciples they should now carry a sword, and verse 38 says they have two. They mistook the remark to be about fighting in defense. John 18:10 names the reacting disciple as Peter and the one struck as Malchus. Matthew has the reaction with more detail. The disciple struck the slave on the ear. Jesus told the disciple to take back his ("your") sword. The "your" here is singular. First, Jesus initially stopped any effort to fight back.

Second, there would be no violence. Those who lived by the sword would die by it (Prov. 22:8; Isa. 50:11, also the Targum on this verse; and Hos. 10:13 are similar in spirit). Here was proof Jesus was no threat for violence.

Third, Jesus then noted that he could call for twelve legions of angels, but he would not. A legion was six thousand soldiers, so the picture was of a huge army of 72,000-plus angels. The rhetorical force is not about the number of angels but of the size of force not to be applied. Once again, Jesus was no threat. He refused to use whatever power he had at the time.

Finally, he noted all of these events were taking place to fulfill Scripture. It had to be that he suffer. This is a generic reference to Scripture. Konradt (2020, 400–401) argues numerous texts and a theme are in view: citations from Zechariah already made in Matthew 26:31 and to be made in 27:9–10, as well as to allusions to violence against the prophets in 21:35–36 and 23:37, alongside appeals to the suffering righteous (Pss. 37:32; 22; 69; Wis. 2:10–20) and the Suffering Servant of Isaiah 52:13–53:12 and Isaiah 50:6. The inclusion of Gentiles is noted in Matthew 12:18–21 and its appeal to Isaiah 42:1–4. There was a divine plan at work. Once again Jesus acted to accept his calling to go to his death so all of this could be accomplished.

26:55–56a. Jesus now addressed the crowd and made two points (Mark 14:48–49; Luke 22:52–53). The first point was a rebuke for the hypocrisy of arresting him as a criminal. Daily he had been available, teaching in the temple, and they did not arrest him there amid the public. The term here is λῃστής, which can mean "robber" or "revolutionary" (BAGD s.v. "λῃστής" 1, 594). Jesus's point was that he had never given any indication he was a threat to public peace. Would a hostile subversive conduct himself so publicly?

The second point was that the arrest fulfilled Scripture, a point the Marcan parallel makes but Luke does not as he had noted the theme earlier in Luke 22:37 that Jesus would be reckoned as a criminal. Luke 22:53 adds the hour of darkness had come. The picture of his rejection was in view. Allusions are likely to Isaiah 53, the righteous sufferer psalms, like Psalm 22 or 69, and to Zechariah 11–14.

In sum, Jesus had three reasons for his response. Violence often led to counterviolence. God could help him if Jesus desired it. Scripture had called for his arrest and death. He was doing God's will (Keener 2009, 644).

26:56b. Bowing to the pressure and fear, the disciples all fled (Mark 14:50). Mark 15:51–52 speaks of a young man fleeing naked. Luke lacks this note about any fleeing. This scattering was just as Jesus predicted in Matthew 26:31, using Scripture from Zechariah 13:7 to make the prophecy. Jesus faced death alone, a point John shows Jesus predicted in John 16:32.

THEOLOGICAL FOCUS

The exegetical idea (as a result of Judas's betrayal and after committing himself to God's will to accept his death, Jesus refused to fight and was arrested as a common criminal in fulfillment of Scripture) shapes this theological truth: God's plan leads to Jesus's arrest and his accepting the way of God in suffering for others.

This scene is about contrasts. Jesus submitted to the Father's will as he prayed before him about what was to come. There was to be no violence, no fighting. What the divine plan and Scripture called for was the path he would walk. The disciples struggled to get this. Judas, one of the Twelve, betrayed him. The others failed to keep watch as the moment approached. They fled when Jesus was arrested. In one sense the unit is simple. Jesus, dependent on the Father and knowing the Scriptures, obediently faced death. The disciples, tired and overwhelmed, failed to respond well. Events marched ahead. Although he was their hope, Jesus was misunderstood by those who arrested him as a threat. Now Jesus faced what the narrative portrayed as an unjust death. He was an innocent and righteous sufferer on behalf of people who were slow to get what was going on. That is what sin does. Still, Jesus was in God's will. Those who arrested him were sinners showing their opposition to God's chosen one. The rest of us are spectators to what took place, but we are left with the choice of who was doing right.

PREACHING AND TEACHING STRATEGIES

Exegetical and Theological Synthesis

The exegetical section describes the depth of Jesus's emotional life. He was fully human, and the threat of God's wrath weighed heavily on him. Though the duration of his Gethsemane prayer is not specified, three cycles of surrender certainly captured the gravity of the scene. Cross-references to Luke's version (22:39–46) and exposition in Hebrews 5:7–8 emphasize Jesus's bodily suffering. The pressure led him to perspire sweat like drops of blood (Luke 22:44)! Matthew emphasized Jesus's deep sorrow. Jesus's lament reflected many of the psalms, where the righteous sufferer cried out to God in his pain.

Although sorrow is perfectly acceptable in prayer, it should not dominate our praying. Typically, psalms of lament followed a complaint with a declaration of trust. "I surrender" follows "I am sad." Our sorrow opens the door to deeper trust. If we cannot be honest with God about our feelings, we are unlikely to trust him with healing. Our God cares about our cares (Matt. 6:25–34; 1 Peter 5:7). Casting our cares on him is cathartic; it lifts the anchor of our sorrow. Then we can move forward in surrender. Then we can say, "Not my will but yours be done."

Preaching Idea

The higher the pressure, the harder we pray.

Contemporary Connections

What does it mean?

This preaching idea should be straightforward. When pressures in our lives increase, our praying should intensify. Jesus modeled this way of praying, evident in his regular prayer retreats at turning points or moments of crisis (Matt. 14:23; 26:36–46; Luke 5:16; 6:12; 9:18, 28) and his cries from the cross (Matt. 27:46, 50; Luke 23:46). Jesus's example fit with his instruction on prayer (Matt. 6:5–15; 7:7–12; Luke 11:1–13; 18:1–14).

Not only do we see Jesus praying hard in high-pressure moments, but we have also felt this pull to pray hard. College students pray harder when finals approach and their grades hang in the balance. Parents pray harder whenever their children cross a new milestone: potty training, going to preschool, baseball tryouts, going through puberty, getting a license, college, marriage, having a child. We pray harder when bad news breaks: war, terror, or suicide of a local teenager bring us to our knees. And we pray harder when bad news hits home: a sewer line breaks, the tumor is malignant, or our spouse wants a divorce.

Is it true?

High pressure should lead us to prayer; however, that is not always our first response. For many of us, high pressure provokes high performance. Instead of praying, we get to work. We try to troubleshoot our way out of the pressure. We search for solutions online or consult a friend. We spend money on products, services, or devices that will alleviate the pressure. We resolve to solve our high-pressure situation by better diet, exercise, time management, financial stewardship, or plain old grit. Prayer eludes us.

Of course, not everyone faces high pressure with such motivation. Some of us hide from it. We retreat to Netflix. We vomit our problems on social media, hoping for a lifeline. We self-medicate with sleeping pills, alcohol, or online shopping. We get defensive, make excuses, and give the pressure power over us rather than pray it away.

We cannot forget that no human is exempt from pressure. Life is hard. Hard work and hiding cannot overcome the pressures. Praying hard keeps that pressure from crushing us.

Now what?

The passage and preaching idea encourage us to follow Jesus's model of praying hard when the pressure is high. He faced betrayal, arrest, desertion, persecution, God's wrath, and death. I cannot imagine a higher-pressure situation. And prayer sustained him. Therefore, we follow his footsteps in naming the pressures, praying hard, inviting others to pray with us, and surrendering.

First, we name the pressure. We should be clear on the specific pressures facing us. If it's relational pressure, we should name the people involved. If it's work-related pressure, we should specify the situation. If it's faith-related pressure, we should name the area of our faith being affected. Often, the very act of articulating a pressure relieves it of some of its power.

Naming Pressures

- "The extra hours at work are killing me. I'm exhausted and agitated all the time. I need rest."
- "My husband criticizes everything I say or do. It's paralyzing. We need counseling."
- "My friends expect me to be on my phone all the time. Texting. Posting. Commenting. I can't keep up, and I don't want to. But I'm afraid to be left out. I don't have other friends."
- "I keep hearing at church that I should be sharing my faith. I don't know how to share it. I'm not even convinced I believe everything in my faith."
- "I have no money. Everything I make goes to bills, most of it debt. I can't get ahead."

Second, we pray hard about the pressure. Naming it begins the prayer. When we name the pressure, we first complain to God. Then we urge God to intervene. We tell him what we want or need. This is not a one-time request. Like the persistent widow in Jesus's parable (Luke 18:1–8), we grovel, beg, and persevere in our prayer. Praying hard means we pray earnestly, repeatedly, and consistently over time.

Third, we invite others to pray. Although Jesus's inner circle failed to intercede for him, this does not invalidate the importance of intercessory prayer. We need others to surround us in prayer. Paul often requested prayer in high-pressure situations (Rom. 15:30–31; Eph. 6:19–20; Col. 4:2–4; 2 Thess. 3:1–2). We should invite others to pray for us when trying to reconnect with a prodigal child, searching for a job, battling anxiety, going on a short-term mission trip, undergoing surgery, or preparing for a sermon on any given Sunday. The list of high-pressure situations provides endless opportunities to invite others to pray.

Finally, we surrender to God. All of the steps above should lead to a posture of surrender. Otherwise, naming our pressures, praying hard, and recruiting interceders merely become attempts at control. As long as we remain in control, the pressure will remain. Like Jesus did in Gethsemane, we must yield to the Father's will ("May it be done on earth as it is in heaven"). We can physically represent surrender by opening our hands, palms toward heaven, and saying to God, "Take this pressure. I surrender."

Creativity in Presentation

For this sermon, you can illustrate the danger of too much pressure with a balloon. Describe a series of high-pressure situations: a deadline at work, an argument at home, a first date, an unexpected bill. After naming each pressure, blow into the balloon. As the pressures add up, the balloon will swell to a dangerous size. Unless some pressure is released, it may burst. Let your congregation know prayer is a way to release the pressure. As you model a prayer, let out some air. (Note: For this illustration, you may want someone else to blow up the balloon. Moreover, you may substitute the balloon for an electric tea kettle that gets to a boiling point or a steamy cup of coffee—unless you open the valve of the tea kettle or remove the lid of the coffee cup, the heat will overwhelm. You need to release the pressure to let out some heat. Prayer does this.)

Paul admonished the church in Thessalonica to "pray without ceasing" (1 Thess. 5:17). Not only does this imperative undergird the 24-7 Prayer movement, but it also inspired one of the most iconic Christian shirts from my (Tim's) high school years. Beneath a black and white picture of a pair of jeans with giant holes worn through the knees was the caption "Pray Hard." Despite its cheesy design, the image has stuck with me. You can find the picture easily enough with an online search. Better yet, consider wearing a copy of the shirt, replete with torn jeans while preaching. Beware, however, some may frown upon a preacher in tattered pants. Just remind them you are a living picture of holey-ness.

Church history boasts an amazing cast of people who have prayed hard. We see earnest prayer in the early church (Acts 4:23–31; 12:5–17). We also have records of numerous Christians dedicated to praying hard in the face of pressure. Consider highlighting any of these notable figures and their prayer practice:

- George Mueller prayed for God's provision to supply needs of his orphanages and expand the gospel. Allegedly, during his lifetime he had 50,000 prayers answered.[1]
- Martin Luther, a critical voice in the Protestant Reformation, was known for praying hard. He wrote about prayer regularly and allegedly prayed for two hours a day. Prayer kept his focus on God and diverted the devil's distractions.[2]
- Evangelist D. L. Moody was known for praying hard. For example, he carried a list of one hundred friends who he daily prayed would come to know Jesus. He was a model of persistence (Staton 2022, 145–47).
- Pearle Goode is one of many women who prayed hard for Billy Graham's ministry. From 1949 to 1972 she interceded for his crusades, traveling widely and praying through the night for God's salvation.[3]
- For more than two decades, the 24-7 Prayer movement has facilitated nonstop prayer for God's global work in evangelism, justice, and renewal. They provide helpful resources for praying hard.[4]

You may add to one of these stories a testimony from someone in your life or church who has lived as a model of praying hard when the pressures are high.

Finally, you may point out the redeeming role of high pressure. On a base level, we appreciate pressure cookers for a quick meal. You might even have an Instapot or rice cooker on the stage. High pressure keeps our tires safe and sends streams of water powerful enough to clean the sides of our homes. We also know that wine comes from pressed grapes, diamonds come from carbon under pressure from the earth's core, and hydrolic pressure can lift heavy vehicles into the air with ease. For Christians, the pressure of Gethsemane created the cleansing of Golgotha.

Ultimately, you want your sermon to communicate that God's plan leads to Jesus's arrest and his accepting the way of God in suffering for others. And the higher the pressure, the harder we pray.

---

1 For a summary of Mueller's life, see: https://www.georgemuller.org/uploads/4/8/6/5/48652749/prayer-filled-life.pdf (accessed July 24, 2024).

2 For a summary of his teaching on prayer, see: https://digitalcommons.luthersem.edu/cgi/viewcontent.cgi?referer=&httpsredir=1&article=1093&context=faculty_articles#:~:text=Luther%20used%20the%20Lord's%20Prayer,and%20forthright%20conversation%20with%20God (accessed July 24, 2024).

3 For her story (and others like it), see: https://billygrahamlibrary.org/blog-womens-history-month-pearl-goode (accessed July 24, 2024).

4 See https://www.24-7prayer.com (accessed July 24, 2024).

- As pressure rises high, Jesus prays hard (26:36–46).
- As pressure comes near, Jesus stands firm (26:47–56).

DISCUSSION QUESTIONS

1. What was the "cup" Jesus prayed for his Father to take away?
2. How does Matthew describe Jesus's emotional state? What does that tell us about Jesus's human nature?
3. What "temptation" did Jesus warn his disciples about? Does their "drowsy oblivion" (Turner 2008, 630) bring you any comfort as a disciple? Explain.
4. In your own words, describe the drama of Jesus's arrest. Consider all players.
5. What does this arrest scene suggest about Jesus's authority? His character?

Matthew 26:57–75

EXEGETICAL IDEA

Alongside Peter's three denials, Jesus predicted his exaltation by God in response to a question about being the Messiah, a view the Jewish leaders took to be blasphemy.

THEOLOGICAL FOCUS

Jesus's claim to be the seated Son of Man produces a choice about him, either blasphemy or exaltation—a dispute Jesus predicts God will resolve in resurrection.

PREACHING IDEA

With God as his witness, Jesus can't lose.

PREACHING POINTERS

The godless plot of the religious leaders moved forward. Jesus stood trial before them. A parade of witnesses presented hollow claims of Jesus's subversive teaching. Then the high priest questioned Jesus directly about his messianic identity. Jesus bore witness to his unique heavenly authority: God would exalt him and seat him in heaven. In this claim, Jesus sealed his fate. The priest condemned Jesus for blasphemy. Meanwhile, his intrepid disciple, Peter, stood outside the court denying inquiries about knowing Jesus. After a third denial, the rooster crowed and Peter wept. Matthew captured the drama of this midnight mock trial. Despite the false charges and denials, Jesus stood firm knowing God was his witness. The original audience would read this section having to decide whether they would side with God's verdict on Jesus or popular opinion.

Jesus remains on trial today. False witnesses misrepresent him. They call him a social justice warrior, revolutionary, or political liberal. The challenge here is that Jesus is some of this, but that is not all he is. Sometimes there is a grain of truth that still misleads. Others call him mystical, magical, or ascetic. Others simply reject Jesus. They ignore his teachings. They view his crucifixion as nothing more than a tragic death, made more tragic by his followers who insist it was necessary to pay for sin and appease God's wrath. Sadly, this impulse to deny Jesus lives in all of us. Peter's bravado is a cautionary tale. Many of us go mute about Jesus when our comfort or reputation is on the line. Few of us brim with confidence when questioned about our faith. All of us fail to represent Jesus's love, mercy, and sacrifice. Fortunately, his verdict does not rest on our virtue. This sermon reminds us that with God as his witness, Jesus can't lose.

JESUS ACCEPTS THE CLAIM OF BEING MESSIAH AND PETER DENIES HIM (26:57–75)

LITERARY STRUCTURE AND THEMES (26:57–75)

This unit has two core parts: (1) the examination of Jesus by the leadership leading into Jesus's acknowledgment of his position and claims of exaltation and vindication from God (Matt. 26:57–68), and (2) the denials of Peter (Matt. 26:69–75). The leadership took the remark as blasphemous and translated the charge into sedition that they could take to Rome. The remark also led to mocking disrespect. At the same time, Peter was denying Jesus—just as Jesus had predicted. Jesus would suffer alone. Both scenes involve dialogues. Jesus's examination worked up to his bold pronouncement that he would sit at God's right hand and ride the clouds in judgment. Peter's passage ended with him whimpering at his failure to stand strong. The contrast was intentional.

Jesus's examination by the Jewish leadership also appears in Mark 14:53–65, Luke 22:54–55, and 66–71. Parallels of the short mocking sequence of Matthew 26:67–68 are in Mark 14:65 and Luke 22:63–65. John 18:13–14, 19–24 has a shorter Jewish questioning by Annas.

Peter's denials have important parallels in Mark 14:66–72, Luke 22:56–62, and John 18:25–27. John's account is abbreviated, moving quickly through the denials. Luke presents the denials and then gives the summary of Jesus's examination. Matthew and Mark have the reverse order.

Matthew made the narrative choice to tell about the trial and then present Peter's denials. Mark did the same. Luke chose to interlace the denials. These are differences of editorial organization and narrative choice.

Davies and Allison (1997, 519) note the trial had a series of mostly pairs: verses 57–58, Jesus and Peter; verses 59–61, false witnesses; verses 61–64, two questions from the high priest; verses 65–66, two judgments; and verses 67–68, two acts of mocking.

Key themes include the leaders' failure to appreciate who Jesus was and a principal disciple's failure. Humanity was not doing well in responding to the hope of Jesus's presence. The first theme rotates around the claims of Jesus to be the Son of Man seated at God's right hand (Ps. 110:1) and riding the clouds (Dan. 7:13–14). This significant Christology and its clash with the leaders' judgment that Jesus blasphemed set out the unit's core theme. The cultural background to the issue of whether Jesus blasphemed when he made his claims of exaltation is fully examined in my work on this scene in the parallel of Mark 14 (Bock 1998). Issues of historicity are also in this monograph, as also in Bock (2012, 156–72), Bock and Webb (2009, 589–667)), and Keener (2009, 644–46). The injustice of what was taking place was highlighted by two elements: the false witnesses and the mocking, which was no way to treat a prisoner whose crime had yet to be established. The irony of what was being done to the one God had sent runs through the entire scene. That someone could be charged or even executed during a feast day with no delay was possible in exceptional circumstances (*m. Sanh.* 11.4).

Mishnah on Execution on a Festival Day

***Sanhedrin* 11.4:** "They put him to death not in the court in his own town or in the court which is in Yabneh, but they bring him up to the high court in Jerusalem. And they keep him until the festival, and they put him to death on the festival, as it is said, 'And all the people shall hear and fear and no more do presumptuously (Dt. 17:13),' the words of R. Aqiba. R. Judah says, 'They do not delay the judgment of this one, but they put him to death at once. And they write messages and send them with messengers to every place: "Mr. So-and-so, son of Mr. So-and-so, has been declared liable to the death penalty by the court."'"

EXPOSITION (26:57–75)

This is one of most important scenes in Matthew. It explains how Jesus made it to the cross and surfaces the ultimate theological issue that was a core dispute between the new movement and the Jewish leadership: the claim that God was so behind Jesus's work that he would give his Son a place at his side in heaven. This leaves no room for options. Either Jesus was who he claimed to be, or this was blasphemy. Matthew will argue later that God's vote on the dispute came with the empty tomb. The example of a calm Jesus meeting his calling also received attention. In fact, it is his own word that led into the movement to the cross, because the leadership did not accept his claim. This was how committed Jesus was to dealing with sin on our behalf.

Alongside Peter's three denials, Jesus predicted his exaltation by God in response to a question about being the Messiah, a view the Jewish leaders took to be blasphemy.

26:57–58. Jesus was brought to the home of the high priest Caiaphas for examination (on the house, Rupprecht 1991; Wilkins 2004, 862; Rousseau and Arav s.v. "Jerusalem, Caiaphas's House," 1995, 136–39—for the diagram of the location, but their questioning of the scene as a later addition and not possible on a feast day will be dealt with below; Mark 14:53). This was likely a mansion that housed both Caiaphas and his father-in-law Annas. A courtyard area may have given a glimpse into a part of the home. There scribes and elders were gathered to help, the only place we get this combination in Matthew. This was not a formal trial, as the Jews could not execute Jesus and thus could not give a decisive verdict followed by a sanctioned action. This was why appeals to violating legal standards like those in the later Mishnah should not be pressed (France 2007, 1019; for a list of violations, Keener 2009, 446–48). They were gathering evidence to take to Pilate, who could crucify him if they found Jesus guilty of a possible crime. Romans kept the power to execute to themselves except in a limited case of Gentiles who violated temple space (Davies and Allison 1997, 524–25; John 18:31; Josephus, *B.J.* 6.126 and 6.303). The stoning of Stephen in Acts 7 was a mob act, and the execution of James got a rebuke from the Romans (Josephus, *A.J.* 20.200). This examination was done with some formality, including witnesses and testimony, but not the full formality of a full trial since no sanction could be placed with the verdict. Josephus did note that Jewish leaders had a role in Jesus's death (*A.J.* 18.63–64). The Josephus citation makes it clear that Jesus (1) existed, (2) had a ministry that involved unusual works, (3) was crucified under Pilate under pressure from Jewish leadership, and (4) had followers who proclaimed resurrection (on the dispute whether this note from Josephus is authentic versus a fabrication and what is likely original in it, Webb in Bock and Webb 2009, 685–86; see chart below).

Roman Authority on Severe Crimes, Including the Death Penalty Except in the Temple Area

Josephus, *Jewish War* 6.124–26: "Now Titus was deeply affected with this state of things, and reproached John and his party, and said to them, 'Have not you, vile wretches that you are, by our permission, put up this partition-wall before your sanctuary? Have not you been allowed to put up

Replica of a Typical Home with a Courtyard Area.

the pillars thereto belonging at due distances, and on it to engrave in Greek, and in your own letters, this prohibition, that no foreigner should go beyond that wall? Have not we given you leave to kill such as go beyond it, though he were a Roman? And what do you do now, you pernicious villains? Why do you trample upon dead bodies in this temple? And why do you pollute this holy house with the blood both of foreigners and Jews themselves?'"

Josephus, *Jewish War* 6.303 [about Jesus, son of Ananus, during the later Jewish revolt when Albinus was procurator]: "Hereupon our rulers supposing, as the case proved to be, that this was a sort of divine fury in the man, brought him to the Roman procurator."

Peter had trailed behind (Mark 14:54; Luke 22:54–55). He at least had the courage to stay close. He went to the high priest's courtyard and sat with the guards to observe what was taking place. The location has options, given the normal design of such homes. This was either likely a central courtyard area as was common in such homes or it sat on the outside edge of the home. He was but one of many potential witnesses to aspects of these events who could have passed on what took place. Joseph of Arimathea, Nicodemus, any of the Jews present who later told what took place in defense of what the Jewish leadership did, or Paul would have known what took place here.

Josephus on Jesus[1] (brackets indicate later additions that are not Josephus)

***Antiquities* 18:63–64:** "Now, there was about this time Jesus, a wise man, [if it be lawful to call him a man], for he was a doer of wonderful works—a teacher of such men as receive the truth with pleasure. He drew over to him both many of the Jews, and many of the Gentiles. [He was the Christ;] and when Pilate, at the suggestion of the principal men amongst us, had condemned him to the cross, those that loved him at the first did not forsake him, for he appeared to them alive again the third day, [as the divine prophets had foretold these and ten thousand other wonderful things concerning him;] and the tribe of Christians, so named from him, are not extinct at this day."

How did Peter get in? Given how many leaders were present, it is likely slaves from other houses also had come. Peter made it in through this mix (Nolland 2005, 1124). John 18:16 also notes the beloved disciple was known and helped them get in.

26:59–61. The chief priests and whole council were gathering evidence and witnesses against Jesus (Mark 14:55–56). The term used here is συνέδριον, "council" or "Sanhedrin" (BDAG s.v. "συνέδριον" 1c, 967—opting for Sanhedrin). Whether or not this was what the Mishnah called the Sanhedrin is discussed (Davies and Allison 1997, 524; Keener 2009, 614–16, refers

1 "Josephus on Jesus." For a wonderful summary of the discussion of this text by classical scholars, see Chris Forbes's exposition at https://www.publicchristianity.org/josephs-and-jesus-a-christian-forgery.

to it as a municipal aristocracy with a mix of rabbis and wealthy landowners; Culpepper 2021, 531–32, argues a formal Sanhedrin did not yet exist). At the least, this was obviously some formal group of civic and religious leaders who had influence on affairs tied to Jews in the city. Matthew says there were false witnesses present. It recalls the work of stealth and trapping Jesus noted earlier by Matthew (Konradt 2020, 403; Matt. 22:15–40; 26:4). Gathering such witnesses violated Torah (Exod. 20:16; Deut. 5:20). Apparently, many came forward in a way that could be closely examined but nothing was corroborated by a second witness, except a remark about the temple.

The cryptic remarks of Jesus about the destruction of the temple shows the problem and helps explain Matthew's claim about false witnesses (Mark 14:57–60). There is no public saying like this in the Synoptic Gospels, but John 2:18–22 does have a remark about Jesus's own body which others mistook to be about the temple. The charge was that "this fellow" said he could ("I am able to") destroy the temple and raise it in three days (also Mark 14:58, which states the claim slightly more strongly, claiming that Jesus said he would destroy the temple). The mocking of Matthew 27:40 repeats this temple charge. Jesus had been speaking of his body being raised after three days, not the physical temple as these witnesses presented his claim. Jesus also did not personally predict he would be the one to destroy this temple, but that it would be destroyed. Had Jesus spoken a word of violence against the temple, this would have been seen as religious blasphemy by the Jews and been a basis for charging him before Pilate with sedition or, at least, disturbing the peace, which Pilate would have been responsible for preserving. Precedent for that concern is seen in Jeremiah 26:1–19 (also Josephus, *B.J.* 6.300–309—of Jesus son of Ananus and his cry against the city and temple; Culpepper 2021, 533). Turner (2008, 639) notes that Jesus's recent temple act may have lent credibility to raising this issue. At least two witnesses (= Mark 14:57, "some") showed the attempt to reach legal standards (Deut. 17:6; 19:15). So, one charge got some attention. Matthew saw this one as serious enough to note in more detail.

It was very important for the leadership to get right the charge and this one opportunity before Pilate. It could not fail, as nothing could have been worse than for such a charge to be examined by Pilate and dismissed. The leadership needed to be confident they could make the case against Jesus in a persuasive way.

26:62–63a. The high priest pressed Jesus to respond to the charges against him as Jesus remained silent. Even after being pressed, Jesus remained silent (Mark 14:61; cf. Isa. 53:7; Isa. 50:6; Acts 8:32).

26:63b. The high priest now moved things along. The temple charge was not clearly established so he asked a direct question. With the support of an oath, the high priest asked Jesus if he was the Christ, the Son of God (Mark 14:61). It is likely all Caiaphas meant by Son of God was a query about being the Messiah (2 Sam. 7:14; Pss. 2:7; 89:26–27; Turner 2008, 639). Caiaphas held to strict monotheism common in Judaism, so the query should not be read in a Christian perspective. It was a natural question given how Jesus had entered the city accepting messianic praise (Matt. 21:9, 15–16) and the question Jesus had raised about Messiah and Psalm 110:1 in Matthew 22:42–45. If they could get Jesus to confess he was a messianic claimant, then they could take that claim of kingship to Rome and ask for a verdict of sedition, since Rome appointed kings in her empire and was not supportive of self-appointed kings.

26:64. Jesus's initial response used the idiom "you say." It means "yes, but not quite as you mean it in asking," just as in Matthew 26:25 and 27:11 (BDAG s.v. "λέγω" 2e, 588–90, "maintain," "declare"). It was so, but not exactly as they thought. Then Jesus elaborated with a crucial remark that sealed his fate.

He assured them that hereafter they would see the Son of Man seated at the right hand of the Power—a careful, even respectful way to refer to God. The reference to the Power is a circumlocution for God, given as a way to show deference and respect as Jesus made his shocking claim. This response implied that God would vindicate him, regardless of what they might decide or do, and would give him the right to share in God's rule based on Psalm 110:1. What Jesus said was not just a response but a prediction about God's action and views of the current dispute. The Son of Man also would come on the clouds. This was a major self-disclosure by Jesus, the most important one made in Matthew. This expression about riding the clouds as Son of Man is from Daniel 7:13–14. In the Old Testament, only God rode the clouds (Deut. 33:26; Pss. 68:4; 104:3; Isa. 19:1). This was a picture of receiving judgment authority from God. The image is also like 1 Enoch 62:5 in the Matthean text as the Son of Man was said to sit on a throne of glory. Jesus was claiming more than being a political Messiah. He was arguing he would share in God's rule and presence from heaven. He would share God's throne. Even more, God's act would place him there. They may have him in for a judgment, but one day he would be back and be their judge! The reference to hereafter meant they would see this soon, as the claim was wrapped up in a predicted vindication God would give to Jesus after he was crucified by raising him from the dead.

Deuteronomy 33:26: "There is no one like God, O Jeshurun, who rides through the sky to help you, on the clouds in majesty."

Psalm 68:4: "Sing to God! Sing praises to his name. Exalt the one who rides on the clouds. For the Lord is his name. Rejoice before him."

Isaiah 19:1: "This is an oracle about Egypt: Look, the Lord rides on a swift-moving cloud and approaches Egypt. The idols of Egypt tremble before him; the Egyptians lose their courage."

Daniel 7:13–14: "I was watching in the night visions, And with the clouds of the sky one like a son of man was approaching. He went up to the Ancient of Days and was escorted before him. To him was given ruling authority, honor, and sovereignty. All peoples, nations, and language groups were serving him. His authority is eternal and will not pass away. His kingdom will not be destroyed."

1 Enoch 62:5: "One half portion of them shall glance at the other half; they shall be terrified and dejected; and pain shall seize them when they see that Son of Man sitting on the throne of his glory."

In effect, Jesus was not just answering the question; he was making a prediction of what God will do. Shockingly, one day Jesus would be their judge, and God would make it so for him, regardless of what they did to him now. The debate about whether Jesus was referring to exaltation-ascension or a second coming is a bit misleading (Davies and Allison 1997, 531, opts for a reference to the return). Jesus's point was a declaration of Jesus's rule as one who would be vindicated by God, a point that included both events on each end. However, the short time frame for the leaders' seeing what was to take place, suggested by "hereafter," means Jesus's point aimed at what would start the sequence, the empty tomb and resurrection (France 2007, 1028). Morris (1992, 684) claims this was not seen and so the reference must be further in the future, but God's power enacted for Jesus was seen in the aftermath of the empty tomb and the work of the Spirit that came soon after. With this true but challenging testimony, Jesus signed his death warrant. Jesus provided the testimony that eventually yielded his death. It is one of the greatest ironies of this scene. It freed the leadership to take a charge of sedition to Pilate. Jesus died for telling the truth.

Jesus's response answered the question he raised about Psalm 110:1 back in Matthew 22:45. David called Messiah "Lord" because God would give this special son of David God's glory, rule, presence, and power. A fuller development of Jesus's answer is in Bock (2012, 163–73). More than David's son, the Messiah is David's Lord, and this coming vindication would show that to be the case.

Mark 14:62 has Jesus reply positively with a simple yes. That was the force of his entire answer, even in Matthew. Then Jesus elaborated, appealing to a seat at the right hand of Power and riding the clouds as described in Matthew. Luke 22:67–71 has a slightly different exchange in the morning. This was a meeting Matthew also notes in Matthew 27:1, but all Matthew gives was its conclusion: Jesus would die. In Luke, when Jesus was asked if he was the Christ, he responded that if he said so they would not believe and if he asked they would not answer. But then Jesus spoke of the Son of Man being at the right hand of the power of God. Luke's version does not mention the clouds because "Son of Man" already alluded to Daniel 7 and the key exaltation starting point was made with Jesus seated at God's right hand. When the high priest asked if Jesus was the Son of God, Jesus replied, "You say that I am," a response much like Matthew's "You say." This led to the council's response of no longer needing further witnesses. Each of these descriptions summarized a much longer and complex exchange.

26:65–66. The remark struck the high priest as blasphemous, so he tore his clothes (Mark 14:63–64), saying Jesus had slandered God. The high priest could not accept that God would share his glory and power with this Galilean teacher. In his view, Jesus "insults the majesty of God" (Davies and Allison 1997, 533). Bock (1998, 234–36) argues that the leadership saw blasphemy in Jesus's claim to share God's presence (and in even more detail, Bock 2009a, 656–61, with the entire article defending historicity of the scene). If Jesus were not who he claimed to be, they would have been correct. "Blasphemy" was slander against God or an act that attacked God's uniqueness, such as acts of idolatry (Exod. 22:20; Lev. 24:10–16; *m. Sanh.* 6.4—on hanging the blasphemer; 7.5—blasphemy is only for misusing God's name). The passage offers a stark choice, either God would exalt Jesus vindicating who he was or Jesus uttered blasphemy. There is no middle option of Jesus being a religious great of some sort, whether prophet or Messiah. Either Jesus belonged at God's side or not. The resurrection was the answer to that difference of view and provided God's vote in the dispute through his action of raising Jesus.

Leviticus 24:11, 15–16a: "The Israelite woman's son misused the Name and cursed, so they brought him to Moses. . . . Moreover, you are to tell the Israelites, 'If any man curses his God he will bear responsibility for his sin, and one who misuses the name of the Lord must surely be put to death.'"

Mishnah, *Sanhedrin* 7:5: "He who blasphemes is liable only when he will have fully pronounced the divine Name."

Tearing clothes was a sign of displeasure, dismay, or grief (Gen. 37:29; 1 Sam. 15:27–28; 2 Kings 18:37–19:1; Job 1:20; Acts 14:14; Jdt. 14:19; 1 Macc. 11:71; *m. Sanh.* 7.5; Josephus, *A.J.* 2.316; Turner 2008, 640). Here it is displeasure at what was allegedly blasphemy. Caiaphas asked why they needed any further witnesses. They had what they needed. He repeated the idea that Jesus had blasphemed and asked what they thought should be done. This perception of Jesus blaspheming goes back to Matthew 9:3. What they were suspicious of then has been confirmed now in their view. The council answered that Jesus was guilty, worthy of death.

They would take Jesus to Pilate. The religious charge of blasphemy would be converted into the political charge of claiming to be a king, a king Rome did not appoint. In other words, the legal charge before Rome would be sedition.

26:67–68. Next, they disrespected Jesus by mocking him (Mark 14:65; Luke 22:63–65). Some spat at him. Others slapped him. They asked him to name who it was who was striking him, to prophesy. The injustice and inhumanity were deep. The allusion was to Isaiah 50:6, a servant song. Such taunting also would take place during the crucifixion (Matt. 27:29, 40, 42–43).

26:69–70. In contrast to Jesus's strong testimony, Peter now began his fall into the denials (Luke 22:56–57). Mark and Matthew do not tell us how long all of this took, but John has a long break between the first two denials (John 18:17, 25), and Luke 22:59 has an hour between the second and third denials (Morris 1992, 687). There is another contrast besides Jesus's declaration and Peter's denials: Jesus spoke before the leaders, while Peter denied him before servants (Osborne 2010, 1000).

The first denial was to a slave girl who recognized Peter and said he was with Jesus of Galilee. Mark 14:66–67 has the girl tie Jesus to being a Nazarene. Peter denied it in front of all of those present, saying he did not know what she was talking about. In Mark 14:68 the first rooster crow took place here. In Mark, Jesus had predicted two rooster crows for the denials. This was an indirect, not a direct, denial of Jesus by Peter, but a direct one was coming.

26:71–72. Peter moved to the gateway. There another slave girl said Peter had been with Jesus of Nazareth. Now Peter uttered an oath that he did not know Jesus. This placed Peter at risk of violating Matthew 10:33 (Konradt 2020, 407) and thus being denied by Jesus. As we shall see, Jesus will be merciful to Peter because he knows his heart (Luke 22:31). Peter's failure here was one of nerve. Luke 22:58 simply has someone else make the challenge, while Mark 14:69–70 has the same girl address Peter a second time. There is a crowd involved in this, with many participating in dealing with Peter.

26:73–75. Others standing there came up to Peter. They said he was with Jesus because his speech—that is, his accent—made it clear he was from Galilee and was associated with Jesus (Mark 14:70–71). Luke 22:59–60 has another single person make the challenge. Peter's denial became more emphatic. He cursed and said again with an oath that he did not know the man. Then a rooster crowed. Mark 14:72 notes a second crowing and also recalls that Jesus had predicted this would take place. Luke 22:61–62 has the Lord turn and look at Peter, causing him to weep. Peter recalled Jesus's prediction that before the rooster crowed, there would be three denials. Jesus knew the situation and Peter's nerve better than Peter did. Jesus may have been regarded as having made false theological claims by the leadership, but here his true knowledge appears as a contrast.

Peter departed weeping tears of regret and shame that he failed to stand up for Jesus and stand with him in his time of suffering (2 Cor. 7:10; France 2007, 1034; Keener 2009, 656). In effect, Peter had deserted Jesus (Turner 2008, 642). Konradt (2020, 408) calls these tears "his repentance." Peter had made it further than the others but still had failed. His fear overtook his commitment to Jesus. He was restored in John 21:15–19 and showed a different heart in the book of Acts. He learned from his failure. This is the last reference to Peter in Matthew, yet all of Matthew's audience surely knew of his turnaround as a key figure in the church.

THEOLOGICAL FOCUS

The exegetical idea (alongside Peter's three denials, Jesus predicted his exaltation by God in response to a question about being the Messiah, a view the Jewish leaders took to be blasphemy) leads to this theological focus: Jesus's claim to be the seated Son of Man produces a choice about him, either blasphemy or exaltation—a dispute Jesus predicts God will resolve in resurrection.

Jesus's confession that he would be vindicated by God and be the judge of the Jewish leadership met with cries of blasphemy and mocking. Even Peter denied Jesus three times.

The entire narrative of Matthew's gospel comes to a head here. Opposition to Jesus had been rising from those who denied he was who he claimed to be. Jesus was resolute. When asked about being the Messiah, Son of God, Jesus affirmed that God would vindicate him as Son of Man. He would have a place at God's side and ride the clouds in judgment. The confession of Jesus seated at God's right hand runs through the New Testament. This position of Jesus became the theme of Peter's key speech in Acts 2, as the Christ distributed the Spirit. Jesus received the martyr Stephen from the right hand of God in Acts 7:56. Jesus intercedes for us from the right hand (Rom. 8:34). We are to seek the things above as Jesus is seated at the right hand (Col. 3:1). Clearly this text made a deep impression on the church. It points to our connection to the person at the center of salvation, who shares authority with the Father. Jesus is worthy to be called Lord (Ps. 110:1).

The key idea of the right hand and the riding on the clouds conveys the authority God gives to Jesus. The expression is in most ancient creeds. This is a declaration about divine vindication, a prediction of God's vote in the current dispute. The empty tomb meant God has spoken on Jesus's behalf. Jesus was and is who he claimed to be and whom God the Father showed the Son to be.

On the other end of the spectrum is Peter's failure. Here we see that no amount of self-confidence can prop up someone who fears men over God. Without dependence on God, failure will come. Peter had been among those who had failed to be diligent in prayer at Gethsemane. Now with his chance to step forward for Jesus, he denied him and finally fled. Peter would grow from this, as the Lord's restoration and provision of the Spirit would give him the heart he needs. In the meantime, Jesus now faced his death all alone.

PREACHING AND TEACHING STRATEGIES

Exegetical and Theological Synthesis

The exegetical section highlights the theologically profound statement Jesus made in his defense. His exaltation and return would be clear evidence not only of his messianic identity but also God's vindication. Whereas the false witnesses could not piece together a coherent case against Jesus, the Mighty One of heaven would (1) seat Jesus and (2) send him back in the clouds. The imagery draws from Psalm 110:1 (seated) and Daniel 7:13–14 (clouds). By applying Son of Man from Daniel 7 to himself, Jesus made a bold statement about his divine-human identity.

While the religious leaders rejected Jesus's bold claim, we should take Jesus at his word. God is his witness (cf. Gen 31:50; Deut. 31:26; Josh. 22:34; 24:27; Jer. 42:5). Likewise, the Spirit and Scriptures are witnesses (John 5:31–40). Finally, he calls his followers to be his witnesses (Matt. 28:18–20; Luke 24:45–48; Acts 1:8; 2:32; 3:15; 5:32; 10:41; 1 Cor. 15:15). Bearing witness to Jesus means telling others about his works (i.e., evangelism) and living like kingdom citizens (i.e., ethically). We will do this imperfectly. Like Peter, we will have lapses of courage. Like Paul, we may struggle with our flesh (2 Cor. 12:7–10; 1 Tim. 1:12–14). Fear and moral failure are forgiveable. What we must avoid is persistent rejection of Jesus. In a haunting passage, Paul warned that denial of Jesus results in his denying us (2 Tim. 2:12).

Preaching Idea

With God as his witness, Jesus can't lose.

Contemporary Connection

What does it mean?

What does it mean that with God as his witness, Jesus can't lose? First, Jesus recognized that his Mighty Father was on his side. God sent Jesus. He verbally validated Jesus at his baptism and transfiguration. He anointed him with the Spirit. He gave him orders to suffer and die for the sins of the world. And he promised to raise him from the dead. Jesus's resurrection would precede his ascension, where he would take a seat at God's right hand. Throughout Jesus's earthly ministry, the Heavenly Father stood by his Son.

Second, the Father's witness pointed past Jesus's present sufferings to his eternal glory. The cross was not the last word: God raised him. He reversed Jesus's sentence, restored his good name (Rom. 1:4; Phil. 2:9–11), and reserved him a seat in heaven (Dan. 7:13–14; Matt. 26:64; Heb. 1:3). What a glorious reversal!

Finally, God's witness should be a source of confidence for us. As followers of Jesus, we are vicariously woven into his story. He has included us in his death, resurrection, and heavenly seat (Eph. 2:4–7; Col. 2:9–15). With both the Father and Son on our side, who can be against us (Rom. 8:31–39)? We have a heavenly witness who assures us we will win, because Jesus has won. This should steel our faith in the face of persecution, reassure us when misunderstood by friends, and steady us when dealing with a terminal disease.

Is it true?

Is it true that with God as his witness, Jesus can't lose? Absolutely. His resurrection was the first sign of a full-scale victory still to come. We must not forget that we live between the times—the "last days" loom as the "new age" slowly dawns. We await King Jesus to come on the clouds and execute judgment (Rev. 19–20). We await Jesus's coming rule and the new heavens and earth (Rev. 21–22). According to his own testimony, Jesus will come soon (Rev. 22:20).

In the meantime, we must "be ready and stay steady" (Matt. 24:36–25:30). Waiting requires not only patience but also perspective. Jesus's delay is deliberate: more people can come to faith the longer we wait for his return (2 Peter 3:8–9). As we wait, we should bear witness to our victorious King. We can share boldly—with God as our witness—knowing that he always leads us in triumph (2 Cor. 2:14–17). We preach; he controls the outcomes (1 Cor. 3:5–9).

Lastly, it is worth noting that our victory in Jesus should provoke humility, not triumphalism. We did not earn it any more than we helped our favorite sports team win a championship. Jesus's victory is something to receive gratefully and celebrate. We must avoid treating it as a trump card or license to trample on others. That Jesus will win does not guarantee a Christian in the White House. That Jesus will win does not excuse bad money management. That Jesus will win does not mean Christians can dispense with civility when talking about charged issues (e.g., sexual identity, racism, religion). That Jesus will win should make us more winsome, not less.

Now what?

This dramatic passage prompts three related responses. First, we should side with Jesus. When it comes to Jesus, there is no neutral ground. We are either with him or against him. The final chapters of Matthew are rife with examples of ways to oppose Jesus: betray, desert, deny, or ridicule. Siding with Jesus means we resist all these forms of opposition. When people slander Jesus, we should stand up for him. When people reject Jesus, we should revere him. When people ignore Jesus, we should exalt him. With God as our witness, we should side with Jesus.

Second, we should savor the victory Jesus secured. Although his arrest, trial, death, and burial covered several dark days, God vindicated Jesus on the third day. His resurrection broke the power of sin, death, and Satan and launched a new age. We have forgiveness of sins. We are indwelled by the Holy Spirit. Jesus placed us in a spiritual family and sent us to make disciples. Victory in Jesus means a new identity, community, and mission. We should celebrate this good news.

Finally, we should stay winsome. This characteristic is mission-critical. As we await Jesus's full victory, our fractured world groans. Sin still stings, injustice lingers, and suffering remains. Winsome Christians do not deny this. Rather, they admit fault, extend justice, and walk humbly with their God. Winsome Christians start conversations, not arguments. They emanate hope, not hubris. Their confidence is centered in God's plan, not politics. Thus, they pray, "Come, Lord Jesus. Come" (1 Cor. 16:22; Rev. 22:20).

Creativity in Presentation

The Bible contains many riveting legal dramas. In each case, when God stands as a witness to his people, they cannot lose. Consider reading the following biblical cases and their verdict:

- In **Potiphar v. Joseph,** the defendant's sentence was reversed when God provided new revelation (Gen. 39–41).
- In **Moses v. Pharoah**, the plaintiff won his people's release after God extended his mighty hand (Exod. 6–14).
- In **King Darius v. Daniel**, the defendant survived his fatal punishment when God closed the mouths of the lions in the pit (Dan. 6).
- In **Jerusalem v. Paul**, the defendant appealed to Rome after the Lord assured him of his strong testimony (Acts 22–28, esp. 23:11).
- In **Jerusalem v. Jesus**, the defendant claimed his messianic identity, knowing crucifixion would precede God's ultimate verdict: his resurrection, ascension, and seat at God's right hand.

At some point in each of these cases, the attorney should stand tall, pause, and confidently announce: "Your honor, for our next witness, we call God to the stand." Case closed!

In a court case, not all witnesses are created equal. Most of us have seen courtroom dramas where witnesses are dismissed because of character flaws or inconsistencies in their testimony. Fortunately, God does not suffer from character flaws or inconsistencies! He is the perfect witness. Moreover, God fits all categories of witness. There are four kinds of witnesses: (1) expert witnesses, (2) eyewitnesses, (3) character witnesses, and (4) fact witnesses.[2] The website theperfectwitness.com offers descriptions of each, stressing the importance of getting the right witnesses on the stand to win a case. For Jesus, God was the perfect witness—an expert who saw it all, knew Jesus's heart, and could report on the facts. Jesus's victory was a foregone conclusion.

Peter's weak witness contrasts with God's winning witness. Consider giving people a closer look at Peter's faltering faith in the courtyard. Dramatic renditions of this scene abound, as evident from a YouTube search. The one from *The Passion of the Christ* (directed by Mel Gibson, 2004) offers a poignant reenactment. Likewise, *The Jesus Film*, commonly used in evangelistic settings, provides a vivid, two-minute interpretation of Peter's denials. Finally, a sixteenth-century Italian poet, Luigi Tansillo, wrote a gripping poem called "The Tears of St. Peter."[3]

---

2 See https://theperfectwitness.com/witness-depositions-testimony (accessed July 24, 2024).

3 Credit goes to the following blog post for presenting an excerpt from this poem and an interpretation: https://mapeel.blogspot.com/2012/04/good-friday-saint-peters-worst-day.html. The blogger also references

Finally, this sermon invites stories of bearing witness from you or people at your church. These stories should focus on witnessing winsomely and how to face opposition in evangelism. Consider recruiting a high school student who shares her faith with classmates, someone who shares his faith with coworkers, or a person who has suffered backlash from family members when talking about faith but remains winsome in her efforts to bear witness.

As you sort through the creative elements for the sermon, be sure to communicate that Jesus's claim to be the seated Son of Man produces a choice about him, either blasphemy or exaltation, a dispute Jesus predicts God will resolve in resurrection. Indeed, with God as his witness, Jesus can't lose.

- Jesus stands firm while standing trial (26:57–68).
- Peter falters while facing pressure (26:69–75).

DISCUSSION QUESTIONS

1. What role did witnesses play in legal situations in Jesus's day? Why were witnesses so important in ancient trials?
2. How did the Jewish leaders manipulate their law to conduct Jesus's trial?
3. Why was Jesus's statement considered blasphemy?
4. How will you explain the variations between the Gospels related to Peter's denials? What are the differences in Matthew's account?
5. What do you think was going on in Peter's mind in this scene? Be specific.
6. When have you recently been a witness for Jesus? What was your level of confidence when bearing witness? How was your testimony received?

Rembrandt's famous picture of Peter's denial, which could be presented while reading portions of this poem A translation of the text can be found here: https://canticasacra.org/?page_id=11227 (accessed July 24, 2024).

Matthew 27:1–31

EXEGETICAL IDEA

With Judas acknowledging Jesus's innocence and the Jewish leaders and crowd applying pressure, Pilate sent Jesus to be crucified.

THEOLOGICAL FOCUS

Under pressure, Pilate sentences Jesus to an unjust death, despite his sense that Jesus is innocent.

PREACHING IDEA

Cowards cave when crowds rage.

PREACHING POINTERS

The religious leaders handed Jesus over to Pilate for his death sentence. Only the Roman governor had the authority to execute Jesus for sedition. Matthew's retelling of Jesus's second (and more official) trial shifts focus from the religious leaders to Judas to Pilate to the crowds. Each perspective provides a contrasting perspective on Jesus's innocence. Judas felt remorse and hanged himself. Religious leaders remained opposed to Jesus and convinced the crowd to call for Barabbas's release. Pilate thought Jesus was innocent but conceded to the crowd. The scene concludes with Roman guards mocking and beating Jesus before leading him to his death. For the original audience, the cast of characters and their responses to Jesus would have highlighted the scandal of his death: an innocent man silently suffered while the mob went mad, and a governor gave into its pressure.

Mob justice is not just an ancient problem. In fact, with the rise of social media, mob justice has experienced a revival. Online masses can immediately form and shame people for anything ranging from shoe styles to political opinion to sexual misconduct. In our age, pastors get canceled addressing the rights of a fetus in being pro-life, following government mandates during a pandemic, speaking up for injustice to minorities, and platforming women during a worship service. Mob justice has plagued higher academia. Students protest "dangerous" guest speakers and demand the resignation of faculty who "trigger" them. A raging crowd stormed the U.S. Capitol building to try and overturn the 2020 presidential election results. Once these masses gain momentum, they become a terrifying force. "Both sides" do it. Few will stand in their way. This sermon illustrates that cowards cave when crowds rage.

JEWISH LEADERS AND A CROWD PRESSURE PILATE TO SENTENCE JESUS TO CRUCIFIXION (27:1–31)

LITERARY STRUCTURE AND THEMES (27:1–31)

This unit has a complex narrative sequence. There is the taking of Jesus to Pilate (Matt. 27:1–2), the scene of Judas' reaction (Matt. 27:3–10), and then the brief examination by Pilate (Matt. 27:11–14). This is followed by Pilate giving the choice to the crowd between Jesus and Barabbas (Matt. 27:15–26) and concludes with a scene of mocking (Matt. 27:27–31).

This unit is a composite of many scenes. But two scenes dominate: (1) Judas's return of the money and the discussion it generated, and (2) the discussion before the crowd about whether they would have Jesus or Barabbas freed. The contrast is important in setting the themes and the irony tied to the crucifixion. Judas as Jesus's betrayer now saw he had betrayed innocent blood. This did not stop the leadership from pursuing Jesus's death. They moved ahead. Pilate also had a sense Jesus was innocent and sought to release him by giving the crowd a choice, having been warned by his wife who related a dream she had experienced. This scene has two cycles of questions from Pilate: first his own and then from others about the charges. Then follows the interaction with the crowd over whether to free Jesus or Barabbas. This also involves two cycles of exchanges and there are two declarations of innocence from Pilate. The pairs made the scene easier to remember in an oral culture.

All of this made the case that Jesus was innocent as he went to his death. The execution he experienced was unjust. Events unfolded, driven by the resolve of the leadership and then of the crowd. All the scenes involve historical narration.

The key theme of Pilate's examination focuses on Jesus going to death as an innocent, an injustice in human terms. The leaders were resolute in dealing with Jesus, while Pilate decided to follow his Jewish advisors despite having a sense something was not right. Both approaches point to injustice, but of different types. One involved a misjudgment about religious matters, the other was a factor of social pressure and indifference, being complicit in the act of others who were more aggressive than Pilate was.

There also is the fact that events tied to the examination fulfilled Scripture, as did the purchase of the field with the blood money. Jesus's silence recalls the imagery of the Suffering Servant (Isa. 50:6; 53:7), as does the theme of injustice (Isa. 53:8). There is an unsavoriness to what was taking place. Jesus's predictions were also being realized when Jesus was handed over to Pilate, just as Jesus had predicted he would be given over (Matt. 17:22; 20:19; 26:2).

The Suffering Servant Suffers Injustice

Isaiah 53:8: "He was led away after an unjust trial—but who even cared? Indeed, he was cut off from the land of the living; because of the rebellion of his own people he was wounded."

Another theme is how the crowd accepted responsibility for what they were doing. The judgment on Israel for covenantal unfaithfulness that Matthew narrates elsewhere (Matt. 23:38–39) represents an outcome of this choice.

The scene involving Judas's return of the money is unique to Matthew. This does not mean it was constructed artificially by Matthew (but so Konradt 2020, 410–11). Konradt makes too much of the difference between Matthew and Acts 1:16–20. The accounts agree on Judas's ignominious end.

Everything else has parallels. Luke 22:66–71 has a longer development of the morning decision that Jesus should die, also reflected in Matthew 27:1. Mark 15:1 also fits here and notes the taking to Pilate as well, paralleled by Luke 23:1 and John 18:28. Luke 23:2 also explicitly lists the charges the leaders brought to Pilate: Jesus twisted customs, denied paying taxes to Caesar, and claimed to be Christ the king. Only the latter charge was true.

The short examination by Pilate is like Luke 23:3–5 and Mark 15:2–5. The Barabbas scene is noted in Luke 23:18–25, following Luke uniquely having an examination by Herod Antipas with Pilate's report that covers Luke 23:6–15. The Barabbas scene is also in Mark 15:6–15. The soldiers leading Jesus away is in Mark 15:16–20. Luke lacks this sequence.

EXPOSITION (27:1–31)

The religious charge that Jesus received from the Jewish leadership now became a political charge before Pilate as they presented him as a king Rome did not appoint. Pilate's role was to protect Caesar's interests and so the charge was formed as something Pilate must deal with in order to uphold Roman authority to appoint vassal rulers. Matthew's portrayal has Pilate struggle to make this decision. Jesus did not seem to be a threat to Roman power, and the ruler's wife had warned him not to pursue this. Only the pressure of the leadership and crowd in their seemingly strange choice of a revolutionary over the teacher cleared the path to the cross. The rejection of Jesus had now run its course. An innocent was headed to his death, executed as a felon in a clear sinner's place. A divine work lay ahead.

With Judas acknowledging Jesus's innocence and the Jewish leaders and crowd applying pressure, Pilate sent Jesus to be crucified.

27:1–2. In the morning, the leadership took counsel and formalized the decision to seek Jesus's death. Luke 22:66–71 has a longer version of this scene that repeats the testimony seen in Matthew. Mark 15:1 also notes this without detail. The morning scene for Luke may have been a review of the earlier testimony in Matthew and Mark (Davies and Allison 1997, 553; France 2007, 1018–19); or there was a repeat of the testimony in the morning to make the examination more official, as examinations normally were not to take place at night (Blomberg 1992, 406; Wilkins 2004, 868). It may simply be that the meeting started in the evening and went into the morning (Nolland 2005, 1146). Any of these options is possible.

Jesus was taken to Pilate (Mark 15:1; Luke 23:1; John 18:28), just as Jesus had predicted (Matt. 20:18–19) and as the leaders had been planning (Matt. 12:14; 22:15). Only Pilate could execute Jesus legally (John 18:31). Rome reserved the right for her leaders to give a death penalty sentence. The Jewish leaders tied Jesus up and led him away for the trip, probably to make Jesus look potentially dangerous to the prefect (Nolland 2005, 1146).

Pilate was prefect for Rome in Judea from A.D. 26 to 36. Caiaphas was always the high priest working with him and appointed by him. Pilate was working with someone he had selected. Pilate could be insensitive to Jewish customs and races in the region (see chart below; Josephus, *A.J.* 18.35—Pilate came to Judea; 18.55–62—effigies in the city; aqueduct paid for with temple funds, 85–89—after Jesus's time, Pilate sent home for treatment of Samaritans; *B.J.* 2.169–77—effigies and aqueduct accounts retold). With Jesus he appeared to be more careful, perhaps because he did not see an unarmed teacher as a threat to Rome (Davies and Allison 1997, 554; Turner 2008, 646). A full treatment of historicity on the Roman examination appears in Webb (Bock and Webb 2009, 669–773), summarized in Bock (2012, 174–89).

These verses were another short transition unit for Matthew, making the transition from the Jewish examination to the trial before Pilate. That narrative picks up again in Matthew 27:11 after a look at what happened with Judas.

Josephus on Pilate's Insensitivity to Jews and Others

***Antiquities* 18.55–62:** "But now Pilate, the procurator of Judea, removed the army from Caesarea to Jerusalem, to take their winter quarters there, in order to abolish the Jewish laws. So he introduced Caesar's effigies, which were upon the ensigns, and brought them into the city; whereas our law forbids us the very making of images; on which account the former procurators were wont to make their entry into the city with such ensigns as had not those ornaments. Pilate was the first who brought those images to Jerusalem, and set them up there; which was done without the knowledge of the people, because it was done in the nighttime; but as soon as they knew it, they came in multitudes to Caesarea, and interceded with Pilate many days, that he would remove the images; and when he would not grant their requests, because it would tend to the injury of Caesar, while yet they persevered in their request, on the sixth day he ordered his soldiers to have their weapons privately, while he came and sat upon his judgment seat, which seat was so prepared in the open place of the city, that it concealed the army that lay ready to oppress them: and when the Jews petitioned him again, he gave a signal to the soldiers to encompass them round, and threatened that their punishment should be no less than immediate death, unless they would leave off disturbing him, and go their ways home. But they threw themselves upon the ground, and laid their necks bare, and said they would take their death very willingly, rather than the wisdom of their laws should be transgressed; upon which Pilate was deeply affected with their firm resolution to keep their laws inviolable, and presently commanded the images to be carried back from Jerusalem to Caesarea.

"But Pilate undertook to bring a current of water to Jerusalem, and did it with the sacred money, and derived the origin of the stream from the distance of two hundred furlongs. However the Jews were not pleased with what had been done about this water; and many ten thousands of the people got together, and made a clamor against him, and insisted that he should leave off that design. Some of them also used reproaches, and abused the man, as crowds of such people usually do. So he habited a great number of his soldiers in their habit, who carried daggers under their garments, and sent them to a place where they might surround them. So he bade the Jews himself go away; but they boldly casting reproaches upon him, he gave the soldiers that signal which had been beforehand agreed on; who laid upon them much greater blows than Pilate had commanded them, and equally punished those that were tumultuous, and those that were not, nor did they spare them in the least; and since the people were unarmed, and were caught by men prepared for what they were about, there were a great number of them slain by this means, and others of them ran away wounded; and thus an end was put to this sedition."

***Antiquities* 18.85–89:** "But the nation of the Samaritans did not escape without tumults. The man who excited them to it, was one who thought lying a thing of little consequence, and who contrived everything so, that the multitude might be pleased; so he bade them get together upon Mount Gerizim, which is by them looked upon as the most holy of all mountains, and assured them that, when they were come thither, he would show them those sacred vessels which were laid under that place, because Moses put them there. So they came thither armed, and thought the discourse of the man probable; and as they abode at a certain village, which was called Tirathaba, they got the rest together to them, and desired to go up the mountain in a great multitude together. But Pilate prevented their going up, by seizing upon the roads with a great band of horsemen and footmen, who fell upon those that were gotten together in the village; and when they came to an action, some of them they slew, and others of them they put to flight, and took a great many alive, the principal of whom, and also the most potent of those that fled away, Pilate ordered to be slain.

"But when this tumult was appeased, the Samaritan senate sent an embassy to Vitellius, a man that had been consul, and who was now president of Syria, and accused Pilate of the murder of those that were killed; for that they did not go to Tirathaba in order to revolt from the Romans, but to escape the violence of Pilate.

"So Vitellius sent Marcellus, a friend of his, to take care of the affairs of Judea, and ordered Pilate to go to Rome, to answer before the emperor to the accusation of the Jews. So Pilate, when he had tarried ten years in Judea, made haste to Rome, and this in obedience to the orders of Vitellius, which he durst not contradict; but before he could get to Rome, Tiberius was dead."

27:3–4. Judas's response and his desire to return the money is unique to Matthew. The condemnation of Jesus had reached Judas and struck him as unjust. Judas regretted having betrayed Jesus. The term here is μεταμέλομαι (BDAG s.v. "μεταμέλομαι" 1, 639). It means "to regret" something, but is not the standard word for repentance in the New Testament (Keener 2009, 658–60; Turner 2008, 650; Wilkins 2004, 869). Matthew 21:32 is the only other use of this term with that meaning in the Gospels, and the word is used rarely in the New Testament, appearing only six times total (Matt 21:29, simply meaning a change of mind; 2 Cor. 7:8 [2x]; Heb. 7:21). Judas saw that he had made a mistake turning Jesus in, but it is not clear what he thought of Jesus at this point (for the idea repentance may be in view, see Davies and Allison 1997, 561–63). Nolland (2005, 1153) even sees Matthew as having Judas restored beyond this life, a scenario exceedingly unlikely given Jesus's curse in Matthew 26:24, not to mention John 6:64, 70–71. These kinder views of the fate of Judas seem problematic. What Judas may have known was that one who betrayed innocent blood was cursed (Deut. 27:25; Turner 2008, 649). He may have thought Jesus would be punished and simply stopped, not sent for execution.

Betraying Innocent Blood

Deuteronomy 27:25: "'Cursed is the one who takes a bribe to kill an innocent person.' Then all the people will say, 'Amen!'"

Judas returned the thirty pieces of silver to the leaders, confessing he had betrayed innocent blood. The amount recalls Zechariah 11:12–13. The leaders should have stopped everything leading to Jesus's death with such a confession, but they did not. Matthew was indicating again that Jesus's death was unjust. The leaders had no interest in taking the money back. Their hardness of heart in resisting Jesus was even stronger than the double-mindedness of Judas. They told Judas to see to the money himself. They denied justice to Jesus, mercy to Judas, and any kind of responsibility (Bruner 2004b, 706).

This detail shows this event likely had been relocated to an earlier point. The leaders were in the temple area here, not in the process of taking Jesus before Pilate. This was a topical placement, so that Matthew could tell the crucifixion-to-resurrection account uninterrupted. It likely took place later than its placement here (France 2007, 1038).

27:5. Judas tossed the money into the temple. He had no desire to keep it and wanted to be as far from it as possible. He then departed and hanged himself. Acts 1:18–19 tells of Judas acquiring the field with his money and dying there as his body burst open. This report may conflate Judas as the source for the money with the purchase of the field (Osborne 2010, 1012; Wilkins 2004, 870). Matthew's language of departing and hanging recalls 2 Samuel 17:23 LXX and the experience of Ahithophel, another well-known traitor. Perhaps the curse of Jesus was ringing in his mind (Matt. 26:24). Judas died completely alone and abandoned.

27:6–8. The leaders considered what do to with the money. They did not wish to place such stained money in the treasury, for it was blood money. Tarnished money from other acts is noted in Deuteronomy 23:19 (23:18 English). First Chronicles 22:8 seems to have a similar idea: shed blood and the temple do not mix in terms of purity (Nolland 2005, 1154). Their scruples here are ironic, given what had been done already. They had chosen purity over justice (Matt. 23:23; Turner 2008, 649). They went and bought a field, known as the Potter's Field, to turn into a burial place for foreigners. "Unclean money buys an unclean place for unclean people" (Blomberg 1992, 408). Tradition has its locale on the east end of the Valley of Hinnom. It is known as *Akeldamach* or *Akeldama*. Matthew alludes to Zechariah 11:13 and Jeremiah 19:1–13 with mention of the temple treasure, the potter's field, and field of blood. The fact it was called the field of blood in Matthew 27:8 associated it with Jesus's death. It was another way to suggest Jesus was innocent. The fact the leaders used the money showed they were even more responsible for what was taking place. Blood haunts the entire scene and chapter.

27:9–10. Matthew cited Jeremiah but also used Zechariah. He may have cited Jeremiah as the more prominent of the two writers (Morris 1991, 696; Osborne 2010, 1013). He named Jeremiah and cited Zechariah to reveal the linkage. The text is a conflation of ideas from Jeremiah 18:2–6; 19:1, 2–4; 32:6–15, as well as citing Zechariah 11:13 (Carson 2010, 629–33; Davies and Allison 1997, 568; Hanger 1995, 811 see chart below). Just how woven together these texts were in Matthew 27:3–10 is developed by Davies and Allison (1997, 558–59). Keener (2009, 657) speaks of the linkage of two passages here known in Jewish hermeneutics as *gezerah shewah*. A similar conflation of ideas is in Matthew 2:23, but without naming a specific source (Wilkins 2004, 871); in Mark 1:2, where Isaiah is the more prominent source cited out of a conflated text between Isaiah and Malachi; and in Romans 9:27, where Hosea and Isaiah are tied to one prophet (Davies and Allison 1997, 569).

Potter and Field Texts

Jeremiah 18:2–6; 19:1: "'Go down at once to the potter's house. I will speak to you further there.' So I went down to the potter's house and found him working at his wheel. Now and then there would be something wrong with the pot he was molding from the clay with his hands. So he would rework the clay into another kind of pot as he saw fit. Then the Lord's message came to me, 'I, the Lord, say: "O nation of Israel, can I not deal with you as this potter deals with the clay? In my hands, you, O nation of Israel, are just like the clay in this potter's hand."' . . . The Lord told Jeremiah, 'Go and buy a clay jar from a potter. Take with you some of the leaders of the people and some of the leaders of the priests.'"

Jeremiah 32:14–15: "'The Lord of Heaven's Armies, the God of Israel says, "Take these documents, both the sealed copy of the deed of purchase and the unsealed copy. Put them in a clay jar so that they may be preserved for a long time to come."' For the Lord of Heaven's Armies, the God of Israel, says, 'Houses, fields, and vineyards will again be bought in this land.'"

> **Zechariah 11:12–13:** "Then I said to them, 'If it seems good to you, pay me my wages, but if not, forget it.' So they weighed out my payment—thirty pieces of silver. The Lord then said to me, 'Throw to the potter that exorbitant sum at which they valued me!' So I took the thirty pieces of silver and threw them to the potter at the temple of the Lord."

This use offers another point about divine design in these culminating events. In Zechariah (thirty pieces of silver), the messenger of God or God himself was undervalued, worth only the price of a slave. He was thrown away for nothing. That pattern pictured Jesus in his death. In Jeremiah we have a promise of restoration to Israel in Jeremiah 32 (field purchase), as well as judgment for her in Jeremiah 18–19, especially 19:1–13 (its themes: visit to a potter, potter jar involved picturing judgment, and innocent blood). It is a pattern prophecy, likely with these three elements. Current events were like the events of old rhetorically strung together.

This is the last of ten fulfillment formula texts in Matthew (Matt. 1:22; 2:15, 17, 23; 4:14; 8:17; 12:17; 13:35; 21:4). Many of these texts are pattern prophecies (Matt. 1:22; 2:15, 17). Events tied to Jesus were part of a divine plan from start to finish. Zechariah 9–13 was important to Matthew, appearing in Matthew 21:4–5 with Zechariah 9:9–10, Matthew 24:30 with Zechariah 12:10–14, and Matthew 26:31 with Zechariah 13:7 (France 2007, 1045).

27:11. Returning to where Matthew left Jesus in Matthew 27:2, Pilate asked if Jesus was king of the Jews. The point was important because Jesus was not being asked if he was merely a prophet. The challenge was for claiming to be a king, with an implication that he would rule and so was at the center of God's program. Politically, Pilate was doing his job of protecting the interests of Caesar. Rome appointed kings, so the question was really a probe into the charge of sedition. It was a very serious question Pilate was asking. This set up the naming of the charge in Matthew 27:37 on the placard that went with Jesus to the cross. Pilate did deal directly with such a challenge from a Samaritan who had gathered forces, seeking out the rebellious leader and killing him (Josephus, *A.J.* 18.85–89, see chart at 27:1–2). Nolland (2005, 1161) notes only the leaders' insistence brought Jesus to Pilate's attention.

Jesus replied with the ambiguous, "You say so." We have seen this reply twice before: when Judas denied he was the betrayer (Matt. 26:25), and when Jesus answered the question about being the Christ (Matt. 26:64). It was an affirmative reply, but not in the sense the questioner expected. Blomberg (1992, 410) says it means "your words, not mine." Unlike at the Jewish examination, Jesus gave no elaboration to this response. Mark 15:2 is parallel as is Luke 23:3 to the entire verse.

27:12–14. The chief priests and elders accused Jesus before the prefect, but Jesus gave no reply. Jesus's silence was in line with the Suffering Servant of Isaiah 42:4, 50:6, and 53:7. This silence caused Pilate to ask if Jesus had any response, but Jesus did not answer a single charge. This left Pilate completely amazed. Pilate surely saw Jesus as no grave threat to Rome, as "too impotent to be dangerous" (Davies and Allison 1997, 582). Jesus had no standing army nor was he gathering one. His following was not violent. Davies and Allison (1997, 578) note that Jesus "quietly turns the other cheek" in this entire scene.

> **Silence of the Suffering Servant**
>
> **Isaiah 53:7:** "He was treated harshly and afflicted, but he did not even open his mouth. Like a lamb led to the slaughtering block, like a sheep silent before her shearers, he did not even open his mouth."

Mark 15:3–5 is parallel. Luke has no parallel to this but instead has the leaders press when Pilate expressed Jesus's innocence. In Luke, the Jewish leaders noted that Jesus had stirred up people in Judea and Galilee (Luke 23:5).

27:15–16. Matthew turned to the policy of amnesty where Pilate often released a prisoner of the people's choice once a year. We have no outside evidence of this practice. However, all we have about Pilate is mostly limited to a few remarks about his rule from Josephus. We do have a couple of examples of this kind of thing, either done or requested, from Josephus (*A.J.* 17.204; 20.208–9, 215; Blomberg 1992, 410; Culpepper 2021, 544; Davies and Allison 1997, 583; France 2007, 1052; Merritt 1985; Nolland 2005, 1167). Matthew notes an infamous, even notorious, prisoner the other gospels identify as named Barabbas (Mark 15:7; Luke 23:18; John 18:40). We are not told what made him so well known, but the other gospels describe him in terms of being a revolutionary (Mark 15:7; John 18:40). His name "Barabbas" simply means "the son of a father." Pilate set up a choice, apparently to get the people to free Jesus in the face of the alternative. Mark 15:6–7 is a parallel, while Luke simply recounts the discussion with no setup of it.

Examples of the Release of One for Another

Josephus, *Antiquities* 20.208–9, 215: "But now the sicarii went into the city by night, just before the festival, which was now at hand, and took the scribe belonging to the governor of the temple, whose name was Eleazar, who was the son of Ananus (Ananias) the high priest, and bound him, and carried him away with them; (20.9.3) after which they sent to Ananias, and said that they would send the scribe to him, if he would persuade Albinus to release ten of those prisoners which he had caught of their party; so Ananias was plainly forced to persuade Albinus, and gained his request of him. . . . But when Albinus heard that Gessius Florus was coming to succeed him, he was desirous to appear to do somewhat that might be grateful to the people of Jerusalem; so he brought out all those prisoners who seemed to him to be the most plainly worthy of death, and ordered them to be put to death accordingly. But as to those who had been put into prison on some trifling occasion, he took money of them, and dismissed them; by which means the prisons were indeed emptied, but the country was filled with robbers."

The scene is full of characters: Pilate, the chief priests and elders, Pilate's wife, the crowd, Barabbas, and Jesus. The scene is all about Jesus who has said next to nothing. Opinions about him abounded. The narration allows for development of the points of view on Jesus in thinking about the passage. The theme of the injustice to Jesus is developed in this characterization. Rome had a leader in Pilate who seemed to see Jesus as innocent but allowed him to go to the cross. This was hardly an endorsement of Roman justice. He preferred expediency to justice (Keener 2009, 665). The Roman examination is different in tone than the Jewish examination, but on justice it did as poorly, just in a different way. The scene also suggests that Jesus never should have made it to the cross, but he did. The forces working against him were successful in getting him there. Even the help of a dream was ignored. This was the one dream in Matthew that was ignored, in contrast to the many dreams in the infancy material.

27:17–18. So early in the morning, the normal time for such events, Pilate offered a choice to the crowd of whom they wanted to release. Did they wish to free Jesus Barabbas or Jesus who is called the Christ? The offer was made in part because Pilate sensed envy on the part of the leaders. They were jealous of Jesus's sway over the populace, hardly a crime. Pilate assumed Jesus would be released (Luke 23:20).

Mark 15:8–10 is the parallel here. In Mark, Pilate asked if they wanted the king of the Jews released to them. The crowd also initiated the request for a prisoner to be released (for locations, see map of Jerusalem at Matt. 26:57–58).

27:19. While at the raised *bēma* (judgment seat) before the crowd, Pilate received a message from his wife about a dream she had had that tormented her. John 19:13 calls the locale *Gabbatha,* the stone pavement. Its location has been discussed, with the Antonia fortress or Herod's palace as the two most common suggested locales. Either is possible and there is no clear way to decide, although many favor Herod's palace. Nolland (2005, 1171) prefers the palace because it was where Pilate likely stayed (Wilkins 2004, 875). To bother him during this process showed how urgent his wife thought this was. Her advice was to do nothing with this innocent man. The term here is δίκαιος, meaning "innocent" or "righteous" (BDAG s.v. "δίκαιος" 1bβ, 246–47; Osborne 2010, 1018). One means the other. The same Greek term shows up in the mouth of a soldier at the cross in Luke 23:47.

This detail about the dream is unique to Matthew. He had noted dreams before in the infancy material (Matt. 1:20; 2:12, 13, 19). They were seen as a way of direction. Pilate did not heed the dream, unlike Joseph and the magi in those early chapters. Pilate's wife was another non-Jewish woman who had a sense of who Jesus was (Davies and Allison 1997, 586). Morris (1992, 704) argues for historicity here and says Pilate's hesitation to deal with Jesus may have been motivated by his wife's concern.

27:20. The chief priests and elders had persuaded the crowd to ask for Barabbas and seek crucifixion for Jesus. Davies and Allison (1997, 588) speak of the blind leading the blind here. Mark 15:11 is parallel, as Mark notes the leaders had stirred up the crowd to ask for Barabbas.

27:21–23. So Pilate asked the crowd whom they wished to have released. They responded asking for Barabbas. Then Pilate asked what they wished to be done with Jesus who was called the Christ. They all responded, "Crucify him." There was unanimity in the crowd. Pilate objected, asking what wrong Jesus had done, which was an implied declaration of innocence. There may be an allusion to Isaiah 53:9 and associating the servant with criminals in the raising of this question (Nolland 2005, 1176). They did not answer the query, as there is no clear answer in the narrative, but merely shouted more insistently to let him be crucified. This detail adds to the notes Matthew made of injustice in the action.

The Servant Associated with Criminals

Isaiah 53:9: "They intended to bury him with criminals, but he ended up in a rich man's tomb, because he had committed no violent deeds, nor had he spoken deceitfully."

The popularity of Jesus on his entry was not present here (Matt. 21:9; 11, 26; 26:5). Two explanations for the change of view about Jesus are possible. One is that Jesus's arrest had persuaded the crowd that Jesus would not lead them into freedom (Davies and Allison 1997, 588; Turner 2008, 654). Another is that this crowd was vastly different in makeup than the crowd of the entry (Blomberg 1992, 412, and France 2007, 1055, allow for both). Might the favoritism Pilate now showed Jesus also be in play by generating a reaction because Rome appeared to be for him (so Nolland 2005, 1174)? Either way, things have reversed quickly. Despite the dream, the Jewish leaders' envy, and nothing surfacing in his examination, Pilate moved ahead because of the crowd. Justice was not served; instead, Jesus was served up.

Some challenge this narrative and argue Pilate was out of character here. He was not sensitive to Jewish concerns and threw his power around to demonstrate Roman sovereignty, especially when it came to Jews. However, Keener (2009, 665–67) has a long discussion about cases where various Roman governors showed care in how they decided sensitive cases. In addition, Pilate's past insensitivities had gotten him into trouble with the emperor Tiberius. So he may have been more careful this time. Add in his wife's concern, and he was being very careful.

Mark 15:12–14 is the parallel here. The only difference is that Pilate asked about the king of the Jews and not the Christ here, a difference that merely explained the title. In addition, in the scene itself, Mark notes the priests had stirred the pot earlier than Matthew does, a difference one should not make too much of as it was a question of when to present the background cause of what was going on. Luke 23:21–23 is also parallel in a more summary form. There, Pilate proclaimed Jesus's innocence as well as pleaded with the crowd about their choice. He offered to flog and release Jesus, but that proposal did not sway the crowd. John 18:39–40 is also a summary asking that Barabbas be freed.

27:24. In another unique Matthean detail, Pilate feared a riot from the crowd and washed his hands of the affair (Deut. 21:1–9; Pss. 26:6; 73:13; Ep. Arist. 305–6; Davies and Allison 1997, 590). He declared himself innocent of this man's blood while sending Jesus to his death. The act was completely contradictory to the pursuit of justice. If Pilate really saw Jesus as innocent enough for Pilate not to want to have anything to do with his death, Jesus should have been released. The act did not absolve Pilate but reflected self-deception, an abdication of justice, and complicity with the voices of those who more aggressively wished to deal with Jesus. As Konradt (2020, 417) says, "Matthew reveals Pilate's attempt to renounce his responsibility cannot stand." Who wants a judge who sees one as innocent to say, "You can die anyway"? Though less hostile, Pilate, and Rome with him, share a role in Jesus's death.

27:25. In another unique Matthean detail, the crowd responded, taking responsibility for the judgment. The crowd said that Jesus's blood should be on them and their children. What Pilate shied away from, the crowd accepted. This has often been taken as a Matthean anti-Semitic remark, but it is not. Turner (2008, 655–56) has a long discussion on this issue, noting this was the language of accepting responsibility. The response also was not a carefully reasoned theological proposition. It was made in the heat of the moment. It was made by a limited group, but an important one: the leaders in Jerusalem and the crowd (Matt. 23:37; Konradt 2020, 418–19). They represent those who reject Jesus, not all of Israel. The expression is simply an idiomatic way of vividly saying, "We take responsibility for urging Jesus's death" (Lev. 20:9; Deut. 19:10; Josh. 2:19; 2 Sam. 1:16; Jer. 26:15; 51:35; Ezek. 18:13; 33:4; Acts 5:28; 18:6; 20:26; Turner 2008, 654). The mention of children recognized that taking such responsibility could have lingering consequences (Jer. 31:29; Lam. 5:7; Ezek. 18:2). For Matthew, A.D. 70 or even the threat of something like it may have been one of those consequences (Davies and Allison 1997, 592). This point emerges whether one dates Matthew before or after the city's being overrun by Rome, as it is either a prediction of such, a reflection of it having taken place, or both. In noting the idiom present, the verse was abused in later church history to justify attacks on Jewish people in a manner having nothing to do with its original meaning (France 2007, 1057; Morris 1992, 708; Nolland 2005, 1179).

Blood on Someone's Head as Taking Responsibility

Leviticus 20:9: "If anyone curses his father or mother he must be put to death. He has cursed his father or mother; his blood guilt is on himself."

2 Samuel 1:16: "David said to him, 'Your blood be on your own head! Your own mouth has testified against you, saying "I have put the Lord's anointed to death."'"

Jeremiah 51:35: "The person who lives in Zion says, 'May Babylon pay for the violence done to me and to my relatives.' Jerusalem says, 'May those living in Babylonia pay for the bloodshed of my people.'"

27:26. Pilate had Barabbas released and sent Jesus to be scourged in preparation for crucifixion. This whipping involved leather cords laced with nails, bone, or other types of metal chips. The beating was designed to get the blood flowing, to make the death more gruesome and speed its arrival through a loss of blood (Josephus, *B.J.* 2.306, 308—in a period after Jesus, Florus even does this to members of the equestrian order; 5.449; 6.304; 7.200–202; Philo, *Flacc.* 10.75; T. Benj. 2:2–4; Turner 2008, 654). The victim was tied to a pole for the beating.

Examples of a Whipping and Then Crucifixion

Josephus, *Jewish War* 2.305b–308: "So the soldiers, taking this exhortation of their commander in a sense agreeable to their desire of gain, did not only plunder the place they were sent to, but forcing themselves into every house, they slew its inhabitants; so the citizens fled along the narrow lanes, and the soldiers slew those that they caught, and no method of plunder was omitted; they also caught many of the quiet people, and brought them before Florus, whom he first chastised with stripes, and then crucified. Accordingly, the whole number of those that were destroyed that day, with their wives and children (for they did not spare even the infants themselves), was about three thousand and six hundred; and what made this calamity the heavier, was this new method of Roman barbarity; for Florus ventured then to what no one had done before, that is, to have men of the equestrian order whipped, and nailed to the cross before his tribunal; who, although they were by birth Jews, yet were they of Roman dignity notwithstanding."

Josephus, *Jewish War* 5.449: "So they were first whipped, and then tormented with all sorts of tortures before they died, and were then crucified before the wall of the city."

Josephus, *Jewish War* 6.304—of another figure named Jesus: "Where he was whipped till his bones were laid bare; yet did he not make any supplication for himself, nor shed any tears, but turning his voice to the most lamentable tone possible, at every stroke of the whip his answer was, 'Woe, woe to Jerusalem!'"

Mark 15:15 is the parallel here. Luke 23:16 and 22 speak of Pilate's earlier intent to flog Jesus and release him, but did not otherwise note the flogging. Luke 23:25 simply says Pilate handed Jesus over to their will.

27:27–31. In the praetorium, the residence of the provincial governor, Jesus was given over to the soldiers, who continued their mocking of him as was predicted in Matthew 20:19. As already noted, this was either at Antonia or in Herod's palace. A cohort was six hundred to one thousand men, mostly non-Jewish, Syro-Palestinian auxiliaries (Josephus, *A.J.* 14.204; 19.365; Davies and Allison 1997, 601). The soldiers' public abuse of prisoners was not unusual (Keener 2009, 674).

They put Jesus in a scarlet robe, gave him a crown of thorns, placed a reed in his hand, bowed before him and addressed him with "Hail, king of the Jews." It was a mocking coronation, replacing the golden crown of a king (1 Macc. 10:20) and his staff (Konradt 2020, 421). There was no rule here, just shame (thorns) and powerlessness (reed). Scarlet was the color of a Roman soldier's cloak, which explains where it came from as well. Mark 15:20 speaks of purple, making a royal allusion. The difference is not significant, as the symbolism of mocking a king is clearly the point (Nolland 2005, 1182). The soldiers spat on him, struck him with the reed, and then dressed him for crucifixion, leading him away. Romans showed sensitivity to Jewish feelings about public nudity by having victims of crucifixion go to the cross clothed.

The allusions in the mocking are to Psalm 22:7 and Isaiah 50:6. Again, the irony is that one day the mocking will be reversed, in a judgment Jesus will lead. Luke lacks this scene, while Mark 15:16–20 is parallel. John 19:1–5 narrates mocking earlier in the sequence of events.

THEOLOGICAL FOCUS

The exegetical idea (with Judas acknowledging Jesus's innocence and the Jewish leaders and crowd applying pressure, Pilate sent Jesus to be crucified) translates into this theological one: under pressure, Pilate sentences Jesus to an unjust death, despite his sense that Jesus is innocent.

Jesus is sent to his death with mocking in the midst of Pilate and his wife's declarations of innocence, showing his death to be unjust even as it also fulfilled Scripture. In all of this, the crowd took responsibility for calling for him to die over Barabbas.

A series of themes swirl around Pilate's examination of Jesus. Some of them are filled with deep irony. Jesus's silence was in fulfillment of Scripture, as was Judas and the leaders' handling of the thirty pieces of silver (Isa. 50:6; Zech. 13:7). God's messenger was worth no more than a slave. Injustice abounded. Hints of Jesus's innocence appeared throughout the passage. Judas realized his betrayal of Jesus was wrong. Pilate did not sense that Jesus was guilty, as he asked what wrong Jesus had done. Pilate's wife warned him, as a dream caused her to tell Pilate not to mess with this righteous man. As the ruler Pilate made a decision he was responsible for, he washed his hands of that responsibility, even though it was his decision that sealed Jesus's fate. The only ones clamoring for Jesus's death were the chief priests and elders who had persuaded the crowd that Jesus should be put to death. The crowd accepted responsibility for this when they chose Barabbas over Jesus. Every step of this said Jesus should be released, but each step also took him closer to death. The description highlighted the injustice of what was taking place. Jesus suffered as a righteous innocent.

Another key image was the substitution of Jesus for Barabbas. Jesus's death made possible the release and continued life of a notorious sinner. This exchange pictured precisely what Jesus's death provided. He died so others could live.

The responsibility the crowd took for the death is not a case of Matthew being anti-Semitic, but rather points to the awareness that they had called for Jesus to die. Matthew's gospel portrays such a decision as covenantal unfaithfulness in line with past acts of Israel (parable of the Wicked Tenants). It led Matthew to suggest that the temple's coming destruction was a judgment for such unfaithfulness, a reflection of Jesus declaring Israel's house desolate in Matthew 23:37–39. The scene had set the table for Jesus's death. All that was left was to tell the story of the cross and its decisive aftermath.

PREACHING AND TEACHING STRATEGIES

Exegetical and Theological Synthesis

The exegetical section demonstrates the power of crowds. The Jewish mob forces Pilate's hand to execute Jesus. Crowds are culpable for their actions (Acts 2:23). Pilate is not the only political figure swayed by popular opinion. Similarly, leaders of schools, businesses, NGOs, and churches often cater to crowds. When enough people join hands and make noise, they pressure the powers that be into change. They make us complicit and justice disappears.

On the other hand, the passage exposes the weakness of crowds. They are easy to manipulate. They are rarely animated by the best information or pure motives. In Matthew's account, the Jewish mob blindly followed their religious leaders. They indiscriminately echoed the priests' plea for crucifixion. Sadly, very little thinking is involved in groupthink, hence Petersen's (2011, 157) observation that crowds are dangerous: they destroy the spirit and impede growth.

Followers of Jesus are called to resist the crowds. We are strangers, pilgrims, and citizens of heaven (Phil. 3:20; 1 Peter 1:1). During our earthly sojourn we are to embody heavenly values, living as salt, light, and royal priests (Matt. 5–7; Phil. 2:14–15; 1 Peter 2:9–17). The early church modeled this in their exclusive worship of the triune God (Matt. 28:19; 1 Cor. 8:6; 2 Cor. 13:13) and commitment to godly households (Eph. 5:22–6:9; Col. 3:18–4:1; 1 Tim. 3–5; Titus 2; 1 Peter 2:18–3:7) and church community (Rom. 12–14; 1 Cor. 12–14; Eph. 2:11–22; 4:1–16). Healthy Christian community, both in the home and church, helps us resist the crowds.

Preaching Idea

Cowards cave when crowds rage.

Contemporary Connections

What does it mean?

A coward is someone who lacks the courage to do what he knows is right. Fear seizes him and he compromises his values or beliefs as a result. This is caving. Pilate is the example here and Jesus paid the price. The fears may be driven by peer pressure, a need to please others, or a desire to save face. Most of us are familiar with these fears on a personal level. For example, a teenager may smoke his first joint because he fears his friends will think him a prude. A woman may compromise her body because she does not want her boyfriend to dump her.

Crowds exacerbate our fears. Their volume and intensity make compromise appealing. For example, a pastor may avoid preaching about racial injustice, knowing it may incite outrage and rumors that he has succumbed to critical race theory. A social media "influencer" may edit or remove a post when its content receives negative feedback from her followers. Networks may revive a canceled TV series when enough fans demand its return. College administrators may fire a professor given enough pressure from students, parents, trustees, and (especially) donors.

Is it true?

It is certainly true that cowards cave when crowds rage. We have seen many examples of companies, church leaders, politicians, and celebrities backpedaling when confronted by the mob. However, not every concession is compromise. Not every apology, avoided topic, or edited comment is an example of caving to crowds. In fact, sometimes what looks like cowardice may be wisdom. For example, the so-called coward may have gained new information that caused a change of mind. This may have been the case with the CDC in the early stages of the COVID pandemic. Rather than caving to the crowds, medical experts gained new insights about the novel virus and amended their guidelines. Likewise, churches and denominations that have recently responded to allegations of sexual abuse may not simply be caving to social justice warriors but taking seriously their responsibility to protect their people.

A second caveat is worth noting: namely, sometimes what passes as courage is stubbornness. The parent who refuses to listen to his children may be stubborn. The senator who never works with colleagues from the opposing party may be stubborn. The Christian who withdraws from all secular institutions may be stubborn. According to C. S. Lewis (1996b, 104),

> Courage is not simply *one* of the virtues, but the form of every virtue at the testing point, which means at the point of highest reality. A chastity or honesty or mercy which yields

> to danger will be chaste or honest or merciful only on conditions. Pilate was merciful till it became risky.[1]

Courage is meant to bolster other virtues, not simply keep us from caving.

Now what?

This passage and preaching idea prompt several responses. First, we should take stock of our fear of others. Where have we caved to peer pressure? What crowds cause us anxiety? How are we saving face? What values or beliefs have we compromised? When we reflect on our fears, we must be brutally honest. We may also benefit from the feedback of a trusted friend or mentor, since we may be prone to self-deception.

Second, we should reframe our fear of others as opportunities to grow in virtue. Review Lewis's quotation. When our values and beliefs are tested, we have two primary choices: be courageous or cave. When we choose courage, an increase of faith follows. When we choose cowardice, it is "purely painful—horrible to anticipate, horrible to feel, horrible to remember" (Lewis 1996b, 104). According to Lewis we do not remain in the pain of cowardice. It may push us to despair like Judas, indifference like Pilate, or repentance like Peter.

Finally, we must seek community instead of crowds. Crowds are fleeting—they flash into existence and quickly disappear. Crowds are violent—they shout, wreak havoc, and trample people in their path. Crowds are impersonal—nameless mobs drag a person's name through the mud. They publicly shame others and call for their blood. In contrast, community abides, extends grace, and knows one another by name. By establishing a biblical, countercultural community, followers of Jesus can resist the crowd.

Creativity in Presentation

Since the rise of the smartphone, the influence of crowds has been on steady display in the U.S. Examples are many: from boycotts of Starbucks and Chick-fil-A, to protests about police brutality, to the storming of the U.S. Capitol after the 2020 elections, to anti-Semitism marches tied to the Israel-Palestine conflict, to countless examples of cancel culture, and to some forms of activism on university campuses. Pick your poison. Show some images. Describe the fervor and effects of the crowd. And expect a little pushback for any example you select![2]

Draw from some haunting examples of caving to the crowd in film and literature. William Golding's disturbing classic *Lord of the Flies* paints a picture of human depravity. In a tragic scene on the beach, a crowd of boys stranded on an island has turned savage. They surrounded Robert. They circle him. One boy begins to poke him. They start chanting, "Kill the pig! Cut his throat. Kill the pig! Bash him in!" Their frenzy nearly becomes fatal. The crowd jeers and snorts. Golding (2006, 114–15) writes, "The desire to squeeze and hurt was over-mastering." The scene illustrates how crowds hijack our thinking.

You may also want to provide examples of courage. Some humorous examples could be the (de)motivational poster of one fish, swimming upstream against all the other fish; soccer players standing with hands crossed for a penalty kick, or a man standing in the street facing a giant Domo doll or standing before a tank to stop its progress.

A personal story may be fitting here, as well. My (Tim's) daughter had an interesting experience in her high school politics class. In a debate about gun control, she took the side of more restrictions for gun sales. She stood alone,

---

1 This excerpt comes from Screwtape's twenty-ninth letter to Wormword (emphasis original). Lewis provides a thoughtful reflection on courage and cowardice. It is worth reading in its entirety.

2 For more on mob mentality in higher academia, see Lukianoff and Haidt (2018). Read the introduction here: https://www.thecoddling.com/copy-of-read-ch-1-on-antifragility (accessed July 24, 2024).

presenting her case and responding to counterarguments. At the end of class, popular opinion prevailed. My daughter felt tired and alone but did not cave. It was a helpful exercise for her. Another high school student shared a similar testimony when she represented her pro-life view at her public high school on the *Love Thy Neighborhood* podcast.[3] Perhaps you have similar stories in your congregation about courageously standing against popular opinion. Share them.

In the end, be sure your sermon shows how, under pressure, Pilate sentences Jesus to an unjust death despite his sense that Jesus is innocent. Indeed, cowards cave when crowds rage.[4]

- Persistent opponents stick to their plot (27:1–2).
- A remorseful betrayer ends his life (27:3–10).
- A curious governor examines Jesus (27:11–14).
- A raging crowd demands Jesus's death (27:15–26).
- Savage soldiers mock "King" Jesus (27:27–31).

DISCUSSION QUESTIONS

1. How do you interpret Judas's actions? What was he thinking and feeling?
2. Compare Jesus's response to Pilate with his response to the chief priests. How are they similar? Different?
3. What details do the other gospel writers bring into this encounter? What was Matthew's aim in his account?
4. Is Matthew sympathetic to Pilate? Explain.
5. Throughout the gospel, Matthew has not taken kindly to crowds. How does this penultimate scene with a crowd further this theme?
6. When have you experienced the rage of crowds?
7. What should we make of the recent uptick in crowd activism and mob mentality?

---

3 For Episode 80: "Where the Gospel Reaches Teenagers," go to: https://lovethyneighborhood.org/80-where-the-gospel-meets-teenagers (accessed July 24, 2024).

4 Frederick Buechner (1977, 8–14) provides a wonderful interpretation of Pilate's interaction with Jesus. Certain imagery and phrases from his description may help you describe Pilate's mindset as he wrestled with truth and Jesus's fate.

Matthew 27:32–66

EXEGETICAL IDEA

Amid mocking, scriptural fulfillment, and heavenly portents that witnesses observed, Jesus was crucified as king of the Jews, confessed as God's Son, given a burial, and had his tomb guarded to prevent the body being stolen.

THEOLOGICAL FOCUS

Jesus dies as king of the Jews and God's Son, in fulfillment of God's plan.

PREACHING IDEA

The cross is a cosmic witness to the work of God.

PREACHING POINTS

Matthew reached a climax in God's redemptive story. Jesus, the promised Son—born of a virgin and sent as a ransom for sins—mounted the cross and died. Matthew describes two types of witnesses: mockers and confessors. Crowds, religious leaders, and criminals mocked him. The centurion, female disciples, and Joseph of Arimathea confessed him. Added to this kaleidoscope of cameos, Matthew describes the cosmic witness affected by Jesus's death: darkness, earthquake, torn veil, and open graves. Jesus's suffering was profound but not without purpose. The Son of God fulfilled Scripture. And the preservation of his body in Joseph's tomb remained a point of interest to his followers and the religious authorities, who anticipated God had not finished the work he began in Jesus. For Matthew's audience, themes of fulfillment, opposition, salvation, and witness came to a head. The cross was a turning point in human history.

The cross remains a core image of Christian faith. Whereas other ancient iconography has lost its potency, the cross is a timeless witness to God's work. The cross testifies to Jesus's suffering, divine forgiveness, and scriptural fulfillment. Today many believers wear cross tattoos, earrings, and pendants to express their faith in Jesus. Likewise, crosses mark Protestant church buildings or adorn pulpits and stages. A cross is the most common etching on the front of a Bible. Perhaps the ubiquity of the cross numbs us to its original brutality. Alas, Jesus sacrificed dearly for our sins. The cross is a profound witness. A wordless and wonderful witness. Or, as this sermon indicates, the cross is a cosmic witness to the work of God.

JESUS IS CRUCIFIED AND BURIED (27:32–66)

LITERARY STRUCTURE AND THEMES (27:32–66)

This unit has many parts we have labeled as cameos. First, Jesus was brought to the cross (Matt. 27:32–37). Then Jesus was mocked (Matt. 27:38–44). As creation went dark, Jesus cried out (Matt. 27:45–50). As Jesus was dying, a torn veil, earthquake, and empty tombs led to a soldier's confession of Jesus as Son of God (Matt. 27:51–56). With women witnesses watching, Jesus was buried by Joseph of Arimathea (Matt. 27:57–61). Out of fear for the body being stolen with claims of resurrection, the Jewish leaders caused guards to be posted at the tomb (Matt. 27:62–66).

The crucifixion scene is a collection of short observations about many different things that took place. It reads like a grocery list, shifting quickly from one angle to another point of view. Many distinct points are made, but all point to the confession of Jesus as Son of God. Despite the mocking and the helpless position of Jesus, he was and is who he claimed to be. Scriptural language showed this, as did the creation.

The parallels to the crucifixion are Mark 15:21–41, Luke 23:26–49, and John 19:16b–37. Each has its own unique observations along with items that overlap with the other passages.

With notes naming witnesses of the crucifixion and describing the burial, Matthew transitions to the tomb. The parallels to the burial are Mark 15:42–47, Luke 23:50–56, and John 19:38–42. However, only Matthew notes the guarding of the tomb.

The quick shifts in perspective make for less of a sustained development of specific characters than for a sense of the wide variety of responses the cross engendered. The role of scriptural language and the responses of creation in many ways occupy a most dominant role. They stand in stark contrast to the seeming indifference or hostility of many people who were present. An irony is that for many, nothing of great significance was taking place, when in fact this death was of momentous importance. The one exception to this in Matthew was the climactic response of the soldiers, who sense from everything going on around them that Jesus was the Son of God. This conclusion was this was something surely the heavenly portents in particular generated, as the earthquake was said to be the cause of their response. This cosmic response encapsulated the theme of the crucifixion's narration. Those with eyes to see would understand what was taking place, even as the creation pointed to an earth-shattering event.

The burial scene showed that not all Jews rejected Jesus. Some even provided for a burial to give him a place of rest. They did so, not anticipating a resurrection to come. Women witnessed this expression of care for Jesus. In ironic contrast, the Jewish leaders sought to make sure nothing could take place that would allow the fabrication of the claim that Jesus was raised from the dead. Guards were placed at the tomb. If anything happened, it would have to be of God. (For discussion of issues of historicity tied to the tomb and burial, see Osborne in Bock and Webb 2009, 775–823; Bock 2012, 190–210; and Evans 2012, 470–71).

EXPOSITION (27:32–66)

Matthew presented the cross in simple but quickly moving terms. The innocent one went to his death for others. Most did not appreciate and were oblivious to what was taking place, but creation knew. Matthew wanted his readers to be reassured heaven knew what was taking place and stood behind it.

Amid mocking, scriptural fulfillment, and heavenly portents that witnesses observed, Jesus was crucified as king of the Jews, confessed as God's Son, given a burial, and had his tomb guarded to prevent the body being stolen.

27:32. The beating Jesus took made him unable to bear the cross. Simon of Cyrene was impressed to carry it for him. Cyrene was in modern Libya; the locale appears in Acts 6:9; 11:20; 13:1. There was a significant Jewish presence there, up to a quarter of the city (Josephus, *A.J.* 14.115–18; C. Ap. 2.44; Keener 2009, 677; Nolland 2005, 1188). Normally the condemned carried his own cross, but Jesus was apparently too weak to do this. Simon likely was a diaspora Jew there for the feast.

Mark 15:21 has detail Matthew lacks, while Luke 23:26 is much like Matthew. Simon was the father of Alexander and Rufus, whose names were dropped in a way that makes them look like they were well known to Mark's audience. Luke 23:27–31 uniquely has the weeping women. Jesus warned them, saying they should not weep for him but for themselves because of what was coming for the spiritually dead nation of Israel, a nation compared to a piece of dead wood.

27:33. They brought the crossbeam, also known as the *patibulum*, to a place known as Golgotha, the place of the skull, a name appropriate with what was taking place as a skull pointed to death. The Aramaic term is *gûlgaltā*ʾ (France 2007, 1065). This site is tied to the Church of the Holy Sepulchre in tradition, which is possible but not certain. It is a more likely locale than the Garden Tomb (especially Wilkins 2004, 898; also Barkay 1986; France 2007, 1065). This was in part because the Garden Tomb does not give evidence of having been used as a burial location in the first century, and the tomb there actually gives evidence of being a tomb centuries older than the unused tomb in which Jesus was placed.[1] The Latin term for "skull" is *calvaria*; the well-known name of Calvary for the crucifixion site comes from this. If Jesus was coming from Herod's palace, then this walk was less than a half mile. If he came from Antonia, then it was much further. Mark 15:22 is the parallel verse and is very similar. John 19:17 also mentions Golgotha.

27:34. Jesus was offered wine mixed with gall, but after tasting it he refused the drink. This would have had a sedative effect (Prov. 31:6; Sanh. 43a), but the gall would have made it bitter, so there may be an element of mocking in this offer (Davies and Allison 1997, 612–13). Jesus intended to go through all the pain of the suffering. The language recalls Psalm 69:21 (68:22 LXX). That psalm pointed to Jesus as suffering in the model of a righteous sufferer.

Wine Mixed with Gall for the Righteous Sufferer

Psalm 69:21: "They put bitter poison into my food, and to quench my thirst they give me vinegar to drink."

Mark 15:23 refers to wine mixed with myrrh. Blomberg (1992, 416) suggests myrrh was what was in the wine, while gall described its effect. John 19:29–30 has Jesus take sour wine just before he died. Luke lacks any mention of the wine.

27:35. Having hung Jesus up on the cross, the soldiers divided his clothes by casting lots.

1 For a good summary: https://biblearchaeologyreport.com/2019/04/20/three-tombs-of-jesus-which-is-the-real-one (accessed Feb 24, 2024).

The language is from Psalm 22:18, another righteous-sufferer psalm. No description was given as to how the crucifixion was done. Jesus apparently was nailed by his wrists with his feet together below him. One died from being unable to take a breath, that is, if the loss of blood from the whipping did not kill the victim first. It is discussed whether Jesus was crucified naked, as was the custom, or if there was a loin cloth out of sensitivity to Jewish concerns about public nudity. The issue is discussed in Mishnah, *Sanhedrin* 6.3 (Nolland 2005, 1193). The likelihood is that he was crucified nude, as part of the point of the event was to make it shameful (Keener 2009, 679; Osborne 2010, 1033). On feelings about crucifixion and other cultural details, see Hengel (1977).

Casting Lots and Execution in the Nude

Psalm 22:18: "They are dividing up my clothes among themselves; they are rolling dice for my garments."

***Mishnah Sanhedrin* 6:3b:** "'In the case of a man, they cover him up in front, and in the case of a woman, they cover her up in front and behind,' the words of R. Judah. And sages say, 'A man is stoned naked, but a woman is not stoned naked.'"

Mark 15:24 is parallel and similar, while 15:25 gives a time note of the third hour. Matthew 27:45 has a time note that from noon to three there was darkness. John 19:23–24 has much more detail, noting the tunic was seamless, the soldiers did not want to tear it, and citing the psalm. Luke 23:34b mentions this briefly and has Jesus ask God to forgive them, for they do not know what they are doing.

27:36–37. Then the soldiers sat and guarded the cross as they awaited the inevitable death to come. This remark is unique to Matthew.

Above Jesus's head was a sign that gave the cause of his death, defining the charge against Jesus: "This is Jesus, the king of the Jews." This was called the *titulus*. He died as king of the Jews, claiming to be a king Rome did not appoint. Stated legally, his crime was sedition. It is an important detail. Jesus was not executed merely for being a prophet. The regal charge pointed in the direction of messianism as a public issue tied to Jesus. The detail may also suggest a standard t-shape to the cross, so the *titulus* could be displayed (Davies and Allison 1997, 613). In the second century, Irenaeus in *Haer.* 2.24.4 describes the shape of the cross as having five extremities (two up, two across, one middle; think of a capital X with a line through the middle). The t-shape is more likely.

Mark 15:26 is parallel. John 19:19–22 also notes the trilingual (Aramaic, Latin, and Greek) inscription as "Jesus of Nazareth, King of the Jews". John discusses the controversy with the Jewish leaders it engendered. Luke 23:38 has simply, "This is the king of the Jews." The variation looks like varying summaries from oral tradition (Davies and Allison 1997, 615). Matthew's reference to "this is" recalls a likely redaction he made of the voice from heaven at Jesus's baptism by John, when he goes with "this is my beloved Son" versus "you are my beloved Son." (Matt. 3:17 in comparison to Mark 1:11; Luke 3:22). Seen as a speech act, this is what the *titulus* does, identifies. Since Luke also has this wording, it may reflect the memory of the tradition.

27:38. Jesus was crucified in the midst of two robbers. The term here is λῃστής, which appears in Matthew 26:55 (BDAG s.v. "λῃστής" 1, 594; also John 18:40). Jesus was numbered among the transgressors. Isaiah 53:12 is conceptually similar, but there is a lack of verbal overlap. The reference to these robbers brackets this scene as they reappear in Matthew 27:44.

Numbered Among the Transgressors

Isaiah 53:12: "So I will assign him a portion with the multitudes, he will divide the spoils of victory with the powerful, because he willingly submitted to death and was numbered with the rebels, when he lifted up the sin of many and intervened on behalf of the rebels."

Mark 15:27 is parallel and very similar, as is John 19:18.

27:39–40. Three sets of people reviled Jesus. Two groups focused on the idea of the Son of God. They may have felt free to mock Jesus because the one who was executed on a tree was accursed (Deut. 21:22–23; Gal. 3:13; Davies and Allison 1997, 616). Crucifixion took place in a very public place as a deterrent. Jesus's death brought a series of reactions. First were the passers-by, who wagged their heads blaspheming or slandering Jesus. The term here is βλασφημέω (BDAG s.v. "βλασφημέω" bє, 178; Matt. 15:19 says this reflects the heart). It refers to "slander" or some form of verbal disrespect. That disrespect was blasphemy when God was involved. Technically, the people would not have seen their remarks as being an insult to the divinity, but that was likely how Matthew saw it. Morris (1992, 717) says, "It is indeed blasphemy when mortals in this way dictate to the Son of God how he should exercise his divine sonship." The heads wagging alluded to Psalm 22:7, a sign of derision (Ps. 109:25; Jer. 18:16; Lam. 2:15; Turner 2008, 662).

Mocking of the Righteous Sufferer

Psalm 22:7: "All who see me taunt me; they mock me and shake their heads."

They urged him if he was the Son of God to save himself, since he said he could rebuild the temple in three days (Matt. 26:61). They urged him to come down and show himself to be the son. The "if you are the Son" taunt is like Satan's temptation challenges (Matt. 4:3, 6). If Jesus had done this, then no one would have died for sin. Instead, Jesus would suffer and then rule (Davies and Allison 1997, 619). The one who called for people to lose their lives to gain them served as the example (Matt. 16:25; Blomberg 1992, 417; Nolland 2005, 1197).

Mark 15:29–30 also notes those who passed by and mocked. Luke 23:35 has those standing by and watching, while the rulers scoffed and called on Jesus to save himself. Luke 23:36 has the soldiers scoff in a similar manner, calling him to save himself as they offered sour wine.

27:41–43. Religious leaders joined in. The second group of mockers were chief priests, scribes, and elders. The chief priests and elders had been the major opponents in the last week. Their taunt was that Jesus saved others but could not save himself. If he would come down from the cross, then they would believe. It was one more false claim to seek a sign and dictate how things should proceed. Multiple times Jesus had already shown who he was, as the miracles attested. This also is an ironic statement because Jesus was vindicated from the cross by God at the resurrection; yet few believed even after that. God was to deliver him, they said mockingly, as they dripped satire on his claim to be God's Son. Ironically, God would deliver him and show him to be God's Son. In fact, these sarcastic uses of "Son of God" contrast with the sincere confession to come in Matthew 27:54 and look back to the controversy over the title in Matthew 26:63. Another irony is the seeming absence of deliverance for a sufferer trusting God, but it was because something greater was being done. The theme Matthew was raising can be seen in Wisdom 2:12–20, where the wicked plot against the righteous man who claimed to be a child of God—they challenged him to be vindicated by God as a demonstration that the righteous one was who he claimed to be (France 2007, 1071). Matthew was pointing to this cynicism.

Culpepper (2021, 558) sees a picture like that Isaiah 6:9–10 describes, seeing but not perceiving. Matthew 27:43 is unique to Matthew and alludes to Psalm 22:8, pointing again to the righteous sufferer theme. Mark 15:31–32a notes the chief priests and scribes mocking.

Mocking of the Righteous Sufferer to Be Delivered by God

Psalm 22:8: "They say, 'Commit yourself to the Lord! Let the Lord rescue him! Let the Lord deliver him, for he delights in him.'"

Wisdom 2:18–20: "For if the righteous man is God's child, he will help him, and will deliver him from the hand of his adversaries. Let us test him with insult and torture, so that we may find out how gentle he is, and make trial of his forbearance. Let us condemn him to a shameful death, for, according to what he says, he will be protected."

27:44. A third group, the robbers crucified with him, joined in the reviling. Jesus was not only suffering pain; he was being shamed by those around him. Irony is in all the mocking. The temple would be destroyed, but the temple of Jesus's body would become alive in three days. Jesus would be saved as Son and vindicated by God's work and, through that act of divine restoration, would save others. Jesus was the king despite what the mockers were doing. God would challenge and reverse their sarcasm. All participated in the mocking from soldiers to leaders, both Jew and Gentile. Jesus was surrounded by antagonism as he died (Morris 1992, 719).

Three groups have engaged in insults described as blaspheming (v. 39), mocking (v. 41), and reviling (v. 44). It is quite possible the totality of the mocking reflects the kinds of objections people had to the preaching of Jesus as the Son of God. How could the Son of God die and be crucified? That question may have fueled why many did not accept Jesus as the Messiah. Of course, the entire passion narrative is Matthew's reply.

Mark 15:32b also notes mocking from the others being crucified with him. Luke 23:39–43 has one criminal mock Jesus, also calling on him to save himself and them; the other crucified criminal rebuked the scoffer and asked Jesus to remember him when Jesus came into his kingdom, probably looking to the future resurrection. Jesus promised him paradise that very day in response. This detail is unique to Luke, as Mark does not report a positive response from either of those crucified with Jesus. John's gospel has no mocking.

27:45. From reviling, we turn to creation's testimony, a complete change of perspective. There was no mocking here, only foreboding lament. The land went dark from the sixth to ninth hour. Since the day was reckoned from the sun's rising, this was noon to three in the afternoon. The darkness pictures creation speaking of the tragic death of an innocent and the consequences of sin. It also reflects judgment imagery of the day of the Lord (Joel 2:2, 31; 3:14–15; Amos 8:9; Zeph. 1:15). This is creation "speaking," a cosmic commentary. Davies and Allison (1997, 623) refer to a similar example tied to Caesar's death as showing such was possible and would be appreciated by ancient readers (Plutarch, *Caesar* 69.5—dull sun and feeble heat; for other texts, Culpepper 2021, 560–61). This is the first of three ways nature spoke to the event in Matthew (veil rending, tombs opened).

Mark 15:33 and Luke 23:44 are parallel. Luke 23:45a notes the sun's light failed, and 23:45b presents the tearing of the temple veil, something Matthew has slightly later.

27:46. At about the ninth hour, or three in the afternoon, Jesus cried out in the language of Psalm 22:1 and in Aramaic, "My God, My God, why have you forsaken me?" That psalm opens with this cry of despair, beginning a lament that ends in a renewed trust of God. This was Jesus's first remark since Matthew 27:11. Was Jesus recognizing the testimony of the creation?

Mark reflects a different rendering of the Aramaic transliteration that has the same meaning, but with a link to the Hebrew (Davies and Allison 1997, 624). Matthew's translation into Greek explained the meaning, but the original language was cited as a last word and because it explained the perception of those around the cross that Jesus was calling for Elijah. It was the cry of someone being left to suffer alone, a theme Matthew had been developing (Matt. 13:53–58; 26:56, 69–75; 27:15–26; Davies and Allison 1997, 625). The despair here was deep and real. It should not be underappreciated. The darkness of the creation was real. As France (2007, 1076) notes, this "expresses not a loss of faith, but a (temporary) loss of contact." Also, Jesus suffered but trusted, crying out "my" God. This is Jesus's only word from the cross in Matthew, one of seven sayings across the Gospels (= Mark 15:34; Luke 23:34, 43, 46; John 19:26, 27, 28, 30).

The moment pictures Jesus's bearing sin and sensing a separation from God, becoming sin on our behalf (2 Cor. 5:21; Gal. 3:13; Wilkins 2004, 902). How this worked exactly is a mystery (Hagner 1995, 845). Although the passion narrative did not develop it in discussing the death, Matthew had developed the issue of death for sin (Matt. 1:21; 20:28; 26:28; and the picture with Barabbas). Psalm 22 had also been alluded to already elsewhere (Matt. 27:35–36, 39, 43).

Mark 15:34 is parallel. Mark 15:25 has the movement toward crucifixion start with the third hour or 9 a.m. (France 2007, 1074). This made the whole crucifixion last six hours.

27:47–49. Some in the crowd thought Jesus was calling for Elijah. The psalm beginning with *'Ēlî* might have led to this misunderstanding. Someone went and filled a sponge with drink to give aid to Jesus. An allusion to Psalm 69:22 LXX (69:21 Eng) makes another suffering-righteous connection (see chart with Matt. 27:34). This was likely one of the few acts of compassion in the midst of Jesus's dying and feeling forsaken (Morris 1992, 723), although Luke 23:36 ties it to the soldiers' mocking. We may have a case here of dealing with different ways of summarizing more complex sets of interactions, some of which may have had mixed motives. Jesus was not being abandoned completely. Some tried to stop this man's act of compassion, urging him to see if Elijah did come. There is irony here, since Elijah had already come to point to Jesus in the person of John the Baptist at the transfiguration (Matt. 3:11–17; 11:1–19). In other words, he had come already to point to Jesus.Mark 15:35–36 is parallel.

27:50. Jesus cried out a second time, but Matthew does not report what was said. Then Jesus gave up his spirit (Sir. 38:23; Wis. 16:14; Nolland 2005, 1210). The feeling is of a voluntary giving up of life. He had now died on the cross.

Mark 15:37 is parallel. Luke 23:46a has Jesus use the language of Psalm 31:5 and details what Jesus said here as "into your hands I commit my Spirit." There is no stark contrast between a Marcan and Matthean appeal of despair with the use of Psalm 22 and a Lucan note of trust in his use of Psalm 31. Luke is simply noting how Jesus trusted God at the end in a moment of deep suffering. Then Jesus breathed his last. John 19:25–27 says Jesus placed the care of his mother in the hands of the beloved disciple. Then in John 19:28, Jesus said he thirsted. John 18:29–30a has Jesus take a sip of sour wine. Then in John 19:30b, he said it was finished, bowed his head, and gave up his spirit.

27:51–53. Two more cosmic signs surfaced. They should be seen as a response to Jesus's prayer and Jesus's work on the cross. New life had come and creation responded (Konradt 2020, 428). An earthquake has multiple effects and illustrates judgment (Joel 3:16; Nah. 1:5–6). The rending of the temple veil is a detail shared with Mark 15:38 and Luke 23:45. It is not certain if this was the inner veil that separated the holy of holies or the veil in front of the holy place (Exod. 26:1–36).

What did it signify? It is unlikely it signified the permanent end of the temple (France 2007, 1081), for the sacrifices continued to A.D. 70 and there are Old Testament texts that tie the temple to the final part of the eschaton (Isa. 2:1–4). The tearing of the veil could refer to the short-term destruction of A.D. 70, provided that did not translate into a permanent destruction of the temple. The point then was not about the temple, but a rebuke of Israel's current leaders (Davies and Allison 1997, 631–32). It did point to the vindication of Jesus (Turner 2008, 670) and to God moving out from the temple into the world (Davies and Allison 1997, 630). Nolland (2005, 1212) sees temple destruction and God moving out to act as the points. Ephesians 2:14 may be a comment on this (Blomberg 1992, 421).

Which veil was meant? An act visible to the public would refer to the outer veil (Osborne 2010, 1043), but the inner veil is more important to picture God's new way (Heb. 9:3; 10:20; so Wilkins 2004, 904–5), so it is hard to be sure which was meant. With a different order, Luke narrates that detail before describing Jesus's death.

The earthquake and open tombs are unique to Matthew. Those who rested in the tombs were raised. They appeared to many in Jerusalem after the resurrection. Matthew did not see this as merely symbolic, as the other signs of the chapter were not symbols (correctly Turner 2008, 670, and Wilkins 2004, 907; against Davies and Allison 1997, 632). This was part of creation's visible testimony for Jesus and in response to him. It also showed how Jesus conquered death even for those who had already died. Konradt (2020, 429) sees Ezekiel 37:7, 12–13, and Zechariah 14:4–5 as perhaps in the background. Matthew mentions an earthquake and empty tombs here, and not just resurrection, to show that Jesus's death and bearing of sin were what opened the door to new life.

27:54. The earthquake moved the centurion and others standing around to respond. They confessed that truly Jesus was the Son of God. Unlike so many in Israel, these Gentiles were sensitive to what the signs around them were indicating (Matt. 8:11–12). God was with Jesus, not against him. They saw that his position was the correct one, not the religious leaders' view of Jesus. In a sense the entire crucifixion scene had been driving toward this pronouncement of how one should respond to the signs God had left. One should consider what is meant here by those who made the confession in reaction to what had taken place. The soldiers probably did not mean it in the full sense Matthew used the term. It was rather a declaration of vindication about Jesus. Jesus was the attested king of the Jews, with a special connection to God. Such rulers were sometimes seen as divine by Gentiles. It was a step of faith, rejecting what they had shared in doing (Wilkins 2004, 908). To understand what Son of God really meant, Jesus's testimony and those who knew him were to be trusted (France 2007, 1084–85; Nolland 2005, 1220).

Mark 15:39 and Luke 23:47 have the confession of a single figure. In Mark it is that Jesus was the Son of God, while in Luke it is that Jesus was innocent/righteous (BDAG s.v. "δίκαιος" 1bβ, 246). Luke's term is ambiguous, and the difference is not great as one meaning yields the other idea by implication. Matthew is suggesting that what was said by one in Mark and Luke was also felt by others. There are multiple witnesses who saw what all of this meant, testifying to its truth. This kind of multiplication, here of witnesses, we also saw in the healing of Matthew 8:28 and in the riding into Jerusalem involving two animals in Matthew 21:1–5.

27:55–56. Matthew closes the crucifixion scene with a note about female disciples from

Galilee who were witnesses (Deut. 19:15). Their loyalty, in contrast to fleeing male disciples, is noted. They watched what was taking place from a distance. Women as witnesses in this culture would not be expected and normally would not be of cultural value, so this detail reflects the event's authenticity versus being made up.

Three women are named: Mary Magdalene (Luke 8:2–3), Mary the mother of James and Joses (= wife Cleopas of John 13:55?), and the mother of the sons of Zebedee (Matt. 20:20–21 = Salome of Mark 15:40). For Matthew, Mary Magdalene and Mary the mother of James and Joses were witnesses of the cross, burial, and empty tomb.

Mark 15:40–41 has a similar note. Here Mary Magdalene, Mary (the mother of James the younger and Joses), and Salome are named. There is a note that many other women were with them in Jerusalem. Luke 23:49 simply mentions that women from Galilee stood at a distance and saw these things; no names are given. Luke 24:10 mentions Mary Magdalene, Joanna, Mary the mother of James, and other women as having gone to the tomb.

27:57–58. A rich man and disciple, Joseph of Arimathea, asked for Jesus's body. Konradt (2020, 432) notes he is not noted anywhere else in the NT outside of this scene, so he is "to be taken as a true historical reminiscence." Pilate granted the request. We know almost nothing about the location of Arimathea. If it was Ramathaim-zophim of 1 Samuel 1:1, then it was twenty-two miles northwest of Jerusalem (Blomberg 1992, 23). However, Nolland (2005, 1228–29) says we do not know, noting four candidates (the just-noted Ramathaim-zophim; Remphis, nine miles northeast of Lydda; Rathamin of 1 Macc. 11:34 tied to Lydda; and Beit Rimeh, five miles east of Rentis and twelve miles northwest of Bethel). The family tomb would have been just outside of Jerusalem, given Joseph had moved there.

To end up in a rich man's tomb alludes to Isaiah 53:9, but only in terms of his innocent death. Jesus's tomb was not among the wicked but he was buried as a criminal, one allegedly guilty of sedition because he did not end up in a family tomb (see chart at Matt. 27:21–23; Davies and Allison 1997, 648). In Judaism, a felon could not be buried in his own family's tomb as a way of dishonoring him. Joseph's act also fit this Jewish custom in providing a non-family tomb (*m. Sanh.* 6.5). Here was a rich man who did well. Such a tomb would be outside the city walls to prevent uncleanness (B. Bat. 2.9).

Felon Not Buried in a Family Tomb

***Mishnah, Sanhedrin* 6.5:** "And they did not bury [the felon] in the burial grounds of his ancestors."

With the soldiers and the female witnesses, Joseph was the third figure in a row who reflected support for Jesus after his death. Added to the creation, there are four witnesses for Jesus in this account. These details counter the three earlier set of mockers (Nolland 2005, 1227). Nolland (2005, 1230–31) defends the request as historical and reflecting sensitivity to Jewish concerns.

John 19:38 describes Joseph as a secret disciple out of fear of the Jews. Mark 15:43 describes him as a member of the council and says he was looking for the kingdom. Mark 15:44–45 notes how Pilate checked with the centurion and found that Jesus surprisingly was already dead. Pilate gave Joseph the body. Luke 23:50–52 also notes Joseph belonged to the council and describes him as a good and righteous man. He also says Joseph did not agree with their decision to seek Jesus's death and was looking for the kingdom. In Luke, Joseph also asks for the body.

27:59–60. Joseph took the body and wrapped it in a clean linen cloth to cover it. He placed it in a new tomb cut in the rock. Hachlili (2005,

29–74) describes such tombs. Osborne (2010, 1050) notes the stone would have been four to six feet high, while niches for the bodies would be six feet long and two feet high. These entrances were not large, only a few feet in diameter. Then Joseph rolled a great stone across its entrance and departed. Likely a hewn boulder, it would have had a disk shape and been placed in a channel to make it roll more easily. It would take several people normally to roll it away to open the tomb.

Photo of a Rolling Stone Tomb.

The body was buried before sunset as the Law required (Deut. 21:22–23). Such labor was seen as honorable (Tob. 1:17–18; on burials, Keener 2009, 691–95, who also sees the Holy Sepulchre locale as likely). Had Jesus not been given a tomb, he would have been deposited in a trash heap for criminals. Matthew says nothing of spices or anointing, possibly because Jesus had already been prepared for burial in the narrative (Matt. 26:6–13; France 2007, 1090).

Mark 15:46 has Joseph take the body down from the cross and wrap it in a linen shroud. He laid him in the tomb cut from the rock and rolled the stone shut. Mark is very similar to Matthew, as also is Luke 23:53. These descriptions are minimal as the body would have been washed and anointed as well. Luke only adds that no one had been in the tomb previously. This detail is important, as there would be no confusion about bodies or whether the tomb was empty. Luke 23:54 adds it was the day of preparation, that is, a day before the Sabbath even though it already was a holy holiday. There was the issue of burying on a feast day and the question of whether the Passover would be broken by burying a dead body (Oliver 2013, 147–69, along with all the issues tied to burial the purchase of spices and anointing). Oliver contends that the succession of two consecutive holy days meant burial would not be prohibited in such a situation, to prevent impurity during the feast time. The minor tractate *Semahot* 7.5 suspends mourning until the weeklong festival is over (Passover and Tabernacles ran for at least seven days), which by implication seems to assume a burial and participation in purity (see also Mo'ed Qat. 19b–20a, which elaborates on the older tradition). These texts are later than the time here but may indicate the kinds of concerns death and feast days generated.

John 19:39–41 notes that Nicodemus came with Joseph. John has more detail that completes the picture. The two men prepared seventy-five pounds of myrrh and aloes, a size fit for a king. John 19:40 refers in the plural to strips of linen versus the singular linen of Matthew, likely including the face cloth (Osborne 2010, 1050). He notes the tomb was in a garden and that no one had been laid in that tomb. John 19:42 also observes that it was the day of preparation and the tomb, being close in location to the cross, made it possible to lay him there.

On Issues Tied to Death and Burial During a Feast

Minor Tractate, *Semahot* 7.5 [trans. Sefaria]: "[If the death occurs] two days within the Festival, *Passover or Tabernacles,* he interrupts [the mourning] for all the Festival and counts seven [days] after it, and people occupy themselves with him for the five days after the Festival. [If the death occurs] seven days within the Festival, he interrupts [the mourning] for all the Festival and counts [seven days] after the Festival, and the community do not occupy themselves with him at all after the Festival."

Babylonian Talmud, Mo'ed Qatan 19b–20a: "Abaye inquired of Rava: If one buried his dead relative on the Festival itself, does the Festival count toward his thirty-day period of mourning, or does the Festival not count toward his thirty-day period of mourning? Abaye elaborated on his question: I do not ask whether or not the Festival counts toward his seven-day period of mourning because the obligation to observe seven days of mourning does not apply at all during the Festival, and therefore he must certainly observe the seven-day mourning period, beginning from after the Festival. What I am asking is with regard to the thirty-day period of mourning, because certain aspects of the mitzva of the thirty-day mourning period do in fact apply during the Festival, e.g., the prohibitions to launder clothes and cut hair. What, then, is the *halakha*: Do the days of the Festival count toward the thirty days or not? Rava said to him: The Festival does not count toward the thirty days. Abaye raised an objection to Rava's opinion from the following *baraita*: If one buries his dead relative two days before a Festival, he must count five days of mourning after the Festival, and during this period his work is performed for him by others. And his menservants and maidservants do this work in private inside his house, and the public need not occupy themselves with him by coming to console him, for they already occupied themselves with him when they came to console him during the Festival. The general principle with regard to the matter is as follows: Any activity that is prohibited to the mourner because it is an expression of mourning is interrupted by the Festival and remains prohibited afterward. And anything that involves the public's occupation with the mourner, e.g., coming to the mourner to offer him comfort and condolence, is not interrupted by the Festival, for people console the mourner during the Festival as well."

27:61. Two female disciples sat opposite the tomb and watched: Mary Magdalene and the other Mary. They knew Jesus was dead and where he was buried. They could later verify the right tomb was empty. They were named in a role as witnesses, a role the church would not have made up since women generally were not witnesses in the culture (Josephus, *A.J.* 4.219). There were exceptions made for cases of sexual abuse or where other witnesses did not exist. The point is if one had made up the story, male witnesses would have likely been provided to bring cultural credibility to the challenging concept of resurrection. The women were in the story because the women were in the event (Keener 2009, 689).

On Women Not Being Witnesses

Josephus, *Antiquities* 4.219: "But let not a single witness be credited; but three, or two at the least, and those such whose testimony is confirmed by their good lives. But let not the testimony of women be admitted, on account of the levity and boldness of their sex, nor let servants be admitted to give testimony on account of the ignobility of their soul; since it is probable that they may not speak truth, either out of hope of gain, or fear of punishment. But if anyone be believed to have borne false witness, let him, when he is convicted, suffer all the very same punishments which he against whom he bore witness was to have suffered."

Mark 15:47 describes Mary Magdalene and Mary the mother of Joses as seeing where Jesus was placed. Luke 23:55–56 says only the women who came from Galilee followed, saw the tomb, and where the body was laid. They returned and prepared spices with ointments to return later. Law-abiding, they rested on the Sabbath.

27:62–65. In a text unique to Matthew, the author shares a visit the chief priests and Pharisees made to Pilate to tell him of Jesus's prediction of resurrection. It is the Sabbath, a Saturday, as it was after the day of preparation. They could do this on the Sabbath as long as they did not walk too far, about two thousand cubits or just more than a half-mile, and did not enter Pilate's house (Wilkins 2004, 914).

Some see this event as pure apologetic and not a real historical event (Davies and Allison 1997, 653; Konradt 2020, 433). The singular testimony of Matthew is the main reason. However, it is not surprising that Matthew's gospel, which was most concerned with the dispute with Jews, would note in a more detailed manner how the leaders reacted after Jesus's death. Throughout, they have been a detailed focus of his. This was not as important a concern for the other gospel writers. It is hard to see the value of making up such a claim if it did not happen. For such a local gospel, it was a detail that could not be effectively fabricated if Matthew's gospel were to maintain any credibility as it circulated in the region (Craig, 1984, 273–81; Morris 1992, 730; France 2007, 1093). Someone like Joseph would have come to know about this meeting, but the women may not have known about guards being posted on the Sabbath (Keener 2009, 696).

The leaders sought Pilate's approval out of respect for the ruler and to be sure the sensitive situation was taken care of in an appropriate manner. He also could take care of it without any other issues of it being a feast time being a concern. It also put Pilate on notice and meant Pilate would be aware if anything happened or anyone complained about the guards' presence. Pilate had washed his hands of this situation, but he was still involved as the leaders kept him in the loop.

They shared how Jesus had predicted he would rise after three days. How they heard of this prediction is not clear, since Jesus's predictions were to the disciples. Did Judas tell them? Did word leak out otherwise? Did they figure it out from the word about Jonah (Matt. 12:38–40; 16:4; so Wilkins 2004, 914)? We do not know (Turner 2008, 676, notes the options). That Pharisees would be present for this request is not surprising since they believed in a resurrection and the Sadducees did not (Matt. 22:23–33; Josephus, *A.J.* 18.14, 16—see chart on the Sadducees and Pharisees at Matt. 22:23–28). The Pharisees have been absent since Matthew 23. The leaders referred to Jesus as "that deceiver," a description we also see in later Jewish discussion of Jesus (Justin, *Dial.* 69, 108; Sanh. 43a, 107b; Davies and Allison 1997, 654). They requested that guards secure the tomb for three days. Later Judaism believed after three days the soul had clearly left the body (Sanh. 90b–91a). They feared the disciples would steal the body and then preach resurrection, deceiving the people beyond what they thought had already taken place. The irony is that in refusing to be open to resurrection, the deception was on the side of those who accused Jesus's followers of potential deception.

Pilate granted the request, but it is not clear if temple police (France 2007, 1094) or Roman soldiers were involved since he said, "You have soldiers." However, their ultimate need to report to Pilate in Matthew 28:14 made it likely Roman soldiers were involved, as does the term used in Matthew 27:27, which refers to Roman soldiers (Davies and Allison 1997, 655; Turner 2008, 677). Although the soldiers originally reported to the chief priests about the empty tomb in Matthew 28:11, they still had to satisfy Pilate, showing he was in charge. Also favoring a Roman guard is that the word for solider is a Latin loanword (BDAG s.v. "κουστωδία" 563; Osborne 2010, 1061).

27:66. So the leaders and soldiers went to the tomb and secured it. They also placed a seal on the entrance to show it had not been entered. The seal, with wax, would have had the imperial seal and may have had a cord running from the stone covering to the rock edge to detect movement. The only way out for Jesus was if God did something.

THEOLOGICAL FOCUS

The exegetical idea (amid mocking, scriptural fulfillment, and heavenly portents that witnesses observed, Jesus was crucified as king of the Jews, confessed as God's Son, given a burial, and had his tomb guarded to prevent the body being stolen) points to this theological focus: Jesus dies as king of the Jews and God's Son in fulfillment of God's plan.

Jesus was crucified and buried amid mockers, witnesses, and the testimony of creation and Scripture. He died as a righteous sufferer, innocent of the crime he was accused of committing and bearing sin for the many. Psalms 22 and 69 were fulfilled as Jesus died. Those who sought his death mocked him. But creation spoke to the darkness of what was happening, as well as to the cataclysmic act Jesus performed over death, pointing to God's presence. It was a kaleidoscope of themes placed side by side. Death on a cross was a grim thing, and Jesus's death looked very glum. But the righteous suffering allowed Jesus to bear being forsaken by God, so others could be reconnected to him. It was the grace of substitution.

Some have complained that God sending his own Son to his death was immoral, like a suicide, not worthy of religious respect. The taunt is like that of the mockers and fails to see that what the cross shows is that sin has a cost. Sin means death and debt. The mocking charge also fails to appreciate that death is not the end of the story, but resurrection and life are. The drama was not done when Jesus was crucified and laid in a sealed tomb with guards and witnesses. God still had one act to perform. It would be the narrative's climax and showed that death was not the end, but the turning point to a new beginning.

PREACHING AND TEACHING STRATEGIES

Exegetical and Theological Synthesis

The exegetical section highlighted the tragedy of Jesus's death. He was physically beaten, publicly humiliated, relationally abandoned, and forsaken by God. Predicting his death did not make the experience more bearable for Jesus. He suffered greatly. Matthew's repeated allusions to Psalm 22, Isaiah 53, and Zechariah 13 reinforced Jesus's desolate state. When we reflect on this section of Matthew and the parallel passages in Mark, Luke, and John, as well as the thoughts of Hebrews 2:10–18 and 5:7–8, we cannot overstate the horror of Jesus's death.

Jesus's excruciating death should result in some cognitive dissonance. On one hand, we should be grateful for Jesus's death. He undid Adam's death sentence over us and gave us his righteousness (Rom. 5). He paid a debt we were incapable of paying and gave us eternal life (Rom. 6:23). He freed us from the power of the flesh and gave us his Spirit (Gal. 2:20). We rejoice in the cross. On the other hand, the cross is a stark reminder of our sin, which plagues all of us (Rom. 3:23). The cross reminds us of our folly, weakness, limitation, and need for mercy. We feel remorse at the cross.

Preaching Idea

The cross is a cosmic witness to the work of God.

Contemporary Connections

What does it mean?

The cross is a powerful metaphor. Before dying on a cross, Jesus used the image to connote a life of sacrifice (Matt. 10:38; 16:24). A disciple denied himself and carried his cross daily (Mark 8:34; Luke 9:23). After his vicarious death and resurrection, the cross became an essential detail of gospel proclamation (Acts 2:23; 5:30; 10:39; 13:29). It became a sturdy witness to Jesus's sacrifice (Phil. 2:8; 1 Peter 2:24). Ironically, a symbol of imperial power and death became an object of Jesus's triumph and God's wisdom (1 Cor. 1:17–18; Col. 2:14–15).

With its vertical and horizontal beams, the cross reaches up to heaven and out to humanity.

The cross's very shape bears witness to God's work of reconciliation between God (Col. 1:20) and humankind (Eph. 2:16). Not only does the cross have a universal reach—Jew and Gentile, male and female—but a cosmic one—heaven and earth, the dead and darkness. The cross reaches all creation with God's offer of reconciliation.

What this means for us is that no one is exempt from the offer of God's grace. The cross can turn an alcoholic father into a Christ-follower. The cross can transform a pious Muslim into a practicing Christian. The cross can proclaim God's great love to an unreached people group in remote regions of Brazil or the slums of India. And the cross can offer assurance to us, in our own ongoing struggle with sin, that grace abounds (Rom. 5:20).

Is it true?

It is true that the cross is a cosmic witness to the work of God. However, a reliable witness does not guarantee those who hear it will believe it. Testimonies are tested. Belief follows. As evident in Matthew's account of the crucifixion, Jesus's death provoked divided reactions. Some mocked him; others confessed he was God's Son.

The cosmic, cruciform testimony still stands. We must decide whether we trust its witness. Those who embrace the cross will confess their sins, repent, accept God's forgiveness, and commit themselves to Jesus. Embracing the cross leads us to carry our own. We follow in Jesus's footsteps, learning from him and living his humble, sacrificial way (Matt. 11:29–30; 16:24; Phil. 2:5–8). Those who reject the testimony of the cross dismiss Jesus's teachings and deem his death a tragic misunderstanding. They view God's plan as unknowable, arbitrary, capricious, or nonexistent. They reject God and exalt themselves.

Now what?

First, the cross compels us to repent of sin. Jesus died to free us not only of sin's eternal consequence but its present hold on us. Sin is reckless and selfish; it denies God's authority and indulges our desires. The cross is evidence that God has released us from the power of sin. Repentance secures this freedom. When we repent from bitterness, we exchange our negative feelings toward others with mercy. When we repent from lust, we submit our sexual cravings to God's expectation for holiness.

Second, the cross invites us to rejoice. The work of the cross is comprehensive. We are forgiven, redeemed, set free from the penalty of sin. We are cleansed, made new, justified by Jesus's crucifixion. Moreover, the work of the cross is inclusive. The cross beckons all types of people—Jew and Gentiles, young and old, male and female, religious and secular, privileged and oppressed. The horizontal arms of the cross depict Jesus's wide embrace: He "is the savior of all people, especially of those who believe" (1 Tim. 4:10 NIV). Such comprehensive and inclusive ramifications of the cross naturally result in joy!

Third, the cross should turn its beneficiaries into witnesses. Those whose lives have been changed by God's forgiveness have a story to share. Our salvation story may be as simple as "I once was lost, but now am found." It may be more elaborate, describing a life of addiction or abuse turned upside down by God's grace. We are not the heroes of our testimonies; Jesus is. Testimonies point to his saving and sustaining work in our lives.

Simple Testimonies Supported by Scripture

- "I was lost, but now I am found" (Luke 19:10).
- "I was dead, but not I am alive" (Eph. 2:1–5).
- "I was God's enemy, but now I am his friend" (Rom. 5:10).
- "I was orphaned, but now I am a child of God" (Rom. 8).
- "I was living in darkness, but now I walk in God's light" (Col. 1:13–14).

- "I was foolish, disobedient, and enslaved, but now I am saved" (Titus 3:3–5).
- "I was against God, but now I am for him" (1 Tim. 1:12–14).

Creativity in Presentation

The cross has inspired beautiful art throughout history. Both the historic event and aesthetic interpretation bear witness to Jesus's great sacrifice. Consider presenting a few of the following images, inviting people to visually appreciate the cross.

The Crucifixion. Painting by Bartolomé Estebán Murillo.

See also:

- Rembrandt's "Descent from the Cross"
- Velasquez's "The Crucified Christ"

In addition to paintings about the cross, you may want worship songs focused on Jesus's crucifixion. Your options are abundant, but below are a few favorites:

Hymns: "The Old Rugged Cross"; "Jesus Paid It All"; "Were You There"; "At the Cross"; "In Christ Alone"; "How Deep the Father's Love"

Contemporary Praise: "At the Cross (Love Ran Red)"; "Once Again"; "The Wonderful Cross"; "Lead Me to the Cross"; "Man of Sorrows."

To illustrate the ubiquitous witness of the cross, consider putting together a slideshow or display of crosses you find around your church,

The Crucifixion. Painting by Fra Angelico.

home, or town. You will likely find them on jewelry, stationery, tattoos, T-shirts, Bibles, church buildings, bumper stickers, and bookshelves. You might even invite people in advance to post pictures of crosses on social media with the hashtag #CrossBearsWitness or #CrossSighting. Then you can include others in your slideshow or display.

To illustrate the cosmic witness of the cross, consider showing a clip from Louie Giglio's film *Indescribable* (2010). The relevant portion comes toward the end (36:30–38:45), after Giglio describes the "astronomical grace" of Jesus displayed on the cross. Then Giglio shows a final series of images from space, zooming into the Whirlpool Galaxy, thirty-one million light years away. At its core is a cruciform image. Giglio says, "Wow. . . . It's Jesus everywhere! . . . It's mercy when you least expect to find it. It's God laughing in heaven when we finally got the Hubble aimed in the right place. And he goes: 'Check this out! It's me! It's grace! It's mercy, it's kindness, it's forgiveness, everywhere you look.'" God truly has left a cosmic witness!

Ultimately, you want your sermon to communicate that Jesus dies as king of the Jews and God's Son in fulfillment of God's plan. Therefore, the cross is a cosmic witness to the work of God.

- Cameo 1: Jesus bears the cross (27:32–37).
- Cameo 2: Multitudes mock Jesus (27:38–44).
- Cameo 3: Darkness and death seize Jesus (27:45–50).
- Cameo 4: Creation and soldiers confess Jesus (27:51–56).
- Cameo 5: Followers take care of Jesus's burial (27:57–61).
- Cameo 6: Authorities send guards to Jesus's tomb (27:62–66).

DISCUSSION QUESTIONS

1. Who are the various cameos in this climactic scene? How does each one represent a different response to Jesus?
2. How did Matthew's account of the crucifixion differ from the others?
3. How does this scene tie into Matthew's opening two chapters? Be specific.
4. What role did Jesus's followers play at the cross?
5. Describe your relationship to the cross. When did you first encounter it? How does it continue to shape you?
6. In what ways have you served as a witness to Jesus? How can you grow in this?

Matthew 28:1–20

EXEGETICAL IDEA
Despite the guards, God raised Jesus, who commissioned his followers to make disciples in all the world and affirmed he would be with them until the end of the age.

THEOLOGICAL FOCUS
The resurrection is God's vindication of Jesus as Son, leading to a commission to take the gospel into the world and make disciples.

PREACHING IDEA
Our mission: Reach out. Bring in. Build up. Repeat.

PREACHING POINTERS
In the final chapter, the risen Jesus appeared and commissioned his followers to continue his kingdom-building work. Matthew describes the empty tomb, opened by an earthquake and visited by various witnesses—angels, women, and Jesus himself. Jesus spoke to the women, giving them orders for the eleven disciples to return to Galilee. Meanwhile, the soldiers tasked with guarding the tomb were dumbfounded and afraid. They reported to the high priests who, by helping them fabricate a story of Jesus's body being stolen, inadvertently testified to the empty tomb. Finally, Jesus met his disciples to reassure them and deliver what has become known as the Great Commission. Matthew recorded these final words as a mandate for his readers and for followers of Jesus in every age. Under Jesus's authority, the church must fulfill her disciple-making mission throughout the world.

Jesus's mandate to make disciples remains relevant today. Without the Great Commission, we grow insular. Church growth experts often envision a bell curve when describing the life cycle of a local congregation. When a church launches, it looks outward. It reaches new people, raises them up, and develops them for ministry. As the body grows, it creates more structures, systems, and programs geared toward those within. Then the church reaches a tipping point. Its mission becomes self-preservation: feeding and maintaining its structures, systems, and programs. Within a few decades, the church begins to decline. The mission of reaching the lost and least is long forgotten. Instead of making disciples, the church drifts into being a social club for spiritual clones. This sermon is an echo of Jesus's timeless mandate to reach out, bring in, build up, and repeat in our disciple-making mission.

GOD'S RESURRECTION OF JESUS VINDICATES THE SON (28:1–20)

LITERARY STRUCTURE AND THEMES (28:1–20)

This final unit has three scenes. There is the discovery of the empty tomb by the women, with the declaration that Jesus was raised and an instruction to meet him in Galilee (Matt. 28:1–10). The guards reported the empty tomb, leading to the claim the disciples stole the body at night (Matt. 28:11–15). There is the meeting in Galilee that produced the Great Commission to make disciples of all nations (Matt. 28:16–20).

There are two appearance scenes that open and close the unit (Matt. 28:1–10, 16–20), with a report of the Jewish response sandwiched in between (Matt. 28:11–15). The first scene comes with an angelic announcement of the resurrection.

There is no effort to describe the resurrection itself. Everything is about how people experienced its effect. This is an element that points to authenticity. Contrast this with the description in the apocryphal Gospel of Peter 9:34–11:44 below, with a large cross and a large Jesus proceeding out of the tomb (see chart below; Osborne 2010, 1065). Keener (2009, 697) speaks of independent sources at work in the various details that were in the canonical Gospels.

Resurrection in the Gospel of Peter

Gospel of Peter 9:34–11:44 [trans. Evans]: "Early in the morning, when the Sabbath had dawned, there came a crowd from Jerusalem and the surrounding countryside to see the tomb that had been sealed. Now in the night in which the Lord's day dawned, when the soldiers, two by two in every watch, were keeping guard, a loud sound rang out in heaven, and they saw the heavens opened and two men come down from there in a great brightness and draw near to the tomb. That stone which had been laid against the entrance to the tomb started of itself to roll and gave way to the side, and the tomb was opened, and both the young men entered. When now those soldiers saw this, they awoke the centurion and the elders (for they also were there keeping watch). And while they were relating what they had seen, they saw again three men come out from the tomb, and two of them sustaining the other, and a cross following them, and the heads of the two reaching to heaven, but that of him who was led by them by the hand overpassing the heavens. And they heard a voice out of the heavens saying, 'Have you preached to them that sleep?' And from the cross there was heard the answer, 'Yes.' Those ones therefore took counsel with each other to go and report these things to Pilate. And while yet deliberating, again the heavens were seen opened and a man having descended and having entered the tomb."

The women were at the center of the first appearance scene. Their presence was culturally surprising. Women were not normally presented as major witnesses (see Matt. 27:61 discussion; Davies and Allison 1997, 662). Matthew 28:9 looks like a summary of a more extensive appearance scene like that in Luke 24:36–49 or John 20:19–23, except it is of the women, not the disciples as a whole. The hugging of Jesus sounds like John 20:17. All of this has the feel of a staccato summary, moving quickly from one act to another. The joy of the appearance is juxtaposed with the plot's sinister nature to deny a resurrection. Opposition continued despite Jesus's surviving after the cross and proving some of the things Jesus was mocked about on the cross. The taunts of Matthew 27:42 are shown to be empty lies of an unwillingness to change one's mind. Besides the obvious theme of resurrection and divine vindication for Jesus, we see the stubbornness of unbelief in this text with the plot to deny the resurrection.

The gospel of Matthew ends with the call to carry out the mission of making disciples of all nations. In many ways, the subsequent history of disciples was and is the extension of the gospel's story. The commission showed the intent for the gospel is for people of every nation. It is a formal commission scene (Davies and Allison 1997, 676). It has an introduction, a note of some opposition, claim of authority, commission, and assurance. Gentile inclusion is stressed here, in the word going to all nations. This final declaration of Jesus was to those who ministered with him. The call of discipleship was and is to obey Jesus in all he has commanded. Baptism and the things associated with it take place in the name and authority of the Father, Son, and Spirit. This gospel ends with a Trinitarian note about where salvation resides and who is responsible for the spiritual washing baptism pictures.

The multiple witnesses to the resurrection include the God who does it, the angels who announce it, the creation that helps to clear the way for it, the women who hear about it, the guards who are afraid of it, ironically the soldiers who report it, and the disciples who get to see it when they experience a risen Lord.

The parallels to the empty tomb's discovery are Mark 16:1–8 and Luke 24:1–12. John 20:1–2 is a very reduced summarized account that simply notes that Mary Magdalene found the tomb empty and reported she did not know where the body was. The last two scenes are unique to Matthew, although Luke 24:44–49 has a variation on the call to go to all the nations.

EXPOSITION (28:1–20)

For Matthew there is only one conclusion about this final segment of his gospel. God raised Jesus from the dead, a divine vindication of everything Jesus's ministry represented. This act of new life was the ultimate reply to the debate with the Jewish leaders about who Jesus was and is. All that was left was for believers to carry out the call to make disciples. It also meant that everyone needed to decide how they would respond to the invitation to salvation based on what Matthew has said about Jesus and the promised kingdom program of God.

Despite the guards, God raised Jesus, who commissioned the disciples to make disciples in all the world and affirmed he would be with them until the end of the age.

28:1. Mary and the other Mary, who had seen Jesus buried in Matthew 27:55–61, now went in the early Sunday morning to visit the tomb. The timing is presented with two phrases "late on the Sabbath" and "as it was dawning the first day of the week." The point was to highlight that they went as soon as they could as one day flowed into another.

They went to see the tomb, giving the most general description of why the women were there. As is typical, Matthew's report is much shorter than that in Mark 16:1–4, which says they went to anoint the body and were discussing how they could roll away the heavy stone, only to find a man in a white robe announcing the resurrection (on angels described as men: 2 Macc. 3:26–30, 33; Acts 1:10; 10:30; Josephus, *A.J.* 5:277; 1 En. 62:15–16—humans wearing garments of glory; 71:1; 87:2; Davies and Allison 1997, 665). Mark has Salome present as well. Matthew only needed two women to make the witness motif point (Deut. 19:15). Luke 24:1–4 also notes their taking spices for the body, discovering the stone rolled away, and encountering two men in dazzling clothes who announced the resurrection. Luke 24:10 notes

Joanna and others were with the women. John 20:12 also has two angels. The dazzling-clothes description in Luke is to make us think of angels (see the next verse).

Descriptions of Angels

2 Maccabees 3:26–30, of Heliodorus attacked as he sought to desecrate the temple: "Two young men also appeared to him, remarkably strong, gloriously beautiful and splendidly dressed, who stood on either side of him and flogged him continuously, inflicting many blows on him. When he suddenly fell to the ground and deep darkness came over him, his men took him up, put him on a stretcher, and carried him away—this man who had just entered the aforesaid treasury with a great retinue and all his bodyguard but was now unable to help himself. They recognized clearly the sovereign power of God. While he lay prostrate, speechless because of the divine intervention and deprived of any hope of recovery, they praised the Lord who had acted marvelously for his own place."

1 Enoch 62:15–16: "The righteous and elect ones shall rise from the earth and shall cease being of downcast face. They shall wear the garments of glory. These garments of yours shall become the garments of life from the Lord of the Spirits. Neither shall your garments wear out, nor your glory come to an end before the Lord of the Spirits."

1 Enoch 71:1: "(Thus) it happened after this that my spirit passed out of sight and ascended into the heavens. And I saw the sons of the holy angels walking upon the flame of fire; their garments were white—and their overcoats—and the light of their faces was like snow."

1 Enoch 87:2: "And I lifted my eyes unto heaven and saw a vision: And behold, there came forth from heaven (a being) in the form of a snow-white person—one came out of that place and three (others) with him."

Josephus, *Antiquities* 5.277, of an experience by Manoah's wife: "Now, he was fond of his wife to a degree of madness, and on that account was unmeasurably jealous of her. Now when his wife was once alone, an apparition was seen by her: it was an angel of God, and resembled a young man, beautiful and tall, and brought her the good news, that she should have a son, born by God's providence, that should be a goodly child, of great strength: by whom, when he was grown up to man's estate, the Philistines should be afflicted."

28:2–4. Matthew loved to discuss how creation reacted to Jesus-events. This is one of four unique Matthean details about the event; the others are the angel rolling the stone away, the impact on the guards, and Jesus appearing to the women as they returned (France 2007, 1097). Here, an earthquake shook the ground, and an angel came to open the entrance to the tomb by rolling away the stone. Was this an aftershock of the earlier earthquake (so Blomberg 1992, 427)? What is not clear is if this took place just before the women arrived or as they arrived. This act means Matthew has bookends, since angels opened the account of Jesus's birth (Matt. 1:20, 24; 2:13, 19). The infancy and resurrection are the only two places in Matthew where an angel appeared, outside of angels helping Jesus in Matthew 4:11 (France 2007, 1100). The angel had a bright appearance like lightning. The picture is of a glorified or transcendent being (Matt. 17:2). The bright clothes are another feature pointing in the same direction (Dan. 10:6; 12:6; Acts 1:10; Rev. 10:1; 15:6).

The guards reacted with terror at the angel's appearance. They were so afraid that they froze like dead men. The text says they "were shaken" or "trembled" (Rev. 1:17). The passive verb, ἐσείσθησαν, indicated how the event had an effect on them (BDAG s.v. "σείω" b, 918). This likely was either a reference to fainting from fear (Turner 2008, 681) or simply being in a stunned stupor, an emotional paralysis (Blomberg 1992,

427). They were too afraid to act. Hagner (1995, 869) describes the irony well: "The ones assigned to guard the dead themselves appear dead while the dead one has been made alive."

28:5–7. The angel told the women not to fear. He knew they had come to see Jesus, who had been crucified. Jesus was no longer present in the tomb but had been raised from the dead as he had said. The passive verb speaks of God the Father's act. Resurrection was God's vindication of Jesus and his vote for him in this religious dispute with the Jewish leadership. Jesus had predicted this repeatedly (Matt. 12:40; 16:21; 17:9, 23; 20:19; 26:32). The crucified one was now the resurrected one (Wilkins 2004, 938). The effect of sin had been reversed; death had been conquered. The force of the announcement was "Jesus has been raised" (Culpepper 2021, 576). The resurrection was a done deal. The angel invited them to look and see where he had been laid. Nothing was there. He told them to go and tell the disciples that Jesus was raised. They were to know that he would meet them in Galilee (Matt. 26:32; 28:10, 16). The women now knew all they needed to know to make that report.

Mark 16:5–7 has a young man in a white robe present, causing the women to be alarmed. He told them not to be alarmed. The Jesus they sought who was crucified has risen. He told them to look where he had been laid as proof. Mark is very close to Matthew at this point. The angel then told them to tell the disciples and Peter that Jesus was going to Galilee before them. Interestingly, Peter, who was prominent in Matthew, was not singled out here by Matthew as he was in Mark. The disciples would see Jesus in Galilee, just as he had said before, an allusion to Jesus predicting his resurrection. Luke 24:5–7 has two angels report and ask why the women were searching for the living among the dead. They proclaimed Jesus risen and that he had told them in Galilee that the Son of Man must be delivered into the hands of sinful men, be crucified, and on the third day, rise.

28:8–10. So they left with fear and joy to tell the disciples immediately. As they went, Jesus appeared to them and greeted them. The whole appearance is very understated, simply presented as an "of course" event. He simply showed up and said hello. This is one of two appearances Matthew recorded.

The women hugged his feet, likely having fallen to their knees (France 2007, 1102), and worshiped him. Matthew 4:9–10 says only God should be worshiped, so the action pointed to their high regard for Jesus. Angels (Rev. 22:8–9) and apostles (Acts 10:25–26; 14:11–15) refused to allow this when it was directed toward them (Wilkins 2004, 941). Jesus was different and accepted such honor. Matthew notes such worship on occasion (Matt. 2:2, 8, 11; 14:33; Osborne 2010, 1069). The hugging showed the resurrection as a physical event, not a hallucination nor a mere rising of a soul (Morris 1992, 739). This fit Jewish expectation of a physical resurrection (Dan. 12:2; 2 Macc. 7—see chart at Matt. 22:23–28 for these first two texts; also 1 En. 22:13; 2 Bar. 30:1; Apoc. Ezek. introduction; L.A.B. 3:10; Pss. Sol. 3:12; 15:12–13; T. Ab. 7B; T. Jud. 25:1–4; T. Zeb. 10:2; Keener 2009, 711). Keener (2009, 703–9) defends the resurrection account against claims of fabrication, myth, and efforts to argue the teaching reflected ancient mystery religions. Keener (2009, 704) notes one would hardly proclaim this "in Jerusalem if people knew of a tomb still containing Jesus's body." They also would be hesitant to do it if Jesus had been left in a criminal's corporate grave site.

Jewish Hope of Resurrection

Psalms of Solomon 3:12: "This is the share of sinners forever, but those who fear the Lord shall rise up to eternal life, and their life shall be in the Lord's light, and it shall never end."

Psalms of Solomon 15:12–13: "And sinners shall perish forever in the day of the Lord's judgment, when God oversees the earth at his judgment. But those who fear the Lord shall find mercy in it and shall live by their God's mercy; but sinners shall perish for all time."

2 Baruch 30:1: "And it will happen after these things when the time of the appearance of the Anointed One has been fulfilled and he returns with glory, that then all who sleep in hope of him will rise."

Pseudo-Philo 3:10: "But when the years appointed for the world have been fulfilled, then the light will cease and the darkness will fade away. And I will bring the dead to life and raise up those who are sleeping from the earth. And hell will pay back its debt, and the place of perdition will return its deposit so that I may render to each according to his works and according to the fruits of his own devices, until I judge between soul and flesh. And the world will cease, and death will be abolished, and hell will shut its mouth. And the earth will not be without progeny or sterile for those inhabiting it; and no one who has been pardoned by me will be tainted. And there will be another earth and another heaven, an everlasting dwelling place."

Testament of Judah 25:3–4: "And you shall be one people of the Lord, with one language. There shall no more be Beliar's spirit of error, because he will be thrown into eternal fire. And those who died in sorrow shall be raised in joy; and those who died in poverty for the Lord's sake shall be made rich; those who died on account of the Lord shall be wakened to life."

Jesus confirmed the angelic instructions and told them not to be afraid but to tell the brothers to go to Galilee where they would see him. Galilee was the central location for Jesus's ministry. The women heard from two witnesses about the resurrection: the angel and Jesus (Davies and Allison 1997, 669; Deut. 19:15). As Turner (2008, 683) observes, the resurrection demonstrated who Jesus was and is, taking him from being an exemplary martyr only dying an honorable death to being the Messiah, Son of God, exalted to God's right hand (Rom 1:2–4). He was all he claimed to be.

The mention of the disciples as brothers showed Jesus restoring those who had scattered (Matt. 26:31–32; France 2007, 1103). He was preparing them to lead in the effort to take the message to the world. They would overcome their past failure. They were family (Matt. 12:49–50).

We are not told that the women obeyed, nor do we need to be told. Jesus's announcement was enough. The next time we see the disciples in Matthew, they will be in Galilee as Jesus commanded.

Mark 16:8, in the likely original short ending, has the women flee the tomb in fear and saying nothing because of that fear. This likely is Mark's open-ended ending, asking people what they would do with the resurrection. It is clear the women overcame their initial fear and reported about the tomb or else no one would know about the event (Blomberg 1992, 428). Luke 24:8–9 has the women recall the words and go report to the disciples. Luke 24:10 names Mary Magdalene, Joanna, Mary the mother of James, and other women. In Luke 24:11, the disciples did not respond well to the initial report, thinking the overwrought women had told a tale. In Luke 24:12, Peter ran to the tomb to see it empty with only the grave cloths. John 20:11–18 has a similar-sounding account only involving Mary, even asking for a report to the brothers in John 20:17.

28:11–14. This scene through Matthew 28:15 is unique to Matthew. In fact, everything from here on in Matthew is unique to his gospel. The guards connect back to Matthew 27:62–66 and 28:2–4. As the women returned to tell the disciples, some of the guards went into the city to tell the high priests all that had taken place. There was no body to guard anymore, given "everything that had happened." As Konradt (2020, 438) says, "The security measures attempted by the high priests have become a boomerang." The priests gathered with the elders and formed a plan. This combination of priests and elders had been the lead group of opposition for the leadership in these final events (Matt. 26:3–4, 47; 27:1, 7, 12, 20). They never contemplated giving the events credence. Resurrection had not changed minds set in stone (Luke 16:31). Sin can be stubborn. The claim of Matthew 27:42 was shown to be mere bravado (Davies and Allison 1997, 671). They only sought to block what had taken place. They had seen Jesus as satanically motivated and continued with that concern (Wilkins 2004, 944; Matt. 12:22–32). They gave the soldiers silver, called a sufficient or large amount (ἱκανά), just as they had with Judas (Matt. 26:15; BDAG s.v. "ἱκανός" 3b, 472). The leaders told the guards to say that the disciples stole the body overnight as the soldiers slept. The irony is the story they tried to prevent from developing was the one they now circulated (Morris 1992, 741).

How the guards knew the body was stolen by disciples, if they were unconscious, is not clear (Turner 2008, 686). It would be at best a guess or a deduction. This does not even raise the issue of how they heard the stone being moved if they were asleep, not to mention the moving of the stone not waking them. Nor does it show awareness that the disciples had fled when Jesus was arrested, thinking it was all over (Wilkins 2004, 945).

The one worry was what might happen if Pilate heard about these events. The chief priests and elders promised to protect the guards and persuade Pilate not to do anything. That persuasion could be verbal or might also likely involve a bribe to help with the persuasion. The point is not clear between those options, but more than words was likely required. The soldiers were to have no worries about their vulnerability before Pilate.

France (2007, 1104–5) takes the fact they reported to the high priest as an indication Jewish guards were in view. However, in that case it would not be clear why Pilate would be a concern for the soldiers or the leadership, since then the entire affair would be in the leaders' hands. More likely is that the soldiers knew they needed the Jewish leaders' protection. Those leaders were far more concerned about what happened with Jesus anyway (Osborne 2010, 1075). With the priests' support, they had a buffer before Pilate. Their plan worked in terms of their protection.

28:15. The soldiers took the silver and did as the leaders instructed. They parroted the plot. Resurrection had done nothing to change closed hearts. To deny a real resurrection was an act of deception, what they had accused the disciples of getting ready to do (Matt. 27:64). Matthew reports that this was the story still told in his time among the Jews. It also was told a century later (Justin, *Dial.* 108.2). Oddly enough, it was a story that confirmed an empty tomb. Jesus's body was nowhere to be found, and remains were never produced (Morris 1992, 743). The options were a grave robbery by bandits (with a grave that was guarded!) or resurrection.

Konradt (2020, 440) has an aside that the resurrection does not require an empty tomb nor an apologetic read like Matthew, and he issues an appeal and warning to what he calls "a problematic theological tendency." He contends that Easter faith goes beyond what history can establish, since faith goes beyond what can be proven in the strictest sense and that 1 Corinthians 15:35–53 looks to a transformation into an imperishable "spiritual" corporeality that need not require an empty tomb. This argues for too much distinction. Yes, faith does not ask us to prove everything (Heb. 11:1), but these accounts, not to mention Paul's own experience including on the Damascus Road, argue for a physicality to the resurrection, even if the raised body has a new form. As a Pharisee, Paul would have held to a form of physical resurrection. Jesus also taught such a physical resurrection hope in contrast to the denial of such by the Sadducees (Matt. 22:23–32). An empty tomb is a natural result of such. An empty tomb is almost a requirement to create the debated climate about Jesus in Jerusalem, as a missing body would have been a key element all would have had to cope with. When Paul defends the resurrection as a necessity in 1 Corinthians 15, he surely is also defending church resurrection traditions like those that referred to an empty tomb, even though he refers only to appearances. Appearances of a raised person assume an empty tomb, since we are not discussing hallucinations or anything like them.

28:16. This final commission scene is unique to Matthew, although Luke 24:44–49 has a similar kind of call to take the message into the world, given in Jerusalem. That there are two locales for such appearances is not surprising, as the disciples originally had come to Jerusalem as pilgrims expecting to return to Galilee. So they likely went back to Galilee to settle things for a longer stay in Jerusalem. Luke's instruction to remain in Jerusalem is speaking to where the new mission would start from once the Spirit came (Luke 24:49). A return to Jerusalem after going back to Galilee to prepare for a longer stay in Jerusalem is not surprising as they get ready for the start of their mission.

Meanwhile, the eleven had headed to Galilee, as Jesus had instructed through the women. They were in the mountain location Jesus had specified. Note that τὸ ὄρος is singular, a specific locale is in view (BDAG s.v. "ὄρος" 725). Revelation would come on a mountain, as it did on Sinai at the end of Moses's life where God called Moses to prepare for Joshua's commissioning (Davies and Allison 1997, 679–80, points to this latter scene; Deut. 31:14–15). This was the first time the Twelve were called the eleven, indicating the loss of Judas (Matt. 27:3–5).

As just noted, that they returned to Galilee for a time is not surprising since they had gone to Jerusalem for a pilgrimage, not intending to stay long-term (France 2007, 1110). No previous Matthean text gave us this detail about the specific location of a mountain in Jesus's instruction to go to Galilee. It is another indication of how selective the tradition was and that it did not backfill holes in the various pieces of what circulated orally. It would have been easy to fix the Galilee instruction above with such an earlier detail (Matt. 26:32 mentions Galilee only). Rather, it was left as it was. The ministry ended in Matthew where it began, in Galilee of the Gentiles (Matt. 4:15–16).

28:17. Jesus appeared to them and received a mixed response. The appearance is merely summarized with no detail, unlike scenes we see in Luke 24:36–49 and in John 20–21. Matthew often was brief. He made no exception here in his style. The only thing that mattered were Jesus's last words and commission. It was not the experience of the risen Jesus that mattered to him as much as what the calling of that risen Jesus was and is.

They worship, and there was doubt or hesitation as well. Wilkins (2004, 948–49) and Morris (1992, 745) opt for others than the eleven being noted as doubters here—a view, though possible, less likely than that the eleven are in view here. To see those outside the eleven would require that we see more than those named as present here as involved. Hagner (1995, 884–85) argues all the eleven were noted as the Greek construction makes no distinctions. We prefer a more complicated way of seeing how the eleven were responding, reflecting a spectrum of emotional embrace about what was taking place. Whether all the eleven were in this state or only some of them, they are presented as a group. The scene involving the doubting Thomas in John's gospel showed that the idea of Jesus being raised took time to sink in for some (John 20:24–29). Whether there were distinctions within them is not clear from the construction, as it reads literally, "Seeing him, they worshiped but they doubted." Matthew was indicating that resurrection led to faith but in a complicated response, as the disciples grew used to what resurrection really meant. It also could simply rhetorically mean that they could hardly believe it was him.

The worship points back to Matthew 14:33 and the moment Jesus's work on creation made an initial deep impression on the disciples about who Jesus was (France 2007, 1110). Others now worshiped as the women had in Matthew 28:9.

The Matthew 28 scene noting doubt is like the one John narrates about an appearance and the doubt of Thomas (John 20:19–29), except this Matthean scene is in Galilee, seemingly later, so it is a distinct case where some doubt. This doubt also involved more than one person. The term here is διστάζω. It refers to a wavering or uncertain response, to be in two minds (BDAG s.v. "διστάζω" 1, 252; Matt. 14:31 is its only other use). It may be that what was doubted was not that Jesus was in some sense alive, but that he had appeared to them and showed himself to be alive more than once. They were having trouble accepting what to make of all of these post-resurrection events, including how omnipresent Jesus really was. When Jesus appeared in Luke 24:36–38, his appearance also startled them and he had to give reassurance. Luke 24:11 also reports initial doubt at the women's report. The disciples were not portrayed as credulous about such an unusual event. The appearances took time to register as real versus an emotional expression of hope.

20:18–20. Jesus now issued a commission that was to function as marching orders for the church. He did so out of a comprehensive authority he possessed from the Father. This was not a new authority, but now it was being exercised in the new entity of fulfilled promise he was commissioned to bring: the kingdom of God. Nolland (2005, 1263–65), in detail, shows a new authority was not meant here. Jesus was not passive and waiting for God to bring him victory as he worked from his new throne seated by God. He was exercising messianic authority over his kingdom as king and as the vindicated Son of Man and Son of God. The resurrection meant Jesus was divinely vindicated and enthroned, so now the king issued his instructions. For Matthew, these were Jesus's last words that were to linger on for those who followed him.

The word "all" dominates the Matthean passage: all authority, all nations, obey all, and Jesus being with the disciples all the days (Turner 2008, 687). The commission shows that the disciples, who had deserted Jesus, were now fully restored (France 2007, 1107).

Turner (2008, 689) speaks of authority like that portrayed in Daniel 7:13–14 where the Ancient of Days gave authority to the Son of Man. This was not new authority, because Jesus had proclaimed as much when he forgave sin in Matthew 9:6–8 and in other remarks in Matthew 11:27 (implied in Matt. 13:37–43 by what the future promises; Davies and Allison 1997, 682). It was kingdom authority that he had and had exercised on occasion during his ministry (Matt. 12:28; Luke 11:20–22). That authority would continue and now extends into eternity (Eph. 1:20–23; Col. 1:12–20; 1 Peter 3:22). Jesus died as king of the Jews, but he was raised to be King of the world as the one who directed God's kingdom. Osborne (2010, 1079) notes how Jesus's authority had been a theme in Matthew (Matt. 4:23–24; 7:29; 8:9, 29–32; 9:6, 8, 35; 10:1; 12:22; 13:41; 17:18; 21:23–27).

Given that Jesus had authority over all, there was now a mission to go into all the world (Davies and Allison 1997, 684). They were to go and make disciples of all nations, that is, all peoples (Keener 2009, 719). There were to be no racial divides among the people of God (Rev. 5:13; 7:9–10). Jesus was to be followed by disciples who would come from every nation, showing a move beyond Israel but still including them, as the book of Acts shows and Paul declares (Rom. 1:16–17; 9–11). Going does not need mean traveling to another land, but going and making disciples wherever God has you. The assumption here was that those in the community would venture out of it to gather people from outside the community, inviting them into a new sacred space to receive blessings that otherwise they would not possess (Bock 2020a, 6–7). This commission also assumed a church that would be engaged with the world. They would go and call people in it into a new world of new life that the world could not supply. The mission of the church was not to make the world into the church, but to be the church in the world as it invited others to join in. The book of Acts shows it took a while for the church to implement this call to go to the nations. The Spirit had to intervene in Acts 10. Likely they may have expected the nations to be brought in through the bringing in of other Jewish believers out of the diaspora, but this did not happen (Hagner 1995, 887). God directly incorporating the Gentiles was what was in mind, as the book of Acts shows. In other words, the gospel had built into it a call for reconciliation where the church would model God's presence and power by doing something the world struggled to accomplish, bringing estranged people of diverse backgrounds into the same family. This move was controversial, as Jews and Gentiles had a deep history of severe conflict. Only the gospel could reverse that hostility (Eph 2:8–22—the first good work of salvation is this reconciliation found in Christ).

A disciple is one who follows Jesus. The original disciples were "to make disciples." A disciple is a pupil or "learner" who sits at the teacher's feet to take instruction (BDAG s.v. "μαθητεύω" 2, 609—"cause one to be a pupil, teach"). The call to make disciples is primary, being the only main verb in the sentence. All the other elements are supportive participles, so "going (a participle in Greek) . . . make disciples, baptizing (participle) . . . and teaching (participle). . ." Everything Jesus had done in instructing his followers showed how this was to be done and what was to be taught. In a sense, the Gospels were discipleship manuals. The church in part existed for the sake of those outside it. There was to be an invitation to enter into sacred space. There was to be initiative in the church to make that happen. There was to be a witness to it in word and deed that showed this divine and corporate reconciliation work was possible. The commission did not know of such a thing as huddled believers or believers staying in their own bubble nor only associating with their own kind.

They were to baptize those disciples in the name of the Father, Son, and Holy Spirit, indicating that the Trinity was involved in their cleansing and entry into the community. This rite pictured spiritual cleansing and washing for those now reconnected to life and the living God (*Did.* 7:1, 3). The phrase "in the name" is singular, even as the Father, Son, and Spirit are noted. Here is an example of the three in one teaching so central to Christian theology proper. Wilkins (2004, 955) notes other early Trinitarian expressions in Matthew 12:28, Galatians 4:4–7, 1 Corinthians 12:4–6, and 2 Corinthians 13:13 as a defense of its early roots and authenticity; note also Jude 20–21 and 1 Peter 1:2. This baptism portrayed their washing by Jesus and entry into new life, not a washing of water but the portrait of a cleansed conscience (Rom. 6:1–4; 1 Peter 3:21). It was not the rite that saved but what the rite represented. The Father had sent the Son to mediate that forgiveness and had given the Spirit to bring life and enablement to those who knew him. They had become cleansed vessels, indwelt by God's Spirit (Acts 2:16–40). They had spiritual purity through Christ. Luke calls this enablement "power" (Luke 24:49). This threefold naming was not so much about a liturgical formula as it was about how God was involved in the making of disciples and their cleansing (France 2007, 1118). The enabling power of the Spirit is something people lack without a relationship with God. The

Spirit restores the image of God to a potential for fullness. The indwelling Spirit is a core gift of the gospel of grace. Nolland (2005, 1268) notes that the variation in early church practice of using the name of Jesus (Acts 2:38; 8:16; 19:5) or this formula with baptism shows a set formula was not the point (also Wilkins 2004, 955). The point was "the action of the Father through the Son and by means of the Spirit" (Nolland 2005, 1269).

Didache on Baptism

***Didache* 7:1–3:** "Now concerning baptism, baptize as follows: after you have reviewed all these things, baptize in the name of the Father and of the Son and of the Holy Spirit in running water. But if you have no running water, then baptize in some other water; and if you are not able to baptize in cold water, then do so in warm. But if you have neither, then pour water on the head three times in the name of Father and Son and Holy Spirit."

They were to instruct disciples to obey all Jesus had commanded them. He would lead them into the spiritual growth they needed to walk with God. This assumed that those who followed Jesus engaged actively in the community of his followers. This activity took place in his church operating with his presence out of his authority, with baptism in his name (France 2007, 1108). Jesus was at the center of it all. A disciple without community is hardly a disciple.

Followers of Jesus were to follow his instruction. This surely alludes back to all Jesus had taught in this gospel, especially in the five key Matthean discourses from the ethics of the Sermon on the Mount to the promise of a return in the Olivet Discourse. As the gospel itself emphasizes, they were to hear and do what Jesus taught (Matt. 7:24–27).

The commission is similar in thrust to Luke 24:44–49, where Jesus reviewed how the Hebrew Scripture said the Christ would suffer, die, and then be raised so that repentance for the forgiveness of sins would be preached in all the world, beginning from Jerusalem. Then Jesus noted the Spirit would be provided as power to enable this mission to be accomplished (Luke 24:49). The book of Acts traces the start of that mission with that power, making the commission a reality. Culpepper (2021, 585) argues there is no need for an ascension account in Matthew and as Luke 24 and Acts 1 recount, because Jesus was always with them.

In Matthew, Jesus closed assuring them that he was, is, and will be with them always until the consummation of the age. When that moment comes, the rest of what God had promised through Jesus will be accomplished. Certainly, Jesus is Immanuel, "God with us" (Matt. 1:23; Isa. 7:14; Turner 2008, 690). He brought and is bringing the Spirit to do the work (Matt. 3:16–17). He would be both present and aiding the disciples. This is like what Jesus taught in the upper room about the Spirit (John 14–16), but here Matthew focuses on how Jesus would be present with them even from heaven. Jesus is active from the right hand of God. Responding to Jesus means embracing the call the disciples are to make to the world. It means moving outside the community to build the community. Faithful disciples live out and disclose that call to a needy world. When Jesus returns, he will have fulfilled all God had sent him to accomplish. The full victory that the disciples had anticipated in this initial part of Jesus's ministry will be accomplished then. Matthew ends the account of Jesus's earthly ministry looking to its sequel—the carrying out of that mission (Davies and Allison 1997, 688). The church is not to sit and wait for heaven but to introduce it to others by the way they live in this life. The end of this gospel was a beginning of a new era of ministry, leading to the completion of all promised hope.

THEOLOGICAL FOCUS

The exegetical idea (despite the guards, God raised Jesus, who commissioned his followers to make disciples in all the world and affirmed he would with them until the end of the age) leads to this theological focus: the resurrection is God's vindication of Jesus as Son, leading to a commission to take the gospel into the world and make disciples. His followers are called to minister in the midst of his presence until Jesus completes the program God has for him.

Resurrection was about two very fundamental things: vindication to establish the kingdom and the kingdom mission that would grow out of its presence in and distinct from the world. Matthew's three scenes about the resurrection touch on both of these.

The first two scenes showed to the disciples that God had done as Jesus had promised by vindicating him and his claims. Jesus was now raised and back with the Father. The Son of Man was now at God's right hand, ready to rule and judge. All authority was and is placed in his hands. Death had been conquered. Sin could be forgiven. The King was in place to lead afresh. The promise was initially realized. Resurrection was about far more than merely showing death had no sting and that there was life after death. Resurrection was about showing who Jesus was and is and where he is.

The exalted position of Jesus is why the world must come to grips with who he is, even though there often is stubborn opposition, as this gospel consistently shows. The efforts of the tomb guards and Jewish leaders showed even resurrection does not convince some. Sin and rebellion before God can be blind and stubborn, not willing to see what God has done. It can make up stories to avoid facing up to God. That is what we see from Jesus's opponents in this final unit.

Jesus's final words in this gospel show that the gospel message is for the nations. The church had, and has, a commission to fulfill because Jesus is raised. That kingdom message mission is to make disciples, those who learn Jesus's ways. Jesus's followers are to go and make these disciples. This calling requires an active and engaging ministry, involving all the followers of Jesus to represent him wherever God has placed them. The initiative to make God and his kingdom program known lies not just with preachers or vocational leaders in the church. It is with everyone who follows the risen Son of God in every space where they live and every space in which they function. Every believer is a royal believer-priest (1 Peter 2:9). Going, these disciples are to show how what God has done through Jesus leads into life in the Spirit of God. They are to invite people into a fresh sacred space where the Spirit uniquely indwells and equips people. That community is in the world but not of the world. Their assignment is not to shape the world through politics or ideology, but to do it with a new faith in a distinct community that has evidence of divine presence. To confuse the kingdom with the world is to confuse the mission and miss the distinct place the community has in God's plan. They do this through their identification with the cleansing Jesus has done on behalf of God and by living amid an array of people from all nations in the way he called it to be lived. The Son gave the Spirit to enable disciples to engage in mission and live in this way that honors God. They do this by obeying all that Jesus has commanded his disciples to do. They do this knowing they are not alone and that when the end of the age comes, Jesus will certainly finish what the Father and the Son have started through the Spirit. The commission is the King's last word in Matthew. It leads to the continuing work of the kingdom within the world. Matthew ends with a message for the world that disciples are to make known in word and deed, where forgiveness, new life, Spirit, character, and a serving community make all the difference for the world.

PREACHING AND TEACHING STRATEGIES

Exegetical and Theological Synthesis

The exegetical section stresses the mission Jesus handed off to his disciples. Although his atoning work was complete—he paid the ransom for sin on the cross (Matt. 20:28; 26:28)—his mission to reach the nations had just begun. The Great Commission extends Jesus's grace to the Gentile world. As mentioned above, Luke recorded this global mission in Acts; the apostles carried forth Jesus's work (Acts 1:1–2).

Crossing ethnic barriers with the gospel did not come without friction in the early church, as evident in Peter's dream (Acts 10) and the Jerusalem Council (Acts 15). Many Jews in the first century took pride in their Jewish heritage. They disparaged Samaritans, Romans, and other non-Jews. Their posture reflected the elitism challenged by Isaiah, who reminded Israel of her calling to be a light to the nations (Isa. 42:6; 49:6; 51:4; 60:3). Ethnic and moral superiority run against the grain of Abram's covenant (Gen. 12:1–3), Israel's calling (Exod. 19:5–6), Zechariah's eschatological vision (Zech. 14), and Jesus's Great Commission (Matt. 28:18–20). Matthew's gospel consistently subverts any trace of elitism and inward focus among Christians. Jesus is the exclusive Son of God, Messiah, and Risen King who extends his offer of salvation to the world.

Preaching Idea

Our mission: Reach out. Bring in. Build up. Repeat.

Contemporary Connections

What does it mean?

The Great Commission remains the core task of the church today. Jesus recruited faithful followers to reproduce faithful followers. It is our mission to multiply. This mission comprises four elements.

First, we reach out. Disciples do not retreat from the world or create exclusive clubs; rather, we engage the world with the message of Jesus's kingdom, grace, a new way of life, and abiding presence. Reaching out includes both natural expressions of our faith, word and deed together (e.g., sharing a testimony, posting Bible verses online, praying for a coworker), as well as organized efforts with other believers (e.g., food pantry, outreach event, prayer walk).

Second, we bring in new disciples. Followers of Jesus belong to the family of God, made up of many tribes and nations; they are part of the worldwide, baptized community of believers. This is the global church. One of the greatest dangers to faith is isolation. When followers of Jesus do not have a specific spiritual community, their faith suffers from discouragement, lack of accountability, and strange readings of the Bible.

Third, we build up each other. The local church is a formative community centered on the teachings of Jesus. Certainly, churches provide regular teaching and preaching. However, building up goes beyond delivering content. Anyone can find good (and bad) Bible teaching in the digital age. The genius of the Great Commission is its emphasis on obedience to Jesus's word. We build up disciples by modeling obedience, fellowshipping and praying with one another, making it normal, and showing how Jesus's teachings apply to everyday life.

Finally, we repeat the process. As disciples mature, they become disciple-makers. They realize their growth is for the good of others. Their growth in confidence may compel them to share their faith more often. Their deeper understanding of the Bible can help them address the doubts of unbelievers. Their developing compassion may help them gently lead a lost soul to Jesus. Regardless of the way a faithful disciple reaches someone new, she will be sure to bring her in and build her up to keep Jesus's mission moving.

Is it true?

It is true that Jesus gave the Great Commission. Two caveats are worth noting. First, the mission is not for elite disciples but every Christian. It is not reserved for pastors, evangelists, or super-Christians. Anyone who follows Jesus can help reach out, bring in, and build up others. A grandchild may reach out to an unsaved grandparent. A teenager may bring a friend and her family into the faith community. An older man may build up a young father in his faith. Every disciple can help make disciples because they serve under Jesus's authority and by the Spirit's enablement.

First, the mission is to make disciples *of Jesus*. As obvious as this sounds, we often miss the mark on this front. Too often we make disciples in our own image. We teach them to follow our convictions, pray according to our template, and mimic our values. We ask them to pursue ideas that make the church less than central. What we end up with are vague imitations of Jesus. Similarly, churches can set denominational loyalty over discipleship to Jesus. We tie church membership to creeds, covenants, and statements of faith rather than obedience to the Sermon on the Mount. Jesus is the subject and *telos* of our discipleship. He will never leave us; our loyalty belongs to him.

Now what?

The preaching idea lends itself to four practices: reach out, bring in, build up, and repeat. Of course, a prerequisite to making disciples is being a disciple. Once someone has decided to follow Jesus, repenting of sins, and believing he is Christ the Lord, the four movements of the Great Commission apply to him.

Second, we go out. Followers of Jesus must engage their neighbors, coworkers, and family members. The mission of God extends beyond the walls of our church. Sadly, for many Christians, the longer they have walked with Jesus, the more insular they become. Going out requires intentionality. We can volunteer at our public school, coach sports teams, be conscious of reflecting our faith in our work, or get involved in an exercise group or garden club in our community. We can invite coworkers to lunch or neighbors to dinner. To reach people we must go out to meet them.

Second, we bring people in. Isolation plagues the Western world. For years, church growth experts have been citing sociologists and saying people need to "belong before they believe." Bringing people in does not merely mean inviting people to a worship service. Discipleship to Jesus requires more than an hour in a room for a Christian event. Disciples need friends, small groups, and safe places to ask questions, share doubts, and celebrate growth. Bringing people in means connecting them to a spiritual community.

Third, we build people up. Christian faith is dynamic. God wants his people to grow into Christlikeness (Eph. 4:14–16). Jesus viewed his teaching as training in resiliency (Matt. 7:24–27). To build up disciples is to train them in the way of Jesus. We teach people how to pray, interpret Scripture, and turn the other cheek. We train people in mercy, kindness, and sacrificial love. We develop a "curriculum of Christlikeness" (Willard 1997, 311–73) that makes sense of and models the teachings of Jesus. And, to be clear, building others up goes beyond giving them information. We relate to and care for them, test them, assess them, and help them make adjustments as they walk with Jesus.

Finally, we repeat the process. Any disciple can make disciples. Until Christ returns, he expects us to go out, bring in, and build up faithful followers of Jesus. So press on!

Creativity in Presentation

The Great Commission led to the expansion of the church. Disciples made disciples who made disciples. You may want to illustrate the numeric rise of the church in numbers or icons, using Luke's numbers in Acts or Sittser's (2019, 6) noted increase from 5,000 in A.D. 40 to 5,000,000 by A.D. 300.[1]

1 According to Sittser (2019, 186), a critical factor in the rise of the early church was its deliberate discipleship process. Namely, early church leaders developed a catechumenate to help form believers into faithful disciples.

Chart: Growth of the Early Church			
120	**3,000**	**5,000**	**Great Increase**
Acts 1:15	**Acts 2:41**	**Acts 4:4**	**Acts 6:7**
Acts 9:31; 16:5; 21:20			

You may also illustrate the power of multiplication using raw math or graphs to picture what Jesus envisioned with the Great Commission.

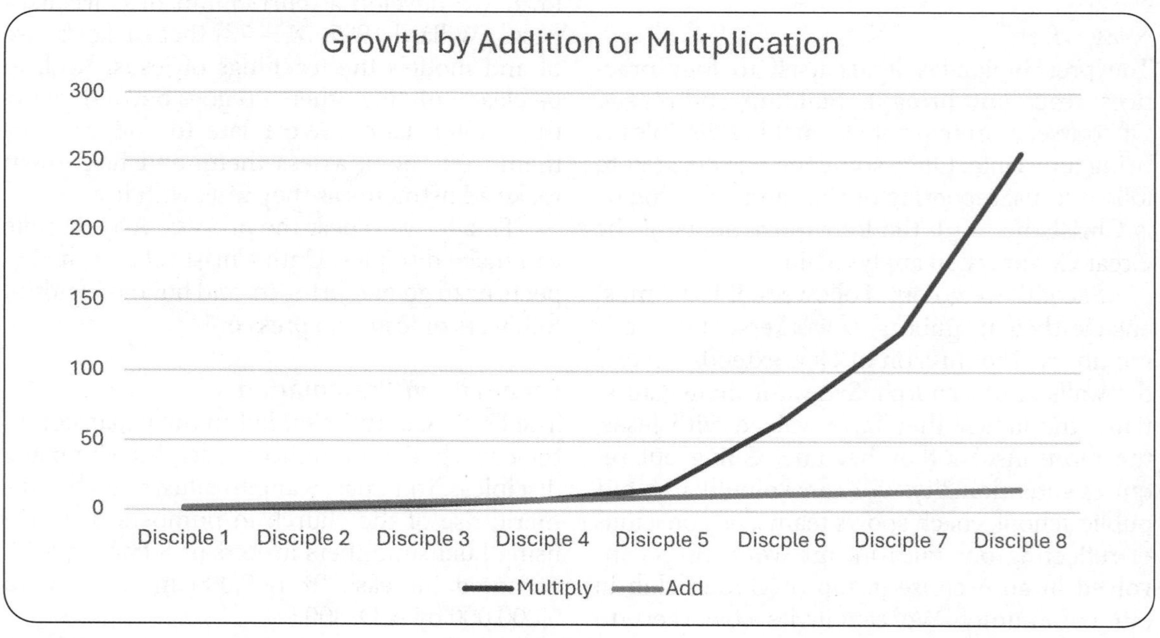

Sittser writes, "Conversion to Christ implied conformity to Christ. . . . Not every Christian became a serious disciple. Still, standards were high because the identity of Christ was clear. Christians believed he was Lord."

Finally, an interactive way to illustrate the need to multiply disciple-makers is to play two rounds of "Disciple Tag." In round one, a volunteer has thirty seconds to tag as many people in the congregation as possible. This depicts the discipleship-by-addition model. In round two, another volunteer has thirty seconds to tag others; however, every person tagged becomes another tagger. Who knows, you may tag the entire congregation in the thirty-second slot. After two rounds of Disciple Tag, ask your congregation the obvious question: "Which version of this game do you think Jesus envisioned: discipleship by addition or multiplication?" Encourage them to respond out loud. Once they say, "Multiplication," you may follow up with, "Exactly. And guess what? Tag. You're it!"

Another way to illustrate our disciple-making commission is to feature one of the many discipleship organizations dedicated to helping the church. Below are a few discipleship programs and details from their work.[2]

Navigators: This organization comes alongside churches to instruct them on making disciple-makers. The cornerstone of their approach is The Wheel, created by Dawson Trotman, the founder of the Navigators. The Wheel has a center (Christ) and four spokes (the Word, witnessing, prayer, and fellowship); it is surrounded by "the obedient Christian in action."[3]

CRU: This college-age ministry seeks to develop disciples on college campuses. They break disciples into four categories: The Follower, The Discipler, The Multiplier, and The Ambassador. See https://www.cru.org/ for more information.

Exponential: This church planning and growth movement offers an assessment tool with five levels of disciple-making: https://exponential.org/disciple-maker-assessment.

Discipleship Dynamics: This organization provides an assessment tool for church leaders that looks at five dimensions and thirty-five outcomes of a "healthy disciple." The dimensions are spiritual formation, personal wholeness, healthy relationships, vocational clarity, and economics/work. For an infographic, see https://discipleshipdynamics.com/making-healthy-disciples-a-guide-for-leaders.

The Master Plan of Evangelism: This classic book by Robert Coleman (1993) draws from Jesus's ministry an eight-step process for discipleship: selection, association, consecration, impartation, demonstration, delegation, supervision, and reproduction.[4]

Finally, to fix the language of the preaching idea into people's memory, consider holding up signs (or slides) with each phrase and an accompanying arrow. Have them repeat the mandate when you show the sign (or slide). You could even have postcards created to give people on their way out the door.

No matter what creative elements you adopt or adapt, be sure that your sermon clarifies that the resurrection is God's vindication of Jesus as Son, leading to a commission to take the gospel into the world and make disciples. This is our mission: Reach out. Bring in. Build up. Repeat.

2 It is worth repeating that our discipleship is to Jesus not a church, denomination, or other Christian. Any discipleship program that focuses more on systems or strategies than a relationship with Jesus misses the mark.

3 For this visual aid, see: https://www.navigators.org/resource/the-wheel-illustration (accessed July 24, 2024).

4 A more contemporary author who has popularized discipleship is Robby Gallaty. He has written and taught extensively on the topic of discipleship, disciple-making, developing a discipleship culture in the church, and D(iscipleship)-Groups. Resources from his ministry can be found here: https://replicate.org/.

- An amazing discovery: He is risen (28:1–10).
- A desperate conspiracy: He is hidden (28:11–15).
- A Great Commission: Make disciples (28:16–20).

DISCUSSION QUESTIONS

1. What makes the women as first witnesses to the resurrection so shocking?
2. How does the conspiracy of the guards and religious leaders corroborate the resurrection story?
3. How do you harmonize the disciples' return to Galilee with their other encounters of the resurrected Jesus in Jerusalem according to Luke?
4. Explain the mixed thoughts of the disciples upon meeting Jesus in Jerusalem.
5. What are the theological implications of the resurrection?
6. How have you seen discipleship programs or strategies be effective? Be specific.
7. What does a healthy disciple look like? How are you making disciples?

REFERENCES

(Asterisk indicates key sources for this commentary—a kind of select bibliography.)

Allberry, Sam. 2019. *7 Myths about Singleness*. Wheaton, IL: Crossway.

Anderson, Neil T. 1990. *Victory over the Darkness: Realize the Power of Your Identity in Christ*. Ventura, CA: Regal.

Aune, David. 1987. *The New Testament in Its Literary Environment*. LEC. Philadelphia: Westminster.

Bailey, M. L. 1998a. "The Parable of the Sower and the Soils." *BSac* 155:172–88.

Bailey, M. L. 1998b. "The Parable of the Tares." *BSac* 155:266–79.

Bailey, M. L. 1998c. "The Parable of the Mustard Seed." *BSac* 155:449–59.

Bailey, M. L. 1999a. "The Parable of the Leavening Process." *BSac* 155:62–71.

Bailey, M. L. 1999b. "The Parables of the Hidden Treasure and the Pearl Merchant." *BSac* 156:175–89.

Bailey, M. L. 1999c. "The Parables of the Dragnet and Householder." *BSac* 156:282–96.

Bailey, M. L. 1999d. "The Doctrine of the Kingdom in Matthew 13." *BSac* 155:444–451.

Banks, Robert. 1974. "Matthew's Understanding of the Law: Authenticity and Interpretation in Matthew 5:17–20." *JBL* 93:226–42.

Barkay, G. 1986. "The Garden Tomb—Was Jesus Buried There?" *BAR* 12:40–57.

Barton, Ruth Haley. 2022. *Embracing Rhythms of Work and Rest: From Sabbath to Sabbatical and Back Again*. Downers Grove, IL: InterVarsity Press.

Bateman, Herbert IV. 2017. *Jude: Evangelical Exegetical Commentary*. Bellingham, WA: Lexham Academic.

*Bateman, Herbert IV, Gordon Johnston, and Darrell L. Bock. 2012. *Jesus the Messiah: Tracing the Promises, Expectations, and Coming of Israel's King*. Grand Rapids: Kregel.

Bauckham, Richard. 1995. "Tamar's Ancestry and Rahab's Marriage." *NovT* 37 313–29.

Bauer, J. B. 1980. "Bemerkungen zu den matthäischen Unzuchtsklauseln (Mt. 5, 32; 19, 9)." In *Begegnung mit dem Wort*, edited by J. Zmijewski and E. Nellessen, 26–27. Bonn: Hanstein.

Baumgarten, A. I. 1984. "Korban and the Pharisaic Paradosis." *JANES* 16:5–17.

Bayer, Hans. 1986. *Jesus's Predictions of Vindication and Resurrection: The Provenance, Meaning and Correlation of the Synoptic Predictions*. WUNT 2.20. Tübingen: Mohr/Siebeck.

Beasley-Murray, G. R. 1962. *Baptism in the New Testament*. Grand Rapids: Eerdmans.

Beaton, Richard. 1999. "Messiah and Justice: A Key to Matthew's Use of Isaiah 42.1–4?" *JSNT* 22:5–23.

Bennett, Thomas J. 1987. "Matthew 7:6—A New Interpretation." *WTJ* 49:372–86.

Berenstain, Stan, and Jan Berenstain. 1983. *The Berenstain Bears and the Messy Room*. New York: First Time Books.

Berger, Klaus. 1973. "Die königlichen Messiastraditionen des Neuen Testaments." *NTS* 20:1–44.

Betz, Han Dieter. 1995. *The Sermon on the Mount*. Hermenia. Minneapolis: Fortress.

Blaising, Craig A. 2012. "The Day of the Lord and the Seventieth Week of Daniel." *BSac* 169:131–42.

Blomberg, Craig. 1987. *The Historical Reliability of the New Testament*. Downers Grove, IL: InterVarsity Press.

Blomberg, Craig. 1990. "Marriage, Divorce, Remarriage, and Celibacy: An Exegesis of Matthew 19:3–12." *TJ* n.s. 11:161–196.

*Blomberg, Craig. 1992. *Matthew.* NAC. Nashville: Broadman.

Blomberg, Craig. 2005. *Contagious Holiness: Jesus's Meals with Sinners.* Downers Grove, IL: InterVarsity Press.

Blomberg, Craig. 2009a. "The Authenticity and Significance of Jesus's Table Fellowship with Sinners." In *Key Events in the Life of the Historical Jesus: A Collaborative Exploration of Context and Coherence,* edited by Darrell L. Bock and Robert L. Webb, 215–50. WUNT 247. Tübingen: Mohr Siebeck.

Blomberg, Craig. 2009b. "Jesus, Sinners and Table Fellowship." *BBR* 19:35–62.

Bock, Darrell L. 1987. *Proclamation from Prophecy and Pattern: Lucan Old Testament Christology.* JSNTSup 12. Sheffield: Sheffield Academic Press.

Bock, Darrell L. 1994. *Luke 1:1–9:50.* BECNT. Grand Rapids: Baker.

Bock, Darrell L. 1998. *Blasphemy and Exaltation in Judaism and the Final Examination of Jesus.* WUNT 2 106. Tübingen: Mohr Siebeck.

Bock, Darrell L., ed. 1999. *Three Views on the Millennium and Beyond.* Grand Rapids: Zondervan.

Bock, Darrell L. 2002. *Jesus according to Scripture: Restoring the Portrait from the Gospel.* Grand Rapids: Baker.

Bock, Darrell L. 2009. "Blasphemy and the Jewish Examination of Jesus." In *Key Events in the Life of the Historical Jesus: A Collaborative Exploration of Context and Coherence,* edited by Darrell L. Bock and Robert L. Webb. WUNT 247, 589–667. Tübingen: Mohr Siebeck.

*Bock, Darrell L. 2012. *Who Is Jesus? Linking the Historical Jesus with the Christ of Faith.* New York: Howard.

Bock, Darrell L. 2013. "The Restoration of Israel in Luke-Acts." In *Introduction to Messianic Judaism: Its Ecclesial Context and Biblical Foundations,* edited by David Rudolph and Joel Willets 168–77. Grand Rapids: Zondervan.

Bock, Darrell L. 2020a. *Cultural Intelligence: Living for God in a Diverse, Pluralistic World.* Nashville: Broadman & Holman Academic.

Bock, Darrell L. 2020b. "Jesus from the Earth Up: Thinking about Jesus's Humanity in the Canon." In *Who Do You Say I Am? On the Humanity of Jesus,* edited by George Kalantzis, David Capes, David and Ty Kieser, 60–84. Eugene: Cascade Books.

Bock, Darrell L., and James H. Charlesworth, eds. 2013. *Parables of Enoch: A Paradigm Shift.* T & T Clark Jewish and Christian Texts 11. New York: Bloomsbury.

Bock, Darrell L., and Mitch Glaser. 2012. *The Gospel according to Isaiah 53.* Grand Rapids: Kregel.

Bock, Darrell L., and Mitch Glaser. 2017. *Messiah in the Passover.* Grand Rapids: Kregel.

*Bock, Darrell L., and Benjamin I. Simpson. 2016. *Jesus the God-Man: The Unity and Diversity of the Gospel Portrayals.* Grand Rapids: Baker Academic.

*Bock, Darrell L., and Benjamin I. Simpson. 2017. *Jesus according to Scripture: Restoring the Portrait from the Gospel.* 2nd ed. Grand Rapids: Baker.

*Bock, Darrell L., and Robert L. Webb, eds. 2009. *Key Events in the Life of the Historical Jesus: A Collaborative Exploration of Context and Coherence.* WUNT 247. Tübingen: Mohr Siebeck.

Bockmuehl, Markus. 1989. "Matthew 5.32, 19.9 in the Light of Pre-Rabbinic Halakah." *NTS* 35:291–95.

Bonhoeffer, Dietrich. 1995. *The Cost of Discipleship.* New York: Touchstone.

Bornkamm, Gunther, Gerhard Barth, and Heinz Joachim Held, eds. 1963. *Tradition and Interpretation in Matthew.* Philadelphia. Westminster Press.

Brooks, David. 2015. *The Road to Character.* New York: Random House.

Brown, Raymond. 1968. *The Semitic Background of the Term "Mystery" in the New Testament.* Philadelphia: Fortress.

Bruce, Alexander B. 2009. *The Training of the Twelve.* New York: Cosimo Classics.

Bruce, F. F. 1990. *The Epistle to the Hebrews.* NICNT. Grand Rapids: Eerdmans.

Brueggemann, Walter. 2006. *The Word That Redescribes the World: The Bible and Discipleship.* Minneapolis: Fortress.

*Bruner, Frederick Dale. 2004a (vol. 1)/2004b (vol. 2). *Matthew: A Commentary.* Rev. and expanded version. 2 vols. Grand Rapids: Eerdmans.

Buchanan, Mark. 2007. *The Rest of God: Restoring Your Soul by Restoring Sabbath.* Nashville: Tommy Nelson.

Buechner, Frederick. 1977. *Telling the Truth: The Gospel as Tragedy, Comedy, and Fairy Tale.* San Francisco: HarperSanFrancisco.

Burridge, Richard A. 1992. *What Are the Gospels? A Comparison with Greco-Roman Biography.* SNTSMS. Cambridge: Cambridge University Press.

Byrskog, Samuel. 1994. *Jesus the Only Teacher: Didactic Authority and Transmission in Ancient Israel, Ancient Judaism and the Matthean Community.* CB New Testament Series 24. Stockholm: Almqvist & Wiksell International.

Calvin, John. 1970. *Institutes of the Christian Religion.* 2 vols. Edited by John T. McNeill. Translated by Ford Lewis Battles. Philadelphia: Westminster.

Campbell, K. M. 1978. "The New Jerusalem in Matthew 5:14." *SJT* 31 (1978): 362–63.

Card, Orson Scott. 1999. *Ender's Shadow.* New York: Tom Doherty Associates.

*Carson, D. A. 1978. *The Sermon on the Mount: An Evangelical Exposition of Matthew 5–7.* Grand Rapids: Baker.

*Carson, D. A. 1984. "Matthew." In *The Expositor's Bible Commentar*, vol. 8, edited by F. E. Gaebelein, 1–599. Grand Rapids: Zondervan.

*Carson, D. A. 2010. "Matthew." In *The Expositor's Bible Commentary*, rev. ed., vol. 9, edited by Tremper Longman III and David Garland, 25–670. Grand Rapids: Zondervan.

Carson, D. A., and Douglas Moo. 2005. *Introduction to the New Testament.* Grand Rapids: Zondervan.

Carson, D. A., P. T. O'Brien, and Mark Seifrid, eds. 2001. *Justification and Variegated Nomism: A Fresh Approach of Paul and Second Temple Judaism.* 2 vols. Grand Rapids: Baker.

Carter, Warren. 2000. "Evoking Isaiah: Matthean Soteriology and an Intertextual Reading of Isaiah 7–9 and Matthew 1:23 and 4:15–16." *JBL* 119:503–20.

*Carter, Warren. 2004. *Matthew and the Margins.* London T & T Clark.

Casey, Maurice. 1997. "The Date of the Passover Sacrifices and Mark 14:12." *TynBul* 48:245–48.

Chae, Young S. 2006. *Jesus as the Eschatological Davidic Shepherd.* WUNT 2.216. Tübingen: Mohr Siebeck.

Chancey, Mark, 2002. *The Myth of a Gentile Galilee.* Cambridge: Cambridge University Press.

Chapman, David W. 2000. "Perceptions of Crucifixion among Jews and Christians in the Ancient World." *Tyndale Bulletin* 51:313–16.

Charlesworth, James H., ed. 2006. *Jesus and Archaeology.* Grand Rapids: Eerdmans.

Chilton, Bruce. 1982. "Jesus *ben David* reflections on the *Davidssohnfrage*." *JSNT* 14:97.

Clinton, Robert J. 2012. *The Making of a Leader: Recognizing the Lessons and Stages of Leadership Development*. 2nd ed. Colorado Springs: NavPress.

Cole, Neil. 2011. *Journeys to Significance: Charting a Leadership Course from the Life of Paul.* San Francisco: Jossey-Bass.

Coleman, Robert E. 1993. *The Master Plan of Evangelism*. 2nd ed. Grand Rapids: Spire.

Comer, John Mark. 2019. *The Ruthless Elimination of Hurry*. Colorado Springs: Waterbrook.

Corbett, Steve, and Brian Fikkert. 2014. *When Helping Hurts: How to Alleviate Poverty without Hurting the Poor . . . and Yourself.* Chicago: Moody.

Cousland, J. R. C. 1999. "The Feeding of the Four Thousand *Gentiles* in Matthew? Matthew 15:29–39 as a Test Case." *NovT* 41:1–23.

Covey, Stephen R. 2020. *7 Habits of Highly Effective People. Revised and Updated.* New York: Simon & Schuster.

Craig, William Lane. 1984. "The Guard at the Tomb." *NTS* 30:273–81.

Crouch, Andy. 2022. *The Life We're Looking For: Reclaiming Relationships in a Technological World*. New York: Convergent.

*Culpepper, R. Alan, 2021. *Matthew.* NTL. Louisville: Westminster/John Knox.

Danylak, Barry. 2010. *Redeeming Singleness: How the Storyline of Scripture Affirms the Single Life*. Wheaton, IL: Crossway.

Daube, David. 1972. "Responsibilities of Master and Disciples in the Gospels." *NTS* 19:1–15.

*Davies, W. D., and Dale Allison. 1988, 1991, 1997. *A Critical and Exegetical Commentary on the Gospel according to Saint Matthew.* 3 vols. ICC. Edinburgh: T & T Clark.

Davis, C. T. 1971. "Tradition and Reaction in Matthew 1:18–2:23." *JBL* 90:419.

Deatrick, Eugene P. 1962. "Salt, Soil, Savor." *BA* 25:44–45.

Deines, Roland. 2004. *Die Gerechtigkeit der Tora im Reich des Messias.* WUNT 177. Tübingen: Mohr/Siebeck.

Derrett, J. D. M. 1971. "Law in the New Testament: The Palm Sunday Colt." *NovT* 13: 241–58.

Deutsch, C. 1987. *Hidden Wisdom and the Easy Yoke: Wisdom, Torah, and Discipleship in Matthew.* JSNTSup 18. Sheffield: JSOT Press.

Doering, Lutz. 1999. *Schabbat.* TSAJ 78. Tübingen: Mohr/Siebeck.

Doering, Lutz. 2008. "Much Ado about Nothing? Jesus's Sabbath Healings and Their Halakhic Implications Revisited." In *Judaistik und neutestamentlche Wissenschaft,* edited by Lutz Doering, Hans-Günther Waaubke, and Florian Wilk, 217–41. FRLANT 226. Göttingen: Vandenhoeck & Ruprecht.

Donahue, J. R. 1971. "Tax Collectors and Sinners: An Attempt at Identification." *CBQ* 33:39–61.

Donaldson, Terrance L. 1985. *Jesus on the Mountain: A Study in Matthean Theology.* JSNTSup 8. Sheffield: JSOT Press.

Donaldson, Terrance L. 1995. "The Law That Hangs (Matthew 22:40): Rabbinic Formulation and Matthean Social World." *CBQ* 57: 689–709.

Downing, F. G. 1984. "Cynics and Christians." *NTS* 30:584–92.

Duling, D. C. 1975. "Solomon, Exorcism, and the Son of David." *HTR* 68:235–52.

Duling, D. C. 1978. "The Therapeutic Son of David: An Element in Matthew's Christological Apologetic." *NTS* 24:392–410.

Dunn, James D. G. 1970. *Baptism in the Holy Spirit.* London: SCM.

Dunn, James D. G. 1975. *Jesus and the Spirit.* London: SCM.

Eggerichs, Emerson. 2004. *Love & Respect: The Love She Most Desires; The Respect He Most Desperately Needs.* Nashville: Tommy Nelson.

Eppstein, V. 1964. "The Historicity of the Gospel Account of the Cleansing of the Temple." *ZNW* 55:42–58.

Eusebius. 1926. *Ecclesiastical History*. Vol. 1. Translated by K. Lake. Loeb Classical Library 153. New York: Putnam.

Eusebius. 1932. *Ecclesiastical History*. Vol. 2. Translated by J. E. L. Oulton, taken from the edition published in conjunction with H. J. Lawlor. Loeb Classical Library 265. New York: Putnam.

Evans, Craig. 1989a. "Jesus's Action in the Temple and Evidence of Corruption in the First-Century Temple." In *Society of Biblical Literature 1989 Seminar Papers*, edited by D. J. Lull, 522–39. Atlanta: Society of Biblical Literature.

Evans, Craig. 1989b. *To See and Not Perceive: Isaiah 6.9–10 in Early Jewish and Christian Interpretation*. JSOTSup 64. Sheffield. JSOT Press.

Evans, Craig. 2005. "Inaugurating the Kingdom of God and Defeating the Kingdom of Satan." *BBR* 15:49–75.

Evans, Craig. 2009. "Exorcisms and the Kingdom: Inaugurating the Kingdom of God and Defeating the Kingdom of Satan." In *Key Events in the Life of the Historical Jesus: A Collaborative Exploration of Context and Coherence*, edited by Darrell L. Bock and Robert L. Webb, 151–79. WUNT 247. Tübingen: Mohr Siebeck.

*Evans, Craig. 2012. *Matthew*. New Cambridge Bible Commentary. Cambridge: Cambridge University Press.

Eve, Eric. 2002. *The Jewish Context of Jesus's Miracles*. JSNTSup 231. Sheffield: Sheffield Academic Press.

Fitzpatrick, Elyse M. 2008. *Because He Loves Me: How Christ Transforms Our Daily Life*. Wheaton, IL: Crossway.

France, R. T. 1979. "Herod and the Children of Bethlehem." *NTS* 21:98–120.

France, R. T. 1981. "Scripture, Tradition, and the History of the Infancy Narratives of Matthew." In *Gospel Perspectives: Studies of History and Tradition in the Four Gospels*, edited by R T. France and David Wenham, 239–66. Sheffield: JSOT Press.

France, R. T. 1985. *The Gospel According to Matthew: An Introduction and Commentary*. TNTC. Grand Rapids, Eerdmans.

France, R. T. 1989. *Matthew: Evangelist and Teacher*. Grand Rapids: Zondervan.

*France, R. T. 2007. *The Gospel of Matthew*. NICNT. Grand Rapids: Eerdmans.

French, David. 2020. *Divided We Fall: America's Succession Threat and How to Restore Our Nation*. New York: St. Martin's Press.

Freyne, Sean. 1988. *Galilee, Jesus and the Gospels: Literary Approaches and Historical Investigations*. Philadelphia: Fortress.

Garland, David E. 1979. *The Intention of Matthew 23*. Leiden: Brill.

Garland, David E. 1995. *Reading Matthew: A Literary and Theological Commentary on the First Gospel*. New York: Crossroad.

Geisler, Norman L., and Frank Turek. 2004. *I Don't Have Enough Faith to Be an Atheist*. Wheaton, IL: Crossway.

Gerhardsson, Birger. 1966. *The Testing of God's Son: (Matt 4:1–11 & Par)*. ConBNT 2:1. Lund: Gleerup.

Gibson, J. 1990. "Jesus's Refusal to Produce a 'Sign' (Mark 8:11–13)." *JSNT* 38:37–66.

Gladwell, Malcolm. 2019. *Talking to Strangers: What We Should Know about the People We Don't Know*. New York: Little Brown and Company.

Glaser, Mitch, and Darrell L. Bock. 2012. *The Gospel according to Isaiah 53: Encountering the Suffering Servant in Jewish and Christian Theology*. Grand Rapids: Kregel.

Golding, William. 2006. *Lord of the Flies*. New York: Perigree.

Gottman, John M. 2015. *The Seven Principles for Making Marriage Work: A Practical Guide from the Country's Foremost Relational Expert*. New York: Harmony.

*Green, Joel, Jeanine K. Brown, and Nicholas Perrin, eds. 2013. *Dictionary of Jesus and the Gospels.* 2nd ed. Downers Grove, IL: InterVarsity Press.

*Green, Joel, Scot McKnight and I. Howard Marshall eds. 1992. *Dictionary of Jesus and the Gospels.* Downers Grove, IL: InterVarsity Press.

Greer, Peter, and Chris Horst. 2018. *Rooting for Rivals: How Collaboration and Generosity Increase the Impact of Leaders, Charities, and Churches*. Minneapolis: Bethany House.

*Grundmann, Walter. 1975. *Das Evangelium nach Matthäus.* THKNT. Berlin: Evangelische Verlasanstalt.

*Guelich, Robert A. 1982. *The Sermon on the Mount: A Foundation for Understanding.* Waco, TX: Word.

*Gundry, Robert. 1982. *Matthew: A Commentary on His Literary and Theological Art.* Grand Rapids: Eerdmans.

Gurtner, Daniel M., Joel Willets, Richard A. Burridge, and Chris Keith, eds. 2011. *Jesus, Matthew's Gospel and Early Christianity: Studies in Memory of Graham N. Stanton.* LNTS. London, T& T Clark.

Haacker, Klaus. 1977. "Der Rechtsatz Jesu zum Thema Ehebruch." *BZ* 21:113–16.

Hachlili, Rachel. 2005. *Jewish Funerary Customs, Practices, and Rites in the Second Temple Period*. JSJSup 94. Leiden: Brill.

Hagberg, Janet O., and Robert A. Guelich. 2005. *The Critical Journey: Stages in the Life of Faith*. Salem, WI: Sheffield Publishing.

*Hagner, Donald. 1993. *Matthew 1–13.* WBC. Dallas: Word.

*Hagner, Donald. 1995. *Matthew 14–28.* WBC. Dallas: Word.

Hagner, Donald. 2009. "Jesus and the Synoptic Sabbath Controversies." In *Key Events in the Life of the Historical Jesus: A Collaborative Exploration of Context and Coherence,* edited by Darrell L. Bock and Robert L. Webb, 251–92. WUNT 247. Tübingen: Mohr Siebeck.

Hamner, Curt, John Trent, Rebekah Byrd, Eric Johnson, and Erik Thoennes, eds. 2018. *Marriage: Its Foundation. Theology, and Mission in a Changing World*. Chicago: Moody.

Hannan, Margaret. 2006. *The Nature and Demands of the Sovereign Rule of God in Matthew's Gospel.* JSNTSup 308. London: T & T Clark.

Hansen, Collin. 2023. *Timothy Keller: His Spiritual and Intellectual Formation*. Grand Rapids: Zondervan.

Harley, Willard F., Jr. 2022. *His Needs, Her Needs: Making Romantic Love Last*. Grand Rapids: Revell.

Hari, Johann. 2023. *Stolen Focus: Why You Can't Pay Attention—and How to Think Deeply Again*. New York: Crown.

Hatina, T. R. 2006. "Did Jesus Quote Isaiah 29:13 against the Pharisees? An Unpopular Appraisal." *BBR* 16:79–94.

Hay, D. M. 1973. *Glory at the Right Hand: Psalm 110:1 in Early Christianity.* SBLMS 18. Nashville: Abingdon Press.

Hays, Richard B. 1996. *The Moral Vision of the New Testament: A Contemporary Introduction to New Testament Ethics*. New York: HarperOne.

Heil, J. P. 1981. *Jesus Walking on the Sea.* Rome: Biblical Institute Press.

Hellerman, Joseph H. 2009. *When the Church Was a Family: Recapturing Jesus's Vision for Authentic Community*. Nashville: B&H Academic.

Hemer, Colin. 1984. "ἐπιούσιος." *JSNT* 22:81–94.

Hendriksen, William. 1973. *New Testament Commentary: Exposition of the Gospel according to Matthew.* Grand Rapids: Baker.

Hengel, Martin. 1977. *Crucifixion.* Philadelphia: Fortress.

Hengel, Martin, 1985. *Studies in the Gospel of Mark.* Translated by J. Bowden. Philadelphia: Fortress.

Hengel, Martin. 2000. *The Four Gospels and the One Gospel of Jesus Christ: An Investigation of the Collection and Origin of the Canonical Gospels.* Harrisburg, PA: Trinity Press International.

Hengel, Martin. 1981. *The Charismatic Leader and His Followers.* Edinburgh: T & T Clark.

Heth, William, and Gordon Wenham. 1984. *Jesus and Divorce: Towards an Evangelical Understanding of New Testament Teaching.* London: Hodder & Stoughton.

*Hill, David. 1972. *The Gospel of Matthew.* NCB. London: Oliphants.

Hill, David. 1977–78. "On the Use and Meaning of Hosea VI.6 in Matthew's Gospel." *NTS* 24:107–19.

Hillenbrand, Laura. 2014. *Unbroken: A World War II Story of Survival, Resilience, and Redemption.* New York: Random House.

Hobbs, T. Raymond. 1990. "Crossing Cultural Bridges: The Biblical World." *MMJT* 1:1–21.

Hoehner, Harold W. 1972. *Herod Antipas.* SNTSMS 17. Cambridge: Cambridge University Press.

Hoehner, Harold W. 1977. *Chronological Aspects of the Life of Christ.* Grand Rapids: Zondervan.

Hoehner, Harold W. 1992. "Chronology." In *Dictionary of Jesus and the Gospels.* Edited by Joel Green and Scot McKnight. Downers Grove, IL: InterVarsity Press.

Honore, Carl. 2004. *In Praise of Slowness: How a Worldwide Movement Is Challenging the Cult of Speed.* San Francisco: HarperSanFrancisco.

Horbury, William. 1984. "The Temple Tax." In *Jesus and the Politics of His Day,* edited by E. Bammel and C. F. D. Moule. Cambridge: Cambridge University Press.

Horsley, Richard. 1986. "Ethics and Exegesis: 'Love Your Enemies' and the Doctrine of Non-Violence." *JAAR* 54:3–31.

Howard, Tracy L. 1986. "The Use of Hosea 11:1 in Matthew 2:15: An Alternative Solution." *BSac* 143:314–28.

Hultberg, Alan, ed. 2010. *Three Views of the Rapture: Pretribulation. Prewrath, or Posttribulation.* Grand Rapids: Zondervan.

Instone-Brewer, David. 2001. "Jesus's Last Passover: The Synoptics and John." *ExpT* 112:122–23.

Instone-Brewer, David. 2002. *Divorce and Remarriage in the Bible: The Social and Literary Context.* Grand Rapids: Eerdmans.

Instone-Brewer, David. 2003. *Divorce and Remarriage in the Church: Biblical Solutions for Pastoral Realities.* Downers Grove, IL: InterVarsity Press.

Ito, Akio. 1991. "The Question of the Authenticity of the Ban on Swearing (Matthew 5.33–37)." *JSNT* 43:5–13.

Janzen, David. 2000. "The Meaning of *Porneia* in Matthew 5:32 and 19:9: An Approach from the Study of Ancient Near Eastern Culture." *JSNT* 80:66–80.

Jeremias, Joachim. 1969. *Jerusalem in the Time of Jesus: An Investigation into Economic and Social Conditions during the New Testament Period.* London: SCM.

Josephus. 1958. *Jewish Antiquities, Books XII–XIV.* Vol. 7. Translated by R. Marcus. Loeb Classical Library. Cambridge, MA: Harvard University Press.

Josephus. 1963. *Jewish Antiquities, Books XV–XVII.* Vol. 8. Translated by R. Marcus. Loeb Classical Library. Cambridge, MA: Harvard University Press.

Josephus. 1965. *Jewish Antiquities, Books XVIII–XX.* Vol. 9. Translated by L. H. Feldman. Loeb Classical Library. Cambridge, MA: Harvard University Press.

Josephus. 1978a. *Jewish Antiquities, Books I–IV.* Vol. 4. Translated by H. St. J. Thackeray. Loeb Classical Library. Cambridge, MA: Harvard University Press.

Josephus. 1978b. *Jewish Antiquities, Books IX–XI.* Vol. 6. Translated by R. Marcus. Loeb Classical Library. Cambridge, MA: Harvard University Press.

Josephus. 1989. *The Jewish War, Books I–III.* Vol. 2. Translated by H. St. J. Thackeray. Loeb Classical Library. Cambridge, MA: Harvard University Press.

Josephus. 1990. *The Jewish War, Books IV–VII.* Vol. 3. Translated by H. St. J. Thackeray. Loeb Classical Library. Cambridge, MA: Harvard University Press.

Kalantzis, George, David Capes, and Ty Kiser, eds. 2020. *Who Do You Say I Am? On the Humanity of Jesus.* Eugene, OR: Cascade Books.

*Keener, Craig. 2009. *The Gospel of Matthew: A Socio-Rhetorical Commentary.* Grand Rapids: Eerdmans.

Keener, Craig. 2012. *Miracles: The Credibility of the New Testament Accounts.* 2 vols. Grand Rapids: Baker.

Keller, Timothy. 2008. *The Reason for God: Belief in an Age of Skepticism.* New York: Riverhead.

Keller, Timothy. 2015. *Walking with God through Pain and Suffering.* New York: Penguin.

Keller, Timothy. 2016. *Making Sense of God: An Invitation to the Skeptical.* New York: Viking.

Keller, Timothy. 2021. "Growing My Faith in the Face of Death." *The Atlantic,* 331:1 (January/February).

Kerr, A. J. 1997. "Matthew 13:25: Sowing *Zizania* among Another's Wheat: Realistic or Artificial?" *JTS* 48:108–9.

King, Stephen. 2004. *The Dark Tower: The Dark Tower VII.* New York: Pocket Books.

Kinman, Brent. 2009. "Jesus's Royal Entry into Jerusalem." In *Key Events in the Life of the Historical Jesus: A Collaborative Exploration of Context and Coherence,* edited by Darrell L. Bock and Robert L. Webb, 383–427. WUNT 247. Tübingen: Mohr Siebeck.

Kinnaman, David, and Gabe Lyons. 2012. *unChristian: What a New Generation Really Thinks about Christianity . . . And Why It Matters.* Grand Rapids: Baker.

*Konradt, Matthias. 2020. *The Gospel according to Matthew: A Commentary.* Translated by M. Eugene Boring. Waco, TX: Baylor University Press.

Konradt, Matthias. 2023. *Das Evangelium nach Matthäus.* NDT 1. 2nd Auf. Göttingen: Vandenhoeck & Ruprecht.

Köstenberger, Andreas, L. Scott Kellum, and Charles L. Quarles. 2016. *The Cradle, the Cross, and the Crown: An Introduction to the New Testament.* Nashville: B&H Academic.

Koukl, Gregory. 2009. *Tactics: A Game Plan for Discussing Your Christian Convictions.* Grand Rapids: Zondervan.

Kümmel, W. G. 1957. *Promise and Fulfillment: The Eschatological Message of Jesus.* SBT 23. London: SCM.

Laughlin, John C. H. 1993. "Capernaum: From Jesus's Time and After." *BAR* 19:55–61, 70.

Le Peau, Andrew T. 2019. *Write Better: A Lifelong Editor on Craft, Art, and Spirituality.* Downers Grove, IL: InterVarsity Press.

Levine, L. I. 1996. "The Nature and Origin of the Palestinian Synagogue Reconsidered." *JBL* 115:425–48.

Levine, L. I. 2000. *The Ancient Synagogue: The First Thousand Years.* New Haven, CT: Yale University Press.

Lewis, C. S. 1963. *Miracles.* New York: Scribner.

Lewis, C. S. 1970. *The Horse and His Boy.* New York: Collier Books.

Lewis, C. S. 1996a. *Mere Christianity*. New York: Touchstone.

Lewis, C. S. 1996b. *The Screwtape Letters*. New York: Touchstone.

Liebermann, S. 1942. *Greek in Jewish Palestine: Studies in the Life and Manners of Jewish Palestine in the II–IV Centuries CE*. New York: Jewish Theological Seminary.

Loader, William R. G. 1997. *Jesus's Attitude towards the Law*. WUNT II.97. Tübingen: Mohr Siebeck.

*Luz, Ulrich. 1989. *Matthew 1–7: A Continental Commentary.* Translated by Wilhelm C. Linss. Minneapolis: Fortress.

*Luz, Ulrich. 2001. *Matthew 8–20.* Hermeneia. Minneapolis: Augsburg/Fortress.

*Luz, Ulrich. 2005. *Matthew 21–28.* Hermeneia. Minneapolis: Augsburg/Fortress.

Machen, J. G. 1930. *The Virgin Birth of Christ.* New York: Harper & Row.

MacIntyre, Alasdair. 1988. *Whose Justice? Which Rationality?* Notre Dame, IN: University of Notre Dame Press.

MacLaurin, E. C. B. 1978. "Beelzeboul." *NovT* 20:156–60.

Marshall, I. Howard. 2009. "The Last Supper." In *Key Events in the Life of the Historical Jesus: A Collaborative Exploration of Context and Coherence,* edited by Darrell L. Bock and Robert L. Webb, 481–588. WUNT 247. Tübingen: Mohr Siebeck.

Maynard, A. H. 1985. "TI EMOI KAI ΣOI." *NTS* 31:582–86.

McDermott, J. M. 1984. "Mt. 10:23 in Context." *BZ* 28:230–40.

McDowell, Josh, and Sean McDowell. 2017. *Evidence That Demands a Verdict: Life-Changing Truth for a Skeptical World.* Nashville: Tommy Nelson.

McDowell, Sean. ed. 2009. *Apologetics for a New Generation: A Biblically and Culturally Relevant Approach to Talking about God*. Eugene, OR: Harvest House.

McIver, Robert K. 1994. "One Hundred-Fold Yield—Miraculous or Mundane? Matthew 13.8, 23; Mark 4.8, 20; Luke 8.8." *NTS* 40:606–8.

McKnight, Scot. 1991. *A Light among the Gentiles: Jewish Missionary Activity in the Second Temple Period*. Minneapolis: Fortress.

McKnight, Scot. 2005. *Jesus and His Death: Historiography, the Historical Jesus, and Atonement Theory*. Waco, TX: Baylor University Press.

McKnight, Scot. 2008. *The Blue Parakeet: Rethinking How You Read the Bible*. Grand Rapids: Zondervan.

McKnight, Scot. 2009. "Jesus and the Twelve." In *Key Events in the Life of the Historical Jesus: A Collaborative Exploration of Context and Coherence,* edited by Darrell L. Bock and Robert L. Webb, 181–214. WUNT 247. Tübingen: Mohr Siebeck.

McKnight, Scot, and Laura Barringer. 2020. *A Church Called Tov.* Carol Stream, IL: Tyndale Elevate.

McMinn, Mark R. 2017. *The Science of Virtue: Why Positive Psychology Matters to the Church.* Grand Rapids: Brazos.

*McNeile, A. H. 1915. *The Gospel according to St. Matthew.* London: MacMillan.

Meier, John P. 1976. *Law and History in Matthew's Gospel.* AnBib 71. Rome: Biblical Institute Press.

Menken, M. J. J. 1998. "The Textual Form of the Quotation from Isaiah 8:23–9:1 in Matthew 4:15–16." *RB* 105:526–45.

Merritt, Robert L. 1985. "Jesus Barabbas and the Paschal Pardon." *JBL* 104:53–68.

Metzger, Bruce. 1971. *A Textual Commentary on the New Testament.* New York: United Bible Societies.

Metzger, Bruce. 1994. *A Textual Commentary on the New Testament.* 2nd ed. Stuttgart: Deutsche Bibelgesellschaft.

Moo, Douglas. 1984. "Jesus and the Authority of the Mosaic Law." *JSNT* 20:3–49.

Moreland, J. P. 2019. *Finding Quiet: My Story of Overcoming Anxiety and the Practices that Brought Peace*. Grand Rapids: Zondervan.

*Morris, Leon. 1992. *The Gospel according to Matthew.* PNTC2. Grand Rapids: Eerdmans.

Muehlhoff, Tim, and Richard Langer. 2020. *Winsome Conviction: Disagreeing without Dividing the Church*. Downers Grove, IL: InterVarsity.

Neyrey, J. H. 1982. "The Thematic Use of Isaiah 42,1–4 in Matthew 12." *Bib* 63:457–73.

Noah, Trevor. 2016. *Born a Crime: Stories from a South African Childhood*. London: One World.

*Nolland, John. 2005. *The Gospel of Matthew.* NIGTC. Grand Rapids: Eerdmans.

Novakovic, Lidja. 2003. *Messiah, the Healer of the Sick: A Study of Jesus as the Son of David in the Gospel of Matthew*. WUNT 2.170. Tübingen: Mohr Siebeck.

Öhler, Markus. 1999. "The Expectation of Elijah and the Presence of the Kingdom of God." *JBL* 118:461–76.

Oliver, Issac W. 2013. *Torah Praxis after 70 CE.* WUNT 2.355. Tübingen: Mohr/Siebeck.

Ortberg, John. 2002. *The Life You've Always Wanted: Spiritual Disciplines for Ordinary People*. Grand Rapids: Zondervan.

Ortberg, John. 2014. *Soul Keeping: Caring for the Most Important Part of You*. Grand Rapids: Zondervan.

Ortlund, Dane. 2020. *Gentle and Lowly: The Heart of Christ for Sinners and Sufferers*. Wheaton, IL: Crossway.

Orton, David E. 2004. *The Understanding Scribe: Matthew and the Apocalyptic Ideal.* London: T & T Clark.

Osborne, Grant R. 2009. "Jesus's Empty Tomb and His Appearances in Jerusalem." In *Key Events in the Life of the Historical Jesus: A Collaborative Exploration of Context and Coherence,* edited by Darrell L. Bock and Robert L. Webb, 775–823. WUNT 247. Tübingen: Mohr Siebeck.

*Osborne, Grant R. 2010. *Matthew.* ECNT Grand Rapids: Zondervan.

Osburn, C. D. 1981. "The Present Indicative of Matthew 19:9." *ResQ* 24:193–203.

Page, S. H. T. 1980. "The Authenticity of the Ransom Logion (Mark 10:45b)." In *Gospel Perspectives,* edited by R. T. France and D. Wenham, 1:137–61. Sheffield: JSOT.

Parker, S. Thomas. 1975. "The Decapolis Reviewed." *JBL* 94:437–41.

Parrott, Les, and Leslie Parrott. 2015. *Saving Your Marriage Before It Starts: Seven Questions to Ask Before—and After—You Marry*. Grand Rapids: Zondervan.

Payne, P. B. 1978. "The Order of Sowing and Ploughing in the Parable of the Sower." *NTS* 25:123–29.

Payne, P. B. 1980. "The Authenticity of the Parable of the Sower and Its Interpretation." In *Gospel Perspectives*, 1:163–207. Sheffield: JSOT Press.

Penner, James A. 1995. "Revelation and Discipleship in Matthew's Transfiguration Account." *BSac* 152:201–10.

Pennington, Jonathan. 2007. *Heaven and Earth in the Gospel of Matthew*. Leiden: Brill.

Pennington, Jonathan T. 2017. *The Sermon on the Mount and Human Flourishing: A Theological Commentary*. Grand Rapids: Baker Academic.

Perkins, Larry. 1998. "'Greater Than Solomon' (Matt 12:42)." *TJ* 19:208–17.

Peterson, Eugene H. 1989. *Answering God: The Psalms as Tools for Prayer*. San Francisco: HarperSanFrancisco.

Peterson, Eugene H. 2011. *The Pastor: A Memoir.* New York: HarperOne.

Pink, Daniel. 2011. *Drive: The Surprising Truth about What Motivates Us*. New York: Riverhead.

Piper, John. 1979. *"Love Your Enemies": Jesus's Love Command in the Synoptic Gospels and the Early Christian Paraenesis.* SNTSMS 38. Cambridge: Cambridge University Press.

Pixner, B. 1985. "Searching for the New Testament Site of Bethsaida." *BA* 48:207–16.

Plummer, Alfred. 1910. *An Exegetical Commentary on the Gospel According to S. Matthew.* New York: Charles Scribner's Sons.

Porter, S. E., and P. Buchanan. 1991. "On the Logical Structure of Matt 19.9." *JETS* 34: 335–39.

Powell, Kara E., and Chap Clark. 2011. *Sticky Faith: Everyday Ideas to Build Lasting Faith in Your Kids*. Grand Rapids: Zondervan.

Przybylski, Benno. 1980. *Righteousness in Matthew and in His World of Thought.* SNTSMS 41. Cambridge: Cambridge University Press.

Pusey, K. 1984. "Jewish Proselyte Baptism." *ExpT* 95:141–45.

*Quarles, Charles. 2011. *The Sermon on the Mount: Restoring Christ's Message to the Modern Church.* Nashville: Broadman & Holman.

Reese, Randy, and Rob Loane. 2014. *Deep Mentoring: Guiding Others on Their Spiritual Journey*. Downers Grove, IL: IVP.

Robertson, A. T. 1934. *A Grammar of the Greek New Testament in Light of Historical Research.* Nashville: Broadman.

Rousseau, John J., and Rami Arav. 1995. *Jesus and His World.* Minneapolis: Fortress.

Rupprecht, Arthur 1991. "The House of Annas-Caiaphas." *ABW* 1/1:4–17.

Saldarini, A. J. 1988. *Pharisees, Scribes, and Sadducees in Palestinian Society.* Grand Rapids: Eerdmans.

Saldarini, A. J. 1994. *Matthew's Christian-Jewish Community.* CSHJ. Chicago: University of Chicago Press.

Sanders, E. P. 1983. "Jesus and the Constraints of the Law." *JSNT* 17:19–24.

Sanders, E. P. 1990. *Jewish Law from Jesus to the Mishnah: Five Studies.* Valley Forge, PA: Trinity Press International.

Sauls, Scott. 2020. *A Gentle Answer: Our "Secret Weapon" in an Age of Us against Them*. Nashville: Tommy Nelson.

Scazzero, Peter. 2015. *The Emotionally Healthy Leader: How Transforming Your Inner Life Will Deeply Transform Your Church, Team, and the World.* Grand Rapids: Zondervan.

*Schnabel, Eckhard. 2004. *Early Christian Mission.* 2 vols. Downers Grove, IL: InterVarsity Press.

Schürer, E. 1973–87. *The History of the Jewish People in the Age of Jesus Christ (175 B.C.–A.D. 135).* Rev ed, edited by G. Vermes, F. Millar, and M. Black. 4 vols. Edinburgh: T & T Clark.

Scott, J. Julius. 1990. "Gentiles and the Ministry of Jesus: Further Observations on Matt 10:5–6." *JETS* 33:161–69.

Shanks, Monte. 2013. *Papias and the New Testament.* Eugene, OR: Pickwick.

Sim, David C. 1996. *Apocalyptic Eschatology in the Gospel of Matthew*. SNTSMS 88. Cambridge: Cambridge University Press.

Sittser, Gerald L. 2019. *Resilient Faith: How the Early Christian "Third Way" Changed the World*. Grand Rapids: Brazos.

Smith, Gordon T. 2011. *Courage and Calling: Embracing Your God-Given Potential.* Downers Grove, IL: IVP.

Snodgrass, Klyne. 2009. "The Temple Incident." In *Key Events in the Life of the Historical Jesus: A Collaborative Exploration of Context and Coherence,* edited by Darrell L. Bock and Robert L. Webb, 229–80. WUNT 247. Tübingen: Mohr Siebeck.

Sproule, John A. 1980. "The Problem of the Mustard Seed." *GTJ* 11:37–42.

Staton, Tyler. 2022. *Praying Like Monks, Living Like Fools: An Invitation to the Wonder and Mystery of Prayer*. Nashville: Tommy Nelson.

Stendahl, Krister. 1968. *The School of St. Matthew and Its Use of the Old Testament.* 2nd ed. Philadelphia: Fortress.

Stott, John R. W. 1978. *The Message of the Sermon on the Mount (Matthew 5–7).* Downers Grove, IL: InterVarsity Press.

Strauss, Mark. 2015. *Jesus Behaving Badly: The Puzzling Paradoxes of the Man from Galillee.* Downers Grove, IL: InterVarsity.

Strecker, George. 1988. *The Sermon on the Mount: An Exegetical Commentary.* Nashville: Abingdon.

Strobel, Lee. 2016. *The Case for Christ: A Journalist's Personal Investigation of the Evidence for Jesus.* Grand Rapids: Zondervan.

Stuhlmacher, Peter. 1986. "Vicariously Giving His Life for Many, Mark 10:45 (Matt. 20:28)." In *Reconciliation, Law and Righteousness,* edited by Peter Stuhlmacher, 16–29. Philadelphia: Fortress.

Suetonius. 1914. *The Twelve Caesars.* Vols. 1–2 of *Suetonius.* Translated by J. C. Rolfe. Loeb Classical Library 31, 38. Cambridge, MA: Harvard University Press.

Suetonius. 2007. *The Twelve Caesars.* Translated by R. Graves. Revised with an introduction and notes by J. B. Rives. Penguin Classics. New York: Penguin Books.

Swoboda, A. J. 2018. *Subversive Sabbath: The Surprising Power of Rest in a Nonstop World.* Grand Rapids: Zondervan.

Talbert, Charles. 2004. *Reading the Sermon on the Mount: Character Formation and Decision Making in Matthew 5–7.* Columbia: University of South Carolina Press.

Ten Boom, Corrie. 1980. *Tramp for the Lord.* Old Tappan: Spire Books.

TerKeurst, Lysa. 2022. *Good Boundaries and Goodbyes: Loving Others without Losing the Best of Who You Are.* Nashville: Thomas Nelson.

Thomas, Gary. 2000. *Sacred Marriage: What If God Designed Marriage to Make Us Holy More Than to Make Us Happy?* Grand Rapids: Zondervan.

Thompson. W. G. 1970. *Matthew's Advice to a Divided Community: Matthew 17:22–18:35.* AnBib 44. Rome: Biblical Institute.

Tosato, Angelo. 1979. "Joseph, Being a Just Man (Matt 1:19)." *CBQ* 41:547–51.

*Toussaint, Stanley D. 1980. *Behold the King: A Study of Matthew.* Portland, OR: Multnomah.

Treweek, Danielle. 2023. *The Meaning of Singleness: Retrieving an Eschatological Vision for the Contemporary Church.* Downers Grove, IL: IVP Academic.

Trueman, Carl R. 2020. *The Rise and Triumph of the Modern Self: Cultural Amnesia, Expressive Individualism, and the Road to Sexual Revolution.* Wheaton, IL: Crossway.

*Turner, David L. 2008. *Matthew.* BECNT. Grand Rapids: Baker.

Twelftree, Graham H. 1993. *Jesus the Exorcist: A Contribution to the Study of the Historical Jesus.* WUNT 2.54. Tübingen: Mohr Siebeck.

Vanderkam, James C. 2004. *From Joshua to Caiaphas.* Minneapolis: Fortress.

Vernick, Leslie. 2013. *The Emotionally Destructive Marriage: How to Find Your Voice and Reclaim Your Hope.* Colorado Springs: Waterbrook.

Verseput, D. J. 1986. *The Rejection of the Humble Messianic King: A Study of the Composition of Matthew 11–12.* EuroHoch 23.291. Frankfurt: Lang.

Wallace, Daniel B. 1996. *Greek Grammar: Beyond the Basics—An Exegetical Syntax of the New Testament.* Grand Rapids: Zondervan.

Warren, William F. 1992. "Focuses on Spirituality in the Sermon on the Mount." *ThEd* 46: 121.

Webb, Robert L. 1991. *John the Baptizer and Prophet: A Socio-Historical Study.* Sheffield: JSOT Press.

Webb, Robert L. 2009. "The Roman Examination and Crucifixion of Jesus." In *Key Events in the Life of the Historical Jesus: A Collaborative Exploration of Context and Coherence,* edited by Darrell L. Bock and Robert

L. Webb, 669–773. WUNT 247. Tübingen: Mohr Siebeck.

Wenham, G. J. 1986. "The Syntax of Matthew 19.9." *JSNT* 28:17–23.

Whitney, Donald S. 2014. *Spiritual Disciplines for the Christian Life*. Colorado Springs: NavPress.

Wiebe, P. H. 1989. "Jesus's Divorce Exception." *JETS* 32:327–33.

Wilkins, Michael. 1988. *The Concept of Disciple in Matthew's Gospel*. Leiden: Brill.

Wilkins, Michael J. 1992. *Following the Master: A Biblical Theology of Discipleship*. Grand Rapids: Zondervan.

*Wilkins, Michael. 2004. *Matthew*. NIVAC. Grand Rapids: Zondervan.

Wilkins, Michael. 2009. "Peter's Declaration concerning Jesus's Identity at Caesarea Philipi." In *Key Events in the Life of the Historical Jesus: A Collaborative Exploration of Context and Coherence*, edited by Darrell L. Bock and Robert L. Webb, 293–381. WUNT 247. Tübingen: Mohr Siebeck.

Willard, Dallas. 1991. *The Spirit of the Disciplines: Understanding How God Changes Lives*. New York: HarperOne.

Willard, Dallas. 1997. *The Divine Conspiracy: Rediscovering Our Hidden Life in God*. San Francisco: HarperSanFrancisco.

Winner, Lauren F. 2007. *Mudhouse Sabbath: An Invitation to a Life of Spiritual Disciplines*. Brewster, MA: Paraclete Press.

Winter, Bruce W. 1991. "The Messiah as the Tutor: The Meaning of καθηγητής in Matthew 23:10." *TynBul* 42:152–57.

Wise, M., M. Abegg, and E. Cook. 1996. *The Dead Sea Scrolls: A New Translation*. San Francisco: HarperSanFrancisco.

Wrede, William. 1901. *The Messianic Secret*. Translated by J. C. G. Craig. London: Clarke, 1971.

Yamasaki, Gary. 1998. *John the Baptist in Life and Death: Audience Oriented Criticism of Matthew's Narrative*. JSNTSup 167. Sheffield: Sheffield Academic Press.

Yamauchi, Edwin M. 1989. "The Episode of the Magi." In *Chronos, Kairos, Christos: Nativity and Chronological Studies Presented to Jack Finegan*, edited by J. Vardaman and E. M. Yamauchi, 15–39. Winona Lake, IN: Eisenbrauns.

Yancey, Philip. 2003. *Soul Survivor: How Thirteen Unlikely Mentors Helped My Faith Survive the Church*. New York: Doubleday.

Yang, Yong-Eui. 1997. *Jesus and the Sabbath in Matthew's Gospel*. JSNTSup 139. Sheffield: Sheffield Academic Press.

Yarhouse, Mark, and Julie Sadusky. 2020. *Emerging Gender Identities: Understanding the Diverse Experience of Today's Youth*. Grand Rapids: Brazos.

Yeivin, Z. 1987. "Ancient Chorazin Comes Back to Life." *BAR* 13:22–36.